DILBERT
Gives You the Business

A DILBERT BOOK

BY SCOTT ADAMS

BOXTREE

First published 1999 by Andrews & McMeel Publishing, Kansas City

This edition published 1999 by Boxtree
an imprint of Macmillan Publishers Ltd
25 Eccleston Place London SW1W 9NF
Basingstoke and Oxford

www.macmillan.co.uk

Associated companies throughout the world

ISBN 0 7522 2394 1

www.dilbert.com

9 8 7 6 5 4 3 2 1

A CIP catalogue record for this book is available from
the British Library.

Printed in Great Britain by The Bath Press, Bath.

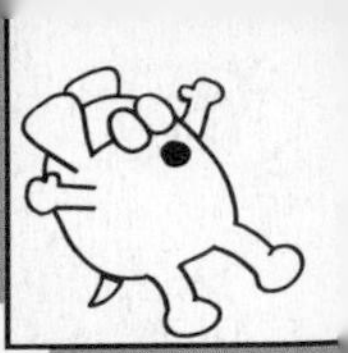

If you're a typical *Dilbert* reader, the question in your mind right now is, "How can I use this book as a weapon to embarrass my enemies?"

I realize that's a gross generalization. The more noble-minded *Dilbert* readers are thinking, "How can I use this book as a weapon to embarrass my friends?" Still others are wondering how they can steal this book from their friends and call it "borrowing."

But whether you have friends or not, I'm here to help.

Responding to an avalanche of suggestions, I have gathered all the most-requested *Dilbert* strips about the business world and organized them by topic. If you want to find all the best *Dilbert* comics on, for example, budgeting, or programming, or performance reviews, or engineering, or marketing, they're here, along with dozens of other topics.

This is a huge improvement over the old method where you might have access to only one or two *Dilbert* comics to make your point. It's nearly impossible to do a thorough job of mocking someone when you are so limited in your choice of comics. Thanks to this book, that will never be a problem again. Now you can show someone a few dozen *Dilbert* strips on the same topic and be certain your message gets across. You'll never again have to deal with the same annoying question, "Are you trying to tell me something?"

It wasn't easy to pull this book together. I stayed up all night, with comics spread around on my furniture and the floor, sorting them into categories. My cat, Sarah, helped by rolling around in the piles until the static electricity made the strips stick to her fur. It wasn't much help, but I don't pay her much either. If you find any duplicates or strips out of place, blame my cat. If the whole book is missing, your friends probably "borrowed" it.

Speaking of friends, you might want to join Dogbert's New Ruling Class and rule by his side when he conquers the planet and makes everyone else our domestic servants. Joining is as easy as signing up for the free *Dilbert* newsletter, published about four times a year whenever I feel like it.

To subscribe, send a blank E-mail to dilbert-text-on@list.unitedmedia.com.
To unsubscribe, send a blank E-mail to dilbert-off@list.unitedmedia.com.
If you have problems with the automated subscription write to newsletter@unitedmedia.com.

You can also subscribe via snail mail:

Dilbert Mailing List
United Media
200 Madison Ave.
New York, NY 10016

S. Adams

Scott Adams

CONTENTS

Jobs

Job Impediments

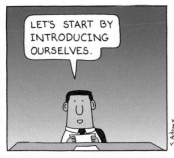

LET'S START BY INTRODUCING OURSELVES.
I'M SUSAN BLOCK FROM I.T.G. I WORK FOR EMILY WOOTEN.
I'M MAX BLUMF. I WORK FOR SUSAN.
I'M ALICE. I WORK FOR ... UH... I ...
AAAGH!!! I'M FILLED WITH SHAME BY ASSOCIATION!!!
WHY ME? WHY WHY WHY
PLEASE TAKE ME TO YOUR GROUP! I'M NOT TAINTED!!!
CAN WE START OVER? I FORGOT WHO THE FIRST THREE PEOPLE ARE.
SOB
S. Adams
2/1/98 © 1998 United Feature Syndicate, Inc.

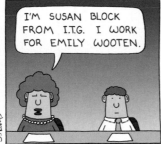

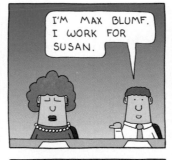

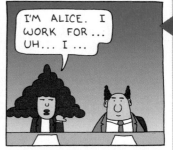

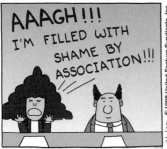

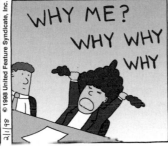

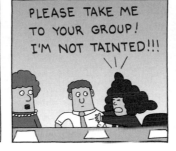

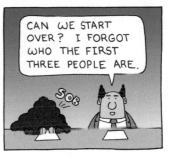

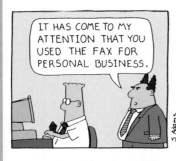

IT HAS COME TO MY ATTENTION THAT YOU USED THE FAX FOR PERSONAL BUSINESS.
I SENT THE FAX DURING LUNCH. IT WAS A LOCAL CALL.
YOU'RE USING UP ALL OF OUR FAX PAPER.
NO, I SENT A FAX. THE PAPER DOESN'T TRAVEL THROUGH THE PHONE LINES.
REALLY?
YOU USED THE COMPANY'S ELECTRICITY.
I HAD A FRIEND FAX US A WAD OF EXTRA ELECTRICITY.
I'M USING IT RIGHT NOW TO POWER MY PC.
DID YOU GET ANY EXTRA ELECTRICITY? MY PC IS OUT.
PRESS THE BUTTON ON THE BACK AND I'LL FAX YOU SOME.
S. Adams
9-25

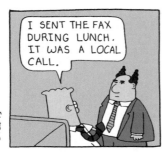

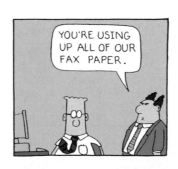

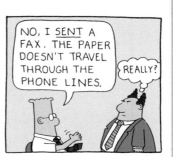

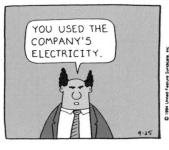

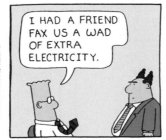

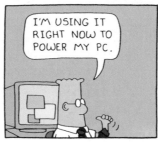

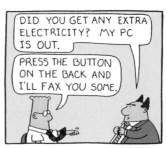

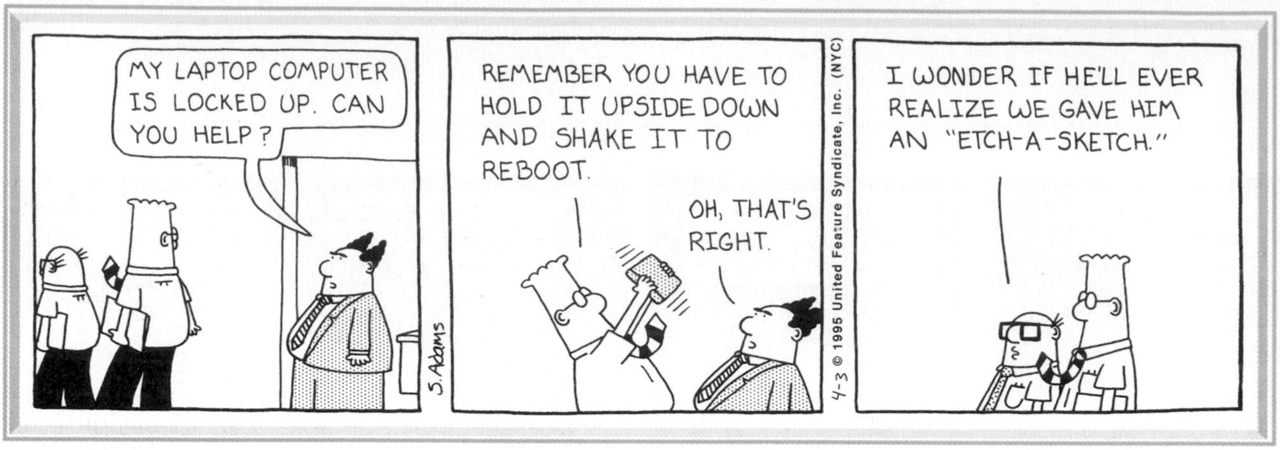
MY LAPTOP COMPUTER IS LOCKED UP. CAN YOU HELP?
S. Adams
REMEMBER YOU HAVE TO HOLD IT UPSIDE DOWN AND SHAKE IT TO REBOOT.
OH, THAT'S RIGHT.
4-3 © 1995 United Feature Syndicate, Inc. (NYC)
I WONDER IF HE'LL EVER REALIZE WE GAVE HIM AN "ETCH-A-SKETCH."

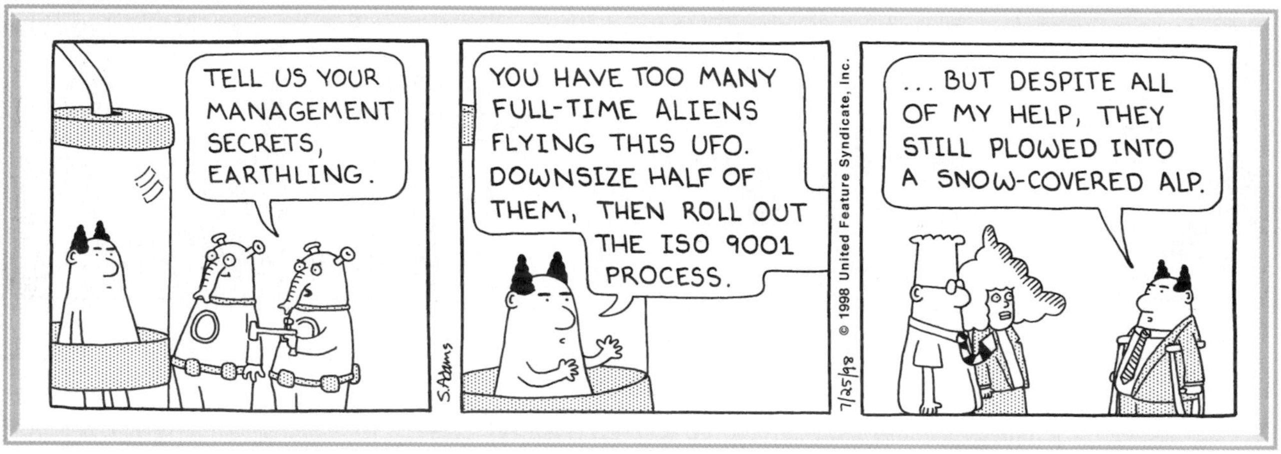
TELL US YOUR MANAGEMENT SECRETS, EARTHLING.
S. Adams
YOU HAVE TOO MANY FULL-TIME ALIENS FLYING THIS UFO. DOWNSIZE HALF OF THEM, THEN ROLL OUT THE ISO 9001 PROCESS.
7/25/98 © 1998 United Feature Syndicate, Inc.
... BUT DESPITE ALL OF MY HELP, THEY STILL PLOWED INTO A SNOW-COVERED ALP.

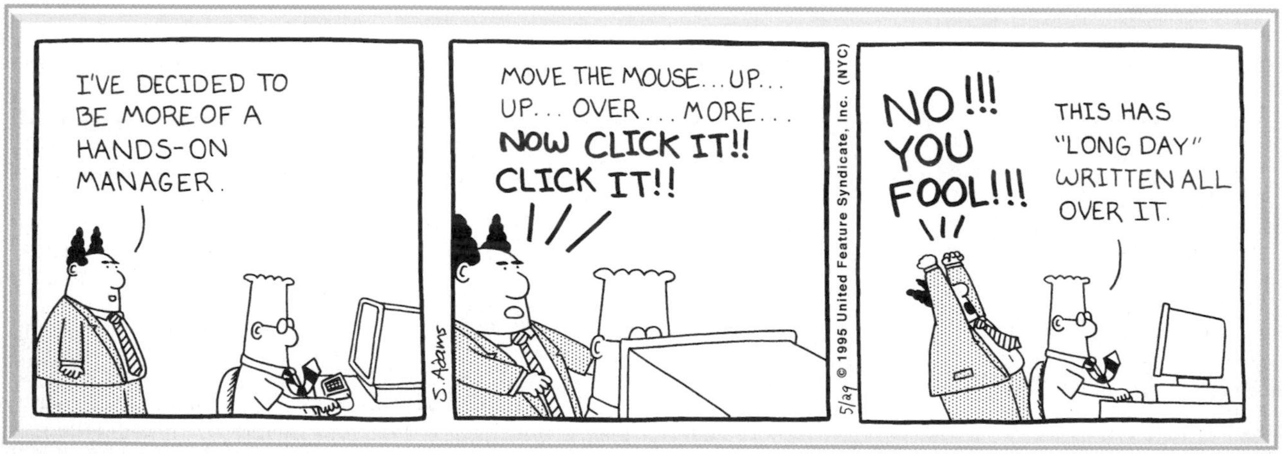
I'VE DECIDED TO BE MORE OF A HANDS-ON MANAGER.
S. Adams
MOVE THE MOUSE... UP... UP... OVER... MORE...
NOW CLICK IT!! CLICK IT!!
5/29 © 1995 United Feature Syndicate, Inc. (NYC)
NO!!! YOU FOOL!!!
THIS HAS "LONG DAY" WRITTEN ALL OVER IT.

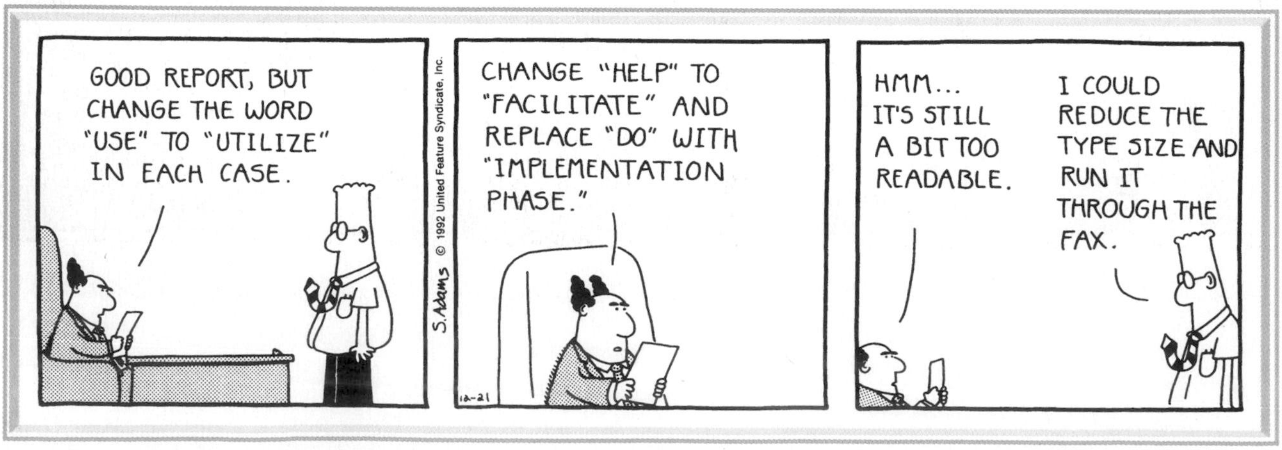
GOOD REPORT, BUT CHANGE THE WORD "USE" TO "UTILIZE" IN EACH CASE.
S. Adams © 1992 United Feature Syndicate, Inc.
CHANGE "HELP" TO "FACILITATE" AND REPLACE "DO" WITH "IMPLEMENTATION PHASE."
12-21
HMM... IT'S STILL A BIT TOO READABLE.
I COULD REDUCE THE TYPE SIZE AND RUN IT THROUGH THE FAX.

YOUR PROPOSAL DOESN'T ADDRESS THE ALTERNATIVES.
THERE AREN'T ANY REASONABLE ALTERNATIVES.
THERE ARE ALWAYS ALTERNATIVES! GIVE ME ALTERNATIVES!!
NO WONDER NOTHING GETS DONE AROUND HERE — NOT ENOUGH ALTERNATIVES.
"WE COULD LOBBY THE GOVERNMENT TO GIVE TAX BREAKS TO ALL IDIOT-RUN BUSINESSES."
"I COULD QUIT THIS STUPID JOB AND START A NEW CAREER HANDING OUT TOWELS AT THE GYM."
"OR WE COULD USE COW CHIPS INSTEAD OF MICROCHIPS AND SAVE MILLIONS."
WHAT'S A COW CHIP?
THIS JOB WOULD BE AN EXAMPLE.
© 1994 United Feature Syndicate, Inc.

THE WORST HE CAN DO IS FIRE ME...
BOSS, I NEED TO TALK TO YOU.
I FEEL YOU DON'T RESPECT ME...
IT'S AN INTANGIBLE THING...
SNEEZE COMING...
I SEE IT IN YOUR BODY LANGUAGE...
AAH...
...AND SOMETIMES THE THINGS YOU SAY...
RRRRIIP
CHOOO
THIS HAS BEEN SOMETHING LESS THAN A VICTORY FOR WORKERS EVERYWHERE.
© 1990 United Feature Syndicate, Inc.

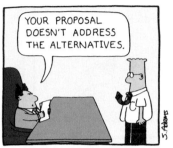

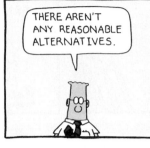

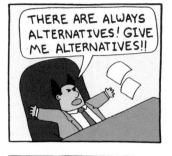

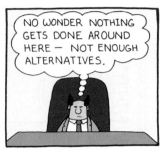

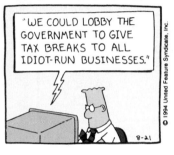

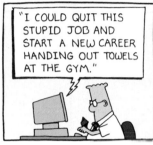

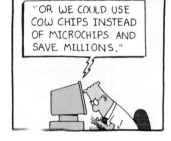

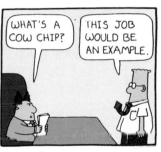

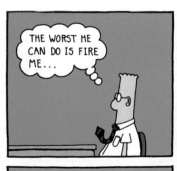

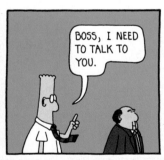

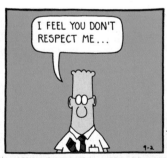

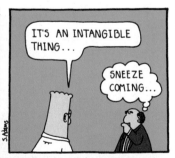

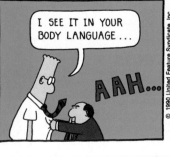

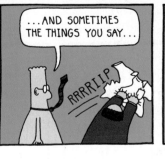

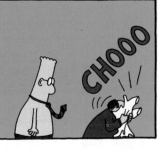

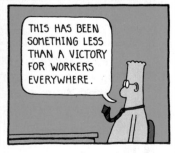

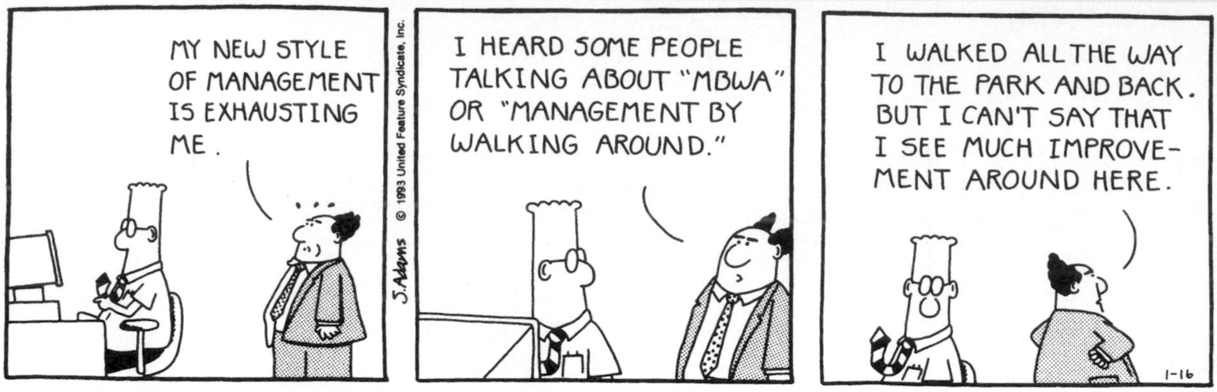
MY NEW STYLE OF MANAGEMENT IS EXHAUSTING ME.
© 1993 United Feature Syndicate, Inc.
I HEARD SOME PEOPLE TALKING ABOUT "MBWA" OR "MANAGEMENT BY WALKING AROUND."
I WALKED ALL THE WAY TO THE PARK AND BACK. BUT I CAN'T SAY THAT I SEE MUCH IMPROVEMENT AROUND HERE.

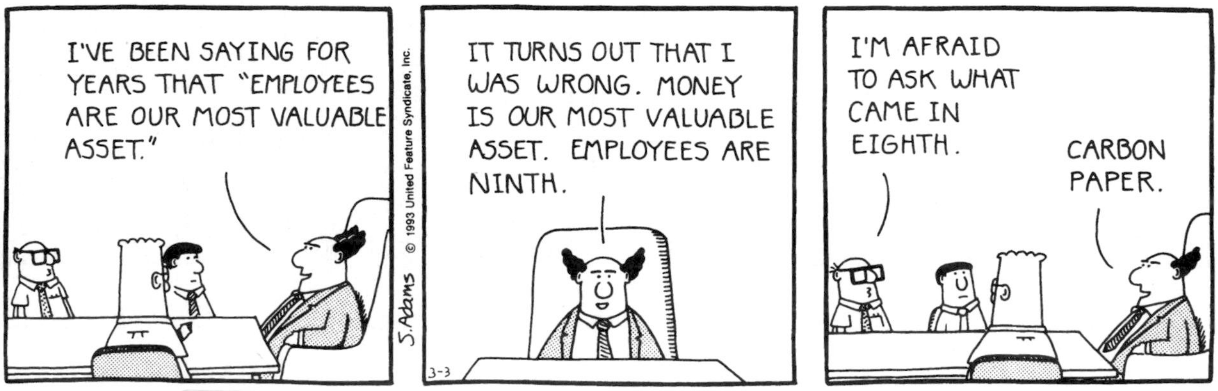
I'VE BEEN SAYING FOR YEARS THAT "EMPLOYEES ARE OUR MOST VALUABLE ASSET."
© 1993 United Feature Syndicate, Inc.
IT TURNS OUT THAT I WAS WRONG. MONEY IS OUR MOST VALUABLE ASSET. EMPLOYEES ARE NINTH.
I'M AFRAID TO ASK WHAT CAME IN EIGHTH.
CARBON PAPER.

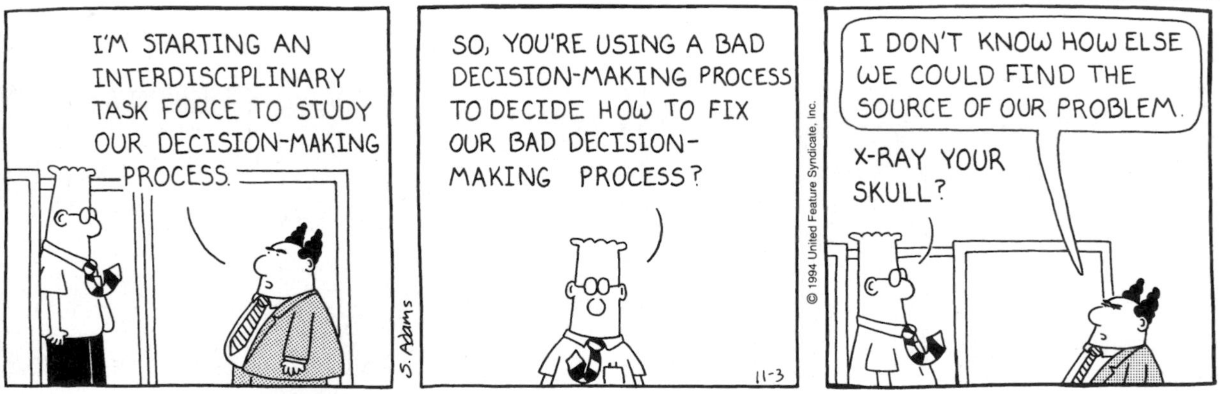
I'M STARTING AN INTERDISCIPLINARY TASK FORCE TO STUDY OUR DECISION-MAKING PROCESS.
SO, YOU'RE USING A BAD DECISION-MAKING PROCESS TO DECIDE HOW TO FIX OUR BAD DECISION-MAKING PROCESS?
© 1994 United Feature Syndicate, Inc.
I DON'T KNOW HOW ELSE WE COULD FIND THE SOURCE OF OUR PROBLEM.
X-RAY YOUR SKULL?

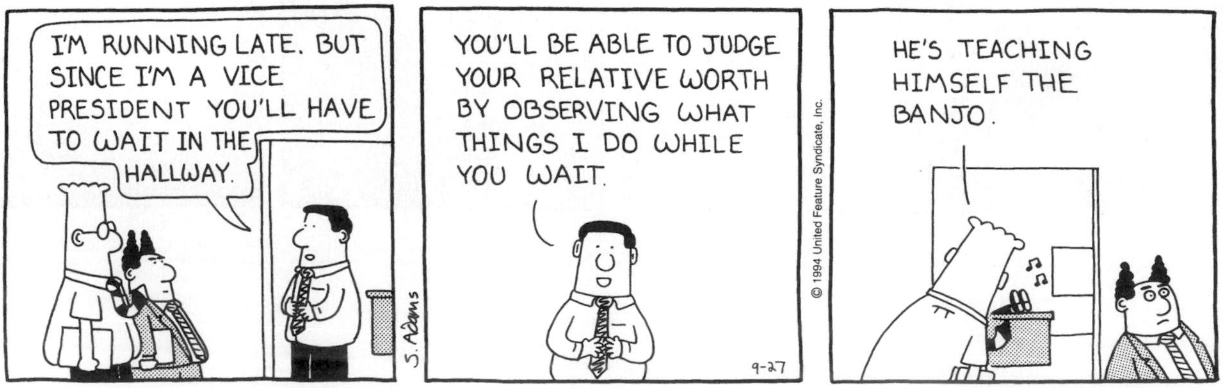
I'M RUNNING LATE. BUT SINCE I'M A VICE PRESIDENT YOU'LL HAVE TO WAIT IN THE HALLWAY.
YOU'LL BE ABLE TO JUDGE YOUR RELATIVE WORTH BY OBSERVING WHAT THINGS I DO WHILE YOU WAIT.
© 1994 United Feature Syndicate, Inc.
HE'S TEACHING HIMSELF THE BANJO.

BOSS TYPES
FIND YOUR BOSS ON THIS HANDY REFERENCE.
S. ADAMS
HOSTAGE TAKER: TRAPS YOU IN YOUR CUBICLE AND TALKS YOUR EARS OFF.
BLAH BLAH
OW!!
FRAUD: USES VIGOROUS HEAD-NODDING TO SIMULATE COMPREHENSION.
THEN WE'LL SUBNET OUR I.P. ADDRESSES.
OH YEAH OH YEAH
MOTIVATIONAL LIAR: HAS NO CLUE WHAT YOU DO BUT SAYS YOU'RE THE BEST.
NOBODY CAN DO WHAT YOU DO!!
EXCEPT A MUSHROOM.
OVER PROMOTED: TRIES TO MASK INCOMPETENCE WITH POOR COMMUNICATION.
LET'S QUALITIZE OUR PARADIGM SO WE DON'T OVER INUNDATE WITH DATUMS.
© 1995 United Feature Syndicate, Inc.
WEASEL: TAKES CREDIT FOR YOUR HARD WORK.
THIS BONUS IS FOR BRILLIANTLY FORCING YOUR STAFF TO WORK 80 HOUR WEEKS.
IT WASN'T EASY!
2-19
MOSES: PERPETUALLY WAITS FOR CLEAR SIGNALS FROM ABOVE.
DON'T DO ANYTHING IMPORTANT YET.
NEVER HAVE.
PERFECT BOSS: DIES OF NATURAL CAUSES ON A THURSDAY AFTERNOON.
SHOULD WE DO SOMETHING?
THREE DAY WEEKEND!

YOU ALL KNOW OUR PRESIDENT, MISTER GOODENRICH. HE'S HERE TO ANSWER ANY QUESTIONS YOU HAVE.
S. Adams
WHY AREN'T THERE ANY WOMEN OR MINORITIES IN SENIOR MANAGEMENT POSITIONS?
WE THINK WOMEN ARE FOR MAKING BABIES. AS FOR MINORITIES, WE FEAR THEM.
HOW CAN YOU JUSTIFY YOUR TEN MILLION DOLLAR SALARY WHEN PROFITS ARE DOWN?
HA HA! THE BOARD OF DIRECTORS ARE FRIENDS OF MINE AND IT'S NOT THEIR MONEY THEY'RE SPEND-ING.
© 1993 United Feature Syndicate, Inc.
WHY DOES THE COMPANY KEEP TALKING ABOUT EMPLOYEE TRAINING WHILE AT THE SAME TIME SLASHING THE TRAINING BUDGET?
WE THINK YOU'RE TOO DUMB TO TRAIN. WE'LL HIRE PEOPLE FROM THE OUTSIDE IF WE NEED TALENT.
7-25
I MUST SAY, YOUR HONESTY IS KIND OF REFRESHING.
AND YOU'RE ALL FIRED FOR ASKING QUESTIONS.

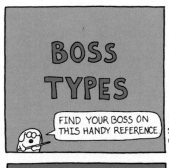

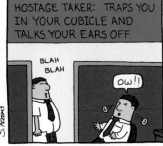

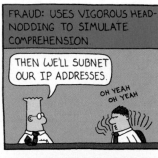

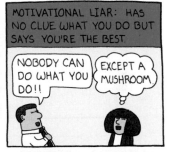

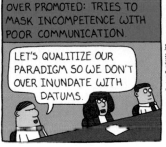

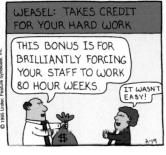

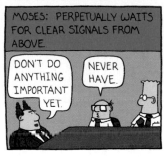

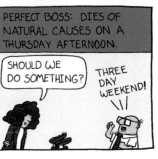

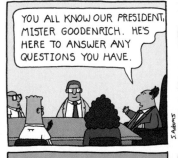

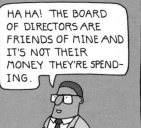

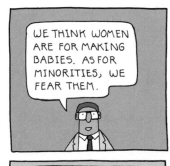

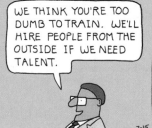

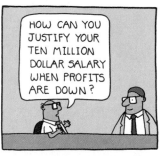

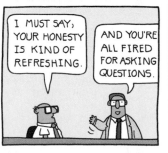

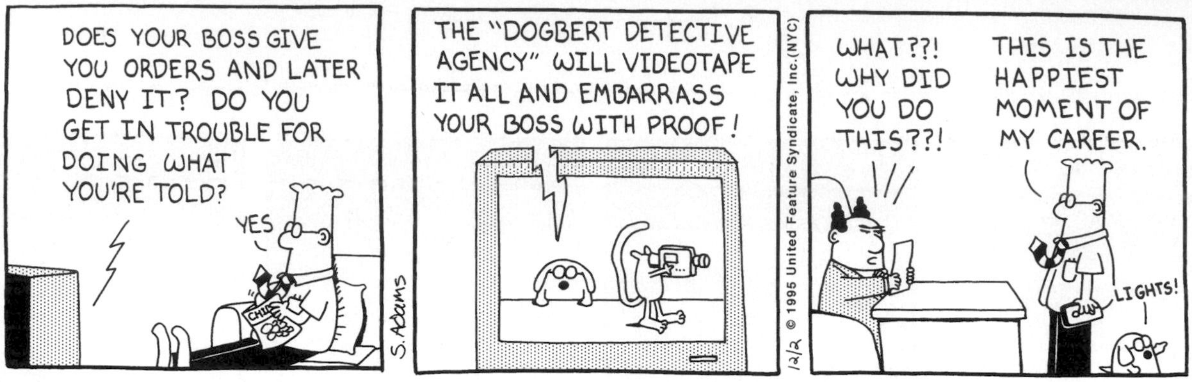
DOES YOUR BOSS GIVE YOU ORDERS AND LATER DENY IT? DO YOU GET IN TROUBLE FOR DOING WHAT YOU'RE TOLD?
YES
S. Adams
THE "DOGBERT DETECTIVE AGENCY" WILL VIDEOTAPE IT ALL AND EMBARRASS YOUR BOSS WITH PROOF!
12/2 © 1995 United Feature Syndicate, Inc.(NYC)
WHAT??! WHY DID YOU DO THIS??!
THIS IS THE HAPPIEST MOMENT OF MY CAREER.
LIGHTS!

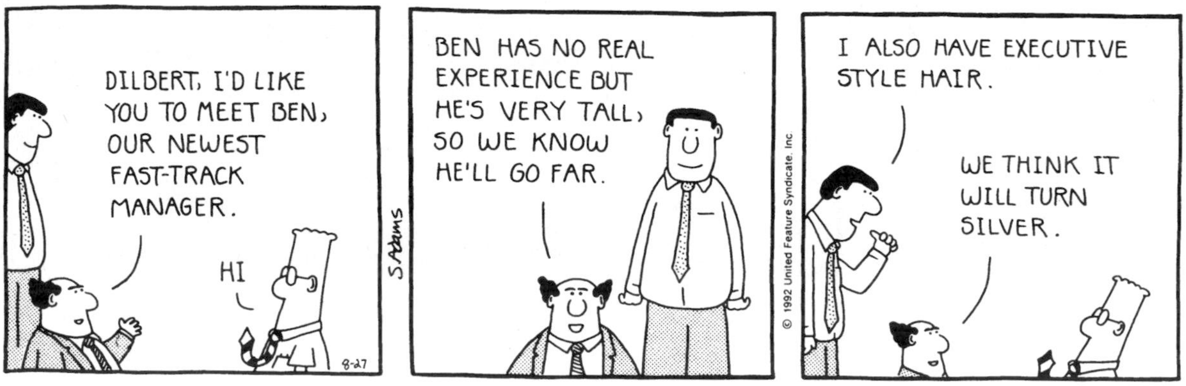
DILBERT, I'D LIKE YOU TO MEET BEN, OUR NEWEST FAST-TRACK MANAGER.
HI
8-27
S. Adams
BEN HAS NO REAL EXPERIENCE BUT HE'S VERY TALL, SO WE KNOW HE'LL GO FAR.
© 1992 United Feature Syndicate, Inc.
I ALSO HAVE EXECUTIVE STYLE HAIR.
WE THINK IT WILL TURN SILVER.

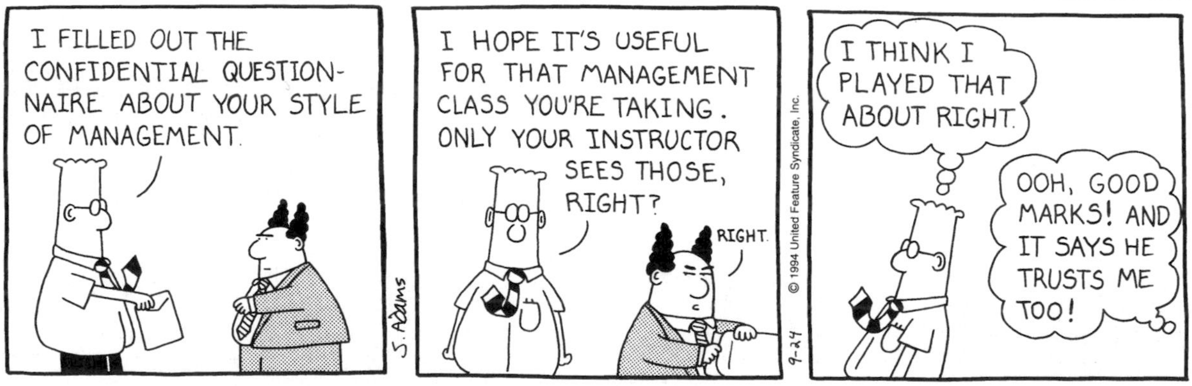
I FILLED OUT THE CONFIDENTIAL QUESTIONNAIRE ABOUT YOUR STYLE OF MANAGEMENT.
S. Adams
I HOPE IT'S USEFUL FOR THAT MANAGEMENT CLASS YOU'RE TAKING. ONLY YOUR INSTRUCTOR SEES THOSE, RIGHT?
RIGHT.
9-24 © 1994 United Feature Syndicate, Inc.
I THINK I PLAYED THAT ABOUT RIGHT.
OOH, GOOD MARKS! AND IT SAYS HE TRUSTS ME TOO!

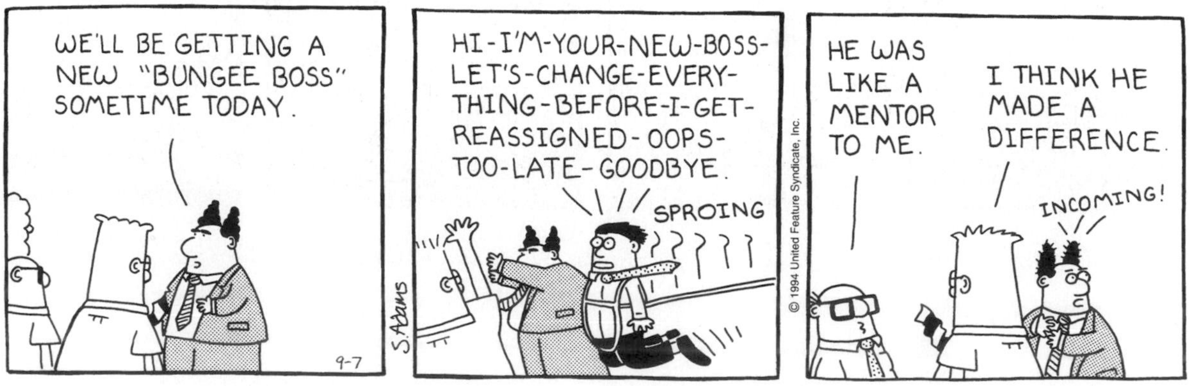
WE'LL BE GETTING A NEW "BUNGEE BOSS" SOMETIME TODAY.
9-7
S. Adams
HI-I'M-YOUR-NEW-BOSS-LET'S-CHANGE-EVERYTHING-BEFORE-I-GET-REASSIGNED-OOPS-TOO-LATE-GOODBYE.
SPROING
© 1994 United Feature Syndicate, Inc.
HE WAS LIKE A MENTOR TO ME.
I THINK HE MADE A DIFFERENCE.
INCOMING!

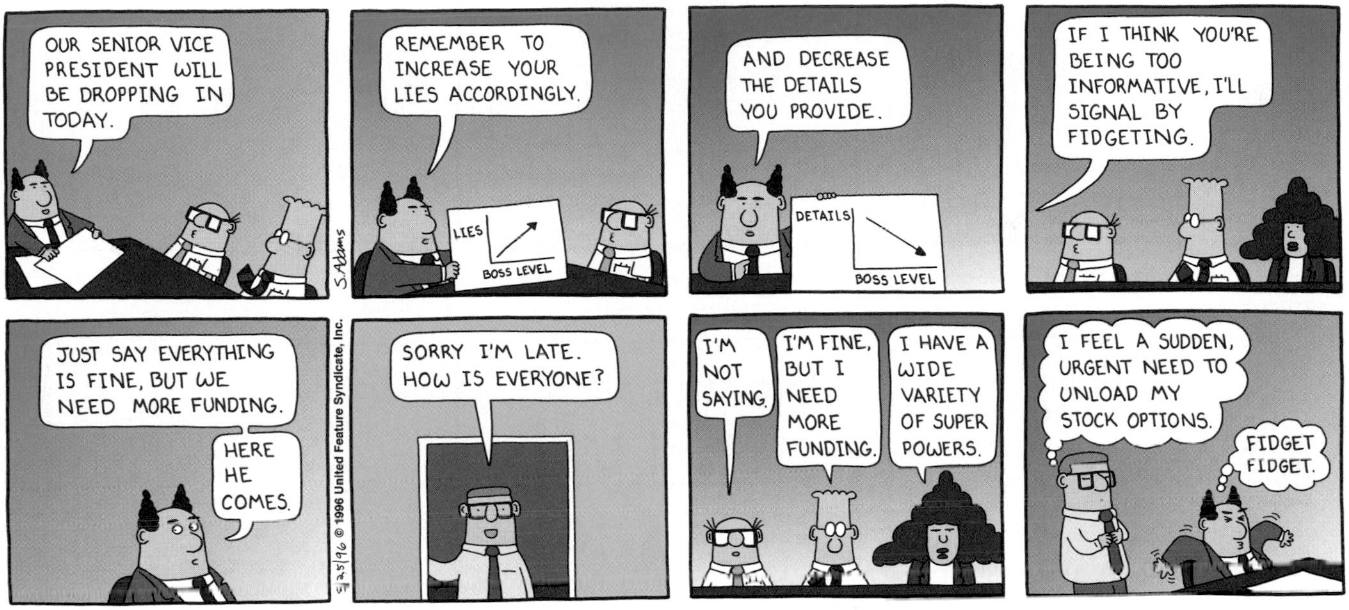
OUR SENIOR VICE PRESIDENT WILL BE DROPPING IN TODAY.
REMEMBER TO INCREASE YOUR LIES ACCORDINGLY.
LIES
BOSS LEVEL
AND DECREASE THE DETAILS YOU PROVIDE.
DETAILS
BOSS LEVEL
IF I THINK YOU'RE BEING TOO INFORMATIVE, I'LL SIGNAL BY FIDGETING.
JUST SAY EVERYTHING IS FINE, BUT WE NEED MORE FUNDING.
HERE HE COMES.
SORRY I'M LATE. HOW IS EVERYONE?
I'M NOT SAYING.
I'M FINE, BUT I NEED MORE FUNDING.
I HAVE A WIDE VARIETY OF SUPER POWERS.
I FEEL A SUDDEN, URGENT NEED TO UNLOAD MY STOCK OPTIONS.
FIDGET FIDGET.
S.Adams
5/25/96 © 1996 United Feature Syndicate, Inc.

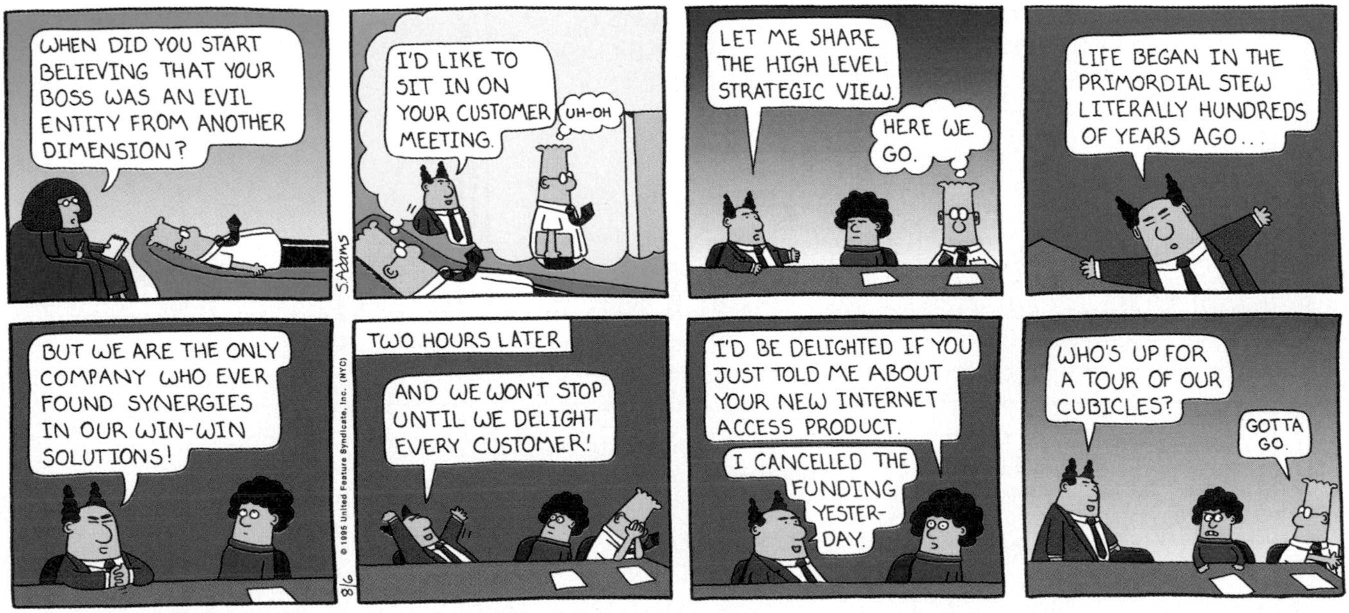
WHEN DID YOU START BELIEVING THAT YOUR BOSS WAS AN EVIL ENTITY FROM ANOTHER DIMENSION?
I'D LIKE TO SIT IN ON YOUR CUSTOMER MEETING.
UH-OH
LET ME SHARE THE HIGH LEVEL STRATEGIC VIEW.
HERE WE GO.
LIFE BEGAN IN THE PRIMORDIAL STEW LITERALLY HUNDREDS OF YEARS AGO...
BUT WE ARE THE ONLY COMPANY WHO EVER FOUND SYNERGIES IN OUR WIN-WIN SOLUTIONS!
TWO HOURS LATER
AND WE WON'T STOP UNTIL WE DELIGHT EVERY CUSTOMER!
I'D BE DELIGHTED IF YOU JUST TOLD ME ABOUT YOUR NEW INTERNET ACCESS PRODUCT.
I CANCELLED THE FUNDING YESTER-DAY.
WHO'S UP FOR A TOUR OF OUR CUBICLES?
GOTTA GO.
S.Adams
8/6 © 1995 United Feature Syndicate, Inc. (NYC)

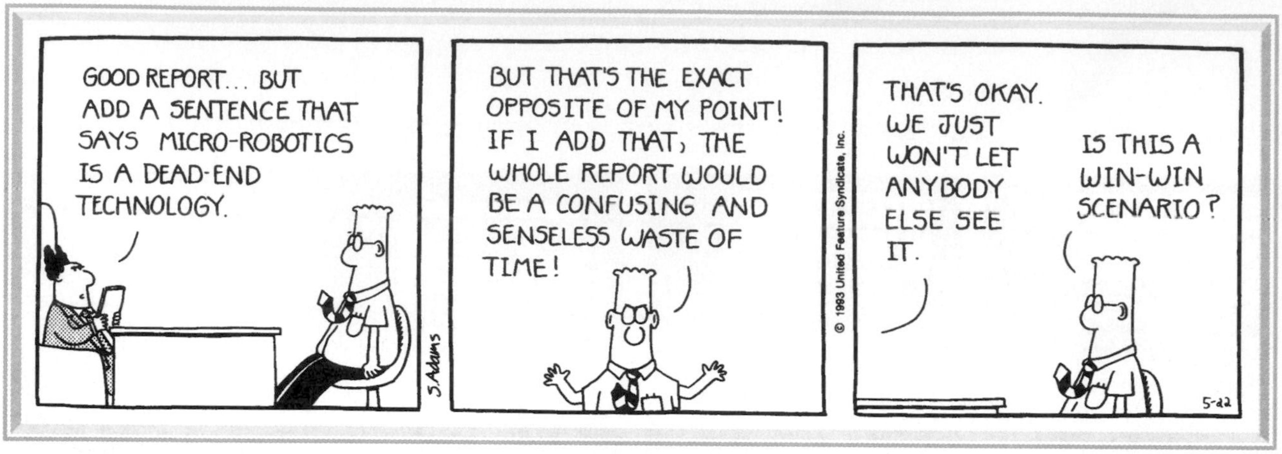
GOOD REPORT... BUT ADD A SENTENCE THAT SAYS MICRO-ROBOTICS IS A DEAD-END TECHNOLOGY.
BUT THAT'S THE EXACT OPPOSITE OF MY POINT! IF I ADD THAT, THE WHOLE REPORT WOULD BE A CONFUSING AND SENSELESS WASTE OF TIME!
THAT'S OKAY. WE JUST WON'T LET ANYBODY ELSE SEE IT.
IS THIS A WIN-WIN SCENARIO?
© 1993 United Feature Syndicate, Inc.

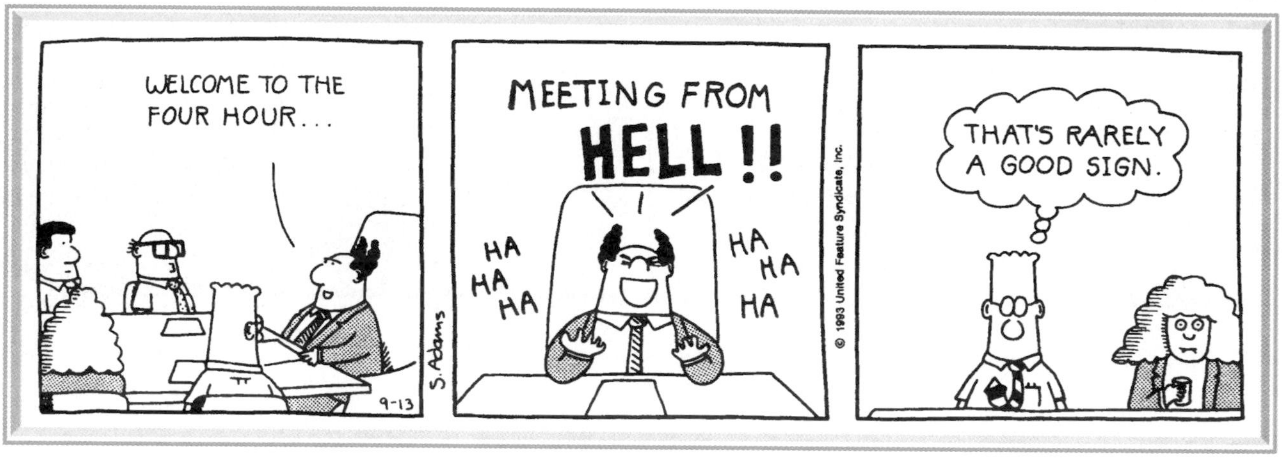
WELCOME TO THE FOUR HOUR...
MEETING FROM HELL!!
HA HA HA
HA HA HA
THAT'S RARELY A GOOD SIGN.
© 1993 United Feature Syndicate, Inc.

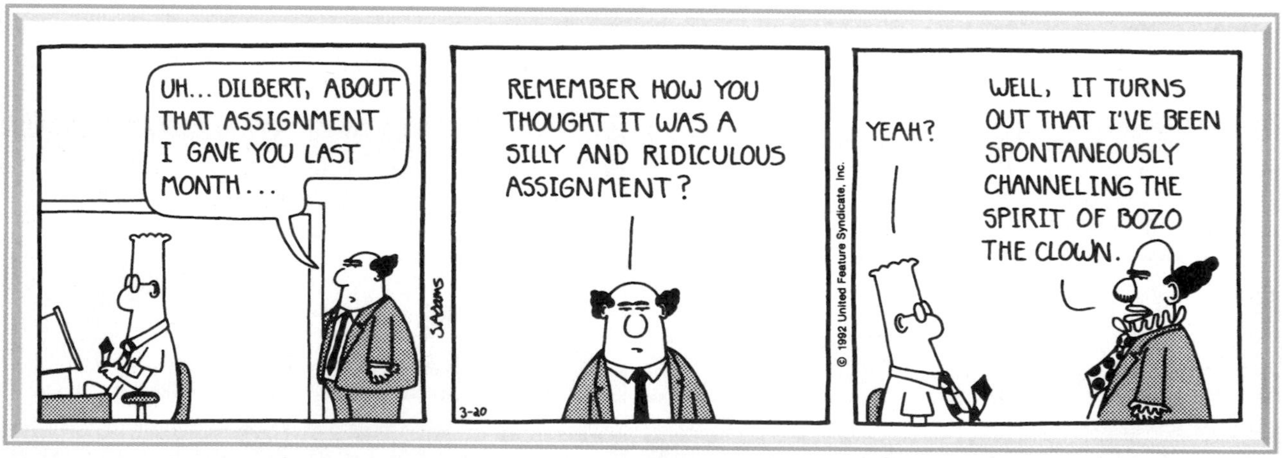
UH... DILBERT, ABOUT THAT ASSIGNMENT I GAVE YOU LAST MONTH...
REMEMBER HOW YOU THOUGHT IT WAS A SILLY AND RIDICULOUS ASSIGNMENT?
YEAH?
WELL, IT TURNS OUT THAT I'VE BEEN SPONTANEOUSLY CHANNELING THE SPIRIT OF BOZO THE CLOWN.
© 1992 United Feature Syndicate, Inc.

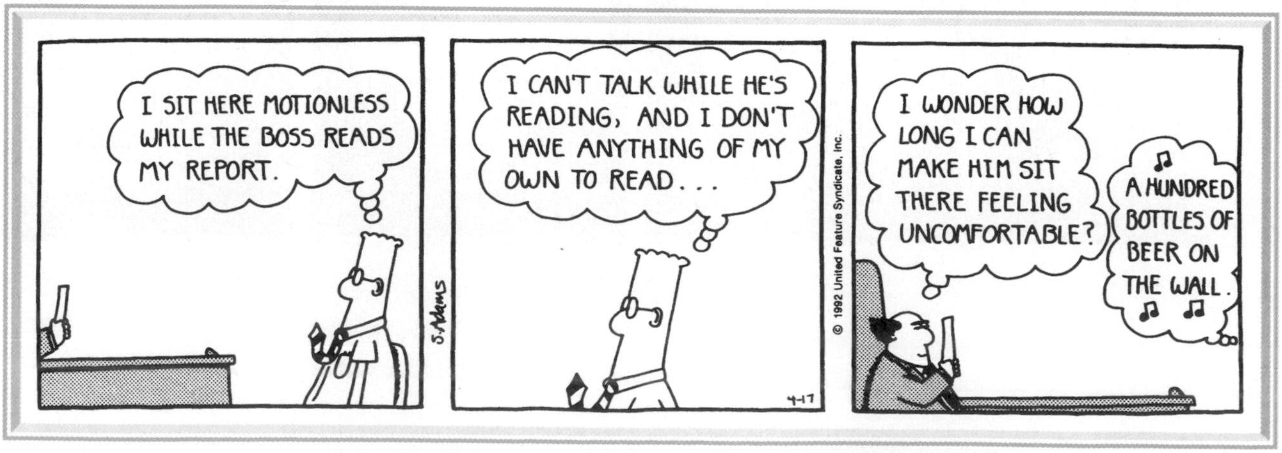
I SIT HERE MOTIONLESS WHILE THE BOSS READS MY REPORT.
I CAN'T TALK WHILE HE'S READING, AND I DON'T HAVE ANYTHING OF MY OWN TO READ...
I WONDER HOW LONG I CAN MAKE HIM SIT THERE FEELING UNCOMFORTABLE?
A HUNDRED BOTTLES OF BEER ON THE WALL.
© 1992 United Feature Syndicate, Inc.

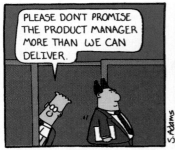

PLEASE DON'T PROMISE THE PRODUCT MANAGER MORE THAN WE CAN DELIVER.
WE NEED A TOTALLY NEW SOFTWARE INTERFACE IN ONE MONTH.
YOU GOT IT!
AND REWRITE THE OPERATING SYSTEM SO WE DOMINATE THE INDUSTRY.
CONCURRENT DEVELOPMENT.
CHECK
SUDDENLY I FEEL OMNIPOTENT.
I WANT ALL NEW HARDWARE, ANTI-GRAVITY PACKAGING, HOLOGRAPHIC AGENTS..
YAWN YAWN
CAN YOUR TEAM REALLY DO THAT IN A MONTH?
LET ME GET THEIR REACTION.
AAAGH!!
PESSIMISM WILL NOT LOOK GOOD ON YOUR PERFORMANCE REVIEW.
TWITCH
S. Adams
8/20
© 1998 United Feature Syndicate, Inc. (NYC)

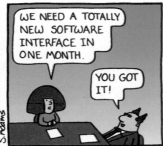

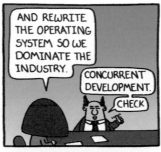

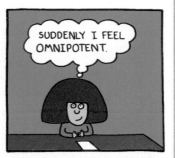

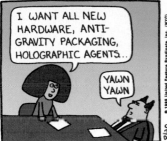

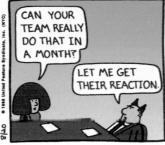

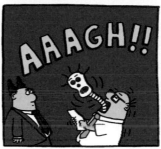

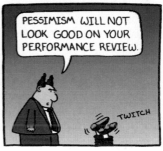

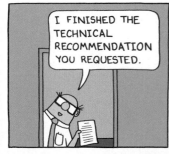

I FINISHED THE TECHNICAL RECOMMENDATION YOU REQUESTED.
AT FIRST I WAS MIFFED THAT YOU TOLD ME WHAT RECOMMENDATION YOU WANTED.
IT MADE ME FEEL USELESS AND WEAK.
BUT RATHER THAN DWELL ON MY POWERLESSNESS...
I DECIDED TO FIND JOY IN THE ONE DECISION I CAN MAKE.
I CHOSE A HELVETICA TYPE FONT.
AND I NEVER LOOKED BACK.
OH, SO THAT'S WHAT'S WRONG WITH IT.
I COACH AND I COACH, BUT THEY STILL WALK OUT OF HERE ALL RUBBER-LEGGED.
2/15/98
© 1998 United Feature Syndicate, Inc.

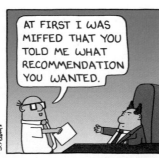

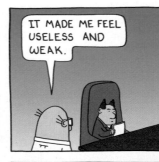

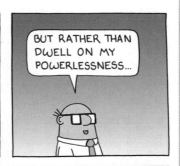

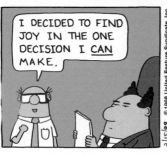

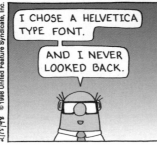

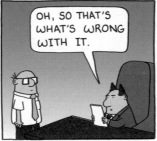

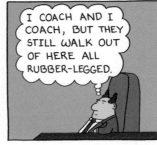

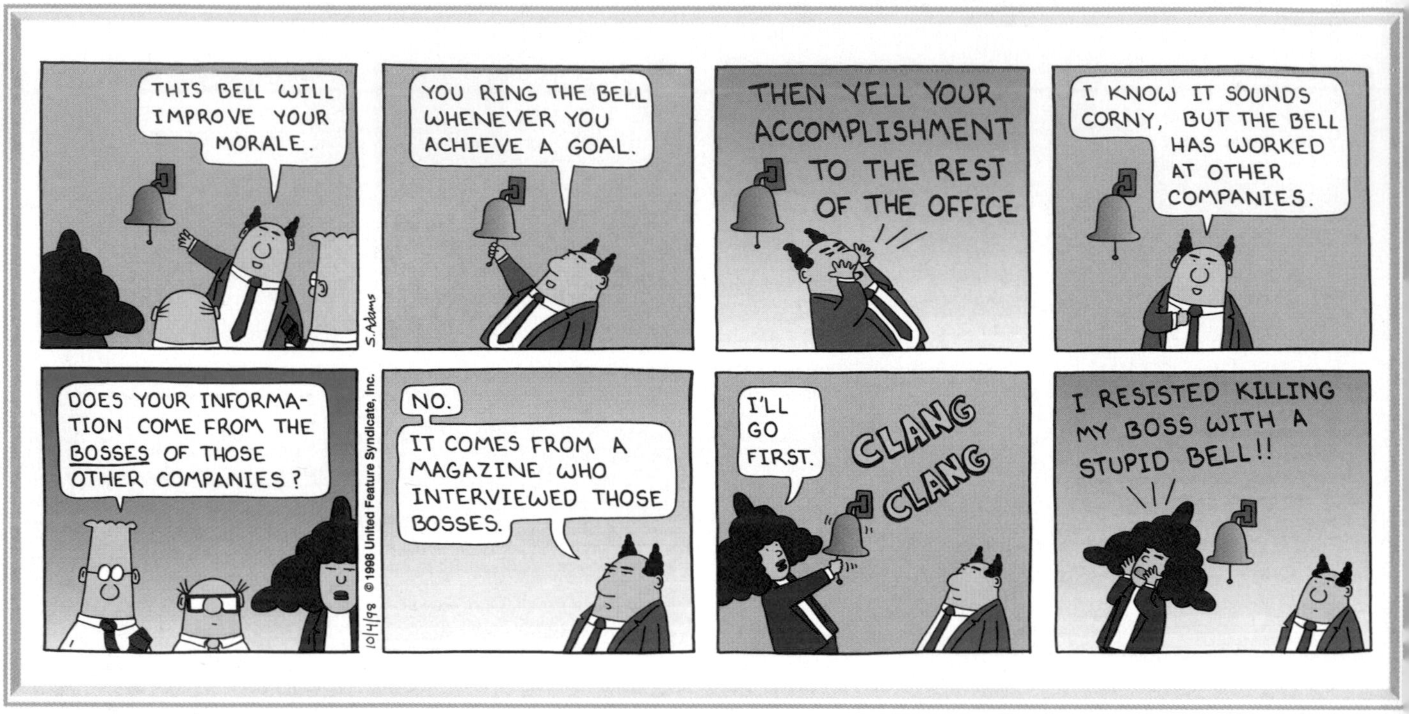
THIS BELL WILL IMPROVE YOUR MORALE.
YOU RING THE BELL WHENEVER YOU ACHIEVE A GOAL.
THEN YELL YOUR ACCOMPLISHMENT TO THE REST OF THE OFFICE
I KNOW IT SOUNDS CORNY, BUT THE BELL HAS WORKED AT OTHER COMPANIES.
DOES YOUR INFORMATION COME FROM THE BOSSES OF THOSE OTHER COMPANIES?
NO.
IT COMES FROM A MAGAZINE WHO INTERVIEWED THOSE BOSSES.
I'LL GO FIRST.
CLANG
CLANG
I RESISTED KILLING MY BOSS WITH A STUPID BELL!!
S. Adams
10/4/98 © 1998 United Feature Syndicate, Inc.

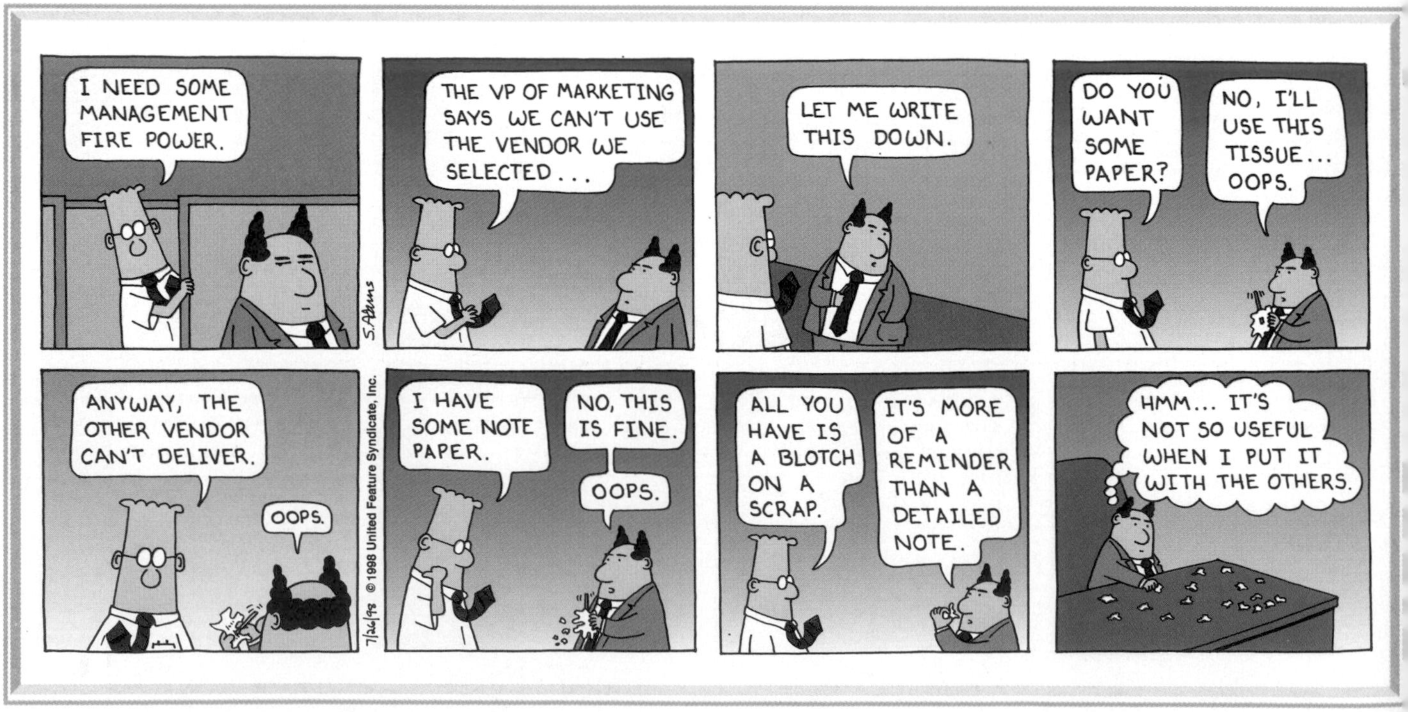
I NEED SOME MANAGEMENT FIRE POWER.
THE VP OF MARKETING SAYS WE CAN'T USE THE VENDOR WE SELECTED...
LET ME WRITE THIS DOWN.
DO YOU WANT SOME PAPER?
NO, I'LL USE THIS TISSUE... OOPS.
ANYWAY, THE OTHER VENDOR CAN'T DELIVER.
OOPS.
I HAVE SOME NOTE PAPER.
NO, THIS IS FINE.
OOPS.
ALL YOU HAVE IS A BLOTCH ON A SCRAP.
IT'S MORE OF A REMINDER THAN A DETAILED NOTE.
HMM... IT'S NOT SO USEFUL WHEN I PUT IT WITH THE OTHERS.
S. Adams
7/26/98 © 1998 United Feature Syndicate, Inc.

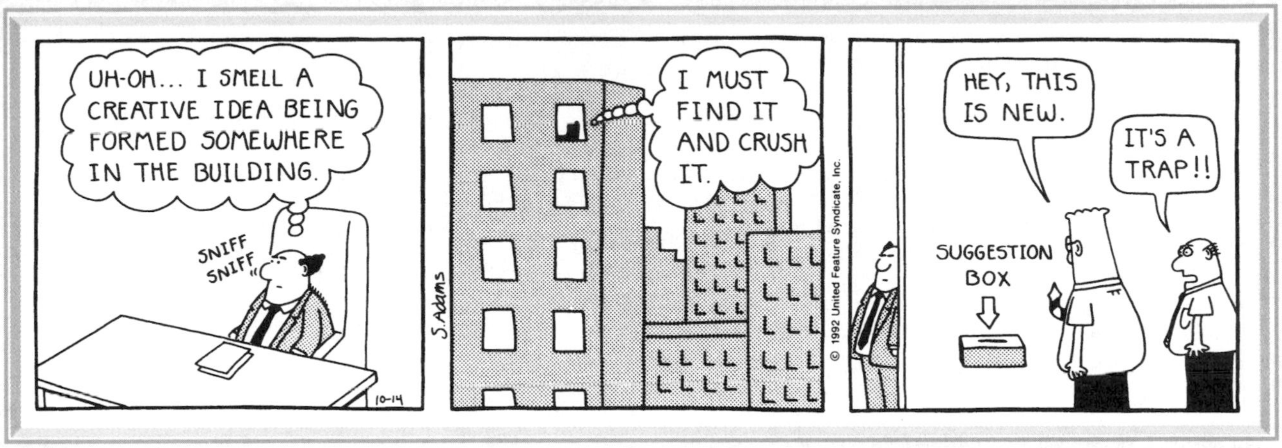
UH-OH... I SMELL A CREATIVE IDEA BEING FORMED SOMEWHERE IN THE BUILDING.
SNIFF SNIFF
I MUST FIND IT AND CRUSH IT.
HEY, THIS IS NEW.
SUGGESTION BOX
IT'S A TRAP!!
© 1992 United Feature Syndicate, Inc.

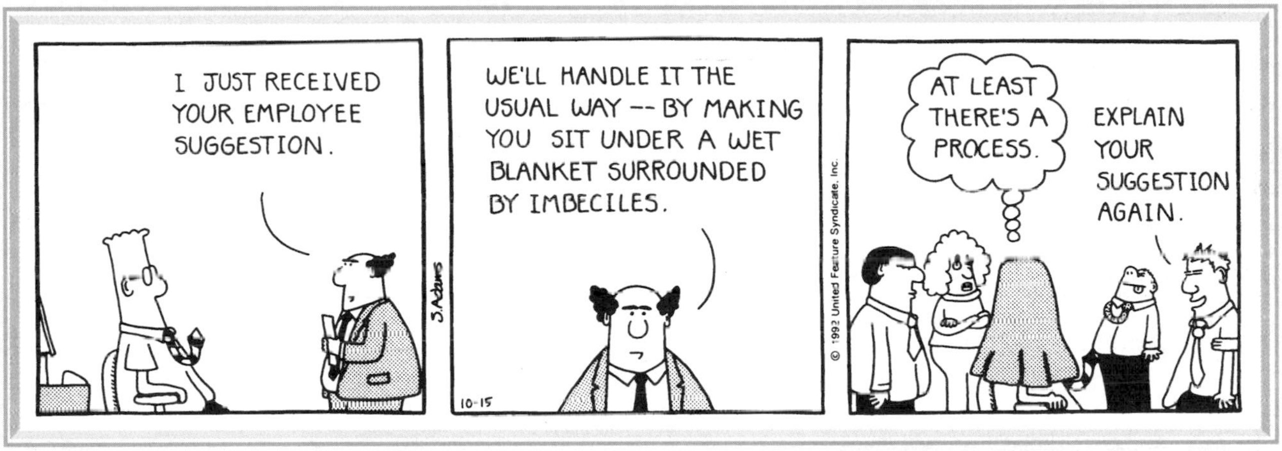
I JUST RECEIVED YOUR EMPLOYEE SUGGESTION.
WE'LL HANDLE IT THE USUAL WAY -- BY MAKING YOU SIT UNDER A WET BLANKET SURROUNDED BY IMBECILES.
AT LEAST THERE'S A PROCESS.
EXPLAIN YOUR SUGGESTION AGAIN.
© 1992 United Feature Syndicate, Inc.

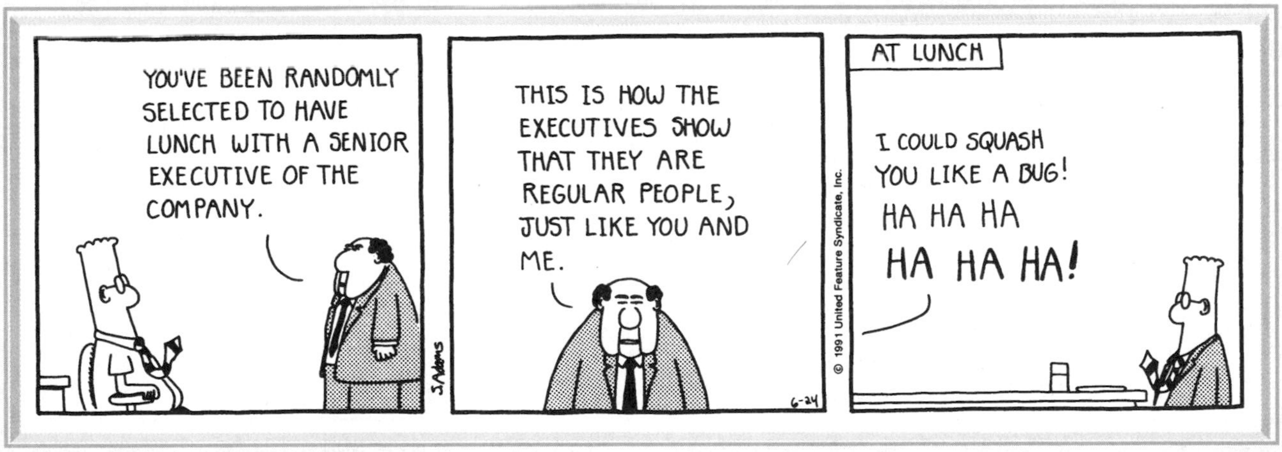
YOU'VE BEEN RANDOMLY SELECTED TO HAVE LUNCH WITH A SENIOR EXECUTIVE OF THE COMPANY.
THIS IS HOW THE EXECUTIVES SHOW THAT THEY ARE REGULAR PEOPLE, JUST LIKE YOU AND ME.
AT LUNCH
I COULD SQUASH YOU LIKE A BUG! HA HA HA HA HA HA!
© 1991 United Feature Syndicate, Inc.

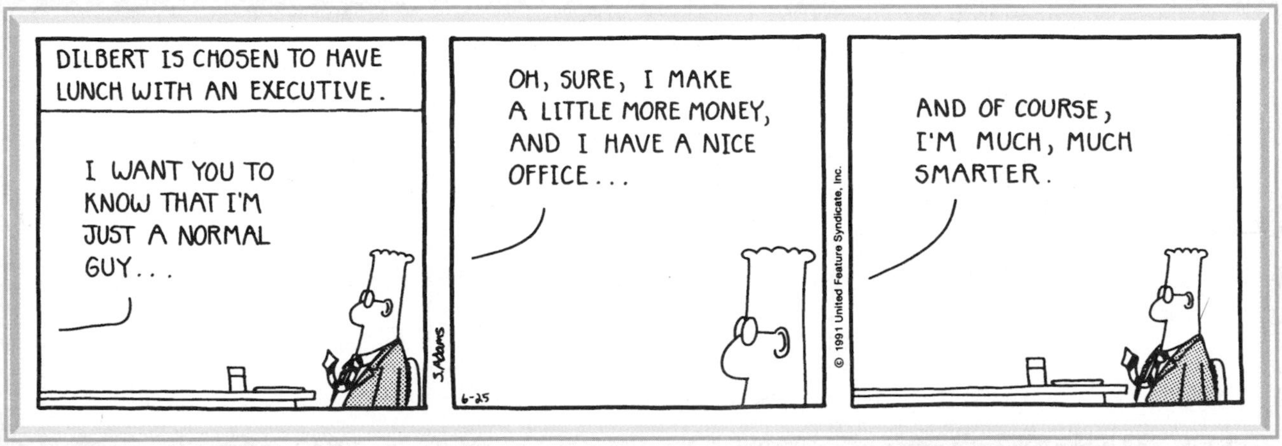
DILBERT IS CHOSEN TO HAVE LUNCH WITH AN EXECUTIVE.
I WANT YOU TO KNOW THAT I'M JUST A NORMAL GUY...
OH, SURE, I MAKE A LITTLE MORE MONEY, AND I HAVE A NICE OFFICE...
AND OF COURSE, I'M MUCH, MUCH SMARTER.
© 1991 United Feature Syndicate, Inc.

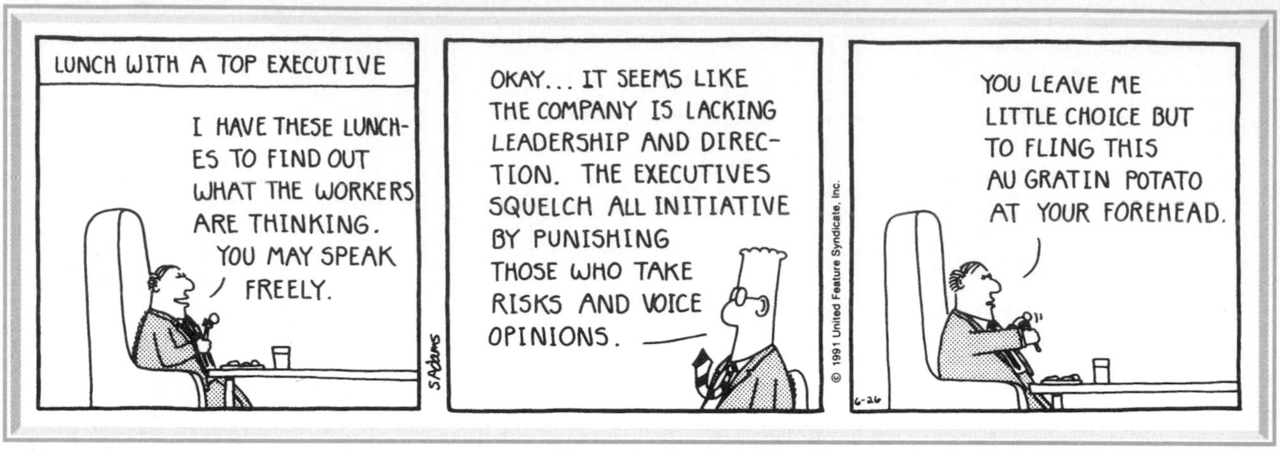
LUNCH WITH A TOP EXECUTIVE
I HAVE THESE LUNCHES TO FIND OUT WHAT THE WORKERS ARE THINKING. YOU MAY SPEAK FREELY.
OKAY... IT SEEMS LIKE THE COMPANY IS LACKING LEADERSHIP AND DIRECTION. THE EXECUTIVES SQUELCH ALL INITIATIVE BY PUNISHING THOSE WHO TAKE RISKS AND VOICE OPINIONS.
YOU LEAVE ME LITTLE CHOICE BUT TO FLING THIS AU GRATIN POTATO AT YOUR FOREHEAD.
© 1991 United Feature Syndicate, Inc.
S.Adams
6-26

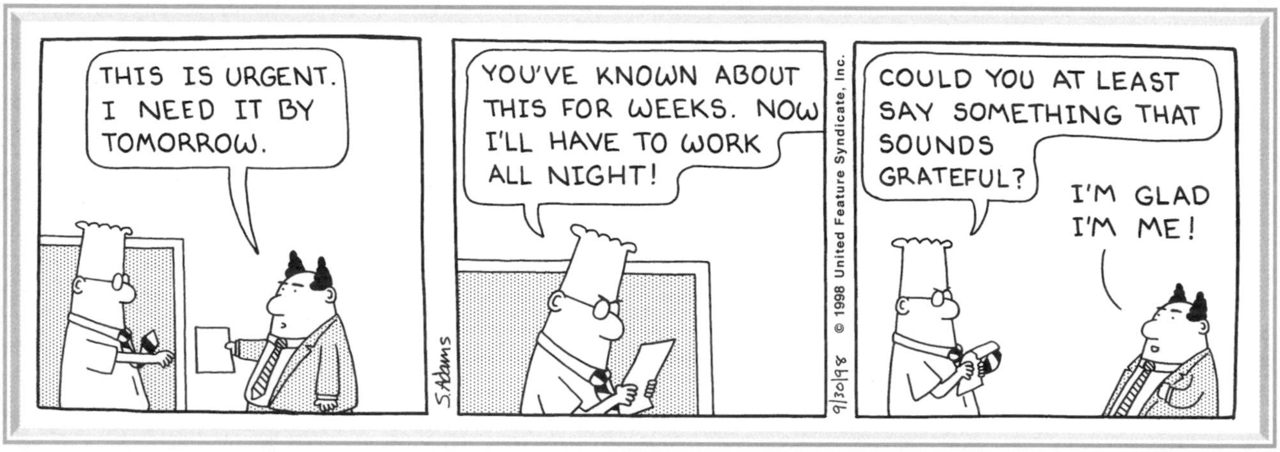
THIS IS URGENT. I NEED IT BY TOMORROW.
YOU'VE KNOWN ABOUT THIS FOR WEEKS. NOW I'LL HAVE TO WORK ALL NIGHT!
COULD YOU AT LEAST SAY SOMETHING THAT SOUNDS GRATEFUL?
I'M GLAD I'M ME!
© 1998 United Feature Syndicate, Inc.
S.Adams
9/30/98

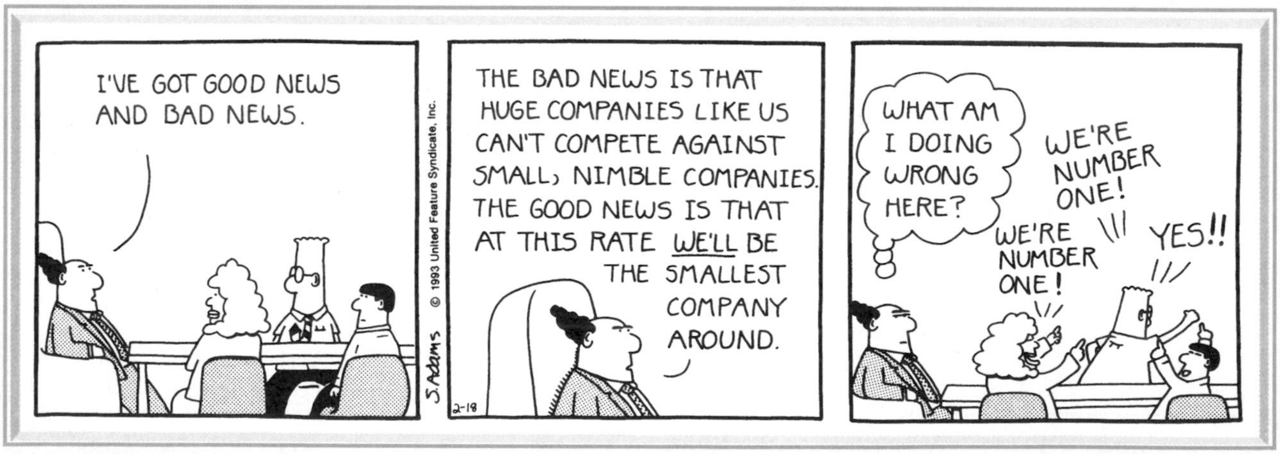
I'VE GOT GOOD NEWS AND BAD NEWS.
THE BAD NEWS IS THAT HUGE COMPANIES LIKE US CAN'T COMPETE AGAINST SMALL, NIMBLE COMPANIES. THE GOOD NEWS IS THAT AT THIS RATE WE'LL BE THE SMALLEST COMPANY AROUND.
WHAT AM I DOING WRONG HERE?
WE'RE NUMBER ONE!
WE'RE NUMBER ONE!
YES!!
© 1993 United Feature Syndicate, Inc.
S.Adams
2-18

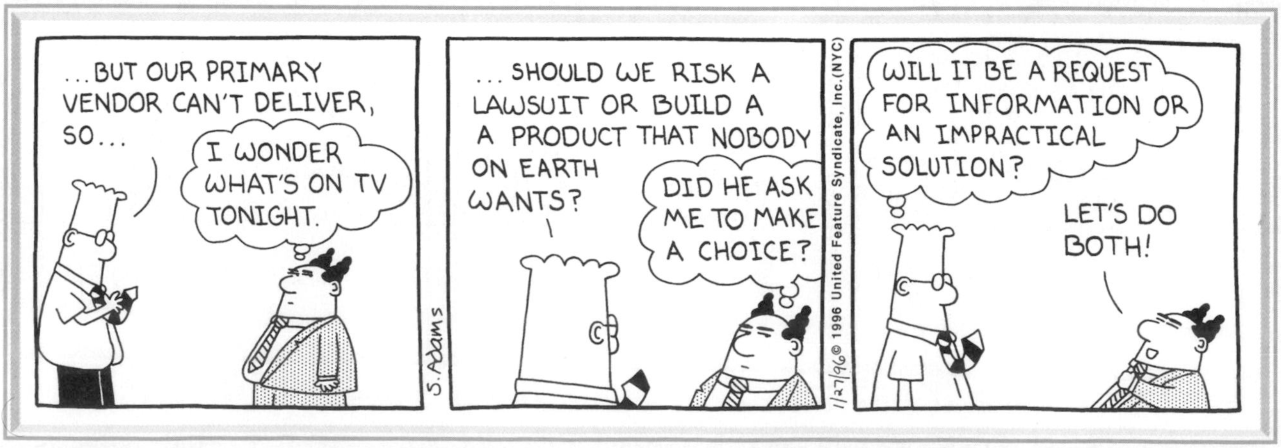
...BUT OUR PRIMARY VENDOR CAN'T DELIVER, SO...
I WONDER WHAT'S ON TV TONIGHT.
...SHOULD WE RISK A LAWSUIT OR BUILD A A PRODUCT THAT NOBODY ON EARTH WANTS?
DID HE ASK ME TO MAKE A CHOICE?
WILL IT BE A REQUEST FOR INFORMATION OR AN IMPRACTICAL SOLUTION?
LET'S DO BOTH!
© 1996 United Feature Syndicate, Inc.(NYC)
S. Adams
1/27/96

IT'S TIME TO GO HOME. THAT MEANS...
HI
RIGHT ON SCHEDULE.
WAIT. LET ME GUESS WHY YOU'RE HERE.
YOU WANT TO DISCUSS A DOCUMENT THAT'S BEEN ON YOUR DESK FOR A MONTH.
IT'S SOMETHING THAT COULD EASILY WAIT UNTIL TOMORROW.
BUT YOU'LL INSIST THAT I HANDLE IT NOW BECAUSE YOU'RE A SOCIOPATH.
WRONG. I MAJORED IN ANTHROPOLOGY.
BUT THAT WAS A SPOOKILY ACCURATE GUESS ABOUT THE DOCUMENT.
S.Adams
1/25/98 © 1998 United Feature Syndicate, Inc.

DID YOU KNOW THAT TWENTY PERCENT OF ALL MICROFLEEMS ARE SUBRADIANTE?
UH-OH. THE BOSS HAS LATCHED ONTO SOME OBSCURE ENGINEERING FACT.
THIS IS GOING TO BE PAINFUL.
JUST THINK OF THE IMPLICATIONS. IT MEANS EIGHTY PERCENT OF MICROFLEEMS ARE NOT SUBRADIANTE.
MAYBE I CAN HIDE UNDER THE DESK UNTIL THIS BLOWS OVER.
DON'T YOU THINK IT'S FASCINATING? I MEAN, WHAT WITH THE IMPLICATIONS AND ALL...
OKAY, OKAY. I ACKNOWLEDGE YOUR INCREDIBLE GRASP OF TECH-NOLOGY ISSUES.
IT ALMOST MAKES ME CURIOUS WHAT A MICROFLEEM IS.
S.Adams
© 1993 United Feature Syndicate, Inc.
5-9

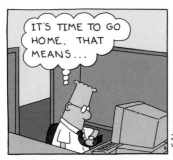

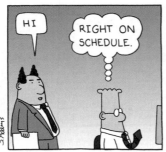

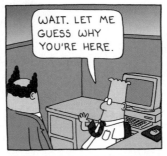

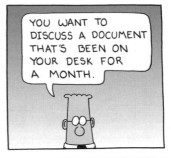

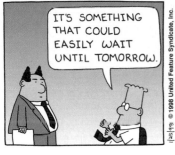

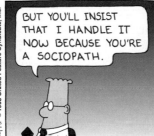

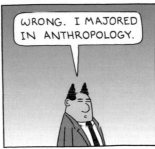

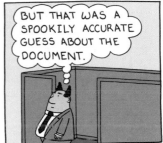

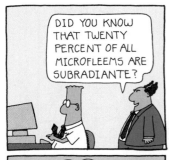

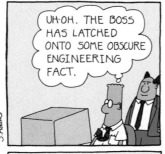

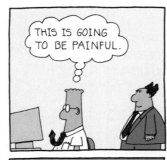

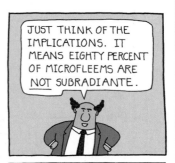

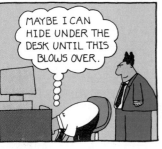

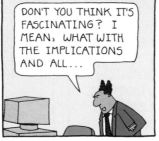

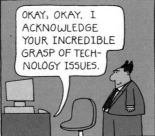

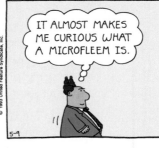

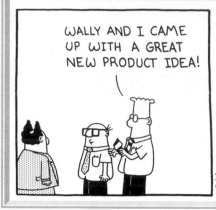

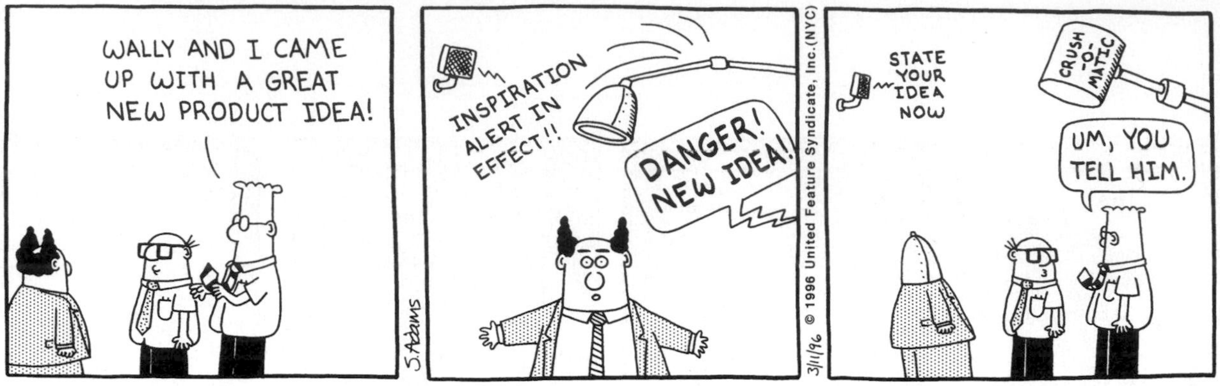
WALLY AND I CAME UP WITH A GREAT NEW PRODUCT IDEA!
INSPIRATION ALERT IN EFFECT!!
DANGER! NEW IDEA!
S. Adams
3/11/96 © 1996 United Feature Syndicate, Inc.(NYC)
STATE YOUR IDEA NOW
CRUSH-O-MATIC
UM, YOU TELL HIM.

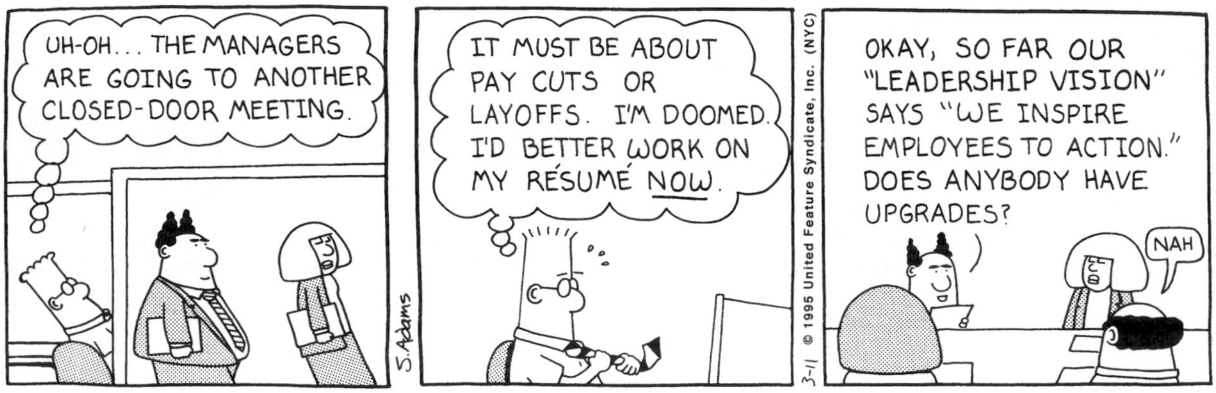
UH-OH... THE MANAGERS ARE GOING TO ANOTHER CLOSED-DOOR MEETING.
S. Adams
IT MUST BE ABOUT PAY CUTS OR LAYOFFS. I'M DOOMED. I'D BETTER WORK ON MY RÉSUMÉ NOW.
3-11 © 1995 United Feature Syndicate, Inc. (NYC)
OKAY, SO FAR OUR "LEADERSHIP VISION" SAYS "WE INSPIRE EMPLOYEES TO ACTION." DOES ANYBODY HAVE UPGRADES?
NAH

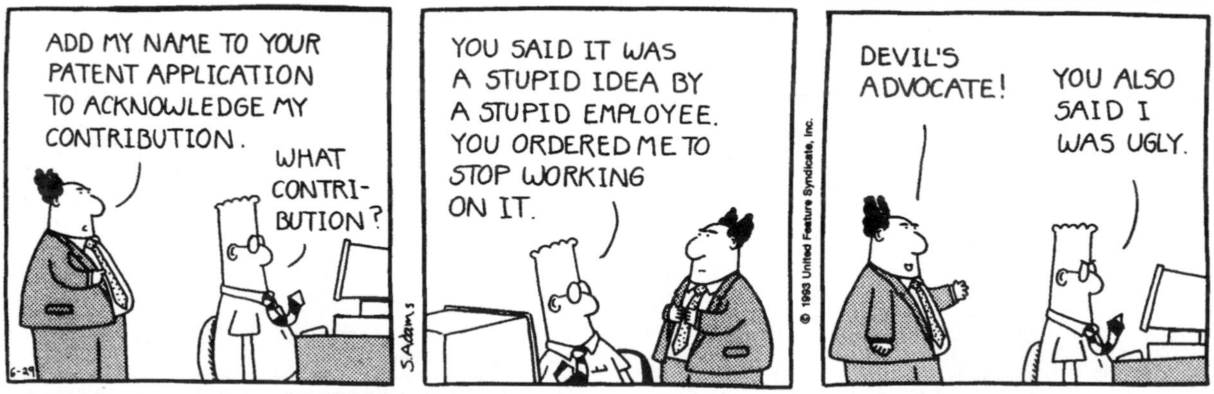
ADD MY NAME TO YOUR PATENT APPLICATION TO ACKNOWLEDGE MY CONTRIBUTION.
WHAT CONTRI-BUTION?
6-29
S. Adams
YOU SAID IT WAS A STUPID IDEA BY A STUPID EMPLOYEE. YOU ORDERED ME TO STOP WORKING ON IT.
© 1993 United Feature Syndicate, Inc.
DEVIL'S ADVOCATE!
YOU ALSO SAID I WAS UGLY.

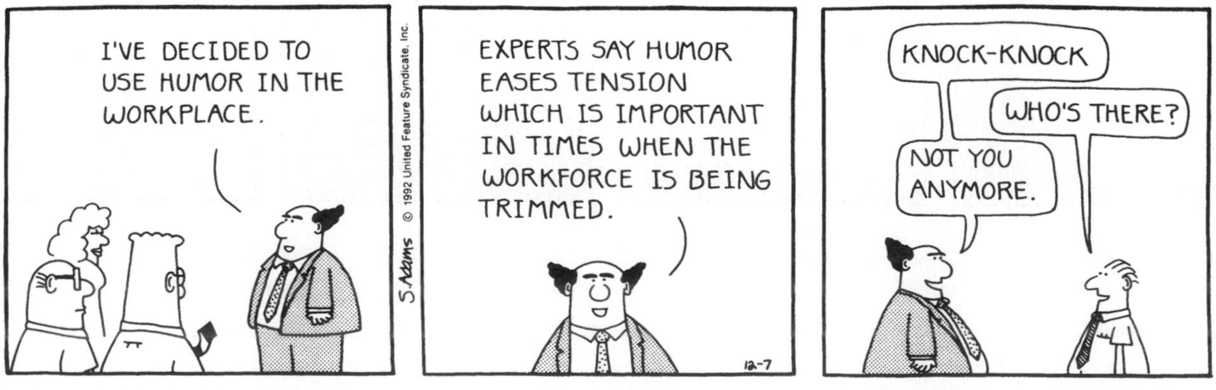
I'VE DECIDED TO USE HUMOR IN THE WORKPLACE.
S. Adams © 1992 United Feature Syndicate, Inc.
EXPERTS SAY HUMOR EASES TENSION WHICH IS IMPORTANT IN TIMES WHEN THE WORKFORCE IS BEING TRIMMED.
12-7
KNOCK-KNOCK
WHO'S THERE?
NOT YOU ANYMORE.

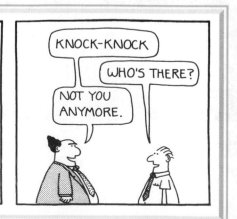

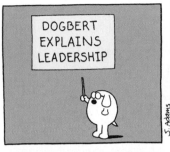

DOGBERT EXPLAINS LEADERSHIP
S. Adams
LEADERS START THEIR CAREERS AS MORONS.
THEY ARE DRAWN TO MEETINGS LIKE MOTHS TO A PORCH LIGHT.
THE SUCCESSFUL MORON WILL HAVE A VERY HIGH BLADDER-TO-BRAIN RATIO.
BRAIN
BLADDER
THEY PREVAIL IN ALL DECISIONS BECAUSE THEY ARE IMPERVIOUS TO LOGIC OR COFFEE.
LET'S DO IT MY WAY!
OKAY!
© 1995 United Feature Syndicate, Inc.
THESE QUALITIES ARE PERCEIVED AS LEADERSHIP.
YOU'RE PROMOTED!
2-5
AFTER SEVERAL PROMOTIONS THEIR JOB TENDS TO MATCH THEIR TALENTS.
I AWARD YOU THIS AWARD.
CONCLUSION: LEADERSHIP IS NATURE'S WAY OF REMOVING MORONS FROM THE PRODUCTIVE FLOW.

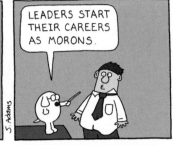

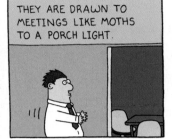

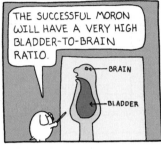

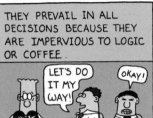

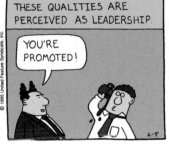

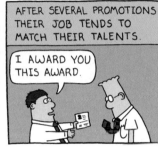

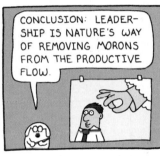

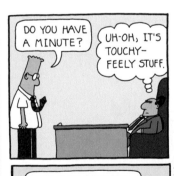

DO YOU HAVE A MINUTE?
UH-OH, IT'S TOUCHY-FEELY STUFF.
WHAT'S GOING TO HAPPEN TO OUR DEPARTMENT? THE RUMORS ARE FLYING.
WHAT HAVE YOU HEARD?
RUMOR HAS IT THAT FLYING LIZARDS FROM THE PLANET ZORB WILL BUY THE COMPANY.
THEY PLAN TO TURN THE EMPLOYEES INTO GIANT CORN DOGS ON STICKS.
S. Adams © 1993 United Feature Syndicate, Inc.
DON'T WORRY ABOUT RUMORS. IT'S BUSINESS AS USUAL FOR NOW.
3-28
GULP
I THINK I HANDLED THAT PRETTY WELL.
ARE YOU SURE THIS WILL IMPRESS THE ZORBIANS?
I HEAR THEY LIKE TEAM PLAYERS.

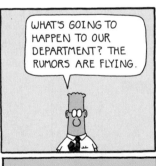

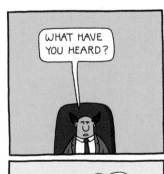

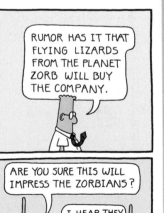

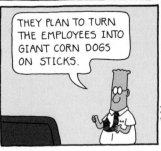

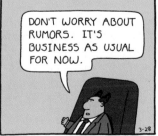

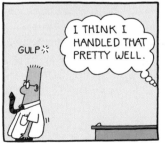

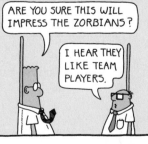

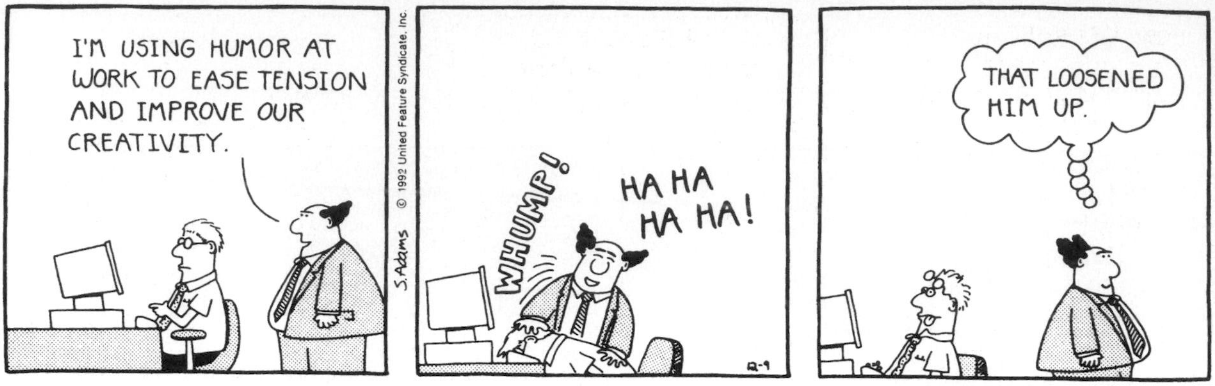
I'M USING HUMOR AT WORK TO EASE TENSION AND IMPROVE OUR CREATIVITY.
© 1992 United Feature Syndicate, Inc.
WHUMP!
HA HA HA HA!
THAT LOOSENED HIM UP.

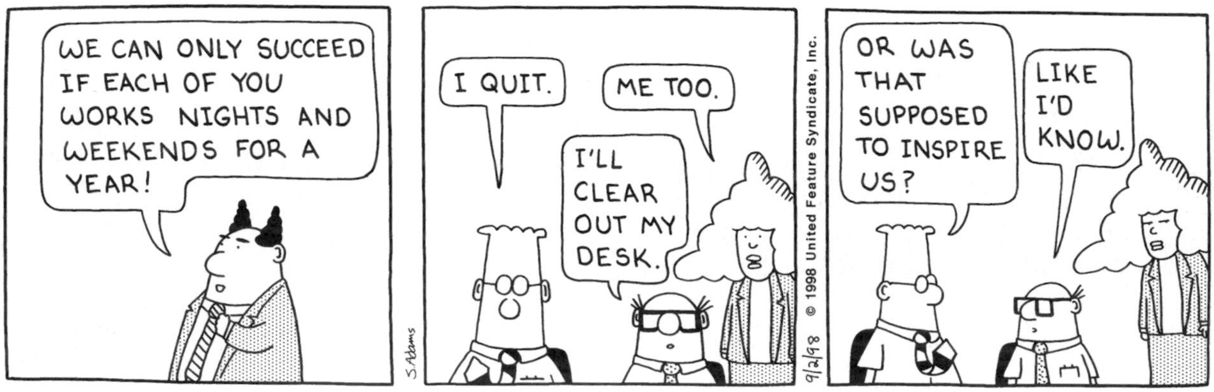
WE CAN ONLY SUCCEED IF EACH OF YOU WORKS NIGHTS AND WEEKENDS FOR A YEAR!
I QUIT.
ME TOO.
I'LL CLEAR OUT MY DESK.
© 1998 United Feature Syndicate, Inc.
OR WAS THAT SUPPOSED TO INSPIRE US?
LIKE I'D KNOW.

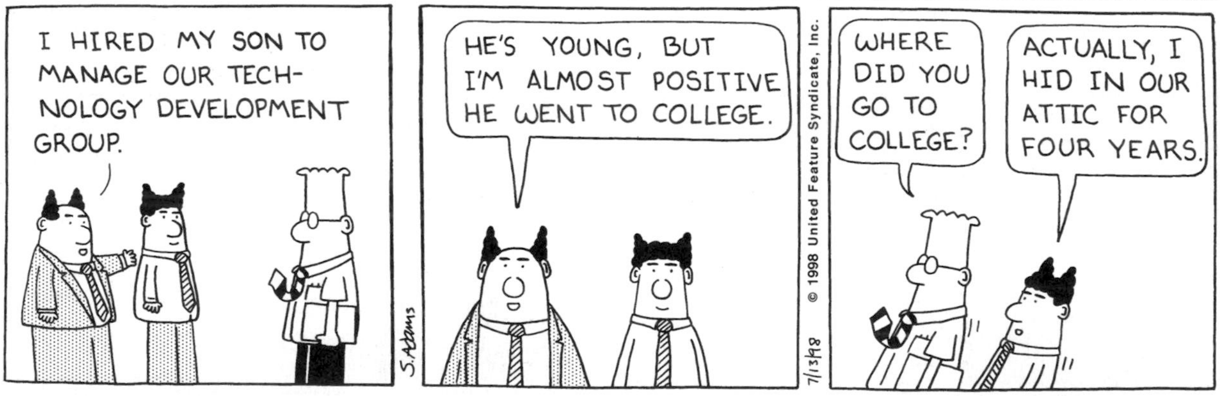
I HIRED MY SON TO MANAGE OUR TECH-NOLOGY DEVELOPMENT GROUP.
HE'S YOUNG, BUT I'M ALMOST POSITIVE HE WENT TO COLLEGE.
© 1998 United Feature Syndicate, Inc.
WHERE DID YOU GO TO COLLEGE?
ACTUALLY, I HID IN OUR ATTIC FOR FOUR YEARS.

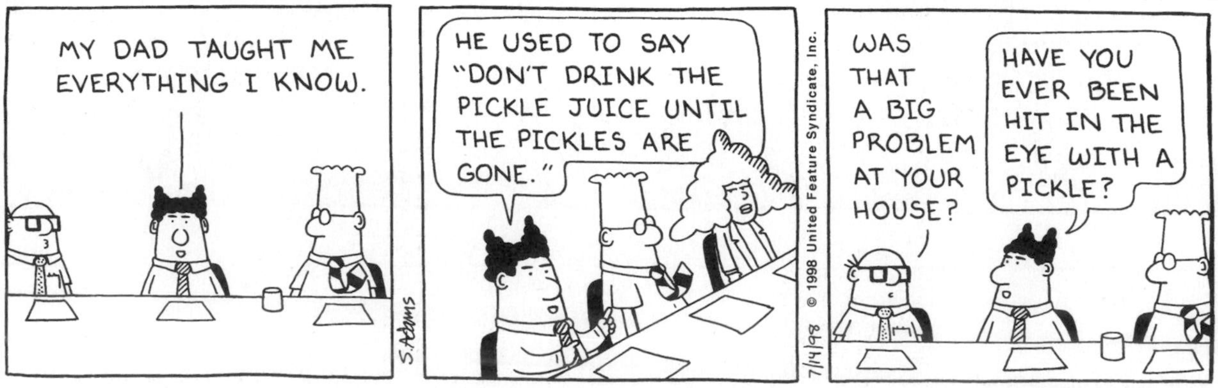
MY DAD TAUGHT ME EVERYTHING I KNOW.
HE USED TO SAY "DON'T DRINK THE PICKLE JUICE UNTIL THE PICKLES ARE GONE."
© 1998 United Feature Syndicate, Inc.
WAS THAT A BIG PROBLEM AT YOUR HOUSE?
HAVE YOU EVER BEEN HIT IN THE EYE WITH A PICKLE?

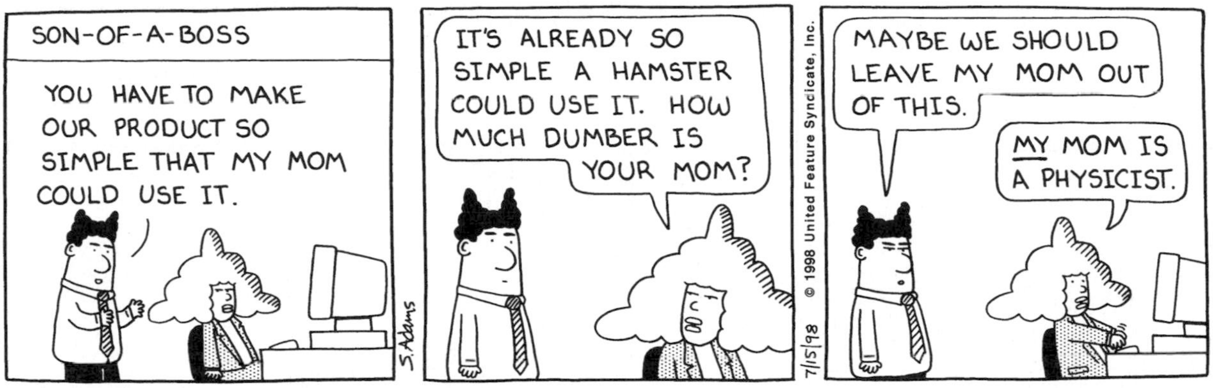
SON-OF-A-BOSS
YOU HAVE TO MAKE OUR PRODUCT SO SIMPLE THAT MY MOM COULD USE IT.
IT'S ALREADY SO SIMPLE A HAMSTER COULD USE IT. HOW MUCH DUMBER IS YOUR MOM?
MAYBE WE SHOULD LEAVE MY MOM OUT OF THIS.
MY MOM IS A PHYSICIST.
S. Adams
7/15/98
© 1998 United Feature Syndicate, Inc.

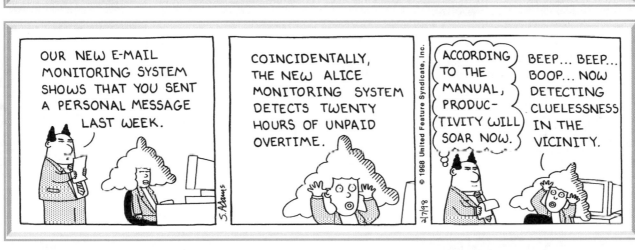

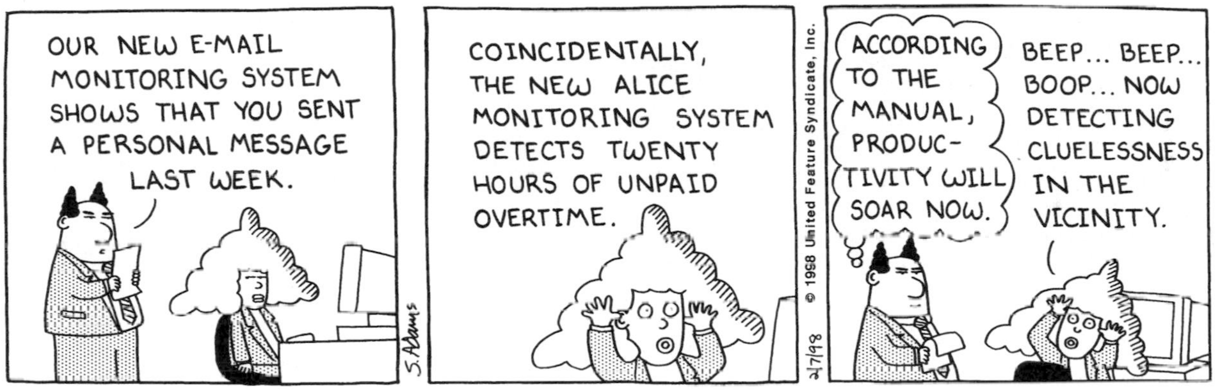
OUR NEW E-MAIL MONITORING SYSTEM SHOWS THAT YOU SENT A PERSONAL MESSAGE LAST WEEK.
COINCIDENTALLY, THE NEW ALICE MONITORING SYSTEM DETECTS TWENTY HOURS OF UNPAID OVERTIME.
ACCORDING TO THE MANUAL, PRODUC-TIVITY WILL SOAR NOW.
BEEP... BEEP... BOOP... NOW DETECTING CLUELESSNESS IN THE VICINITY.
S. Adams
2/7/98
© 1998 United Feature Syndicate, Inc.

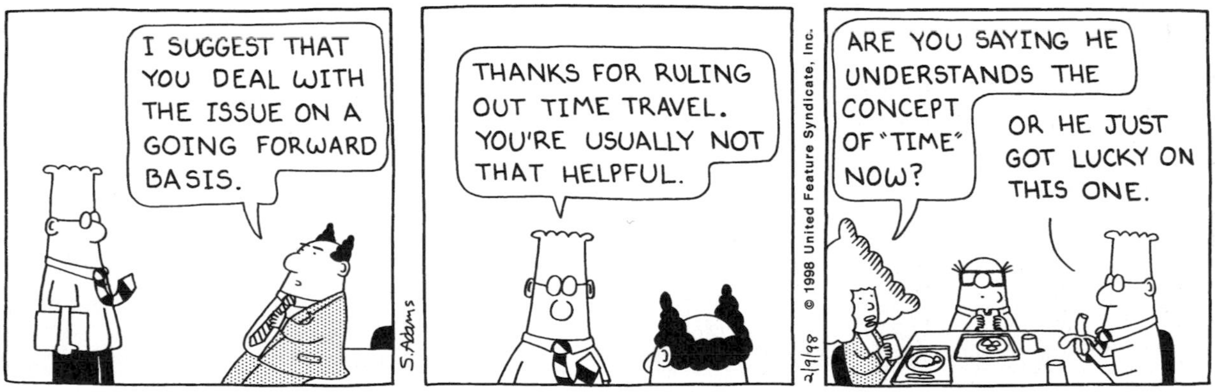
I SUGGEST THAT YOU DEAL WITH THE ISSUE ON A GOING FORWARD BASIS.
THANKS FOR RULING OUT TIME TRAVEL. YOU'RE USUALLY NOT THAT HELPFUL.
ARE YOU SAYING HE UNDERSTANDS THE CONCEPT OF "TIME" NOW?
OR HE JUST GOT LUCKY ON THIS ONE.
S. Adams
2/9/98
© 1998 United Feature Syndicate, Inc.

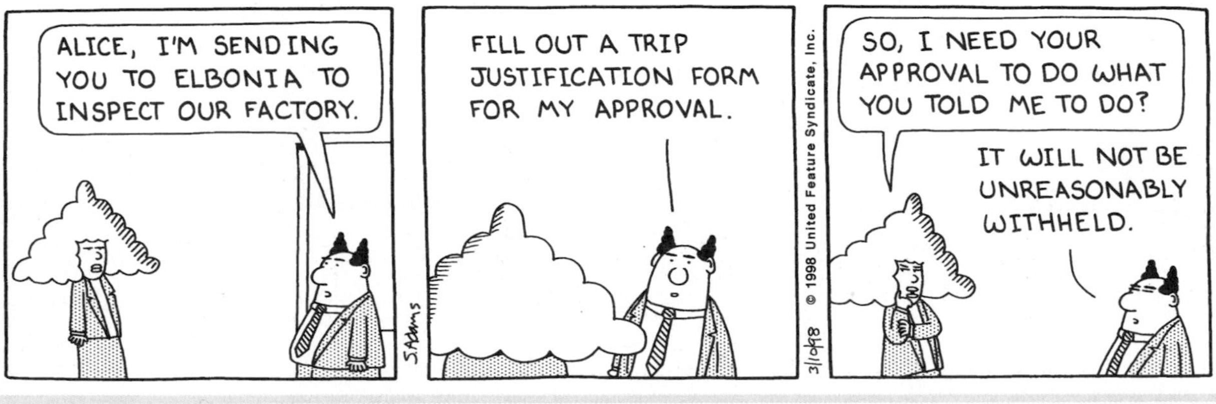
ALICE, I'M SENDING YOU TO ELBONIA TO INSPECT OUR FACTORY.
FILL OUT A TRIP JUSTIFICATION FORM FOR MY APPROVAL.
SO, I NEED YOUR APPROVAL TO DO WHAT YOU TOLD ME TO DO?
IT WILL NOT BE UNREASONABLY WITHHELD.
S. Adams
3/10/98
© 1998 United Feature Syndicate, Inc.

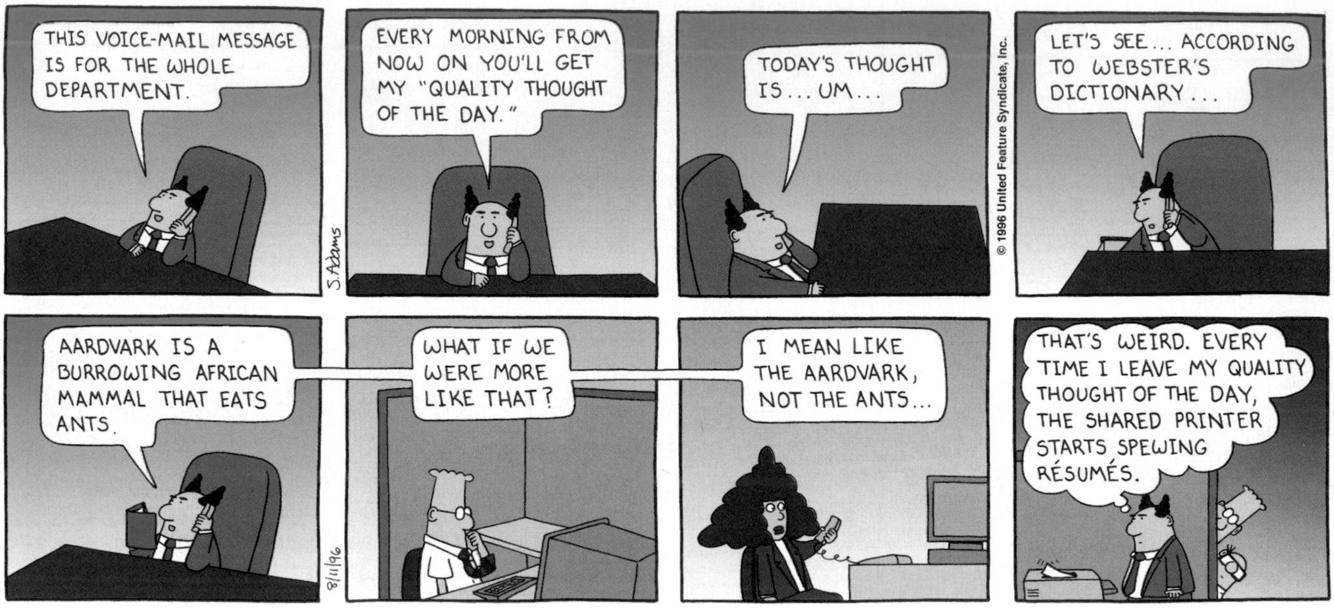
THIS VOICE-MAIL MESSAGE IS FOR THE WHOLE DEPARTMENT.
EVERY MORNING FROM NOW ON YOU'LL GET MY "QUALITY THOUGHT OF THE DAY."
S. Adams
TODAY'S THOUGHT IS... UM...
© 1996 United Feature Syndicate, Inc.
LET'S SEE... ACCORDING TO WEBSTER'S DICTIONARY...
AARDVARK IS A BURROWING AFRICAN MAMMAL THAT EATS ANTS.
WHAT IF WE WERE MORE LIKE THAT?
8/11/96
I MEAN LIKE THE AARDVARK, NOT THE ANTS...
THAT'S WEIRD. EVERY TIME I LEAVE MY QUALITY THOUGHT OF THE DAY, THE SHARED PRINTER STARTS SPEWING RÉSUMÉS.

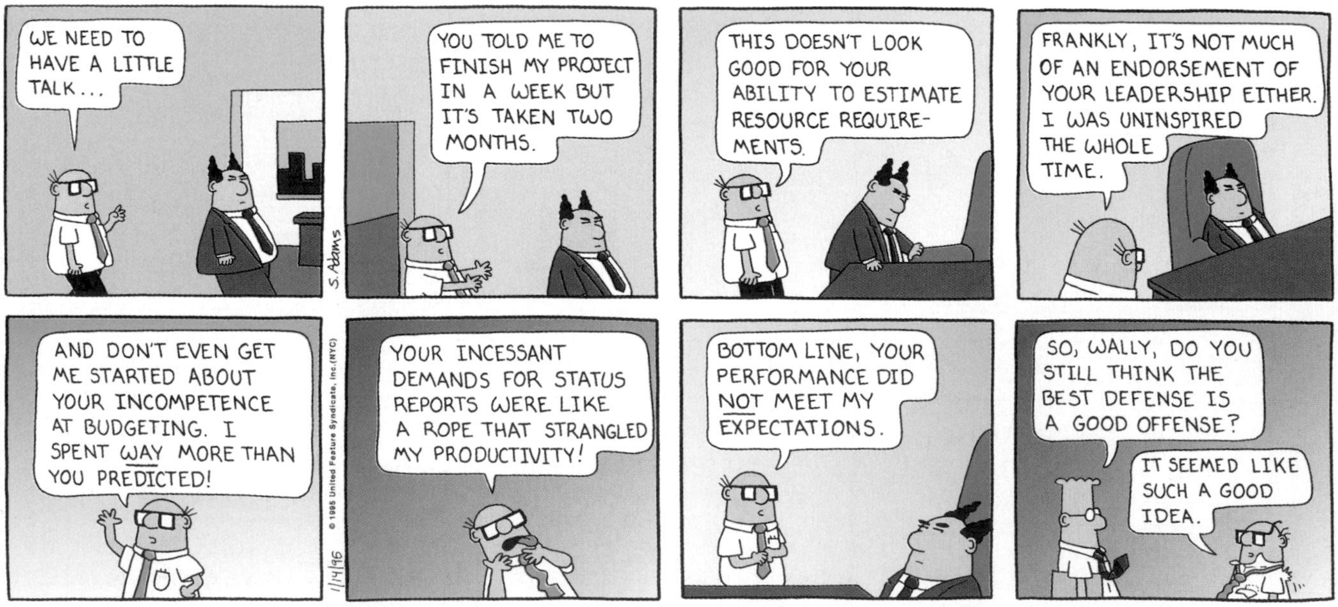
WE NEED TO HAVE A LITTLE TALK...
YOU TOLD ME TO FINISH MY PROJECT IN A WEEK BUT IT'S TAKEN TWO MONTHS.
S. Adams
THIS DOESN'T LOOK GOOD FOR YOUR ABILITY TO ESTIMATE RESOURCE REQUIRE-MENTS.
FRANKLY, IT'S NOT MUCH OF AN ENDORSEMENT OF YOUR LEADERSHIP EITHER. I WAS UNINSPIRED THE WHOLE TIME.
AND DON'T EVEN GET ME STARTED ABOUT YOUR INCOMPETENCE AT BUDGETING. I SPENT WAY MORE THAN YOU PREDICTED!
© 1995 United Feature Syndicate, Inc.(NYC)
1/14/96
YOUR INCESSANT DEMANDS FOR STATUS REPORTS WERE LIKE A ROPE THAT STRANGLED MY PRODUCTIVITY!
BOTTOM LINE, YOUR PERFORMANCE DID NOT MEET MY EXPECTATIONS.
SO, WALLY, DO YOU STILL THINK THE BEST DEFENSE IS A GOOD OFFENSE?
IT SEEMED LIKE SUCH A GOOD IDEA.

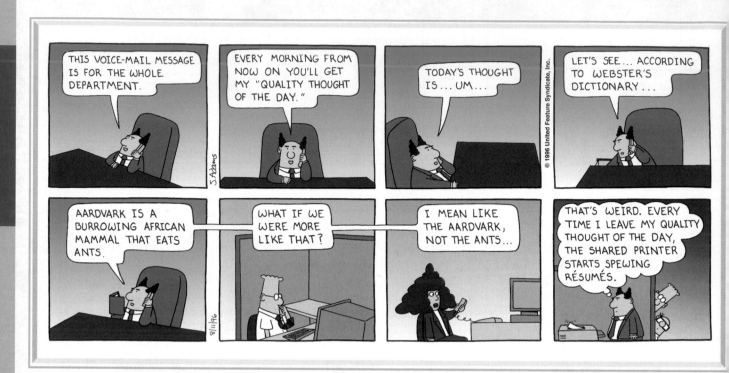

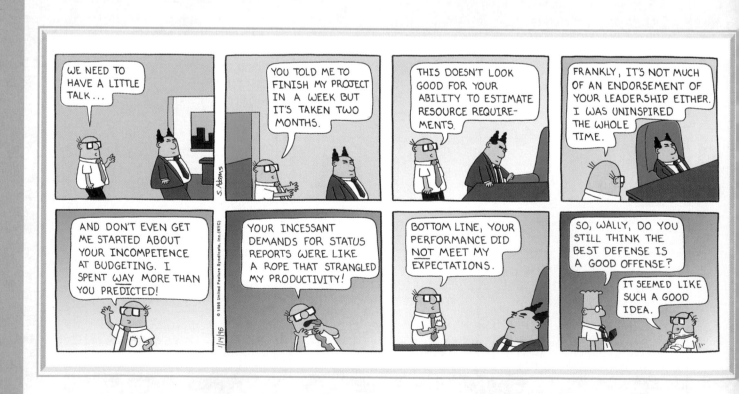

OUR NEW VP SAYS HE HAS AN "OPEN DOOR POLICY." LET'S CHECK IT OUT.

KNOCK KNOCK

HI HO. NOTHING IMPORTANT. WE JUST WANTED TO DROP IN.

THIS OPEN DOOR POLICY IS GREAT. OUR LAST VP WAS ALOOF.

ARE THOSE SOURBALLS?

LOOK AT ALL THE FURNITURE IN HERE!

I CALL COUCH!

IS THERE SOMETHING I CAN DO FOR YOU?

WELL...SOMETIMES OUR CUBICLES ARE TOO HOT.

COULD YOU HAVE SOMEBODY LOOK INTO IT?

BOY, THOSE SOURBALLS SURE LULL YOU INTO A FALSE SENSE OF SECURITY.

THE MAN IS LIKE A HUGE INSINCERE SPIDER.

© 1995 United Feature Syndicate, Inc. 7-30

WHAT WE NEED IS MORE COMMUNICATION BETWEEN MANAGEMENT AND...WHATEVER YOU ARE.

SO, ONCE A MONTH I'LL HAVE "OPEN DOOR DAY."

YOU CAN DROP BY AND WHINE ABOUT ANYTHING YOU WANT.

I'LL LISTEN WITH A CONCERNED EXPRESSION LIKE THIS.

THEN I'LL EXPLAIN WHY EVERYTHING IS FINE JUST THE WAY IT IS.

© 1993 United Feature Syndicate, Inc.

THEN, MORALE WILL IMPROVE, PROFITS WILL SKYROCKET AND MY STOCK OPTIONS WILL MAKE ME RICH!!

8-29

MAY I MAKE SOME OBSERVATIONS ABOUT YOUR PLAN?

UH... FORGET IT.

DO YOU NOTICE HOW CONCERNED I LOOK?

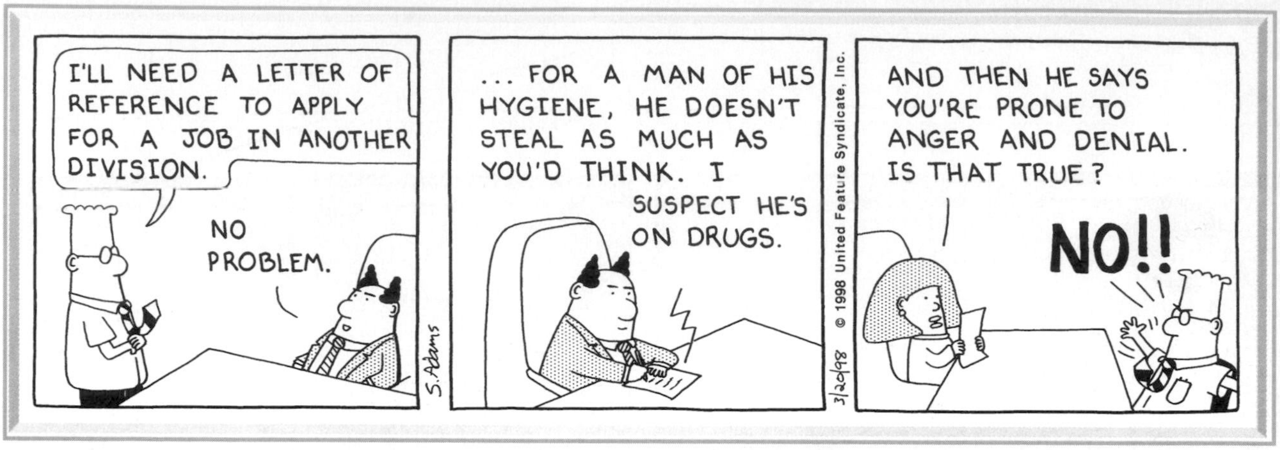
I'LL NEED A LETTER OF REFERENCE TO APPLY FOR A JOB IN ANOTHER DIVISION.
NO PROBLEM.
S. Adams
... FOR A MAN OF HIS HYGIENE, HE DOESN'T STEAL AS MUCH AS YOU'D THINK. I SUSPECT HE'S ON DRUGS.
3/20/98 © 1998 United Feature Syndicate, Inc.
AND THEN HE SAYS YOU'RE PRONE TO ANGER AND DENIAL. IS THAT TRUE?
NO!!

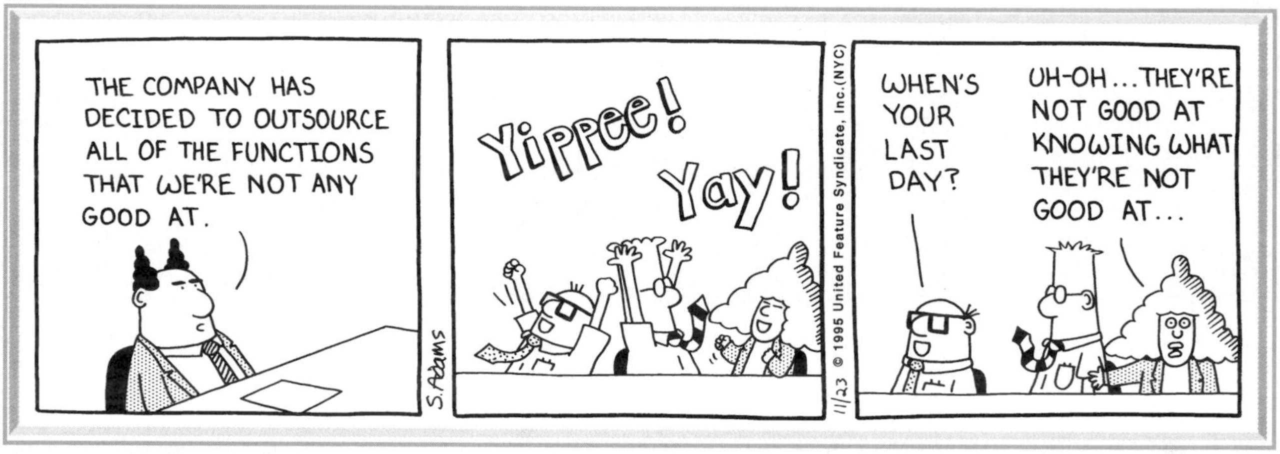
THE COMPANY HAS DECIDED TO OUTSOURCE ALL OF THE FUNCTIONS THAT WE'RE NOT ANY GOOD AT.
S. Adams
Yippee!
Yay!
11/23 © 1995 United Feature Syndicate, Inc.(NYC)
WHEN'S YOUR LAST DAY?
UH-OH ... THEY'RE NOT GOOD AT KNOWING WHAT THEY'RE NOT GOOD AT ...

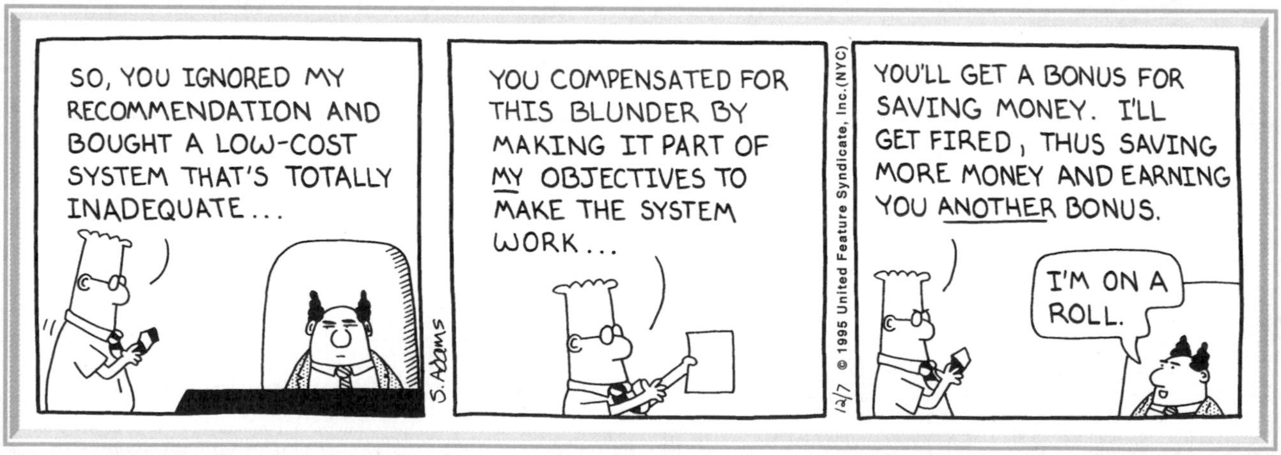
SO, YOU IGNORED MY RECOMMENDATION AND BOUGHT A LOW-COST SYSTEM THAT'S TOTALLY INADEQUATE ...
S. Adams
YOU COMPENSATED FOR THIS BLUNDER BY MAKING IT PART OF MY OBJECTIVES TO MAKE THE SYSTEM WORK ...
12/7 © 1995 United Feature Syndicate, Inc.(NYC)
YOU'LL GET A BONUS FOR SAVING MONEY. I'LL GET FIRED, THUS SAVING MORE MONEY AND EARNING YOU ANOTHER BONUS.
I'M ON A ROLL.

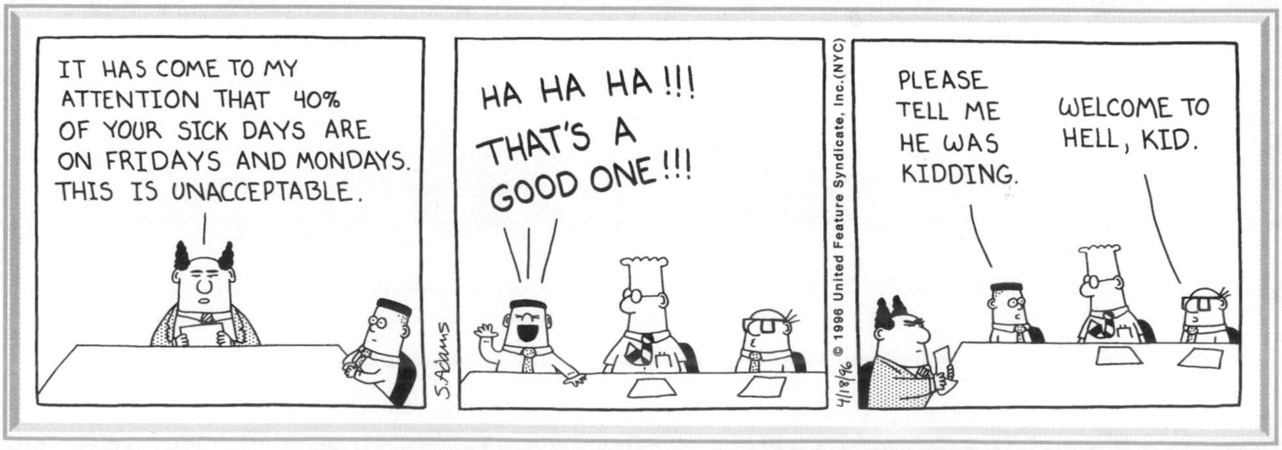
IT HAS COME TO MY ATTENTION THAT 40% OF YOUR SICK DAYS ARE ON FRIDAYS AND MONDAYS. THIS IS UNACCEPTABLE.
S. Adams
HA HA HA!!! THAT'S A GOOD ONE!!!
4/18/96 © 1996 United Feature Syndicate, Inc.(NYC)
PLEASE TELL ME HE WAS KIDDING.
WELCOME TO HELL, KID.

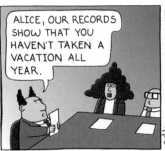

ALICE, OUR RECORDS SHOW THAT YOU HAVEN'T TAKEN A VACATION ALL YEAR.
COMPANY POLICY REQUIRES YOU TO USE YOUR VACATION DAYS.
HOW?? YOU TOLD ME TO WORK SEVEN DAYS A WEEK TO PREPARE THE PROJECT FOR YOUR BOSS'S YEAR-END REVIEW.
DO YOU WANT ME TO MEET THE ARTIFICIAL PROJECT TARGET OR THE ARTIFICIAL VACATION TARGET?
HELLO!!! THESE ARE MUTUALLY EXCLUSIVE GOALS!!! HELLO!!!
OOH... SORRY. I USUALLY JUST THINK THAT LAST PART IN SILENT FRUSTRATION.
MOVING RIGHT ALONG... KUDOS TO WALLY FOR USING ALL OF HIS VACATION DAYS AHEAD OF SCHEDULE.
GET OVER IT, ALICE. WE CAN'T ALL BE SUPERSTARS.
S. Adams
© 1995 United Feature Syndicate, Inc.(NYC)
12/17/95

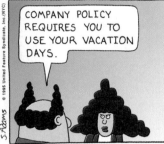

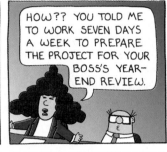

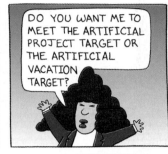

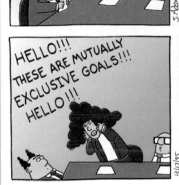

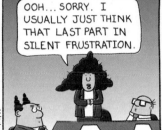

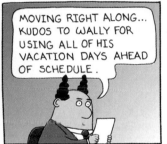

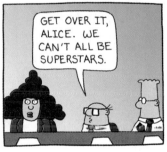

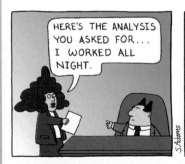

HERE'S THE ANALYSIS YOU ASKED FOR... I WORKED ALL NIGHT.
BUT YOU SAID THIS WAS VITAL FOR YOUR MEETING TODAY SO I KNOW IT WAS WORTH THE EFFORT.
THIS IS EXCELLENT WORK, ALICE.
A RARE COMPLIMENT; IT WAS ALL WORTH-WHILE.
MMM
I'LL USE IT AS BACKUP MATERIAL.
BACKUP?!! NOBODY LOOKS AT BACKUP MATERIAL!
I'M GOING TO GRAB YOUR POINTY HAIR, YANK YOU OUT OF THAT CHEAP SUIT AND FLING YOUR NAKED BODY DOWN THE HALL.
SHE'S ALWAYS IRRITABLE THE WEEK BEFORE HER PERFORMANCE REVIEW CYCLE.
HER DISTANCE IMPROVED THIS YEAR.
OW
S. Adams
© 1996 United Feature Syndicate, Inc.(NYC)
3/24/96

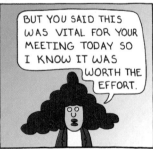

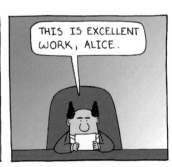

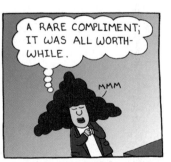

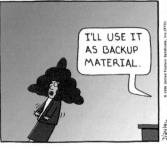

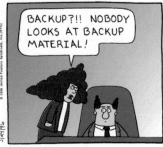

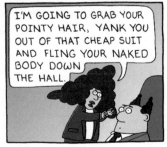

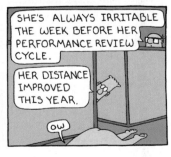

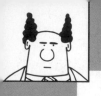

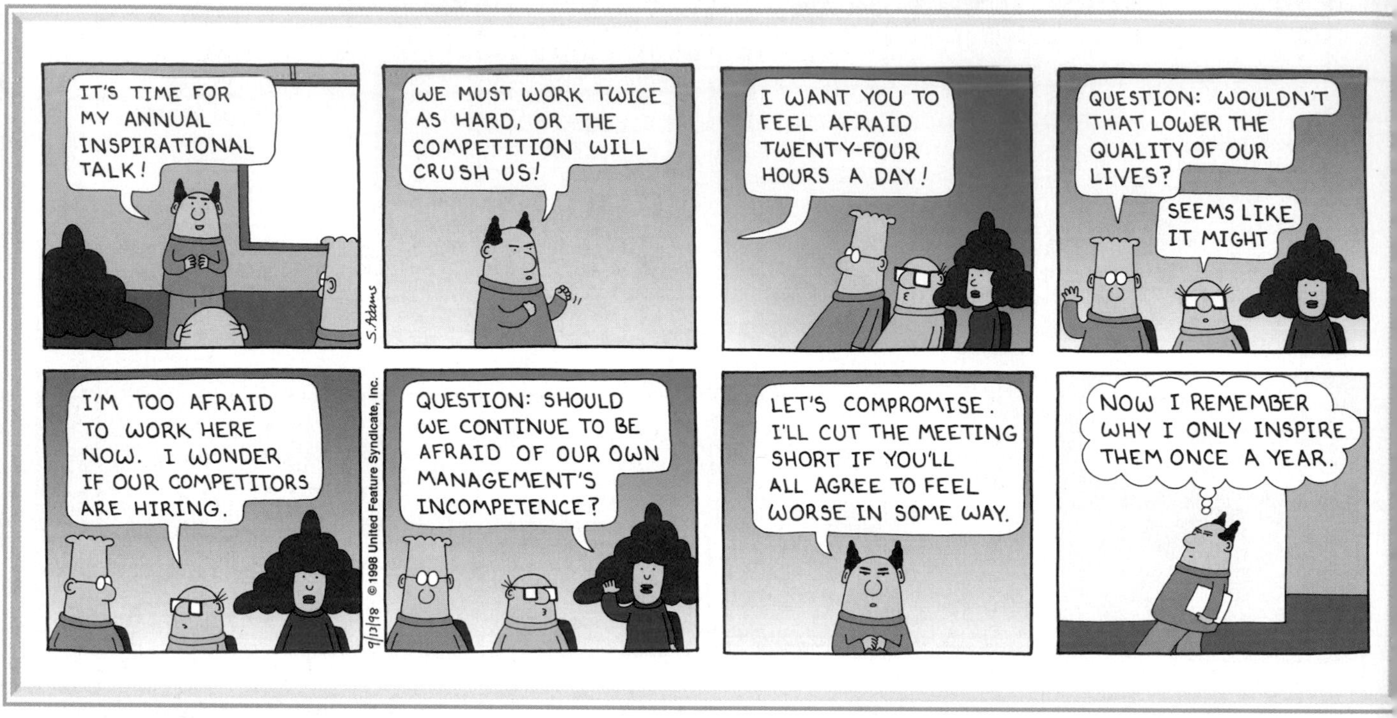
IT'S TIME FOR MY ANNUAL INSPIRATIONAL TALK!
WE MUST WORK TWICE AS HARD, OR THE COMPETITION WILL CRUSH US!
I WANT YOU TO FEEL AFRAID TWENTY-FOUR HOURS A DAY!
QUESTION: WOULDN'T THAT LOWER THE QUALITY OF OUR LIVES?
SEEMS LIKE IT MIGHT
I'M TOO AFRAID TO WORK HERE NOW. I WONDER IF OUR COMPETITORS ARE HIRING.
QUESTION: SHOULD WE CONTINUE TO BE AFRAID OF OUR OWN MANAGEMENT'S INCOMPETENCE?
LET'S COMPROMISE. I'LL CUT THE MEETING SHORT IF YOU'LL ALL AGREE TO FEEL WORSE IN SOME WAY.
NOW I REMEMBER WHY I ONLY INSPIRE THEM ONCE A YEAR.
S. Adams
9/13/98 © 1998 United Feature Syndicate, Inc.

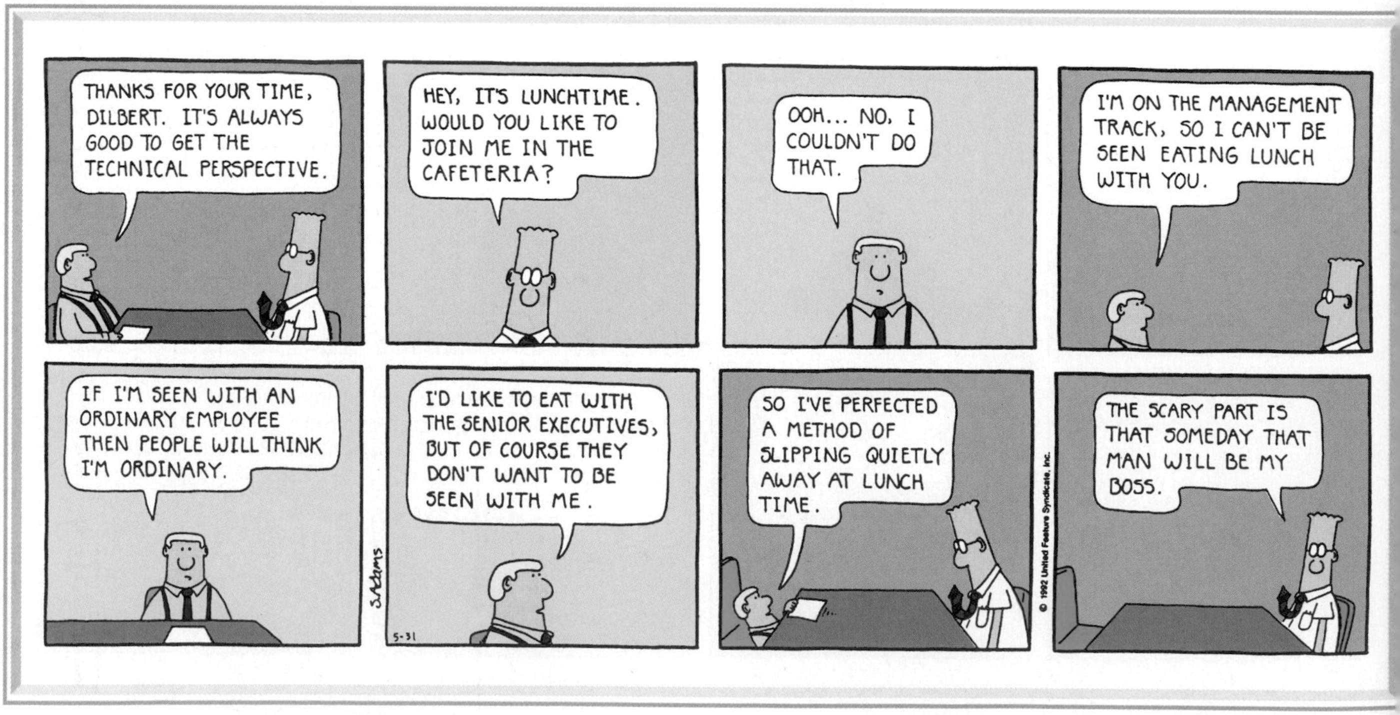
THANKS FOR YOUR TIME, DILBERT. IT'S ALWAYS GOOD TO GET THE TECHNICAL PERSPECTIVE.
HEY, IT'S LUNCHTIME. WOULD YOU LIKE TO JOIN ME IN THE CAFETERIA?
OOH... NO, I COULDN'T DO THAT.
I'M ON THE MANAGEMENT TRACK, SO I CAN'T BE SEEN EATING LUNCH WITH YOU.
IF I'M SEEN WITH AN ORDINARY EMPLOYEE THEN PEOPLE WILL THINK I'M ORDINARY.
I'D LIKE TO EAT WITH THE SENIOR EXECUTIVES, BUT OF COURSE THEY DON'T WANT TO BE SEEN WITH ME.
SO I'VE PERFECTED A METHOD OF SLIPPING QUIETLY AWAY AT LUNCH TIME.
THE SCARY PART IS THAT SOMEDAY THAT MAN WILL BE MY BOSS.
S. Adams
5-31
© 1992 United Feature Syndicate, Inc.

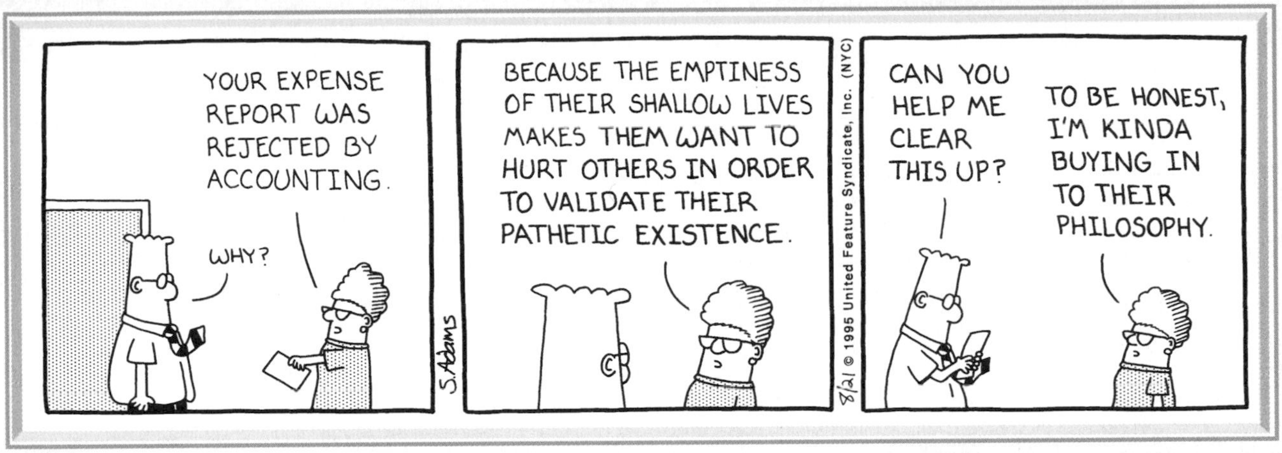
YOUR EXPENSE REPORT WAS REJECTED BY ACCOUNTING.
WHY?
S. Adams
BECAUSE THE EMPTINESS OF THEIR SHALLOW LIVES MAKES THEM WANT TO HURT OTHERS IN ORDER TO VALIDATE THEIR PATHETIC EXISTENCE.
8/21 © 1995 United Feature Syndicate, Inc. (NYC)
CAN YOU HELP ME CLEAR THIS UP?
TO BE HONEST, I'M KINDA BUYING IN TO THEIR PHILOSOPHY.

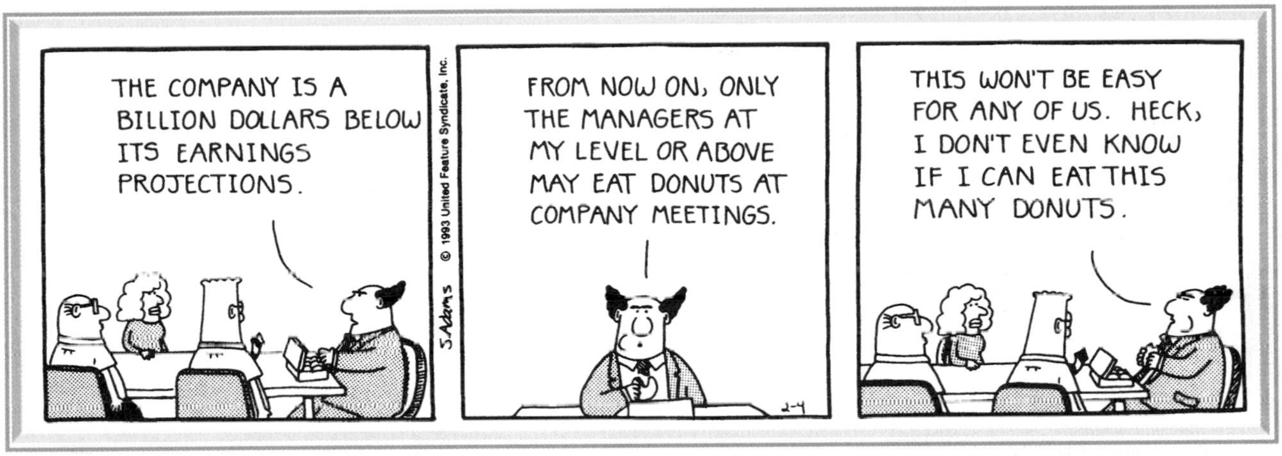
THE COMPANY IS A BILLION DOLLARS BELOW ITS EARNINGS PROJECTIONS.
S. Adams © 1993 United Feature Syndicate, Inc.
FROM NOW ON, ONLY THE MANAGERS AT MY LEVEL OR ABOVE MAY EAT DONUTS AT COMPANY MEETINGS.
2-4
THIS WON'T BE EASY FOR ANY OF US. HECK, I DON'T EVEN KNOW IF I CAN EAT THIS MANY DONUTS.

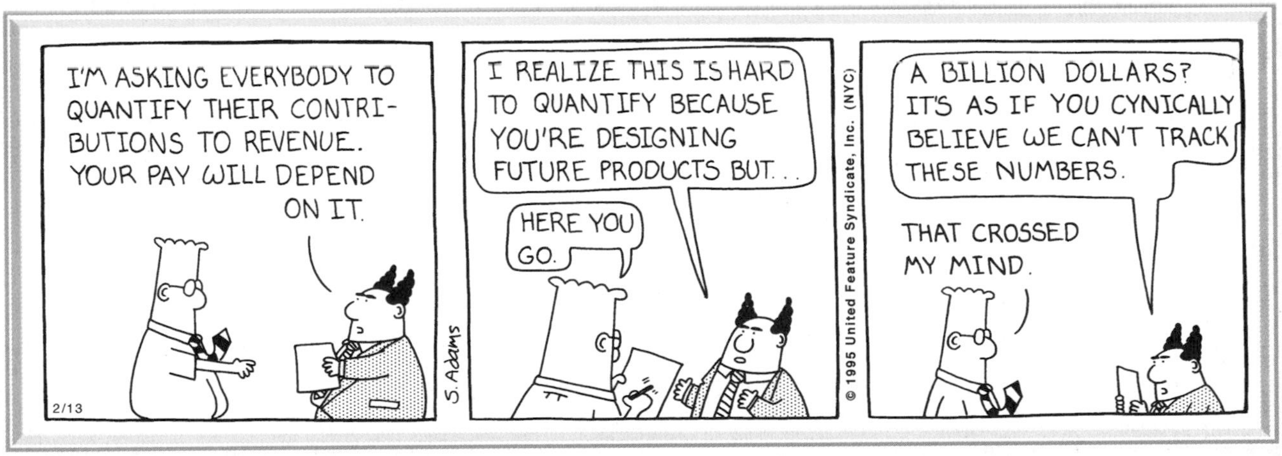
I'M ASKING EVERYBODY TO QUANTIFY THEIR CONTRIBUTIONS TO REVENUE. YOUR PAY WILL DEPEND ON IT.
2/13
S. Adams
I REALIZE THIS IS HARD TO QUANTIFY BECAUSE YOU'RE DESIGNING FUTURE PRODUCTS BUT...
HERE YOU GO.
© 1995 United Feature Syndicate, Inc. (NYC)
A BILLION DOLLARS? IT'S AS IF YOU CYNICALLY BELIEVE WE CAN'T TRACK THESE NUMBERS.
THAT CROSSED MY MIND.

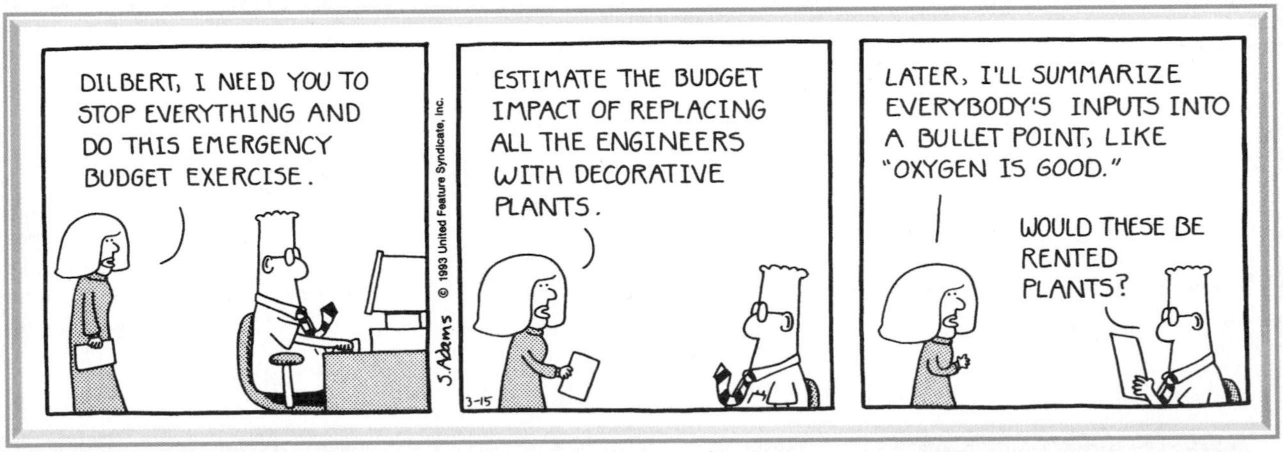
DILBERT, I NEED YOU TO STOP EVERYTHING AND DO THIS EMERGENCY BUDGET EXERCISE.
S. Adams © 1993 United Feature Syndicate, Inc.
ESTIMATE THE BUDGET IMPACT OF REPLACING ALL THE ENGINEERS WITH DECORATIVE PLANTS.
3-15
LATER, I'LL SUMMARIZE EVERYBODY'S INPUTS INTO A BULLET POINT, LIKE "OXYGEN IS GOOD."
WOULD THESE BE RENTED PLANTS?

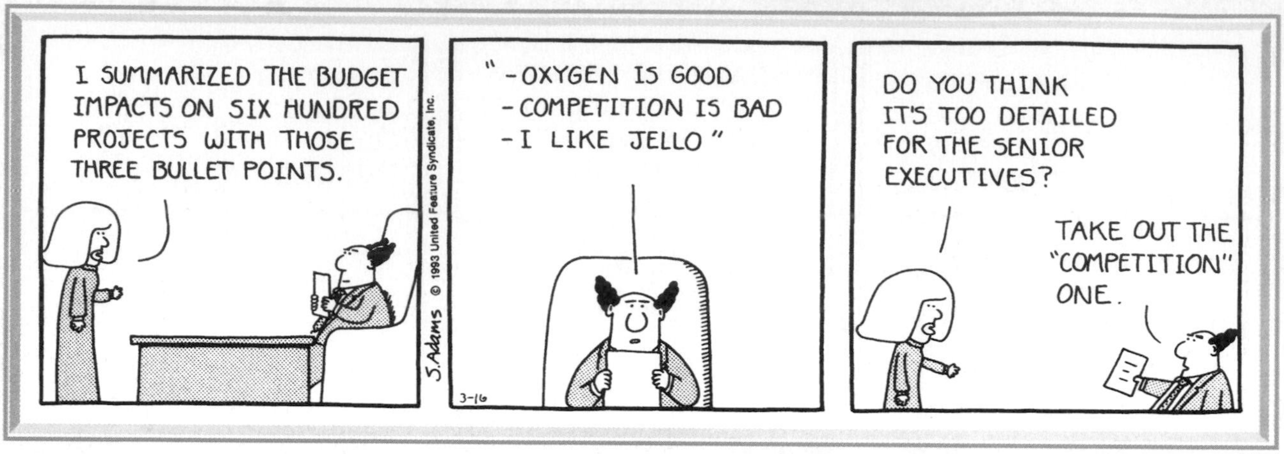
I SUMMARIZED THE BUDGET IMPACTS ON SIX HUNDRED PROJECTS WITH THOSE THREE BULLET POINTS.
© 1993 United Feature Syndicate, Inc.
S. Adams 3-16
"-OXYGEN IS GOOD -COMPETITION IS BAD -I LIKE JELLO"
DO YOU THINK IT'S TOO DETAILED FOR THE SENIOR EXECUTIVES?
TAKE OUT THE "COMPETITION" ONE.

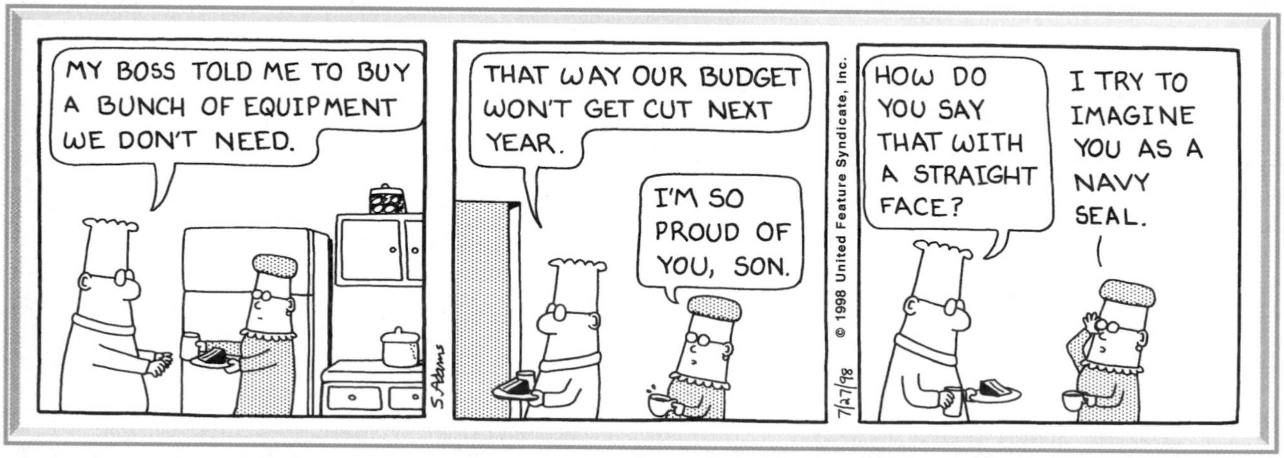
MY BOSS TOLD ME TO BUY A BUNCH OF EQUIPMENT WE DON'T NEED.
S. Adams
THAT WAY OUR BUDGET WON'T GET CUT NEXT YEAR.
I'M SO PROUD OF YOU, SON.
© 1998 United Feature Syndicate, Inc.
7/27/98
HOW DO YOU SAY THAT WITH A STRAIGHT FACE?
I TRY TO IMAGINE YOU AS A NAVY SEAL.

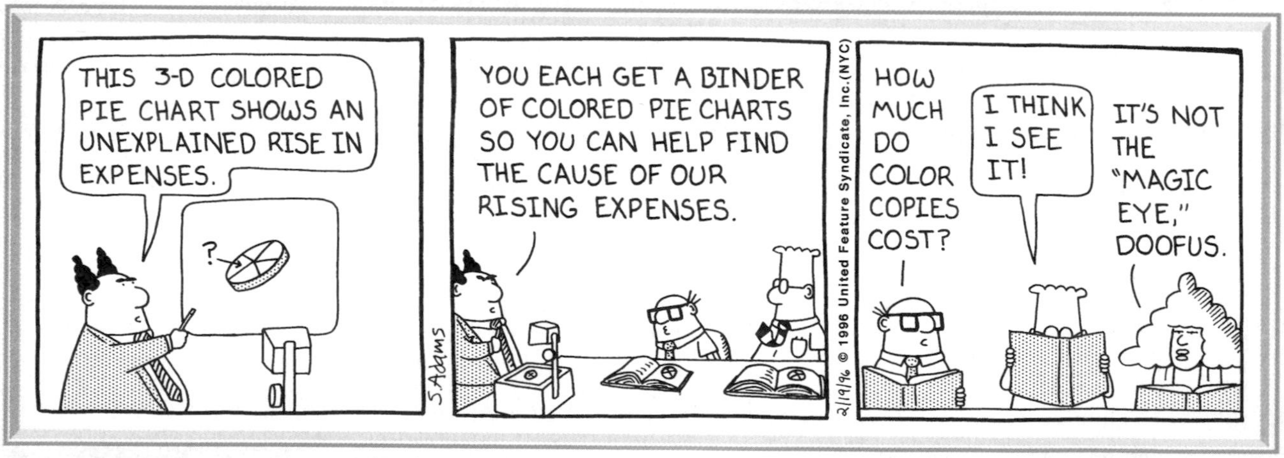
THIS 3-D COLORED PIE CHART SHOWS AN UNEXPLAINED RISE IN EXPENSES.
?
S. Adams
YOU EACH GET A BINDER OF COLORED PIE CHARTS SO YOU CAN HELP FIND THE CAUSE OF OUR RISING EXPENSES.
2/19/96 © 1996 United Feature Syndicate, Inc.(NYC)
HOW MUCH DO COLOR COPIES COST?
I THINK I SEE IT!
IT'S NOT THE "MAGIC EYE," DOOFUS.

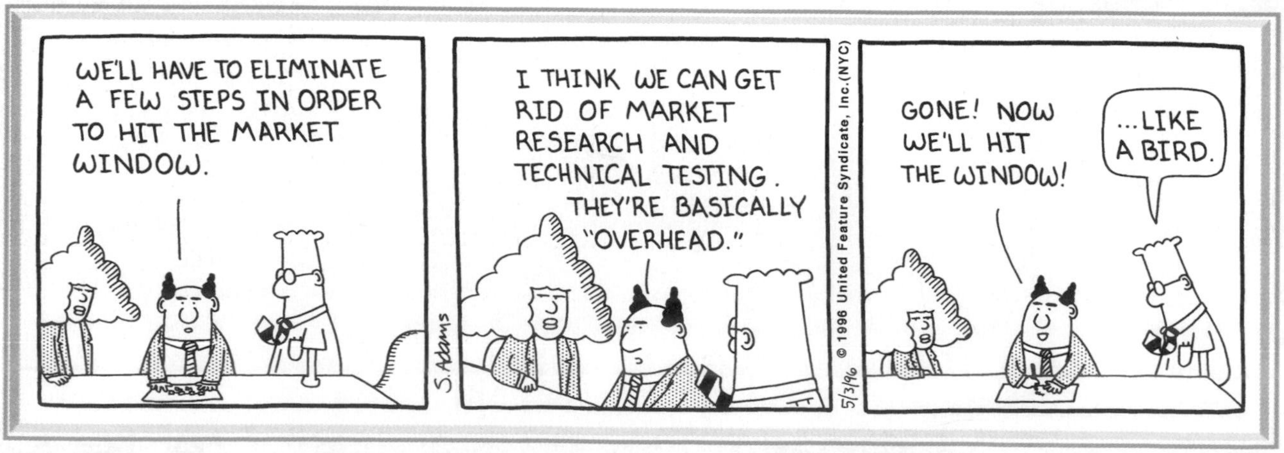
WE'LL HAVE TO ELIMINATE A FEW STEPS IN ORDER TO HIT THE MARKET WINDOW.
S. Adams
I THINK WE CAN GET RID OF MARKET RESEARCH AND TECHNICAL TESTING. THEY'RE BASICALLY "OVERHEAD."
5/3/96 © 1996 United Feature Syndicate, Inc.(NYC)
GONE! NOW WE'LL HIT THE WINDOW!
...LIKE A BIRD.

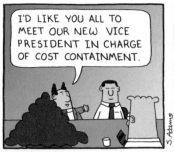

I'D LIKE YOU ALL TO MEET OUR NEW VICE PRESIDENT IN CHARGE OF COST CONTAINMENT.
MY FIRST PRIORITY IS TO REDUCE OUR SPIRALING EXPENSES FOR OFFICE SUPPLIES.
FROM NOW ON, YOUR SUPPLY CABINET WILL BE LOCKED.
THE ONLY KEY WILL BE UNDER THE CONTROL OF YOUR BITTER AND INEFFICIENT SECRETARY.
QUESTIONS?
I AM ONLY AN INTERN SO PLEASE EXCUSE THIS NAIVE QUESTION...
I'VE NOTICED THAT THE EMPLOYEES ARE ALL DISPIRITED HOLLOW SHELLS, MANAGEMENT IS RANDOM AND OUR PRODUCTS ARE SHODDY.
HOW ARE YOU GOING TO SOLVE THAT BY MAKING IT HARD TO GET SUPPLIES?
I THOUGHT YOU SAID THEY LIKE HONESTY.
ASK HOW MUCH HE'S PAID. IT SHOWS YOU CARE.
S. Adams
5/12/96 © 1996 United Feature Syndicate, Inc.

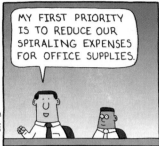

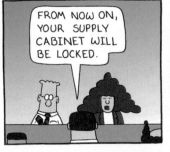

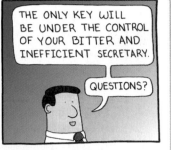

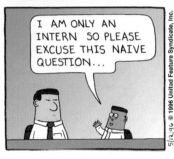

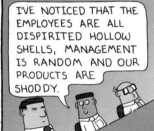

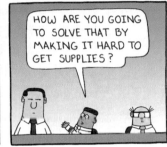

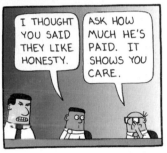

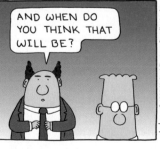

IT'S TIME TO DELEGATE.
DILBERT, I WANT YOU TO GIVE ME A NEW CASH FLOW ESTIMATE FOR YOUR PROJECT.
OKAY, FINE.
WHEN WILL I GET IT?
WHEN DO YOU NEED IT?
AS SOON AS POSSIBLE!
OKAY.
AND WHEN DO YOU THINK THAT WILL BE?
I USUALLY WAIT A FEW DAYS TO SEE IF YOU CHANGE YOUR MIND.
THEN I'LL GIVE YOU LAST YEAR'S CASH FLOW AS A TEST TO SEE IF YOU READ IT.
THE MORE EXPERIENCE THEY GET, THE WORSE THEY ARE.
S. Adams
10/18/98 © 1998 United Feature Syndicate, Inc.

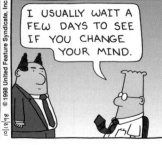

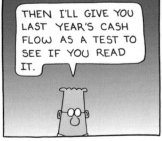

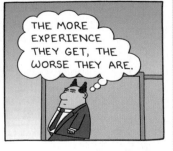

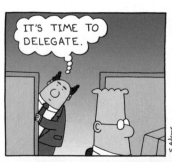

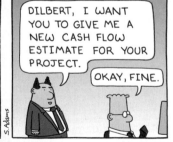

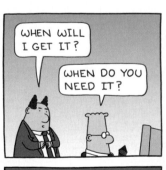

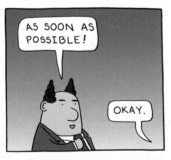

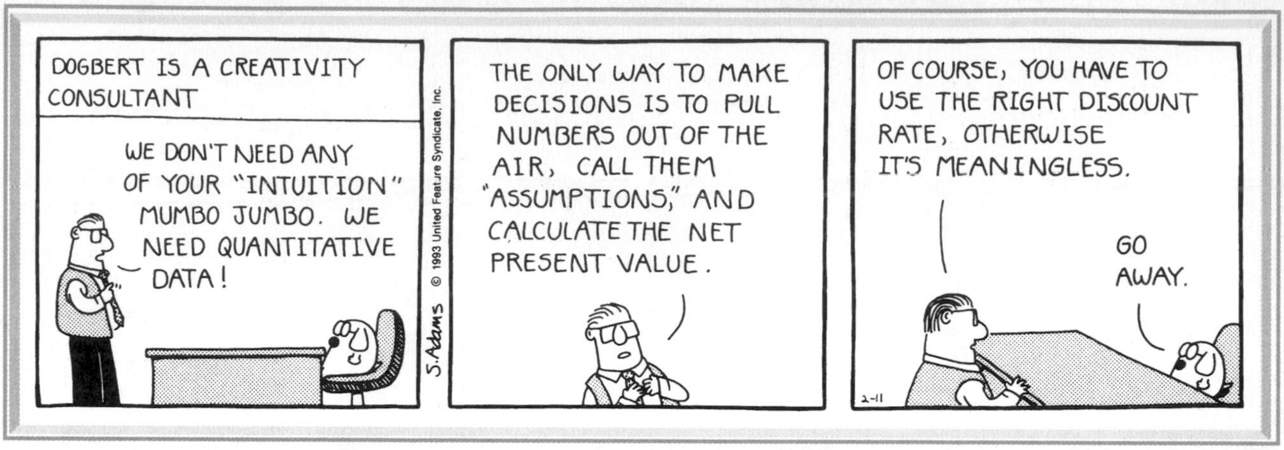
DOGBERT IS A CREATIVITY CONSULTANT
WE DON'T NEED ANY OF YOUR "INTUITION" MUMBO JUMBO. WE NEED QUANTITATIVE DATA!
THE ONLY WAY TO MAKE DECISIONS IS TO PULL NUMBERS OUT OF THE AIR, CALL THEM "ASSUMPTIONS," AND CALCULATE THE NET PRESENT VALUE.
OF COURSE, YOU HAVE TO USE THE RIGHT DISCOUNT RATE, OTHERWISE IT'S MEANINGLESS.
GO AWAY.
S. Adams © 1993 United Feature Syndicate, Inc.
2-11

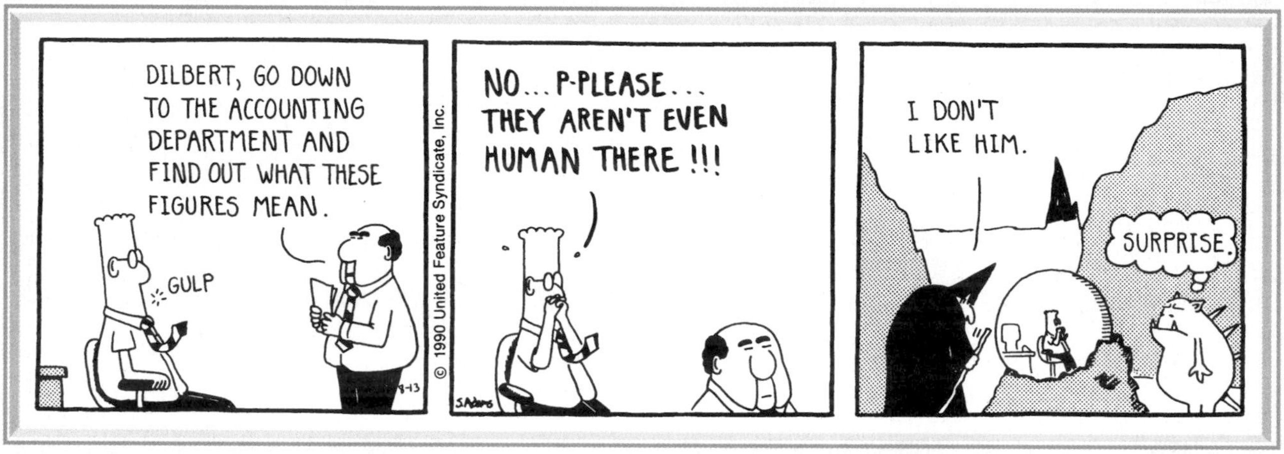
DILBERT, GO DOWN TO THE ACCOUNTING DEPARTMENT AND FIND OUT WHAT THESE FIGURES MEAN.
GULP
8-13
NO... P-PLEASE... THEY AREN'T EVEN HUMAN THERE !!!
© 1990 United Feature Syndicate, Inc.
S. Adams
I DON'T LIKE HIM.
SURPRISE.

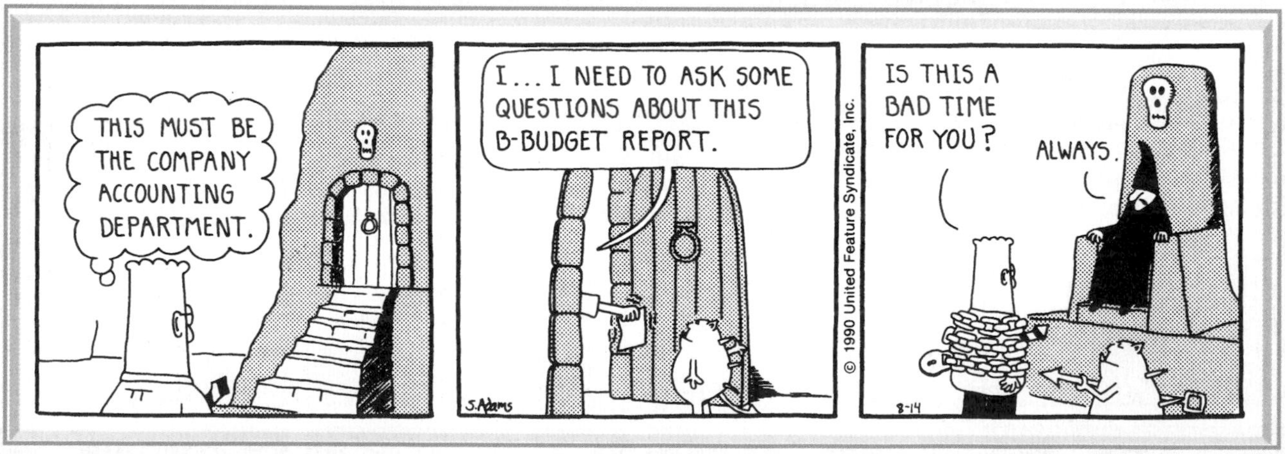
THIS MUST BE THE COMPANY ACCOUNTING DEPARTMENT.
I... I NEED TO ASK SOME QUESTIONS ABOUT THIS B-BUDGET REPORT.
S. Adams
© 1990 United Feature Syndicate, Inc.
IS THIS A BAD TIME FOR YOU?
ALWAYS.
8-14

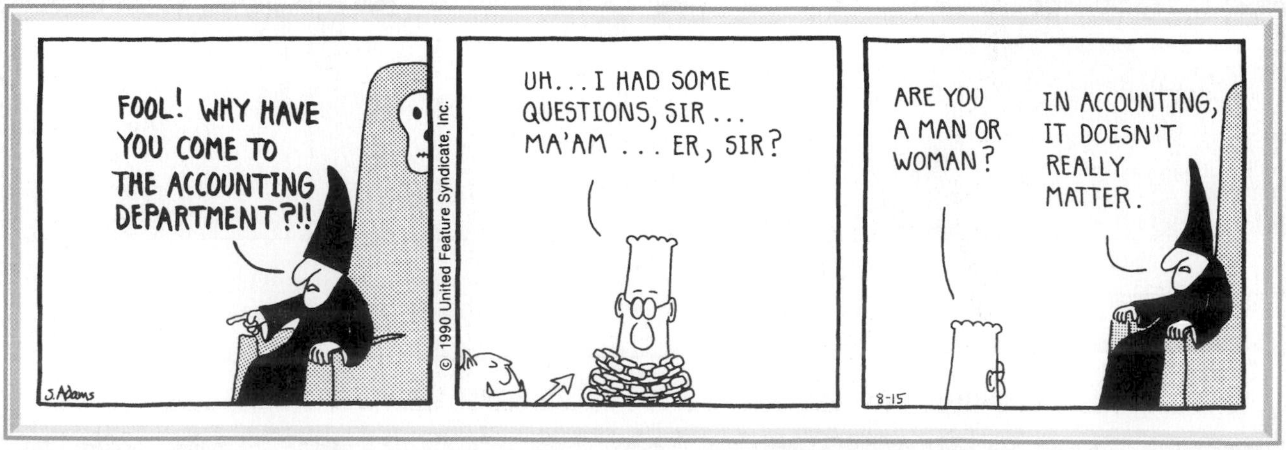
FOOL! WHY HAVE YOU COME TO THE ACCOUNTING DEPARTMENT?!!
S. Adams
© 1990 United Feature Syndicate, Inc.
UH... I HAD SOME QUESTIONS, SIR... MA'AM... ER, SIR?
ARE YOU A MAN OR WOMAN?
IN ACCOUNTING, IT DOESN'T REALLY MATTER.
8-15

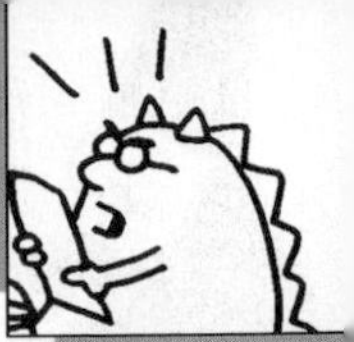

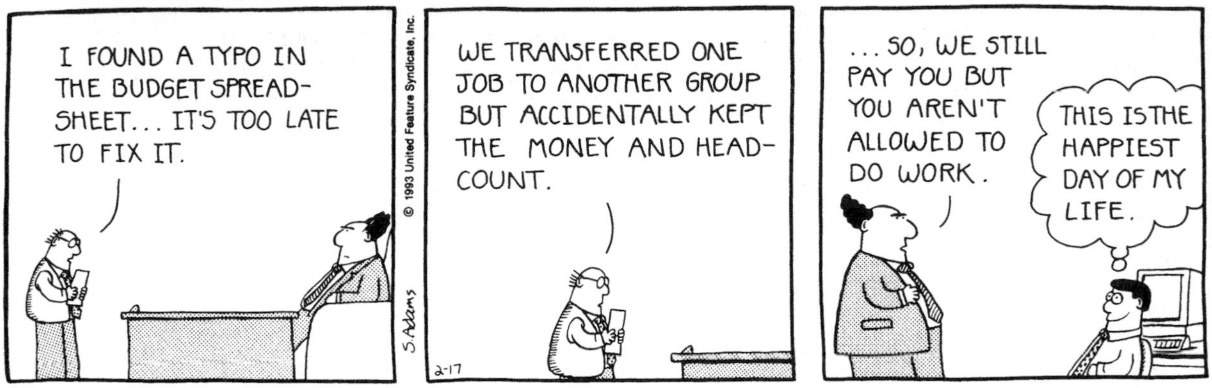
I FOUND A TYPO IN THE BUDGET SPREAD-SHEET... IT'S TOO LATE TO FIX IT.
© 1993 United Feature Syndicate, Inc.
S. Adams 2-17
WE TRANSFERRED ONE JOB TO ANOTHER GROUP BUT ACCIDENTALLY KEPT THE MONEY AND HEAD-COUNT.
...SO, WE STILL PAY YOU BUT YOU AREN'T ALLOWED TO DO WORK.
THIS IS THE HAPPIEST DAY OF MY LIFE.

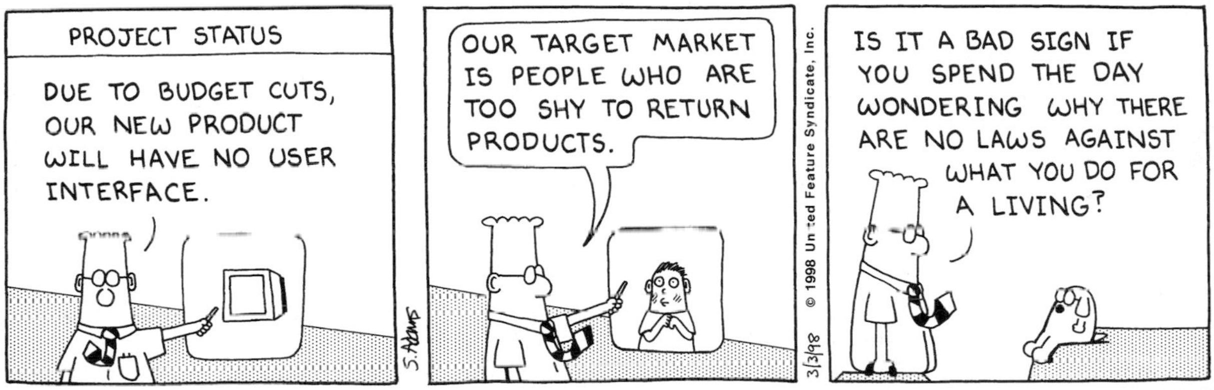
PROJECT STATUS
DUE TO BUDGET CUTS, OUR NEW PRODUCT WILL HAVE NO USER INTERFACE.
S. Adams
OUR TARGET MARKET IS PEOPLE WHO ARE TOO SHY TO RETURN PRODUCTS.
3/3/98 © 1998 United Feature Syndicate, Inc.
IS IT A BAD SIGN IF YOU SPEND THE DAY WONDERING WHY THERE ARE NO LAWS AGAINST WHAT YOU DO FOR A LIVING?

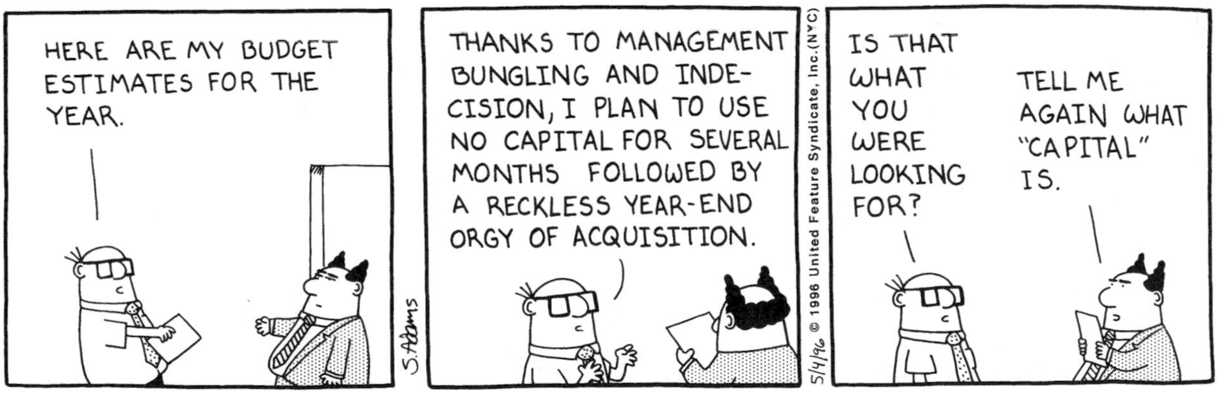
HERE ARE MY BUDGET ESTIMATES FOR THE YEAR.
S. Adams
THANKS TO MANAGEMENT BUNGLING AND INDE-CISION, I PLAN TO USE NO CAPITAL FOR SEVERAL MONTHS FOLLOWED BY A RECKLESS YEAR-END ORGY OF ACQUISITION.
5/4/96 © 1996 United Feature Syndicate, Inc.(NYC)
IS THAT WHAT YOU WERE LOOKING FOR?
TELL ME AGAIN WHAT "CAPITAL" IS.

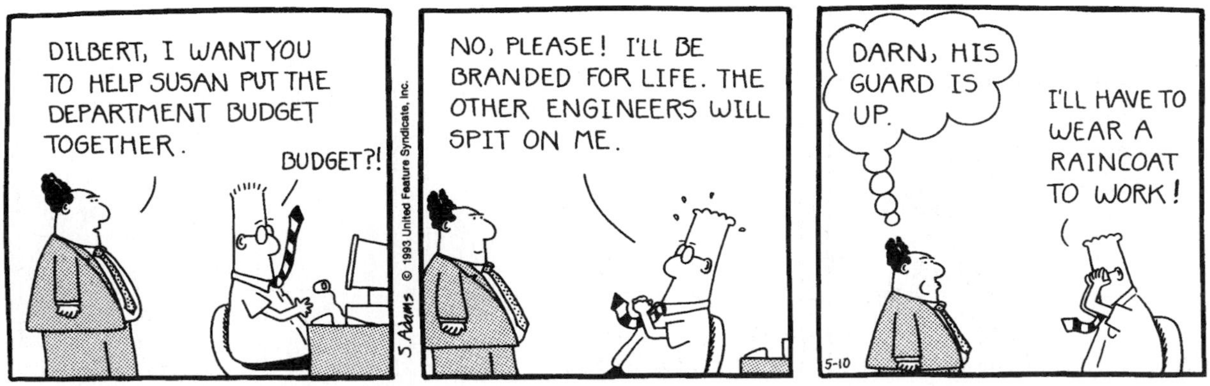
DILBERT, I WANT YOU TO HELP SUSAN PUT THE DEPARTMENT BUDGET TOGETHER.
BUDGET?!
S. Adams © 1993 United Feature Syndicate, Inc.
NO, PLEASE! I'LL BE BRANDED FOR LIFE. THE OTHER ENGINEERS WILL SPIT ON ME.
DARN, HIS GUARD IS UP.
I'LL HAVE TO WEAR A RAINCOAT TO WORK!
5-10

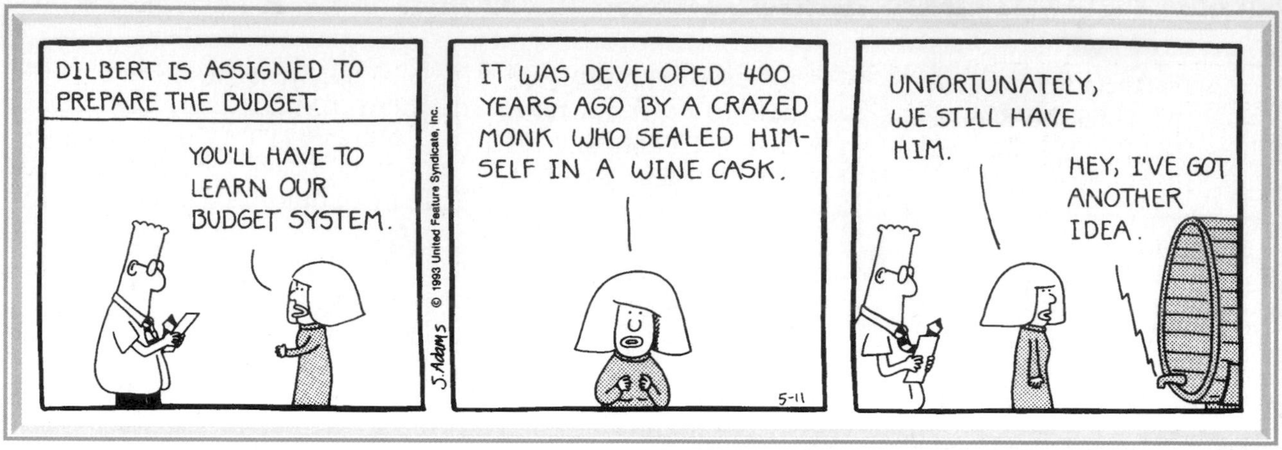
DILBERT IS ASSIGNED TO PREPARE THE BUDGET.
YOU'LL HAVE TO LEARN OUR BUDGET SYSTEM.
S. Adams © 1993 United Feature Syndicate, Inc.
IT WAS DEVELOPED 400 YEARS AGO BY A CRAZED MONK WHO SEALED HIMSELF IN A WINE CASK.
5-11
UNFORTUNATELY, WE STILL HAVE HIM.
HEY, I'VE GOT ANOTHER IDEA.

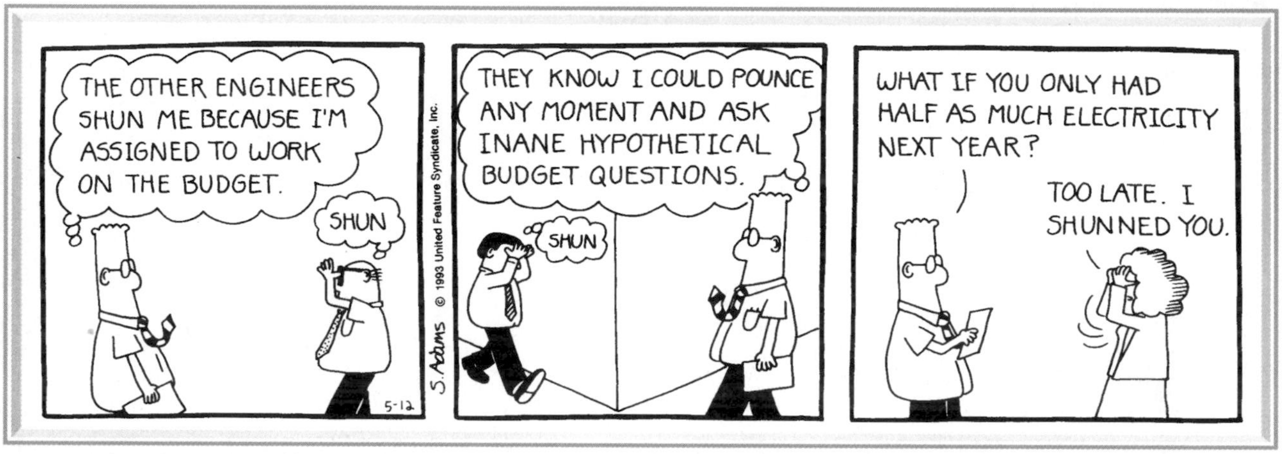
THE OTHER ENGINEERS SHUN ME BECAUSE I'M ASSIGNED TO WORK ON THE BUDGET.
SHUN
5-12
S. Adams © 1993 United Feature Syndicate, Inc.
THEY KNOW I COULD POUNCE ANY MOMENT AND ASK INANE HYPOTHETICAL BUDGET QUESTIONS.
SHUN
WHAT IF YOU ONLY HAD HALF AS MUCH ELECTRICITY NEXT YEAR?
TOO LATE. I SHUNNED YOU.

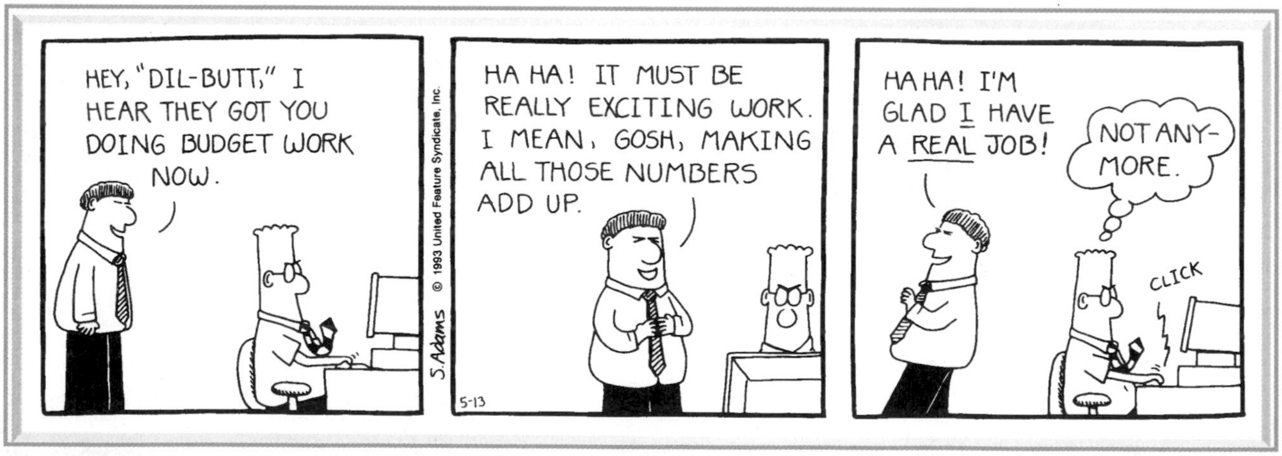
HEY, "DIL-BUTT," I HEAR THEY GOT YOU DOING BUDGET WORK NOW.
S. Adams © 1993 United Feature Syndicate, Inc.
HA HA! IT MUST BE REALLY EXCITING WORK. I MEAN, GOSH, MAKING ALL THOSE NUMBERS ADD UP.
5-13
HA HA! I'M GLAD I HAVE A REAL JOB!
NOT ANY-MORE.
CLICK

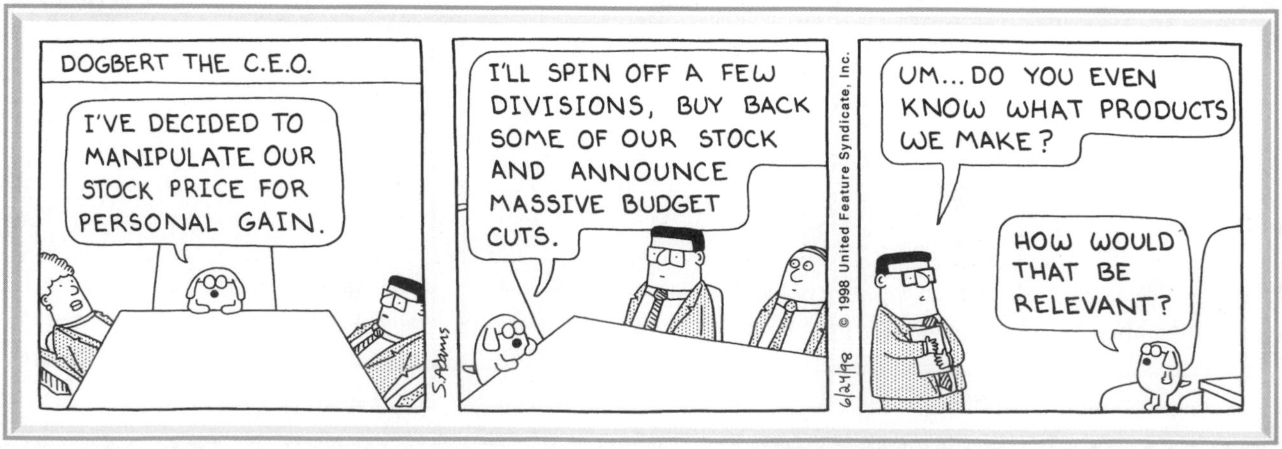
DOGBERT THE C.E.O.
I'VE DECIDED TO MANIPULATE OUR STOCK PRICE FOR PERSONAL GAIN.
S. Adams
I'LL SPIN OFF A FEW DIVISIONS, BUY BACK SOME OF OUR STOCK AND ANNOUNCE MASSIVE BUDGET CUTS.
6/24/98 © 1998 United Feature Syndicate, Inc.
UM... DO YOU EVEN KNOW WHAT PRODUCTS WE MAKE?
HOW WOULD THAT BE RELEVANT?

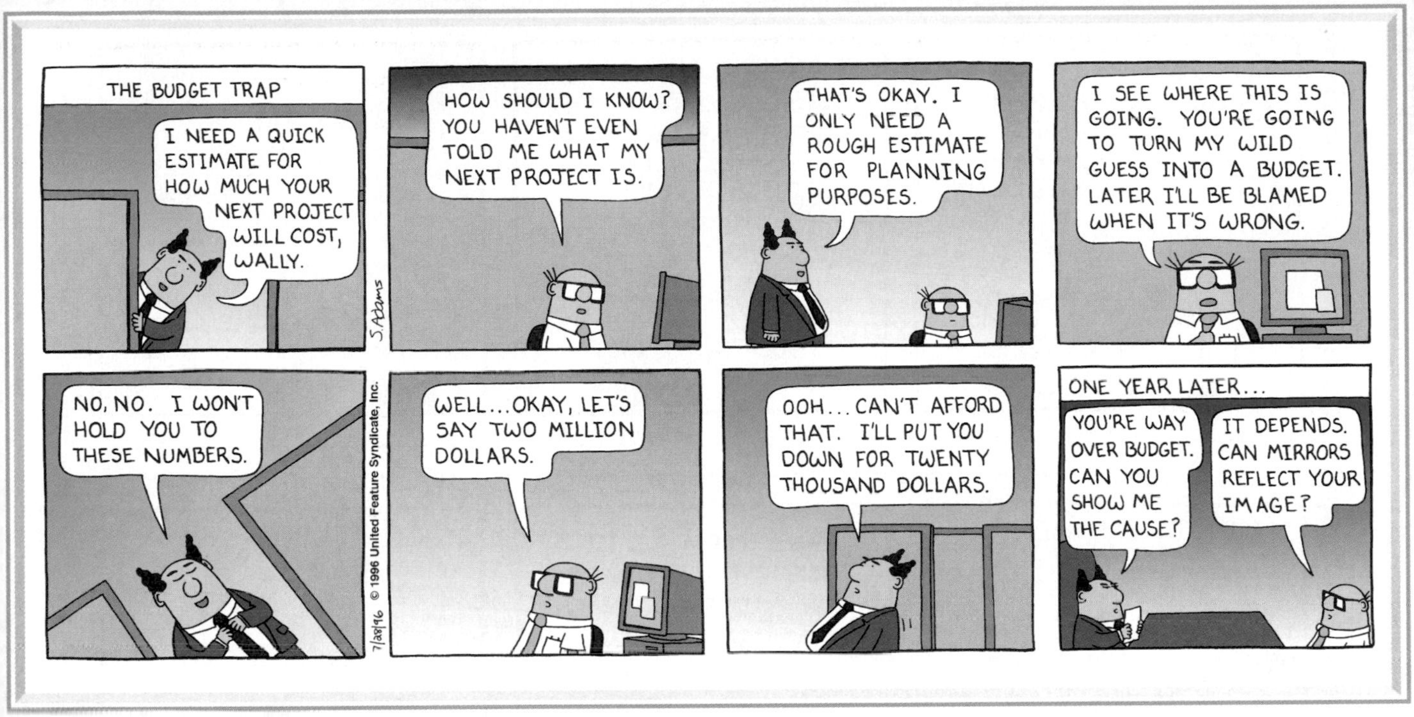
THE BUDGET TRAP
I NEED A QUICK ESTIMATE FOR HOW MUCH YOUR NEXT PROJECT WILL COST, WALLY.
HOW SHOULD I KNOW? YOU HAVEN'T EVEN TOLD ME WHAT MY NEXT PROJECT IS.
THAT'S OKAY. I ONLY NEED A ROUGH ESTIMATE FOR PLANNING PURPOSES.
I SEE WHERE THIS IS GOING. YOU'RE GOING TO TURN MY WILD GUESS INTO A BUDGET. LATER I'LL BE BLAMED WHEN IT'S WRONG.
NO, NO. I WON'T HOLD YOU TO THESE NUMBERS.
WELL...OKAY, LET'S SAY TWO MILLION DOLLARS.
OOH... CAN'T AFFORD THAT. I'LL PUT YOU DOWN FOR TWENTY THOUSAND DOLLARS.
ONE YEAR LATER...
YOU'RE WAY OVER BUDGET. CAN YOU SHOW ME THE CAUSE?
IT DEPENDS. CAN MIRRORS REFLECT YOUR IMAGE?
S. Adams
7/28/96 © 1996 United Feature Syndicate, Inc.

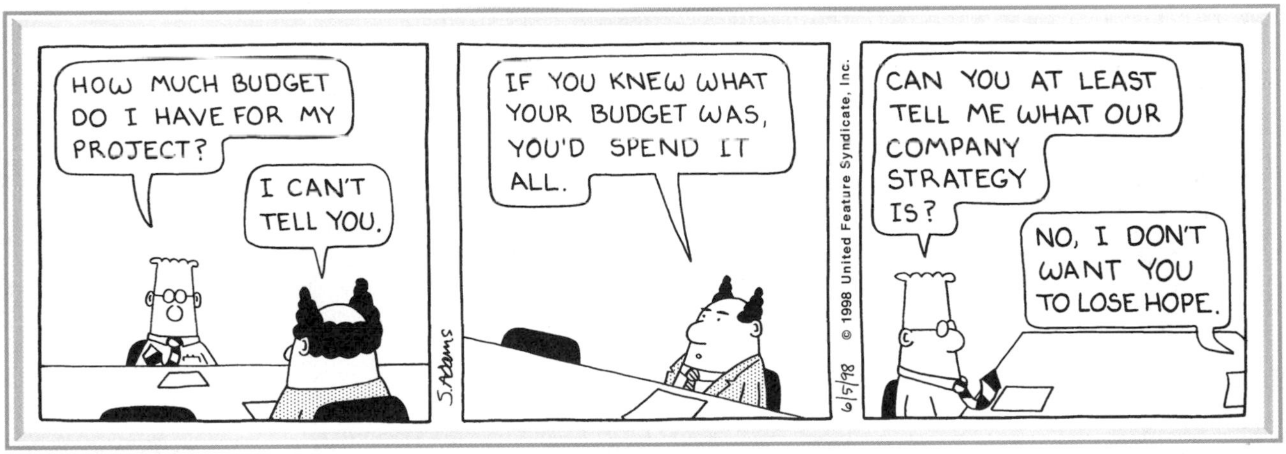
HOW MUCH BUDGET DO I HAVE FOR MY PROJECT?
I CAN'T TELL YOU.
IF YOU KNEW WHAT YOUR BUDGET WAS, YOU'D SPEND IT ALL.
CAN YOU AT LEAST TELL ME WHAT OUR COMPANY STRATEGY IS?
NO, I DON'T WANT YOU TO LOSE HOPE.
S. Adams
6/5/98 © 1998 United Feature Syndicate, Inc.

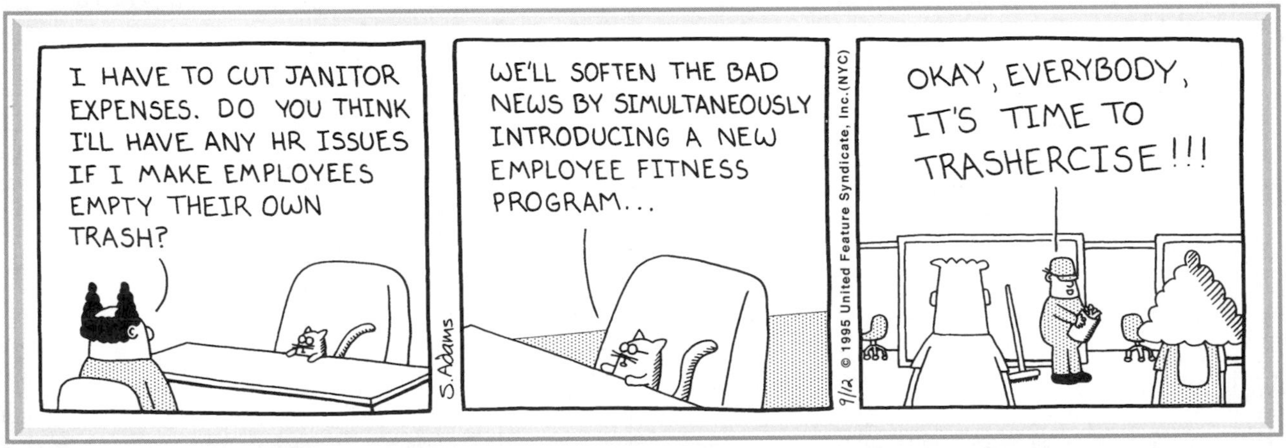
I HAVE TO CUT JANITOR EXPENSES. DO YOU THINK I'LL HAVE ANY HR ISSUES IF I MAKE EMPLOYEES EMPTY THEIR OWN TRASH?
WE'LL SOFTEN THE BAD NEWS BY SIMULTANEOUSLY INTRODUCING A NEW EMPLOYEE FITNESS PROGRAM...
OKAY, EVERYBODY, IT'S TIME TO TRASHERCISE!!!
S. Adams
9/12 © 1995 United Feature Syndicate, Inc.(NYC)

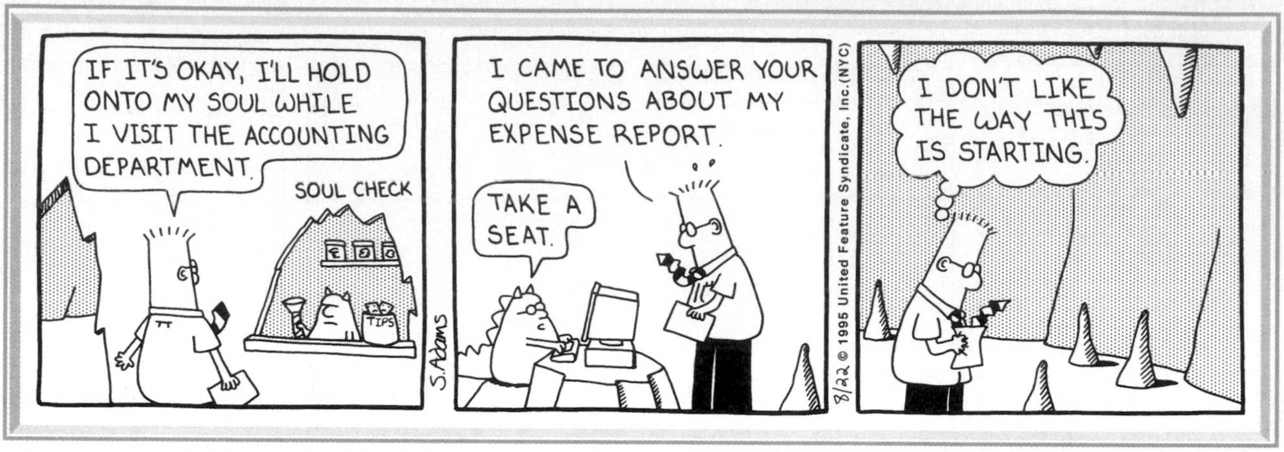
IF IT'S OKAY, I'LL HOLD ONTO MY SOUL WHILE I VISIT THE ACCOUNTING DEPARTMENT.
SOUL CHECK
TIPS
S. Adams
I CAME TO ANSWER YOUR QUESTIONS ABOUT MY EXPENSE REPORT.
TAKE A SEAT.
8/22 © 1995 United Feature Syndicate, Inc.(NYC)
I DON'T LIKE THE WAY THIS IS STARTING.

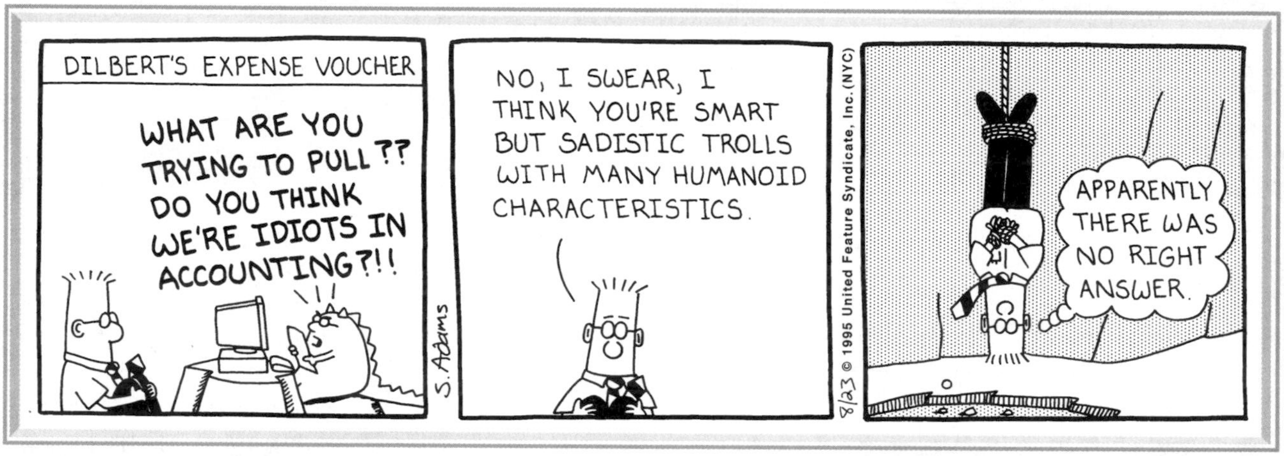
DILBERT'S EXPENSE VOUCHER
WHAT ARE YOU TRYING TO PULL?? DO YOU THINK WE'RE IDIOTS IN ACCOUNTING?!!
S. Adams
NO, I SWEAR, I THINK YOU'RE SMART BUT SADISTIC TROLLS WITH MANY HUMANOID CHARACTERISTICS.
8/23 © 1995 United Feature Syndicate, Inc.(NYC)
APPARENTLY THERE WAS NO RIGHT ANSWER.

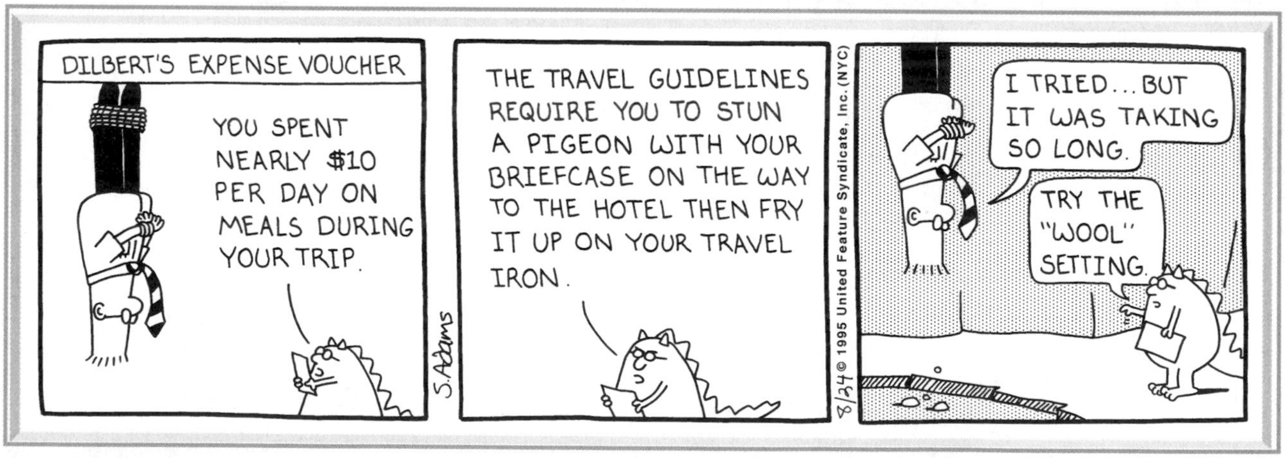
DILBERT'S EXPENSE VOUCHER
YOU SPENT NEARLY $10 PER DAY ON MEALS DURING YOUR TRIP.
S. Adams
THE TRAVEL GUIDELINES REQUIRE YOU TO STUN A PIGEON WITH YOUR BRIEFCASE ON THE WAY TO THE HOTEL THEN FRY IT UP ON YOUR TRAVEL IRON.
8/24 © 1995 United Feature Syndicate, Inc.(NYC)
I TRIED... BUT IT WAS TAKING SO LONG.
TRY THE "WOOL" SETTING.

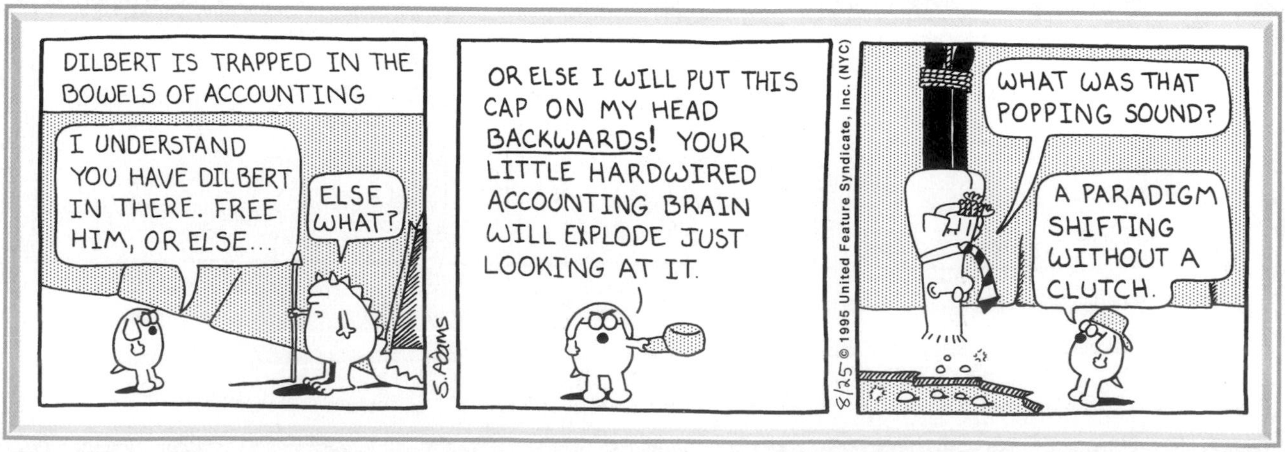
DILBERT IS TRAPPED IN THE BOWELS OF ACCOUNTING
I UNDERSTAND YOU HAVE DILBERT IN THERE. FREE HIM, OR ELSE...
ELSE WHAT?
S. Adams
OR ELSE I WILL PUT THIS CAP ON MY HEAD BACKWARDS! YOUR LITTLE HARDWIRED ACCOUNTING BRAIN WILL EXPLODE JUST LOOKING AT IT.
8/25 © 1995 United Feature Syndicate, Inc.(NYC)
WHAT WAS THAT POPPING SOUND?
A PARADIGM SHIFTING WITHOUT A CLUTCH.

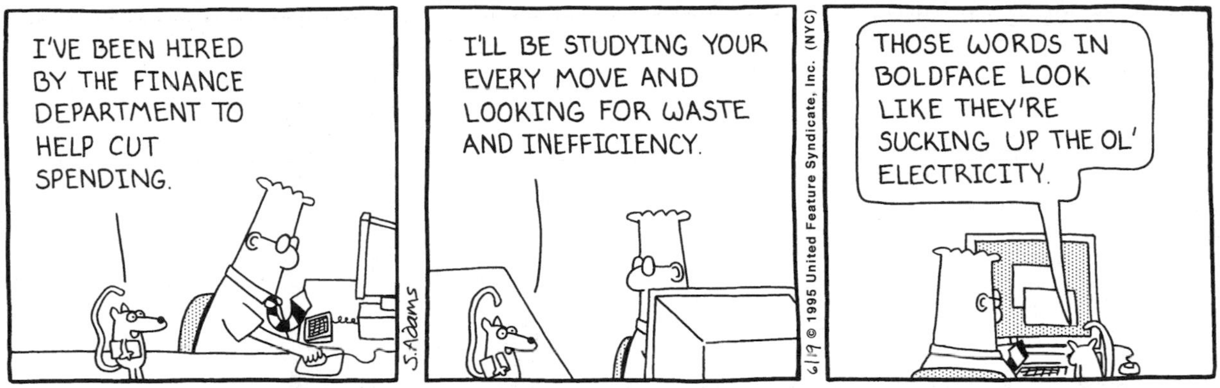
I'VE BEEN HIRED BY THE FINANCE DEPARTMENT TO HELP CUT SPENDING.
S. Adams
I'LL BE STUDYING YOUR EVERY MOVE AND LOOKING FOR WASTE AND INEFFICIENCY.
6/19 © 1995 United Feature Syndicate, Inc. (NYC)
THOSE WORDS IN BOLDFACE LOOK LIKE THEY'RE SUCKING UP THE OL' ELECTRICITY.

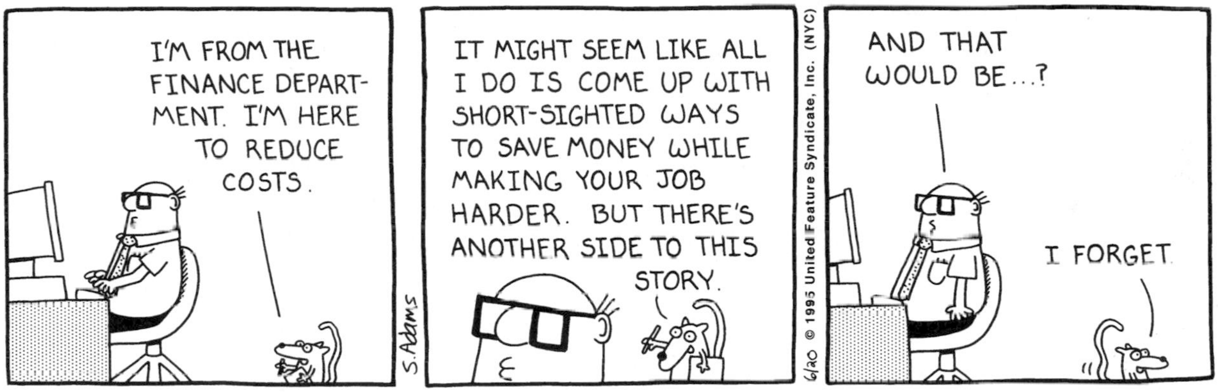
I'M FROM THE FINANCE DEPARTMENT. I'M HERE TO REDUCE COSTS.
S. Adams
IT MIGHT SEEM LIKE ALL I DO IS COME UP WITH SHORT-SIGHTED WAYS TO SAVE MONEY WHILE MAKING YOUR JOB HARDER. BUT THERE'S ANOTHER SIDE TO THIS STORY.
6/20 © 1995 United Feature Syndicate, Inc. (NYC)
AND THAT WOULD BE...?
I FORGET.

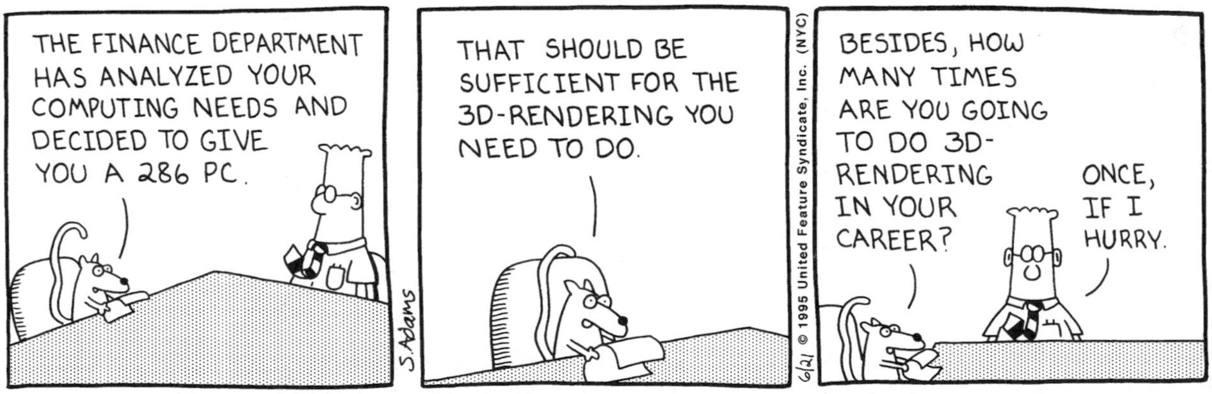
THE FINANCE DEPARTMENT HAS ANALYZED YOUR COMPUTING NEEDS AND DECIDED TO GIVE YOU A 286 PC.
S. Adams
THAT SHOULD BE SUFFICIENT FOR THE 3D-RENDERING YOU NEED TO DO.
6/21 © 1995 United Feature Syndicate, Inc. (NYC)
BESIDES, HOW MANY TIMES ARE YOU GOING TO DO 3D-RENDERING IN YOUR CAREER?
ONCE, IF I HURRY.

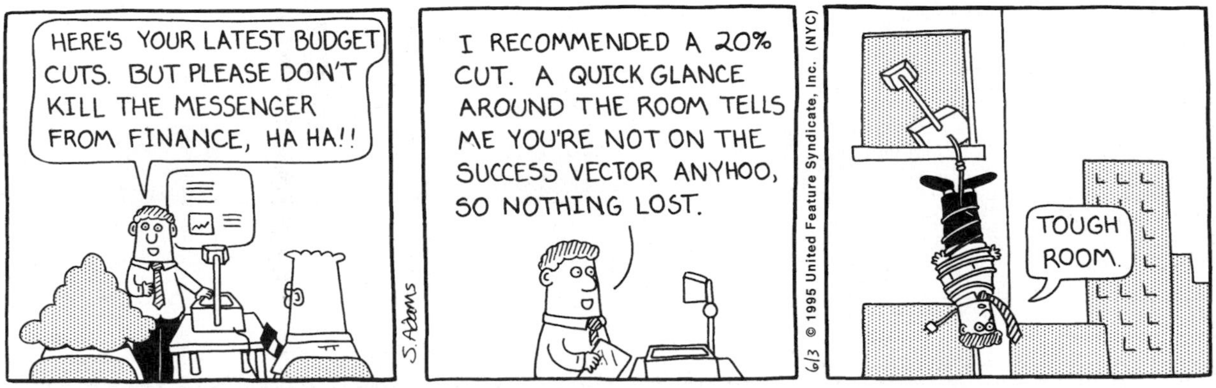
HERE'S YOUR LATEST BUDGET CUTS. BUT PLEASE DON'T KILL THE MESSENGER FROM FINANCE, HA HA!!
S. Adams
I RECOMMENDED A 20% CUT. A QUICK GLANCE AROUND THE ROOM TELLS ME YOU'RE NOT ON THE SUCCESS VECTOR ANYHOO, SO NOTHING LOST.
6/3 © 1995 United Feature Syndicate, Inc. (NYC)
TOUGH ROOM.

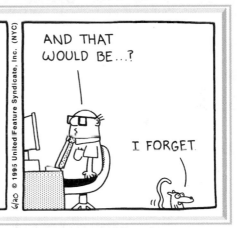

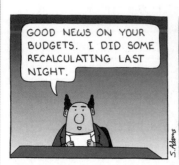

GOOD NEWS ON YOUR BUDGETS. I DID SOME RECALCULATING LAST NIGHT.
I FOUND A WAY TO GIVE MORE MONEY TO EVERY PROJECT WITHOUT INCREASING THE TOTAL BUDGET FOR PROJECTS!
S. Adams
QUESTION: DOES YOUR NEW WAY INVOLVE POOR MATH SKILLS?
IGNORE THE SKEPTIC.
HEY, I HAVE A SUGGESTION!
?
MAYBE YOU COULD RECALCULATE OUR SALARY BUDGET NEXT.
3/1/98 © 1998 United Feature Syndicate, Inc.
AND WHEN WAS THE LAST TIME YOU RECALCULATED OUR VACATION DAYS?
I CALCULATE THAT WE HAVE AN HOUR LEFT FOR THIS MEETING.
BUT I'M INTERESTED IN YOUR CALCULATION.
I THINK WE GOT GREEDY WHEN WE ASKED IF HE HAD CHANGE FOR A FIVE.

HERE'S THE GOAL THAT WILL MOTIVATE YOU FOR THE NEXT YEAR.
"BUILD A GLOBAL SATELLITE NETWORK. BUDGET: $12,000."
S. Adams
MOTIVATION FEELS MUCH DIFFERENT FROM WHAT I IMAGINED.
I WAS EXPECTING A LIGHT, ENERGETIC FEELING.
BUT IT'S MORE LIKE BEING PINNED UNDER A BURNING COUCH.
7/19/98 © 1998 United Feature Syndicate, Inc.
WHOO! I'M GETTING DIZZY.
I'D BETTER LIE DOWN UNTIL THE MOTIVATION WEARS OFF.
HE'S GOING TO BE TROUBLE DURING THE NEXT ROUND OF BUDGET CUTS.

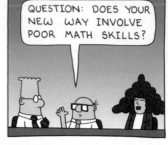

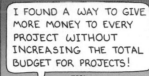

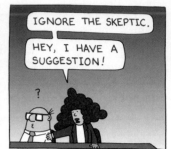

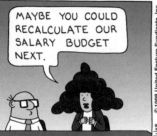

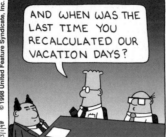

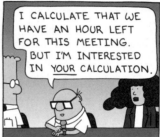

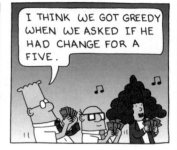

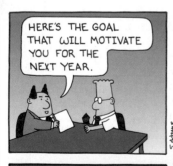

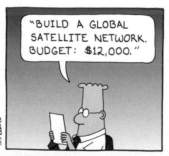

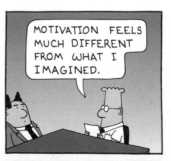

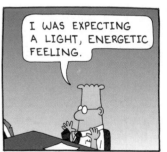

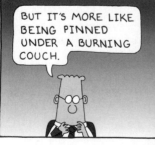

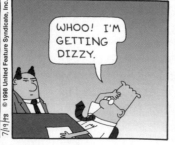

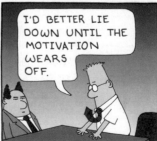

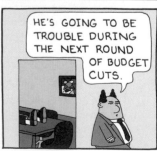

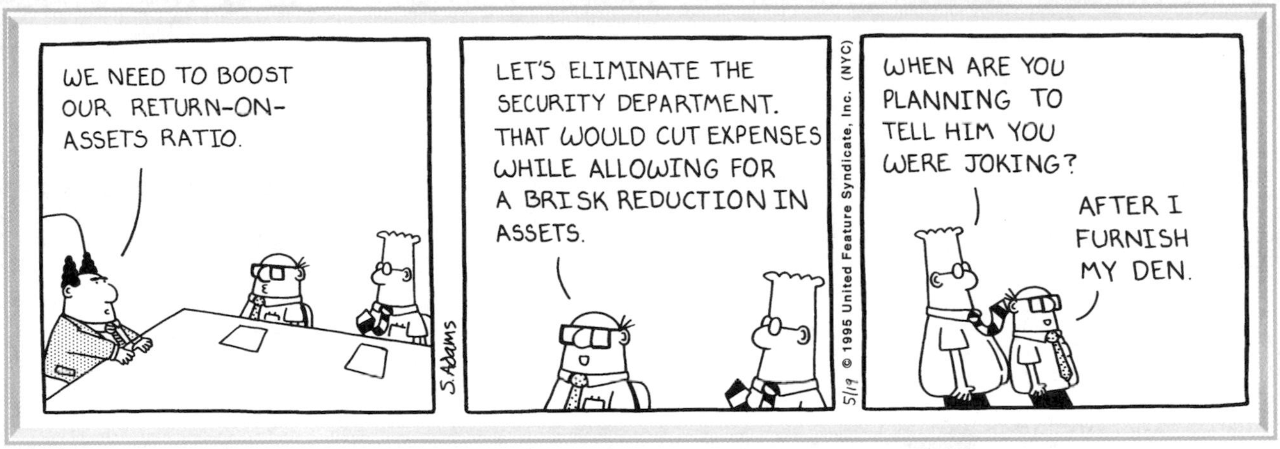
WE NEED TO BOOST OUR RETURN-ON-ASSETS RATIO.
LET'S ELIMINATE THE SECURITY DEPARTMENT. THAT WOULD CUT EXPENSES WHILE ALLOWING FOR A BRISK REDUCTION IN ASSETS.
WHEN ARE YOU PLANNING TO TELL HIM YOU WERE JOKING?
AFTER I FURNISH MY DEN.
S. Adams
5/19 © 1995 United Feature Syndicate, Inc. (NYC)

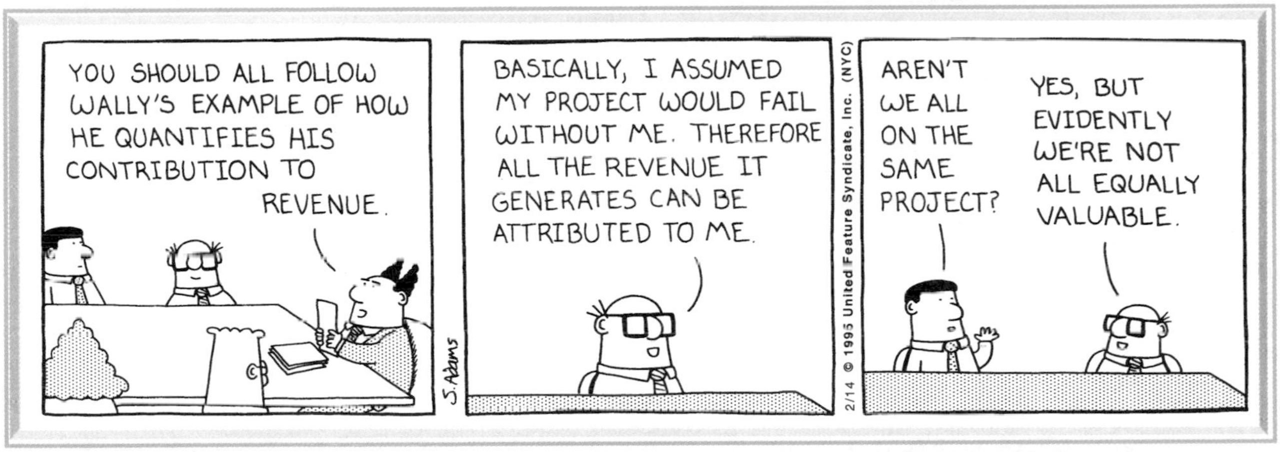
YOU SHOULD ALL FOLLOW WALLY'S EXAMPLE OF HOW HE QUANTIFIES HIS CONTRIBUTION TO REVENUE.
BASICALLY, I ASSUMED MY PROJECT WOULD FAIL WITHOUT ME. THEREFORE ALL THE REVENUE IT GENERATES CAN BE ATTRIBUTED TO ME.
AREN'T WE ALL ON THE SAME PROJECT?
YES, BUT EVIDENTLY WE'RE NOT ALL EQUALLY VALUABLE.
S. Adams
2/14 © 1995 United Feature Syndicate, Inc. (NYC)

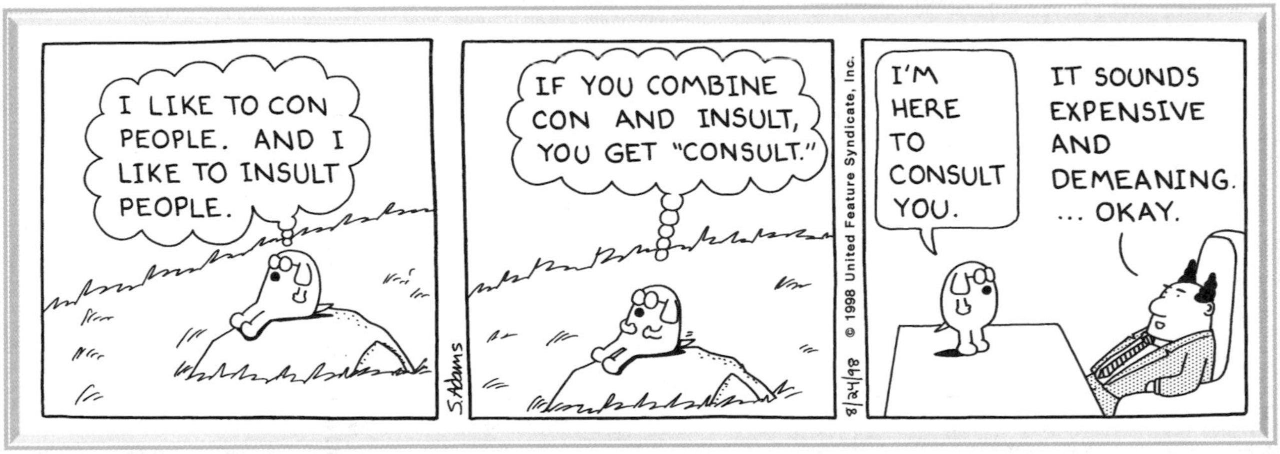
I LIKE TO CON PEOPLE. AND I LIKE TO INSULT PEOPLE.
IF YOU COMBINE CON AND INSULT, YOU GET "CONSULT."
I'M HERE TO CONSULT YOU.
IT SOUNDS EXPENSIVE AND DEMEANING. ... OKAY.
S. Adams
8/24/98 © 1998 United Feature Syndicate, Inc.

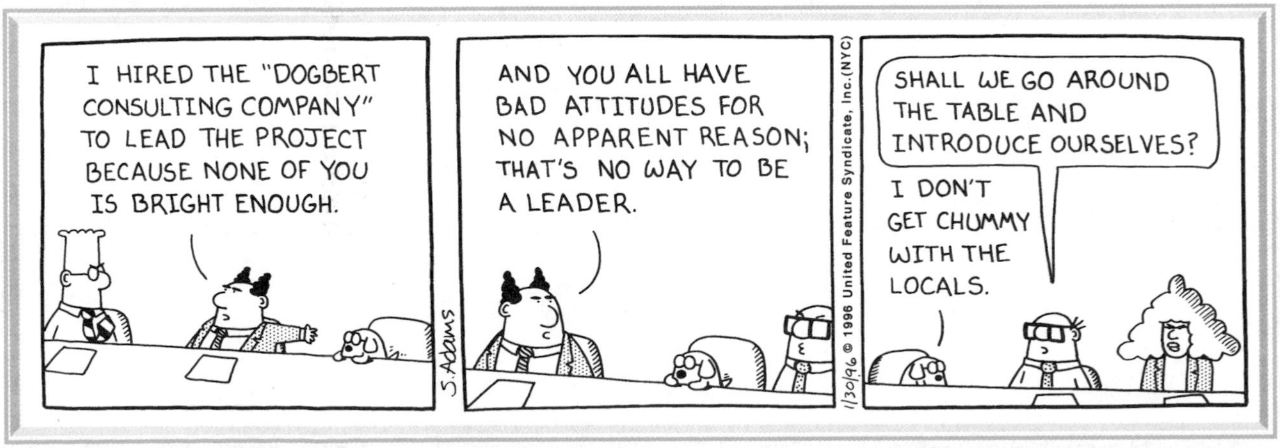
I HIRED THE "DOGBERT CONSULTING COMPANY" TO LEAD THE PROJECT BECAUSE NONE OF YOU IS BRIGHT ENOUGH.
AND YOU ALL HAVE BAD ATTITUDES FOR NO APPARENT REASON; THAT'S NO WAY TO BE A LEADER.
SHALL WE GO AROUND THE TABLE AND INTRODUCE OURSELVES?
I DON'T GET CHUMMY WITH THE LOCALS.
S. Adams
1/30/96 © 1996 United Feature Syndicate, Inc. (NYC)

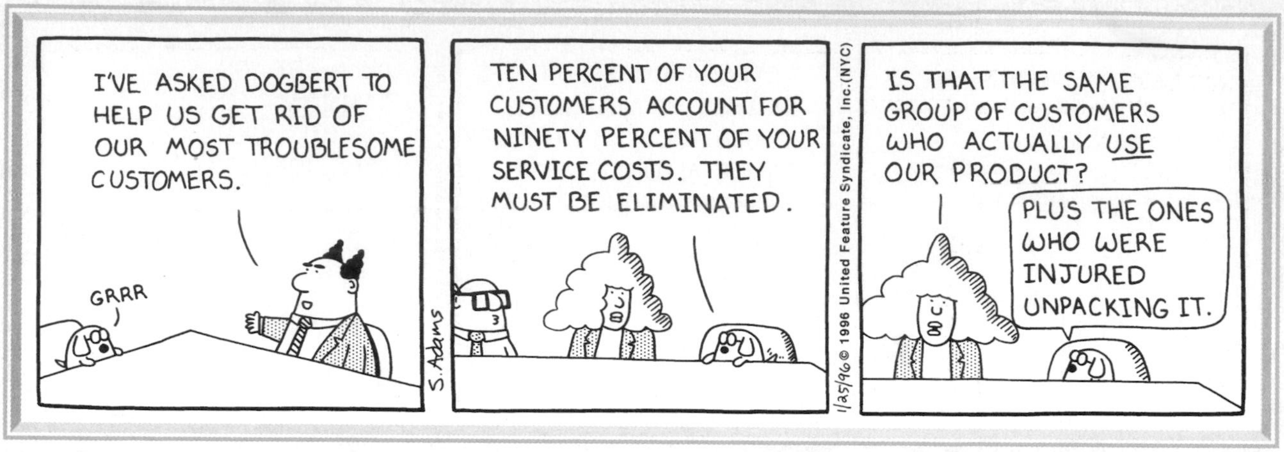
I'VE ASKED DOGBERT TO HELP US GET RID OF OUR MOST TROUBLESOME CUSTOMERS.
GRRR
TEN PERCENT OF YOUR CUSTOMERS ACCOUNT FOR NINETY PERCENT OF YOUR SERVICE COSTS. THEY MUST BE ELIMINATED.
S. Adams
1/25/96 © 1996 United Feature Syndicate, Inc.(NYC)
IS THAT THE SAME GROUP OF CUSTOMERS WHO ACTUALLY USE OUR PRODUCT?
PLUS THE ONES WHO WERE INJURED UNPACKING IT.

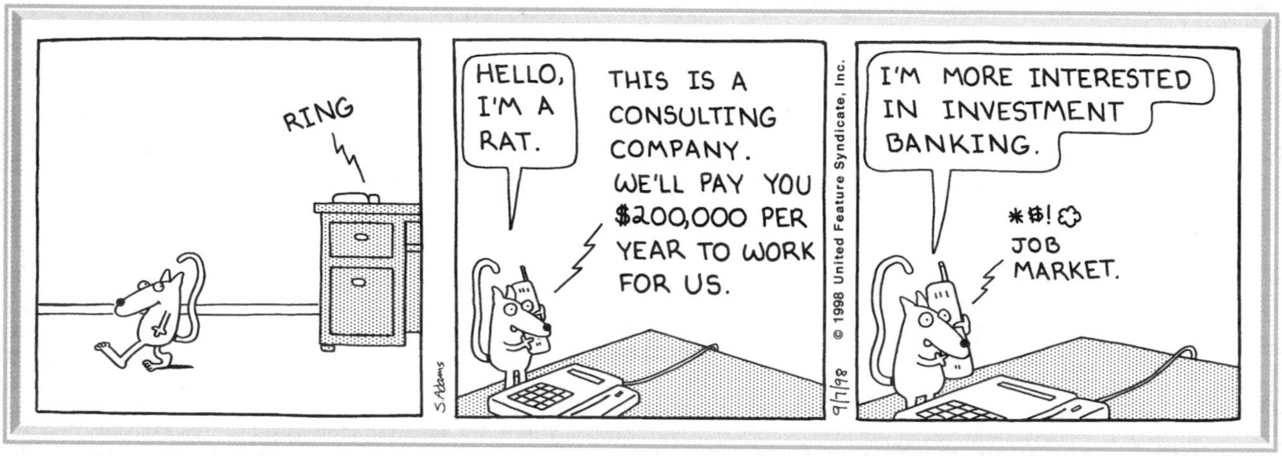
RING
HELLO, I'M A RAT.
THIS IS A CONSULTING COMPANY. WE'LL PAY YOU $200,000 PER YEAR TO WORK FOR US.
S. Adams
9/7/98 © 1998 United Feature Syndicate, Inc.
I'M MORE INTERESTED IN INVESTMENT BANKING.
*$! JOB MARKET.

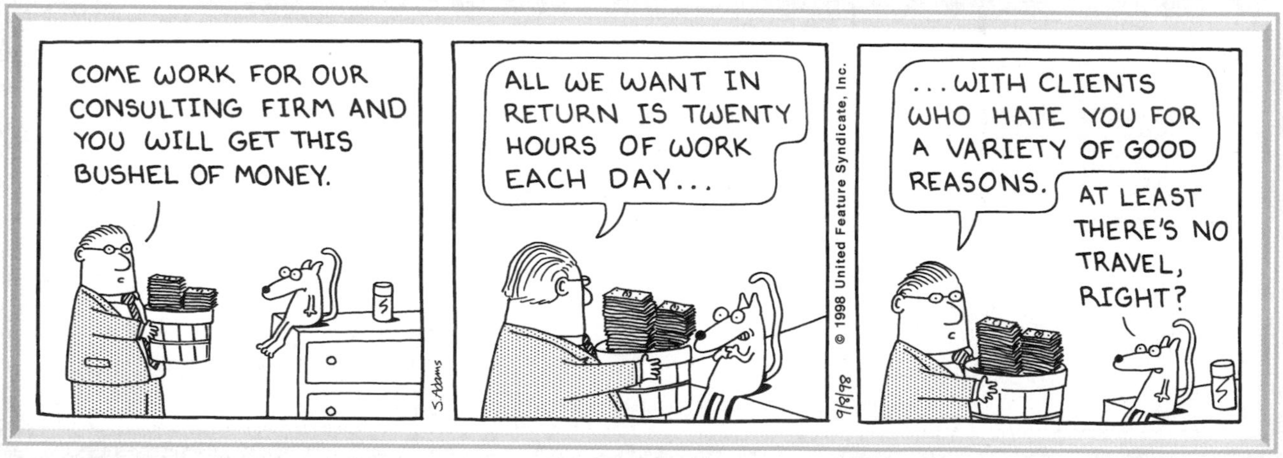
COME WORK FOR OUR CONSULTING FIRM AND YOU WILL GET THIS BUSHEL OF MONEY.
ALL WE WANT IN RETURN IS TWENTY HOURS OF WORK EACH DAY...
S. Adams
9/8/98 © 1998 United Feature Syndicate, Inc.
...WITH CLIENTS WHO HATE YOU FOR A VARIETY OF GOOD REASONS.
AT LEAST THERE'S NO TRAVEL, RIGHT?

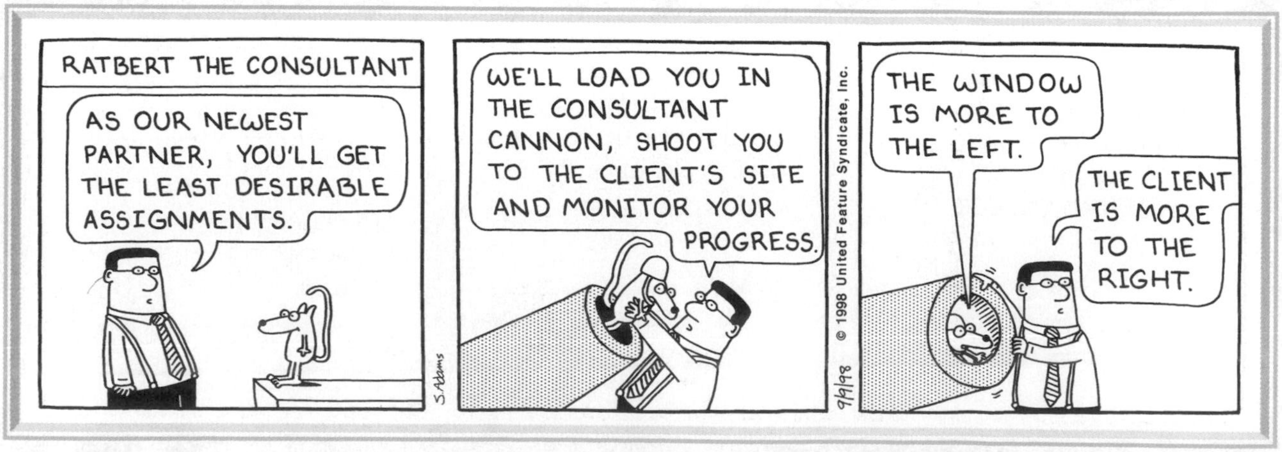
RATBERT THE CONSULTANT
AS OUR NEWEST PARTNER, YOU'LL GET THE LEAST DESIRABLE ASSIGNMENTS.
WE'LL LOAD YOU IN THE CONSULTANT CANNON, SHOOT YOU TO THE CLIENT'S SITE AND MONITOR YOUR PROGRESS.
S. Adams
9/9/98 © 1998 United Feature Syndicate, Inc.
THE WINDOW IS MORE TO THE LEFT.
THE CLIENT IS MORE TO THE RIGHT.

CONSULTING

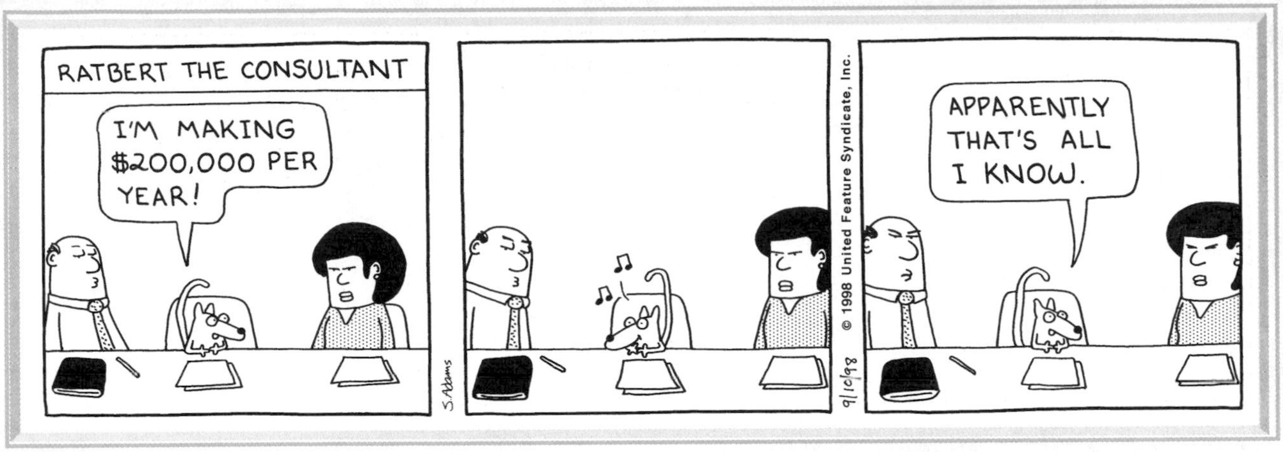
RATBERT THE CONSULTANT
I'M MAKING $200,000 PER YEAR!
APPARENTLY THAT'S ALL I KNOW.
© 1998 United Feature Syndicate, Inc.

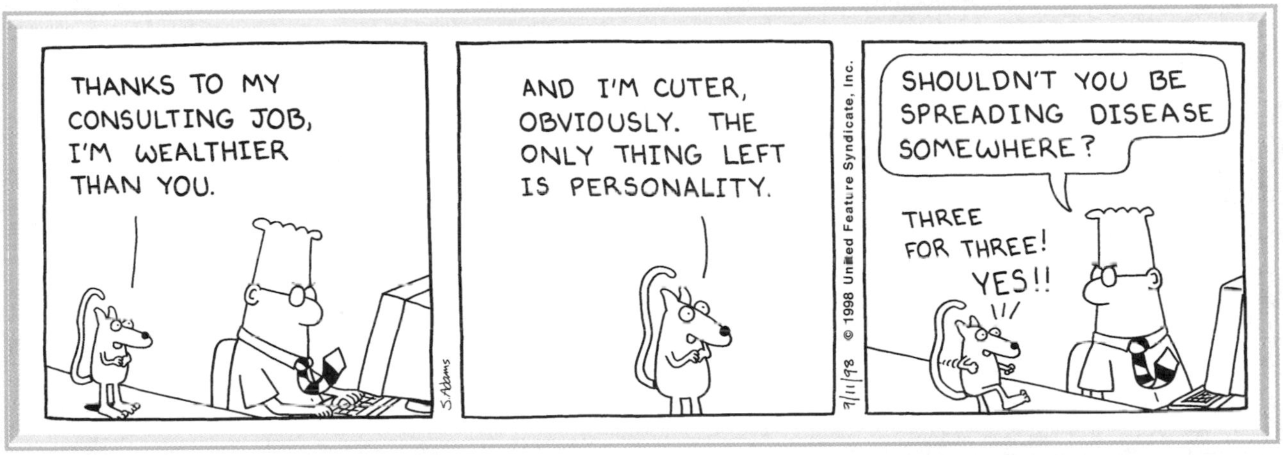
THANKS TO MY CONSULTING JOB, I'M WEALTHIER THAN YOU.
AND I'M CUTER, OBVIOUSLY. THE ONLY THING LEFT IS PERSONALITY.
SHOULDN'T YOU BE SPREADING DISEASE SOMEWHERE?
THREE FOR THREE!
YES!!
© 1998 United Feature Syndicate, Inc.

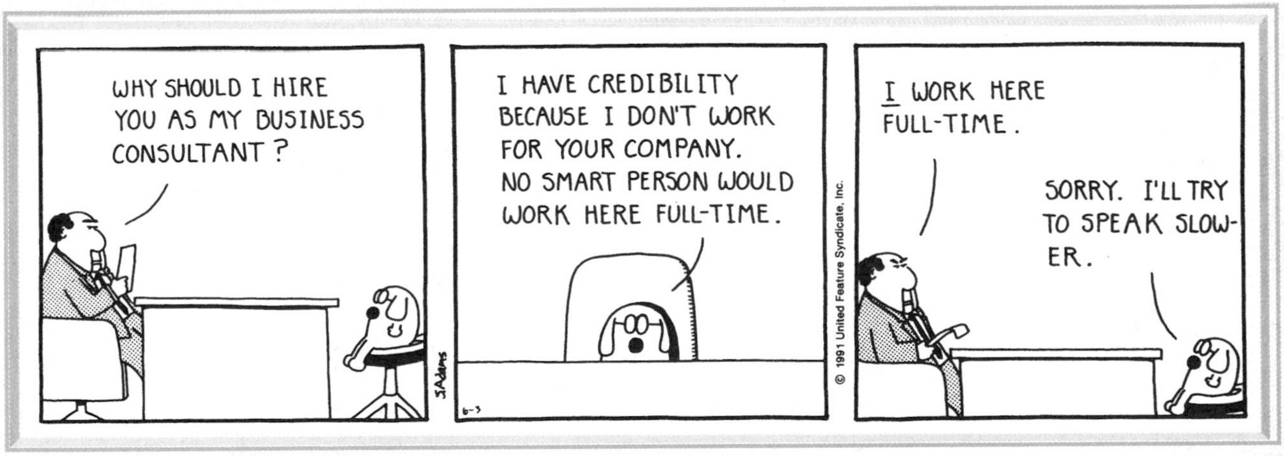
WHY SHOULD I HIRE YOU AS MY BUSINESS CONSULTANT?
I HAVE CREDIBILITY BECAUSE I DON'T WORK FOR YOUR COMPANY. NO SMART PERSON WOULD WORK HERE FULL-TIME.
I WORK HERE FULL-TIME.
SORRY. I'LL TRY TO SPEAK SLOW-ER.
© 1991 United Feature Syndicate, Inc.

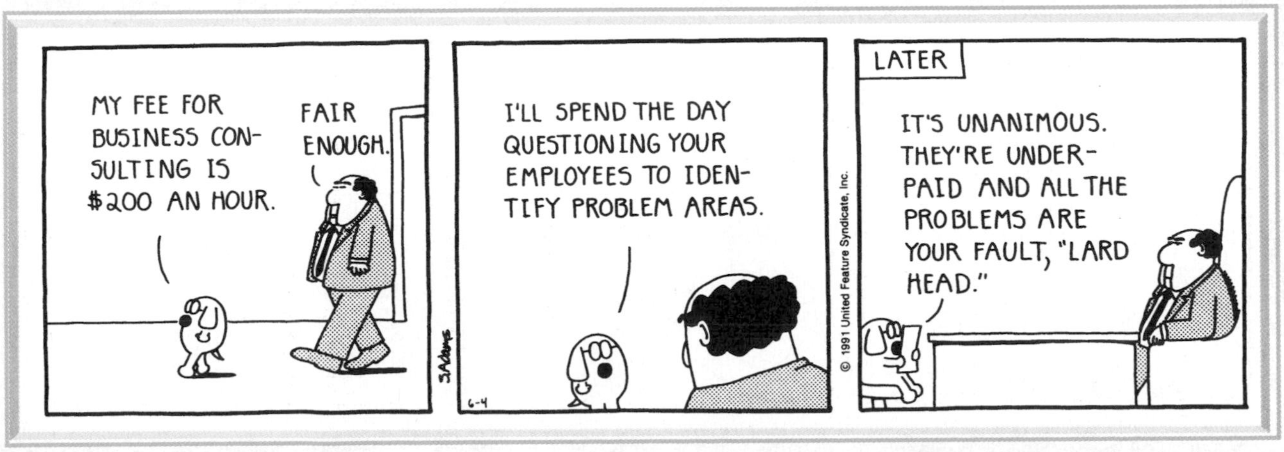
MY FEE FOR BUSINESS CON-SULTING IS $200 AN HOUR.
FAIR ENOUGH.
I'LL SPEND THE DAY QUESTIONING YOUR EMPLOYEES TO IDEN-TIFY PROBLEM AREAS.
LATER
IT'S UNANIMOUS. THEY'RE UNDER-PAID AND ALL THE PROBLEMS ARE YOUR FAULT, "LARD HEAD."
© 1991 United Feature Syndicate, Inc.

CONSULTING

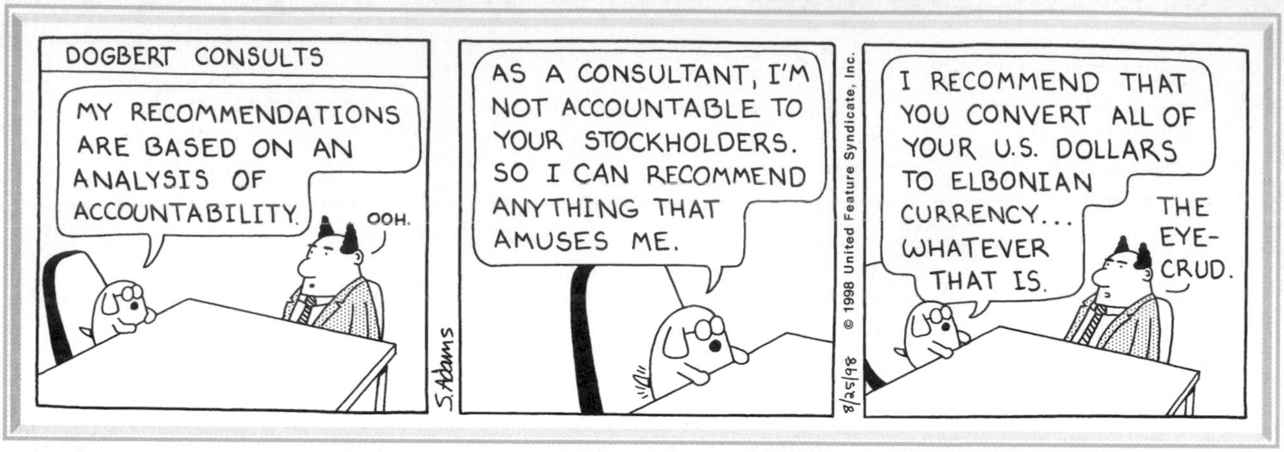
DOGBERT CONSULTS
MY RECOMMENDATIONS ARE BASED ON AN ANALYSIS OF ACCOUNTABILITY.
OOH.
AS A CONSULTANT, I'M NOT ACCOUNTABLE TO YOUR STOCKHOLDERS. SO I CAN RECOMMEND ANYTHING THAT AMUSES ME.
I RECOMMEND THAT YOU CONVERT ALL OF YOUR U.S. DOLLARS TO ELBONIAN CURRENCY... WHATEVER THAT IS.
THE EYE-CRUD.
S. Adams
8/25/98 © 1998 United Feature Syndicate, Inc.

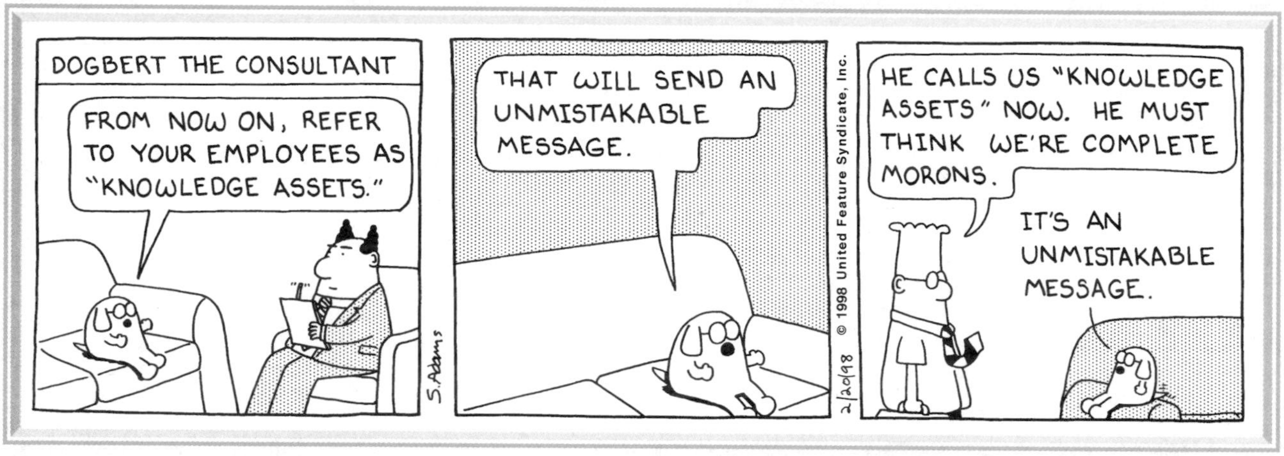
DOGBERT THE CONSULTANT
FROM NOW ON, REFER TO YOUR EMPLOYEES AS "KNOWLEDGE ASSETS."
THAT WILL SEND AN UNMISTAKABLE MESSAGE.
HE CALLS US "KNOWLEDGE ASSETS" NOW. HE MUST THINK WE'RE COMPLETE MORONS.
IT'S AN UNMISTAKABLE MESSAGE.
S. Adams
2/20/98 © 1998 United Feature Syndicate, Inc.

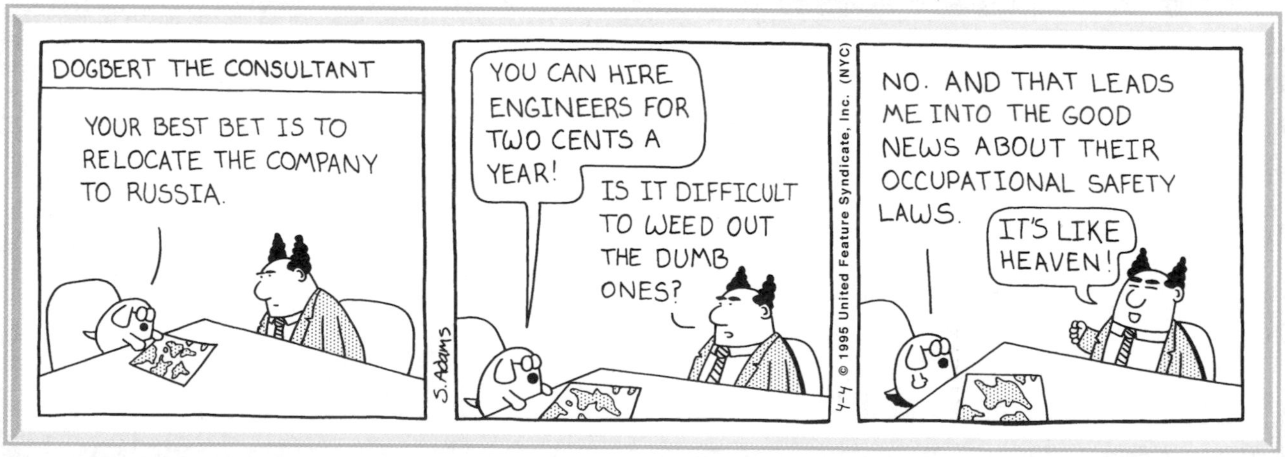
DOGBERT THE CONSULTANT
YOUR BEST BET IS TO RELOCATE THE COMPANY TO RUSSIA.
YOU CAN HIRE ENGINEERS FOR TWO CENTS A YEAR!
IS IT DIFFICULT TO WEED OUT THE DUMB ONES?
NO. AND THAT LEADS ME INTO THE GOOD NEWS ABOUT THEIR OCCUPATIONAL SAFETY LAWS.
IT'S LIKE HEAVEN!
S. Adams
4-4 © 1995 United Feature Syndicate, Inc. (NYC)

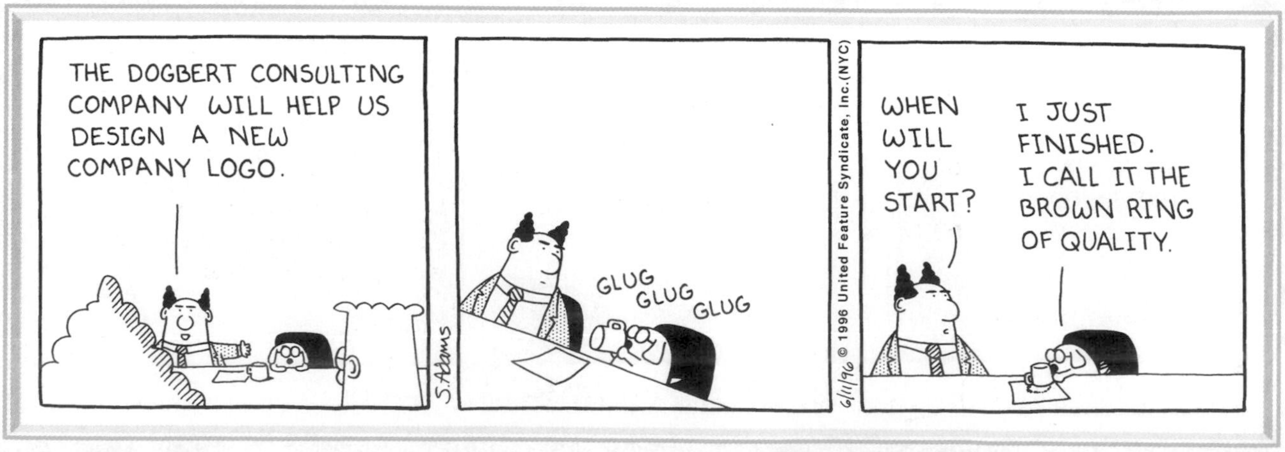
THE DOGBERT CONSULTING COMPANY WILL HELP US DESIGN A NEW COMPANY LOGO.
GLUG GLUG GLUG
WHEN WILL YOU START?
I JUST FINISHED. I CALL IT THE BROWN RING OF QUALITY.
S. Adams
6/11/96 © 1996 United Feature Syndicate, Inc.(NYC)

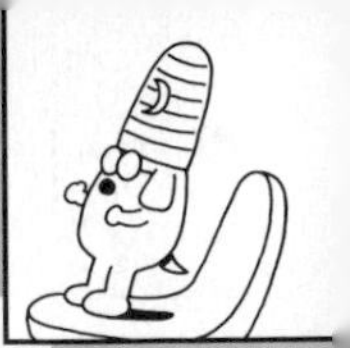

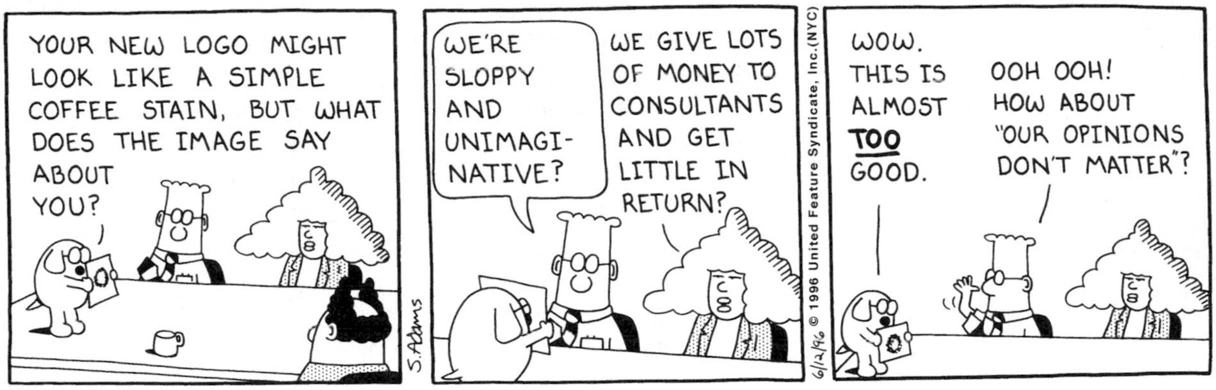
YOUR NEW LOGO MIGHT LOOK LIKE A SIMPLE COFFEE STAIN, BUT WHAT DOES THE IMAGE SAY ABOUT YOU?
WE'RE SLOPPY AND UNIMAGINATIVE?
WE GIVE LOTS OF MONEY TO CONSULTANTS AND GET LITTLE IN RETURN?
WOW. THIS IS ALMOST TOO GOOD.
OOH OOH! HOW ABOUT "OUR OPINIONS DON'T MATTER"?
S. Adams
6/12/96 © 1996 United Feature Syndicate, Inc.(NYC)

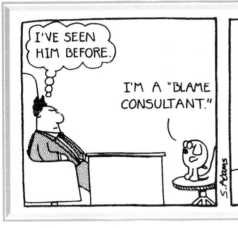

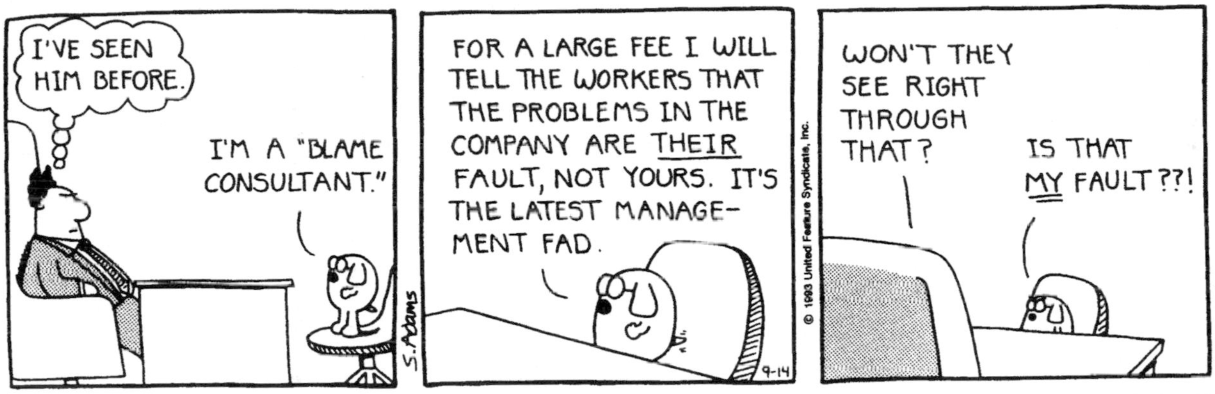
I'VE SEEN HIM BEFORE.
I'M A "BLAME CONSULTANT."
FOR A LARGE FEE I WILL TELL THE WORKERS THAT THE PROBLEMS IN THE COMPANY ARE THEIR FAULT, NOT YOURS. IT'S THE LATEST MANAGEMENT FAD.
WON'T THEY SEE RIGHT THROUGH THAT?
IS THAT MY FAULT??!
S. Adams
9-14
© 1993 United Feature Syndicate, Inc.

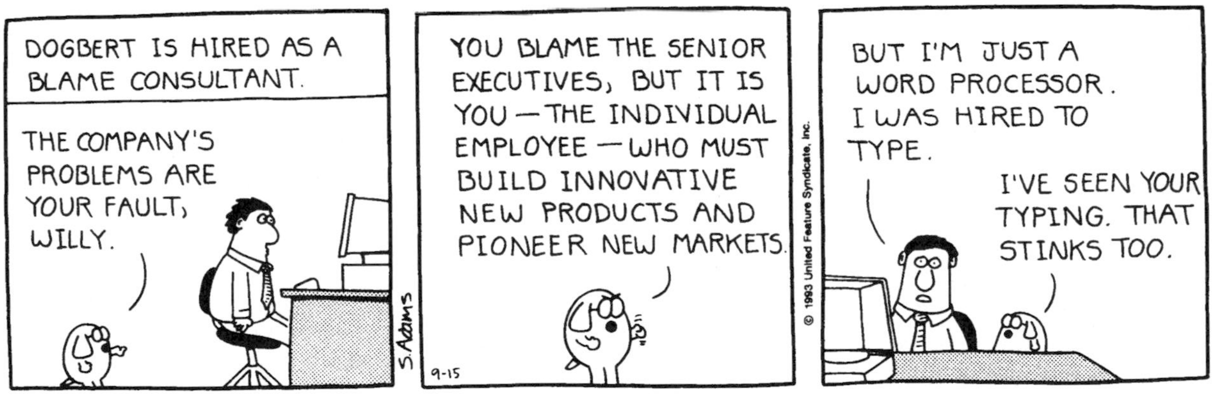
DOGBERT IS HIRED AS A BLAME CONSULTANT.
THE COMPANY'S PROBLEMS ARE YOUR FAULT, WILLY.
YOU BLAME THE SENIOR EXECUTIVES, BUT IT IS YOU — THE INDIVIDUAL EMPLOYEE — WHO MUST BUILD INNOVATIVE NEW PRODUCTS AND PIONEER NEW MARKETS.
BUT I'M JUST A WORD PROCESSOR. I WAS HIRED TO TYPE.
I'VE SEEN YOUR TYPING. THAT STINKS TOO.
S. Adams
9-15
© 1993 United Feature Syndicate, Inc.

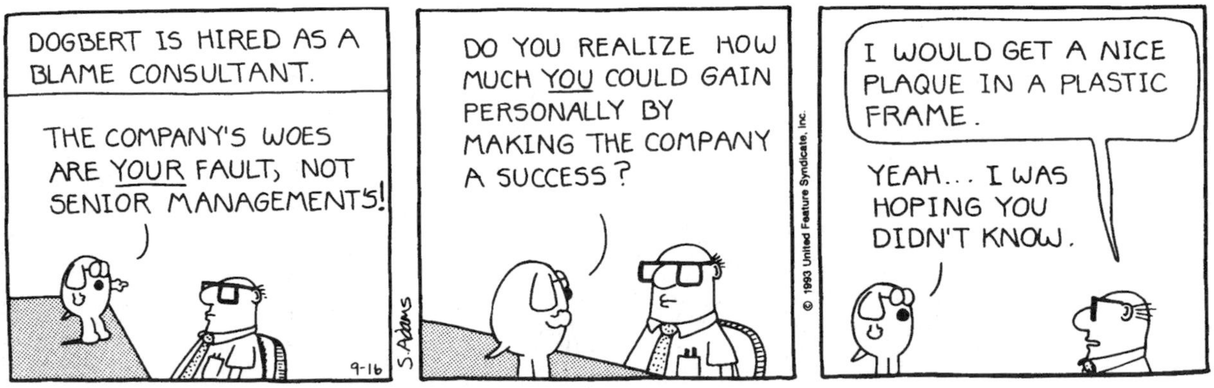
DOGBERT IS HIRED AS A BLAME CONSULTANT.
THE COMPANY'S WOES ARE YOUR FAULT, NOT SENIOR MANAGEMENT'S!
DO YOU REALIZE HOW MUCH YOU COULD GAIN PERSONALLY BY MAKING THE COMPANY A SUCCESS?
I WOULD GET A NICE PLAQUE IN A PLASTIC FRAME.
YEAH... I WAS HOPING YOU DIDN'T KNOW.
S. Adams
9-16
© 1993 United Feature Syndicate, Inc.

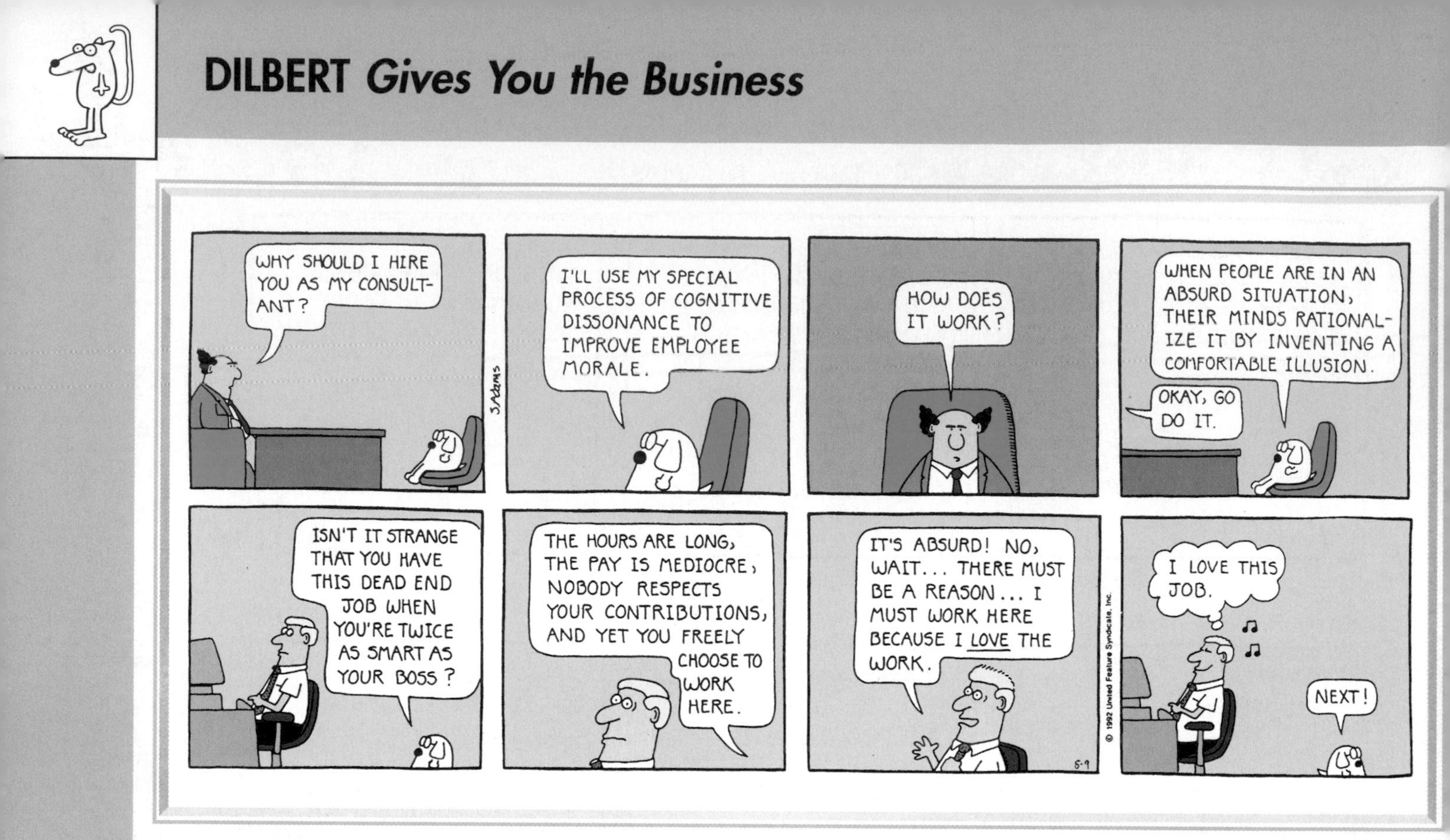
WHY SHOULD I HIRE YOU AS MY CONSULTANT?
I'LL USE MY SPECIAL PROCESS OF COGNITIVE DISSONANCE TO IMPROVE EMPLOYEE MORALE.
HOW DOES IT WORK?
WHEN PEOPLE ARE IN AN ABSURD SITUATION, THEIR MINDS RATIONALIZE IT BY INVENTING A COMFORTABLE ILLUSION.
OKAY, GO DO IT.
ISN'T IT STRANGE THAT YOU HAVE THIS DEAD END JOB WHEN YOU'RE TWICE AS SMART AS YOUR BOSS?
THE HOURS ARE LONG, THE PAY IS MEDIOCRE, NOBODY RESPECTS YOUR CONTRIBUTIONS, AND YET YOU FREELY CHOOSE TO WORK HERE.
IT'S ABSURD! NO, WAIT... THERE MUST BE A REASON... I MUST WORK HERE BECAUSE I LOVE THE WORK.
I LOVE THIS JOB.
NEXT!
© 1992 United Feature Syndicate, Inc.

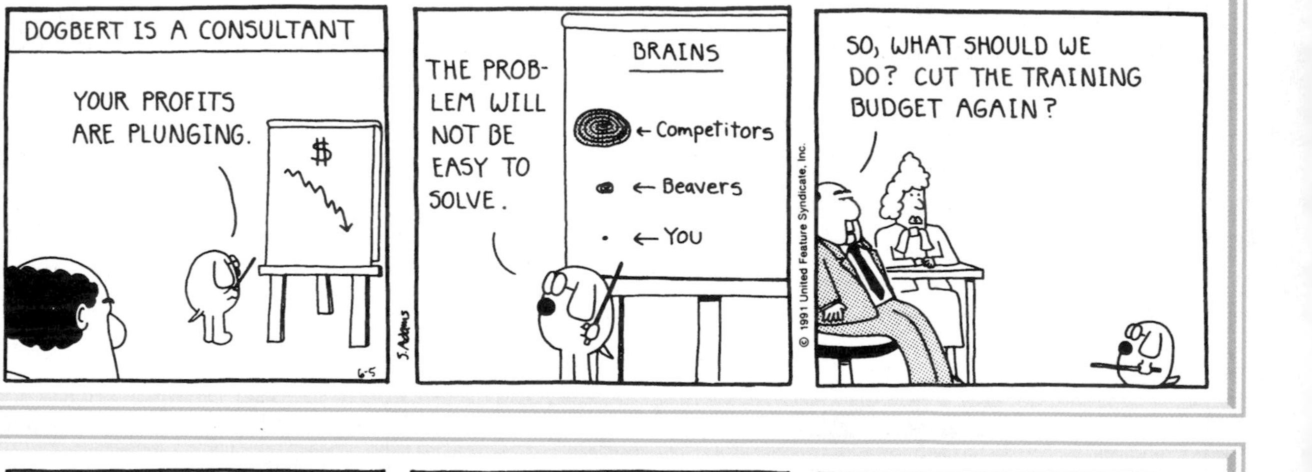
DOGBERT IS A CONSULTANT
YOUR PROFITS ARE PLUNGING.
$
THE PROBLEM WILL NOT BE EASY TO SOLVE.
BRAINS
← Competitors
← Beavers
← You
SO, WHAT SHOULD WE DO? CUT THE TRAINING BUDGET AGAIN?
© 1991 United Feature Syndicate, Inc.

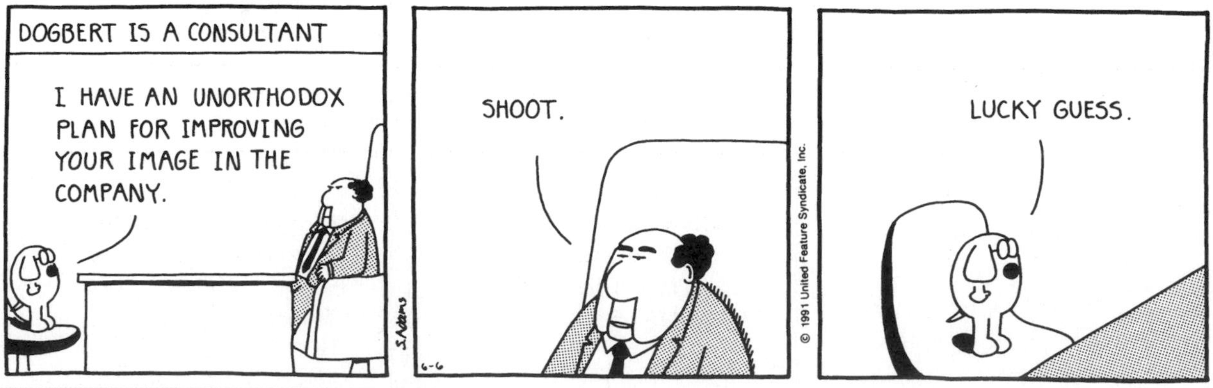
DOGBERT IS A CONSULTANT
I HAVE AN UNORTHODOX PLAN FOR IMPROVING YOUR IMAGE IN THE COMPANY.
SHOOT.
LUCKY GUESS.
© 1991 United Feature Syndicate, Inc.

CONSULTING

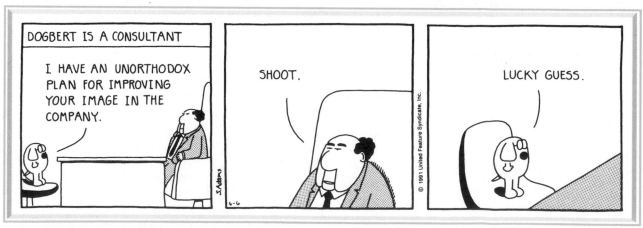

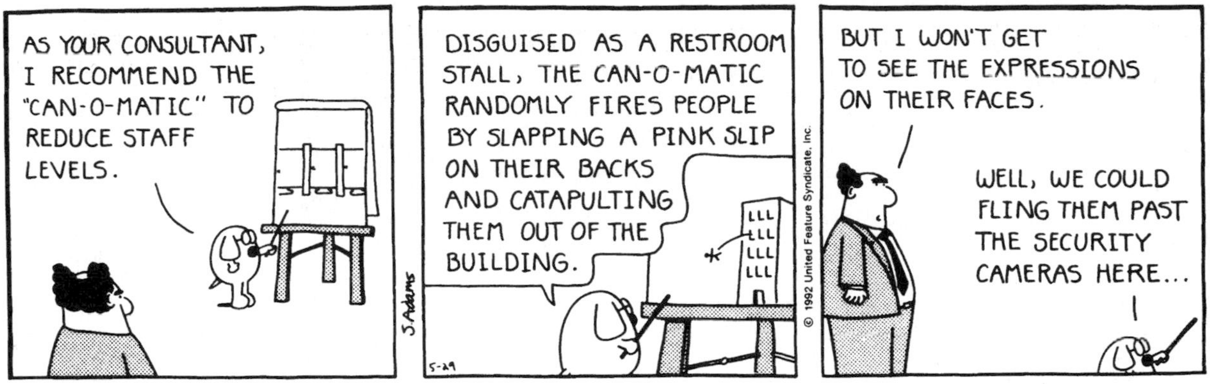
AS YOUR CONSULTANT, I RECOMMEND THE "CAN-O-MATIC" TO REDUCE STAFF LEVELS.
DISGUISED AS A RESTROOM STALL, THE CAN-O-MATIC RANDOMLY FIRES PEOPLE BY SLAPPING A PINK SLIP ON THEIR BACKS AND CATAPULTING THEM OUT OF THE BUILDING.
BUT I WON'T GET TO SEE THE EXPRESSIONS ON THEIR FACES.
WELL, WE COULD FLING THEM PAST THE SECURITY CAMERAS HERE...
© 1992 United Feature Syndicate, Inc.

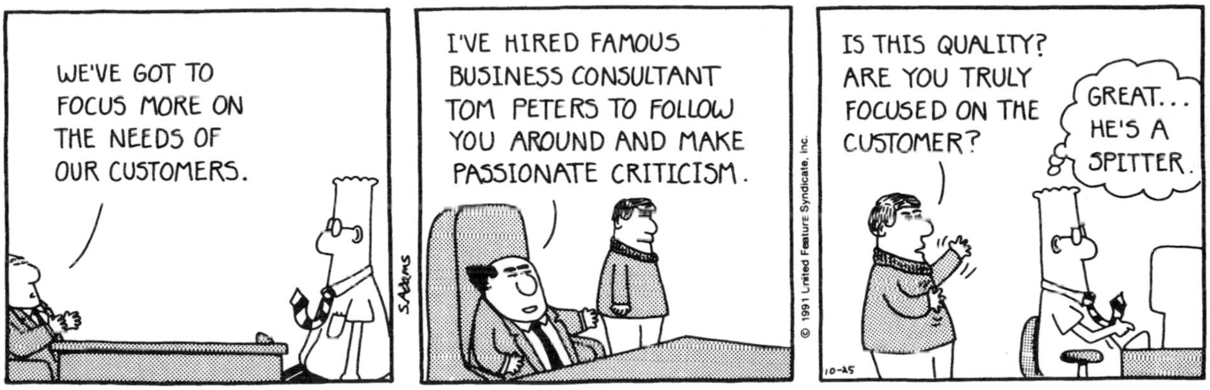
WE'VE GOT TO FOCUS MORE ON THE NEEDS OF OUR CUSTOMERS.
I'VE HIRED FAMOUS BUSINESS CONSULTANT TOM PETERS TO FOLLOW YOU AROUND AND MAKE PASSIONATE CRITICISM.
IS THIS QUALITY? ARE YOU TRULY FOCUSED ON THE CUSTOMER?
GREAT... HE'S A SPITTER.
© 1991 United Feature Syndicate, Inc.

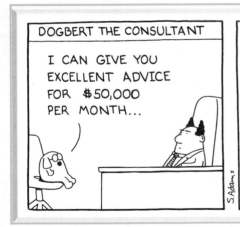

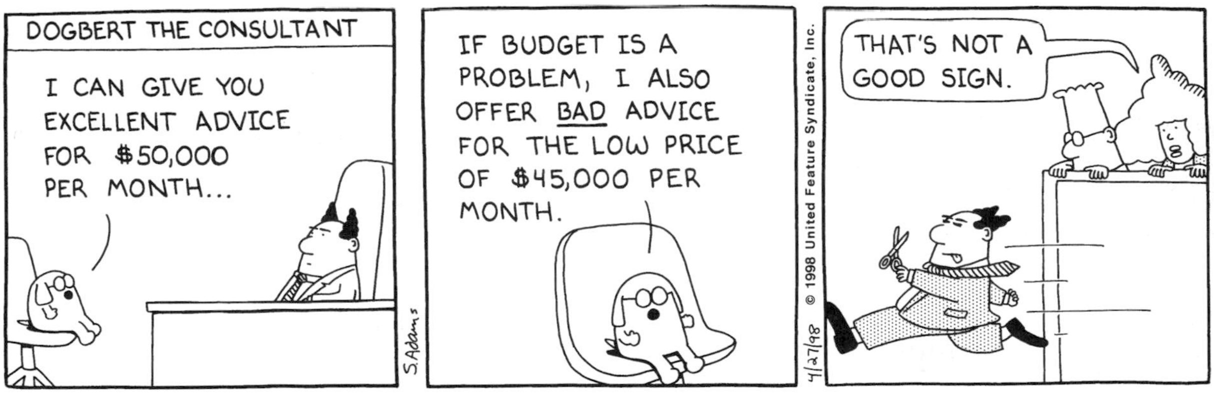
DOGBERT THE CONSULTANT
I CAN GIVE YOU EXCELLENT ADVICE FOR $50,000 PER MONTH...
IF BUDGET IS A PROBLEM, I ALSO OFFER BAD ADVICE FOR THE LOW PRICE OF $45,000 PER MONTH.
THAT'S NOT A GOOD SIGN.
© 1998 United Feature Syndicate, Inc.

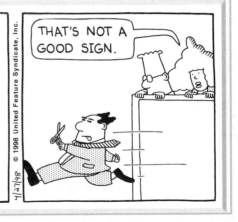

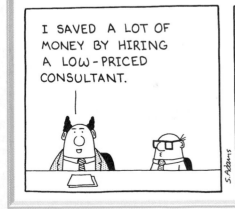

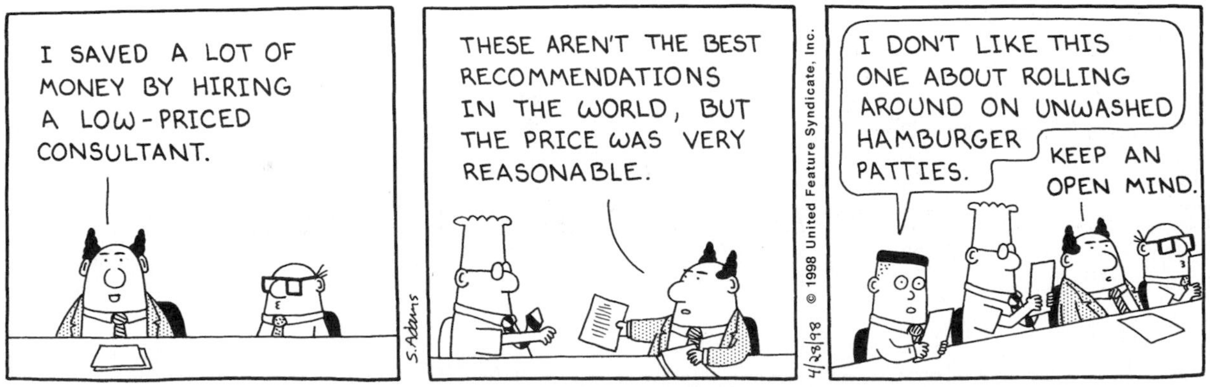
I SAVED A LOT OF MONEY BY HIRING A LOW-PRICED CONSULTANT.
THESE AREN'T THE BEST RECOMMENDATIONS IN THE WORLD, BUT THE PRICE WAS VERY REASONABLE.
I DON'T LIKE THIS ONE ABOUT ROLLING AROUND ON UNWASHED HAMBURGER PATTIES.
KEEP AN OPEN MIND.
© 1998 United Feature Syndicate, Inc.

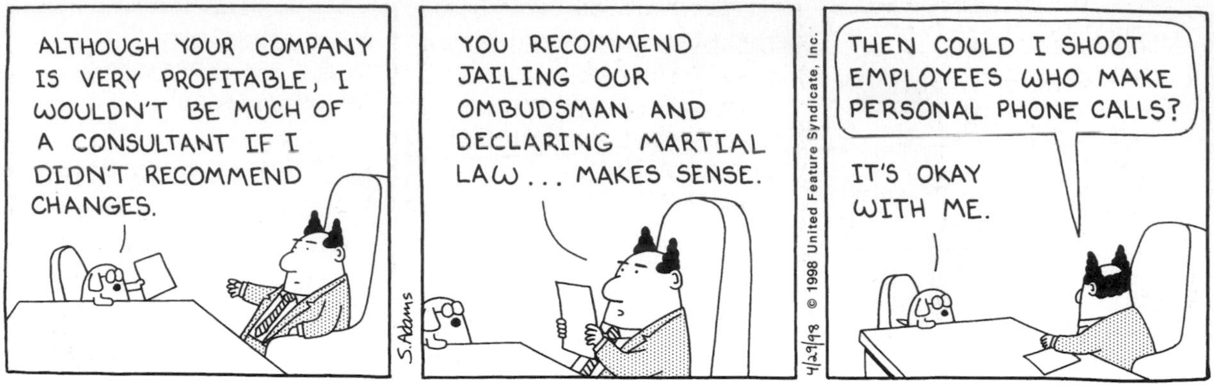
ALTHOUGH YOUR COMPANY IS VERY PROFITABLE, I WOULDN'T BE MUCH OF A CONSULTANT IF I DIDN'T RECOMMEND CHANGES.
YOU RECOMMEND JAILING OUR OMBUDSMAN AND DECLARING MARTIAL LAW... MAKES SENSE.
S. Adams
4/29/98 © 1998 United Feature Syndicate, Inc.
THEN COULD I SHOOT EMPLOYEES WHO MAKE PERSONAL PHONE CALLS?
IT'S OKAY WITH ME.

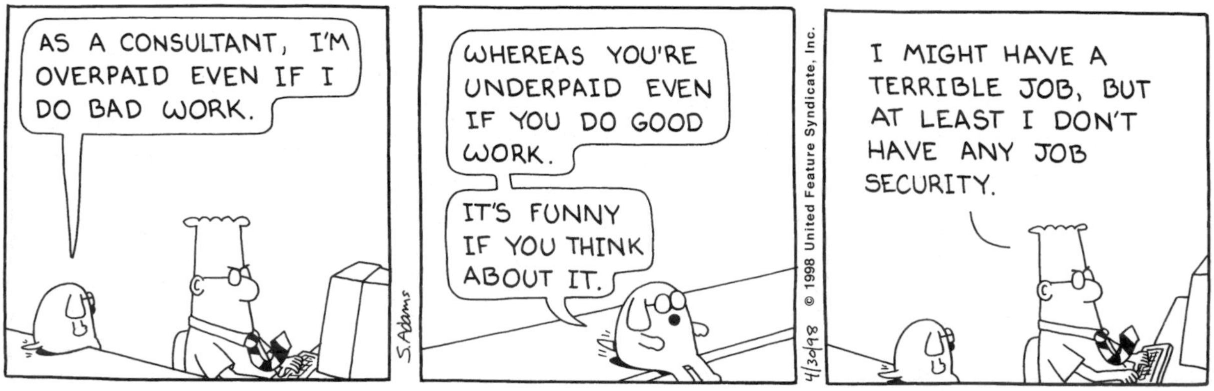
AS A CONSULTANT, I'M OVERPAID EVEN IF I DO BAD WORK.
WHEREAS YOU'RE UNDERPAID EVEN IF YOU DO GOOD WORK.
IT'S FUNNY IF YOU THINK ABOUT IT.
S. Adams
4/30/98 © 1998 United Feature Syndicate, Inc.
I MIGHT HAVE A TERRIBLE JOB, BUT AT LEAST I DON'T HAVE ANY JOB SECURITY.

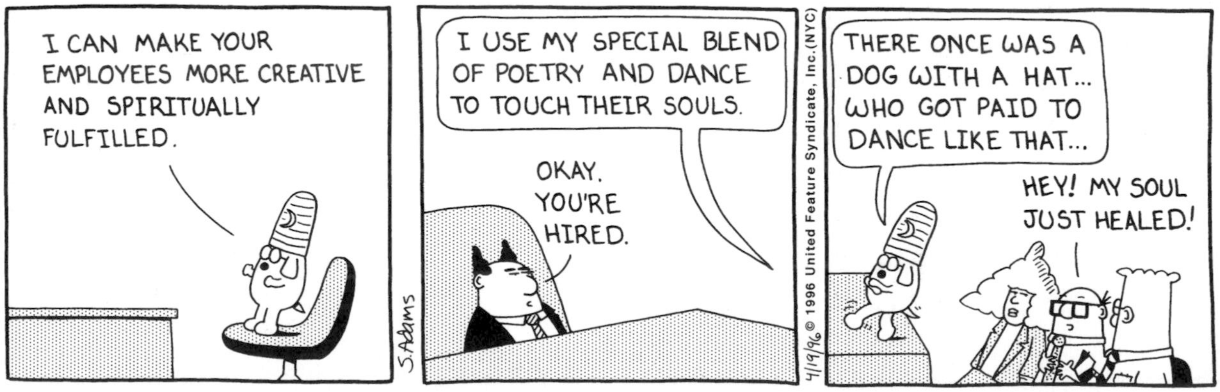
I CAN MAKE YOUR EMPLOYEES MORE CREATIVE AND SPIRITUALLY FULFILLED.
I USE MY SPECIAL BLEND OF POETRY AND DANCE TO TOUCH THEIR SOULS.
OKAY. YOU'RE HIRED.
S. Adams
4/19/96 © 1996 United Feature Syndicate, Inc.(NYC)
THERE ONCE WAS A DOG WITH A HAT... WHO GOT PAID TO DANCE LIKE THAT...
HEY! MY SOUL JUST HEALED!

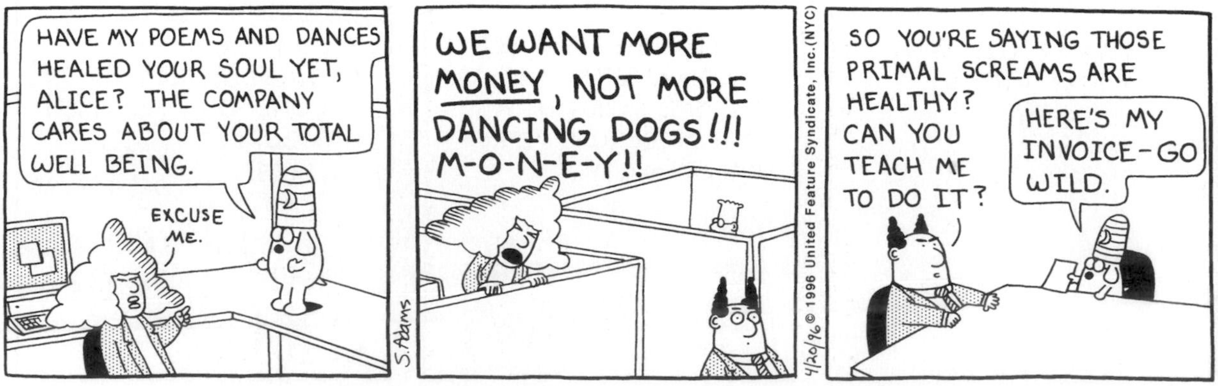
HAVE MY POEMS AND DANCES HEALED YOUR SOUL YET, ALICE? THE COMPANY CARES ABOUT YOUR TOTAL WELL BEING.
EXCUSE ME.
WE WANT MORE MONEY, NOT MORE DANCING DOGS!!! M-O-N-E-Y!!
S. Adams
4/20/96 © 1996 United Feature Syndicate, Inc.(NYC)
SO YOU'RE SAYING THOSE PRIMAL SCREAMS ARE HEALTHY? CAN YOU TEACH ME TO DO IT?
HERE'S MY INVOICE–GO WILD.

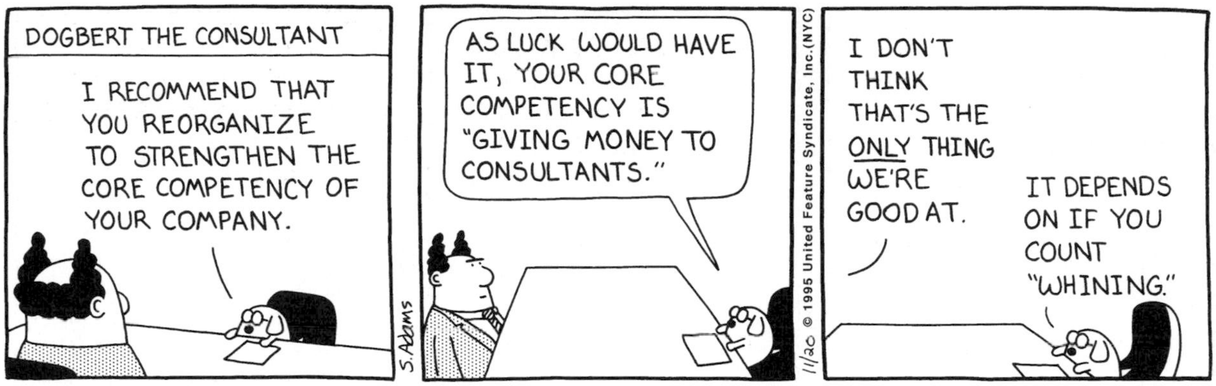
DOGBERT THE CONSULTANT
I RECOMMEND THAT YOU REORGANIZE TO STRENGTHEN THE CORE COMPETENCY OF YOUR COMPANY.
AS LUCK WOULD HAVE IT, YOUR CORE COMPETENCY IS "GIVING MONEY TO CONSULTANTS."
I DON'T THINK THAT'S THE ONLY THING WE'RE GOOD AT.
IT DEPENDS ON IF YOU COUNT "WHINING."
S. Adams
11/20 © 1995 United Feature Syndicate, Inc.(NYC)

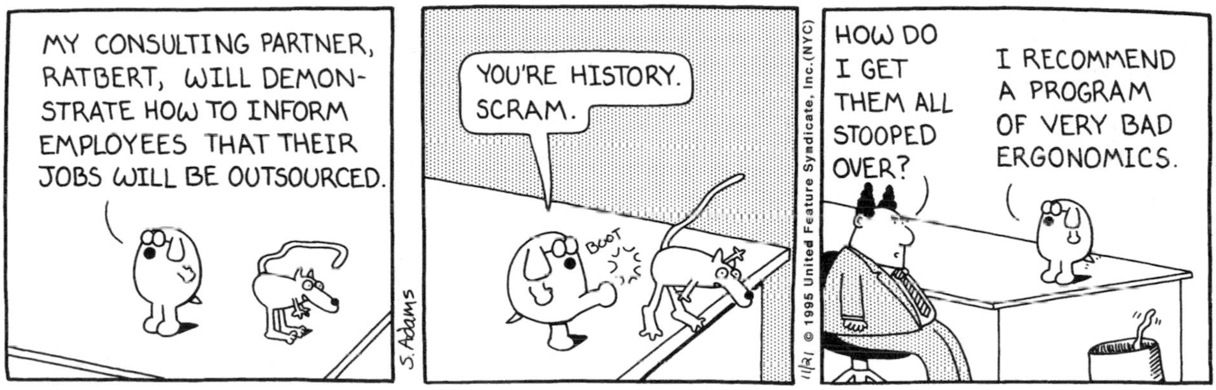
MY CONSULTING PARTNER, RATBERT, WILL DEMONSTRATE HOW TO INFORM EMPLOYEES THAT THEIR JOBS WILL BE OUTSOURCED.
YOU'RE HISTORY. SCRAM.
BOOT
HOW DO I GET THEM ALL STOOPED OVER?
I RECOMMEND A PROGRAM OF VERY BAD ERGONOMICS.
S. Adams
11/21 © 1995 United Feature Syndicate, Inc.(NYC)

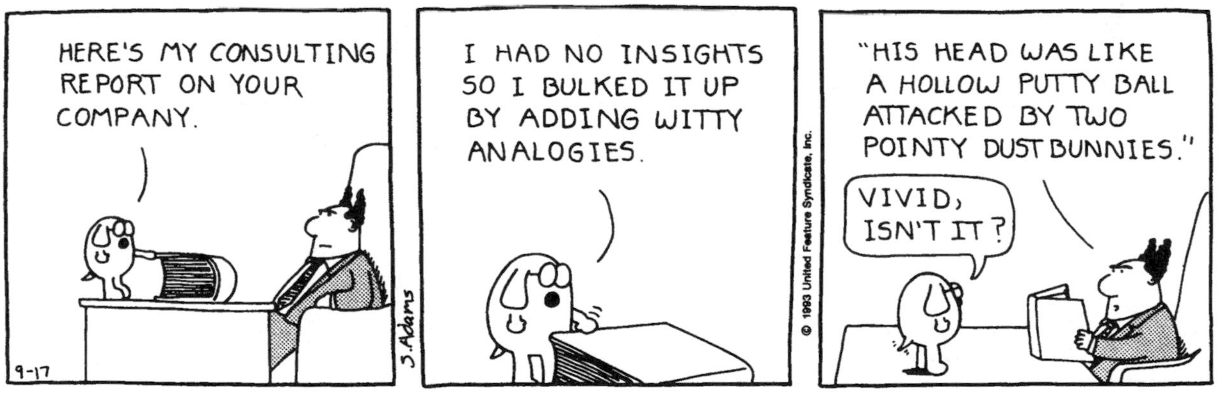
HERE'S MY CONSULTING REPORT ON YOUR COMPANY.
9-17
I HAD NO INSIGHTS SO I BULKED IT UP BY ADDING WITTY ANALOGIES.
S. Adams
© 1993 United Feature Syndicate, Inc.
"HIS HEAD WAS LIKE A HOLLOW PUTTY BALL ATTACKED BY TWO POINTY DUST BUNNIES."
VIVID, ISN'T IT?

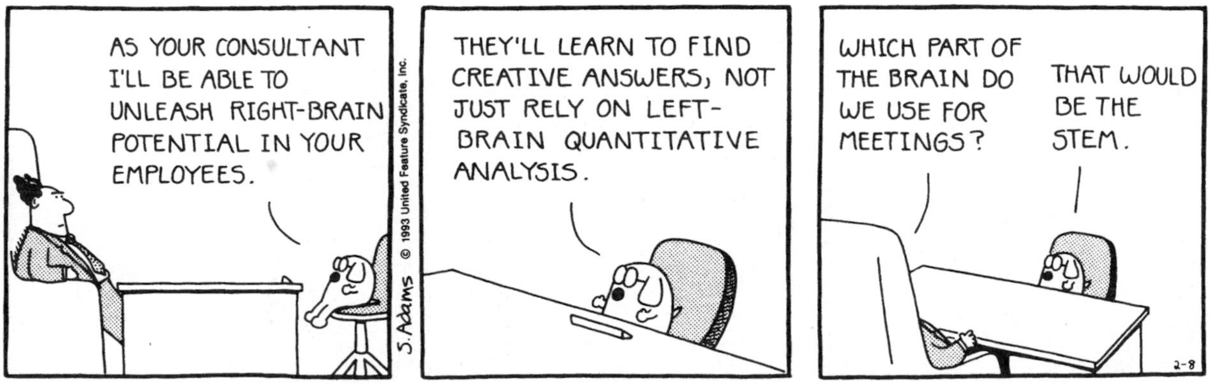
AS YOUR CONSULTANT I'LL BE ABLE TO UNLEASH RIGHT-BRAIN POTENTIAL IN YOUR EMPLOYEES.
S. Adams
© 1993 United Feature Syndicate, Inc.
THEY'LL LEARN TO FIND CREATIVE ANSWERS, NOT JUST RELY ON LEFT-BRAIN QUANTITATIVE ANALYSIS.
WHICH PART OF THE BRAIN DO WE USE FOR MEETINGS?
THAT WOULD BE THE STEM.
2-8

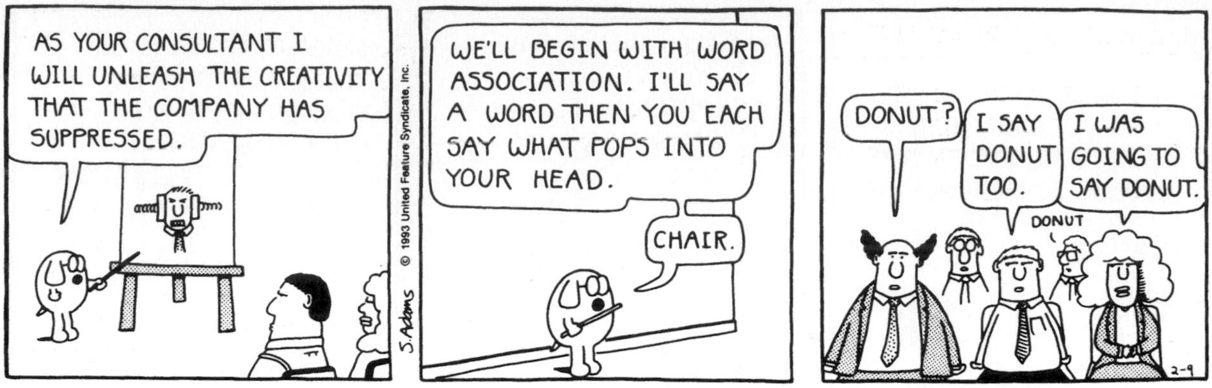
AS YOUR CONSULTANT I WILL UNLEASH THE CREATIVITY THAT THE COMPANY HAS SUPPRESSED.
S. Adams © 1993 United Feature Syndicate, Inc.
WE'LL BEGIN WITH WORD ASSOCIATION. I'LL SAY A WORD THEN YOU EACH SAY WHAT POPS INTO YOUR HEAD.
CHAIR.
DONUT?
I SAY DONUT TOO.
I WAS GOING TO SAY DONUT.
DONUT
2-9

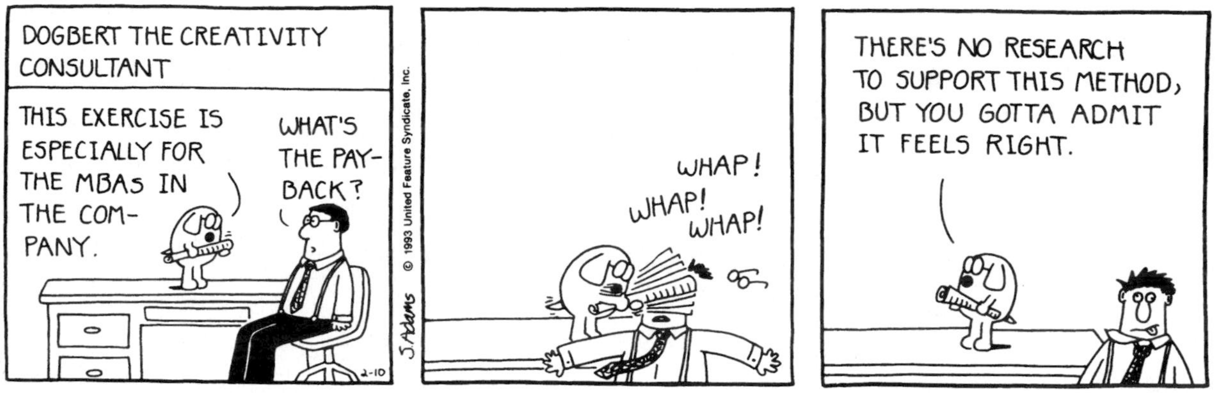
DOGBERT THE CREATIVITY CONSULTANT
THIS EXERCISE IS ESPECIALLY FOR THE MBAS IN THE COMPANY.
WHAT'S THE PAY-BACK?
2-10
S. Adams © 1993 United Feature Syndicate, Inc.
WHAP! WHAP! WHAP!
THERE'S NO RESEARCH TO SUPPORT THIS METHOD, BUT YOU GOTTA ADMIT IT FEELS RIGHT.

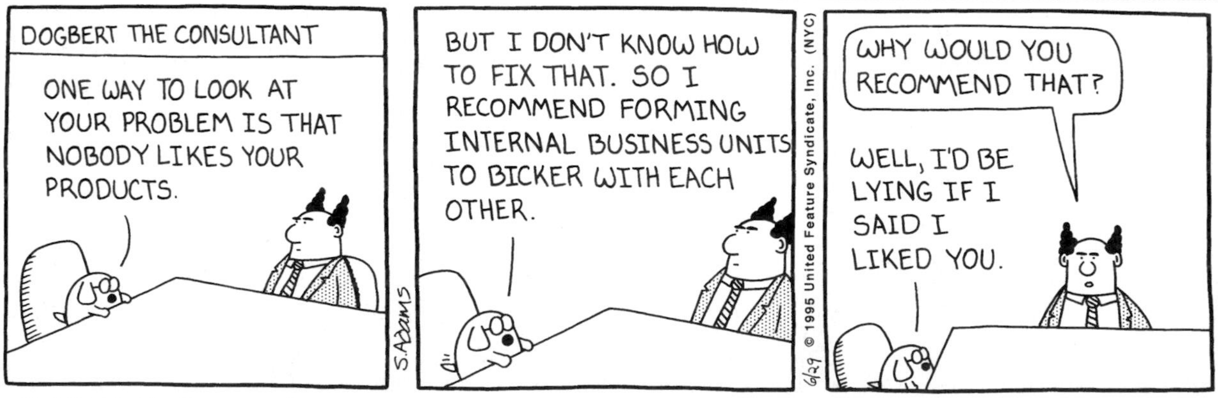
DOGBERT THE CONSULTANT
ONE WAY TO LOOK AT YOUR PROBLEM IS THAT NOBODY LIKES YOUR PRODUCTS.
S. Adams
BUT I DON'T KNOW HOW TO FIX THAT. SO I RECOMMEND FORMING INTERNAL BUSINESS UNITS TO BICKER WITH EACH OTHER.
6/29 © 1995 United Feature Syndicate, Inc. (NYC)
WHY WOULD YOU RECOMMEND THAT?
WELL, I'D BE LYING IF I SAID I LIKED YOU.

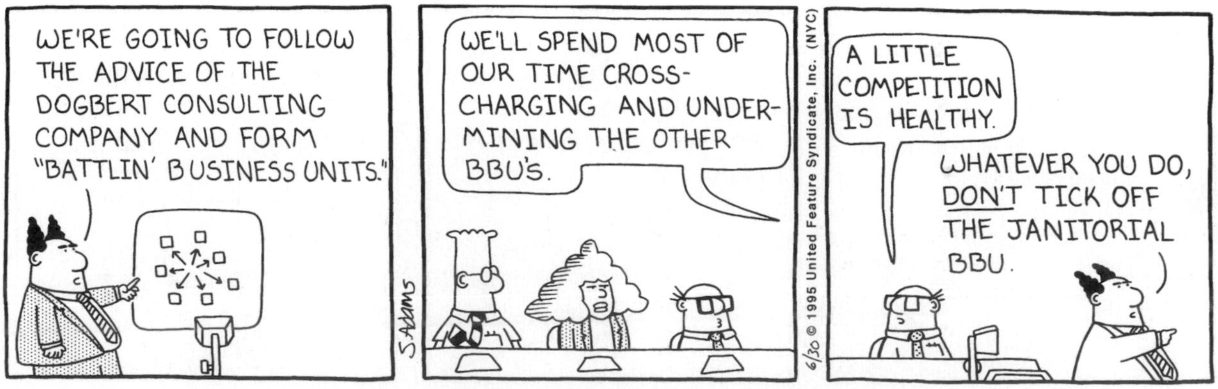
WE'RE GOING TO FOLLOW THE ADVICE OF THE DOGBERT CONSULTING COMPANY AND FORM "BATTLIN' BUSINESS UNITS."
S. Adams
WE'LL SPEND MOST OF OUR TIME CROSS-CHARGING AND UNDER-MINING THE OTHER BBU'S.
6/30 © 1995 United Feature Syndicate, Inc. (NYC)
A LITTLE COMPETITION IS HEALTHY.
WHATEVER YOU DO, DON'T TICK OFF THE JANITORIAL BBU.

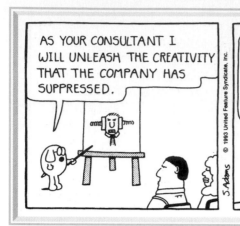

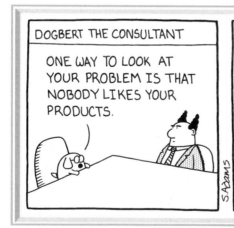

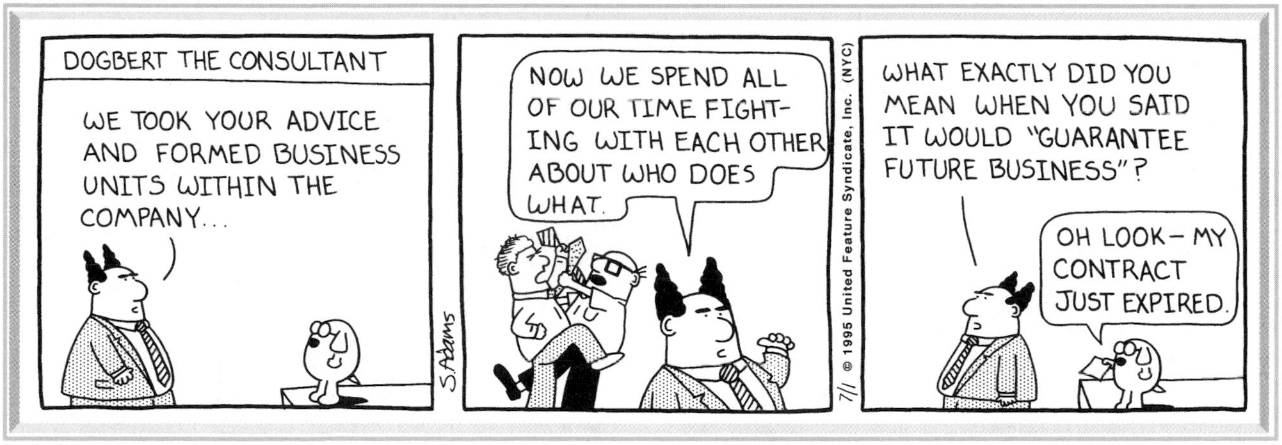
DOGBERT THE CONSULTANT
WE TOOK YOUR ADVICE AND FORMED BUSINESS UNITS WITHIN THE COMPANY...
S. Adams
NOW WE SPEND ALL OF OUR TIME FIGHTING WITH EACH OTHER ABOUT WHO DOES WHAT.
7/1 © 1995 United Feature Syndicate, Inc. (NYC)
WHAT EXACTLY DID YOU MEAN WHEN YOU SAID IT WOULD "GUARANTEE FUTURE BUSINESS"?
OH LOOK – MY CONTRACT JUST EXPIRED.

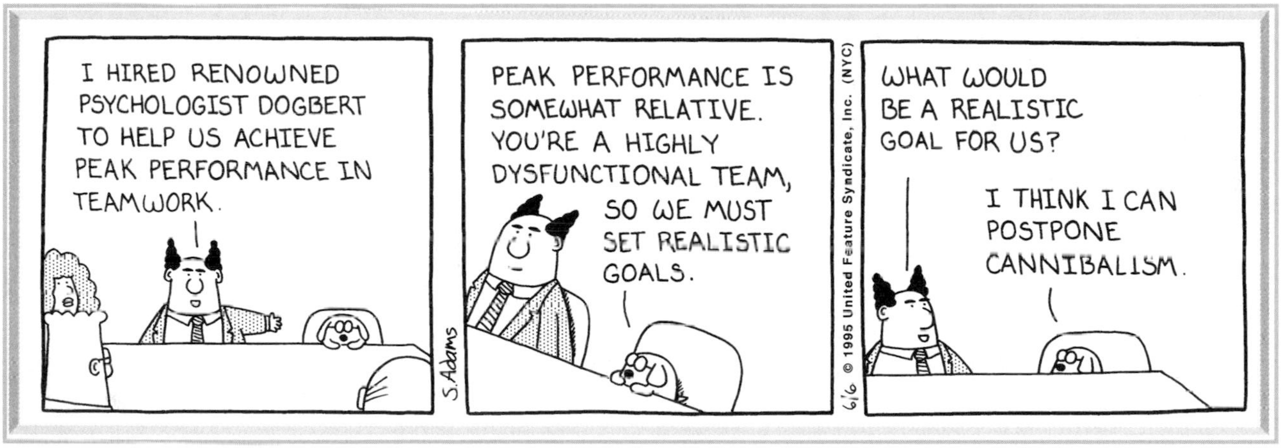
I HIRED RENOWNED PSYCHOLOGIST DOGBERT TO HELP US ACHIEVE PEAK PERFORMANCE IN TEAMWORK.
S. Adams
PEAK PERFORMANCE IS SOMEWHAT RELATIVE. YOU'RE A HIGHLY DYSFUNCTIONAL TEAM,
SO WE MUST SET REALISTIC GOALS.
6/6 © 1995 United Feature Syndicate, Inc. (NYC)
WHAT WOULD BE A REALISTIC GOAL FOR US?
I THINK I CAN POSTPONE CANNIBALISM.

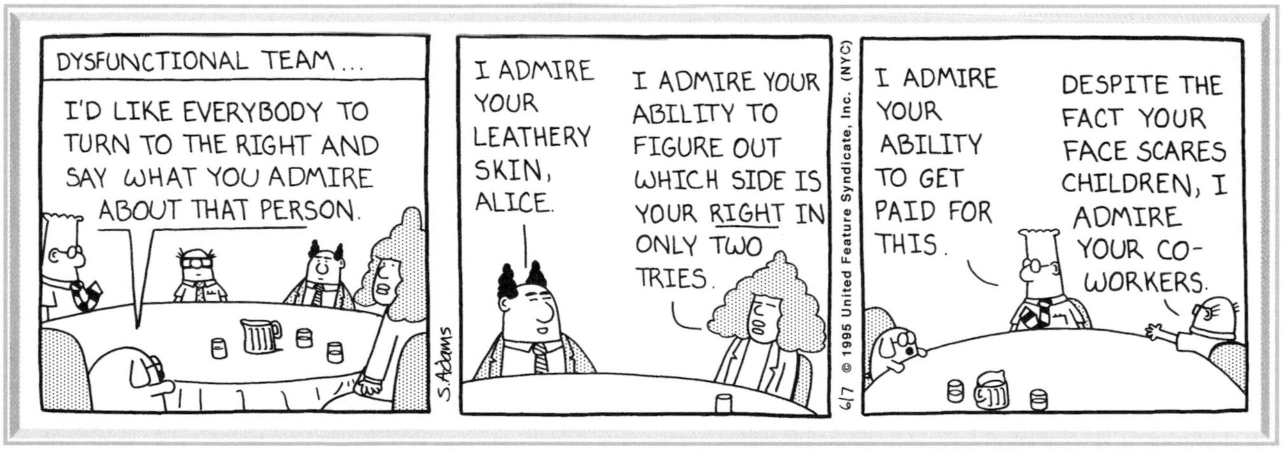
DYSFUNCTIONAL TEAM...
I'D LIKE EVERYBODY TO TURN TO THE RIGHT AND SAY WHAT YOU ADMIRE ABOUT THAT PERSON.
S. Adams
I ADMIRE YOUR LEATHERY SKIN, ALICE.
I ADMIRE YOUR ABILITY TO FIGURE OUT WHICH SIDE IS YOUR RIGHT IN ONLY TWO TRIES.
6/7 © 1995 United Feature Syndicate, Inc. (NYC)
I ADMIRE YOUR ABILITY TO GET PAID FOR THIS.
DESPITE THE FACT YOUR FACE SCARES CHILDREN, I ADMIRE YOUR CO-WORKERS.

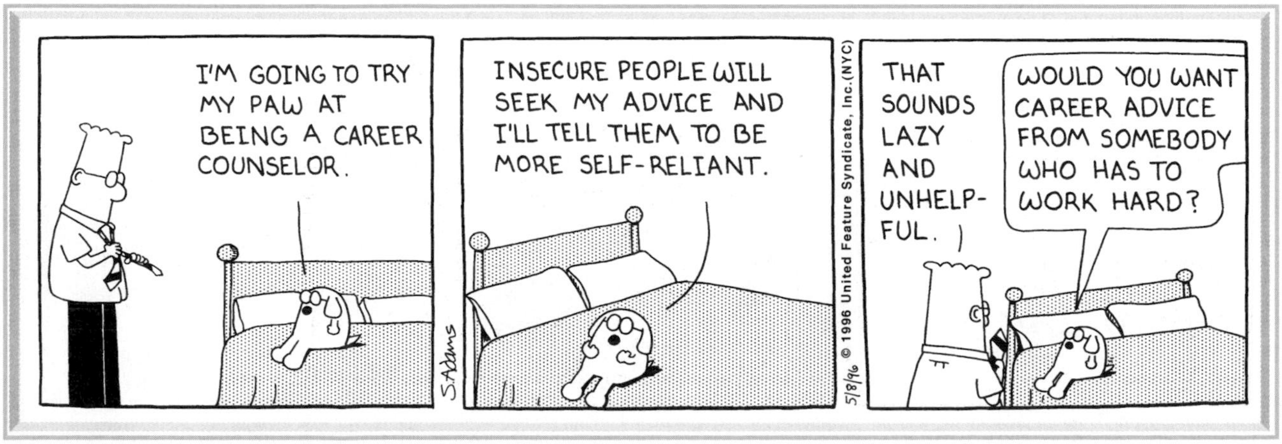
I'M GOING TO TRY MY PAW AT BEING A CAREER COUNSELOR.
S. Adams
INSECURE PEOPLE WILL SEEK MY ADVICE AND I'LL TELL THEM TO BE MORE SELF-RELIANT.
5/8/96 © 1996 United Feature Syndicate, Inc. (NYC)
THAT SOUNDS LAZY AND UNHELPFUL.
WOULD YOU WANT CAREER ADVICE FROM SOMEBODY WHO HAS TO WORK HARD?

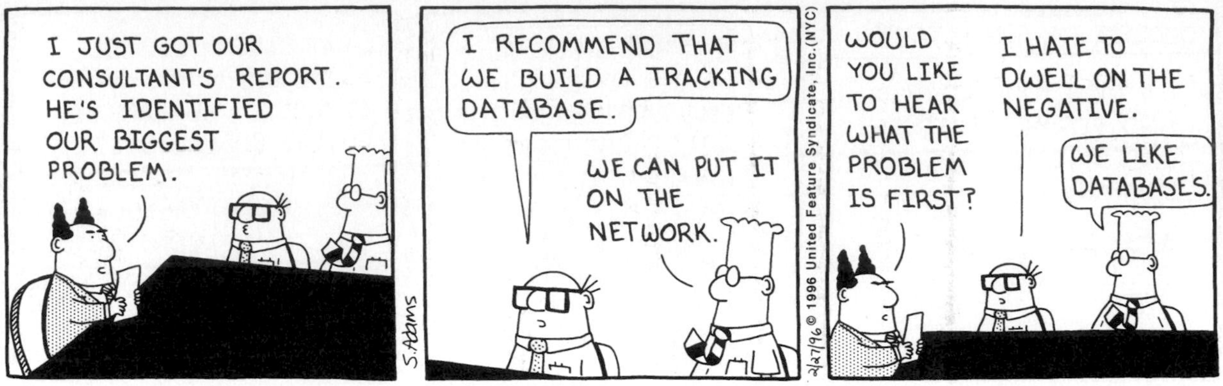
I JUST GOT OUR CONSULTANT'S REPORT. HE'S IDENTIFIED OUR BIGGEST PROBLEM.
I RECOMMEND THAT WE BUILD A TRACKING DATABASE.
WE CAN PUT IT ON THE NETWORK.
WOULD YOU LIKE TO HEAR WHAT THE PROBLEM IS FIRST?
I HATE TO DWELL ON THE NEGATIVE.
WE LIKE DATABASES.
2/27/96 © 1996 United Feature Syndicate, Inc.(NYC)

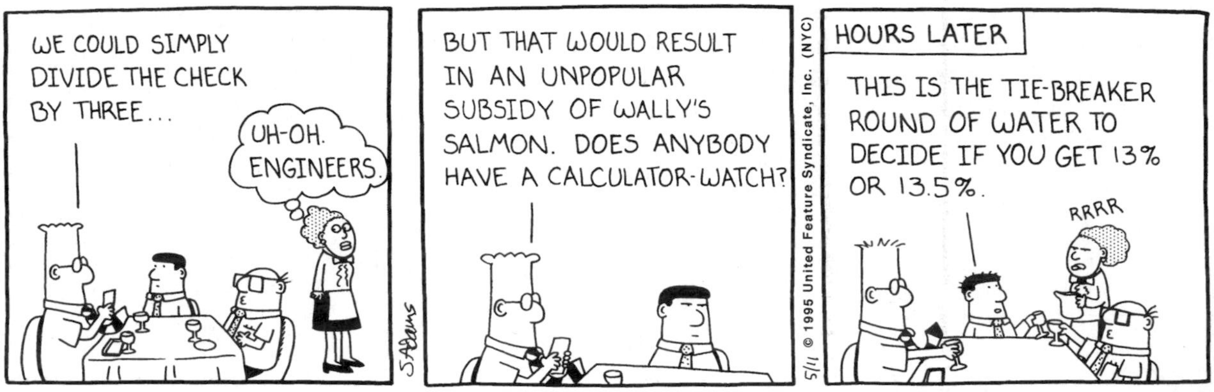
WE COULD SIMPLY DIVIDE THE CHECK BY THREE...
UH-OH. ENGINEERS.
BUT THAT WOULD RESULT IN AN UNPOPULAR SUBSIDY OF WALLY'S SALMON. DOES ANYBODY HAVE A CALCULATOR-WATCH?
HOURS LATER
THIS IS THE TIE-BREAKER ROUND OF WATER TO DECIDE IF YOU GET 13% OR 13.5%.
RRRR
5/11 © 1995 United Feature Syndicate, Inc. (NYC)

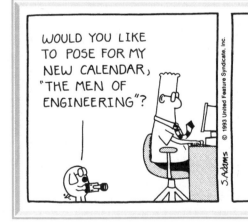

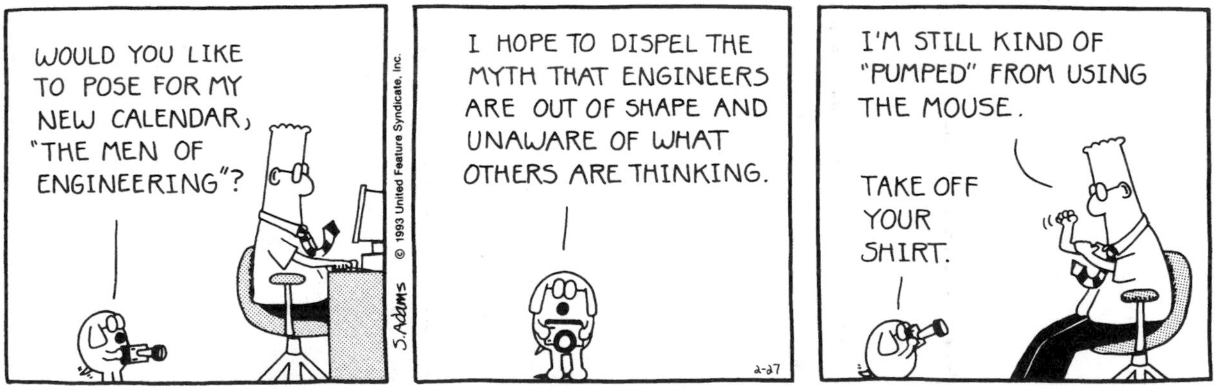
WOULD YOU LIKE TO POSE FOR MY NEW CALENDAR, "THE MEN OF ENGINEERING"?
© 1993 United Feature Syndicate, Inc.
I HOPE TO DISPEL THE MYTH THAT ENGINEERS ARE OUT OF SHAPE AND UNAWARE OF WHAT OTHERS ARE THINKING.
I'M STILL KIND OF "PUMPED" FROM USING THE MOUSE.
TAKE OFF YOUR SHIRT.

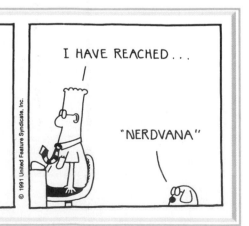

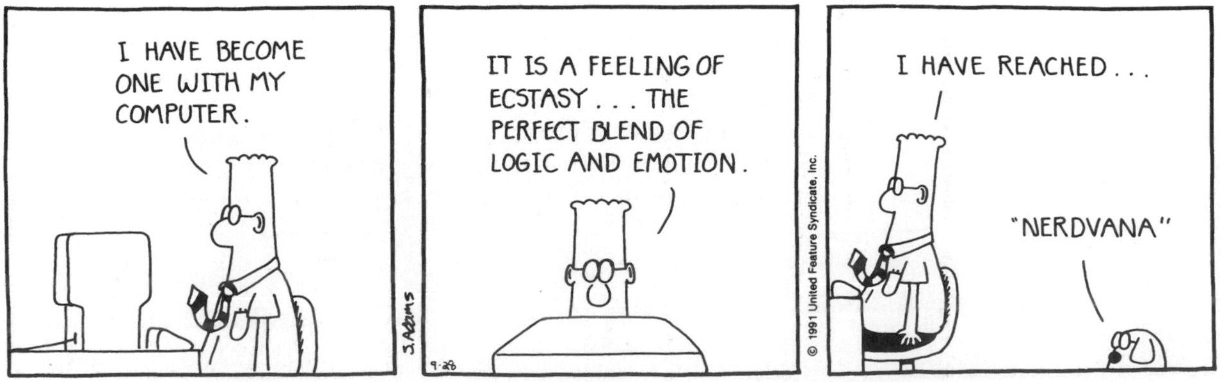
I HAVE BECOME ONE WITH MY COMPUTER.
IT IS A FEELING OF ECSTASY . . . THE PERFECT BLEND OF LOGIC AND EMOTION.
I HAVE REACHED . . .
"NERDVANA"
© 1991 United Feature Syndicate, Inc.

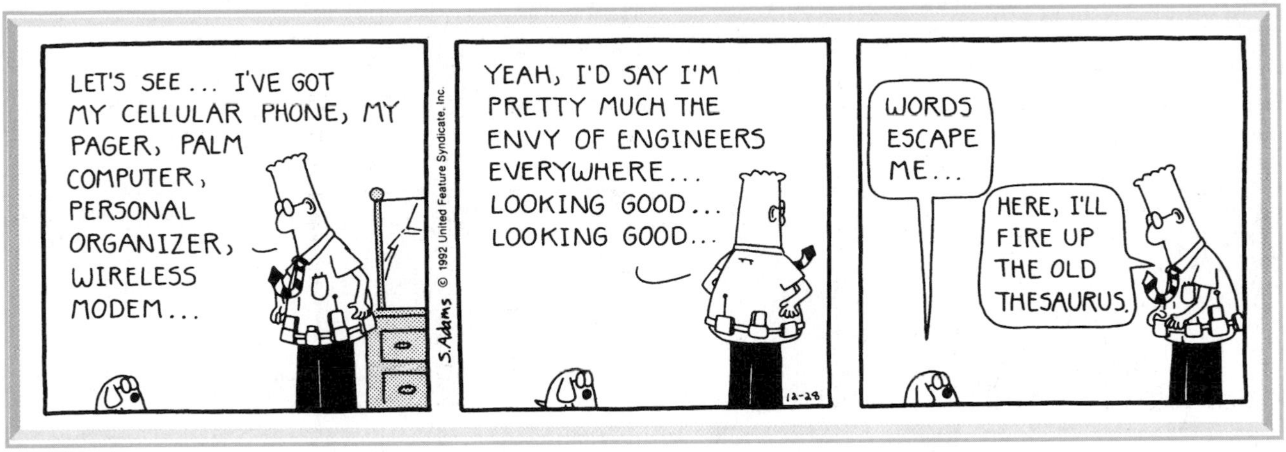
LET'S SEE... I'VE GOT MY CELLULAR PHONE, MY PAGER, PALM COMPUTER, PERSONAL ORGANIZER, WIRELESS MODEM...
S. Adams © 1992 United Feature Syndicate, Inc.
YEAH, I'D SAY I'M PRETTY MUCH THE ENVY OF ENGINEERS EVERYWHERE... LOOKING GOOD... LOOKING GOOD...
12-28
WORDS ESCAPE ME...
HERE, I'LL FIRE UP THE OLD THESAURUS.

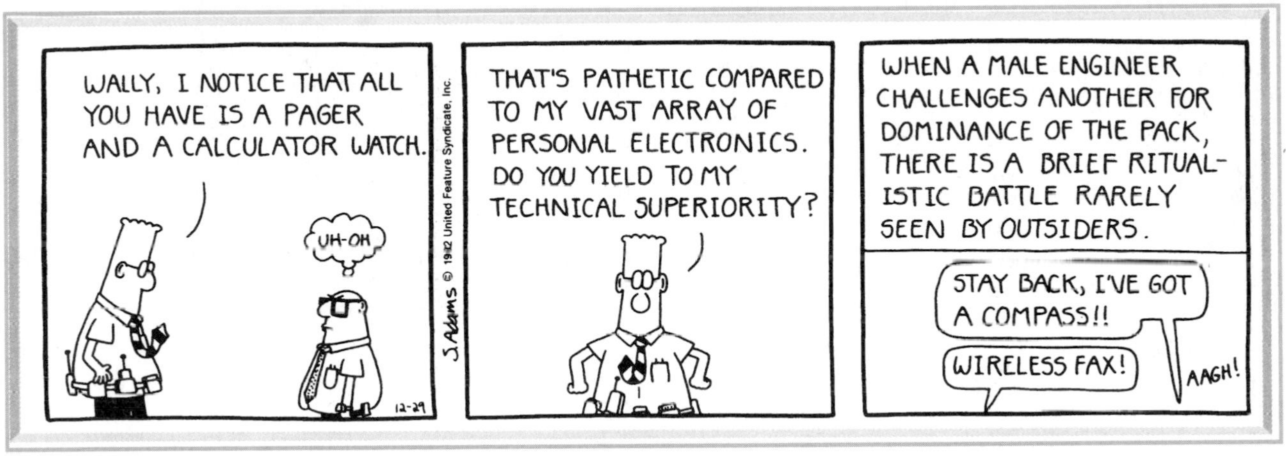
WALLY, I NOTICE THAT ALL YOU HAVE IS A PAGER AND A CALCULATOR WATCH.
UH-OH
12-29
S. Adams © 1992 United Feature Syndicate, Inc.
THAT'S PATHETIC COMPARED TO MY VAST ARRAY OF PERSONAL ELECTRONICS. DO YOU YIELD TO MY TECHNICAL SUPERIORITY?
WHEN A MALE ENGINEER CHALLENGES ANOTHER FOR DOMINANCE OF THE PACK, THERE IS A BRIEF RITUALISTIC BATTLE RARELY SEEN BY OUTSIDERS.
STAY BACK, I'VE GOT A COMPASS!!
WIRELESS FAX!
AAGH!

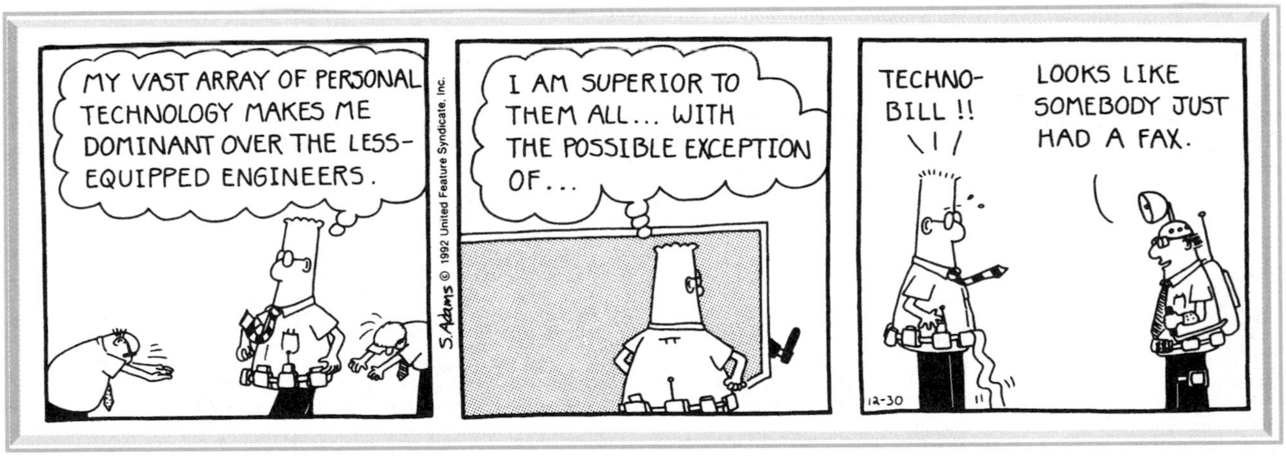
MY VAST ARRAY OF PERSONAL TECHNOLOGY MAKES ME DOMINANT OVER THE LESS-EQUIPPED ENGINEERS.
S. Adams © 1992 United Feature Syndicate, Inc.
I AM SUPERIOR TO THEM ALL... WITH THE POSSIBLE EXCEPTION OF...
TECHNO-BILL !!
LOOKS LIKE SOMEBODY JUST HAD A FAX.
12-30

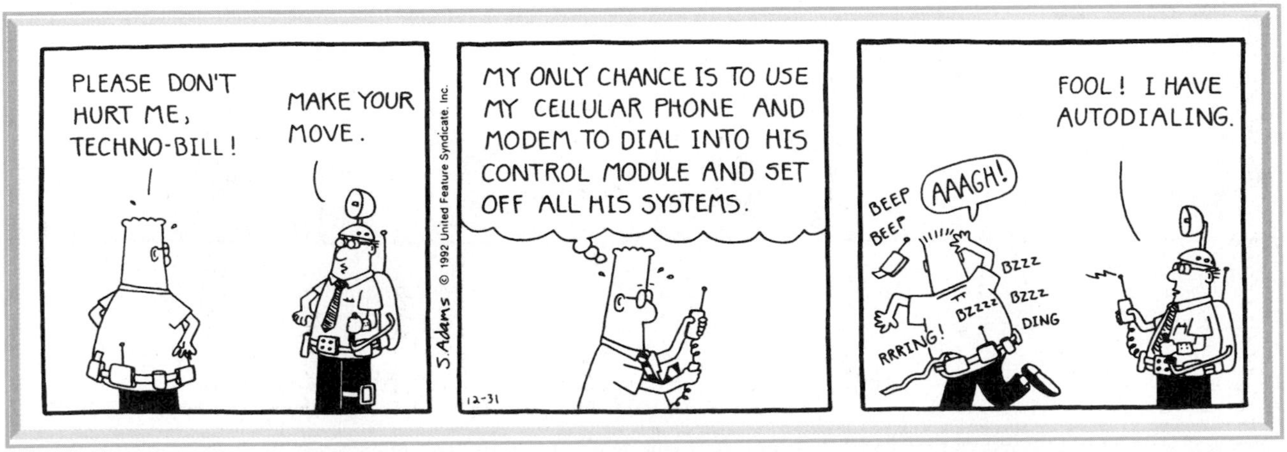
PLEASE DON'T HURT ME, TECHNO-BILL!
MAKE YOUR MOVE.
S. Adams © 1992 United Feature Syndicate, Inc.
MY ONLY CHANCE IS TO USE MY CELLULAR PHONE AND MODEM TO DIAL INTO HIS CONTROL MODULE AND SET OFF ALL HIS SYSTEMS.
12-31
FOOL! I HAVE AUTODIALING.
BEEP BEEP
AAAGH!
BZZZ
BZZZZ
BZZZ
DING
RRRING!

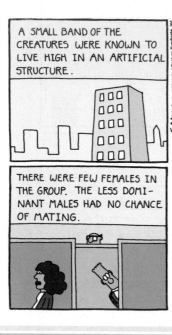

A SMALL BAND OF THE CREATURES WERE KNOWN TO LIVE HIGH IN AN ARTIFICIAL STRUCTURE.
S.ADAMS © 1993 United Feature Syndicate, Inc.
ON MY WAY TO STUDY THEM I TOOK NOTE OF THE NATIVE VEGETATION.
RENTED
THE YOUNGER MALES WERE AT PLAY. THEY BECAME SELF-CONSCIOUS WHEN WATCHED.
THE DOMINANT MALE HAD A GRAY BACK. HE CONTROLLED THE OTHERS BY WAVING LITTLE ENVELOPES.
THERE WERE FEW FEMALES IN THE GROUP. THE LESS DOMINANT MALES HAD NO CHANCE OF MATING.
UNLIKE OTHER SPECIES THEY HAD NO INSTINCT FOR GROOMING.
WANT TO GROOM?
DROP DEAD.
4-11
MY TIME WAS UP. BUT I WILL MISS THEM, THOSE...
ENGINEERS IN THE MIST
HOW LONG ARE YOU SUPPOSED TO MICROWAVE POPCORN?

DILBERT, I WANT YOU TO INTERVIEW THE JOB APPLICANT WHO'S COMING IN TODAY.
S.ADAMS
SEE IF HE'S GOT WHAT IT TAKES TO BE AN ENGINEER.
HI, KARL. WE'LL START WITH THE STANDARD ENGINEERING TEST.
OKEY-DOKEY.
I HAVE THIRTY-FIVE PENS AND PENCILS HERE. HOW MANY ARE REALLY NEEDED TO PERFORM YOUR JOB?
ALL OF THEM.
CORRECT... NOW, WHAT IS THE PROPER WAY TO CARRY THEM WITH YOU?
2-14
© 1993 United Feature Syndicate, Inc.
RIGHT AGAIN. LAST QUESTION: WHAT IS THE ADVANTAGE OF WEARING NATURAL FABRICS?
UH-OH... PANIC SITUATION.
I... I DON'T KNOW.
THAT'S OKAY. I WAS TESTING YOUR HAIR. YOU'RE AN ENGINEER.

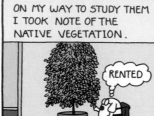

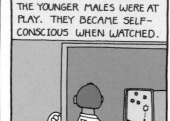

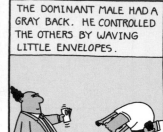

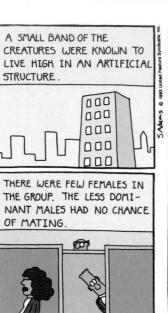

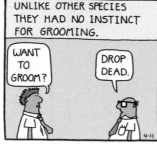

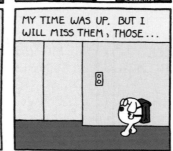

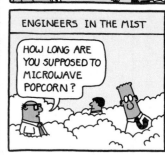

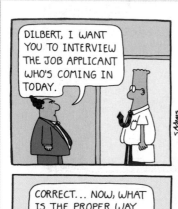

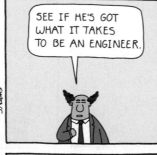

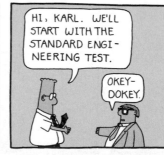

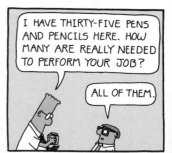

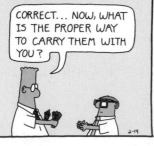

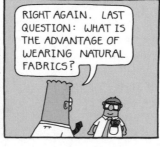

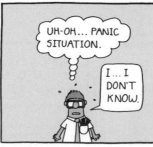

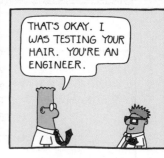

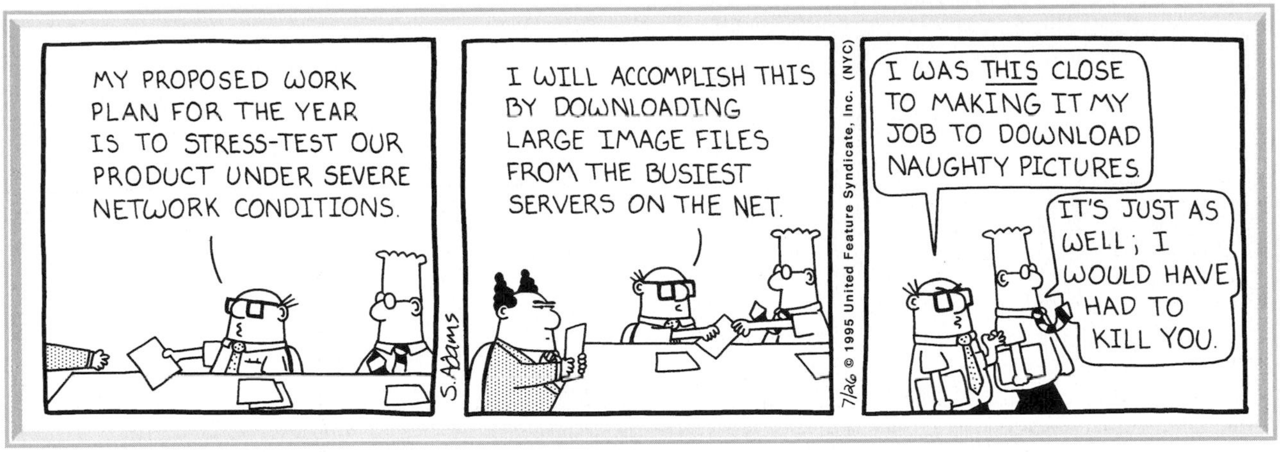
MY PROPOSED WORK PLAN FOR THE YEAR IS TO STRESS-TEST OUR PRODUCT UNDER SEVERE NETWORK CONDITIONS.
I WILL ACCOMPLISH THIS BY DOWNLOADING LARGE IMAGE FILES FROM THE BUSIEST SERVERS ON THE NET.
I WAS THIS CLOSE TO MAKING IT MY JOB TO DOWNLOAD NAUGHTY PICTURES.
IT'S JUST AS WELL; I WOULD HAVE HAD TO KILL YOU.
© 1995 United Feature Syndicate, Inc. (NYC)

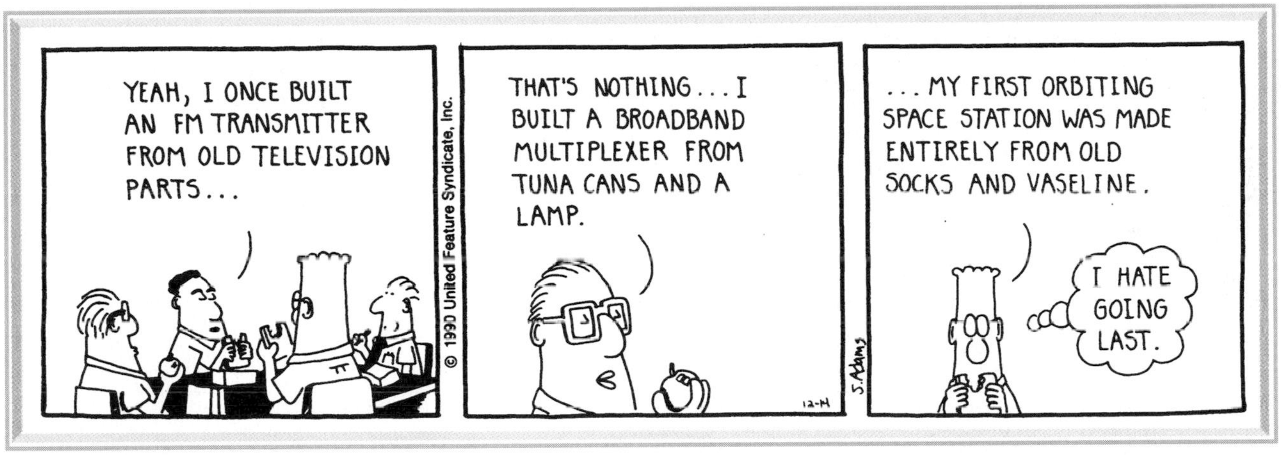
YEAH, I ONCE BUILT AN FM TRANSMITTER FROM OLD TELEVISION PARTS...
THAT'S NOTHING... I BUILT A BROADBAND MULTIPLEXER FROM TUNA CANS AND A LAMP.
...MY FIRST ORBITING SPACE STATION WAS MADE ENTIRELY FROM OLD SOCKS AND VASELINE.
I HATE GOING LAST.
© 1990 United Feature Syndicate, Inc.

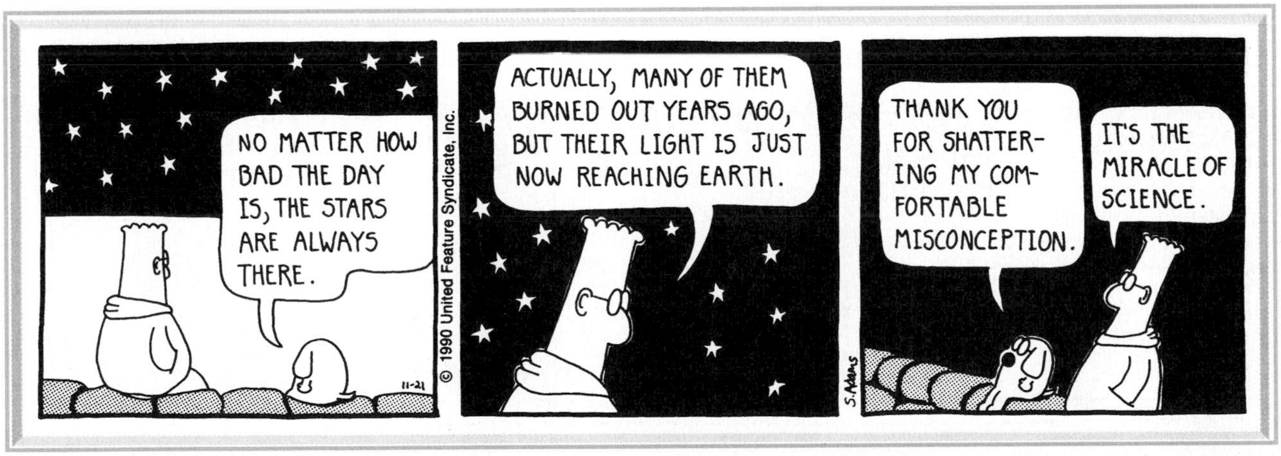
NO MATTER HOW BAD THE DAY IS, THE STARS ARE ALWAYS THERE.
ACTUALLY, MANY OF THEM BURNED OUT YEARS AGO, BUT THEIR LIGHT IS JUST NOW REACHING EARTH.
THANK YOU FOR SHATTER-ING MY COM-FORTABLE MISCONCEPTION.
IT'S THE MIRACLE OF SCIENCE.
© 1990 United Feature Syndicate, Inc.

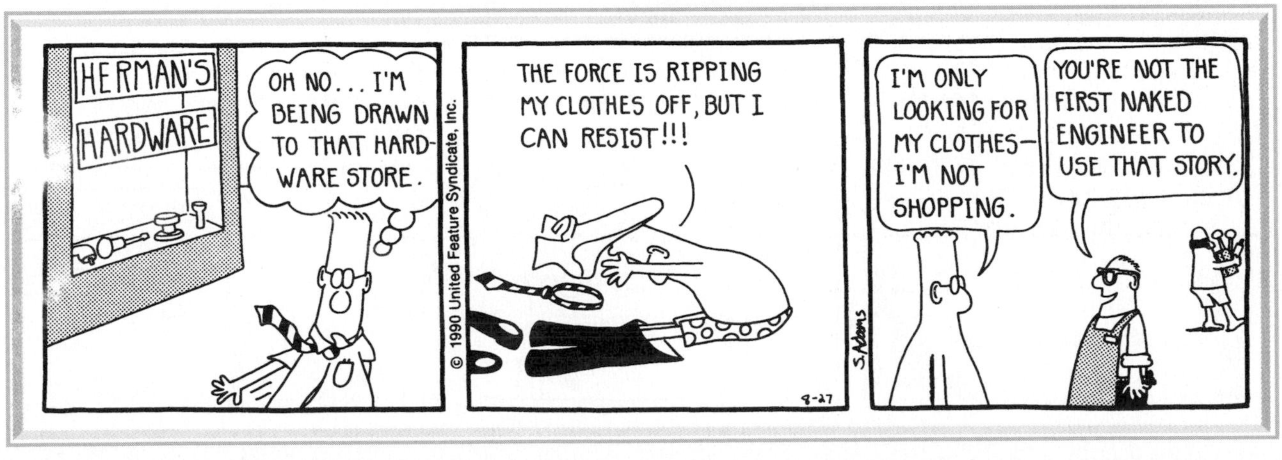
HERMAN'S
HARDWARE
OH NO... I'M BEING DRAWN TO THAT HARD-WARE STORE.
THE FORCE IS RIPPING MY CLOTHES OFF, BUT I CAN RESIST!!!
I'M ONLY LOOKING FOR MY CLOTHES— I'M NOT SHOPPING.
YOU'RE NOT THE FIRST NAKED ENGINEER TO USE THAT STORY.
© 1990 United Feature Syndicate, Inc.

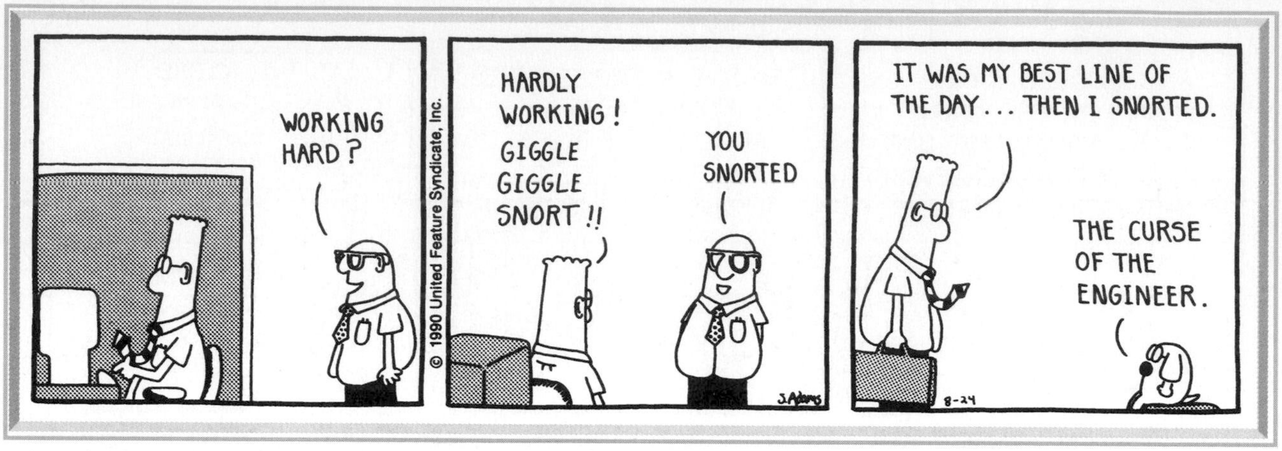
WORKING HARD?
HARDLY WORKING! GIGGLE GIGGLE SNORT!!
YOU SNORTED
IT WAS MY BEST LINE OF THE DAY... THEN I SNORTED.
THE CURSE OF THE ENGINEER.
© 1990 United Feature Syndicate, Inc.

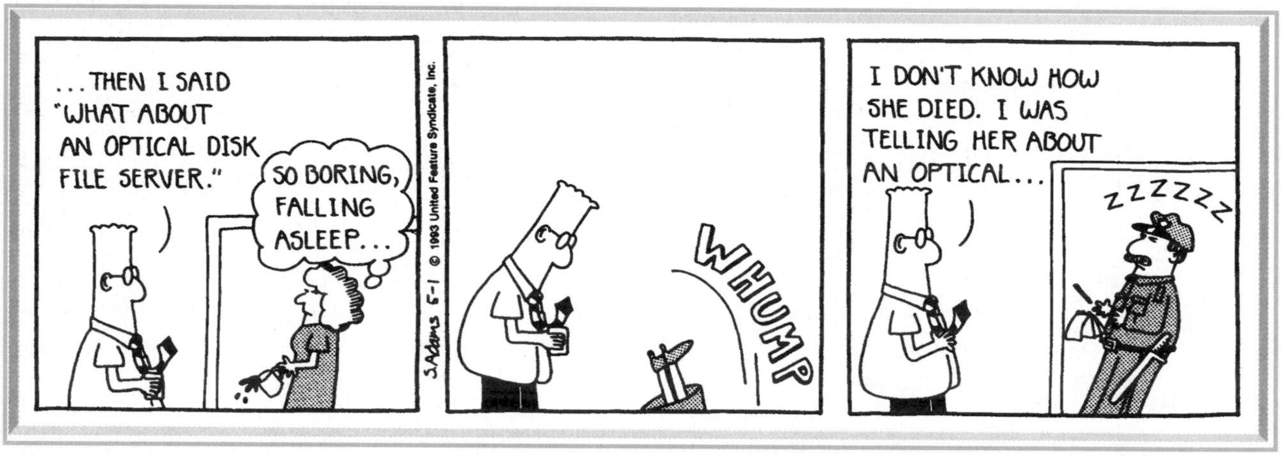
...THEN I SAID "WHAT ABOUT AN OPTICAL DISK FILE SERVER."
SO BORING, FALLING ASLEEP...
WHUMP
I DON'T KNOW HOW SHE DIED. I WAS TELLING HER ABOUT AN OPTICAL...
ZZZZZZ
© 1993 United Feature Syndicate, Inc.

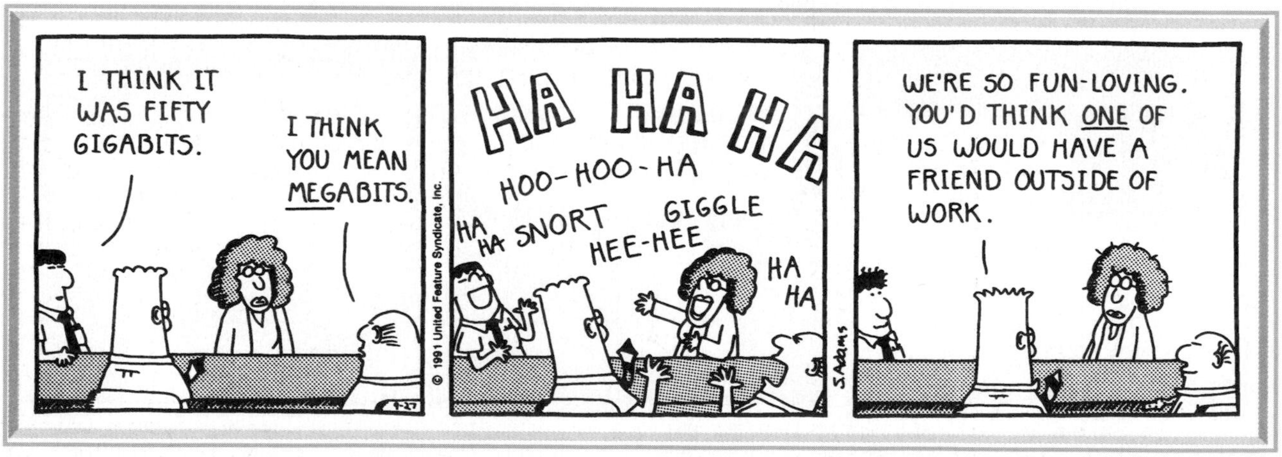
I THINK IT WAS FIFTY GIGABITS.
I THINK YOU MEAN MEGABITS.
HA HA HA
HOO-HOO-HA
HA HA SNORT
GIGGLE
HEE-HEE
HA HA
WE'RE SO FUN-LOVING. YOU'D THINK ONE OF US WOULD HAVE A FRIEND OUTSIDE OF WORK.
© 1991 United Feature Syndicate, Inc.

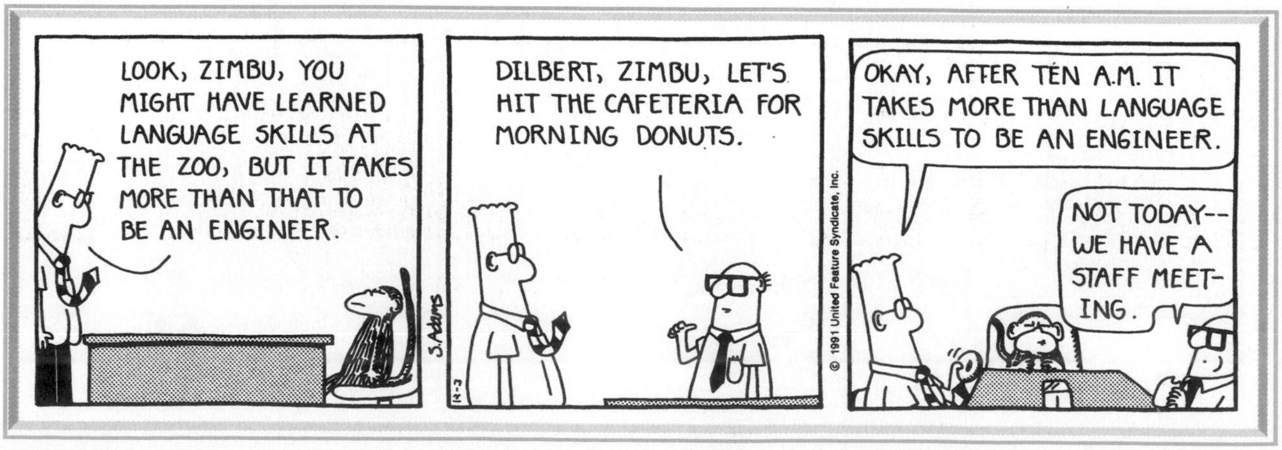
LOOK, ZIMBU, YOU MIGHT HAVE LEARNED LANGUAGE SKILLS AT THE ZOO, BUT IT TAKES MORE THAN THAT TO BE AN ENGINEER.
DILBERT, ZIMBU, LET'S HIT THE CAFETERIA FOR MORNING DONUTS.
OKAY, AFTER TEN A.M. IT TAKES MORE THAN LANGUAGE SKILLS TO BE AN ENGINEER.
NOT TODAY-- WE HAVE A STAFF MEET-ING.
© 1991 United Feature Syndicate, Inc.

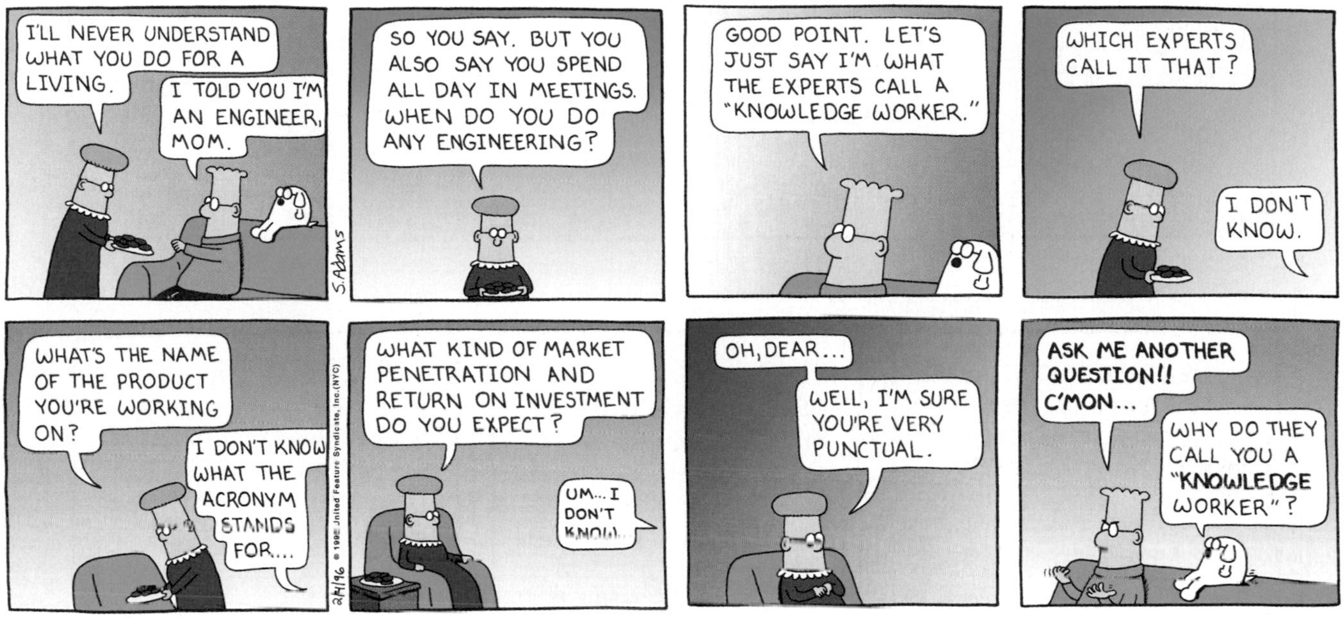
I'LL NEVER UNDERSTAND WHAT YOU DO FOR A LIVING.
I TOLD YOU I'M AN ENGINEER, MOM.
S. Adams
SO YOU SAY. BUT YOU ALSO SAY YOU SPEND ALL DAY IN MEETINGS. WHEN DO YOU DO ANY ENGINEERING?
GOOD POINT. LET'S JUST SAY I'M WHAT THE EXPERTS CALL A "KNOWLEDGE WORKER."
WHICH EXPERTS CALL IT THAT?
I DON'T KNOW.
WHAT'S THE NAME OF THE PRODUCT YOU'RE WORKING ON?
I DON'T KNOW WHAT THE ACRONYM STANDS FOR...
2/4/96 © 1996 United Feature Syndicate, Inc.(NYC)
WHAT KIND OF MARKET PENETRATION AND RETURN ON INVESTMENT DO YOU EXPECT?
UM... I DON'T KNOW...
OH, DEAR...
WELL, I'M SURE YOU'RE VERY PUNCTUAL.
ASK ME ANOTHER QUESTION!! C'MON...
WHY DO THEY CALL YOU A "KNOWLEDGE WORKER"?

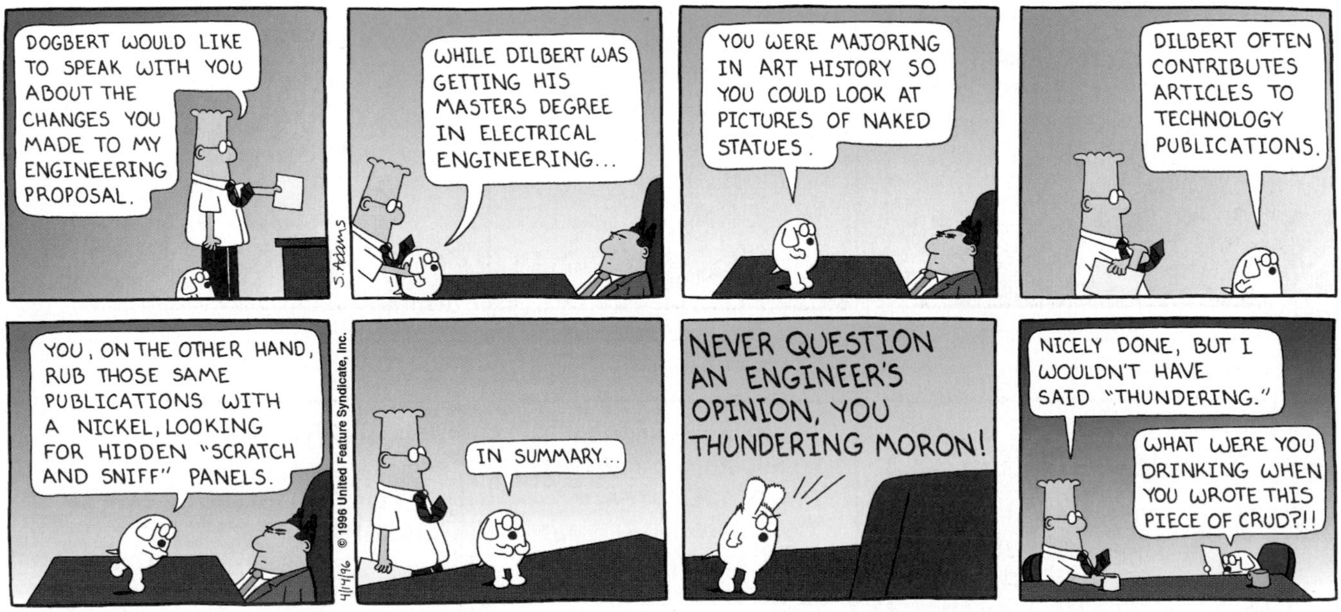
DOGBERT WOULD LIKE TO SPEAK WITH YOU ABOUT THE CHANGES YOU MADE TO MY ENGINEERING PROPOSAL.
S. Adams
WHILE DILBERT WAS GETTING HIS MASTERS DEGREE IN ELECTRICAL ENGINEERING...
YOU WERE MAJORING IN ART HISTORY SO YOU COULD LOOK AT PICTURES OF NAKED STATUES.
DILBERT OFTEN CONTRIBUTES ARTICLES TO TECHNOLOGY PUBLICATIONS.
YOU, ON THE OTHER HAND, RUB THOSE SAME PUBLICATIONS WITH A NICKEL, LOOKING FOR HIDDEN "SCRATCH AND SNIFF" PANELS.
4/14/96 © 1996 United Feature Syndicate, Inc.
IN SUMMARY...
NEVER QUESTION AN ENGINEER'S OPINION, YOU THUNDERING MORON!
NICELY DONE, BUT I WOULDN'T HAVE SAID "THUNDERING."
WHAT WERE YOU DRINKING WHEN YOU WROTE THIS PIECE OF CRUD?!!

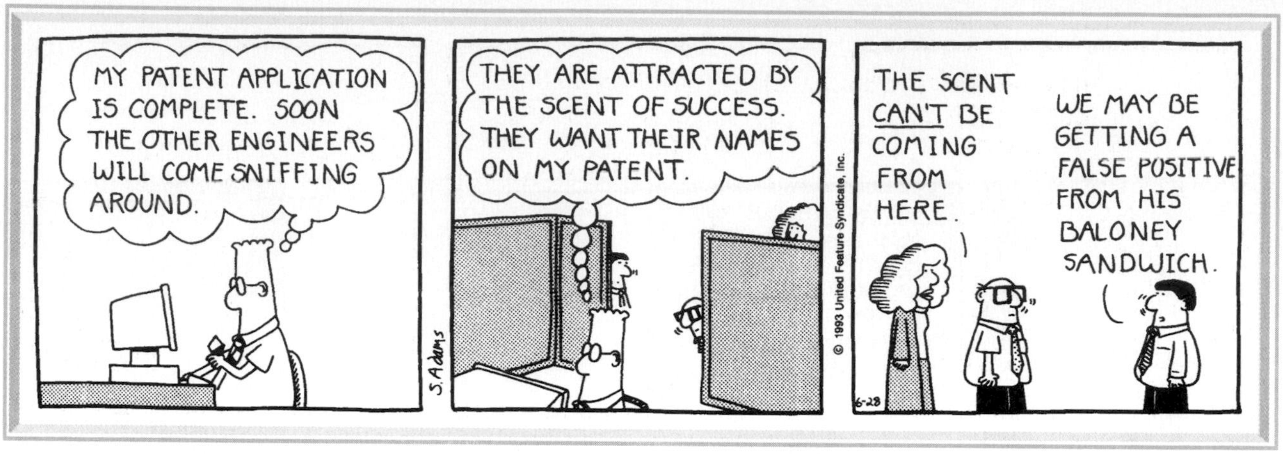
MY PATENT APPLICATION IS COMPLETE. SOON THE OTHER ENGINEERS WILL COME SNIFFING AROUND.
THEY ARE ATTRACTED BY THE SCENT OF SUCCESS. THEY WANT THEIR NAMES ON MY PATENT.
THE SCENT CAN'T BE COMING FROM HERE.
WE MAY BE GETTING A FALSE POSITIVE FROM HIS BALONEY SANDWICH.
© 1993 United Feature Syndicate, Inc.

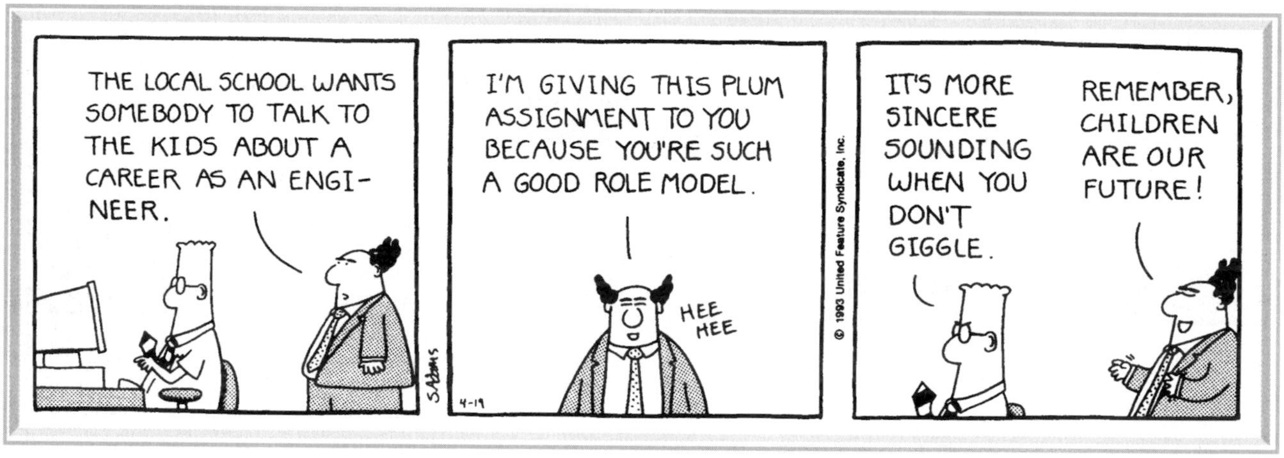
THE LOCAL SCHOOL WANTS SOMEBODY TO TALK TO THE KIDS ABOUT A CAREER AS AN ENGI-NEER.
I'M GIVING THIS PLUM ASSIGNMENT TO YOU BECAUSE YOU'RE SUCH A GOOD ROLE MODEL.
HEE HEE
IT'S MORE SINCERE SOUNDING WHEN YOU DON'T GIGGLE.
REMEMBER, CHILDREN ARE OUR FUTURE!
© 1993 United Feature Syndicate, Inc.

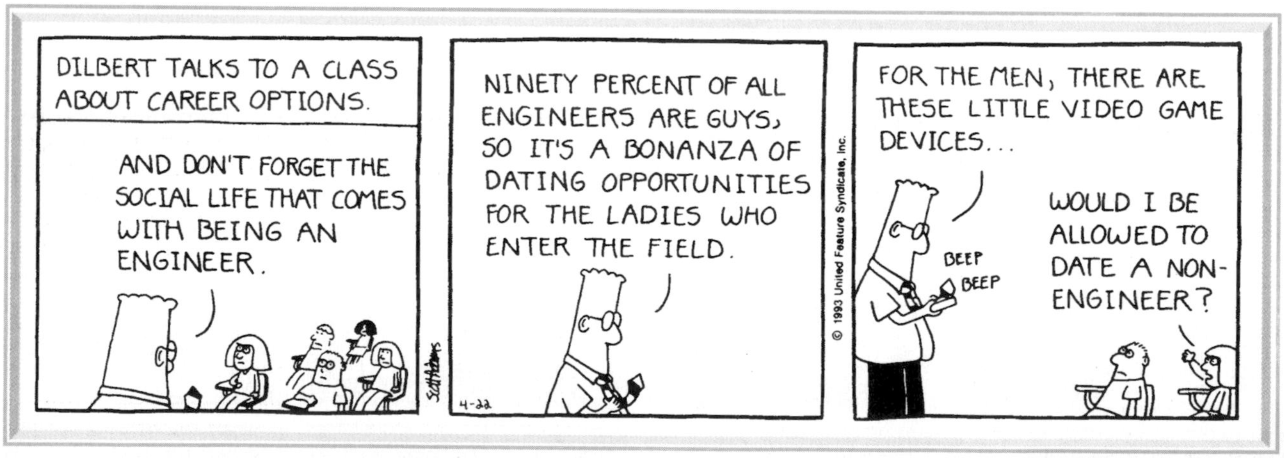
DILBERT TALKS TO A CLASS ABOUT CAREER OPTIONS.
AND DON'T FORGET THE SOCIAL LIFE THAT COMES WITH BEING AN ENGINEER.
NINETY PERCENT OF ALL ENGINEERS ARE GUYS, SO IT'S A BONANZA OF DATING OPPORTUNITIES FOR THE LADIES WHO ENTER THE FIELD.
FOR THE MEN, THERE ARE THESE LITTLE VIDEO GAME DEVICES...
BEEP BEEP
WOULD I BE ALLOWED TO DATE A NON-ENGINEER?
© 1993 United Feature Syndicate, Inc.

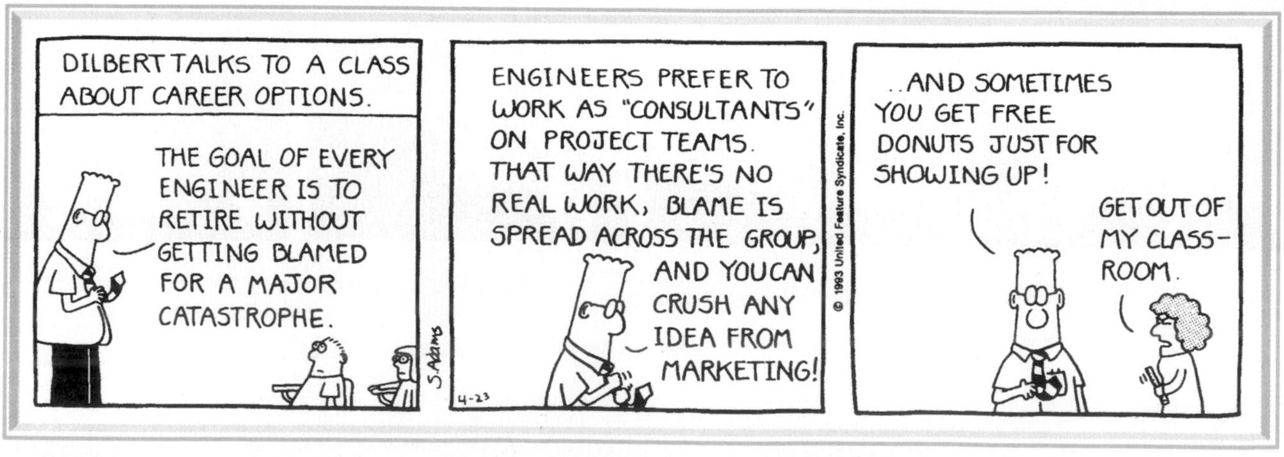
DILBERT TALKS TO A CLASS ABOUT CAREER OPTIONS.
THE GOAL OF EVERY ENGINEER IS TO RETIRE WITHOUT GETTING BLAMED FOR A MAJOR CATASTROPHE.
ENGINEERS PREFER TO WORK AS "CONSULTANTS" ON PROJECT TEAMS. THAT WAY THERE'S NO REAL WORK, BLAME IS SPREAD ACROSS THE GROUP,
AND YOU CAN CRUSH ANY IDEA FROM MARKETING!
...AND SOMETIMES YOU GET FREE DONUTS JUST FOR SHOWING UP!
GET OUT OF MY CLASS-ROOM.
© 1993 United Feature Syndicate, Inc.

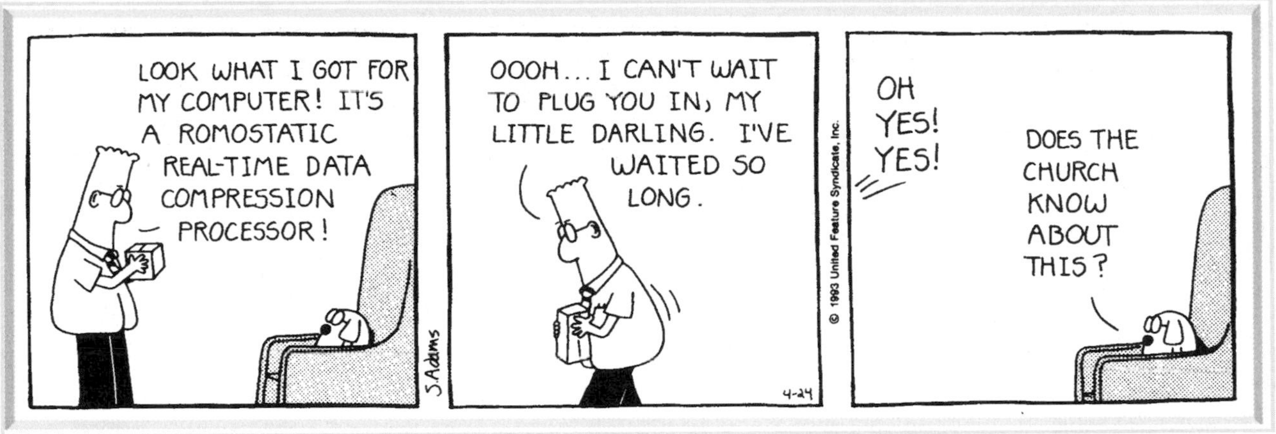
LOOK WHAT I GOT FOR MY COMPUTER! IT'S A ROMOSTATIC REAL-TIME DATA COMPRESSION PROCESSOR!
S. Adams
OOOH... I CAN'T WAIT TO PLUG YOU IN, MY LITTLE DARLING. I'VE WAITED SO LONG.
4-24
© 1993 United Feature Syndicate, Inc.
OH YES! YES!
DOES THE CHURCH KNOW ABOUT THIS?

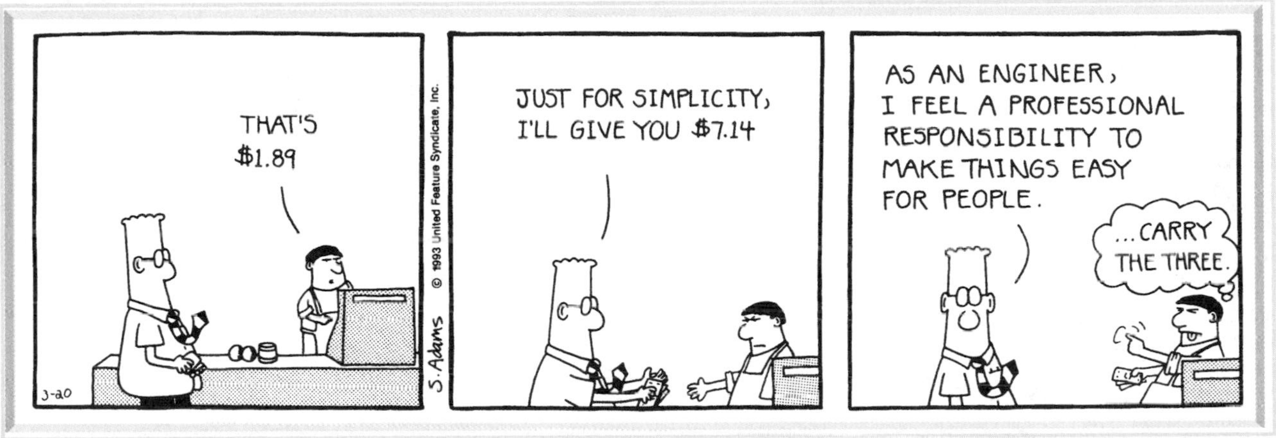
THAT'S $1.89
3-20
S. Adams
© 1993 United Feature Syndicate, Inc.
JUST FOR SIMPLICITY, I'LL GIVE YOU $7.14
AS AN ENGINEER, I FEEL A PROFESSIONAL RESPONSIBILITY TO MAKE THINGS EASY FOR PEOPLE.
...CARRY THE THREE.

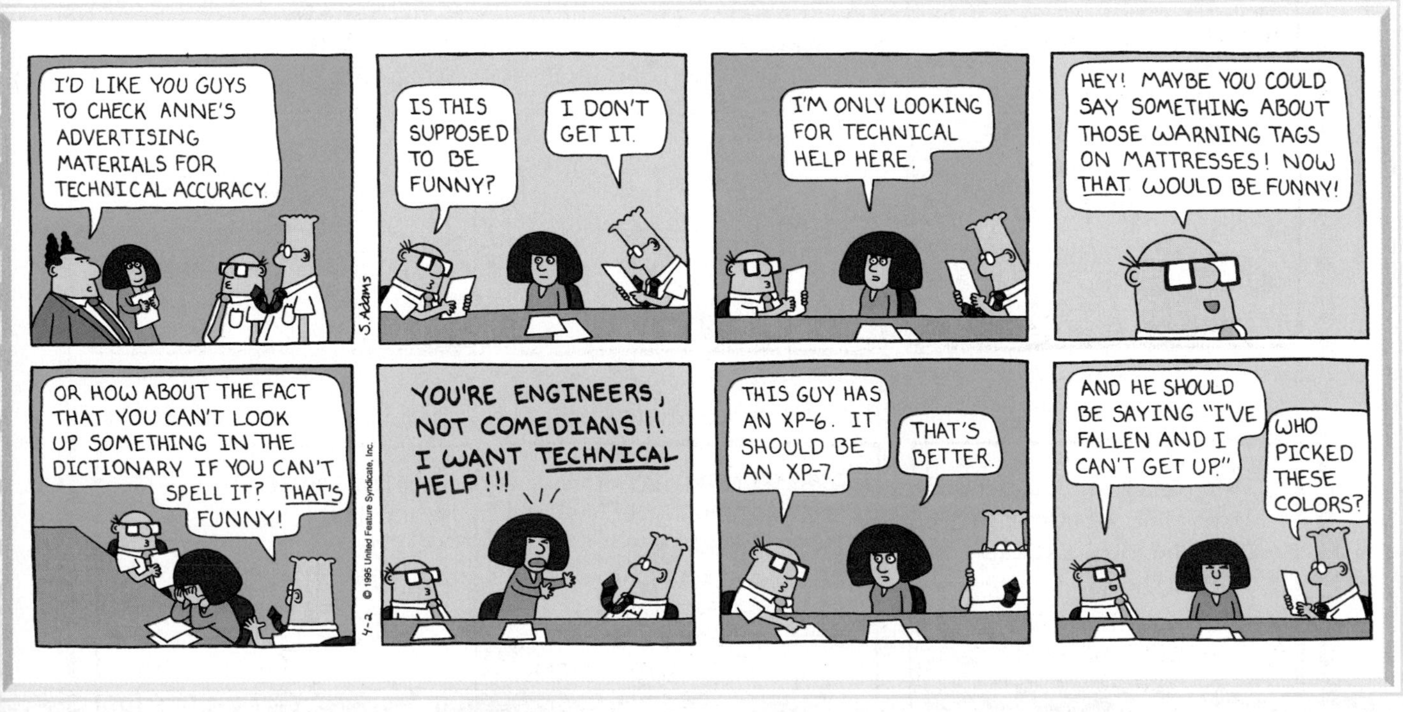
I'D LIKE YOU GUYS TO CHECK ANNE'S ADVERTISING MATERIALS FOR TECHNICAL ACCURACY.
S. Adams
IS THIS SUPPOSED TO BE FUNNY?
I DON'T GET IT.
I'M ONLY LOOKING FOR TECHNICAL HELP HERE.
HEY! MAYBE YOU COULD SAY SOMETHING ABOUT THOSE WARNING TAGS ON MATTRESSES! NOW THAT WOULD BE FUNNY!
OR HOW ABOUT THE FACT THAT YOU CAN'T LOOK UP SOMETHING IN THE DICTIONARY IF YOU CAN'T SPELL IT? THAT'S FUNNY!
4-2
© 1995 United Feature Syndicate, Inc.
YOU'RE ENGINEERS, NOT COMEDIANS!! I WANT TECHNICAL HELP!!!
THIS GUY HAS AN XP-6. IT SHOULD BE AN XP-7.
THAT'S BETTER.
AND HE SHOULD BE SAYING "I'VE FALLEN AND I CAN'T GET UP."
WHO PICKED THESE COLORS?

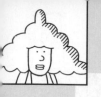

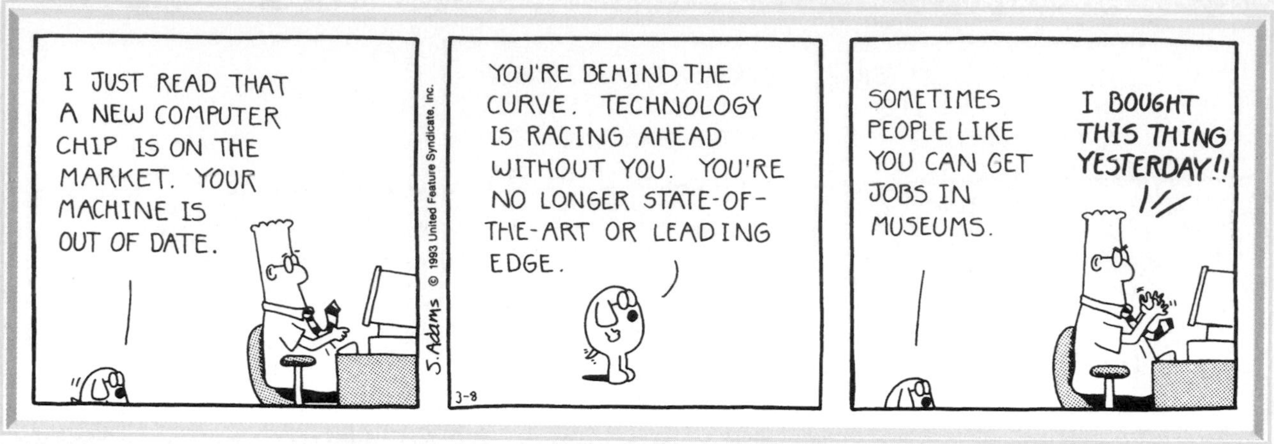
I JUST READ THAT A NEW COMPUTER CHIP IS ON THE MARKET. YOUR MACHINE IS OUT OF DATE.
S.Adams © 1993 United Feature Syndicate, Inc.
YOU'RE BEHIND THE CURVE. TECHNOLOGY IS RACING AHEAD WITHOUT YOU. YOU'RE NO LONGER STATE-OF-THE-ART OR LEADING EDGE.
3-8
SOMETIMES PEOPLE LIKE YOU CAN GET JOBS IN MUSEUMS.
I BOUGHT THIS THING YESTERDAY!!

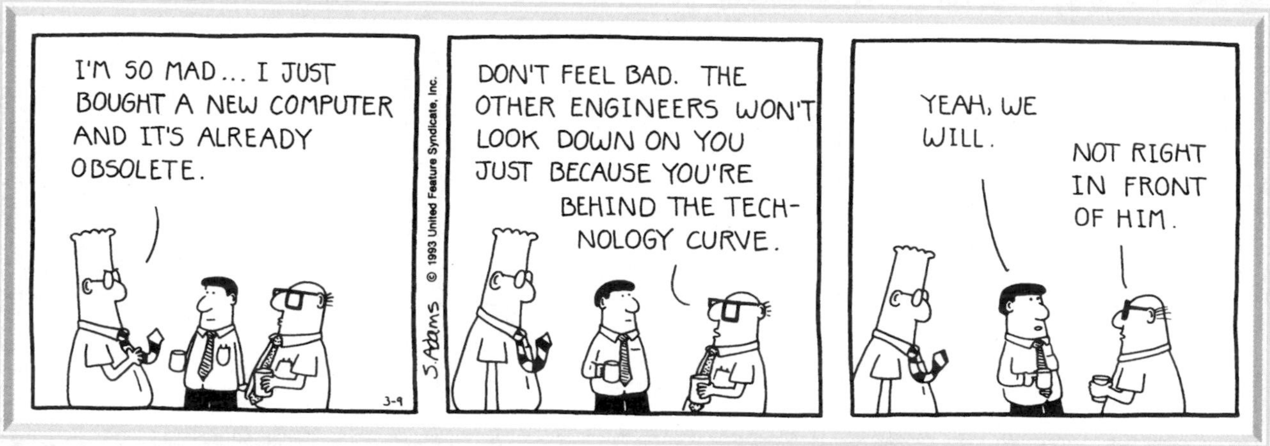
I'M SO MAD... I JUST BOUGHT A NEW COMPUTER AND IT'S ALREADY OBSOLETE.
3-9
S.Adams © 1993 United Feature Syndicate, Inc.
DON'T FEEL BAD. THE OTHER ENGINEERS WON'T LOOK DOWN ON YOU JUST BECAUSE YOU'RE BEHIND THE TECHNOLOGY CURVE.
YEAH, WE WILL.
NOT RIGHT IN FRONT OF HIM.

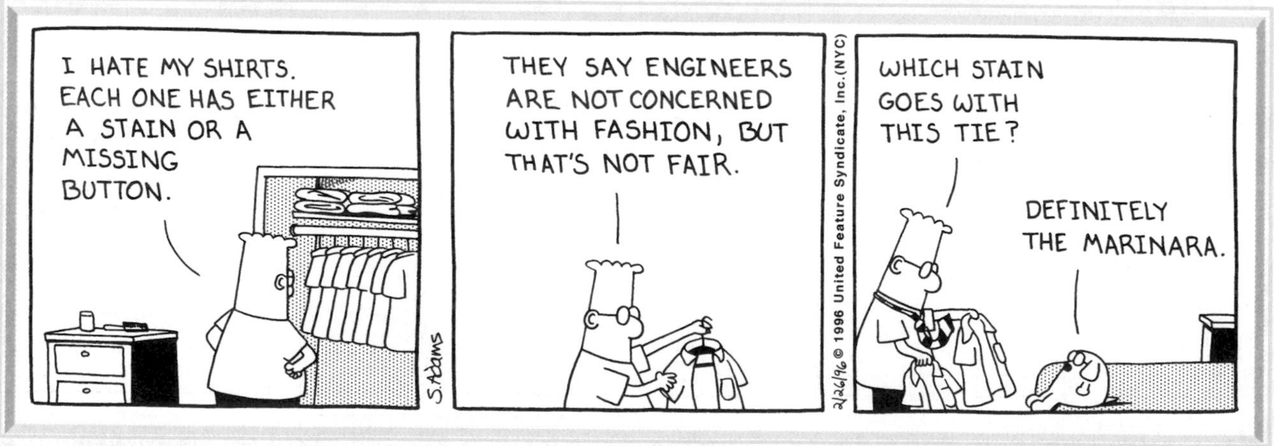
I HATE MY SHIRTS. EACH ONE HAS EITHER A STAIN OR A MISSING BUTTON.
S.Adams
THEY SAY ENGINEERS ARE NOT CONCERNED WITH FASHION, BUT THAT'S NOT FAIR.
2/26/96 © 1996 United Feature Syndicate, Inc.(NYC)
WHICH STAIN GOES WITH THIS TIE?
DEFINITELY THE MARINARA.

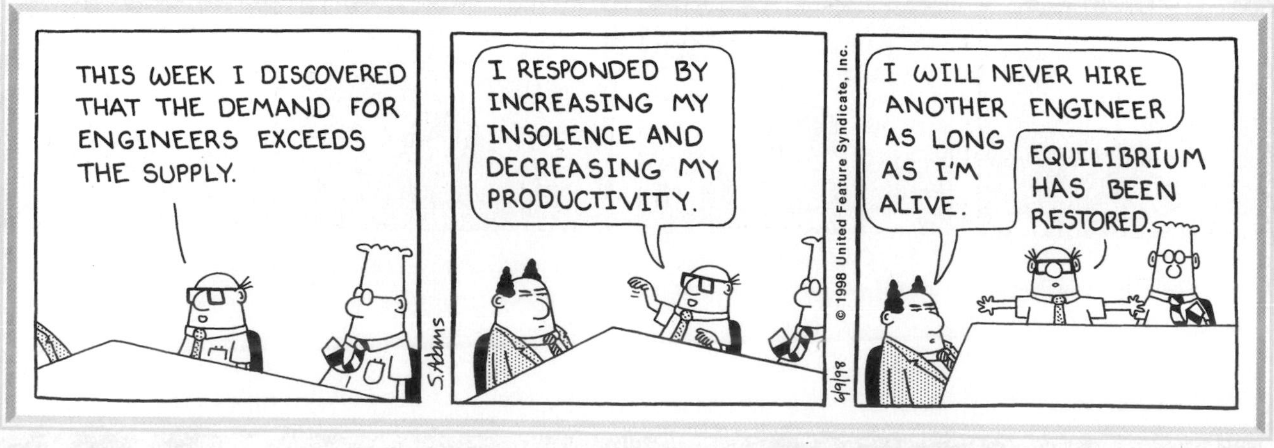
THIS WEEK I DISCOVERED THAT THE DEMAND FOR ENGINEERS EXCEEDS THE SUPPLY.
S.Adams
I RESPONDED BY INCREASING MY INSOLENCE AND DECREASING MY PRODUCTIVITY.
6/9/98 © 1998 United Feature Syndicate, Inc.
I WILL NEVER HIRE ANOTHER ENGINEER AS LONG AS I'M ALIVE.
EQUILIBRIUM HAS BEEN RESTORED.

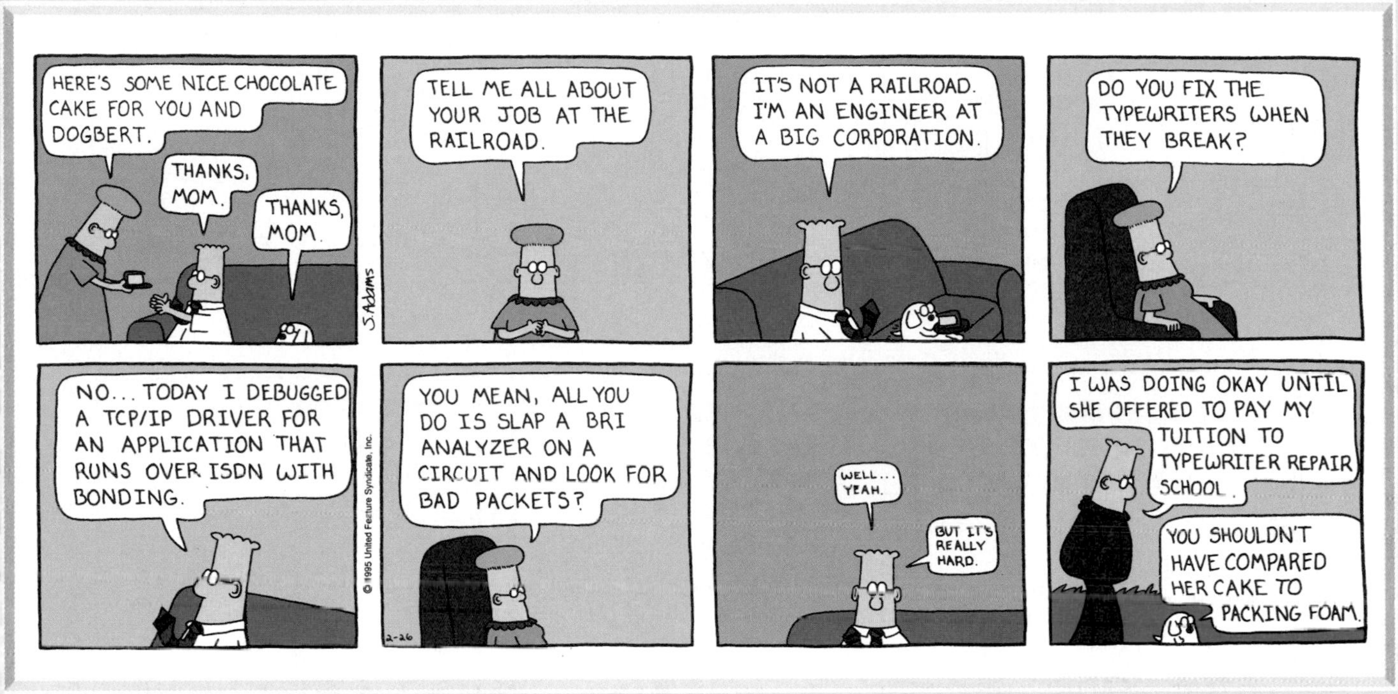
HERE'S SOME NICE CHOCOLATE CAKE FOR YOU AND DOGBERT.
THANKS, MOM.
THANKS, MOM.
S. Adams
TELL ME ALL ABOUT YOUR JOB AT THE RAILROAD.
IT'S NOT A RAILROAD. I'M AN ENGINEER AT A BIG CORPORATION.
DO YOU FIX THE TYPEWRITERS WHEN THEY BREAK?
NO... TODAY I DEBUGGED A TCP/IP DRIVER FOR AN APPLICATION THAT RUNS OVER ISDN WITH BONDING.
© 1995 United Feature Syndicate, Inc.
2-26
YOU MEAN, ALL YOU DO IS SLAP A BRI ANALYZER ON A CIRCUIT AND LOOK FOR BAD PACKETS?
WELL... YEAH.
BUT IT'S REALLY HARD.
I WAS DOING OKAY UNTIL SHE OFFERED TO PAY MY TUITION TO TYPEWRITER REPAIR SCHOOL.
YOU SHOULDN'T HAVE COMPARED HER CAKE TO PACKING FOAM.

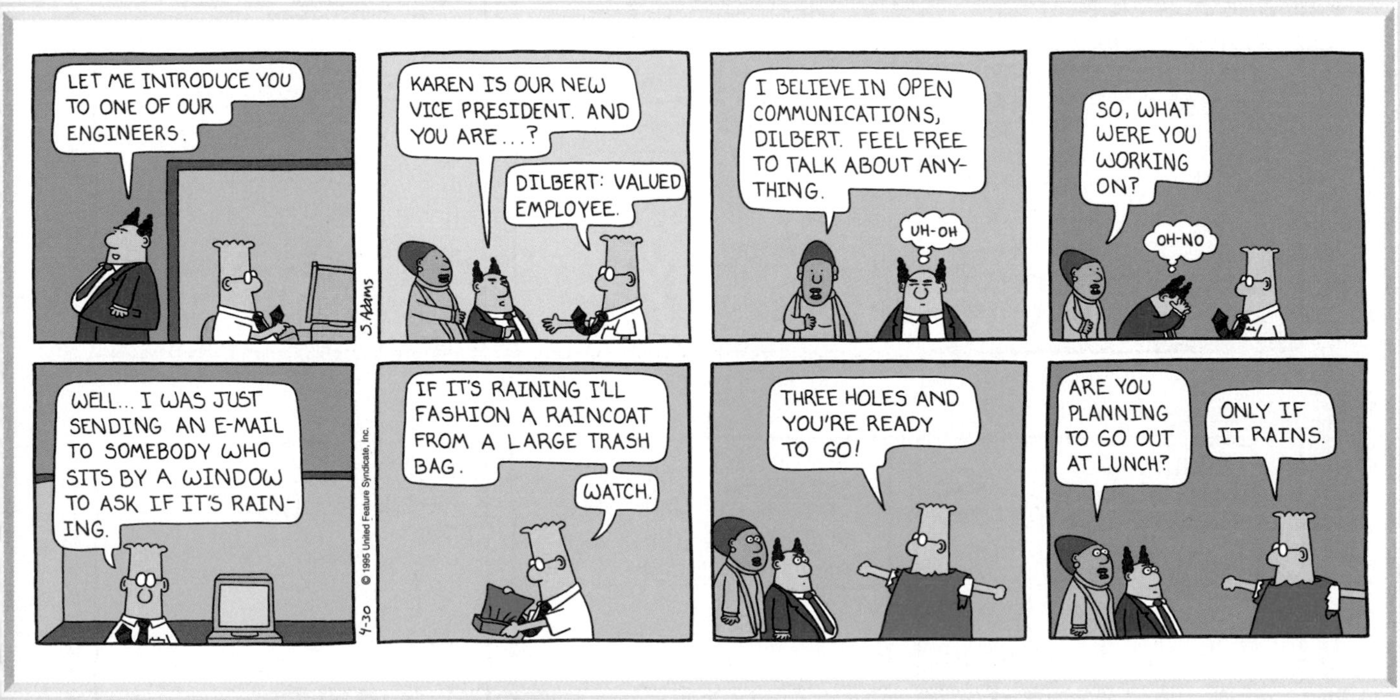
LET ME INTRODUCE YOU TO ONE OF OUR ENGINEERS.
S. Adams
KAREN IS OUR NEW VICE PRESIDENT. AND YOU ARE...?
DILBERT: VALUED EMPLOYEE.
I BELIEVE IN OPEN COMMUNICATIONS, DILBERT. FEEL FREE TO TALK ABOUT ANY-THING.
UH-OH
SO, WHAT WERE YOU WORKING ON?
OH-NO
WELL... I WAS JUST SENDING AN E-MAIL TO SOMEBODY WHO SITS BY A WINDOW TO ASK IF IT'S RAIN-ING.
© 1995 United Feature Syndicate, Inc.
4-30
IF IT'S RAINING I'LL FASHION A RAINCOAT FROM A LARGE TRASH BAG.
WATCH.
THREE HOLES AND YOU'RE READY TO GO!
ARE YOU PLANNING TO GO OUT AT LUNCH?
ONLY IF IT RAINS.

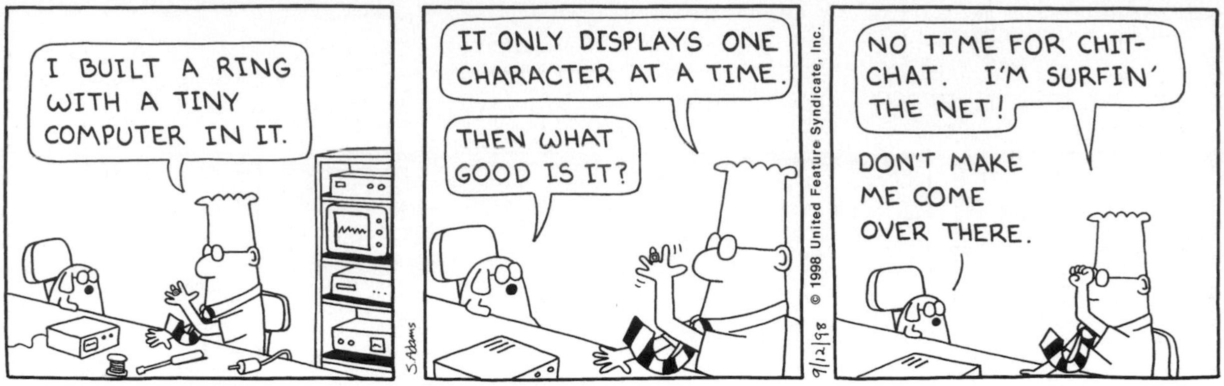
I BUILT A RING WITH A TINY COMPUTER IN IT.
IT ONLY DISPLAYS ONE CHARACTER AT A TIME.
THEN WHAT GOOD IS IT?
NO TIME FOR CHIT-CHAT. I'M SURFIN' THE NET!
DON'T MAKE ME COME OVER THERE.

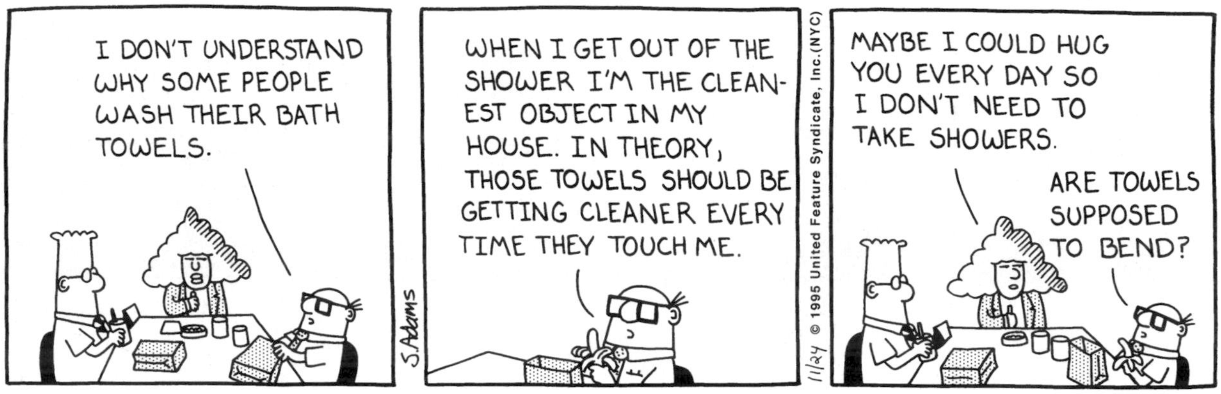
I DON'T UNDERSTAND WHY SOME PEOPLE WASH THEIR BATH TOWELS.
WHEN I GET OUT OF THE SHOWER I'M THE CLEAN-EST OBJECT IN MY HOUSE. IN THEORY, THOSE TOWELS SHOULD BE GETTING CLEANER EVERY TIME THEY TOUCH ME.
MAYBE I COULD HUG YOU EVERY DAY SO I DON'T NEED TO TAKE SHOWERS.
ARE TOWELS SUPPOSED TO BEND?

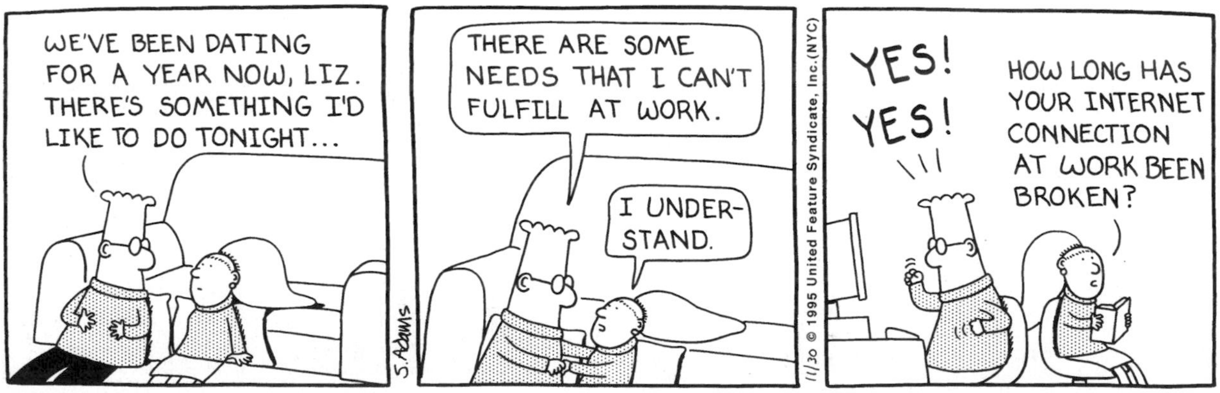
WE'VE BEEN DATING FOR A YEAR NOW, LIZ. THERE'S SOMETHING I'D LIKE TO DO TONIGHT...
THERE ARE SOME NEEDS THAT I CAN'T FULFILL AT WORK.
I UNDER-STAND.
YES! YES!
HOW LONG HAS YOUR INTERNET CONNECTION AT WORK BEEN BROKEN?

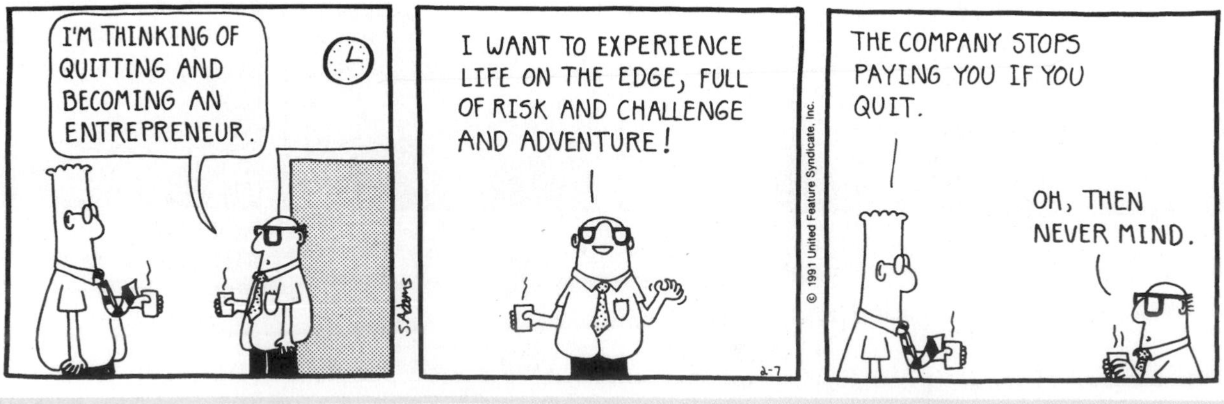
I'M THINKING OF QUITTING AND BECOMING AN ENTREPRENEUR.
I WANT TO EXPERIENCE LIFE ON THE EDGE, FULL OF RISK AND CHALLENGE AND ADVENTURE!
THE COMPANY STOPS PAYING YOU IF YOU QUIT.
OH, THEN NEVER MIND.

ENTREPRENEURS AND VENTURE CAPITALISTS

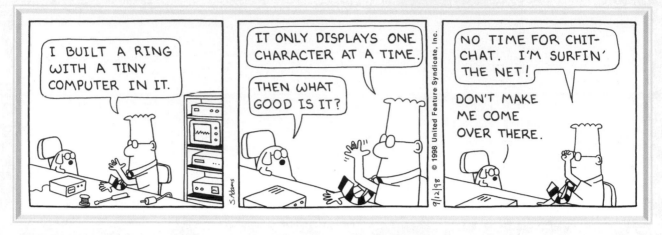

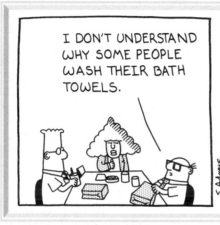

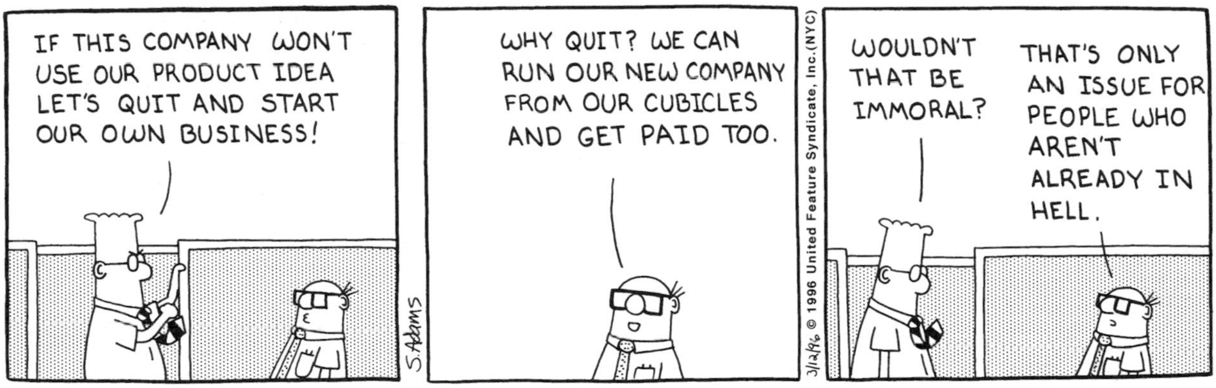
IF THIS COMPANY WON'T USE OUR PRODUCT IDEA LET'S QUIT AND START OUR OWN BUSINESS!
S.Adams
WHY QUIT? WE CAN RUN OUR NEW COMPANY FROM OUR CUBICLES AND GET PAID TOO.
3/12/96 © 1996 United Feature Syndicate, Inc.(NYC)
WOULDN'T THAT BE IMMORAL?
THAT'S ONLY AN ISSUE FOR PEOPLE WHO AREN'T ALREADY IN HELL.

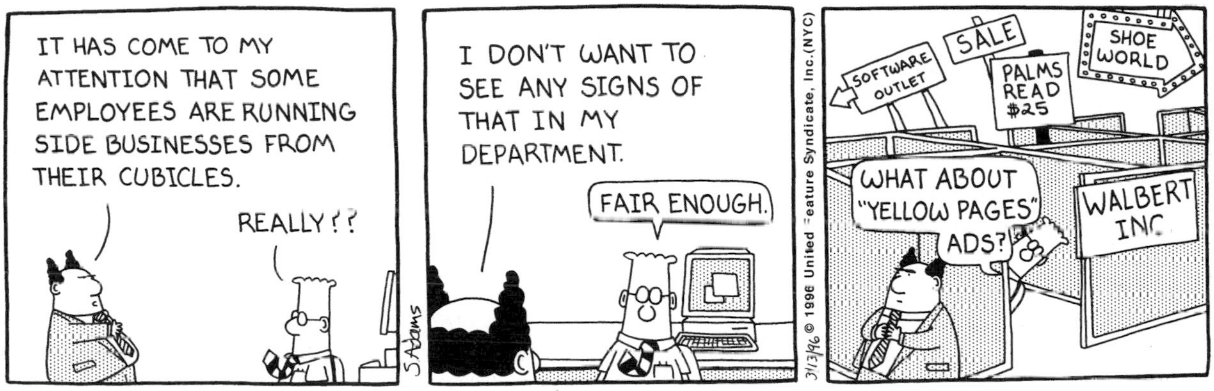
IT HAS COME TO MY ATTENTION THAT SOME EMPLOYEES ARE RUNNING SIDE BUSINESSES FROM THEIR CUBICLES.
REALLY??
S.Adams
I DON'T WANT TO SEE ANY SIGNS OF THAT IN MY DEPARTMENT.
FAIR ENOUGH.
3/13/96 © 1996 United Feature Syndicate, Inc.(NYC)
SOFTWARE OUTLET
SALE
PALMS READ $25
SHOE WORLD
WHAT ABOUT "YELLOW PAGES" ADS?
WALBERT INC

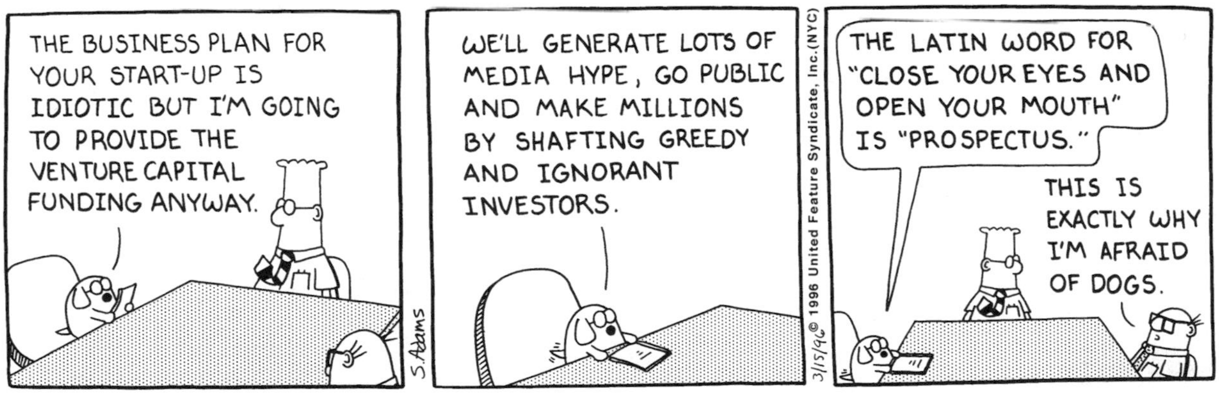
THE BUSINESS PLAN FOR YOUR START-UP IS IDIOTIC BUT I'M GOING TO PROVIDE THE VENTURE CAPITAL FUNDING ANYWAY.
S.Adams
WE'LL GENERATE LOTS OF MEDIA HYPE, GO PUBLIC AND MAKE MILLIONS BY SHAFTING GREEDY AND IGNORANT INVESTORS.
3/15/96 © 1996 United Feature Syndicate, Inc.(NYC)
THE LATIN WORD FOR "CLOSE YOUR EYES AND OPEN YOUR MOUTH" IS "PROSPECTUS."
THIS IS EXACTLY WHY I'M AFRAID OF DOGS.

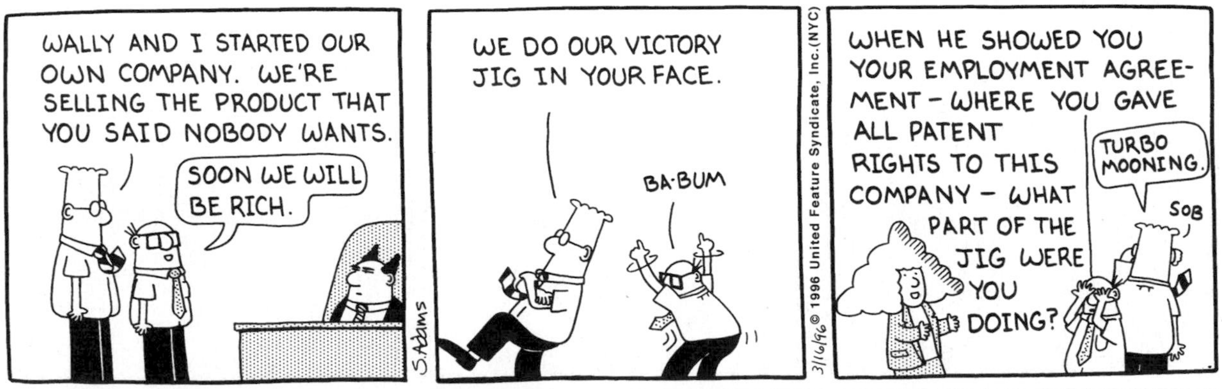
WALLY AND I STARTED OUR OWN COMPANY. WE'RE SELLING THE PRODUCT THAT YOU SAID NOBODY WANTS.
SOON WE WILL BE RICH.
S.Adams
WE DO OUR VICTORY JIG IN YOUR FACE.
BA-BUM
3/16/96 © 1996 United Feature Syndicate, Inc.(NYC)
WHEN HE SHOWED YOU YOUR EMPLOYMENT AGREEMENT – WHERE YOU GAVE ALL PATENT RIGHTS TO THIS COMPANY – WHAT PART OF THE JIG WERE YOU DOING?
TURBO MOONING.
SOB

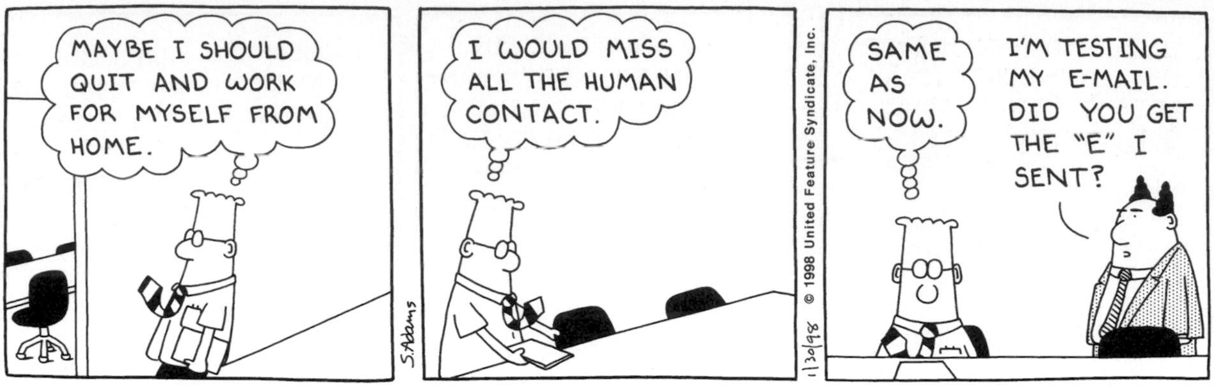
MAYBE I SHOULD QUIT AND WORK FOR MYSELF FROM HOME.
I WOULD MISS ALL THE HUMAN CONTACT.
S. Adams
1/30/98 © 1998 United Feature Syndicate, Inc.
SAME AS NOW.
I'M TESTING MY E-MAIL. DID YOU GET THE "E" I SENT?

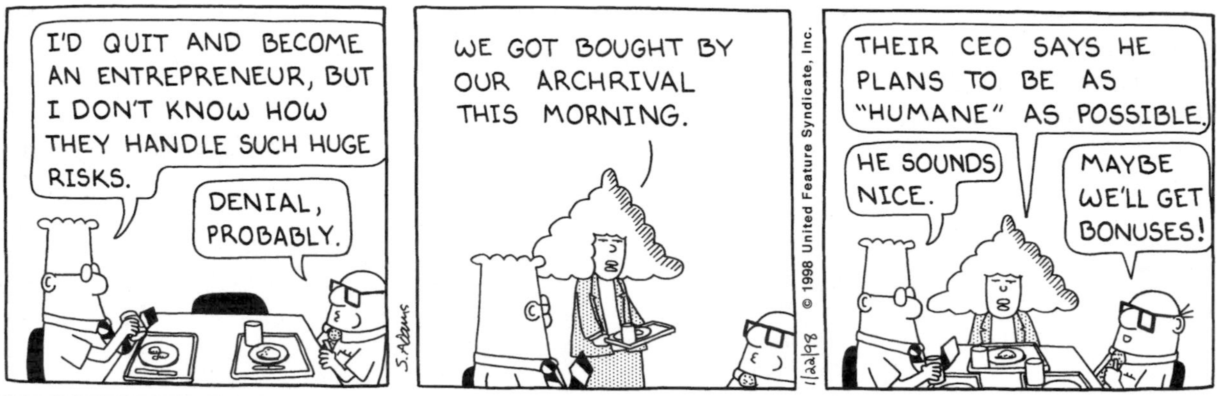
I'D QUIT AND BECOME AN ENTREPRENEUR, BUT I DON'T KNOW HOW THEY HANDLE SUCH HUGE RISKS.
DENIAL, PROBABLY.
S. Adams
WE GOT BOUGHT BY OUR ARCHRIVAL THIS MORNING.
1/22/98 © 1998 United Feature Syndicate, Inc.
THEIR CEO SAYS HE PLANS TO BE AS "HUMANE" AS POSSIBLE.
HE SOUNDS NICE.
MAYBE WE'LL GET BONUSES!

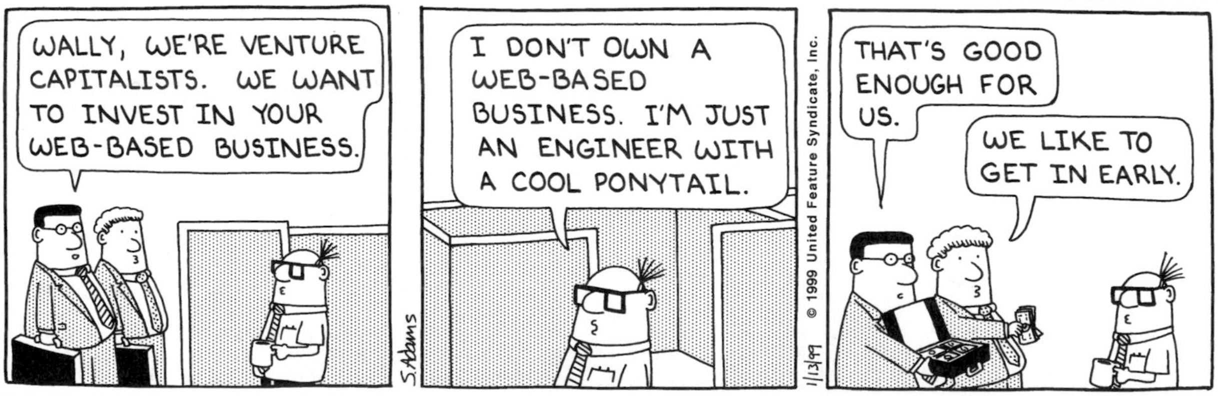
WALLY, WE'RE VENTURE CAPITALISTS. WE WANT TO INVEST IN YOUR WEB-BASED BUSINESS.
S. Adams
I DON'T OWN A WEB-BASED BUSINESS. I'M JUST AN ENGINEER WITH A COOL PONYTAIL.
1/13/99 © 1999 United Feature Syndicate, Inc.
THAT'S GOOD ENOUGH FOR US.
WE LIKE TO GET IN EARLY.

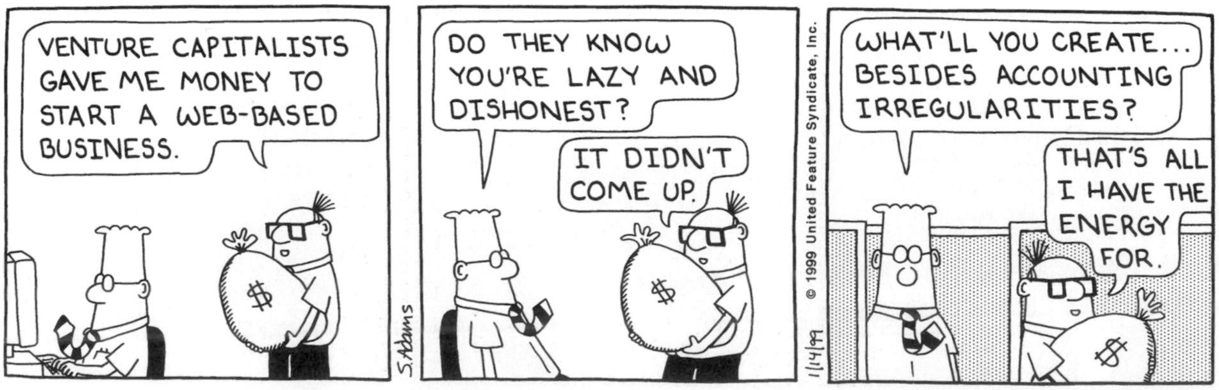
VENTURE CAPITALISTS GAVE ME MONEY TO START A WEB-BASED BUSINESS.
S. Adams
DO THEY KNOW YOU'RE LAZY AND DISHONEST?
IT DIDN'T COME UP.
1/14/99 © 1999 United Feature Syndicate, Inc.
WHAT'LL YOU CREATE... BESIDES ACCOUNTING IRREGULARITIES?
THAT'S ALL I HAVE THE ENERGY FOR.

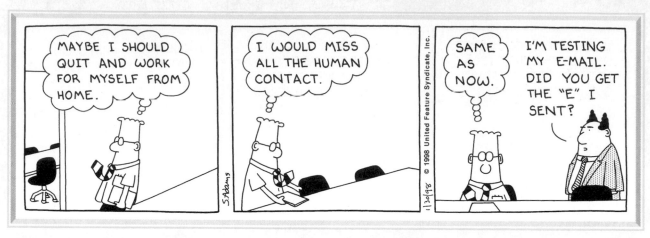

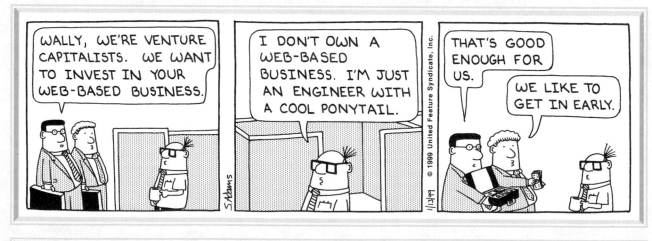

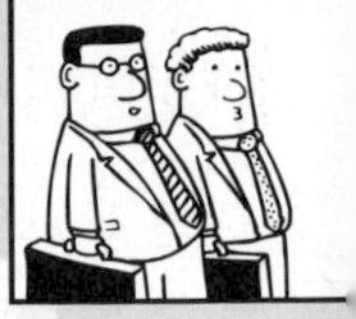

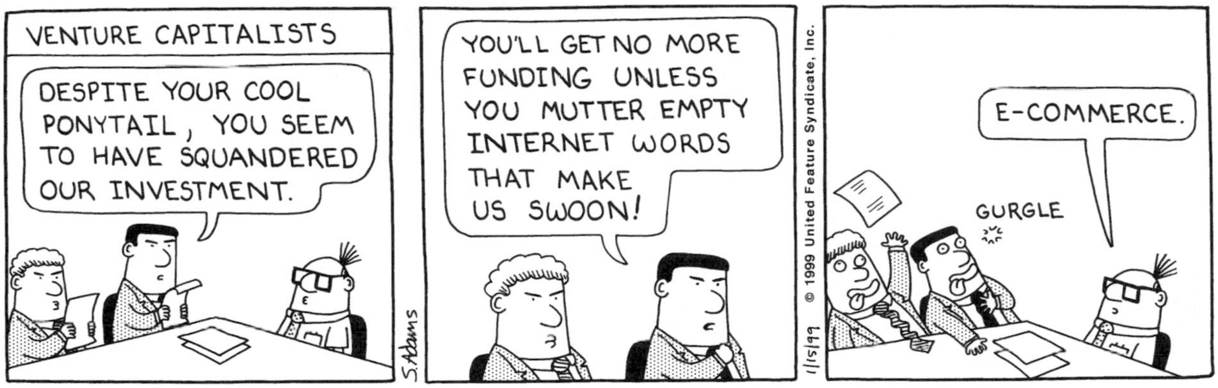
VENTURE CAPITALISTS
DESPITE YOUR COOL PONYTAIL, YOU SEEM TO HAVE SQUANDERED OUR INVESTMENT.
YOU'LL GET NO MORE FUNDING UNLESS YOU MUTTER EMPTY INTERNET WORDS THAT MAKE US SWOON!
E-COMMERCE.
GURGLE
© 1999 United Feature Syndicate, Inc.

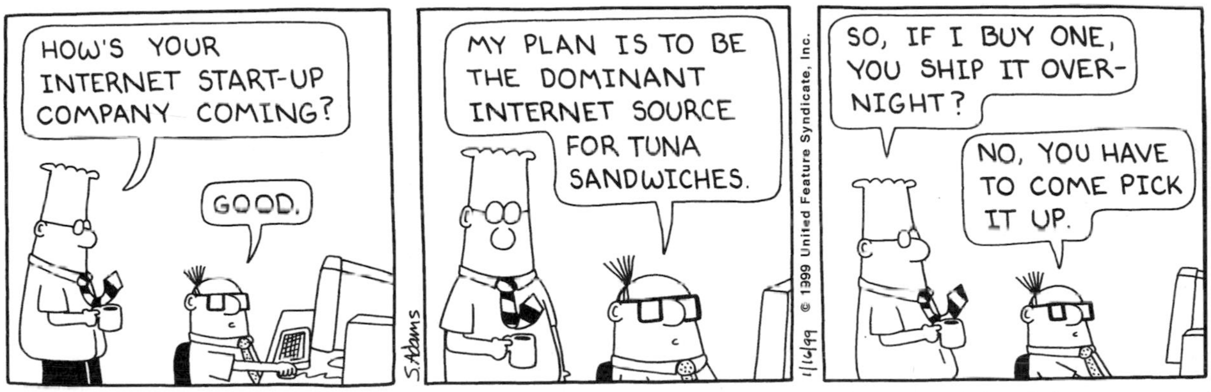
HOW'S YOUR INTERNET START-UP COMPANY COMING?
GOOD.
MY PLAN IS TO BE THE DOMINANT INTERNET SOURCE FOR TUNA SANDWICHES.
SO, IF I BUY ONE, YOU SHIP IT OVER-NIGHT?
NO, YOU HAVE TO COME PICK IT UP.
© 1999 United Feature Syndicate, Inc.

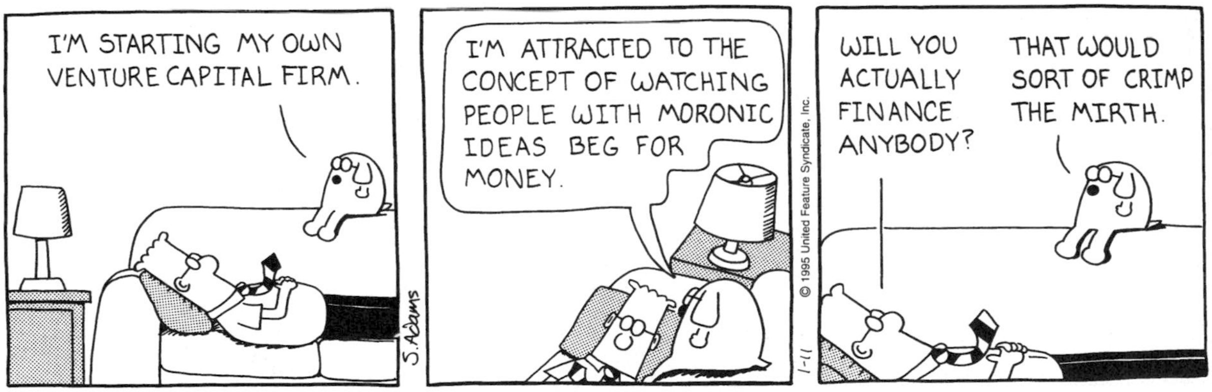
I'M STARTING MY OWN VENTURE CAPITAL FIRM.
I'M ATTRACTED TO THE CONCEPT OF WATCHING PEOPLE WITH MORONIC IDEAS BEG FOR MONEY.
WILL YOU ACTUALLY FINANCE ANYBODY?
THAT WOULD SORT OF CRIMP THE MIRTH.
© 1995 United Feature Syndicate, Inc.

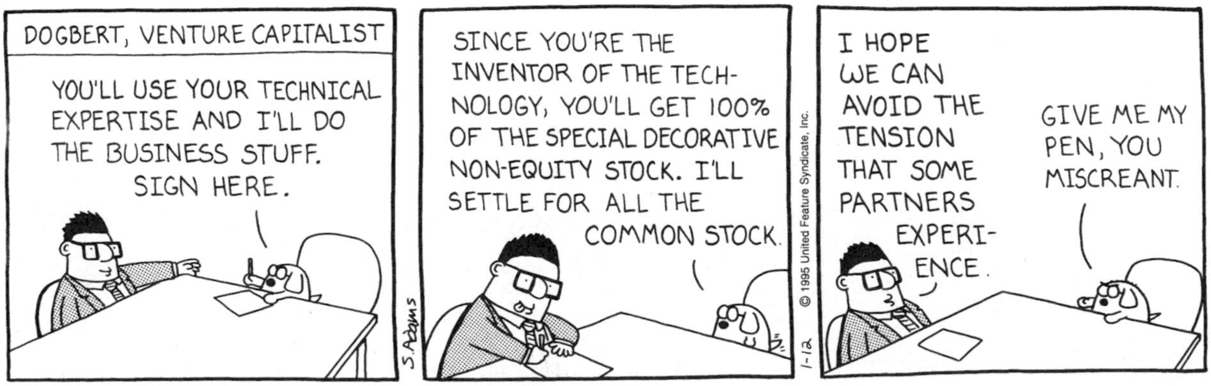
DOGBERT, VENTURE CAPITALIST
YOU'LL USE YOUR TECHNICAL EXPERTISE AND I'LL DO THE BUSINESS STUFF. SIGN HERE.
SINCE YOU'RE THE INVENTOR OF THE TECH-NOLOGY, YOU'LL GET 100% OF THE SPECIAL DECORATIVE NON-EQUITY STOCK. I'LL SETTLE FOR ALL THE COMMON STOCK.
I HOPE WE CAN AVOID THE TENSION THAT SOME PARTNERS EXPERI-ENCE.
GIVE ME MY PEN, YOU MISCREANT.
© 1995 United Feature Syndicate, Inc.

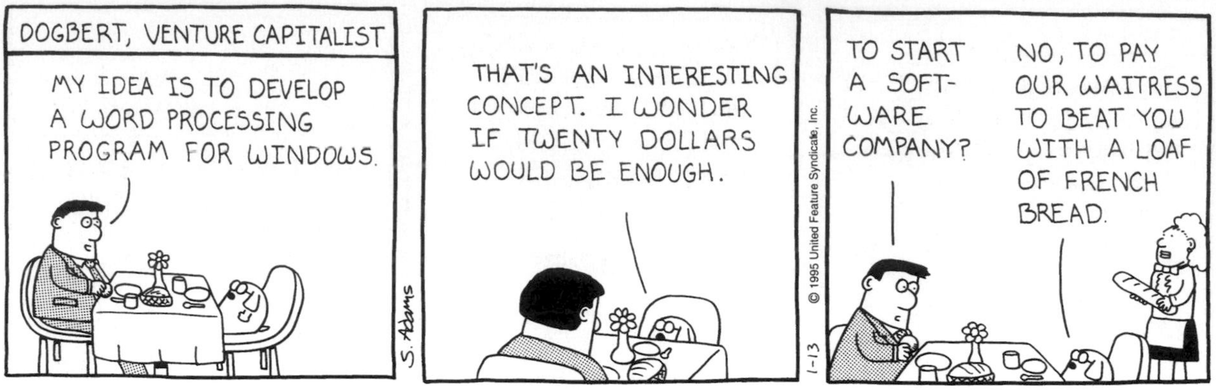
DOGBERT, VENTURE CAPITALIST
MY IDEA IS TO DEVELOP A WORD PROCESSING PROGRAM FOR WINDOWS.
THAT'S AN INTERESTING CONCEPT. I WONDER IF TWENTY DOLLARS WOULD BE ENOUGH.
TO START A SOFT-WARE COMPANY?
NO, TO PAY OUR WAITRESS TO BEAT YOU WITH A LOAF OF FRENCH BREAD.
S. Adams
1-13
© 1995 United Feature Syndicate, Inc.

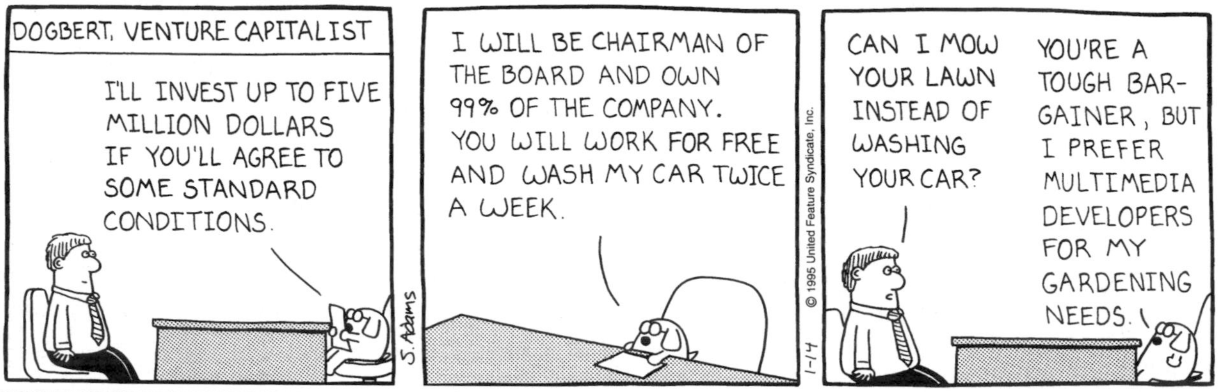
DOGBERT, VENTURE CAPITALIST
I'LL INVEST UP TO FIVE MILLION DOLLARS IF YOU'LL AGREE TO SOME STANDARD CONDITIONS.
I WILL BE CHAIRMAN OF THE BOARD AND OWN 99% OF THE COMPANY. YOU WILL WORK FOR FREE AND WASH MY CAR TWICE A WEEK.
CAN I MOW YOUR LAWN INSTEAD OF WASHING YOUR CAR?
YOU'RE A TOUGH BAR-GAINER, BUT I PREFER MULTIMEDIA DEVELOPERS FOR MY GARDENING NEEDS.
S. Adams
1-14
© 1995 United Feature Syndicate, Inc.

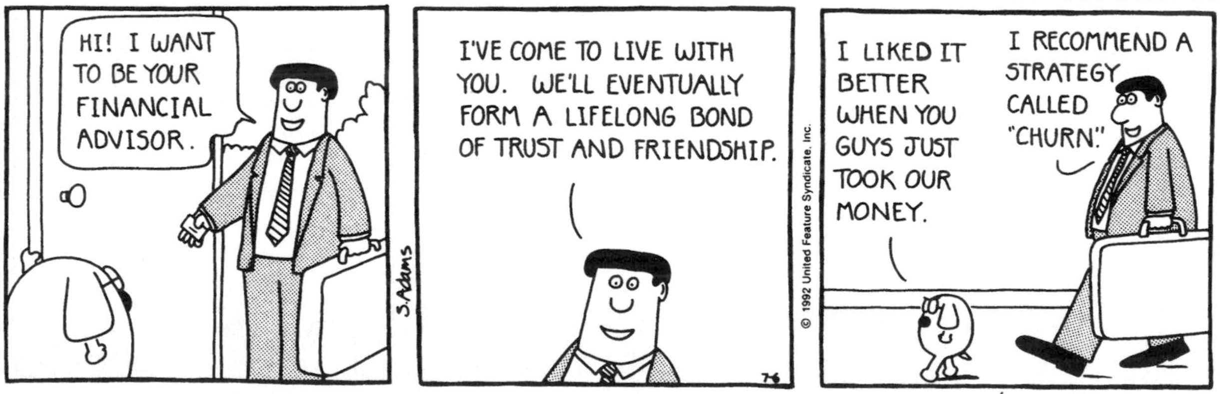
HI! I WANT TO BE YOUR FINANCIAL ADVISOR.
I'VE COME TO LIVE WITH YOU. WE'LL EVENTUALLY FORM A LIFELONG BOND OF TRUST AND FRIENDSHIP.
I LIKED IT BETTER WHEN YOU GUYS JUST TOOK OUR MONEY.
I RECOMMEND A STRATEGY CALLED "CHURN."
S. Adams
7-6
© 1992 United Feature Syndicate, Inc.

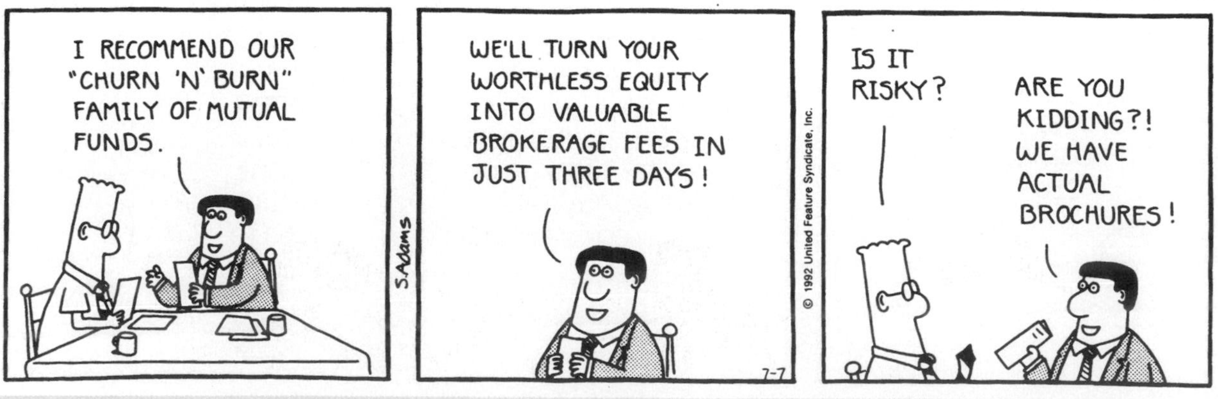
I RECOMMEND OUR "CHURN 'N' BURN" FAMILY OF MUTUAL FUNDS.
WE'LL TURN YOUR WORTHLESS EQUITY INTO VALUABLE BROKERAGE FEES IN JUST THREE DAYS!
IS IT RISKY?
ARE YOU KIDDING?! WE HAVE ACTUAL BROCHURES!
S. Adams
7-7
© 1992 United Feature Syndicate, Inc.

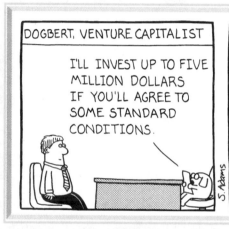

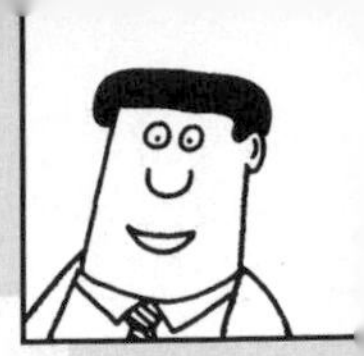

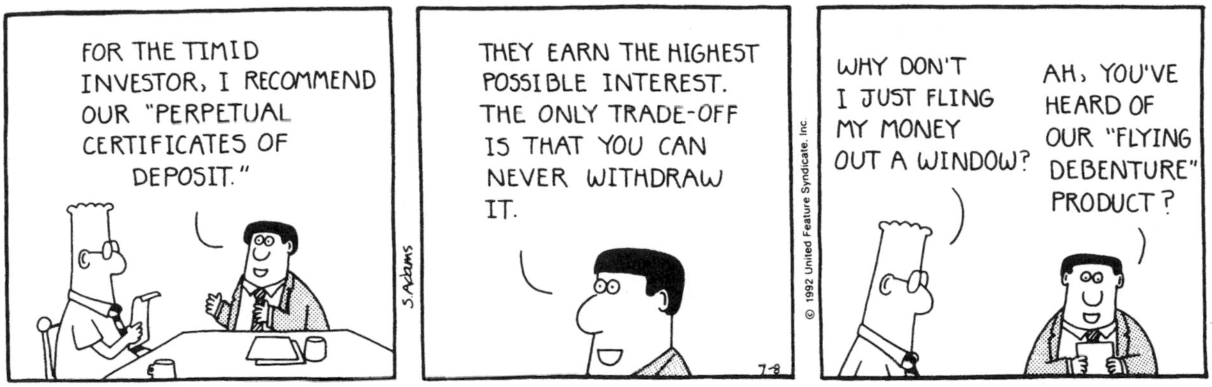
FOR THE TIMID INVESTOR, I RECOMMEND OUR "PERPETUAL CERTIFICATES OF DEPOSIT."
S. Adams
THEY EARN THE HIGHEST POSSIBLE INTEREST. THE ONLY TRADE-OFF IS THAT YOU CAN NEVER WITHDRAW IT.
7-8
© 1992 United Feature Syndicate, Inc.
WHY DON'T I JUST FLING MY MONEY OUT A WINDOW?
AH, YOU'VE HEARD OF OUR "FLYING DEBENTURE" PRODUCT?

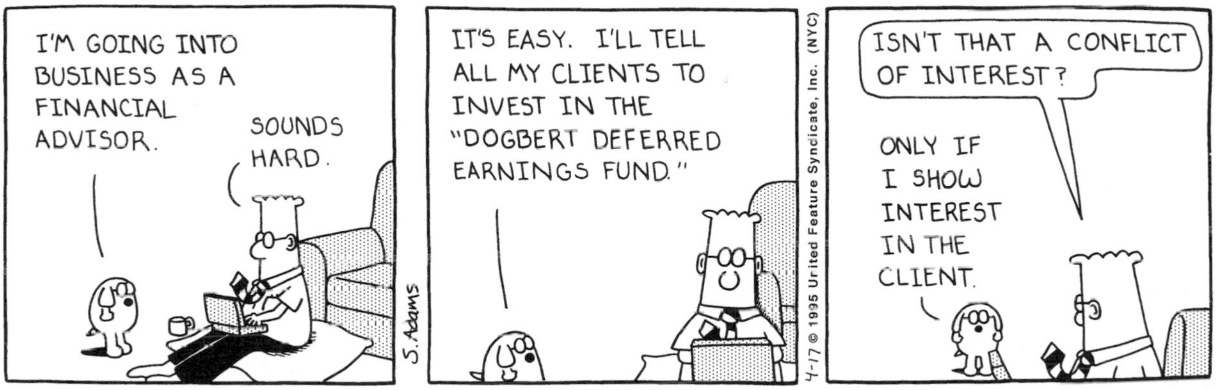
I'M GOING INTO BUSINESS AS A FINANCIAL ADVISOR.
SOUNDS HARD.
S. Adams
IT'S EASY. I'LL TELL ALL MY CLIENTS TO INVEST IN THE "DOGBERT DEFERRED EARNINGS FUND."
4-17 © 1995 United Feature Syndicate, Inc. (NYC)
ISN'T THAT A CONFLICT OF INTEREST?
ONLY IF I SHOW INTEREST IN THE CLIENT.

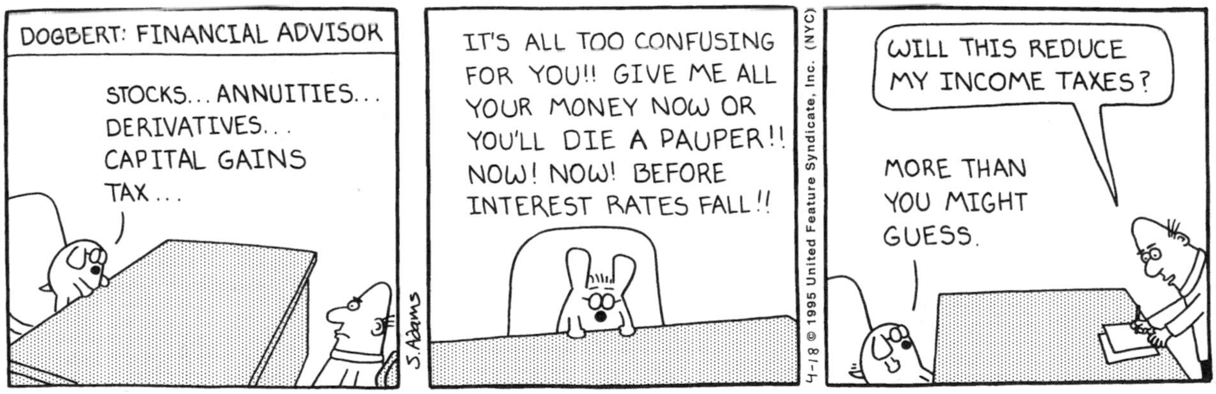
DOGBERT: FINANCIAL ADVISOR
STOCKS... ANNUITIES... DERIVATIVES... CAPITAL GAINS TAX...
S. Adams
IT'S ALL TOO CONFUSING FOR YOU!! GIVE ME ALL YOUR MONEY NOW OR YOU'LL DIE A PAUPER!! NOW! NOW! BEFORE INTEREST RATES FALL!!
4-18 © 1995 United Feature Syndicate, Inc. (NYC)
WILL THIS REDUCE MY INCOME TAXES?
MORE THAN YOU MIGHT GUESS.

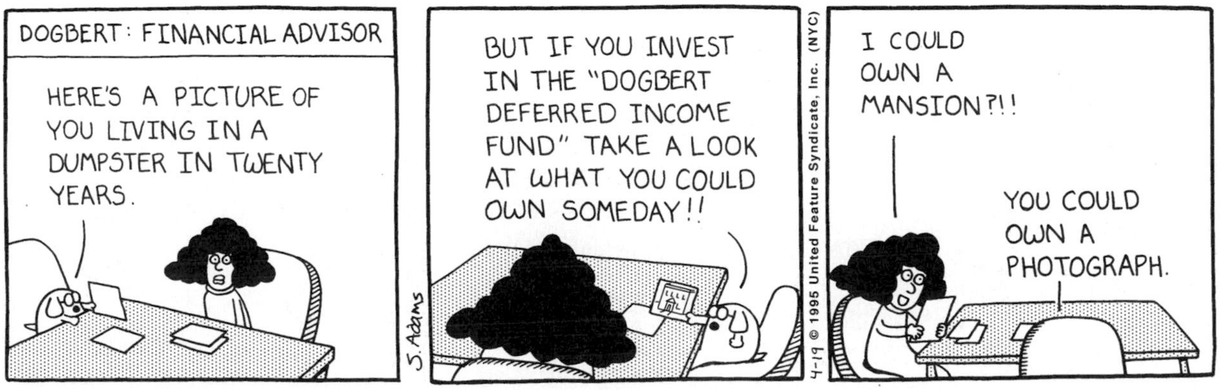
DOGBERT: FINANCIAL ADVISOR
HERE'S A PICTURE OF YOU LIVING IN A DUMPSTER IN TWENTY YEARS.
S. Adams
BUT IF YOU INVEST IN THE "DOGBERT DEFERRED INCOME FUND" TAKE A LOOK AT WHAT YOU COULD OWN SOMEDAY!!
4-19 © 1995 United Feature Syndicate, Inc. (NYC)
I COULD OWN A MANSION?!!
YOU COULD OWN A PHOTOGRAPH.

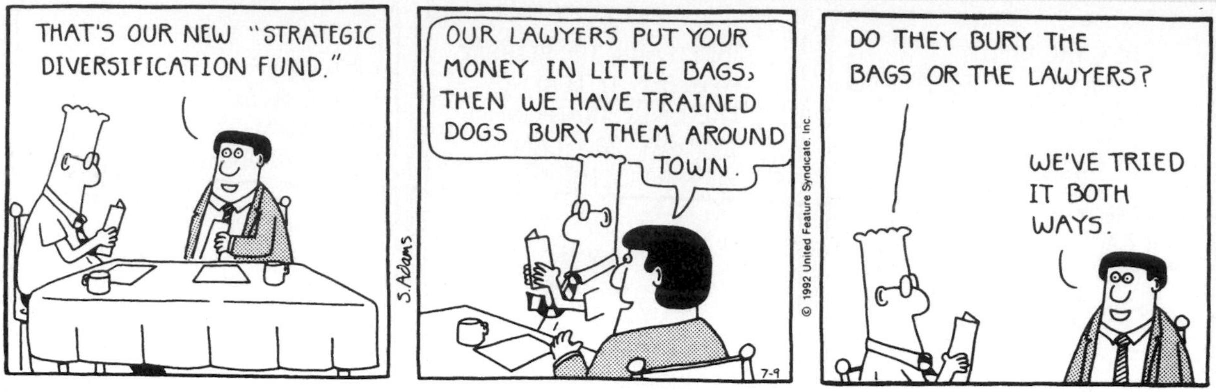
THAT'S OUR NEW "STRATEGIC DIVERSIFICATION FUND."
OUR LAWYERS PUT YOUR MONEY IN LITTLE BAGS, THEN WE HAVE TRAINED DOGS BURY THEM AROUND TOWN.
DO THEY BURY THE BAGS OR THE LAWYERS?
WE'VE TRIED IT BOTH WAYS.
S. Adams
7-9
© 1992 United Feature Syndicate, Inc.

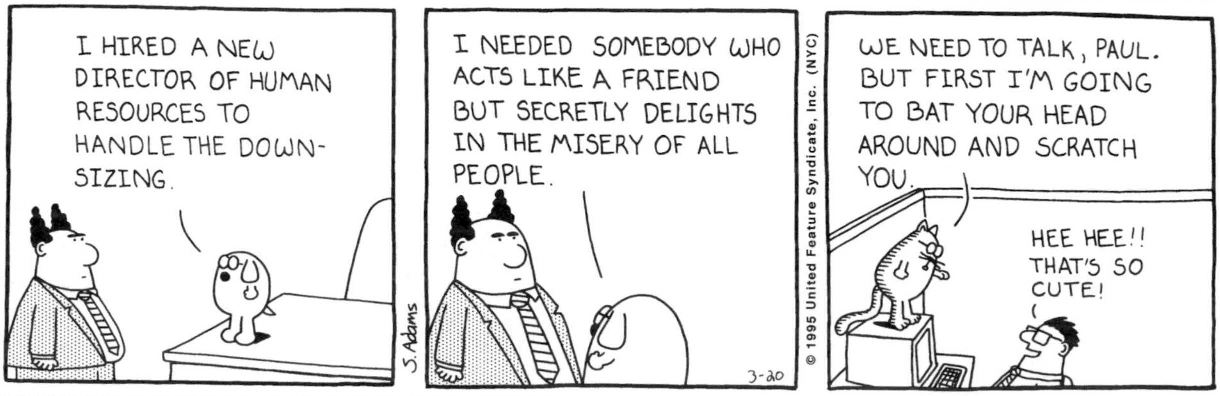
I HIRED A NEW DIRECTOR OF HUMAN RESOURCES TO HANDLE THE DOWN-SIZING.
I NEEDED SOMEBODY WHO ACTS LIKE A FRIEND BUT SECRETLY DELIGHTS IN THE MISERY OF ALL PEOPLE.
WE NEED TO TALK, PAUL. BUT FIRST I'M GOING TO BAT YOUR HEAD AROUND AND SCRATCH YOU.
HEE HEE!! THAT'S SO CUTE!
S. Adams
3-20
© 1995 United Feature Syndicate, Inc. (NYC)

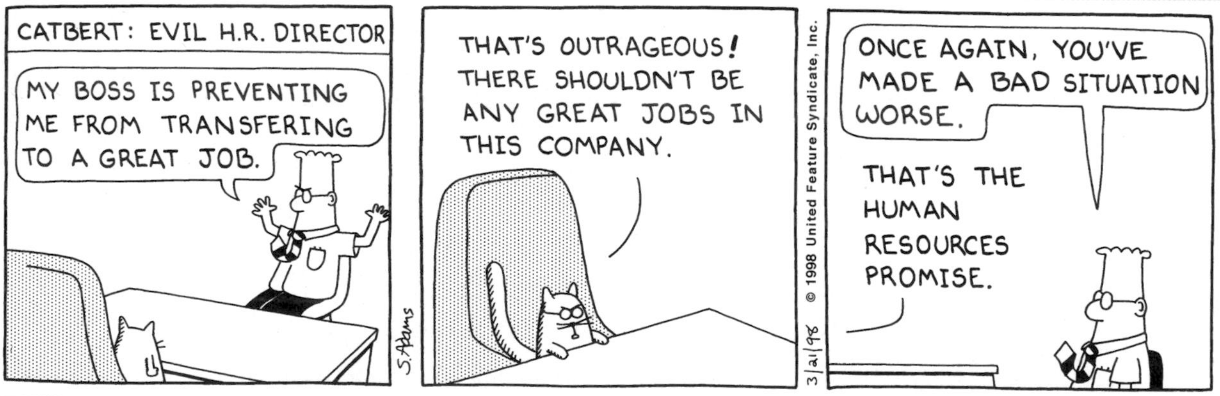
CATBERT: EVIL H.R. DIRECTOR
MY BOSS IS PREVENTING ME FROM TRANSFERING TO A GREAT JOB.
THAT'S OUTRAGEOUS! THERE SHOULDN'T BE ANY GREAT JOBS IN THIS COMPANY.
ONCE AGAIN, YOU'VE MADE A BAD SITUATION WORSE.
THAT'S THE HUMAN RESOURCES PROMISE.
S. Adams
3/21/98
© 1998 United Feature Syndicate, Inc.

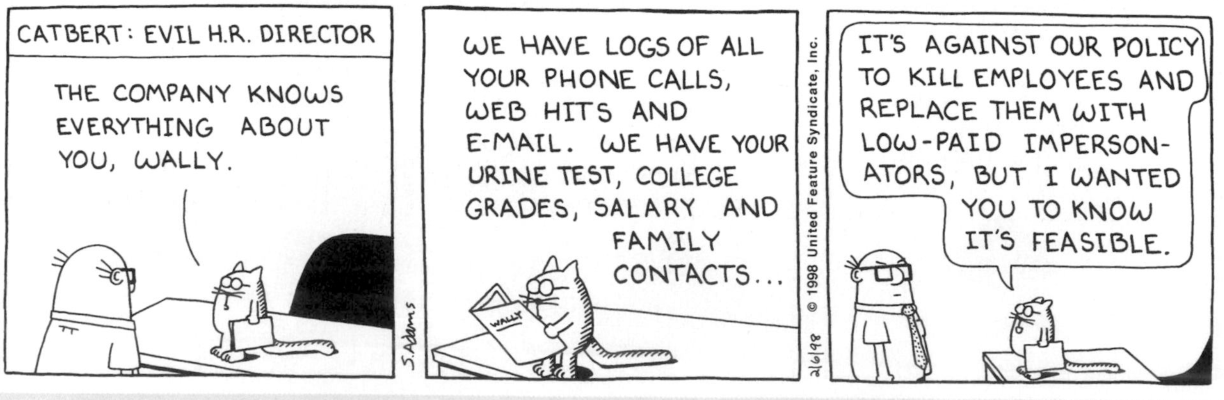
CATBERT: EVIL H.R. DIRECTOR
THE COMPANY KNOWS EVERYTHING ABOUT YOU, WALLY.
WE HAVE LOGS OF ALL YOUR PHONE CALLS, WEB HITS AND E-MAIL. WE HAVE YOUR URINE TEST, COLLEGE GRADES, SALARY AND FAMILY CONTACTS...
WALLY
IT'S AGAINST OUR POLICY TO KILL EMPLOYEES AND REPLACE THEM WITH LOW-PAID IMPERSON-ATORS, BUT I WANTED YOU TO KNOW IT'S FEASIBLE.
S. Adams
2/6/98
© 1998 United Feature Syndicate, Inc.

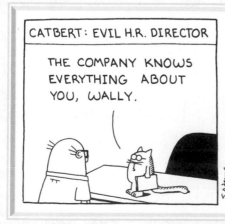

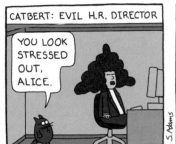

CATBERT: EVIL H.R. DIRECTOR
YOU LOOK STRESSED OUT, ALICE.
I COULD FIX THAT BY BECOMING A CHAMPION FOR IMPROVEMENTS IN THE WORKPLACE.
OR I COULD GIVE YOU A LITTLE BOOKLET CALLED "STRESS NO MORE."
HMM... I WONDER WHICH WAY IS BEST.
S. Adams
4/19/98
© 1998 United Feature Syndicate, Inc.
"STRESS IS YOUR BODY'S WAY OF SAYING..."
"... YOU HAVEN'T WORKED ENOUGH UNPAID OVERTIME."
I'VE NEVER SEEN A WOMAN'S FOREHEAD IGNITE HER HAIR BEFORE.

MISTER CATBERT WILL EXPLAIN OUR NEW "TOTAL COMPENSATION PLAN" FOR EXCELLENCE.
WE NO LONGER VIEW COMPENSATION IN THE NARROW TERMS OF SALARY ALONE.
DANGER! DANGER!
IF EMPLOYEE BENEFITS GO UP, THEN SALARIES CAN GO DOWN AND IT ALL BALANCES OUT.
S. Adams
FOR EXAMPLE, DID YOU KNOW YOU COULD LOWER YOUR BLOOD PRESSURE BY RUBBING MY SOFT, FURRY BELLY?
© 1995 United Feature Syndicate, Inc.(NYC)
1/12
IT MIGHT BE A TRICK!
WHAT'S THE WORST THING THAT COULD HAPPEN?
HA HA HA!!! IT'S A HEALTH BENEFIT! NOW I'LL CUT EVERYBODY'S SALARY!
I'VE NOTICED THAT THE MORE HEALTH BENEFITS I GET, THE WORSE I FEEL.

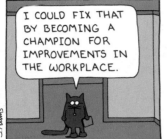

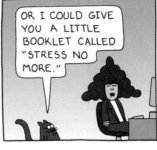

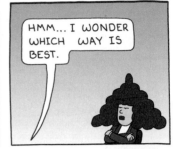

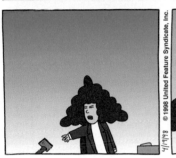

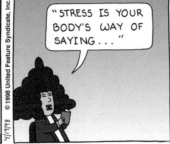

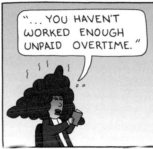

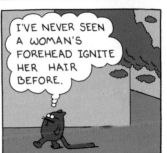

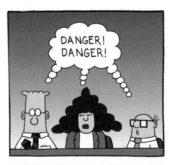

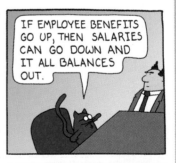

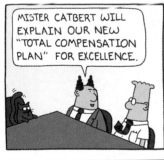

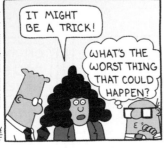

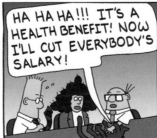

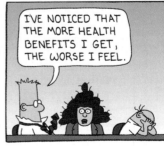

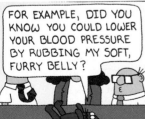

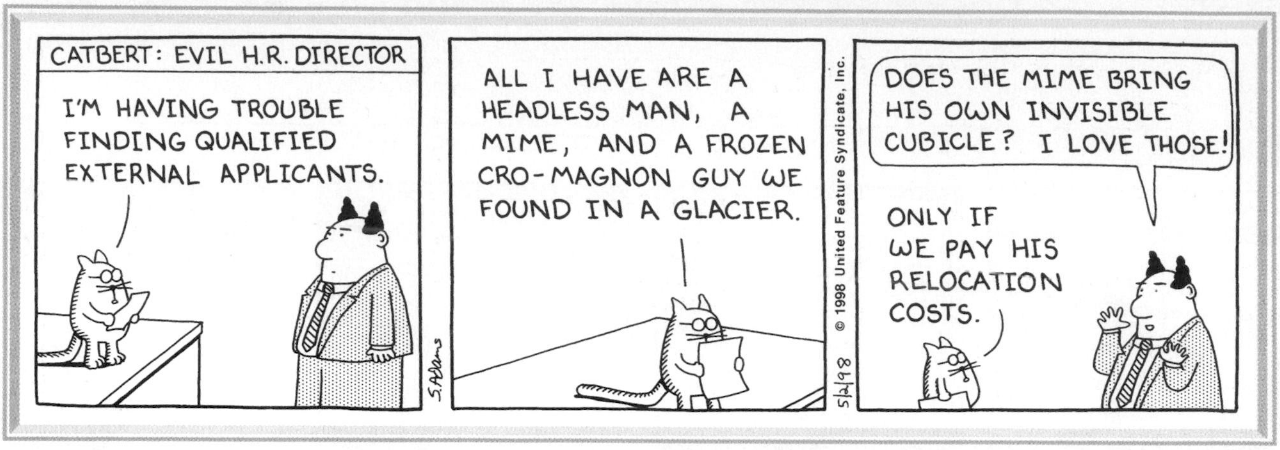
CATBERT: EVIL H.R. DIRECTOR
I'M HAVING TROUBLE FINDING QUALIFIED EXTERNAL APPLICANTS.
S. Adams
ALL I HAVE ARE A HEADLESS MAN, A MIME, AND A FROZEN CRO-MAGNON GUY WE FOUND IN A GLACIER.
5/2/98 © 1998 United Feature Syndicate, Inc.
DOES THE MIME BRING HIS OWN INVISIBLE CUBICLE? I LOVE THOSE!
ONLY IF WE PAY HIS RELOCATION COSTS.

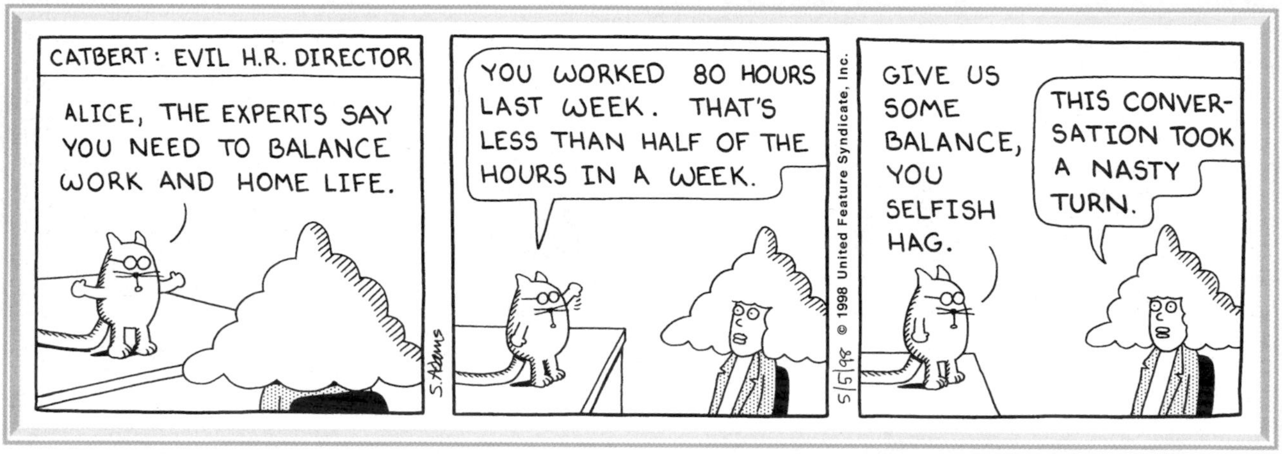
CATBERT: EVIL H.R. DIRECTOR
ALICE, THE EXPERTS SAY YOU NEED TO BALANCE WORK AND HOME LIFE.
S. Adams
YOU WORKED 80 HOURS LAST WEEK. THAT'S LESS THAN HALF OF THE HOURS IN A WEEK.
5/5/98 © 1998 United Feature Syndicate, Inc.
GIVE US SOME BALANCE, YOU SELFISH HAG.
THIS CONVERSATION TOOK A NASTY TURN.

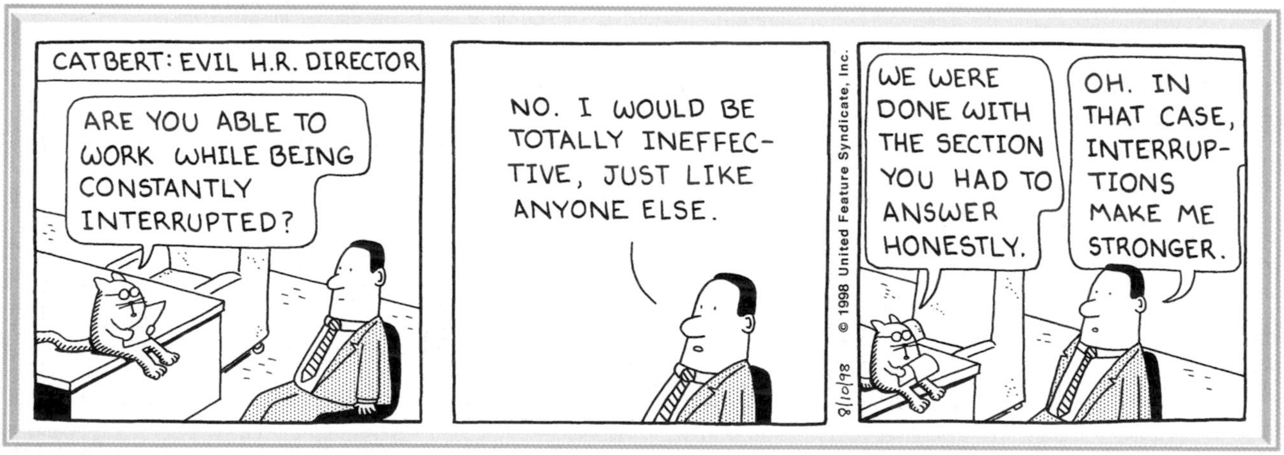
CATBERT: EVIL H.R. DIRECTOR
ARE YOU ABLE TO WORK WHILE BEING CONSTANTLY INTERRUPTED?
NO. I WOULD BE TOTALLY INEFFECTIVE, JUST LIKE ANYONE ELSE.
8/10/98 © 1998 United Feature Syndicate, Inc.
WE WERE DONE WITH THE SECTION YOU HAD TO ANSWER HONESTLY.
OH. IN THAT CASE, INTERRUPTIONS MAKE ME STRONGER.

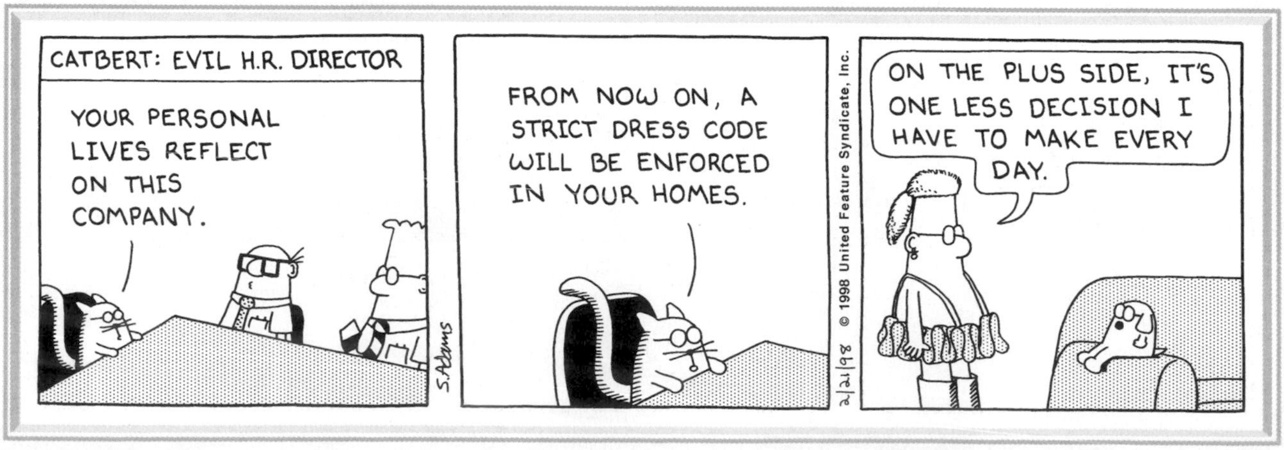
CATBERT: EVIL H.R. DIRECTOR
YOUR PERSONAL LIVES REFLECT ON THIS COMPANY.
S. Adams
FROM NOW ON, A STRICT DRESS CODE WILL BE ENFORCED IN YOUR HOMES.
2/21/98 © 1998 United Feature Syndicate, Inc.
ON THE PLUS SIDE, IT'S ONE LESS DECISION I HAVE TO MAKE EVERY DAY.

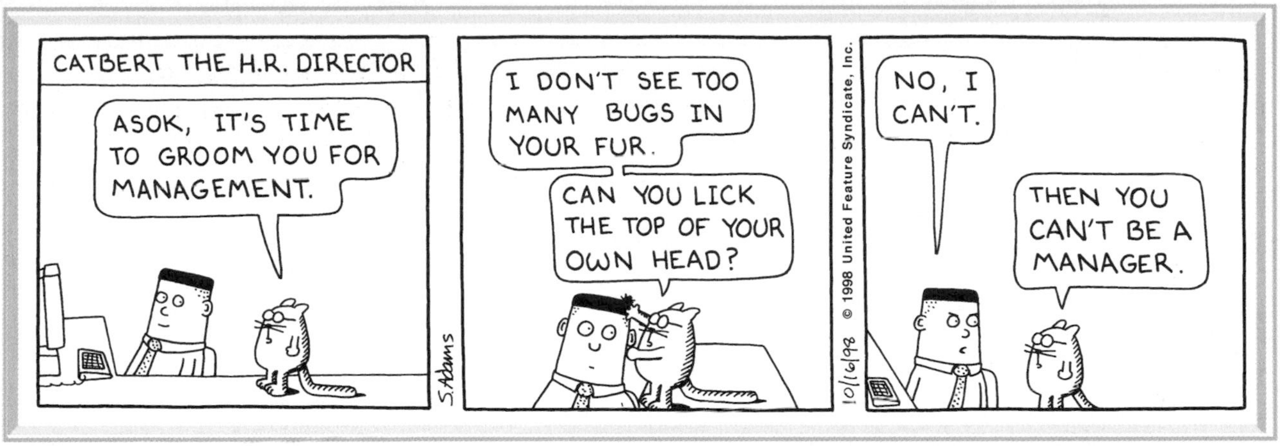
CATBERT THE H.R. DIRECTOR
ASOK, IT'S TIME TO GROOM YOU FOR MANAGEMENT.
I DON'T SEE TOO MANY BUGS IN YOUR FUR.
CAN YOU LICK THE TOP OF YOUR OWN HEAD?
NO, I CAN'T.
THEN YOU CAN'T BE A MANAGER.
S.Adams
10/16/98 © 1998 United Feature Syndicate, Inc.

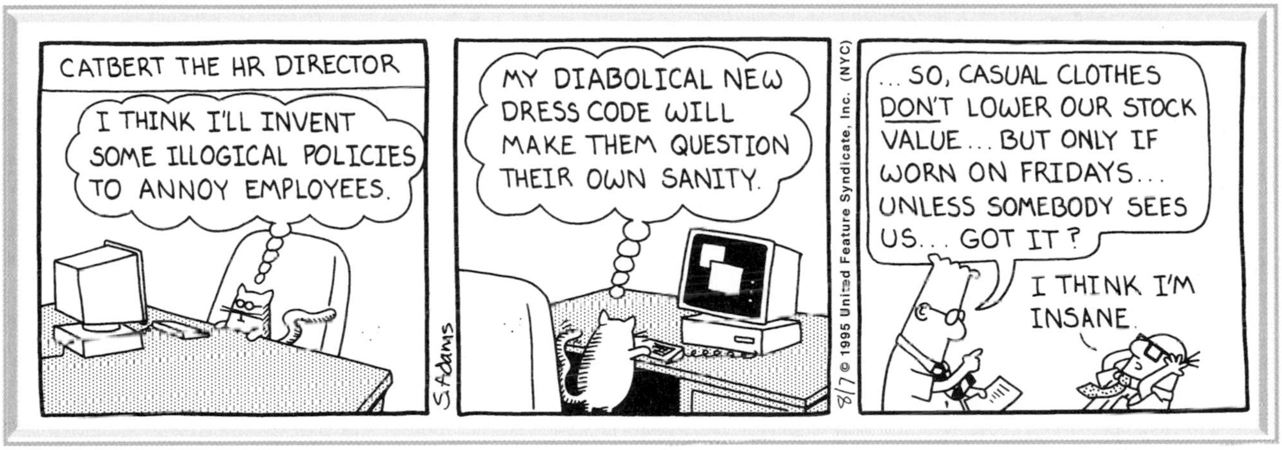
CATBERT THE HR DIRECTOR
I THINK I'LL INVENT SOME ILLOGICAL POLICIES TO ANNOY EMPLOYEES.
MY DIABOLICAL NEW DRESS CODE WILL MAKE THEM QUESTION THEIR OWN SANITY.
... SO, CASUAL CLOTHES DON'T LOWER OUR STOCK VALUE... BUT ONLY IF WORN ON FRIDAYS... UNLESS SOMEBODY SEES US... GOT IT?
I THINK I'M INSANE.
S.Adams
8/7 © 1995 United Feature Syndicate, Inc. (NYC)

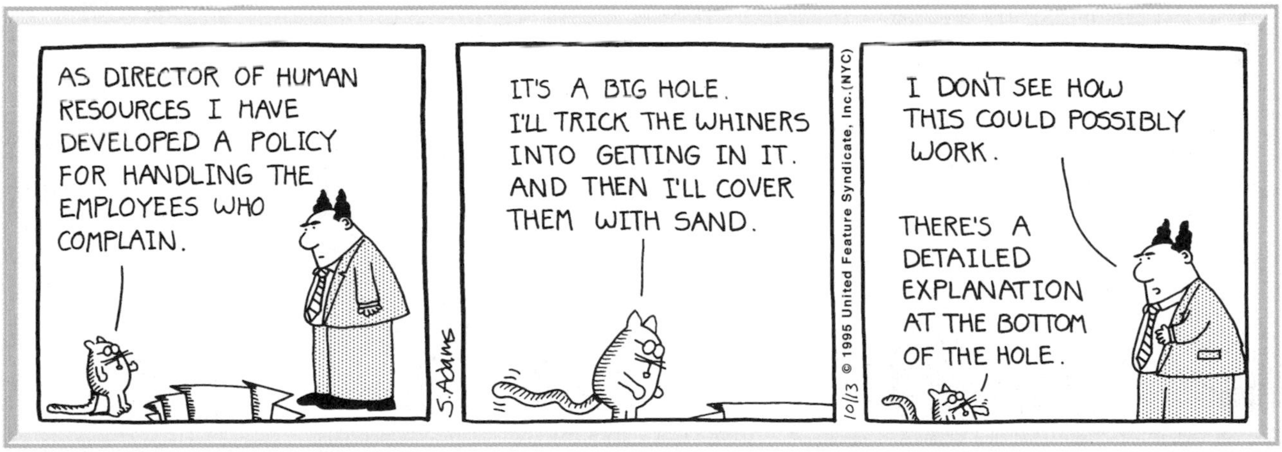
AS DIRECTOR OF HUMAN RESOURCES I HAVE DEVELOPED A POLICY FOR HANDLING THE EMPLOYEES WHO COMPLAIN.
IT'S A BIG HOLE. I'LL TRICK THE WHINERS INTO GETTING IN IT. AND THEN I'LL COVER THEM WITH SAND.
I DON'T SEE HOW THIS COULD POSSIBLY WORK.
THERE'S A DETAILED EXPLANATION AT THE BOTTOM OF THE HOLE.
S.Adams
10/13 © 1995 United Feature Syndicate, Inc. (NYC)

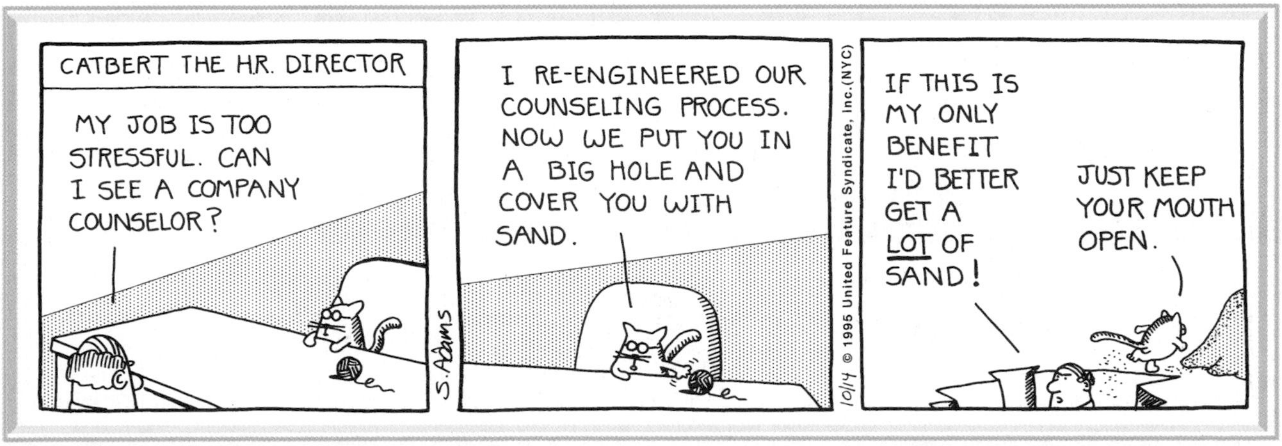
CATBERT THE HR. DIRECTOR
MY JOB IS TOO STRESSFUL. CAN I SEE A COMPANY COUNSELOR?
I RE-ENGINEERED OUR COUNSELING PROCESS. NOW WE PUT YOU IN A BIG HOLE AND COVER YOU WITH SAND.
IF THIS IS MY ONLY BENEFIT I'D BETTER GET A LOT OF SAND!
JUST KEEP YOUR MOUTH OPEN.
S.Adams
10/14 © 1995 United Feature Syndicate, Inc. (NYC)

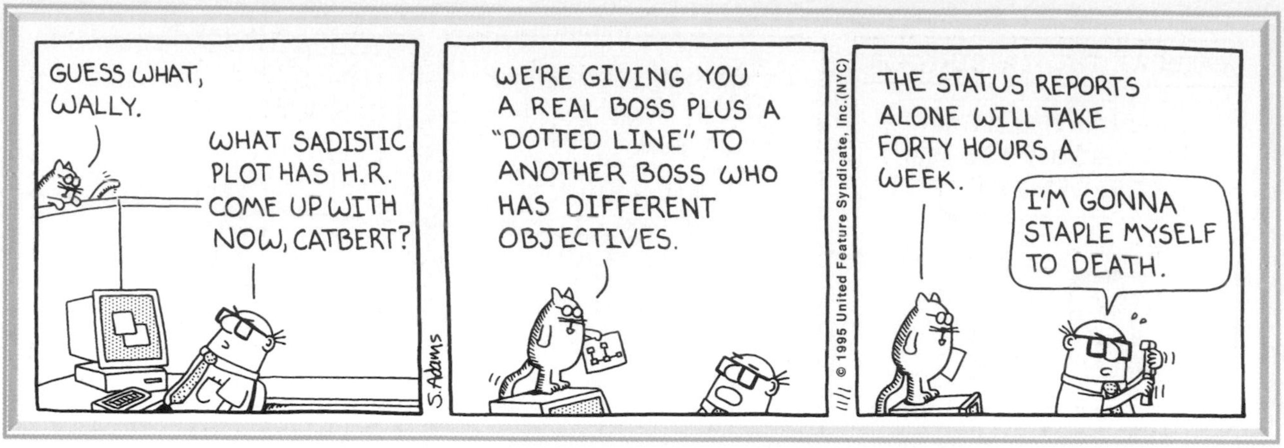
GUESS WHAT, WALLY.
WHAT SADISTIC PLOT HAS H.R. COME UP WITH NOW, CATBERT?
S. Adams
WE'RE GIVING YOU A REAL BOSS PLUS A "DOTTED LINE" TO ANOTHER BOSS WHO HAS DIFFERENT OBJECTIVES.
1/1 © 1995 United Feature Syndicate, Inc.(NYC)
THE STATUS REPORTS ALONE WILL TAKE FORTY HOURS A WEEK.
I'M GONNA STAPLE MYSELF TO DEATH.

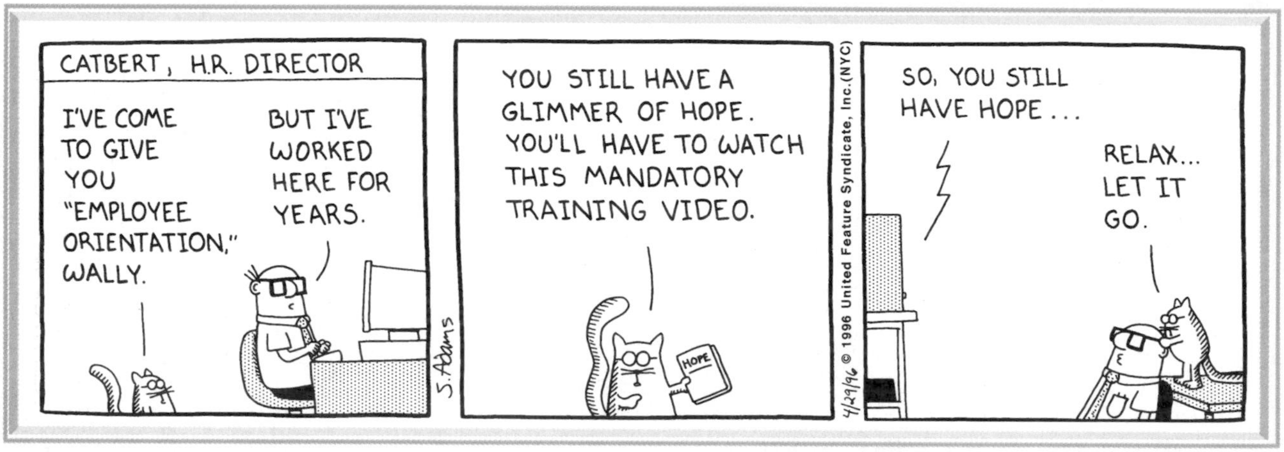
CATBERT, H.R. DIRECTOR
I'VE COME TO GIVE YOU "EMPLOYEE ORIENTATION," WALLY.
BUT I'VE WORKED HERE FOR YEARS.
S. Adams
YOU STILL HAVE A GLIMMER OF HOPE. YOU'LL HAVE TO WATCH THIS MANDATORY TRAINING VIDEO.
HOPE
4/29/96 © 1996 United Feature Syndicate, Inc.(NYC)
SO, YOU STILL HAVE HOPE . . .
RELAX... LET IT GO.

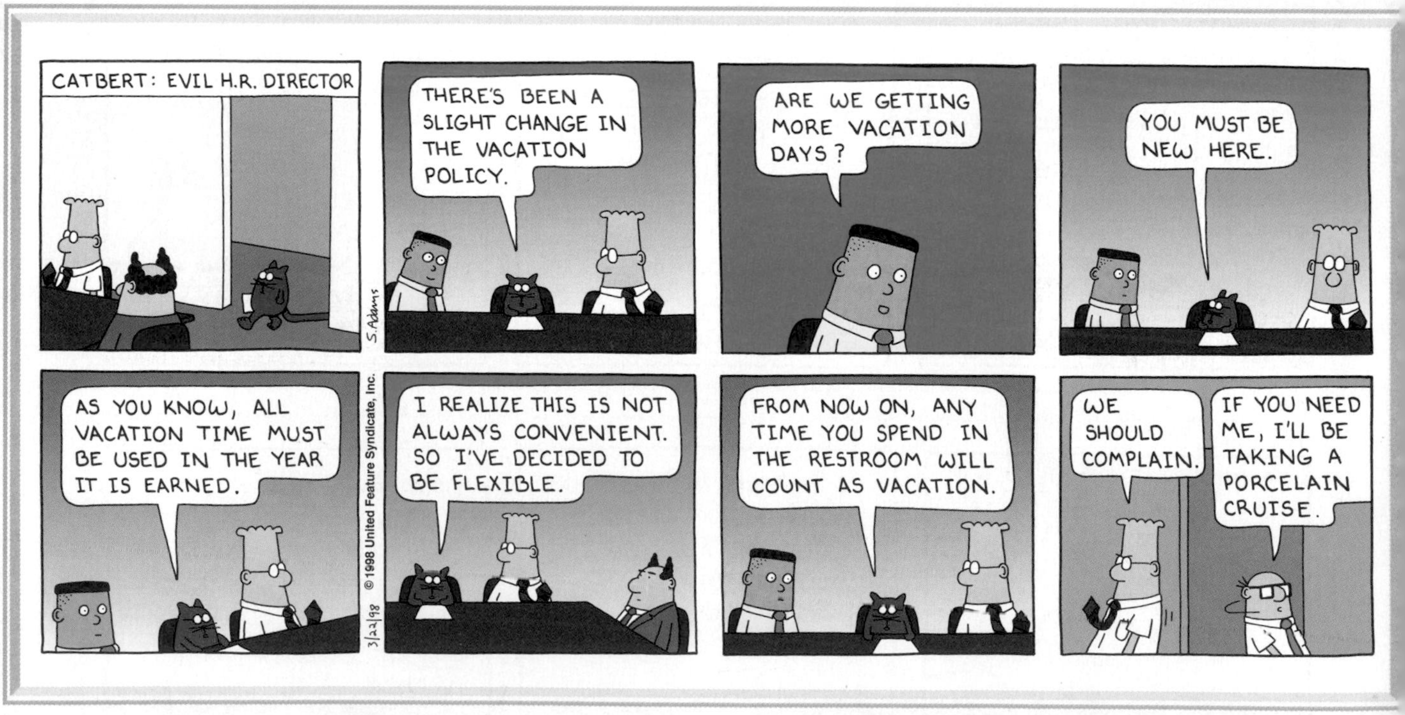
CATBERT: EVIL H.R. DIRECTOR
S. Adams
THERE'S BEEN A SLIGHT CHANGE IN THE VACATION POLICY.
ARE WE GETTING MORE VACATION DAYS?
YOU MUST BE NEW HERE.
AS YOU KNOW, ALL VACATION TIME MUST BE USED IN THE YEAR IT IS EARNED.
3/22/98 © 1998 United Feature Syndicate, Inc.
I REALIZE THIS IS NOT ALWAYS CONVENIENT. SO I'VE DECIDED TO BE FLEXIBLE.
FROM NOW ON, ANY TIME YOU SPEND IN THE RESTROOM WILL COUNT AS VACATION.
WE SHOULD COMPLAIN.
IF YOU NEED ME, I'LL BE TAKING A PORCELAIN CRUISE.

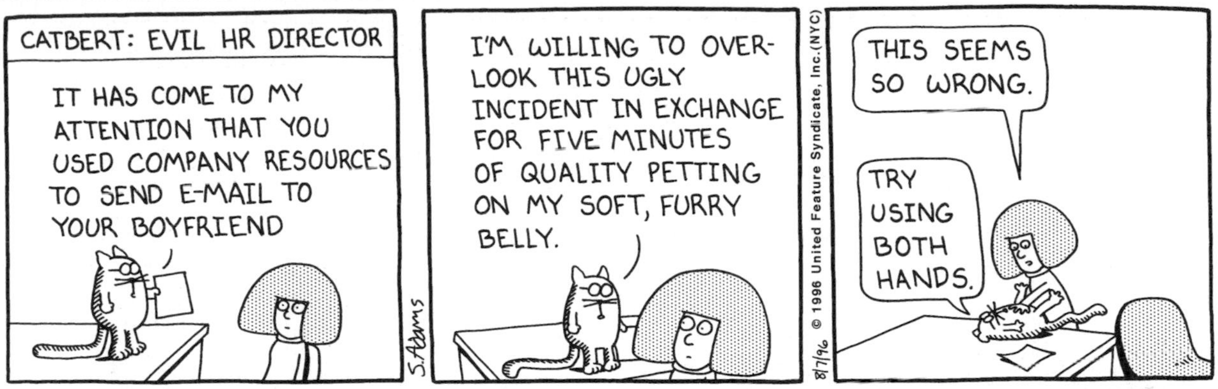
CATBERT: EVIL HR DIRECTOR
IT HAS COME TO MY ATTENTION THAT YOU USED COMPANY RESOURCES TO SEND E-MAIL TO YOUR BOYFRIEND
I'M WILLING TO OVERLOOK THIS UGLY INCIDENT IN EXCHANGE FOR FIVE MINUTES OF QUALITY PETTING ON MY SOFT, FURRY BELLY.
THIS SEEMS SO WRONG.
TRY USING BOTH HANDS.
S. Adams
8/7/96 © 1996 United Feature Syndicate, Inc.(NYC)

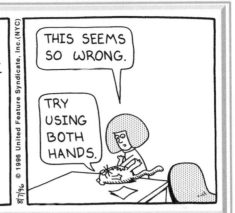

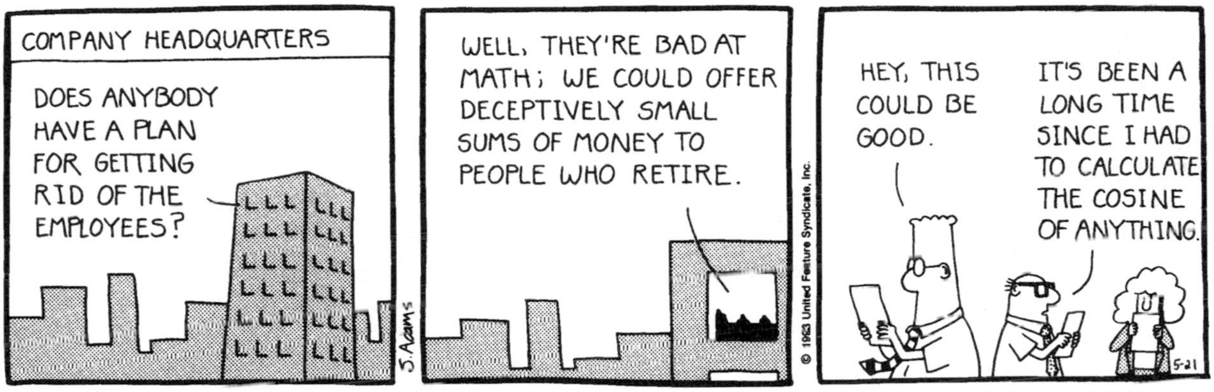
COMPANY HEADQUARTERS
DOES ANYBODY HAVE A PLAN FOR GETTING RID OF THE EMPLOYEES?
WELL, THEY'RE BAD AT MATH; WE COULD OFFER DECEPTIVELY SMALL SUMS OF MONEY TO PEOPLE WHO RETIRE.
HEY, THIS COULD BE GOOD.
IT'S BEEN A LONG TIME SINCE I HAD TO CALCULATE THE COSINE OF ANYTHING.
S. Adams
© 1993 United Feature Syndicate, Inc.
5-21

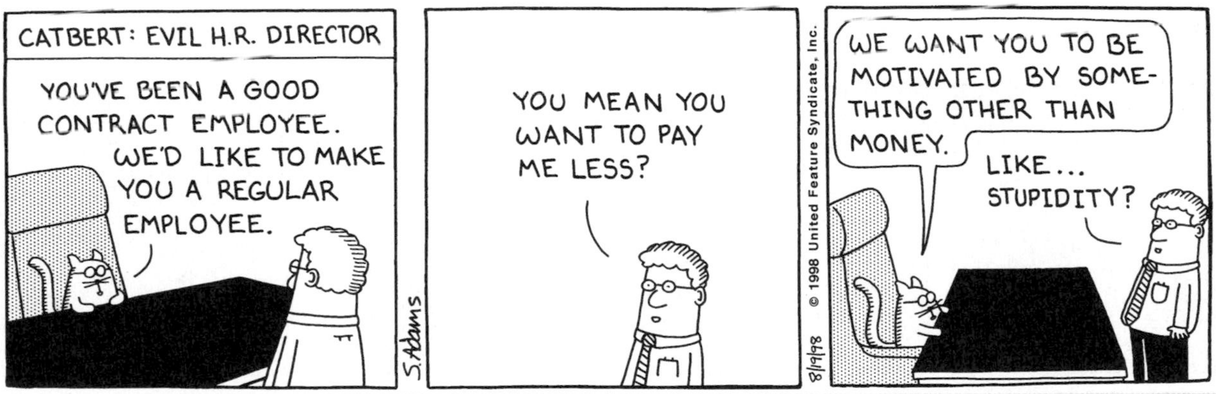
CATBERT: EVIL H.R. DIRECTOR
YOU'VE BEEN A GOOD CONTRACT EMPLOYEE.
WE'D LIKE TO MAKE YOU A REGULAR EMPLOYEE.
YOU MEAN YOU WANT TO PAY ME LESS?
WE WANT YOU TO BE MOTIVATED BY SOMETHING OTHER THAN MONEY.
LIKE... STUPIDITY?
S. Adams
8/9/98 © 1998 United Feature Syndicate, Inc.

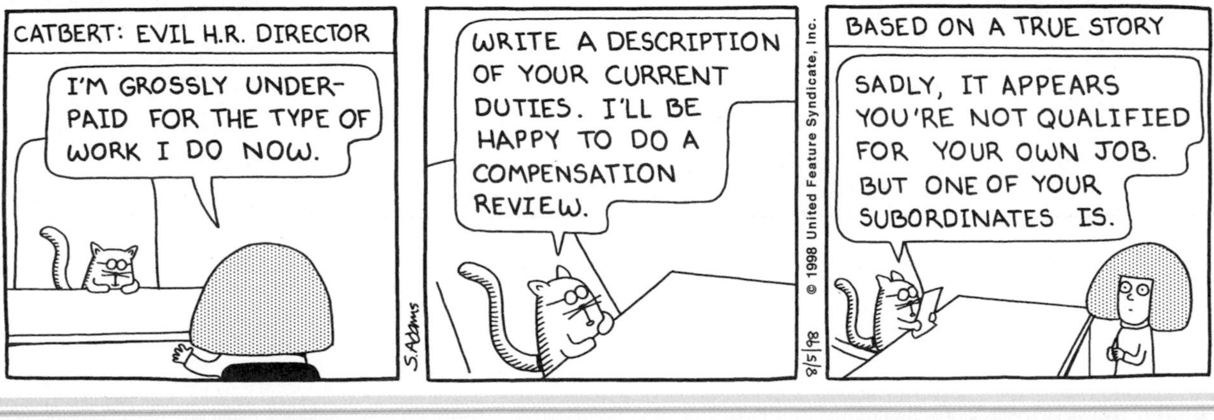
CATBERT: EVIL H.R. DIRECTOR
I'M GROSSLY UNDERPAID FOR THE TYPE OF WORK I DO NOW.
WRITE A DESCRIPTION OF YOUR CURRENT DUTIES. I'LL BE HAPPY TO DO A COMPENSATION REVIEW.
BASED ON A TRUE STORY
SADLY, IT APPEARS YOU'RE NOT QUALIFIED FOR YOUR OWN JOB. BUT ONE OF YOUR SUBORDINATES IS.
S. Adams
8/5/98 © 1998 United Feature Syndicate, Inc.

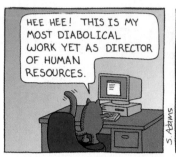

HEE HEE! THIS IS MY MOST DIABOLICAL WORK YET AS DIRECTOR OF HUMAN RESOURCES.
THANKS TO E-MAIL I CAN PLAY WITH HUNDREDS OF EMPLOYEES AT ONCE!
S. Adams
UH-OH... A MESSAGE FROM THE EVIL MISTER CATBERT.
"IN ORDER TO REDUCE OUR JANITORIAL EXPENSES..."
THAT'S A PHRASE YOU DON'T WANT TO SEE.
"EVERY ENGINEER WILL BE REQUIRED TO STRAP A BROOM TO HIS OR HER..."
1/21/96 © 1996 United Feature Syndicate, Inc.(NYC)
"...BUTTOCKS."
ON THE POSITIVE SIDE, MARKETING INVITES US TO A LOT MORE MEETINGS NOW.
FIVE MINUTES; WE'RE STILL EATING COOKIES.

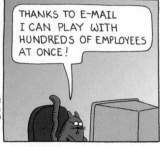

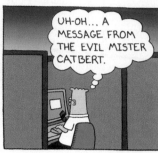

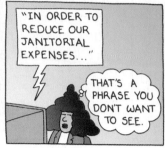

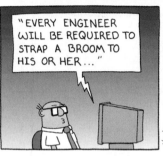

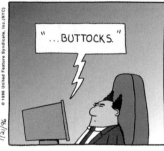

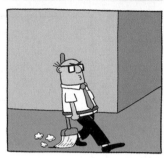

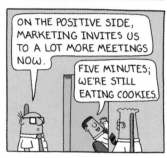

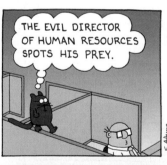

THE EVIL DIRECTOR OF HUMAN RESOURCES SPOTS HIS PREY.
S. Adams
WALLY, YOU HAVEN'T FILLED OUT A VACATION REQUEST FORM YET.
IF WE DON'T GET IT BY TOMORROW, YOU LOSE YOUR VACATION.
WHERE DO I GET A FORM?
WE'RE ALL OUT.
DID THEY EVER EXIST?
8/16/98 © 1998 United Feature Syndicate, Inc.
WALLY, DOES ANYTHING REALLY EXIST, OR IS IT ALL JUST SHADOWS ON A CUBICLE WALL?
I LEAVE YOU WITH THAT THOUGHT.
WHO SAYS PHILOSOPHY IS USELESS?
BONK
BONK

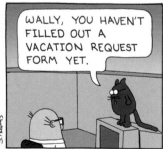

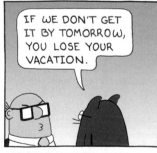

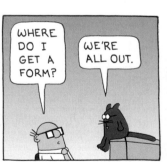

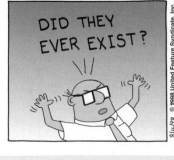

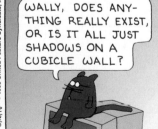

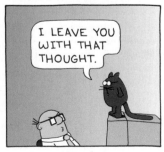

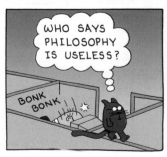

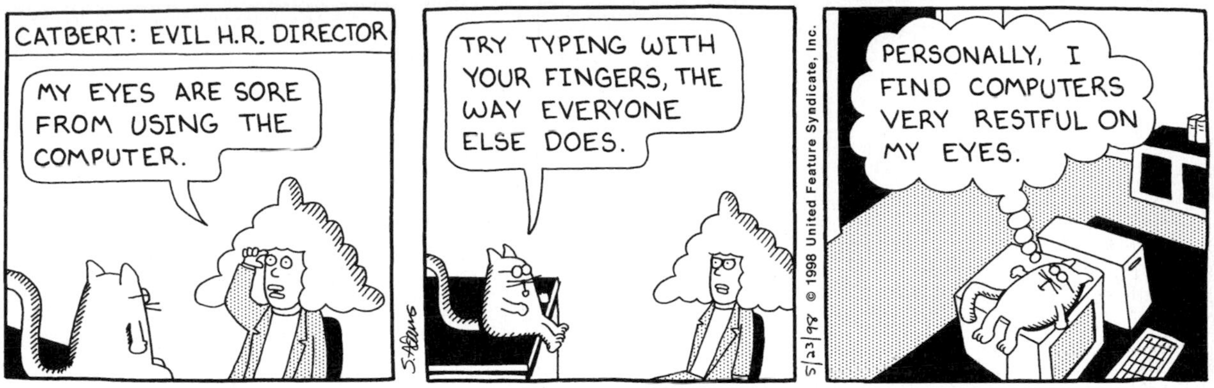
CATBERT: EVIL H.R. DIRECTOR
MY EYES ARE SORE FROM USING THE COMPUTER.
TRY TYPING WITH YOUR FINGERS, THE WAY EVERYONE ELSE DOES.
PERSONALLY, I FIND COMPUTERS VERY RESTFUL ON MY EYES.
S. Adams
5/23/98
© 1998 United Feature Syndicate, Inc.

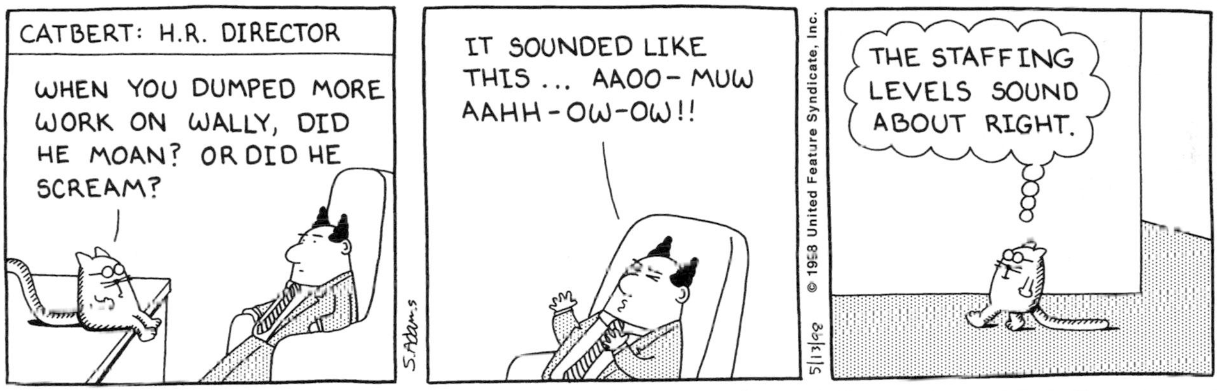
CATBERT: H.R. DIRECTOR
WHEN YOU DUMPED MORE WORK ON WALLY, DID HE MOAN? OR DID HE SCREAM?
IT SOUNDED LIKE THIS ... AAOO-MUW AAHH-OW-OW!!
THE STAFFING LEVELS SOUND ABOUT RIGHT.
S. Adams
5/13/98
© 1998 United Feature Syndicate, Inc.

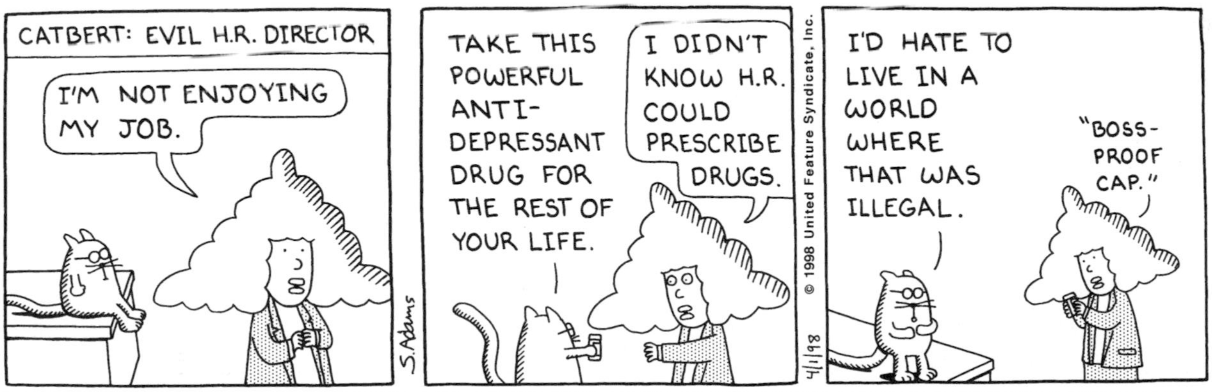
CATBERT: EVIL H.R. DIRECTOR
I'M NOT ENJOYING MY JOB.
TAKE THIS POWERFUL ANTI-DEPRESSANT DRUG FOR THE REST OF YOUR LIFE.
I DIDN'T KNOW H.R. COULD PRESCRIBE DRUGS.
I'D HATE TO LIVE IN A WORLD WHERE THAT WAS ILLEGAL.
"BOSS-PROOF CAP."
S. Adams
4/1/98
© 1998 United Feature Syndicate, Inc.

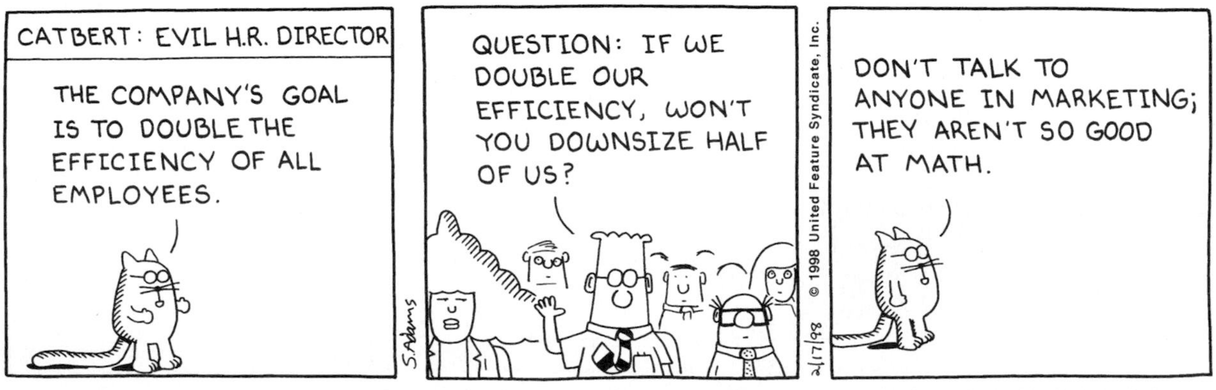
CATBERT: EVIL H.R. DIRECTOR
THE COMPANY'S GOAL IS TO DOUBLE THE EFFICIENCY OF ALL EMPLOYEES.
QUESTION: IF WE DOUBLE OUR EFFICIENCY, WON'T YOU DOWNSIZE HALF OF US?
DON'T TALK TO ANYONE IN MARKETING; THEY AREN'T SO GOOD AT MATH.
S. Adams
2/17/98
© 1998 United Feature Syndicate, Inc.

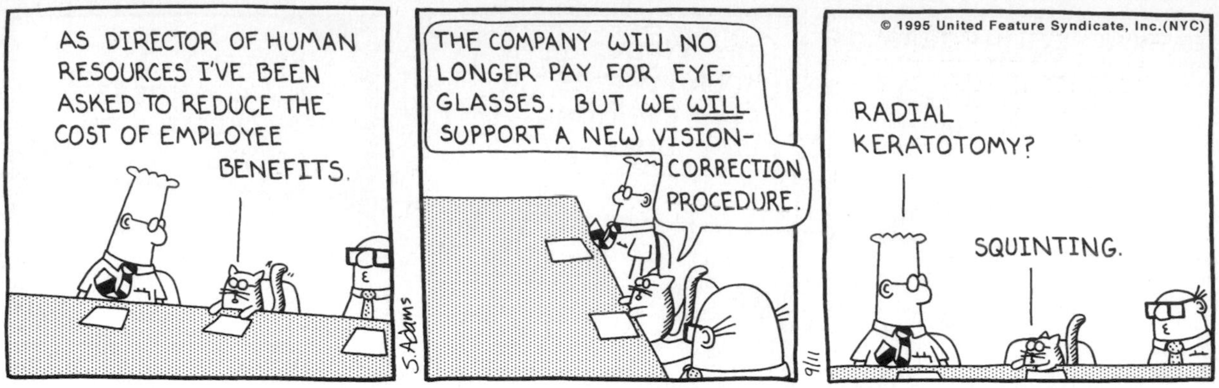
AS DIRECTOR OF HUMAN RESOURCES I'VE BEEN ASKED TO REDUCE THE COST OF EMPLOYEE BENEFITS.
THE COMPANY WILL NO LONGER PAY FOR EYE-GLASSES. BUT WE WILL SUPPORT A NEW VISION-CORRECTION PROCEDURE.
© 1995 United Feature Syndicate, Inc.(NYC)
RADIAL KERATOTOMY?
SQUINTING.
S. Adams
9/11

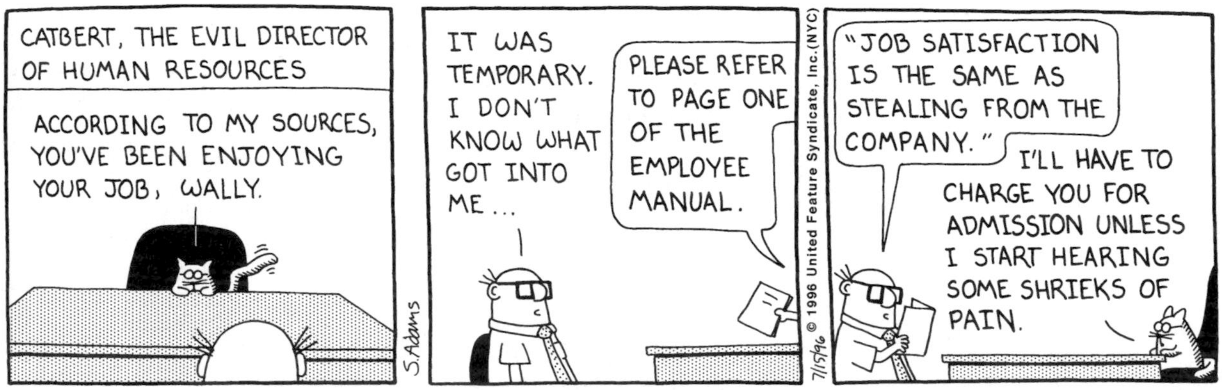
CATBERT, THE EVIL DIRECTOR OF HUMAN RESOURCES
ACCORDING TO MY SOURCES, YOU'VE BEEN ENJOYING YOUR JOB, WALLY.
IT WAS TEMPORARY. I DON'T KNOW WHAT GOT INTO ME...
PLEASE REFER TO PAGE ONE OF THE EMPLOYEE MANUAL.
"JOB SATISFACTION IS THE SAME AS STEALING FROM THE COMPANY."
I'LL HAVE TO CHARGE YOU FOR ADMISSION UNLESS I START HEARING SOME SHRIEKS OF PAIN.
S. Adams
7/15/96 © 1996 United Feature Syndicate, Inc.(NYC)

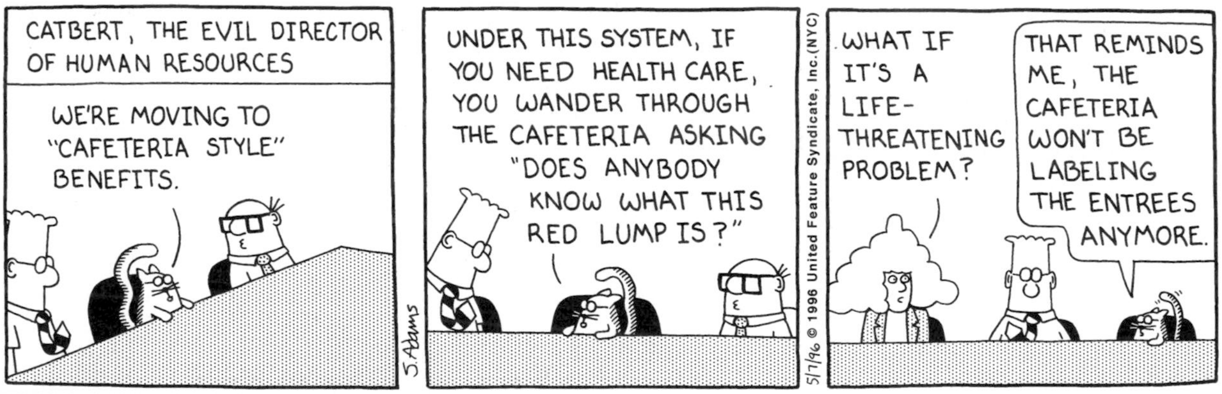
CATBERT, THE EVIL DIRECTOR OF HUMAN RESOURCES
WE'RE MOVING TO "CAFETERIA STYLE" BENEFITS.
UNDER THIS SYSTEM, IF YOU NEED HEALTH CARE, YOU WANDER THROUGH THE CAFETERIA ASKING "DOES ANYBODY KNOW WHAT THIS RED LUMP IS?"
WHAT IF IT'S A LIFE-THREATENING PROBLEM?
THAT REMINDS ME, THE CAFETERIA WON'T BE LABELING THE ENTREES ANYMORE.
S. Adams
5/1/96 © 1996 United Feature Syndicate, Inc.(NYC)

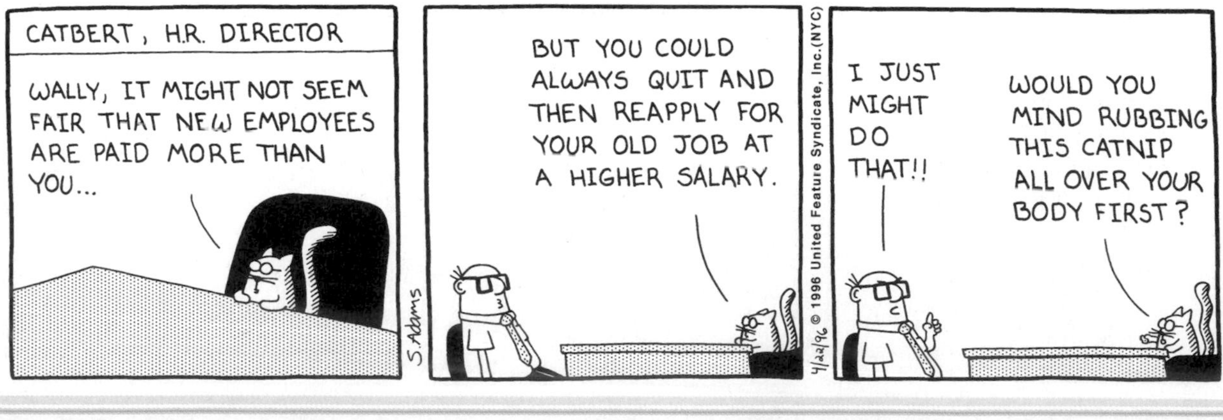
CATBERT, H.R. DIRECTOR
WALLY, IT MIGHT NOT SEEM FAIR THAT NEW EMPLOYEES ARE PAID MORE THAN YOU...
BUT YOU COULD ALWAYS QUIT AND THEN REAPPLY FOR YOUR OLD JOB AT A HIGHER SALARY.
I JUST MIGHT DO THAT!!
WOULD YOU MIND RUBBING THIS CATNIP ALL OVER YOUR BODY FIRST?
S. Adams
4/22/96 © 1996 United Feature Syndicate, Inc.(NYC)

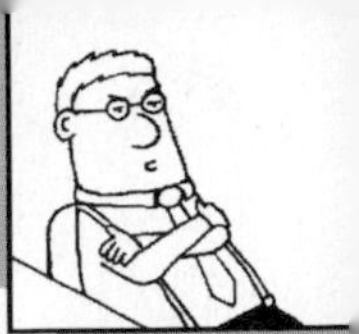

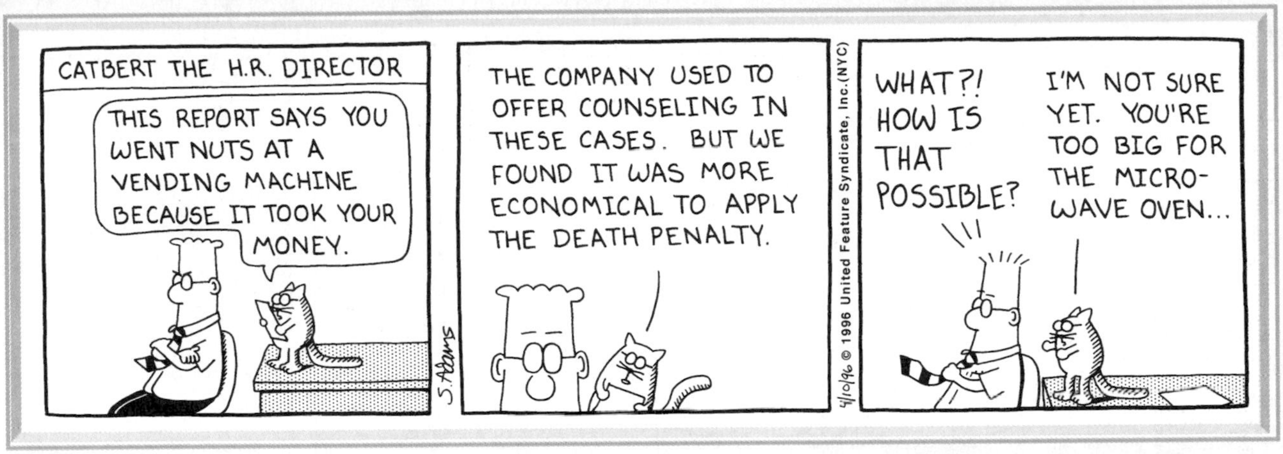
CATBERT THE H.R. DIRECTOR
THIS REPORT SAYS YOU WENT NUTS AT A VENDING MACHINE BECAUSE IT TOOK YOUR MONEY.
THE COMPANY USED TO OFFER COUNSELING IN THESE CASES. BUT WE FOUND IT WAS MORE ECONOMICAL TO APPLY THE DEATH PENALTY.
WHAT?! HOW IS THAT POSSIBLE?
I'M NOT SURE YET. YOU'RE TOO BIG FOR THE MICRO-WAVE OVEN...
S. Adams
4/10/96 © 1996 United Feature Syndicate, Inc.(NYC)

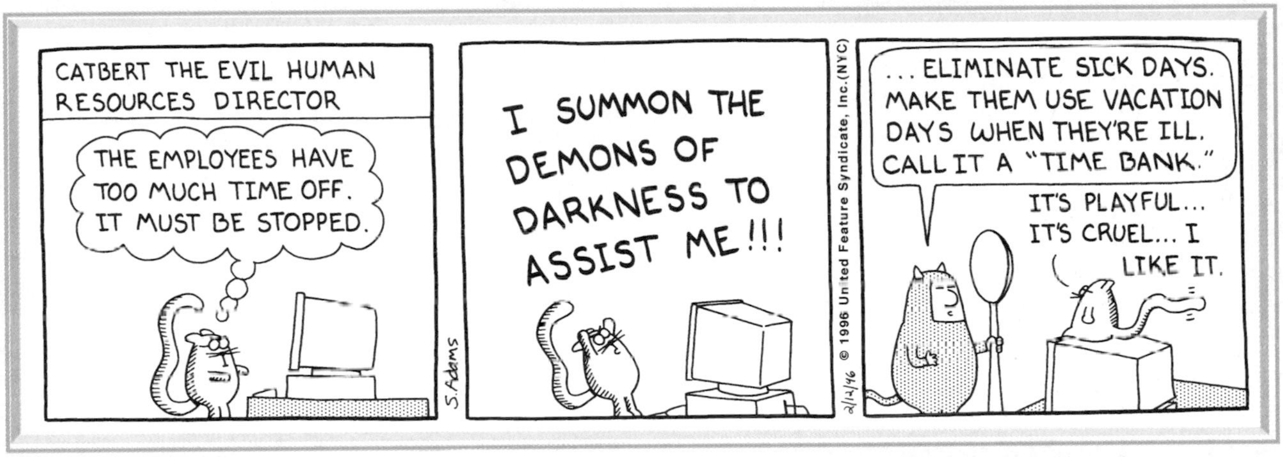
CATBERT THE EVIL HUMAN RESOURCES DIRECTOR
THE EMPLOYEES HAVE TOO MUCH TIME OFF. IT MUST BE STOPPED.
I SUMMON THE DEMONS OF DARKNESS TO ASSIST ME!!!
...ELIMINATE SICK DAYS. MAKE THEM USE VACATION DAYS WHEN THEY'RE ILL. CALL IT A "TIME BANK."
IT'S PLAYFUL... IT'S CRUEL... I LIKE IT.
S. Adams
2/14/96 © 1996 United Feature Syndicate, Inc.(NYC)

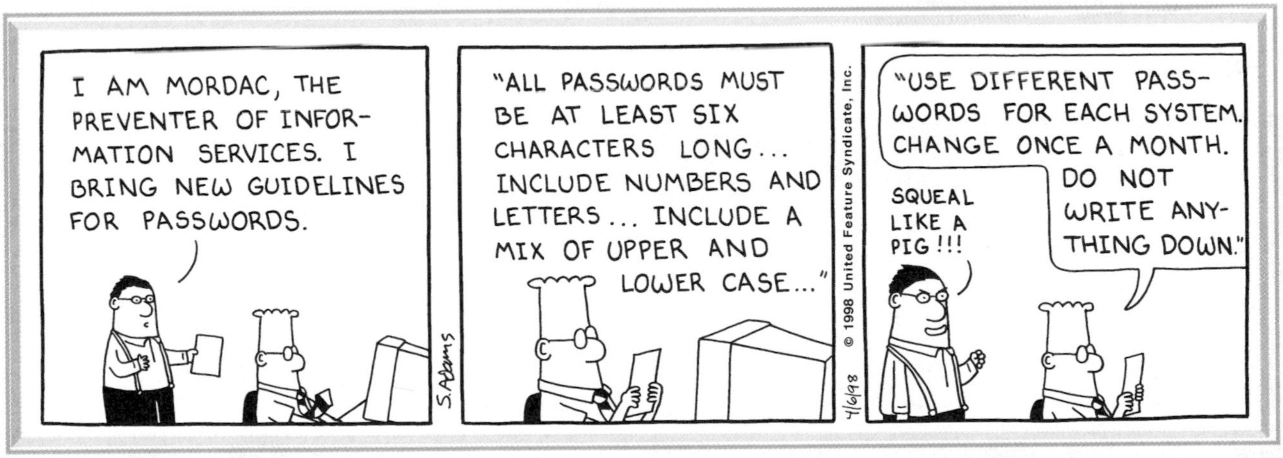
I AM MORDAC, THE PREVENTER OF INFOR-MATION SERVICES. I BRING NEW GUIDELINES FOR PASSWORDS.
"ALL PASSWORDS MUST BE AT LEAST SIX CHARACTERS LONG... INCLUDE NUMBERS AND LETTERS... INCLUDE A MIX OF UPPER AND LOWER CASE..."
"USE DIFFERENT PASS-WORDS FOR EACH SYSTEM. CHANGE ONCE A MONTH. DO NOT WRITE ANY-THING DOWN."
SQUEAL LIKE A PIG!!!
S. Adams
4/6/98 © 1998 United Feature Syndicate, Inc.

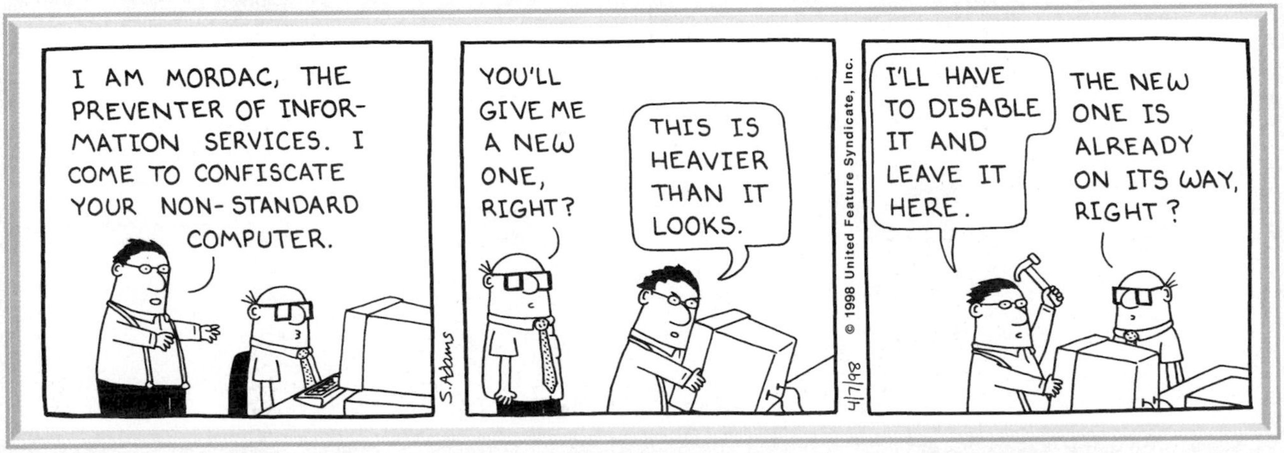
I AM MORDAC, THE PREVENTER OF INFOR-MATION SERVICES. I COME TO CONFISCATE YOUR NON-STANDARD COMPUTER.
YOU'LL GIVE ME A NEW ONE, RIGHT?
THIS IS HEAVIER THAN IT LOOKS.
I'LL HAVE TO DISABLE IT AND LEAVE IT HERE.
THE NEW ONE IS ALREADY ON ITS WAY, RIGHT?
S. Adams
4/7/98 © 1998 United Feature Syndicate, Inc.

INFORMATION SERVICES

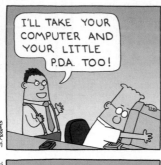

I AM MORDAC, THE PREVENTER OF INFORMATION SERVICES!
I'LL TAKE YOUR COMPUTER AND YOUR LITTLE P.D.A. TOO!
DO YOU RECOGNIZE THIS?
AAAGH! THAT'S MY NETWORK CABLE!
WHAT DO YOU WANT FROM ME?!
MORDAC, IT IS I, CATBERT, THE EVIL DIRECTOR OF HUMAN RESOURCES!
YOU MADE MY PERSONAL PRINTER A SHARED DEVICE!
GRRRR!!
AAAGH!!
TWO WRONGS MADE A RIGHT.
WELCOME TO MY REALITY.
S. Adams
2/7/99
© 1999 United Feature Syndicate, Inc.

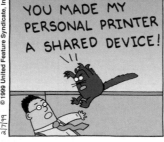

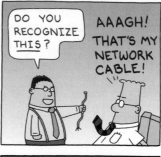

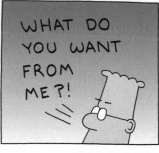

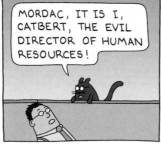

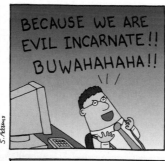

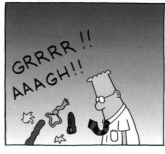

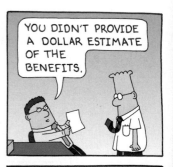

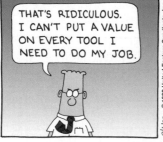

WHY DID THE I.S. DEPARTMENT DENY MY REQUEST FOR A PC UPGRADE?
BECAUSE WE ARE EVIL INCARNATE!! BUWAHAHAHA!!
I WAS LOOKING FOR SOMETHING MORE SPECIFIC.
YOU DIDN'T PROVIDE A DOLLAR ESTIMATE OF THE BENEFITS.
THAT'S RIDICULOUS. I CAN'T PUT A VALUE ON EVERY TOOL I NEED TO DO MY JOB.
IF YOU CAN'T QUANTIFY IT, THEN IT MUST NOT BE NECESSARY.
THEN WHY DOES THE COMPANY GIVE ME A CHAIR? I CAN'T QUANTIFY THAT EITHER?
HERE'S ONE MORE REASON WHY IT STINKS TO BE ME.
S. Adams
9/6/98
© 1998 United Feature Syndicate, Inc.

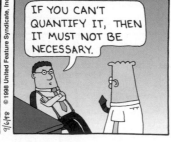

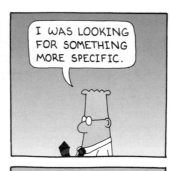

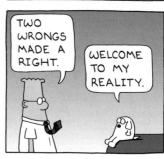

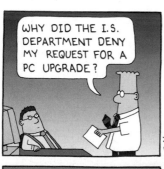

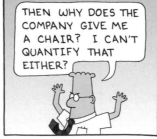

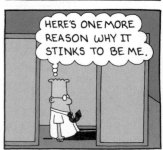

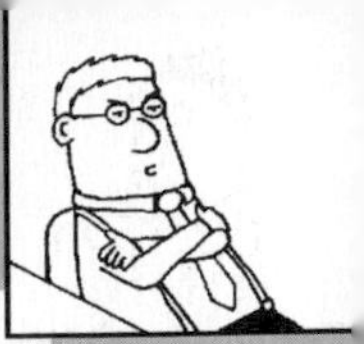

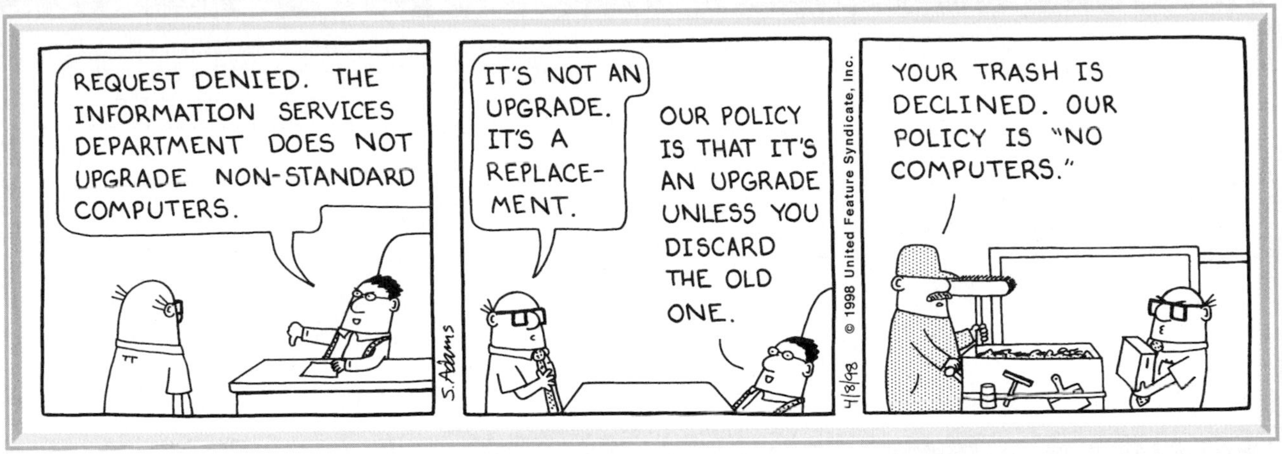
REQUEST DENIED. THE INFORMATION SERVICES DEPARTMENT DOES NOT UPGRADE NON-STANDARD COMPUTERS.
IT'S NOT AN UPGRADE. IT'S A REPLACEMENT.
OUR POLICY IS THAT IT'S AN UPGRADE UNLESS YOU DISCARD THE OLD ONE.
YOUR TRASH IS DECLINED. OUR POLICY IS "NO COMPUTERS."
S. Adams
© 1998 United Feature Syndicate, Inc.
4/8/98

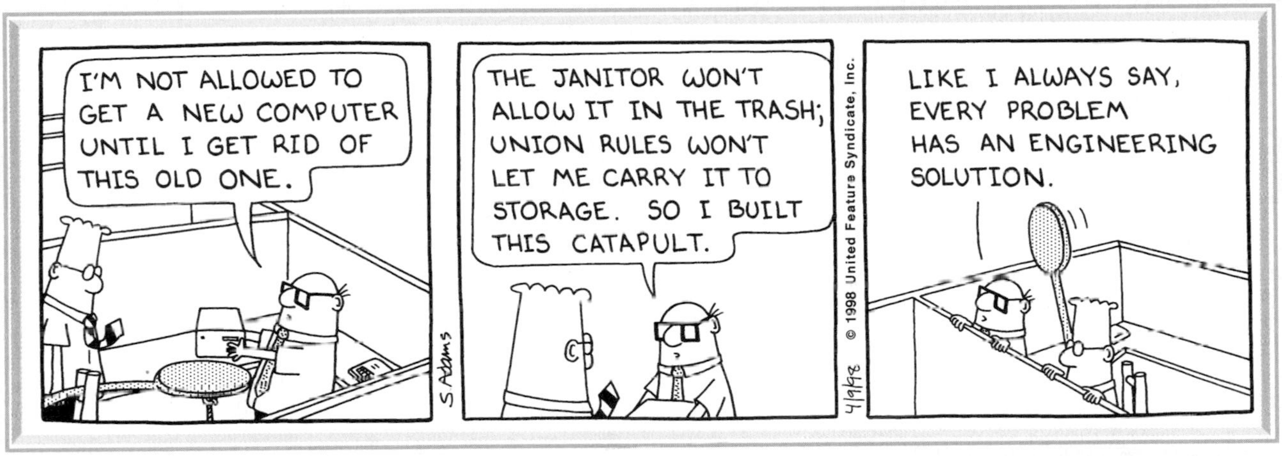
I'M NOT ALLOWED TO GET A NEW COMPUTER UNTIL I GET RID OF THIS OLD ONE.
THE JANITOR WON'T ALLOW IT IN THE TRASH; UNION RULES WON'T LET ME CARRY IT TO STORAGE. SO I BUILT THIS CATAPULT.
LIKE I ALWAYS SAY, EVERY PROBLEM HAS AN ENGINEERING SOLUTION.
S. Adams
© 1998 United Feature Syndicate, Inc.
4/9/98

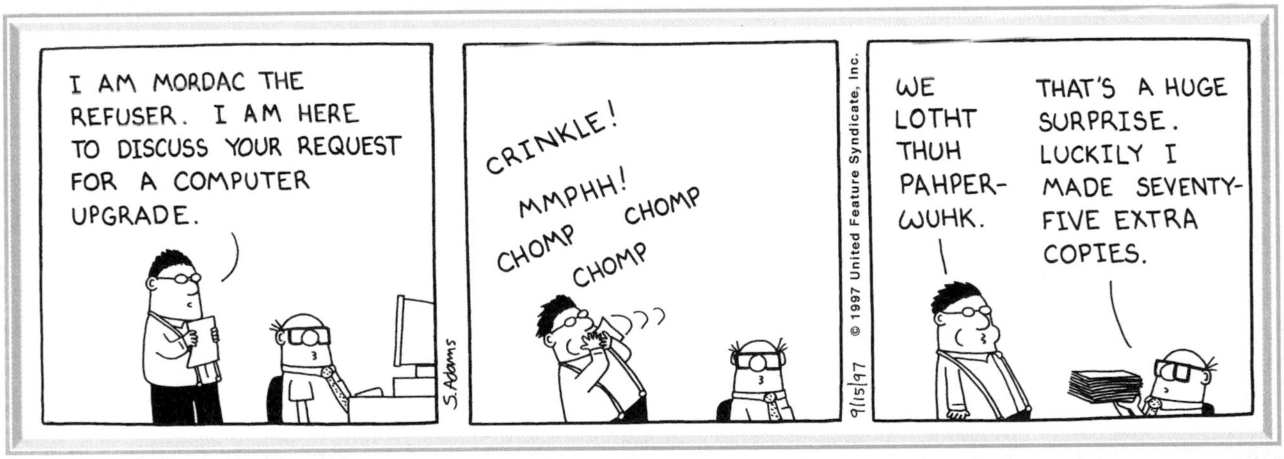
I AM MORDAC THE REFUSER. I AM HERE TO DISCUSS YOUR REQUEST FOR A COMPUTER UPGRADE.
CRINKLE!
MMPHH!
CHOMP CHOMP
CHOMP
WE LOTHT THUH PAHPER-WUHK.
THAT'S A HUGE SURPRISE. LUCKILY I MADE SEVENTY-FIVE EXTRA COPIES.
S. Adams
© 1997 United Feature Syndicate, Inc.
9/15/97

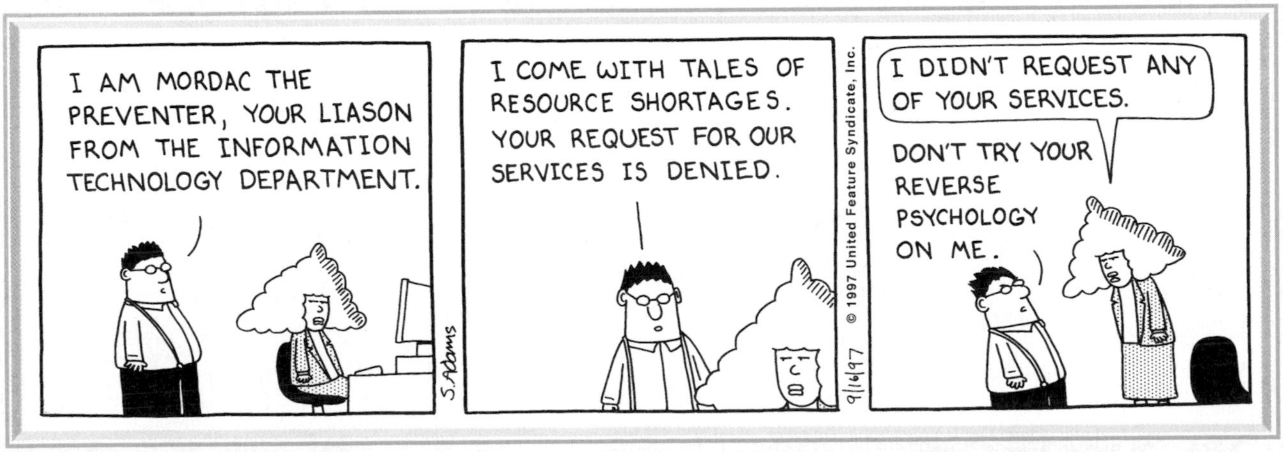
I AM MORDAC THE PREVENTER, YOUR LIASON FROM THE INFORMATION TECHNOLOGY DEPARTMENT.
I COME WITH TALES OF RESOURCE SHORTAGES. YOUR REQUEST FOR OUR SERVICES IS DENIED.
I DIDN'T REQUEST ANY OF YOUR SERVICES.
DON'T TRY YOUR REVERSE PSYCHOLOGY ON ME.
S. Adams
© 1997 United Feature Syndicate, Inc.
9/16/97

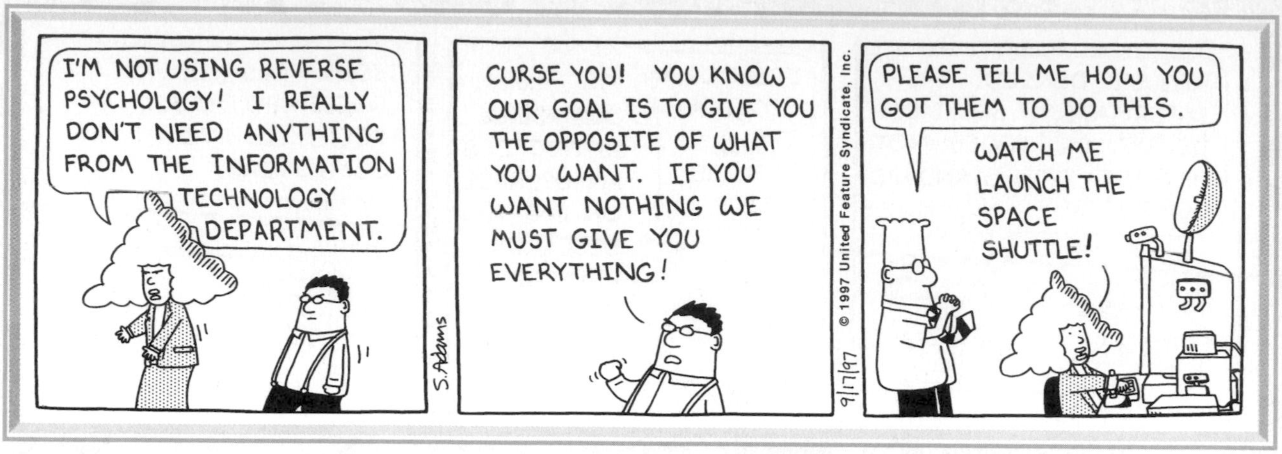
I'M NOT USING REVERSE PSYCHOLOGY! I REALLY DON'T NEED ANYTHING FROM THE INFORMATION TECHNOLOGY DEPARTMENT.
CURSE YOU! YOU KNOW OUR GOAL IS TO GIVE YOU THE OPPOSITE OF WHAT YOU WANT. IF YOU WANT NOTHING WE MUST GIVE YOU EVERYTHING!
PLEASE TELL ME HOW YOU GOT THEM TO DO THIS.
WATCH ME LAUNCH THE SPACE SHUTTLE!
S. Adams
9/17/97
© 1997 United Feature Syndicate, Inc.

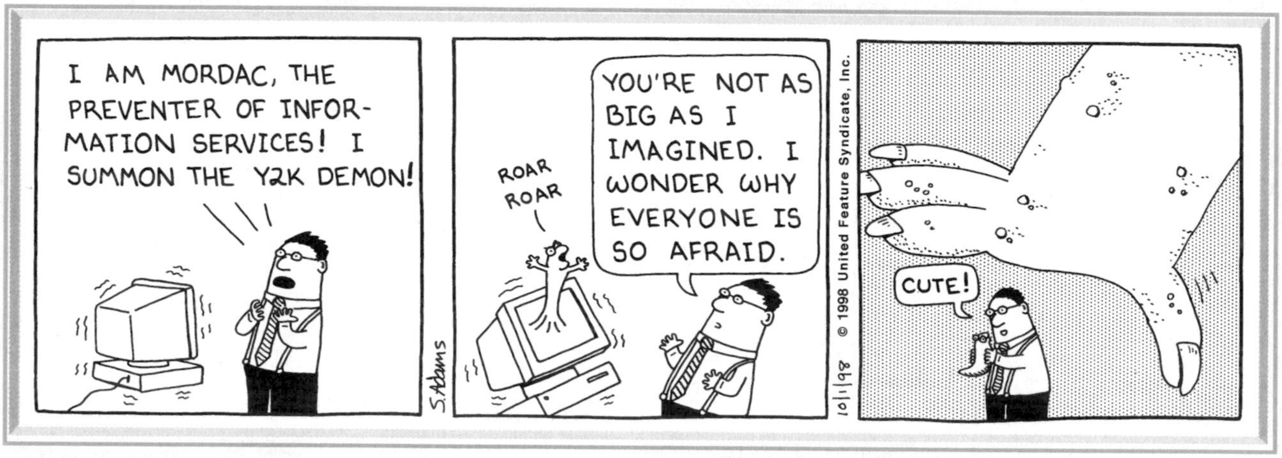
I AM MORDAC, THE PREVENTER OF INFORMATION SERVICES! I SUMMON THE Y2K DEMON!
ROAR ROAR
YOU'RE NOT AS BIG AS I IMAGINED. I WONDER WHY EVERYONE IS SO AFRAID.
CUTE!
S. Adams
10/1/98
© 1998 United Feature Syndicate, Inc.

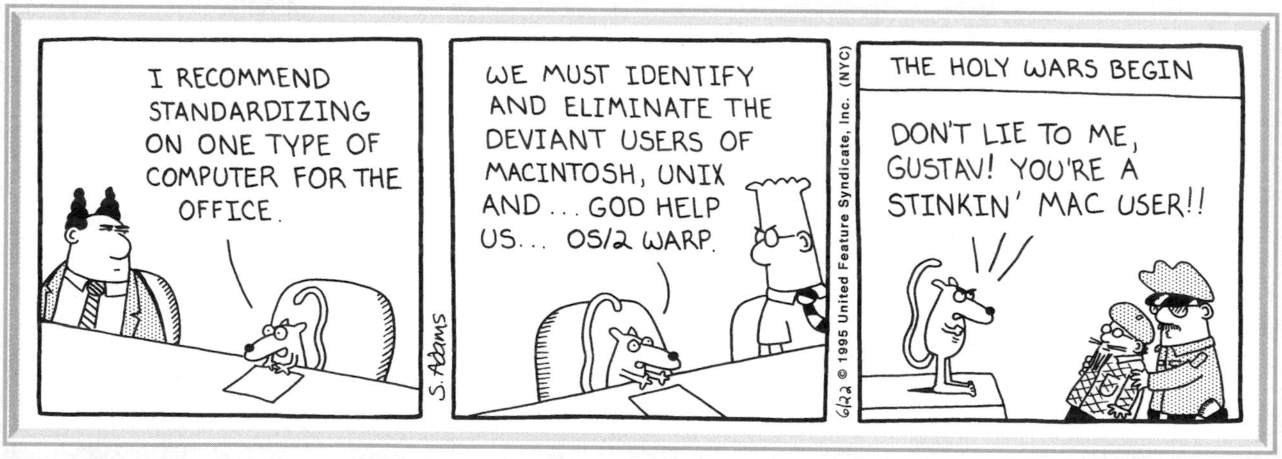
I RECOMMEND STANDARDIZING ON ONE TYPE OF COMPUTER FOR THE OFFICE.
WE MUST IDENTIFY AND ELIMINATE THE DEVIANT USERS OF MACINTOSH, UNIX AND... GOD HELP US... OS/2 WARP.
THE HOLY WARS BEGIN
DON'T LIE TO ME, GUSTAV! YOU'RE A STINKIN' MAC USER!!
S. Adams
6/22
© 1995 United Feature Syndicate, Inc. (NYC)

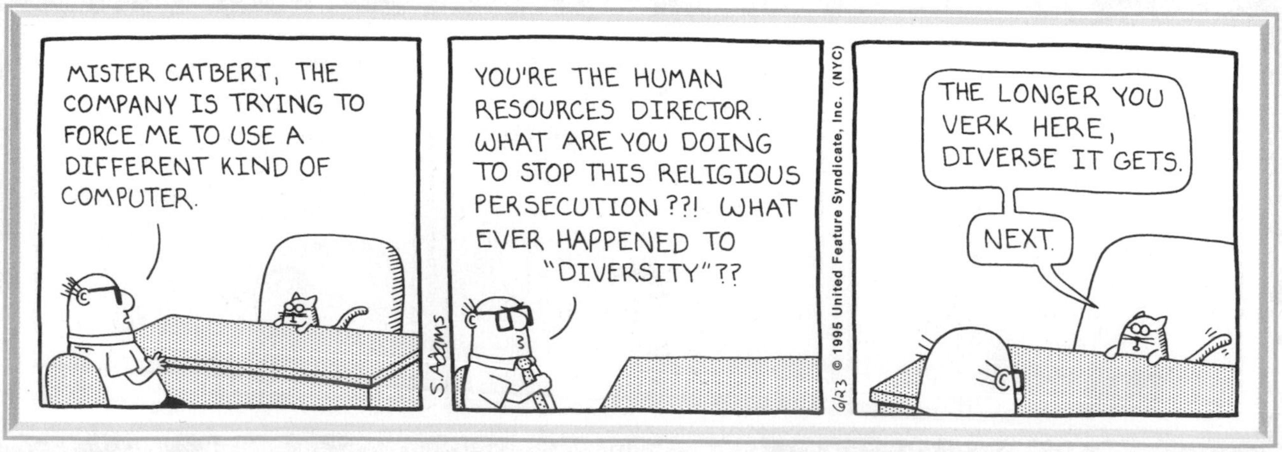
MISTER CATBERT, THE COMPANY IS TRYING TO FORCE ME TO USE A DIFFERENT KIND OF COMPUTER.
YOU'RE THE HUMAN RESOURCES DIRECTOR. WHAT ARE YOU DOING TO STOP THIS RELIGIOUS PERSECUTION??! WHAT EVER HAPPENED TO "DIVERSITY"??
THE LONGER YOU VERK HERE, DIVERSE IT GETS.
NEXT.
S. Adams
6/23
© 1995 United Feature Syndicate, Inc. (NYC)

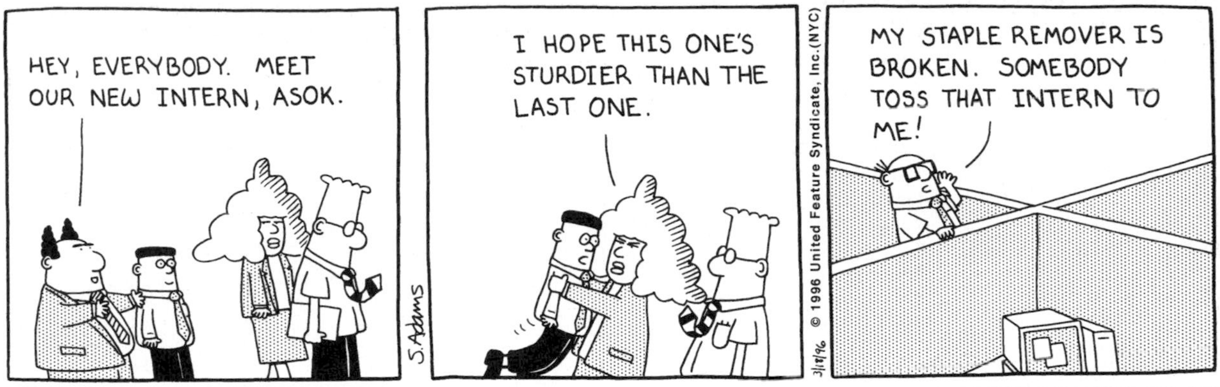
HEY, EVERYBODY. MEET OUR NEW INTERN, ASOK.
I HOPE THIS ONE'S STURDIER THAN THE LAST ONE.
MY STAPLE REMOVER IS BROKEN. SOMEBODY TOSS THAT INTERN TO ME!
S. Adams
© 1996 United Feature Syndicate, Inc.(NYC)

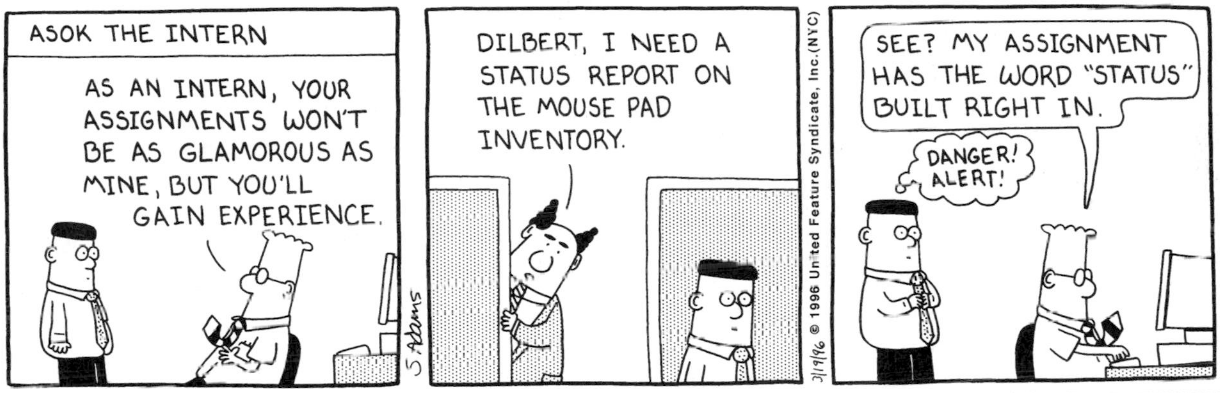
ASOK THE INTERN
AS AN INTERN, YOUR ASSIGNMENTS WON'T BE AS GLAMOROUS AS MINE, BUT YOU'LL GAIN EXPERIENCE.
DILBERT, I NEED A STATUS REPORT ON THE MOUSE PAD INVENTORY.
SEE? MY ASSIGNMENT HAS THE WORD "STATUS" BUILT RIGHT IN.
DANGER! ALERT!
S. Adams
© 1996 United Feature Syndicate, Inc.(NYC)

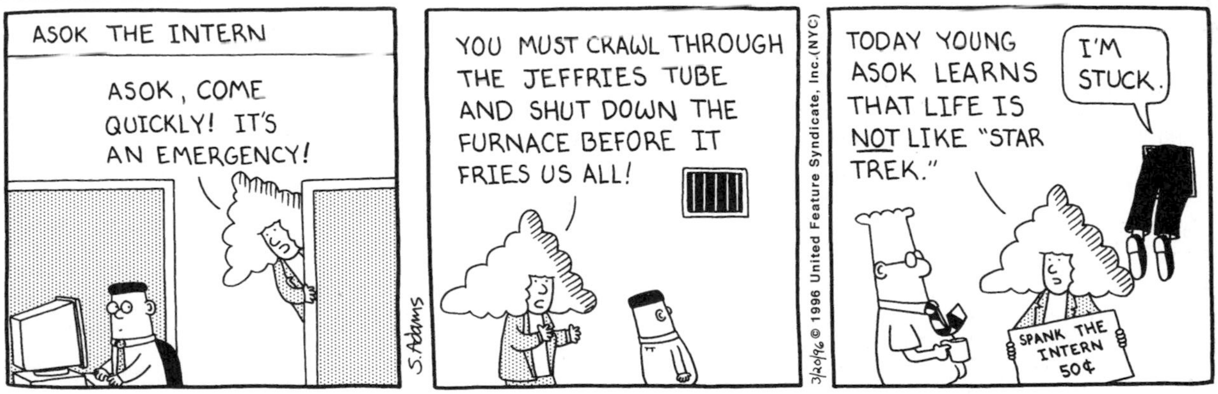
ASOK THE INTERN
ASOK, COME QUICKLY! IT'S AN EMERGENCY!
YOU MUST CRAWL THROUGH THE JEFFRIES TUBE AND SHUT DOWN THE FURNACE BEFORE IT FRIES US ALL!
TODAY YOUNG ASOK LEARNS THAT LIFE IS NOT LIKE "STAR TREK."
I'M STUCK.
SPANK THE INTERN 50¢
S. Adams
© 1996 United Feature Syndicate, Inc.(NYC)

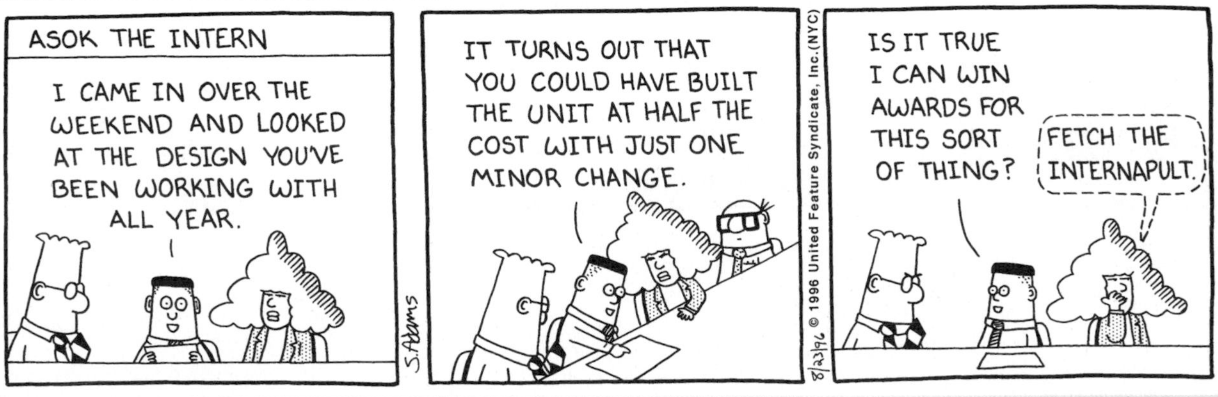
ASOK THE INTERN
I CAME IN OVER THE WEEKEND AND LOOKED AT THE DESIGN YOU'VE BEEN WORKING WITH ALL YEAR.
IT TURNS OUT THAT YOU COULD HAVE BUILT THE UNIT AT HALF THE COST WITH JUST ONE MINOR CHANGE.
IS IT TRUE I CAN WIN AWARDS FOR THIS SORT OF THING?
FETCH THE INTERNAPULT.
S. Adams
© 1996 United Feature Syndicate, Inc.(NYC)

DILBERT *Gives You the Business*

I WON'T ALWAYS BE AROUND TO BE YOUR MENTOR, ASOK.
SO I'VE CAPTURED ALL OF MY CAREER WISDOM IN THIS SOFTWARE, WHICH I CALL THE "AUTOMENTOR."
AUTOMENTOR, HOW CAN I ACHIEVE JOB SATISFACTION?
TRY GIVING YOURSELF A MASSAGE IN YOUR CUBICLE.
AUTOMENTOR, HOW CAN I MAKE SURE MY ACCOMPLISHMENTS GET NOTICED?
THAT'S NOT A PROBLEM AT THIS COMPANY; NOBODY ACCOMPLISHES ANYTHING.
SHOULD I LOOK FOR A NEW JOB?
TOO LATE. THEY DON'T CALL THIS PLACE THE "RÉSUMÉ STAIN" FOR NOTHING.
HOW DO YOU HANDLE ALL THE HOPELESSNESS?
I GIVE IT TO THE NEW GUY.
6/23/96 © 1996 United Feature Syndicate, Inc.

I'D LIKE YOU ALL TO MEET OUR NEW CO-OP EMPLOYEE.
WE DON'T PAY HIM. HE WORKS FOR FREE TO GAIN VALUABLE JOB EXPERIENCE.
I'M PUTTING YOU IN CHARGE OF THE PTG PROJECT!
WOW! WHAT IS IT?!!
PTG STANDS FOR "PAPER TOWEL GUY."
IF SOMEBODY SPILLS COFFEE IT'S YOUR JOB TO THROW YOUR BODY ON IT BEFORE IT REACHES ONE OF US.
OOPS
FIRE IN THE HOLE!!!
HOW'D I DO?
NOT SO GOOD, KID. THAT WAS TEA.
© 1995 United Feature Syndicate, Inc.

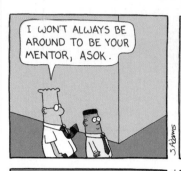

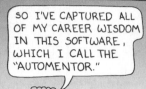

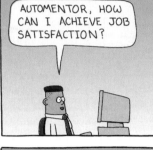

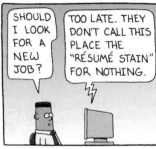

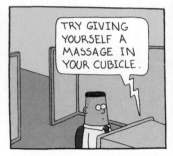

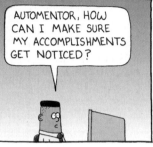

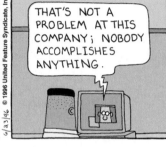

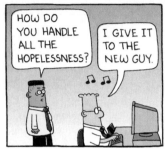

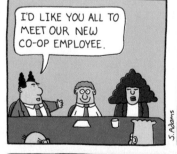

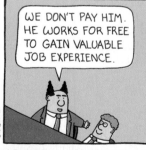

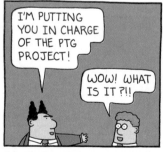

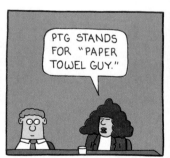

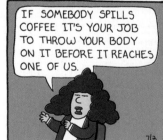

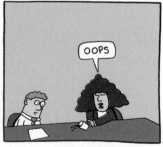

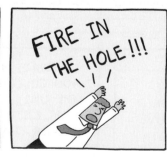

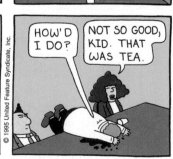

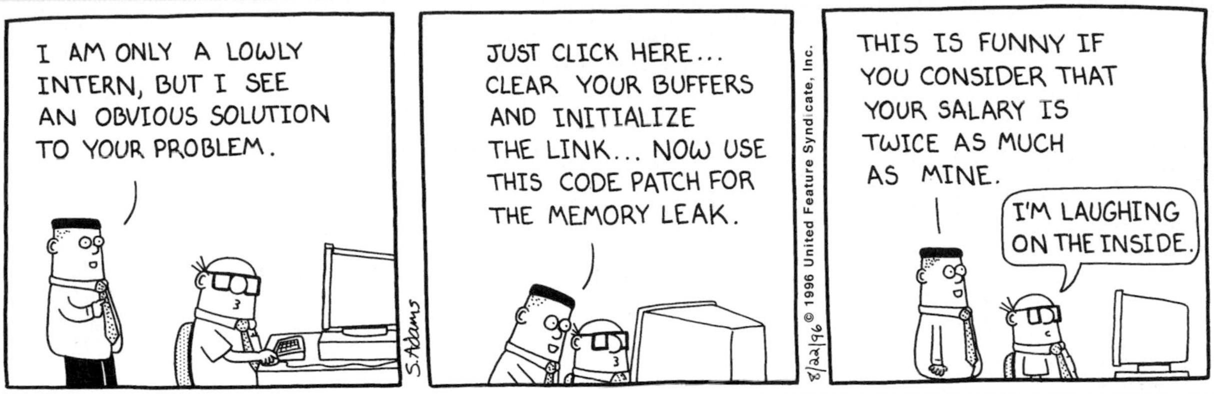
I AM ONLY A LOWLY INTERN, BUT I SEE AN OBVIOUS SOLUTION TO YOUR PROBLEM.
JUST CLICK HERE... CLEAR YOUR BUFFERS AND INITIALIZE THE LINK... NOW USE THIS CODE PATCH FOR THE MEMORY LEAK.
THIS IS FUNNY IF YOU CONSIDER THAT YOUR SALARY IS TWICE AS MUCH AS MINE.
I'M LAUGHING ON THE INSIDE.
S. Adams
8/22/96 © 1996 United Feature Syndicate, Inc.

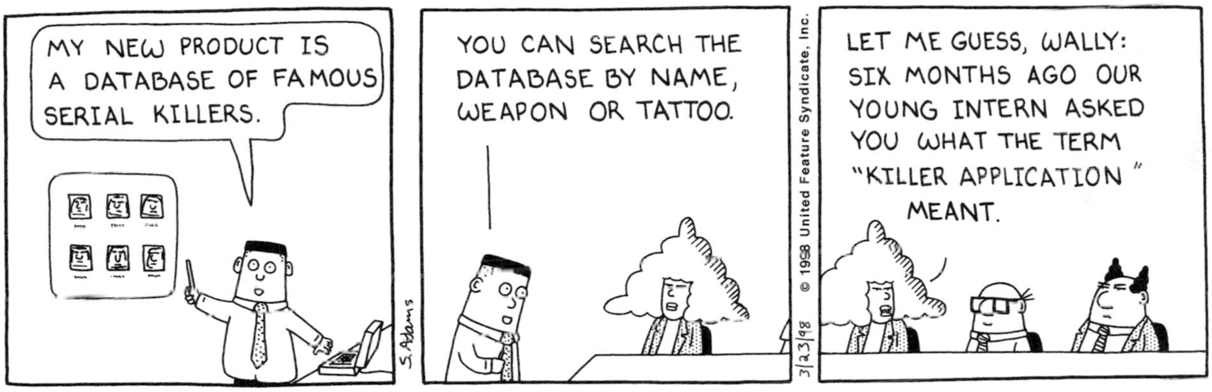
MY NEW PRODUCT IS A DATABASE OF FAMOUS SERIAL KILLERS.
YOU CAN SEARCH THE DATABASE BY NAME, WEAPON OR TATTOO.
LET ME GUESS, WALLY: SIX MONTHS AGO OUR YOUNG INTERN ASKED YOU WHAT THE TERM "KILLER APPLICATION" MEANT.
S. Adams
3/23/98 © 1998 United Feature Syndicate, Inc.

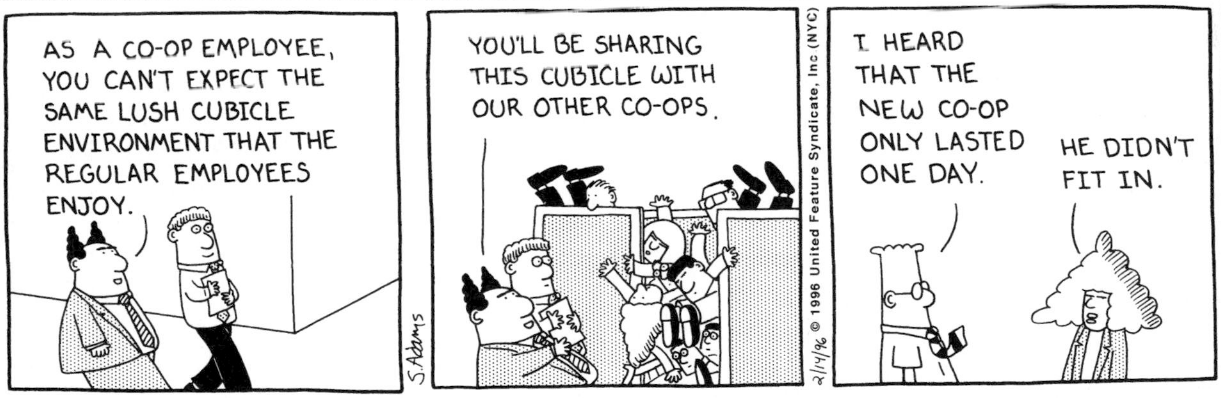
AS A CO-OP EMPLOYEE, YOU CAN'T EXPECT THE SAME LUSH CUBICLE ENVIRONMENT THAT THE REGULAR EMPLOYEES ENJOY.
YOU'LL BE SHARING THIS CUBICLE WITH OUR OTHER CO-OPS.
I HEARD THAT THE NEW CO-OP ONLY LASTED ONE DAY.
HE DIDN'T FIT IN.
S. Adams
2/14/96 © 1996 United Feature Syndicate, Inc (NYC)

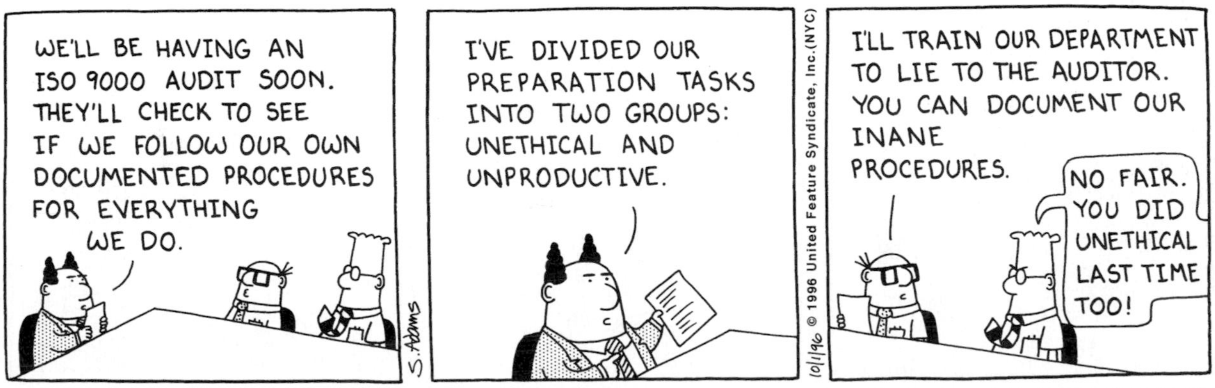
WE'LL BE HAVING AN ISO 9000 AUDIT SOON. THEY'LL CHECK TO SEE IF WE FOLLOW OUR OWN DOCUMENTED PROCEDURES FOR EVERYTHING WE DO.
I'VE DIVIDED OUR PREPARATION TASKS INTO TWO GROUPS: UNETHICAL AND UNPRODUCTIVE.
I'LL TRAIN OUR DEPARTMENT TO LIE TO THE AUDITOR. YOU CAN DOCUMENT OUR INANE PROCEDURES.
NO FAIR. YOU DID UNETHICAL LAST TIME TOO!
S. Adams
10/1/96 © 1996 United Feature Syndicate, Inc.(NYC)

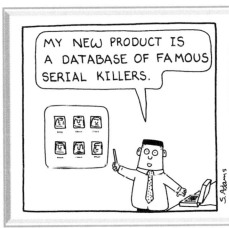

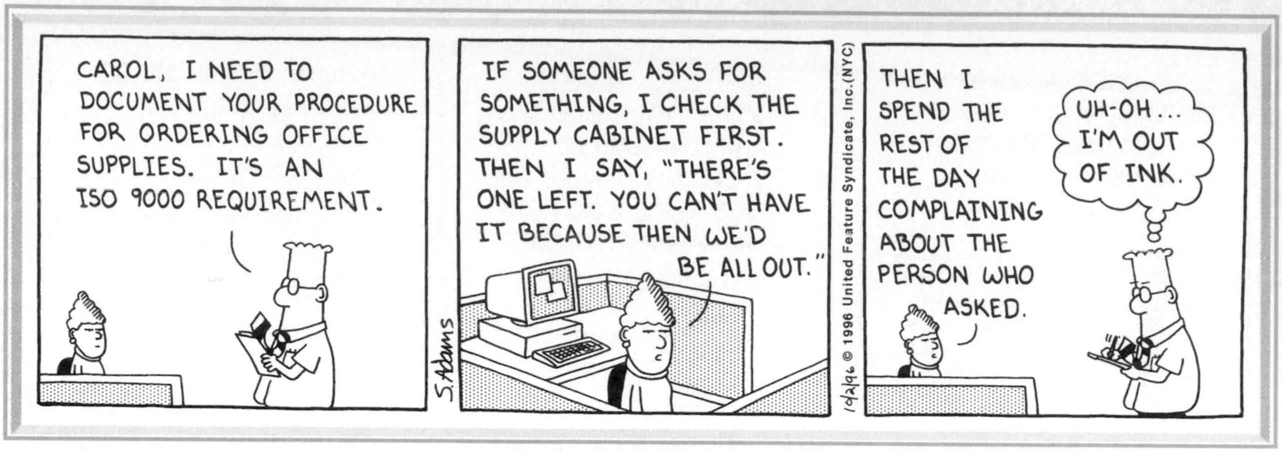
CAROL, I NEED TO DOCUMENT YOUR PROCEDURE FOR ORDERING OFFICE SUPPLIES. IT'S AN ISO 9000 REQUIREMENT.
IF SOMEONE ASKS FOR SOMETHING, I CHECK THE SUPPLY CABINET FIRST. THEN I SAY, "THERE'S ONE LEFT. YOU CAN'T HAVE IT BECAUSE THEN WE'D BE ALL OUT."
THEN I SPEND THE REST OF THE DAY COMPLAINING ABOUT THE PERSON WHO ASKED.
UH-OH... I'M OUT OF INK.
S. Adams
10/2/96 © 1996 United Feature Syndicate, Inc.(NYC)

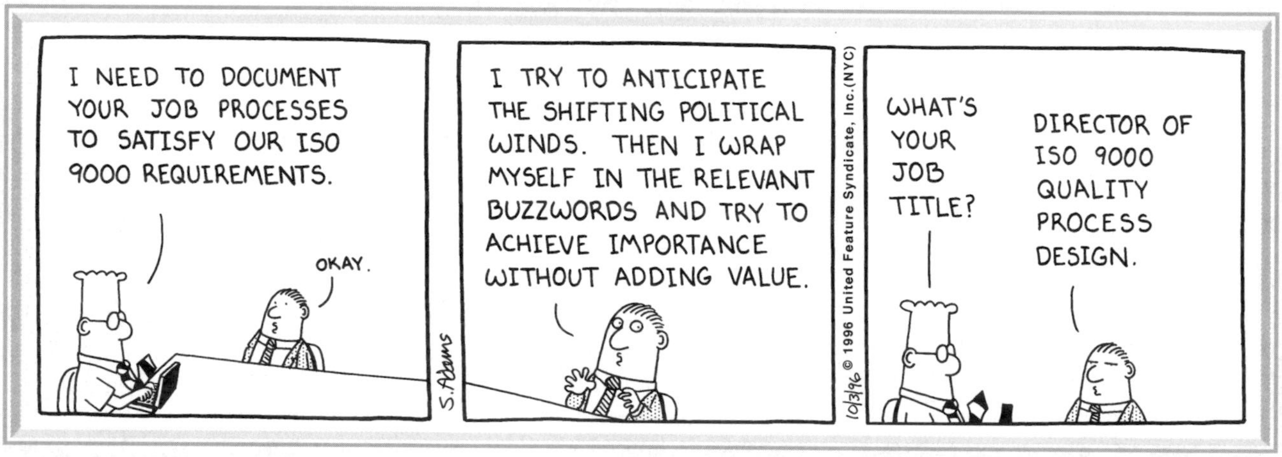
I NEED TO DOCUMENT YOUR JOB PROCESSES TO SATISFY OUR ISO 9000 REQUIREMENTS.
OKAY.
I TRY TO ANTICIPATE THE SHIFTING POLITICAL WINDS. THEN I WRAP MYSELF IN THE RELEVANT BUZZWORDS AND TRY TO ACHIEVE IMPORTANCE WITHOUT ADDING VALUE.
WHAT'S YOUR JOB TITLE?
DIRECTOR OF ISO 9000 QUALITY PROCESS DESIGN.
S. Adams
10/3/96 © 1996 United Feature Syndicate, Inc.(NYC)

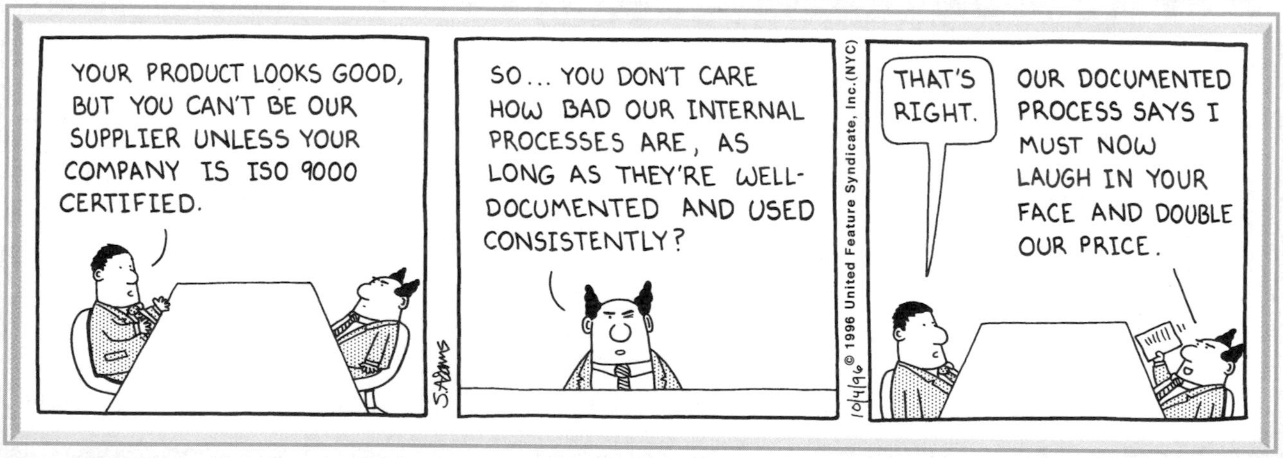
YOUR PRODUCT LOOKS GOOD, BUT YOU CAN'T BE OUR SUPPLIER UNLESS YOUR COMPANY IS ISO 9000 CERTIFIED.
SO... YOU DON'T CARE HOW BAD OUR INTERNAL PROCESSES ARE, AS LONG AS THEY'RE WELL-DOCUMENTED AND USED CONSISTENTLY?
THAT'S RIGHT.
OUR DOCUMENTED PROCESS SAYS I MUST NOW LAUGH IN YOUR FACE AND DOUBLE OUR PRICE.
S. Adams
10/4/96 © 1996 United Feature Syndicate, Inc.(NYC)

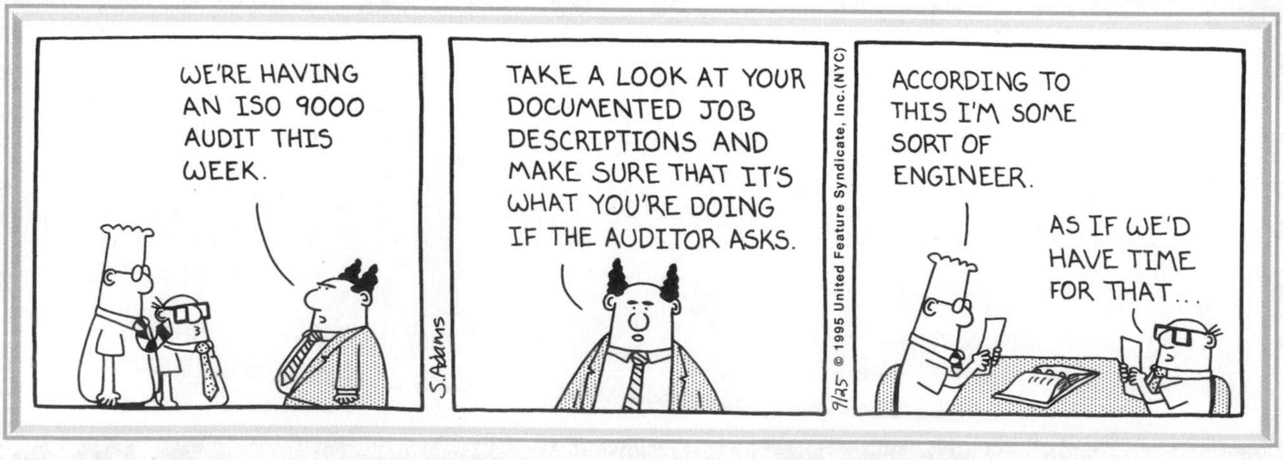
WE'RE HAVING AN ISO 9000 AUDIT THIS WEEK.
TAKE A LOOK AT YOUR DOCUMENTED JOB DESCRIPTIONS AND MAKE SURE THAT IT'S WHAT YOU'RE DOING IF THE AUDITOR ASKS.
ACCORDING TO THIS I'M SOME SORT OF ENGINEER.
AS IF WE'D HAVE TIME FOR THAT...
S. Adams
9/25 © 1995 United Feature Syndicate, Inc.(NYC)

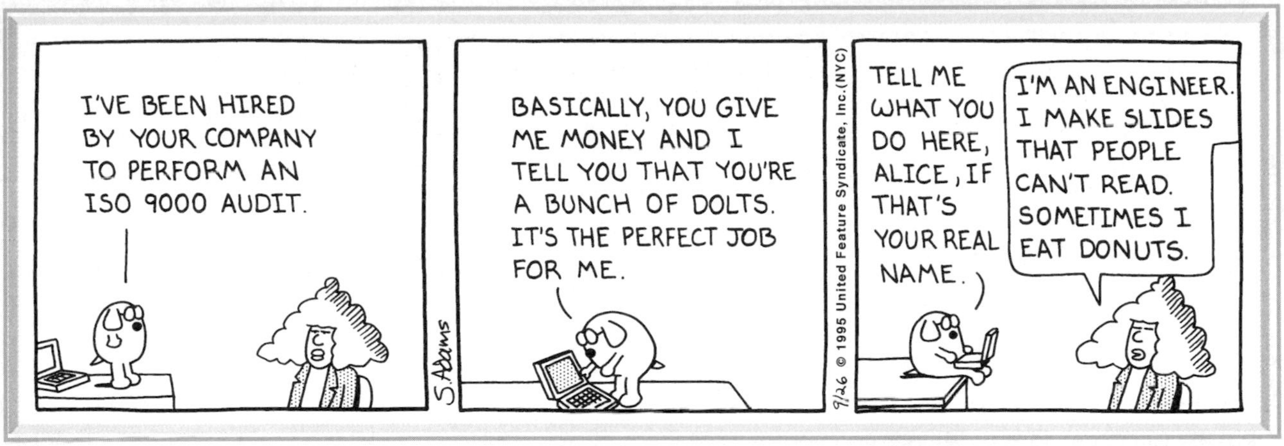
I'VE BEEN HIRED BY YOUR COMPANY TO PERFORM AN ISO 9000 AUDIT.
BASICALLY, YOU GIVE ME MONEY AND I TELL YOU THAT YOU'RE A BUNCH OF DOLTS. IT'S THE PERFECT JOB FOR ME.
TELL ME WHAT YOU DO HERE, ALICE, IF THAT'S YOUR REAL NAME.
I'M AN ENGINEER. I MAKE SLIDES THAT PEOPLE CAN'T READ. SOMETIMES I EAT DONUTS.
S. Adams
9/26 © 1995 United Feature Syndicate, Inc.(NYC)

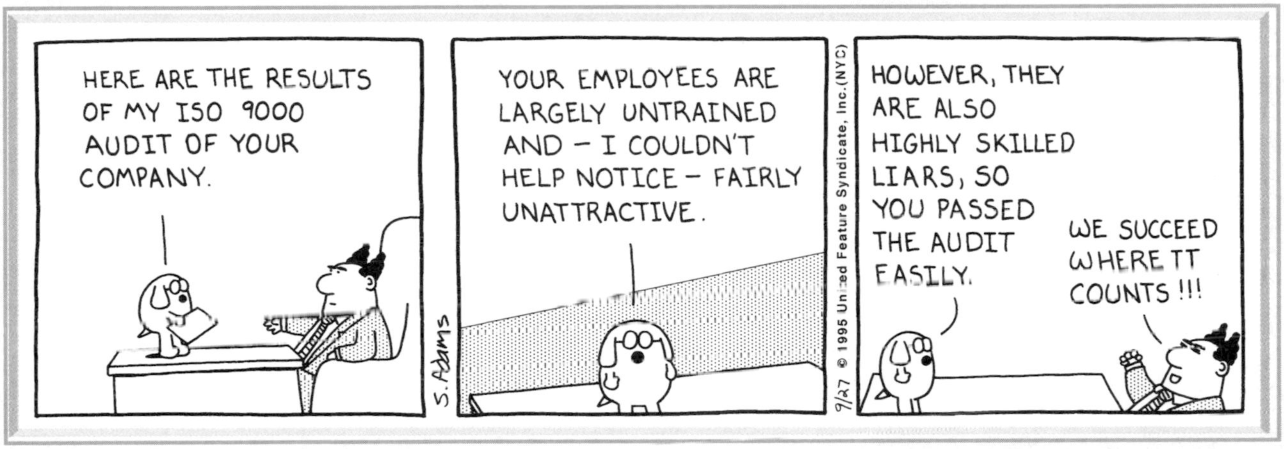
HERE ARE THE RESULTS OF MY ISO 9000 AUDIT OF YOUR COMPANY.
YOUR EMPLOYEES ARE LARGELY UNTRAINED AND – I COULDN'T HELP NOTICE – FAIRLY UNATTRACTIVE.
HOWEVER, THEY ARE ALSO HIGHLY SKILLED LIARS, SO YOU PASSED THE AUDIT EASILY.
WE SUCCEED WHERE IT COUNTS !!!
S. Adams
9/27 © 1995 United Feature Syndicate, Inc.(NYC)

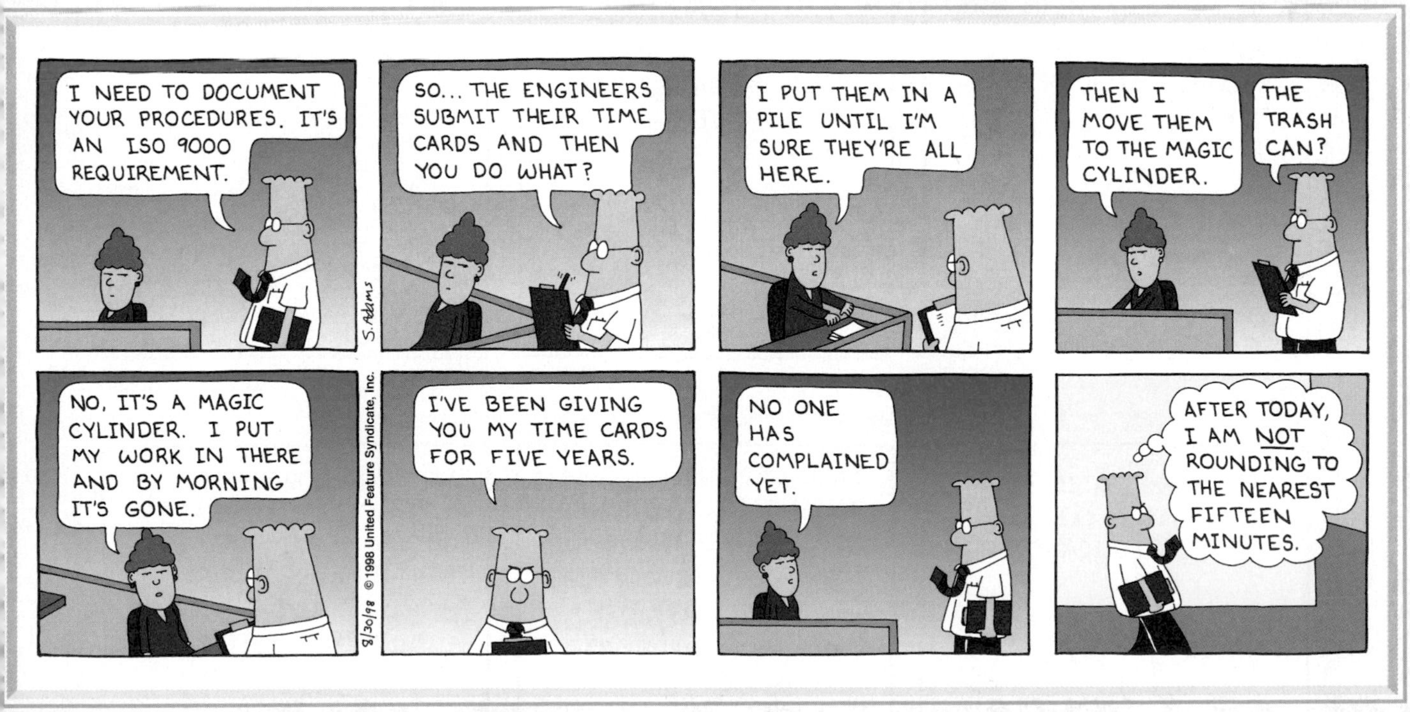
I NEED TO DOCUMENT YOUR PROCEDURES. IT'S AN ISO 9000 REQUIREMENT.
SO... THE ENGINEERS SUBMIT THEIR TIME CARDS AND THEN YOU DO WHAT?
I PUT THEM IN A PILE UNTIL I'M SURE THEY'RE ALL HERE.
THEN I MOVE THEM TO THE MAGIC CYLINDER.
THE TRASH CAN?
NO, IT'S A MAGIC CYLINDER. I PUT MY WORK IN THERE AND BY MORNING IT'S GONE.
I'VE BEEN GIVING YOU MY TIME CARDS FOR FIVE YEARS.
NO ONE HAS COMPLAINED YET.
AFTER TODAY, I AM NOT ROUNDING TO THE NEAREST FIFTEEN MINUTES.
S. Adams
8/30/98 © 1998 United Feature Syndicate, Inc.

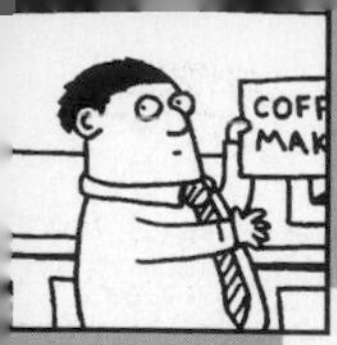

COFF
MAK

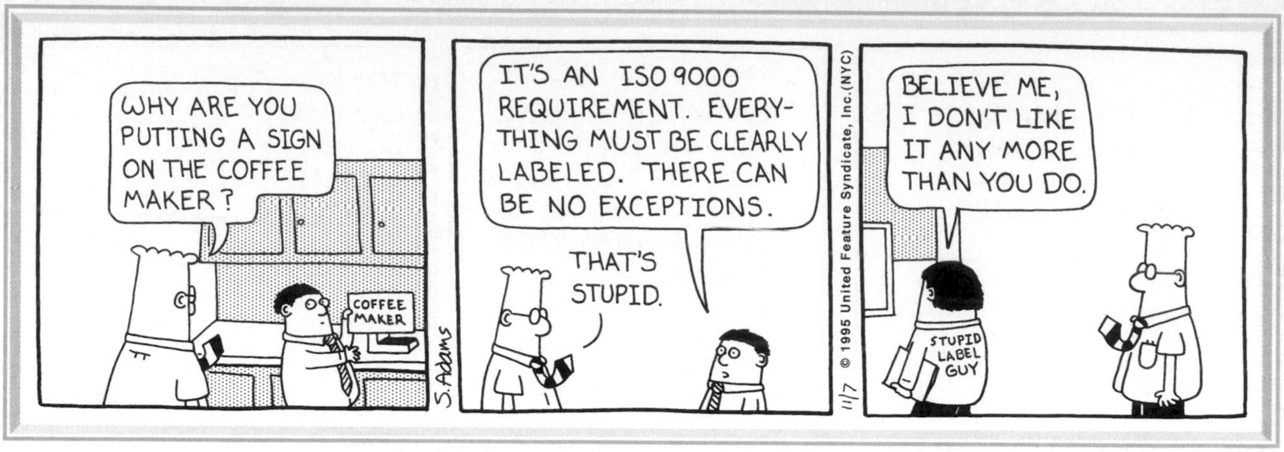

WHY ARE YOU PUTTING A SIGN ON THE COFFEE MAKER?
COFFEE MAKER
S. Adams
IT'S AN ISO 9000 REQUIREMENT. EVERYTHING MUST BE CLEARLY LABELED. THERE CAN BE NO EXCEPTIONS.
THAT'S STUPID.
11/7 © 1995 United Feature Syndicate, Inc.(NYC)
BELIEVE ME, I DON'T LIKE IT ANY MORE THAN YOU DO.
STUPID LABEL GUY

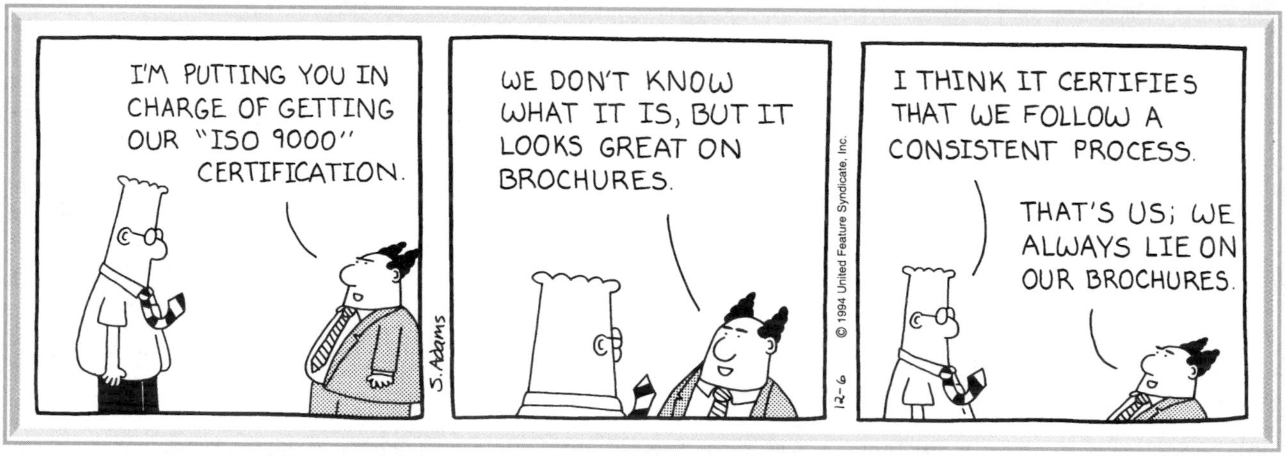

I'M PUTTING YOU IN CHARGE OF GETTING OUR "ISO 9000" CERTIFICATION.
S. Adams
WE DON'T KNOW WHAT IT IS, BUT IT LOOKS GREAT ON BROCHURES.
12-6 © 1994 United Feature Syndicate, Inc.
I THINK IT CERTIFIES THAT WE FOLLOW A CONSISTENT PROCESS.
THAT'S US; WE ALWAYS LIE ON OUR BROCHURES.

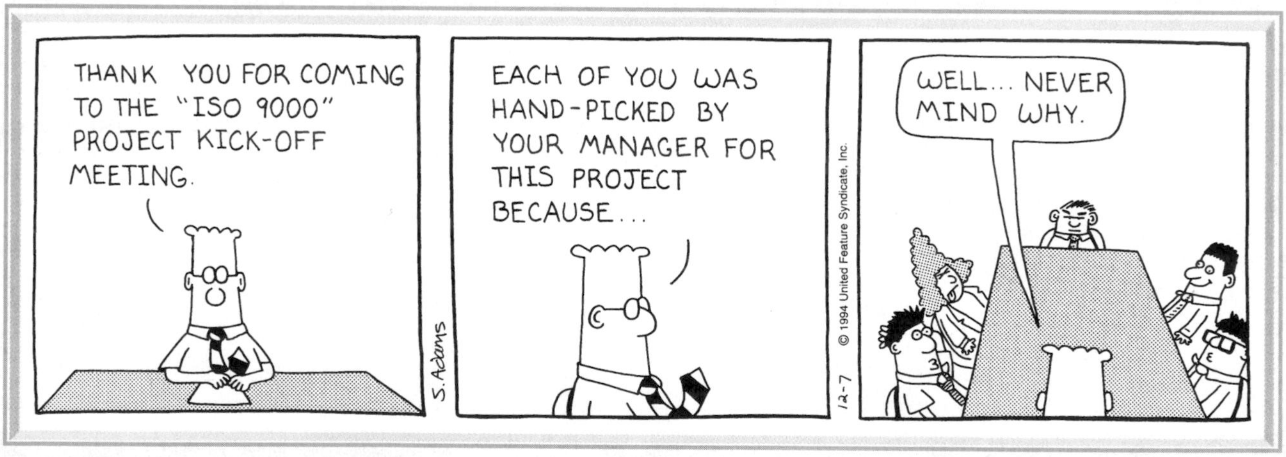

THANK YOU FOR COMING TO THE "ISO 9000" PROJECT KICK-OFF MEETING.
S. Adams
EACH OF YOU WAS HAND-PICKED BY YOUR MANAGER FOR THIS PROJECT BECAUSE...
12-7 © 1994 United Feature Syndicate, Inc.
WELL... NEVER MIND WHY.

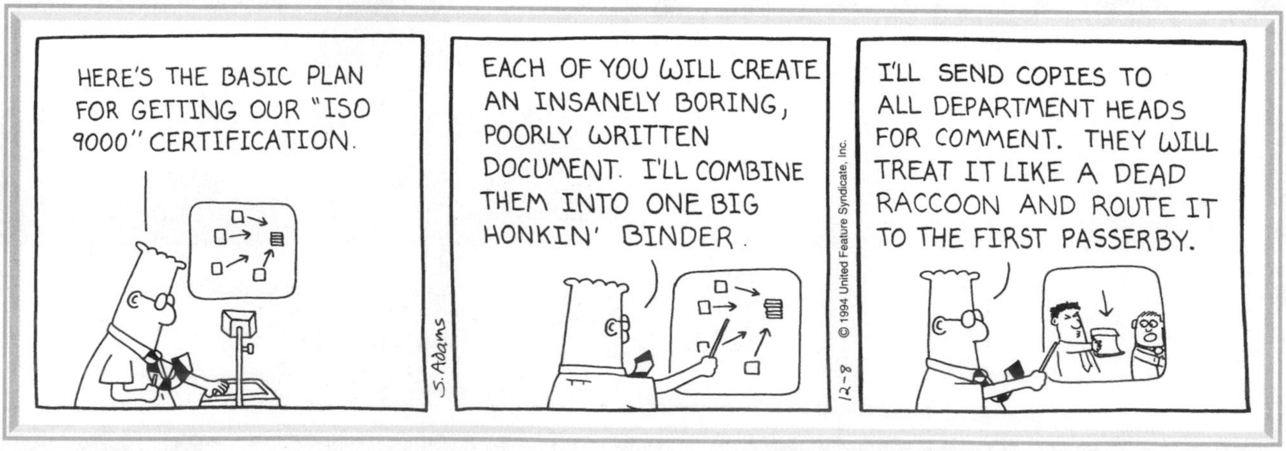

HERE'S THE BASIC PLAN FOR GETTING OUR "ISO 9000" CERTIFICATION.
S. Adams
EACH OF YOU WILL CREATE AN INSANELY BORING, POORLY WRITTEN DOCUMENT. I'LL COMBINE THEM INTO ONE BIG HONKIN' BINDER.
12-8 © 1994 United Feature Syndicate, Inc.
I'LL SEND COPIES TO ALL DEPARTMENT HEADS FOR COMMENT. THEY WILL TREAT IT LIKE A DEAD RACCOON AND ROUTE IT TO THE FIRST PASSERBY.

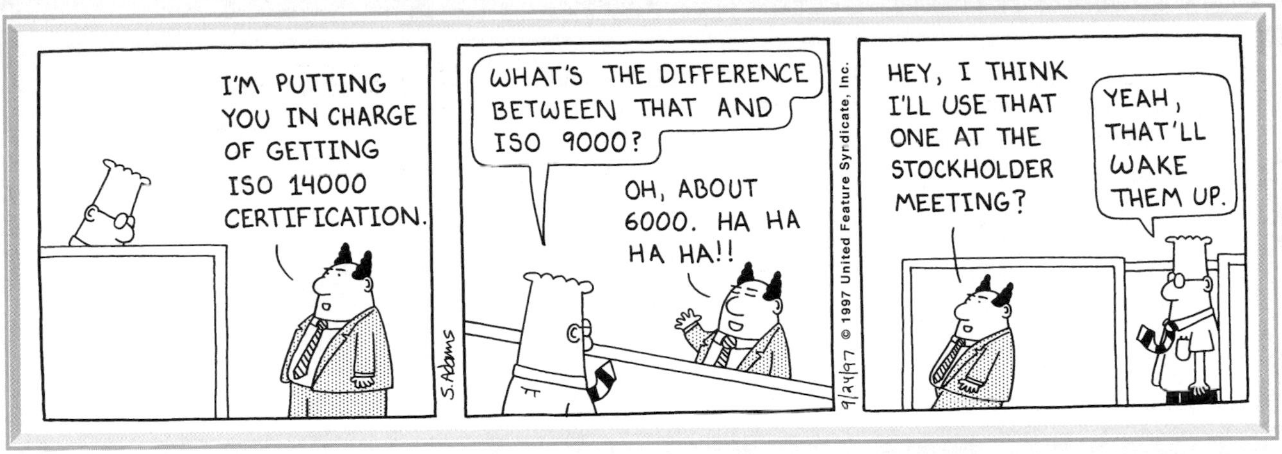
I'M PUTTING YOU IN CHARGE OF GETTING ISO 14000 CERTIFICATION.
WHAT'S THE DIFFERENCE BETWEEN THAT AND ISO 9000?
OH, ABOUT 6000. HA HA HA HA!!
HEY, I THINK I'LL USE THAT ONE AT THE STOCKHOLDER MEETING?
YEAH, THAT'LL WAKE THEM UP.
S. Adams
9/24/97 © 1997 United Feature Syndicate, Inc.

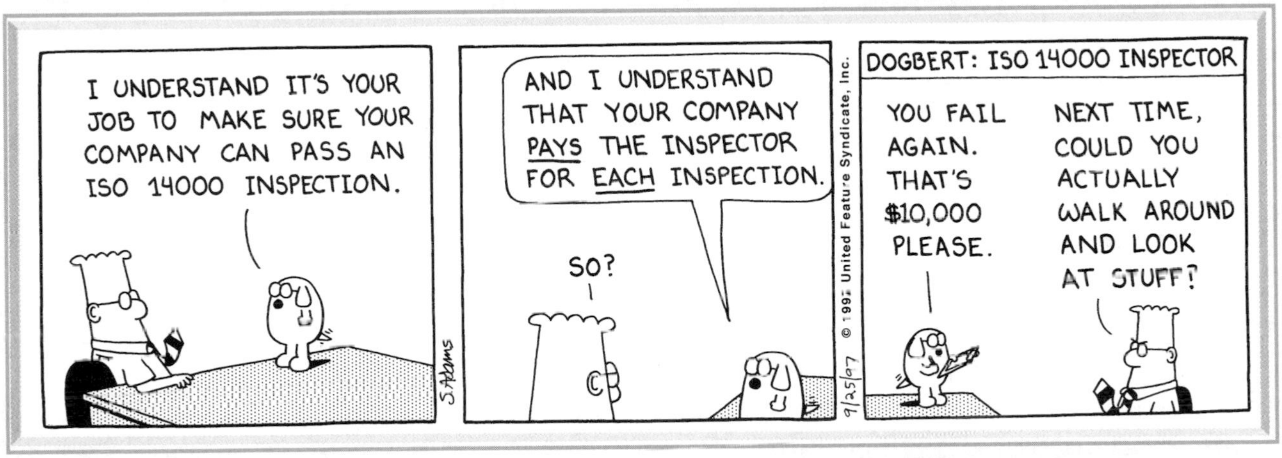
I UNDERSTAND IT'S YOUR JOB TO MAKE SURE YOUR COMPANY CAN PASS AN ISO 14000 INSPECTION.
AND I UNDERSTAND THAT YOUR COMPANY PAYS THE INSPECTOR FOR EACH INSPECTION.
SO?
DOGBERT: ISO 14000 INSPECTOR
YOU FAIL AGAIN. THAT'S $10,000 PLEASE.
NEXT TIME, COULD YOU ACTUALLY WALK AROUND AND LOOK AT STUFF?
S. Adams
9/25/97

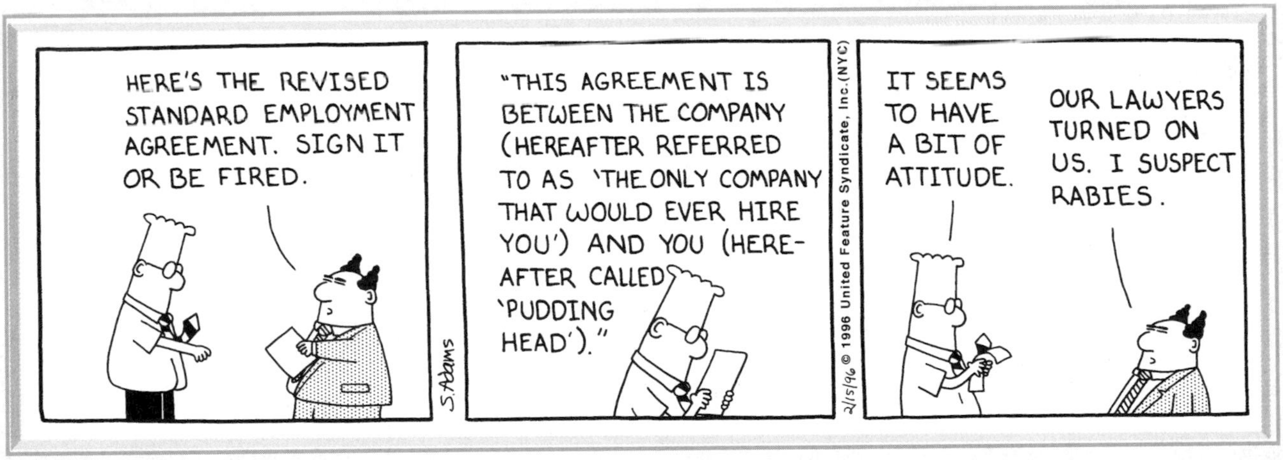
HERE'S THE REVISED STANDARD EMPLOYMENT AGREEMENT. SIGN IT OR BE FIRED.
"THIS AGREEMENT IS BETWEEN THE COMPANY (HEREAFTER REFERRED TO AS 'THE ONLY COMPANY THAT WOULD EVER HIRE YOU') AND YOU (HEREAFTER CALLED 'PUDDING HEAD')."
IT SEEMS TO HAVE A BIT OF ATTITUDE.
OUR LAWYERS TURNED ON US. I SUSPECT RABIES.
S. Adams
2/15/96 © 1996 United Feature Syndicate, Inc.(NYC)

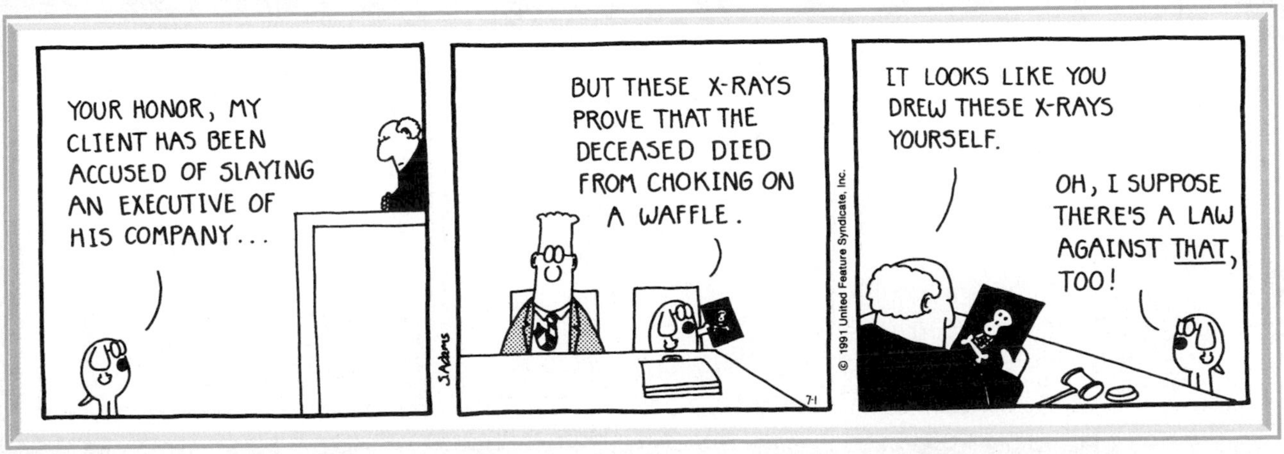
YOUR HONOR, MY CLIENT HAS BEEN ACCUSED OF SLAYING AN EXECUTIVE OF HIS COMPANY...
BUT THESE X-RAYS PROVE THAT THE DECEASED DIED FROM CHOKING ON A WAFFLE.
IT LOOKS LIKE YOU DREW THESE X-RAYS YOURSELF.
OH, I SUPPOSE THERE'S A LAW AGAINST THAT, TOO!
S. Adams
© 1991 United Feature Syndicate, Inc.

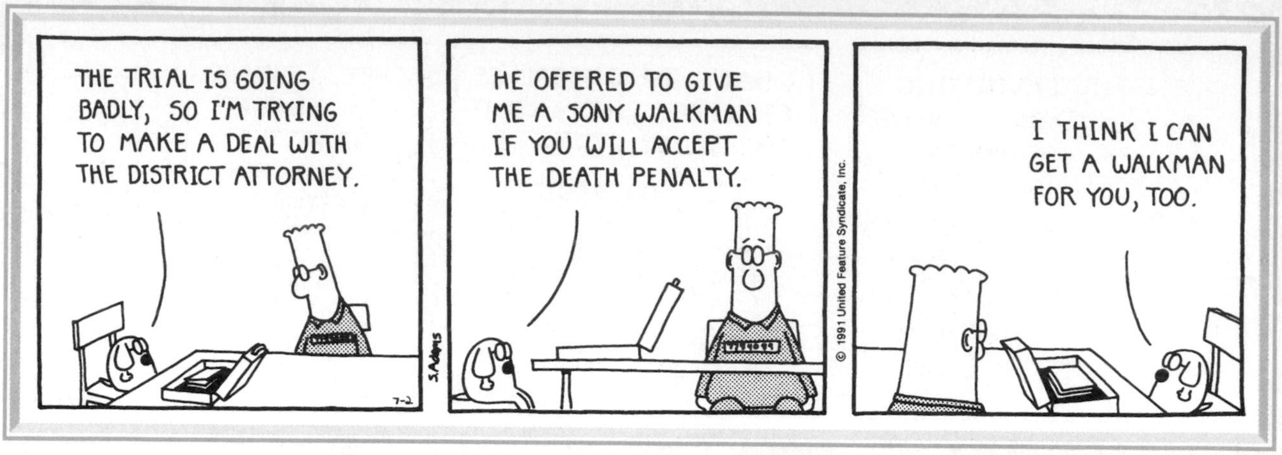
THE TRIAL IS GOING BADLY, SO I'M TRYING TO MAKE A DEAL WITH THE DISTRICT ATTORNEY.
HE OFFERED TO GIVE ME A SONY WALKMAN IF YOU WILL ACCEPT THE DEATH PENALTY.
I THINK I CAN GET A WALKMAN FOR YOU, TOO.
© 1991 United Feature Syndicate, Inc.

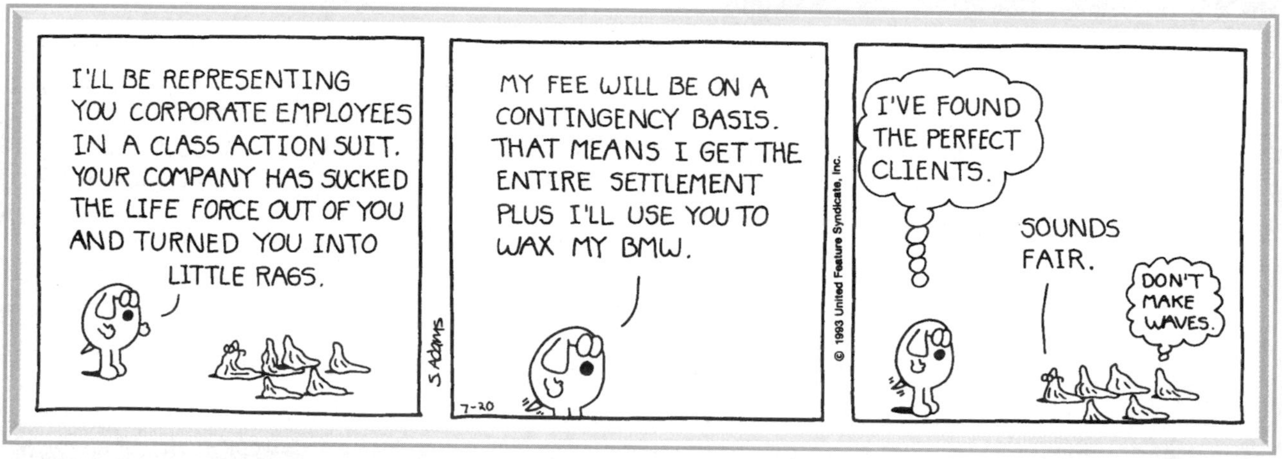
I'LL BE REPRESENTING YOU CORPORATE EMPLOYEES IN A CLASS ACTION SUIT. YOUR COMPANY HAS SUCKED THE LIFE FORCE OUT OF YOU AND TURNED YOU INTO LITTLE RAGS.
MY FEE WILL BE ON A CONTINGENCY BASIS. THAT MEANS I GET THE ENTIRE SETTLEMENT PLUS I'LL USE YOU TO WAX MY BMW.
I'VE FOUND THE PERFECT CLIENTS.
SOUNDS FAIR.
DON'T MAKE WAVES.
© 1993 United Feature Syndicate, Inc.

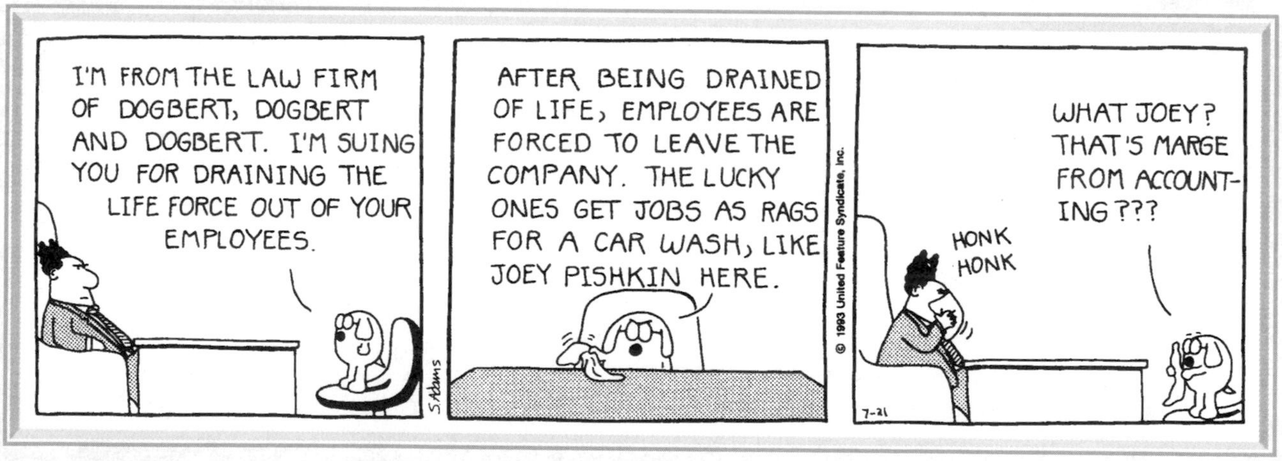
I'M FROM THE LAW FIRM OF DOGBERT, DOGBERT AND DOGBERT. I'M SUING YOU FOR DRAINING THE LIFE FORCE OUT OF YOUR EMPLOYEES.
AFTER BEING DRAINED OF LIFE, EMPLOYEES ARE FORCED TO LEAVE THE COMPANY. THE LUCKY ONES GET JOBS AS RAGS FOR A CAR WASH, LIKE JOEY PISHKIN HERE.
HONK HONK
WHAT JOEY? THAT'S MARGE FROM ACCOUNTING???
© 1993 United Feature Syndicate, Inc.

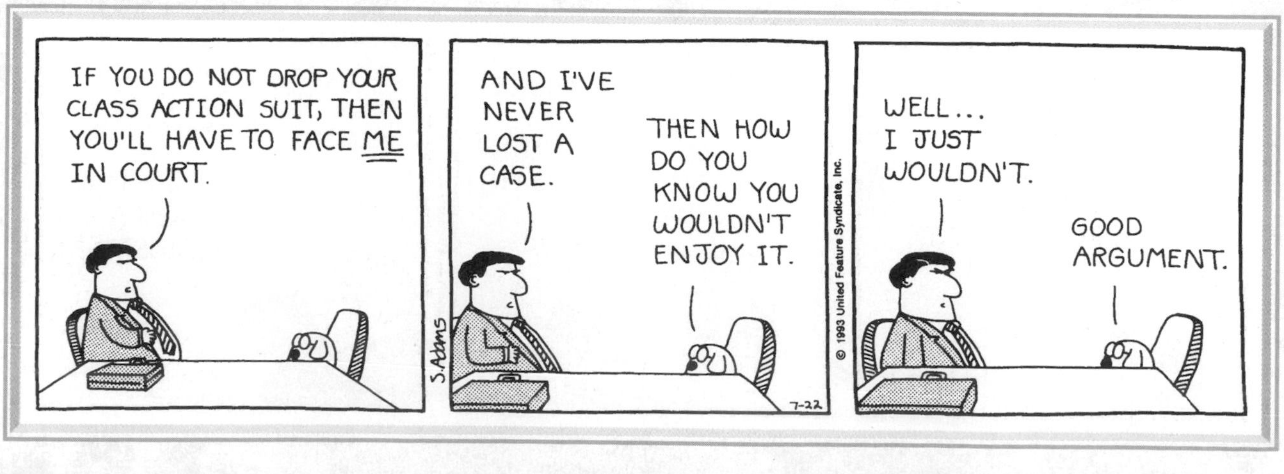
IF YOU DO NOT DROP YOUR CLASS ACTION SUIT, THEN YOU'LL HAVE TO FACE ME IN COURT.
AND I'VE NEVER LOST A CASE.
THEN HOW DO YOU KNOW YOU WOULDN'T ENJOY IT.
WELL... I JUST WOULDN'T.
GOOD ARGUMENT.
© 1993 United Feature Syndicate, Inc.

LAWYERS

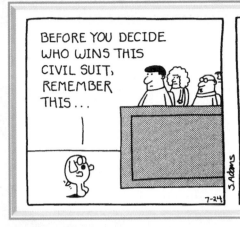

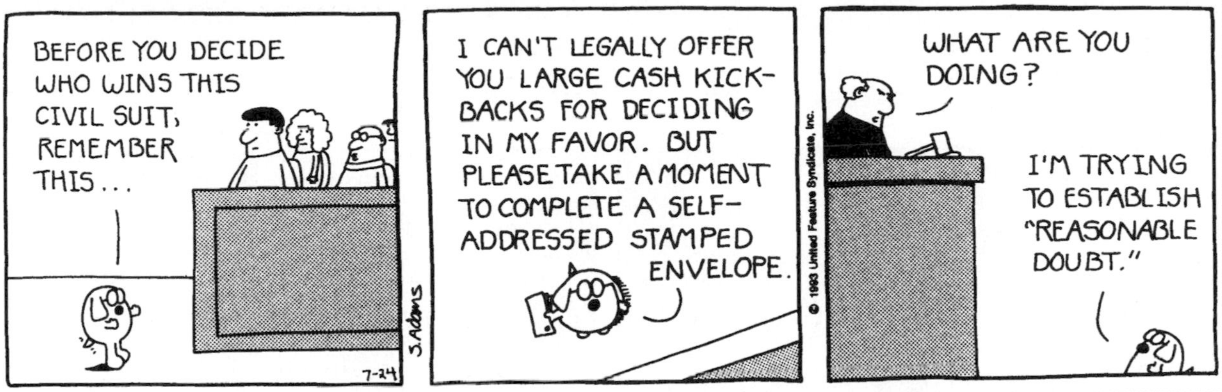
BEFORE YOU DECIDE WHO WINS THIS CIVIL SUIT, REMEMBER THIS...
7-24
S. Adams
I CAN'T LEGALLY OFFER YOU LARGE CASH KICK-BACKS FOR DECIDING IN MY FAVOR. BUT PLEASE TAKE A MOMENT TO COMPLETE A SELF-ADDRESSED STAMPED ENVELOPE.
© 1993 United Feature Syndicate, Inc.
WHAT ARE YOU DOING?
I'M TRYING TO ESTABLISH "REASONABLE DOUBT."

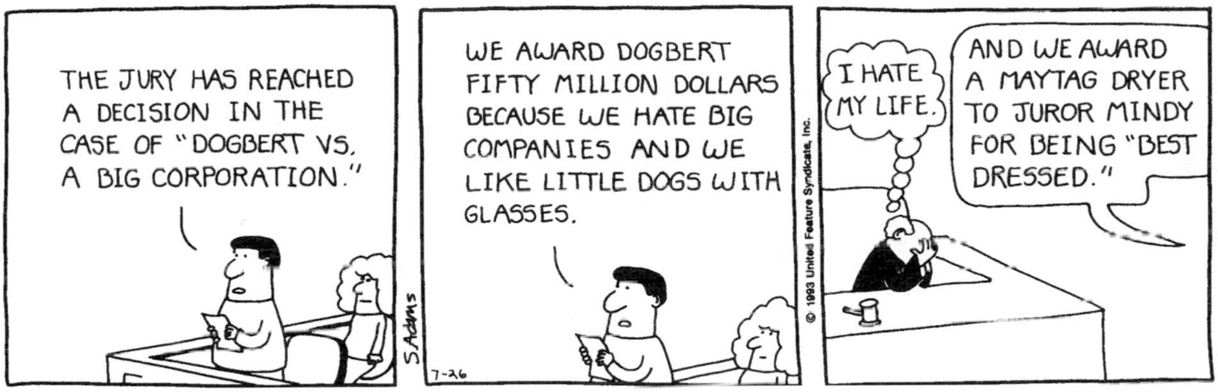
THE JURY HAS REACHED A DECISION IN THE CASE OF "DOGBERT VS. A BIG CORPORATION."
S. Adams
7-26
WE AWARD DOGBERT FIFTY MILLION DOLLARS BECAUSE WE HATE BIG COMPANIES AND WE LIKE LITTLE DOGS WITH GLASSES.
© 1993 United Feature Syndicate, Inc.
I HATE MY LIFE.
AND WE AWARD A MAYTAG DRYER TO JUROR MINDY FOR BEING "BEST DRESSED."

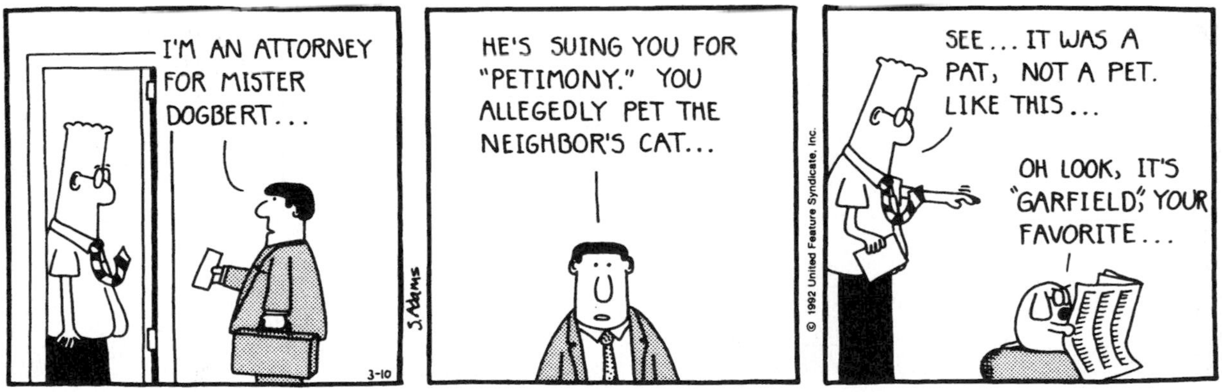
I'M AN ATTORNEY FOR MISTER DOGBERT...
3-10
S. Adams
HE'S SUING YOU FOR "PETIMONY." YOU ALLEGEDLY PET THE NEIGHBOR'S CAT...
© 1992 United Feature Syndicate, Inc.
SEE... IT WAS A PAT, NOT A PET. LIKE THIS...
OH LOOK, IT'S "GARFIELD," YOUR FAVORITE...

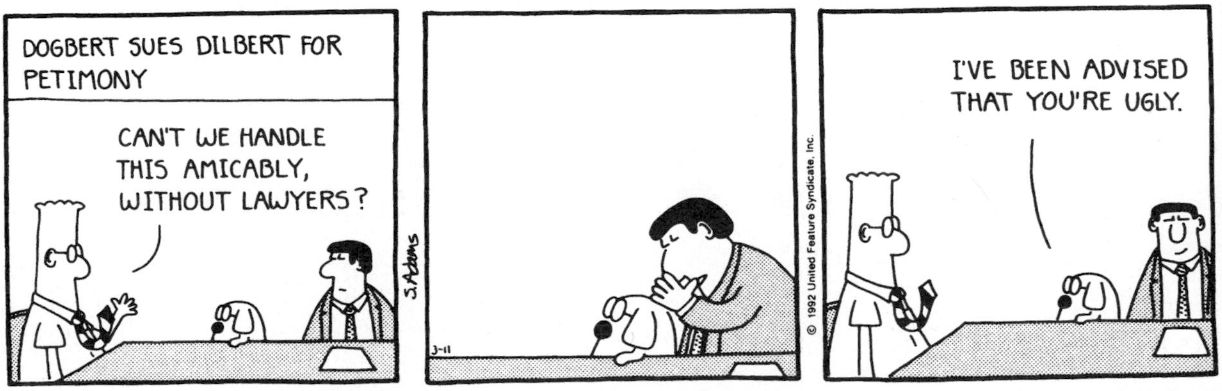
DOGBERT SUES DILBERT FOR PETIMONY
CAN'T WE HANDLE THIS AMICABLY, WITHOUT LAWYERS?
S. Adams
3-11
© 1992 United Feature Syndicate, Inc.
I'VE BEEN ADVISED THAT YOU'RE UGLY.

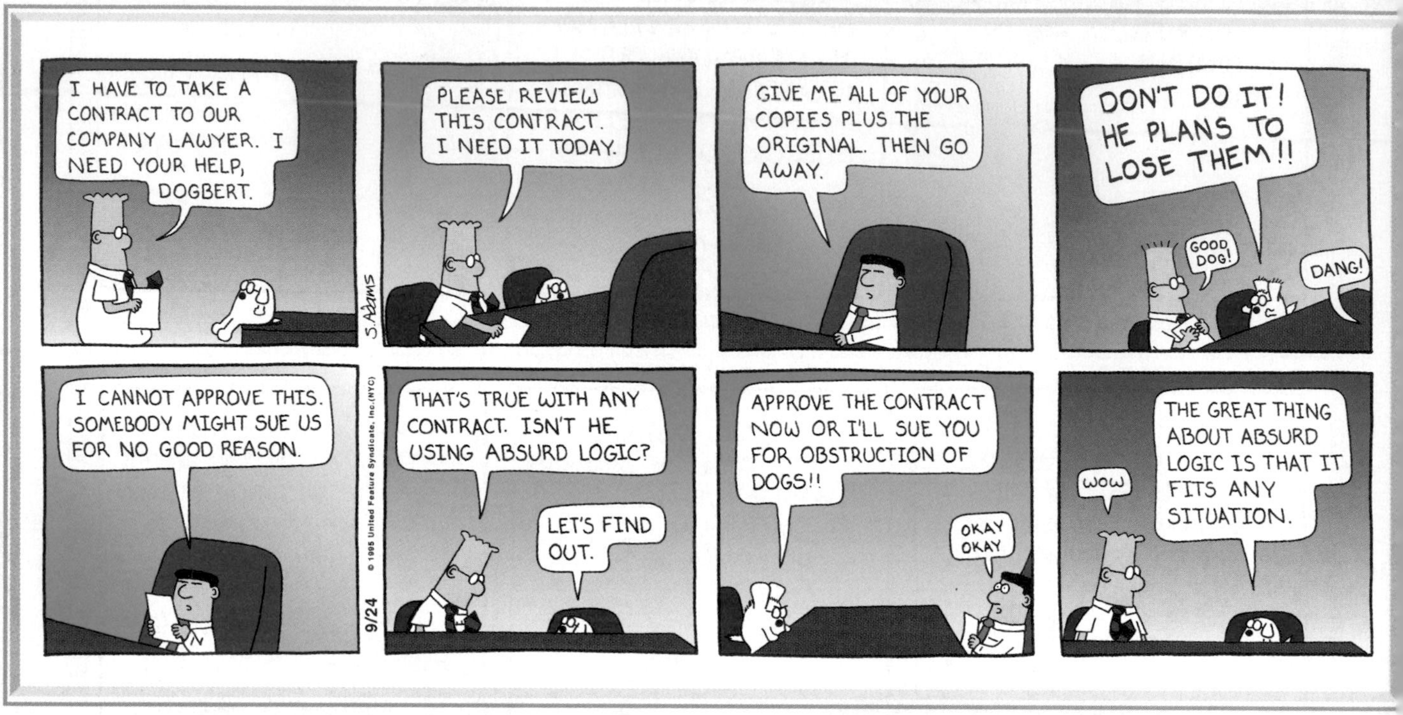
I HAVE TO TAKE A CONTRACT TO OUR COMPANY LAWYER. I NEED YOUR HELP, DOGBERT.
S. Adams
PLEASE REVIEW THIS CONTRACT. I NEED IT TODAY.
GIVE ME ALL OF YOUR COPIES PLUS THE ORIGINAL. THEN GO AWAY.
DON'T DO IT! HE PLANS TO LOSE THEM!!
GOOD DOG!
DANG!
I CANNOT APPROVE THIS. SOMEBODY MIGHT SUE US FOR NO GOOD REASON.
9/24
© 1995 United Feature Syndicate, Inc.(NYC)
THAT'S TRUE WITH ANY CONTRACT. ISN'T HE USING ABSURD LOGIC?
LET'S FIND OUT.
APPROVE THE CONTRACT NOW OR I'LL SUE YOU FOR OBSTRUCTION OF DOGS!!
OKAY OKAY
WOW
THE GREAT THING ABOUT ABSURD LOGIC IS THAT IT FITS ANY SITUATION.

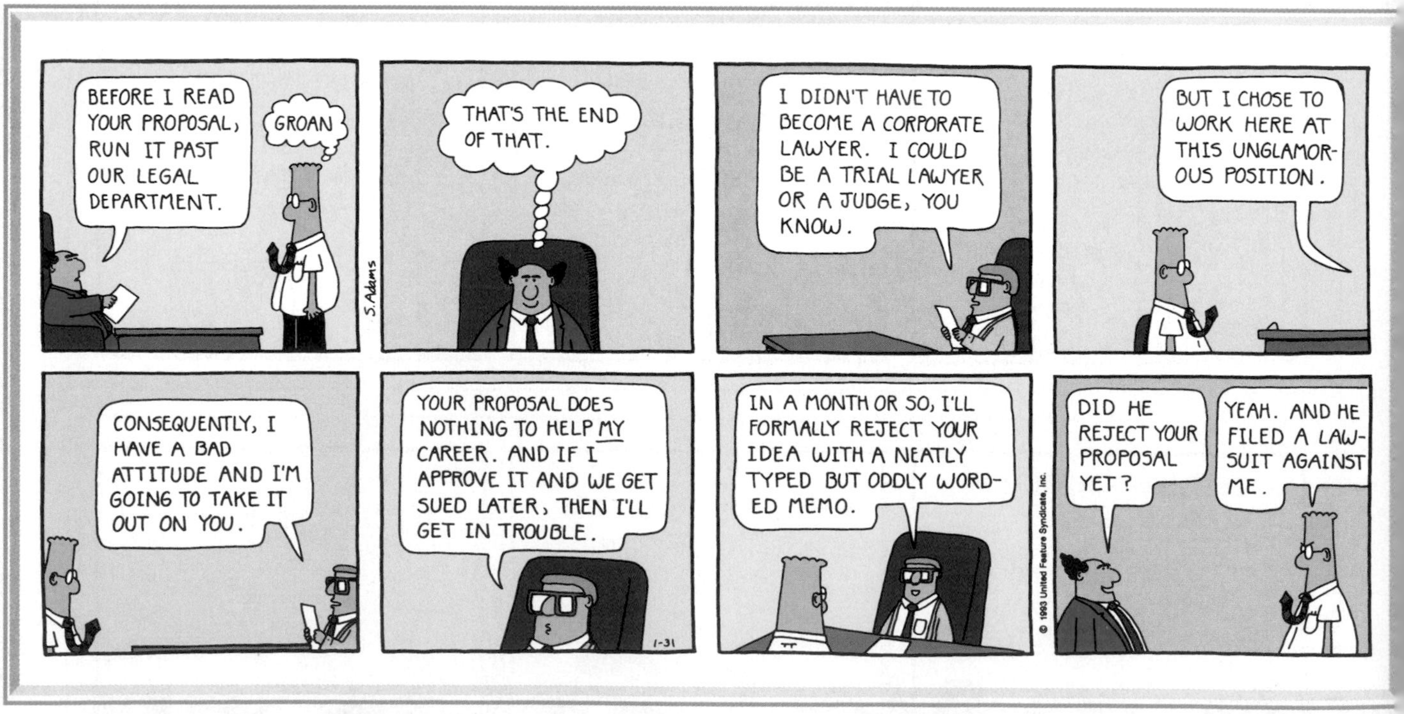
BEFORE I READ YOUR PROPOSAL, RUN IT PAST OUR LEGAL DEPARTMENT.
GROAN
S. Adams
THAT'S THE END OF THAT.
I DIDN'T HAVE TO BECOME A CORPORATE LAWYER. I COULD BE A TRIAL LAWYER OR A JUDGE, YOU KNOW.
BUT I CHOSE TO WORK HERE AT THIS UNGLAMOROUS POSITION.
CONSEQUENTLY, I HAVE A BAD ATTITUDE AND I'M GOING TO TAKE IT OUT ON YOU.
YOUR PROPOSAL DOES NOTHING TO HELP MY CAREER. AND IF I APPROVE IT AND WE GET SUED LATER, THEN I'LL GET IN TROUBLE.
1-31
IN A MONTH OR SO, I'LL FORMALLY REJECT YOUR IDEA WITH A NEATLY TYPED BUT ODDLY WORDED MEMO.
© 1993 United Feature Syndicate, Inc.
DID HE REJECT YOUR PROPOSAL YET?
YEAH. AND HE FILED A LAWSUIT AGAINST ME.

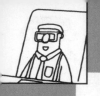

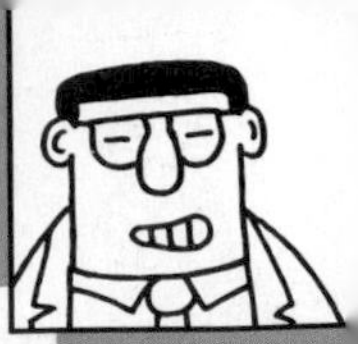

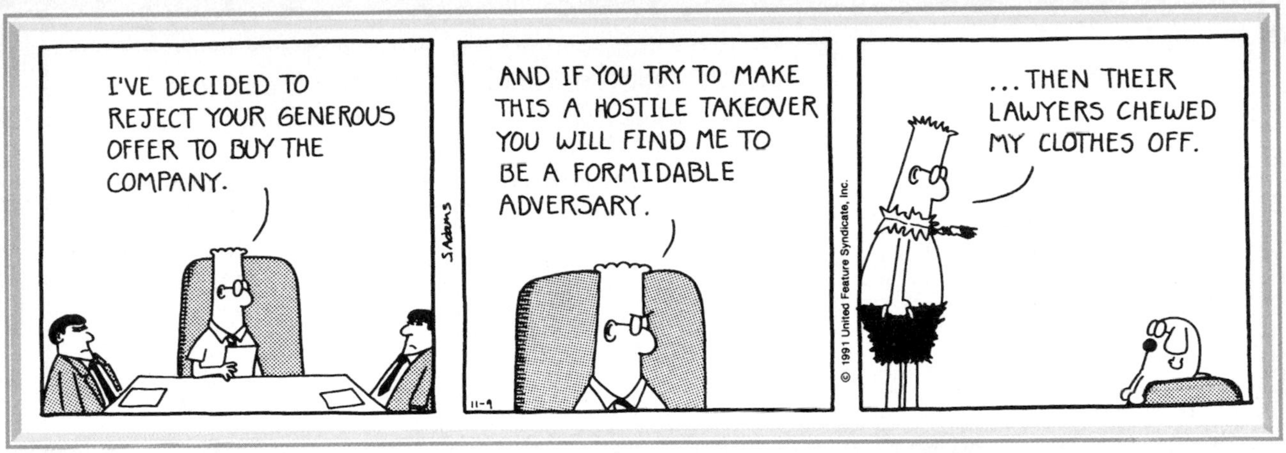
I'VE DECIDED TO REJECT YOUR GENEROUS OFFER TO BUY THE COMPANY.
AND IF YOU TRY TO MAKE THIS A HOSTILE TAKEOVER YOU WILL FIND ME TO BE A FORMIDABLE ADVERSARY.
...THEN THEIR LAWYERS CHEWED MY CLOTHES OFF.
S. Adams
11-9
© 1991 United Feature Syndicate, Inc.

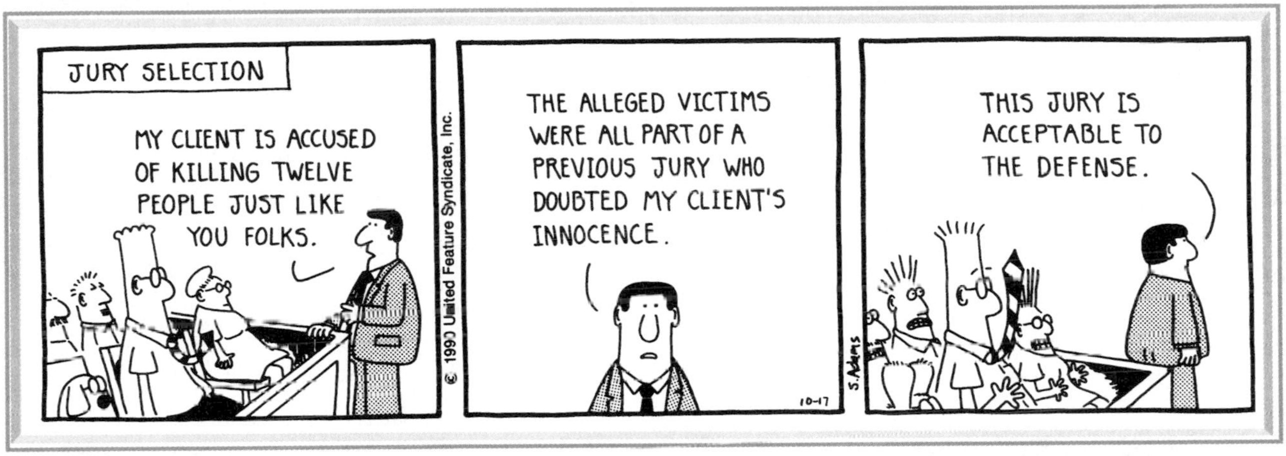
JURY SELECTION
MY CLIENT IS ACCUSED OF KILLING TWELVE PEOPLE JUST LIKE YOU FOLKS.
© 1990 United Feature Syndicate, Inc.
THE ALLEGED VICTIMS WERE ALL PART OF A PREVIOUS JURY WHO DOUBTED MY CLIENT'S INNOCENCE.
10-17
THIS JURY IS ACCEPTABLE TO THE DEFENSE.
S. Adams

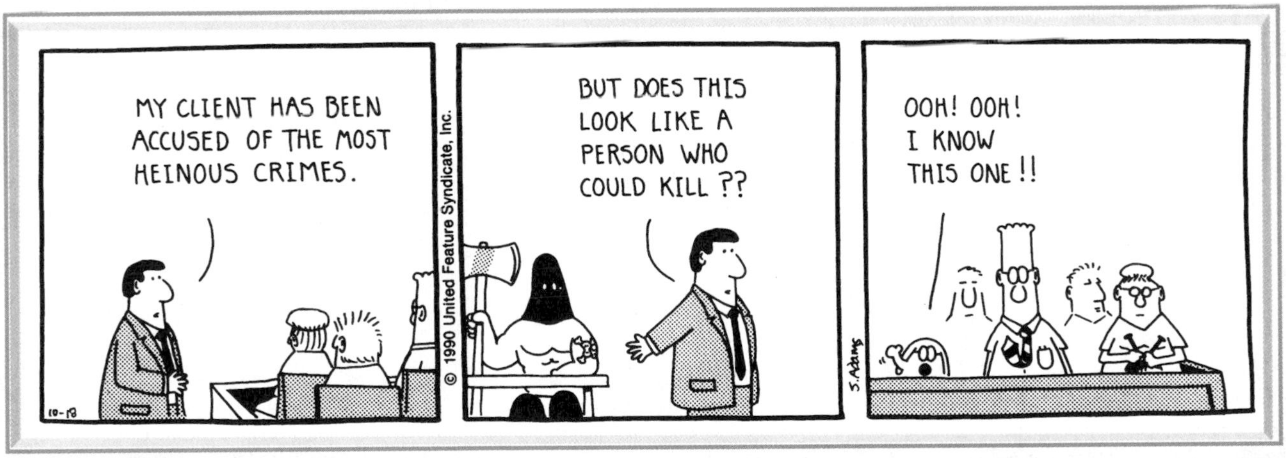
MY CLIENT HAS BEEN ACCUSED OF THE MOST HEINOUS CRIMES.
10-18
© 1990 United Feature Syndicate, Inc.
BUT DOES THIS LOOK LIKE A PERSON WHO COULD KILL ??
OOH! OOH! I KNOW THIS ONE !!
S. Adams

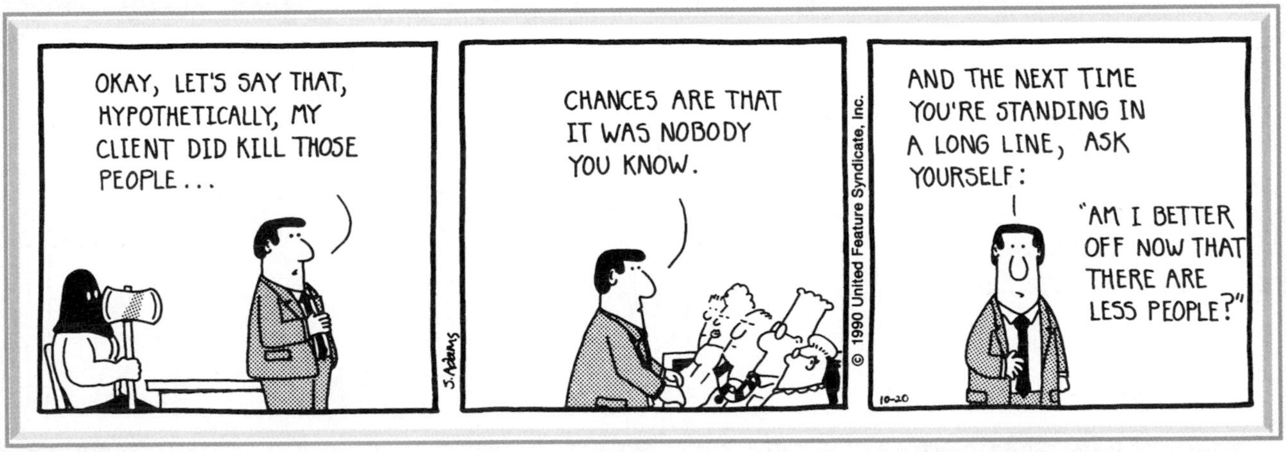
OKAY, LET'S SAY THAT, HYPOTHETICALLY, MY CLIENT DID KILL THOSE PEOPLE...
S. Adams
CHANCES ARE THAT IT WAS NOBODY YOU KNOW.
© 1990 United Feature Syndicate, Inc.
AND THE NEXT TIME YOU'RE STANDING IN A LONG LINE, ASK YOURSELF:
"AM I BETTER OFF NOW THAT THERE ARE LESS PEOPLE?"
10-20

LAWYERS

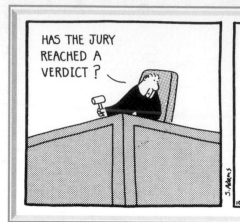

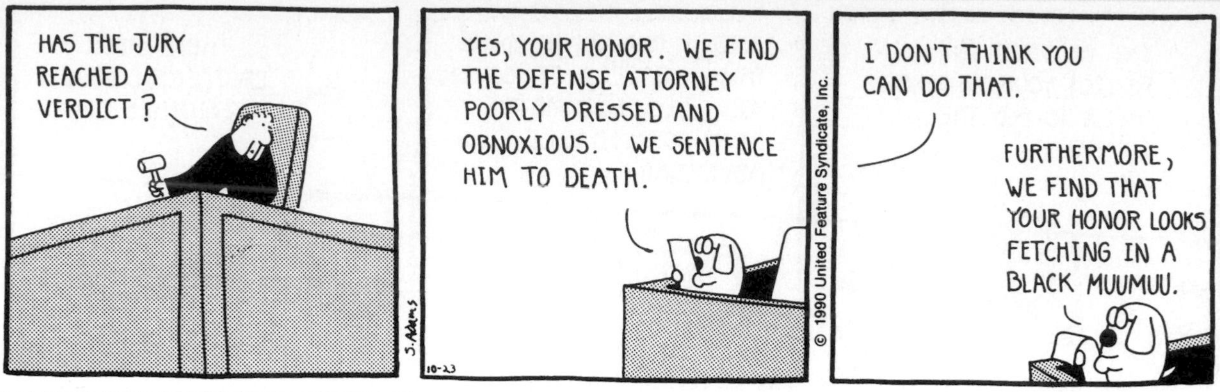
HAS THE JURY REACHED A VERDICT?
YES, YOUR HONOR. WE FIND THE DEFENSE ATTORNEY POORLY DRESSED AND OBNOXIOUS. WE SENTENCE HIM TO DEATH.
I DON'T THINK YOU CAN DO THAT.
FURTHERMORE, WE FIND THAT YOUR HONOR LOOKS FETCHING IN A BLACK MUUMUU.
© 1990 United Feature Syndicate, Inc.

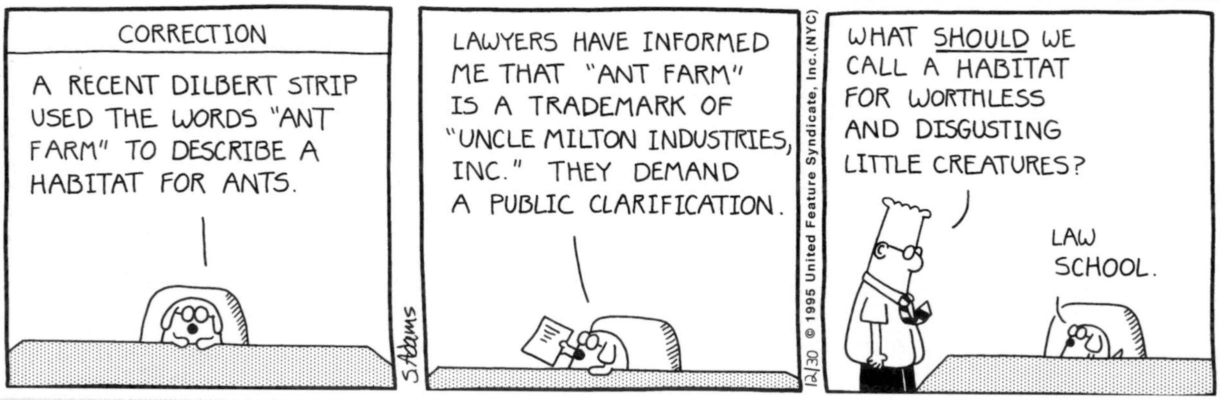
CORRECTION
A RECENT DILBERT STRIP USED THE WORDS "ANT FARM" TO DESCRIBE A HABITAT FOR ANTS.
LAWYERS HAVE INFORMED ME THAT "ANT FARM" IS A TRADEMARK OF "UNCLE MILTON INDUSTRIES, INC." THEY DEMAND A PUBLIC CLARIFICATION.
WHAT SHOULD WE CALL A HABITAT FOR WORTHLESS AND DISGUSTING LITTLE CREATURES?
LAW SCHOOL.
© 1995 United Feature Syndicate, Inc.(NYC)

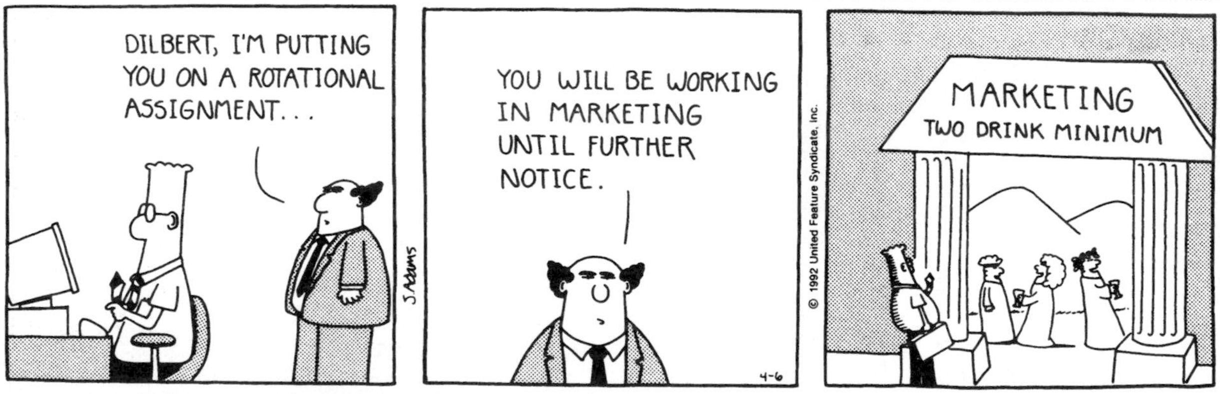
DILBERT, I'M PUTTING YOU ON A ROTATIONAL ASSIGNMENT...
YOU WILL BE WORKING IN MARKETING UNTIL FURTHER NOTICE.
MARKETING
TWO DRINK MINIMUM
© 1992 United Feature Syndicate, Inc.

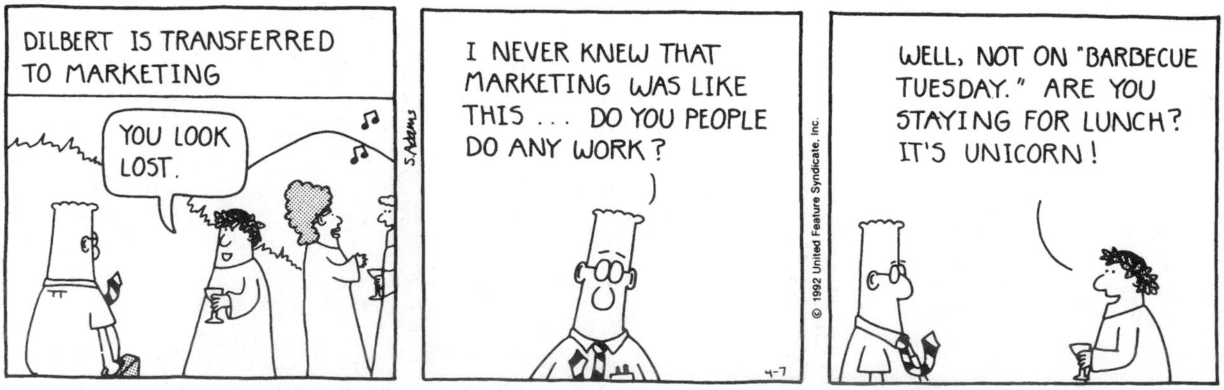
DILBERT IS TRANSFERRED TO MARKETING
YOU LOOK LOST.
I NEVER KNEW THAT MARKETING WAS LIKE THIS... DO YOU PEOPLE DO ANY WORK?
WELL, NOT ON "BARBECUE TUESDAY." ARE YOU STAYING FOR LUNCH? IT'S UNICORN!
© 1992 United Feature Syndicate, Inc.

MARKETING

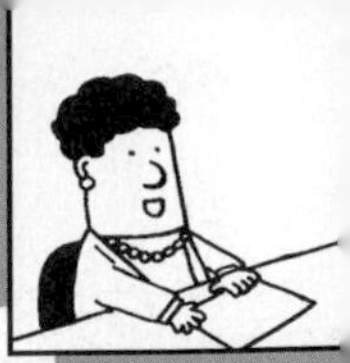

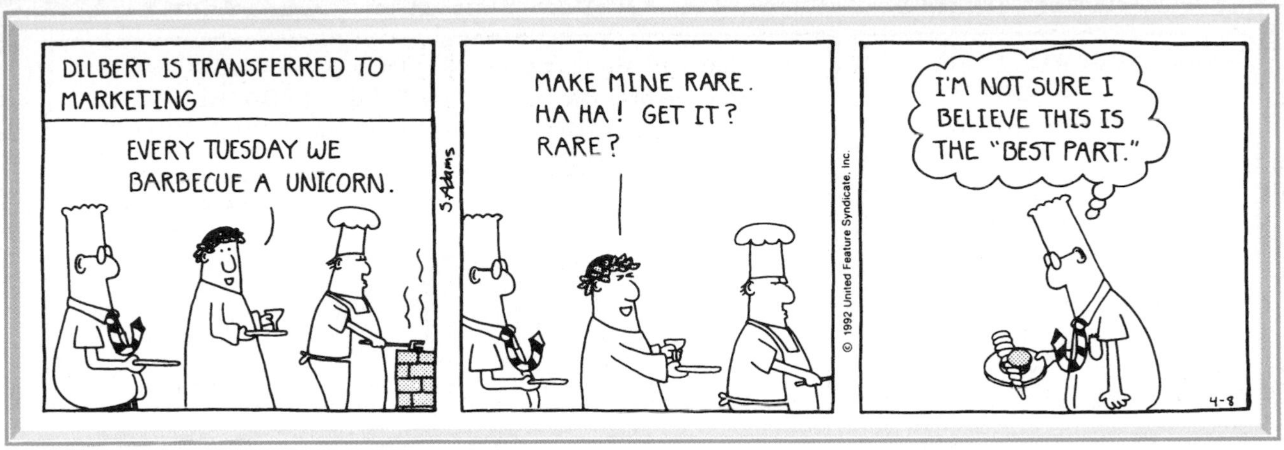
DILBERT IS TRANSFERRED TO MARKETING
EVERY TUESDAY WE BARBECUE A UNICORN.
MAKE MINE RARE. HA HA! GET IT? RARE?
I'M NOT SURE I BELIEVE THIS IS THE "BEST PART."
© 1992 United Feature Syndicate, Inc.

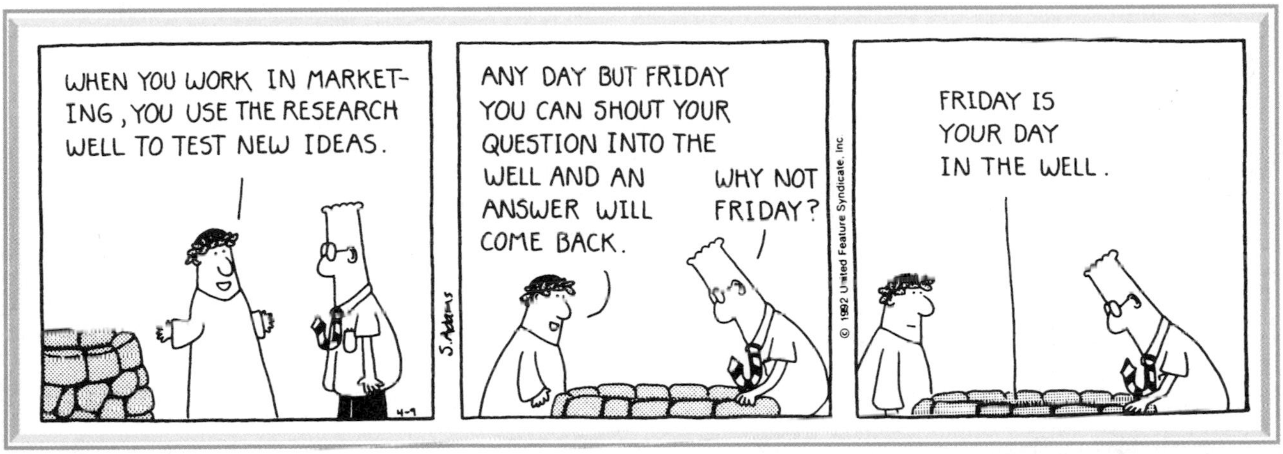
WHEN YOU WORK IN MARKETING, YOU USE THE RESEARCH WELL TO TEST NEW IDEAS.
ANY DAY BUT FRIDAY YOU CAN SHOUT YOUR QUESTION INTO THE WELL AND AN ANSWER WILL COME BACK.
WHY NOT FRIDAY?
FRIDAY IS YOUR DAY IN THE WELL.
© 1992 United Feature Syndicate, Inc.

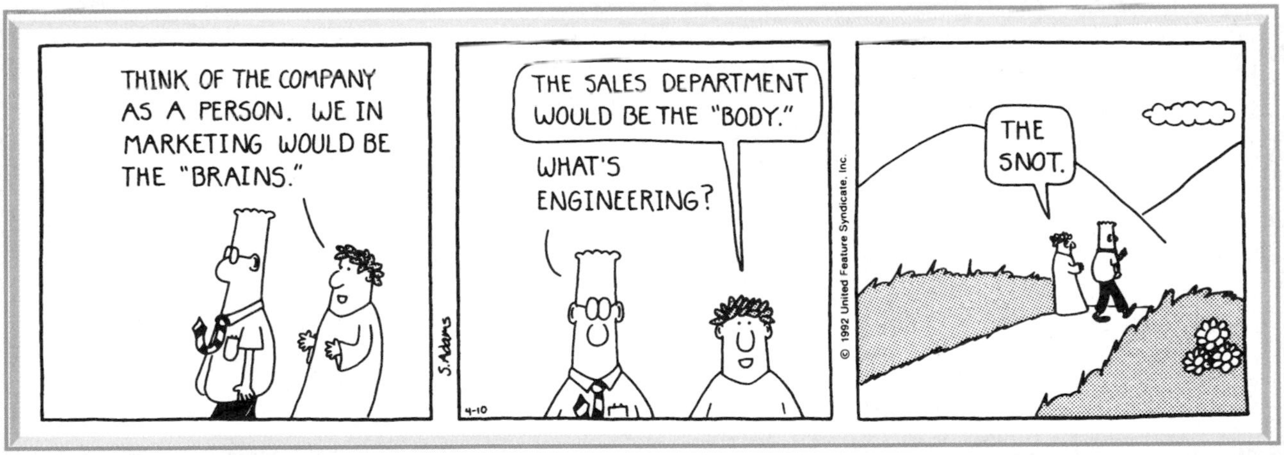
THINK OF THE COMPANY AS A PERSON. WE IN MARKETING WOULD BE THE "BRAINS."
THE SALES DEPARTMENT WOULD BE THE "BODY."
WHAT'S ENGINEERING?
THE SNOT.
© 1992 United Feature Syndicate, Inc.

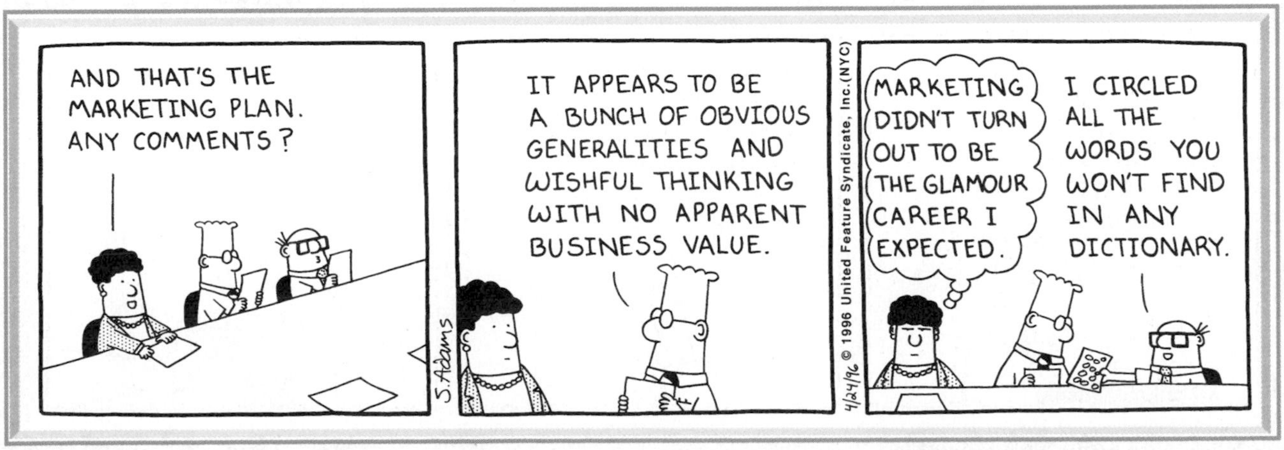
AND THAT'S THE MARKETING PLAN. ANY COMMENTS?
IT APPEARS TO BE A BUNCH OF OBVIOUS GENERALITIES AND WISHFUL THINKING WITH NO APPARENT BUSINESS VALUE.
MARKETING DIDN'T TURN OUT TO BE THE GLAMOUR CAREER I EXPECTED.
I CIRCLED ALL THE WORDS YOU WON'T FIND IN ANY DICTIONARY.
© 1996 United Feature Syndicate, Inc.(NYC)

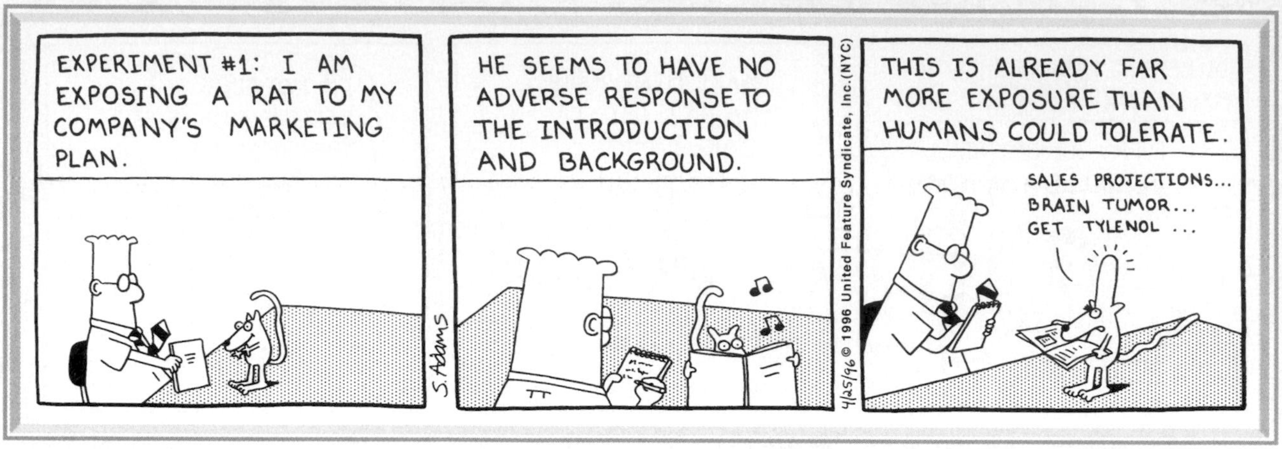
EXPERIMENT #1: I AM EXPOSING A RAT TO MY COMPANY'S MARKETING PLAN.
S. Adams
HE SEEMS TO HAVE NO ADVERSE RESPONSE TO THE INTRODUCTION AND BACKGROUND.
4/25/96 © 1996 United Feature Syndicate, Inc.(NYC)
THIS IS ALREADY FAR MORE EXPOSURE THAN HUMANS COULD TOLERATE.
SALES PROJECTIONS... BRAIN TUMOR... GET TYLENOL...

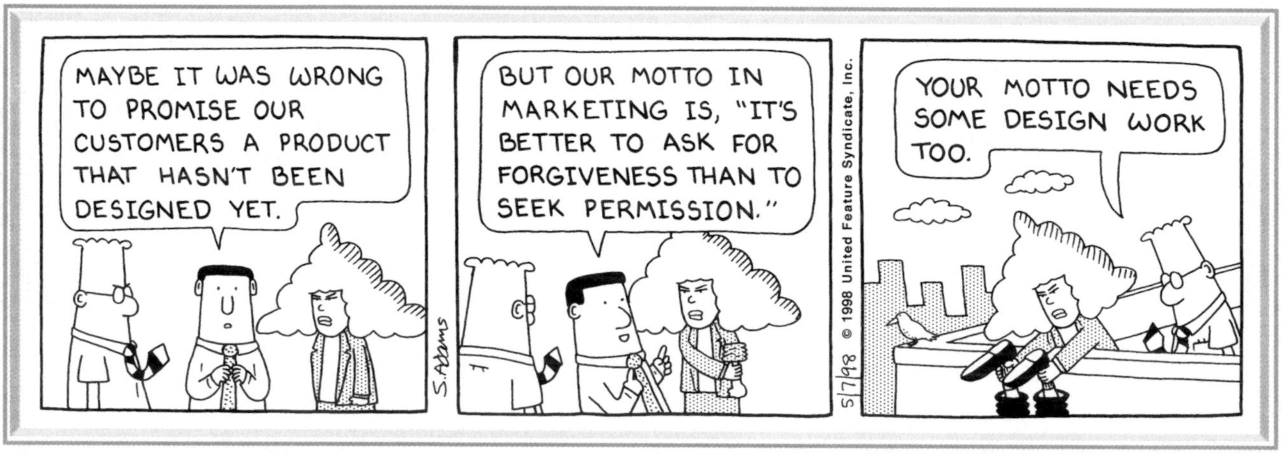
MAYBE IT WAS WRONG TO PROMISE OUR CUSTOMERS A PRODUCT THAT HASN'T BEEN DESIGNED YET.
S. Adams
BUT OUR MOTTO IN MARKETING IS, "IT'S BETTER TO ASK FOR FORGIVENESS THAN TO SEEK PERMISSION."
5/7/98 © 1998 United Feature Syndicate, Inc.
YOUR MOTTO NEEDS SOME DESIGN WORK TOO.

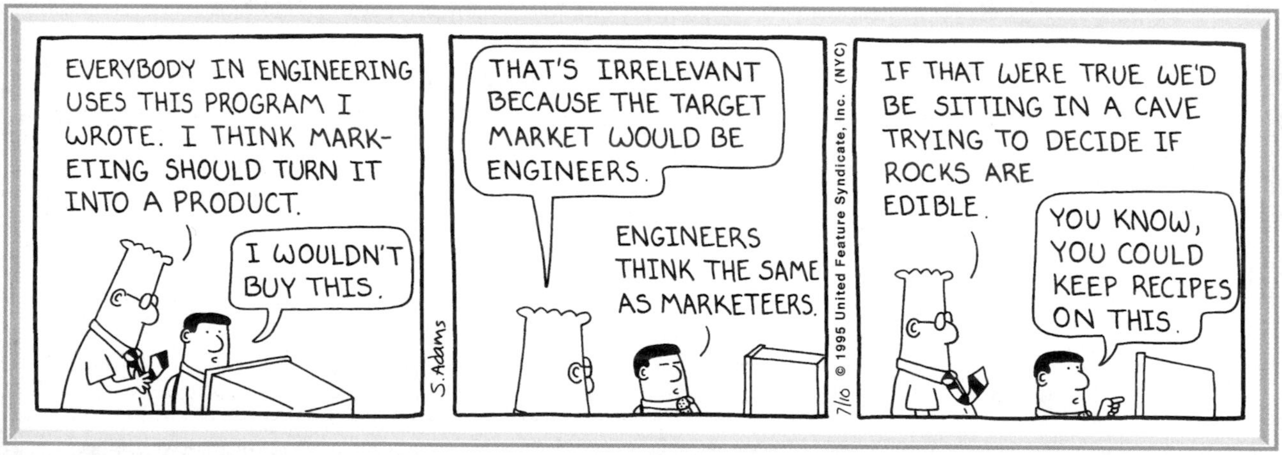
EVERYBODY IN ENGINEERING USES THIS PROGRAM I WROTE. I THINK MARK-ETING SHOULD TURN IT INTO A PRODUCT.
I WOULDN'T BUY THIS.
S. Adams
THAT'S IRRELEVANT BECAUSE THE TARGET MARKET WOULD BE ENGINEERS.
ENGINEERS THINK THE SAME AS MARKETEERS.
7/10 © 1995 United Feature Syndicate, Inc. (NYC)
IF THAT WERE TRUE WE'D BE SITTING IN A CAVE TRYING TO DECIDE IF ROCKS ARE EDIBLE.
YOU KNOW, YOU COULD KEEP RECIPES ON THIS.

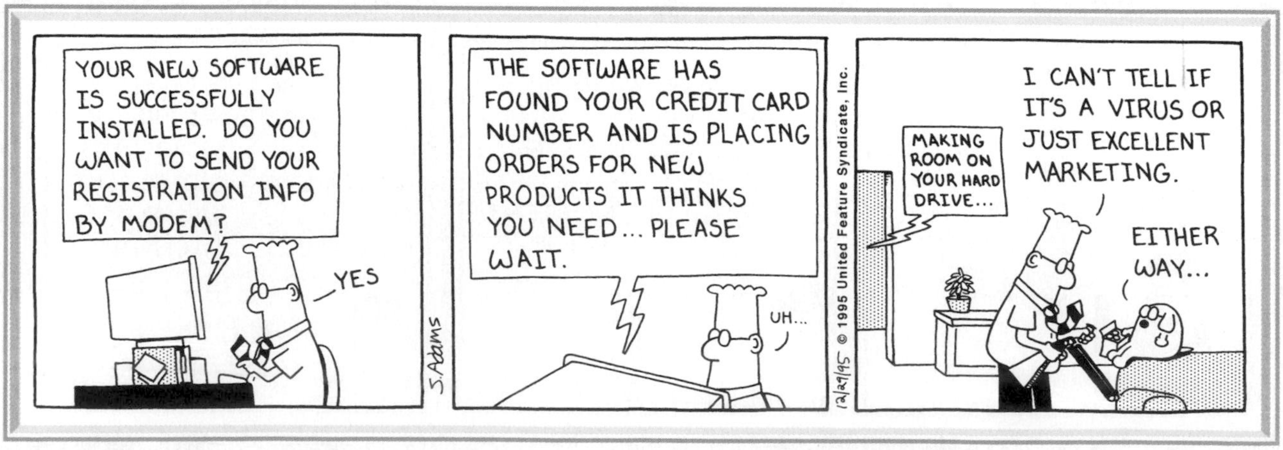
YOUR NEW SOFTWARE IS SUCCESSFULLY INSTALLED. DO YOU WANT TO SEND YOUR REGISTRATION INFO BY MODEM?
YES
S. Adams
THE SOFTWARE HAS FOUND YOUR CREDIT CARD NUMBER AND IS PLACING ORDERS FOR NEW PRODUCTS IT THINKS YOU NEED... PLEASE WAIT.
UH...
12/29/95 © 1995 United Feature Syndicate, Inc.
MAKING ROOM ON YOUR HARD DRIVE...
I CAN'T TELL IF IT'S A VIRUS OR JUST EXCELLENT MARKETING.
EITHER WAY...

MARKETING

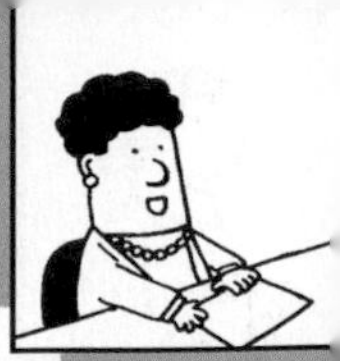

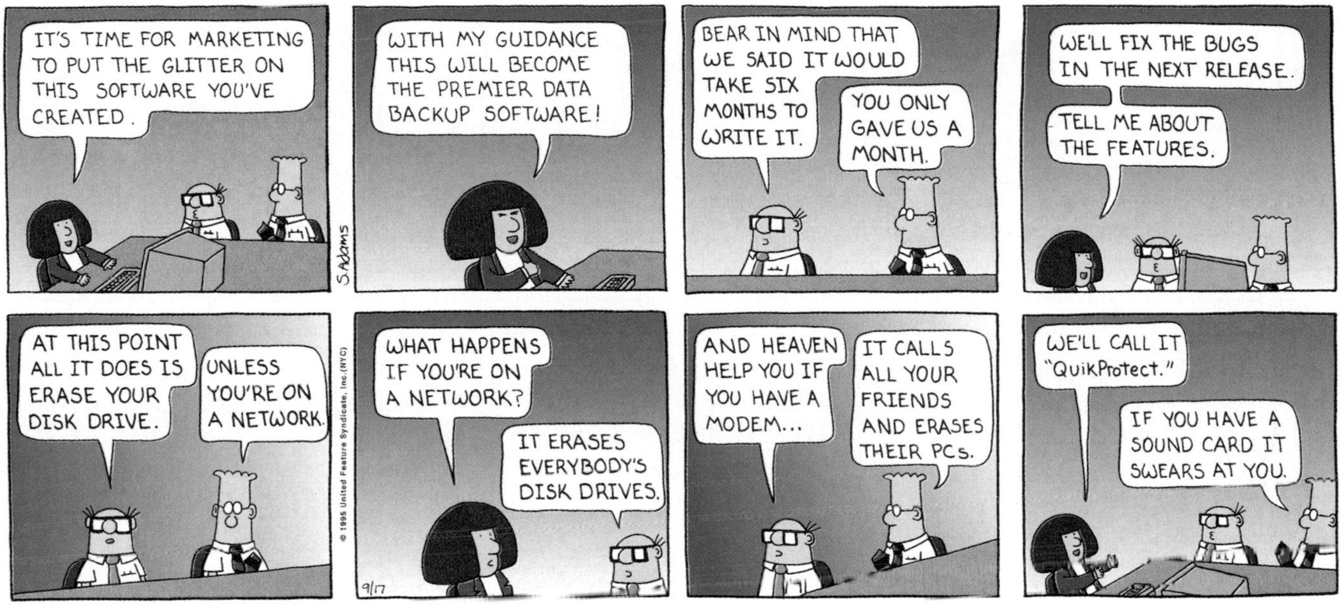
IT'S TIME FOR MARKETING TO PUT THE GLITTER ON THIS SOFTWARE YOU'VE CREATED.
WITH MY GUIDANCE THIS WILL BECOME THE PREMIER DATA BACKUP SOFTWARE!
BEAR IN MIND THAT WE SAID IT WOULD TAKE SIX MONTHS TO WRITE IT.
YOU ONLY GAVE US A MONTH.
WE'LL FIX THE BUGS IN THE NEXT RELEASE.
TELL ME ABOUT THE FEATURES.
AT THIS POINT ALL IT DOES IS ERASE YOUR DISK DRIVE.
UNLESS YOU'RE ON A NETWORK.
WHAT HAPPENS IF YOU'RE ON A NETWORK?
IT ERASES EVERYBODY'S DISK DRIVES.
AND HEAVEN HELP YOU IF YOU HAVE A MODEM...
IT CALLS ALL YOUR FRIENDS AND ERASES THEIR PCs.
WE'LL CALL IT "QuikProtect."
IF YOU HAVE A SOUND CARD IT SWEARS AT YOU.
S.Adams
© 1995 United Feature Syndicate, Inc.(NYC)
9/17

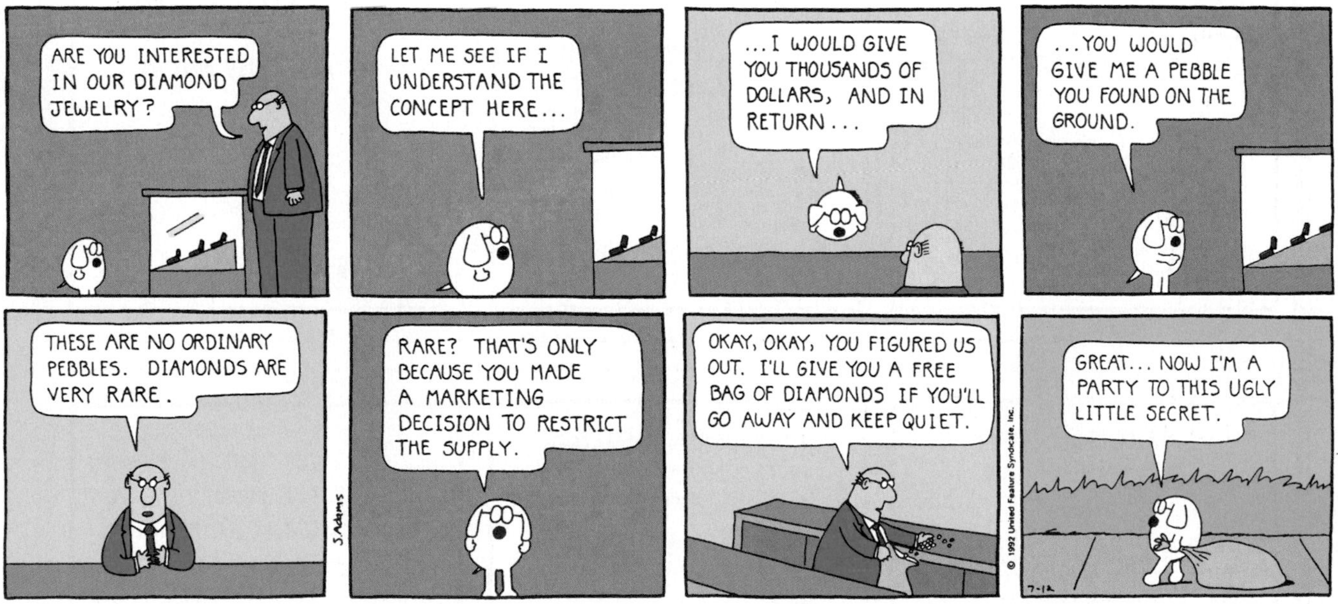
ARE YOU INTERESTED IN OUR DIAMOND JEWELRY?
LET ME SEE IF I UNDERSTAND THE CONCEPT HERE...
...I WOULD GIVE YOU THOUSANDS OF DOLLARS, AND IN RETURN...
...YOU WOULD GIVE ME A PEBBLE YOU FOUND ON THE GROUND.
THESE ARE NO ORDINARY PEBBLES. DIAMONDS ARE VERY RARE.
RARE? THAT'S ONLY BECAUSE YOU MADE A MARKETING DECISION TO RESTRICT THE SUPPLY.
OKAY, OKAY, YOU FIGURED US OUT. I'LL GIVE YOU A FREE BAG OF DIAMONDS IF YOU'LL GO AWAY AND KEEP QUIET.
GREAT... NOW I'M A PARTY TO THIS UGLY LITTLE SECRET.
S.Adams
© 1992 United Feature Syndicate, Inc.
7-12

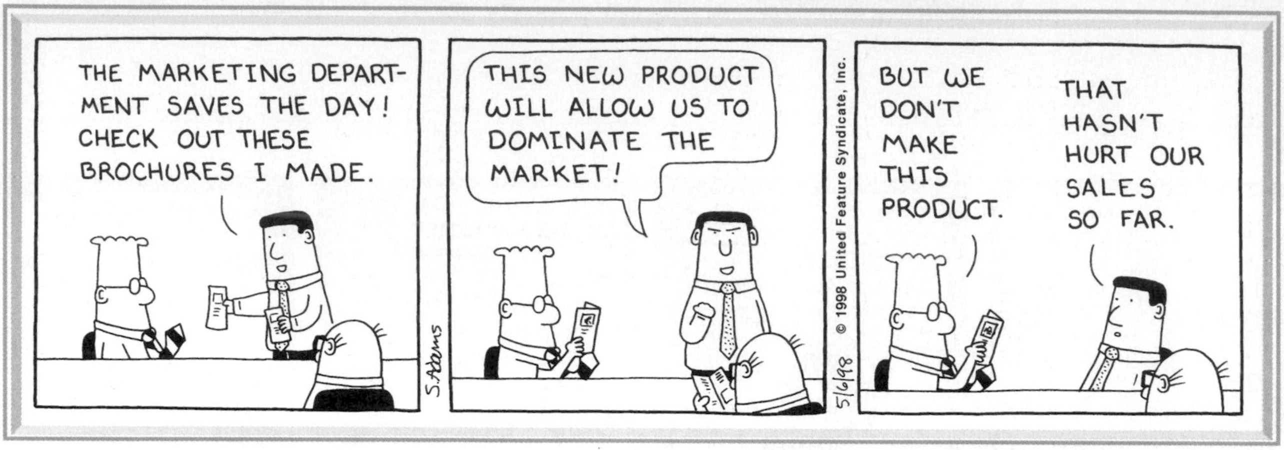
THE MARKETING DEPARTMENT SAVES THE DAY! CHECK OUT THESE BROCHURES I MADE.
THIS NEW PRODUCT WILL ALLOW US TO DOMINATE THE MARKET!
BUT WE DON'T MAKE THIS PRODUCT.
THAT HASN'T HURT OUR SALES SO FAR.
© 1998 United Feature Syndicate, Inc.
5/6/98

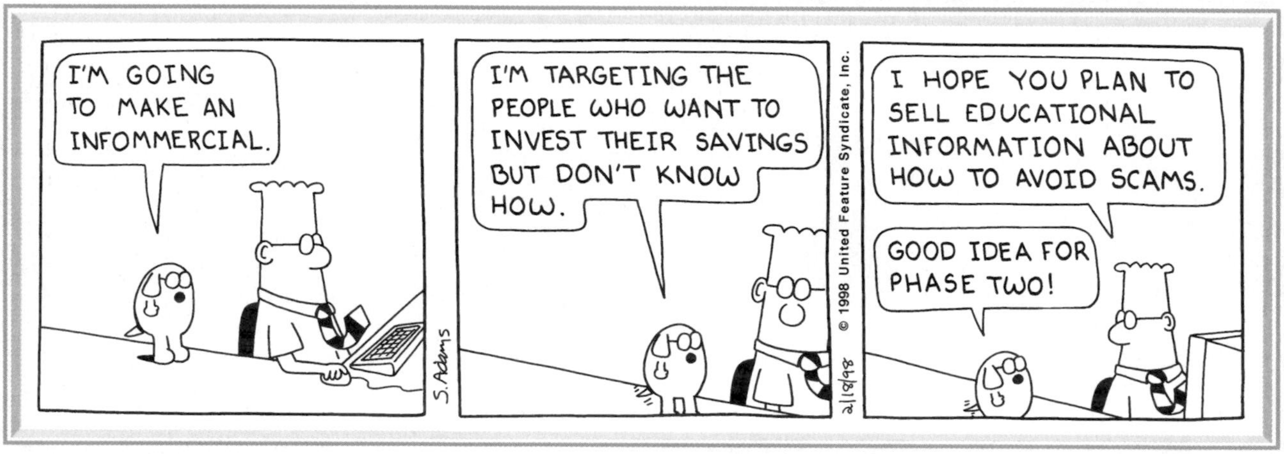
I'M GOING TO MAKE AN INFOMMERCIAL.
I'M TARGETING THE PEOPLE WHO WANT TO INVEST THEIR SAVINGS BUT DON'T KNOW HOW.
I HOPE YOU PLAN TO SELL EDUCATIONAL INFORMATION ABOUT HOW TO AVOID SCAMS.
GOOD IDEA FOR PHASE TWO!
© 1998 United Feature Syndicate, Inc.
2/19/98

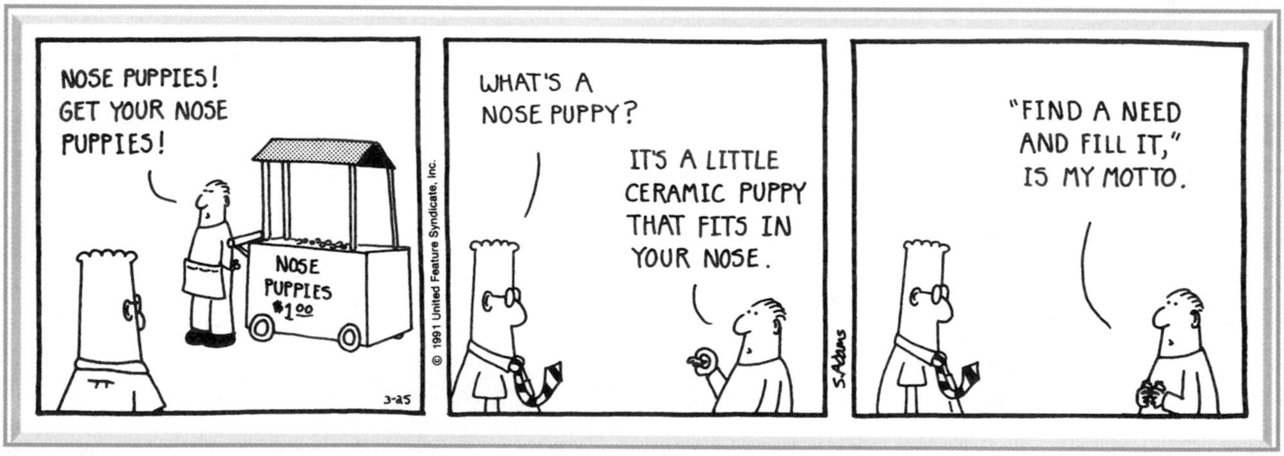
NOSE PUPPIES! GET YOUR NOSE PUPPIES!
NOSE PUPPIES $1.00
3-25
© 1991 United Feature Syndicate, Inc.
WHAT'S A NOSE PUPPY?
IT'S A LITTLE CERAMIC PUPPY THAT FITS IN YOUR NOSE.
"FIND A NEED AND FILL IT," IS MY MOTTO.

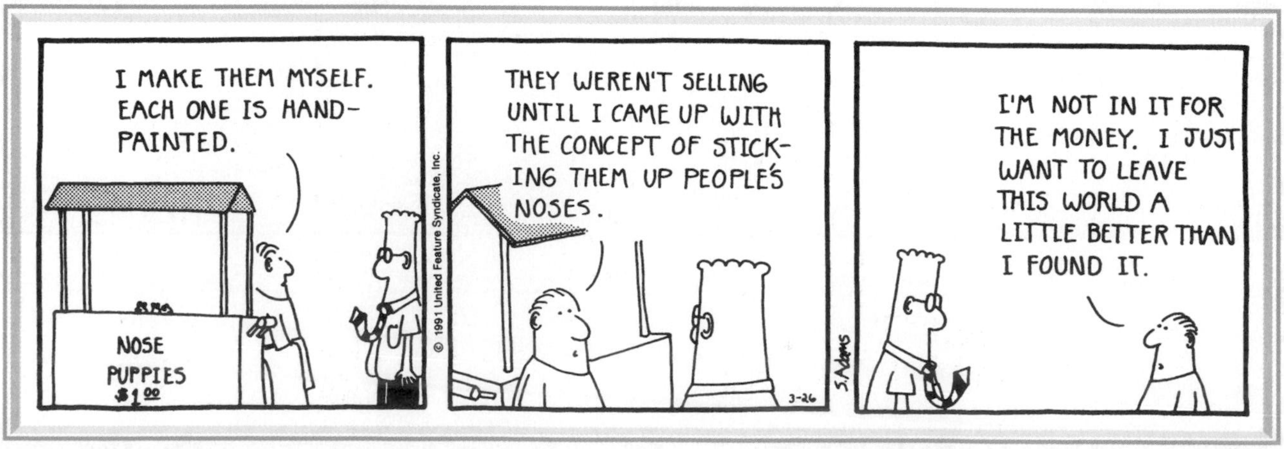
I MAKE THEM MYSELF. EACH ONE IS HAND-PAINTED.
NOSE PUPPIES $1.00
© 1991 United Feature Syndicate, Inc.
THEY WEREN'T SELLING UNTIL I CAME UP WITH THE CONCEPT OF STICKING THEM UP PEOPLE'S NOSES.
3-26
I'M NOT IN IT FOR THE MONEY. I JUST WANT TO LEAVE THIS WORLD A LITTLE BETTER THAN I FOUND IT.

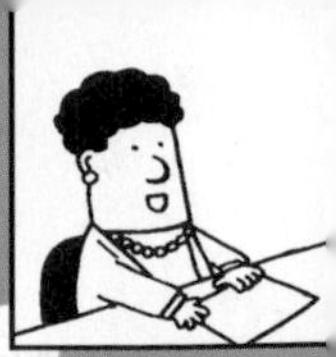

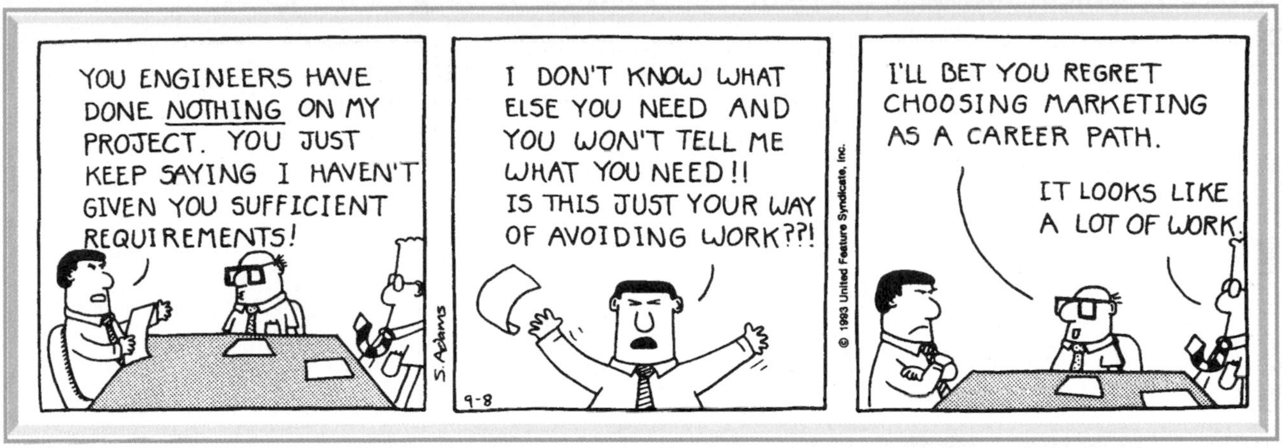
YOU ENGINEERS HAVE DONE NOTHING ON MY PROJECT. YOU JUST KEEP SAYING I HAVEN'T GIVEN YOU SUFFICIENT REQUIREMENTS!
S. Adams
I DON'T KNOW WHAT ELSE YOU NEED AND YOU WON'T TELL ME WHAT YOU NEED!! IS THIS JUST YOUR WAY OF AVOIDING WORK??!
9-8
© 1993 United Feature Syndicate, Inc.
I'LL BET YOU REGRET CHOOSING MARKETING AS A CAREER PATH.
IT LOOKS LIKE A LOT OF WORK.

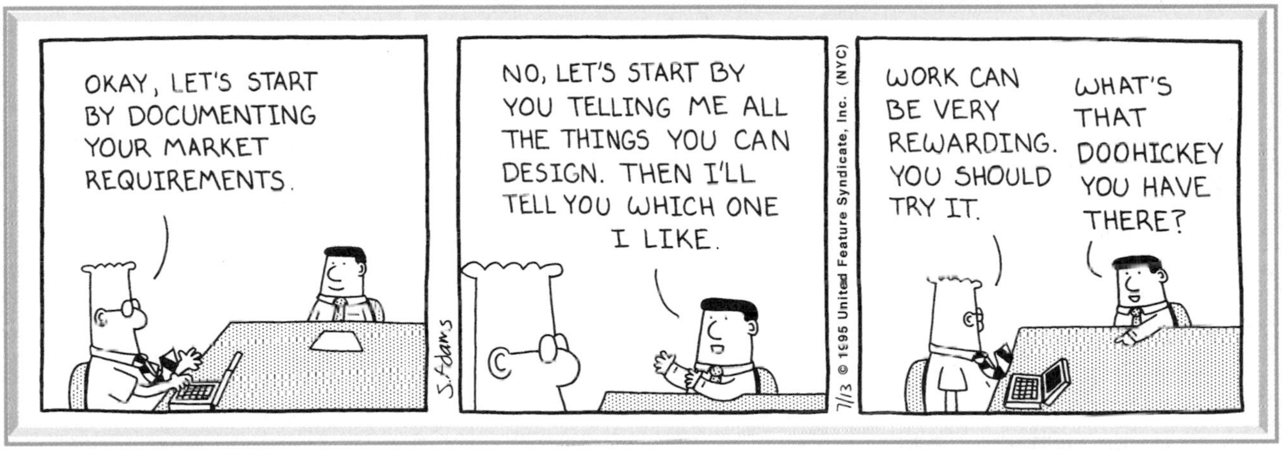
OKAY, LET'S START BY DOCUMENTING YOUR MARKET REQUIREMENTS.
S. Adams
NO, LET'S START BY YOU TELLING ME ALL THE THINGS YOU CAN DESIGN. THEN I'LL TELL YOU WHICH ONE I LIKE.
7/3 © 1995 United Feature Syndicate, Inc. (NYC)
WORK CAN BE VERY REWARDING. YOU SHOULD TRY IT.
WHAT'S THAT DOOHICKEY YOU HAVE THERE?

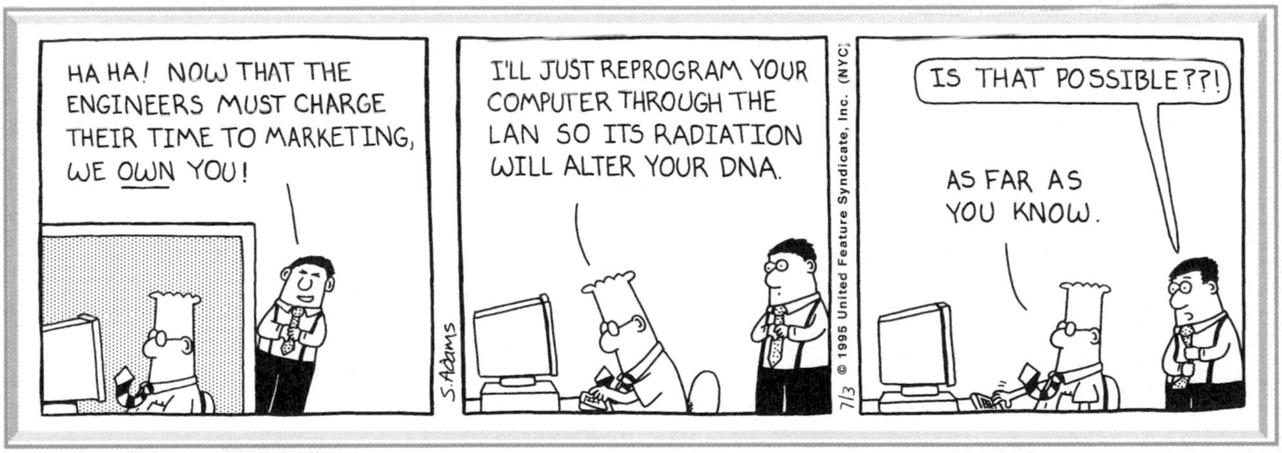
HA HA! NOW THAT THE ENGINEERS MUST CHARGE THEIR TIME TO MARKETING, WE OWN YOU!
S. Adams
I'LL JUST REPROGRAM YOUR COMPUTER THROUGH THE LAN SO ITS RADIATION WILL ALTER YOUR DNA.
7/3 © 1995 United Feature Syndicate, Inc. (NYC)
IS THAT POSSIBLE??!
AS FAR AS YOU KNOW.

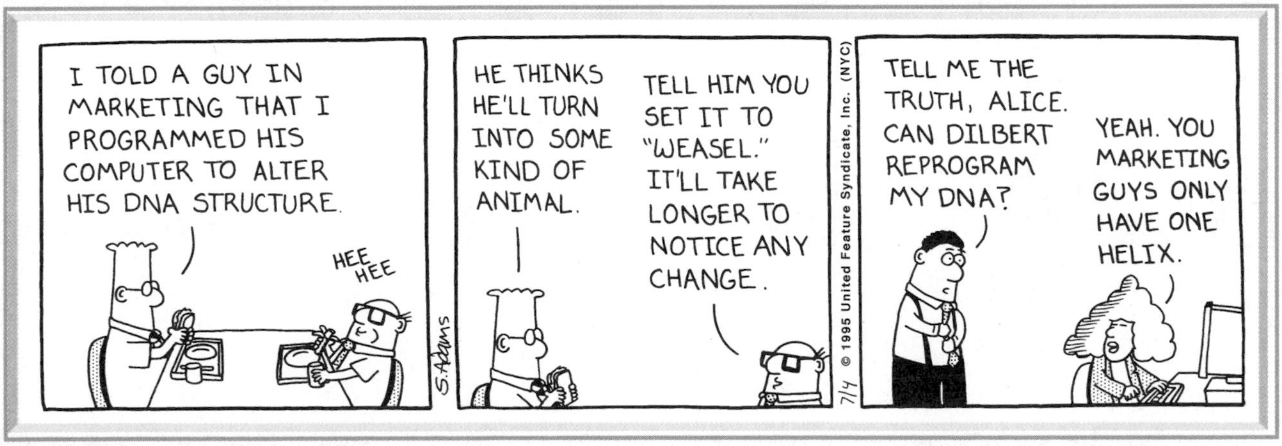
I TOLD A GUY IN MARKETING THAT I PROGRAMMED HIS COMPUTER TO ALTER HIS DNA STRUCTURE.
HEE HEE
S. Adams
HE THINKS HE'LL TURN INTO SOME KIND OF ANIMAL.
TELL HIM YOU SET IT TO "WEASEL." IT'LL TAKE LONGER TO NOTICE ANY CHANGE.
7/4 © 1995 United Feature Syndicate, Inc. (NYC)
TELL ME THE TRUTH, ALICE. CAN DILBERT REPROGRAM MY DNA?
YEAH. YOU MARKETING GUYS ONLY HAVE ONE HELIX.

MARKETING

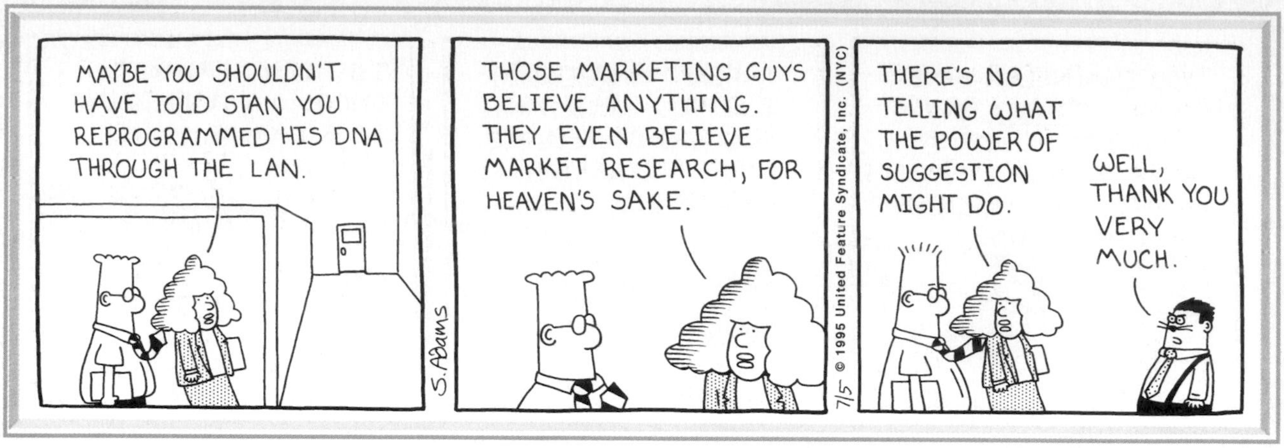
MAYBE YOU SHOULDN'T HAVE TOLD STAN YOU REPROGRAMMED HIS DNA THROUGH THE LAN.
THOSE MARKETING GUYS BELIEVE ANYTHING. THEY EVEN BELIEVE MARKET RESEARCH, FOR HEAVEN'S SAKE.
THERE'S NO TELLING WHAT THE POWER OF SUGGESTION MIGHT DO.
WELL, THANK YOU VERY MUCH.
S. Adams
7/5 © 1995 United Feature Syndicate, Inc. (NYC)

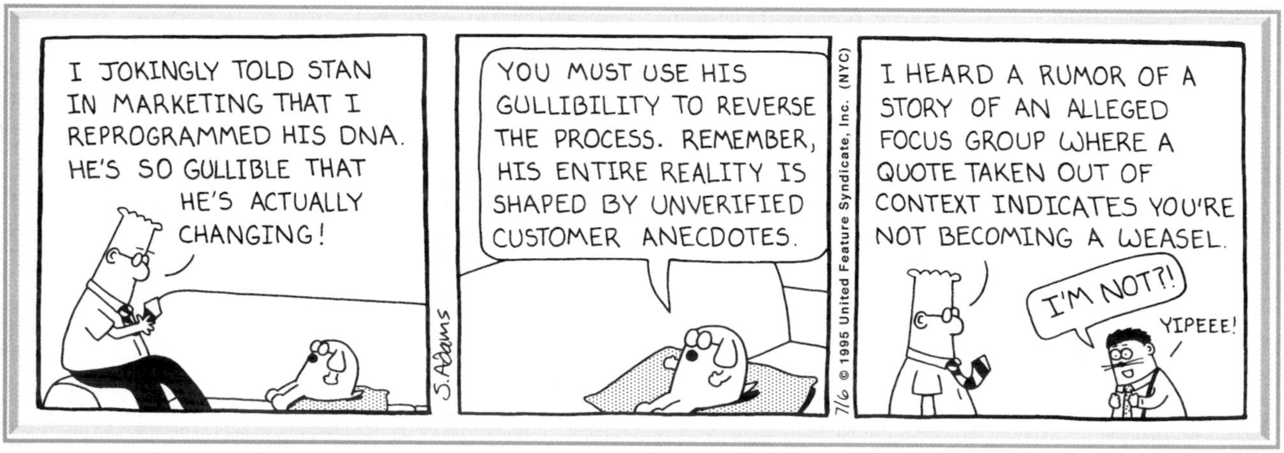
I JOKINGLY TOLD STAN IN MARKETING THAT I REPROGRAMMED HIS DNA. HE'S SO GULLIBLE THAT HE'S ACTUALLY CHANGING!
YOU MUST USE HIS GULLIBILITY TO REVERSE THE PROCESS. REMEMBER, HIS ENTIRE REALITY IS SHAPED BY UNVERIFIED CUSTOMER ANECDOTES.
I HEARD A RUMOR OF A STORY OF AN ALLEGED FOCUS GROUP WHERE A QUOTE TAKEN OUT OF CONTEXT INDICATES YOU'RE NOT BECOMING A WEASEL.
I'M NOT?!
YIPEEE!
S. Adams
7/6 © 1995 United Feature Syndicate, Inc. (NYC)

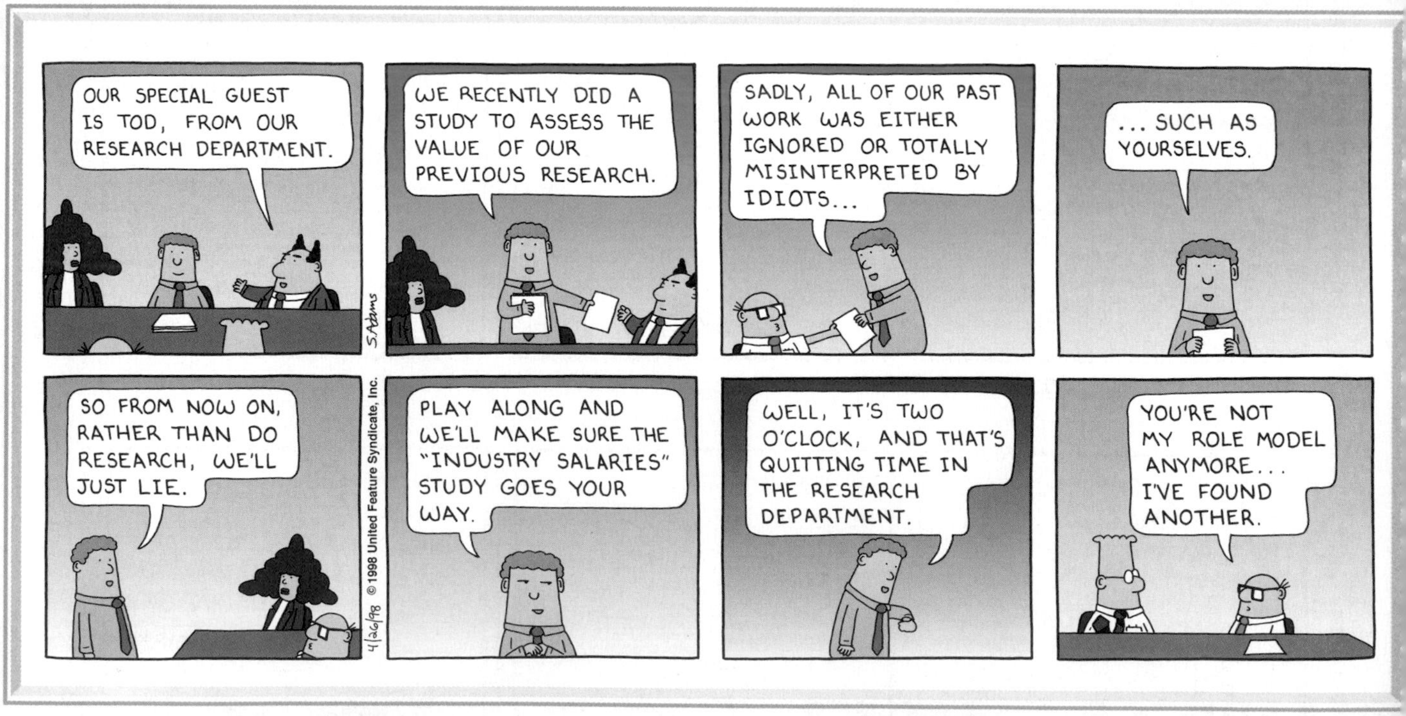
OUR SPECIAL GUEST IS TOD, FROM OUR RESEARCH DEPARTMENT.
WE RECENTLY DID A STUDY TO ASSESS THE VALUE OF OUR PREVIOUS RESEARCH.
SADLY, ALL OF OUR PAST WORK WAS EITHER IGNORED OR TOTALLY MISINTERPRETED BY IDIOTS...
... SUCH AS YOURSELVES.
SO FROM NOW ON, RATHER THAN DO RESEARCH, WE'LL JUST LIE.
PLAY ALONG AND WE'LL MAKE SURE THE "INDUSTRY SALARIES" STUDY GOES YOUR WAY.
WELL, IT'S TWO O'CLOCK, AND THAT'S QUITTING TIME IN THE RESEARCH DEPARTMENT.
YOU'RE NOT MY ROLE MODEL ANYMORE... I'VE FOUND ANOTHER.
S. Adams
4/26/98 © 1998 United Feature Syndicate, Inc.

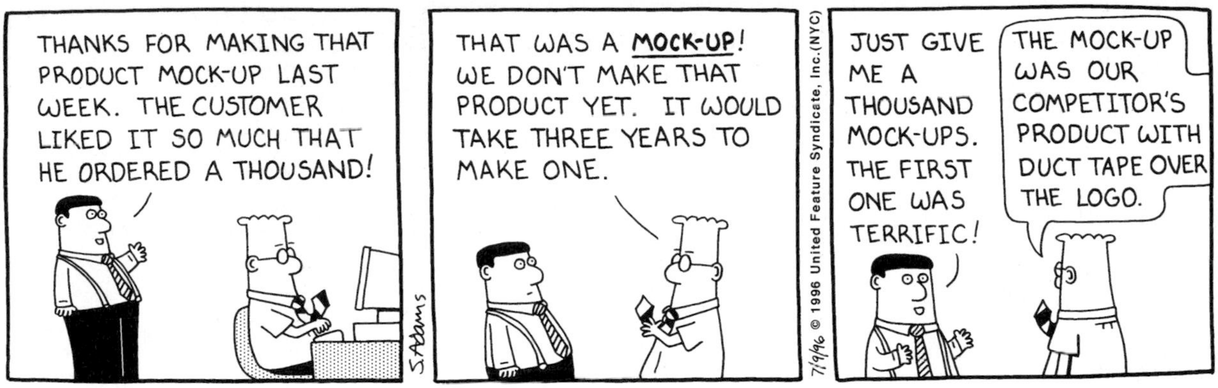
THANKS FOR MAKING THAT PRODUCT MOCK-UP LAST WEEK. THE CUSTOMER LIKED IT SO MUCH THAT HE ORDERED A THOUSAND!
S. Adams
THAT WAS A MOCK-UP! WE DON'T MAKE THAT PRODUCT YET. IT WOULD TAKE THREE YEARS TO MAKE ONE.
7/9/96 © 1996 United Feature Syndicate, Inc.(NYC)
JUST GIVE ME A THOUSAND MOCK-UPS. THE FIRST ONE WAS TERRIFIC!
THE MOCK-UP WAS OUR COMPETITOR'S PRODUCT WITH DUCT TAPE OVER THE LOGO.

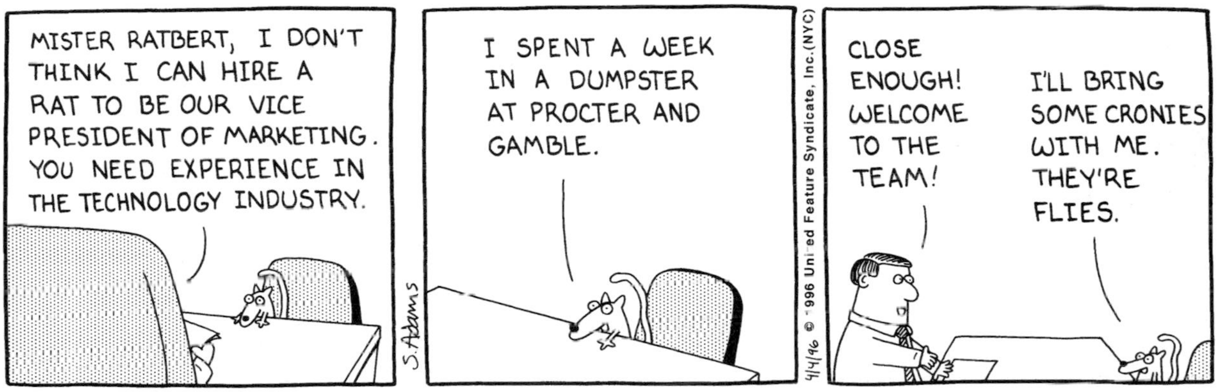
MISTER RATBERT, I DON'T THINK I CAN HIRE A RAT TO BE OUR VICE PRESIDENT OF MARKETING. YOU NEED EXPERIENCE IN THE TECHNOLOGY INDUSTRY.
S. Adams
I SPENT A WEEK IN A DUMPSTER AT PROCTER AND GAMBLE.
4/4/96 © 1996 United Feature Syndicate, Inc.(NYC)
CLOSE ENOUGH! WELCOME TO THE TEAM!
I'LL BRING SOME CRONIES WITH ME. THEY'RE FLIES.

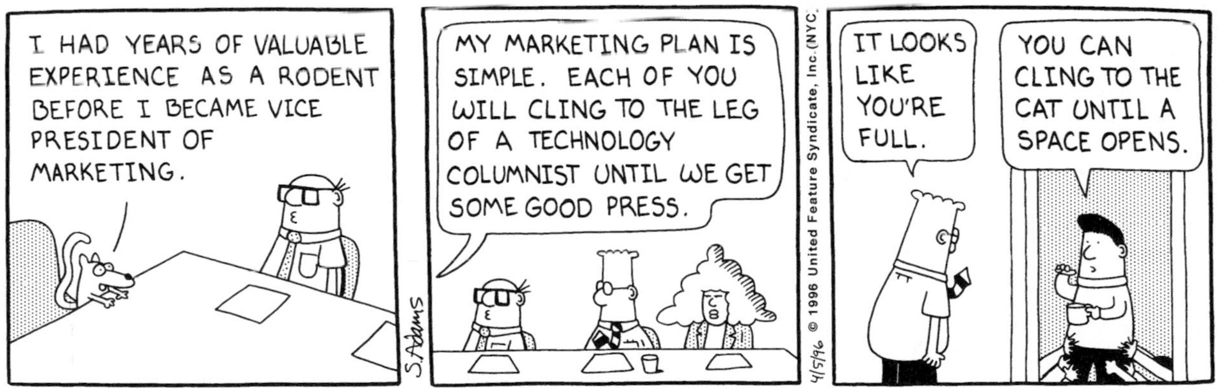
I HAD YEARS OF VALUABLE EXPERIENCE AS A RODENT BEFORE I BECAME VICE PRESIDENT OF MARKETING.
S. Adams
MY MARKETING PLAN IS SIMPLE. EACH OF YOU WILL CLING TO THE LEG OF A TECHNOLOGY COLUMNIST UNTIL WE GET SOME GOOD PRESS.
4/5/96 © 1996 United Feature Syndicate, Inc.(NYC)
IT LOOKS LIKE YOU'RE FULL.
YOU CAN CLING TO THE CAT UNTIL A SPACE OPENS.

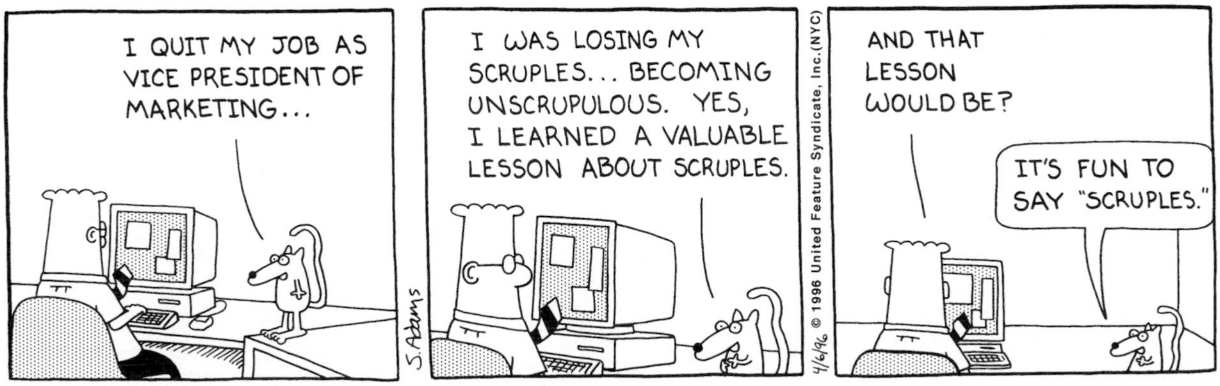
I QUIT MY JOB AS VICE PRESIDENT OF MARKETING...
S. Adams
I WAS LOSING MY SCRUPLES... BECOMING UNSCRUPULOUS. YES, I LEARNED A VALUABLE LESSON ABOUT SCRUPLES.
4/6/96 © 1996 United Feature Syndicate, Inc.(NYC)
AND THAT LESSON WOULD BE?
IT'S FUN TO SAY "SCRUPLES."

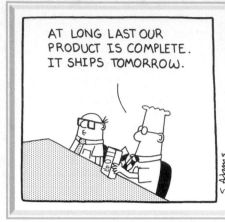

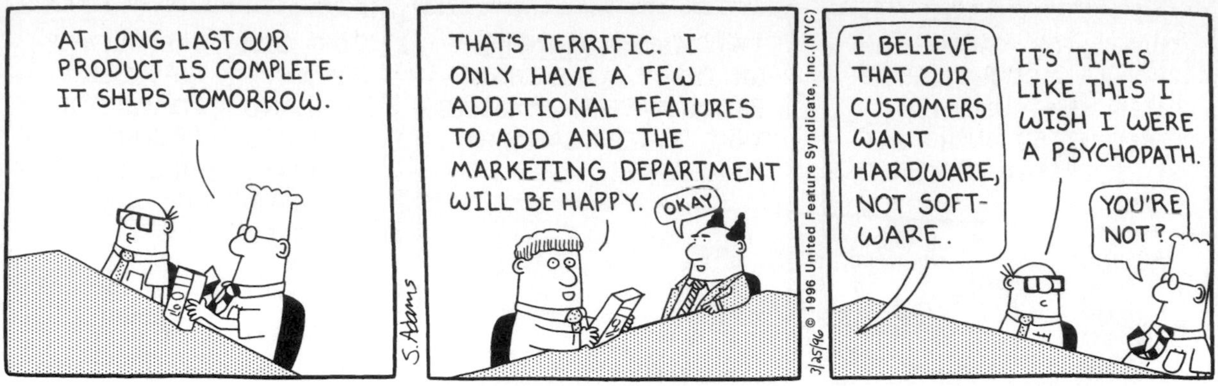
AT LONG LAST OUR PRODUCT IS COMPLETE. IT SHIPS TOMORROW.
THAT'S TERRIFIC. I ONLY HAVE A FEW ADDITIONAL FEATURES TO ADD AND THE MARKETING DEPARTMENT WILL BE HAPPY.
OKAY
S. Adams
3/25/96 © 1996 United Feature Syndicate, Inc.(NYC)
I BELIEVE THAT OUR CUSTOMERS WANT HARDWARE, NOT SOFT-WARE.
IT'S TIMES LIKE THIS I WISH I WERE A PSYCHOPATH.
YOU'RE NOT?

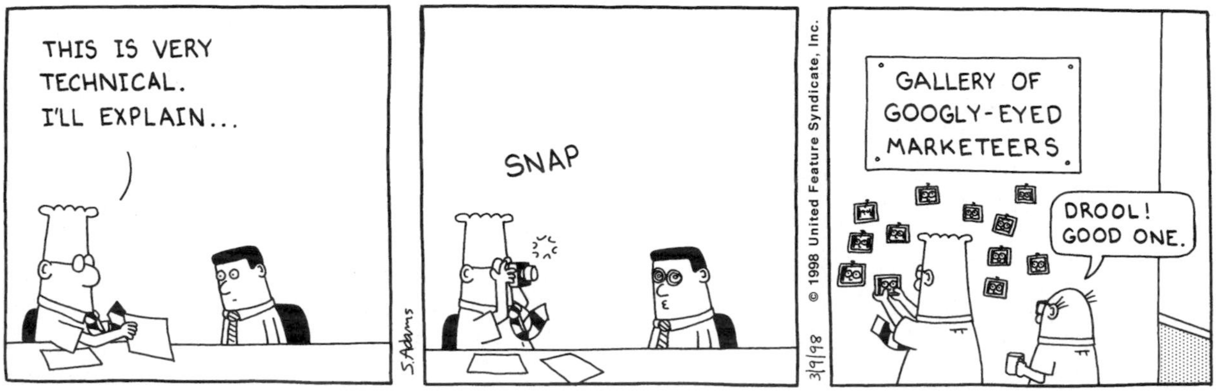
THIS IS VERY TECHNICAL. I'LL EXPLAIN...
S. Adams
SNAP
3/9/98 © 1998 United Feature Syndicate, Inc.
GALLERY OF GOOGLY-EYED MARKETEERS
DROOL! GOOD ONE.

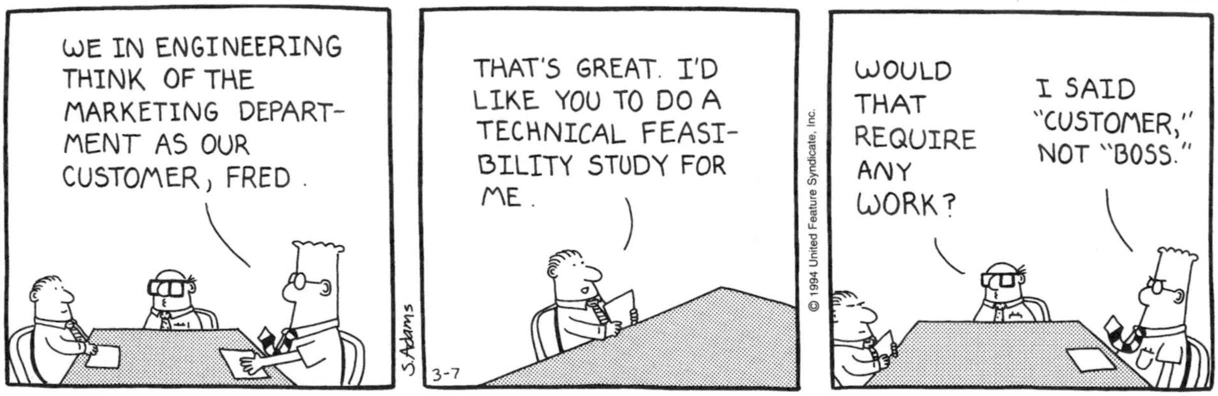
WE IN ENGINEERING THINK OF THE MARKETING DEPART-MENT AS OUR CUSTOMER, FRED.
S. Adams
THAT'S GREAT. I'D LIKE YOU TO DO A TECHNICAL FEASI-BILITY STUDY FOR ME.
3-7
© 1994 United Feature Syndicate, Inc.
WOULD THAT REQUIRE ANY WORK?
I SAID "CUSTOMER," NOT "BOSS."

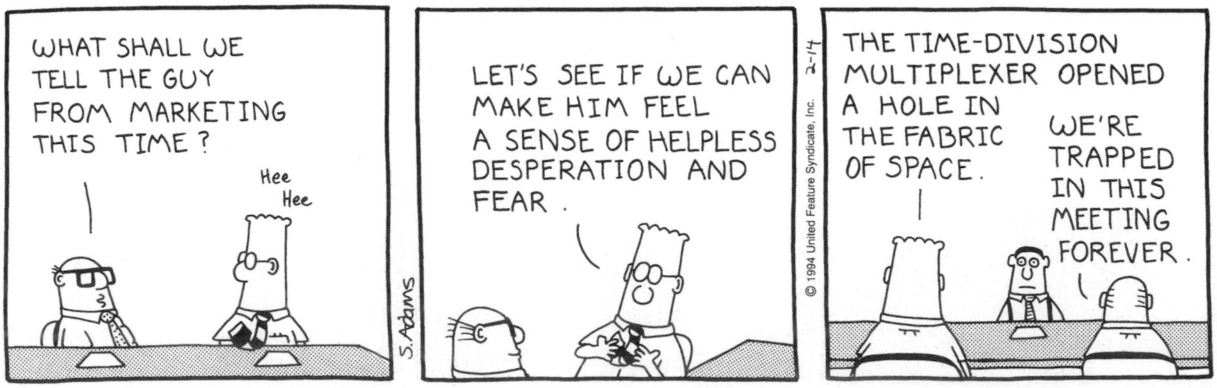
WHAT SHALL WE TELL THE GUY FROM MARKETING THIS TIME?
Hee Hee
S. Adams
LET'S SEE IF WE CAN MAKE HIM FEEL A SENSE OF HELPLESS DESPERATION AND FEAR.
2-14
© 1994 United Feature Syndicate, Inc.
THE TIME-DIVISION MULTIPLEXER OPENED A HOLE IN THE FABRIC OF SPACE.
WE'RE TRAPPED IN THIS MEETING FOREVER.

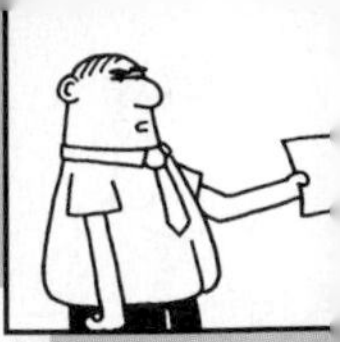

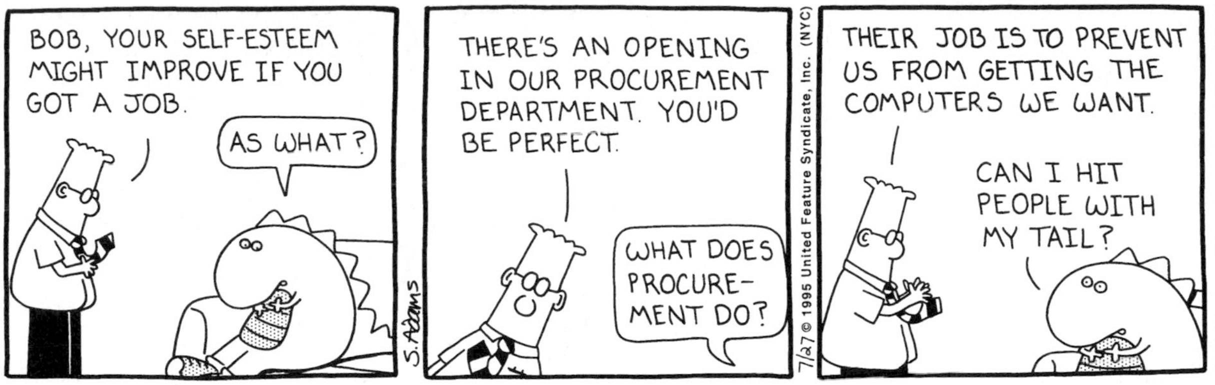
BOB, YOUR SELF-ESTEEM MIGHT IMPROVE IF YOU GOT A JOB.
AS WHAT?
THERE'S AN OPENING IN OUR PROCUREMENT DEPARTMENT. YOU'D BE PERFECT.
WHAT DOES PROCURE-MENT DO?
THEIR JOB IS TO PREVENT US FROM GETTING THE COMPUTERS WE WANT.
CAN I HIT PEOPLE WITH MY TAIL?
7/27 © 1995 United Feature Syndicate, Inc. (NYC)

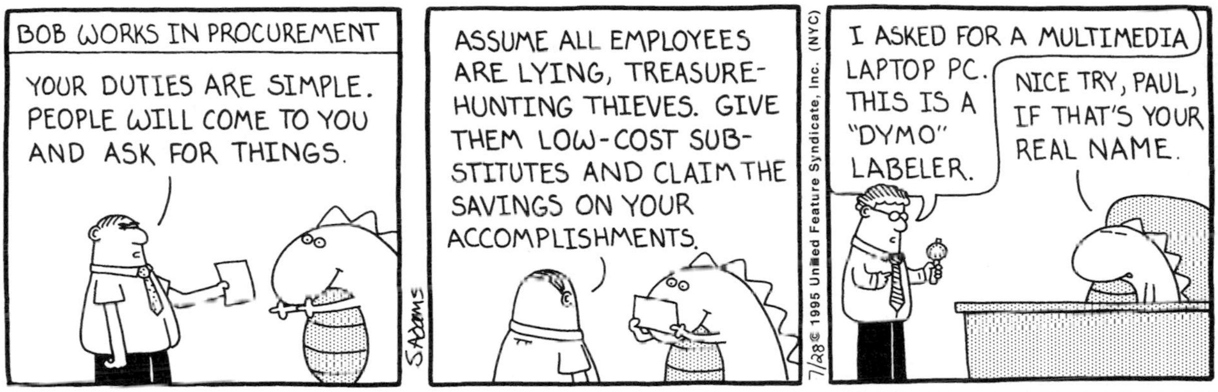
BOB WORKS IN PROCUREMENT
YOUR DUTIES ARE SIMPLE. PEOPLE WILL COME TO YOU AND ASK FOR THINGS.
ASSUME ALL EMPLOYEES ARE LYING, TREASURE-HUNTING THIEVES. GIVE THEM LOW-COST SUB-STITUTES AND CLAIM THE SAVINGS ON YOUR ACCOMPLISHMENTS.
I ASKED FOR A MULTIMEDIA LAPTOP PC. THIS IS A "DYMO" LABELER.
NICE TRY, PAUL, IF THAT'S YOUR REAL NAME.
7/28 © 1995 United Feature Syndicate, Inc. (NYC)

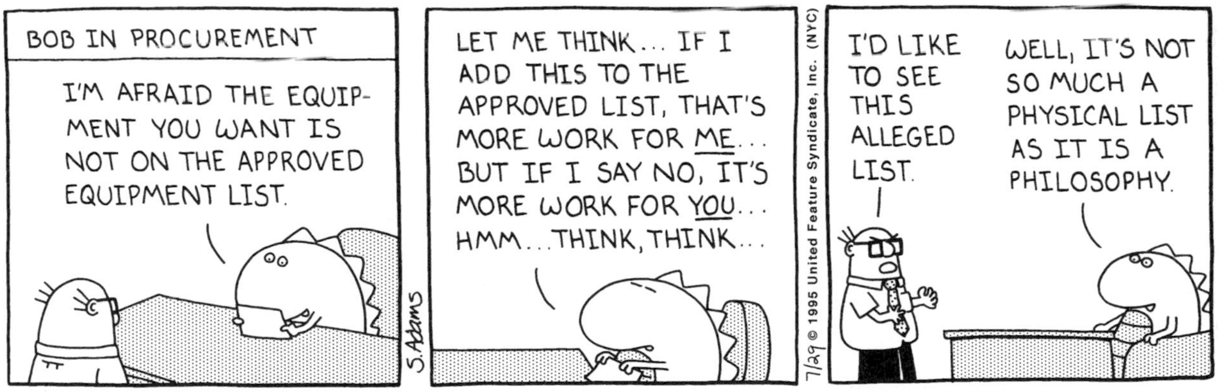
BOB IN PROCUREMENT
I'M AFRAID THE EQUIP-MENT YOU WANT IS NOT ON THE APPROVED EQUIPMENT LIST.
LET ME THINK... IF I ADD THIS TO THE APPROVED LIST, THAT'S MORE WORK FOR ME... BUT IF I SAY NO, IT'S MORE WORK FOR YOU... HMM...THINK, THINK...
I'D LIKE TO SEE THIS ALLEGED LIST.
WELL, IT'S NOT SO MUCH A PHYSICAL LIST AS IT IS A PHILOSOPHY.
7/29 © 1995 United Feature Syndicate, Inc. (NYC)

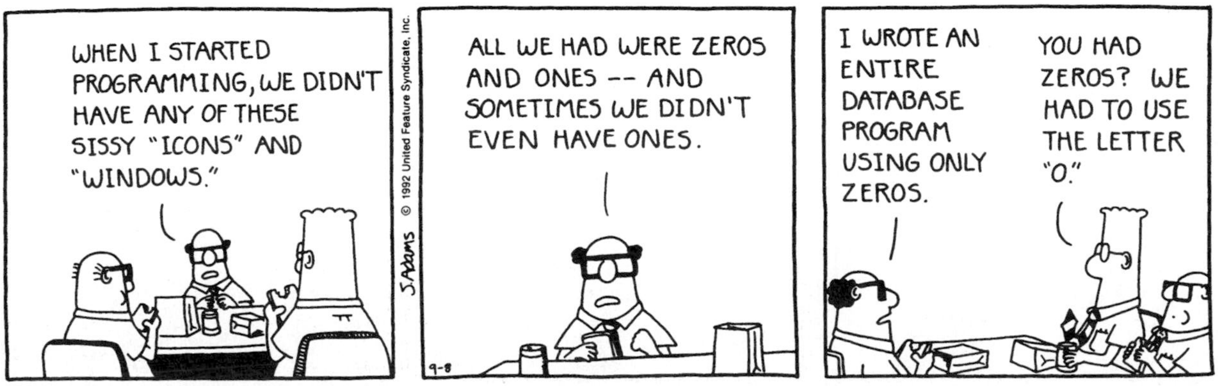
WHEN I STARTED PROGRAMMING, WE DIDN'T HAVE ANY OF THESE SISSY "ICONS" AND "WINDOWS."
ALL WE HAD WERE ZEROS AND ONES -- AND SOMETIMES WE DIDN'T EVEN HAVE ONES.
I WROTE AN ENTIRE DATABASE PROGRAM USING ONLY ZEROS.
YOU HAD ZEROS? WE HAD TO USE THE LETTER "O."
© 1992 United Feature Syndicate, Inc.
9-8

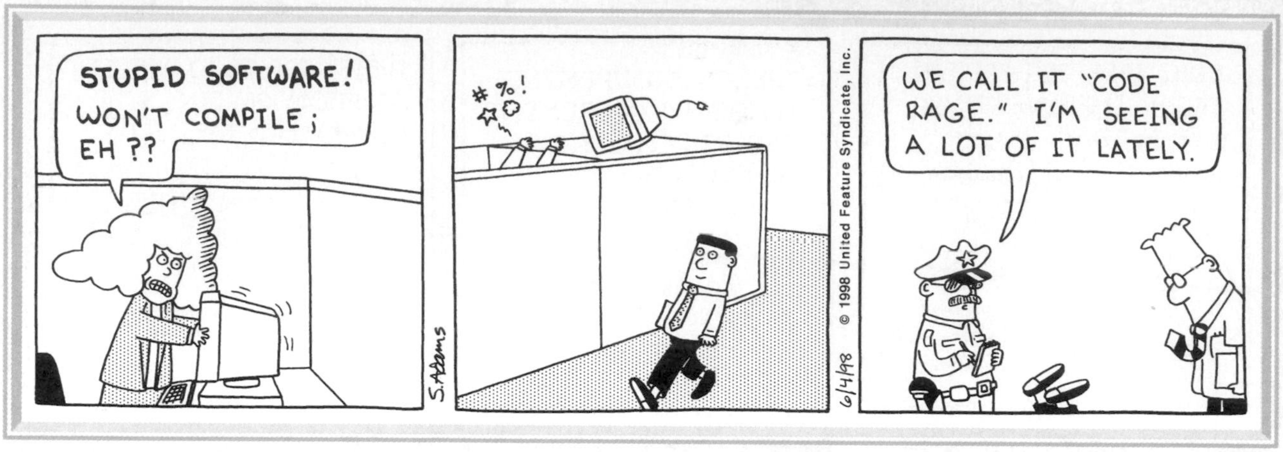
STUPID SOFTWARE! WON'T COMPILE; EH ??
%!
S. Adams
6/4/98 © 1998 United Feature Syndicate, Inc.
WE CALL IT "CODE RAGE." I'M SEEING A LOT OF IT LATELY.

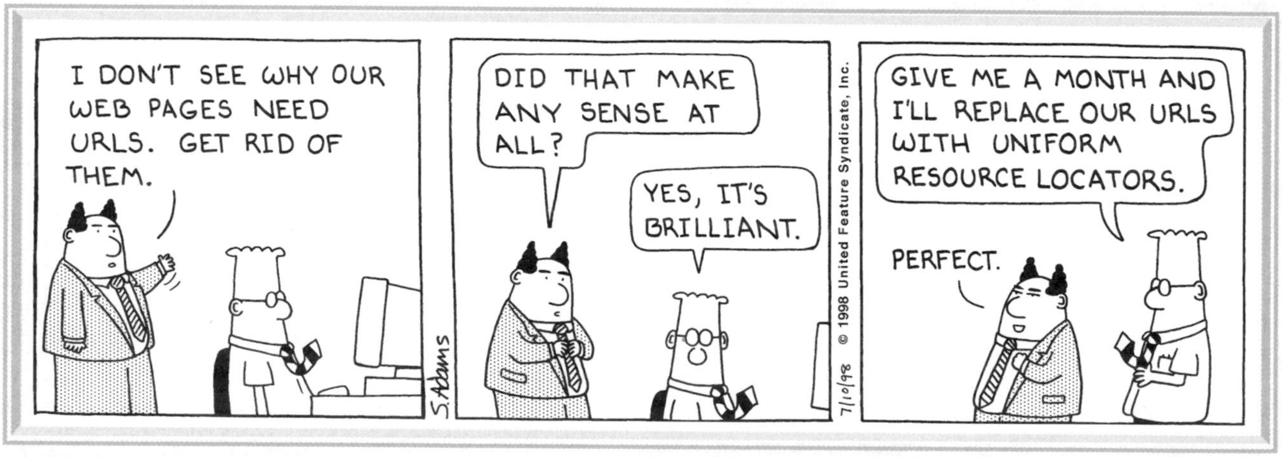
I DON'T SEE WHY OUR WEB PAGES NEED URLS. GET RID OF THEM.
S. Adams
DID THAT MAKE ANY SENSE AT ALL?
YES, IT'S BRILLIANT.
7/10/98 © 1998 United Feature Syndicate, Inc.
GIVE ME A MONTH AND I'LL REPLACE OUR URLS WITH UNIFORM RESOURCE LOCATORS.
PERFECT.

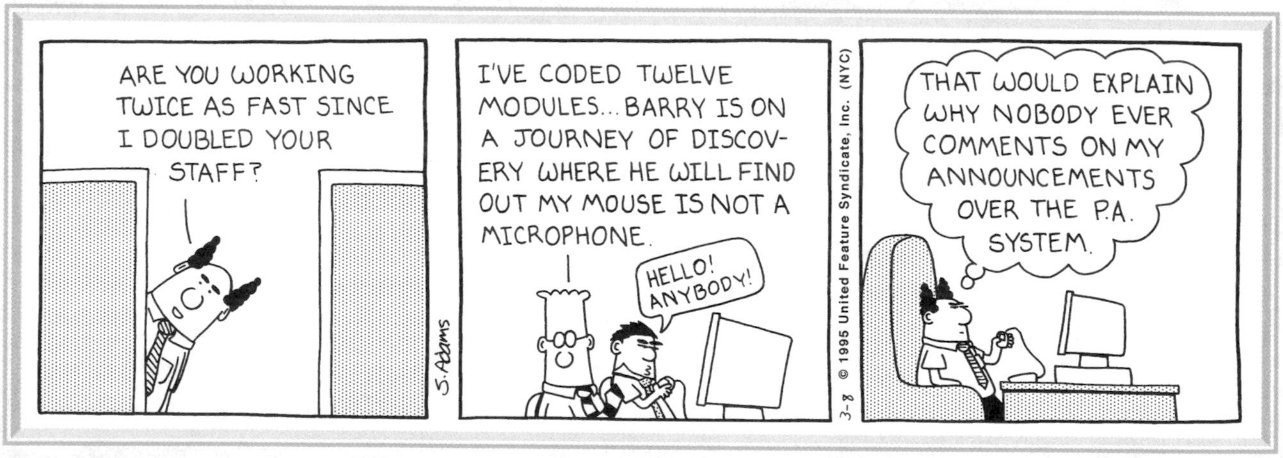
ARE YOU WORKING TWICE AS FAST SINCE I DOUBLED YOUR STAFF?
S. Adams
I'VE CODED TWELVE MODULES... BARRY IS ON A JOURNEY OF DISCOVERY WHERE HE WILL FIND OUT MY MOUSE IS NOT A MICROPHONE.
HELLO! ANYBODY!
3-8 © 1995 United Feature Syndicate, Inc. (NYC)
THAT WOULD EXPLAIN WHY NOBODY EVER COMMENTS ON MY ANNOUNCEMENTS OVER THE P.A. SYSTEM.

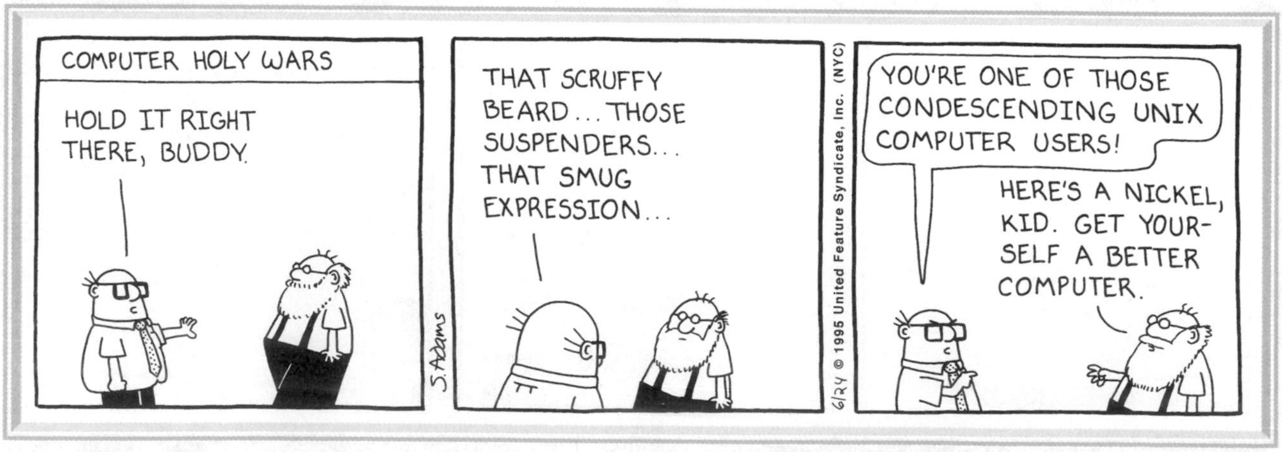
COMPUTER HOLY WARS
HOLD IT RIGHT THERE, BUDDY.
S. Adams
THAT SCRUFFY BEARD... THOSE SUSPENDERS... THAT SMUG EXPRESSION...
6/24 © 1995 United Feature Syndicate, Inc. (NYC)
YOU'RE ONE OF THOSE CONDESCENDING UNIX COMPUTER USERS!
HERE'S A NICKEL, KID. GET YOURSELF A BETTER COMPUTER.

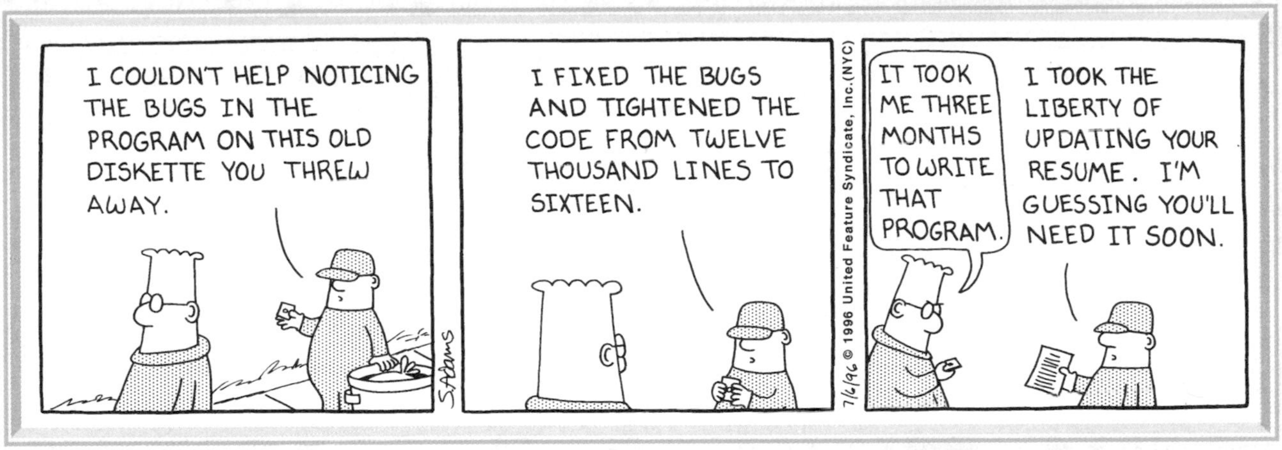
I COULDN'T HELP NOTICING THE BUGS IN THE PROGRAM ON THIS OLD DISKETTE YOU THREW AWAY.
I FIXED THE BUGS AND TIGHTENED THE CODE FROM TWELVE THOUSAND LINES TO SIXTEEN.
IT TOOK ME THREE MONTHS TO WRITE THAT PROGRAM.
I TOOK THE LIBERTY OF UPDATING YOUR RESUME. I'M GUESSING YOU'LL NEED IT SOON.
S.Adams
7/6/96 © 1996 United Feature Syndicate, Inc.(NYC)

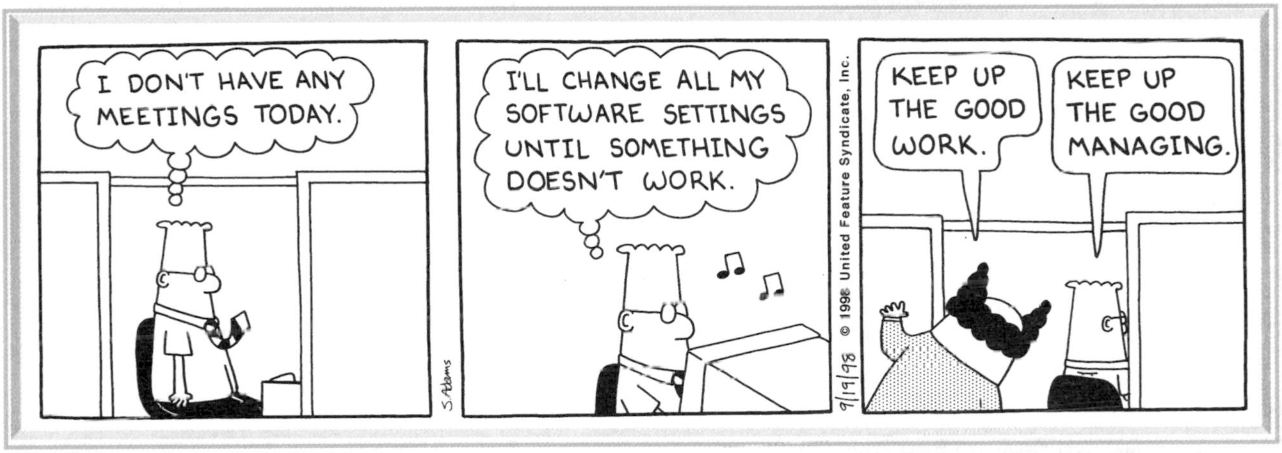
I DON'T HAVE ANY MEETINGS TODAY.
I'LL CHANGE ALL MY SOFTWARE SETTINGS UNTIL SOMETHING DOESN'T WORK.
KEEP UP THE GOOD WORK.
KEEP UP THE GOOD MANAGING.
S.Adams
9/19/98 © 1998 United Feature Syndicate, Inc.

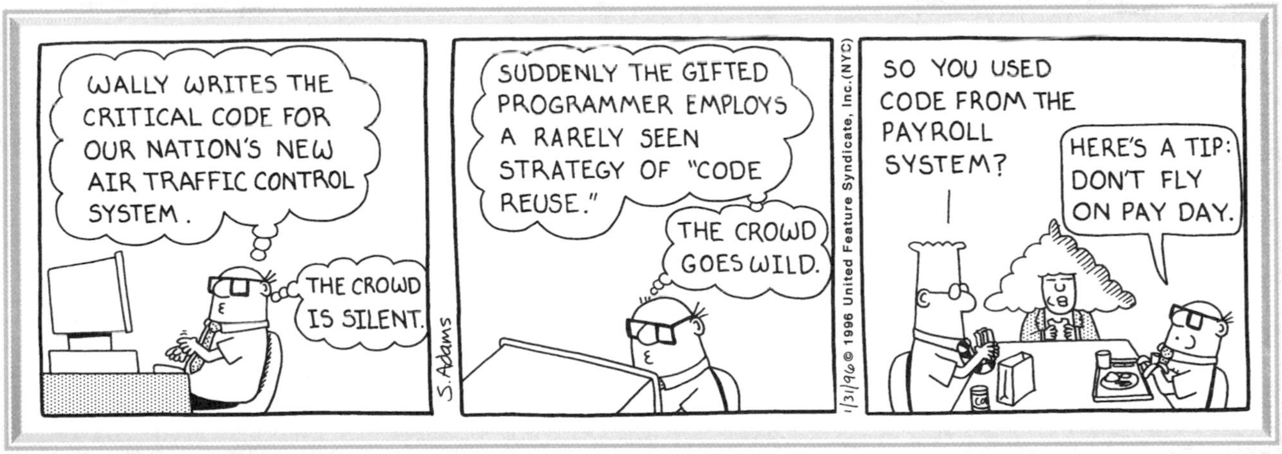
WALLY WRITES THE CRITICAL CODE FOR OUR NATION'S NEW AIR TRAFFIC CONTROL SYSTEM.
THE CROWD IS SILENT.
SUDDENLY THE GIFTED PROGRAMMER EMPLOYS A RARELY SEEN STRATEGY OF "CODE REUSE."
THE CROWD GOES WILD.
SO YOU USED CODE FROM THE PAYROLL SYSTEM?
HERE'S A TIP: DON'T FLY ON PAY DAY.
S.Adams
1/31/96 © 1996 United Feature Syndicate, Inc.(NYC)

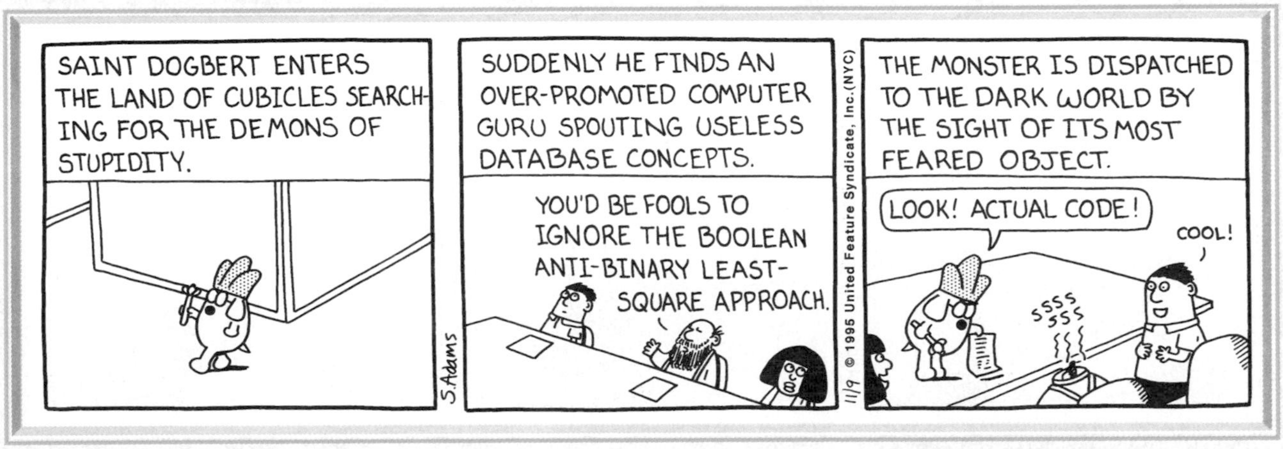
SAINT DOGBERT ENTERS THE LAND OF CUBICLES SEARCHING FOR THE DEMONS OF STUPIDITY.
SUDDENLY HE FINDS AN OVER-PROMOTED COMPUTER GURU SPOUTING USELESS DATABASE CONCEPTS.
YOU'D BE FOOLS TO IGNORE THE BOOLEAN ANTI-BINARY LEAST-SQUARE APPROACH.
THE MONSTER IS DISPATCHED TO THE DARK WORLD BY THE SIGHT OF ITS MOST FEARED OBJECT.
LOOK! ACTUAL CODE!
COOL!
SSSS SSS
S.Adams
11/9 © 1995 United Feature Syndicate, Inc.(NYC)

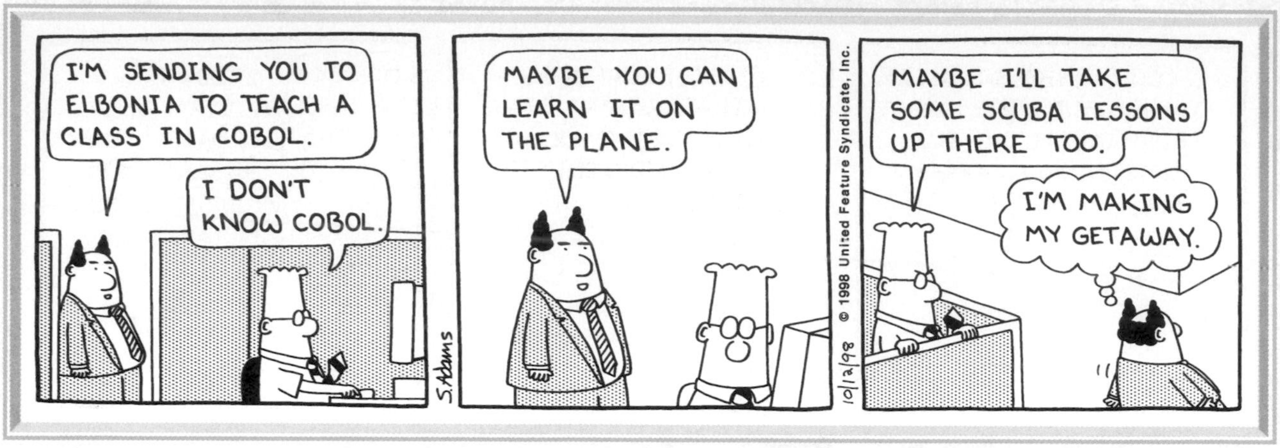
I'M SENDING YOU TO ELBONIA TO TEACH A CLASS IN COBOL.
I DON'T KNOW COBOL.
MAYBE YOU CAN LEARN IT ON THE PLANE.
MAYBE I'LL TAKE SOME SCUBA LESSONS UP THERE TOO.
I'M MAKING MY GETAWAY.
S. Adams
10/12/98 © 1998 United Feature Syndicate, Inc.

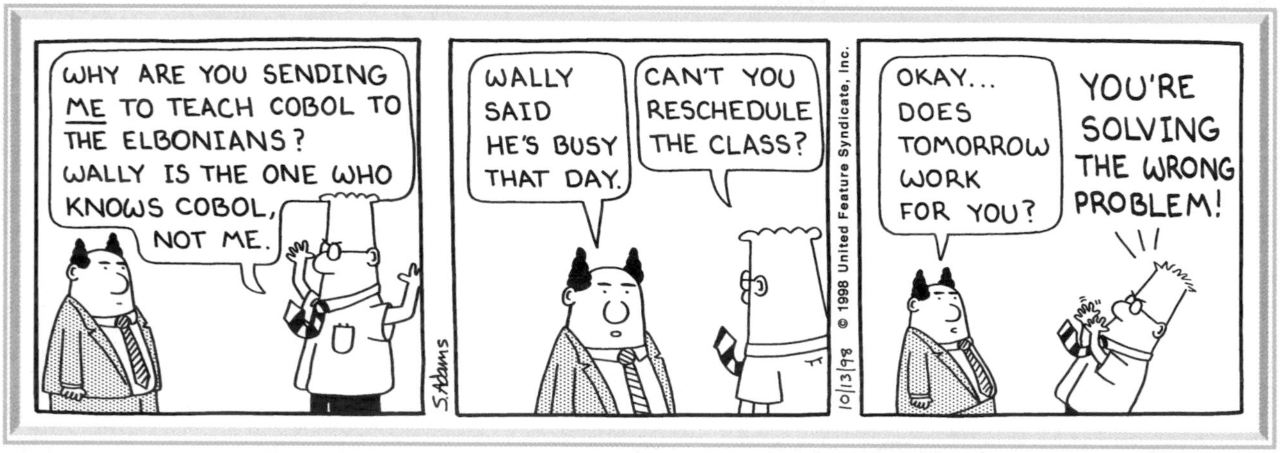
WHY ARE YOU SENDING ME TO TEACH COBOL TO THE ELBONIANS? WALLY IS THE ONE WHO KNOWS COBOL, NOT ME.
WALLY SAID HE'S BUSY THAT DAY.
CAN'T YOU RESCHEDULE THE CLASS?
OKAY... DOES TOMORROW WORK FOR YOU?
YOU'RE SOLVING THE WRONG PROBLEM!
S. Adams
10/13/98 © 1998 United Feature Syndicate, Inc.

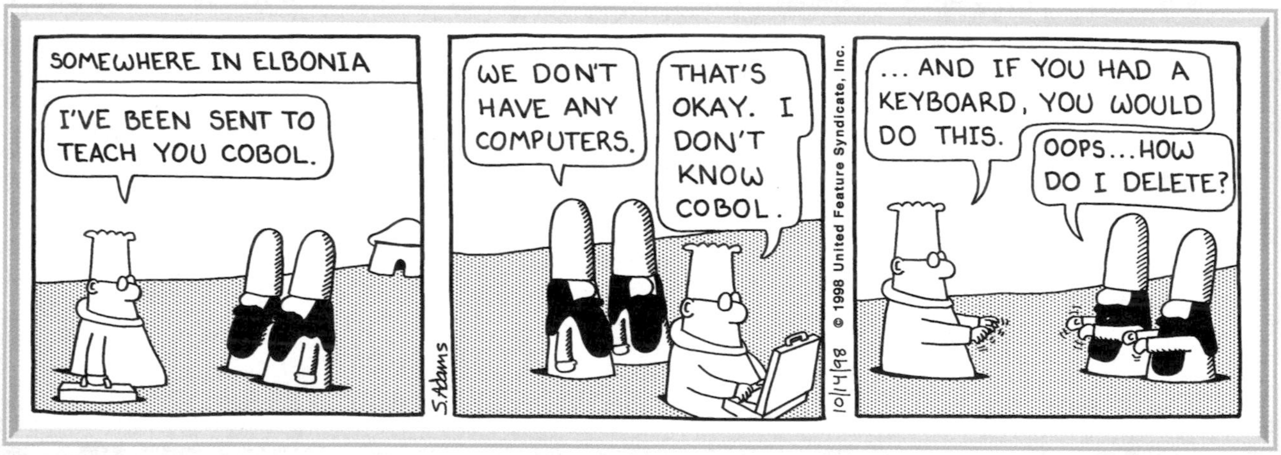
SOMEWHERE IN ELBONIA
I'VE BEEN SENT TO TEACH YOU COBOL.
WE DON'T HAVE ANY COMPUTERS.
THAT'S OKAY. I DON'T KNOW COBOL.
... AND IF YOU HAD A KEYBOARD, YOU WOULD DO THIS.
OOPS... HOW DO I DELETE?
S. Adams
10/14/98 © 1998 United Feature Syndicate, Inc.

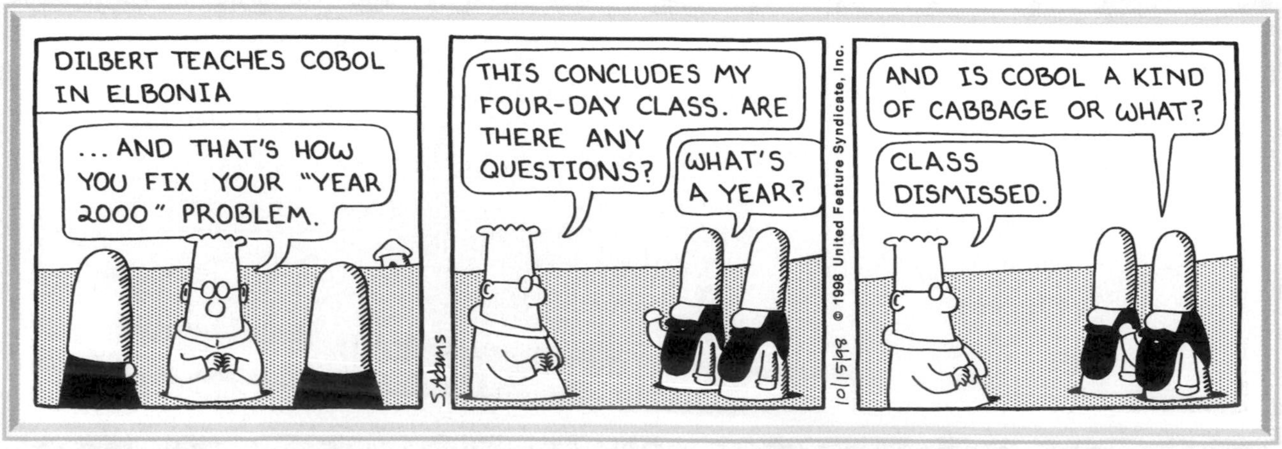
DILBERT TEACHES COBOL IN ELBONIA
... AND THAT'S HOW YOU FIX YOUR "YEAR 2000" PROBLEM.
THIS CONCLUDES MY FOUR-DAY CLASS. ARE THERE ANY QUESTIONS?
WHAT'S A YEAR?
AND IS COBOL A KIND OF CABBAGE OR WHAT?
CLASS DISMISSED.
S. Adams
10/15/98 © 1998 United Feature Syndicate, Inc.

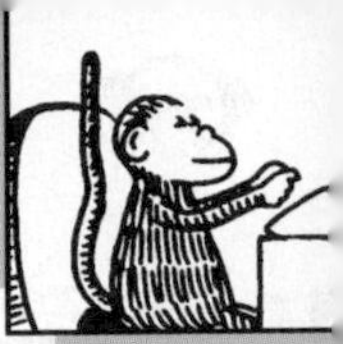

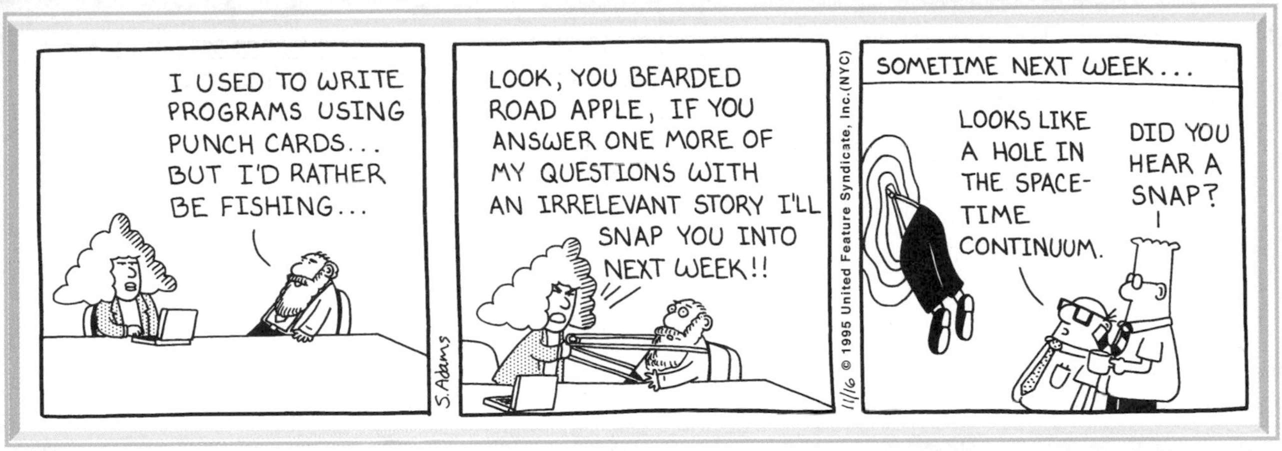
I USED TO WRITE PROGRAMS USING PUNCH CARDS... BUT I'D RATHER BE FISHING...
S. Adams
LOOK, YOU BEARDED ROAD APPLE, IF YOU ANSWER ONE MORE OF MY QUESTIONS WITH AN IRRELEVANT STORY I'LL SNAP YOU INTO NEXT WEEK!!
11/16 © 1995 United Feature Syndicate, Inc.(NYC)
SOMETIME NEXT WEEK...
LOOKS LIKE A HOLE IN THE SPACE-TIME CONTINUUM.
DID YOU HEAR A SNAP?

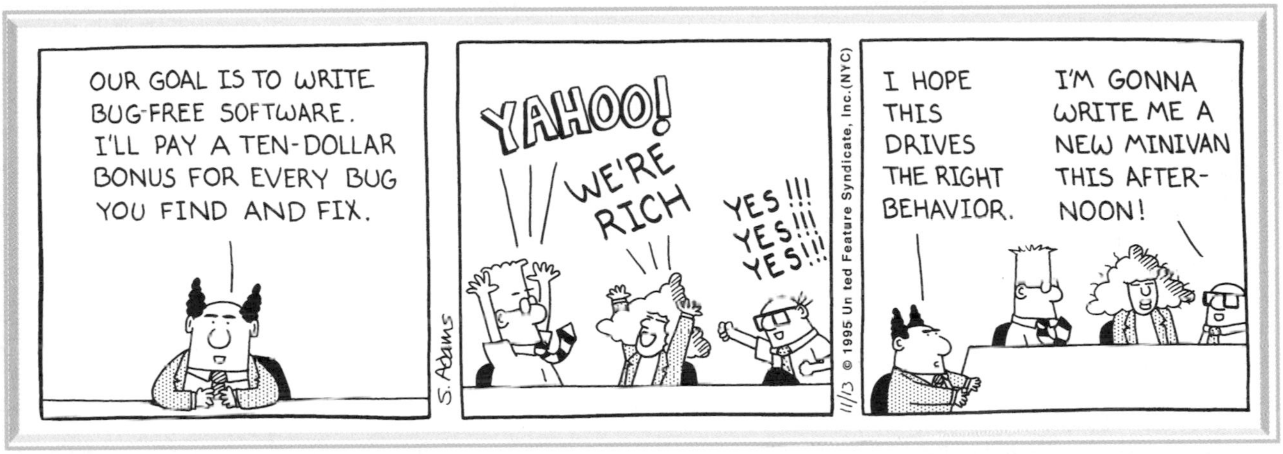
OUR GOAL IS TO WRITE BUG-FREE SOFTWARE. I'LL PAY A TEN-DOLLAR BONUS FOR EVERY BUG YOU FIND AND FIX.
S. Adams
YAHOO!
WE'RE RICH
YES!!! YES!!! YES!!!
11/13 © 1995 United Feature Syndicate, Inc.(NYC)
I HOPE THIS DRIVES THE RIGHT BEHAVIOR.
I'M GONNA WRITE ME A NEW MINIVAN THIS AFTERNOON!

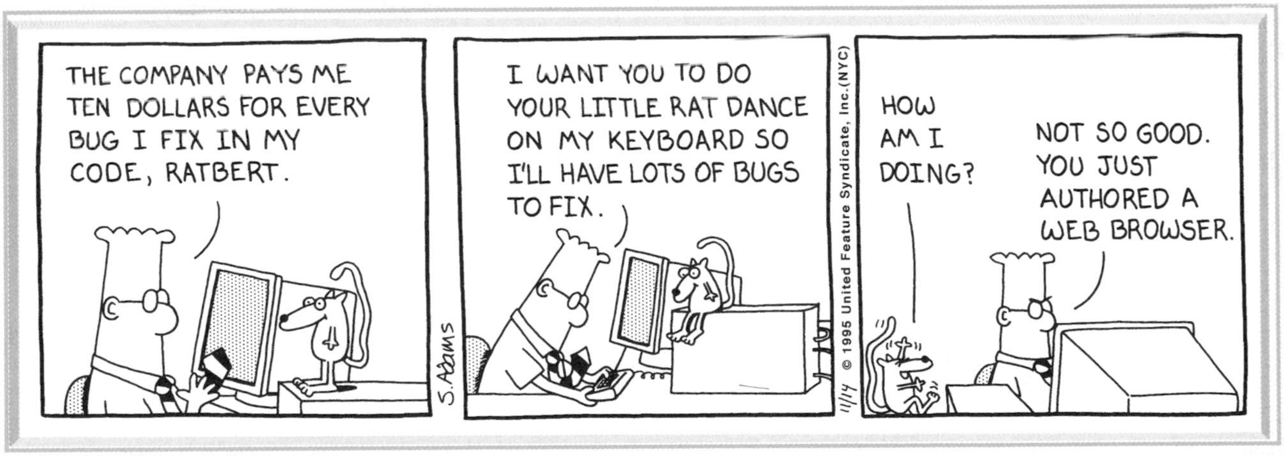
THE COMPANY PAYS ME TEN DOLLARS FOR EVERY BUG I FIX IN MY CODE, RATBERT.
S. Adams
I WANT YOU TO DO YOUR LITTLE RAT DANCE ON MY KEYBOARD SO I'LL HAVE LOTS OF BUGS TO FIX.
11/14 © 1995 United Feature Syndicate, Inc.(NYC)
HOW AM I DOING?
NOT SO GOOD. YOU JUST AUTHORED A WEB BROWSER.

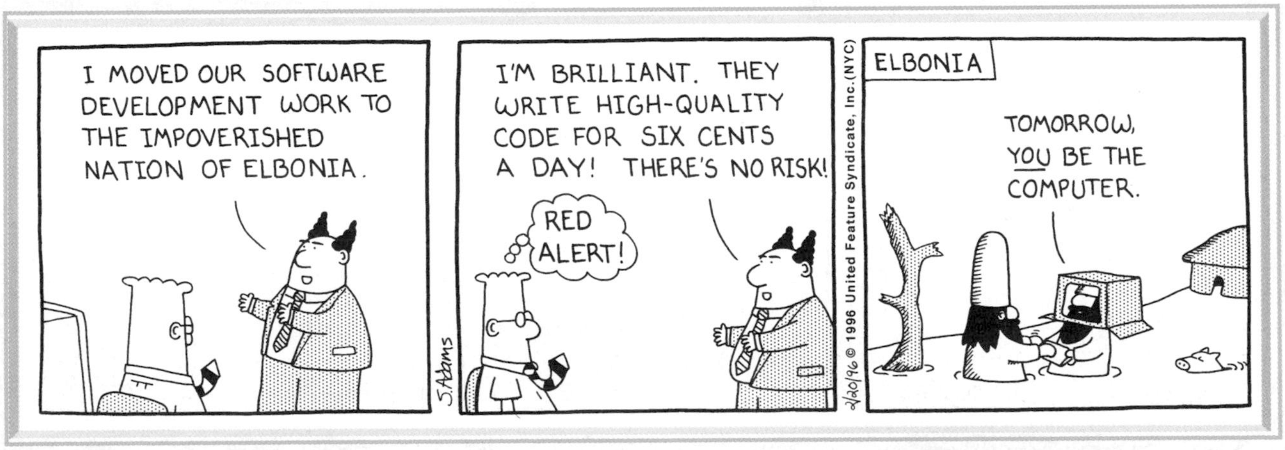
I MOVED OUR SOFTWARE DEVELOPMENT WORK TO THE IMPOVERISHED NATION OF ELBONIA.
S. Adams
I'M BRILLIANT. THEY WRITE HIGH-QUALITY CODE FOR SIX CENTS A DAY! THERE'S NO RISK!
RED ALERT!
2/20/96 © 1996 United Feature Syndicate, Inc.(NYC)
ELBONIA
TOMORROW, YOU BE THE COMPUTER.

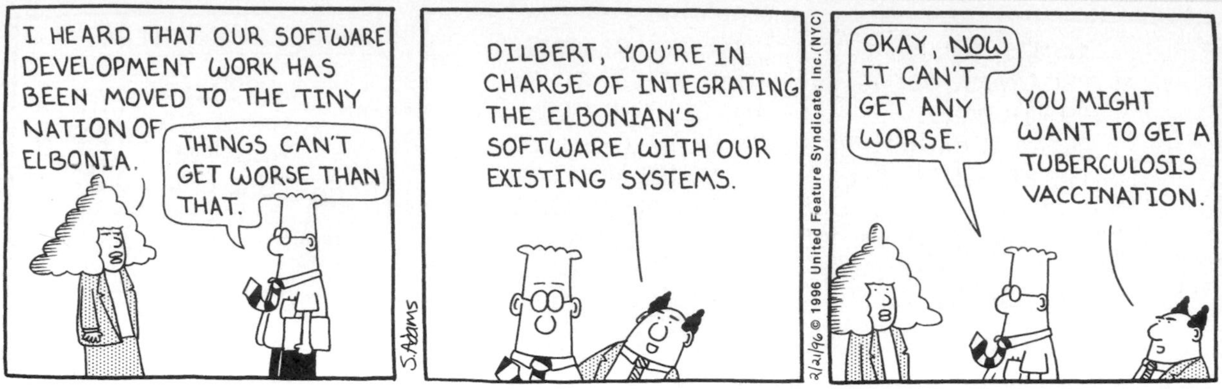
I HEARD THAT OUR SOFTWARE DEVELOPMENT WORK HAS BEEN MOVED TO THE TINY NATION OF ELBONIA.
THINGS CAN'T GET WORSE THAN THAT.
S.Adams
DILBERT, YOU'RE IN CHARGE OF INTEGRATING THE ELBONIAN'S SOFTWARE WITH OUR EXISTING SYSTEMS.
2/21/96 © 1996 United Feature Syndicate, Inc.(NYC)
OKAY, NOW IT CAN'T GET ANY WORSE.
YOU MIGHT WANT TO GET A TUBERCULOSIS VACCINATION.

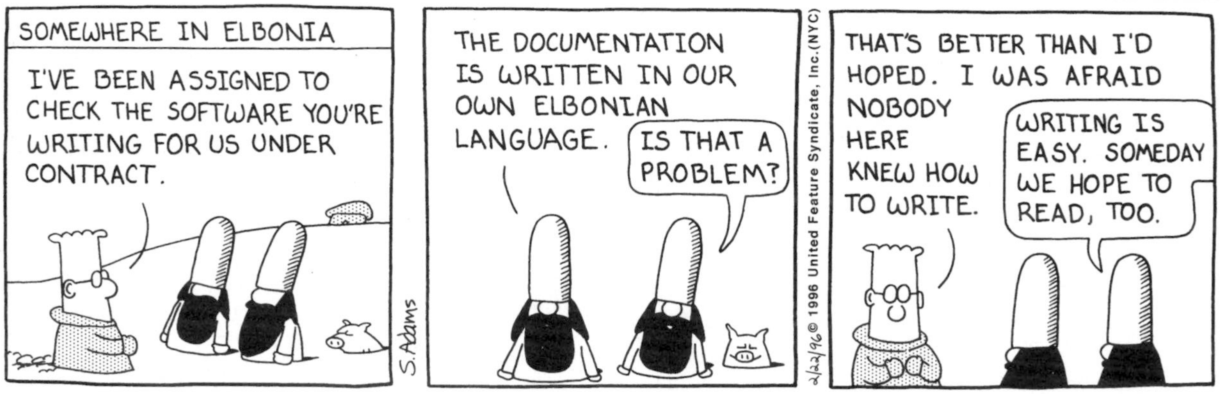
SOMEWHERE IN ELBONIA
I'VE BEEN ASSIGNED TO CHECK THE SOFTWARE YOU'RE WRITING FOR US UNDER CONTRACT.
S.Adams
THE DOCUMENTATION IS WRITTEN IN OUR OWN ELBONIAN LANGUAGE.
IS THAT A PROBLEM?
2/22/96 © 1996 United Feature Syndicate, Inc.(NYC)
THAT'S BETTER THAN I'D HOPED. I WAS AFRAID NOBODY HERE KNEW HOW TO WRITE.
WRITING IS EASY. SOMEDAY WE HOPE TO READ, TOO.

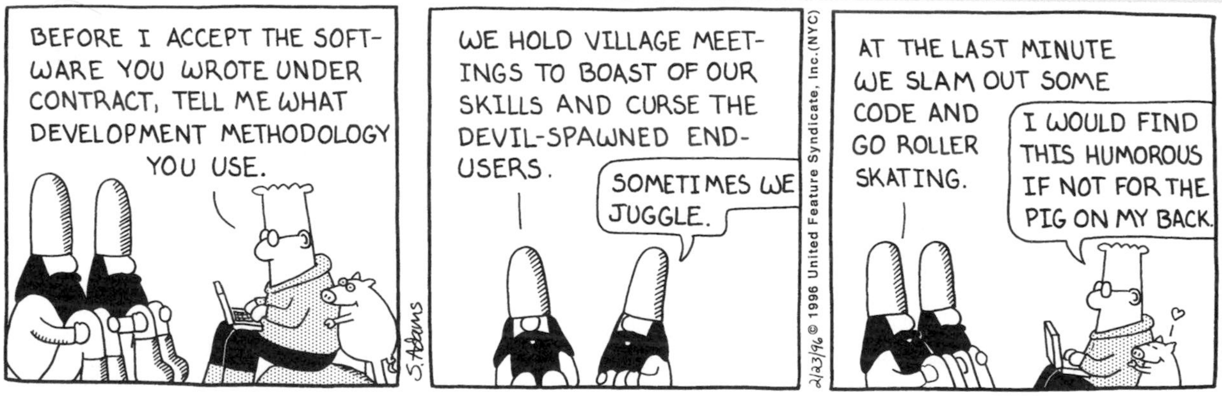
BEFORE I ACCEPT THE SOFTWARE YOU WROTE UNDER CONTRACT, TELL ME WHAT DEVELOPMENT METHODOLOGY YOU USE.
S.Adams
WE HOLD VILLAGE MEETINGS TO BOAST OF OUR SKILLS AND CURSE THE DEVIL-SPAWNED END-USERS.
SOMETIMES WE JUGGLE.
2/23/96 © 1996 United Feature Syndicate, Inc.(NYC)
AT THE LAST MINUTE WE SLAM OUT SOME CODE AND GO ROLLER SKATING.
I WOULD FIND THIS HUMOROUS IF NOT FOR THE PIG ON MY BACK.

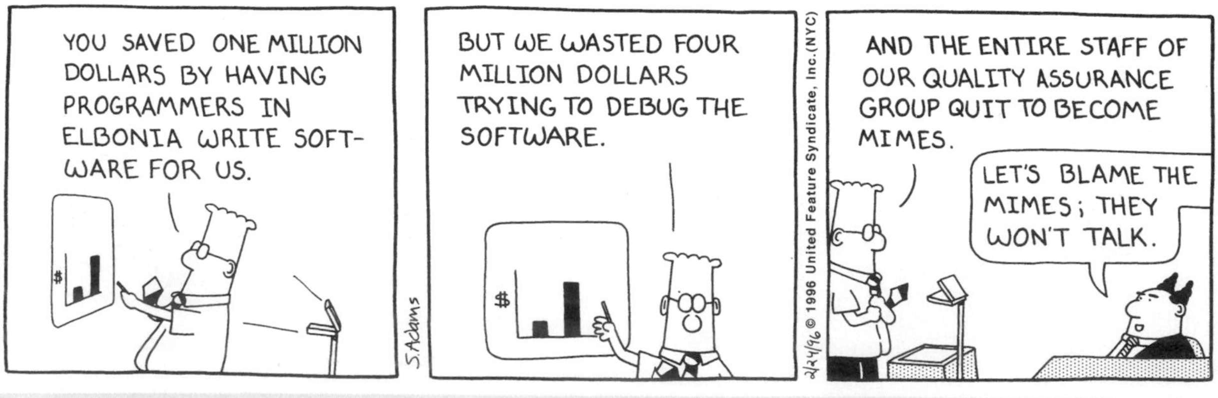
YOU SAVED ONE MILLION DOLLARS BY HAVING PROGRAMMERS IN ELBONIA WRITE SOFTWARE FOR US.
$
S.Adams
BUT WE WASTED FOUR MILLION DOLLARS TRYING TO DEBUG THE SOFTWARE.
$
2/24/96 © 1996 United Feature Syndicate, Inc.(NYC)
AND THE ENTIRE STAFF OF OUR QUALITY ASSURANCE GROUP QUIT TO BECOME MIMES.
LET'S BLAME THE MIMES; THEY WON'T TALK.

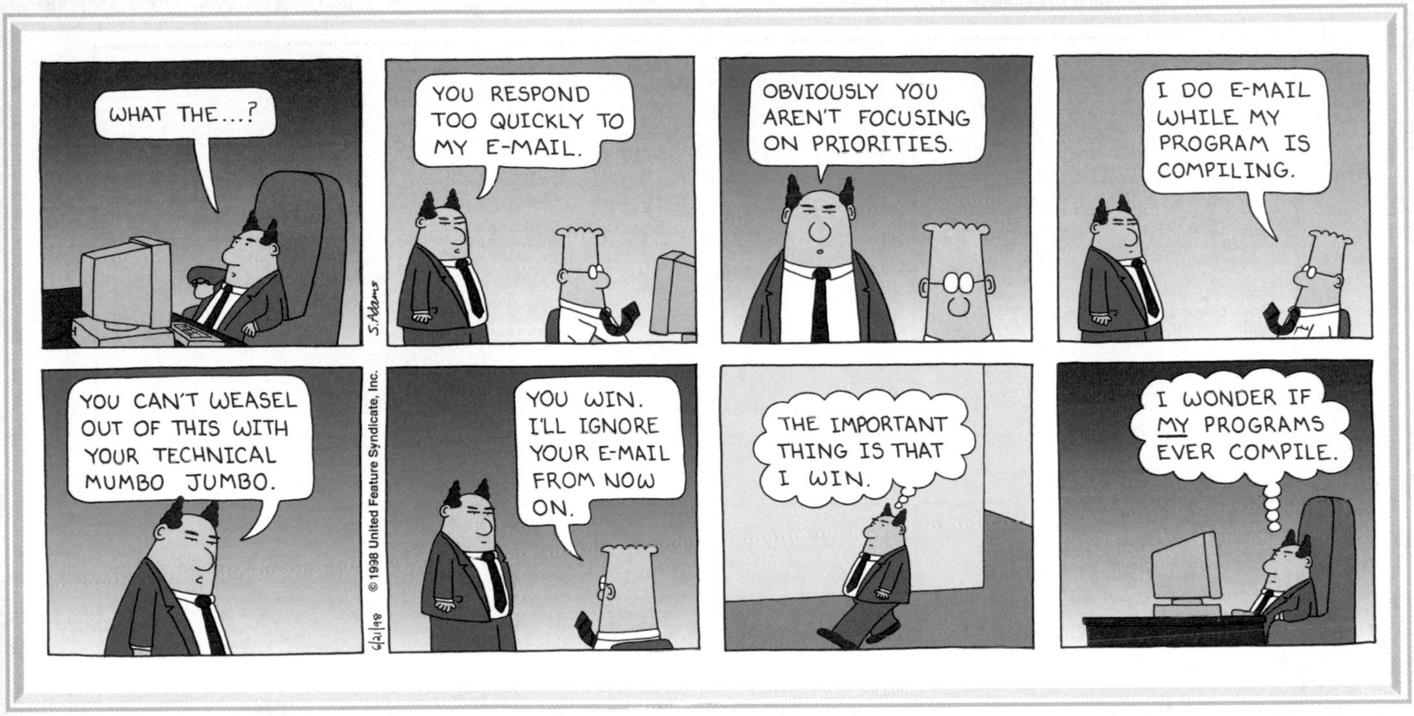
WHAT THE...?
YOU RESPOND TOO QUICKLY TO MY E-MAIL.
OBVIOUSLY YOU AREN'T FOCUSING ON PRIORITIES.
I DO E-MAIL WHILE MY PROGRAM IS COMPILING.
YOU CAN'T WEASEL OUT OF THIS WITH YOUR TECHNICAL MUMBO JUMBO.
YOU WIN. I'LL IGNORE YOUR E-MAIL FROM NOW ON.
THE IMPORTANT THING IS THAT I WIN.
I WONDER IF MY PROGRAMS EVER COMPILE.
S. Adams
© 1998 United Feature Syndicate, Inc.
6/21/98

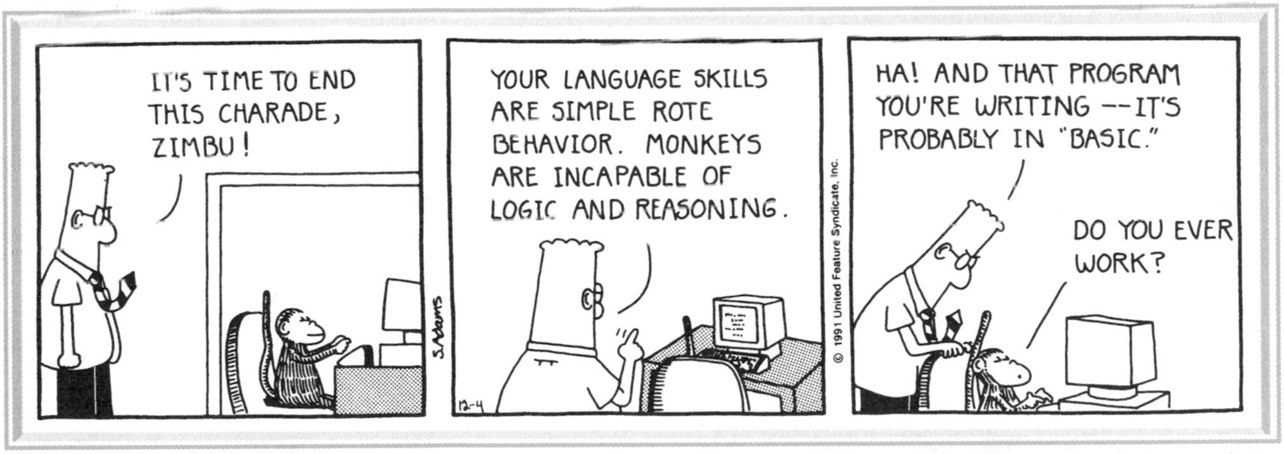
IT'S TIME TO END THIS CHARADE, ZIMBU!
YOUR LANGUAGE SKILLS ARE SIMPLE ROTE BEHAVIOR. MONKEYS ARE INCAPABLE OF LOGIC AND REASONING.
HA! AND THAT PROGRAM YOU'RE WRITING --IT'S PROBABLY IN "BASIC."
DO YOU EVER WORK?
S. Adams
12-4
© 1991 United Feature Syndicate, Inc.

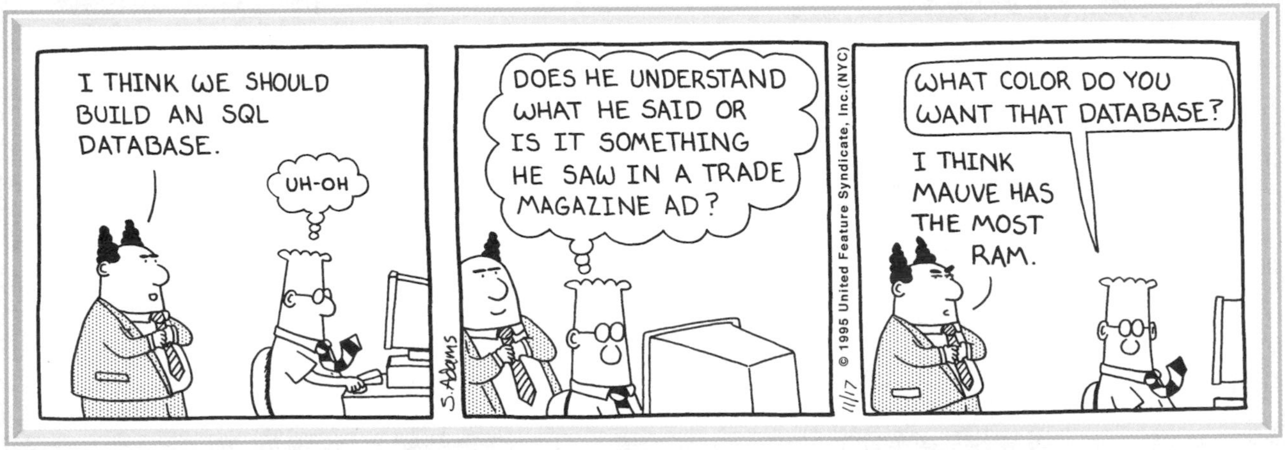
I THINK WE SHOULD BUILD AN SQL DATABASE.
UH-OH
DOES HE UNDERSTAND WHAT HE SAID OR IS IT SOMETHING HE SAW IN A TRADE MAGAZINE AD?
WHAT COLOR DO YOU WANT THAT DATABASE?
I THINK MAUVE HAS THE MOST RAM.
S. Adams
© 1995 United Feature Syndicate, Inc.(NYC)
11/17

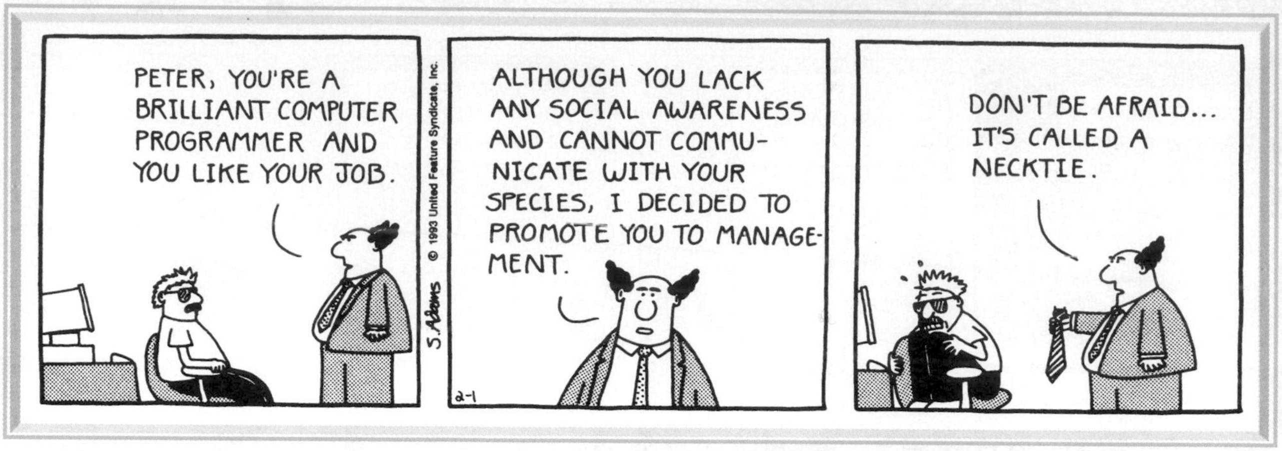
PETER, YOU'RE A BRILLIANT COMPUTER PROGRAMMER AND YOU LIKE YOUR JOB.
© 1993 United Feature Syndicate, Inc.
ALTHOUGH YOU LACK ANY SOCIAL AWARENESS AND CANNOT COMMUNICATE WITH YOUR SPECIES, I DECIDED TO PROMOTE YOU TO MANAGEMENT.
DON'T BE AFRAID... IT'S CALLED A NECKTIE.

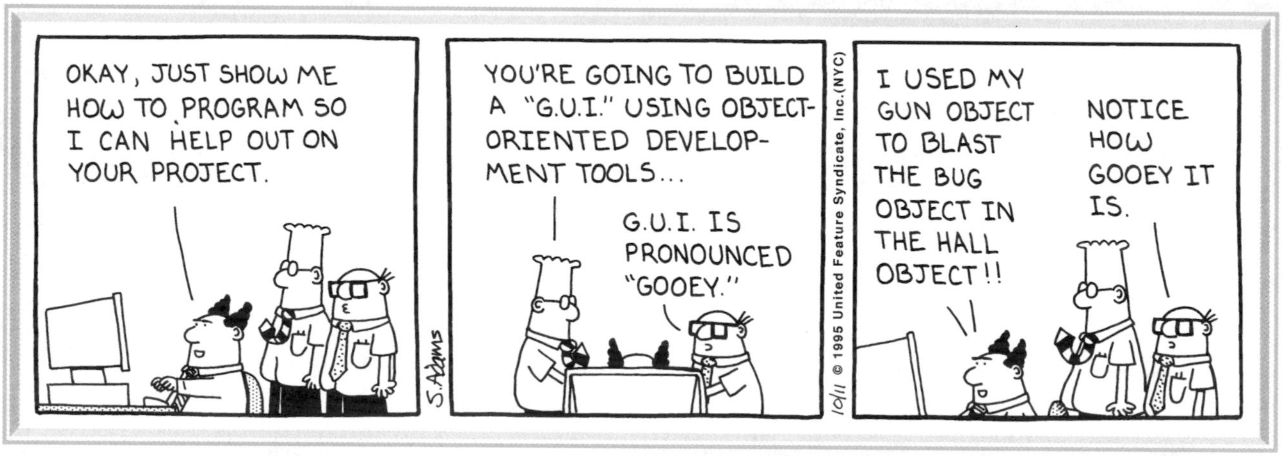
OKAY, JUST SHOW ME HOW TO PROGRAM SO I CAN HELP OUT ON YOUR PROJECT.
YOU'RE GOING TO BUILD A "G.U.I." USING OBJECT-ORIENTED DEVELOPMENT TOOLS...
G.U.I. IS PRONOUNCED "GOOEY."
© 1995 United Feature Syndicate, Inc.(NYC)
I USED MY GUN OBJECT TO BLAST THE BUG OBJECT IN THE HALL OBJECT!!
NOTICE HOW GOOEY IT IS.

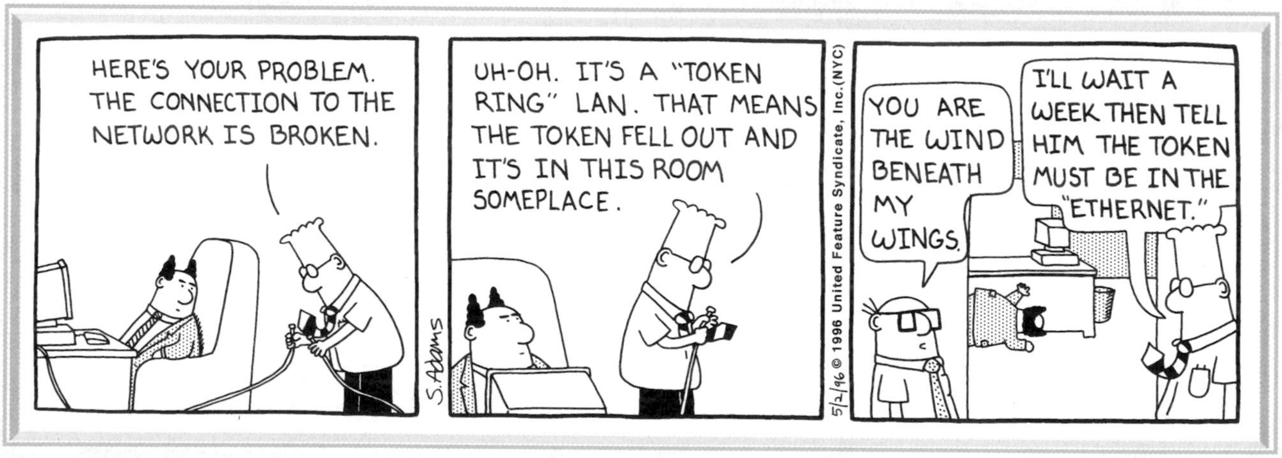
HERE'S YOUR PROBLEM. THE CONNECTION TO THE NETWORK IS BROKEN.
UH-OH. IT'S A "TOKEN RING" LAN. THAT MEANS THE TOKEN FELL OUT AND IT'S IN THIS ROOM SOMEPLACE.
© 1996 United Feature Syndicate, Inc.(NYC)
YOU ARE THE WIND BENEATH MY WINGS.
I'LL WAIT A WEEK THEN TELL HIM THE TOKEN MUST BE IN THE "ETHERNET."

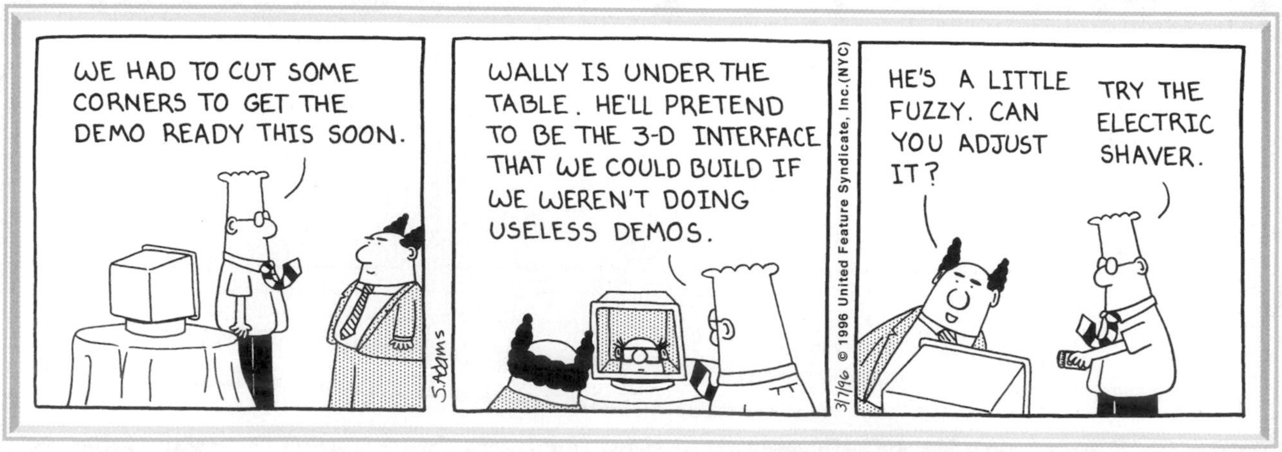
WE HAD TO CUT SOME CORNERS TO GET THE DEMO READY THIS SOON.
WALLY IS UNDER THE TABLE. HE'LL PRETEND TO BE THE 3-D INTERFACE THAT WE COULD BUILD IF WE WEREN'T DOING USELESS DEMOS.
© 1996 United Feature Syndicate, Inc.(NYC)
HE'S A LITTLE FUZZY. CAN YOU ADJUST IT?
TRY THE ELECTRIC SHAVER.

PROGRAMMERS

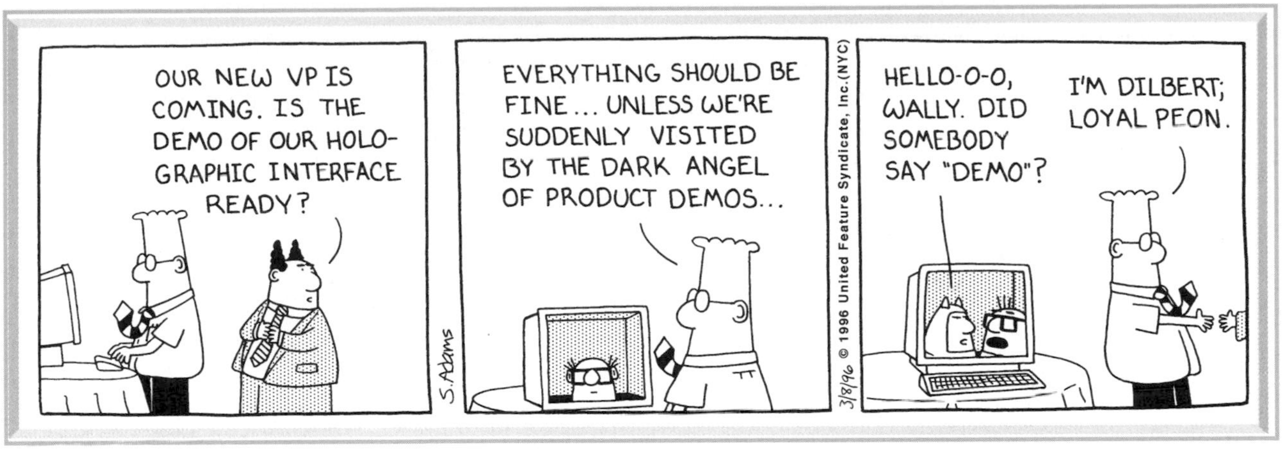
OUR NEW VP IS COMING. IS THE DEMO OF OUR HOLO-GRAPHIC INTERFACE READY?
EVERYTHING SHOULD BE FINE... UNLESS WE'RE SUDDENLY VISITED BY THE DARK ANGEL OF PRODUCT DEMOS...
HELLO-O-O, WALLY. DID SOMEBODY SAY "DEMO"?
I'M DILBERT; LOYAL PEON.
S. Adams
3/8/96 © 1996 United Feature Syndicate, Inc.(NYC)

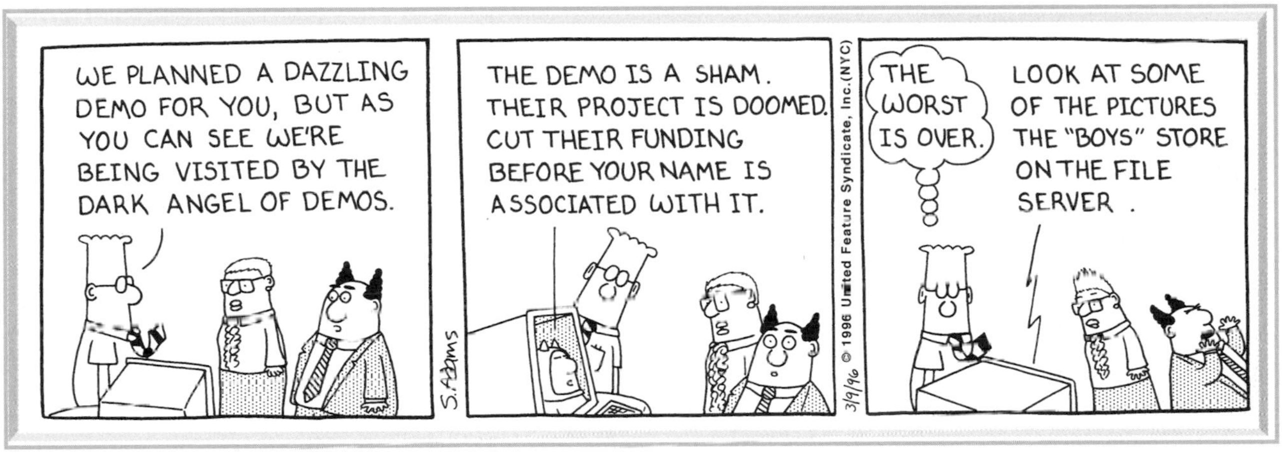
WE PLANNED A DAZZLING DEMO FOR YOU, BUT AS YOU CAN SEE WE'RE BEING VISITED BY THE DARK ANGEL OF DEMOS.
THE DEMO IS A SHAM. THEIR PROJECT IS DOOMED. CUT THEIR FUNDING BEFORE YOUR NAME IS ASSOCIATED WITH IT.
THE WORST IS OVER.
LOOK AT SOME OF THE PICTURES THE "BOYS" STORE ON THE FILE SERVER.
S. Adams
3/9/96 © 1996 United Feature Syndicate, Inc.(NYC)

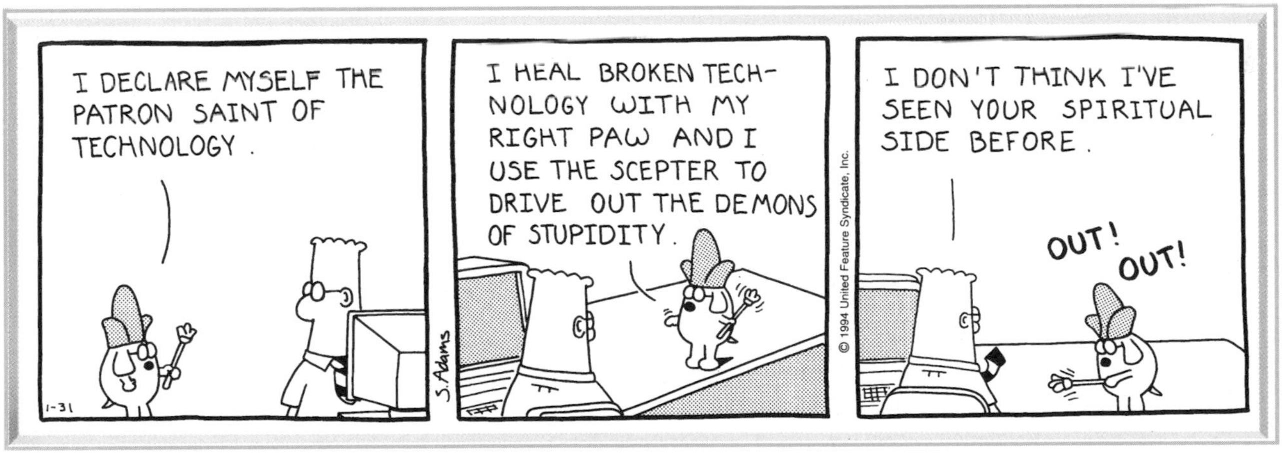
I DECLARE MYSELF THE PATRON SAINT OF TECHNOLOGY.
1-31
I HEAL BROKEN TECH-NOLOGY WITH MY RIGHT PAW AND I USE THE SCEPTER TO DRIVE OUT THE DEMONS OF STUPIDITY.
S. Adams
© 1994 United Feature Syndicate, Inc.
I DON'T THINK I'VE SEEN YOUR SPIRITUAL SIDE BEFORE.
OUT! OUT!

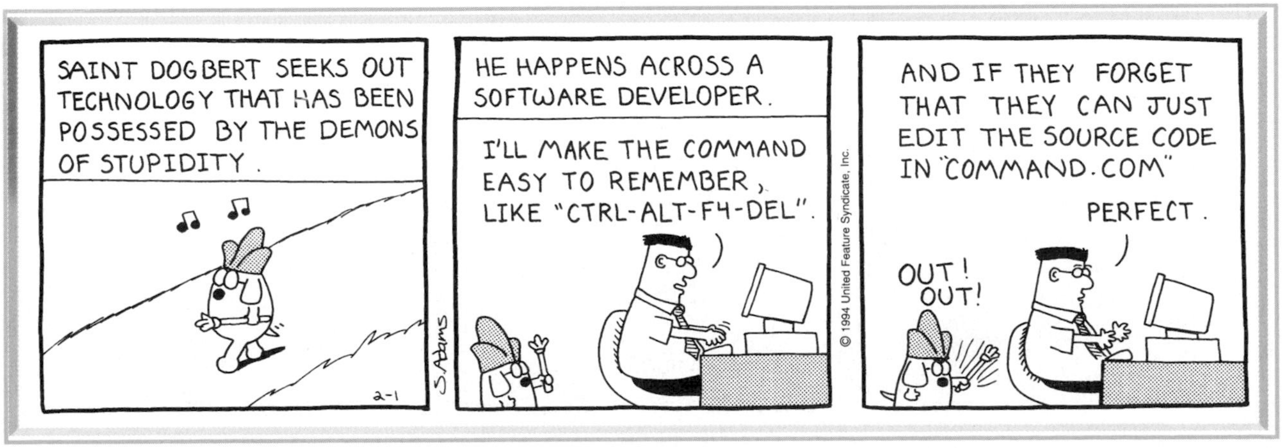
SAINT DOGBERT SEEKS OUT TECHNOLOGY THAT HAS BEEN POSSESSED BY THE DEMONS OF STUPIDITY.
2-1
HE HAPPENS ACROSS A SOFTWARE DEVELOPER.
I'LL MAKE THE COMMAND EASY TO REMEMBER, LIKE "CTRL-ALT-F4-DEL".
S. Adams
© 1994 United Feature Syndicate, Inc.
AND IF THEY FORGET THAT THEY CAN JUST EDIT THE SOURCE CODE IN "COMMAND.COM"
PERFECT.
OUT! OUT!

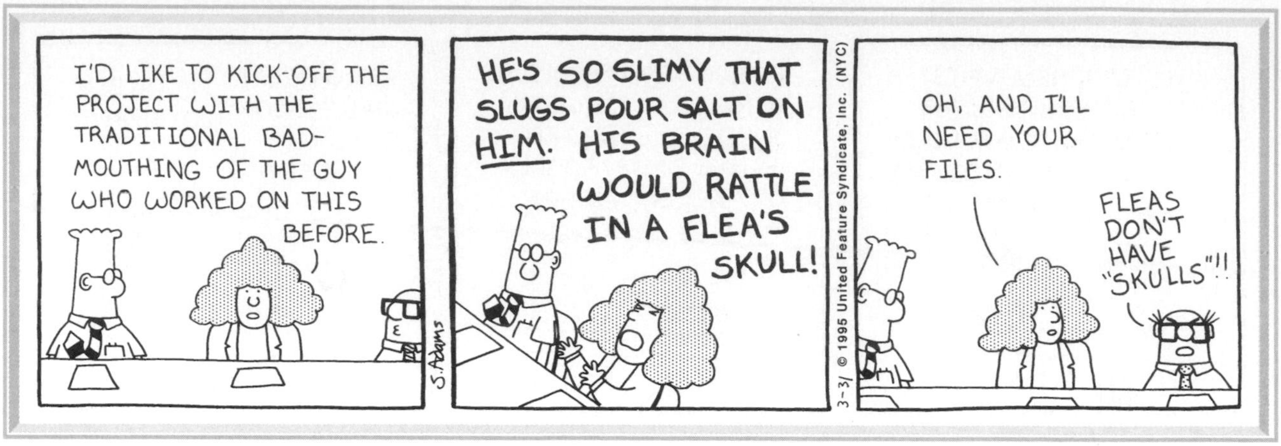
I'D LIKE TO KICK-OFF THE PROJECT WITH THE TRADITIONAL BAD-MOUTHING OF THE GUY WHO WORKED ON THIS BEFORE.
HE'S SO SLIMY THAT SLUGS POUR SALT ON HIM. HIS BRAIN WOULD RATTLE IN A FLEA'S SKULL!
OH, AND I'LL NEED YOUR FILES.
FLEAS DON'T HAVE "SKULLS"!!
© 1995 United Feature Syndicate, Inc. (NYC)

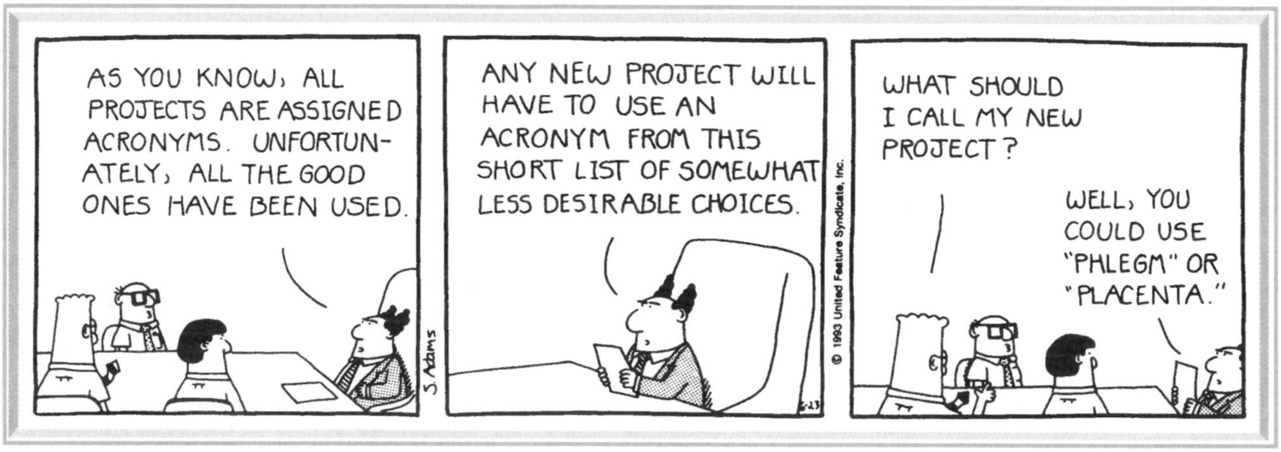
AS YOU KNOW, ALL PROJECTS ARE ASSIGNED ACRONYMS. UNFORTUNATELY, ALL THE GOOD ONES HAVE BEEN USED.
ANY NEW PROJECT WILL HAVE TO USE AN ACRONYM FROM THIS SHORT LIST OF SOMEWHAT LESS DESIRABLE CHOICES.
WHAT SHOULD I CALL MY NEW PROJECT?
WELL, YOU COULD USE "PHLEGM" OR "PLACENTA."
© 1993 United Feature Syndicate, Inc.

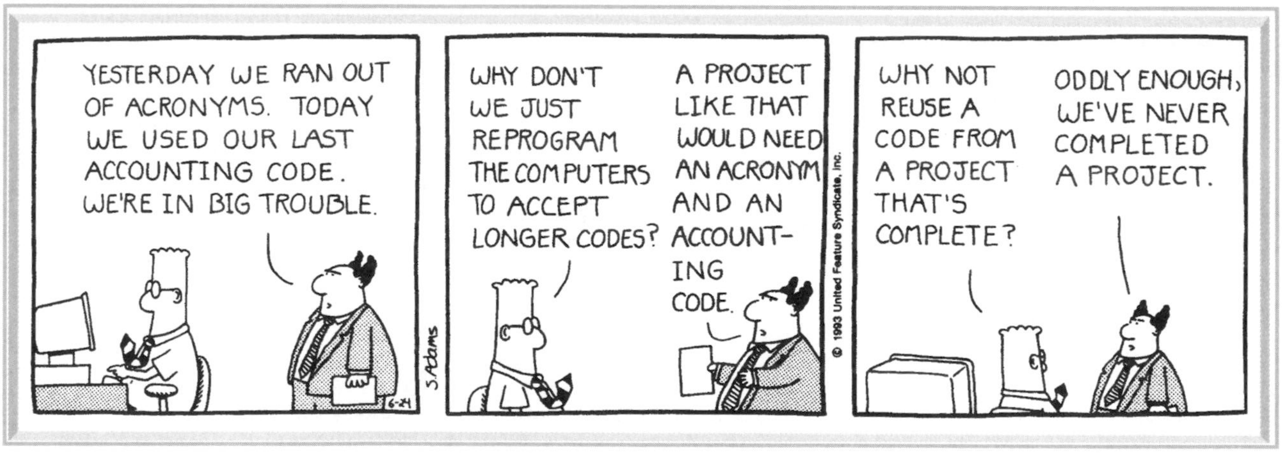
YESTERDAY WE RAN OUT OF ACRONYMS. TODAY WE USED OUR LAST ACCOUNTING CODE. WE'RE IN BIG TROUBLE.
WHY DON'T WE JUST REPROGRAM THE COMPUTERS TO ACCEPT LONGER CODES?
A PROJECT LIKE THAT WOULD NEED AN ACRONYM AND AN ACCOUNTING CODE.
WHY NOT REUSE A CODE FROM A PROJECT THAT'S COMPLETE?
ODDLY ENOUGH, WE'VE NEVER COMPLETED A PROJECT.
© 1993 United Feature Syndicate, Inc.

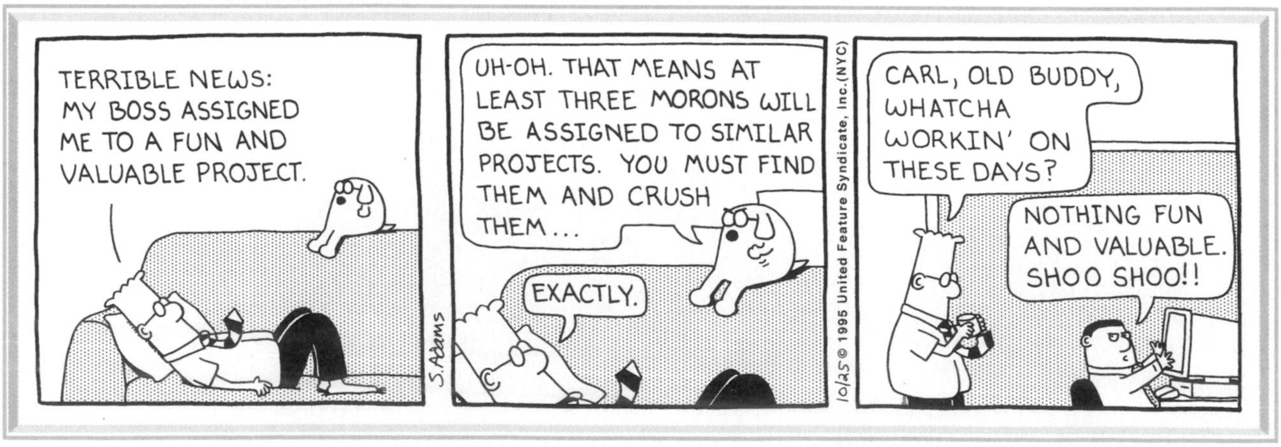
TERRIBLE NEWS: MY BOSS ASSIGNED ME TO A FUN AND VALUABLE PROJECT.
UH-OH. THAT MEANS AT LEAST THREE MORONS WILL BE ASSIGNED TO SIMILAR PROJECTS. YOU MUST FIND THEM AND CRUSH THEM...
EXACTLY.
CARL, OLD BUDDY, WHATCHA WORKIN' ON THESE DAYS?
NOTHING FUN AND VALUABLE. SHOO SHOO!!
© 1995 United Feature Syndicate, Inc. (NYC)

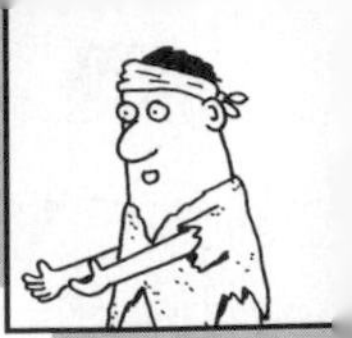

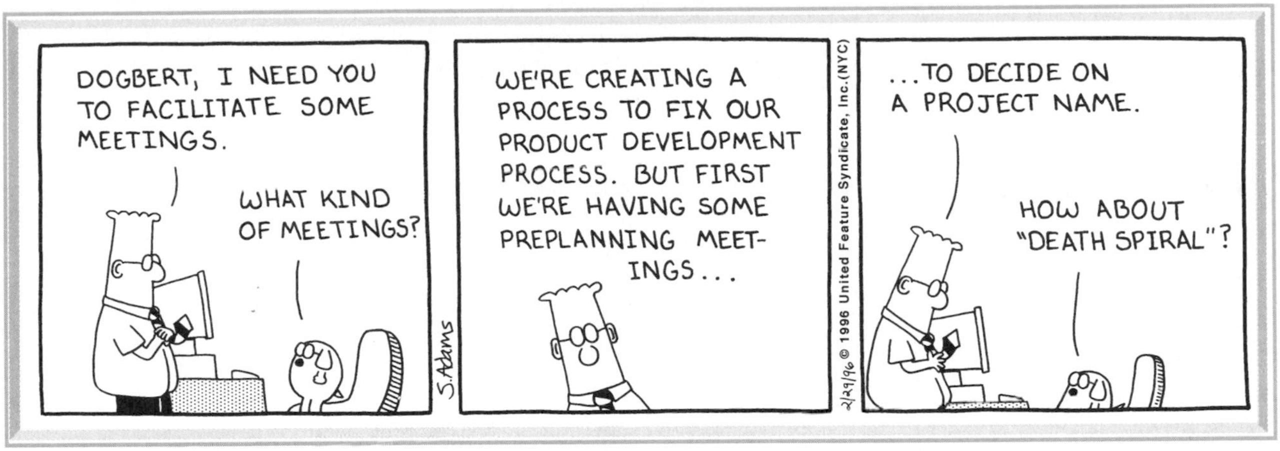
DOGBERT, I NEED YOU TO FACILITATE SOME MEETINGS.
WHAT KIND OF MEETINGS?
S. Adams
WE'RE CREATING A PROCESS TO FIX OUR PRODUCT DEVELOPMENT PROCESS. BUT FIRST WE'RE HAVING SOME PREPLANNING MEETINGS...
2/29/96 © 1996 United Feature Syndicate, Inc.(NYC)
...TO DECIDE ON A PROJECT NAME.
HOW ABOUT "DEATH SPIRAL"?

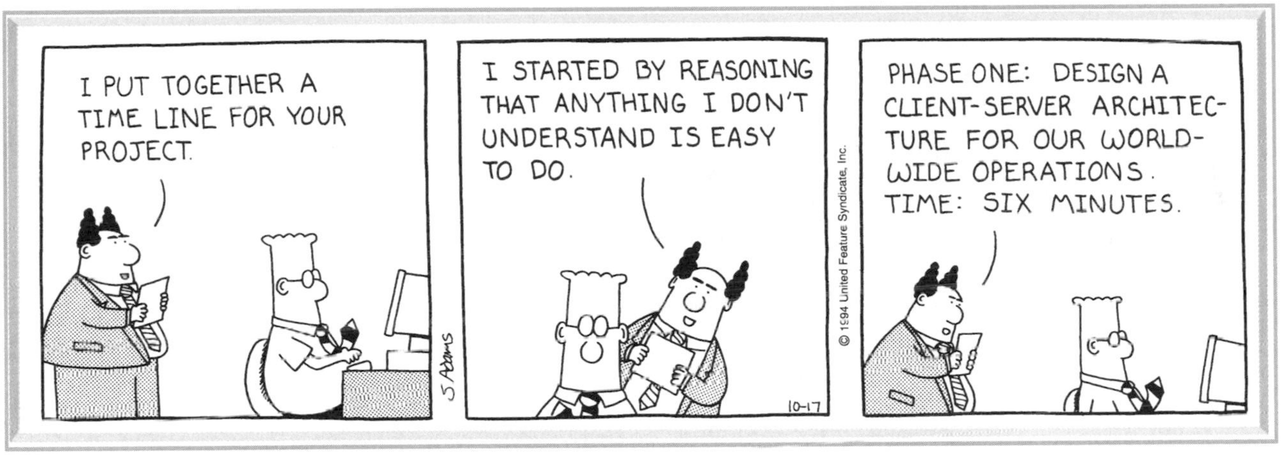
I PUT TOGETHER A TIME LINE FOR YOUR PROJECT.
S. Adams
I STARTED BY REASONING THAT ANYTHING I DON'T UNDERSTAND IS EASY TO DO.
10-17
© 1994 United Feature Syndicate, Inc.
PHASE ONE: DESIGN A CLIENT-SERVER ARCHITECTURE FOR OUR WORLD-WIDE OPERATIONS. TIME: SIX MINUTES.

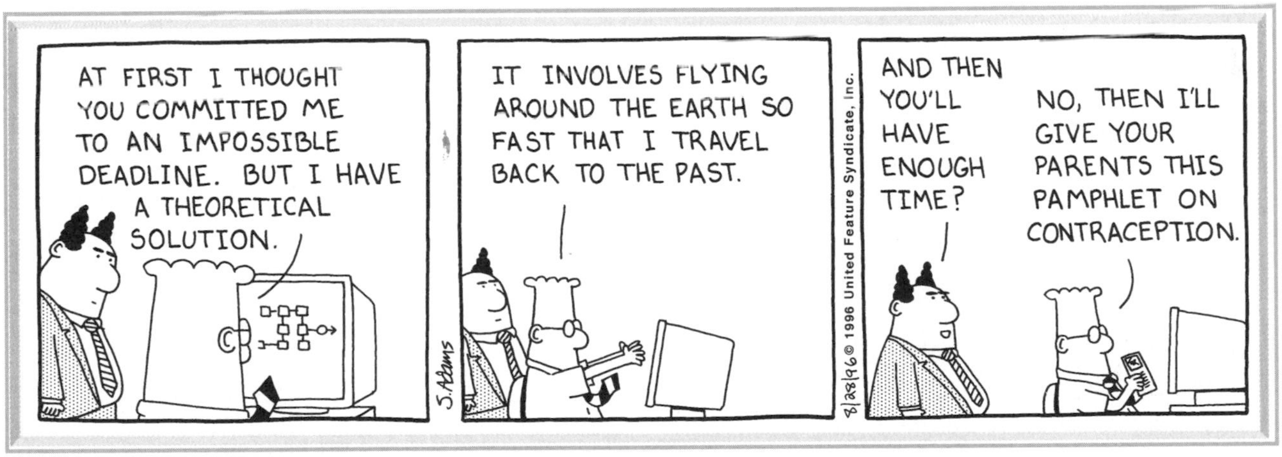
AT FIRST I THOUGHT YOU COMMITTED ME TO AN IMPOSSIBLE DEADLINE. BUT I HAVE A THEORETICAL SOLUTION.
S. Adams
IT INVOLVES FLYING AROUND THE EARTH SO FAST THAT I TRAVEL BACK TO THE PAST.
8/28/96 © 1996 United Feature Syndicate, Inc.
AND THEN YOU'LL HAVE ENOUGH TIME?
NO, THEN I'LL GIVE YOUR PARENTS THIS PAMPHLET ON CONTRACEPTION.

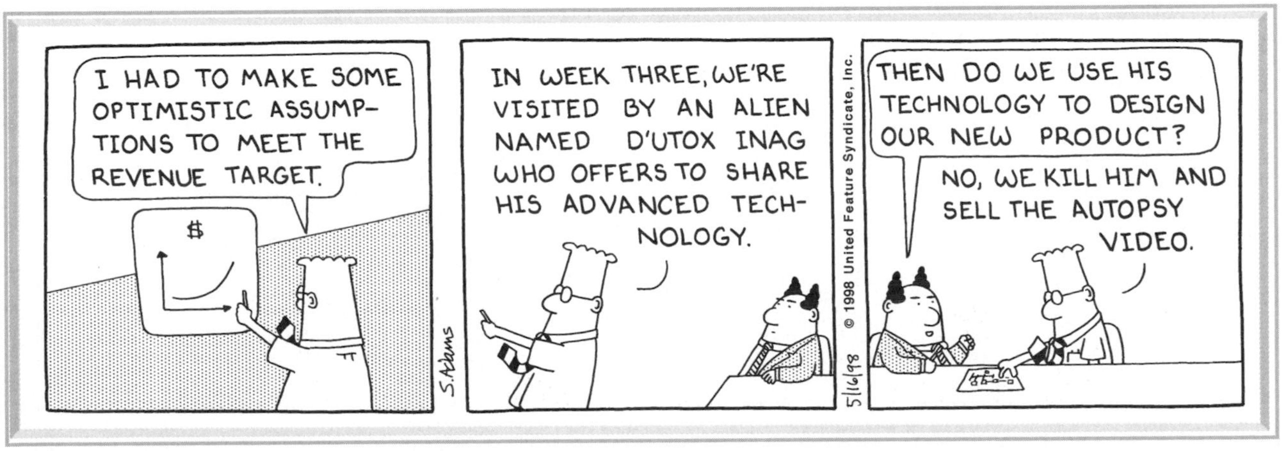
I HAD TO MAKE SOME OPTIMISTIC ASSUMPTIONS TO MEET THE REVENUE TARGET.
$
S. Adams
IN WEEK THREE, WE'RE VISITED BY AN ALIEN NAMED D'UTOX INAG WHO OFFERS TO SHARE HIS ADVANCED TECHNOLOGY.
5/16/98 © 1998 United Feature Syndicate, Inc.
THEN DO WE USE HIS TECHNOLOGY TO DESIGN OUR NEW PRODUCT?
NO, WE KILL HIM AND SELL THE AUTOPSY VIDEO.

OUR NEXT PRODUCT WILL DETERMINE THE FUTURE OF OUR COMPANY!
$
I NEED A PROJECT LEADER WHO HAS A PASSION FOR SUCCESS!
WOULD THAT LEADER GET EXTRA PAY?
IT'S NOT ABOUT MONEY, WALLY. IT'S ABOUT A PASSION FOR SUCCESS!
ALL I HAVE IS A VAGUE PREFERENCE. HOW ABOUT YOU?
YES, I'M FEELING SOMETHING... MAYBE IT'S...
NO, IT'S JUST MY ALLERGY MEDICATION.
WHAT WAS IT LIKE?
IT TINGLED.
S. Adams
6/28/98 © 1998 United Feature Syndicate, Inc.

HERE'S MY PROJECT TIME LINE.
THE "WORK" PORTION WILL TAKE ONE WEEK.
WORK
1 WEEK
I'LL SPEND THREE WEEKS MEETING WITH PEOPLE WHOM YOU SEND TO ME BECAUSE YOU DON'T FEEL LIKE TALKING TO THEM YOURSELF.
3 WEEKS
I'LL SPEND EIGHT WEEKS GETTING COMPETITIVE BIDS FROM COMPANIES THAT I KNOW I WON'T SELECT.
...SIX WEEKS TO GET THE WISDOM AND APPROVAL OF EXECUTIVES WHO ARE TOO BUSY TO UNDERSTAND THE ISSUES.
DURING THAT TIME YOU WILL RANDOMLY REORGANIZE THE DEPARTMENT AND CUT MY FUNDING.
IN THE FINAL PHASE I LEAP TO MY DEATH, A BITTER AND BROKEN SHELL OF A MAN.
EEEE!!!
IS THERE SOME SORT OF MANAGER THING I SHOULD BE DOING NOW?
IF I TIME MY LEAP RIGHT YOU'LL JUST BE LEAVING THE BUILDING.
S. Adams
2/4/96 © 1996 United Feature Syndicate, Inc.(NYC)

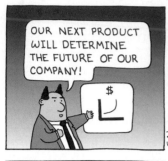

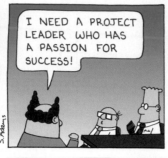

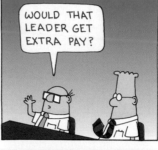

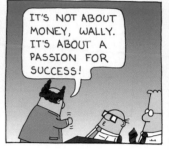

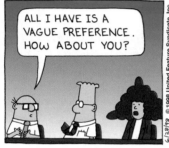

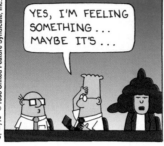

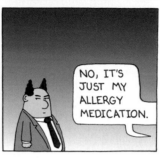

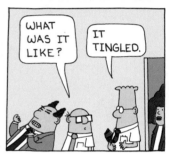

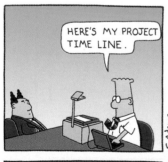

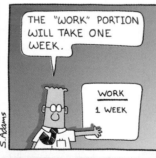

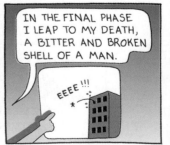

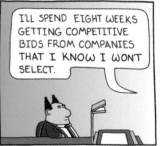

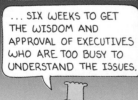

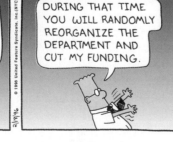

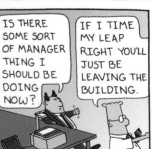

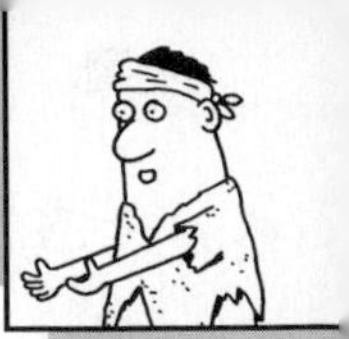

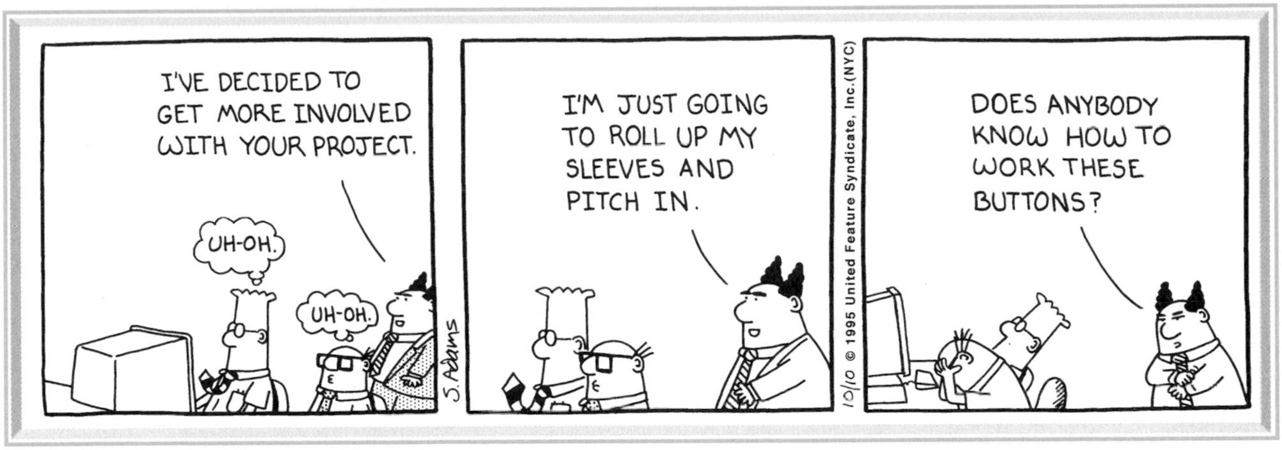
I'VE DECIDED TO GET MORE INVOLVED WITH YOUR PROJECT.
UH-OH.
UH-OH.
S. Adams
I'M JUST GOING TO ROLL UP MY SLEEVES AND PITCH IN.
10/10 © 1995 United Feature Syndicate, Inc.(NYC)
DOES ANYBODY KNOW HOW TO WORK THESE BUTTONS?

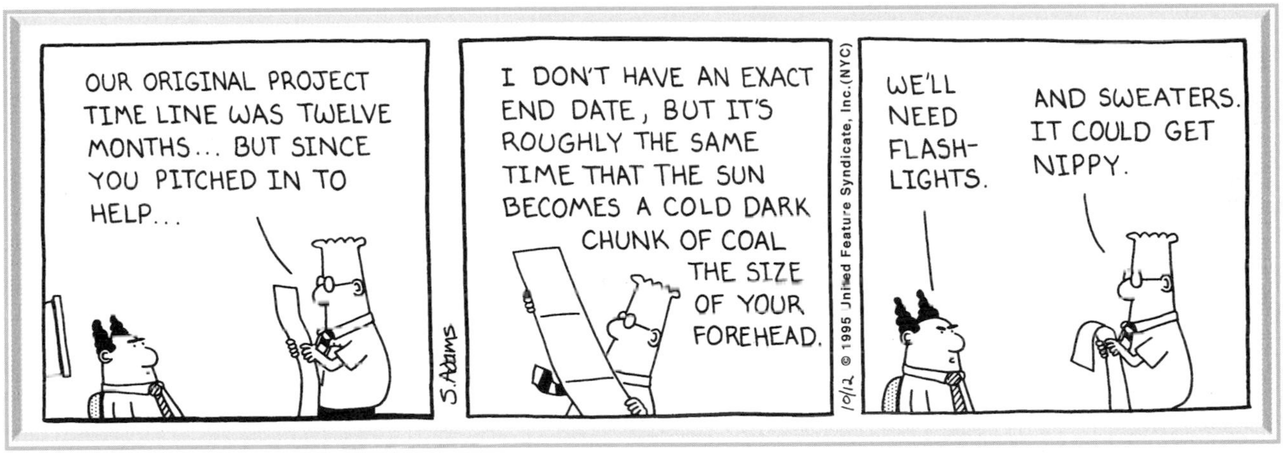
OUR ORIGINAL PROJECT TIME LINE WAS TWELVE MONTHS... BUT SINCE YOU PITCHED IN TO HELP...
S. Adams
I DON'T HAVE AN EXACT END DATE, BUT IT'S ROUGHLY THE SAME TIME THAT THE SUN BECOMES A COLD DARK CHUNK OF COAL THE SIZE OF YOUR FOREHEAD.
10/12 © 1995 United Feature Syndicate, Inc.(NYC)
WE'LL NEED FLASH-LIGHTS.
AND SWEATERS. IT COULD GET NIPPY.

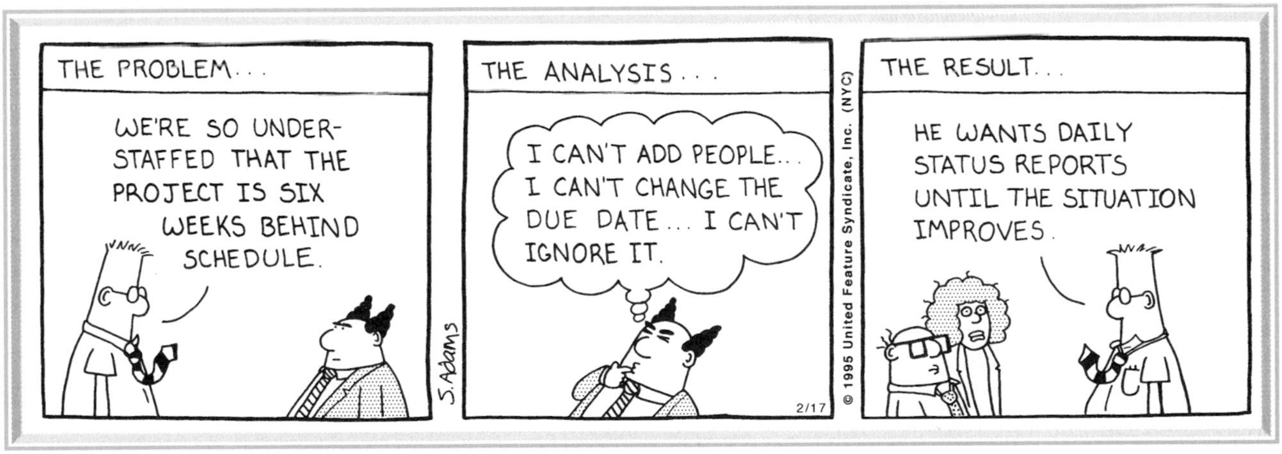
THE PROBLEM...
WE'RE SO UNDER-STAFFED THAT THE PROJECT IS SIX WEEKS BEHIND SCHEDULE.
S. Adams
THE ANALYSIS...
I CAN'T ADD PEOPLE... I CAN'T CHANGE THE DUE DATE... I CAN'T IGNORE IT.
2/17
© 1995 United Feature Syndicate, Inc. (NYC)
THE RESULT...
HE WANTS DAILY STATUS REPORTS UNTIL THE SITUATION IMPROVES.

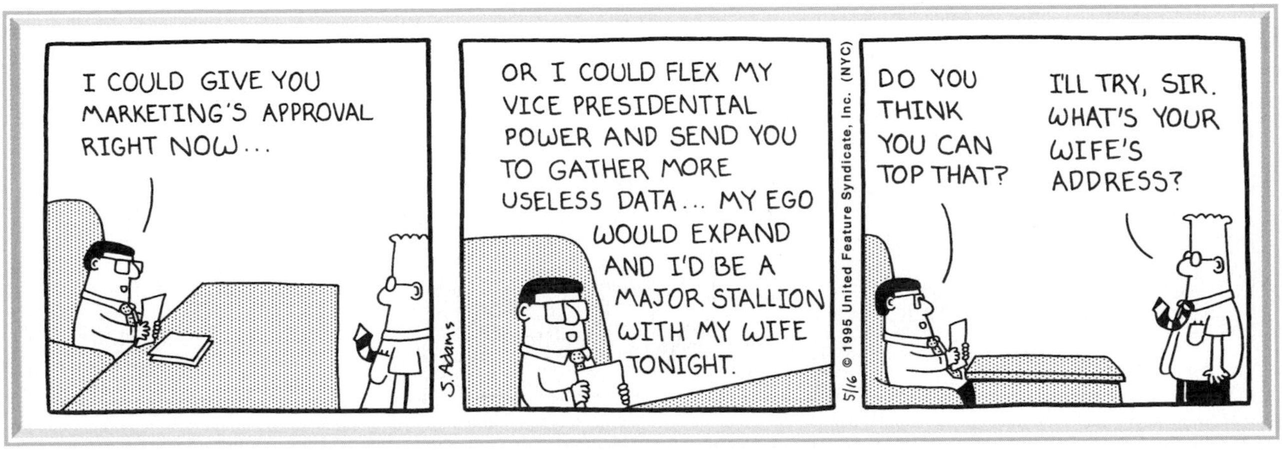
I COULD GIVE YOU MARKETING'S APPROVAL RIGHT NOW...
S. Adams
OR I COULD FLEX MY VICE PRESIDENTIAL POWER AND SEND YOU TO GATHER MORE USELESS DATA... MY EGO WOULD EXPAND AND I'D BE A MAJOR STALLION WITH MY WIFE TONIGHT.
5/6 © 1995 United Feature Syndicate, Inc. (NYC)
DO YOU THINK YOU CAN TOP THAT?
I'LL TRY, SIR. WHAT'S YOUR WIFE'S ADDRESS?

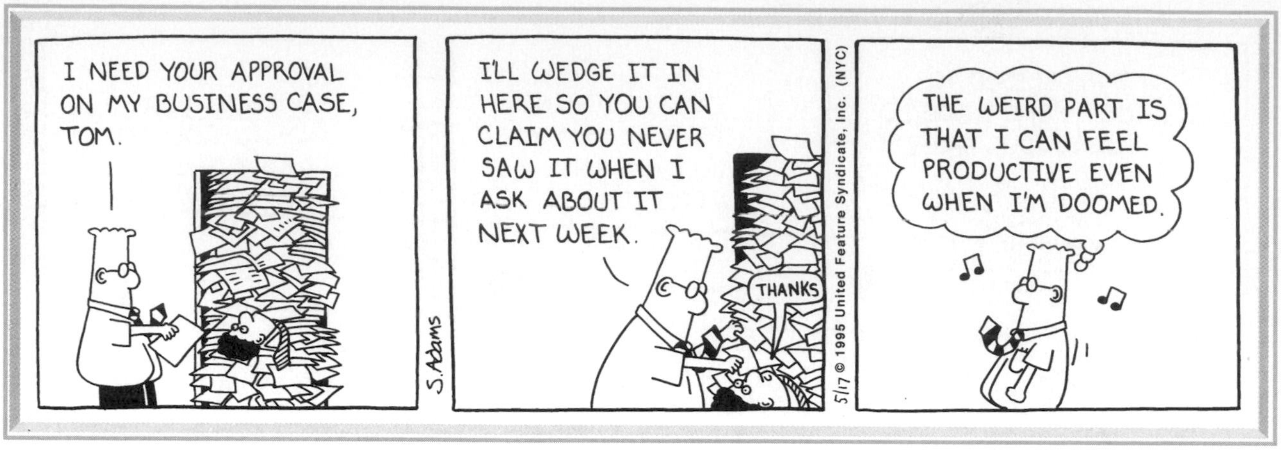
I NEED YOUR APPROVAL ON MY BUSINESS CASE, TOM.
I'LL WEDGE IT IN HERE SO YOU CAN CLAIM YOU NEVER SAW IT WHEN I ASK ABOUT IT NEXT WEEK.
THANKS
THE WEIRD PART IS THAT I CAN FEEL PRODUCTIVE EVEN WHEN I'M DOOMED.
S. Adams
5/17 © 1995 United Feature Syndicate, Inc. (NYC)

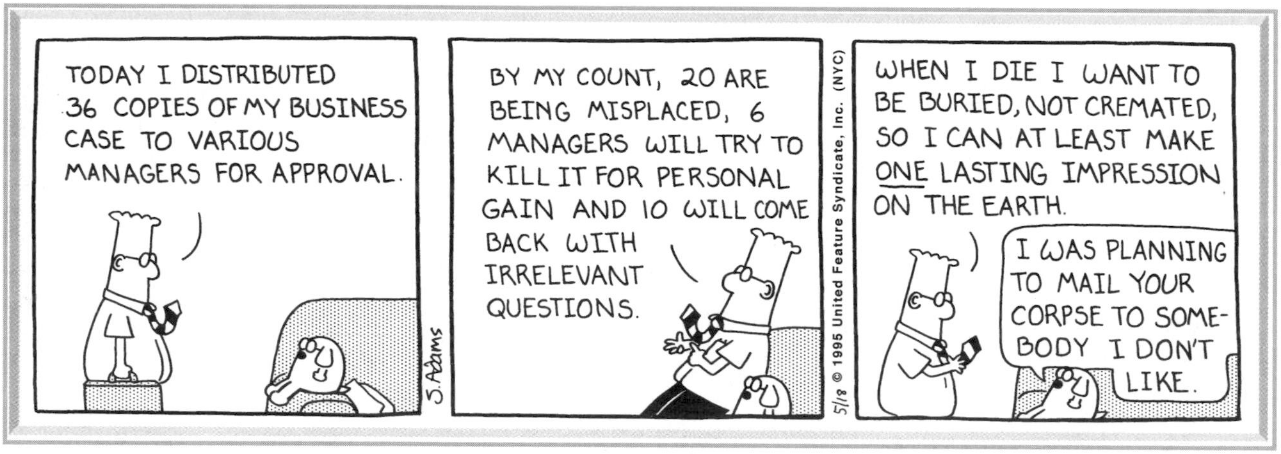
TODAY I DISTRIBUTED 36 COPIES OF MY BUSINESS CASE TO VARIOUS MANAGERS FOR APPROVAL.
BY MY COUNT, 20 ARE BEING MISPLACED, 6 MANAGERS WILL TRY TO KILL IT FOR PERSONAL GAIN AND 10 WILL COME BACK WITH IRRELEVANT QUESTIONS.
WHEN I DIE I WANT TO BE BURIED, NOT CREMATED, SO I CAN AT LEAST MAKE ONE LASTING IMPRESSION ON THE EARTH.
I WAS PLANNING TO MAIL YOUR CORPSE TO SOMEBODY I DON'T LIKE.
S. Adams
5/18 © 1995 United Feature Syndicate, Inc. (NYC)

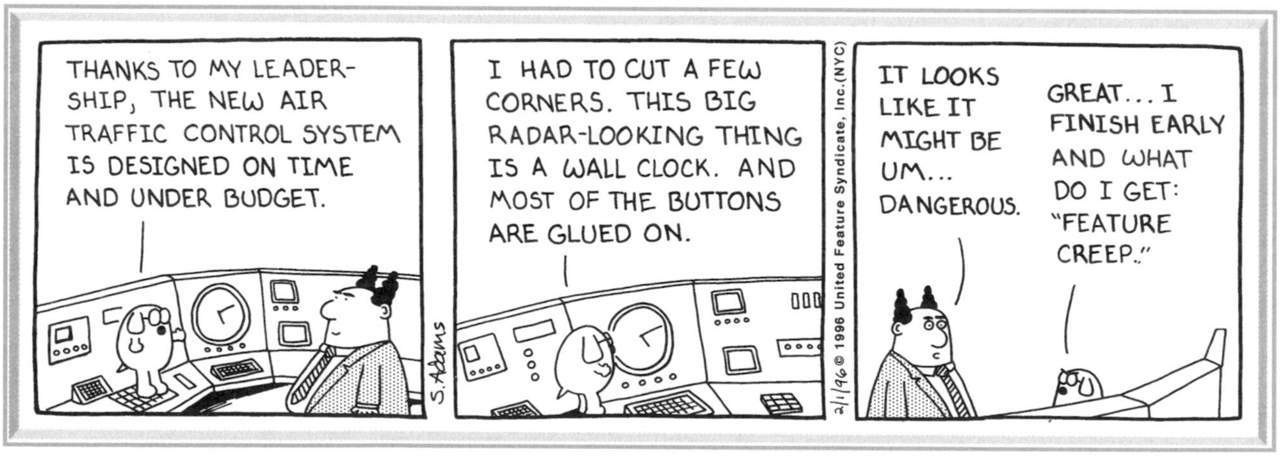
THANKS TO MY LEADERSHIP, THE NEW AIR TRAFFIC CONTROL SYSTEM IS DESIGNED ON TIME AND UNDER BUDGET.
I HAD TO CUT A FEW CORNERS. THIS BIG RADAR-LOOKING THING IS A WALL CLOCK. AND MOST OF THE BUTTONS ARE GLUED ON.
IT LOOKS LIKE IT MIGHT BE UM... DANGEROUS.
GREAT... I FINISH EARLY AND WHAT DO I GET: "FEATURE CREEP."
S. Adams
2/1/96 © 1996 United Feature Syndicate, Inc. (NYC)

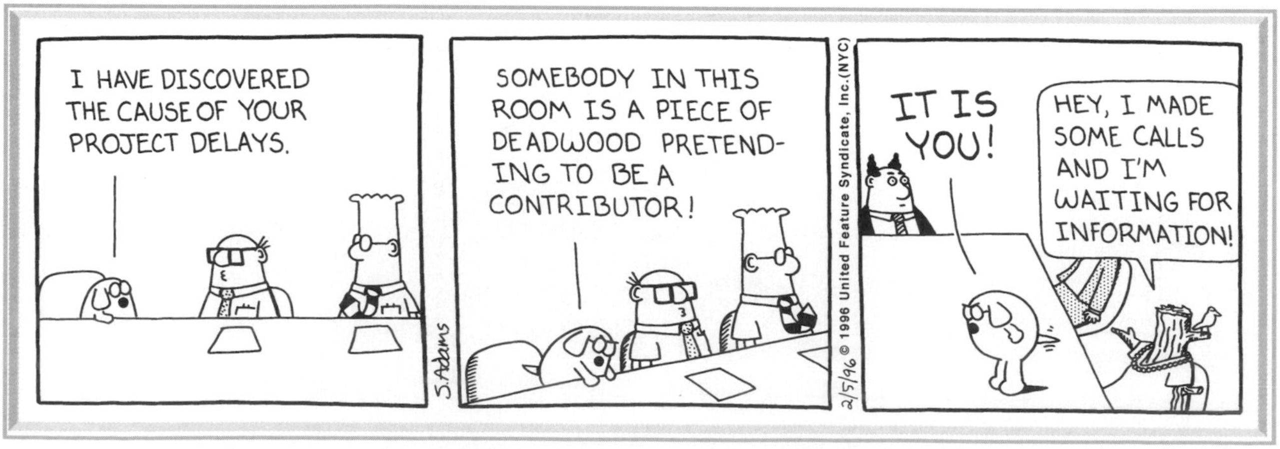
I HAVE DISCOVERED THE CAUSE OF YOUR PROJECT DELAYS.
SOMEBODY IN THIS ROOM IS A PIECE OF DEADWOOD PRETENDING TO BE A CONTRIBUTOR!
IT IS YOU!
HEY, I MADE SOME CALLS AND I'M WAITING FOR INFORMATION!
S. Adams
2/5/96 © 1996 United Feature Syndicate, Inc. (NYC)

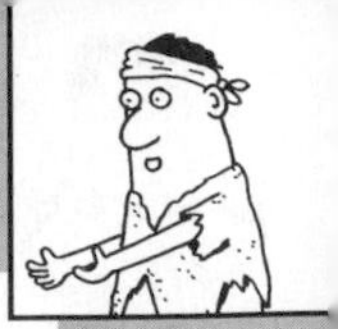

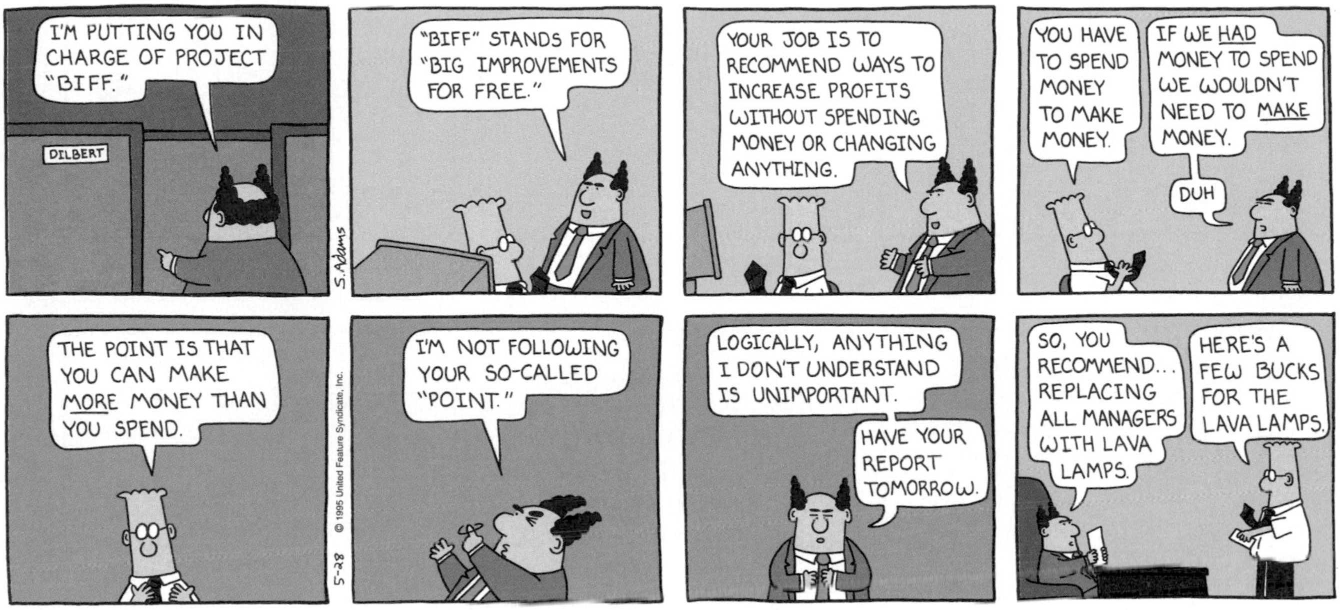
I'M PUTTING YOU IN CHARGE OF PROJECT "BIFF."
DILBERT
"BIFF" STANDS FOR "BIG IMPROVEMENTS FOR FREE."
YOUR JOB IS TO RECOMMEND WAYS TO INCREASE PROFITS WITHOUT SPENDING MONEY OR CHANGING ANYTHING.
YOU HAVE TO SPEND MONEY TO MAKE MONEY.
IF WE HAD MONEY TO SPEND WE WOULDN'T NEED TO MAKE MONEY.
DUH
THE POINT IS THAT YOU CAN MAKE MORE MONEY THAN YOU SPEND.
I'M NOT FOLLOWING YOUR SO-CALLED "POINT."
LOGICALLY, ANYTHING I DON'T UNDERSTAND IS UNIMPORTANT.
HAVE YOUR REPORT TOMORROW.
SO, YOU RECOMMEND... REPLACING ALL MANAGERS WITH LAVA LAMPS.
HERE'S A FEW BUCKS FOR THE LAVA LAMPS.
S. Adams
5-28 © 1995 United Feature Syndicate, Inc.

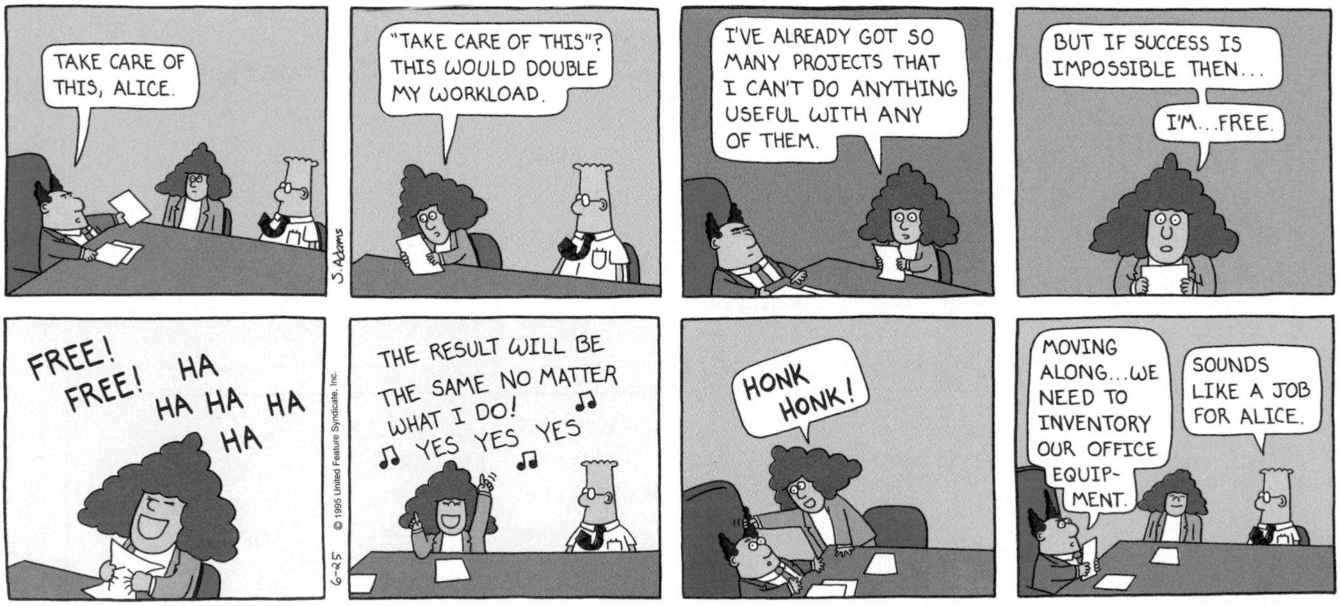
TAKE CARE OF THIS, ALICE.
"TAKE CARE OF THIS"? THIS WOULD DOUBLE MY WORKLOAD.
I'VE ALREADY GOT SO MANY PROJECTS THAT I CAN'T DO ANYTHING USEFUL WITH ANY OF THEM.
BUT IF SUCCESS IS IMPOSSIBLE THEN...
I'M...FREE.
FREE! FREE! HA HA HA HA HA
THE RESULT WILL BE THE SAME NO MATTER WHAT I DO! YES YES YES
HONK HONK!
MOVING ALONG...WE NEED TO INVENTORY OUR OFFICE EQUIP-MENT.
SOUNDS LIKE A JOB FOR ALICE.
S. Adams
6-25 © 1995 United Feature Syndicate, Inc.

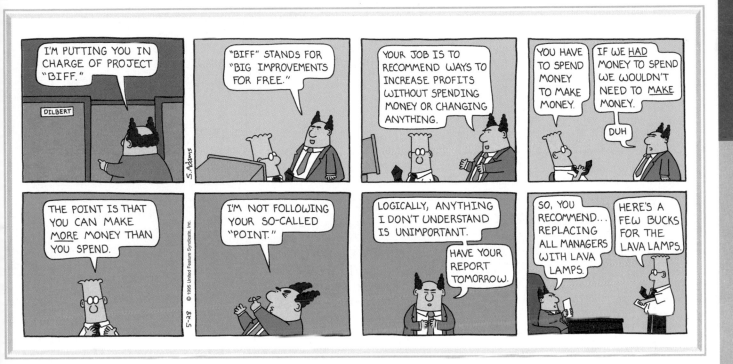

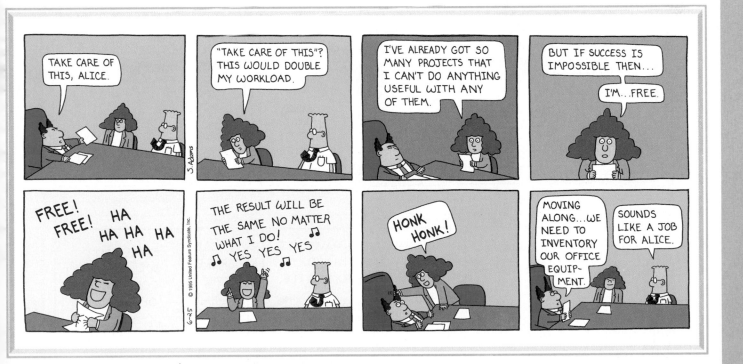

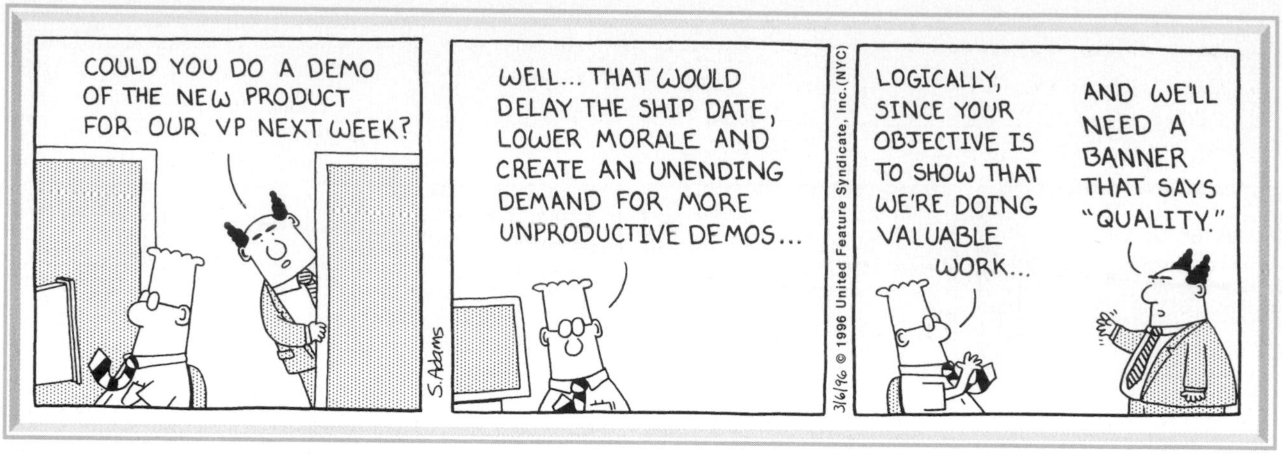
COULD YOU DO A DEMO OF THE NEW PRODUCT FOR OUR VP NEXT WEEK?
WELL... THAT WOULD DELAY THE SHIP DATE, LOWER MORALE AND CREATE AN UNENDING DEMAND FOR MORE UNPRODUCTIVE DEMOS...
S. Adams
3/6/96 © 1996 United Feature Syndicate, Inc.(NYC)
LOGICALLY, SINCE YOUR OBJECTIVE IS TO SHOW THAT WE'RE DOING VALUABLE WORK...
AND WE'LL NEED A BANNER THAT SAYS "QUALITY."

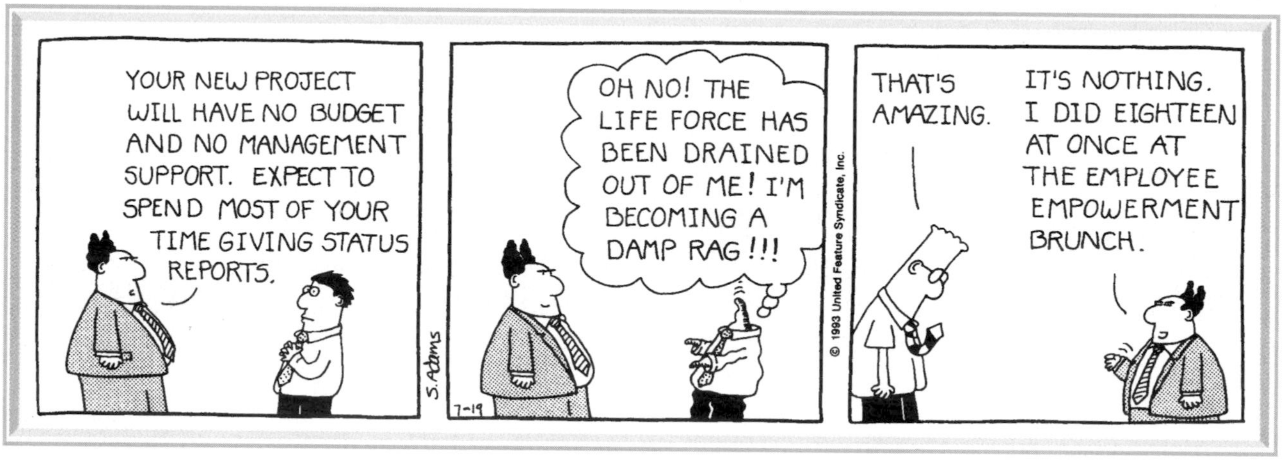
YOUR NEW PROJECT WILL HAVE NO BUDGET AND NO MANAGEMENT SUPPORT. EXPECT TO SPEND MOST OF YOUR TIME GIVING STATUS REPORTS.
S. Adams
7-19
OH NO! THE LIFE FORCE HAS BEEN DRAINED OUT OF ME! I'M BECOMING A DAMP RAG!!!
© 1993 United Feature Syndicate, Inc.
THAT'S AMAZING.
IT'S NOTHING. I DID EIGHTEEN AT ONCE AT THE EMPLOYEE EMPOWERMENT BRUNCH.

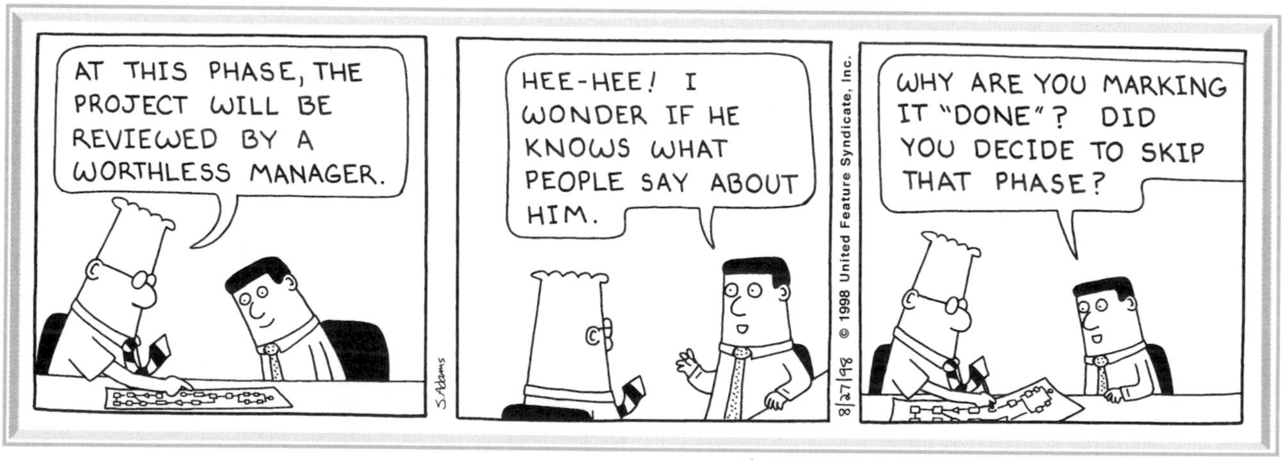
AT THIS PHASE, THE PROJECT WILL BE REVIEWED BY A WORTHLESS MANAGER.
S. Adams
HEE-HEE! I WONDER IF HE KNOWS WHAT PEOPLE SAY ABOUT HIM.
8/27/98 © 1998 United Feature Syndicate, Inc.
WHY ARE YOU MARKING IT "DONE"? DID YOU DECIDE TO SKIP THAT PHASE?

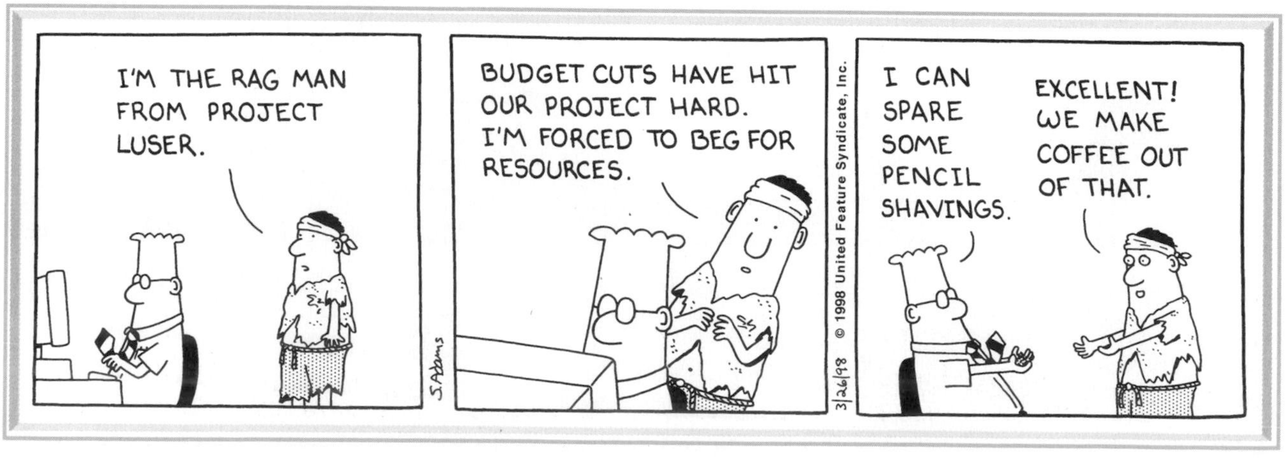
I'M THE RAG MAN FROM PROJECT LUSER.
S. Adams
BUDGET CUTS HAVE HIT OUR PROJECT HARD. I'M FORCED TO BEG FOR RESOURCES.
3/26/98 © 1998 United Feature Syndicate, Inc.
I CAN SPARE SOME PENCIL SHAVINGS.
EXCELLENT! WE MAKE COFFEE OUT OF THAT.

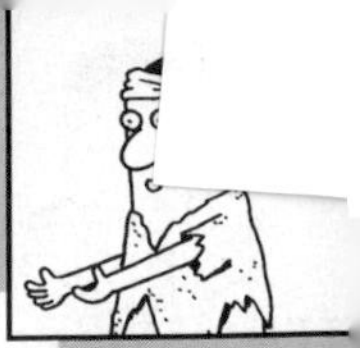

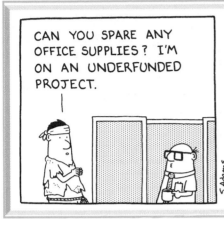

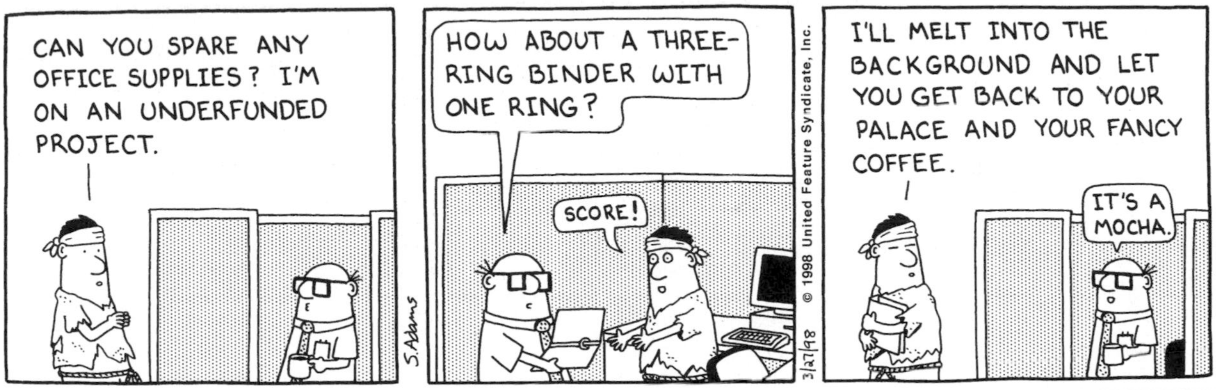
CAN YOU SPARE ANY OFFICE SUPPLIES? I'M ON AN UNDERFUNDED PROJECT.
HOW ABOUT A THREE-RING BINDER WITH ONE RING?
SCORE!
I'LL MELT INTO THE BACKGROUND AND LET YOU GET BACK TO YOUR PALACE AND YOUR FANCY COFFEE.
IT'S A MOCHA.
S. Adams
3/27/98 © 1998 United Feature Syndicate, Inc.

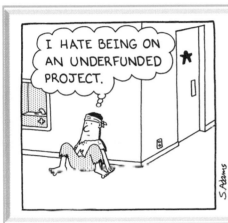

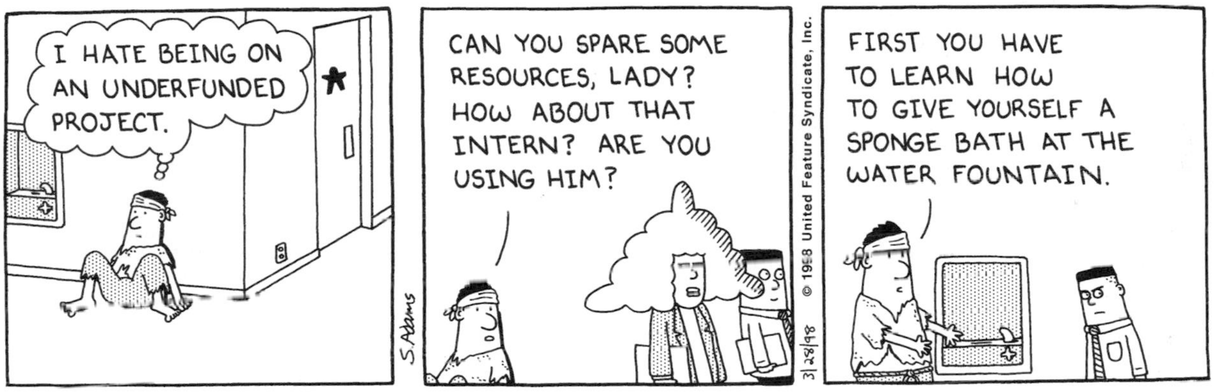
I HATE BEING ON AN UNDERFUNDED PROJECT.
CAN YOU SPARE SOME RESOURCES, LADY? HOW ABOUT THAT INTERN? ARE YOU USING HIM?
FIRST YOU HAVE TO LEARN HOW TO GIVE YOURSELF A SPONGE BATH AT THE WATER FOUNTAIN.
S. Adams
3/28/98 © 1998 United Feature Syndicate, Inc.

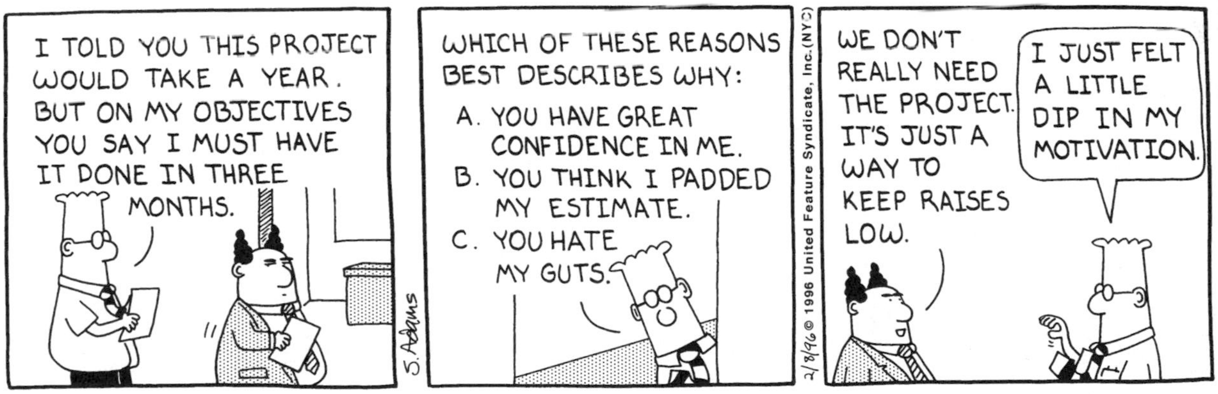
I TOLD YOU THIS PROJECT WOULD TAKE A YEAR. BUT ON MY OBJECTIVES YOU SAY I MUST HAVE IT DONE IN THREE MONTHS.
WHICH OF THESE REASONS BEST DESCRIBES WHY:
A. YOU HAVE GREAT CONFIDENCE IN ME.
B. YOU THINK I PADDED MY ESTIMATE.
C. YOU HATE MY GUTS.
WE DON'T REALLY NEED THE PROJECT. IT'S JUST A WAY TO KEEP RAISES LOW.
I JUST FELT A LITTLE DIP IN MY MOTIVATION.
S. Adams
2/8/96 © 1996 United Feature Syndicate, Inc.(NYC)

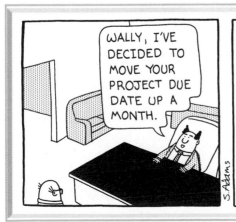

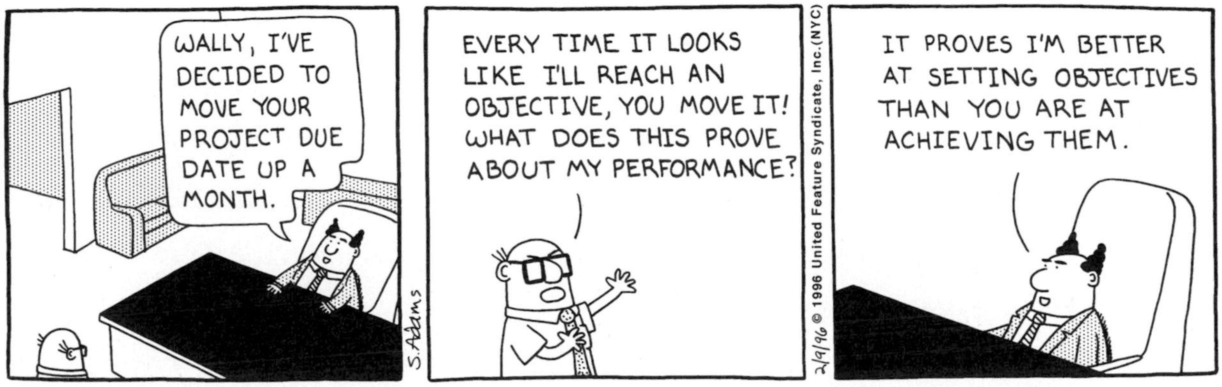
WALLY, I'VE DECIDED TO MOVE YOUR PROJECT DUE DATE UP A MONTH.
EVERY TIME IT LOOKS LIKE I'LL REACH AN OBJECTIVE, YOU MOVE IT! WHAT DOES THIS PROVE ABOUT MY PERFORMANCE?
IT PROVES I'M BETTER AT SETTING OBJECTIVES THAN YOU ARE AT ACHIEVING THEM.
S. Adams
2/9/96 © 1996 United Feature Syndicate, Inc.(NYC)

WE DESPERATELY NEED ANOTHER PERSON ON MY PROJECT!
WE'RE ALREADY OVER HEADCOUNT. GET A CONTRACT EMPLOYEE.
OKAY, BUT THEY COST TWICE AS MUCH.
S. Adams
PLUS WE NEED TO BUY A COMPUTER.
RENT ONE. WE'RE OVER OUR CAPITAL BUDGET.
RENTING IS EXPENSIVE. WE'LL GO OVER OUR EXPENSE BUDGET.
I'LL FIRE WALLY. THAT WILL FREE UP SOME CASH.
WALLY'S ON MY PROJECT!
7/9
FORGET IT! I'LL JUST WORK SIXTEEN HOURS A DAY!!
THAT WORKED OUT PERFECTLY. I THINK I MIGHT BE A GENIUS OR SOMETHING.
© 1995 United Feature Syndicate, Inc.
I WONDER IF I SHOULD HAVE TOLD HIM THE PROJECT WAS CANCELLED LAST WEEK.

WE JUST HIRED JACK AWAY FROM OUR COMPETITOR. HE WAS THEIR BEST MANAGER.
S. Adams
JACK WILL BE IN CHARGE OF PROJECT "GOOSEFOOD."
I'D LIKE YOU TWO TO BRIEF JACK ON THE PROJECT.
PROJECT "GOOSEFOOD" HAS NO BUDGET AND NO MANAGEMENT SUPPORT.
YOUR JOB IS TO BUILD A GLOBAL INFORMATION NETWORK IN TWO WEEKS.
© 1995 United Feature Syndicate, Inc.(NYC)
FAILURE IS CERTAIN. SOON YOU WILL LEAVE THE INDUSTRY IN DISGRACE.
9/10
...JUST LIKE THE OTHER "BEST MANAGERS" WE HIRED FROM OUR COMPETITORS.
JUST OUT OF CURIOSITY, HOW DID THE PROJECT GET ITS NAME?
LET'S JUST SAY THAT YOU'RE THE GOOSE FOOD...

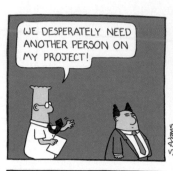

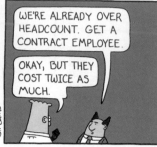

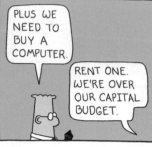

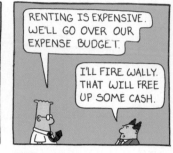

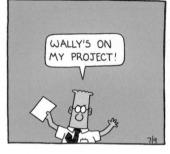

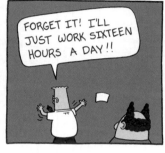

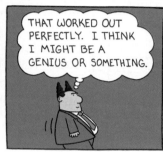

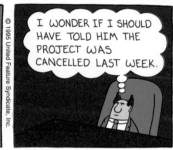

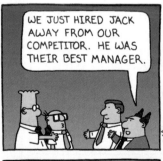

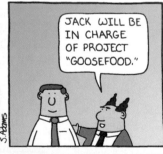

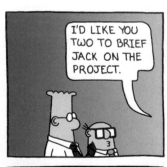

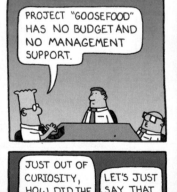

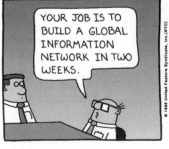

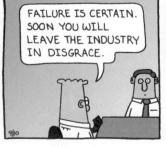

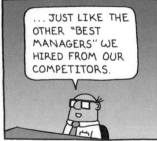

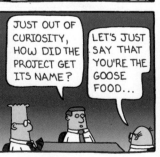

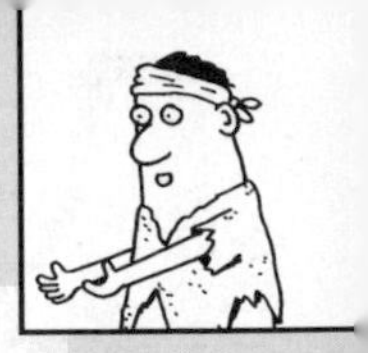

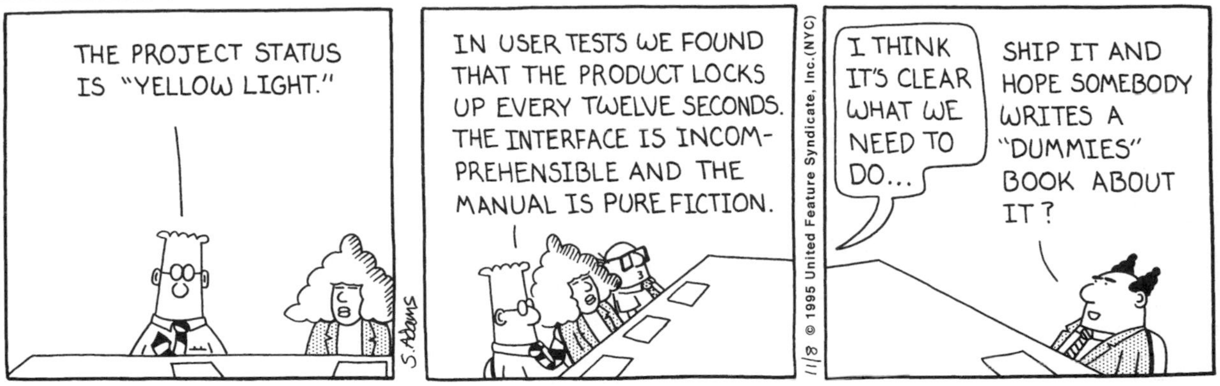
THE PROJECT STATUS IS "YELLOW LIGHT."
IN USER TESTS WE FOUND THAT THE PRODUCT LOCKS UP EVERY TWELVE SECONDS. THE INTERFACE IS INCOMPREHENSIBLE AND THE MANUAL IS PURE FICTION.
I THINK IT'S CLEAR WHAT WE NEED TO DO...
SHIP IT AND HOPE SOMEBODY WRITES A "DUMMIES" BOOK ABOUT IT?
S. Adams
11/8 © 1995 United Feature Syndicate, Inc.(NYC)

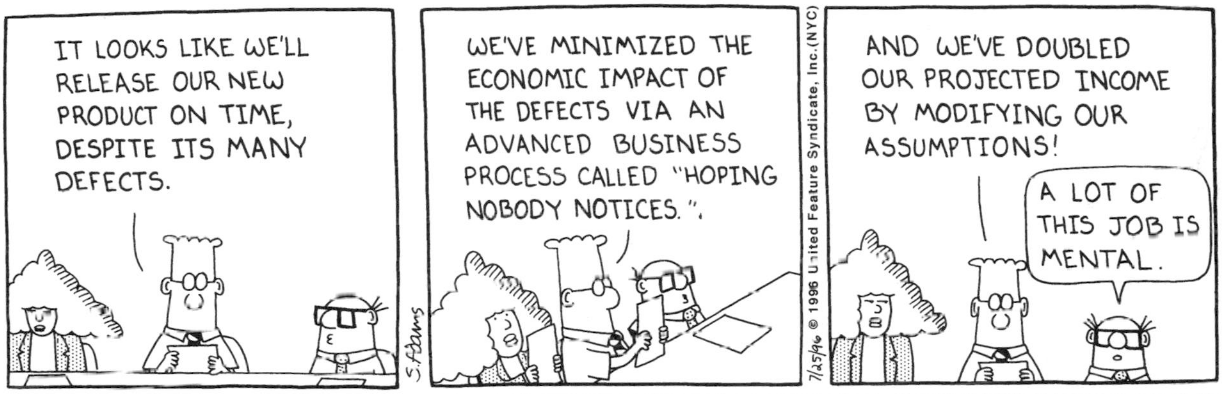
IT LOOKS LIKE WE'LL RELEASE OUR NEW PRODUCT ON TIME, DESPITE ITS MANY DEFECTS.
WE'VE MINIMIZED THE ECONOMIC IMPACT OF THE DEFECTS VIA AN ADVANCED BUSINESS PROCESS CALLED "HOPING NOBODY NOTICES."
AND WE'VE DOUBLED OUR PROJECTED INCOME BY MODIFYING OUR ASSUMPTIONS!
A LOT OF THIS JOB IS MENTAL.
S. Adams
7/25/96 © 1996 United Feature Syndicate, Inc.(NYC)

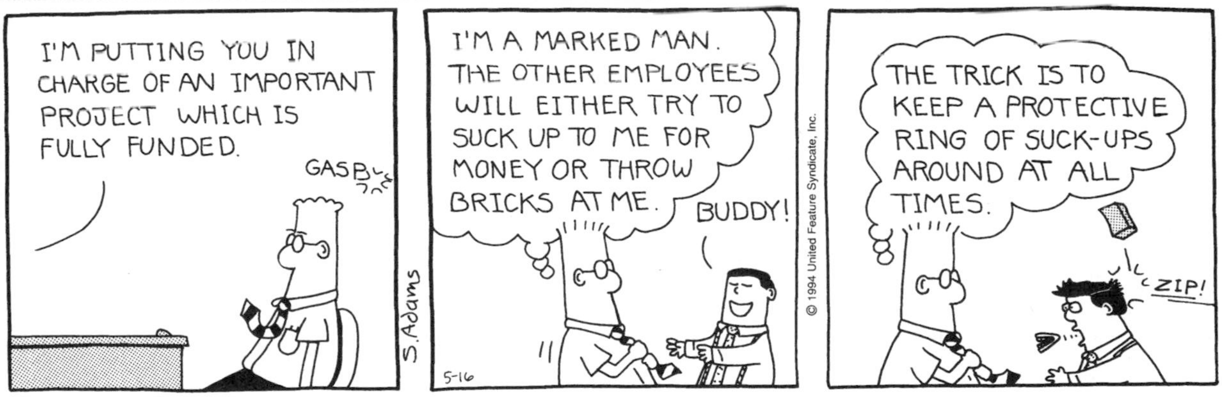
I'M PUTTING YOU IN CHARGE OF AN IMPORTANT PROJECT WHICH IS FULLY FUNDED.
GASP!
I'M A MARKED MAN. THE OTHER EMPLOYEES WILL EITHER TRY TO SUCK UP TO ME FOR MONEY OR THROW BRICKS AT ME.
BUDDY!
THE TRICK IS TO KEEP A PROTECTIVE RING OF SUCK-UPS AROUND AT ALL TIMES.
ZIP!
S. Adams
5-16
© 1994 United Feature Syndicate, Inc.

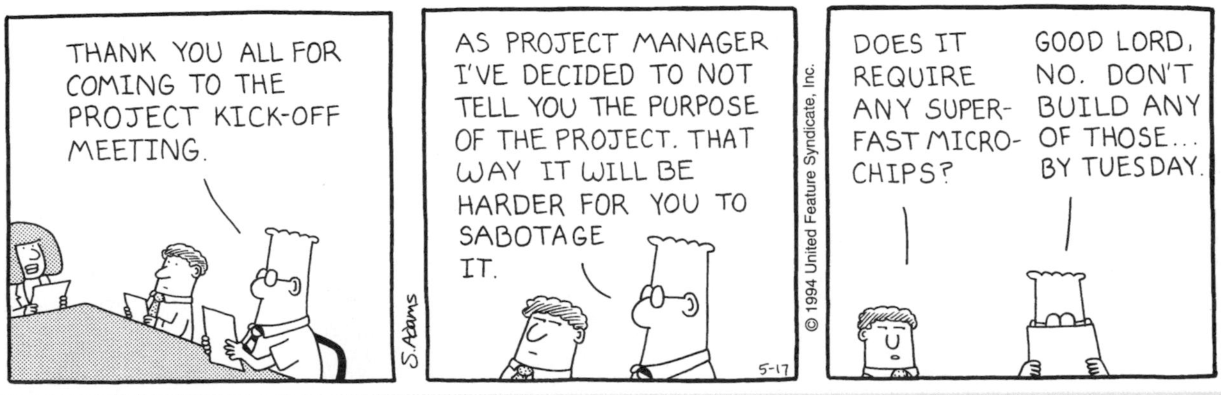
THANK YOU ALL FOR COMING TO THE PROJECT KICK-OFF MEETING.
AS PROJECT MANAGER I'VE DECIDED TO NOT TELL YOU THE PURPOSE OF THE PROJECT. THAT WAY IT WILL BE HARDER FOR YOU TO SABOTAGE IT.
DOES IT REQUIRE ANY SUPER-FAST MICRO-CHIPS?
GOOD LORD, NO. DON'T BUILD ANY OF THOSE... BY TUESDAY.
S. Adams
5-17
© 1994 United Feature Syndicate, Inc.

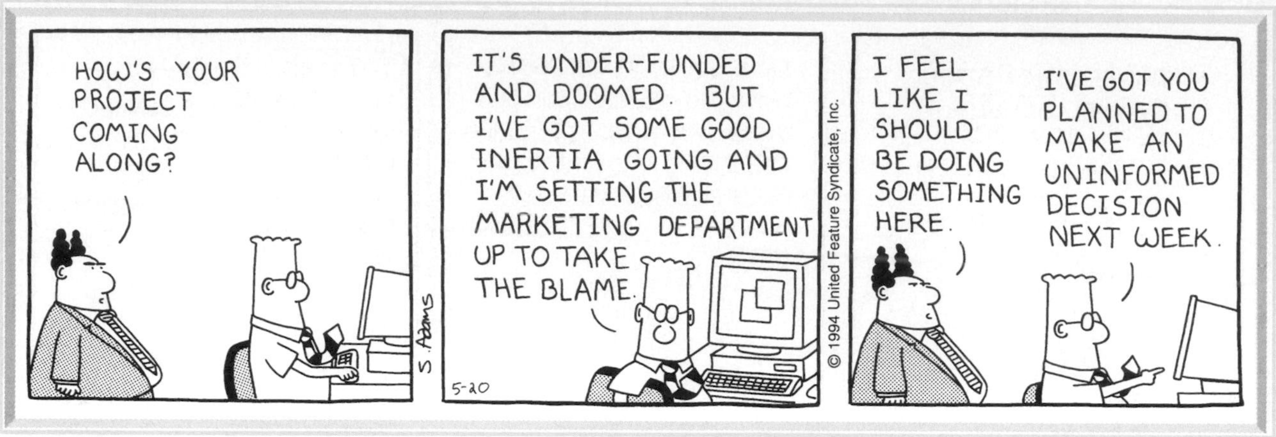
HOW'S YOUR PROJECT COMING ALONG?
IT'S UNDER-FUNDED AND DOOMED. BUT I'VE GOT SOME GOOD INERTIA GOING AND I'M SETTING THE MARKETING DEPARTMENT UP TO TAKE THE BLAME.
I FEEL LIKE I SHOULD BE DOING SOMETHING HERE.
I'VE GOT YOU PLANNED TO MAKE AN UNINFORMED DECISION NEXT WEEK.
© 1994 United Feature Syndicate, Inc.

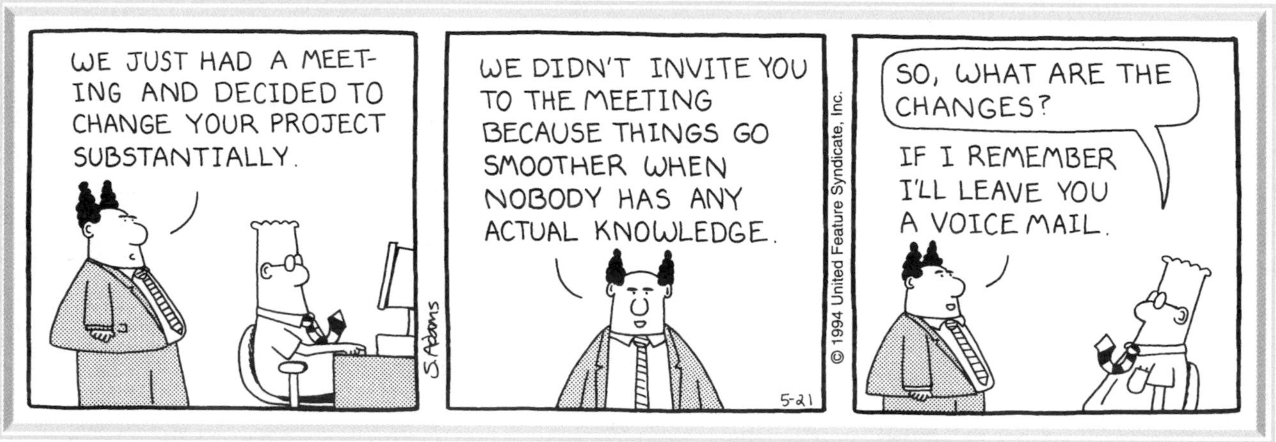
WE JUST HAD A MEETING AND DECIDED TO CHANGE YOUR PROJECT SUBSTANTIALLY.
WE DIDN'T INVITE YOU TO THE MEETING BECAUSE THINGS GO SMOOTHER WHEN NOBODY HAS ANY ACTUAL KNOWLEDGE.
SO, WHAT ARE THE CHANGES?
IF I REMEMBER I'LL LEAVE YOU A VOICE MAIL.
© 1994 United Feature Syndicate, Inc.

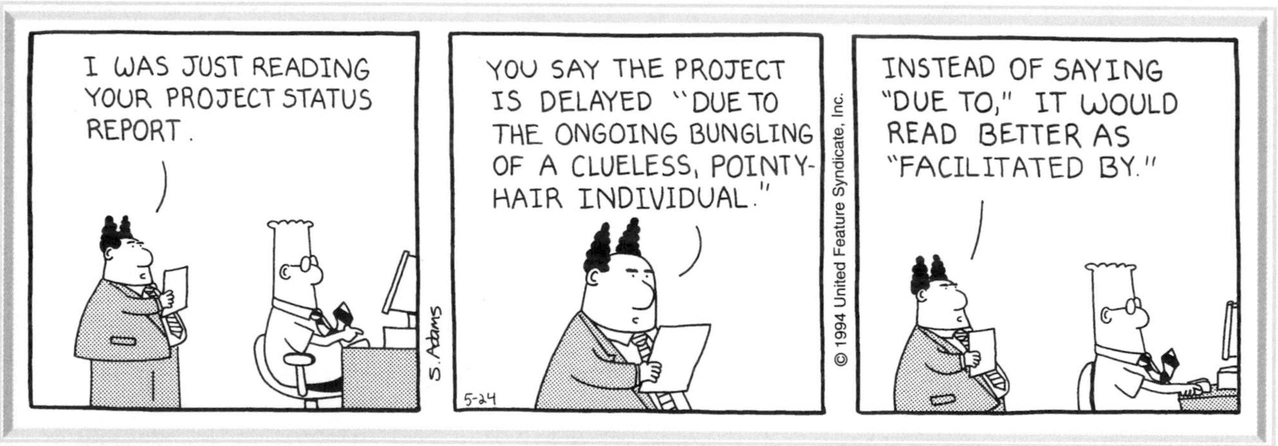
I WAS JUST READING YOUR PROJECT STATUS REPORT.
YOU SAY THE PROJECT IS DELAYED "DUE TO THE ONGOING BUNGLING OF A CLUELESS, POINTY-HAIR INDIVIDUAL."
INSTEAD OF SAYING "DUE TO," IT WOULD READ BETTER AS "FACILITATED BY."
© 1994 United Feature Syndicate, Inc.

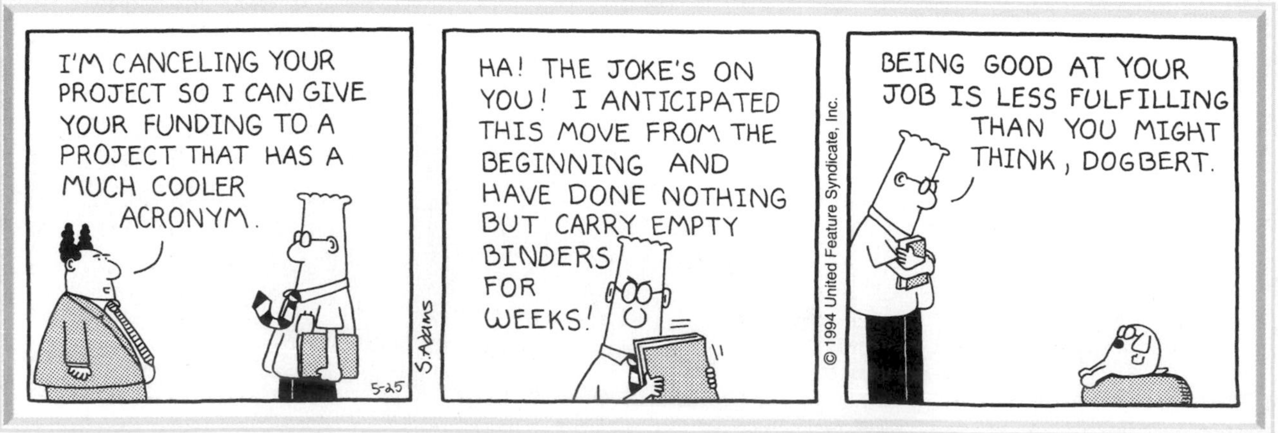
I'M CANCELING YOUR PROJECT SO I CAN GIVE YOUR FUNDING TO A PROJECT THAT HAS A MUCH COOLER ACRONYM.
HA! THE JOKE'S ON YOU! I ANTICIPATED THIS MOVE FROM THE BEGINNING AND HAVE DONE NOTHING BUT CARRY EMPTY BINDERS FOR WEEKS!
BEING GOOD AT YOUR JOB IS LESS FULFILLING THAN YOU MIGHT THINK, DOGBERT.
© 1994 United Feature Syndicate, Inc.

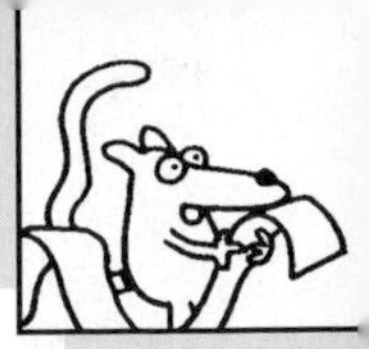

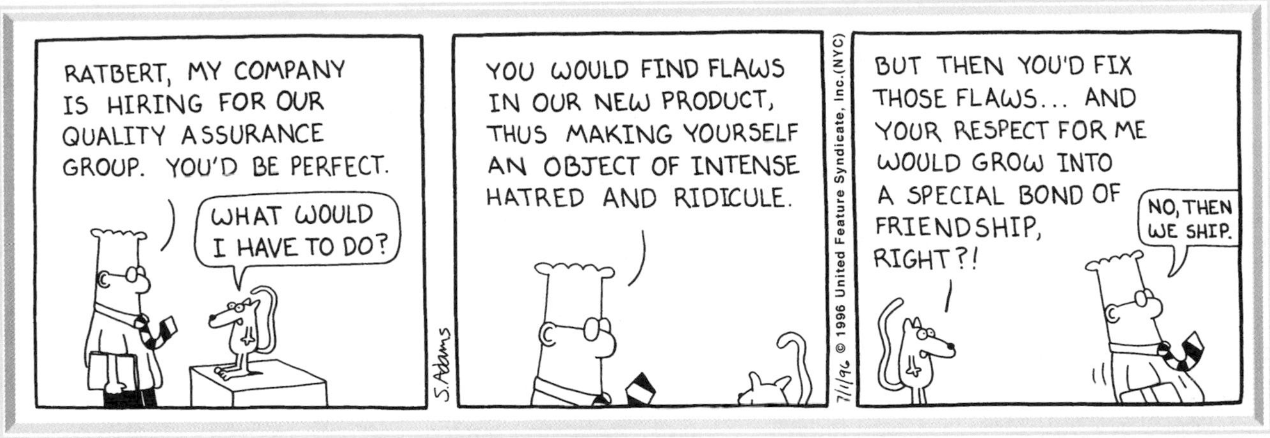
RATBERT, MY COMPANY IS HIRING FOR OUR QUALITY ASSURANCE GROUP. YOU'D BE PERFECT.
WHAT WOULD I HAVE TO DO?
S. Adams
YOU WOULD FIND FLAWS IN OUR NEW PRODUCT, THUS MAKING YOURSELF AN OBJECT OF INTENSE HATRED AND RIDICULE.
7/1/96 © 1996 United Feature Syndicate, Inc.(NYC)
BUT THEN YOU'D FIX THOSE FLAWS... AND YOUR RESPECT FOR ME WOULD GROW INTO A SPECIAL BOND OF FRIENDSHIP, RIGHT?!
NO, THEN WE SHIP.

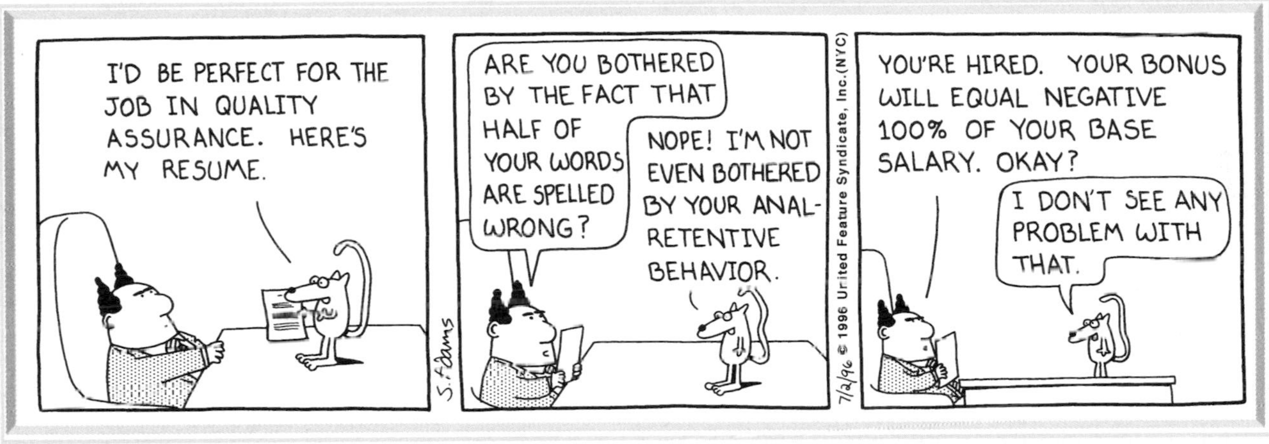
I'D BE PERFECT FOR THE JOB IN QUALITY ASSURANCE. HERE'S MY RESUME.
S. Adams
ARE YOU BOTHERED BY THE FACT THAT HALF OF YOUR WORDS ARE SPELLED WRONG?
NOPE! I'M NOT EVEN BOTHERED BY YOUR ANAL-RETENTIVE BEHAVIOR.
7/2/96 © 1996 United Feature Syndicate, Inc.(NYC)
YOU'RE HIRED. YOUR BONUS WILL EQUAL NEGATIVE 100% OF YOUR BASE SALARY. OKAY?
I DON'T SEE ANY PROBLEM WITH THAT.

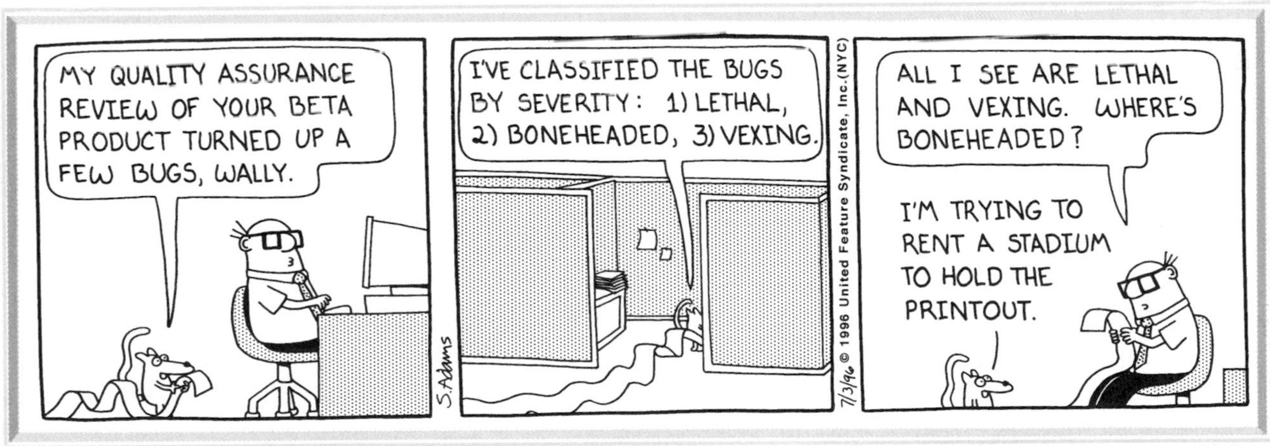
MY QUALITY ASSURANCE REVIEW OF YOUR BETA PRODUCT TURNED UP A FEW BUGS, WALLY.
S. Adams
I'VE CLASSIFIED THE BUGS BY SEVERITY: 1) LETHAL, 2) BONEHEADED, 3) VEXING.
7/3/96 © 1996 United Feature Syndicate, Inc.(NYC)
ALL I SEE ARE LETHAL AND VEXING. WHERE'S BONEHEADED?
I'M TRYING TO RENT A STADIUM TO HOLD THE PRINTOUT.

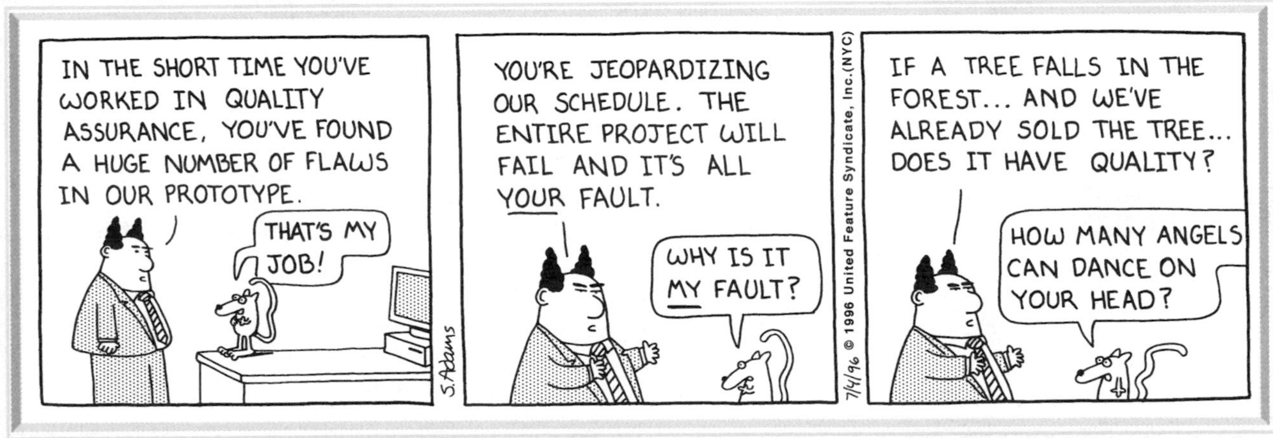
IN THE SHORT TIME YOU'VE WORKED IN QUALITY ASSURANCE, YOU'VE FOUND A HUGE NUMBER OF FLAWS IN OUR PROTOTYPE.
THAT'S MY JOB!
S. Adams
YOU'RE JEOPARDIZING OUR SCHEDULE. THE ENTIRE PROJECT WILL FAIL AND IT'S ALL YOUR FAULT.
WHY IS IT MY FAULT?
7/4/96 © 1996 United Feature Syndicate, Inc.(NYC)
IF A TREE FALLS IN THE FOREST... AND WE'VE ALREADY SOLD THE TREE... DOES IT HAVE QUALITY?
HOW MANY ANGELS CAN DANCE ON YOUR HEAD?

BANK OF ETHEL
NEXT VICTIM.
YOU CHARGED ME A FEE FOR PAYING MY CREDIT CARD BILL A DAY LATE.
SO?
WHY DON'T YOUR COMPUTERS AUTOMATICALLY TRANSFER MONEY FROM MY CHECKING ACCOUNT INSTEAD OF CHARGING A PENALTY?
FRANKLY, WE'RE NOT MUCH INTO THE "CUSTOMER SERVICE" CRAZE.
WE PREFER TO SET LITTLE TRAPS SO CUSTOMERS GET HIT WITH UNEXPECTED PENALTIES.
WELL!! I THINK I'LL JUST TAKE MY BUSINESS ELSEWHERE!
YOU'RE ANNOYING ME. THAT'S A HUNDRED DOLLAR PENALTY!
I DON'T THINK I CAN EVEN CLAIM A MORAL VICTORY HERE.
S. Adams
© 1993 United Feature Syndicate, Inc.

PHARMACY
IS THIS ONE LINE OR TWO?
I'LL HEDGE MY BETS BY STANDING IN THE MIDDLE.
THIS GUY IS CONFUSED TOO.
GET BEHIND ME... GET BEHIND ME... GET BEHIND ME... GET BEHIND ME...
OH-NO! HE'S FORMING A NEW LINE BEHIND THE FAST CASHIER!
#!%*
HE'S DISTRACTED! I TAKE THE ANGLE! I WIN!
STRESS MEDICATIONS ARE THE OTHER LINE.
S. Adams
© 1998 United Feature Syndicate, Inc.

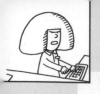

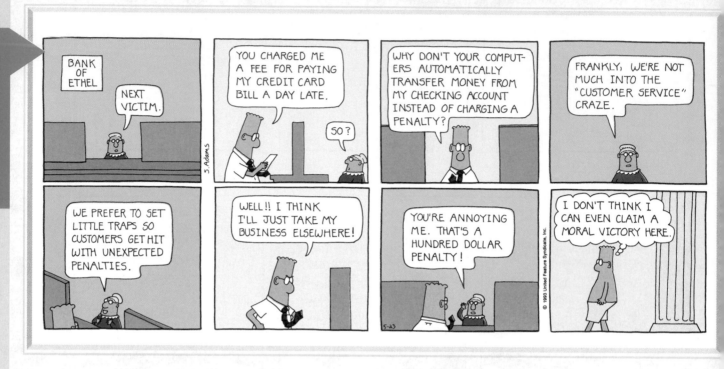

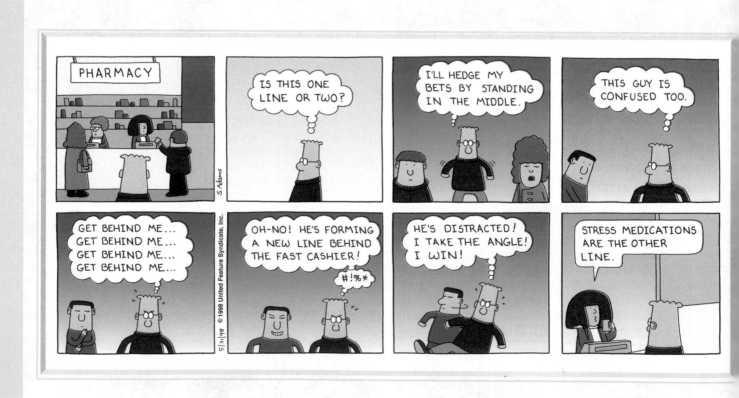

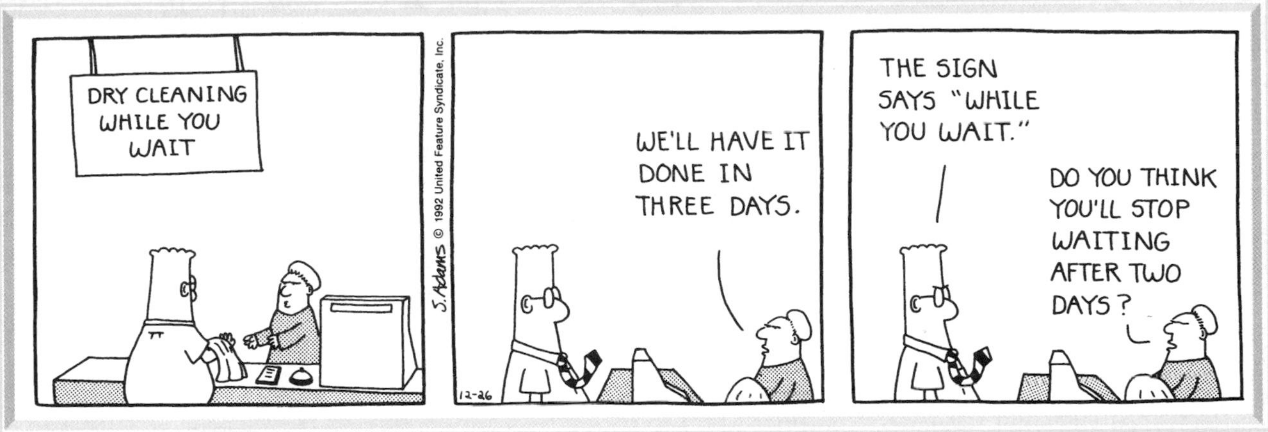
DRY CLEANING WHILE YOU WAIT
WE'LL HAVE IT DONE IN THREE DAYS.
THE SIGN SAYS "WHILE YOU WAIT."
DO YOU THINK YOU'LL STOP WAITING AFTER TWO DAYS?
S. Adams © 1992 United Feature Syndicate, Inc.
12-26

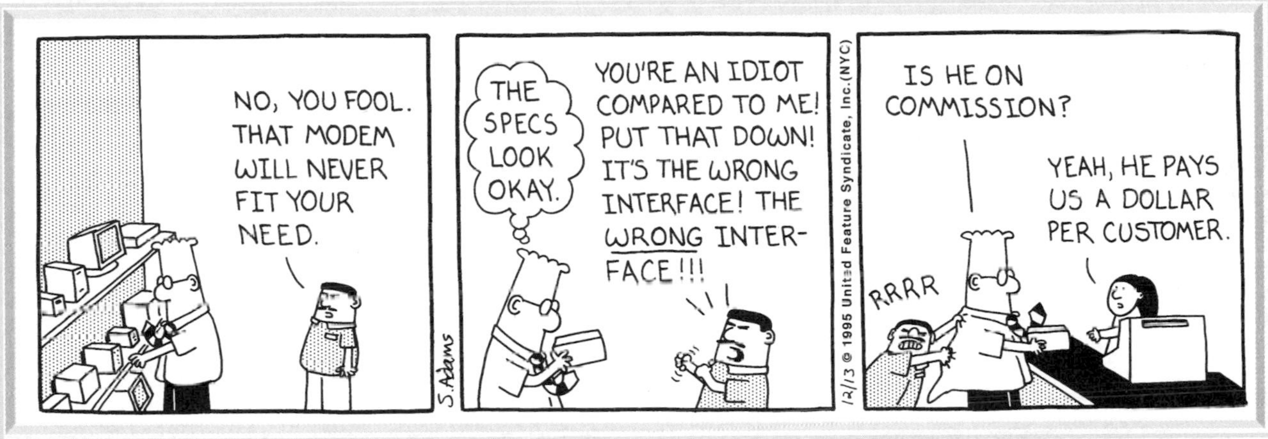
NO, YOU FOOL. THAT MODEM WILL NEVER FIT YOUR NEED.
THE SPECS LOOK OKAY.
YOU'RE AN IDIOT COMPARED TO ME! PUT THAT DOWN! IT'S THE WRONG INTERFACE! THE WRONG INTER-FACE!!!
IS HE ON COMMISSION?
YEAH, HE PAYS US A DOLLAR PER CUSTOMER.
RRRR
S. Adams
12/13 © 1995 United Feature Syndicate, Inc.(NYC)

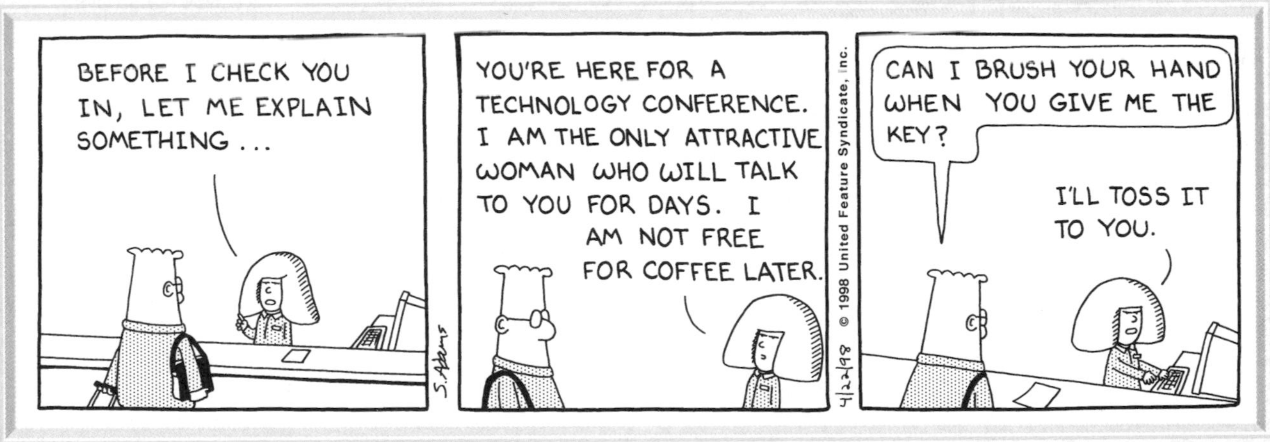
BEFORE I CHECK YOU IN, LET ME EXPLAIN SOMETHING...
YOU'RE HERE FOR A TECHNOLOGY CONFERENCE. I AM THE ONLY ATTRACTIVE WOMAN WHO WILL TALK TO YOU FOR DAYS. I AM NOT FREE FOR COFFEE LATER.
CAN I BRUSH YOUR HAND WHEN YOU GIVE ME THE KEY?
I'LL TOSS IT TO YOU.
S. Adams
4/22/98 © 1998 United Feature Syndicate, Inc.

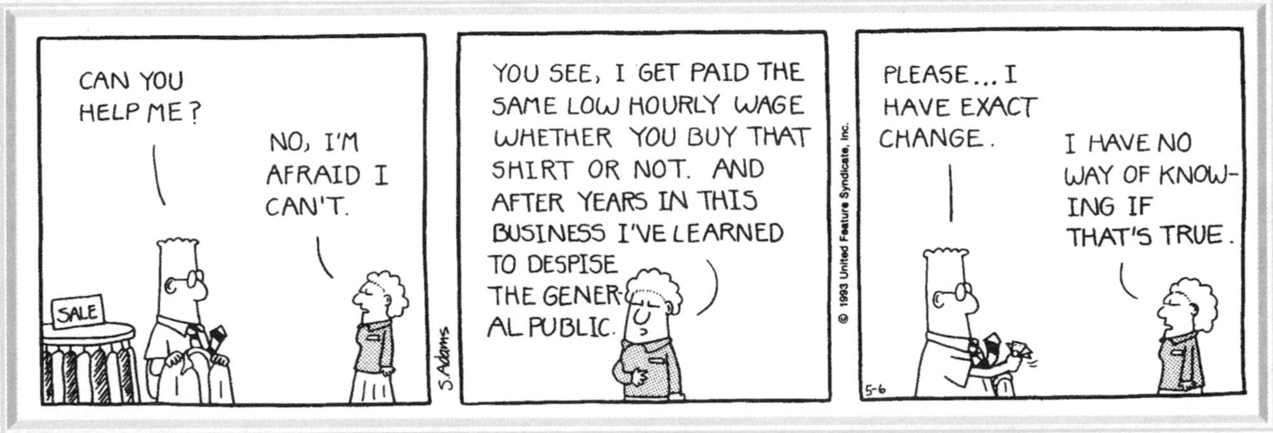
CAN YOU HELP ME?
NO, I'M AFRAID I CAN'T.
SALE
YOU SEE, I GET PAID THE SAME LOW HOURLY WAGE WHETHER YOU BUY THAT SHIRT OR NOT. AND AFTER YEARS IN THIS BUSINESS I'VE LEARNED TO DESPISE THE GENERAL PUBLIC.
PLEASE... I HAVE EXACT CHANGE.
I HAVE NO WAY OF KNOWING IF THAT'S TRUE.
S. Adams
© 1993 United Feature Syndicate, Inc.
5-6

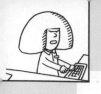

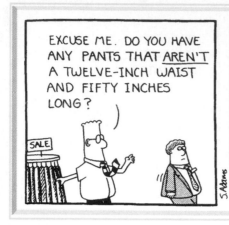

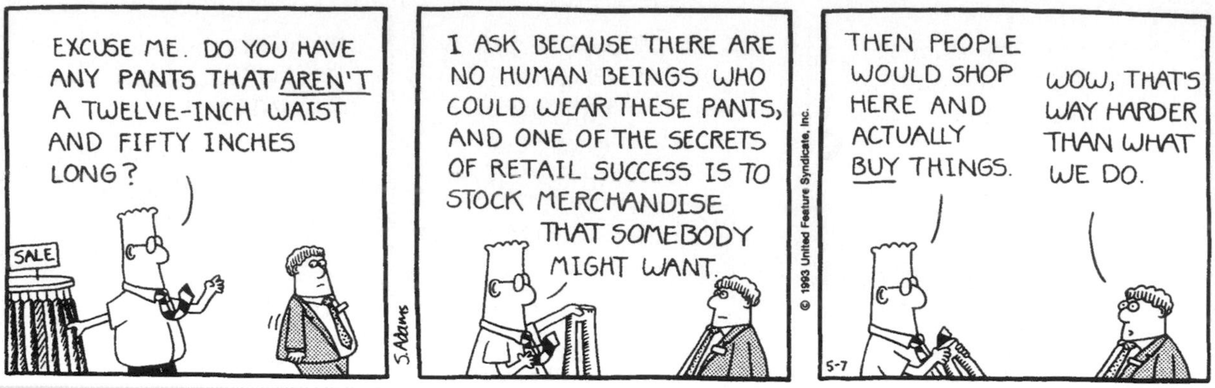
EXCUSE ME. DO YOU HAVE ANY PANTS THAT AREN'T A TWELVE-INCH WAIST AND FIFTY INCHES LONG?
SALE
I ASK BECAUSE THERE ARE NO HUMAN BEINGS WHO COULD WEAR THESE PANTS, AND ONE OF THE SECRETS OF RETAIL SUCCESS IS TO STOCK MERCHANDISE THAT SOMEBODY MIGHT WANT.
THEN PEOPLE WOULD SHOP HERE AND ACTUALLY BUY THINGS.
WOW, THAT'S WAY HARDER THAN WHAT WE DO.
© 1993 United Feature Syndicate, Inc.
5-7

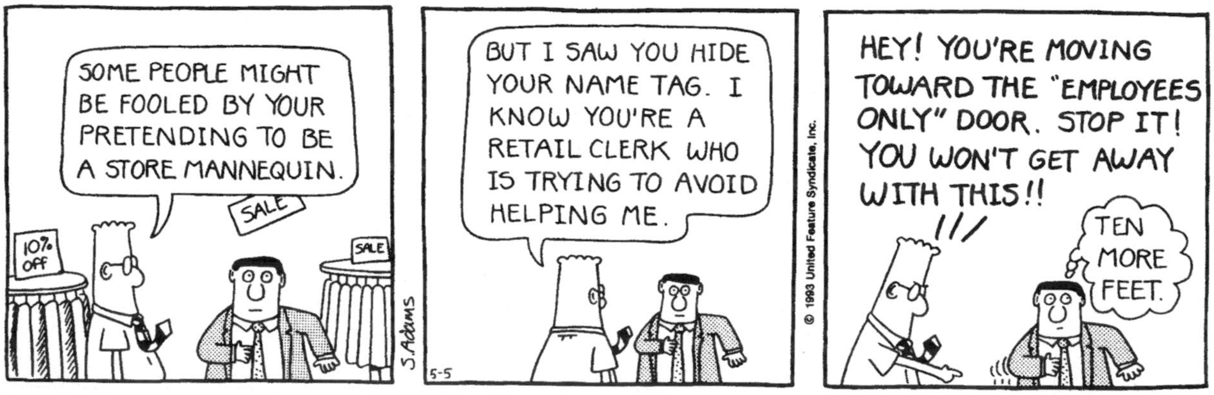
SOME PEOPLE MIGHT BE FOOLED BY YOUR PRETENDING TO BE A STORE MANNEQUIN.
10% OFF
SALE
SALE
BUT I SAW YOU HIDE YOUR NAME TAG. I KNOW YOU'RE A RETAIL CLERK WHO IS TRYING TO AVOID HELPING ME.
5-5
© 1993 United Feature Syndicate, Inc.
HEY! YOU'RE MOVING TOWARD THE "EMPLOYEES ONLY" DOOR. STOP IT! YOU WON'T GET AWAY WITH THIS!!
TEN MORE FEET.

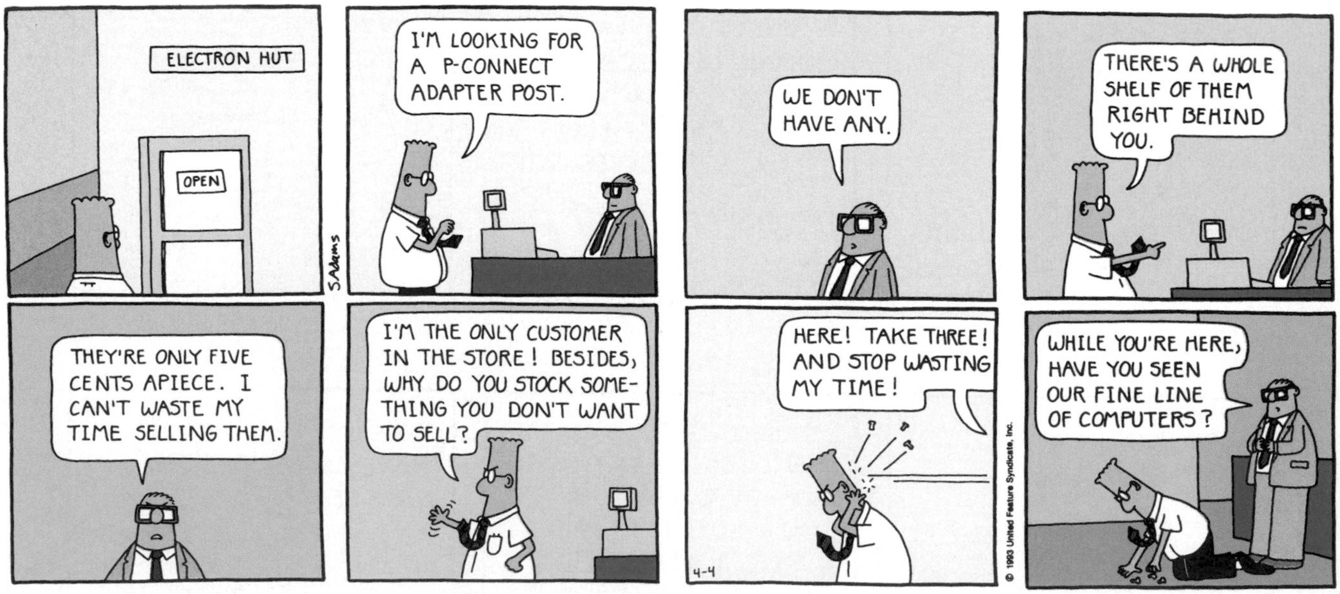
ELECTRON HUT
OPEN
I'M LOOKING FOR A P-CONNECT ADAPTER POST.
WE DON'T HAVE ANY.
THERE'S A WHOLE SHELF OF THEM RIGHT BEHIND YOU.
THEY'RE ONLY FIVE CENTS APIECE. I CAN'T WASTE MY TIME SELLING THEM.
I'M THE ONLY CUSTOMER IN THE STORE! BESIDES, WHY DO YOU STOCK SOMETHING YOU DON'T WANT TO SELL?
HERE! TAKE THREE! AND STOP WASTING MY TIME!
4-4
© 1993 United Feature Syndicate, Inc.
WHILE YOU'RE HERE, HAVE YOU SEEN OUR FINE LINE OF COMPUTERS?

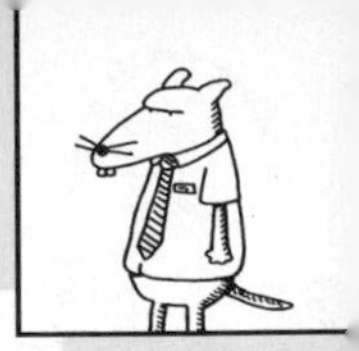

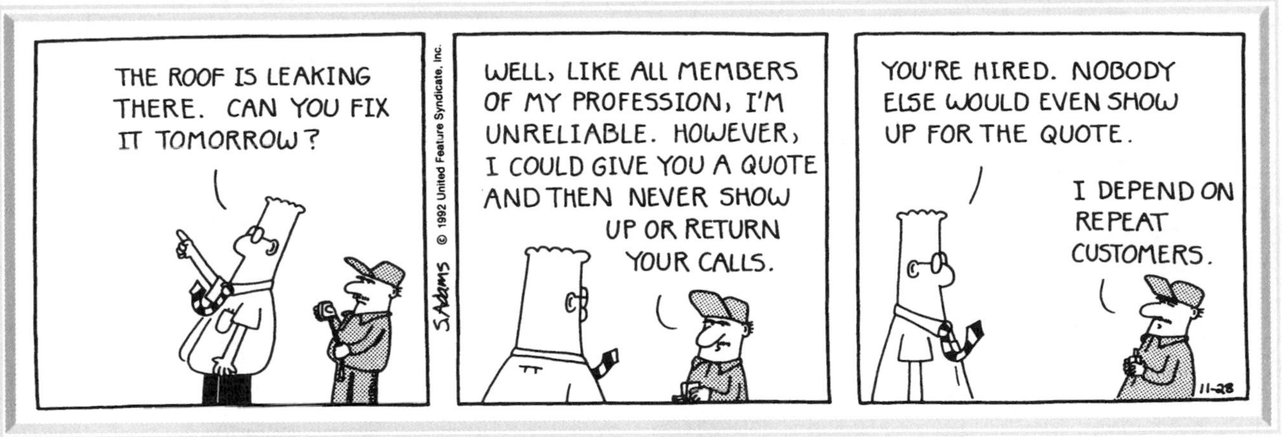
THE ROOF IS LEAKING THERE. CAN YOU FIX IT TOMORROW?
WELL, LIKE ALL MEMBERS OF MY PROFESSION, I'M UNRELIABLE. HOWEVER, I COULD GIVE YOU A QUOTE AND THEN NEVER SHOW UP OR RETURN YOUR CALLS.
YOU'RE HIRED. NOBODY ELSE WOULD EVEN SHOW UP FOR THE QUOTE.
I DEPEND ON REPEAT CUSTOMERS.
© 1992 United Feature Syndicate, Inc.

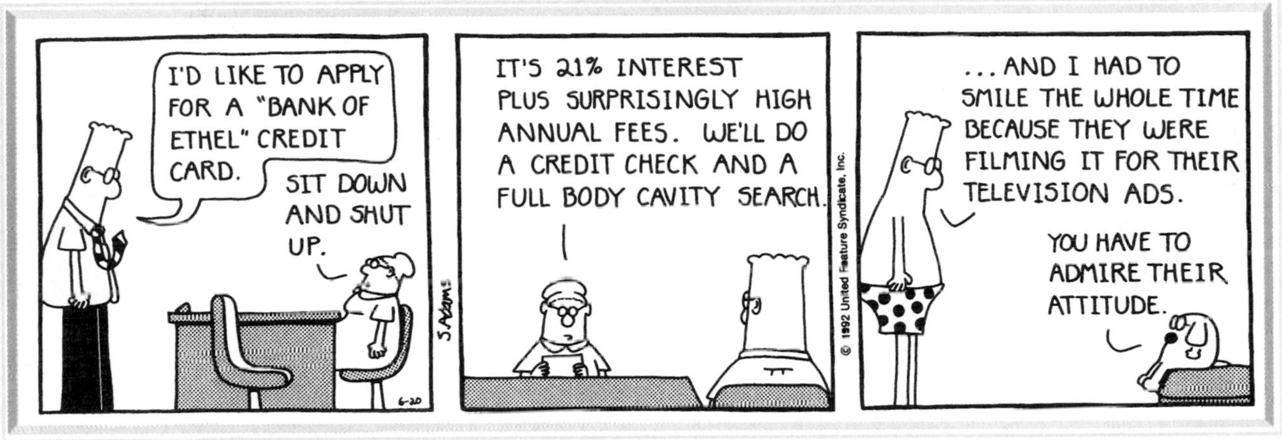
I'D LIKE TO APPLY FOR A "BANK OF ETHEL" CREDIT CARD.
SIT DOWN AND SHUT UP.
IT'S 21% INTEREST PLUS SURPRISINGLY HIGH ANNUAL FEES. WE'LL DO A CREDIT CHECK AND A FULL BODY CAVITY SEARCH.
...AND I HAD TO SMILE THE WHOLE TIME BECAUSE THEY WERE FILMING IT FOR THEIR TELEVISION ADS.
YOU HAVE TO ADMIRE THEIR ATTITUDE.
© 1992 United Feature Syndicate, Inc.

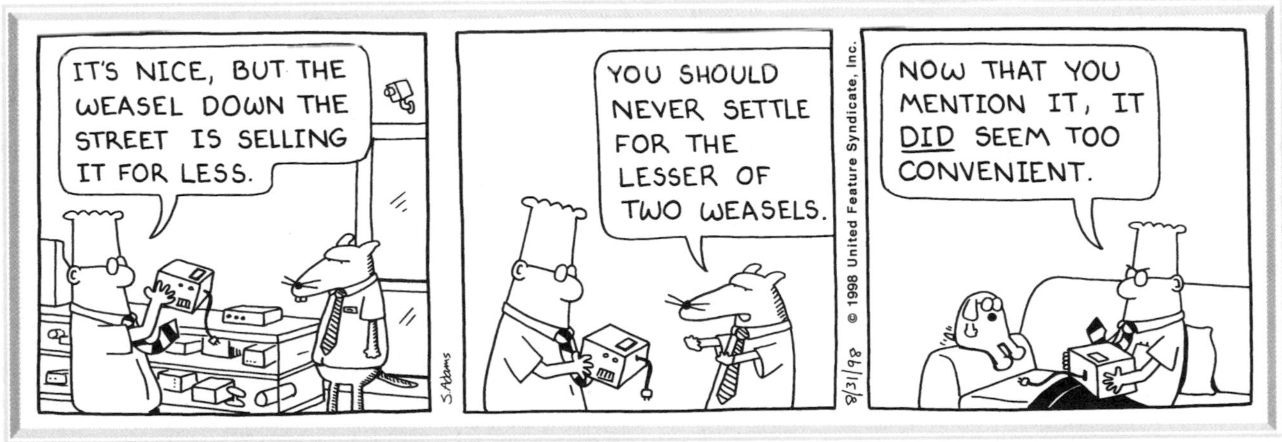
IT'S NICE, BUT THE WEASEL DOWN THE STREET IS SELLING IT FOR LESS.
YOU SHOULD NEVER SETTLE FOR THE LESSER OF TWO WEASELS.
NOW THAT YOU MENTION IT, IT DID SEEM TOO CONVENIENT.
© 1998 United Feature Syndicate, Inc.

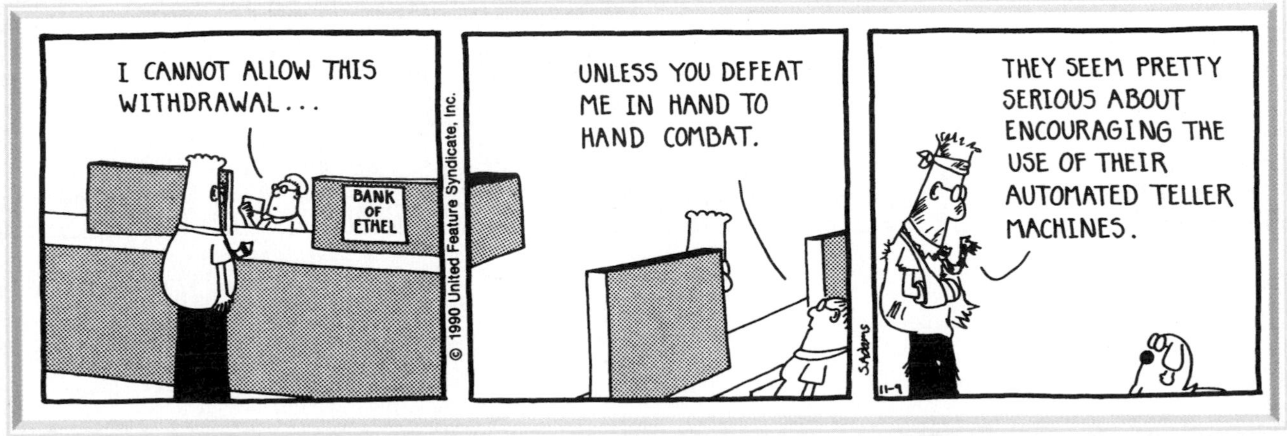
I CANNOT ALLOW THIS WITHDRAWAL...
BANK OF ETHEL
UNLESS YOU DEFEAT ME IN HAND TO HAND COMBAT.
THEY SEEM PRETTY SERIOUS ABOUT ENCOURAGING THE USE OF THEIR AUTOMATED TELLER MACHINES.
© 1990 United Feature Syndicate, Inc.

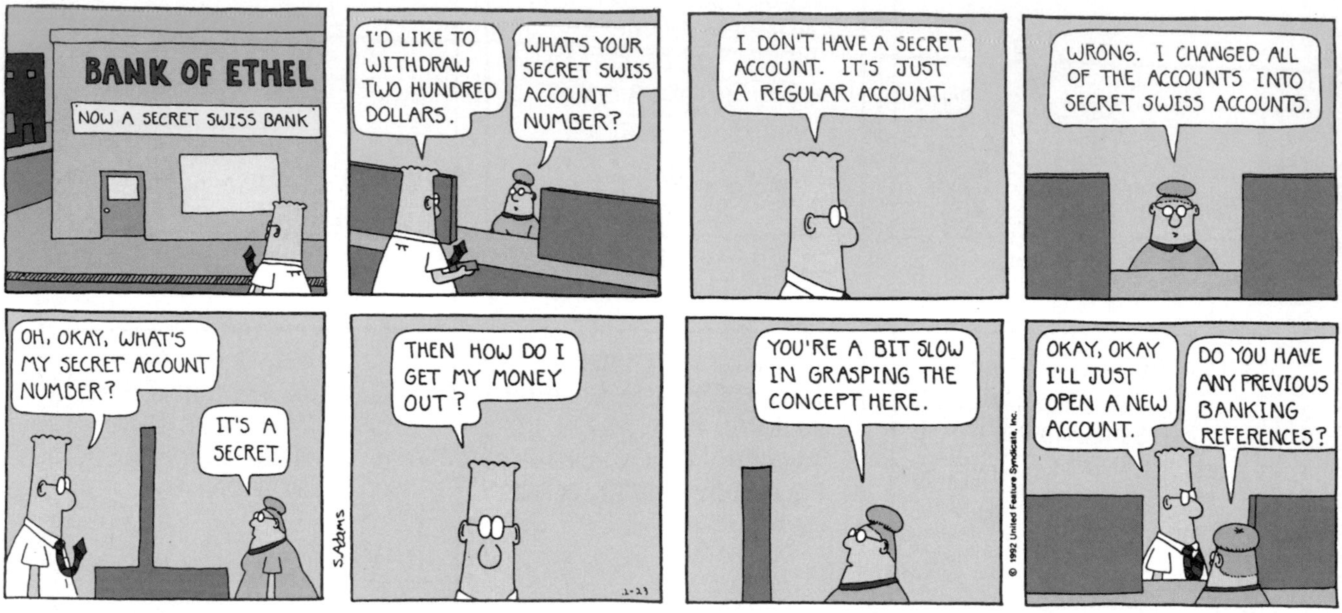
BANK OF ETHEL
NOW A SECRET SWISS BANK
I'D LIKE TO WITHDRAW TWO HUNDRED DOLLARS.
WHAT'S YOUR SECRET SWISS ACCOUNT NUMBER?
I DON'T HAVE A SECRET ACCOUNT. IT'S JUST A REGULAR ACCOUNT.
WRONG. I CHANGED ALL OF THE ACCOUNTS INTO SECRET SWISS ACCOUNTS.
OH, OKAY, WHAT'S MY SECRET ACCOUNT NUMBER?
IT'S A SECRET.
S.Adams
THEN HOW DO I GET MY MONEY OUT?
YOU'RE A BIT SLOW IN GRASPING THE CONCEPT HERE.
© 1992 United Feature Syndicate, Inc.
OKAY, OKAY I'LL JUST OPEN A NEW ACCOUNT.
DO YOU HAVE ANY PREVIOUS BANKING REFERENCES?

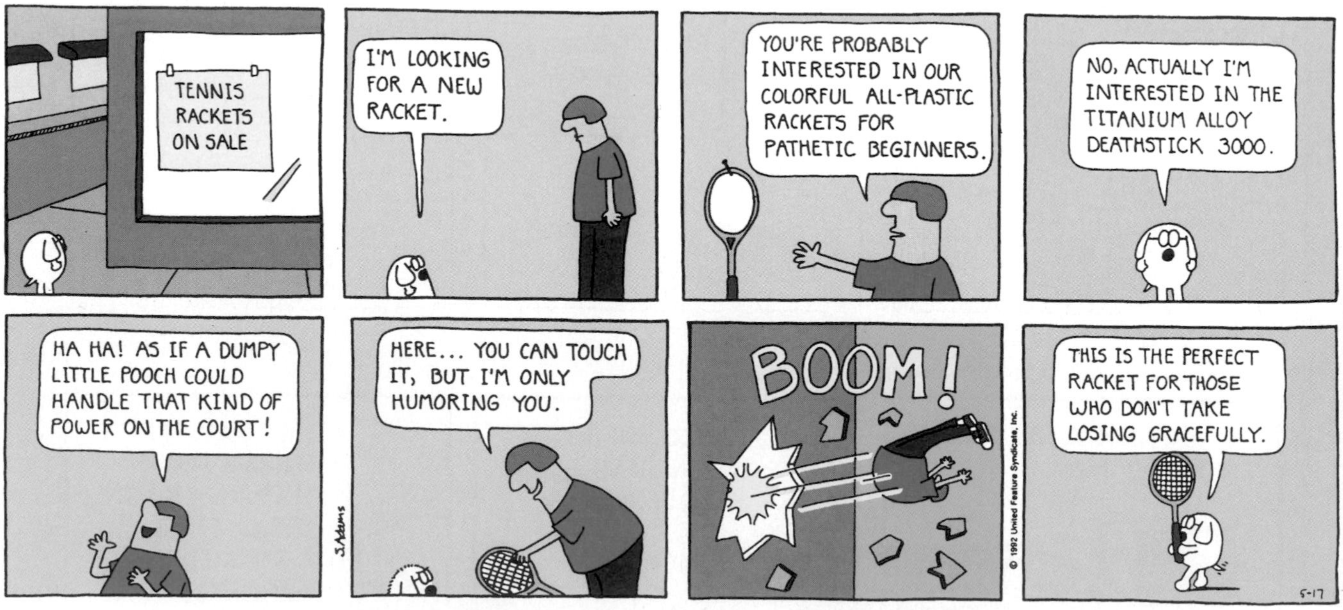
TENNIS RACKETS ON SALE
I'M LOOKING FOR A NEW RACKET.
YOU'RE PROBABLY INTERESTED IN OUR COLORFUL ALL-PLASTIC RACKETS FOR PATHETIC BEGINNERS.
NO, ACTUALLY I'M INTERESTED IN THE TITANIUM ALLOY DEATHSTICK 3000.
HA HA! AS IF A DUMPY LITTLE POOCH COULD HANDLE THAT KIND OF POWER ON THE COURT!
HERE... YOU CAN TOUCH IT, BUT I'M ONLY HUMORING YOU.
S.Adams
BOOM!
© 1992 United Feature Syndicate, Inc.
THIS IS THE PERFECT RACKET FOR THOSE WHO DON'T TAKE LOSING GRACEFULLY.
5-17

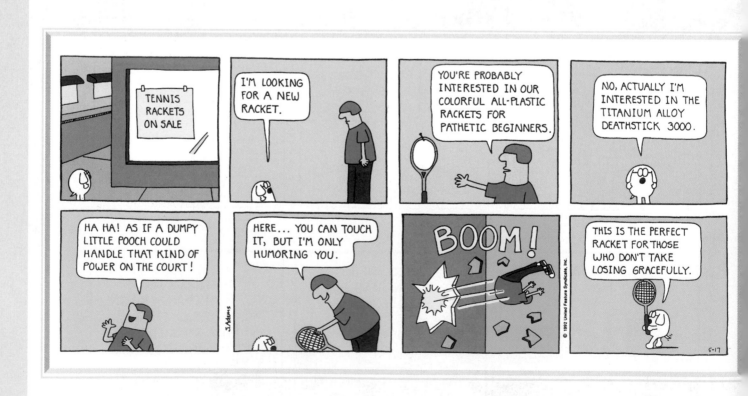

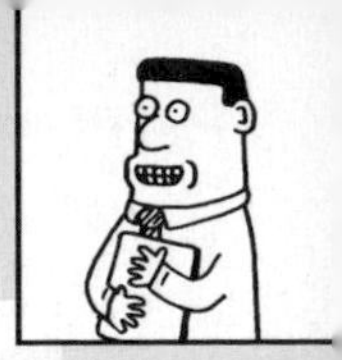

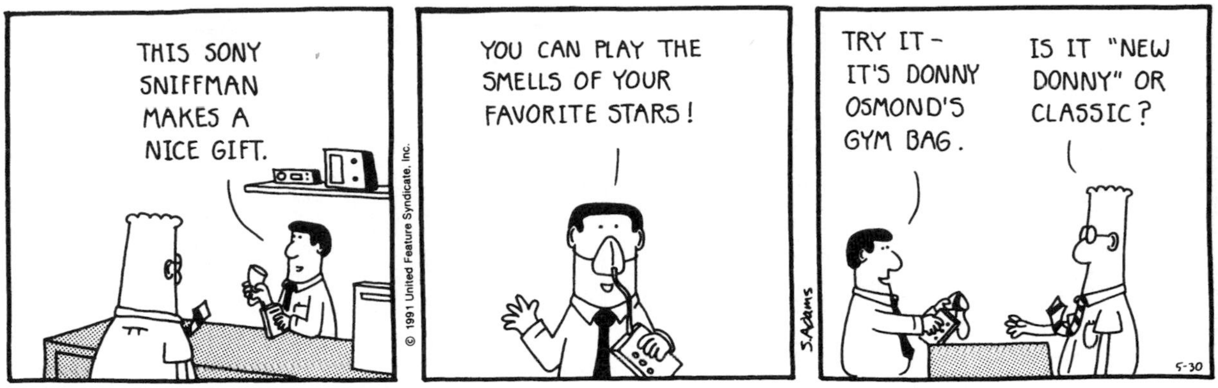
THIS SONY SNIFFMAN MAKES A NICE GIFT.
YOU CAN PLAY THE SMELLS OF YOUR FAVORITE STARS!
TRY IT – IT'S DONNY OSMOND'S GYM BAG.
IS IT "NEW DONNY" OR CLASSIC?
© 1991 United Feature Syndicate, Inc.
S. Adams
5-30

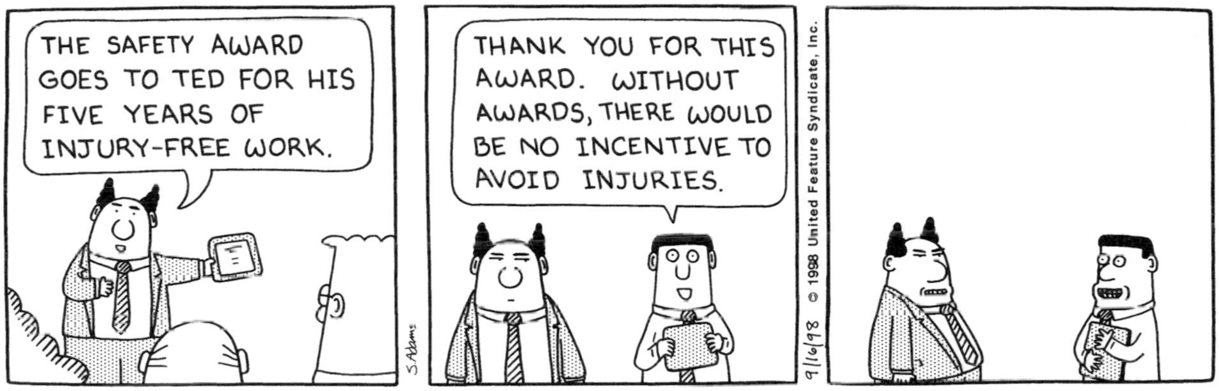
THE SAFETY AWARD GOES TO TED FOR HIS FIVE YEARS OF INJURY-FREE WORK.
S. Adams
THANK YOU FOR THIS AWARD. WITHOUT AWARDS, THERE WOULD BE NO INCENTIVE TO AVOID INJURIES.
9/16/98 © 1998 United Feature Syndicate, Inc.

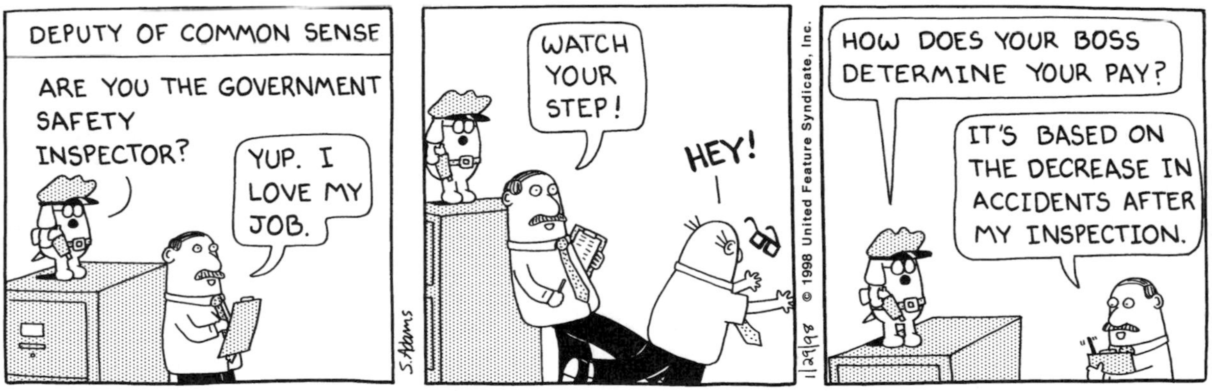
DEPUTY OF COMMON SENSE
ARE YOU THE GOVERNMENT SAFETY INSPECTOR?
YUP. I LOVE MY JOB.
S. Adams
WATCH YOUR STEP!
HEY!
1/29/98 © 1998 United Feature Syndicate, Inc.
HOW DOES YOUR BOSS DETERMINE YOUR PAY?
IT'S BASED ON THE DECREASE IN ACCIDENTS AFTER MY INSPECTION.

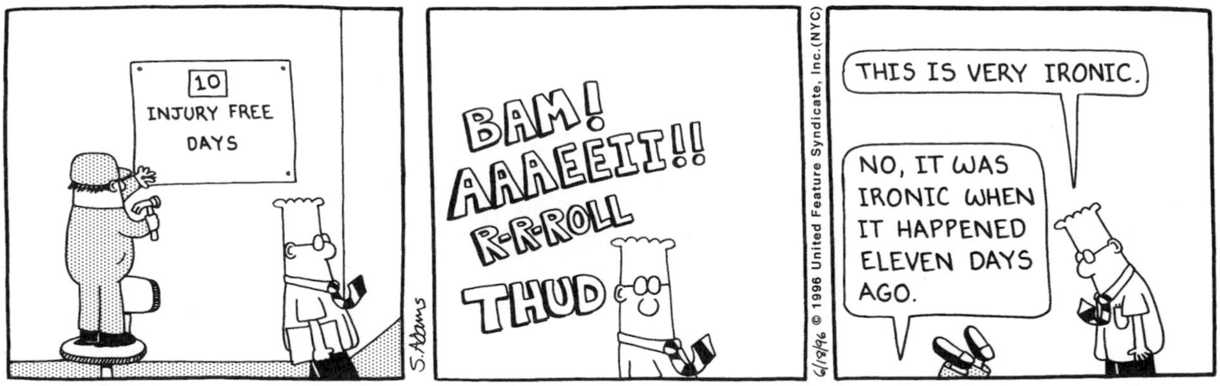
10
INJURY FREE DAYS
S. Adams
BAM!
AAAEEII!!
R-R-ROLL
THUD
6/19/96 © 1996 United Feature Syndicate, Inc.(NYC)
THIS IS VERY IRONIC.
NO, IT WAS IRONIC WHEN IT HAPPENED ELEVEN DAYS AGO.

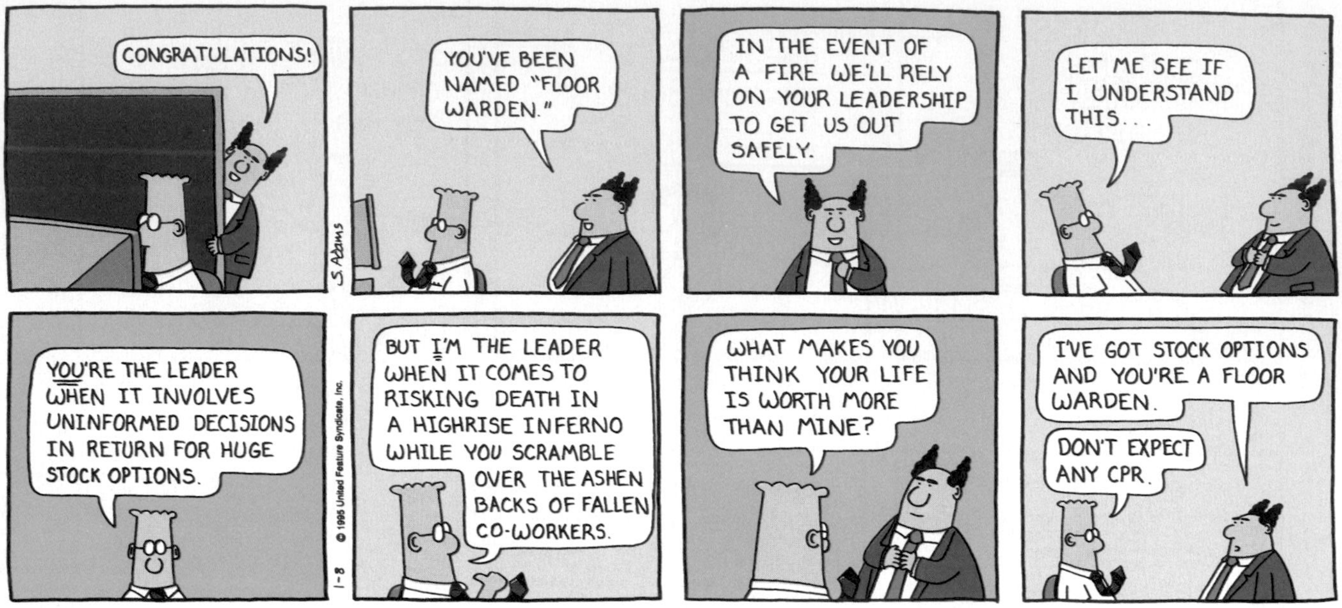
CONGRATULATIONS!
YOU'VE BEEN NAMED "FLOOR WARDEN."
IN THE EVENT OF A FIRE WE'LL RELY ON YOUR LEADERSHIP TO GET US OUT SAFELY.
LET ME SEE IF I UNDERSTAND THIS...
YOU'RE THE LEADER WHEN IT INVOLVES UNINFORMED DECISIONS IN RETURN FOR HUGE STOCK OPTIONS.
BUT I'M THE LEADER WHEN IT COMES TO RISKING DEATH IN A HIGHRISE INFERNO WHILE YOU SCRAMBLE OVER THE ASHEN BACKS OF FALLEN CO-WORKERS.
WHAT MAKES YOU THINK YOUR LIFE IS WORTH MORE THAN MINE?
I'VE GOT STOCK OPTIONS AND YOU'RE A FLOOR WARDEN.
DON'T EXPECT ANY CPR.
S. Adams
1-8 © 1995 United Feature Syndicate, Inc.

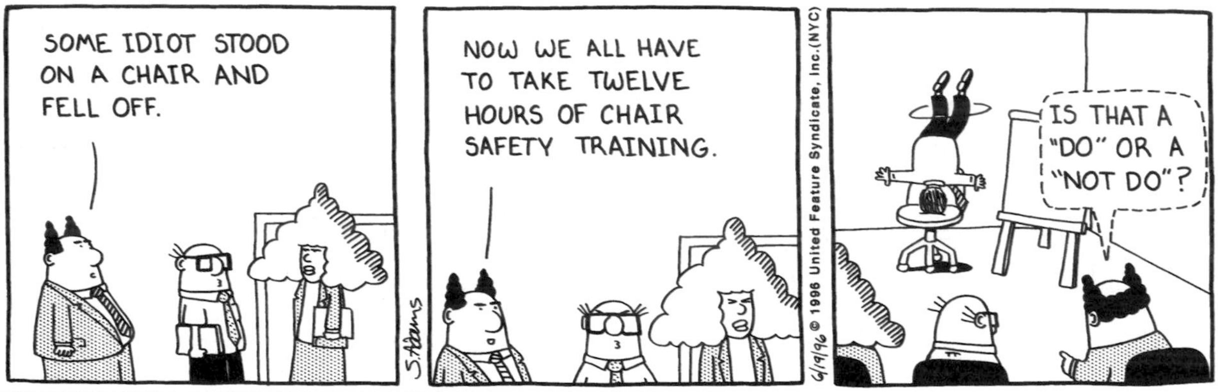
SOME IDIOT STOOD ON A CHAIR AND FELL OFF.
NOW WE ALL HAVE TO TAKE TWELVE HOURS OF CHAIR SAFETY TRAINING.
IS THAT A "DO" OR A "NOT DO"?
S. Adams
6/19/96 © 1996 United Feature Syndicate, Inc.(NYC)

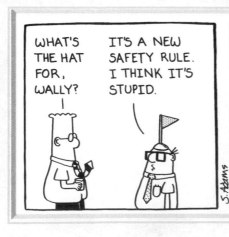

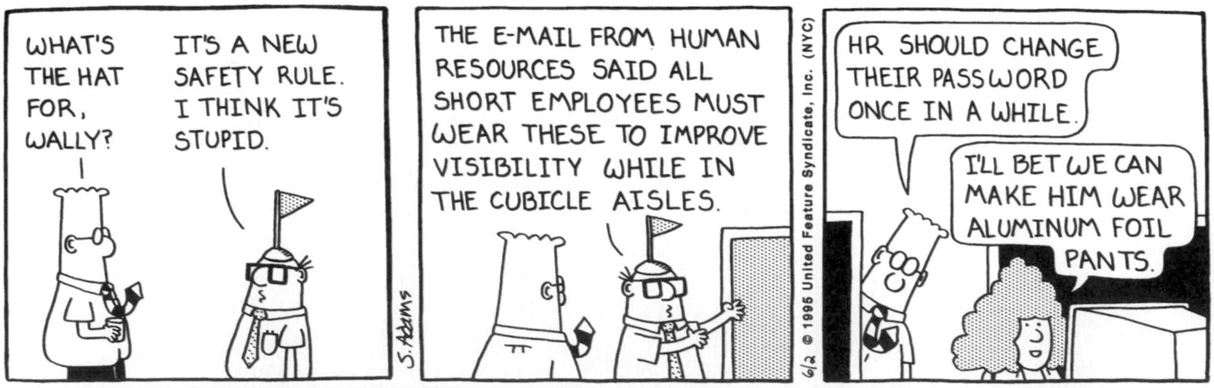
WHAT'S THE HAT FOR, WALLY?
IT'S A NEW SAFETY RULE. I THINK IT'S STUPID.
THE E-MAIL FROM HUMAN RESOURCES SAID ALL SHORT EMPLOYEES MUST WEAR THESE TO IMPROVE VISIBILITY WHILE IN THE CUBICLE AISLES.
HR SHOULD CHANGE THEIR PASSWORD ONCE IN A WHILE.
I'LL BET WE CAN MAKE HIM WEAR ALUMINUM FOIL PANTS.
S. Adams
6/2 © 1995 United Feature Syndicate, Inc. (NYC)

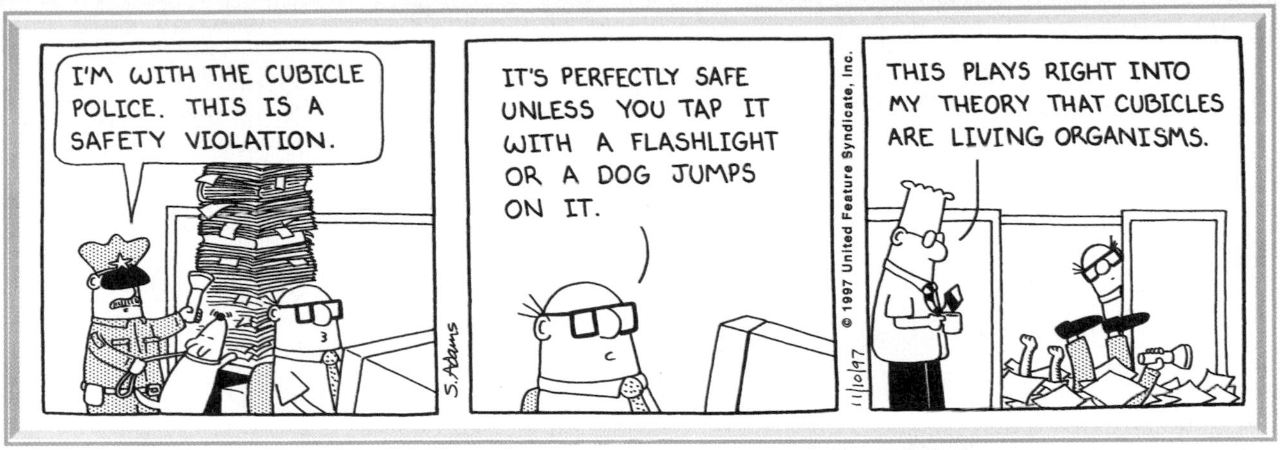
I'M WITH THE CUBICLE POLICE. THIS IS A SAFETY VIOLATION.
IT'S PERFECTLY SAFE UNLESS YOU TAP IT WITH A FLASHLIGHT OR A DOG JUMPS ON IT.
THIS PLAYS RIGHT INTO MY THEORY THAT CUBICLES ARE LIVING ORGANISMS.
S. Adams
11/10/97
© 1997 United Feature Syndicate, Inc.

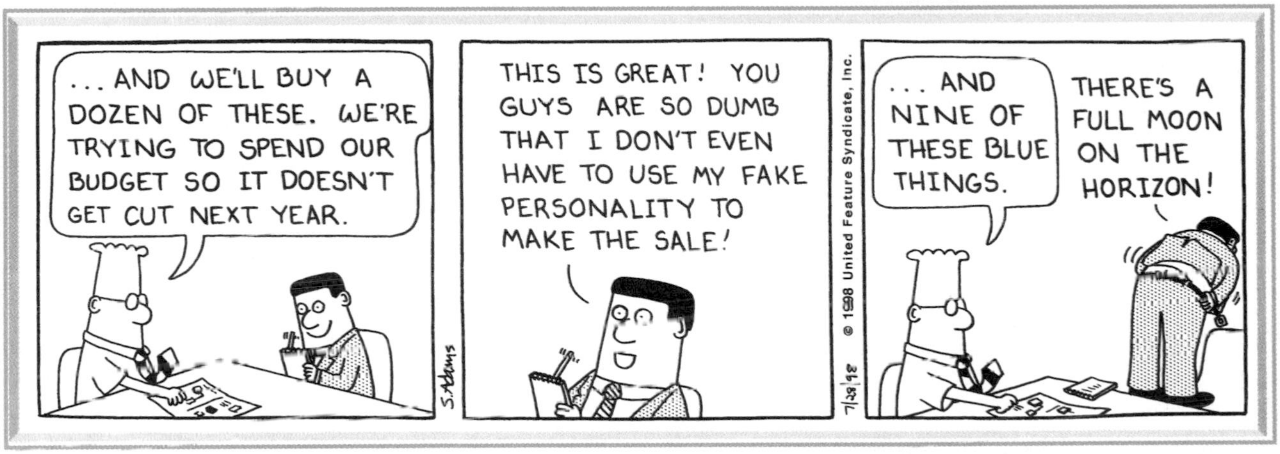
... AND WE'LL BUY A DOZEN OF THESE. WE'RE TRYING TO SPEND OUR BUDGET SO IT DOESN'T GET CUT NEXT YEAR.
THIS IS GREAT! YOU GUYS ARE SO DUMB THAT I DON'T EVEN HAVE TO USE MY FAKE PERSONALITY TO MAKE THE SALE!
... AND NINE OF THESE BLUE THINGS.
THERE'S A FULL MOON ON THE HORIZON!
S. Adams
7/28/98
© 1998 United Feature Syndicate, Inc.

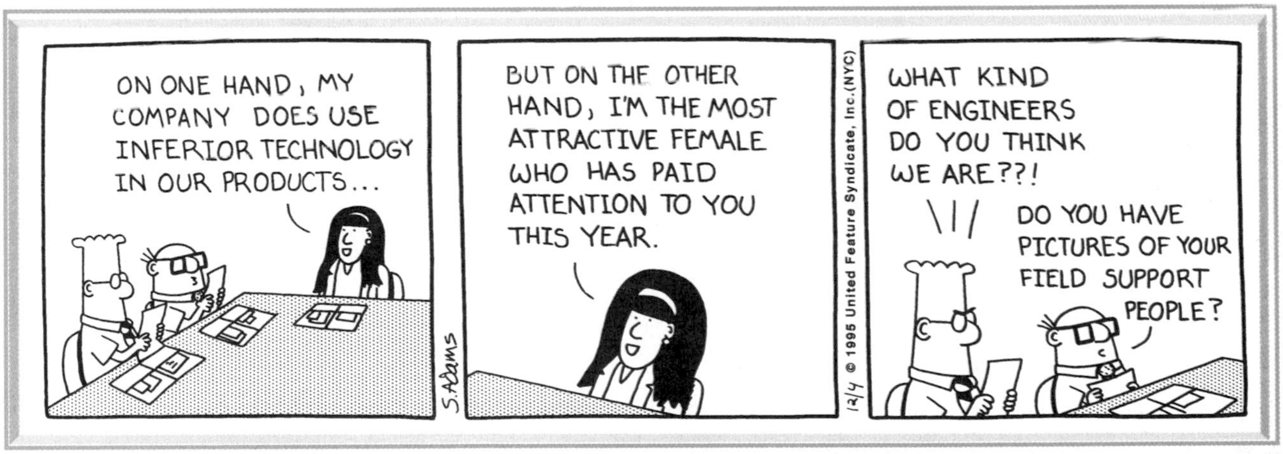
ON ONE HAND, MY COMPANY DOES USE INFERIOR TECHNOLOGY IN OUR PRODUCTS...
BUT ON THE OTHER HAND, I'M THE MOST ATTRACTIVE FEMALE WHO HAS PAID ATTENTION TO YOU THIS YEAR.
WHAT KIND OF ENGINEERS DO YOU THINK WE ARE??!
DO YOU HAVE PICTURES OF YOUR FIELD SUPPORT PEOPLE?
S. Adams
12/4
© 1995 United Feature Syndicate, Inc.(NYC)

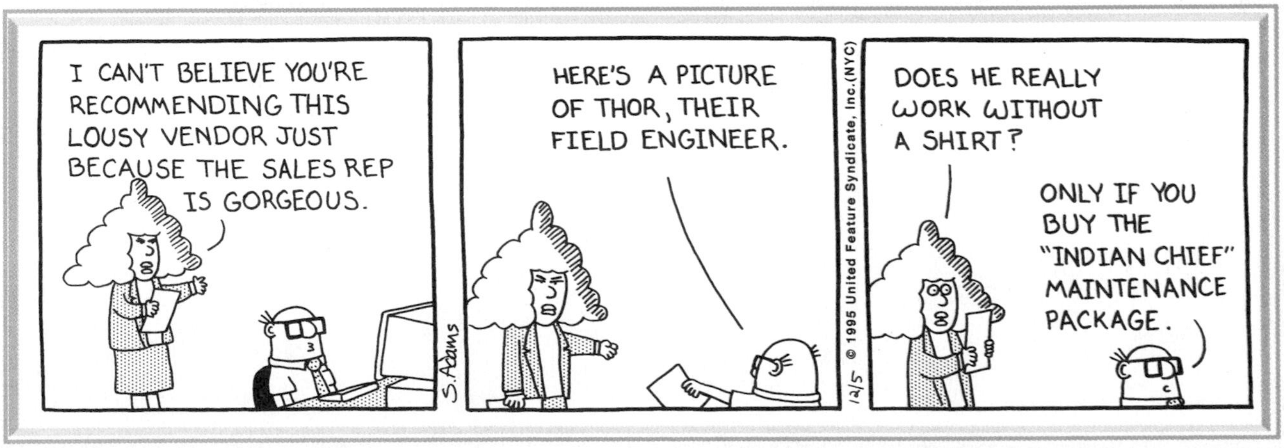
I CAN'T BELIEVE YOU'RE RECOMMENDING THIS LOUSY VENDOR JUST BECAUSE THE SALES REP IS GORGEOUS.
HERE'S A PICTURE OF THOR, THEIR FIELD ENGINEER.
DOES HE REALLY WORK WITHOUT A SHIRT?
ONLY IF YOU BUY THE "INDIAN CHIEF" MAINTENANCE PACKAGE.
S. Adams
12/5
© 1995 United Feature Syndicate, Inc.(NYC)

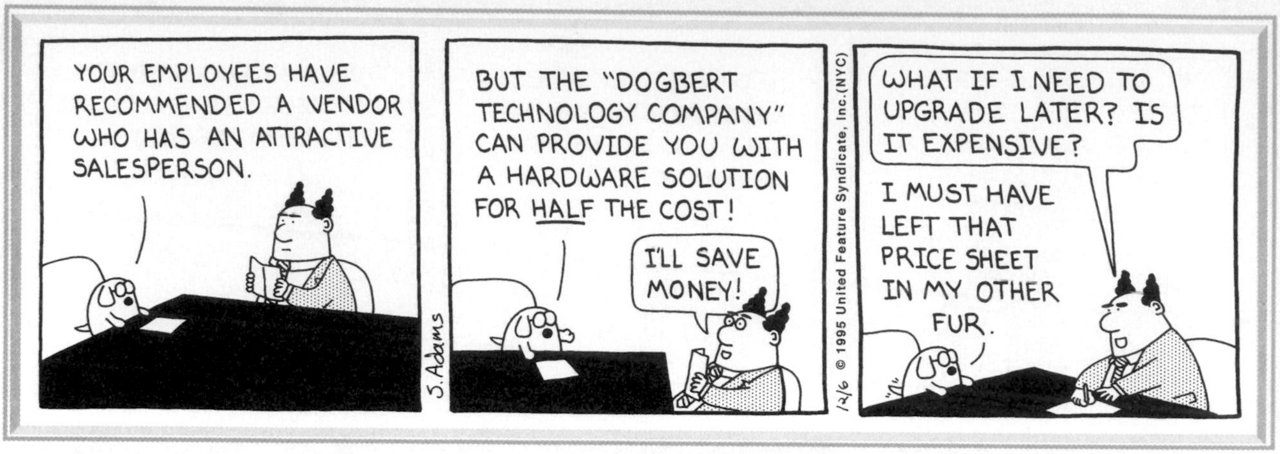
YOUR EMPLOYEES HAVE RECOMMENDED A VENDOR WHO HAS AN ATTRACTIVE SALESPERSON.
BUT THE "DOGBERT TECHNOLOGY COMPANY" CAN PROVIDE YOU WITH A HARDWARE SOLUTION FOR HALF THE COST!
I'LL SAVE MONEY!
WHAT IF I NEED TO UPGRADE LATER? IS IT EXPENSIVE?
I MUST HAVE LEFT THAT PRICE SHEET IN MY OTHER FUR.
S. Adams
12/6 © 1995 United Feature Syndicate, Inc.(NYC)

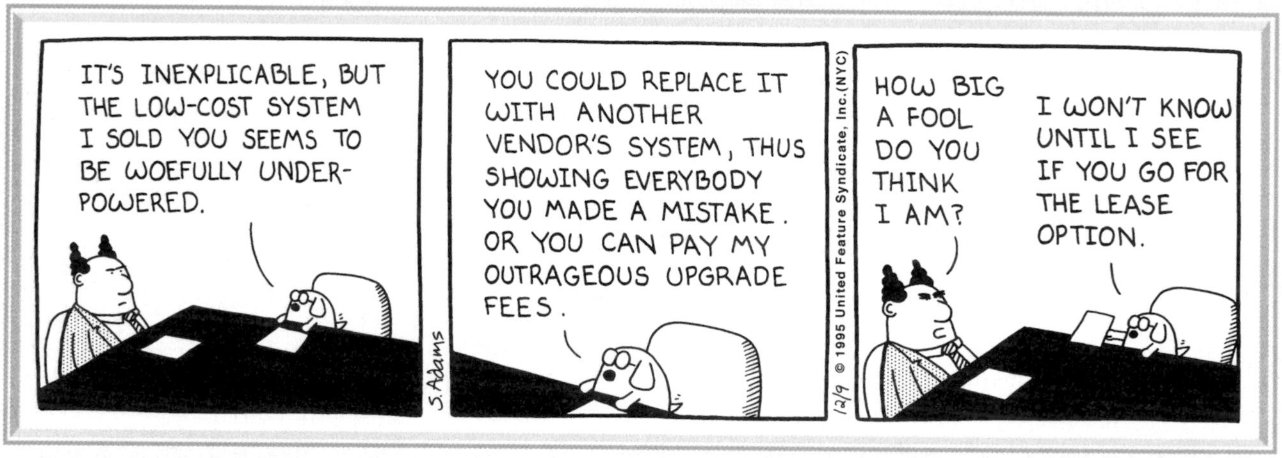
IT'S INEXPLICABLE, BUT THE LOW-COST SYSTEM I SOLD YOU SEEMS TO BE WOEFULLY UNDER-POWERED.
YOU COULD REPLACE IT WITH ANOTHER VENDOR'S SYSTEM, THUS SHOWING EVERYBODY YOU MADE A MISTAKE. OR YOU CAN PAY MY OUTRAGEOUS UPGRADE FEES.
HOW BIG A FOOL DO YOU THINK I AM?
I WON'T KNOW UNTIL I SEE IF YOU GO FOR THE LEASE OPTION.
S. Adams
12/9 © 1995 United Feature Syndicate, Inc.(NYC)

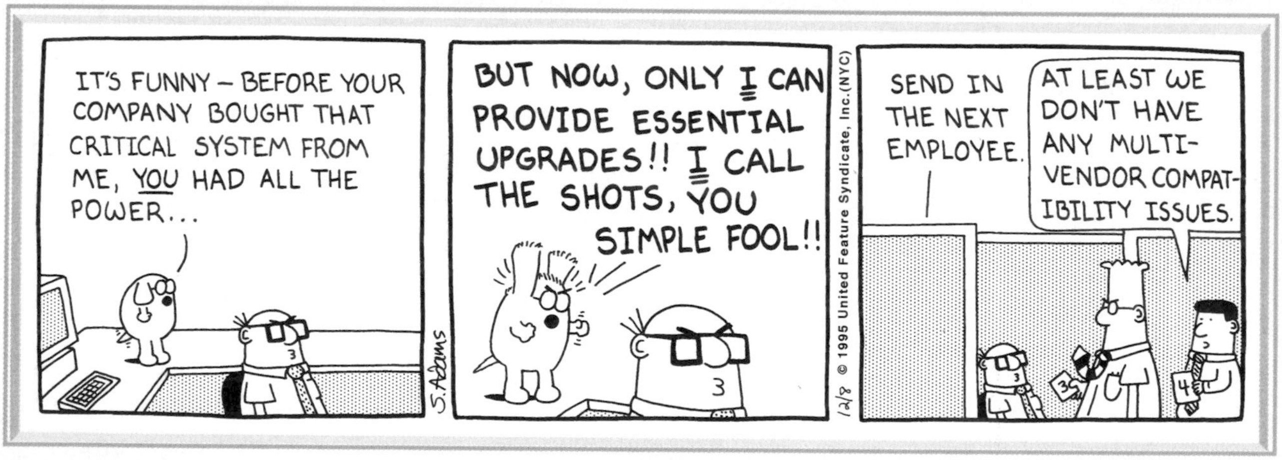
IT'S FUNNY – BEFORE YOUR COMPANY BOUGHT THAT CRITICAL SYSTEM FROM ME, YOU HAD ALL THE POWER...
BUT NOW, ONLY I CAN PROVIDE ESSENTIAL UPGRADES!! I CALL THE SHOTS, YOU SIMPLE FOOL!!
SEND IN THE NEXT EMPLOYEE.
AT LEAST WE DON'T HAVE ANY MULTI-VENDOR COMPAT-IBILITY ISSUES.
S. Adams
12/8 © 1995 United Feature Syndicate, Inc.(NYC)

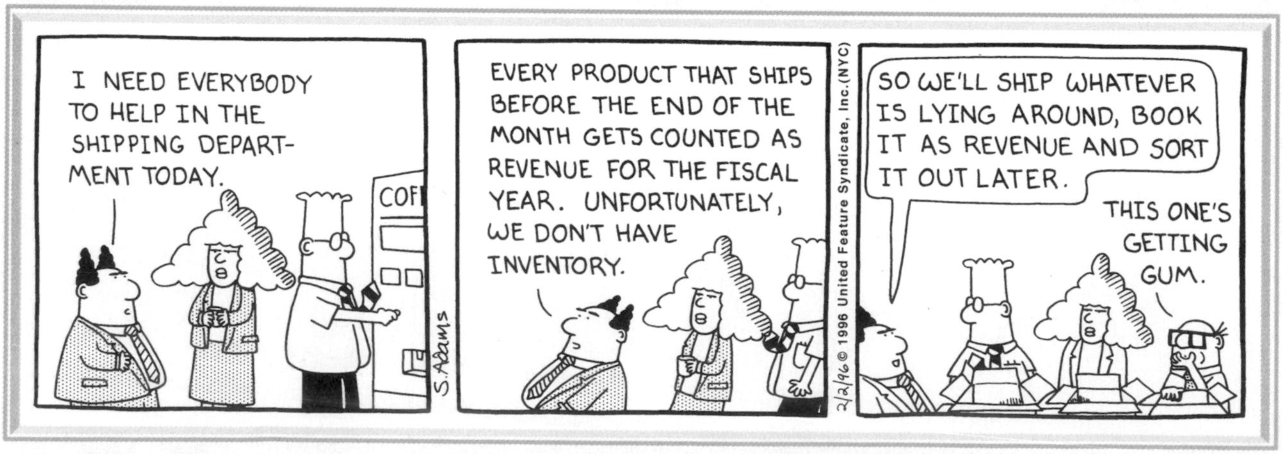
I NEED EVERYBODY TO HELP IN THE SHIPPING DEPART-MENT TODAY.
COF
EVERY PRODUCT THAT SHIPS BEFORE THE END OF THE MONTH GETS COUNTED AS REVENUE FOR THE FISCAL YEAR. UNFORTUNATELY, WE DON'T HAVE INVENTORY.
SO WE'LL SHIP WHATEVER IS LYING AROUND, BOOK IT AS REVENUE AND SORT IT OUT LATER.
THIS ONE'S GETTING GUM.
S. Adams
2/2/96 © 1996 United Feature Syndicate, Inc.(NYC)

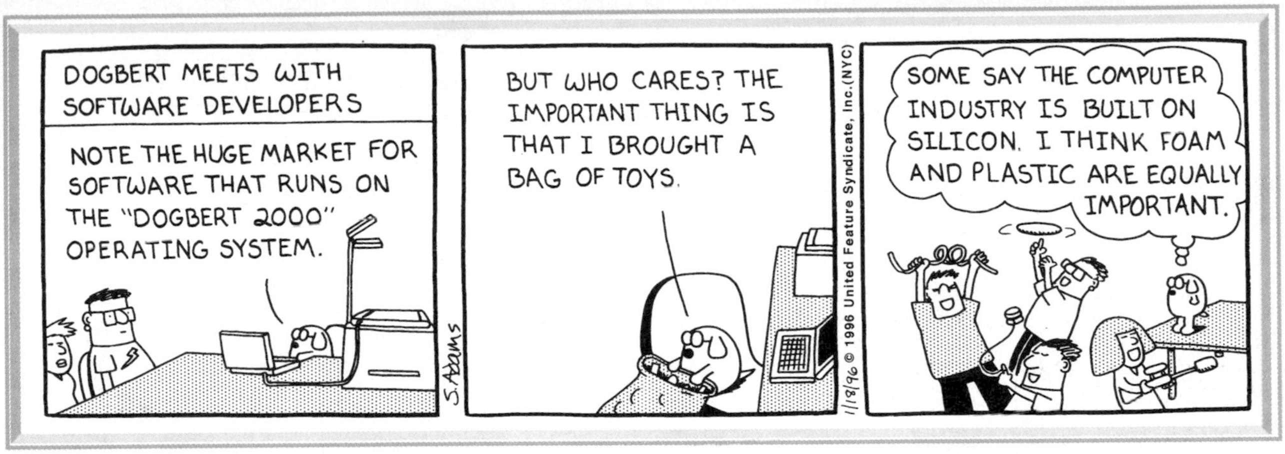
DOGBERT MEETS WITH SOFTWARE DEVELOPERS
NOTE THE HUGE MARKET FOR SOFTWARE THAT RUNS ON THE "DOGBERT 2000" OPERATING SYSTEM.
S. Adams
BUT WHO CARES? THE IMPORTANT THING IS THAT I BROUGHT A BAG OF TOYS.
1/18/96 © 1996 United Feature Syndicate, Inc.(NYC)
SOME SAY THE COMPUTER INDUSTRY IS BUILT ON SILICON. I THINK FOAM AND PLASTIC ARE EQUALLY IMPORTANT.

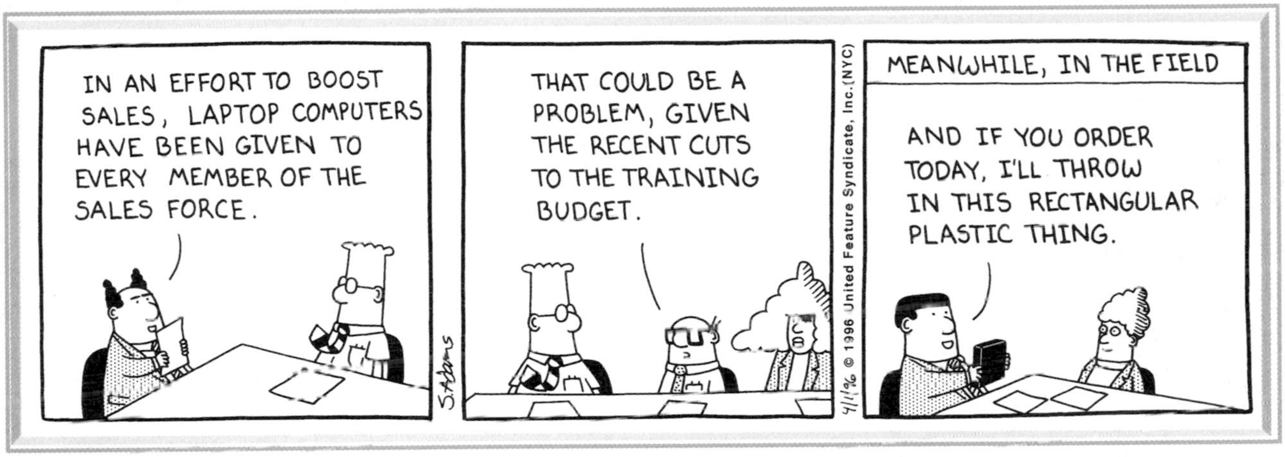
IN AN EFFORT TO BOOST SALES, LAPTOP COMPUTERS HAVE BEEN GIVEN TO EVERY MEMBER OF THE SALES FORCE.
S. Adams
THAT COULD BE A PROBLEM, GIVEN THE RECENT CUTS TO THE TRAINING BUDGET.
4/1/96 © 1996 United Feature Syndicate, Inc.(NYC)
MEANWHILE, IN THE FIELD
AND IF YOU ORDER TODAY, I'LL THROW IN THIS RECTANGULAR PLASTIC THING.

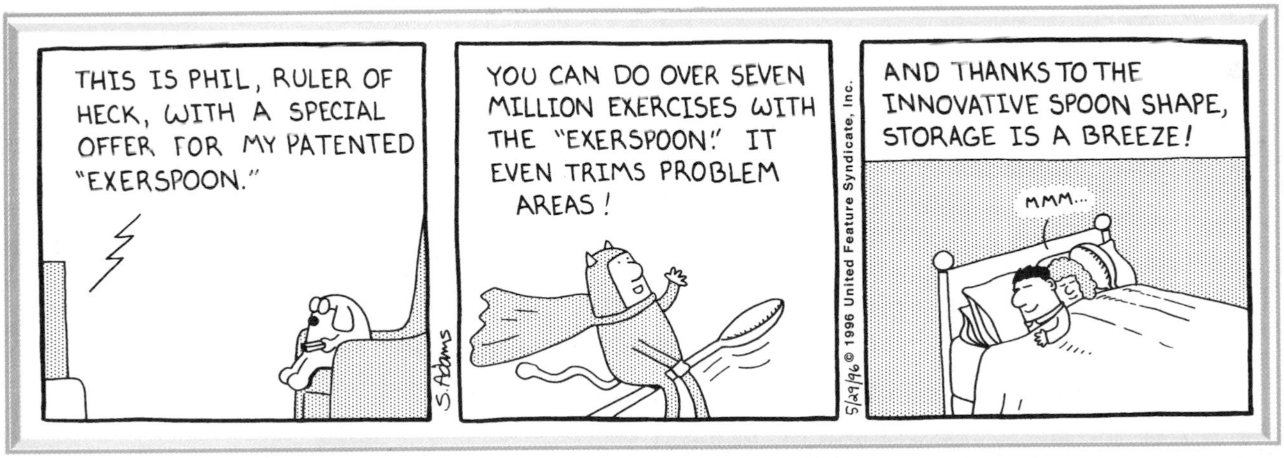
THIS IS PHIL, RULER OF HECK, WITH A SPECIAL OFFER FOR MY PATENTED "EXERSPOON."
S. Adams
YOU CAN DO OVER SEVEN MILLION EXERCISES WITH THE "EXERSPOON." IT EVEN TRIMS PROBLEM AREAS!
5/29/96 © 1996 United Feature Syndicate, Inc.
AND THANKS TO THE INNOVATIVE SPOON SHAPE, STORAGE IS A BREEZE!
MMM...

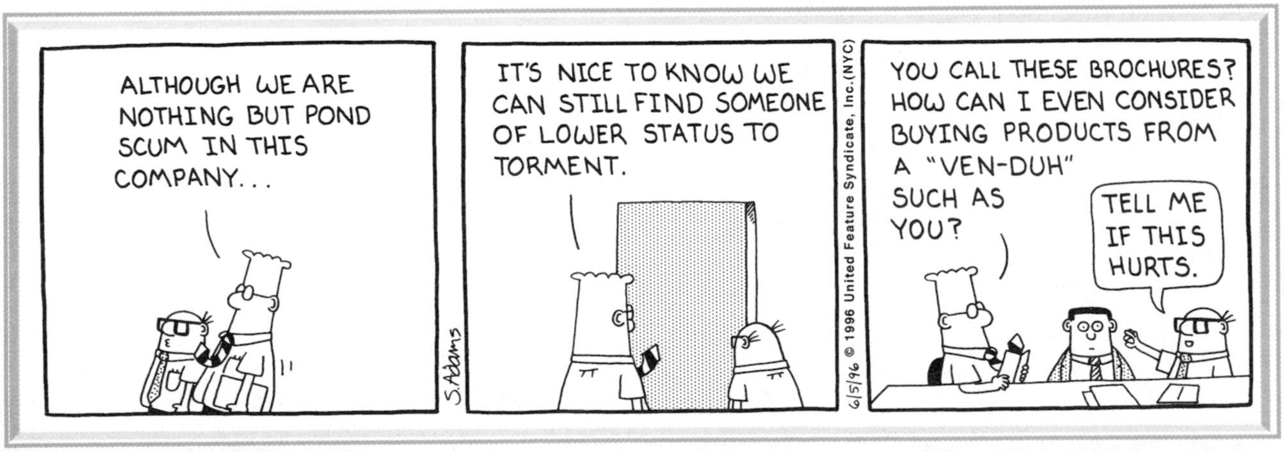
ALTHOUGH WE ARE NOTHING BUT POND SCUM IN THIS COMPANY...
S. Adams
IT'S NICE TO KNOW WE CAN STILL FIND SOMEONE OF LOWER STATUS TO TORMENT.
6/5/96 © 1996 United Feature Syndicate, Inc.(NYC)
YOU CALL THESE BROCHURES? HOW CAN I EVEN CONSIDER BUYING PRODUCTS FROM A "VEN-DUH" SUCH AS YOU?
TELL ME IF THIS HURTS.

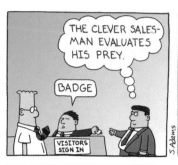

THE CLEVER SALES-MAN EVALUATES HIS PREY.
BADGE
VISITORS SIGN IN
S. Adams
I HOPE HE'S AN IMPORTANT DECISION-MAKER.
TAKE ANY SEAT. I CALL THE GOOD CHAIR.
WARNING! CUBICLE! LOW-RANKING EMPLOYEE!
HERE'S OUR ORGANIZATION CHART: PRESIDENT... SENIOR VICE PRESIDENT... VICE PRESIDENT...
OKAY, LIFT YOUR FOOT. DO YOU SEE THAT COFFEE STAIN ON THE CARPET?
THAT'S YOU?
© 1995 United Feature Syndicate, Inc.(NYC)
NO, THAT'S MY BOSS. I WOULD BE UNDER THE CARPET.
11/26
DO I HAVE ANY HOPE OF TALKING TO SOME-BODY WHO CAN MAKE A DECISION?
LET ME CHECK.
HEY, WALLY. WHAT'S A "DECISION"?
IT SOUNDS LIKE SOMETHING OUR COMPETITORS DO.
SOB

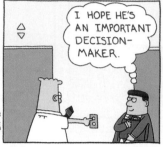

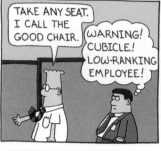

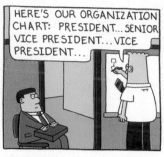

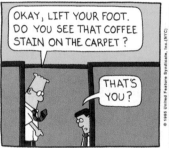

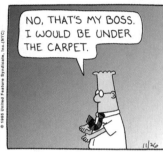

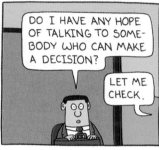

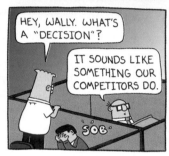

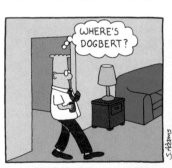

WHERE'S DOGBERT?
S. Adams
UH-OH.
ARE YOU GULLIBLE? DO YOU SPEND MONEY ON STUPID STUFF?
CALL THE "DOGBERT GULLIBLE FRIENDS HOTLINE" FOR HELP. ONLY FOUR DOLLARS PER MINUTE.
HELLO, DOGBERT. I BOUGHT AN EXERCISE MACHINE AND I'M STILL LAZY.
6/9/96 © 1996 United Feature Syndicate, Inc.
PLEASE HOLD.
OKAY!
CALL NOW, AND I'LL REPLACE YOUR OLD TELEVISION WITH A NEW ONE THAT LOOKS JUST LIKE IT, WHILE YOU SLEEP!
IF YOU DON'T HAVE A TOUCH TONE PHONE, STAY ON THE LINE...
UNTIL YOU GET ONE.

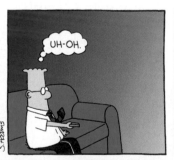

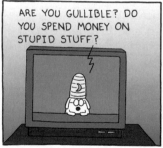

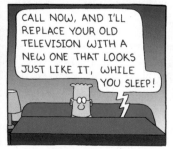

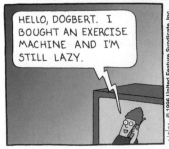

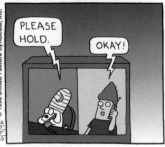

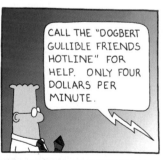

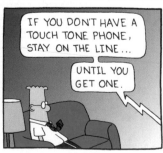

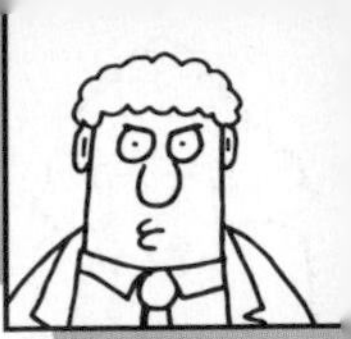

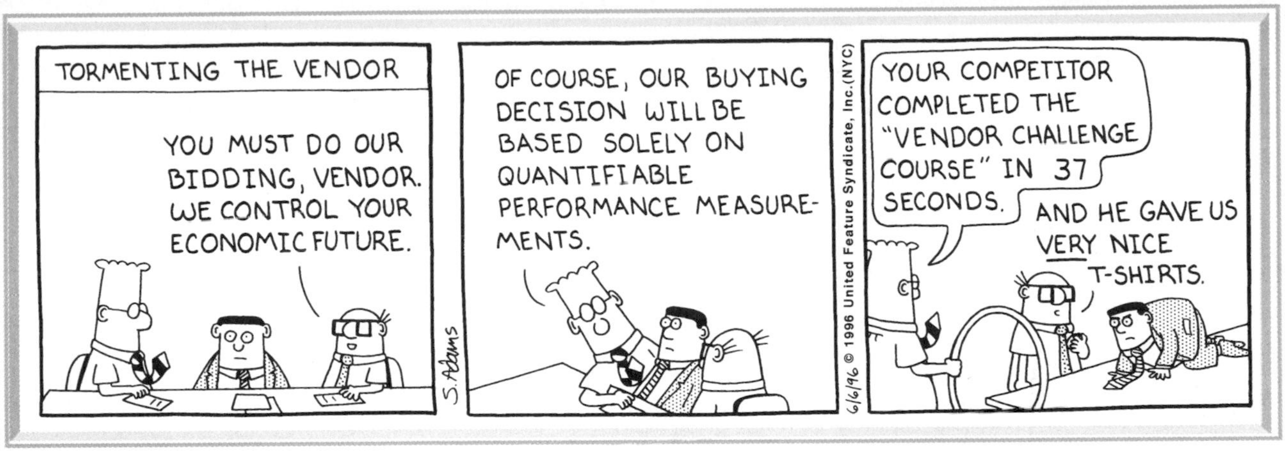
TORMENTING THE VENDOR
YOU MUST DO OUR BIDDING, VENDOR. WE CONTROL YOUR ECONOMIC FUTURE.
OF COURSE, OUR BUYING DECISION WILL BE BASED SOLELY ON QUANTIFIABLE PERFORMANCE MEASUREMENTS.
YOUR COMPETITOR COMPLETED THE "VENDOR CHALLENGE COURSE" IN 37 SECONDS.
AND HE GAVE US VERY NICE T-SHIRTS.
S. Adams
6/6/96 © 1996 United Feature Syndicate, Inc.(NYC)

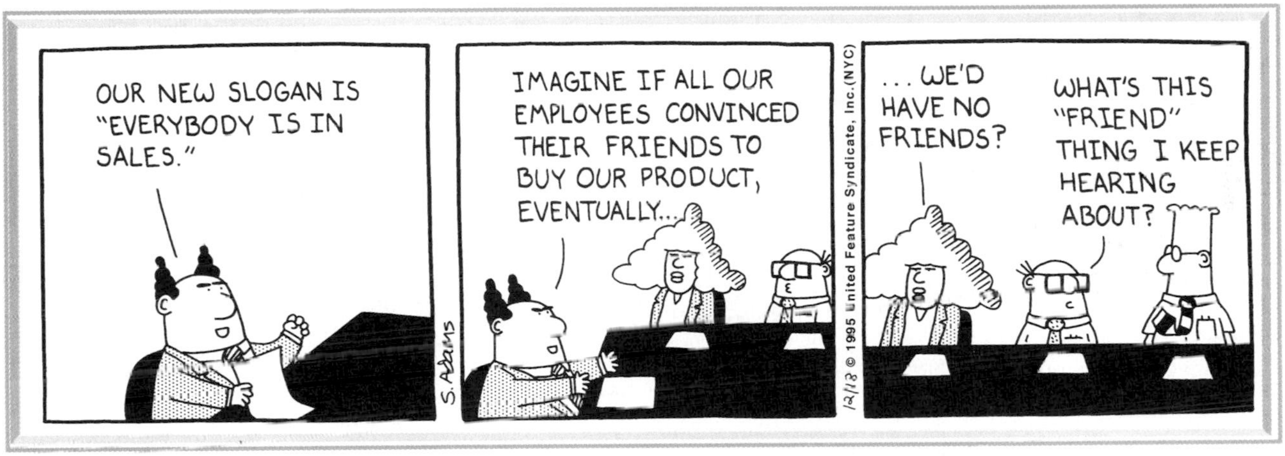
OUR NEW SLOGAN IS "EVERYBODY IS IN SALES."
IMAGINE IF ALL OUR EMPLOYEES CONVINCED THEIR FRIENDS TO BUY OUR PRODUCT, EVENTUALLY...
...WE'D HAVE NO FRIENDS?
WHAT'S THIS "FRIEND" THING I KEEP HEARING ABOUT?
S. Adams
12/18 © 1995 United Feature Syndicate, Inc.(NYC)

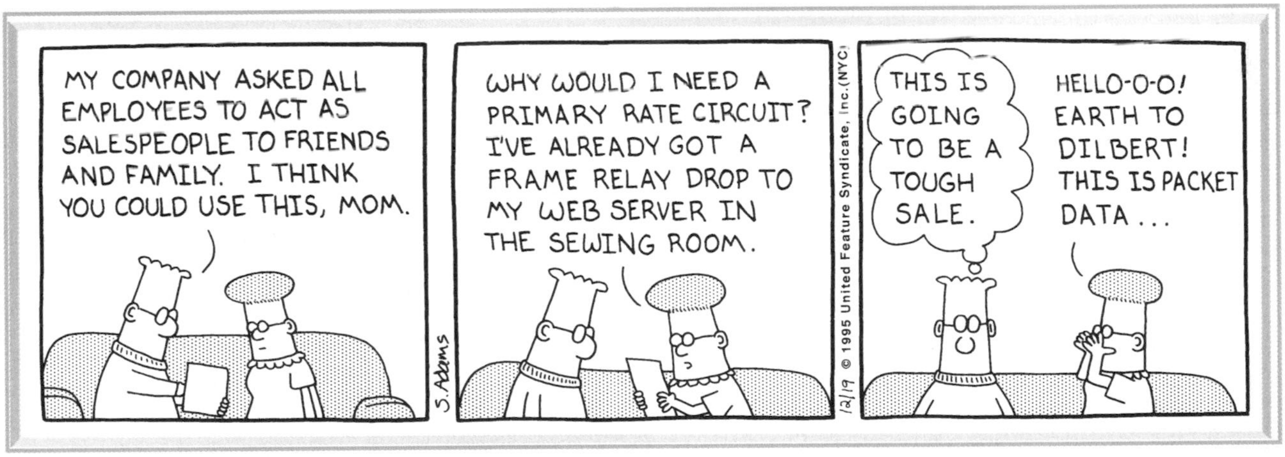
MY COMPANY ASKED ALL EMPLOYEES TO ACT AS SALESPEOPLE TO FRIENDS AND FAMILY. I THINK YOU COULD USE THIS, MOM.
WHY WOULD I NEED A PRIMARY RATE CIRCUIT? I'VE ALREADY GOT A FRAME RELAY DROP TO MY WEB SERVER IN THE SEWING ROOM.
THIS IS GOING TO BE A TOUGH SALE.
HELLO-O-O! EARTH TO DILBERT! THIS IS PACKET DATA...
S. Adams
12/19 © 1995 United Feature Syndicate, Inc.(NYC)

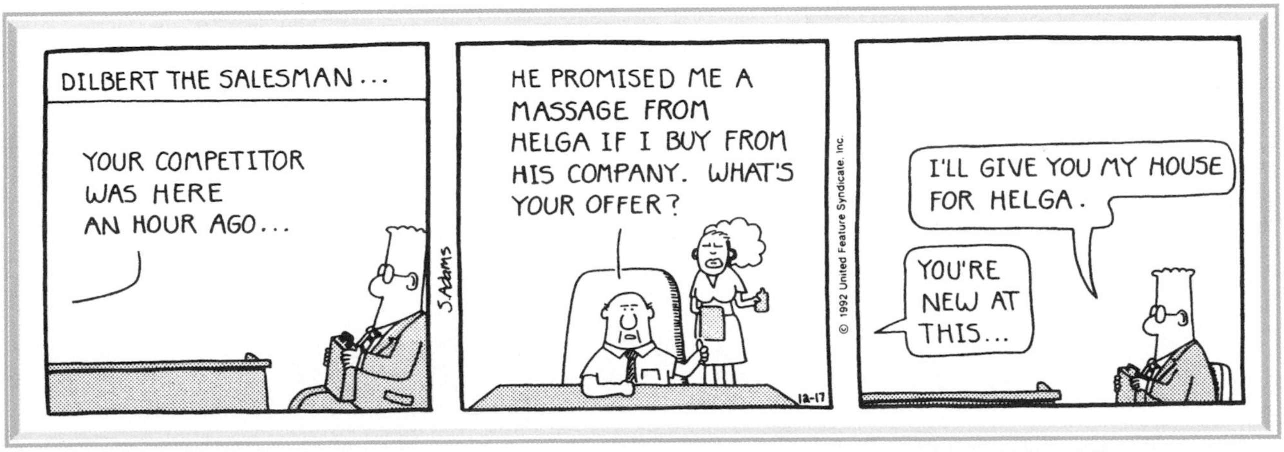
DILBERT THE SALESMAN...
YOUR COMPETITOR WAS HERE AN HOUR AGO...
HE PROMISED ME A MASSAGE FROM HELGA IF I BUY FROM HIS COMPANY. WHAT'S YOUR OFFER?
I'LL GIVE YOU MY HOUSE FOR HELGA.
YOU'RE NEW AT THIS...
S. Adams
© 1992 United Feature Syndicate, Inc.
12-17

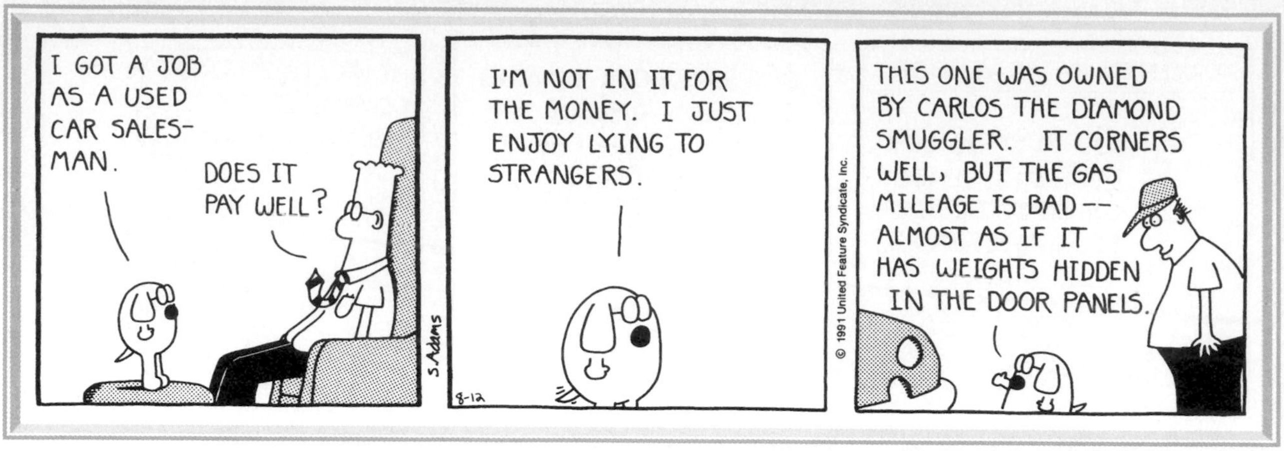
I GOT A JOB AS A USED CAR SALES-MAN.
DOES IT PAY WELL?
I'M NOT IN IT FOR THE MONEY. I JUST ENJOY LYING TO STRANGERS.
THIS ONE WAS OWNED BY CARLOS THE DIAMOND SMUGGLER. IT CORNERS WELL, BUT THE GAS MILEAGE IS BAD -- ALMOST AS IF IT HAS WEIGHTS HIDDEN IN THE DOOR PANELS.
© 1991 United Feature Syndicate, Inc.

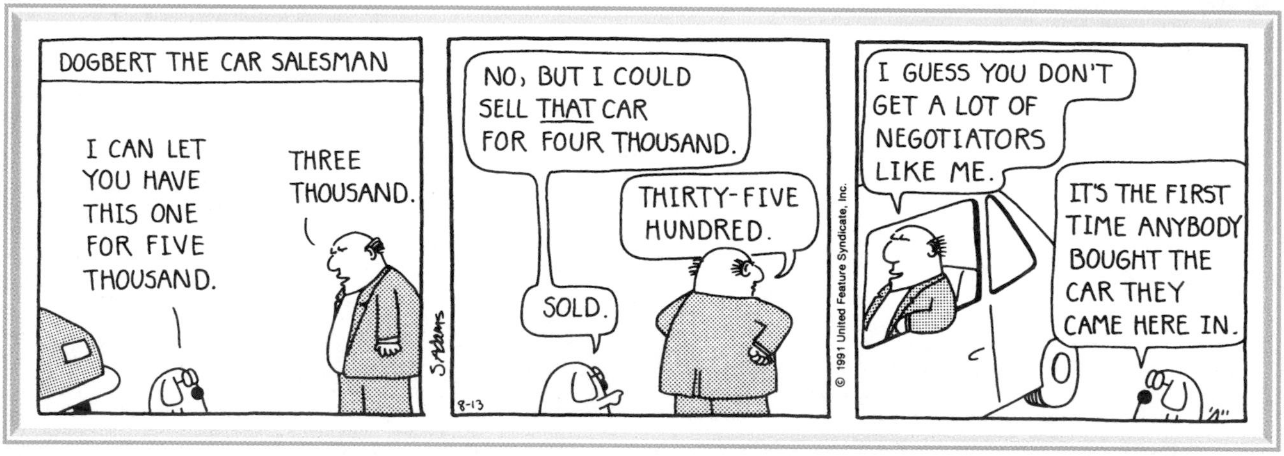
DOGBERT THE CAR SALESMAN
I CAN LET YOU HAVE THIS ONE FOR FIVE THOUSAND.
THREE THOUSAND.
NO, BUT I COULD SELL THAT CAR FOR FOUR THOUSAND.
THIRTY-FIVE HUNDRED.
SOLD.
I GUESS YOU DON'T GET A LOT OF NEGOTIATORS LIKE ME.
IT'S THE FIRST TIME ANYBODY BOUGHT THE CAR THEY CAME HERE IN.
© 1991 United Feature Syndicate, Inc.

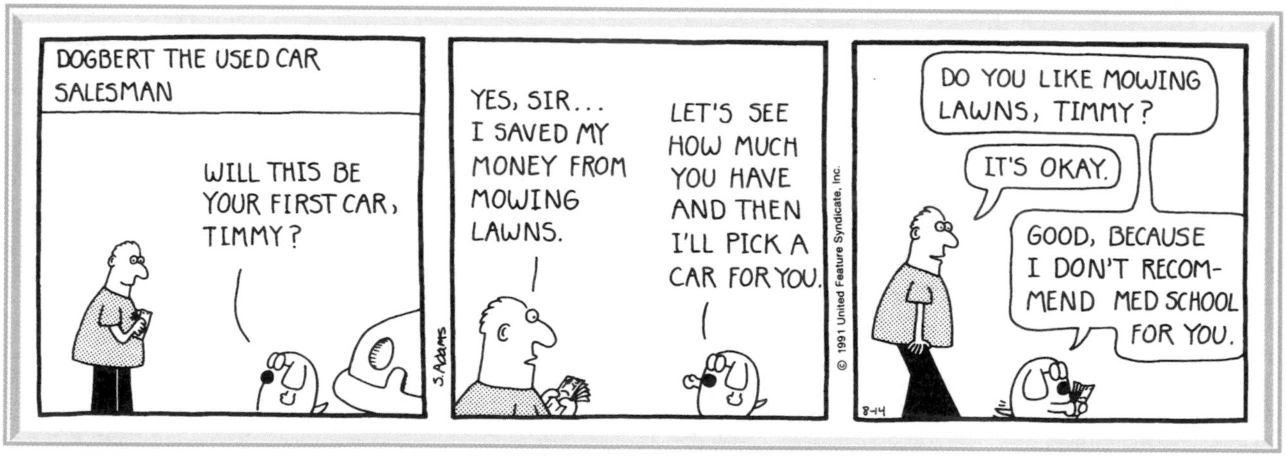
DOGBERT THE USED CAR SALESMAN
WILL THIS BE YOUR FIRST CAR, TIMMY?
YES, SIR... I SAVED MY MONEY FROM MOWING LAWNS.
LET'S SEE HOW MUCH YOU HAVE AND THEN I'LL PICK A CAR FOR YOU.
DO YOU LIKE MOWING LAWNS, TIMMY?
IT'S OKAY.
GOOD, BECAUSE I DON'T RECOM-MEND MED SCHOOL FOR YOU.
© 1991 United Feature Syndicate, Inc.

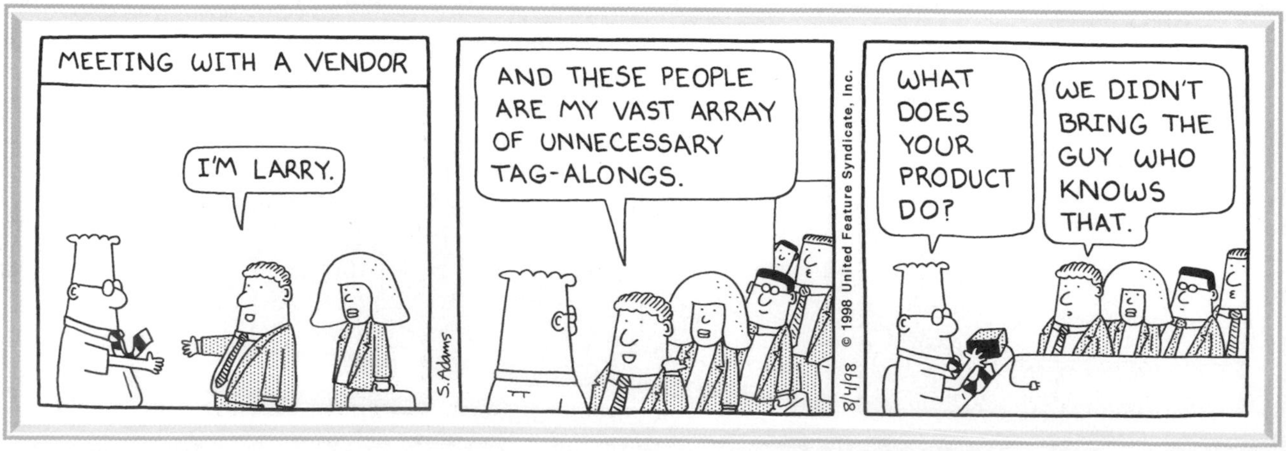
MEETING WITH A VENDOR
I'M LARRY.
AND THESE PEOPLE ARE MY VAST ARRAY OF UNNECESSARY TAG-ALONGS.
WHAT DOES YOUR PRODUCT DO?
WE DIDN'T BRING THE GUY WHO KNOWS THAT.
© 1998 United Feature Syndicate, Inc.

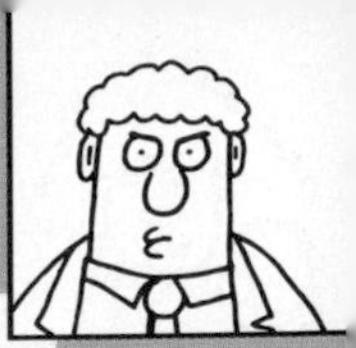

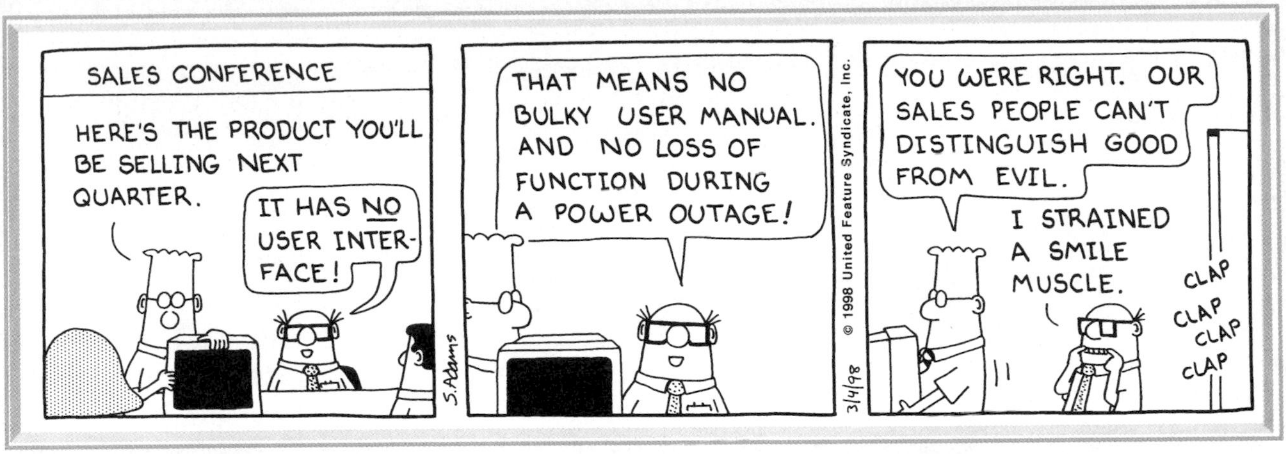
SALES CONFERENCE
HERE'S THE PRODUCT YOU'LL BE SELLING NEXT QUARTER.
IT HAS NO USER INTERFACE!
THAT MEANS NO BULKY USER MANUAL. AND NO LOSS OF FUNCTION DURING A POWER OUTAGE!
YOU WERE RIGHT. OUR SALES PEOPLE CAN'T DISTINGUISH GOOD FROM EVIL.
I STRAINED A SMILE MUSCLE.
CLAP CLAP CLAP CLAP
S. Adams
3/4/98
© 1998 United Feature Syndicate, Inc.

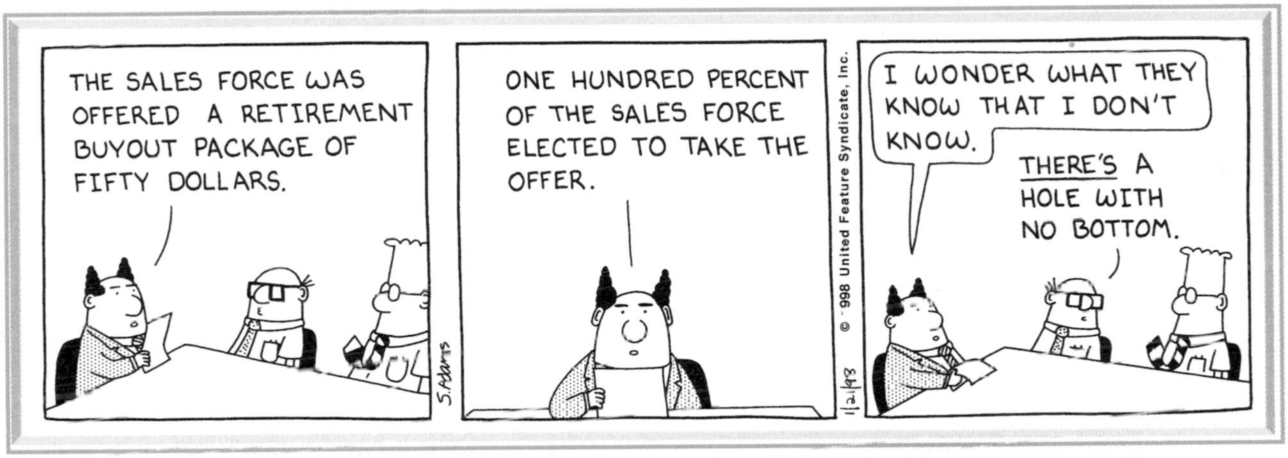
THE SALES FORCE WAS OFFERED A RETIREMENT BUYOUT PACKAGE OF FIFTY DOLLARS.
ONE HUNDRED PERCENT OF THE SALES FORCE ELECTED TO TAKE THE OFFER.
I WONDER WHAT THEY KNOW THAT I DON'T KNOW.
THERE'S A HOLE WITH NO BOTTOM.
S. Adams
© 1998 United Feature Syndicate, Inc.

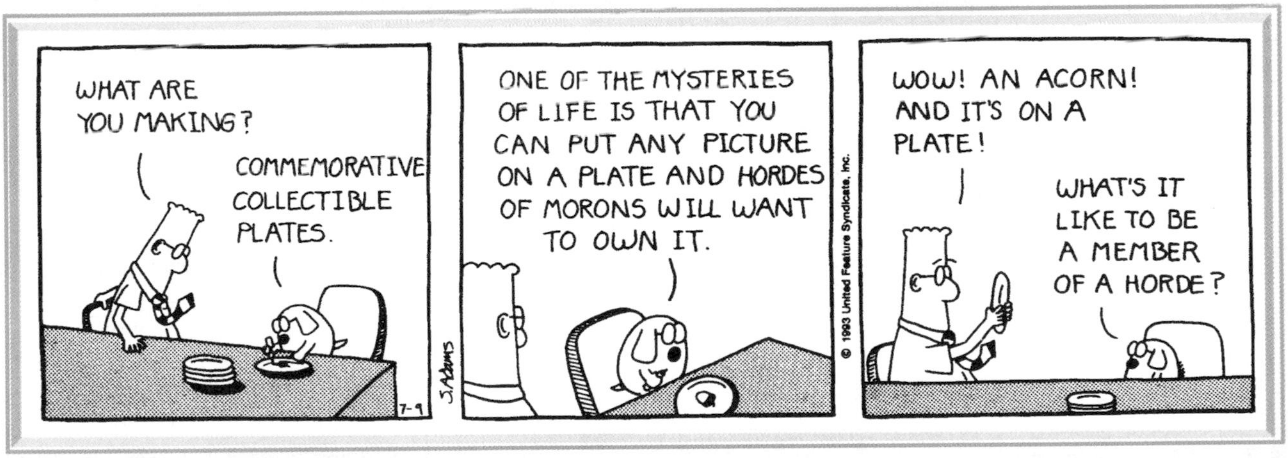
WHAT ARE YOU MAKING?
COMMEMORATIVE COLLECTIBLE PLATES.
ONE OF THE MYSTERIES OF LIFE IS THAT YOU CAN PUT ANY PICTURE ON A PLATE AND HORDES OF MORONS WILL WANT TO OWN IT.
WOW! AN ACORN! AND IT'S ON A PLATE!
WHAT'S IT LIKE TO BE A MEMBER OF A HORDE?
7-9
S. Adams
© 1993 United Feature Syndicate, Inc.

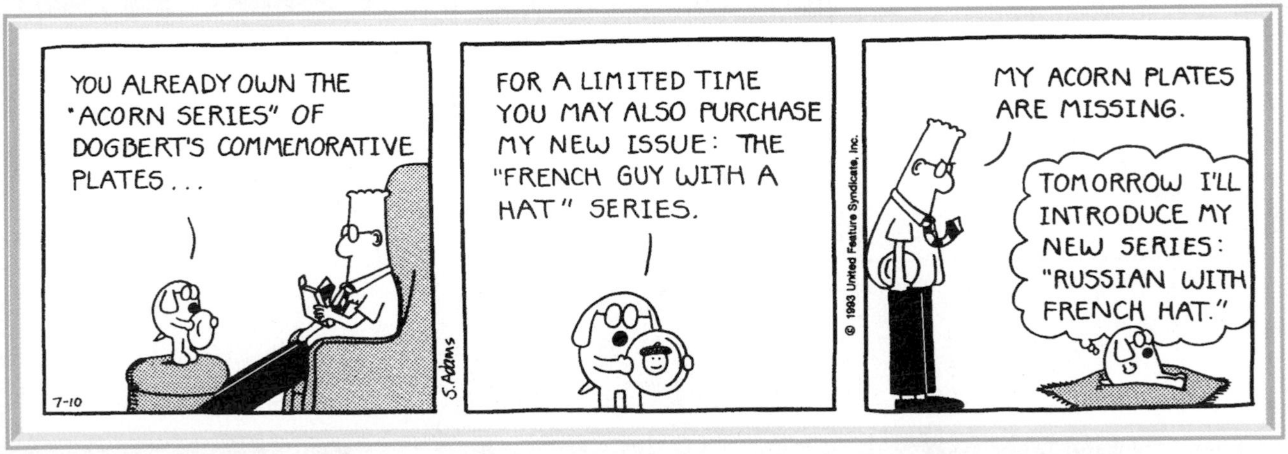
YOU ALREADY OWN THE "ACORN SERIES" OF DOGBERT'S COMMEMORATIVE PLATES...
FOR A LIMITED TIME YOU MAY ALSO PURCHASE MY NEW ISSUE: THE "FRENCH GUY WITH A HAT" SERIES.
MY ACORN PLATES ARE MISSING.
TOMORROW I'LL INTRODUCE MY NEW SERIES: "RUSSIAN WITH FRENCH HAT."
7-10
S. Adams
© 1993 United Feature Syndicate, Inc.

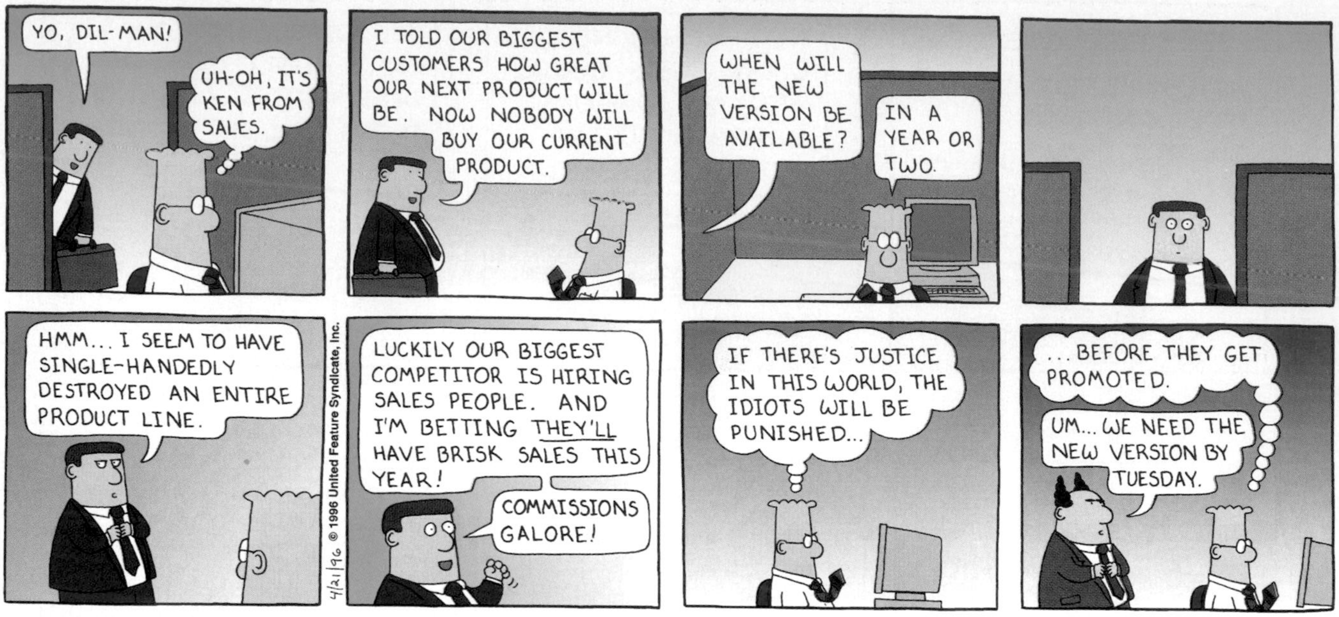
YO, DIL-MAN!
UH-OH, IT'S KEN FROM SALES.
I TOLD OUR BIGGEST CUSTOMERS HOW GREAT OUR NEXT PRODUCT WILL BE. NOW NOBODY WILL BUY OUR CURRENT PRODUCT.
WHEN WILL THE NEW VERSION BE AVAILABLE?
IN A YEAR OR TWO.
HMM... I SEEM TO HAVE SINGLE-HANDEDLY DESTROYED AN ENTIRE PRODUCT LINE.
LUCKILY OUR BIGGEST COMPETITOR IS HIRING SALES PEOPLE. AND I'M BETTING THEY'LL HAVE BRISK SALES THIS YEAR!
COMMISSIONS GALORE!
IF THERE'S JUSTICE IN THIS WORLD, THE IDIOTS WILL BE PUNISHED...
... BEFORE THEY GET PROMOTED.
UM... WE NEED THE NEW VERSION BY TUESDAY.
4/21/96 © 1996 United Feature Syndicate, Inc.

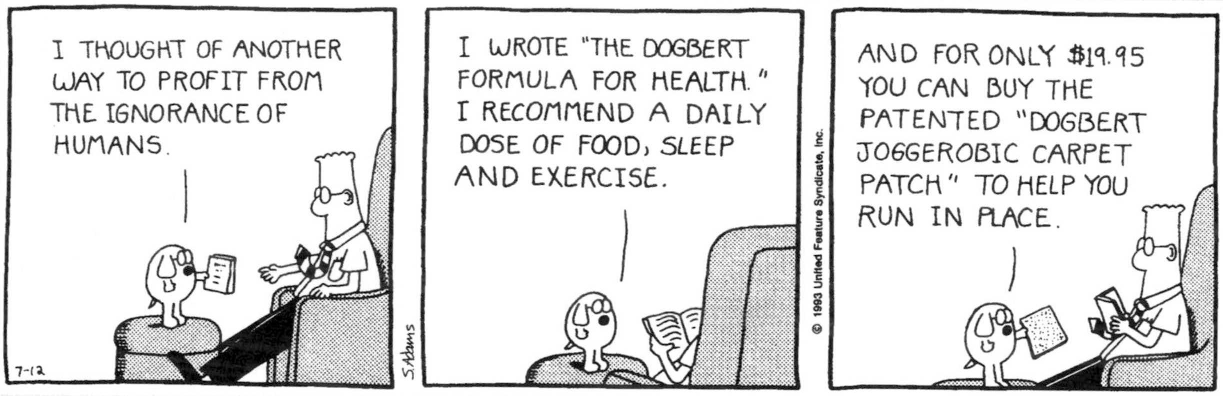
I THOUGHT OF ANOTHER WAY TO PROFIT FROM THE IGNORANCE OF HUMANS.
I WROTE "THE DOGBERT FORMULA FOR HEALTH." I RECOMMEND A DAILY DOSE OF FOOD, SLEEP AND EXERCISE.
AND FOR ONLY $19.95 YOU CAN BUY THE PATENTED "DOGBERT JOGGEROBIC CARPET PATCH" TO HELP YOU RUN IN PLACE.
7-12
S.Adams
© 1993 United Feature Syndicate, Inc.

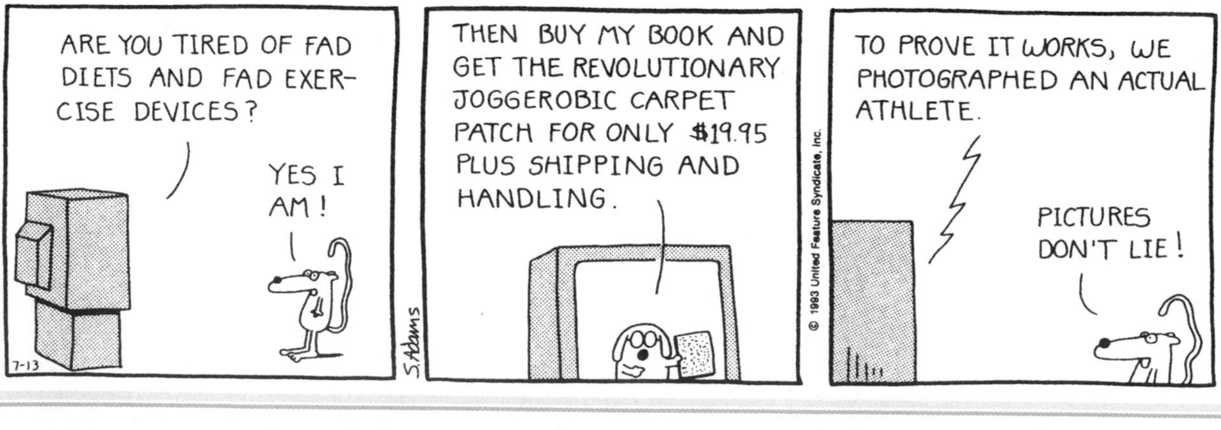
ARE YOU TIRED OF FAD DIETS AND FAD EXERCISE DEVICES?
YES I AM!
THEN BUY MY BOOK AND GET THE REVOLUTIONARY JOGGEROBIC CARPET PATCH FOR ONLY $19.95 PLUS SHIPPING AND HANDLING.
TO PROVE IT WORKS, WE PHOTOGRAPHED AN ACTUAL ATHLETE.
PICTURES DON'T LIE!
7-13
S.Adams
© 1993 United Feature Syndicate, Inc.

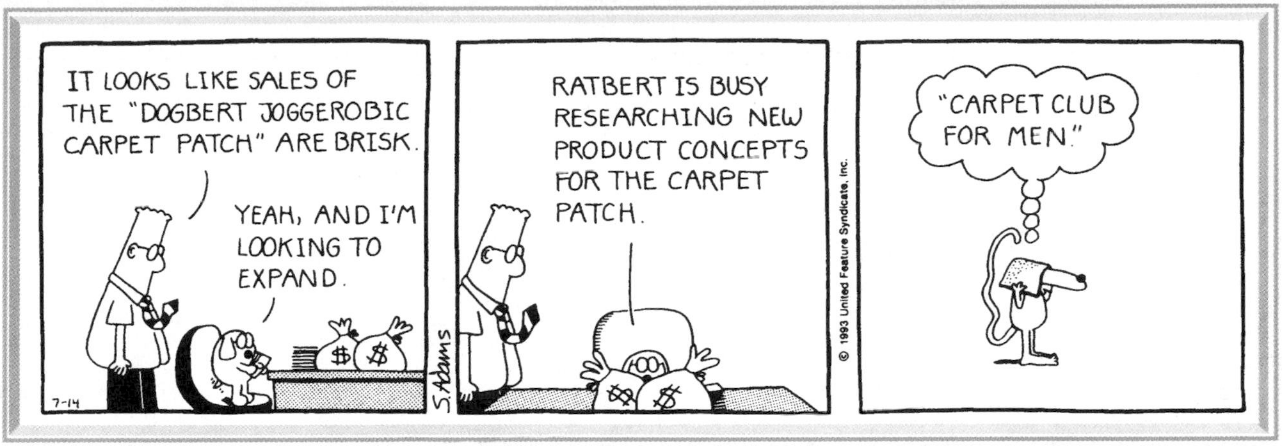
IT LOOKS LIKE SALES OF THE "DOGBERT JOGGEROBIC CARPET PATCH" ARE BRISK.
YEAH, AND I'M LOOKING TO EXPAND.
RATBERT IS BUSY RESEARCHING NEW PRODUCT CONCEPTS FOR THE CARPET PATCH.
"CARPET CLUB FOR MEN."
7-14
S. Adams
© 1993 United Feature Syndicate, Inc.

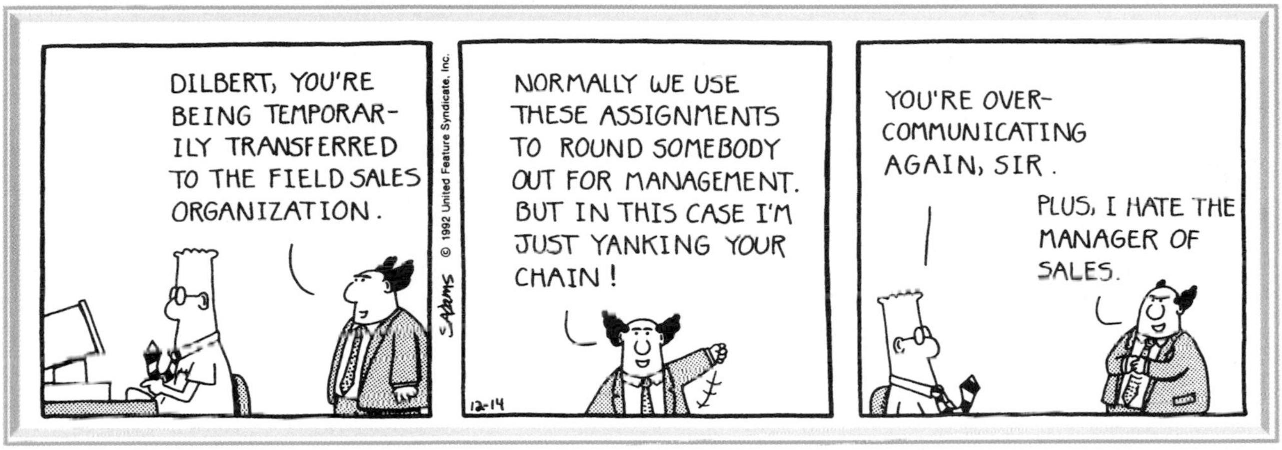
DILBERT, YOU'RE BEING TEMPORARILY TRANSFERRED TO THE FIELD SALES ORGANIZATION.
NORMALLY WE USE THESE ASSIGNMENTS TO ROUND SOMEBODY OUT FOR MANAGEMENT. BUT IN THIS CASE I'M JUST YANKING YOUR CHAIN!
YOU'RE OVER-COMMUNICATING AGAIN, SIR.
PLUS, I HATE THE MANAGER OF SALES.
S. Adams
© 1992 United Feature Syndicate, Inc.
12-14

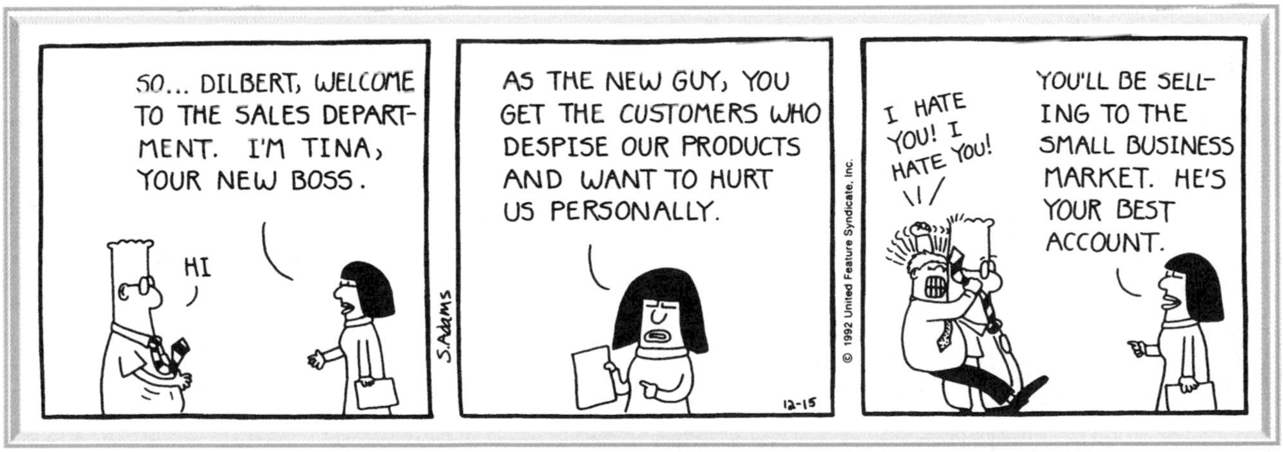
SO... DILBERT, WELCOME TO THE SALES DEPARTMENT. I'M TINA, YOUR NEW BOSS.
HI
AS THE NEW GUY, YOU GET THE CUSTOMERS WHO DESPISE OUR PRODUCTS AND WANT TO HURT US PERSONALLY.
I HATE YOU! I HATE YOU!
YOU'LL BE SELLING TO THE SMALL BUSINESS MARKET. HE'S YOUR BEST ACCOUNT.
S. Adams
12-15
© 1992 United Feature Syndicate, Inc.

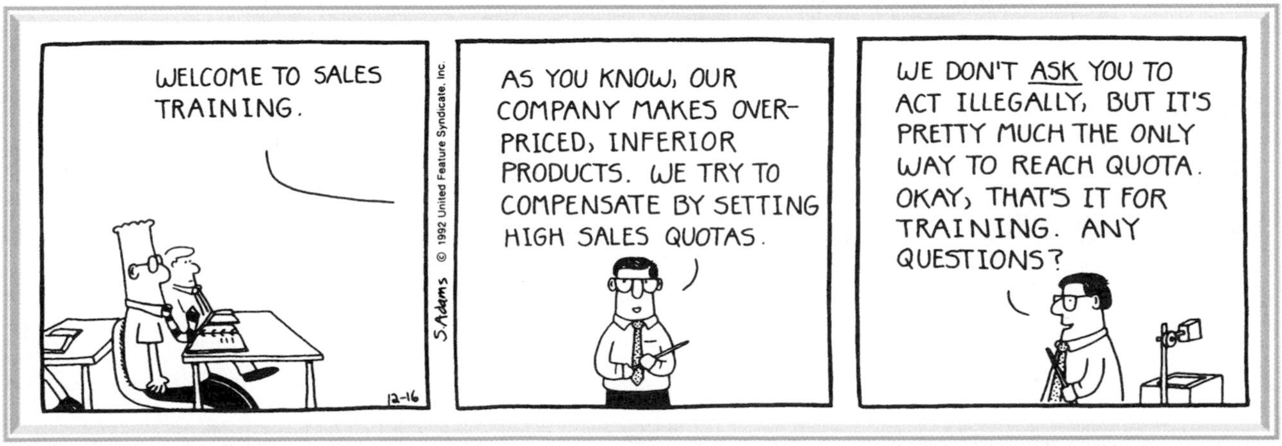
WELCOME TO SALES TRAINING.
AS YOU KNOW, OUR COMPANY MAKES OVERPRICED, INFERIOR PRODUCTS. WE TRY TO COMPENSATE BY SETTING HIGH SALES QUOTAS.
WE DON'T ASK YOU TO ACT ILLEGALLY, BUT IT'S PRETTY MUCH THE ONLY WAY TO REACH QUOTA. OKAY, THAT'S IT FOR TRAINING. ANY QUESTIONS?
12-16
S. Adams
© 1992 United Feature Syndicate, Inc.

YOUR COMPANY MAKES AN ATTRACTIVE LITTLE PRODUCT, JIM.
BUT WE'VE DECIDED TO GO WITH A VENDOR WHOSE PRODUCT ACTUALLY WORKS.
FOOLS!!! I'LL CRUSH YOU!!!
I'LL TELL YOUR BOSS YOU MADE A STUPID DECISION!! YOUR CAREERS WILL BE RUINED AND I'LL GET THE CONTRACT ANYWAY!!
YOU CAN'T SCARE US! DO YOU THINK OUR BOSS WILL BELIEVE A VENDOR OVER HIS OWN LOYAL EMPLOYEES?
MUST... KEEP... A... STRAIGHT... FACE...
HA HA HA HA HA HA HA
WE'LL TAKE A MILLION UNITS.
TAKE TWO MILLION AND I'LL SEE THAT YOU GET NICE RAISES.
© 1995 United Feature Syndicate, Inc.

I'D LIKE YOU TO MEET OUR NEWEST CUSTOMER.
YOU WON'T BE SORRY; WE'RE ONE OF THE TOP FIVE COMPANIES IN THIS FIELD.
I THOUGHT YOU SAID NO ONE ELSE MAKES THIS KIND OF PRODUCT.
NO ONE ELSE MAKES ONE WITH SO FEW FEATURES.
SO... YOUR STRATEGY IS LOW PRICE, RIGHT?
NO, HIGH MARGINS!
YOU!
I'D BETTER ASK SOMEONE WHAT A "MARGIN" IS.
© 1998 United Feature Syndicate, Inc.

SALES

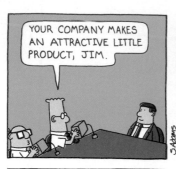

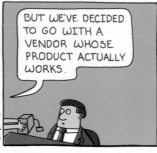

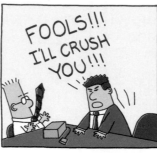

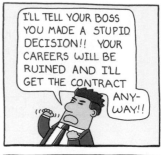

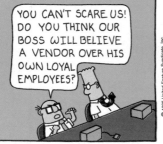

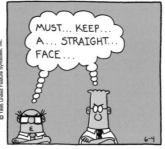

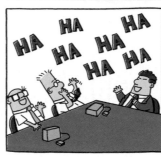

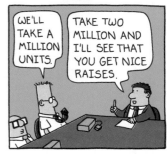

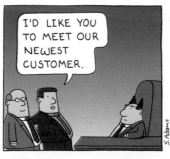

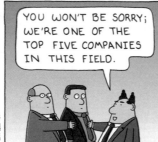

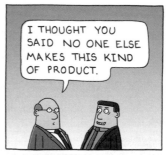

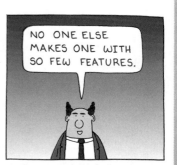

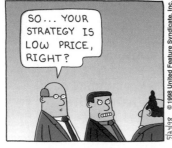

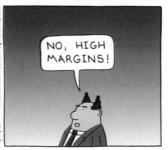

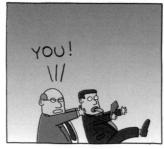

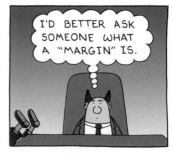

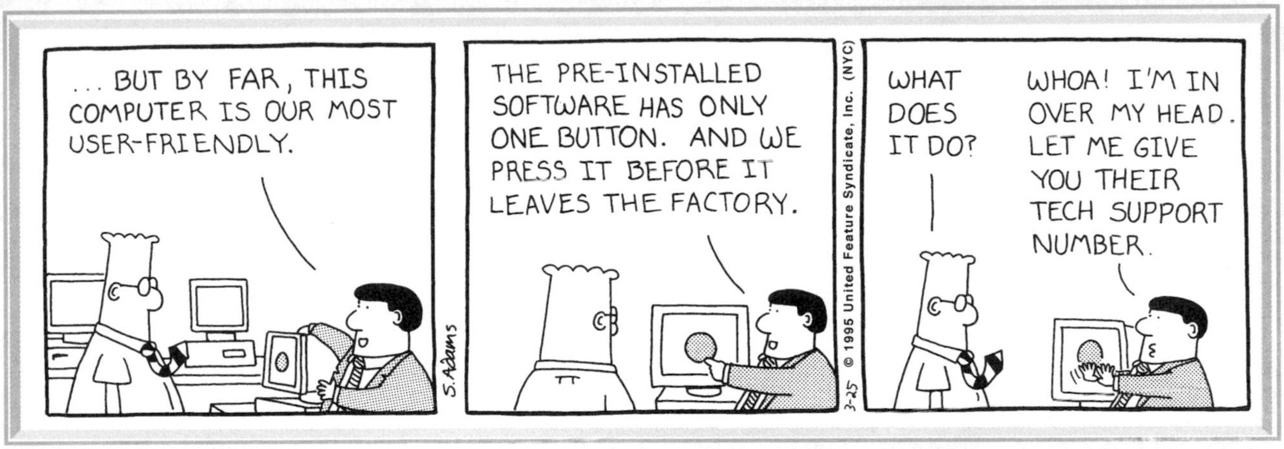

... BUT BY FAR, THIS COMPUTER IS OUR MOST USER-FRIENDLY.
THE PRE-INSTALLED SOFTWARE HAS ONLY ONE BUTTON. AND WE PRESS IT BEFORE IT LEAVES THE FACTORY.
WHAT DOES IT DO?
WHOA! I'M IN OVER MY HEAD. LET ME GIVE YOU THEIR TECH SUPPORT NUMBER.
S. Adams
3-25 © 1995 United Feature Syndicate, Inc. (NYC)

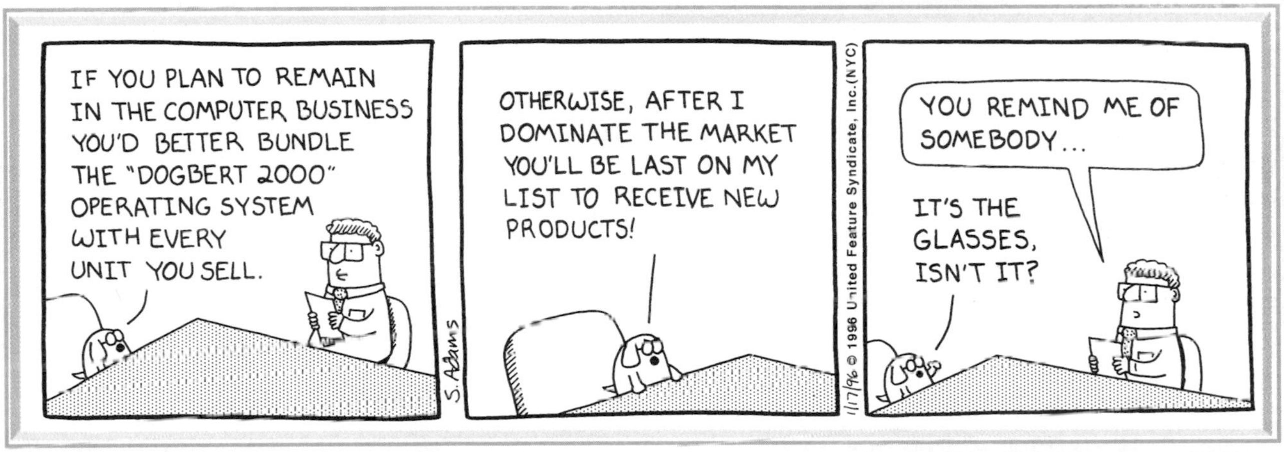

IF YOU PLAN TO REMAIN IN THE COMPUTER BUSINESS YOU'D BETTER BUNDLE THE "DOGBERT 2000" OPERATING SYSTEM WITH EVERY UNIT YOU SELL.
OTHERWISE, AFTER I DOMINATE THE MARKET YOU'LL BE LAST ON MY LIST TO RECEIVE NEW PRODUCTS!
YOU REMIND ME OF SOMEBODY...
IT'S THE GLASSES, ISN'T IT?
S. Adams
1/17/96 © 1996 United Feature Syndicate, Inc.(NYC)

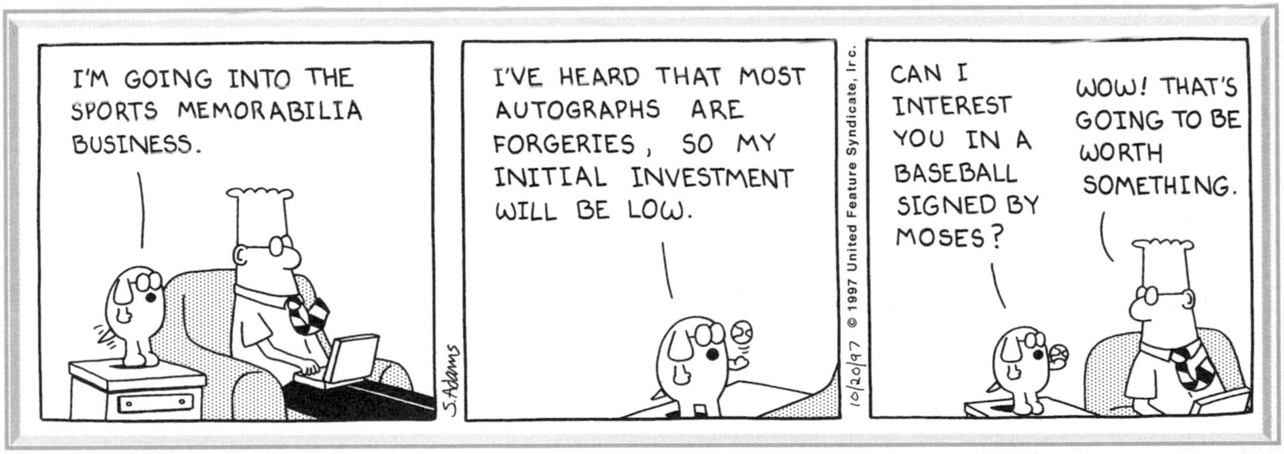

I'M GOING INTO THE SPORTS MEMORABILIA BUSINESS.
I'VE HEARD THAT MOST AUTOGRAPHS ARE FORGERIES, SO MY INITIAL INVESTMENT WILL BE LOW.
CAN I INTEREST YOU IN A BASEBALL SIGNED BY MOSES?
WOW! THAT'S GOING TO BE WORTH SOMETHING.
S. Adams
10/20/97 © 1997 United Feature Syndicate, Inc.

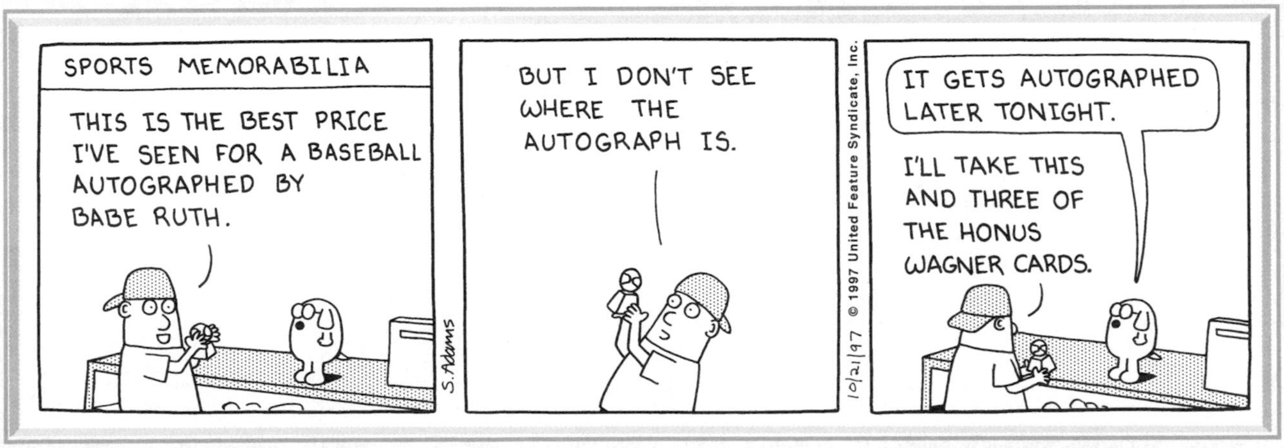

SPORTS MEMORABILIA
THIS IS THE BEST PRICE I'VE SEEN FOR A BASEBALL AUTOGRAPHED BY BABE RUTH.
BUT I DON'T SEE WHERE THE AUTOGRAPH IS.
IT GETS AUTOGRAPHED LATER TONIGHT.
I'LL TAKE THIS AND THREE OF THE HONUS WAGNER CARDS.
S. Adams
10/21/97 © 1997 United Feature Syndicate, Inc.

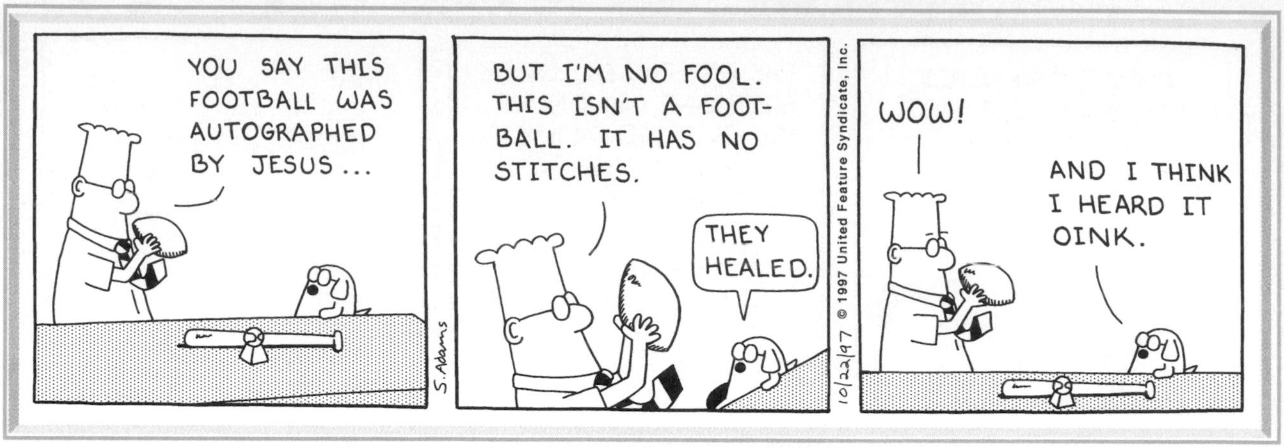
YOU SAY THIS FOOTBALL WAS AUTOGRAPHED BY JESUS...
BUT I'M NO FOOL. THIS ISN'T A FOOT-BALL. IT HAS NO STITCHES.
THEY HEALED.
WOW!
AND I THINK I HEARD IT OINK.
S. Adams
10/22/97
© 1997 United Feature Syndicate, Inc.

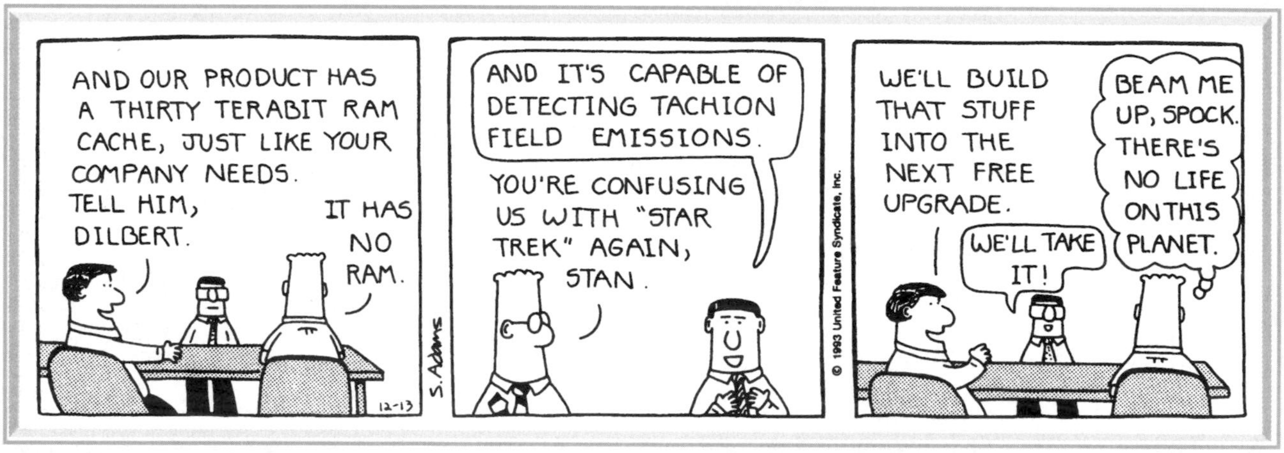
AND OUR PRODUCT HAS A THIRTY TERABIT RAM CACHE, JUST LIKE YOUR COMPANY NEEDS.
TELL HIM, DILBERT.
IT HAS NO RAM.
12-13
S. Adams
AND IT'S CAPABLE OF DETECTING TACHION FIELD EMISSIONS.
YOU'RE CONFUSING US WITH "STAR TREK" AGAIN, STAN.
© 1993 United Feature Syndicate, Inc.
WE'LL BUILD THAT STUFF INTO THE NEXT FREE UPGRADE.
WE'LL TAKE IT!
BEAM ME UP, SPOCK. THERE'S NO LIFE ON THIS PLANET.

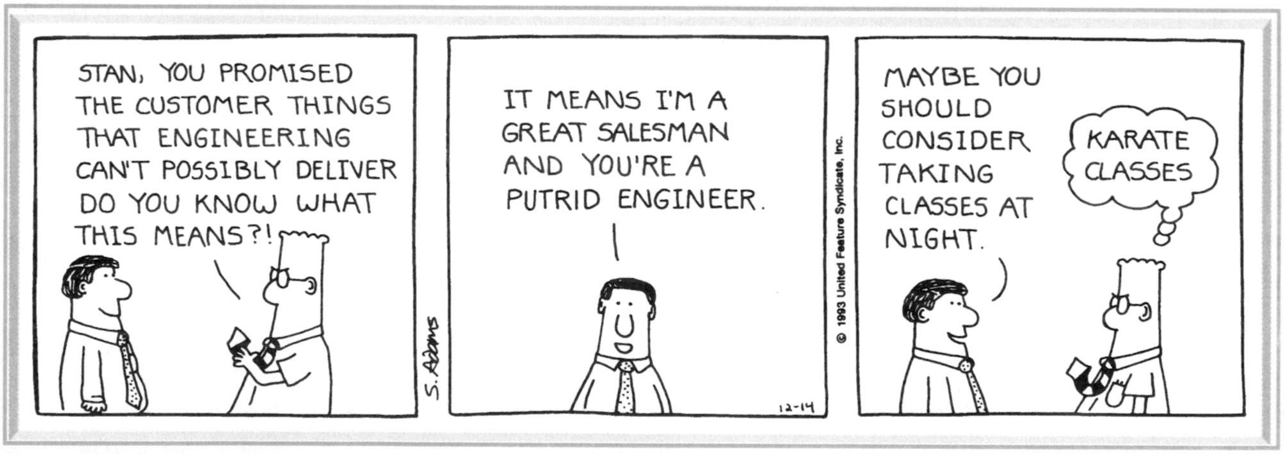
STAN, YOU PROMISED THE CUSTOMER THINGS THAT ENGINEERING CAN'T POSSIBLY DELIVER DO YOU KNOW WHAT THIS MEANS?!
S. Adams
IT MEANS I'M A GREAT SALESMAN AND YOU'RE A PUTRID ENGINEER.
12-14
© 1993 United Feature Syndicate, Inc.
MAYBE YOU SHOULD CONSIDER TAKING CLASSES AT NIGHT.
KARATE CLASSES

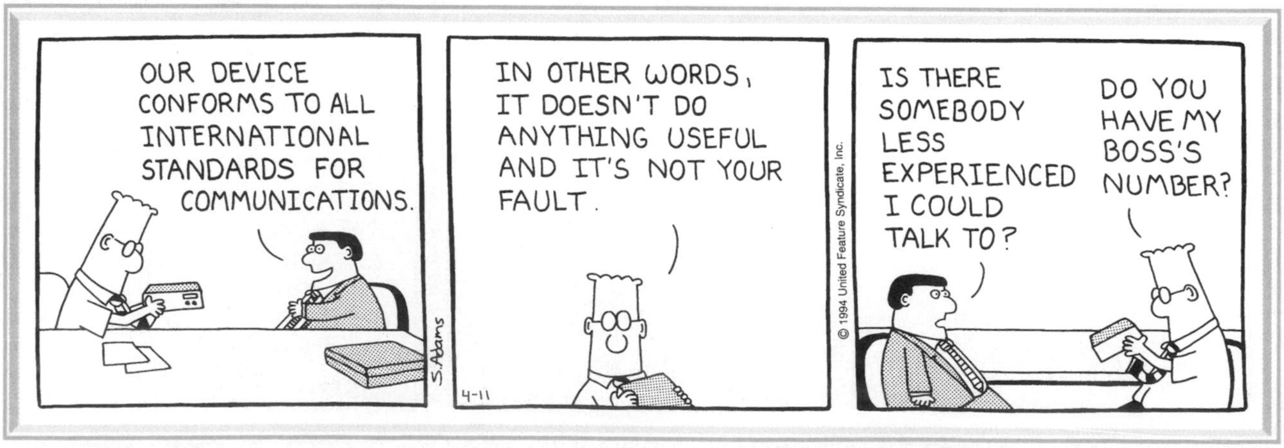
OUR DEVICE CONFORMS TO ALL INTERNATIONAL STANDARDS FOR COMMUNICATIONS.
S. Adams
IN OTHER WORDS, IT DOESN'T DO ANYTHING USEFUL AND IT'S NOT YOUR FAULT.
4-11
© 1994 United Feature Syndicate, Inc.
IS THERE SOMEBODY LESS EXPERIENCED I COULD TALK TO?
DO YOU HAVE MY BOSS'S NUMBER?

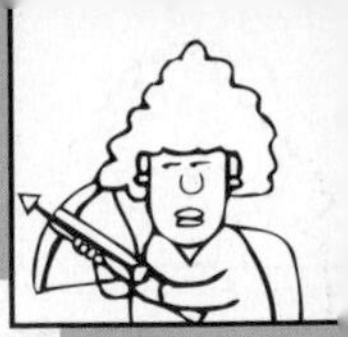

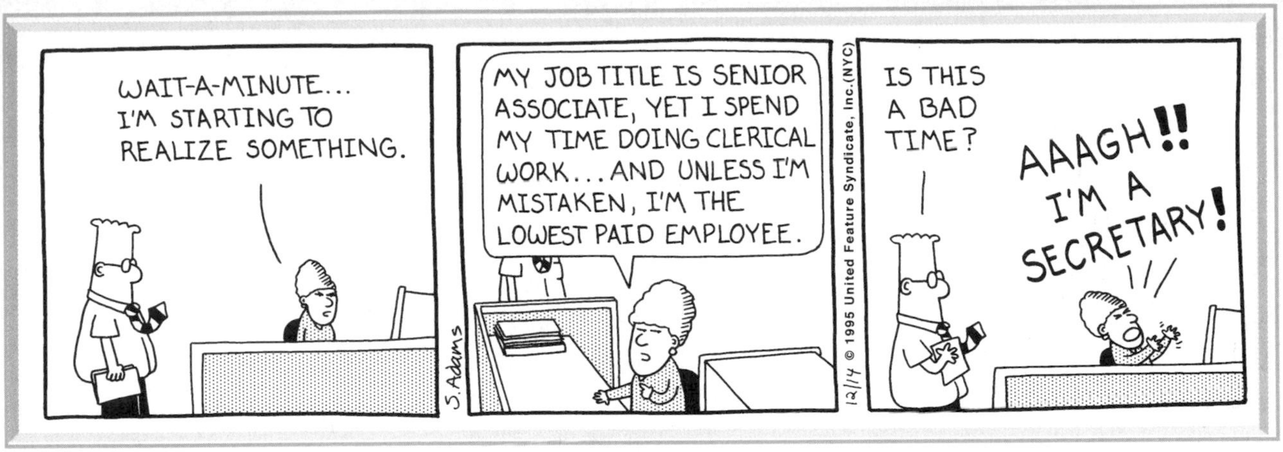
WAIT-A-MINUTE... I'M STARTING TO REALIZE SOMETHING.
MY JOB TITLE IS SENIOR ASSOCIATE, YET I SPEND MY TIME DOING CLERICAL WORK... AND UNLESS I'M MISTAKEN, I'M THE LOWEST PAID EMPLOYEE.
IS THIS A BAD TIME?
AAAGH!! I'M A SECRETARY!
S. Adams
12/14 © 1995 United Feature Syndicate, Inc.(NYC)

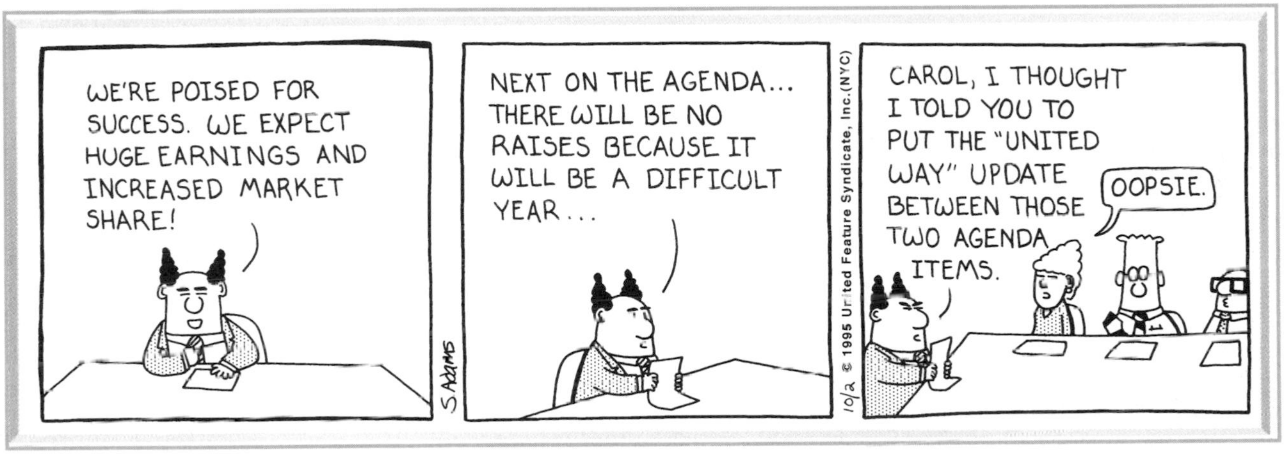
WE'RE POISED FOR SUCCESS. WE EXPECT HUGE EARNINGS AND INCREASED MARKET SHARE!
NEXT ON THE AGENDA... THERE WILL BE NO RAISES BECAUSE IT WILL BE A DIFFICULT YEAR...
CAROL, I THOUGHT I TOLD YOU TO PUT THE "UNITED WAY" UPDATE BETWEEN THOSE TWO AGENDA ITEMS.
OOPSIE.
S. Adams
10/2 © 1995 United Feature Syndicate, Inc.(NYC)

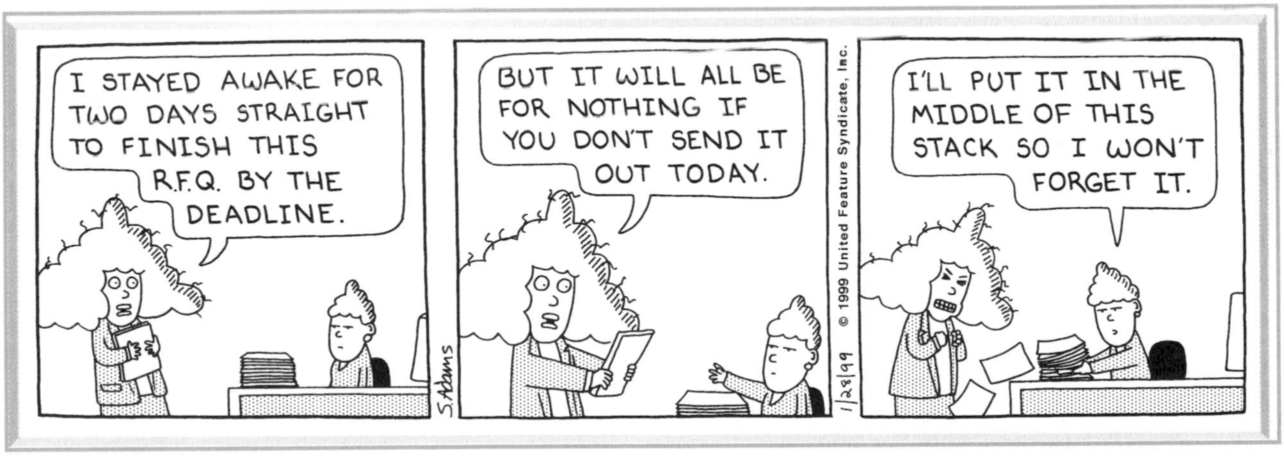
I STAYED AWAKE FOR TWO DAYS STRAIGHT TO FINISH THIS R.F.Q. BY THE DEADLINE.
BUT IT WILL ALL BE FOR NOTHING IF YOU DON'T SEND IT OUT TODAY.
I'LL PUT IT IN THE MIDDLE OF THIS STACK SO I WON'T FORGET IT.
S. Adams
1/28/99 © 1999 United Feature Syndicate, Inc.

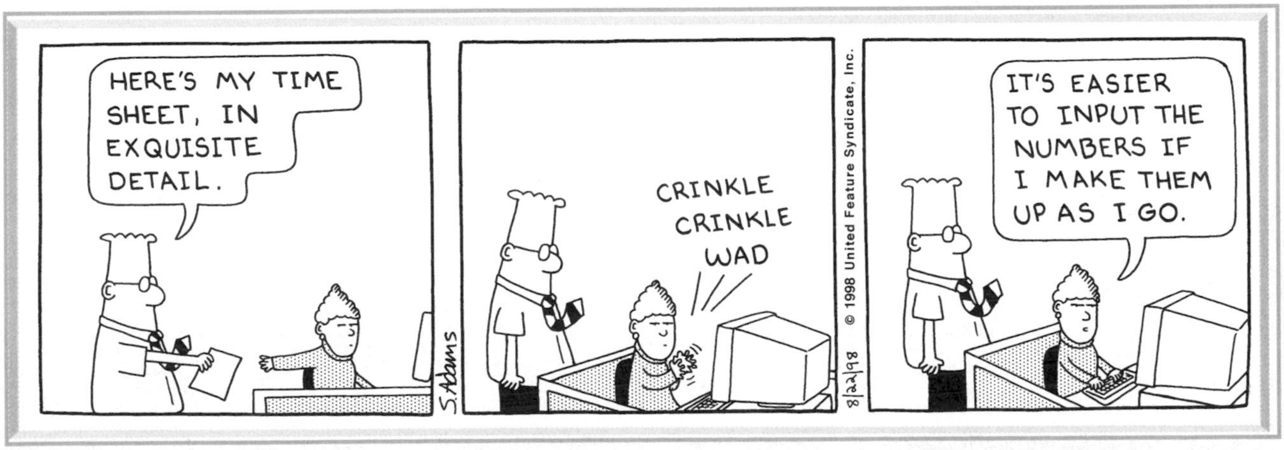
HERE'S MY TIME SHEET, IN EXQUISITE DETAIL.
CRINKLE CRINKLE WAD
IT'S EASIER TO INPUT THE NUMBERS IF I MAKE THEM UP AS I GO.
S. Adams
8/22/98 © 1998 United Feature Syndicate, Inc.

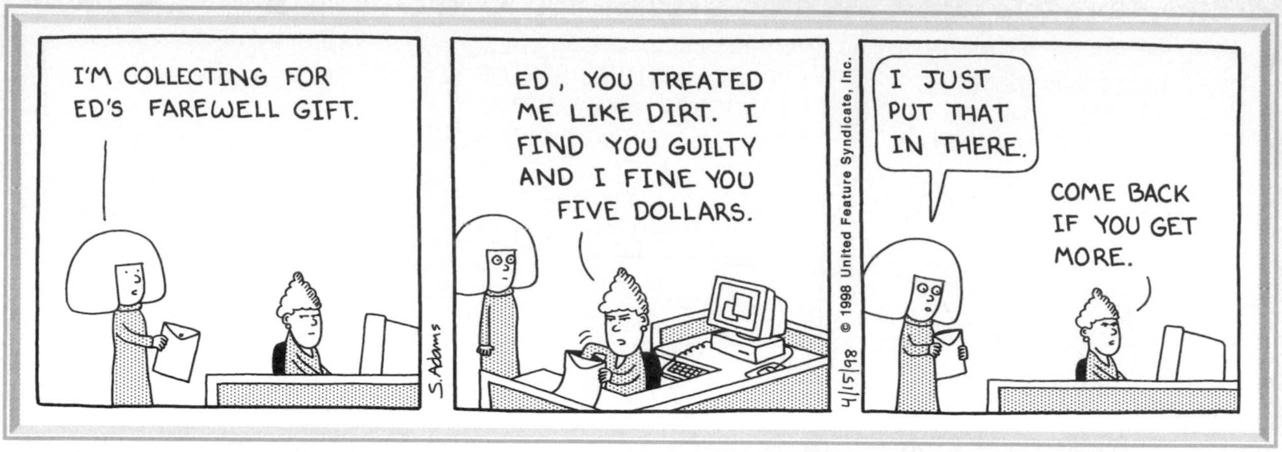
I'M COLLECTING FOR ED'S FAREWELL GIFT.
S. Adams
ED, YOU TREATED ME LIKE DIRT. I FIND YOU GUILTY AND I FINE YOU FIVE DOLLARS.
4/15/98
© 1998 United Feature Syndicate, Inc.
I JUST PUT THAT IN THERE.
COME BACK IF YOU GET MORE.

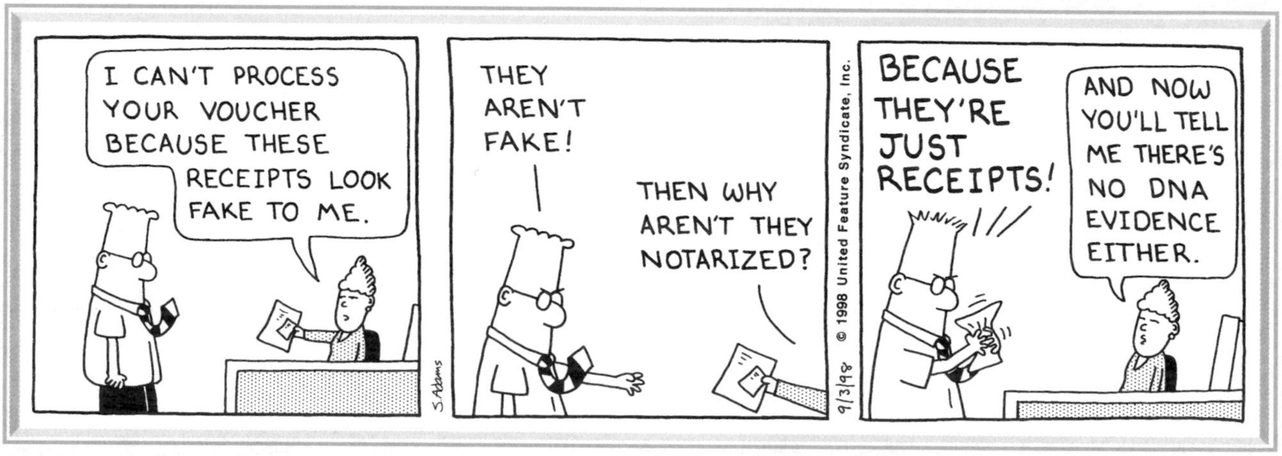
I CAN'T PROCESS YOUR VOUCHER BECAUSE THESE RECEIPTS LOOK FAKE TO ME.
S. Adams
THEY AREN'T FAKE!
THEN WHY AREN'T THEY NOTARIZED?
9/3/98
© 1998 United Feature Syndicate, Inc.
BECAUSE THEY'RE JUST RECEIPTS!
AND NOW YOU'LL TELL ME THERE'S NO DNA EVIDENCE EITHER.

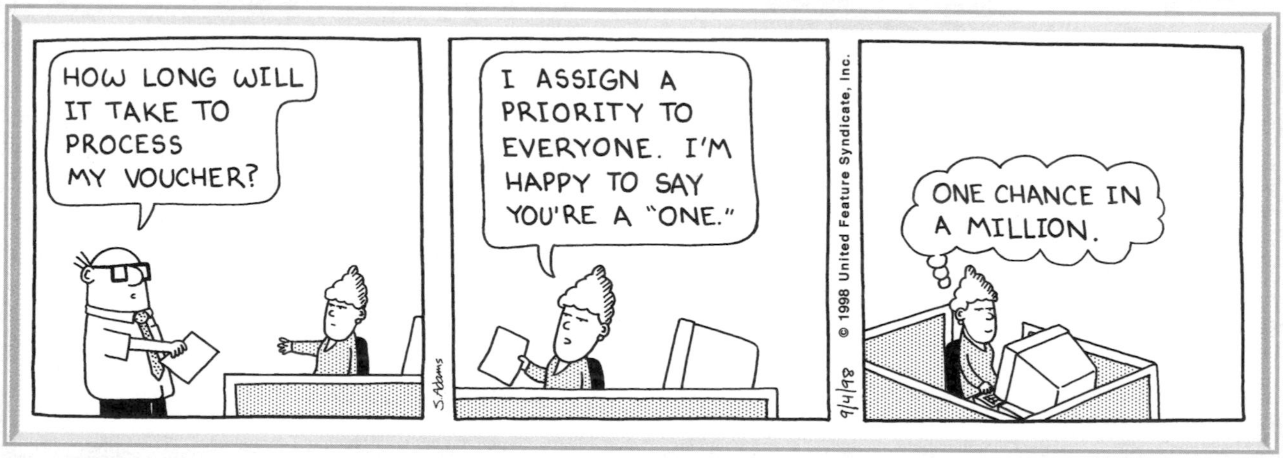
HOW LONG WILL IT TAKE TO PROCESS MY VOUCHER?
S. Adams
I ASSIGN A PRIORITY TO EVERYONE. I'M HAPPY TO SAY YOU'RE A "ONE."
9/4/98
© 1998 United Feature Syndicate, Inc.
ONE CHANCE IN A MILLION.

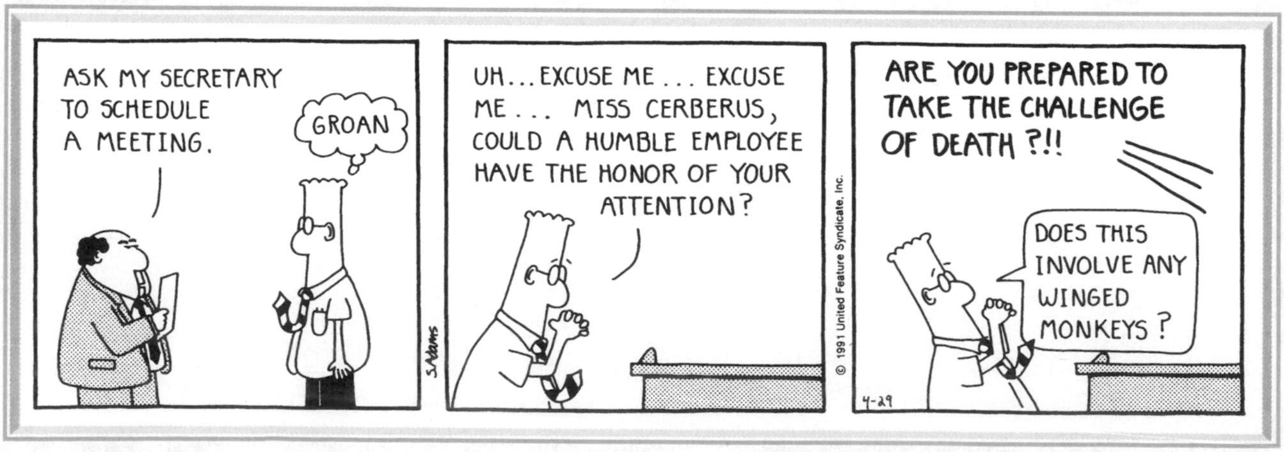
ASK MY SECRETARY TO SCHEDULE A MEETING.
GROAN
S. Adams
UH... EXCUSE ME ... EXCUSE ME ... MISS CERBERUS, COULD A HUMBLE EMPLOYEE HAVE THE HONOR OF YOUR ATTENTION?
© 1991 United Feature Syndicate, Inc.
ARE YOU PREPARED TO TAKE THE CHALLENGE OF DEATH ?!!
DOES THIS INVOLVE ANY WINGED MONKEYS ?
4-29

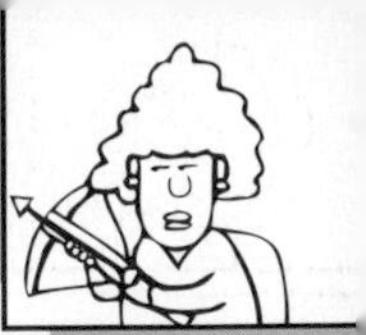

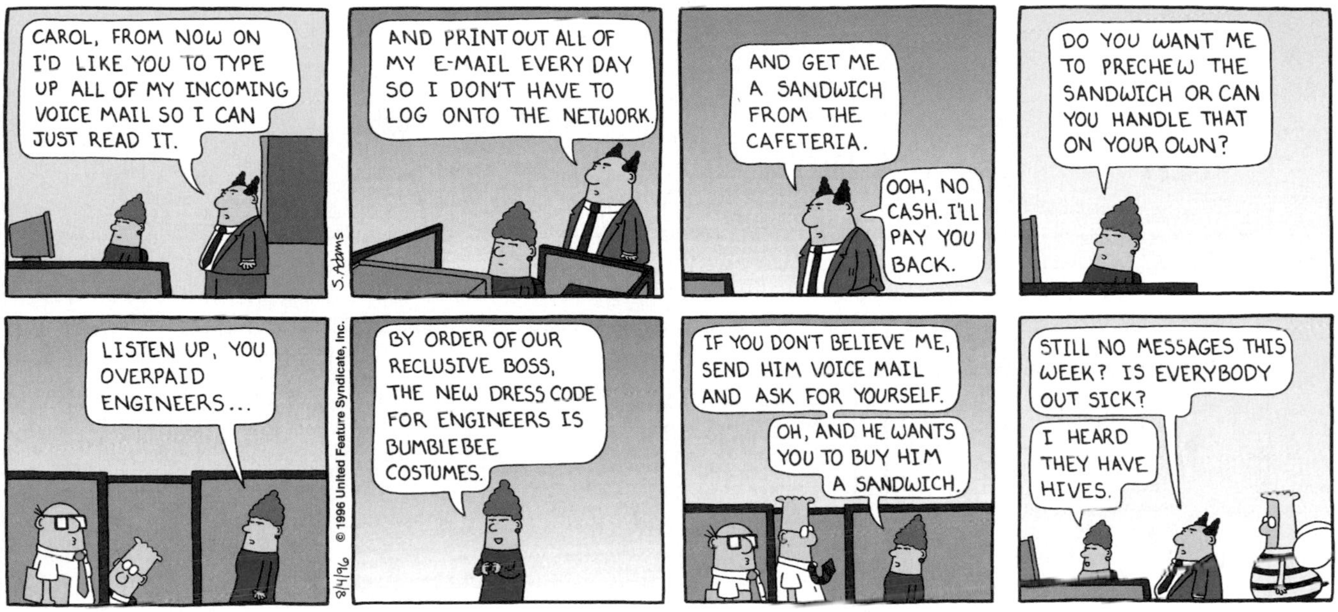
CAROL, FROM NOW ON I'D LIKE YOU TO TYPE UP ALL OF MY INCOMING VOICE MAIL SO I CAN JUST READ IT.
S. Adams
AND PRINT OUT ALL OF MY E-MAIL EVERY DAY SO I DON'T HAVE TO LOG ONTO THE NETWORK.
AND GET ME A SANDWICH FROM THE CAFETERIA.
OOH, NO CASH. I'LL PAY YOU BACK.
DO YOU WANT ME TO PRECHEW THE SANDWICH OR CAN YOU HANDLE THAT ON YOUR OWN?
LISTEN UP, YOU OVERPAID ENGINEERS...
8/4/96 © 1996 United Feature Syndicate, Inc.
BY ORDER OF OUR RECLUSIVE BOSS, THE NEW DRESS CODE FOR ENGINEERS IS BUMBLEBEE COSTUMES.
IF YOU DON'T BELIEVE ME, SEND HIM VOICE MAIL AND ASK FOR YOURSELF.
OH, AND HE WANTS YOU TO BUY HIM A SANDWICH.
STILL NO MESSAGES THIS WEEK? IS EVERYBODY OUT SICK?
I HEARD THEY HAVE HIVES.

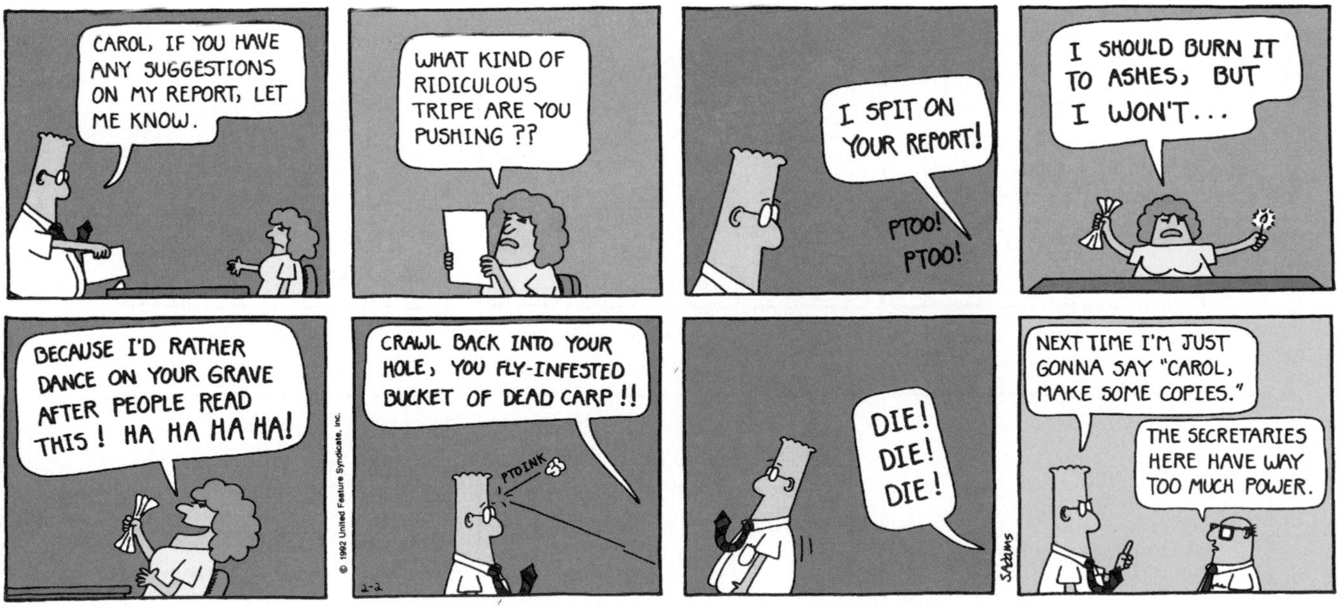
CAROL, IF YOU HAVE ANY SUGGESTIONS ON MY REPORT, LET ME KNOW.
WHAT KIND OF RIDICULOUS TRIPE ARE YOU PUSHING ??
I SPIT ON YOUR REPORT!
PTOO! PTOO!
I SHOULD BURN IT TO ASHES, BUT I WON'T...
BECAUSE I'D RATHER DANCE ON YOUR GRAVE AFTER PEOPLE READ THIS! HA HA HA HA!
© 1992 United Feature Syndicate, Inc.
CRAWL BACK INTO YOUR HOLE, YOU FLY-INFESTED BUCKET OF DEAD CARP !!
PTOINK
2-2
DIE! DIE! DIE!
S. Adams
NEXT TIME I'M JUST GONNA SAY "CAROL, MAKE SOME COPIES."
THE SECRETARIES HERE HAVE WAY TOO MUCH POWER.

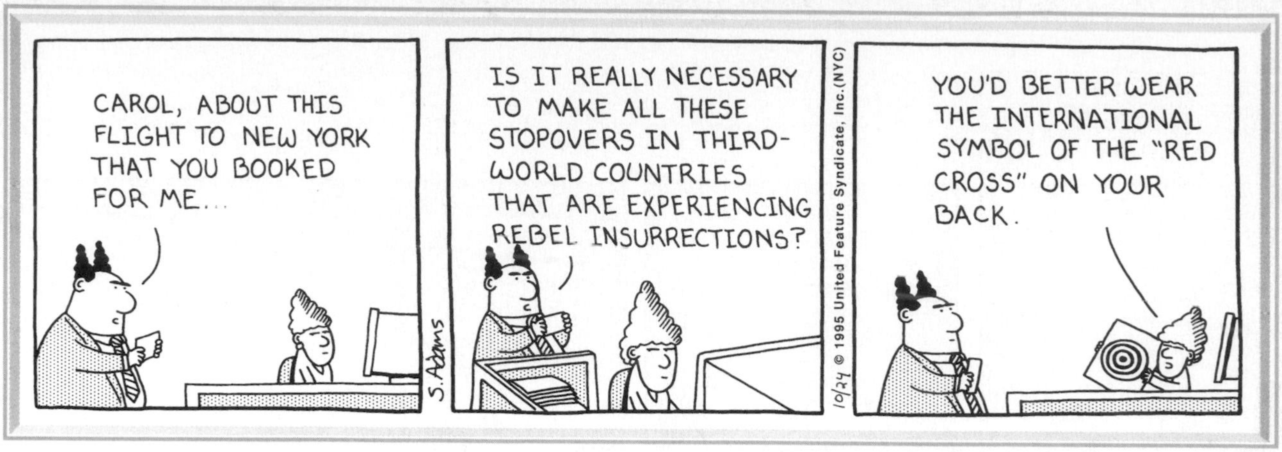
CAROL, ABOUT THIS FLIGHT TO NEW YORK THAT YOU BOOKED FOR ME...
IS IT REALLY NECESSARY TO MAKE ALL THESE STOPOVERS IN THIRD-WORLD COUNTRIES THAT ARE EXPERIENCING REBEL INSURRECTIONS?
YOU'D BETTER WEAR THE INTERNATIONAL SYMBOL OF THE "RED CROSS" ON YOUR BACK.
S. Adams
10/24 © 1995 United Feature Syndicate, Inc.(NYC)

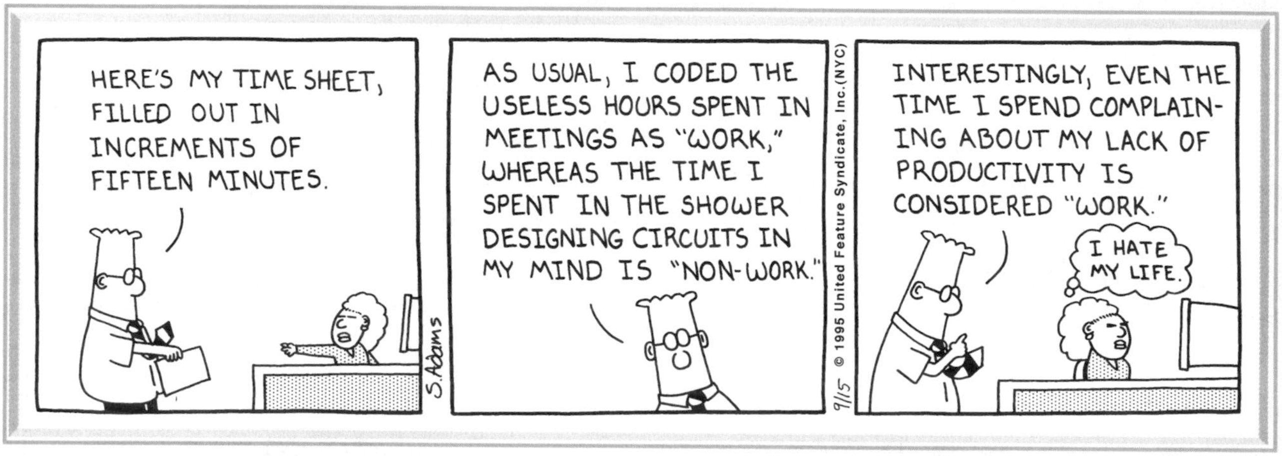
HERE'S MY TIME SHEET, FILLED OUT IN INCREMENTS OF FIFTEEN MINUTES.
AS USUAL, I CODED THE USELESS HOURS SPENT IN MEETINGS AS "WORK," WHEREAS THE TIME I SPENT IN THE SHOWER DESIGNING CIRCUITS IN MY MIND IS "NON-WORK."
INTERESTINGLY, EVEN THE TIME I SPEND COMPLAINING ABOUT MY LACK OF PRODUCTIVITY IS CONSIDERED "WORK."
I HATE MY LIFE.
S. Adams
9/15 © 1995 United Feature Syndicate, Inc.(NYC)

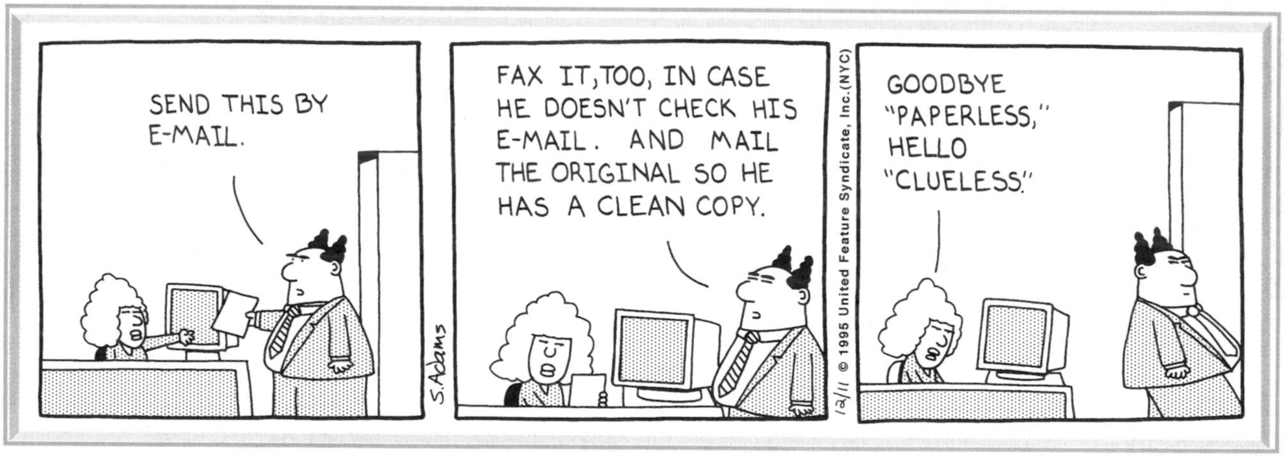
SEND THIS BY E-MAIL.
FAX IT, TOO, IN CASE HE DOESN'T CHECK HIS E-MAIL. AND MAIL THE ORIGINAL SO HE HAS A CLEAN COPY.
GOODBYE "PAPERLESS," HELLO "CLUELESS."
S. Adams
12/11 © 1995 United Feature Syndicate, Inc.(NYC)

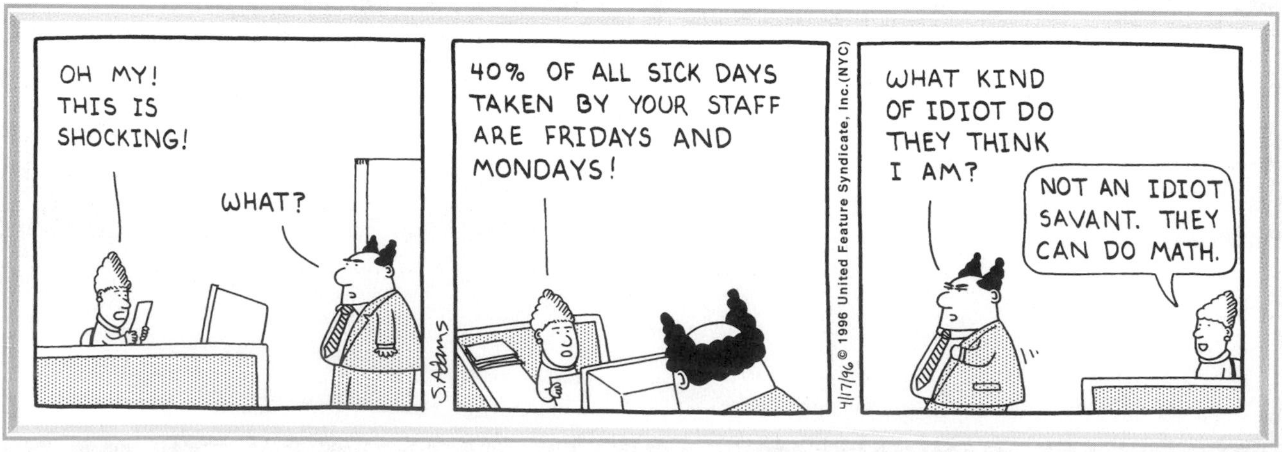
OH MY! THIS IS SHOCKING!
WHAT?
40% OF ALL SICK DAYS TAKEN BY YOUR STAFF ARE FRIDAYS AND MONDAYS!
WHAT KIND OF IDIOT DO THEY THINK I AM?
NOT AN IDIOT SAVANT. THEY CAN DO MATH.
S. Adams
4/17/96 © 1996 United Feature Syndicate, Inc.(NYC)

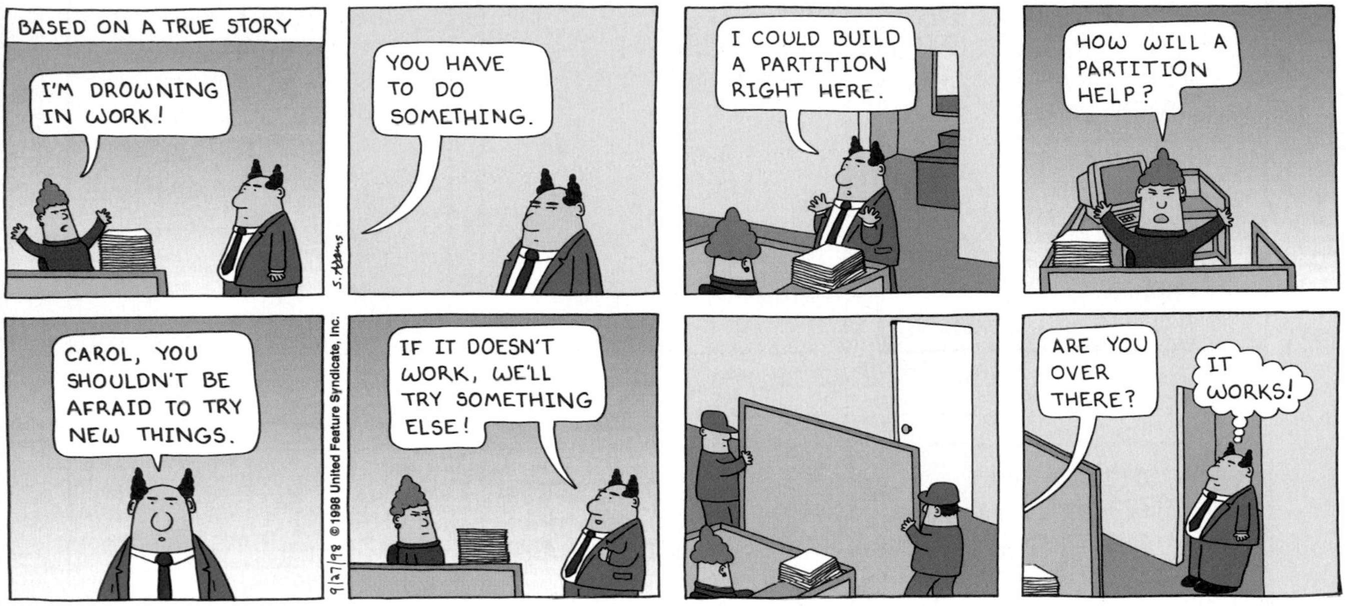
BASED ON A TRUE STORY
I'M DROWNING IN WORK!
YOU HAVE TO DO SOMETHING.
I COULD BUILD A PARTITION RIGHT HERE.
HOW WILL A PARTITION HELP?
CAROL, YOU SHOULDN'T BE AFRAID TO TRY NEW THINGS.
IF IT DOESN'T WORK, WE'LL TRY SOMETHING ELSE!
ARE YOU OVER THERE?
IT WORKS!
9/27/98 © 1998 United Feature Syndicate, Inc.

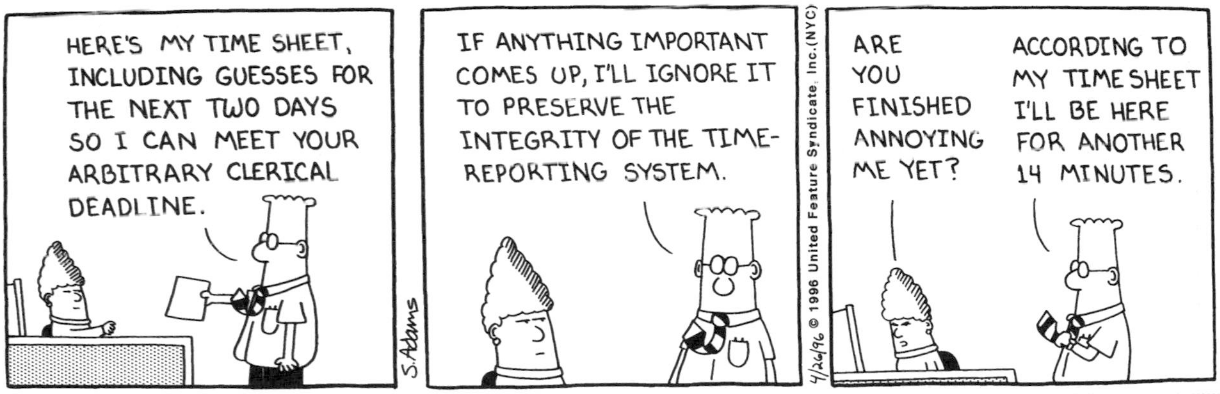
HERE'S MY TIME SHEET, INCLUDING GUESSES FOR THE NEXT TWO DAYS SO I CAN MEET YOUR ARBITRARY CLERICAL DEADLINE.
IF ANYTHING IMPORTANT COMES UP, I'LL IGNORE IT TO PRESERVE THE INTEGRITY OF THE TIME-REPORTING SYSTEM.
ARE YOU FINISHED ANNOYING ME YET?
ACCORDING TO MY TIME SHEET I'LL BE HERE FOR ANOTHER 14 MINUTES.
4/26/96 © 1996 United Feature Syndicate, Inc.(NYC)

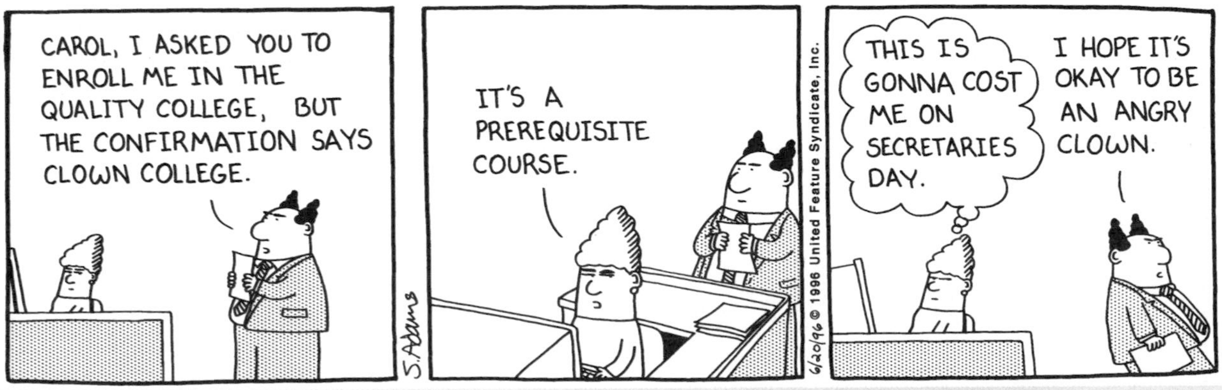
CAROL, I ASKED YOU TO ENROLL ME IN THE QUALITY COLLEGE, BUT THE CONFIRMATION SAYS CLOWN COLLEGE.
IT'S A PREREQUISITE COURSE.
THIS IS GONNA COST ME ON SECRETARIES DAY.
I HOPE IT'S OKAY TO BE AN ANGRY CLOWN.
6/20/96 © 1996 United Feature Syndicate, Inc.

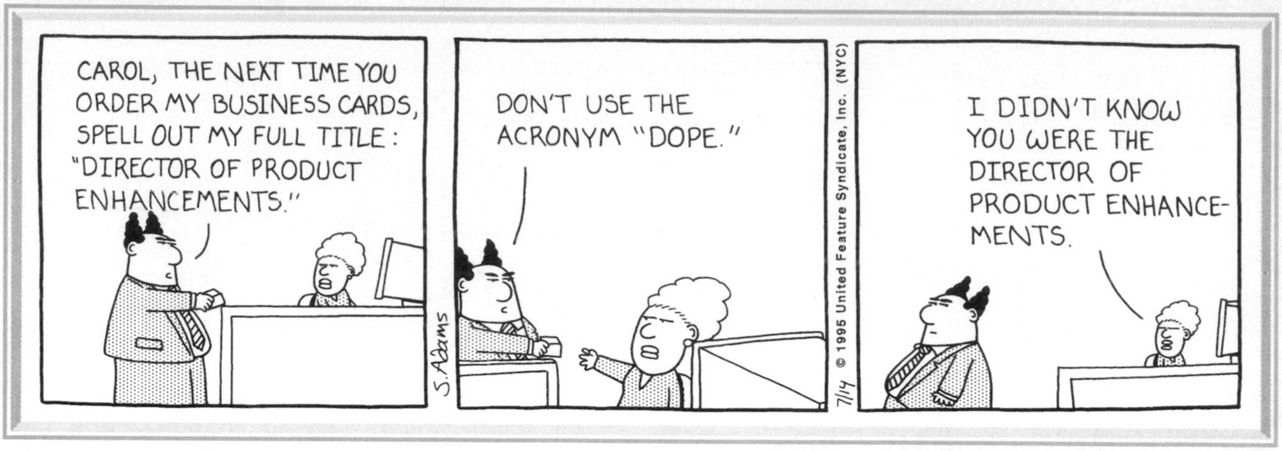
CAROL, THE NEXT TIME YOU ORDER MY BUSINESS CARDS, SPELL OUT MY FULL TITLE: "DIRECTOR OF PRODUCT ENHANCEMENTS."
DON'T USE THE ACRONYM "DOPE."
I DIDN'T KNOW YOU WERE THE DIRECTOR OF PRODUCT ENHANCEMENTS.
S. Adams
7/14 © 1995 United Feature Syndicate, Inc. (NYC)

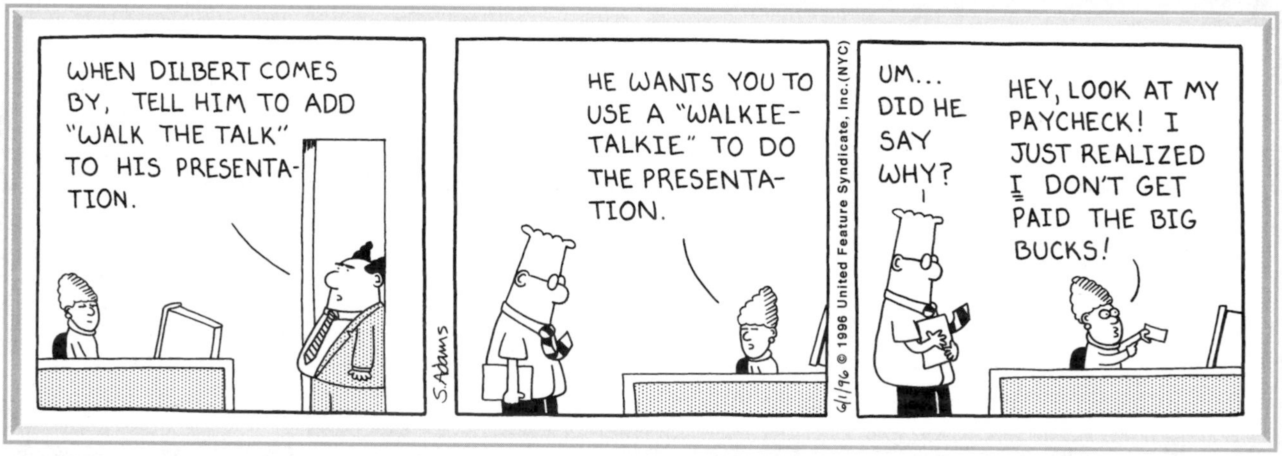
WHEN DILBERT COMES BY, TELL HIM TO ADD "WALK THE TALK" TO HIS PRESENTATION.
HE WANTS YOU TO USE A "WALKIE-TALKIE" TO DO THE PRESENTATION.
UM... DID HE SAY WHY?
HEY, LOOK AT MY PAYCHECK! I JUST REALIZED I DON'T GET PAID THE BIG BUCKS!
S. Adams
6/1/96 © 1996 United Feature Syndicate, Inc.(NYC)

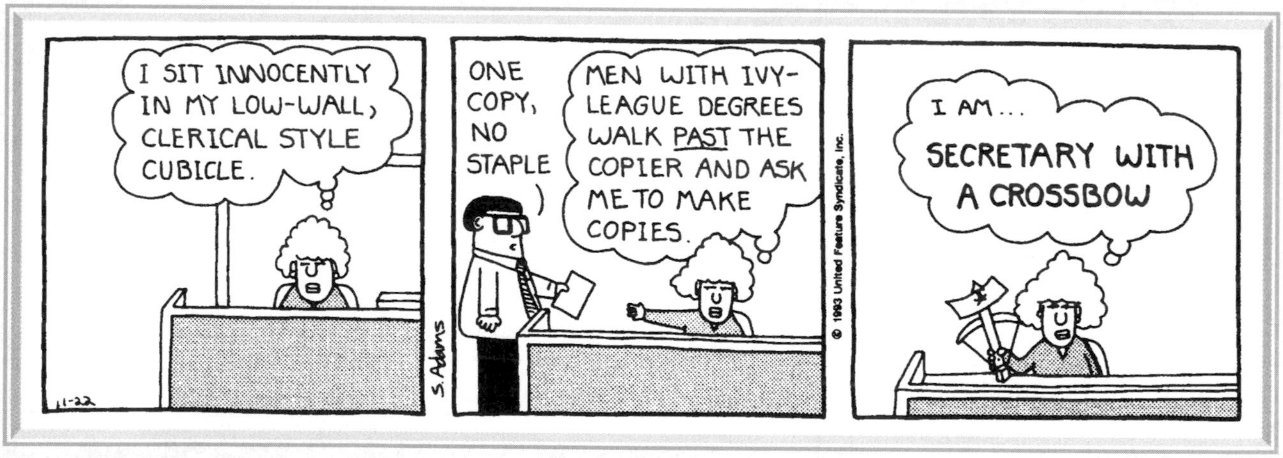
I SIT INNOCENTLY IN MY LOW-WALL, CLERICAL STYLE CUBICLE.
ONE COPY, NO STAPLE
MEN WITH IVY-LEAGUE DEGREES WALK PAST THE COPIER AND ASK ME TO MAKE COPIES.
I AM...
SECRETARY WITH A CROSSBOW
11-22
S. Adams
© 1993 United Feature Syndicate, Inc.

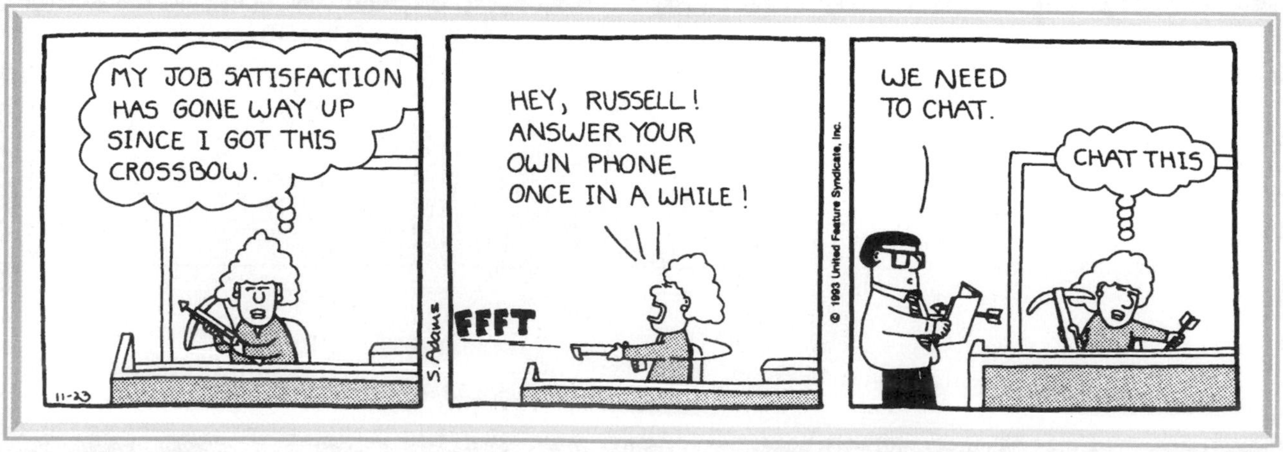
MY JOB SATISFACTION HAS GONE WAY UP SINCE I GOT THIS CROSSBOW.
HEY, RUSSELL! ANSWER YOUR OWN PHONE ONCE IN A WHILE!
FFFT
WE NEED TO CHAT.
CHAT THIS
11-23
S. Adams
© 1993 United Feature Syndicate, Inc.

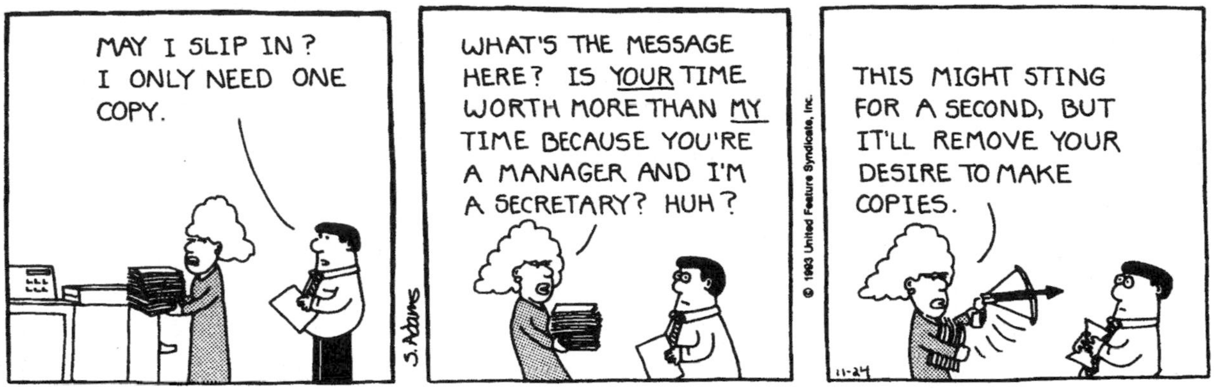
MAY I SLIP IN? I ONLY NEED ONE COPY.
WHAT'S THE MESSAGE HERE? IS YOUR TIME WORTH MORE THAN MY TIME BECAUSE YOU'RE A MANAGER AND I'M A SECRETARY? HUH?
© 1993 United Feature Syndicate, Inc.
THIS MIGHT STING FOR A SECOND, BUT IT'LL REMOVE YOUR DESIRE TO MAKE COPIES.

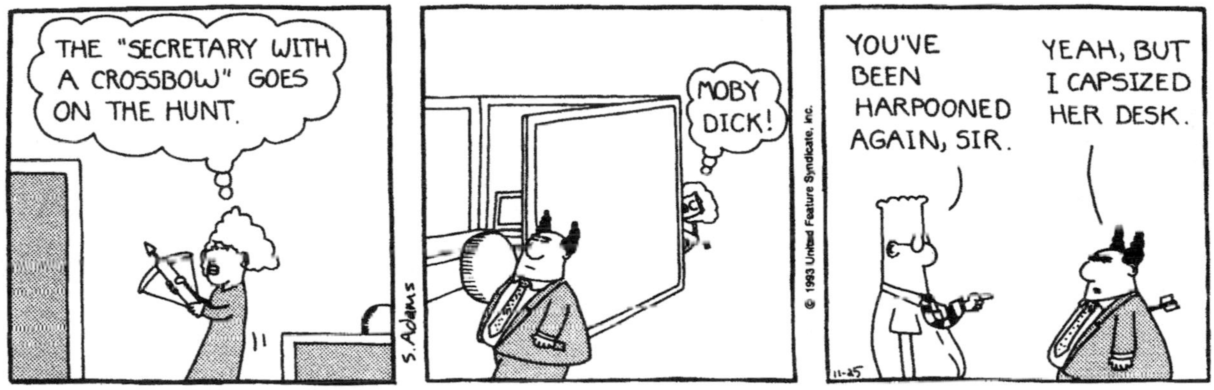
THE "SECRETARY WITH A CROSSBOW" GOES ON THE HUNT.
MOBY DICK!
© 1993 United Feature Syndicate, Inc.
YOU'VE BEEN HARPOONED AGAIN, SIR.
YEAH, BUT I CAPSIZED HER DESK.

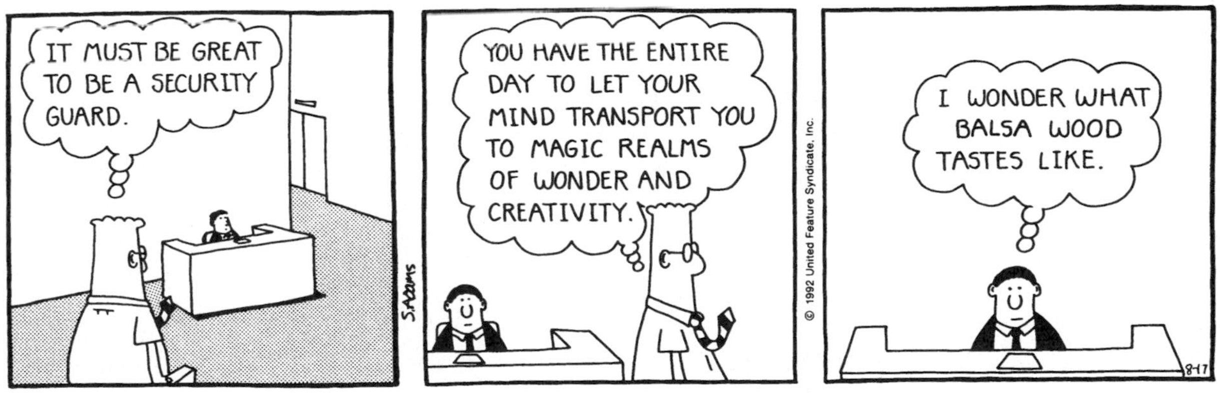
IT MUST BE GREAT TO BE A SECURITY GUARD.
YOU HAVE THE ENTIRE DAY TO LET YOUR MIND TRANSPORT YOU TO MAGIC REALMS OF WONDER AND CREATIVITY.
© 1992 United Feature Syndicate, Inc.
I WONDER WHAT BALSA WOOD TASTES LIKE.

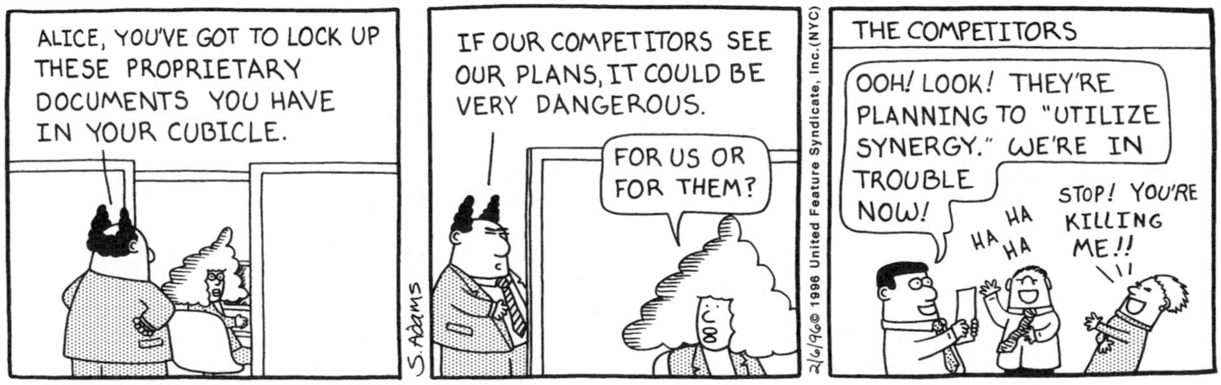
ALICE, YOU'VE GOT TO LOCK UP THESE PROPRIETARY DOCUMENTS YOU HAVE IN YOUR CUBICLE.
IF OUR COMPETITORS SEE OUR PLANS, IT COULD BE VERY DANGEROUS.
FOR US OR FOR THEM?
© 1996 United Feature Syndicate, Inc.(NYC)
THE COMPETITORS
OOH! LOOK! THEY'RE PLANNING TO "UTILIZE SYNERGY." WE'RE IN TROUBLE NOW!
HA HA HA HA
STOP! YOU'RE KILLING ME!!

SECURITY

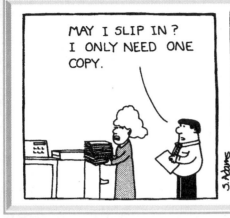

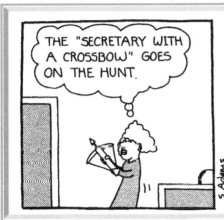

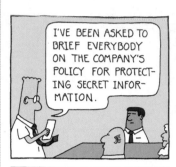

I'VE BEEN ASKED TO BRIEF EVERYBODY ON THE COMPANY'S POLICY FOR PROTECTING SECRET INFORMATION.
ALL SECRET INFORMATION MUST BE LOCKED UP AT NIGHT.
OUR SECRETS COULD BE OF GREAT VALUE TO OUR COMPETITORS.
© 1991 United Feature Syndicate, Inc.
IN FACT, SOME COMPANIES TRY TO BUY THE SECRETS OF THEIR COMPETITORS.
JUST OUT OF CURIOSITY, HOW MUCH WOULD OUR COMPETITORS PAY FOR OUR SECRETS?
S.Adams
OH, I DUNNO... MAYBE SEVERAL TIMES YOUR ANNUAL SALARY.
12-24
I DON'T THINK THIS WAS SOME OF MY BEST WORK.

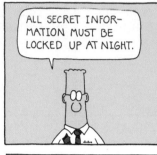

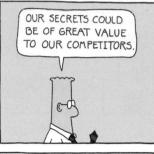

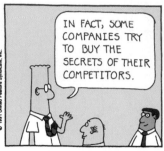

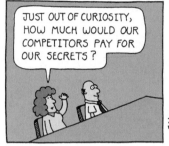

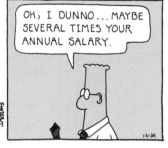

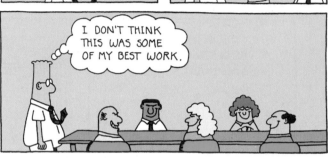

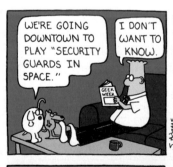

WE'RE GOING DOWNTOWN TO PLAY "SECURITY GUARDS IN SPACE."
I DON'T WANT TO KNOW.
GEEK WEEK
S.Adams
LET'S TRY THAT BUILDING.
LUNCH
I'LL NEED TO SEE YOUR I.D. BADGE, SIR.
LOOK FAST!! THERE IT IS!! NOT A PACK OF MATCHES!!
OKAY
ZIP!
I'LL HAVE TO SEARCH YOUR LUNCH BOX.
© 1995 United Feature Syndicate, Inc.
IT'S JUST A BUNCH OF WIRES AND GIZMOS.
YOU'RE MAKING ME SO HUNGRY.
LUNCH
COULD YOU WATCH MY LUNCH WHILE I TAKE THE CART BACK TO MY CAR?
3-5
I FEEL BAD, BUT IT'S THE ONLY WAY TO TEST IF SPACE TRAVEL IS SAFE FOR US ANIMALS.
I FEEL SAFER ALREADY.

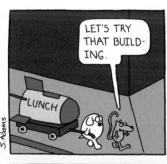

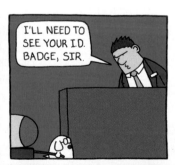

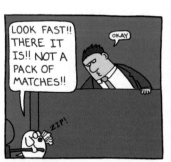

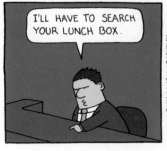

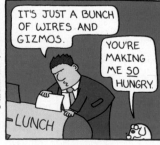

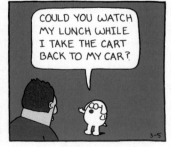

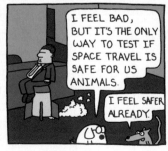

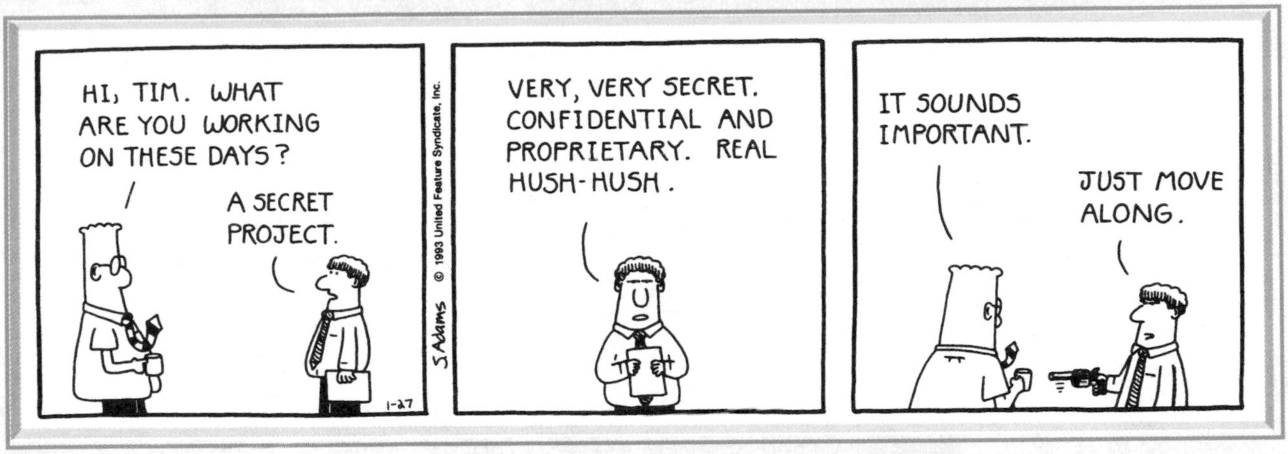
HI, TIM. WHAT ARE YOU WORKING ON THESE DAYS?
A SECRET PROJECT.
© 1993 United Feature Syndicate, Inc.
VERY, VERY SECRET. CONFIDENTIAL AND PROPRIETARY. REAL HUSH-HUSH.
IT SOUNDS IMPORTANT.
JUST MOVE ALONG.

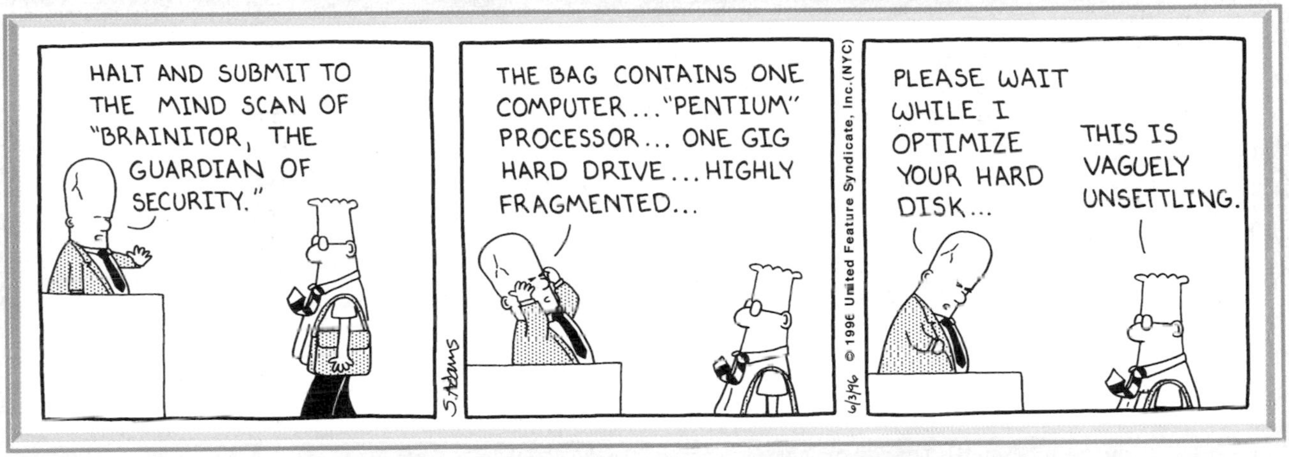
HALT AND SUBMIT TO THE MIND SCAN OF "BRAINITOR, THE GUARDIAN OF SECURITY."
THE BAG CONTAINS ONE COMPUTER... "PENTIUM" PROCESSOR... ONE GIG HARD DRIVE... HIGHLY FRAGMENTED...
© 1996 United Feature Syndicate, Inc.(NYC)
PLEASE WAIT WHILE I OPTIMIZE YOUR HARD DISK...
THIS IS VAGUELY UNSETTLING.

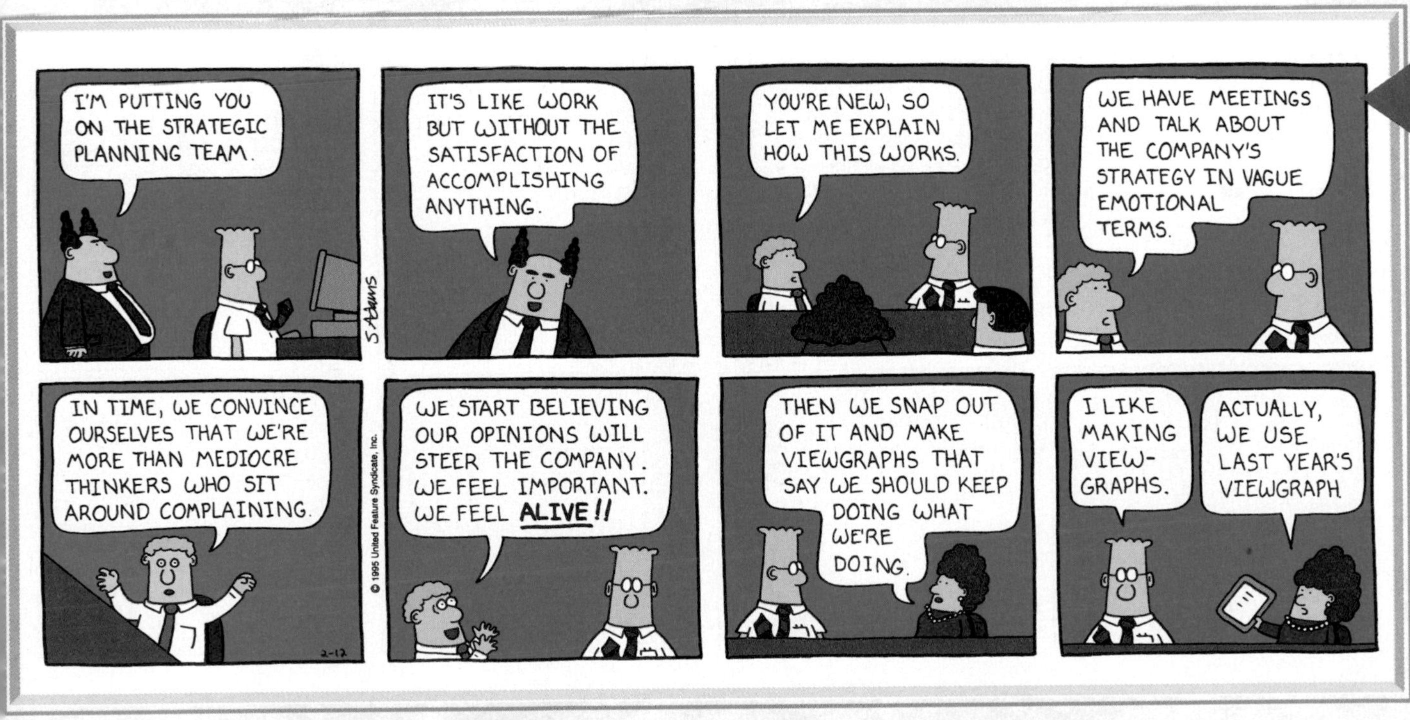
I'M PUTTING YOU ON THE STRATEGIC PLANNING TEAM.
IT'S LIKE WORK BUT WITHOUT THE SATISFACTION OF ACCOMPLISHING ANYTHING.
YOU'RE NEW, SO LET ME EXPLAIN HOW THIS WORKS.
WE HAVE MEETINGS AND TALK ABOUT THE COMPANY'S STRATEGY IN VAGUE EMOTIONAL TERMS.
IN TIME, WE CONVINCE OURSELVES THAT WE'RE MORE THAN MEDIOCRE THINKERS WHO SIT AROUND COMPLAINING.
© 1995 United Feature Syndicate, Inc.
WE START BELIEVING OUR OPINIONS WILL STEER THE COMPANY. WE FEEL IMPORTANT. WE FEEL ALIVE!!
THEN WE SNAP OUT OF IT AND MAKE VIEWGRAPHS THAT SAY WE SHOULD KEEP DOING WHAT WE'RE DOING.
I LIKE MAKING VIEW-GRAPHS.
ACTUALLY, WE USE LAST YEAR'S VIEWGRAPH.

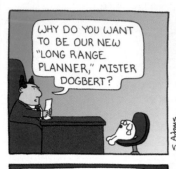

WHY DO YOU WANT TO BE OUR NEW "LONG RANGE PLANNER," MISTER DOGBERT?
BECAUSE "LONG RANGE" IS VERY FAR AWAY...
...THEREFORE IT WILL BE IMPOSSIBLE TO EVALUATE MY PERFORMANCE.
IF IT'S NOT TOO MUCH TO ASK, I'D LIKE TO BE ON FLEX-TIME SO YOU'LL NEVER KNOW IF I'M SUPPOSED TO BE AT WORK.
I'LL NEED AN INTERNET CONNECTION AT HOME SO I CAN TELECOMMUTE AND NOT POLLUTE.
BECAUSE I GIVE A HOOT.
ALSO, I'D LIKE TO BE IN A GROUP WITH LOTS OF LOSERS. THAT WAY I'LL GET THE BIGGEST RAISE WHEN WE'RE RANKED.
YOU'RE HIRED. ALL OF THE OTHER APPLICANTS DEMANDED RELOCATION EXPENSES AND I HAVE NO BUDGET FOR THAT.
WHY DO I HAVE TO WORK WHILE YOU JUST LOOK FOR POODLE GRAPHICS ON THE INTERNET?
DON'T WORK TOO HARD; I'D LIKE A BIG RAISE.
S. Adams
10-15
© 1995 United Feature Syndicate, Inc. (NYC)

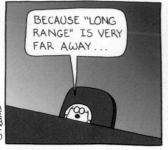

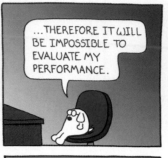

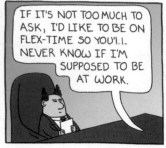

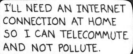

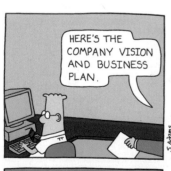

HERE'S THE COMPANY VISION AND BUSINESS PLAN.
"VISION: EMPOWERED EMPLOYEES WORKING TOWARD A COMMON PLAN."
SOUNDS GOOD.
BUT THE BUSINESS PLAN IS BLANK.
IT'S CONFI-DENTIAL.
HOW AM I SUPPOSED TO KNOW WHAT TO DO?
I'LL YELL AT YOU IF YOU DO THE WRONG THING.
I THOUGHT I WAS EMPOWERED.
DON'T BE SO LITERAL.
I'LL JUST KEEP DOING WHAT I WAS DOING.
NO!!! YOU FOOL!!!
WE'RE DOOMED, AREN'T WE?
I DON'T KNOW. I HAVEN'T SEEN THE PLAN.
S. Adams
5-21
© 1995 United Feature Syndicate, Inc.

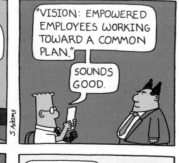

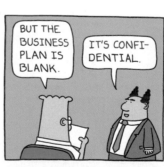

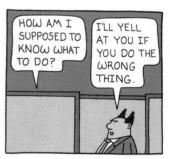

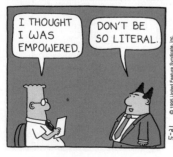

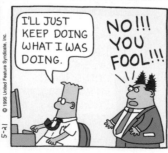

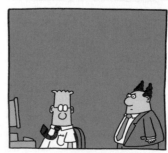

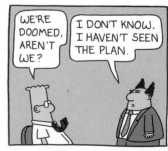

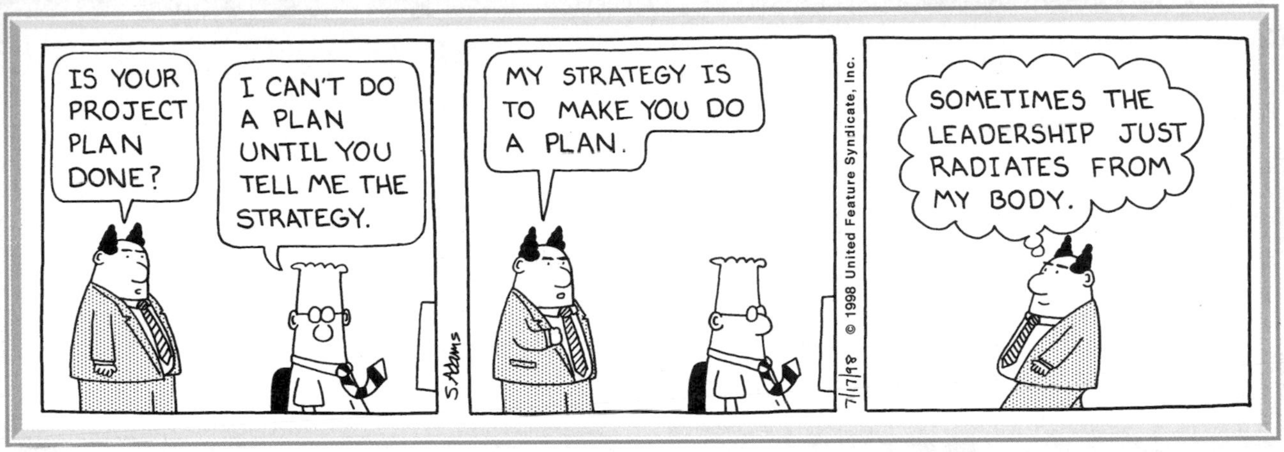
IS YOUR PROJECT PLAN DONE?
I CAN'T DO A PLAN UNTIL YOU TELL ME THE STRATEGY.
S.Adams
MY STRATEGY IS TO MAKE YOU DO A PLAN.
7/17/98 © 1998 United Feature Syndicate, Inc.
SOMETIMES THE LEADERSHIP JUST RADIATES FROM MY BODY.

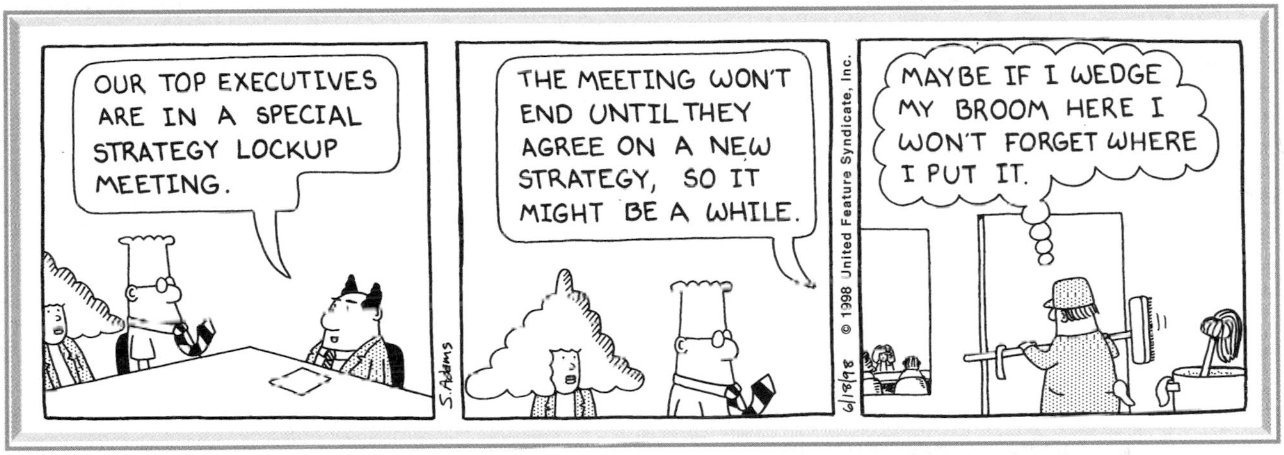
OUR TOP EXECUTIVES ARE IN A SPECIAL STRATEGY LOCKUP MEETING.
S.Adams
THE MEETING WON'T END UNTIL THEY AGREE ON A NEW STRATEGY, SO IT MIGHT BE A WHILE.
6/18/98 © 1998 United Feature Syndicate, Inc.
MAYBE IF I WEDGE MY BROOM HERE I WON'T FORGET WHERE I PUT IT.

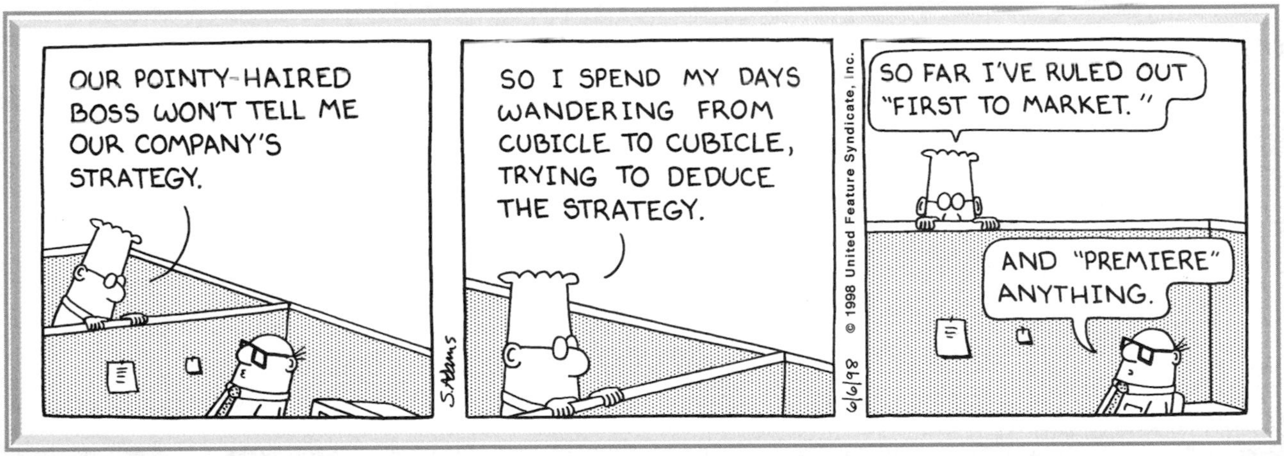
OUR POINTY-HAIRED BOSS WON'T TELL ME OUR COMPANY'S STRATEGY.
S.Adams
SO I SPEND MY DAYS WANDERING FROM CUBICLE TO CUBICLE, TRYING TO DEDUCE THE STRATEGY.
6/6/98 © 1998 United Feature Syndicate, Inc.
SO FAR I'VE RULED OUT "FIRST TO MARKET."
AND "PREMIERE" ANYTHING.

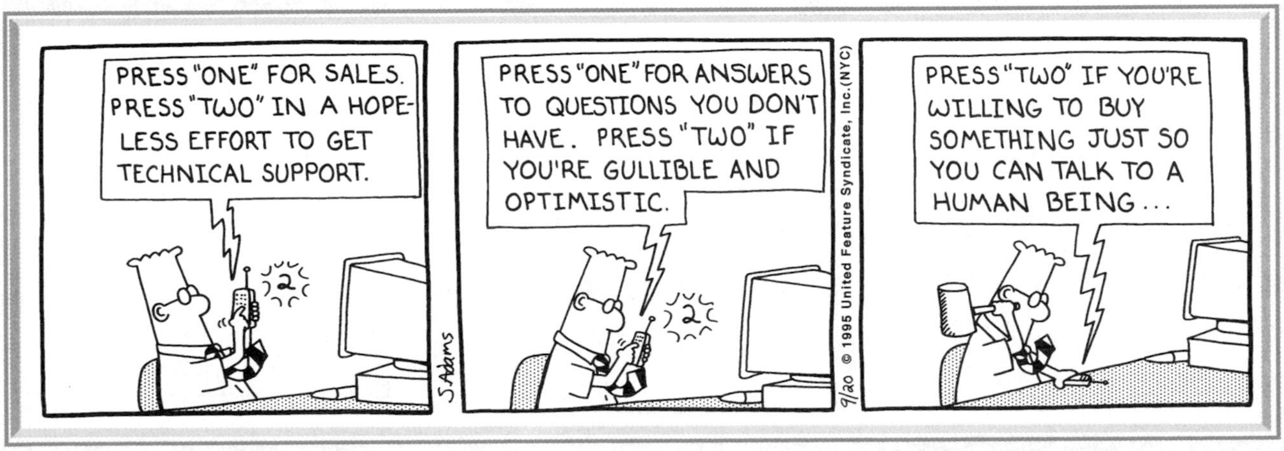
PRESS "ONE" FOR SALES. PRESS "TWO" IN A HOPE-LESS EFFORT TO GET TECHNICAL SUPPORT.
2
S.Adams
PRESS "ONE" FOR ANSWERS TO QUESTIONS YOU DON'T HAVE. PRESS "TWO" IF YOU'RE GULLIBLE AND OPTIMISTIC.
2
9/20 © 1995 United Feature Syndicate, Inc.(NYC)
PRESS "TWO" IF YOU'RE WILLING TO BUY SOMETHING JUST SO YOU CAN TALK TO A HUMAN BEING...

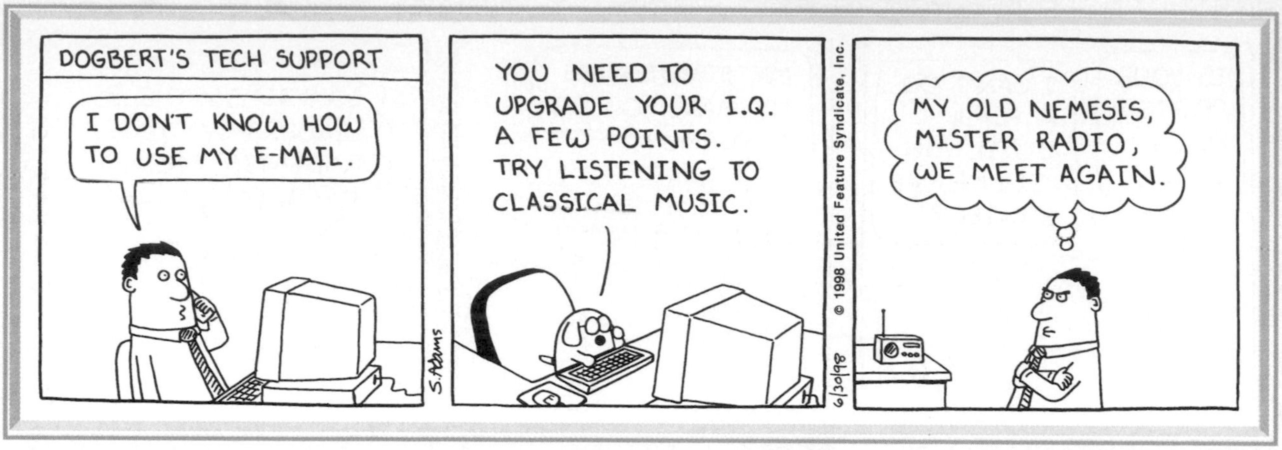
DOGBERT'S TECH SUPPORT
I DON'T KNOW HOW TO USE MY E-MAIL.
YOU NEED TO UPGRADE YOUR I.Q. A FEW POINTS. TRY LISTENING TO CLASSICAL MUSIC.
MY OLD NEMESIS, MISTER RADIO, WE MEET AGAIN.
S.Adams
6/30/98
© 1998 United Feature Syndicate, Inc.

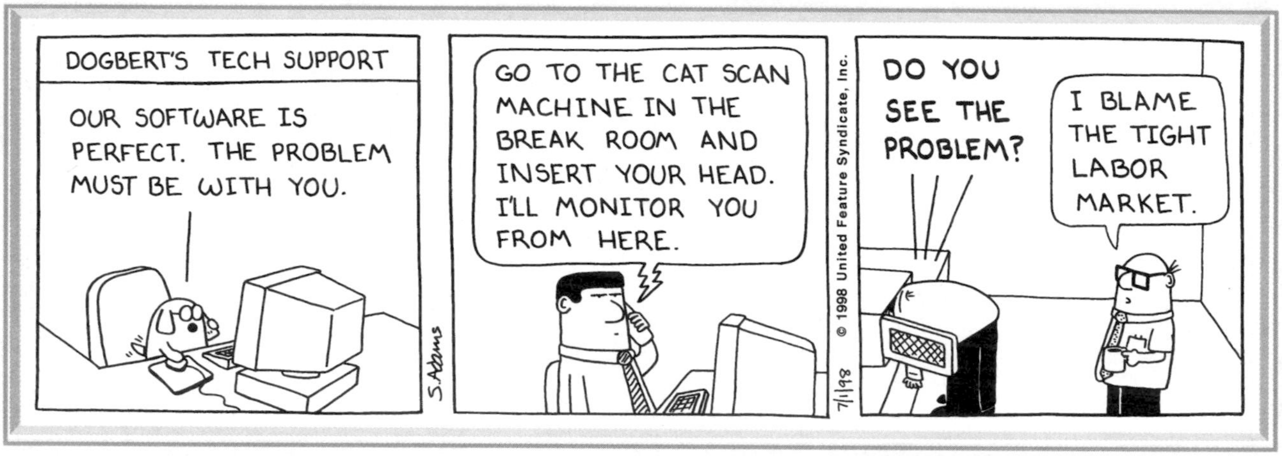
DOGBERT'S TECH SUPPORT
OUR SOFTWARE IS PERFECT. THE PROBLEM MUST BE WITH YOU.
GO TO THE CAT SCAN MACHINE IN THE BREAK ROOM AND INSERT YOUR HEAD. I'LL MONITOR YOU FROM HERE.
DO YOU SEE THE PROBLEM?
I BLAME THE TIGHT LABOR MARKET.
S.Adams
7/1/98
© 1998 United Feature Syndicate, Inc.

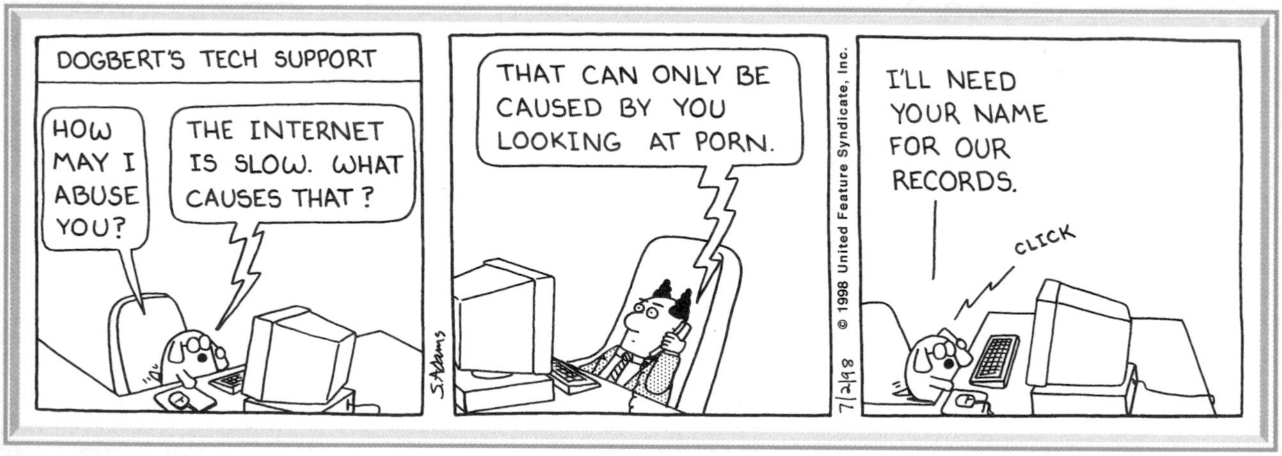
DOGBERT'S TECH SUPPORT
HOW MAY I ABUSE YOU?
THE INTERNET IS SLOW. WHAT CAUSES THAT?
THAT CAN ONLY BE CAUSED BY YOU LOOKING AT PORN.
I'LL NEED YOUR NAME FOR OUR RECORDS.
CLICK
S.Adams
7/2/98
© 1998 United Feature Syndicate, Inc.

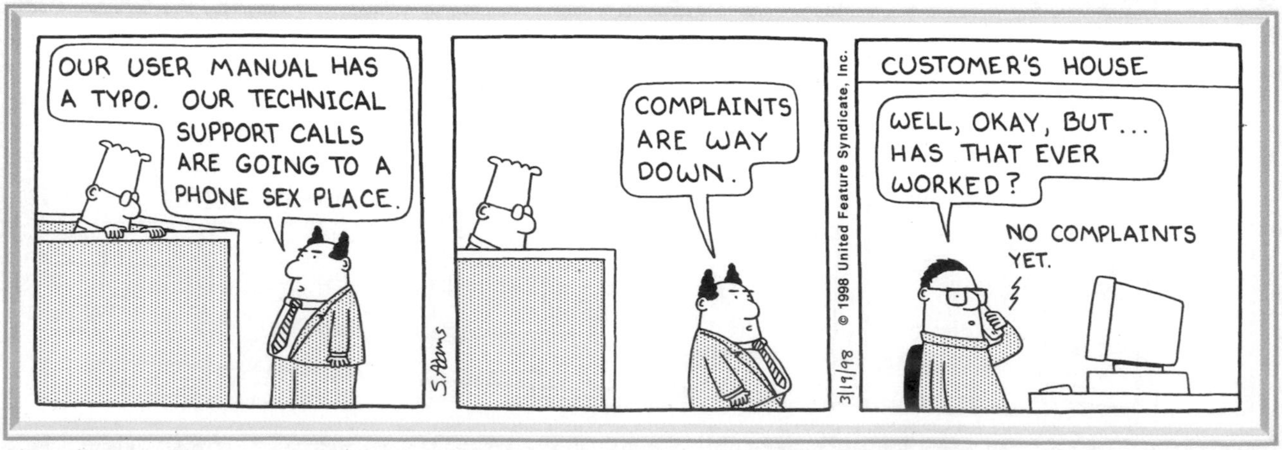
OUR USER MANUAL HAS A TYPO. OUR TECHNICAL SUPPORT CALLS ARE GOING TO A PHONE SEX PLACE.
COMPLAINTS ARE WAY DOWN.
CUSTOMER'S HOUSE
WELL, OKAY, BUT... HAS THAT EVER WORKED?
NO COMPLAINTS YET.
S.Adams
3/19/98
© 1998 United Feature Syndicate, Inc.

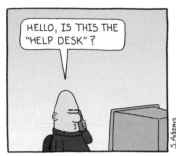

HELLO, IS THIS THE "HELP DESK"?
NO, THAT GROUP GOT REENGINEERED OUT OF EXISTENCE.
I'M THE NEW "NO HELP WHATSOEVER DESK." MY JOB IS TO MAKE SURE YOU NEVER CALL AGAIN.
CAN YOU TELL ME HOW TO MAKE A PIE CHART?
CRUSH YOUR COMPUTER INTO SMALL CHUNKS, ADD FLOUR AND BAKE ONE HOUR.
WHILE YOU'RE WAITING, READ THE FREE NOVEL WE SENT YOU. IT'S A SPANISH STORY ABOUT A GUY NAMED "MANUAL."
REPEAT THE PROCESS UNTIL YOU GET THE DESIRED RESULT.
THIS LOST A LOT IN THE TRANSLATION.
MANUAL
S. Adams
© 1995 United Feature Syndicate, Inc.(NYC)
12/10

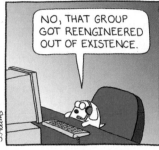

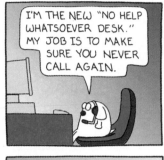

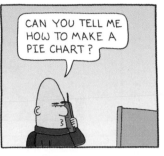

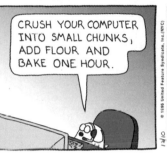

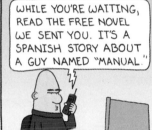

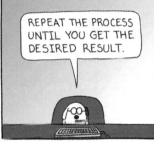

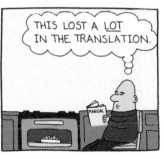

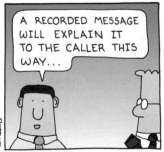

WE'RE DISCONTINUING TECHNICAL SUPPORT OF ALL OUR PRODUCTS.
A RECORDED MESSAGE WILL EXPLAIN IT TO THE CALLER THIS WAY...
"IN ORDER TO SERVE CUSTOMERS BETTER, WE'VE DISCONTINUED TECHNICAL SUPPORT."
HOW DOES THAT SERVE CUSTOMERS BETTER?
WE'LL REDIRECT THOSE RESOURCES TO OTHER AREAS.
WHAT OTHER AREAS?
PROFITS.
THAT MAKES YOUR BONUS LARGER.
ANY OTHER QUESTIONS?
APPARENTLY I'M ENGULFED IN EVIL.
THAT'S THE SPIRIT!
S. Adams
8/9/98

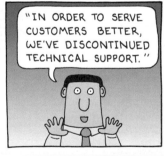

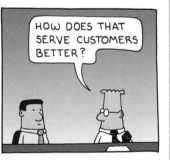

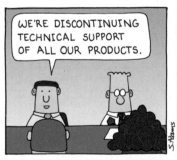

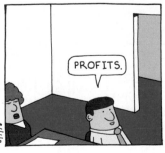

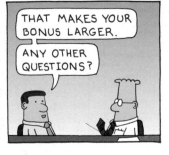

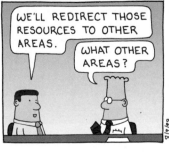

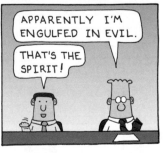

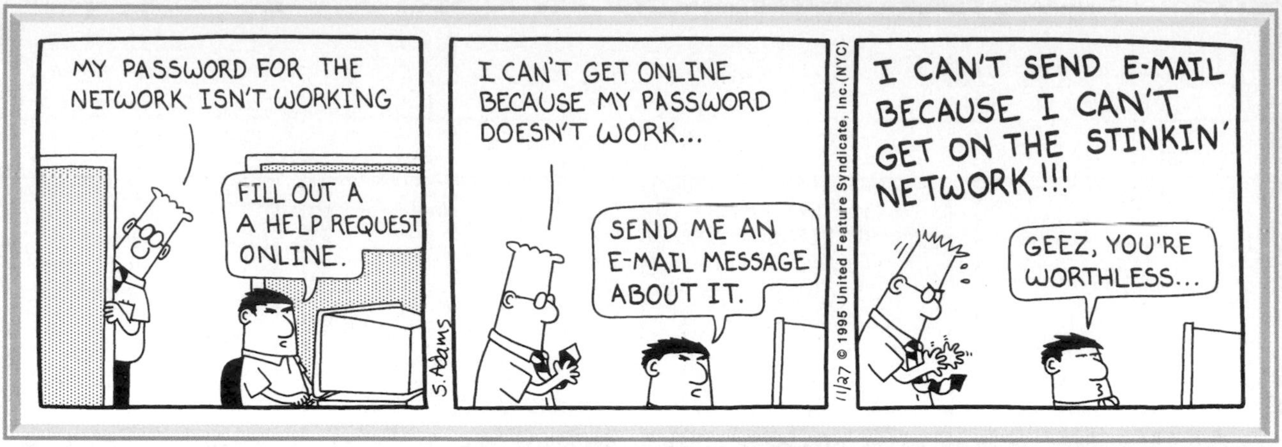
MY PASSWORD FOR THE NETWORK ISN'T WORKING
FILL OUT A A HELP REQUEST ONLINE.
S. Adams
I CAN'T GET ONLINE BECAUSE MY PASSWORD DOESN'T WORK...
SEND ME AN E-MAIL MESSAGE ABOUT IT.
11/27 © 1995 United Feature Syndicate, Inc.(NYC)
I CAN'T SEND E-MAIL BECAUSE I CAN'T GET ON THE STINKIN' NETWORK!!!
GEEZ, YOU'RE WORTHLESS...

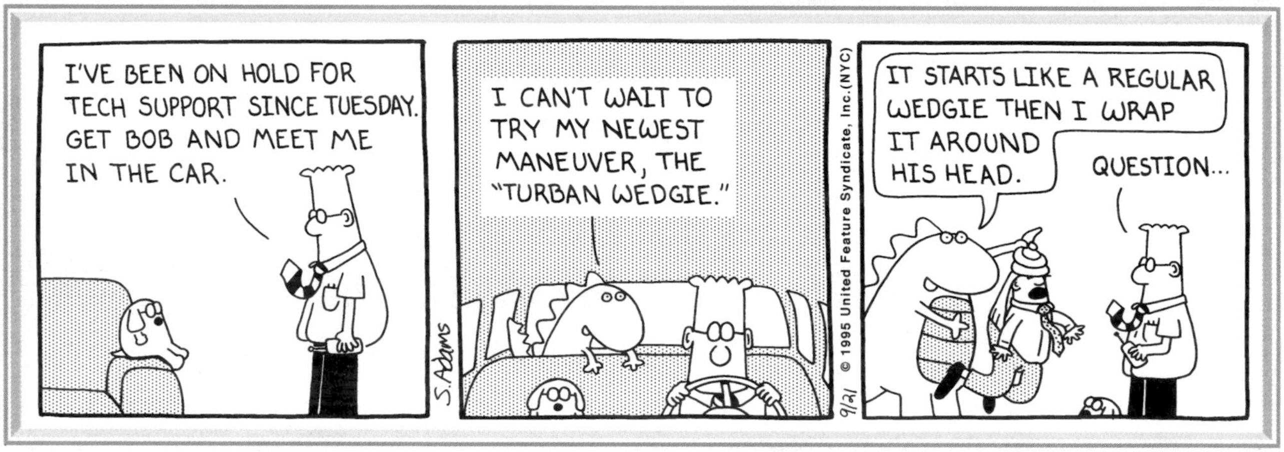
I'VE BEEN ON HOLD FOR TECH SUPPORT SINCE TUESDAY. GET BOB AND MEET ME IN THE CAR.
S. Adams
I CAN'T WAIT TO TRY MY NEWEST MANEUVER, THE "TURBAN WEDGIE."
9/21 © 1995 United Feature Syndicate, Inc.(NYC)
IT STARTS LIKE A REGULAR WEDGIE THEN I WRAP IT AROUND HIS HEAD.
QUESTION...

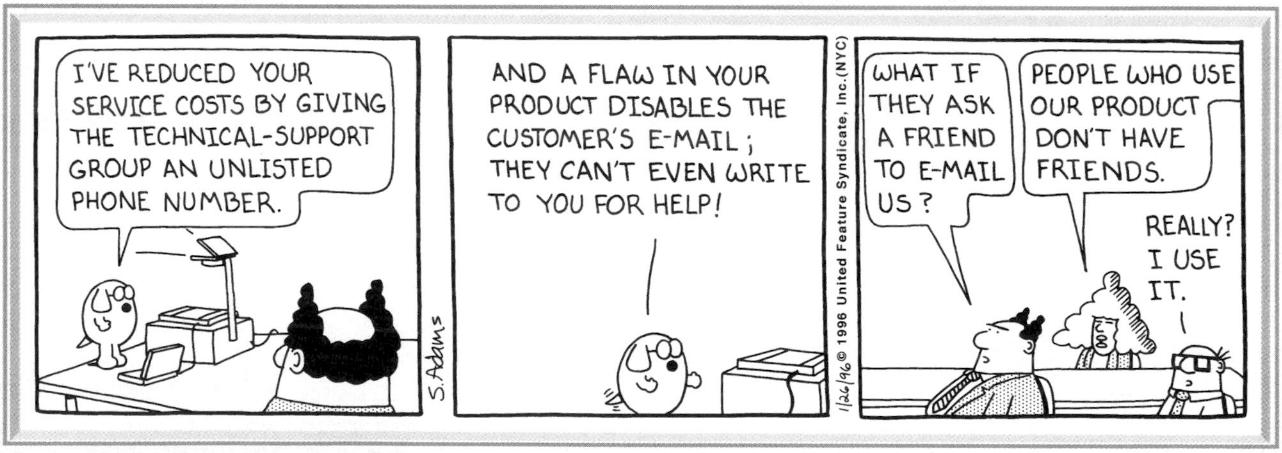
I'VE REDUCED YOUR SERVICE COSTS BY GIVING THE TECHNICAL-SUPPORT GROUP AN UNLISTED PHONE NUMBER.
S. Adams
AND A FLAW IN YOUR PRODUCT DISABLES THE CUSTOMER'S E-MAIL; THEY CAN'T EVEN WRITE TO YOU FOR HELP!
1/26/96 © 1996 United Feature Syndicate, Inc.(NYC)
WHAT IF THEY ASK A FRIEND TO E-MAIL US?
PEOPLE WHO USE OUR PRODUCT DON'T HAVE FRIENDS.
REALLY? I USE IT.

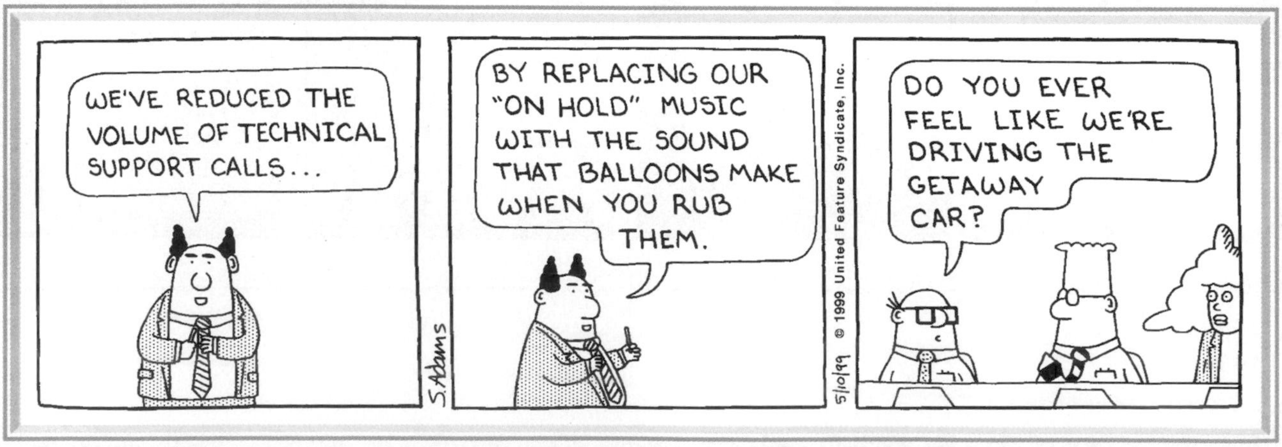
WE'VE REDUCED THE VOLUME OF TECHNICAL SUPPORT CALLS...
S. Adams
BY REPLACING OUR "ON HOLD" MUSIC WITH THE SOUND THAT BALLOONS MAKE WHEN YOU RUB THEM.
5/10/99 © 1999 United Feature Syndicate, Inc.
DO YOU EVER FEEL LIKE WE'RE DRIVING THE GETAWAY CAR?

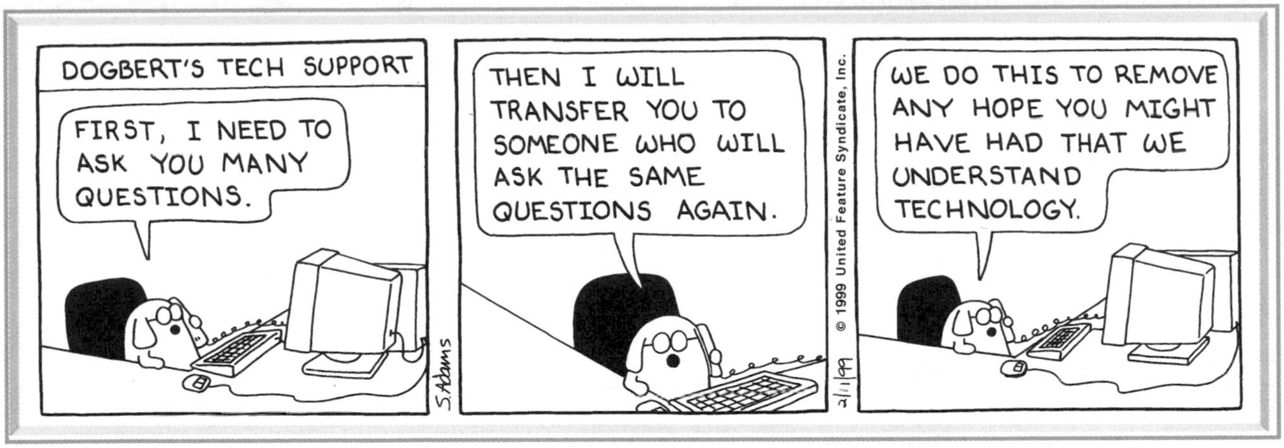
DOGBERT'S TECH SUPPORT
FIRST, I NEED TO ASK YOU MANY QUESTIONS.
S. Adams
THEN I WILL TRANSFER YOU TO SOMEONE WHO WILL ASK THE SAME QUESTIONS AGAIN.
2/1/99
© 1999 United Feature Syndicate, Inc.
WE DO THIS TO REMOVE ANY HOPE YOU MIGHT HAVE HAD THAT WE UNDERSTAND TECHNOLOGY.

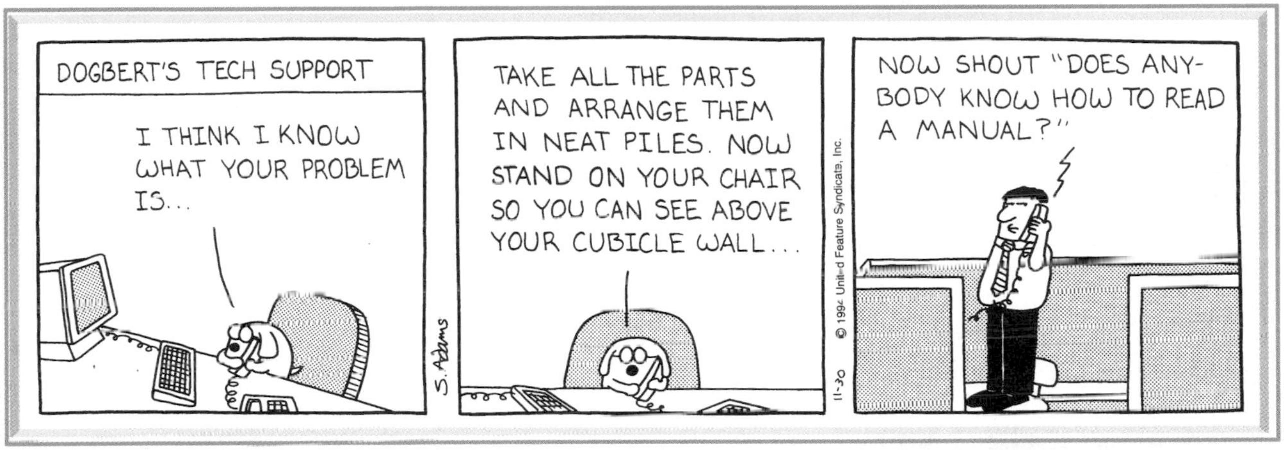
DOGBERT'S TECH SUPPORT
I THINK I KNOW WHAT YOUR PROBLEM IS...
S. Adams
TAKE ALL THE PARTS AND ARRANGE THEM IN NEAT PILES. NOW STAND ON YOUR CHAIR SO YOU CAN SEE ABOVE YOUR CUBICLE WALL...
11-30
© 1994 United Feature Syndicate, Inc.
NOW SHOUT "DOES ANYBODY KNOW HOW TO READ A MANUAL?"

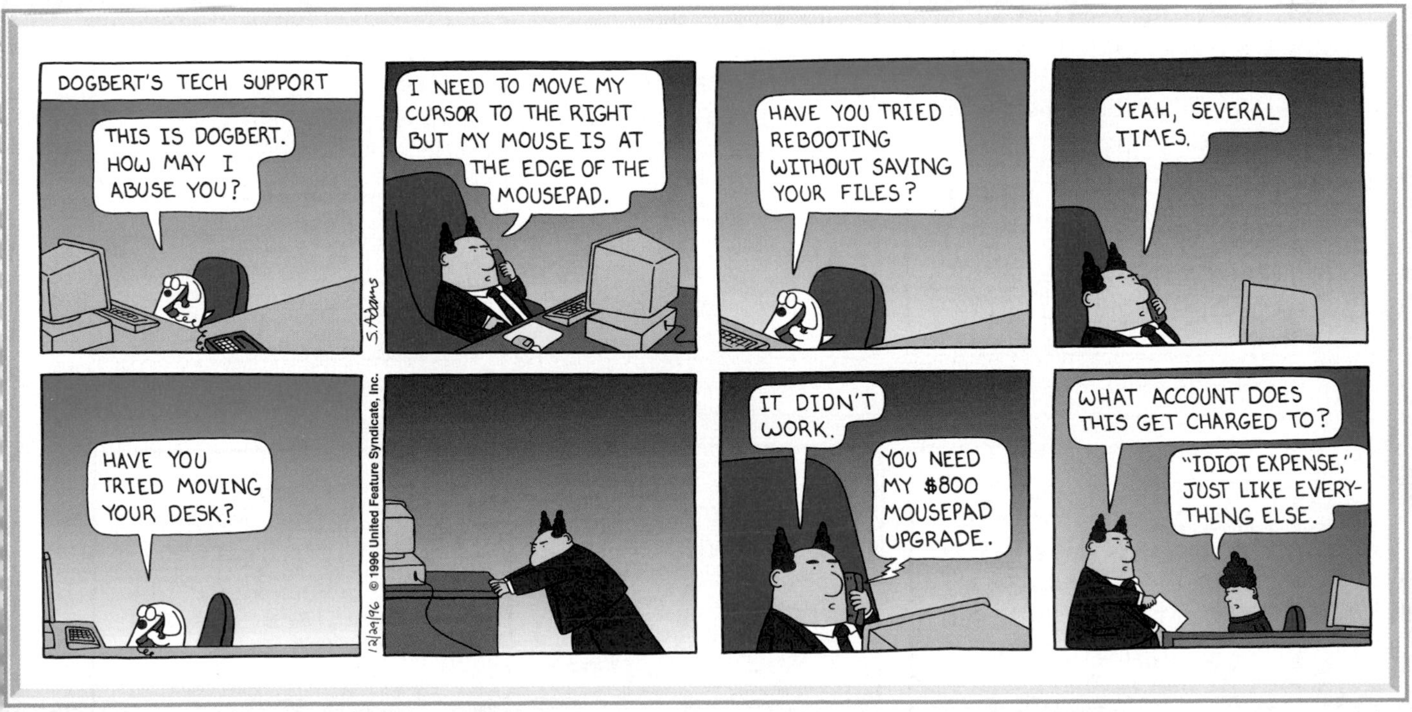
DOGBERT'S TECH SUPPORT
THIS IS DOGBERT. HOW MAY I ABUSE YOU?
S. Adams
I NEED TO MOVE MY CURSOR TO THE RIGHT BUT MY MOUSE IS AT THE EDGE OF THE MOUSEPAD.
HAVE YOU TRIED REBOOTING WITHOUT SAVING YOUR FILES?
YEAH, SEVERAL TIMES.
HAVE YOU TRIED MOVING YOUR DESK?
12/29/96
© 1996 United Feature Syndicate, Inc.
IT DIDN'T WORK.
YOU NEED MY $800 MOUSEPAD UPGRADE.
WHAT ACCOUNT DOES THIS GET CHARGED TO?
"IDIOT EXPENSE," JUST LIKE EVERYTHING ELSE.

DILBERT *Gives You the Business*

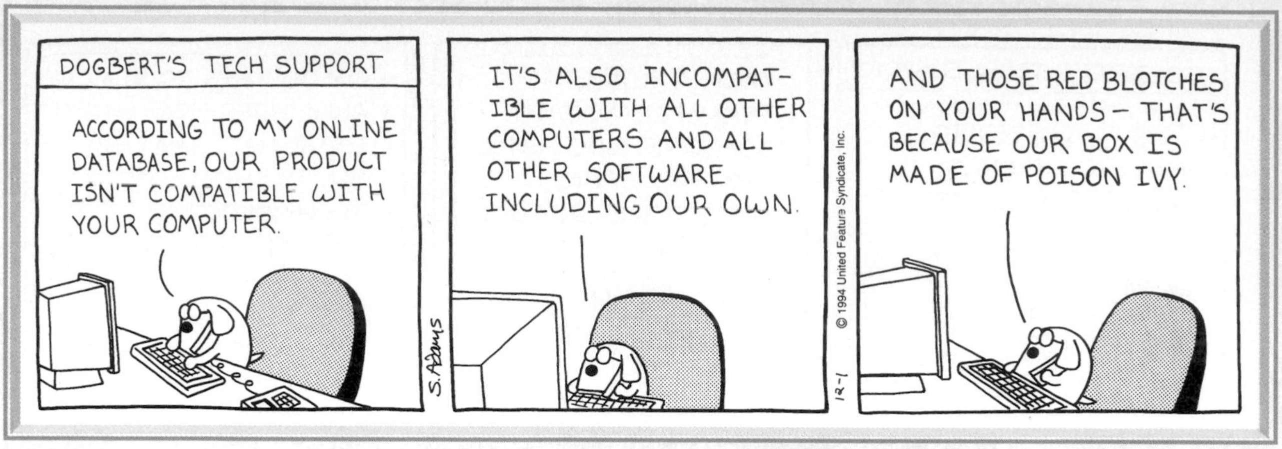
DOGBERT'S TECH SUPPORT
ACCORDING TO MY ONLINE DATABASE, OUR PRODUCT ISN'T COMPATIBLE WITH YOUR COMPUTER.
IT'S ALSO INCOMPATIBLE WITH ALL OTHER COMPUTERS AND ALL OTHER SOFTWARE INCLUDING OUR OWN.
AND THOSE RED BLOTCHES ON YOUR HANDS – THAT'S BECAUSE OUR BOX IS MADE OF POISON IVY.
S. Adams
12-1
© 1994 United Feature Syndicate, Inc.

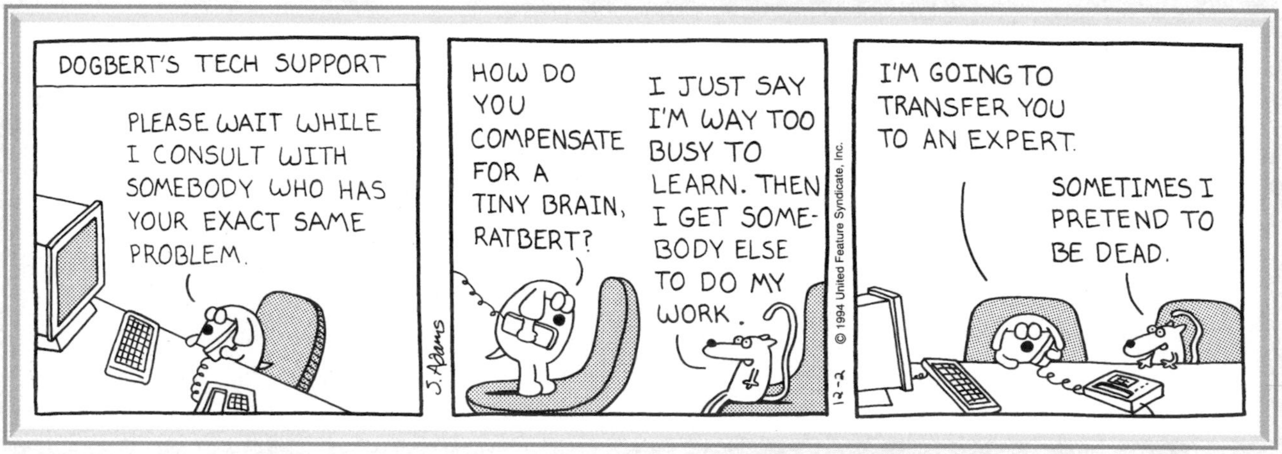
DOGBERT'S TECH SUPPORT
PLEASE WAIT WHILE I CONSULT WITH SOMEBODY WHO HAS YOUR EXACT SAME PROBLEM.
HOW DO YOU COMPENSATE FOR A TINY BRAIN, RATBERT?
I JUST SAY I'M WAY TOO BUSY TO LEARN. THEN I GET SOMEBODY ELSE TO DO MY WORK.
I'M GOING TO TRANSFER YOU TO AN EXPERT.
SOMETIMES I PRETEND TO BE DEAD.
S. Adams
12-2
© 1994 United Feature Syndicate, Inc.

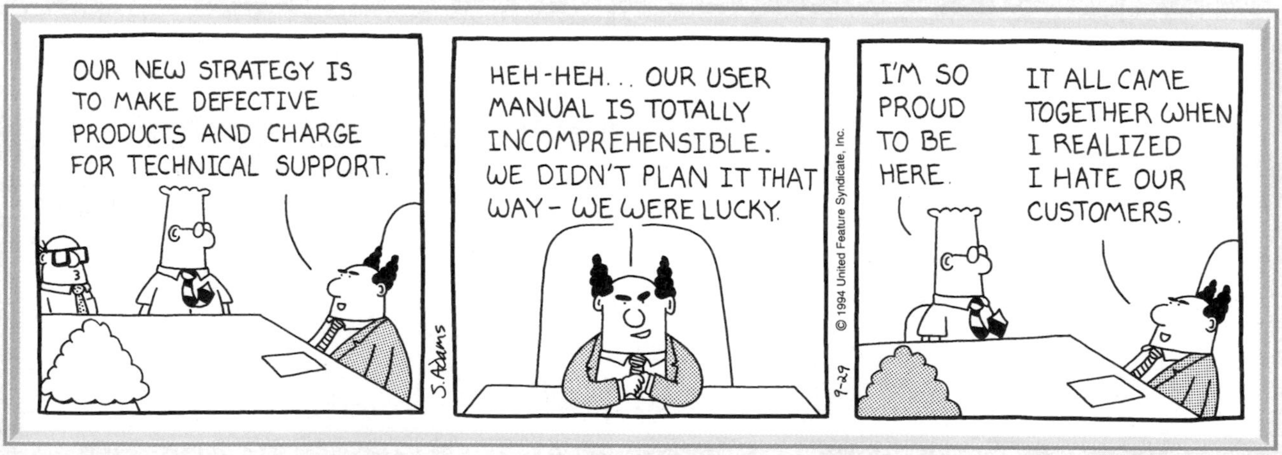
OUR NEW STRATEGY IS TO MAKE DEFECTIVE PRODUCTS AND CHARGE FOR TECHNICAL SUPPORT.
HEH-HEH... OUR USER MANUAL IS TOTALLY INCOMPREHENSIBLE. WE DIDN'T PLAN IT THAT WAY – WE WERE LUCKY.
I'M SO PROUD TO BE HERE.
IT ALL CAME TOGETHER WHEN I REALIZED I HATE OUR CUSTOMERS.
S. Adams
9-29
© 1994 United Feature Syndicate, Inc.

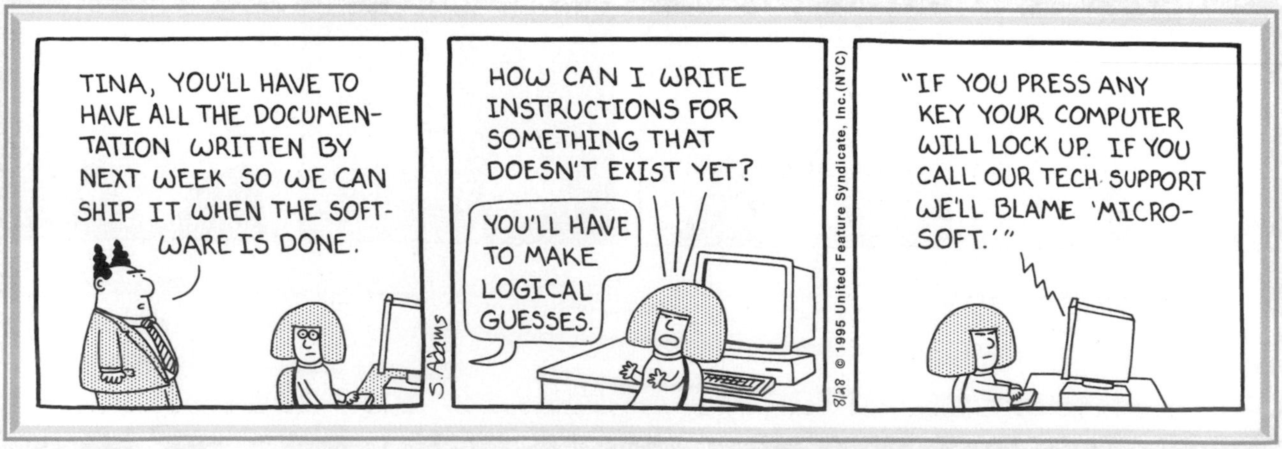
TINA, YOU'LL HAVE TO HAVE ALL THE DOCUMENTATION WRITTEN BY NEXT WEEK SO WE CAN SHIP IT WHEN THE SOFTWARE IS DONE.
HOW CAN I WRITE INSTRUCTIONS FOR SOMETHING THAT DOESN'T EXIST YET?
YOU'LL HAVE TO MAKE LOGICAL GUESSES.
"IF YOU PRESS ANY KEY YOUR COMPUTER WILL LOCK UP. IF YOU CALL OUR TECH SUPPORT WE'LL BLAME 'MICROSOFT.'"
S. Adams
8/28
© 1995 United Feature Syndicate, Inc.(NYC)

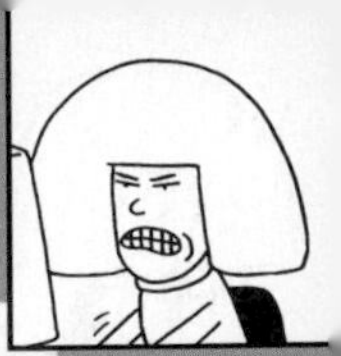

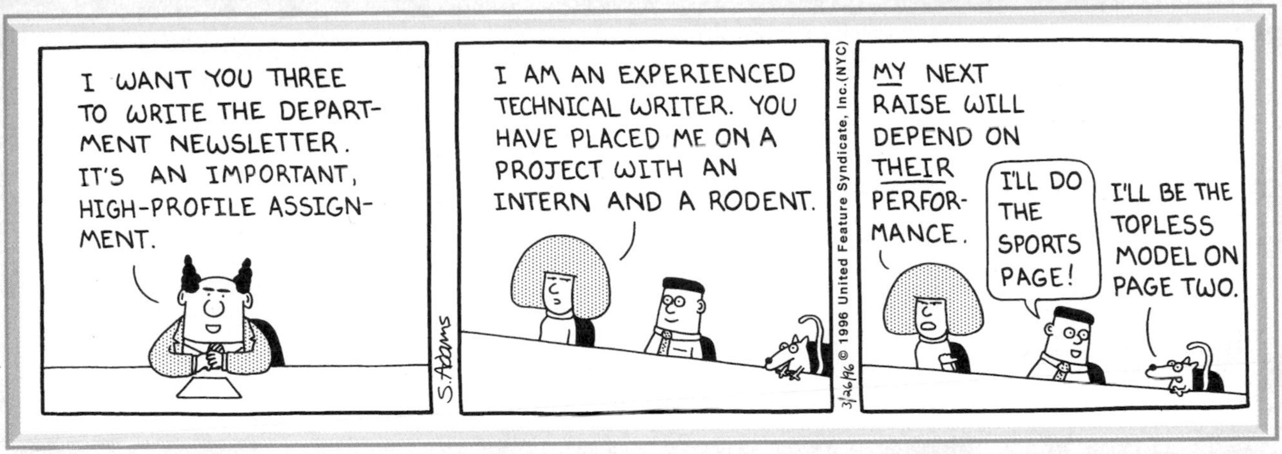
I WANT YOU THREE TO WRITE THE DEPARTMENT NEWSLETTER. IT'S AN IMPORTANT, HIGH-PROFILE ASSIGNMENT.
S. Adams
I AM AN EXPERIENCED TECHNICAL WRITER. YOU HAVE PLACED ME ON A PROJECT WITH AN INTERN AND A RODENT.
3/26/96 © 1996 United Feature Syndicate, Inc.(NYC)
MY NEXT RAISE WILL DEPEND ON THEIR PERFORMANCE.
I'LL DO THE SPORTS PAGE!
I'LL BE THE TOPLESS MODEL ON PAGE TWO.

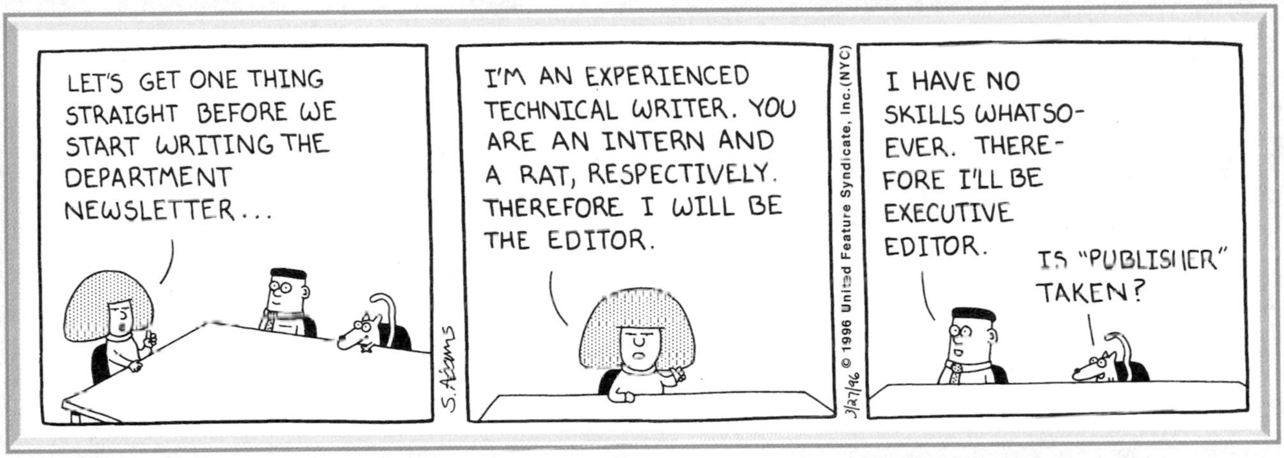
LET'S GET ONE THING STRAIGHT BEFORE WE START WRITING THE DEPARTMENT NEWSLETTER...
S. Adams
I'M AN EXPERIENCED TECHNICAL WRITER. YOU ARE AN INTERN AND A RAT, RESPECTIVELY. THEREFORE I WILL BE THE EDITOR.
3/27/96 © 1996 United Feature Syndicate, Inc.(NYC)
I HAVE NO SKILLS WHATSOEVER. THEREFORE I'LL BE EXECUTIVE EDITOR.
IS "PUBLISHER" TAKEN?

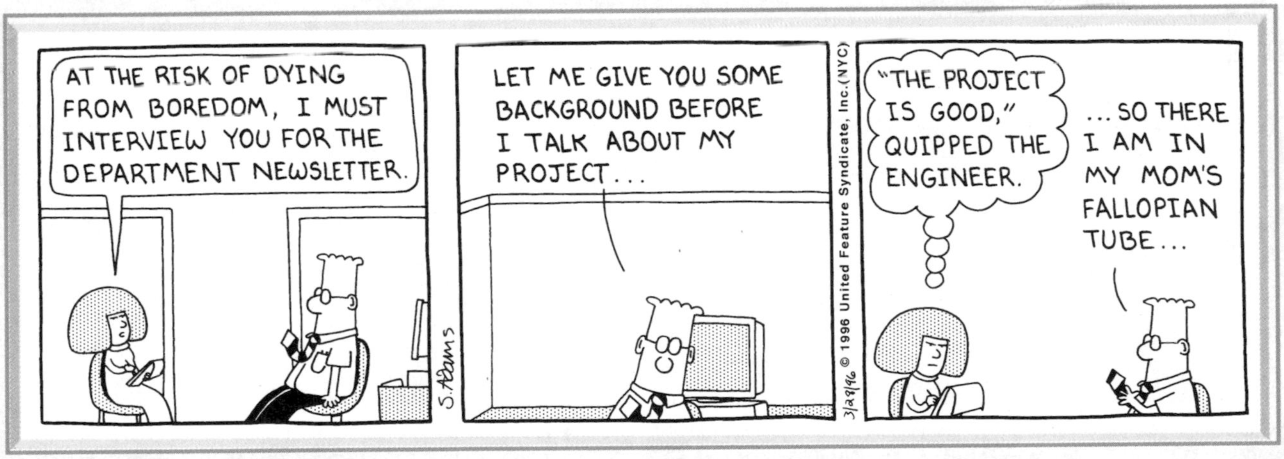
AT THE RISK OF DYING FROM BOREDOM, I MUST INTERVIEW YOU FOR THE DEPARTMENT NEWSLETTER.
S. Adams
LET ME GIVE YOU SOME BACKGROUND BEFORE I TALK ABOUT MY PROJECT...
3/28/96 © 1996 United Feature Syndicate, Inc.(NYC)
"THE PROJECT IS GOOD," QUIPPED THE ENGINEER.
...SO THERE I AM IN MY MOM'S FALLOPIAN TUBE...

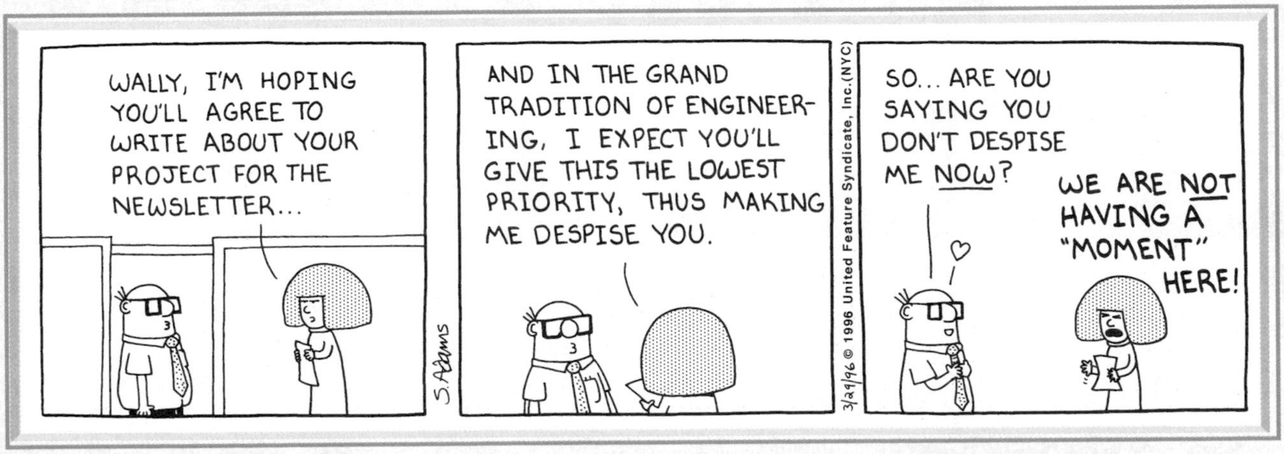
WALLY, I'M HOPING YOU'LL AGREE TO WRITE ABOUT YOUR PROJECT FOR THE NEWSLETTER...
S. Adams
AND IN THE GRAND TRADITION OF ENGINEERING, I EXPECT YOU'LL GIVE THIS THE LOWEST PRIORITY, THUS MAKING ME DESPISE YOU.
3/29/96 © 1996 United Feature Syndicate, Inc.(NYC)
SO... ARE YOU SAYING YOU DON'T DESPISE ME NOW?
WE ARE NOT HAVING A "MOMENT" HERE!

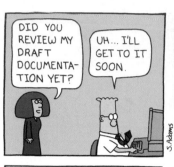

DID YOU REVIEW MY DRAFT DOCUMENTATION YET?
UH... I'LL GET TO IT SOON.
S. Adams
THAT'S WHAT YOU'VE BEEN SAYING SINCE JULY!!
I KNOW I'M ONLY A LOWLY TECHNICAL WRITER AND YOU'RE A BIG IMPORTANT ENGINEER...
BUT IS IT TOO MUCH TO ASK FOR YOU TO GLANCE AT THE FRUITS OF MY LABORS?!!!
FIVE LOUSY MINUTES IS ALL IT WOULD TAKE TO VALIDATE MY VALUE ON THIS PLANET! READ IT, YOU FETID PILE OF COMPOST!!
© 1995 United Feature Syndicate, Inc.
OKAY, OKAY! I'LL READ IT RIGHT NOW!
THESE PAGES ARE BLANK! YOU'VE BEEN BLUFFING FOR MONTHS!
3-12
I THINK I'LL GO HAVE A YUMMY COMPOST SALAD WITH DELICIOUS FETID CHEESE
I'M GOING TO LOOK UP THOSE WORDS.

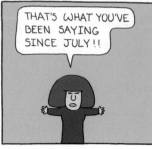

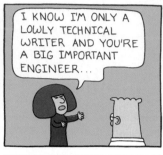

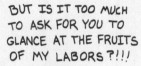

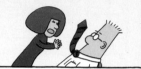

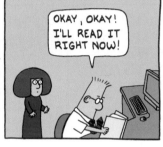

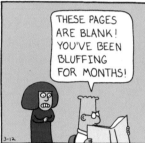

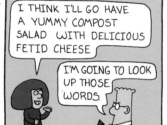

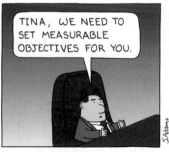

TINA, WE NEED TO SET MEASURABLE OBJECTIVES FOR YOU.
S. Adams
I'M A TECHNICAL WRITER. HOW CAN YOU MEASURE GOOD WRITING?
EVERYTHING IS MEASURABLE IF YOU TRY HARD ENOUGH.
IS THAT YOUR WELL-REASONED OPINION?
OR IS IT THE DOGMATIC BABBLING OF A MANAGER IN TOTAL COGNITIVE SURRENDER?
3/8/98 © 1998 United Feature Syndicate, Inc.
FOR EXAMPLE, WE COULD MEASURE THE NUMBER OF WORDS YOU TYPE.
WE'LL HAVE TO SUBTRACT WORDS YOU DELETE. THAT WAY WE WON'T MOTIVATE THE WRONG BEHAVIOR.
IN THIS EDITION OF TINA'S HOURLY NEWSLETTER, I COMPARE OUR PROJECTS TO VARIOUS TYPES OF WOOD.

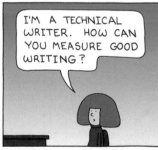

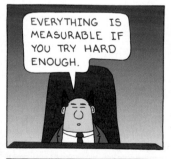

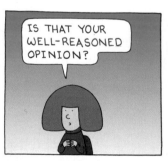

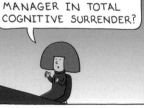

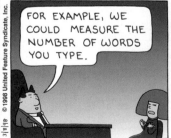

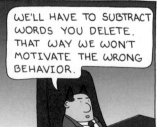

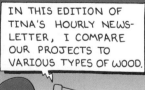

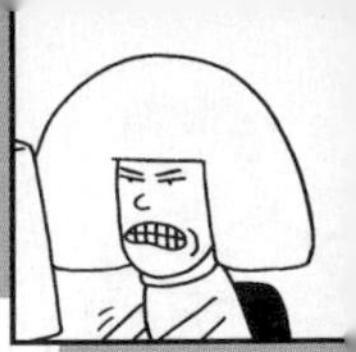

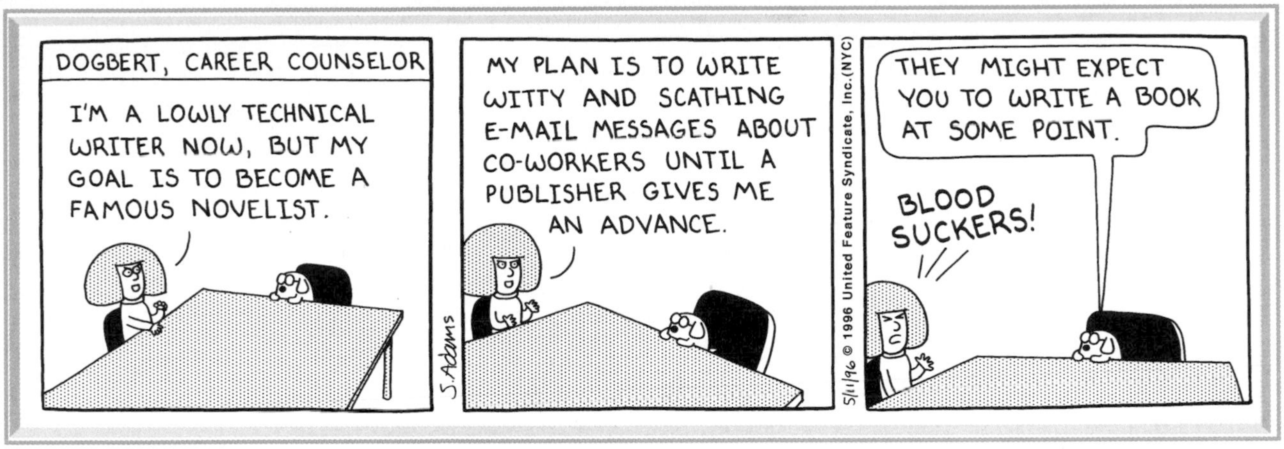
DOGBERT, CAREER COUNSELOR
I'M A LOWLY TECHNICAL WRITER NOW, BUT MY GOAL IS TO BECOME A FAMOUS NOVELIST.
MY PLAN IS TO WRITE WITTY AND SCATHING E-MAIL MESSAGES ABOUT CO-WORKERS UNTIL A PUBLISHER GIVES ME AN ADVANCE.
S. Adams
5/11/96 © 1996 United Feature Syndicate, Inc.(NYC)
THEY MIGHT EXPECT YOU TO WRITE A BOOK AT SOME POINT.
BLOOD SUCKERS!

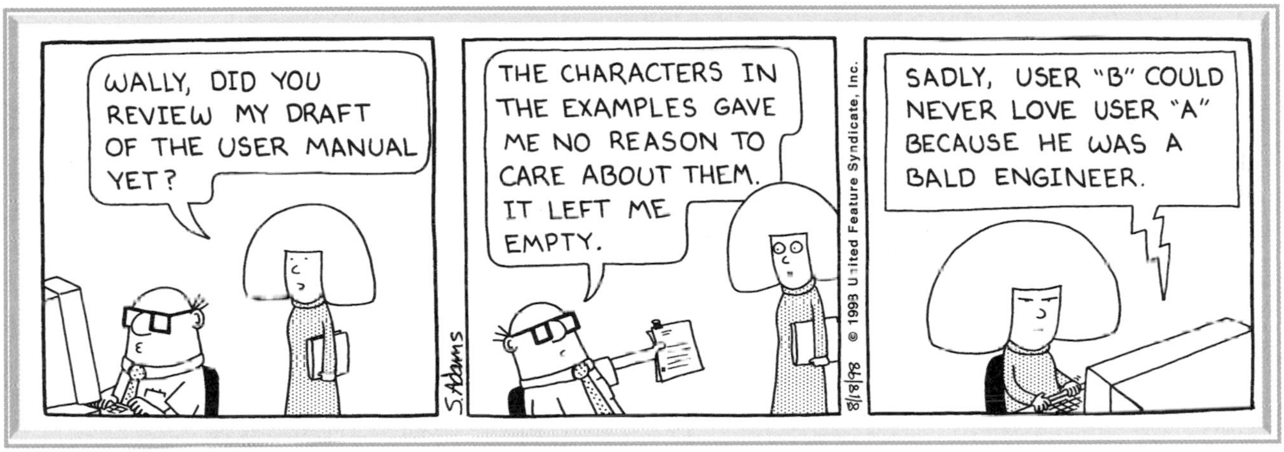
WALLY, DID YOU REVIEW MY DRAFT OF THE USER MANUAL YET?
THE CHARACTERS IN THE EXAMPLES GAVE ME NO REASON TO CARE ABOUT THEM. IT LEFT ME EMPTY.
S. Adams
8/18/98 © 1993 United Feature Syndicate, Inc.
SADLY, USER "B" COULD NEVER LOVE USER "A" BECAUSE HE WAS A BALD ENGINEER.

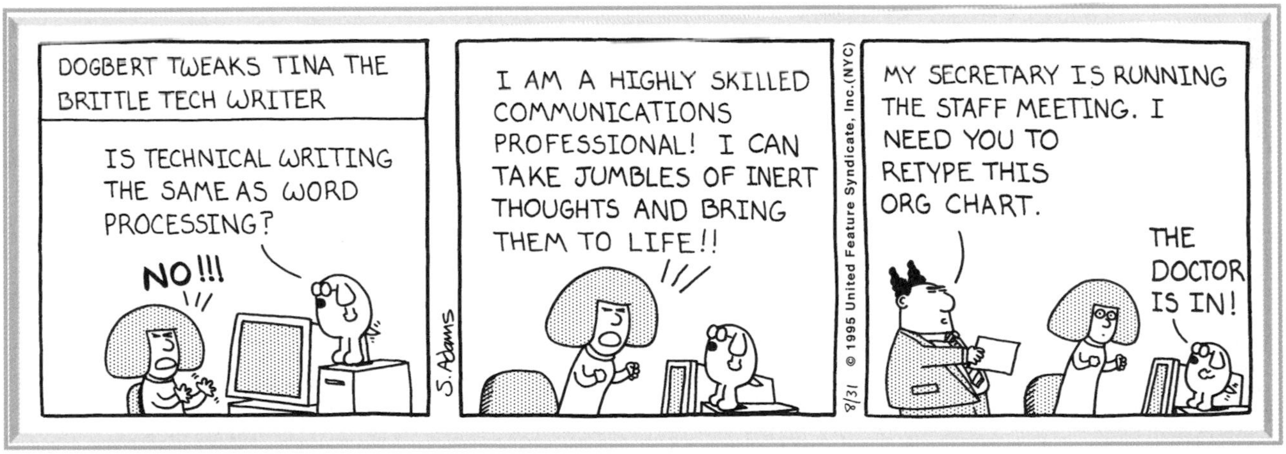
DOGBERT TWEAKS TINA THE BRITTLE TECH WRITER
IS TECHNICAL WRITING THE SAME AS WORD PROCESSING?
NO!!!
I AM A HIGHLY SKILLED COMMUNICATIONS PROFESSIONAL! I CAN TAKE JUMBLES OF INERT THOUGHTS AND BRING THEM TO LIFE!!
S. Adams
8/31 © 1995 United Feature Syndicate, Inc.(NYC)
MY SECRETARY IS RUNNING THE STAFF MEETING. I NEED YOU TO RETYPE THIS ORG CHART.
THE DOCTOR IS IN!

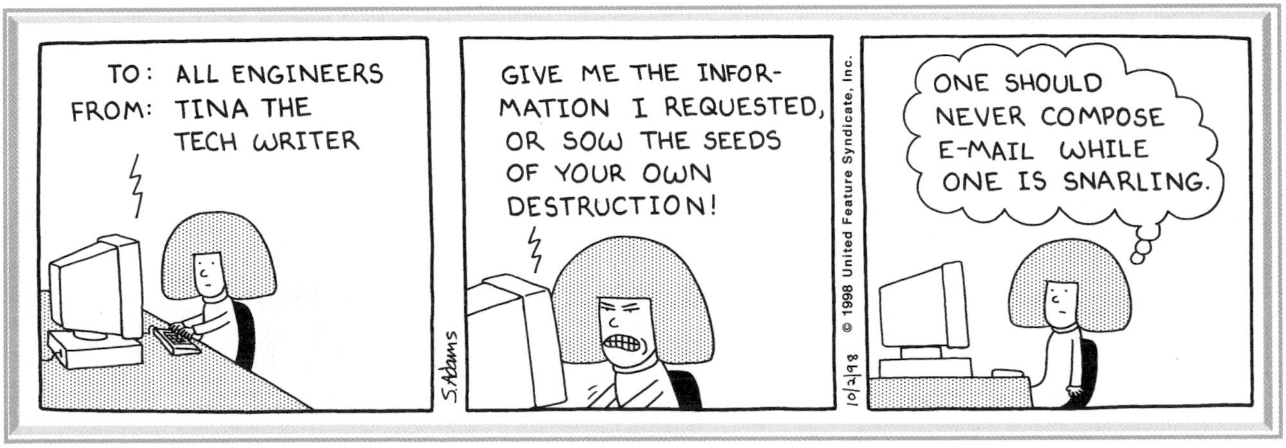
TO: ALL ENGINEERS
FROM: TINA THE TECH WRITER
GIVE ME THE INFORMATION I REQUESTED, OR SOW THE SEEDS OF YOUR OWN DESTRUCTION!
S. Adams
10/2/98 © 1998 United Feature Syndicate, Inc.
ONE SHOULD NEVER COMPOSE E-MAIL WHILE ONE IS SNARLING.

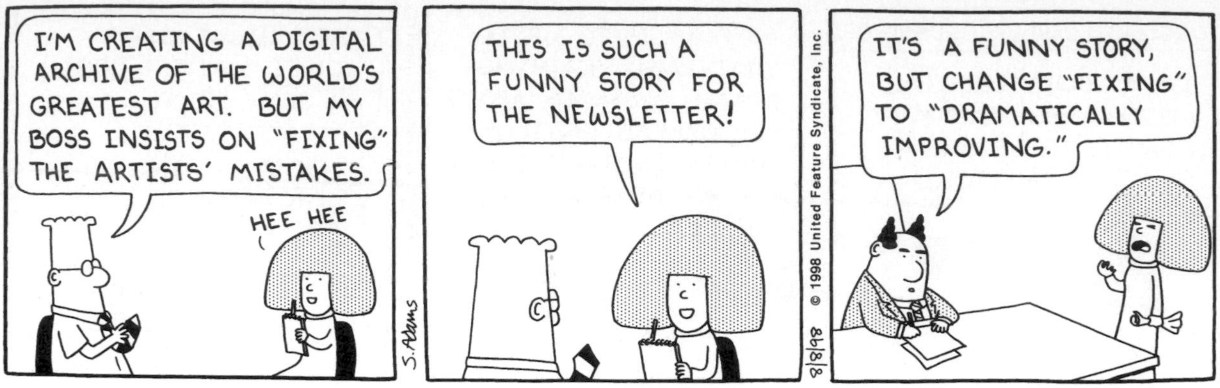
I'M CREATING A DIGITAL ARCHIVE OF THE WORLD'S GREATEST ART. BUT MY BOSS INSISTS ON "FIXING" THE ARTISTS' MISTAKES.
HEE HEE
S. Adams
THIS IS SUCH A FUNNY STORY FOR THE NEWSLETTER!
8/8/98 © 1998 United Feature Syndicate, Inc.
IT'S A FUNNY STORY, BUT CHANGE "FIXING" TO "DRAMATICALLY IMPROVING."

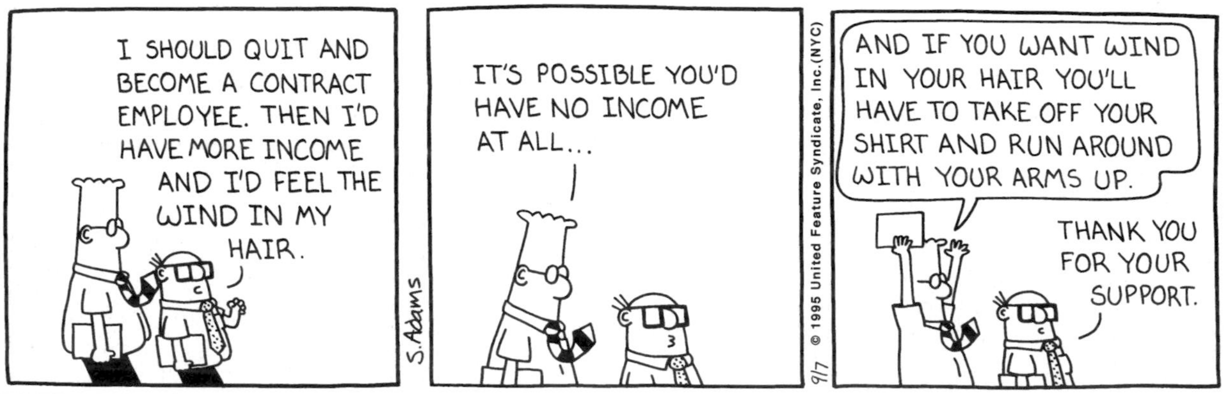
I SHOULD QUIT AND BECOME A CONTRACT EMPLOYEE. THEN I'D HAVE MORE INCOME
AND I'D FEEL THE WIND IN MY HAIR.
S. Adams
IT'S POSSIBLE YOU'D HAVE NO INCOME AT ALL...
9/7 © 1995 United Feature Syndicate, Inc.(NYC)
AND IF YOU WANT WIND IN YOUR HAIR YOU'LL HAVE TO TAKE OFF YOUR SHIRT AND RUN AROUND WITH YOUR ARMS UP.
THANK YOU FOR YOUR SUPPORT.

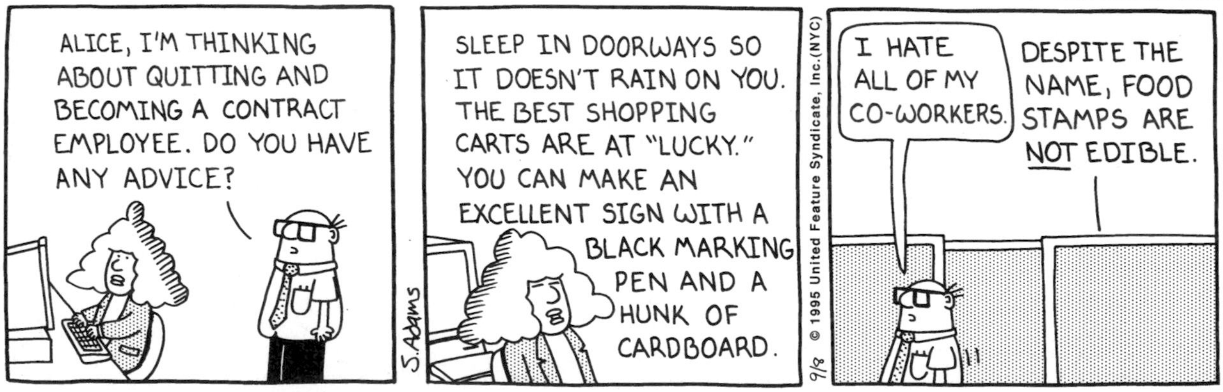
ALICE, I'M THINKING ABOUT QUITTING AND BECOMING A CONTRACT EMPLOYEE. DO YOU HAVE ANY ADVICE?
S. Adams
SLEEP IN DOORWAYS SO IT DOESN'T RAIN ON YOU. THE BEST SHOPPING CARTS ARE AT "LUCKY." YOU CAN MAKE AN EXCELLENT SIGN WITH A BLACK MARKING PEN AND A HUNK OF CARDBOARD.
9/8 © 1995 United Feature Syndicate, Inc.(NYC)
I HATE ALL OF MY CO-WORKERS.
DESPITE THE NAME, FOOD STAMPS ARE NOT EDIBLE.

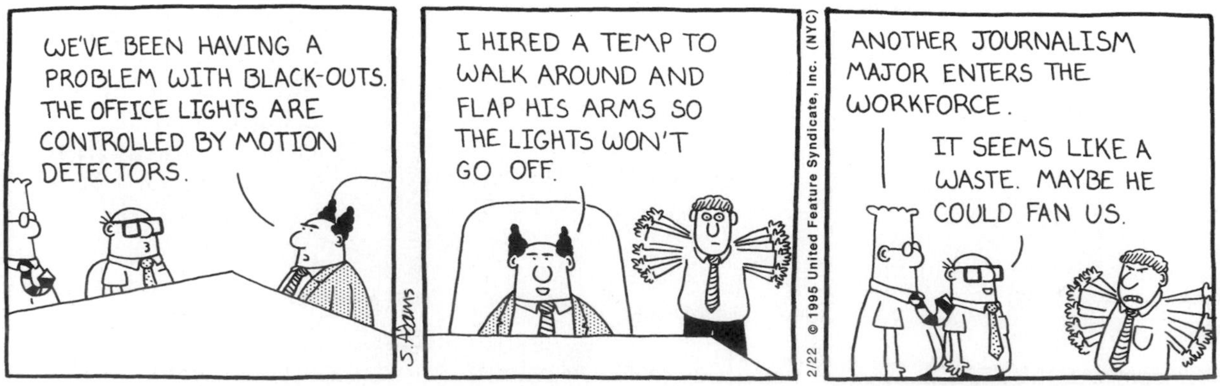
WE'VE BEEN HAVING A PROBLEM WITH BLACK-OUTS. THE OFFICE LIGHTS ARE CONTROLLED BY MOTION DETECTORS.
S. Adams
I HIRED A TEMP TO WALK AROUND AND FLAP HIS ARMS SO THE LIGHTS WON'T GO OFF.
2/22 © 1995 United Feature Syndicate, Inc. (NYC)
ANOTHER JOURNALISM MAJOR ENTERS THE WORKFORCE.
IT SEEMS LIKE A WASTE. MAYBE HE COULD FAN US.

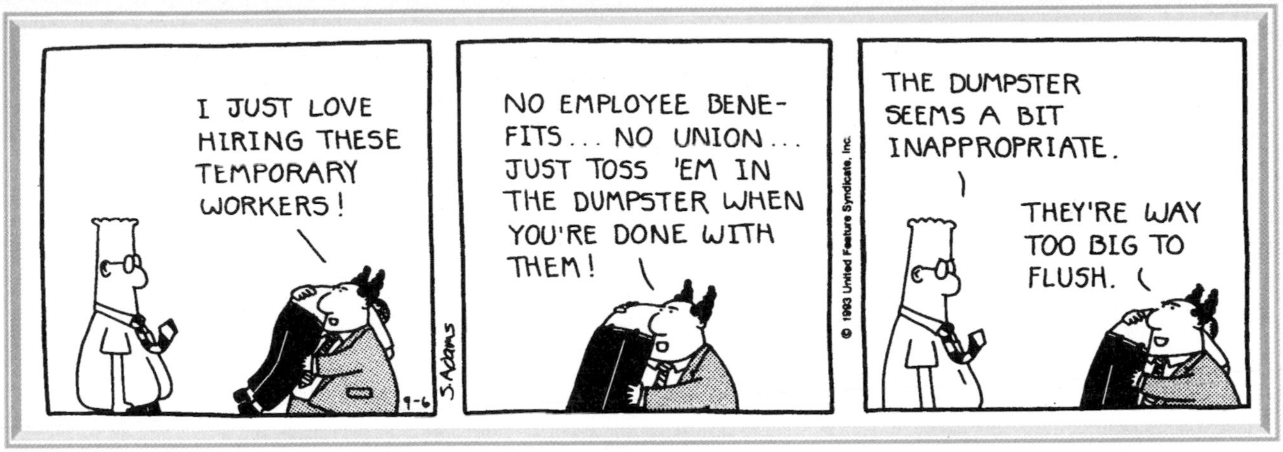
I JUST LOVE HIRING THESE TEMPORARY WORKERS!
NO EMPLOYEE BENEFITS... NO UNION... JUST TOSS 'EM IN THE DUMPSTER WHEN YOU'RE DONE WITH THEM!
THE DUMPSTER SEEMS A BIT INAPPROPRIATE.
THEY'RE WAY TOO BIG TO FLUSH.
© 1993 United Feature Syndicate, Inc.

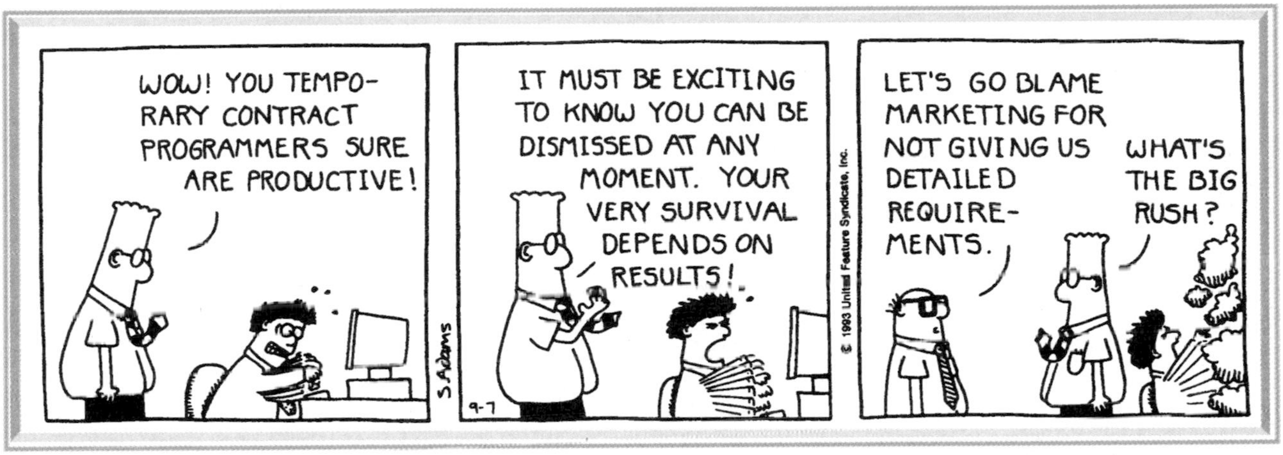
WOW! YOU TEMPORARY CONTRACT PROGRAMMERS SURE ARE PRODUCTIVE!
IT MUST BE EXCITING TO KNOW YOU CAN BE DISMISSED AT ANY MOMENT. YOUR VERY SURVIVAL DEPENDS ON RESULTS!
LET'S GO BLAME MARKETING FOR NOT GIVING US DETAILED REQUIREMENTS.
WHAT'S THE BIG RUSH?
© 1993 United Feature Syndicate, Inc.

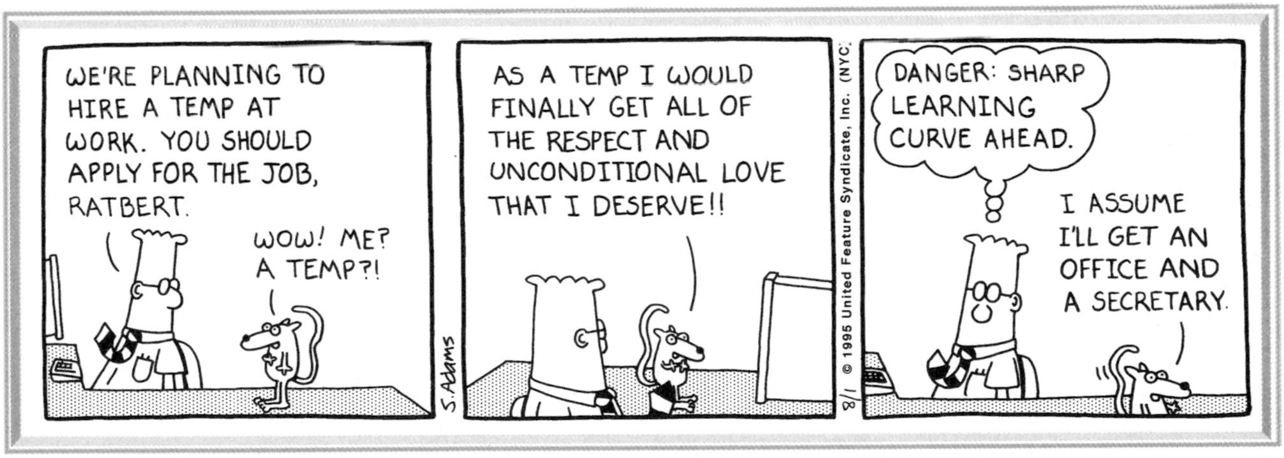
WE'RE PLANNING TO HIRE A TEMP AT WORK. YOU SHOULD APPLY FOR THE JOB, RATBERT.
WOW! ME? A TEMP?!
AS A TEMP I WOULD FINALLY GET ALL OF THE RESPECT AND UNCONDITIONAL LOVE THAT I DESERVE!!
DANGER: SHARP LEARNING CURVE AHEAD.
I ASSUME I'LL GET AN OFFICE AND A SECRETARY.
© 1995 United Feature Syndicate, Inc. (NYC)

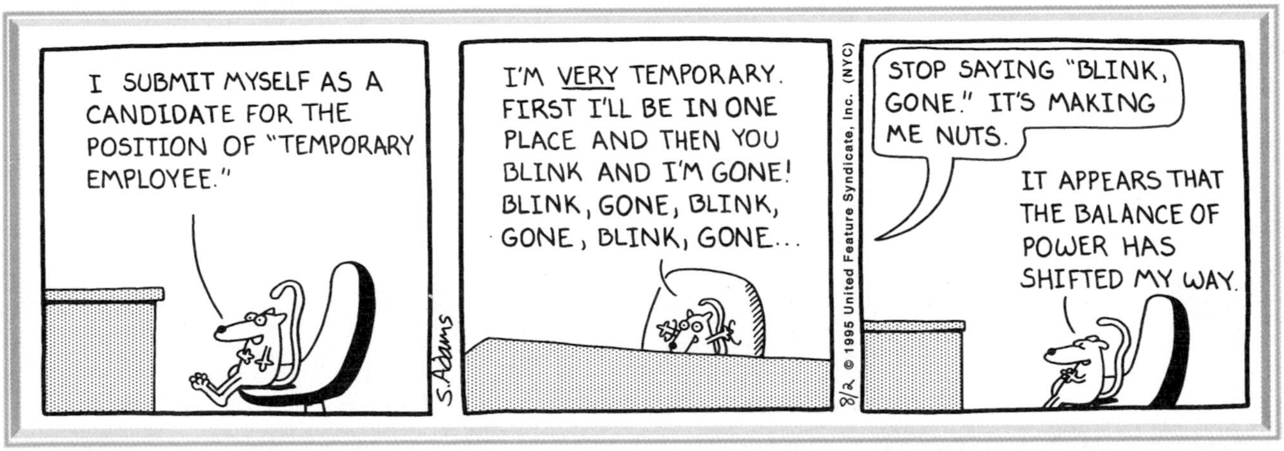
I SUBMIT MYSELF AS A CANDIDATE FOR THE POSITION OF "TEMPORARY EMPLOYEE."
I'M VERY TEMPORARY. FIRST I'LL BE IN ONE PLACE AND THEN YOU BLINK AND I'M GONE! BLINK, GONE, BLINK, GONE, BLINK, GONE...
STOP SAYING "BLINK, GONE." IT'S MAKING ME NUTS.
IT APPEARS THAT THE BALANCE OF POWER HAS SHIFTED MY WAY.
© 1995 United Feature Syndicate, Inc. (NYC)

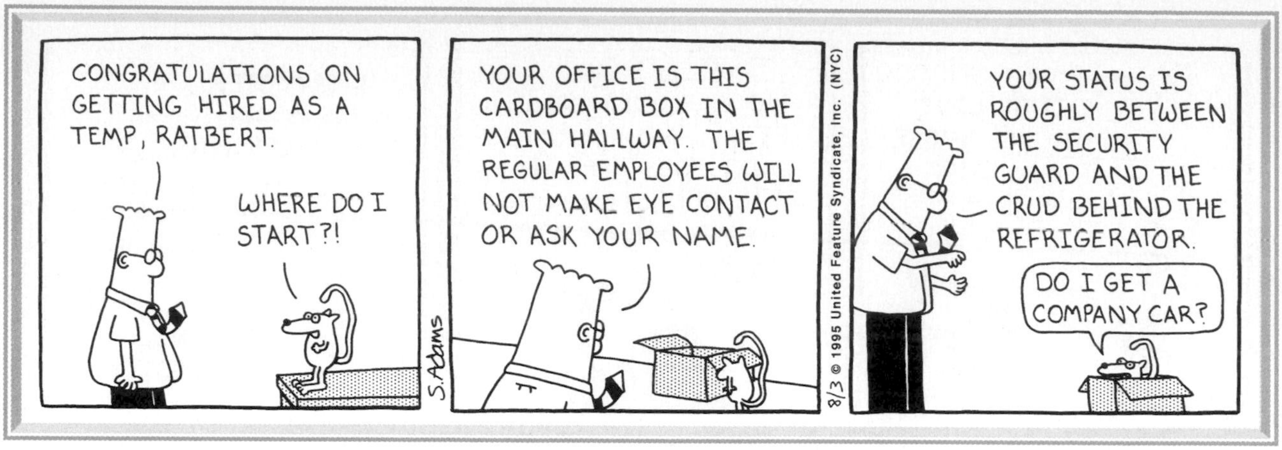

CONGRATULATIONS ON GETTING HIRED AS A TEMP, RATBERT.
WHERE DO I START?!
YOUR OFFICE IS THIS CARDBOARD BOX IN THE MAIN HALLWAY. THE REGULAR EMPLOYEES WILL NOT MAKE EYE CONTACT OR ASK YOUR NAME.
YOUR STATUS IS ROUGHLY BETWEEN THE SECURITY GUARD AND THE CRUD BEHIND THE REFRIGERATOR.
DO I GET A COMPANY CAR?
S.Adams
8/3 © 1995 United Feature Syndicate, Inc. (NYC)

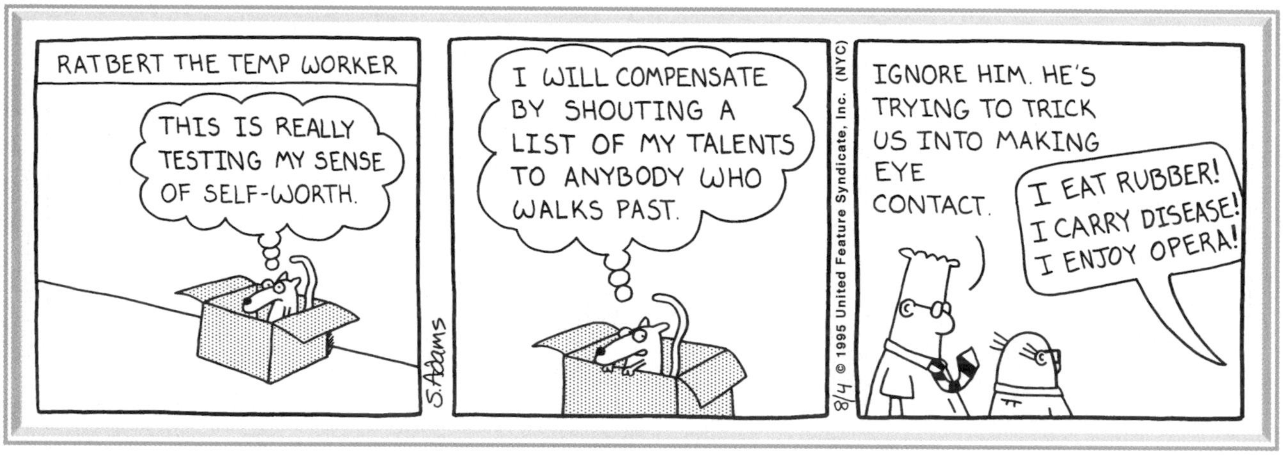

RATBERT THE TEMP WORKER
THIS IS REALLY TESTING MY SENSE OF SELF-WORTH.
I WILL COMPENSATE BY SHOUTING A LIST OF MY TALENTS TO ANYBODY WHO WALKS PAST.
IGNORE HIM. HE'S TRYING TO TRICK US INTO MAKING EYE CONTACT.
I EAT RUBBER! I CARRY DISEASE! I ENJOY OPERA!
S.Adams
8/4 © 1995 United Feature Syndicate, Inc. (NYC)

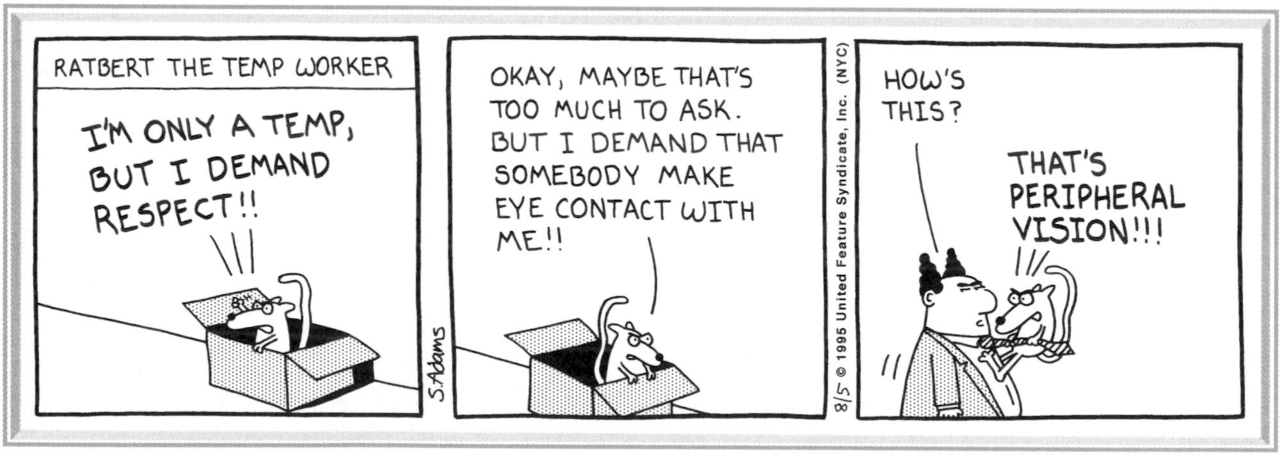

RATBERT THE TEMP WORKER
I'M ONLY A TEMP, BUT I DEMAND RESPECT!!
OKAY, MAYBE THAT'S TOO MUCH TO ASK. BUT I DEMAND THAT SOMEBODY MAKE EYE CONTACT WITH ME!!
HOW'S THIS?
THAT'S PERIPHERAL VISION!!!
S.Adams
8/5 © 1995 United Feature Syndicate, Inc. (NYC)

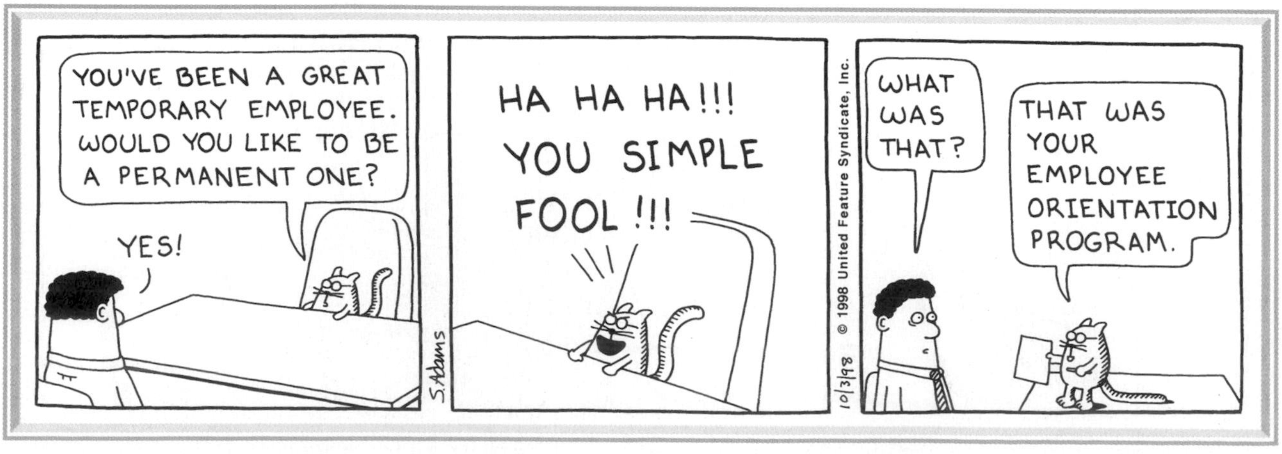

YOU'VE BEEN A GREAT TEMPORARY EMPLOYEE. WOULD YOU LIKE TO BE A PERMANENT ONE?
YES!
HA HA HA!!! YOU SIMPLE FOOL!!!
WHAT WAS THAT?
THAT WAS YOUR EMPLOYEE ORIENTATION PROGRAM.
S.Adams
10/3/98 © 1998 United Feature Syndicate, Inc.

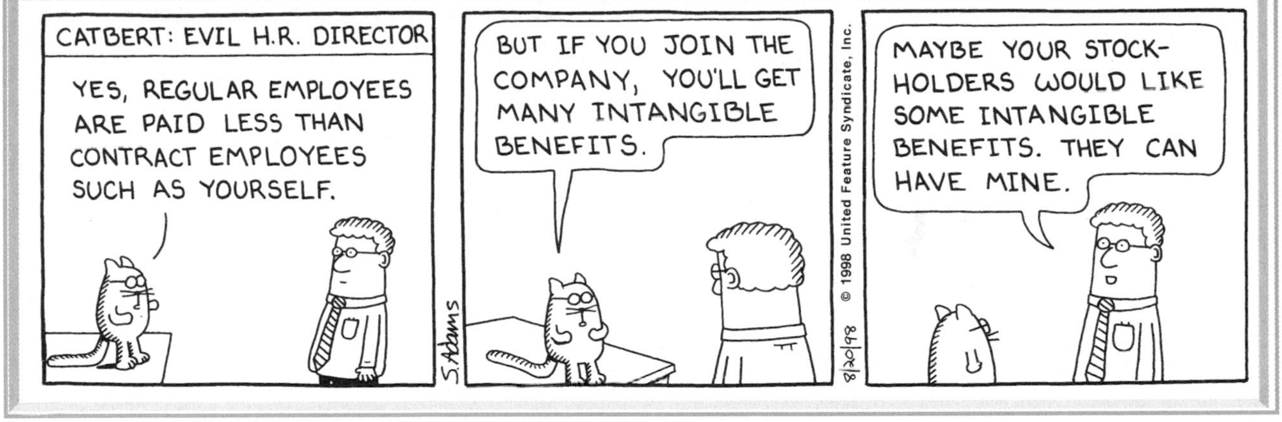
CATBERT: EVIL H.R. DIRECTOR
YES, REGULAR EMPLOYEES ARE PAID LESS THAN CONTRACT EMPLOYEES SUCH AS YOURSELF.
BUT IF YOU JOIN THE COMPANY, YOU'LL GET MANY INTANGIBLE BENEFITS.
© 1998 United Feature Syndicate, Inc.
MAYBE YOUR STOCK-HOLDERS WOULD LIKE SOME INTANGIBLE BENEFITS. THEY CAN HAVE MINE.

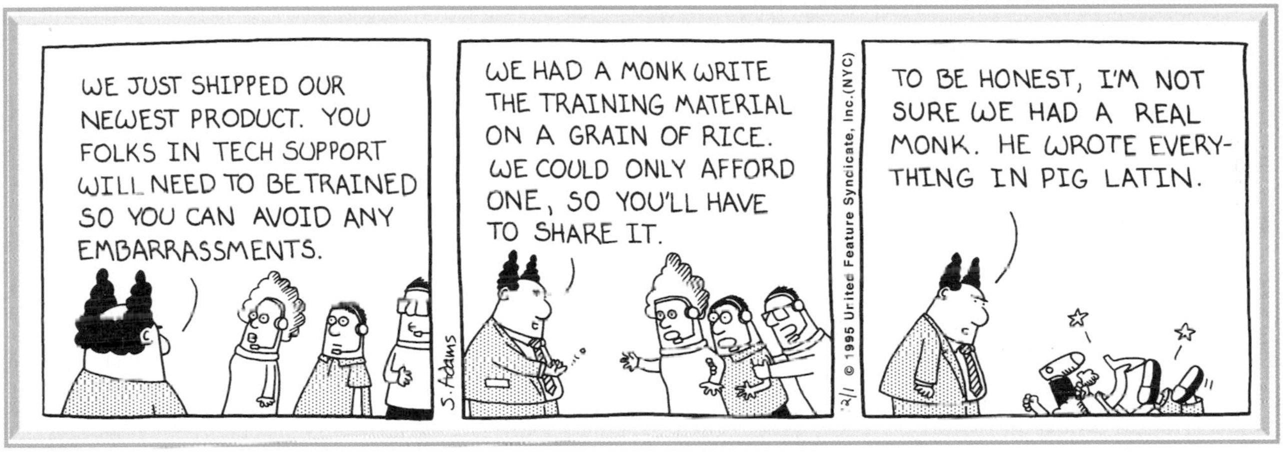
WE JUST SHIPPED OUR NEWEST PRODUCT. YOU FOLKS IN TECH SUPPORT WILL NEED TO BE TRAINED SO YOU CAN AVOID ANY EMBARRASSMENTS.
WE HAD A MONK WRITE THE TRAINING MATERIAL ON A GRAIN OF RICE. WE COULD ONLY AFFORD ONE, SO YOU'LL HAVE TO SHARE IT.
© 1995 United Feature Syndicate, Inc.(NYC)
TO BE HONEST, I'M NOT SURE WE HAD A REAL MONK. HE WROTE EVERY-THING IN PIG LATIN.

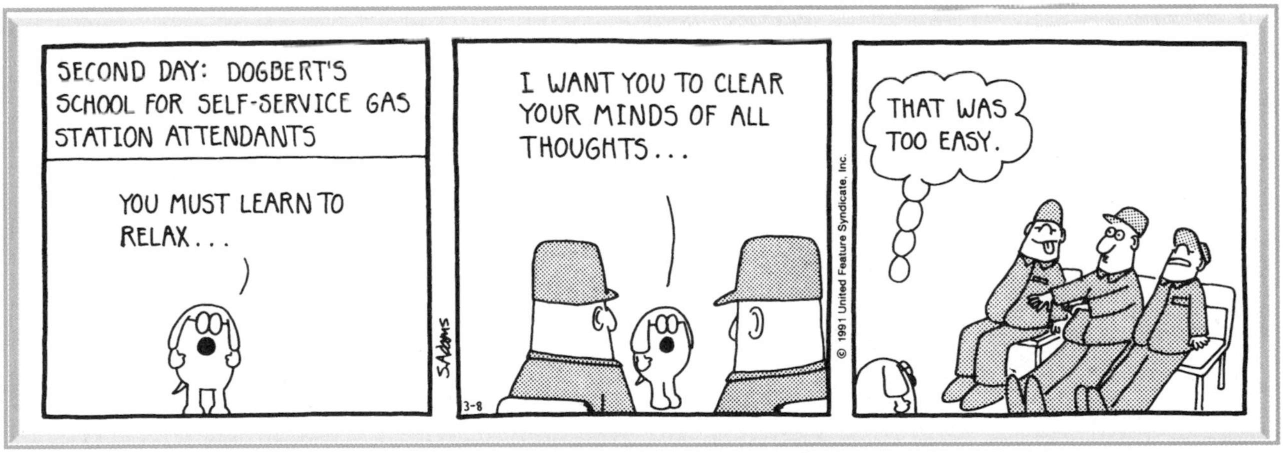
SECOND DAY: DOGBERT'S SCHOOL FOR SELF-SERVICE GAS STATION ATTENDANTS
YOU MUST LEARN TO RELAX...
I WANT YOU TO CLEAR YOUR MINDS OF ALL THOUGHTS...
© 1991 United Feature Syndicate, Inc.
THAT WAS TOO EASY.

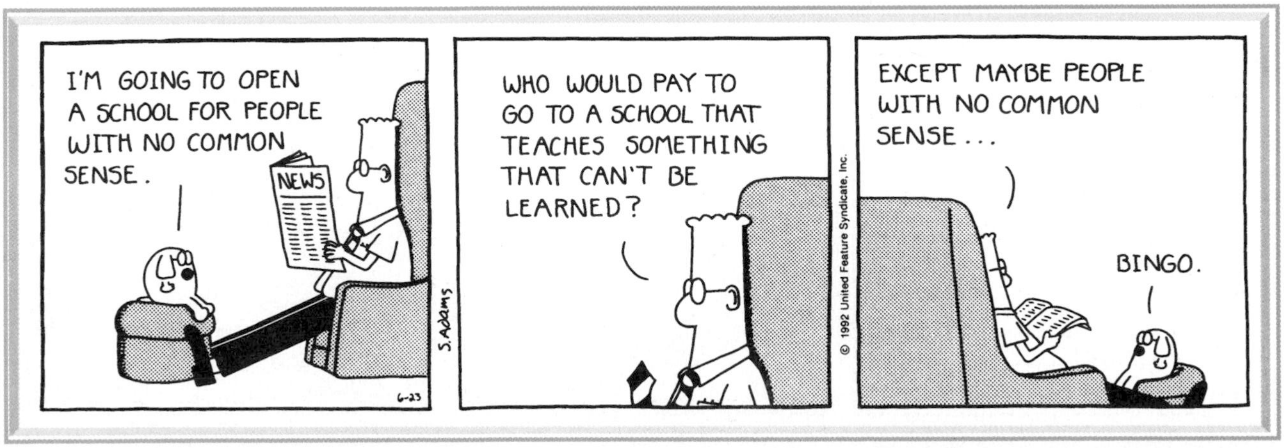
I'M GOING TO OPEN A SCHOOL FOR PEOPLE WITH NO COMMON SENSE.
NEWS
WHO WOULD PAY TO GO TO A SCHOOL THAT TEACHES SOMETHING THAT CAN'T BE LEARNED?
© 1992 United Feature Syndicate, Inc.
EXCEPT MAYBE PEOPLE WITH NO COMMON SENSE...
BINGO.

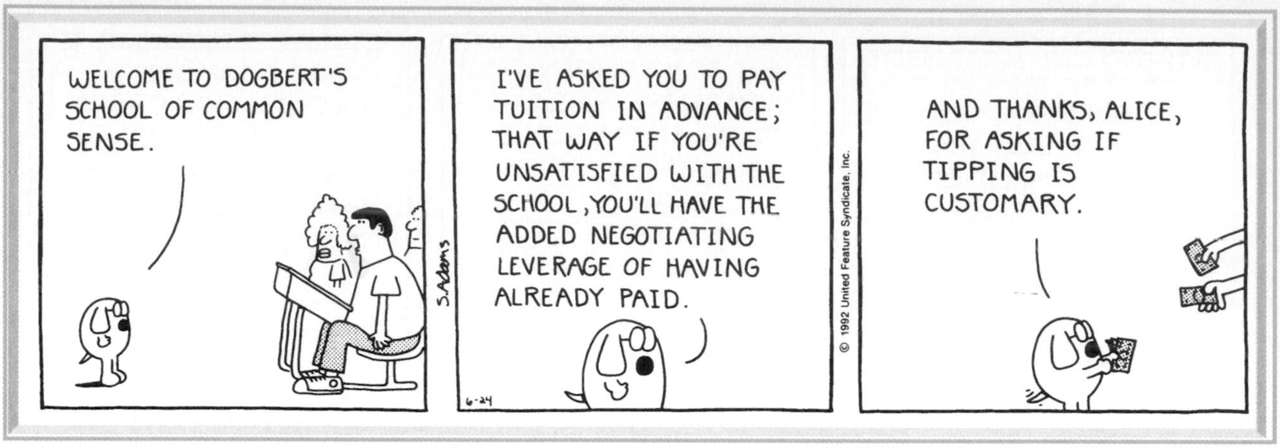
WELCOME TO DOGBERT'S SCHOOL OF COMMON SENSE.
I'VE ASKED YOU TO PAY TUITION IN ADVANCE; THAT WAY IF YOU'RE UNSATISFIED WITH THE SCHOOL, YOU'LL HAVE THE ADDED NEGOTIATING LEVERAGE OF HAVING ALREADY PAID.
AND THANKS, ALICE, FOR ASKING IF TIPPING IS CUSTOMARY.
S. Adams
6-24
© 1992 United Feature Syndicate, Inc.

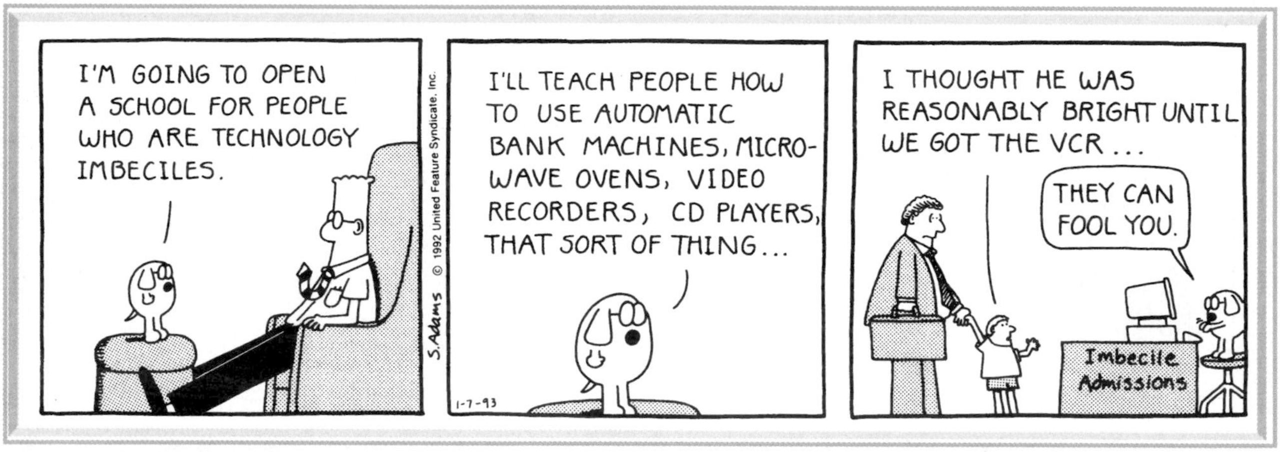
I'M GOING TO OPEN A SCHOOL FOR PEOPLE WHO ARE TECHNOLOGY IMBECILES.
S. Adams
© 1992 United Feature Syndicate, Inc.
I'LL TEACH PEOPLE HOW TO USE AUTOMATIC BANK MACHINES, MICRO-WAVE OVENS, VIDEO RECORDERS, CD PLAYERS, THAT SORT OF THING...
1-7-93
I THOUGHT HE WAS REASONABLY BRIGHT UNTIL WE GOT THE VCR...
THEY CAN FOOL YOU.
Imbecile Admissions

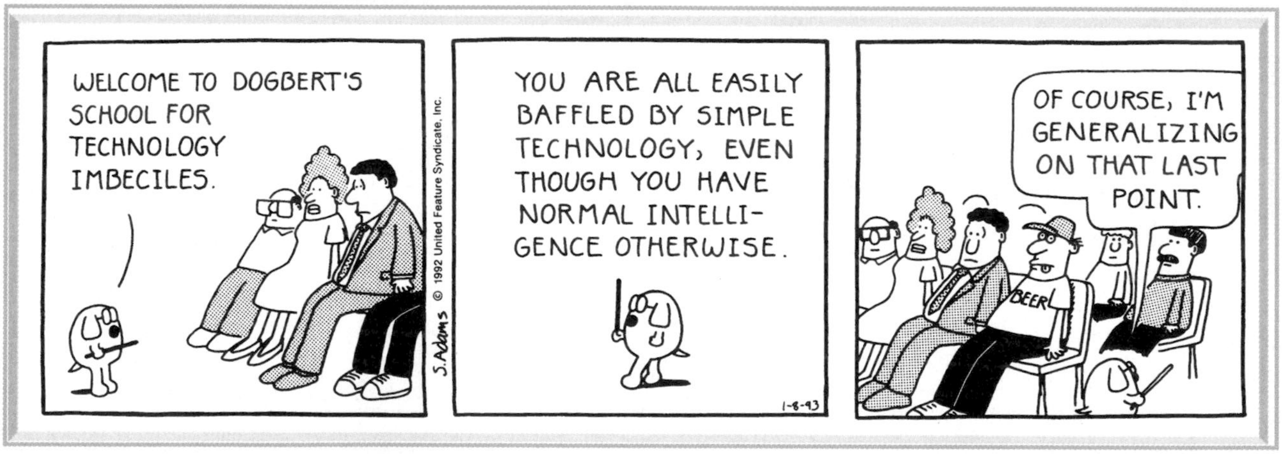
WELCOME TO DOGBERT'S SCHOOL FOR TECHNOLOGY IMBECILES.
S. Adams
© 1992 United Feature Syndicate, Inc.
YOU ARE ALL EASILY BAFFLED BY SIMPLE TECHNOLOGY, EVEN THOUGH YOU HAVE NORMAL INTELLI-GENCE OTHERWISE.
1-8-93
OF COURSE, I'M GENERALIZING ON THAT LAST POINT.
BEER

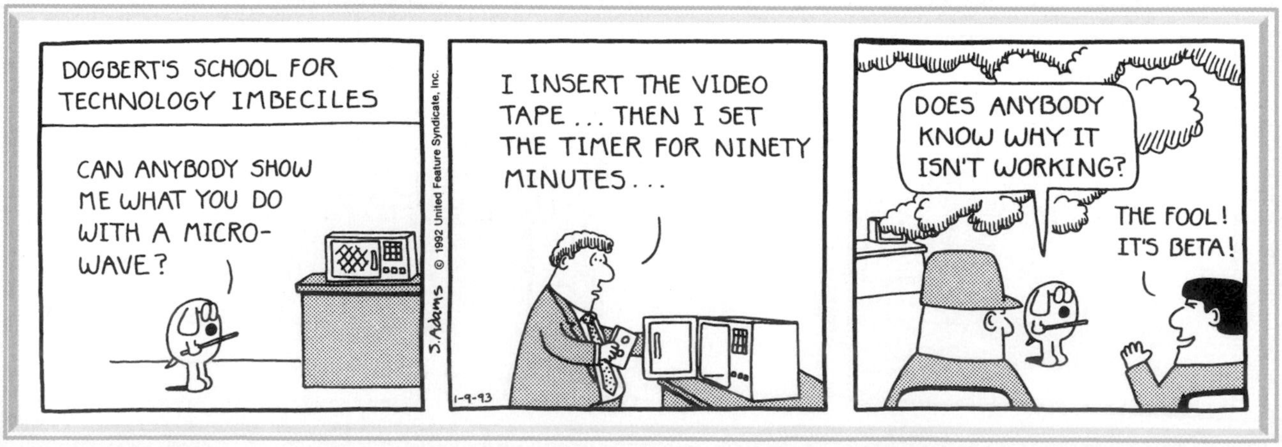
DOGBERT'S SCHOOL FOR TECHNOLOGY IMBECILES
CAN ANYBODY SHOW ME WHAT YOU DO WITH A MICRO-WAVE?
S. Adams
© 1992 United Feature Syndicate, Inc.
I INSERT THE VIDEO TAPE... THEN I SET THE TIMER FOR NINETY MINUTES...
1-9-93
DOES ANYBODY KNOW WHY IT ISN'T WORKING?
THE FOOL! IT'S BETA!

LET'S GO AROUND THE CIRCLE AND SHARE WHAT WE LEARNED IN THE THREE-DAY WORKSHOP.
TEAM
AT FIRST I THOUGHT IT WAS A WASTE OF OUR TRAINING BUDGET...
THEN YOU ASKED US TO FORM TEAMS AND MAKE PAPER AIRPLANES WHILE BLINDFOLDED...
I DON'T KNOW IF IT WAS BECAUSE OF THE DARKNESS OR THE WAY WE SHARED OUR THOUGHTS ABOUT FLIGHT...
BUT SUDDENLY I FOUND UNCONDITIONAL LOVE FOR MY CO-WORKERS.
BE THEY ACCOUNTANTS, BE THEY MARKETEERS OR BE THEY SECRETARIES.
© 1995 United Feature Syndicate, Inc.
AS A RESULT, I'VE BECOME A COMPETITIVE LION, EAGER TO POUNCE ON MY WORKLOAD AND INCREASE STOCK-HOLDER VALUES!!
THANK YOU, WALLY.
DILBERT, WHAT DID YOU LEARN?
I LEARNED THAT YOU SHOULDN'T PUT A LITTLE ERASER-PILOT IN YOUR PAPER AIRPLANE.
SOMEBODY NEEDS A GROUP HUG!

WELCOME TO DOGBERT'S "SCHOOL OF HARD KNOCKS."
THIS IS THE SCHOOL YOU'VE HEARD SO MUCH ABOUT.
CHANCES ARE, ONE OF YOUR PARENTS IS A GRADUATE OF THIS SCHOOL.
© 1991 United Feature Syndicate, Inc.
AT DOGBERT'S SCHOOL OF HARD KNOCKS, YOU WILL GAIN THE WISDOM THAT CAN ONLY BE OBTAINED THROUGH SUFFERING.
THROUGHOUT THE COURSE, I'LL BE WHACKING YOU WITH VARIOUS BLUNT OBJECTS.
IT MAY BE UNPLEASANT AT FIRST, BUT YOU'LL GET USED TO IT.
EVENTUALLY, YOUR BRAIN WILL RATIONALIZE THE WHOLE EXPERIENCE. YOU'LL THINK I'M A DEDICATED TEACHER, AND YOU'LL ACTUALLY BELIEVE YOU LEARNED SOMETHING.
STICK WITH THE BASICS, I SAY.

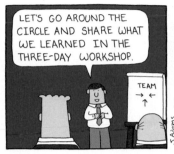

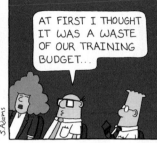

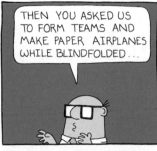

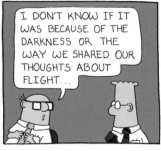

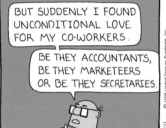

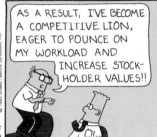

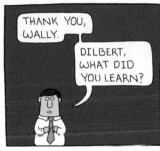

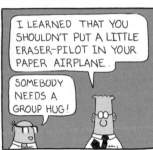

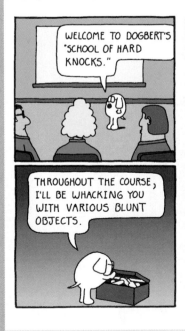

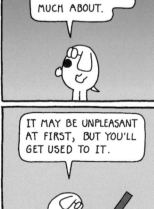

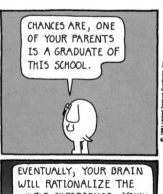

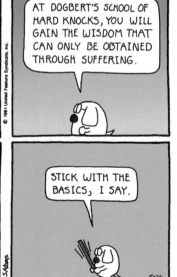

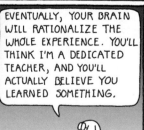

DILBERT® *Gives You the Business*

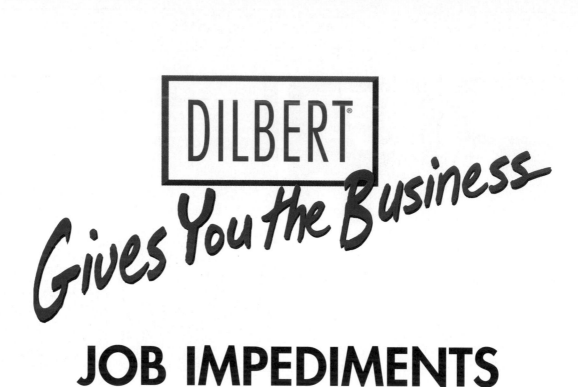

JOB IMPEDIMENTS

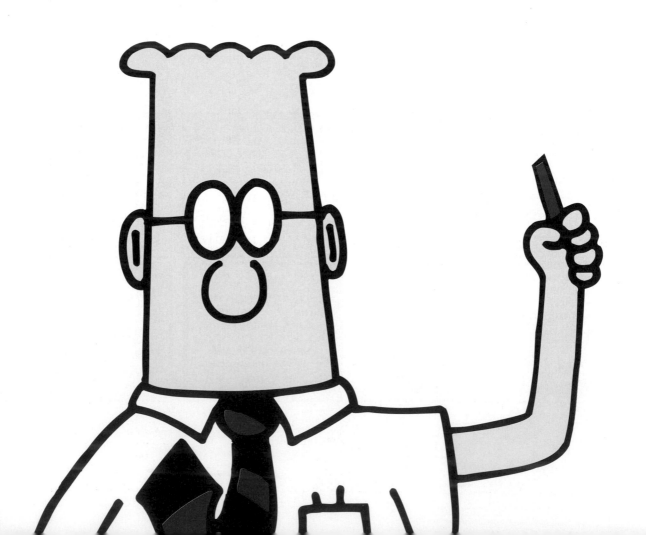

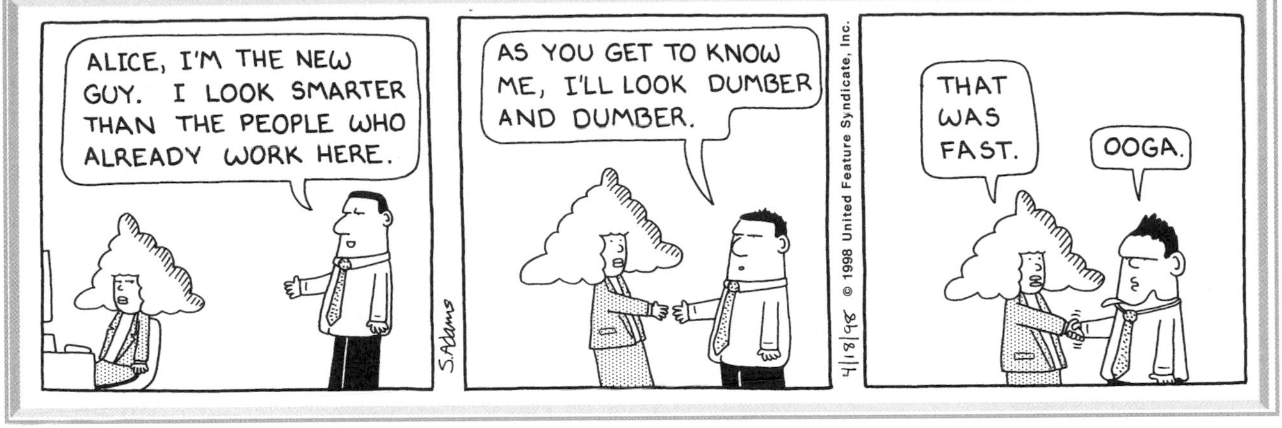
ALICE, I'M THE NEW GUY. I LOOK SMARTER THAN THE PEOPLE WHO ALREADY WORK HERE.
AS YOU GET TO KNOW ME, I'LL LOOK DUMBER AND DUMBER.
THAT WAS FAST.
OOGA.
S. Adams
4/18/98 © 1998 United Feature Syndicate, Inc.

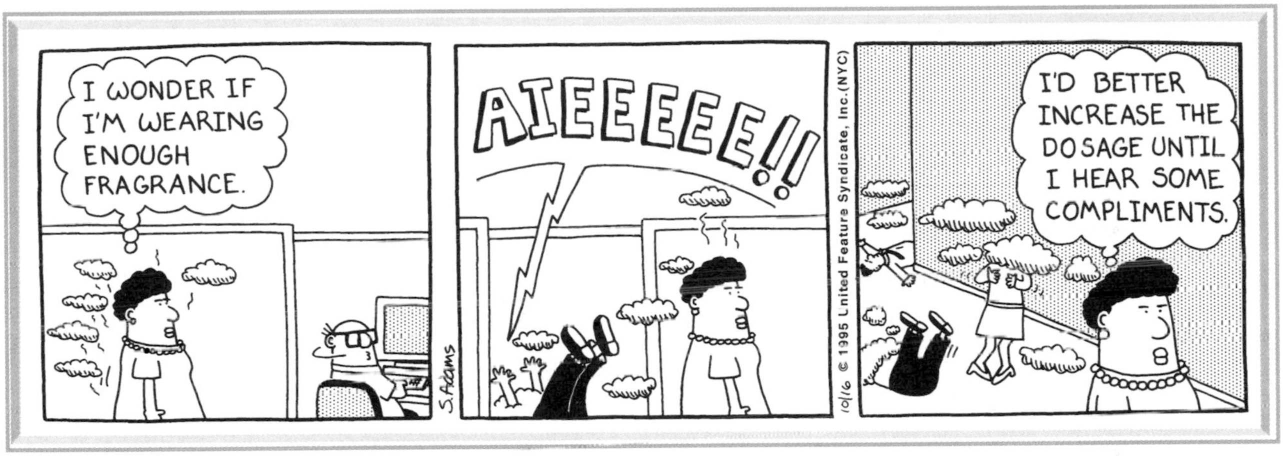
I WONDER IF I'M WEARING ENOUGH FRAGRANCE.
AIEEEEEE!!
I'D BETTER INCREASE THE DOSAGE UNTIL I HEAR SOME COMPLIMENTS.
S. Adams
10/16 © 1995 United Feature Syndicate, Inc.(NYC)

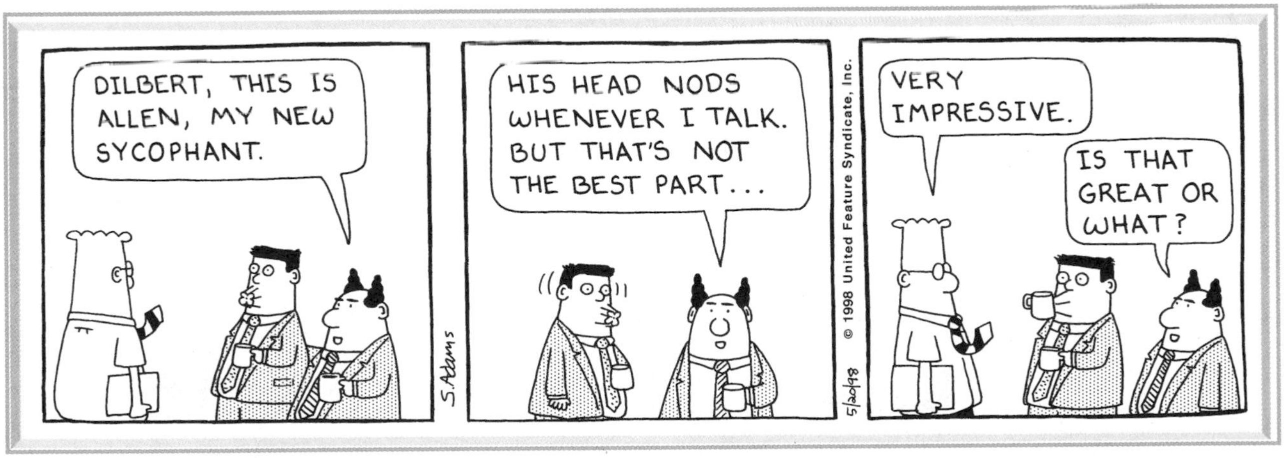
DILBERT, THIS IS ALLEN, MY NEW SYCOPHANT.
HIS HEAD NODS WHENEVER I TALK. BUT THAT'S NOT THE BEST PART...
VERY IMPRESSIVE.
IS THAT GREAT OR WHAT?
S. Adams
5/20/98 © 1998 United Feature Syndicate, Inc.

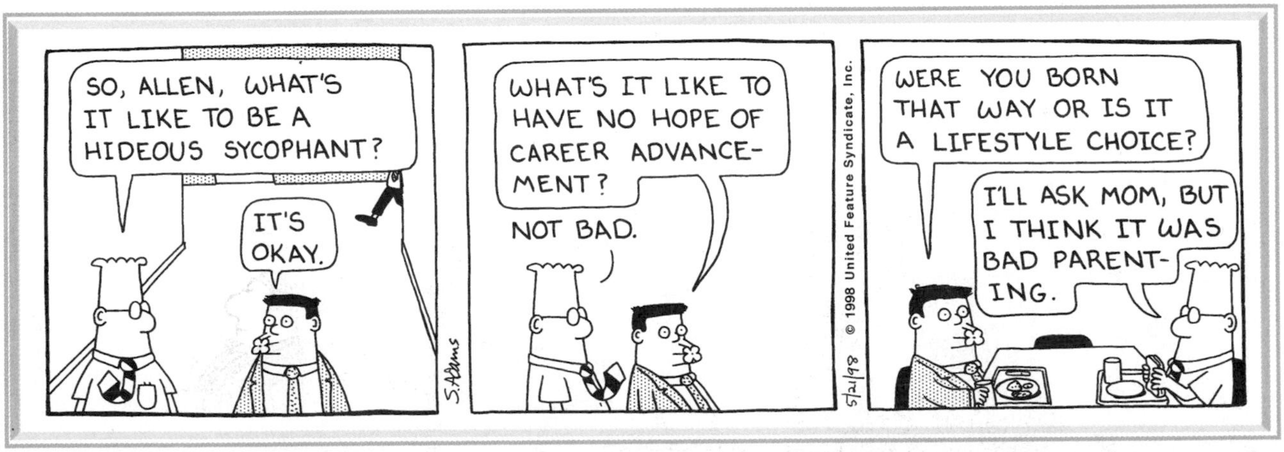
SO, ALLEN, WHAT'S IT LIKE TO BE A HIDEOUS SYCOPHANT?
IT'S OKAY.
WHAT'S IT LIKE TO HAVE NO HOPE OF CAREER ADVANCE- MENT?
NOT BAD.
WERE YOU BORN THAT WAY OR IS IT A LIFESTYLE CHOICE?
I'LL ASK MOM, BUT I THINK IT WAS BAD PARENT- ING.
S. Adams
5/21/98 © 1998 United Feature Syndicate, Inc.

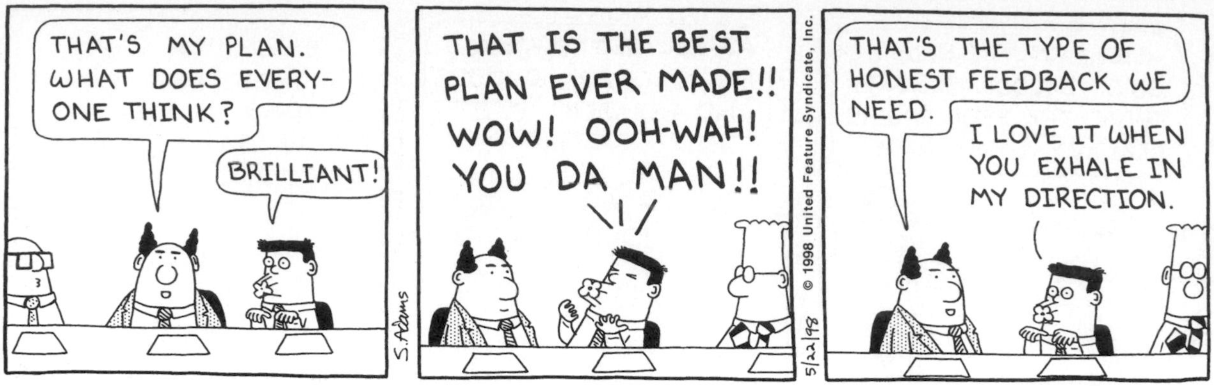
THAT'S MY PLAN. WHAT DOES EVERYONE THINK?
BRILLIANT!
THAT IS THE BEST PLAN EVER MADE!! WOW! OOH-WAH! YOU DA MAN!!
THAT'S THE TYPE OF HONEST FEEDBACK WE NEED.
I LOVE IT WHEN YOU EXHALE IN MY DIRECTION.
S. Adams 5/22/98 © 1998 United Feature Syndicate, Inc.

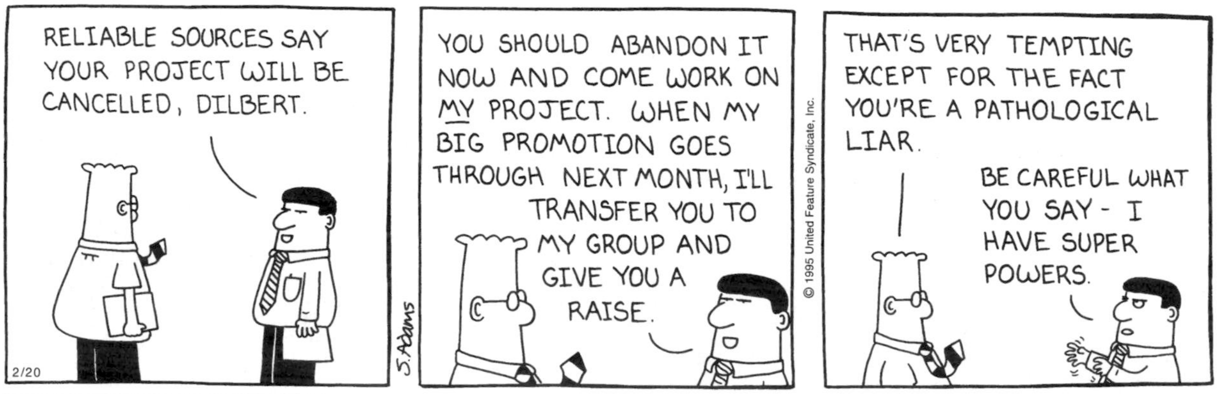
RELIABLE SOURCES SAY YOUR PROJECT WILL BE CANCELLED, DILBERT.
YOU SHOULD ABANDON IT NOW AND COME WORK ON MY PROJECT. WHEN MY BIG PROMOTION GOES THROUGH NEXT MONTH, I'LL TRANSFER YOU TO MY GROUP AND GIVE YOU A RAISE.
THAT'S VERY TEMPTING EXCEPT FOR THE FACT YOU'RE A PATHOLOGICAL LIAR.
BE CAREFUL WHAT YOU SAY - I HAVE SUPER POWERS.
2/20 S. Adams © 1995 United Feature Syndicate, Inc.

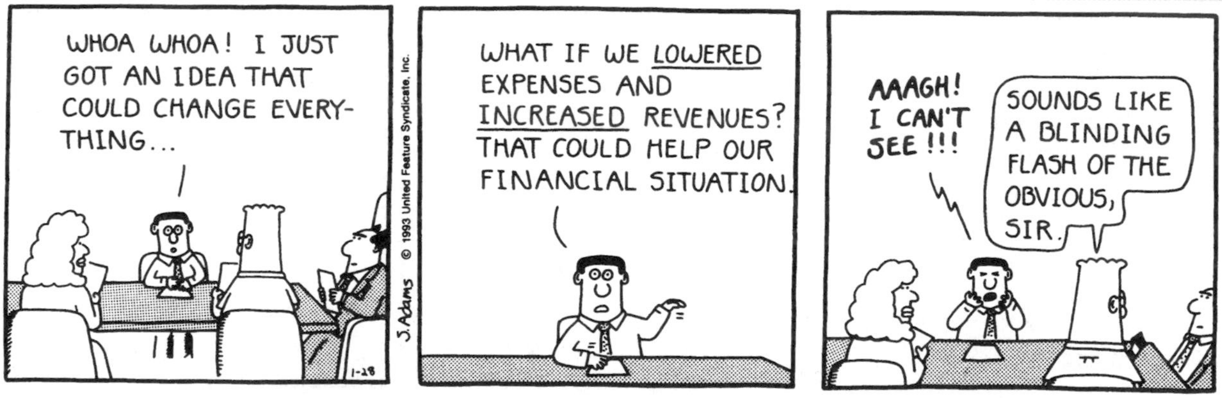
WHOA WHOA! I JUST GOT AN IDEA THAT COULD CHANGE EVERYTHING...
WHAT IF WE LOWERED EXPENSES AND INCREASED REVENUES? THAT COULD HELP OUR FINANCIAL SITUATION.
AAAGH! I CAN'T SEE!!!
SOUNDS LIKE A BLINDING FLASH OF THE OBVIOUS, SIR.
1-28 S. Adams © 1993 United Feature Syndicate, Inc.

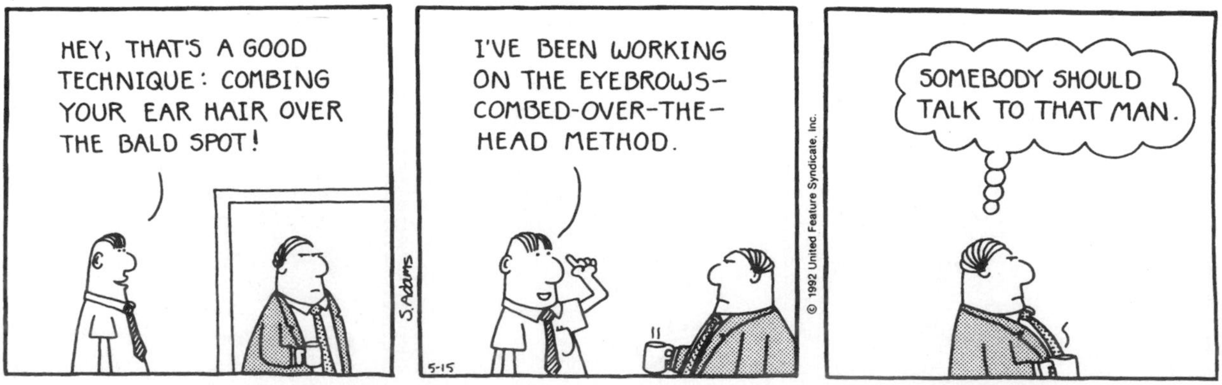
HEY, THAT'S A GOOD TECHNIQUE: COMBING YOUR EAR HAIR OVER THE BALD SPOT!
I'VE BEEN WORKING ON THE EYEBROWS-COMBED-OVER-THE-HEAD METHOD.
SOMEBODY SHOULD TALK TO THAT MAN.
S. Adams 5-15 © 1992 United Feature Syndicate, Inc.

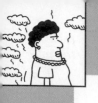

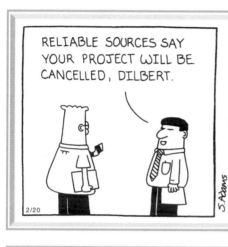

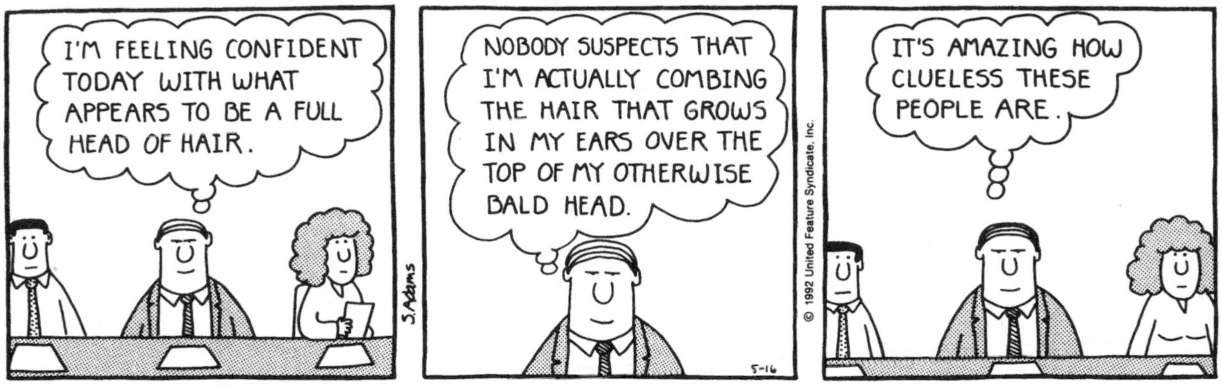
I'M FEELING CONFIDENT TODAY WITH WHAT APPEARS TO BE A FULL HEAD OF HAIR.
NOBODY SUSPECTS THAT I'M ACTUALLY COMBING THE HAIR THAT GROWS IN MY EARS OVER THE TOP OF MY OTHERWISE BALD HEAD.
IT'S AMAZING HOW CLUELESS THESE PEOPLE ARE.
© 1992 United Feature Syndicate, Inc.

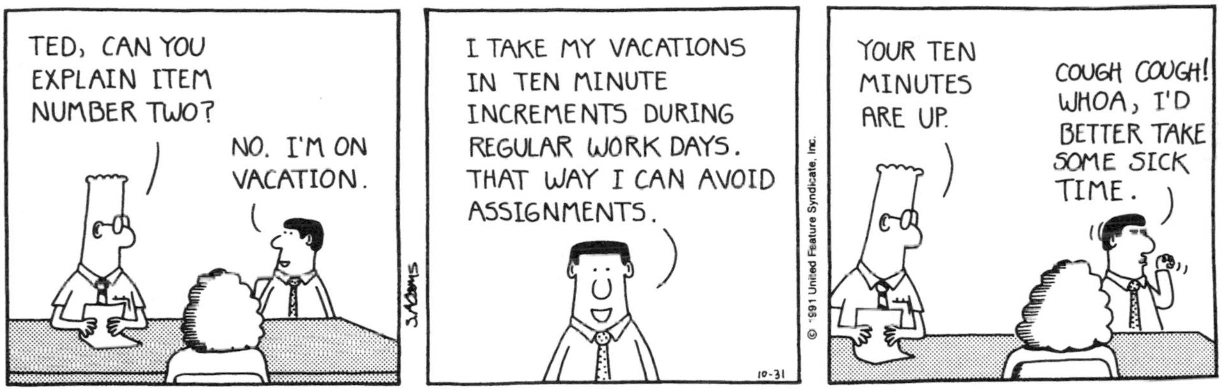
TED, CAN YOU EXPLAIN ITEM NUMBER TWO?
NO. I'M ON VACATION.
I TAKE MY VACATIONS IN TEN MINUTE INCREMENTS DURING REGULAR WORK DAYS. THAT WAY I CAN AVOID ASSIGNMENTS.
YOUR TEN MINUTES ARE UP.
COUGH COUGH! WHOA, I'D BETTER TAKE SOME SICK TIME.
© 1991 United Feature Syndicate, Inc.

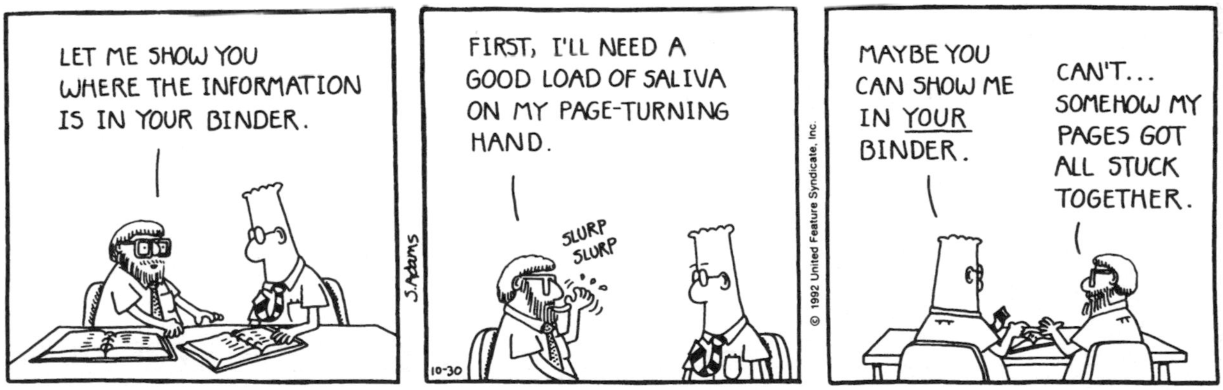
LET ME SHOW YOU WHERE THE INFORMATION IS IN YOUR BINDER.
FIRST, I'LL NEED A GOOD LOAD OF SALIVA ON MY PAGE-TURNING HAND.
SLURP SLURP
MAYBE YOU CAN SHOW ME IN YOUR BINDER.
CAN'T... SOMEHOW MY PAGES GOT ALL STUCK TOGETHER.
© 1992 United Feature Syndicate, Inc.

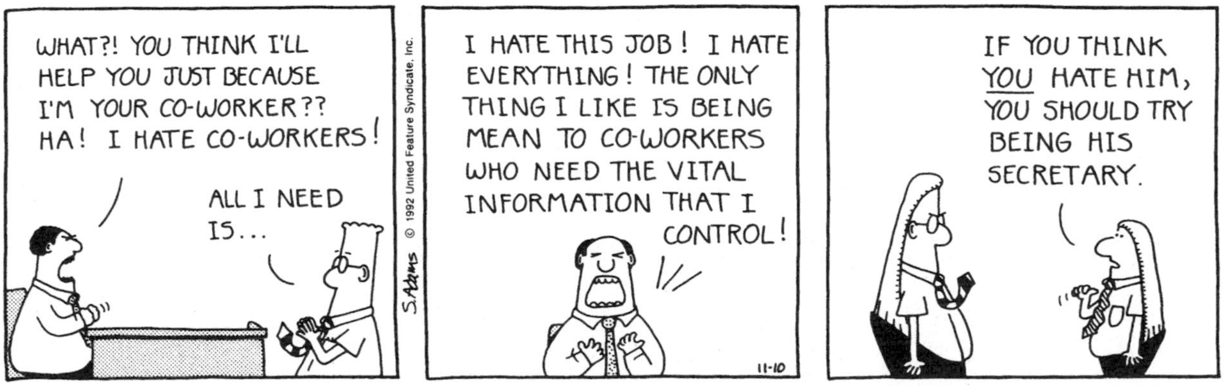
WHAT?! YOU THINK I'LL HELP YOU JUST BECAUSE I'M YOUR CO-WORKER?? HA! I HATE CO-WORKERS!
ALL I NEED IS...
I HATE THIS JOB! I HATE EVERYTHING! THE ONLY THING I LIKE IS BEING MEAN TO CO-WORKERS WHO NEED THE VITAL INFORMATION THAT I CONTROL!
IF YOU THINK YOU HATE HIM, YOU SHOULD TRY BEING HIS SECRETARY.
© 1992 United Feature Syndicate, Inc.

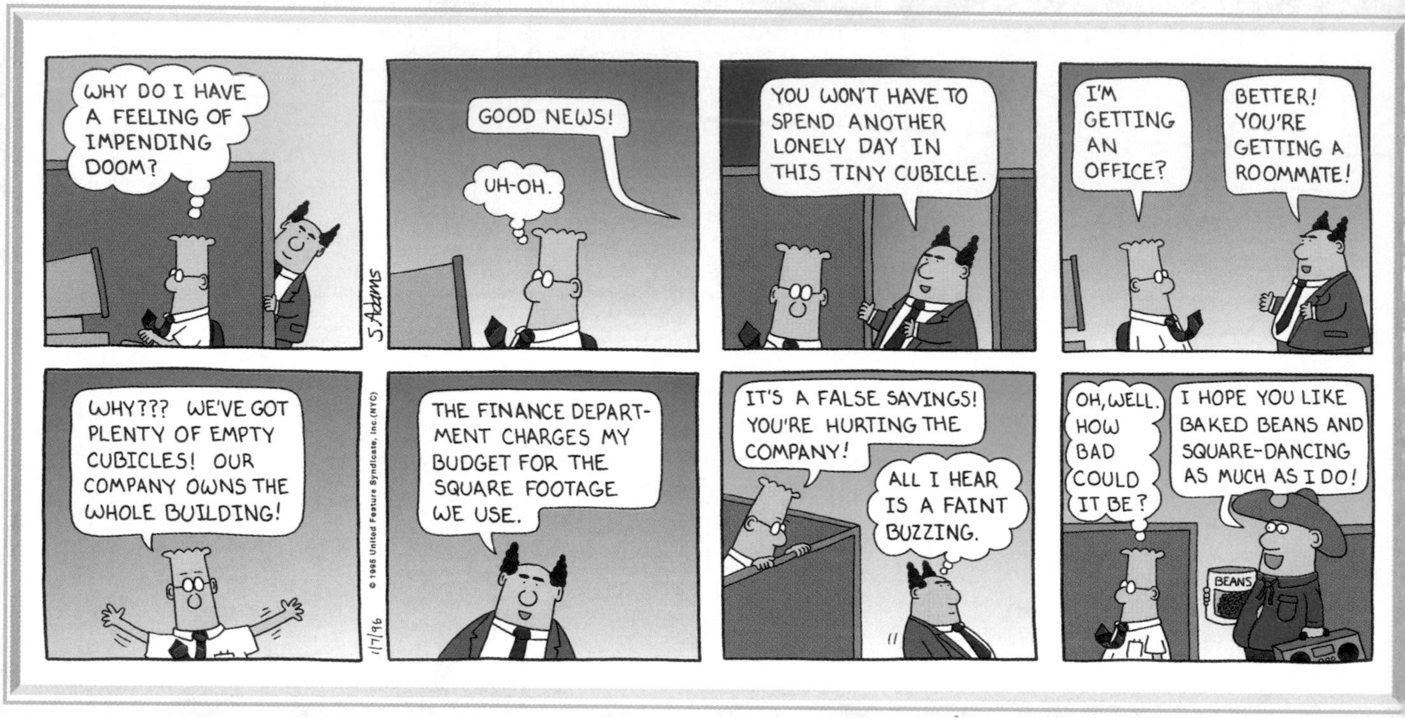
WHY DO I HAVE A FEELING OF IMPENDING DOOM?
GOOD NEWS!
UH-OH.
S. Adams
YOU WON'T HAVE TO SPEND ANOTHER LONELY DAY IN THIS TINY CUBICLE.
I'M GETTING AN OFFICE?
BETTER! YOU'RE GETTING A ROOMMATE!
WHY??? WE'VE GOT PLENTY OF EMPTY CUBICLES! OUR COMPANY OWNS THE WHOLE BUILDING!
© 1995 United Feature Syndicate, Inc.(NYC)
1/7/96
THE FINANCE DEPARTMENT CHARGES MY BUDGET FOR THE SQUARE FOOTAGE WE USE.
IT'S A FALSE SAVINGS! YOU'RE HURTING THE COMPANY!
ALL I HEAR IS A FAINT BUZZING.
OH, WELL. HOW BAD COULD IT BE?
I HOPE YOU LIKE BAKED BEANS AND SQUARE-DANCING AS MUCH AS I DO!
BEANS

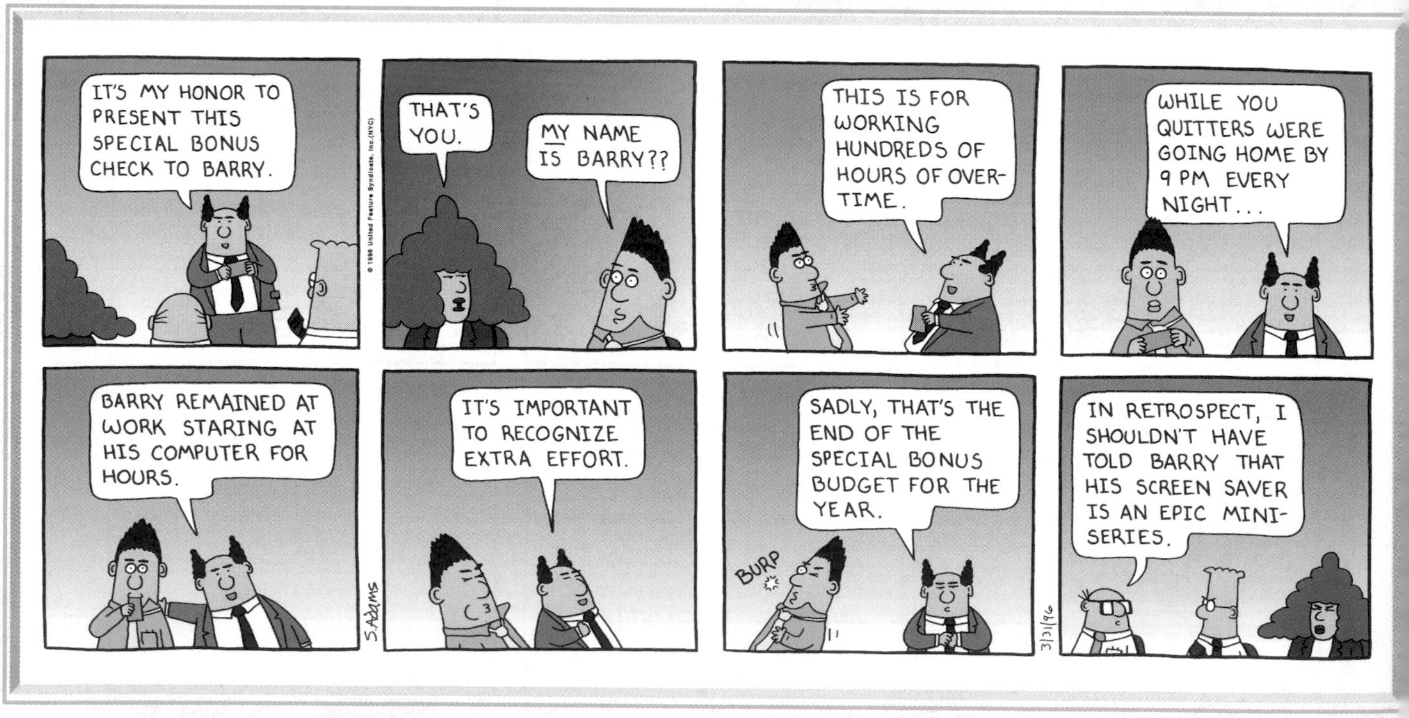
IT'S MY HONOR TO PRESENT THIS SPECIAL BONUS CHECK TO BARRY.
THAT'S YOU.
MY NAME IS BARRY??
THIS IS FOR WORKING HUNDREDS OF HOURS OF OVER-TIME.
WHILE YOU QUITTERS WERE GOING HOME BY 9 PM EVERY NIGHT...
BARRY REMAINED AT WORK STARING AT HIS COMPUTER FOR HOURS.
IT'S IMPORTANT TO RECOGNIZE EXTRA EFFORT.
S. Adams
SADLY, THAT'S THE END OF THE SPECIAL BONUS BUDGET FOR THE YEAR.
BURP
3/31/96
IN RETROSPECT, I SHOULDN'T HAVE TOLD BARRY THAT HIS SCREEN SAVER IS AN EPIC MINI-SERIES.

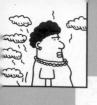

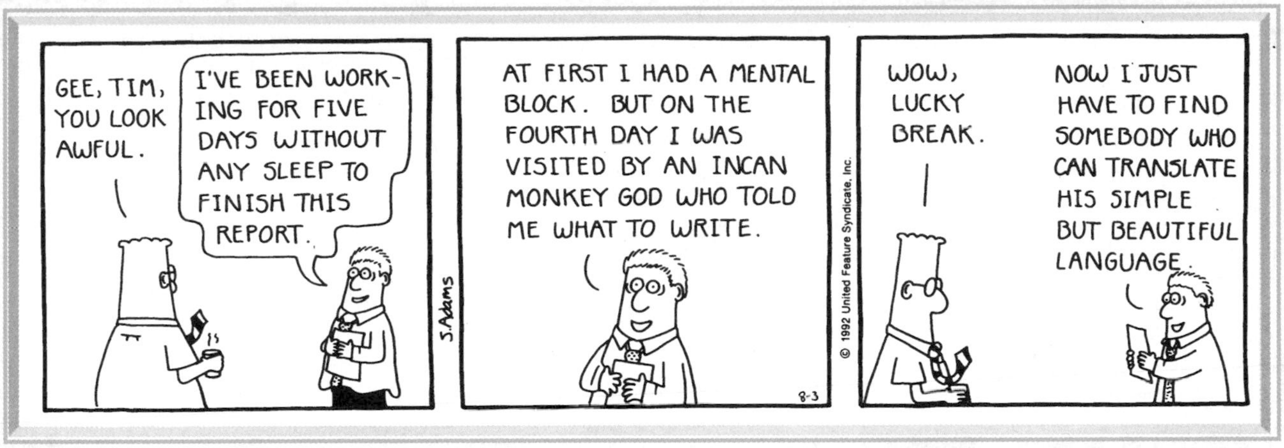
GEE, TIM, YOU LOOK AWFUL.
I'VE BEEN WORKING FOR FIVE DAYS WITHOUT ANY SLEEP TO FINISH THIS REPORT.
AT FIRST I HAD A MENTAL BLOCK. BUT ON THE FOURTH DAY I WAS VISITED BY AN INCAN MONKEY GOD WHO TOLD ME WHAT TO WRITE.
WOW, LUCKY BREAK.
NOW I JUST HAVE TO FIND SOMEBODY WHO CAN TRANSLATE HIS SIMPLE BUT BEAUTIFUL LANGUAGE.
© 1992 United Feature Syndicate, Inc.

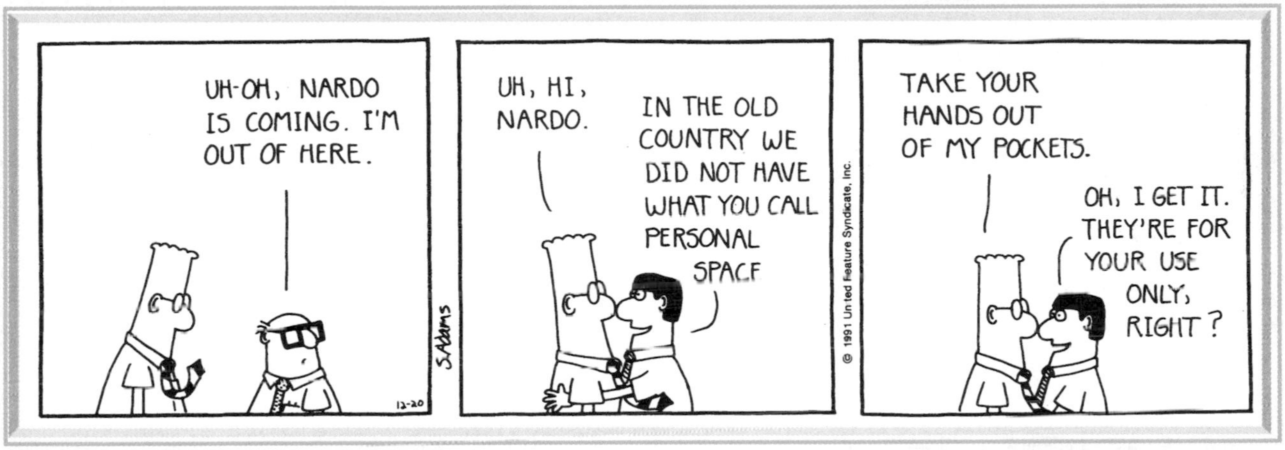
UH-OH, NARDO IS COMING. I'M OUT OF HERE.
UH, HI, NARDO.
IN THE OLD COUNTRY WE DID NOT HAVE WHAT YOU CALL PERSONAL SPACE
TAKE YOUR HANDS OUT OF MY POCKETS.
OH, I GET IT. THEY'RE FOR YOUR USE ONLY, RIGHT?
© 1991 United Feature Syndicate, Inc.

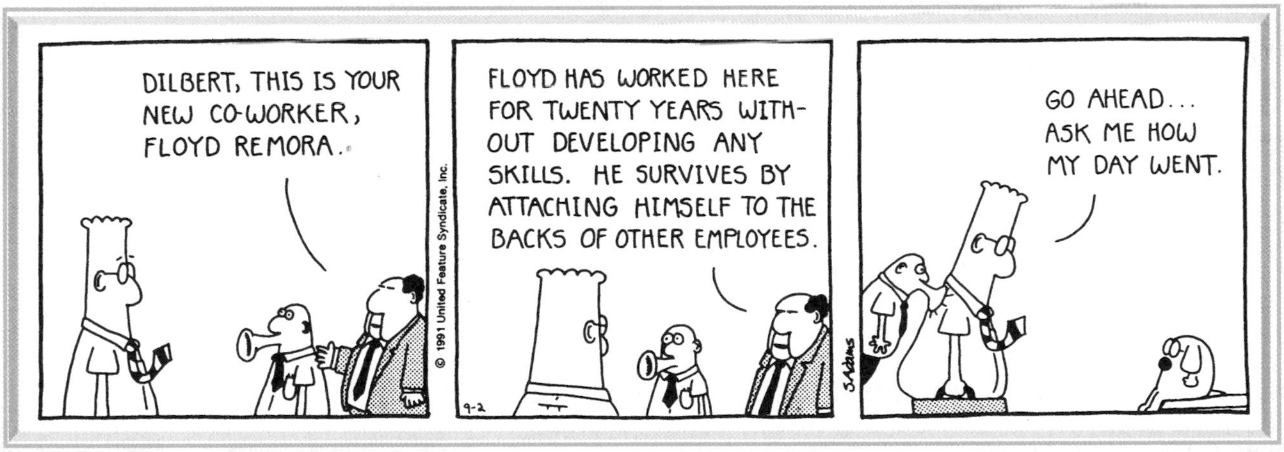
DILBERT, THIS IS YOUR NEW CO-WORKER, FLOYD REMORA.
FLOYD HAS WORKED HERE FOR TWENTY YEARS WITHOUT DEVELOPING ANY SKILLS. HE SURVIVES BY ATTACHING HIMSELF TO THE BACKS OF OTHER EMPLOYEES.
GO AHEAD... ASK ME HOW MY DAY WENT.
© 1991 United Feature Syndicate, Inc.

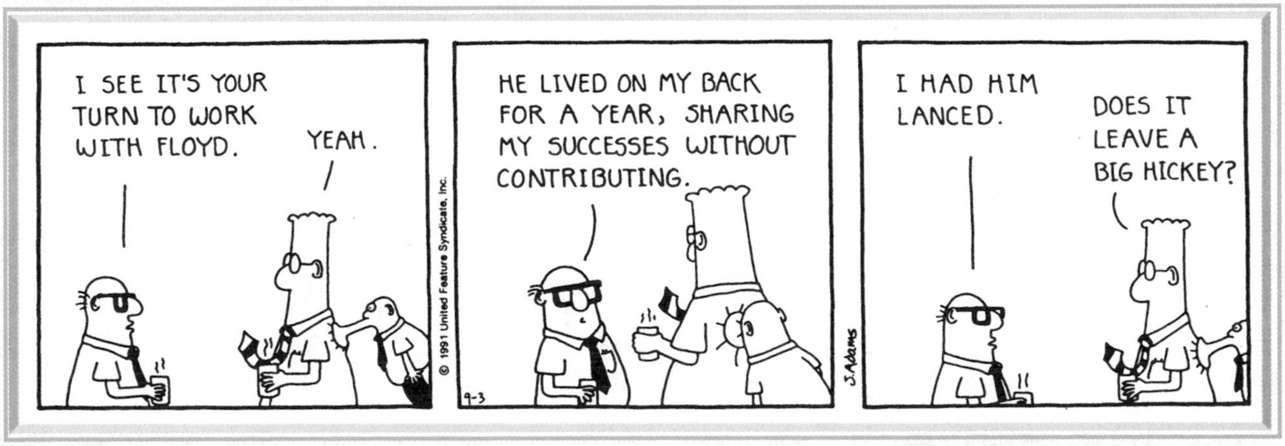
I SEE IT'S YOUR TURN TO WORK WITH FLOYD.
YEAH.
HE LIVED ON MY BACK FOR A YEAR, SHARING MY SUCCESSES WITHOUT CONTRIBUTING.
I HAD HIM LANCED.
DOES IT LEAVE A BIG HICKEY?
© 1991 United Feature Syndicate, Inc.

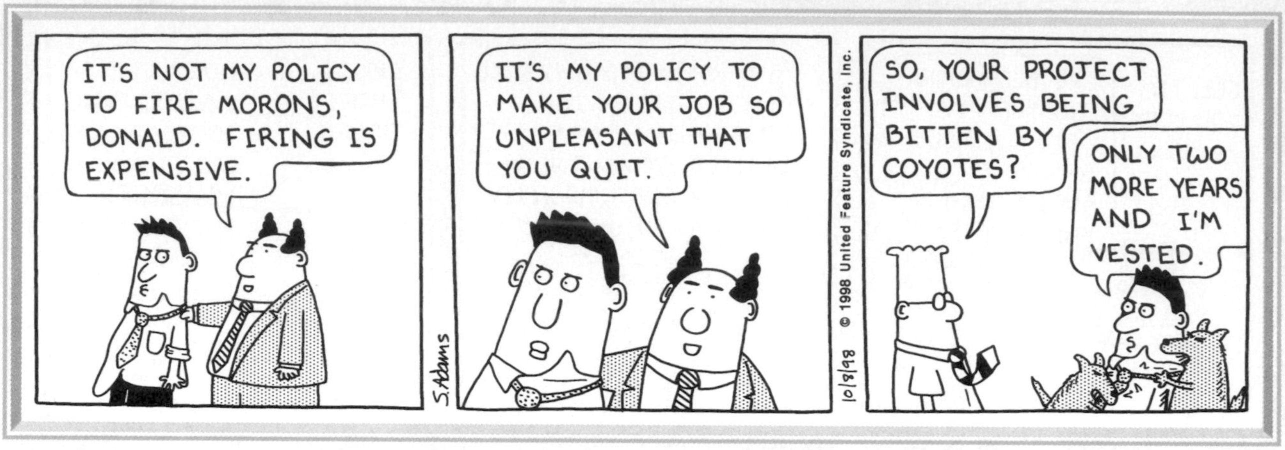

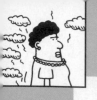

IT'S NOT MY POLICY TO FIRE MORONS, DONALD. FIRING IS EXPENSIVE.
IT'S MY POLICY TO MAKE YOUR JOB SO UNPLEASANT THAT YOU QUIT.
S.Adams
10/8/98
© 1998 United Feature Syndicate, Inc.
SO, YOUR PROJECT INVOLVES BEING BITTEN BY COYOTES?
ONLY TWO MORE YEARS AND I'M VESTED.

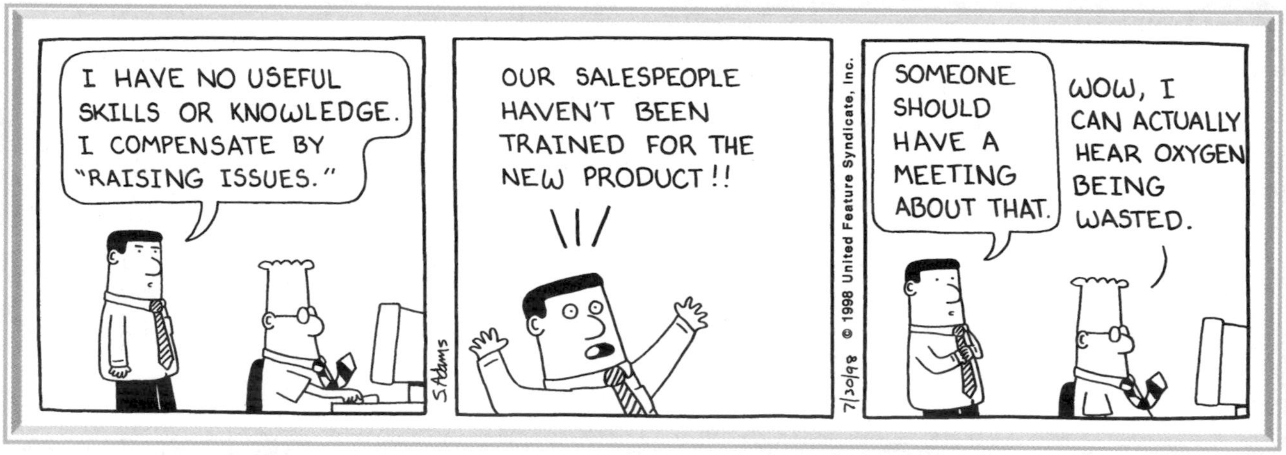

I HAVE NO USEFUL SKILLS OR KNOWLEDGE. I COMPENSATE BY "RAISING ISSUES."
OUR SALESPEOPLE HAVEN'T BEEN TRAINED FOR THE NEW PRODUCT!!
S.Adams
7/30/98
© 1998 United Feature Syndicate, Inc.
SOMEONE SHOULD HAVE A MEETING ABOUT THAT.
WOW, I CAN ACTUALLY HEAR OXYGEN BEING WASTED.

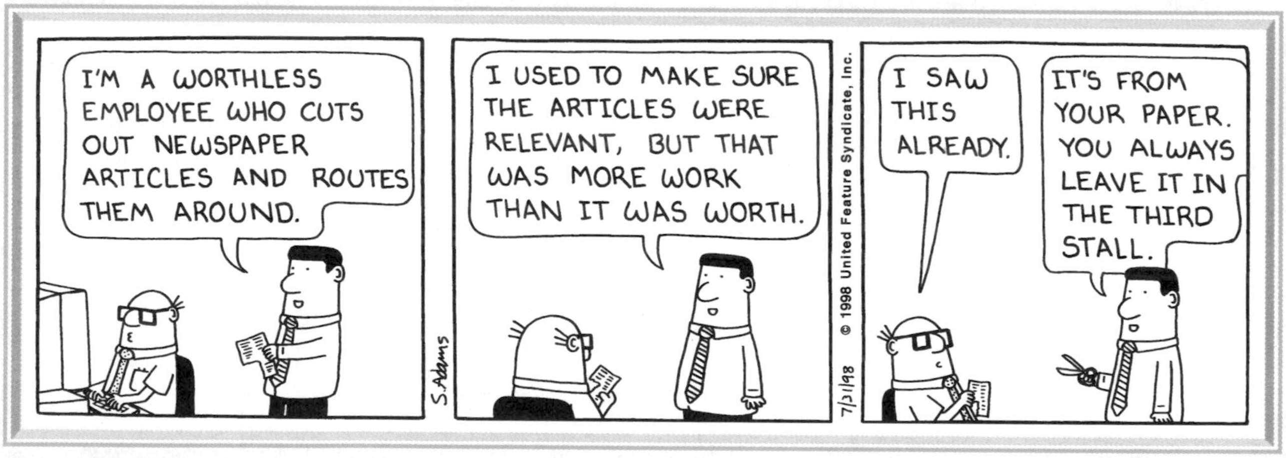

I'M A WORTHLESS EMPLOYEE WHO CUTS OUT NEWSPAPER ARTICLES AND ROUTES THEM AROUND.
I USED TO MAKE SURE THE ARTICLES WERE RELEVANT, BUT THAT WAS MORE WORK THAN IT WAS WORTH.
S.Adams
7/31/98
© 1998 United Feature Syndicate, Inc.
I SAW THIS ALREADY.
IT'S FROM YOUR PAPER. YOU ALWAYS LEAVE IT IN THE THIRD STALL.

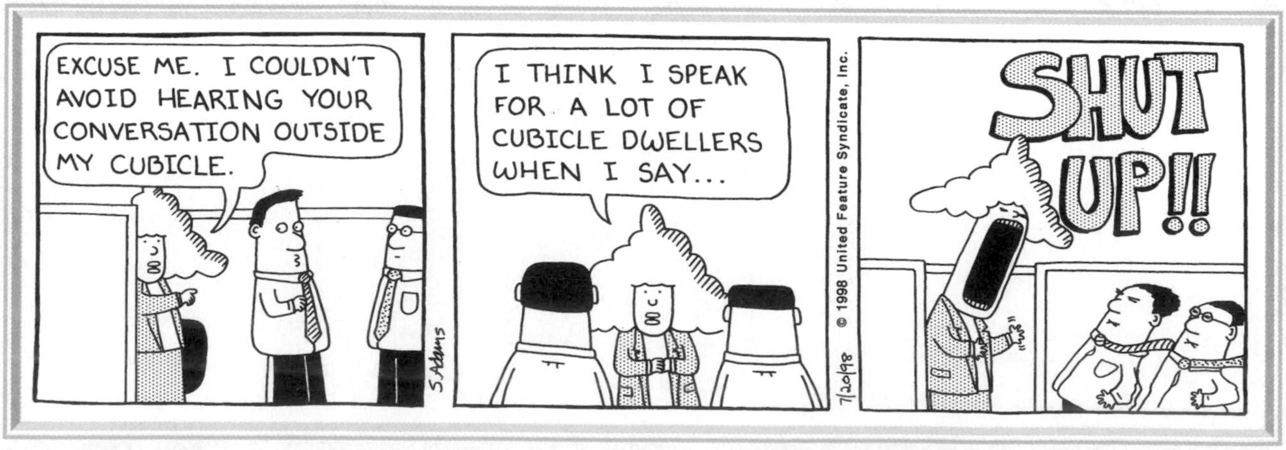

EXCUSE ME. I COULDN'T AVOID HEARING YOUR CONVERSATION OUTSIDE MY CUBICLE.
I THINK I SPEAK FOR A LOT OF CUBICLE DWELLERS WHEN I SAY...
S.Adams
7/20/98
© 1998 United Feature Syndicate, Inc.
SHUT UP!!

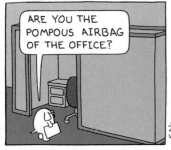

ARE YOU THE POMPOUS AIRBAG OF THE OFFICE?
INDEED.
I'VE BEEN ASKED TO DEFLATE YOU.
MY SOURCES TELL ME THAT YOU COMBINE ARROGANCE WITH TRIVIA AND TRY TO PASS IT OFF AS INTELLIGENCE.
THAT'S BECAUSE I'M SURROUNDED BY FOOLS WHO DON'T EVEN KNOW THE CAPITAL OF ELBONIA!
I HAVE A SIGNED STATEMENT FROM YOUR WIFE...
...THAT YOU PUT WET LAUNDRY IN THE OVEN LAST NIGHT.
THAT EXPLAINS THE CHEWY CASSEROLE SHE SERVED ME THIS MORNING.
S.Adams
5/17/98 © 1998 United Feature Syndicate, Inc.

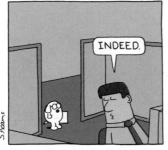

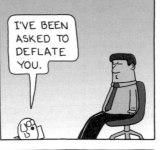

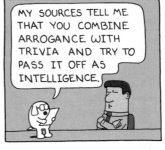

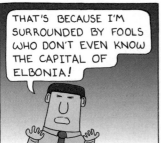

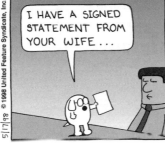

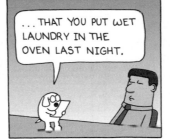

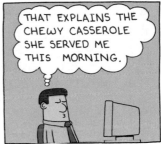

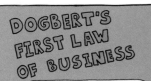

DOGBERT'S FIRST LAW OF BUSINESS
REALITY IS ALWAYS CONTROLLED BY THE PEOPLE WHO ARE MOST INSANE.
6/14/98 © 1998 United Feature Syndicate, Inc.
EXAMPLE
THANKS FOR AGREEING TO WORK ON MY PROJECT.
I NEVER AGREED TO WORK ON YOUR PROJECT.
YOU CAN'T CHANGE YOUR MIND NOW! IT'S TOO LATE TO GET SOMEONE ELSE!
UM... I'M NOT CHANGING MY MIND. I CLEARLY SAID I WOULD NOT WORK ON YOUR PROJECT.
YOU LYING WEASEL! I'LL RUIN YOU!!
OKAY! OKAY! I'LL WORK ON YOUR PROJECT!
WALLY, THANKS FOR AGREEING TO DONATE YOUR COMPUTER TO MY PROJECT.
WHAT?
S.Adams

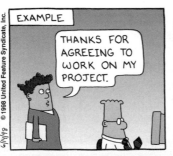

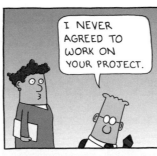

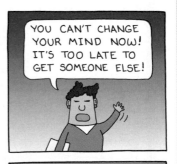

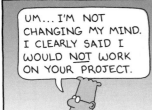

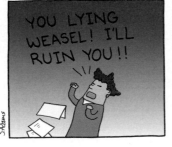

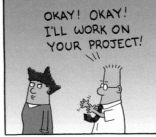

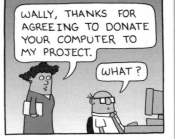

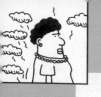

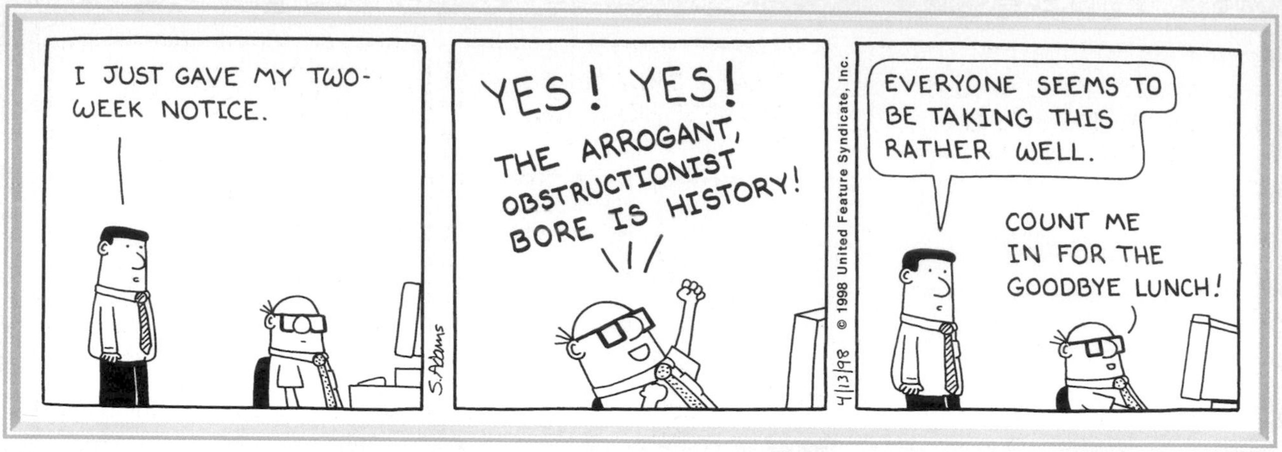
I JUST GAVE MY TWO-WEEK NOTICE.
S. Adams
YES! YES! THE ARROGANT, OBSTRUCTIONIST BORE IS HISTORY!
4/13/98 © 1998 United Feature Syndicate, Inc.
EVERYONE SEEMS TO BE TAKING THIS RATHER WELL.
COUNT ME IN FOR THE GOODBYE LUNCH!

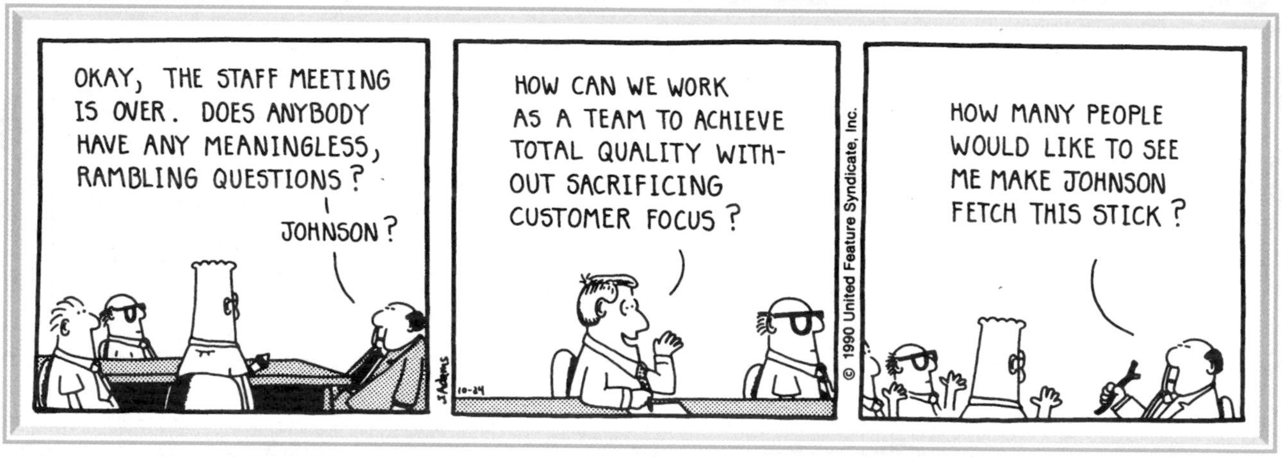
OKAY, THE STAFF MEETING IS OVER. DOES ANYBODY HAVE ANY MEANINGLESS, RAMBLING QUESTIONS?
JOHNSON?
S. Adams 10-24
HOW CAN WE WORK AS A TEAM TO ACHIEVE TOTAL QUALITY WITHOUT SACRIFICING CUSTOMER FOCUS?
© 1990 United Feature Syndicate, Inc.
HOW MANY PEOPLE WOULD LIKE TO SEE ME MAKE JOHNSON FETCH THIS STICK?

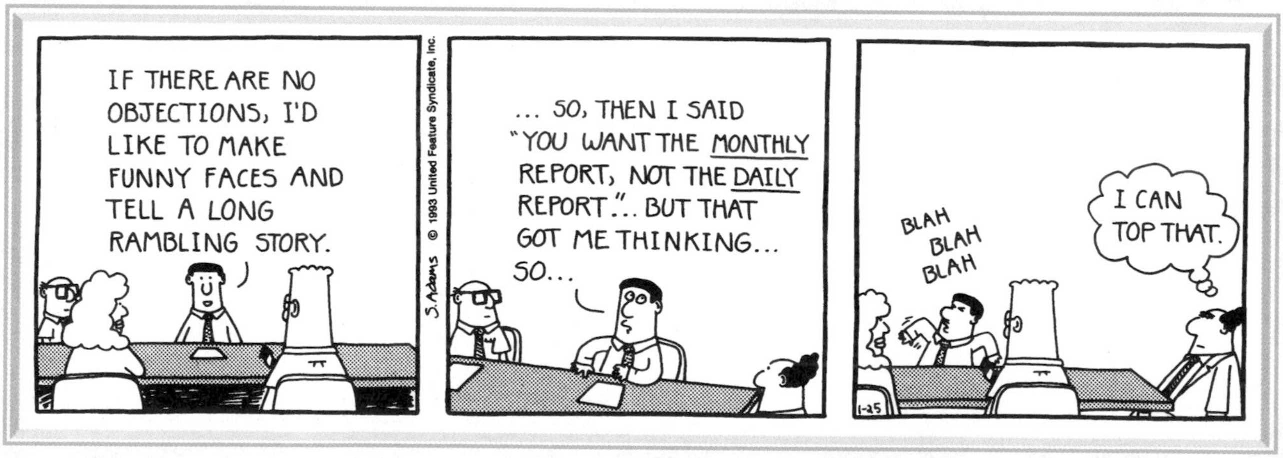
IF THERE ARE NO OBJECTIONS, I'D LIKE TO MAKE FUNNY FACES AND TELL A LONG RAMBLING STORY.
S. Adams © 1993 United Feature Syndicate, Inc.
... SO, THEN I SAID "YOU WANT THE MONTHLY REPORT, NOT THE DAILY REPORT."... BUT THAT GOT ME THINKING... SO...
BLAH BLAH BLAH
I CAN TOP THAT.
1-25

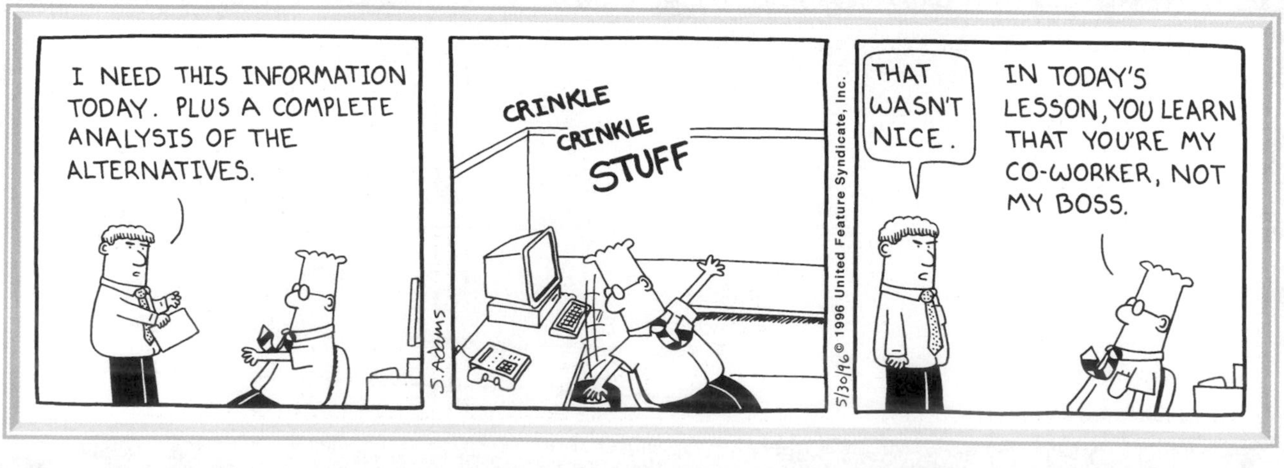
I NEED THIS INFORMATION TODAY. PLUS A COMPLETE ANALYSIS OF THE ALTERNATIVES.
S. Adams
CRINKLE
CRINKLE
STUFF
5/30/96 © 1996 United Feature Syndicate, Inc.
THAT WASN'T NICE.
IN TODAY'S LESSON, YOU LEARN THAT YOU'RE MY CO-WORKER, NOT MY BOSS.

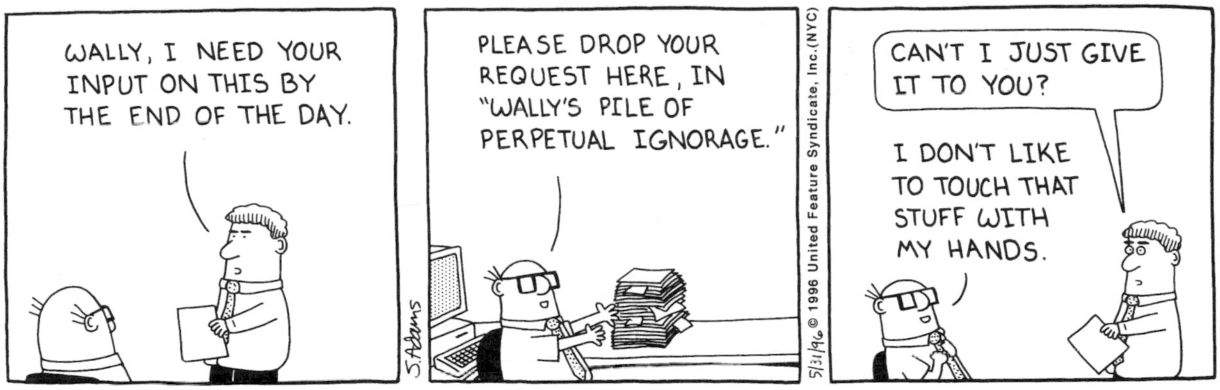
WALLY, I NEED YOUR INPUT ON THIS BY THE END OF THE DAY.
PLEASE DROP YOUR REQUEST HERE, IN "WALLY'S PILE OF PERPETUAL IGNORAGE."
CAN'T I JUST GIVE IT TO YOU?
I DON'T LIKE TO TOUCH THAT STUFF WITH MY HANDS.
5/31/96 © 1996 United Feature Syndicate, Inc.(NYC)

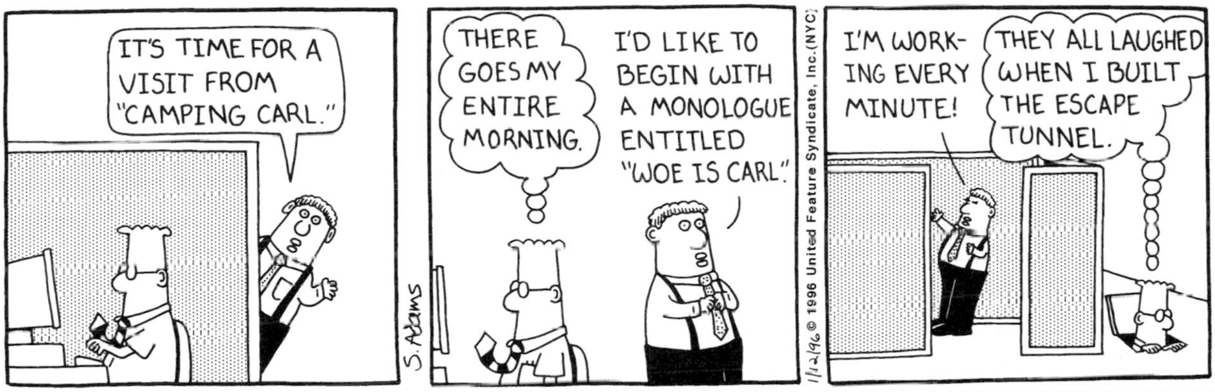
IT'S TIME FOR A VISIT FROM "CAMPING CARL."
THERE GOES MY ENTIRE MORNING.
I'D LIKE TO BEGIN WITH A MONOLOGUE ENTITLED "WOE IS CARL."
I'M WORKING EVERY MINUTE!
THEY ALL LAUGHED WHEN I BUILT THE ESCAPE TUNNEL.
1/12/96 © 1996 United Feature Syndicate, Inc.(NYC)

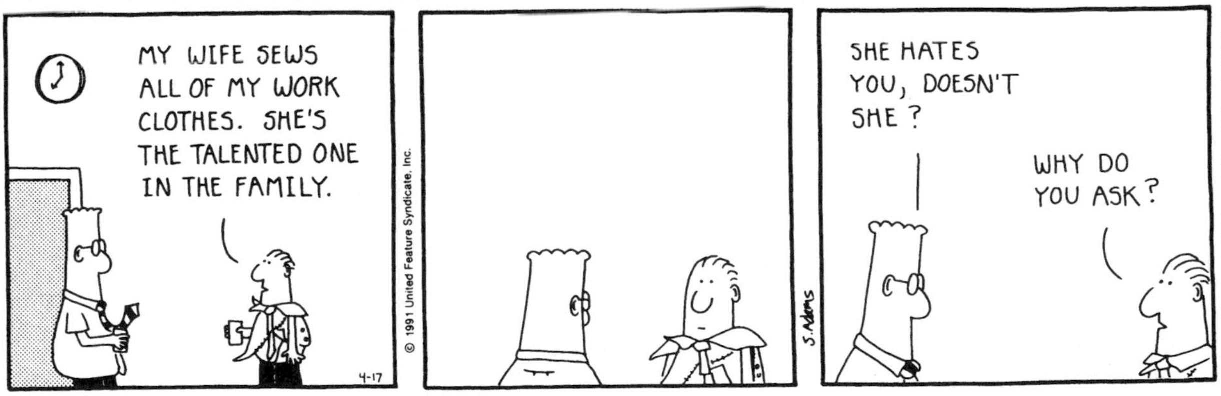
MY WIFE SEWS ALL OF MY WORK CLOTHES. SHE'S THE TALENTED ONE IN THE FAMILY.
4-17
© 1991 United Feature Syndicate, Inc.
SHE HATES YOU, DOESN'T SHE?
WHY DO YOU ASK?

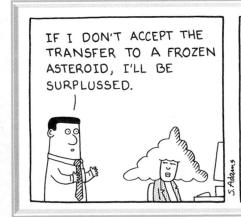

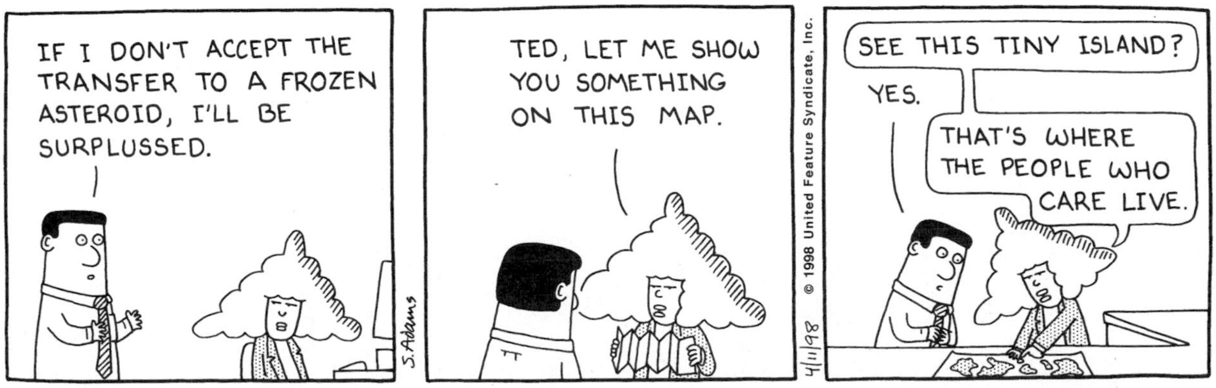
IF I DON'T ACCEPT THE TRANSFER TO A FROZEN ASTEROID, I'LL BE SURPLUSSED.
TED, LET ME SHOW YOU SOMETHING ON THIS MAP.
4/11/98 © 1998 United Feature Syndicate, Inc.
SEE THIS TINY ISLAND?
YES.
THAT'S WHERE THE PEOPLE WHO CARE LIVE.

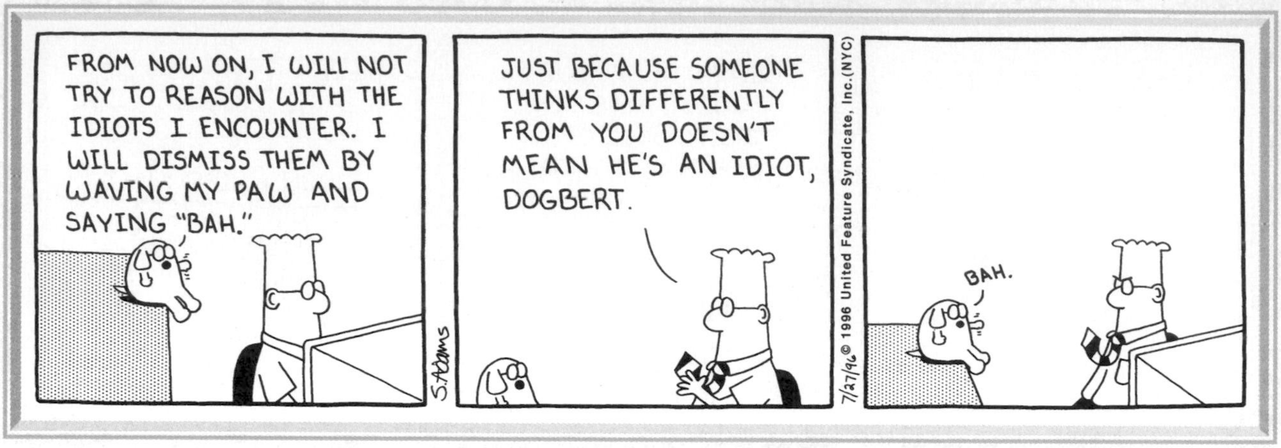
FROM NOW ON, I WILL NOT TRY TO REASON WITH THE IDIOTS I ENCOUNTER. I WILL DISMISS THEM BY WAVING MY PAW AND SAYING "BAH."
S. Adams
JUST BECAUSE SOMEONE THINKS DIFFERENTLY FROM YOU DOESN'T MEAN HE'S AN IDIOT, DOGBERT.
7/27/96 © 1996 United Feature Syndicate, Inc.(NYC)
BAH.

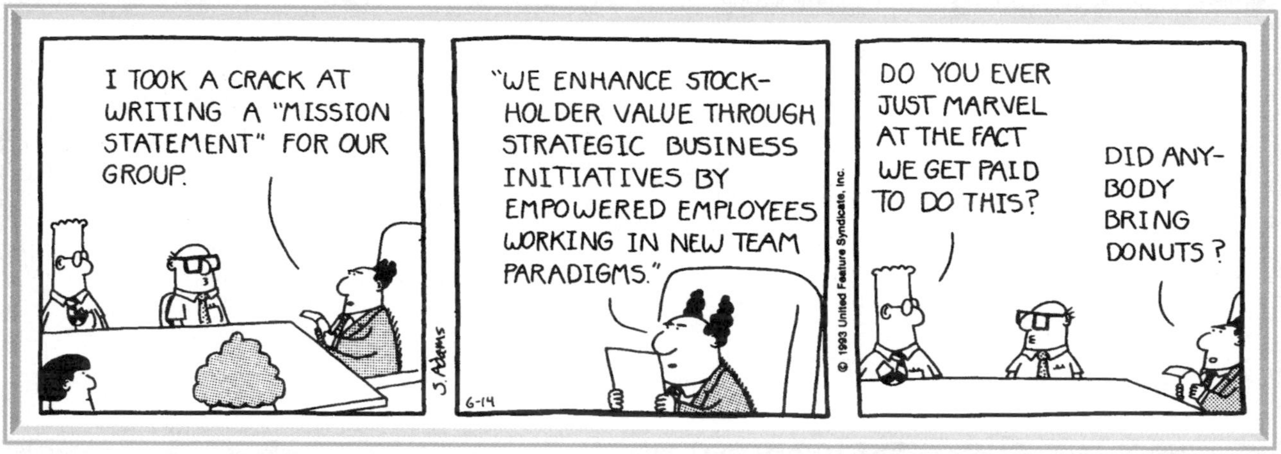
I TOOK A CRACK AT WRITING A "MISSION STATEMENT" FOR OUR GROUP.
S. Adams
6-14
"WE ENHANCE STOCK-HOLDER VALUE THROUGH STRATEGIC BUSINESS INITIATIVES BY EMPOWERED EMPLOYEES WORKING IN NEW TEAM PARADIGMS."
© 1993 United Feature Syndicate, Inc.
DO YOU EVER JUST MARVEL AT THE FACT WE GET PAID TO DO THIS?
DID ANY-BODY BRING DONUTS?

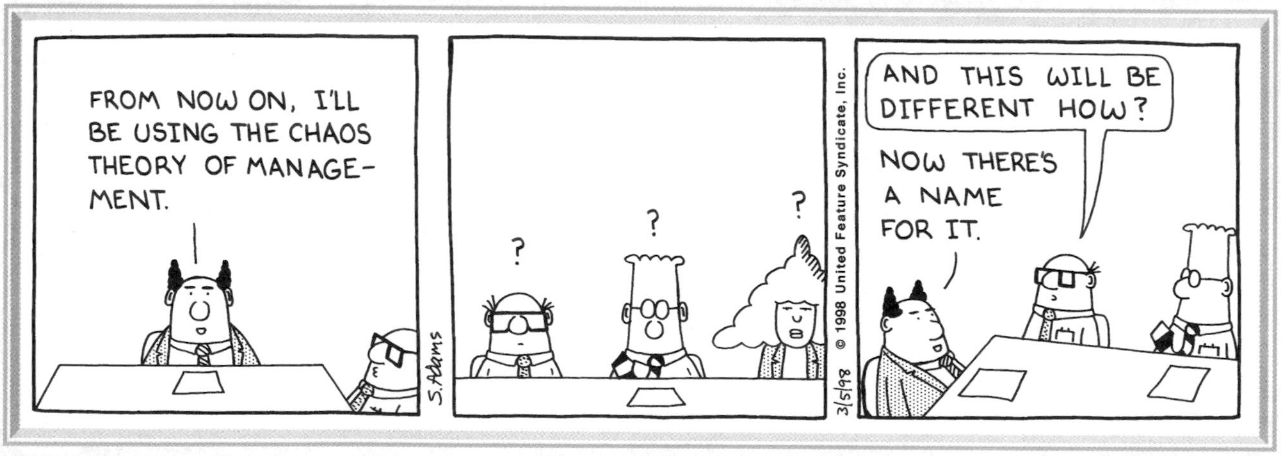
FROM NOW ON, I'LL BE USING THE CHAOS THEORY OF MANAGE-MENT.
S. Adams
? ? ?
3/5/98 © 1998 United Feature Syndicate, Inc.
AND THIS WILL BE DIFFERENT HOW?
NOW THERE'S A NAME FOR IT.

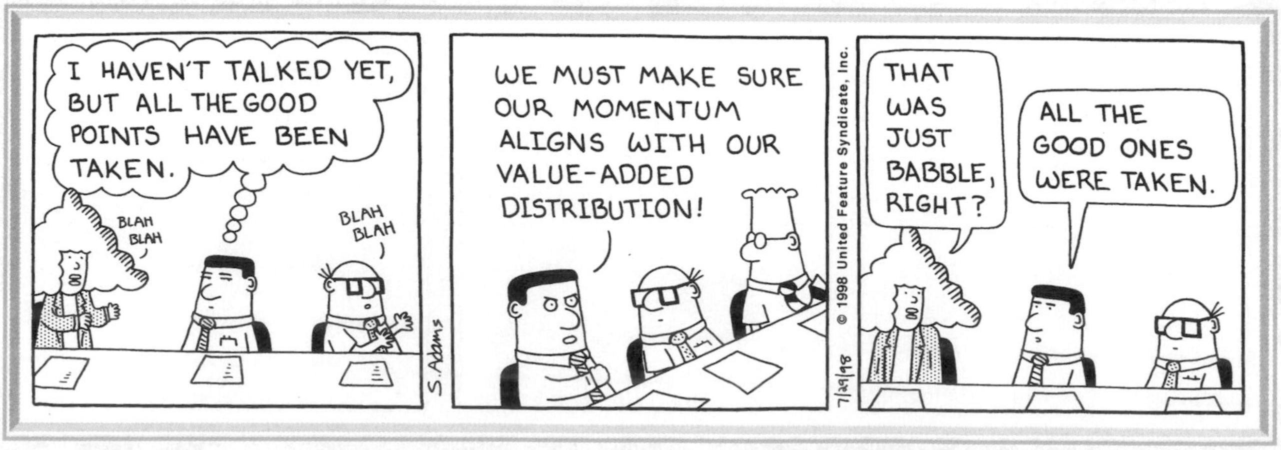
I HAVEN'T TALKED YET, BUT ALL THE GOOD POINTS HAVE BEEN TAKEN.
BLAH BLAH
BLAH BLAH
S. Adams
WE MUST MAKE SURE OUR MOMENTUM ALIGNS WITH OUR VALUE-ADDED DISTRIBUTION!
7/29/98 © 1998 United Feature Syndicate, Inc.
THAT WAS JUST BABBLE, RIGHT?
ALL THE GOOD ONES WERE TAKEN.

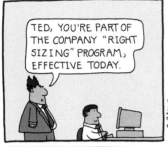

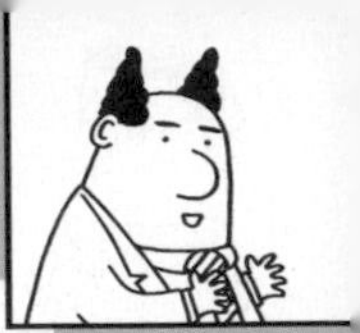

TED, YOU'RE PART OF THE COMPANY "RIGHT SIZING" PROGRAM, EFFECTIVE TODAY.
THANK YOU! IT'S NICE TO GET POSITIVE FEEDBACK FROM THE BOSS!
IT'S NOT FEEDBACK. I'M SAYING YOUR POSITION HAS BEEN "MANAGEMENT ADJUSTED."
SOUNDS GREAT! IS THERE A RAISE INVOLVED?
LISTEN TO ME!! YOU'RE PART OF "MANAGER ATTRITION" STARTING RIGHT NOW!
WOW! IS THAT THE FAST-TRACK PROGRAM FOR MANAGERS?
I HEARD THAT TED GOT PICKED FOR THE "MANAGER ATTRITION" PROGRAM.
WHY NOT US?
SO UNLESS YOU PUT US ON THE "MANAGER ATTRITION" PROGRAM TOO, WE QUIT!
THERE'S NEVER A FLAMETHROWER HANDY WHEN YOU NEED IT.
S. Adams
© 1993 United Feature Syndicate, Inc.

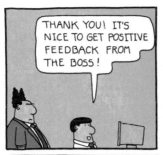

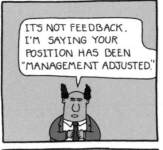

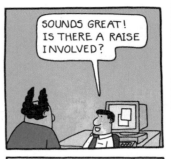

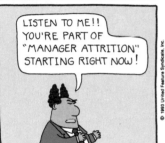

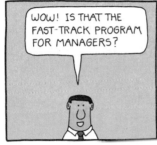

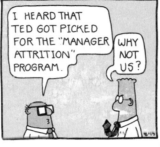

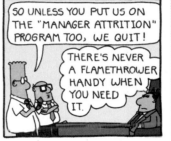

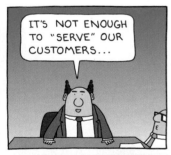

IT'S NOT ENOUGH TO "SERVE" OUR CUSTOMERS...
WE MUST DELIGHT THEM!
YOU MEAN WE HAVE TO STOP PRICE-GOUGING?
NO, I THINK WE CAN STILL DO THAT.
OOH OOH! I KNOW!
WE COULD STOP SELLING PRODUCTS WITH KNOWN DEFECTS.
I'M TALKING ABOUT CUSTOMERS, NOT PRODUCTS!!
DO YOU FEEL LIKE DELIGHTING CUSTOMERS?
I BARELY HAVE THE EMPATHY TO PITY THEM.
10/11/98 © 1998 United Feature Syndicate, Inc.

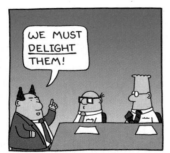

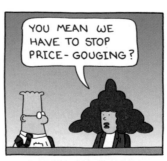

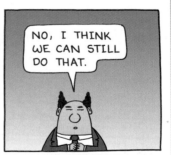

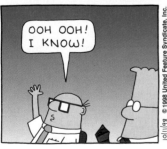

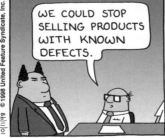

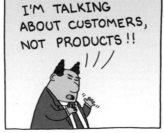

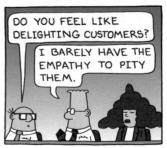

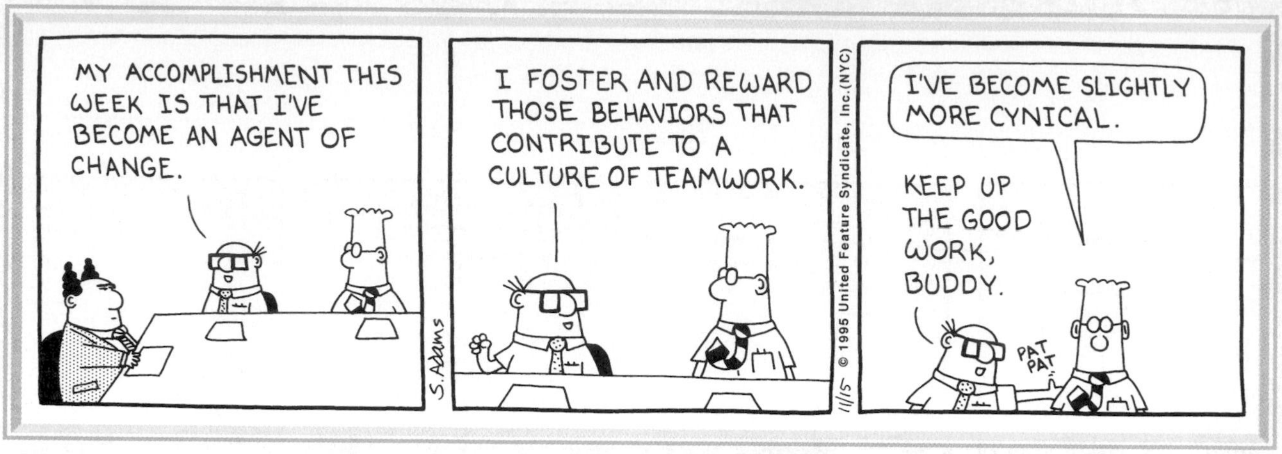
MY ACCOMPLISHMENT THIS WEEK IS THAT I'VE BECOME AN AGENT OF CHANGE.
I FOSTER AND REWARD THOSE BEHAVIORS THAT CONTRIBUTE TO A CULTURE OF TEAMWORK.
I'VE BECOME SLIGHTLY MORE CYNICAL.
KEEP UP THE GOOD WORK, BUDDY.
PAT PAT
S. Adams
11/15 © 1995 United Feature Syndicate, Inc.(NYC)

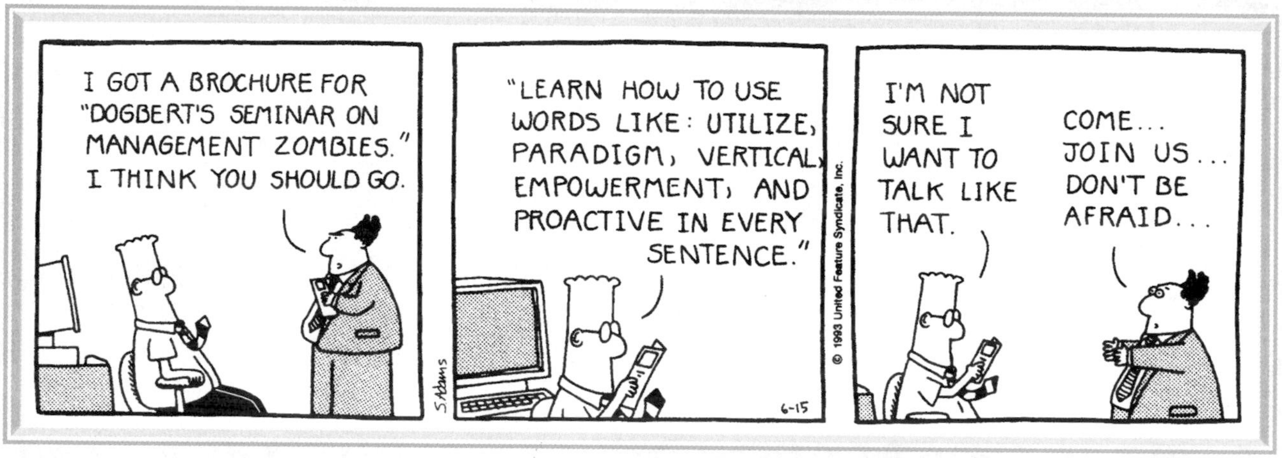
I GOT A BROCHURE FOR "DOGBERT'S SEMINAR ON MANAGEMENT ZOMBIES." I THINK YOU SHOULD GO.
"LEARN HOW TO USE WORDS LIKE: UTILIZE, PARADIGM, VERTICAL, EMPOWERMENT, AND PROACTIVE IN EVERY SENTENCE."
I'M NOT SURE I WANT TO TALK LIKE THAT.
COME... JOIN US... DON'T BE AFRAID...
S. Adams
6-15
© 1993 United Feature Syndicate, Inc.

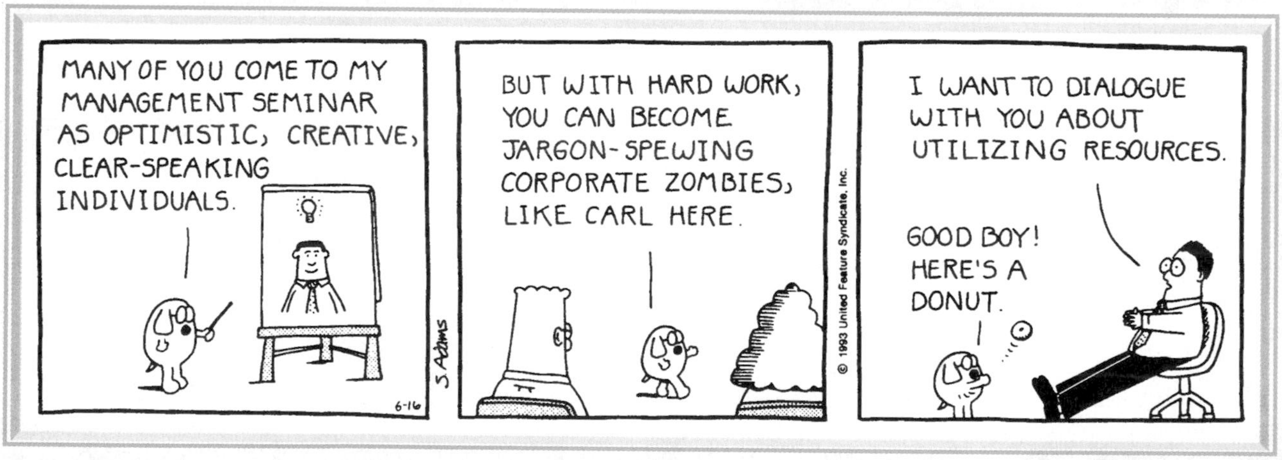
MANY OF YOU COME TO MY MANAGEMENT SEMINAR AS OPTIMISTIC, CREATIVE, CLEAR-SPEAKING INDIVIDUALS.
BUT WITH HARD WORK, YOU CAN BECOME JARGON-SPEWING CORPORATE ZOMBIES, LIKE CARL HERE.
I WANT TO DIALOGUE WITH YOU ABOUT UTILIZING RESOURCES.
GOOD BOY! HERE'S A DONUT.
S. Adams
6-16
© 1993 United Feature Syndicate, Inc.

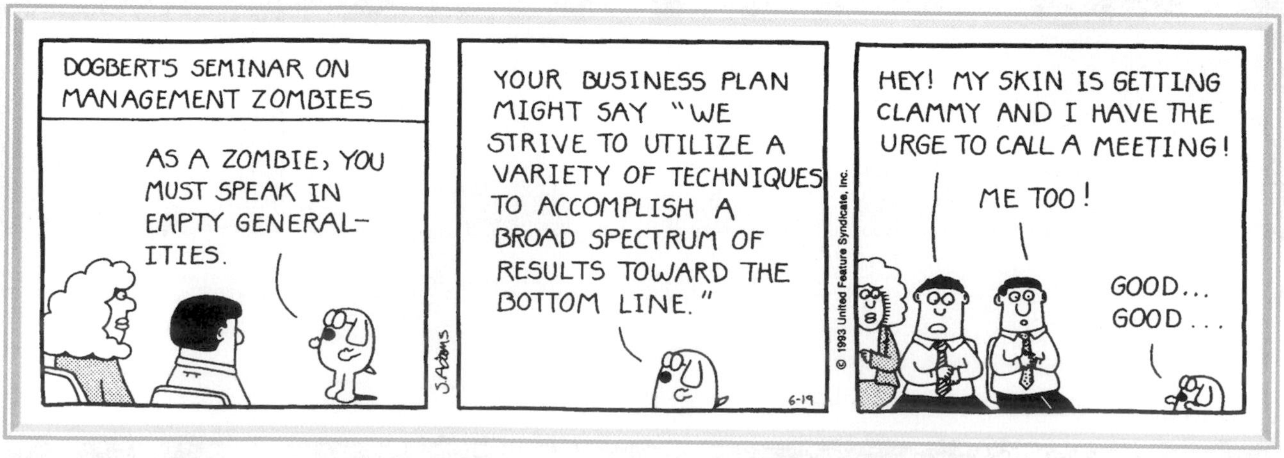
DOGBERT'S SEMINAR ON MANAGEMENT ZOMBIES
AS A ZOMBIE, YOU MUST SPEAK IN EMPTY GENERAL-ITIES.
YOUR BUSINESS PLAN MIGHT SAY "WE STRIVE TO UTILIZE A VARIETY OF TECHNIQUES TO ACCOMPLISH A BROAD SPECTRUM OF RESULTS TOWARD THE BOTTOM LINE."
HEY! MY SKIN IS GETTING CLAMMY AND I HAVE THE URGE TO CALL A MEETING!
ME TOO!
GOOD... GOOD...
S. Adams
6-19
© 1993 United Feature Syndicate, Inc.

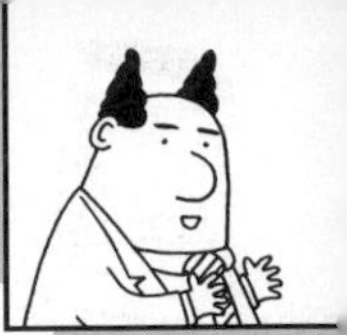

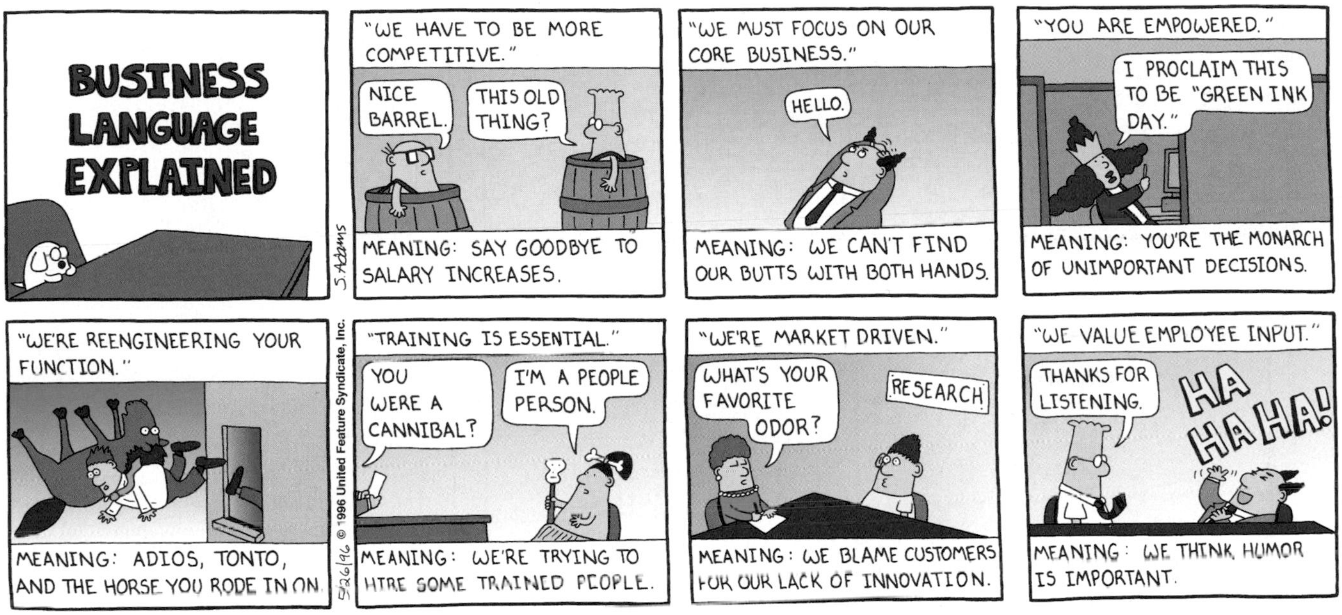
BUSINESS LANGUAGE EXPLAINED
"WE HAVE TO BE MORE COMPETITIVE."
NICE BARREL.
THIS OLD THING?
MEANING: SAY GOODBYE TO SALARY INCREASES.
"WE MUST FOCUS ON OUR CORE BUSINESS."
HELLO.
MEANING: WE CAN'T FIND OUR BUTTS WITH BOTH HANDS.
"YOU ARE EMPOWERED."
I PROCLAIM THIS TO BE "GREEN INK DAY."
MEANING: YOU'RE THE MONARCH OF UNIMPORTANT DECISIONS.
"WE'RE REENGINEERING YOUR FUNCTION."
MEANING: ADIOS, TONTO, AND THE HORSE YOU RODE IN ON.
S. Adams
5/26/96 © 1996 United Feature Syndicate, Inc.
"TRAINING IS ESSENTIAL."
YOU WERE A CANNIBAL?
I'M A PEOPLE PERSON.
MEANING: WE'RE TRYING TO HIRE SOME TRAINED PEOPLE.
"WE'RE MARKET DRIVEN."
WHAT'S YOUR FAVORITE ODOR?
RESEARCH
MEANING: WE BLAME CUSTOMERS FOR OUR LACK OF INNOVATION.
"WE VALUE EMPLOYEE INPUT."
THANKS FOR LISTENING.
HA HA HA!
MEANING: WE THINK HUMOR IS IMPORTANT.

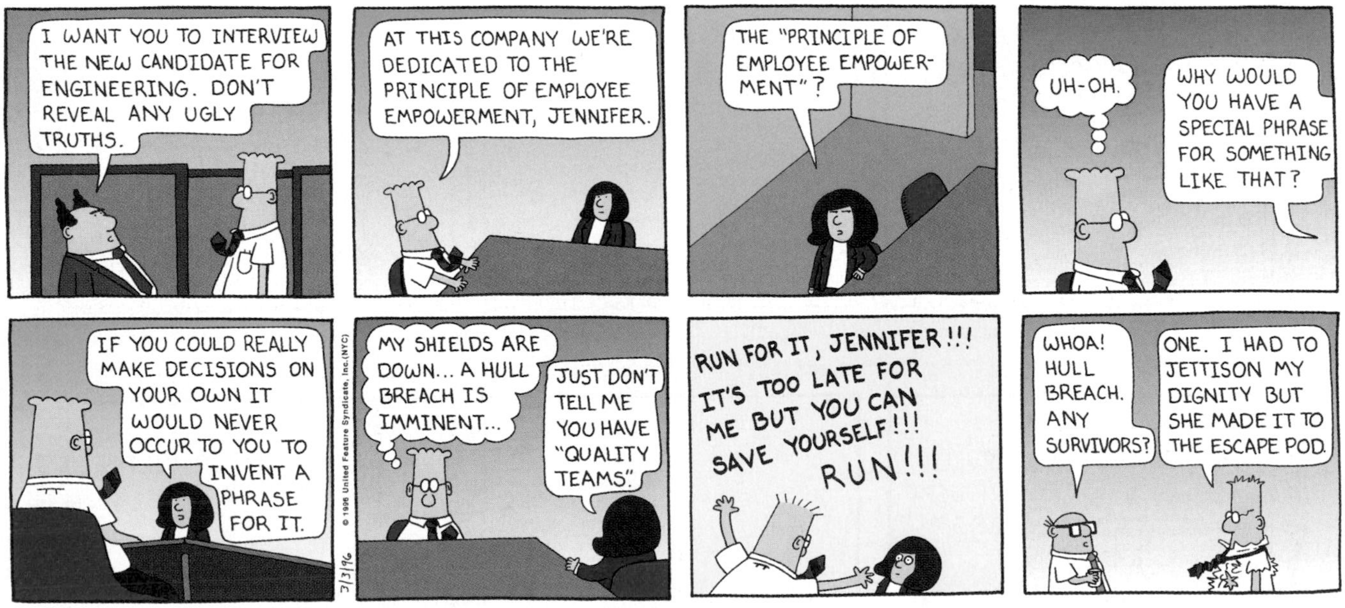
I WANT YOU TO INTERVIEW THE NEW CANDIDATE FOR ENGINEERING. DON'T REVEAL ANY UGLY TRUTHS.
AT THIS COMPANY WE'RE DEDICATED TO THE PRINCIPLE OF EMPLOYEE EMPOWERMENT, JENNIFER.
THE "PRINCIPLE OF EMPLOYEE EMPOWERMENT"?
UH-OH.
WHY WOULD YOU HAVE A SPECIAL PHRASE FOR SOMETHING LIKE THAT?
IF YOU COULD REALLY MAKE DECISIONS ON YOUR OWN IT WOULD NEVER OCCUR TO YOU TO INVENT A PHRASE FOR IT.
7/3/96 © 1996 United Feature Syndicate, Inc.(NYC)
MY SHIELDS ARE DOWN... A HULL BREACH IS IMMINENT...
JUST DON'T TELL ME YOU HAVE "QUALITY TEAMS."
RUN FOR IT, JENNIFER!!! IT'S TOO LATE FOR ME BUT YOU CAN SAVE YOURSELF!!! RUN!!!
WHOA! HULL BREACH. ANY SURVIVORS?
ONE. I HAD TO JETTISON MY DIGNITY BUT SHE MADE IT TO THE ESCAPE POD.

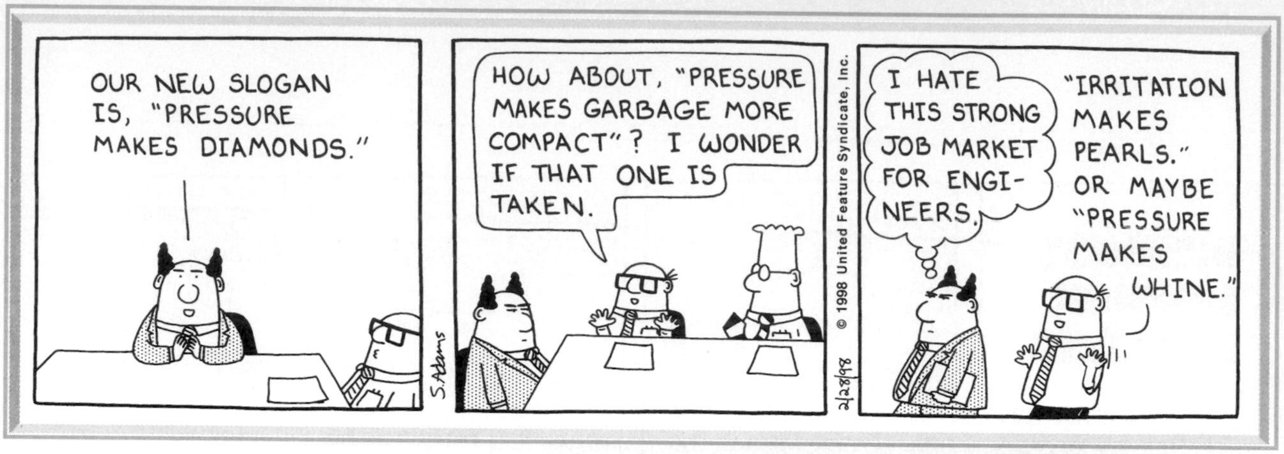
OUR NEW SLOGAN IS, "PRESSURE MAKES DIAMONDS."
HOW ABOUT, "PRESSURE MAKES GARBAGE MORE COMPACT"? I WONDER IF THAT ONE IS TAKEN.
I HATE THIS STRONG JOB MARKET FOR ENGINEERS.
"IRRITATION MAKES PEARLS." OR MAYBE "PRESSURE MAKES WHINE."
S. Adams
2/28/98
© 1998 United Feature Syndicate, Inc.

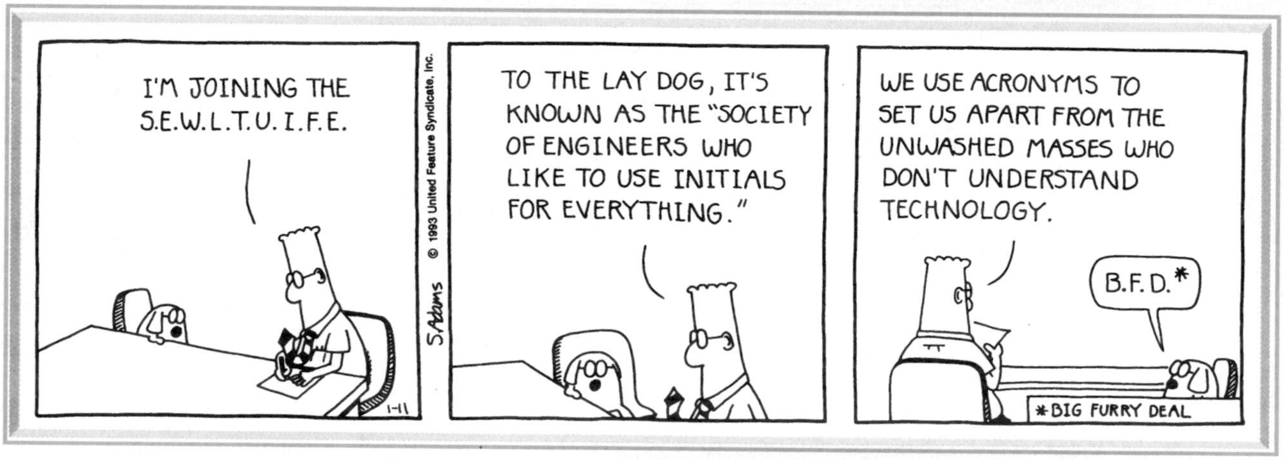
I'M JOINING THE S.E.W.L.T.U.I.F.E.
1-11
S. Adams
© 1993 United Feature Syndicate, Inc.
TO THE LAY DOG, IT'S KNOWN AS THE "SOCIETY OF ENGINEERS WHO LIKE TO USE INITIALS FOR EVERYTHING."
WE USE ACRONYMS TO SET US APART FROM THE UNWASHED MASSES WHO DON'T UNDERSTAND TECHNOLOGY.
B.F.D.*
*BIG FURRY DEAL

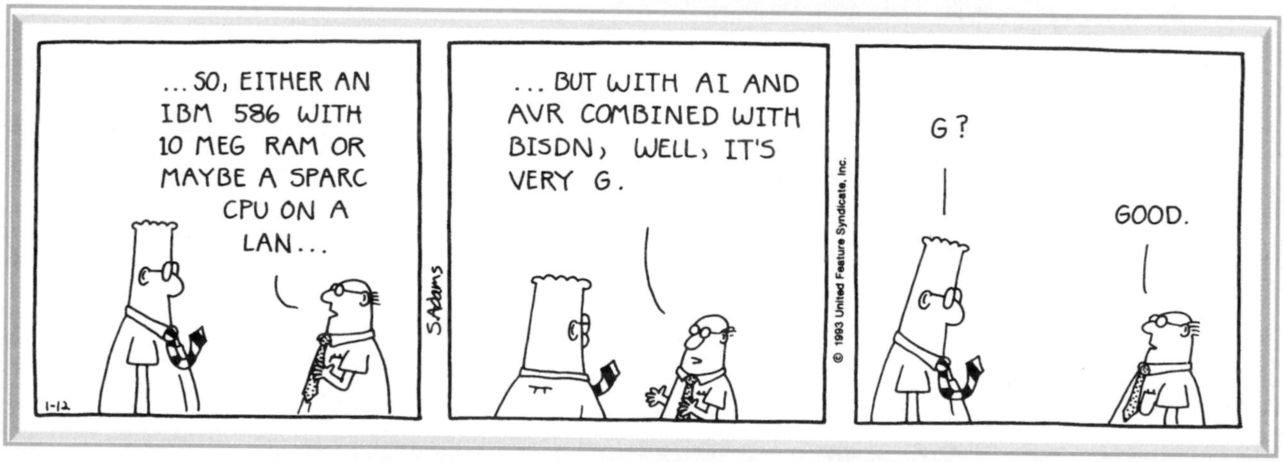
...SO, EITHER AN IBM 586 WITH 10 MEG RAM OR MAYBE A SPARC CPU ON A LAN...
1-12
S. Adams
...BUT WITH AI AND AVR COMBINED WITH BISDN, WELL, IT'S VERY G.
© 1993 United Feature Syndicate, Inc.
G?
GOOD.

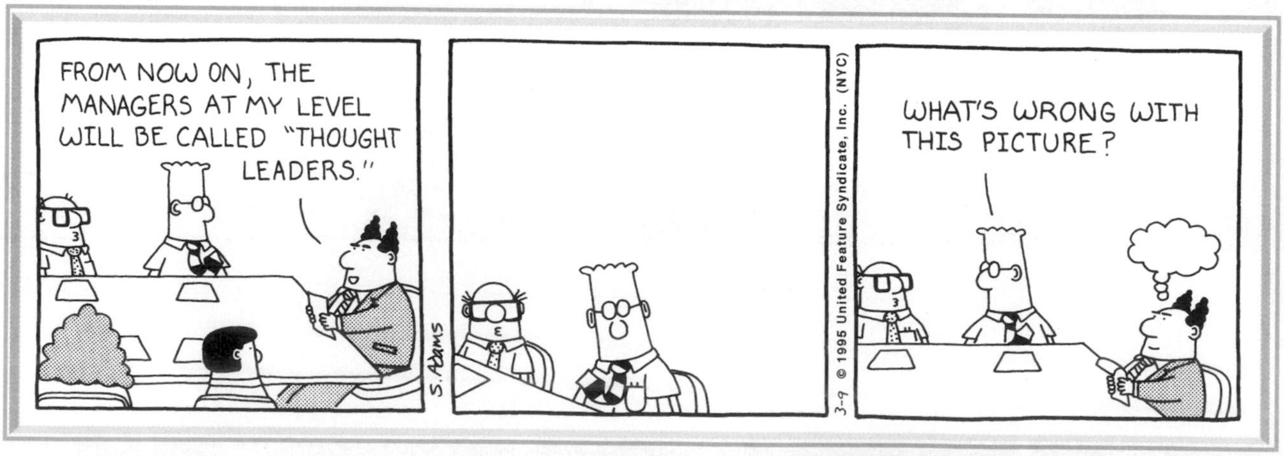
FROM NOW ON, THE MANAGERS AT MY LEVEL WILL BE CALLED "THOUGHT LEADERS."
S. Adams
3-9 © 1995 United Feature Syndicate, Inc. (NYC)
WHAT'S WRONG WITH THIS PICTURE?

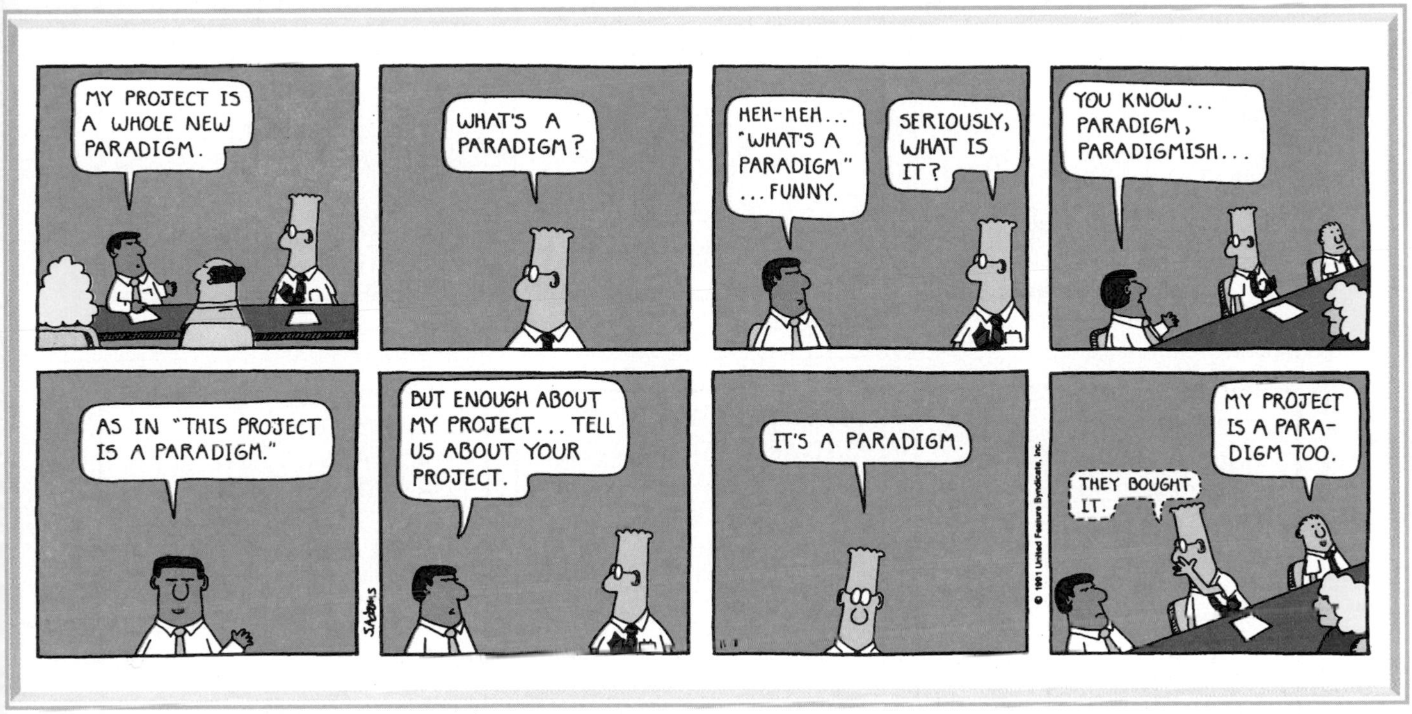
MY PROJECT IS A WHOLE NEW PARADIGM.
WHAT'S A PARADIGM?
HEH-HEH... "WHAT'S A PARADIGM" ...FUNNY.
SERIOUSLY, WHAT IS IT?
YOU KNOW... PARADIGM, PARADIGMISH...
AS IN "THIS PROJECT IS A PARADIGM."
BUT ENOUGH ABOUT MY PROJECT... TELL US ABOUT YOUR PROJECT.
IT'S A PARADIGM.
THEY BOUGHT IT.
MY PROJECT IS A PARA-DIGM TOO.
© 1991 United Feature Syndicate, Inc.

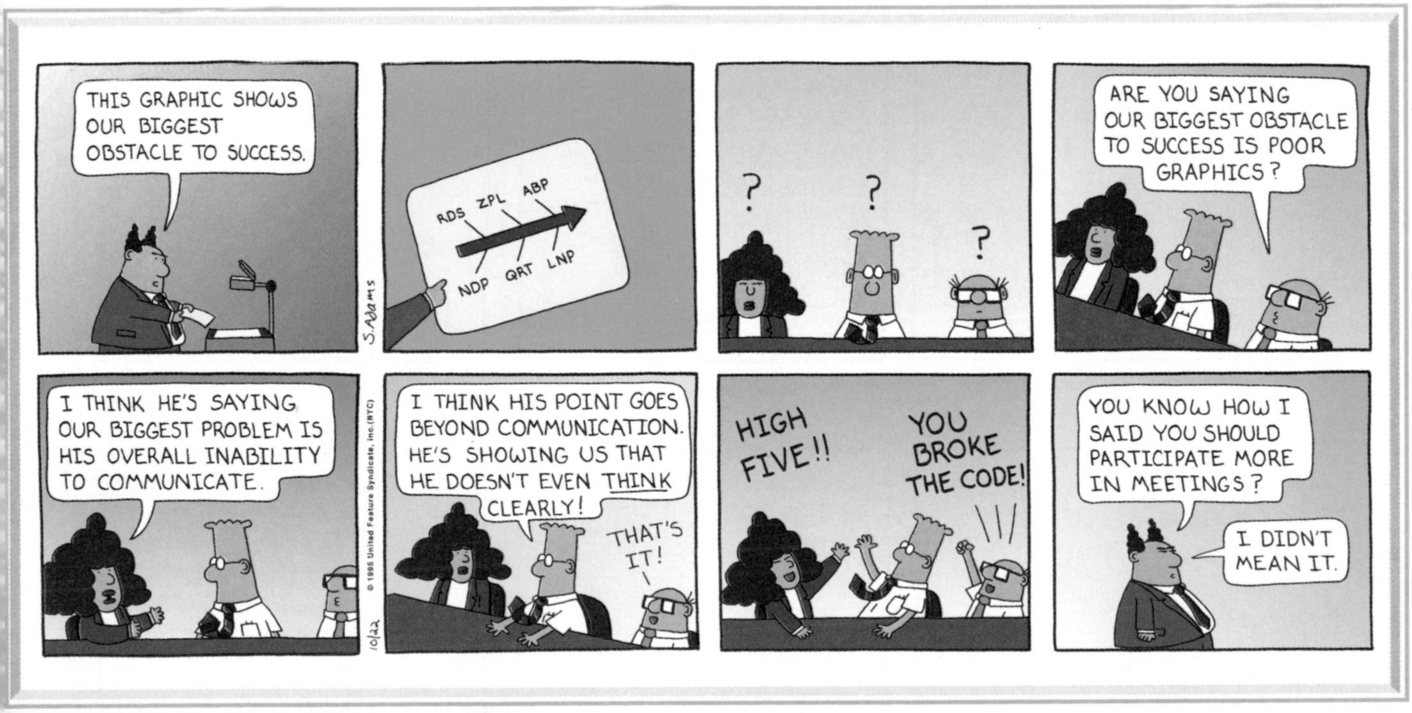
THIS GRAPHIC SHOWS OUR BIGGEST OBSTACLE TO SUCCESS.
RDS
ZPL
ABP
NDP
QRT
LNP
?
?
?
ARE YOU SAYING OUR BIGGEST OBSTACLE TO SUCCESS IS POOR GRAPHICS?
I THINK HE'S SAYING OUR BIGGEST PROBLEM IS HIS OVERALL INABILITY TO COMMUNICATE.
© 1995 United Feature Syndicate, Inc.(NYC)
I THINK HIS POINT GOES BEYOND COMMUNICATION. HE'S SHOWING US THAT HE DOESN'T EVEN THINK CLEARLY!
THAT'S IT!
HIGH FIVE!!
YOU BROKE THE CODE!
YOU KNOW HOW I SAID YOU SHOULD PARTICIPATE MORE IN MEETINGS?
I DIDN'T MEAN IT.

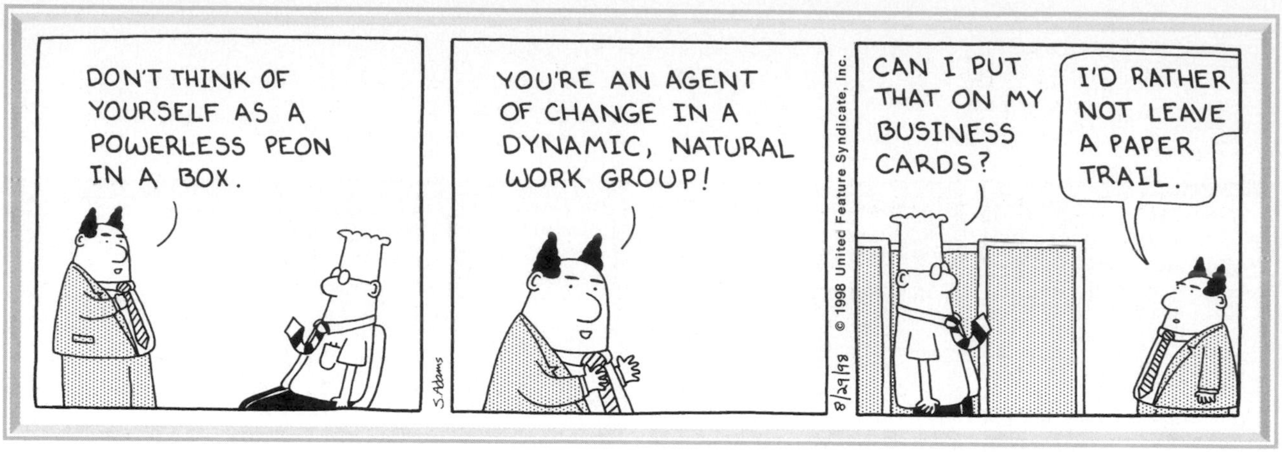
DON'T THINK OF YOURSELF AS A POWERLESS PEON IN A BOX.
YOU'RE AN AGENT OF CHANGE IN A DYNAMIC, NATURAL WORK GROUP!
CAN I PUT THAT ON MY BUSINESS CARDS?
I'D RATHER NOT LEAVE A PAPER TRAIL.
S.Adams
8/29/98 © 1998 United Feature Syndicate, Inc.

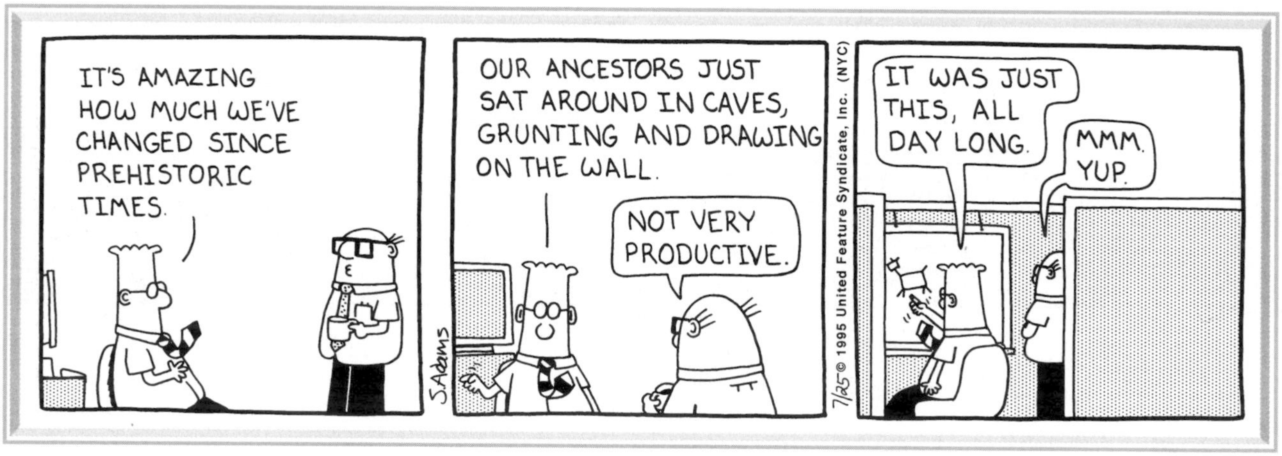
IT'S AMAZING HOW MUCH WE'VE CHANGED SINCE PREHISTORIC TIMES.
OUR ANCESTORS JUST SAT AROUND IN CAVES, GRUNTING AND DRAWING ON THE WALL.
NOT VERY PRODUCTIVE.
IT WAS JUST THIS, ALL DAY LONG.
MMM. YUP.
S.Adams
7/25 © 1995 United Feature Syndicate, Inc. (NYC)

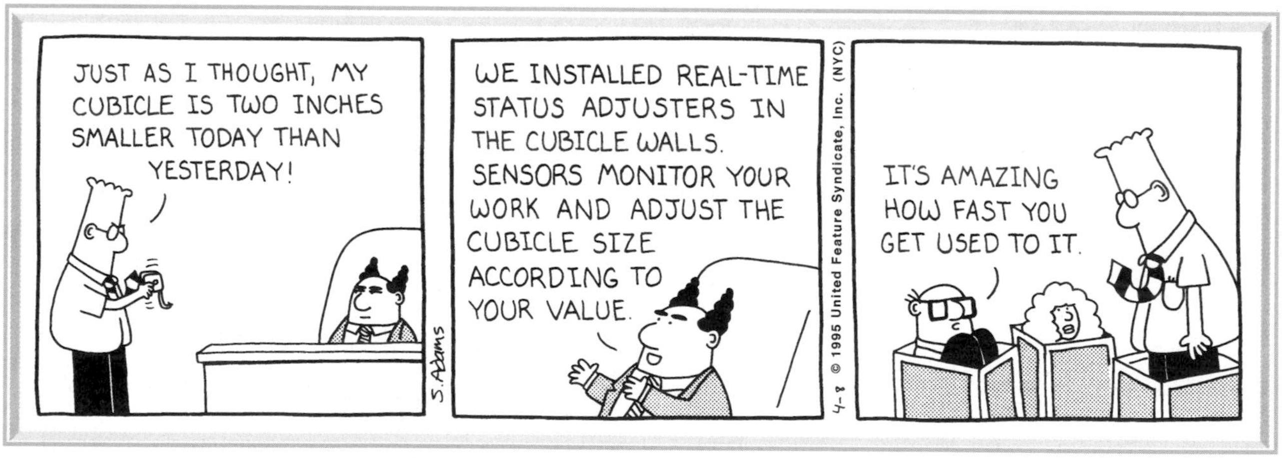
JUST AS I THOUGHT, MY CUBICLE IS TWO INCHES SMALLER TODAY THAN YESTERDAY!
WE INSTALLED REAL-TIME STATUS ADJUSTERS IN THE CUBICLE WALLS. SENSORS MONITOR YOUR WORK AND ADJUST THE CUBICLE SIZE ACCORDING TO YOUR VALUE.
IT'S AMAZING HOW FAST YOU GET USED TO IT.
S.Adams
4-8 © 1995 United Feature Syndicate, Inc. (NYC)

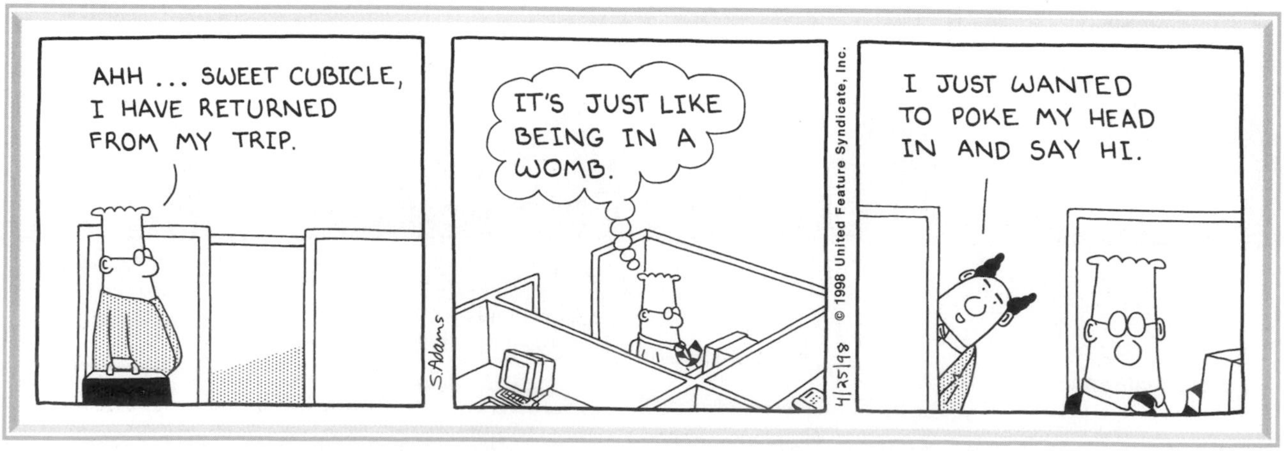
AHH ... SWEET CUBICLE, I HAVE RETURNED FROM MY TRIP.
IT'S JUST LIKE BEING IN A WOMB.
I JUST WANTED TO POKE MY HEAD IN AND SAY HI.
S.Adams
4/25/98 © 1998 United Feature Syndicate, Inc.

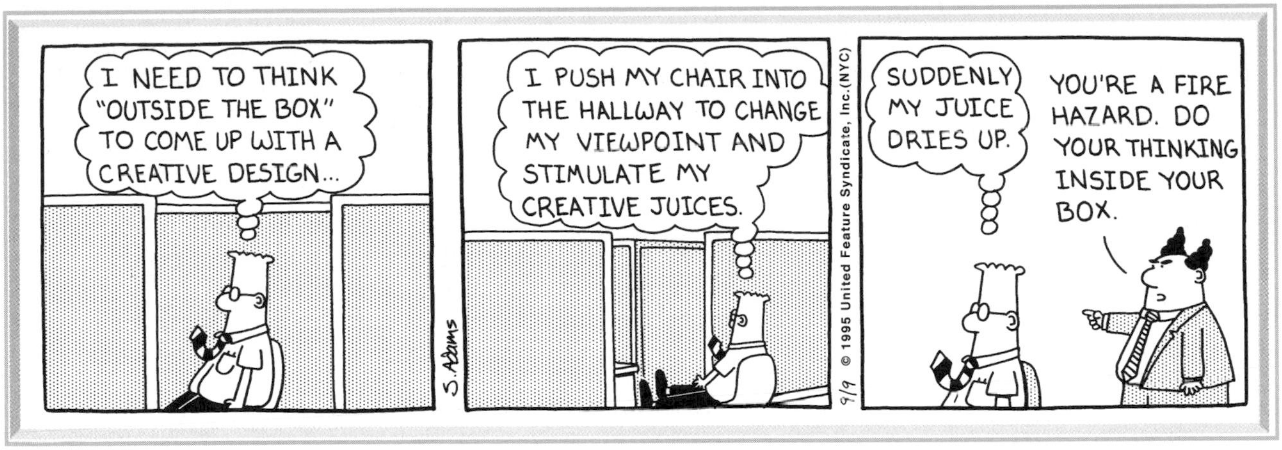
I NEED TO THINK "OUTSIDE THE BOX" TO COME UP WITH A CREATIVE DESIGN...
S. Adams
I PUSH MY CHAIR INTO THE HALLWAY TO CHANGE MY VIEWPOINT AND STIMULATE MY CREATIVE JUICES.
9/9 © 1995 United Feature Syndicate, Inc.(NYC)
SUDDENLY MY JUICE DRIES UP.
YOU'RE A FIRE HAZARD. DO YOUR THINKING INSIDE YOUR BOX.

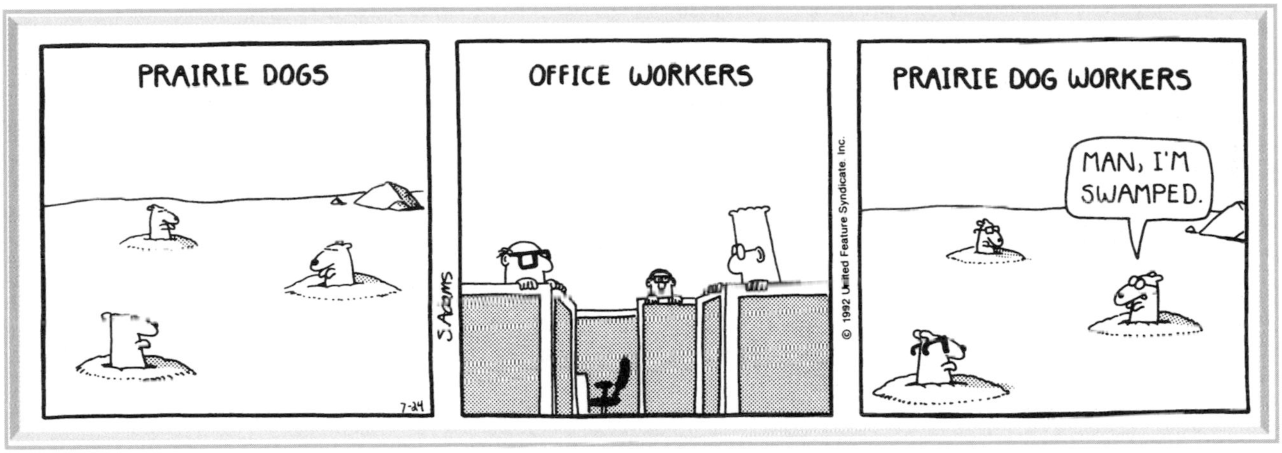
PRAIRIE DOGS
7-24
S. Adams
OFFICE WORKERS
© 1992 United Feature Syndicate Inc.
PRAIRIE DOG WORKERS
MAN, I'M SWAMPED.

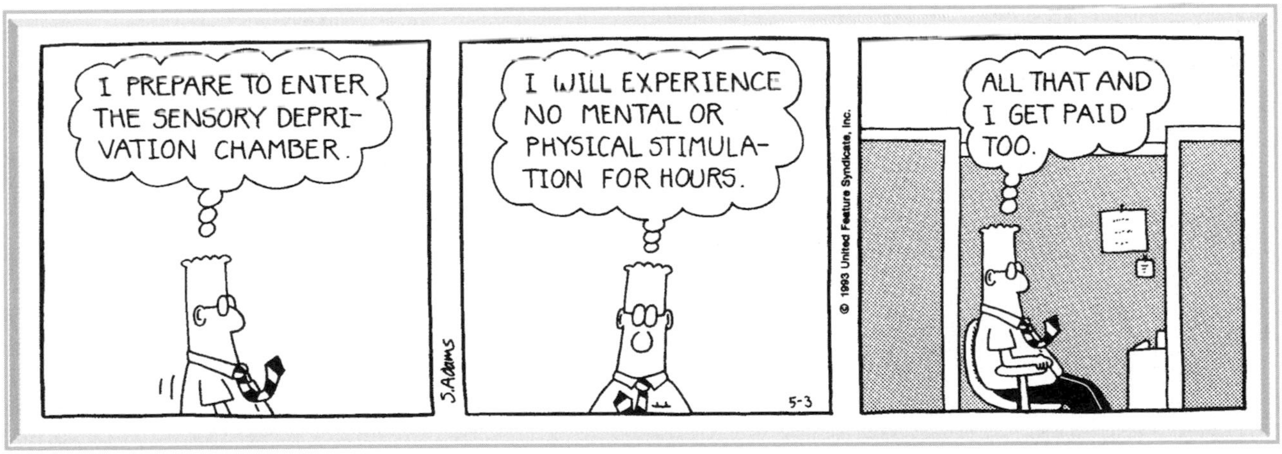
I PREPARE TO ENTER THE SENSORY DEPRIVATION CHAMBER.
S. Adams
I WILL EXPERIENCE NO MENTAL OR PHYSICAL STIMULATION FOR HOURS.
5-3
© 1993 United Feature Syndicate, Inc.
ALL THAT AND I GET PAID TOO.

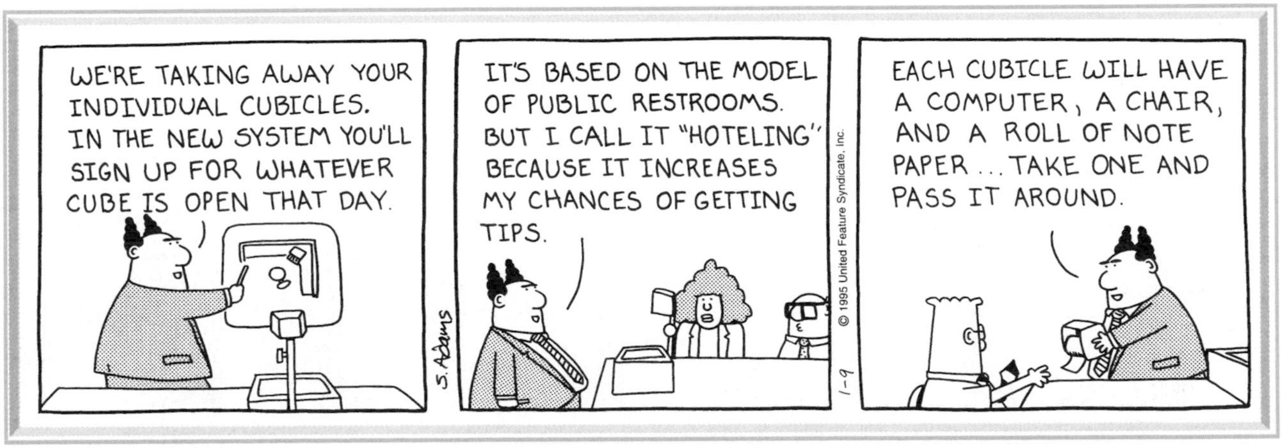
WE'RE TAKING AWAY YOUR INDIVIDUAL CUBICLES. IN THE NEW SYSTEM YOU'LL SIGN UP FOR WHATEVER CUBE IS OPEN THAT DAY.
S. Adams
IT'S BASED ON THE MODEL OF PUBLIC RESTROOMS. BUT I CALL IT "HOTELING" BECAUSE IT INCREASES MY CHANCES OF GETTING TIPS.
1-9 © 1995 United Feature Syndicate, Inc.
EACH CUBICLE WILL HAVE A COMPUTER, A CHAIR, AND A ROLL OF NOTE PAPER ... TAKE ONE AND PASS IT AROUND.

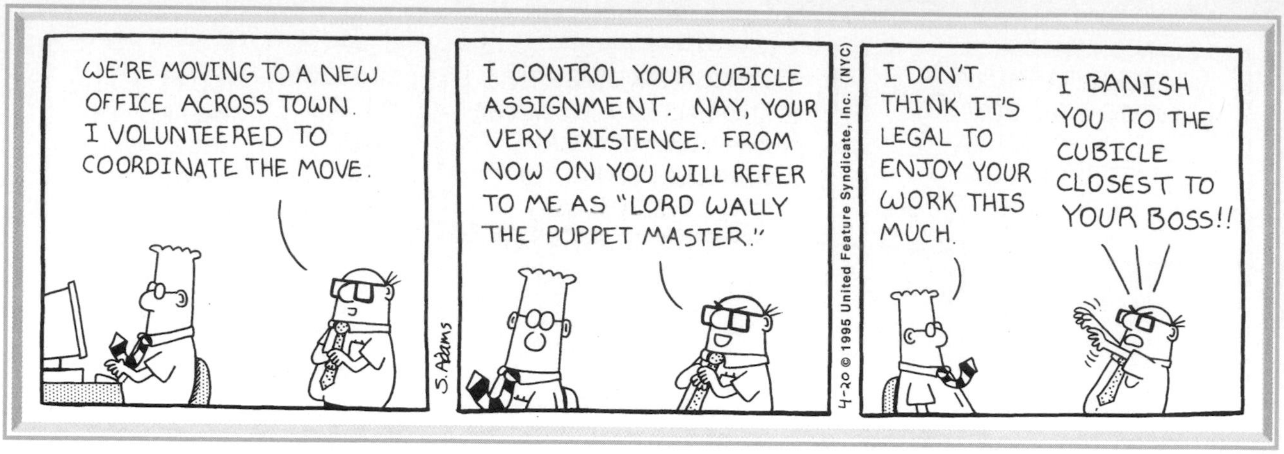
WE'RE MOVING TO A NEW OFFICE ACROSS TOWN. I VOLUNTEERED TO COORDINATE THE MOVE.
I CONTROL YOUR CUBICLE ASSIGNMENT. NAY, YOUR VERY EXISTENCE. FROM NOW ON YOU WILL REFER TO ME AS "LORD WALLY THE PUPPET MASTER."
I DON'T THINK IT'S LEGAL TO ENJOY YOUR WORK THIS MUCH.
I BANISH YOU TO THE CUBICLE CLOSEST TO YOUR BOSS!!
S. Adams
4-20 © 1995 United Feature Syndicate, Inc. (NYC)

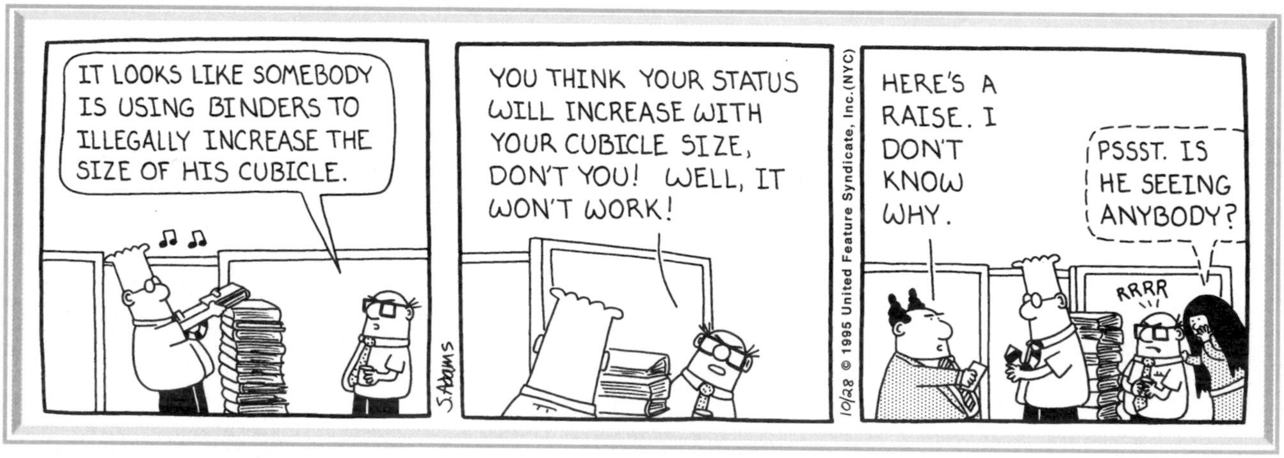
IT LOOKS LIKE SOMEBODY IS USING BINDERS TO ILLEGALLY INCREASE THE SIZE OF HIS CUBICLE.
YOU THINK YOUR STATUS WILL INCREASE WITH YOUR CUBICLE SIZE, DON'T YOU! WELL, IT WON'T WORK!
HERE'S A RAISE. I DON'T KNOW WHY.
PSSST. IS HE SEEING ANYBODY?
RRRR
S. Adams
10/28 © 1995 United Feature Syndicate, Inc. (NYC)

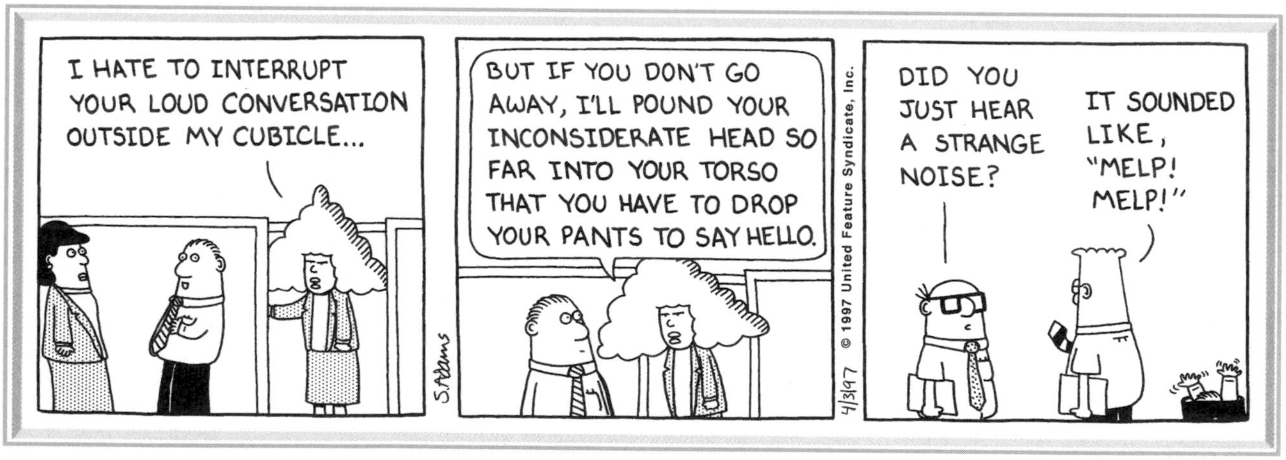
I HATE TO INTERRUPT YOUR LOUD CONVERSATION OUTSIDE MY CUBICLE...
BUT IF YOU DON'T GO AWAY, I'LL POUND YOUR INCONSIDERATE HEAD SO FAR INTO YOUR TORSO THAT YOU HAVE TO DROP YOUR PANTS TO SAY HELLO.
DID YOU JUST HEAR A STRANGE NOISE?
IT SOUNDED LIKE, "MELP! MELP!"
S. Adams
4/3/97 © 1997 United Feature Syndicate, Inc.

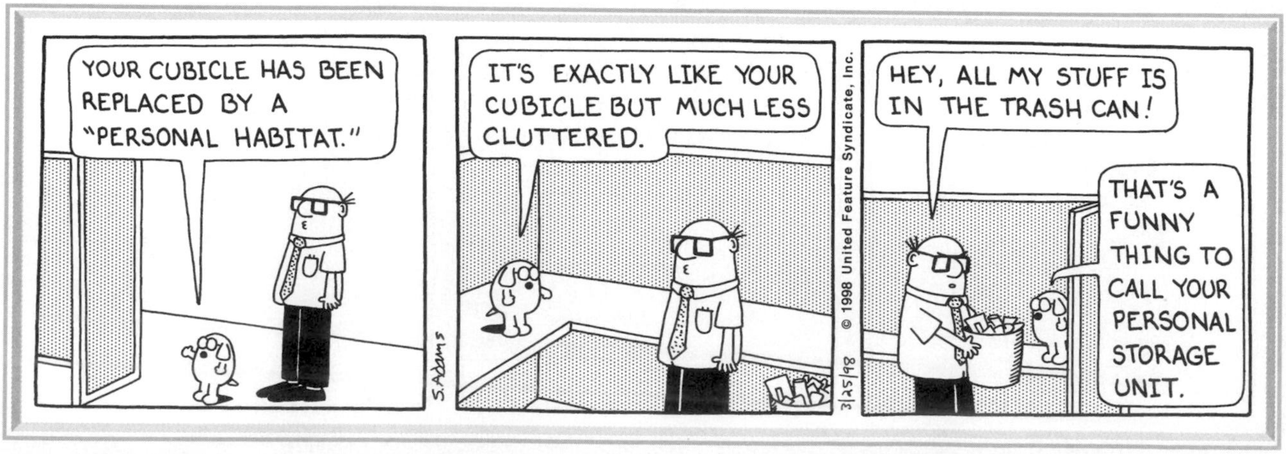
YOUR CUBICLE HAS BEEN REPLACED BY A "PERSONAL HABITAT."
IT'S EXACTLY LIKE YOUR CUBICLE BUT MUCH LESS CLUTTERED.
HEY, ALL MY STUFF IS IN THE TRASH CAN!
THAT'S A FUNNY THING TO CALL YOUR PERSONAL STORAGE UNIT.
S. Adams
3/25/98 © 1998 United Feature Syndicate, Inc.

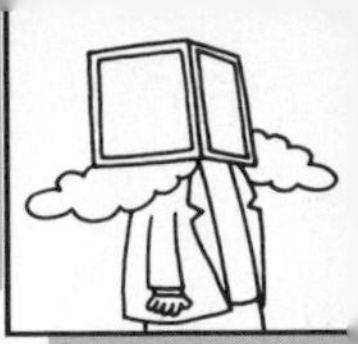

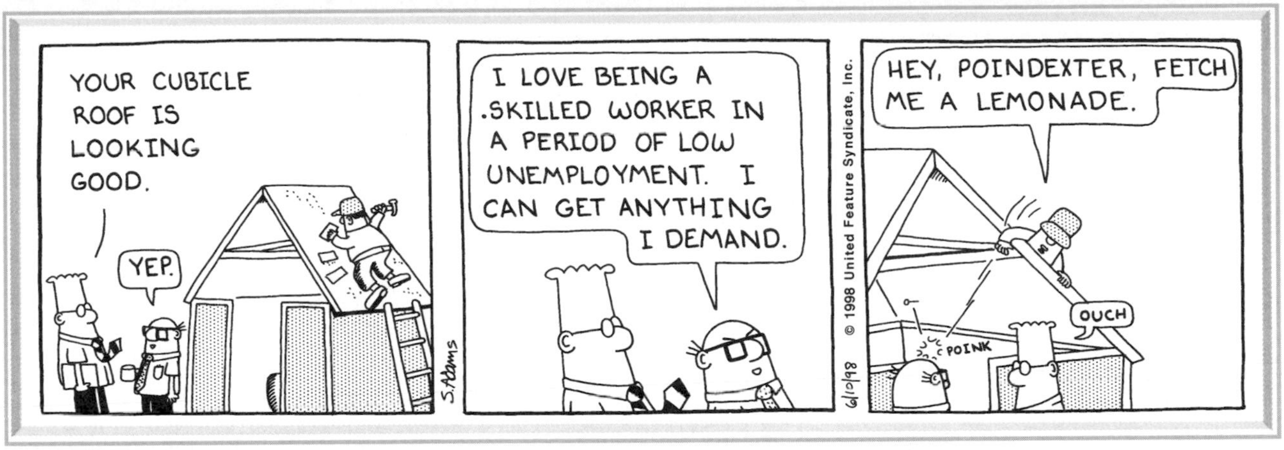
YOUR CUBICLE ROOF IS LOOKING GOOD.
YEP.
I LOVE BEING A SKILLED WORKER IN A PERIOD OF LOW UNEMPLOYMENT. I CAN GET ANYTHING I DEMAND.
HEY, POINDEXTER, FETCH ME A LEMONADE.
OUCH
POINK
S. Adams
6/10/98 © 1998 United Feature Syndicate, Inc.

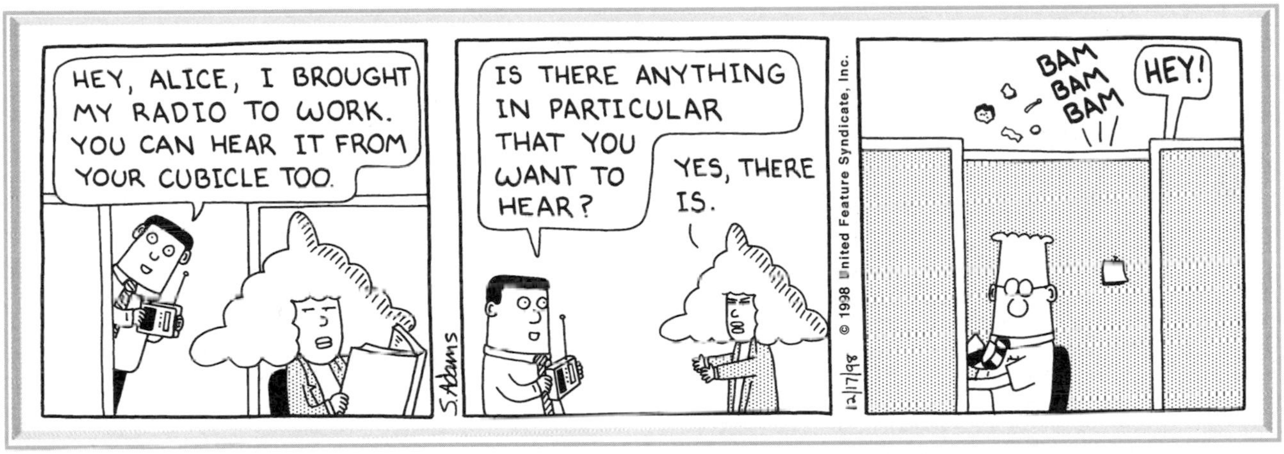
HEY, ALICE, I BROUGHT MY RADIO TO WORK. YOU CAN HEAR IT FROM YOUR CUBICLE TOO.
IS THERE ANYTHING IN PARTICULAR THAT YOU WANT TO HEAR?
YES, THERE IS.
BAM BAM BAM
HEY!
S. Adams
12/17/98 © 1998 United Feature Syndicate, Inc.

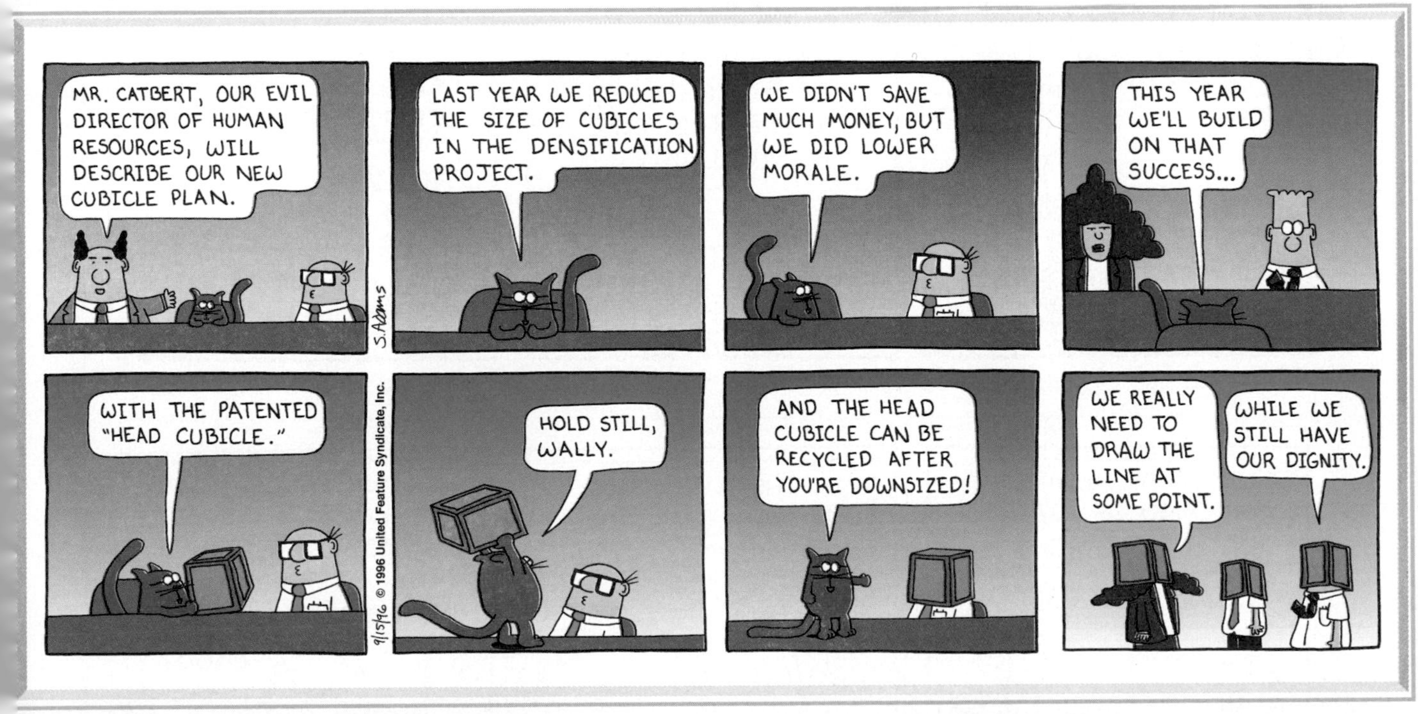
MR. CATBERT, OUR EVIL DIRECTOR OF HUMAN RESOURCES, WILL DESCRIBE OUR NEW CUBICLE PLAN.
LAST YEAR WE REDUCED THE SIZE OF CUBICLES IN THE DENSIFICATION PROJECT.
WE DIDN'T SAVE MUCH MONEY, BUT WE DID LOWER MORALE.
THIS YEAR WE'LL BUILD ON THAT SUCCESS...
WITH THE PATENTED "HEAD CUBICLE."
HOLD STILL, WALLY.
AND THE HEAD CUBICLE CAN BE RECYCLED AFTER YOU'RE DOWNSIZED!
WE REALLY NEED TO DRAW THE LINE AT SOME POINT.
WHILE WE STILL HAVE OUR DIGNITY.
S. Adams
9/15/96 © 1996 United Feature Syndicate, Inc.

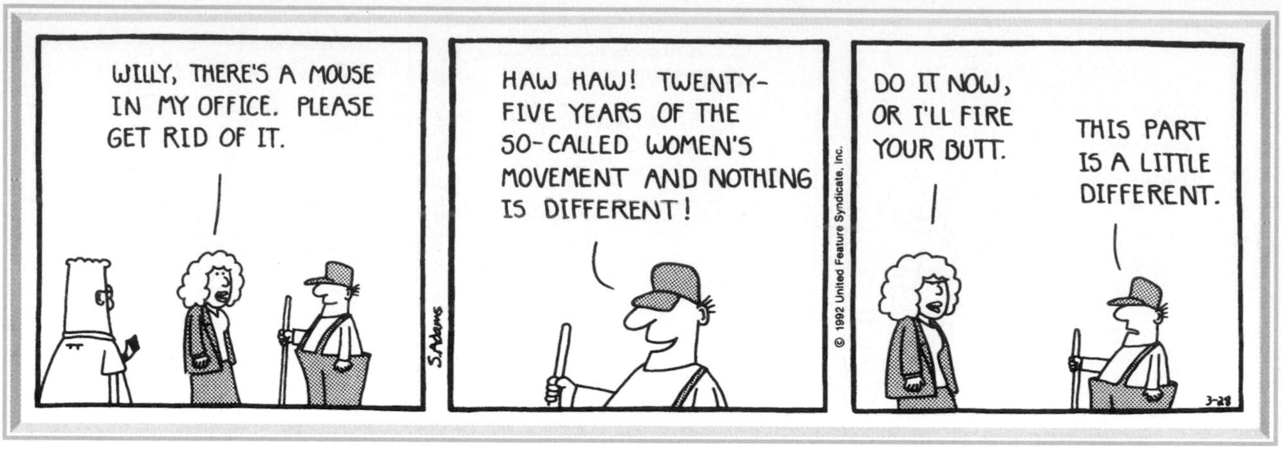
WILLY, THERE'S A MOUSE IN MY OFFICE. PLEASE GET RID OF IT.
HAW HAW! TWENTY-FIVE YEARS OF THE SO-CALLED WOMEN'S MOVEMENT AND NOTHING IS DIFFERENT!
DO IT NOW, OR I'LL FIRE YOUR BUTT.
THIS PART IS A LITTLE DIFFERENT.
© 1992 United Feature Syndicate, Inc.

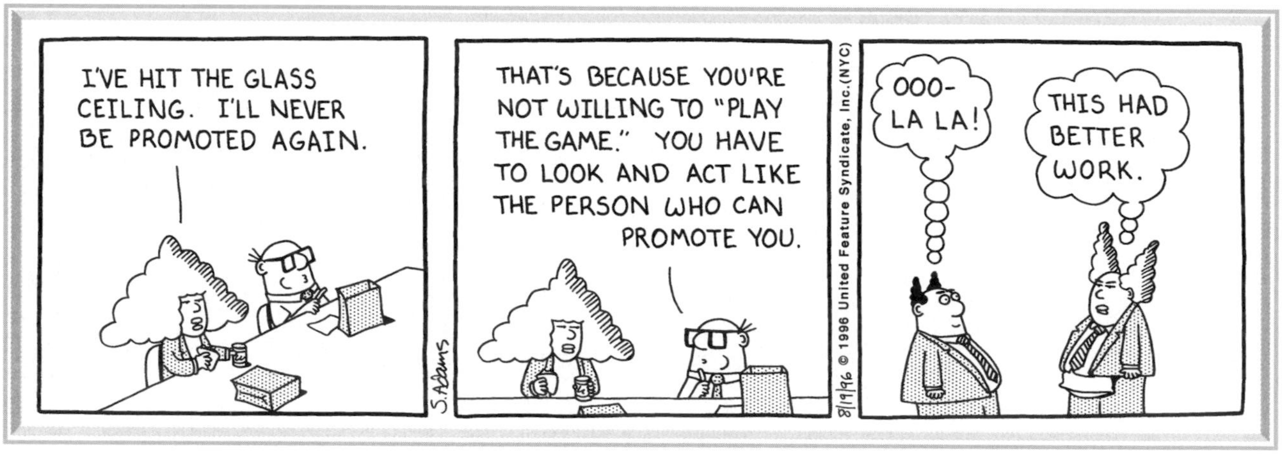
I'VE HIT THE GLASS CEILING. I'LL NEVER BE PROMOTED AGAIN.
THAT'S BECAUSE YOU'RE NOT WILLING TO "PLAY THE GAME." YOU HAVE TO LOOK AND ACT LIKE THE PERSON WHO CAN PROMOTE YOU.
OOO-LA LA!
THIS HAD BETTER WORK.
8/19/96 © 1996 United Feature Syndicate, Inc.(NYC)

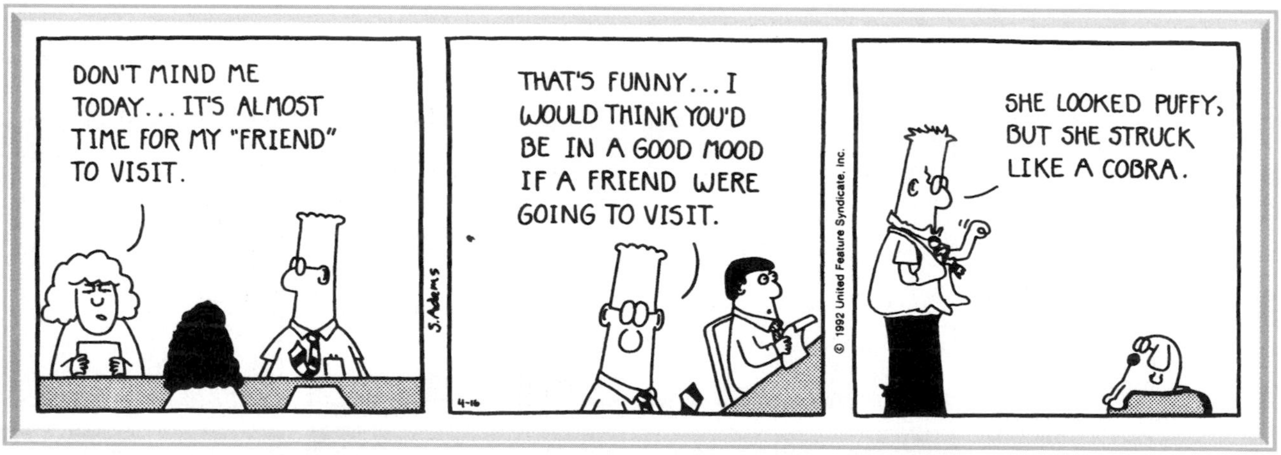
DON'T MIND ME TODAY... IT'S ALMOST TIME FOR MY "FRIEND" TO VISIT.
THAT'S FUNNY... I WOULD THINK YOU'D BE IN A GOOD MOOD IF A FRIEND WERE GOING TO VISIT.
SHE LOOKED PUFFY, BUT SHE STRUCK LIKE A COBRA.
© 1992 United Feature Syndicate, Inc.

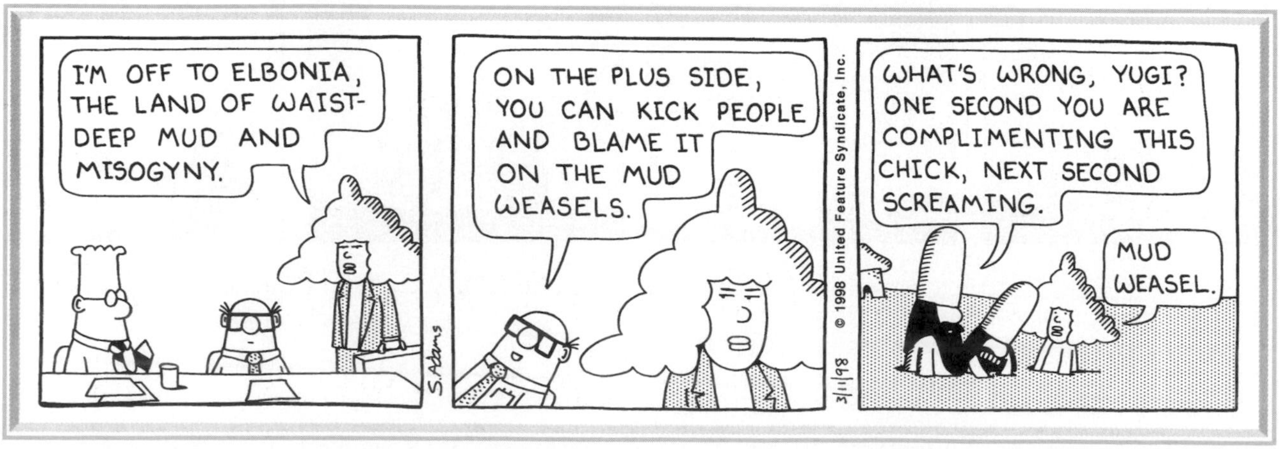
I'M OFF TO ELBONIA, THE LAND OF WAIST-DEEP MUD AND MISOGYNY.
ON THE PLUS SIDE, YOU CAN KICK PEOPLE AND BLAME IT ON THE MUD WEASELS.
WHAT'S WRONG, YUGI? ONE SECOND YOU ARE COMPLIMENTING THIS CHICK, NEXT SECOND SCREAMING.
MUD WEASEL.
3/1/98 © 1998 United Feature Syndicate, Inc.

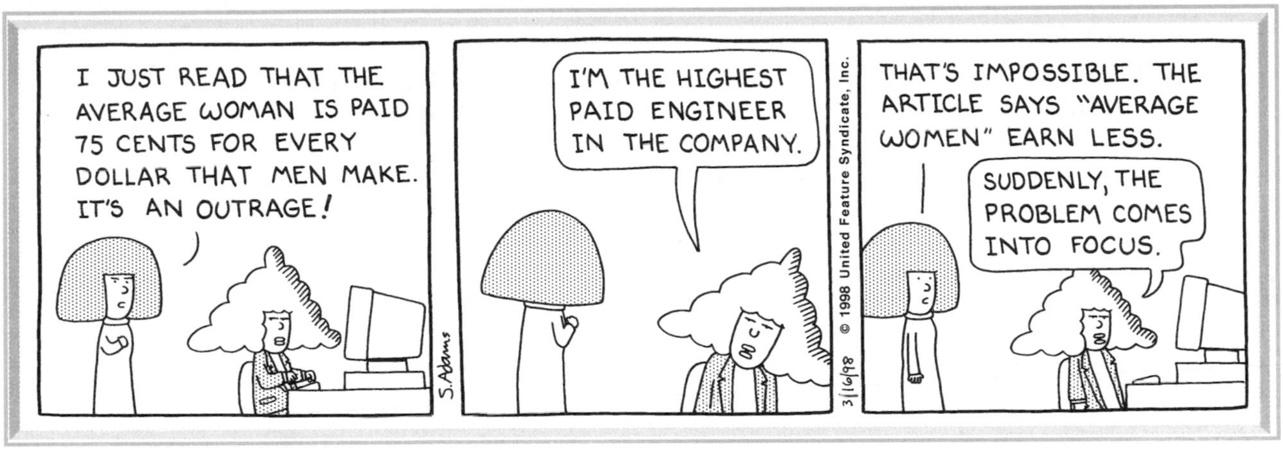
I JUST READ THAT THE AVERAGE WOMAN IS PAID 75 CENTS FOR EVERY DOLLAR THAT MEN MAKE. IT'S AN OUTRAGE!
I'M THE HIGHEST PAID ENGINEER IN THE COMPANY.
THAT'S IMPOSSIBLE. THE ARTICLE SAYS "AVERAGE WOMEN" EARN LESS.
SUDDENLY, THE PROBLEM COMES INTO FOCUS.

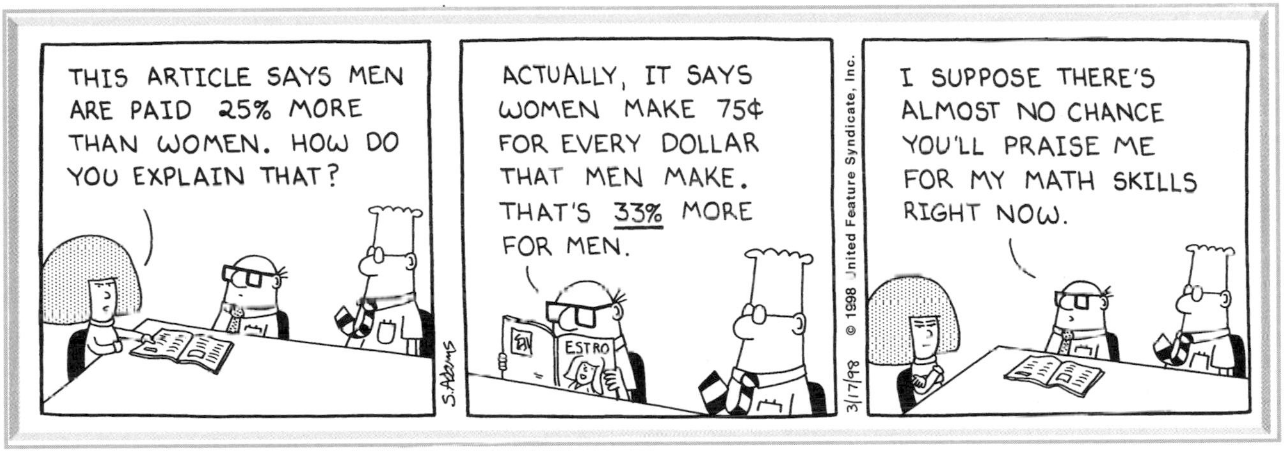
THIS ARTICLE SAYS MEN ARE PAID 25% MORE THAN WOMEN. HOW DO YOU EXPLAIN THAT?
ACTUALLY, IT SAYS WOMEN MAKE 75¢ FOR EVERY DOLLAR THAT MEN MAKE. THAT'S 33% MORE FOR MEN.
ESTRO
I SUPPOSE THERE'S ALMOST NO CHANCE YOU'LL PRAISE ME FOR MY MATH SKILLS RIGHT NOW.

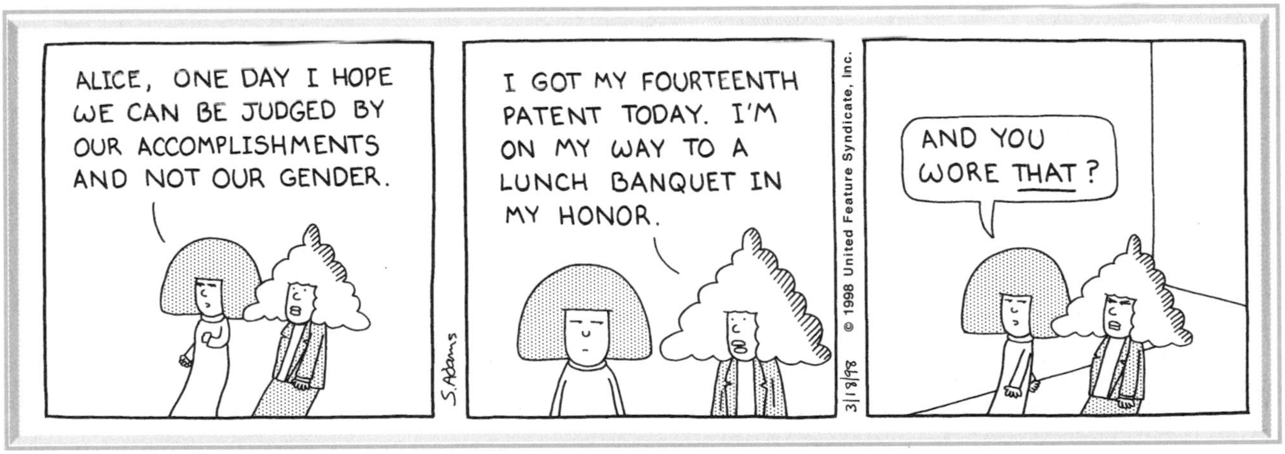
ALICE, ONE DAY I HOPE WE CAN BE JUDGED BY OUR ACCOMPLISHMENTS AND NOT OUR GENDER.
I GOT MY FOURTEENTH PATENT TODAY. I'M ON MY WAY TO A LUNCH BANQUET IN MY HONOR.
AND YOU WORE THAT?

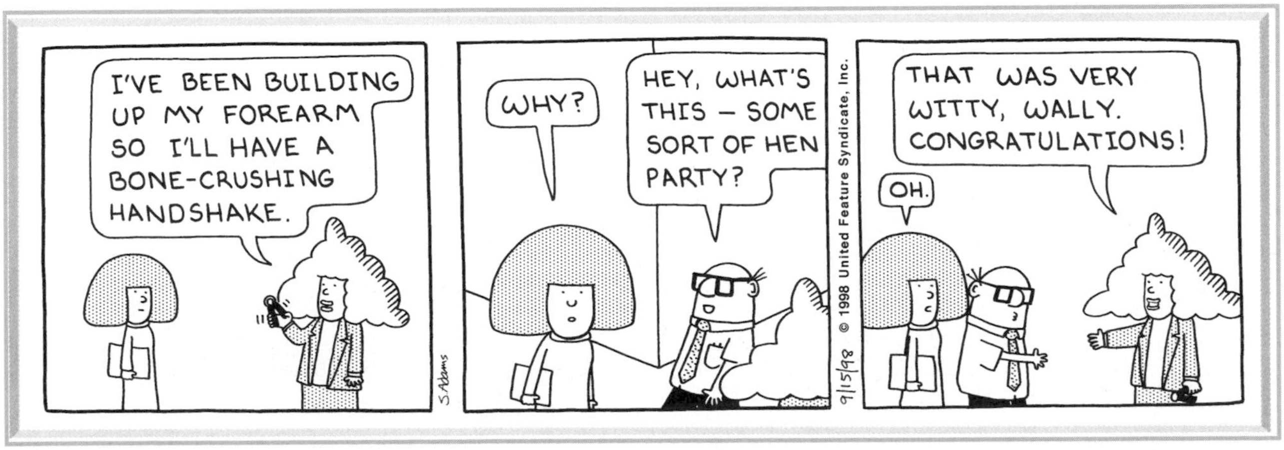
I'VE BEEN BUILDING UP MY FOREARM SO I'LL HAVE A BONE-CRUSHING HANDSHAKE.
WHY?
HEY, WHAT'S THIS – SOME SORT OF HEN PARTY?
THAT WAS VERY WITTY, WALLY. CONGRATULATIONS!
OH.

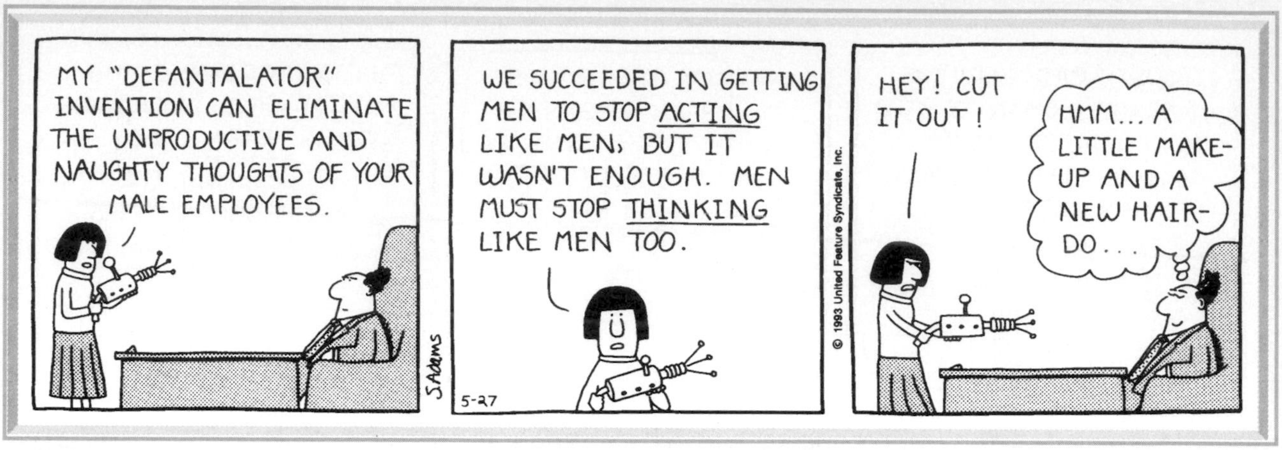
MY "DEFANTALATOR" INVENTION CAN ELIMINATE THE UNPRODUCTIVE AND NAUGHTY THOUGHTS OF YOUR MALE EMPLOYEES.
S.Adams
5-27
WE SUCCEEDED IN GETTING MEN TO STOP ACTING LIKE MEN, BUT IT WASN'T ENOUGH. MEN MUST STOP THINKING LIKE MEN TOO.
© 1993 United Feature Syndicate, Inc.
HEY! CUT IT OUT!
HMM... A LITTLE MAKE-UP AND A NEW HAIR-DO...

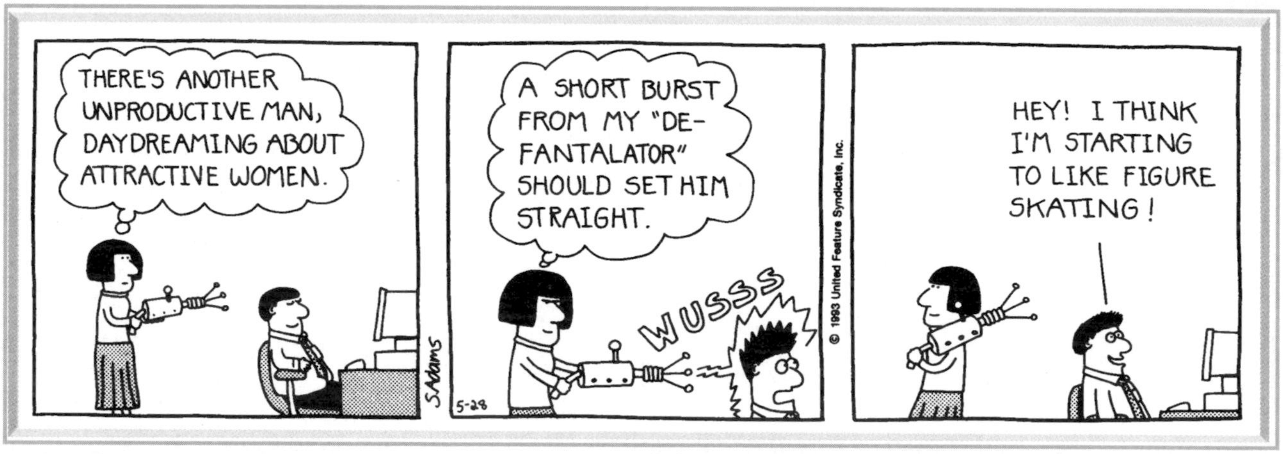
THERE'S ANOTHER UNPRODUCTIVE MAN, DAYDREAMING ABOUT ATTRACTIVE WOMEN.
S.Adams
5-28
A SHORT BURST FROM MY "DE-FANTALATOR" SHOULD SET HIM STRAIGHT.
WUSSS
© 1993 United Feature Syndicate, Inc.
HEY! I THINK I'M STARTING TO LIKE FIGURE SKATING!

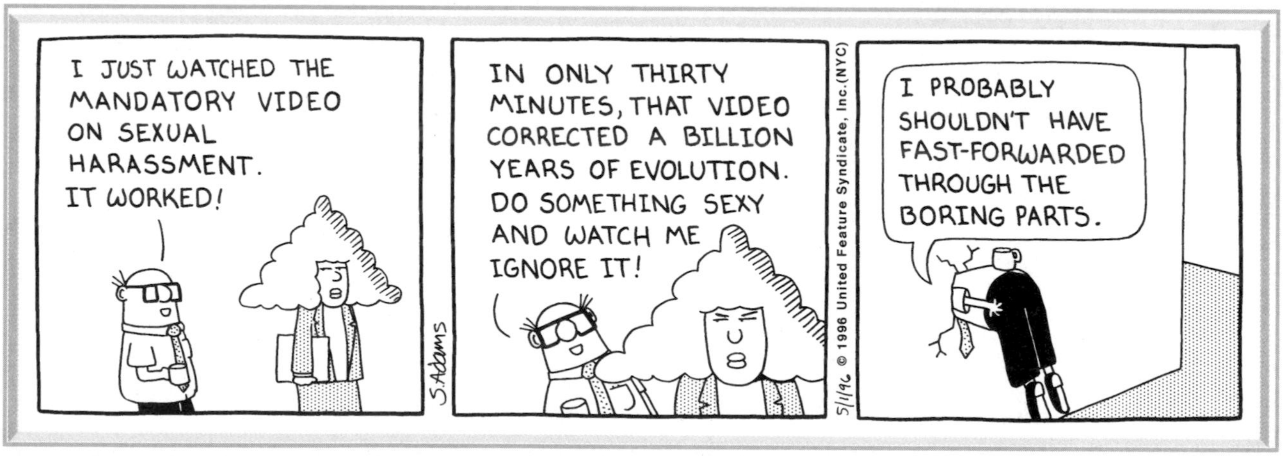
I JUST WATCHED THE MANDATORY VIDEO ON SEXUAL HARASSMENT. IT WORKED!
S.Adams
IN ONLY THIRTY MINUTES, THAT VIDEO CORRECTED A BILLION YEARS OF EVOLUTION. DO SOMETHING SEXY AND WATCH ME IGNORE IT!
5/1/96 © 1996 United Feature Syndicate, Inc.(NYC)
I PROBABLY SHOULDN'T HAVE FAST-FORWARDED THROUGH THE BORING PARTS.

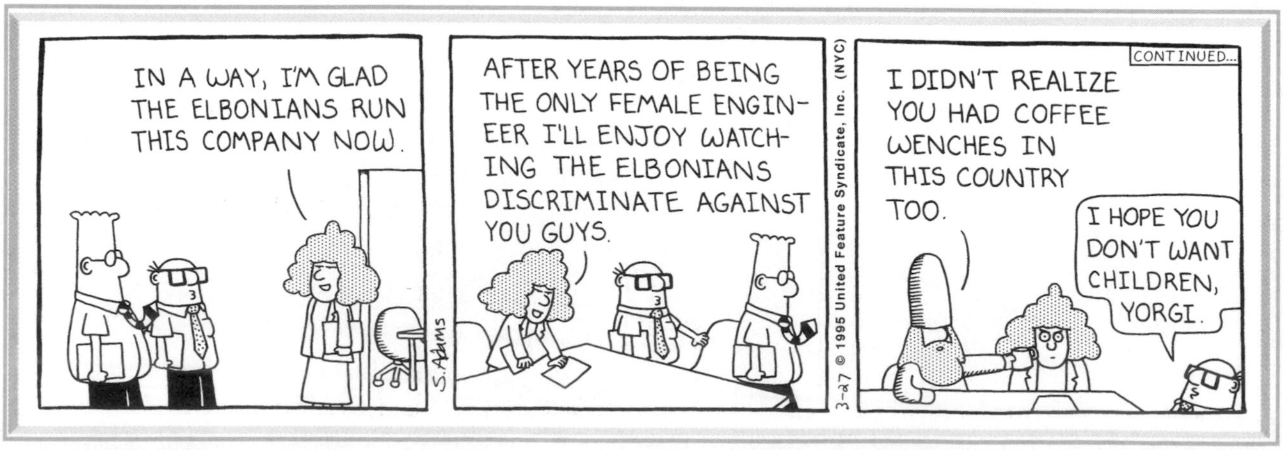
IN A WAY, I'M GLAD THE ELBONIANS RUN THIS COMPANY NOW.
S.Adams
AFTER YEARS OF BEING THE ONLY FEMALE ENGINEER I'LL ENJOY WATCHING THE ELBONIANS DISCRIMINATE AGAINST YOU GUYS.
3-27 © 1995 United Feature Syndicate, Inc. (NYC)
CONTINUED...
I DIDN'T REALIZE YOU HAD COFFEE WENCHES IN THIS COUNTRY TOO.
I HOPE YOU DON'T WANT CHILDREN, YORGI.

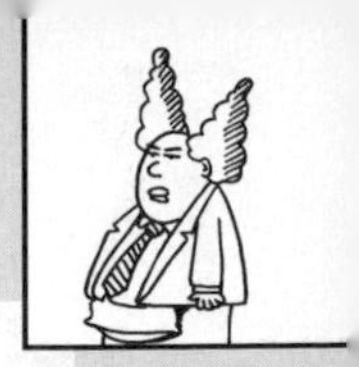

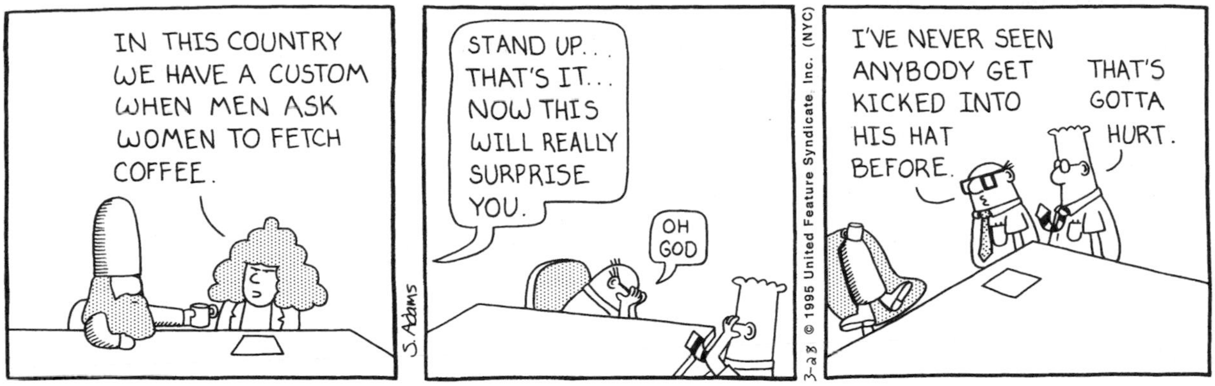
IN THIS COUNTRY WE HAVE A CUSTOM WHEN MEN ASK WOMEN TO FETCH COFFEE.
STAND UP... THAT'S IT... NOW THIS WILL REALLY SURPRISE YOU.
OH GOD
I'VE NEVER SEEN ANYBODY GET KICKED INTO HIS HAT BEFORE.
THAT'S GOTTA HURT.
S. Adams
3-28 © 1995 United Feature Syndicate, Inc. (NYC)

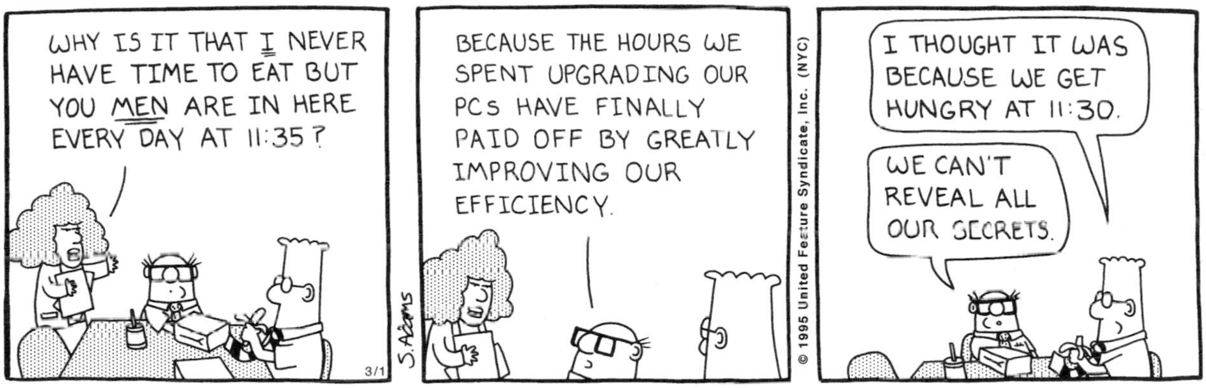
WHY IS IT THAT I NEVER HAVE TIME TO EAT BUT YOU MEN ARE IN HERE EVERY DAY AT 11:35?
3/1
BECAUSE THE HOURS WE SPENT UPGRADING OUR PCs HAVE FINALLY PAID OFF BY GREATLY IMPROVING OUR EFFICIENCY.
S. Adams
© 1995 United Feature Syndicate, Inc. (NYC)
I THOUGHT IT WAS BECAUSE WE GET HUNGRY AT 11:30.
WE CAN'T REVEAL ALL OUR SECRETS.

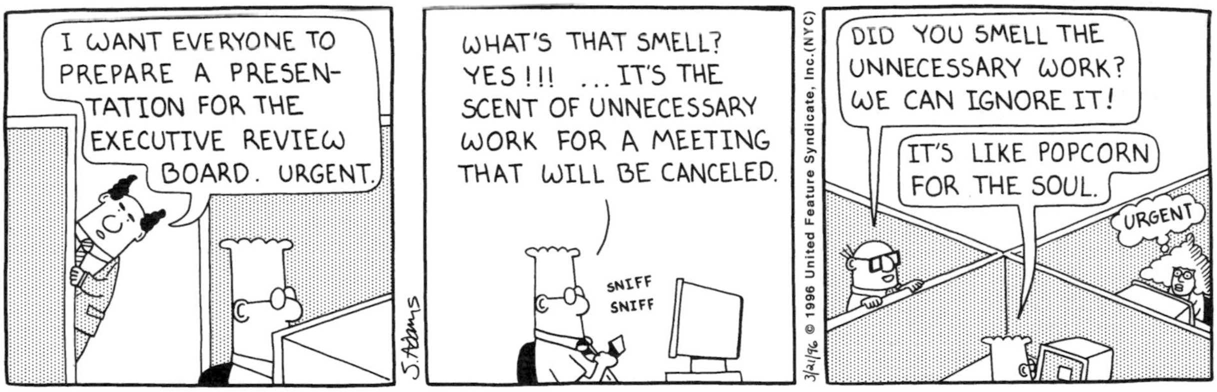
I WANT EVERYONE TO PREPARE A PRESENTATION FOR THE EXECUTIVE REVIEW BOARD. URGENT.
S. Adams
WHAT'S THAT SMELL? YES!!! ...IT'S THE SCENT OF UNNECESSARY WORK FOR A MEETING THAT WILL BE CANCELED.
SNIFF SNIFF
3/21/96 © 1996 United Feature Syndicate, Inc.(NYC)
DID YOU SMELL THE UNNECESSARY WORK? WE CAN IGNORE IT!
IT'S LIKE POPCORN FOR THE SOUL.
URGENT

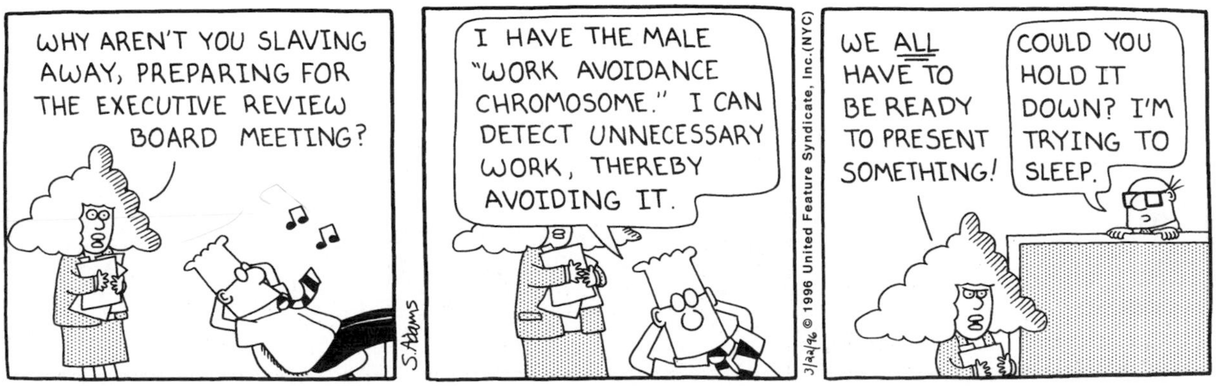
WHY AREN'T YOU SLAVING AWAY, PREPARING FOR THE EXECUTIVE REVIEW BOARD MEETING?
S. Adams
I HAVE THE MALE "WORK AVOIDANCE CHROMOSOME." I CAN DETECT UNNECESSARY WORK, THEREBY AVOIDING IT.
3/22/96 © 1996 United Feature Syndicate, Inc.(NYC)
WE ALL HAVE TO BE READY TO PRESENT SOMETHING!
COULD YOU HOLD IT DOWN? I'M TRYING TO SLEEP.

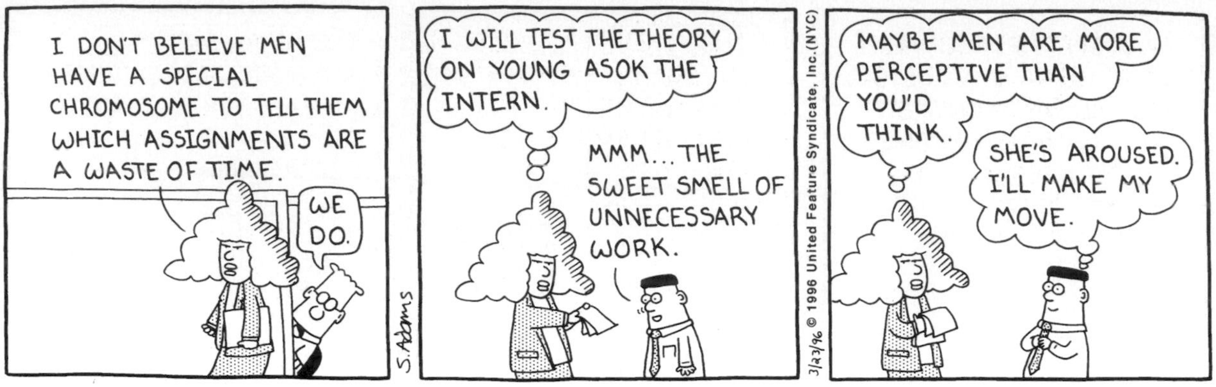
I DON'T BELIEVE MEN HAVE A SPECIAL CHROMOSOME TO TELL THEM WHICH ASSIGNMENTS ARE A WASTE OF TIME.
WE DO.
I WILL TEST THE THEORY ON YOUNG ASOK THE INTERN.
MMM... THE SWEET SMELL OF UNNECESSARY WORK.
MAYBE MEN ARE MORE PERCEPTIVE THAN YOU'D THINK.
SHE'S AROUSED. I'LL MAKE MY MOVE.
S. Adams
3/23/96 © 1996 United Feature Syndicate, Inc.(NYC)

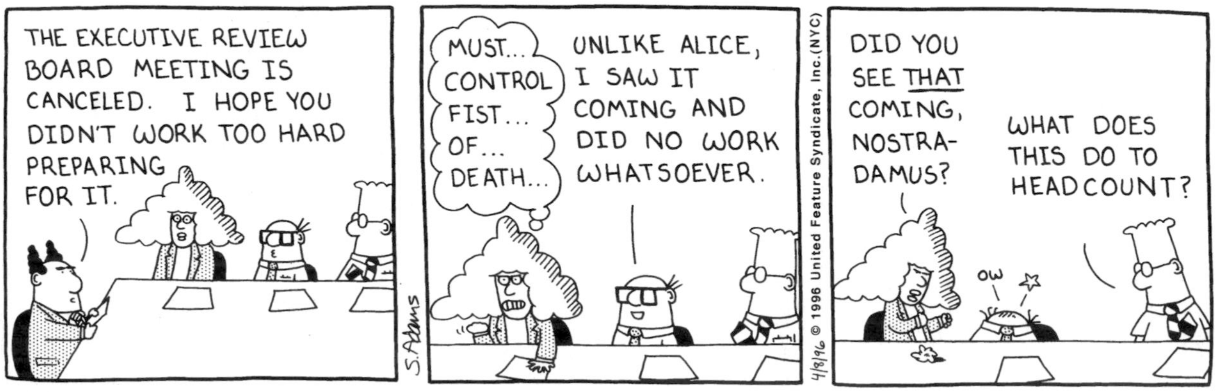
THE EXECUTIVE REVIEW BOARD MEETING IS CANCELED. I HOPE YOU DIDN'T WORK TOO HARD PREPARING FOR IT.
MUST... CONTROL FIST... OF... DEATH...
UNLIKE ALICE, I SAW IT COMING AND DID NO WORK WHATSOEVER.
DID YOU SEE THAT COMING, NOSTRADAMUS?
OW
WHAT DOES THIS DO TO HEADCOUNT?
S. Adams
4/8/96 © 1996 United Feature Syndicate, Inc.(NYC)

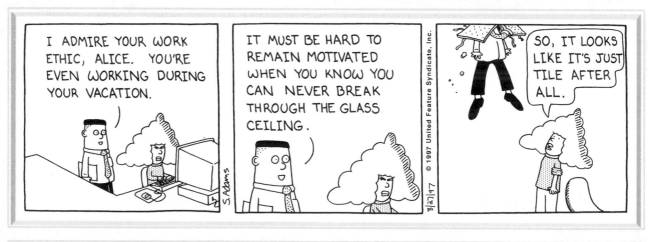

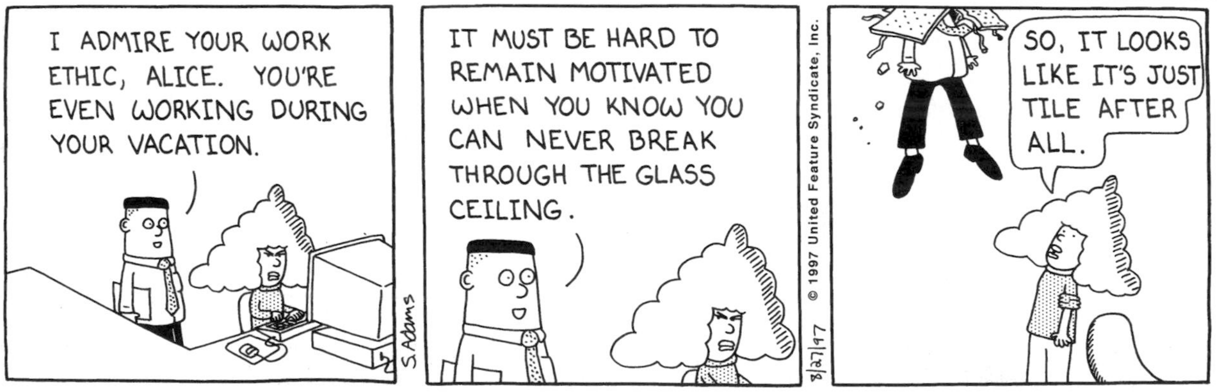
I ADMIRE YOUR WORK ETHIC, ALICE. YOU'RE EVEN WORKING DURING YOUR VACATION.
IT MUST BE HARD TO REMAIN MOTIVATED WHEN YOU KNOW YOU CAN NEVER BREAK THROUGH THE GLASS CEILING.
SO, IT LOOKS LIKE IT'S JUST TILE AFTER ALL.
S. Adams
8/27/97 © 1997 United Feature Syndicate, Inc.

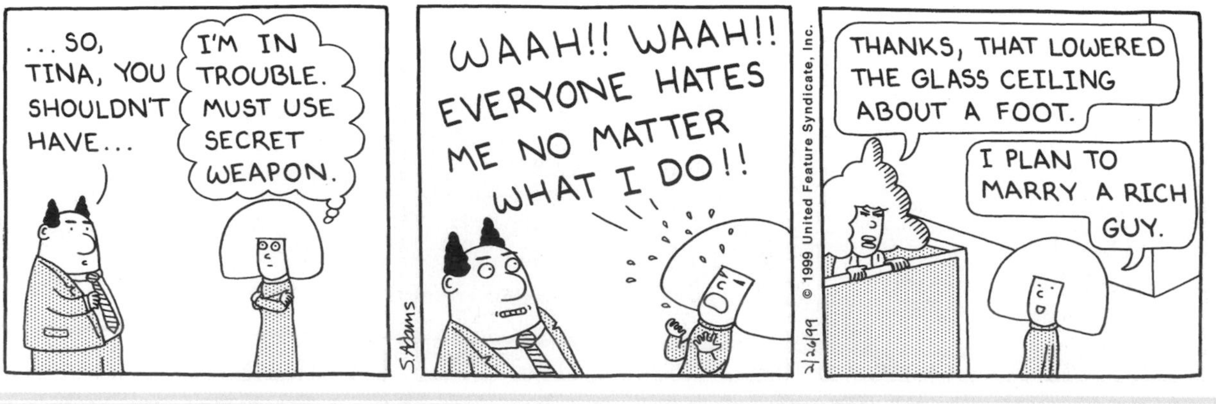
... SO, TINA, YOU SHOULDN'T HAVE...
I'M IN TROUBLE. MUST USE SECRET WEAPON.
WAAH!! WAAH!! EVERYONE HATES ME NO MATTER WHAT I DO!!
THANKS, THAT LOWERED THE GLASS CEILING ABOUT A FOOT.
I PLAN TO MARRY A RICH GUY.
S. Adams
2/26/99 © 1999 United Feature Syndicate, Inc.

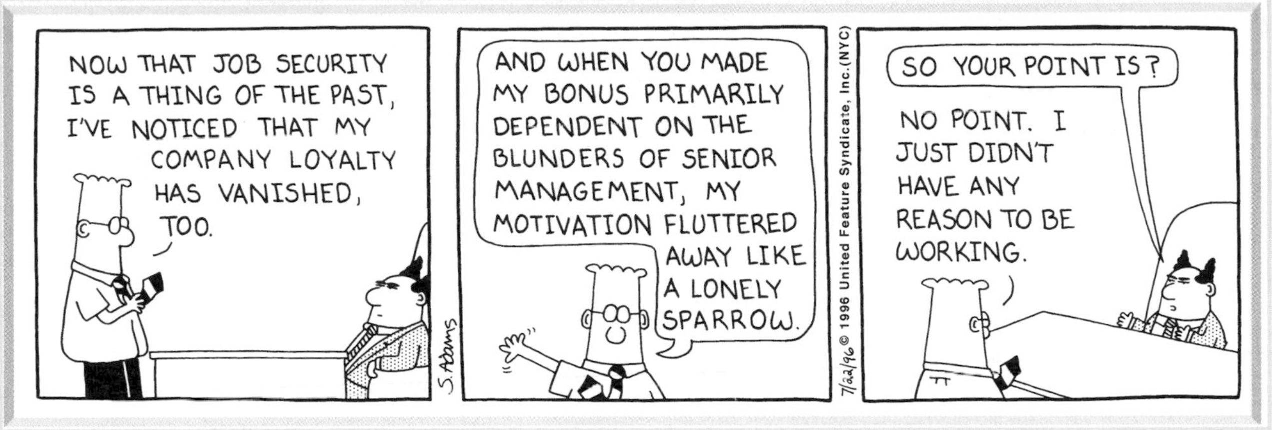
NOW THAT JOB SECURITY IS A THING OF THE PAST, I'VE NOTICED THAT MY COMPANY LOYALTY HAS VANISHED, TOO.
S. Adams
AND WHEN YOU MADE MY BONUS PRIMARILY DEPENDENT ON THE BLUNDERS OF SENIOR MANAGEMENT, MY MOTIVATION FLUTTERED AWAY LIKE A LONELY SPARROW.
7/22/96 © 1996 United Feature Syndicate, Inc.(NYC)
SO YOUR POINT IS?
NO POINT. I JUST DIDN'T HAVE ANY REASON TO BE WORKING.

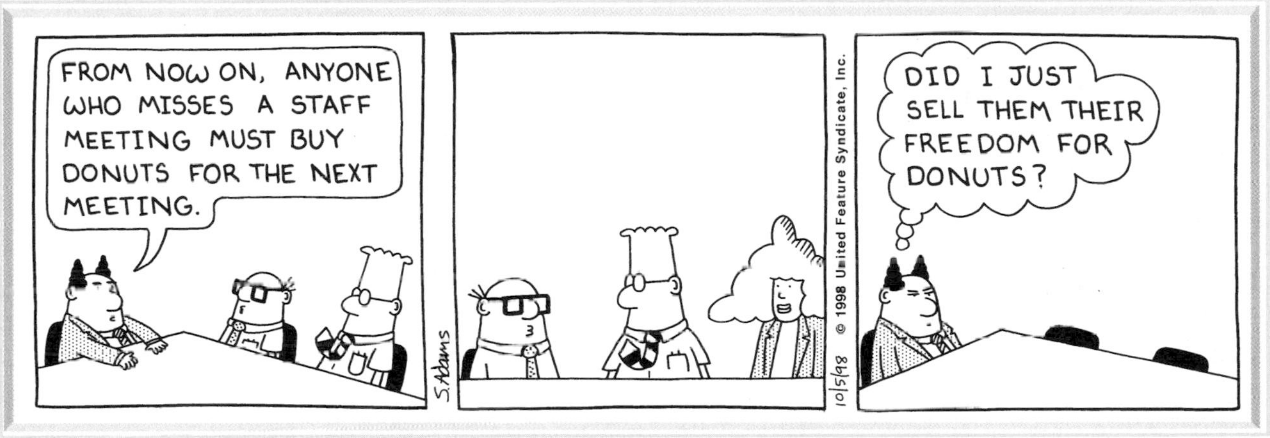
FROM NOW ON, ANYONE WHO MISSES A STAFF MEETING MUST BUY DONUTS FOR THE NEXT MEETING.
S. Adams
10/5/98 © 1998 United Feature Syndicate, Inc.
DID I JUST SELL THEM THEIR FREEDOM FOR DONUTS?

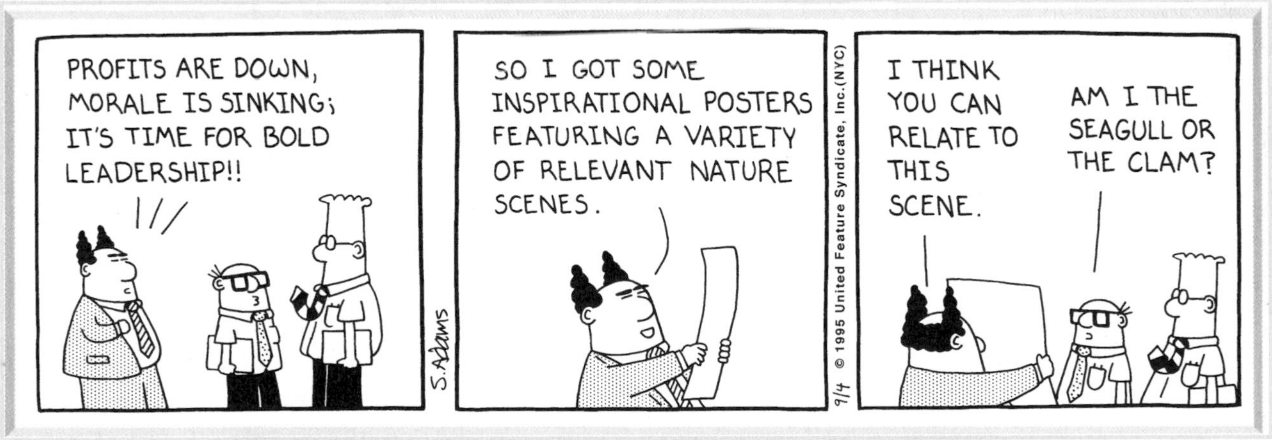
PROFITS ARE DOWN, MORALE IS SINKING; IT'S TIME FOR BOLD LEADERSHIP!!
S. Adams
SO I GOT SOME INSPIRATIONAL POSTERS FEATURING A VARIETY OF RELEVANT NATURE SCENES.
9/4 © 1995 United Feature Syndicate, Inc.(NYC)
I THINK YOU CAN RELATE TO THIS SCENE.
AM I THE SEAGULL OR THE CLAM?

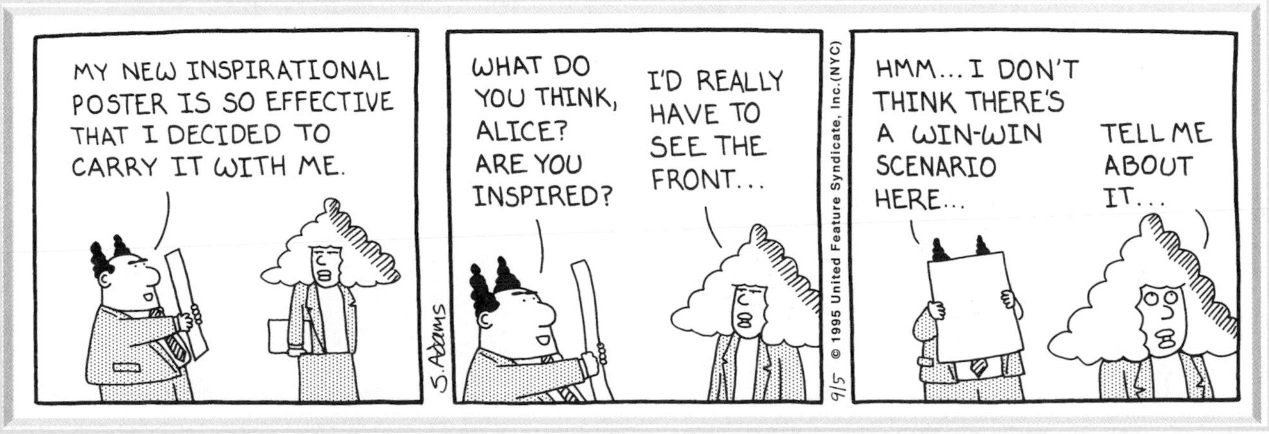
MY NEW INSPIRATIONAL POSTER IS SO EFFECTIVE THAT I DECIDED TO CARRY IT WITH ME.
S. Adams
WHAT DO YOU THINK, ALICE? ARE YOU INSPIRED?
I'D REALLY HAVE TO SEE THE FRONT...
9/5 © 1995 United Feature Syndicate, Inc.(NYC)
HMM... I DON'T THINK THERE'S A WIN-WIN SCENARIO HERE...
TELL ME ABOUT IT...

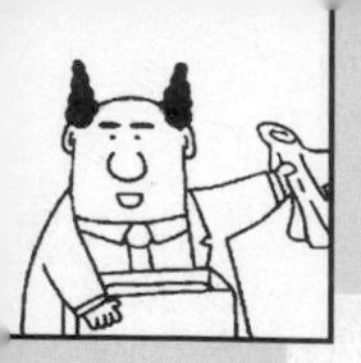

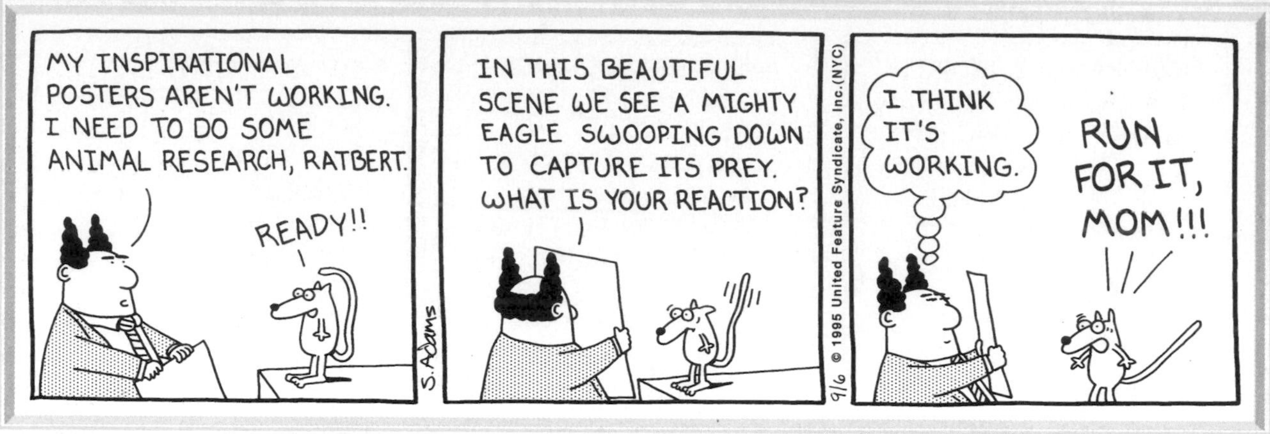
MY INSPIRATIONAL POSTERS AREN'T WORKING. I NEED TO DO SOME ANIMAL RESEARCH, RATBERT.
READY!!
S. Adams
IN THIS BEAUTIFUL SCENE WE SEE A MIGHTY EAGLE SWOOPING DOWN TO CAPTURE ITS PREY. WHAT IS YOUR REACTION?
9/6 © 1995 United Feature Syndicate, Inc.(NYC)
I THINK IT'S WORKING.
RUN FOR IT, MOM!!!

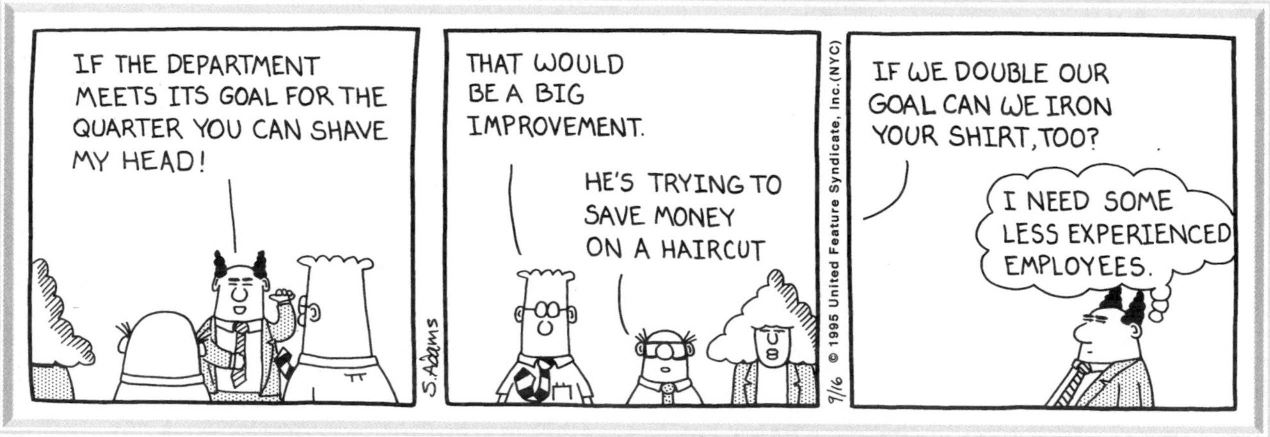
IF THE DEPARTMENT MEETS ITS GOAL FOR THE QUARTER YOU CAN SHAVE MY HEAD!
S. Adams
THAT WOULD BE A BIG IMPROVEMENT.
HE'S TRYING TO SAVE MONEY ON A HAIRCUT
9/16 © 1995 United Feature Syndicate, Inc.(NYC)
IF WE DOUBLE OUR GOAL CAN WE IRON YOUR SHIRT, TOO?
I NEED SOME LESS EXPERIENCED EMPLOYEES.

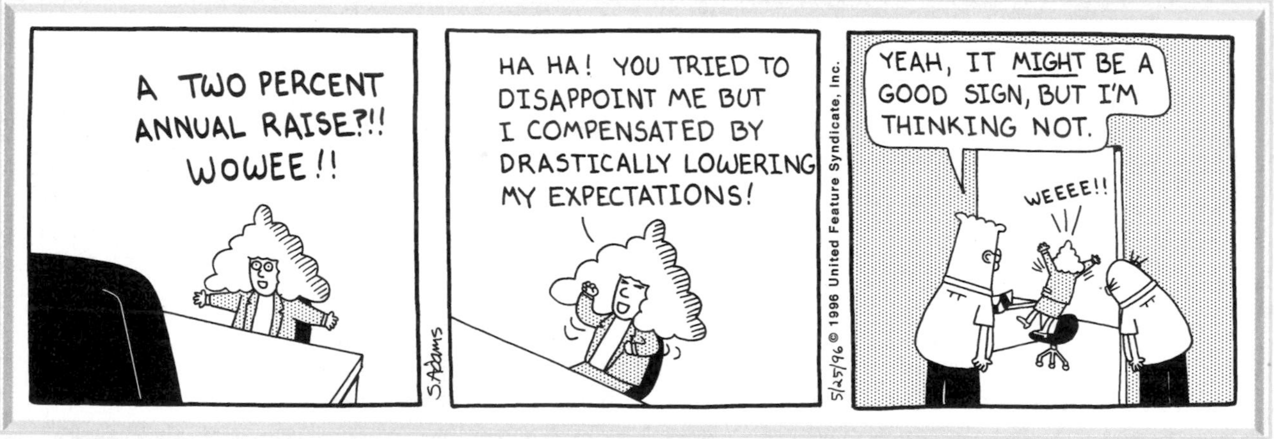
A TWO PERCENT ANNUAL RAISE?!! WOWEE!!
S.Adams
HA HA! YOU TRIED TO DISAPPOINT ME BUT I COMPENSATED BY DRASTICALLY LOWERING MY EXPECTATIONS!
5/25/96 © 1996 United Feature Syndicate, Inc.
YEAH, IT MIGHT BE A GOOD SIGN, BUT I'M THINKING NOT.
WEEEE!!

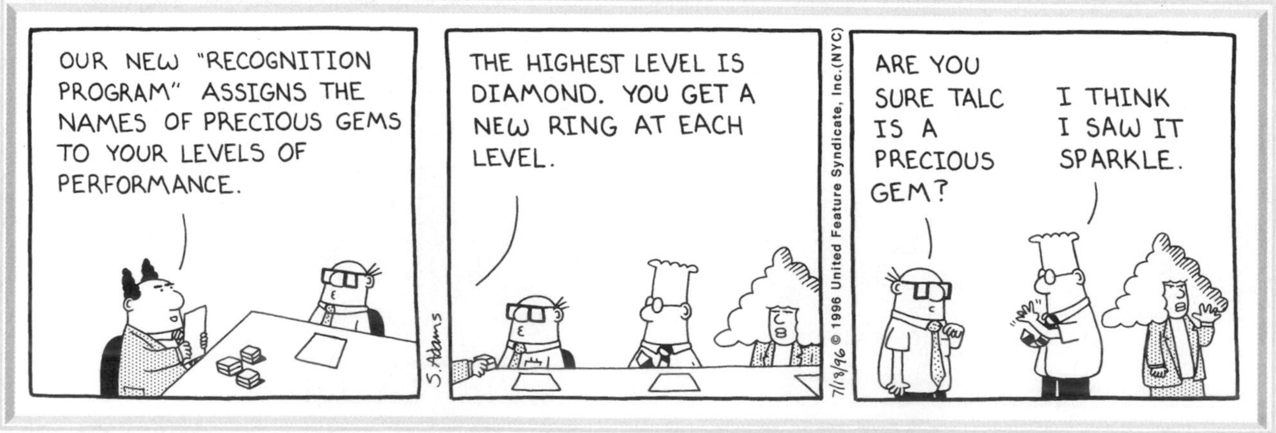
OUR NEW "RECOGNITION PROGRAM" ASSIGNS THE NAMES OF PRECIOUS GEMS TO YOUR LEVELS OF PERFORMANCE.
S. Adams
THE HIGHEST LEVEL IS DIAMOND. YOU GET A NEW RING AT EACH LEVEL.
7/18/96 © 1996 United Feature Syndicate, Inc.(NYC)
ARE YOU SURE TALC IS A PRECIOUS GEM?
I THINK I SAW IT SPARKLE.

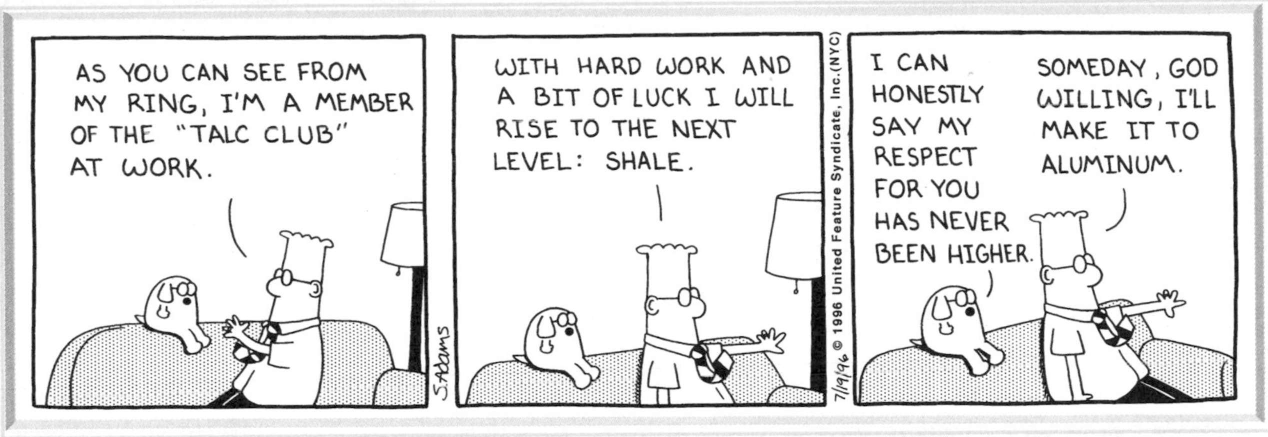
AS YOU CAN SEE FROM MY RING, I'M A MEMBER OF THE "TALC CLUB" AT WORK.
WITH HARD WORK AND A BIT OF LUCK I WILL RISE TO THE NEXT LEVEL: SHALE.
I CAN HONESTLY SAY MY RESPECT FOR YOU HAS NEVER BEEN HIGHER.
SOMEDAY, GOD WILLING, I'LL MAKE IT TO ALUMINUM.
7/9/96 © 1996 United Feature Syndicate, Inc.(NYC)

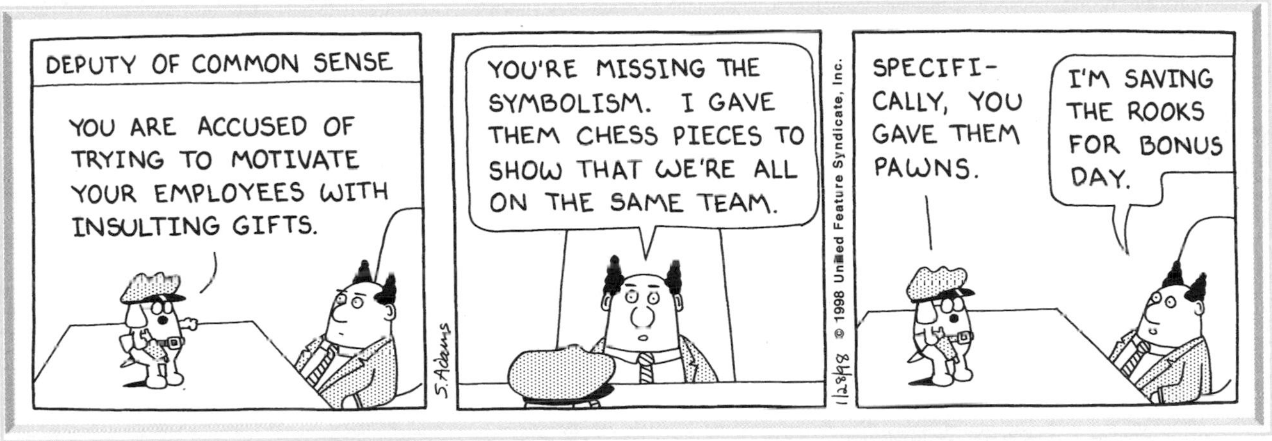
DEPUTY OF COMMON SENSE
YOU ARE ACCUSED OF TRYING TO MOTIVATE YOUR EMPLOYEES WITH INSULTING GIFTS.
YOU'RE MISSING THE SYMBOLISM. I GAVE THEM CHESS PIECES TO SHOW THAT WE'RE ALL ON THE SAME TEAM.
SPECIFI-CALLY, YOU GAVE THEM PAWNS.
I'M SAVING THE ROOKS FOR BONUS DAY.
1/28/98 © 1998 United Feature Syndicate, Inc.

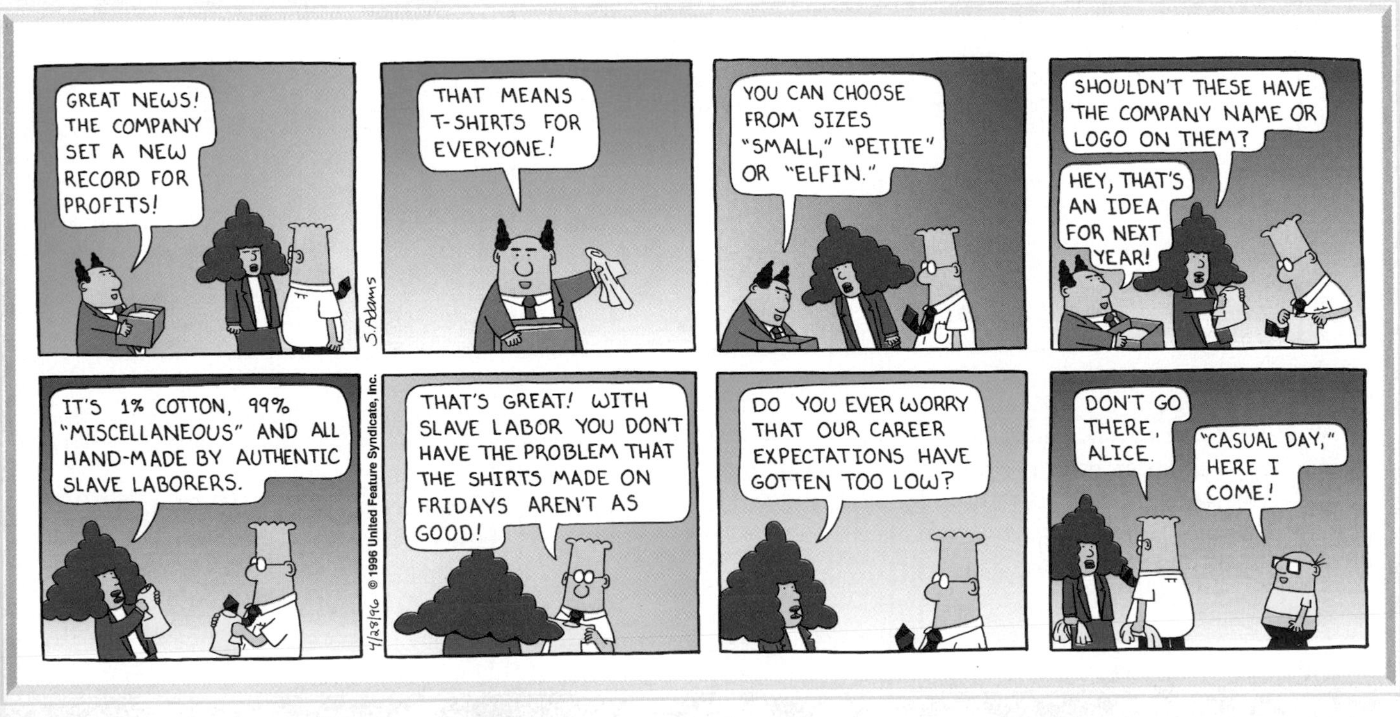
GREAT NEWS! THE COMPANY SET A NEW RECORD FOR PROFITS!
THAT MEANS T-SHIRTS FOR EVERYONE!
YOU CAN CHOOSE FROM SIZES "SMALL," "PETITE" OR "ELFIN."
SHOULDN'T THESE HAVE THE COMPANY NAME OR LOGO ON THEM?
HEY, THAT'S AN IDEA FOR NEXT YEAR!
IT'S 1% COTTON, 99% "MISCELLANEOUS" AND ALL HAND-MADE BY AUTHENTIC SLAVE LABORERS.
THAT'S GREAT! WITH SLAVE LABOR YOU DON'T HAVE THE PROBLEM THAT THE SHIRTS MADE ON FRIDAYS AREN'T AS GOOD!
DO YOU EVER WORRY THAT OUR CAREER EXPECTATIONS HAVE GOTTEN TOO LOW?
DON'T GO THERE, ALICE.
"CASUAL DAY," HERE I COME!
4/28/96 © 1996 United Feature Syndicate, Inc.

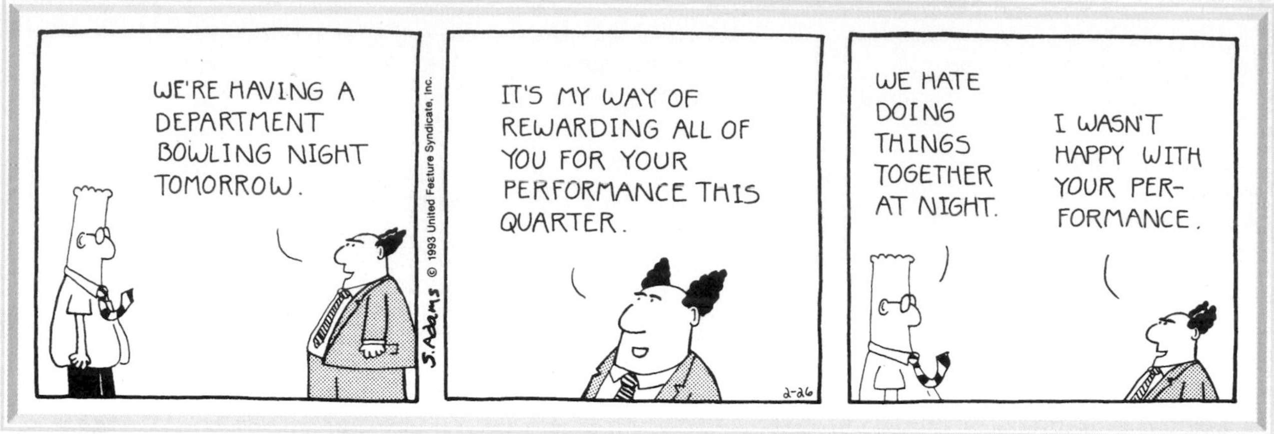
WE'RE HAVING A DEPARTMENT BOWLING NIGHT TOMORROW.
S. Adams © 1993 United Feature Syndicate, Inc.
IT'S MY WAY OF REWARDING ALL OF YOU FOR YOUR PERFORMANCE THIS QUARTER.
2-26
WE HATE DOING THINGS TOGETHER AT NIGHT.
I WASN'T HAPPY WITH YOUR PERFORMANCE.

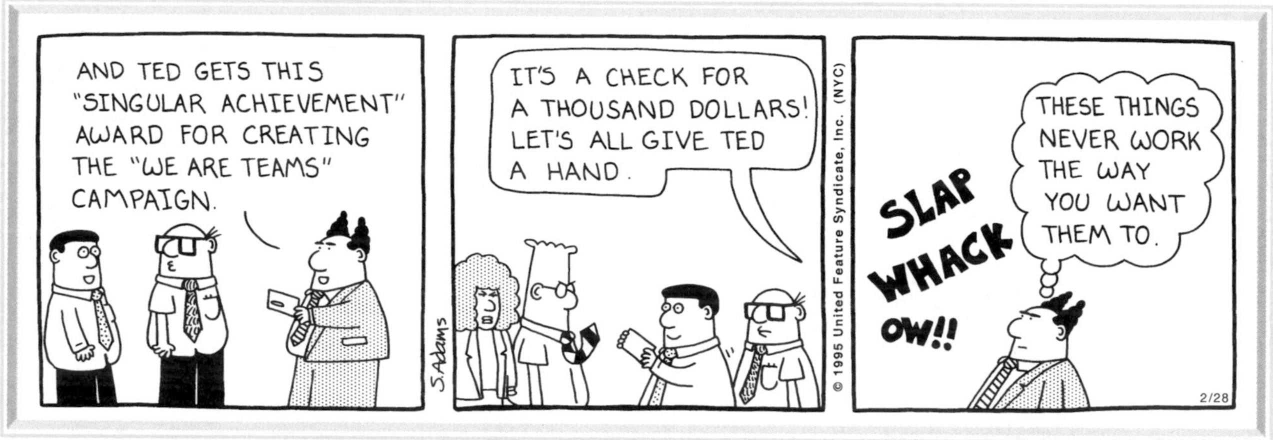
AND TED GETS THIS "SINGULAR ACHIEVEMENT" AWARD FOR CREATING THE "WE ARE TEAMS" CAMPAIGN.
S. Adams
IT'S A CHECK FOR A THOUSAND DOLLARS! LET'S ALL GIVE TED A HAND.
© 1995 United Feature Syndicate, Inc. (NYC)
SLAP
WHACK
OW!!
THESE THINGS NEVER WORK THE WAY YOU WANT THEM TO.
2/28

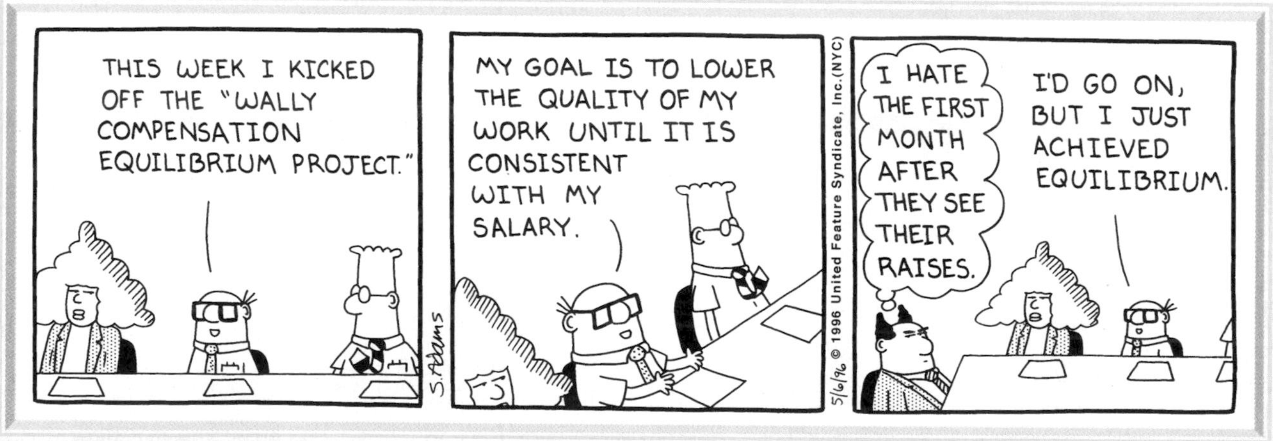
THIS WEEK I KICKED OFF THE "WALLY COMPENSATION EQUILIBRIUM PROJECT."
S. Adams
MY GOAL IS TO LOWER THE QUALITY OF MY WORK UNTIL IT IS CONSISTENT WITH MY SALARY.
5/6/96 © 1996 United Feature Syndicate, Inc.(NYC)
I HATE THE FIRST MONTH AFTER THEY SEE THEIR RAISES.
I'D GO ON, BUT I JUST ACHIEVED EQUILIBRIUM.

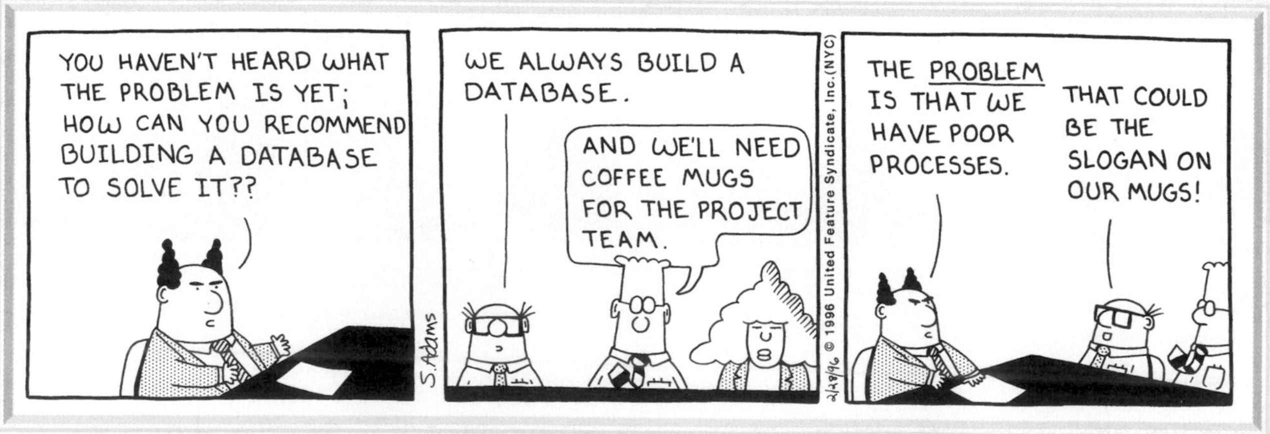
YOU HAVEN'T HEARD WHAT THE PROBLEM IS YET; HOW CAN YOU RECOMMEND BUILDING A DATABASE TO SOLVE IT??
S. Adams
WE ALWAYS BUILD A DATABASE.
AND WE'LL NEED COFFEE MUGS FOR THE PROJECT TEAM.
2/28/96 © 1996 United Feature Syndicate, Inc.(NYC)
THE PROBLEM IS THAT WE HAVE POOR PROCESSES.
THAT COULD BE THE SLOGAN ON OUR MUGS!

BE CANDID, DILBERT. WE HAVE A CORPORATE PHILOSOPHY THAT SAYS WE "DON'T SHOOT THE MESSENGER."
GOOD.
© 1990 United Feature Syndicate, Inc.
HAD YOU CONSULTED WITH THE ENGINEERING DEPARTMENT, YOU NEVER WOULD HAVE LAUNCHED SUCH AN ILL-CONCEIVED PRODUCT.
IT IS DOOMED TO FAIL. YOU WILL ALL BE HUMILIATED AND PROBABLY FIRED.
CAN'T I JUST WING HIM?!!
NO, EILEEN, THAT'S NOT OUR PHI-LOSOPHY.
IT TURNS OUT THE CORPORATE PHILOSOPHY IS A VERY FLEXIBLE DOCUMENT.
YOU'RE GETTING TAR ON THE CARPET.

DILBERT, DO A PRESENTA-TION FOR THE BIG BOSS TOMORROW MORNING ON THE STATUS OF YOUR PROJECT.
THERE ISN'T ANY STATUS. YOU ONLY ASSIGNED THE PROJECT AN HOUR AGO.
WELL THEN, DO A PRESENTATION ON WHY THERE'S NO STATUS.
I DON'T HAVE TIME BEFORE TOMORROW MORNING.
OKAY, THEN JUST DO A PRESENTATION ON WHY THERE'S NO TIME TO DO A PRESENTATION OF THE STATUS.
AND I WANT TO REVIEW IT TWO DAYS BEFORE YOU PRESENT IT.
THAT WOULD BE YESTERDAY.
SHOULD I DO A PRESENTATION ON WHY TOMORROW IS LESS THAN TWO DAYS FROM TODAY?
HMM...GOOD. THE BOSS LIKES THAT ANALYTICAL STUFF.

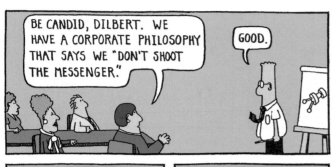

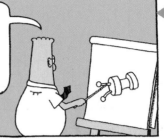

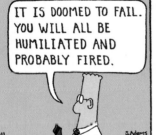

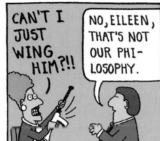

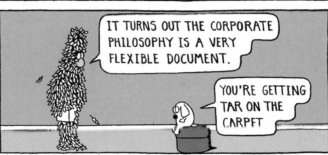

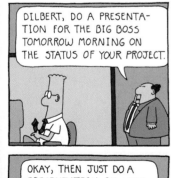

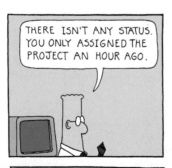

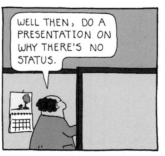

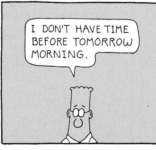

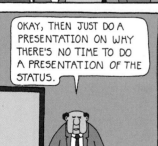

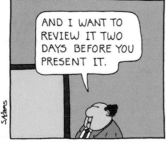

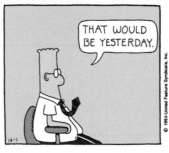

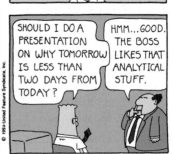

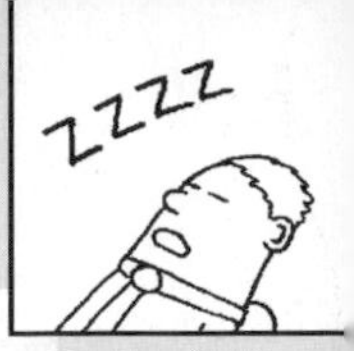

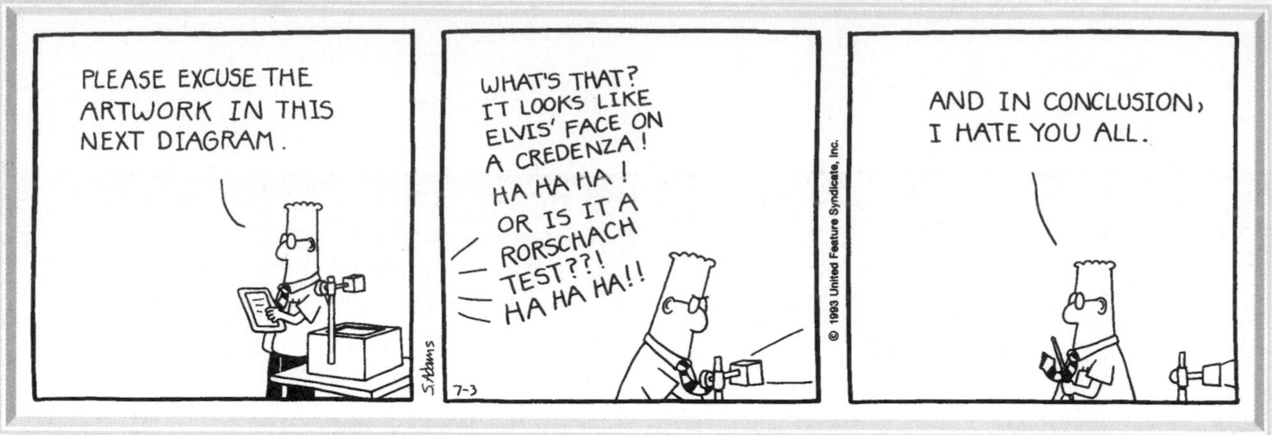
PLEASE EXCUSE THE ARTWORK IN THIS NEXT DIAGRAM.
S.Adams
WHAT'S THAT? IT LOOKS LIKE ELVIS' FACE ON A CREDENZA! HA HA HA! OR IS IT A RORSCHACH TEST??! HA HA HA!!
7-3
© 1993 United Feature Syndicate, Inc.
AND IN CONCLUSION, I HATE YOU ALL.

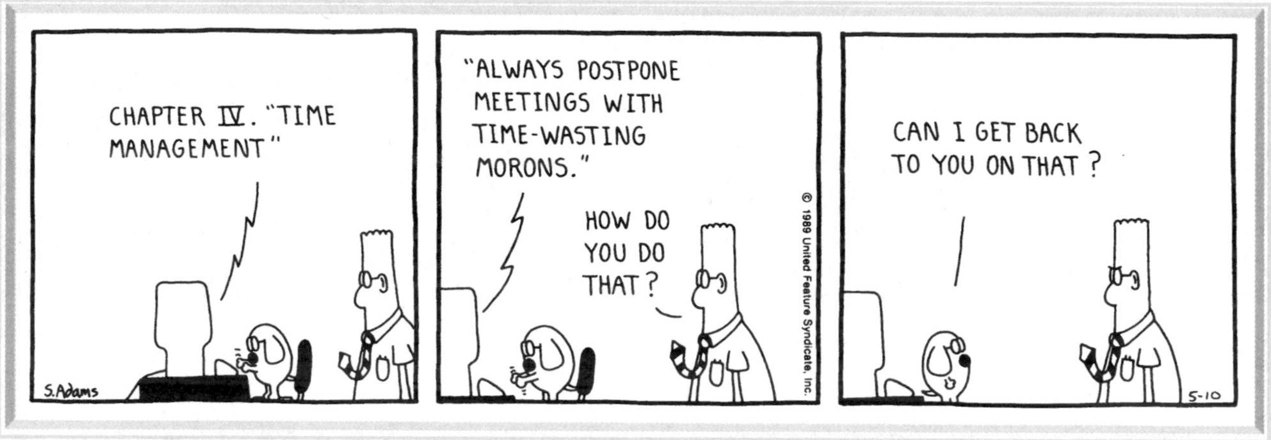
CHAPTER IV. "TIME MANAGEMENT"
S.Adams
"ALWAYS POSTPONE MEETINGS WITH TIME-WASTING MORONS."
HOW DO YOU DO THAT?
© 1989 United Feature Syndicate, Inc.
CAN I GET BACK TO YOU ON THAT?
5-10

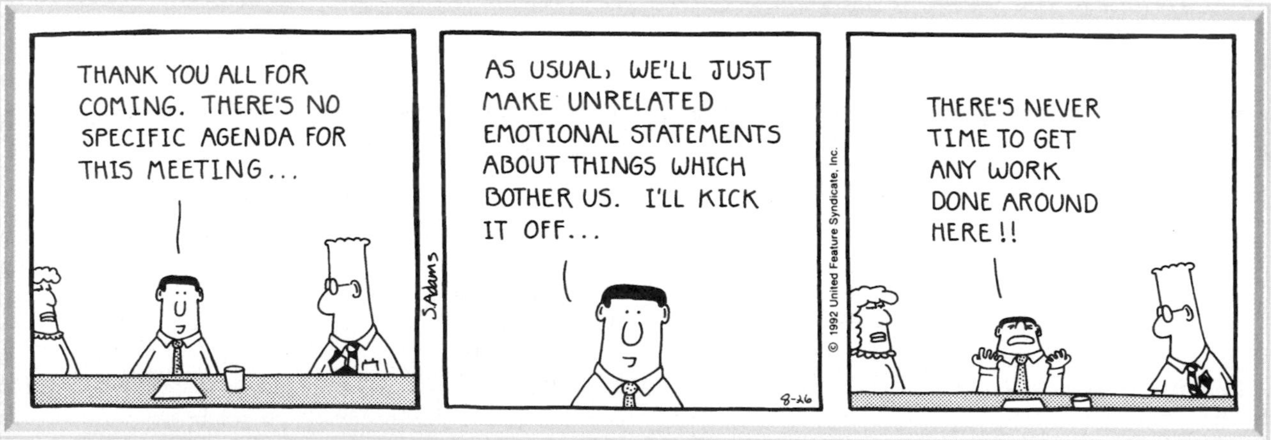
THANK YOU ALL FOR COMING. THERE'S NO SPECIFIC AGENDA FOR THIS MEETING...
S.Adams
AS USUAL, WE'LL JUST MAKE UNRELATED EMOTIONAL STATEMENTS ABOUT THINGS WHICH BOTHER US. I'LL KICK IT OFF...
8-26
© 1992 United Feature Syndicate, Inc.
THERE'S NEVER TIME TO GET ANY WORK DONE AROUND HERE!!

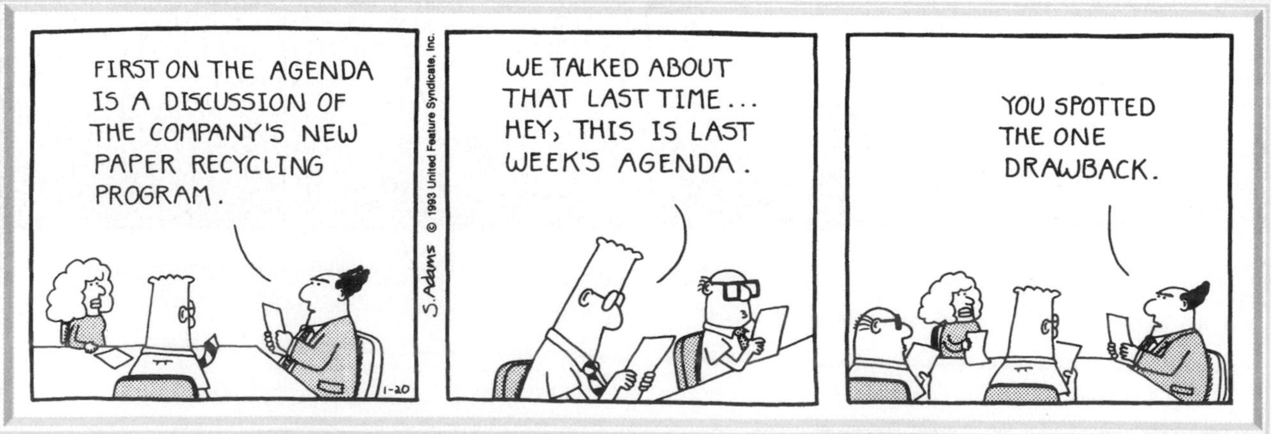
FIRST ON THE AGENDA IS A DISCUSSION OF THE COMPANY'S NEW PAPER RECYCLING PROGRAM.
1-20
S.Adams © 1993 United Feature Syndicate, Inc.
WE TALKED ABOUT THAT LAST TIME... HEY, THIS IS LAST WEEK'S AGENDA.
YOU SPOTTED THE ONE DRAWBACK.

ZZZZ

...THEREFORE, I RECOMMEND THAT WE SWITCH TO THE NEW TECHNOLOGY... ANY QUESTIONS?
DILBERT, ARE YOU WILLING TO BET YOUR CAREER ON THIS?
YES, I WOULD DEFINITELY BET MY CAREER.
YOU WOULD TOO IF YOU HAD MY CAREER.
I HAVE A VIEW GRAPH WHICH ANTICIPATED YOUR QUESTION.
S.Adams
THIS CHART TRACKS MY DECLINING SENSE OF SELF-WORTH AS MY CAREER PROGRESSES.
9-6
AT THE LOW-POINT, HERE, I'M REDUCED TO ANSWERING IMBECILIC QUESTIONS WHILE POINTING A LITTLE STICK AT THE WALL.
© 1992 United Feature Syndicate, Inc.
HOW DID THE PRESENTATION GO?
THERE'S SUCH A THING AS BEING TOO PREPARED.

THIS CONCLUDES MY PROPOSAL TO THE EXECUTIVE COMMITTEE. ANY QUESTIONS?
A
B
NO, I THINK MOST OF US WERE THINKING ABOUT OTHER THINGS.
BUT HERE'S MY IMPRESSION OF WHAT YOU LOOKED LIKE GIVING THE PRESENTATION.
© 1991 United Feature Syndicate, Inc.
FUH FUH FUH FUH
NO, NO, IT WAS MORE LIKE...
S.Adams
FUH FUH FUH FUH
HOW DID YOUR PRESENTATION GO?
DON'T ASK.
FUH FUH DON'T ASK FUH FUH FUH FUH...
4-21

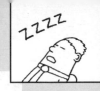

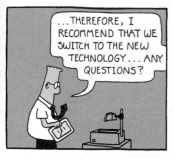

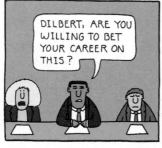

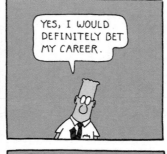

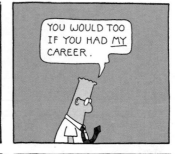

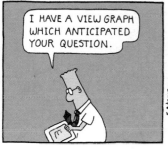

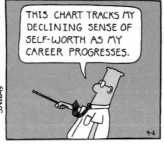

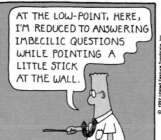

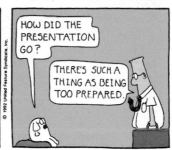

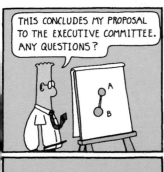

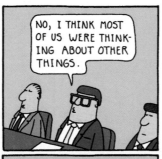

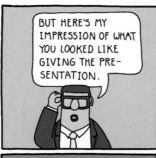

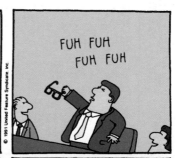

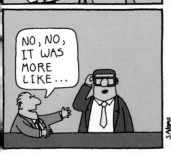

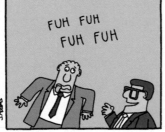

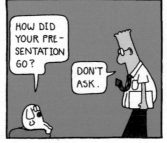

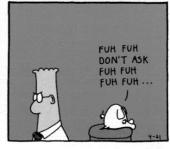

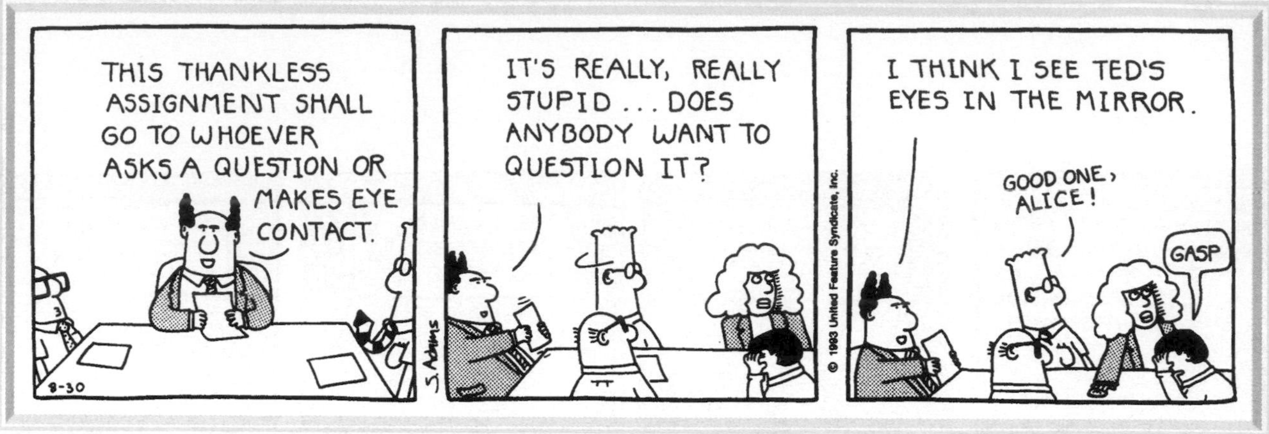
THIS THANKLESS ASSIGNMENT SHALL GO TO WHOEVER ASKS A QUESTION OR MAKES EYE CONTACT.
8-30
S. Adams
IT'S REALLY, REALLY STUPID ... DOES ANYBODY WANT TO QUESTION IT?
© 1993 United Feature Syndicate, Inc.
I THINK I SEE TED'S EYES IN THE MIRROR.
GOOD ONE, ALICE!
GASP

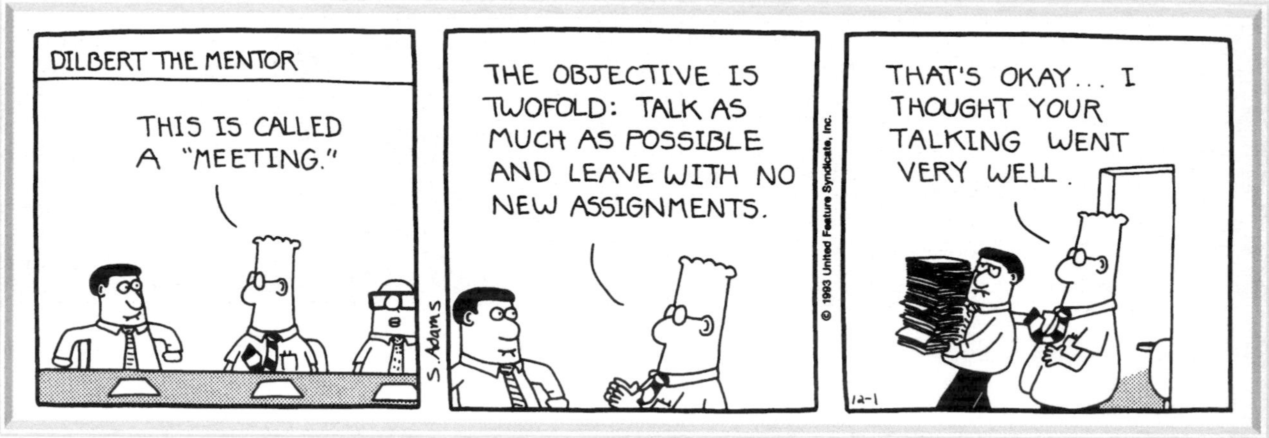
DILBERT THE MENTOR
THIS IS CALLED A "MEETING."
S. Adams
THE OBJECTIVE IS TWOFOLD: TALK AS MUCH AS POSSIBLE AND LEAVE WITH NO NEW ASSIGNMENTS.
© 1993 United Feature Syndicate, Inc.
THAT'S OKAY... I THOUGHT YOUR TALKING WENT VERY WELL.
12-1

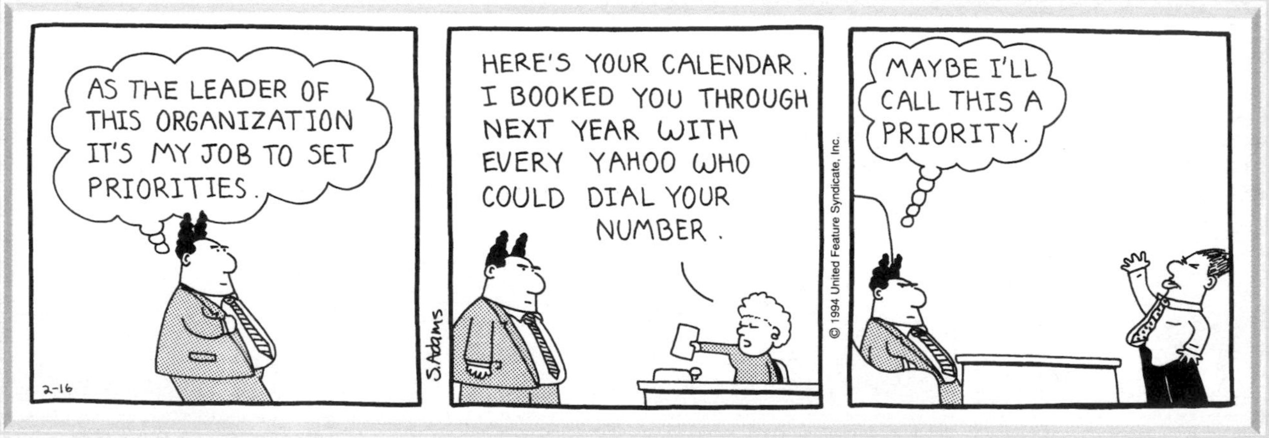
AS THE LEADER OF THIS ORGANIZATION IT'S MY JOB TO SET PRIORITIES.
2-16
S. Adams
HERE'S YOUR CALENDAR. I BOOKED YOU THROUGH NEXT YEAR WITH EVERY YAHOO WHO COULD DIAL YOUR NUMBER.
© 1994 United Feature Syndicate, Inc.
MAYBE I'LL CALL THIS A PRIORITY.

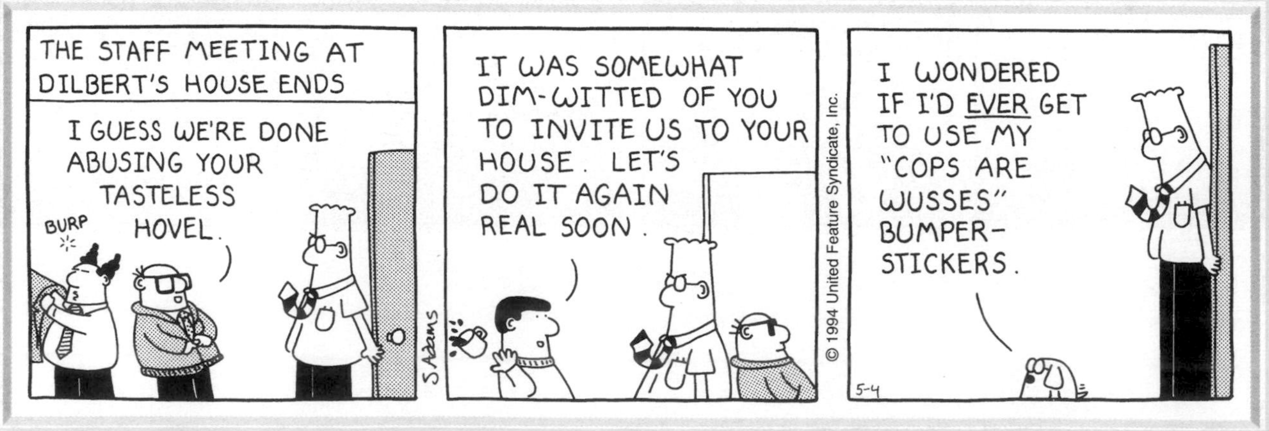
THE STAFF MEETING AT DILBERT'S HOUSE ENDS
I GUESS WE'RE DONE ABUSING YOUR TASTELESS HOVEL.
BURP
S. Adams
IT WAS SOMEWHAT DIM-WITTED OF YOU TO INVITE US TO YOUR HOUSE. LET'S DO IT AGAIN REAL SOON.
© 1994 United Feature Syndicate, Inc.
I WONDERED IF I'D EVER GET TO USE MY "COPS ARE WUSSES" BUMPER-STICKERS.
5-4

THAT'S FOUR HOURS THAT I'D LIKE TO HAVE BACK.
WHO CALLED THAT MEETING ANYWAY?
I MUST HAVE LEFT MY CALENDAR IN THERE.
OOOH
?
I'VE DISCOVERED A PRIMITIVE DONUT-SCAVENGING MAN CLAD ONLY IN YELLOW STICKY NOTES!!
I WAS ONCE LIKE YOU, BEFORE THE GREAT RIF.
BUT RATHER THAN LEAVE IN HUMILIATION I DECIDED TO STAY AND LIVE OFF THE LAND LIKE OUR PROUD ANCESTORS.
TO ENSURE A BOUNTIFUL HARVEST I DO MY DONUT DANCE TO THE GODS.
WHEN THAT DOESN'T WORK I DISTRIBUTE MEETING NOTICES.
YOU'RE THE ONE!!
S. Adams
© 1995 United Feature Syndicate, Inc.(NYC)

I WORKED ALL NIGHT BUT I FINISHED THE PRESENTATION PACKAGE YOU WANTED.
PUT THE PRESENTATION DATE ON EACH PAGE.
THOSE ARE COLOR TRANSPARENCIES. IT WOULD TAKE HOURS AND COST HUNDREDS OF DOLLARS TO REPRINT THEM.
THERE'S NO REASON TO DATE THEM. IN FACT, IT WOULD LIMIT FUTURE USE AND CLUTTER THE PAGE.
BUT SINCE YOU'RE INCAPABLE OF ADMITTING ERROR...
I EAGERLY AWAIT YOUR BIZARRE, OTHER-WORLDLY EXPLANATION FOR PUTTING THE DATE ON EACH PAGE.
SOME PEOPLE MIGHT NOT HAVE CALENDARS. AND WE HAVE TO MAKE SURE IT'S NOT A HOLIDAY.
BAM!
OUCH. MY BRAIN EXPLODED.
THE FIRST PRESENTATION IS FEBRUARY 30TH...
S. Adams
© 1995 United Feature Syndicate, Inc.(NYC)
11/5

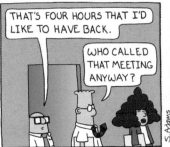

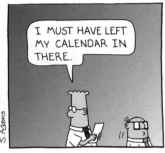

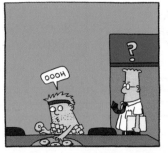

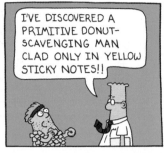

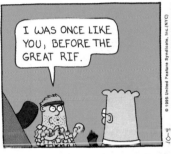

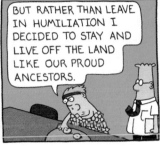

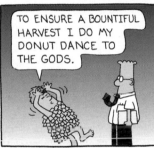

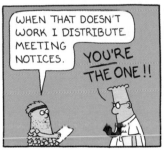

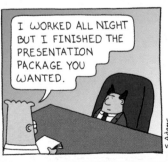

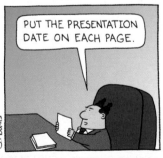

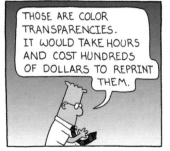

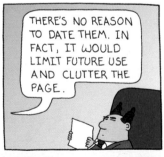

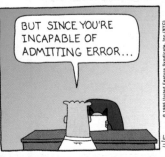

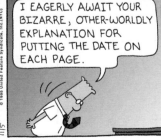

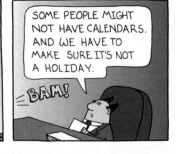

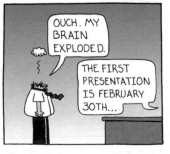

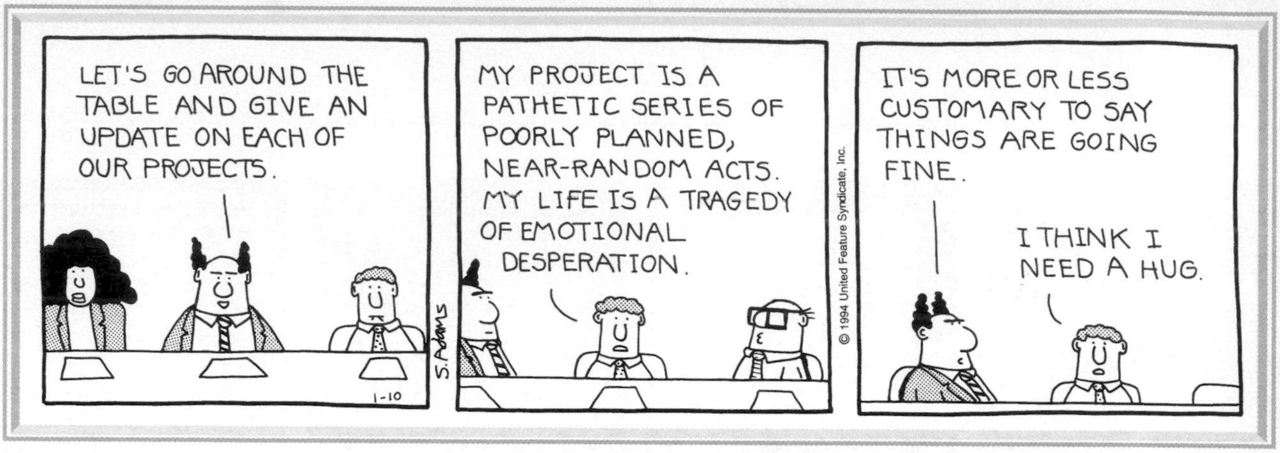
LET'S GO AROUND THE TABLE AND GIVE AN UPDATE ON EACH OF OUR PROJECTS.
MY PROJECT IS A PATHETIC SERIES OF POORLY PLANNED, NEAR-RANDOM ACTS. MY LIFE IS A TRAGEDY OF EMOTIONAL DESPERATION.
IT'S MORE OR LESS CUSTOMARY TO SAY THINGS ARE GOING FINE.
I THINK I NEED A HUG.
© 1994 United Feature Syndicate, Inc.

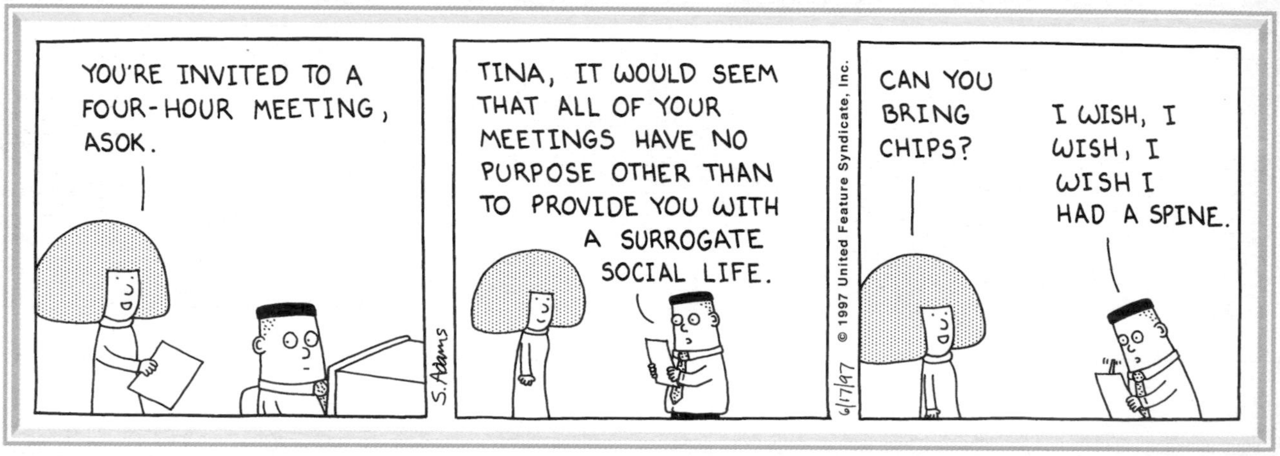
YOU'RE INVITED TO A FOUR-HOUR MEETING, ASOK.
TINA, IT WOULD SEEM THAT ALL OF YOUR MEETINGS HAVE NO PURPOSE OTHER THAN TO PROVIDE YOU WITH A SURROGATE SOCIAL LIFE.
CAN YOU BRING CHIPS?
I WISH, I WISH, I WISH I HAD A SPINE.
© 1997 United Feature Syndicate, Inc.

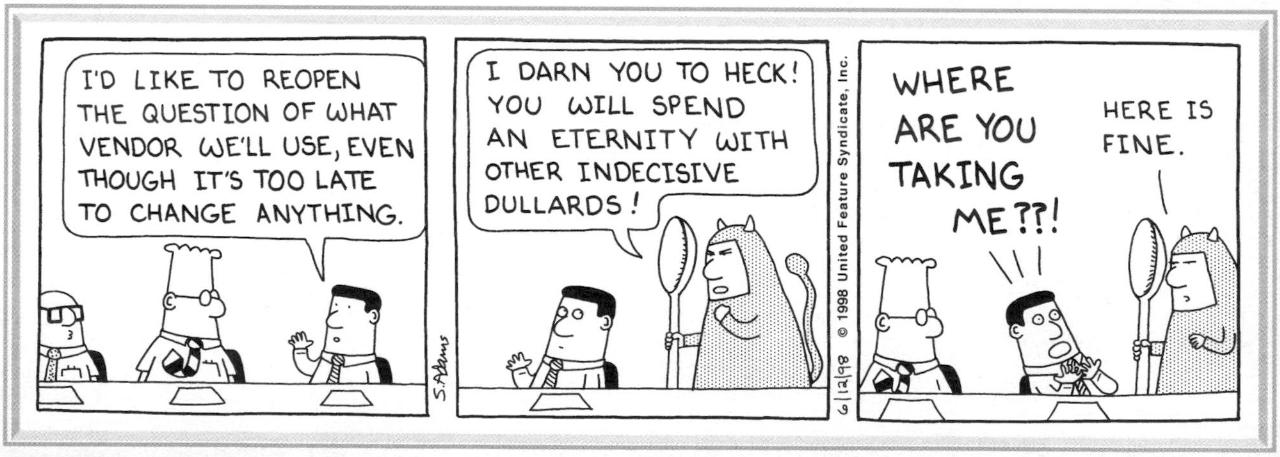
I'D LIKE TO REOPEN THE QUESTION OF WHAT VENDOR WE'LL USE, EVEN THOUGH IT'S TOO LATE TO CHANGE ANYTHING.
I DARN YOU TO HECK! YOU WILL SPEND AN ETERNITY WITH OTHER INDECISIVE DULLARDS!
WHERE ARE YOU TAKING ME??!
HERE IS FINE.
© 1998 United Feature Syndicate, Inc.

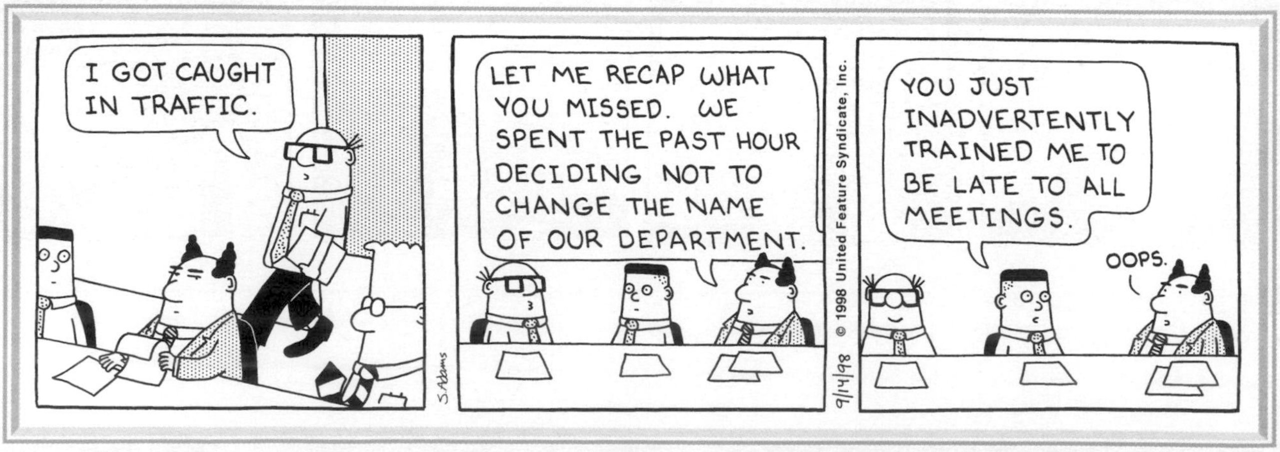
I GOT CAUGHT IN TRAFFIC.
LET ME RECAP WHAT YOU MISSED. WE SPENT THE PAST HOUR DECIDING NOT TO CHANGE THE NAME OF OUR DEPARTMENT.
YOU JUST INADVERTENTLY TRAINED ME TO BE LATE TO ALL MEETINGS.
OOPS.
© 1998 United Feature Syndicate, Inc.

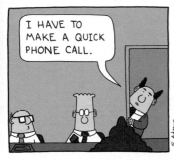

I HAVE TO MAKE A QUICK PHONE CALL.
S. Adams
DO YOU WANT TO MAKE SMALL TALK?
NO.
I BROUGHT A MAGAZINE.
COULD YOU TEAR OUT A FEW PAGES FOR ME TO READ?
THAT WOULDN'T BE RIGHT.
GIVE ME SOME PAGES OR ELSE I'LL ASK ALICE ABOUT PANTY HOSE.
YOU WOULDN'T DARE.
10/12/97 © 1997 United Feature Syndicate, Inc.
SO, ALICE, WHAT DO YOU THINK OF THE CONCEPT OF PANTY HOSE?
AARGH!! WHAT MORON INVENTED LEG COVERS THAT CAN BE DESTROYED BY TOUCHING A TWIG?!
HERE! MAKE IT STOP!!
TOO LATE.
LOOK AT THIS!!!

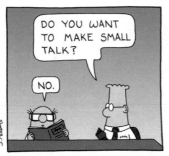

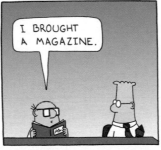

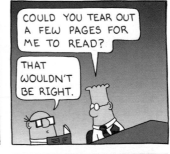

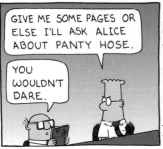

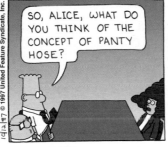

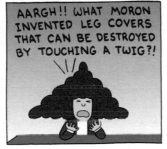

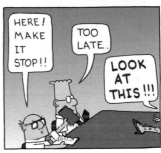

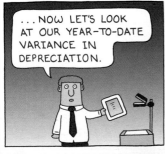

. . . NOW LET'S LOOK AT OUR YEAR-TO-DATE VARIANCE IN DEPRECIATION.
S. Adams
ONLY FIVE MINUTES LEFT OF OUR FOUR HOUR MEETING.
ZZZZZZ
IF HE KEEPS DRONING, THERE WON'T BE ANY TIME FOR MY PRESENTATION.
ZZZZZ
I SPENT A WHOLE WEEK PREPARING MY PRESENTATION.
ZZZZ
ZZZ
EVERYONE ELSE IS ALREADY ASLEEP.
4/5/98 © 1998 United Feature Syndicate, Inc.
MY ONLY HOPE IS TO STUN THE PRESENTER WITH A STALE DONUT.
ZZZZ
AS YOU CAN SEE, THERE'S NOTHING TO REPORT.
$
I WASTED A DONUT.
ZZZZ
ZZZZ

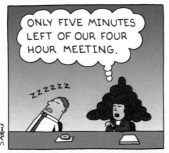

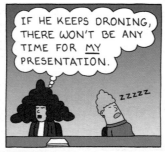

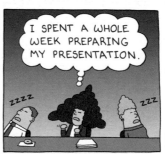

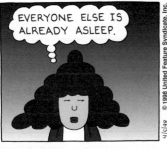

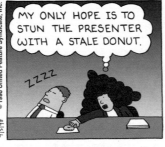

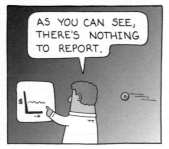

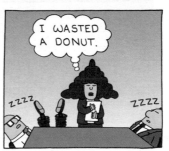

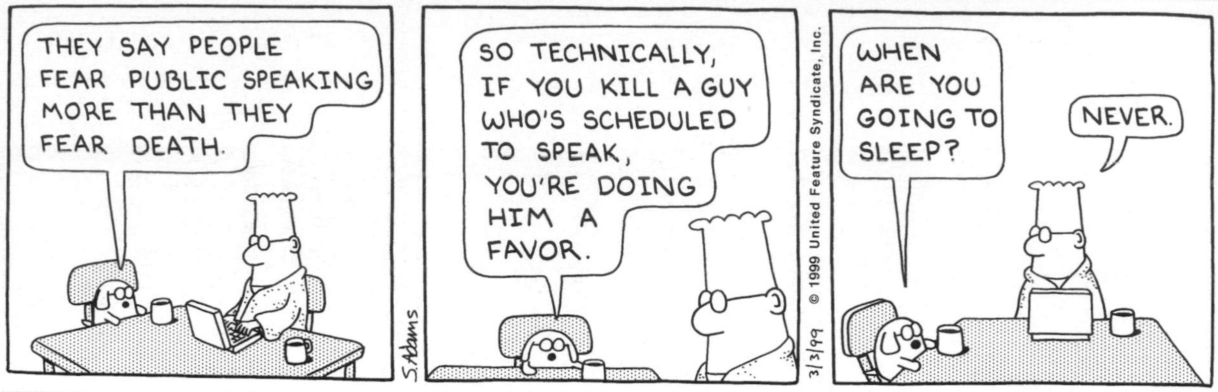
THEY SAY PEOPLE FEAR PUBLIC SPEAKING MORE THAN THEY FEAR DEATH.
SO TECHNICALLY, IF YOU KILL A GUY WHO'S SCHEDULED TO SPEAK, YOU'RE DOING HIM A FAVOR.
WHEN ARE YOU GOING TO SLEEP?
NEVER.
S. Adams
3/3/99 © 1999 United Feature Syndicate, Inc.

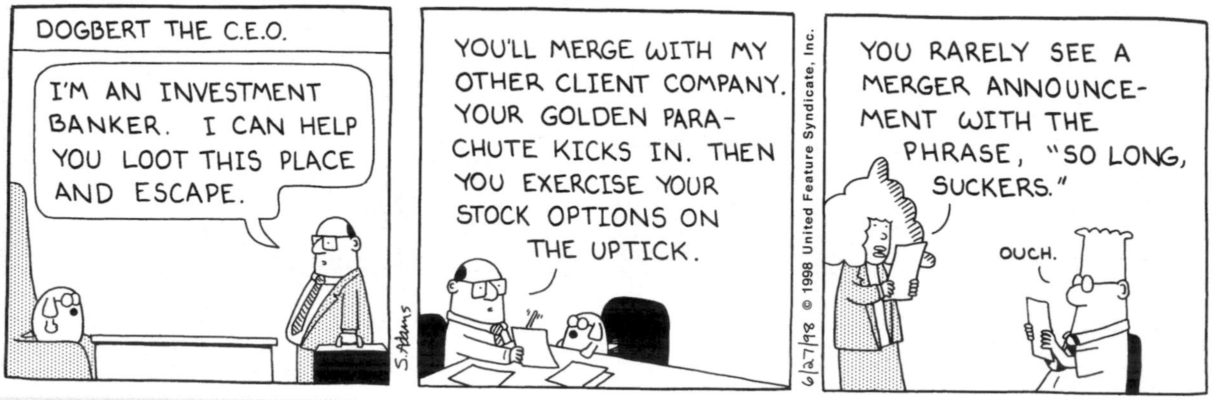
DOGBERT THE C.E.O.
I'M AN INVESTMENT BANKER. I CAN HELP YOU LOOT THIS PLACE AND ESCAPE.
YOU'LL MERGE WITH MY OTHER CLIENT COMPANY. YOUR GOLDEN PARACHUTE KICKS IN. THEN YOU EXERCISE YOUR STOCK OPTIONS ON THE UPTICK.
YOU RARELY SEE A MERGER ANNOUNCEMENT WITH THE PHRASE, "SO LONG, SUCKERS."
OUCH.
S. Adams
6/27/98 © 1998 United Feature Syndicate, Inc.

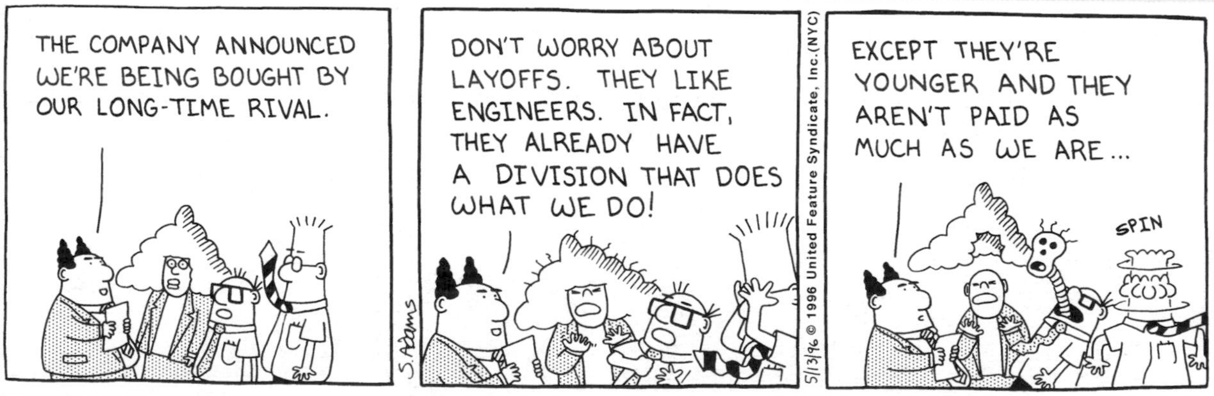
THE COMPANY ANNOUNCED WE'RE BEING BOUGHT BY OUR LONG-TIME RIVAL.
DON'T WORRY ABOUT LAYOFFS. THEY LIKE ENGINEERS. IN FACT, THEY ALREADY HAVE A DIVISION THAT DOES WHAT WE DO!
EXCEPT THEY'RE YOUNGER AND THEY AREN'T PAID AS MUCH AS WE ARE...
SPIN
S. Adams
5/13/96 © 1996 United Feature Syndicate, Inc.(NYC)

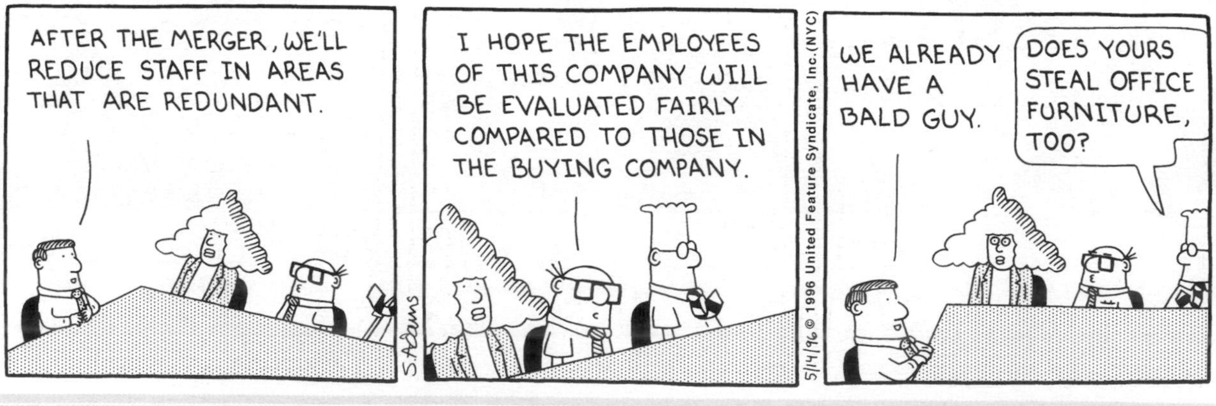
AFTER THE MERGER, WE'LL REDUCE STAFF IN AREAS THAT ARE REDUNDANT.
I HOPE THE EMPLOYEES OF THIS COMPANY WILL BE EVALUATED FAIRLY COMPARED TO THOSE IN THE BUYING COMPANY.
WE ALREADY HAVE A BALD GUY.
DOES YOURS STEAL OFFICE FURNITURE, TOO?
S. Adams
5/14/96 © 1996 United Feature Syndicate, Inc.(NYC)

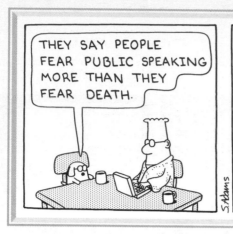

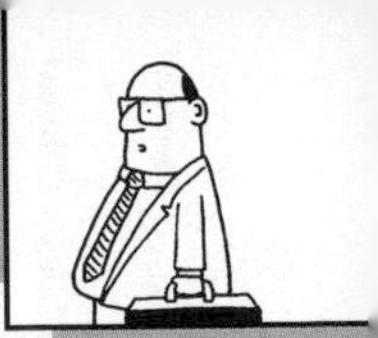

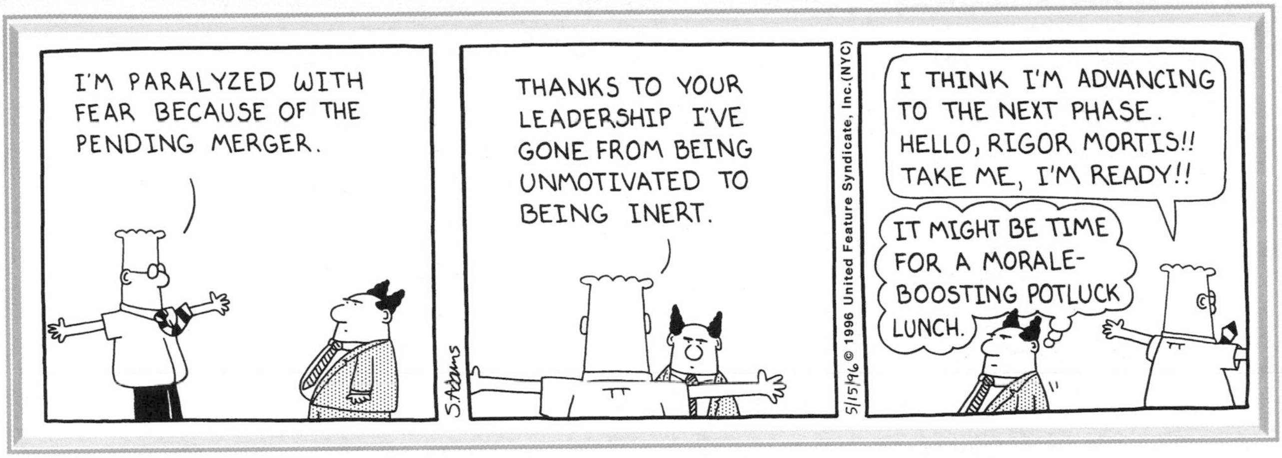
I'M PARALYZED WITH FEAR BECAUSE OF THE PENDING MERGER.
THANKS TO YOUR LEADERSHIP I'VE GONE FROM BEING UNMOTIVATED TO BEING INERT.
I THINK I'M ADVANCING TO THE NEXT PHASE. HELLO, RIGOR MORTIS!! TAKE ME, I'M READY!!
IT MIGHT BE TIME FOR A MORALE-BOOSTING POTLUCK LUNCH.
S. Adams
5/15/96 © 1996 United Feature Syndicate, Inc.(NYC)

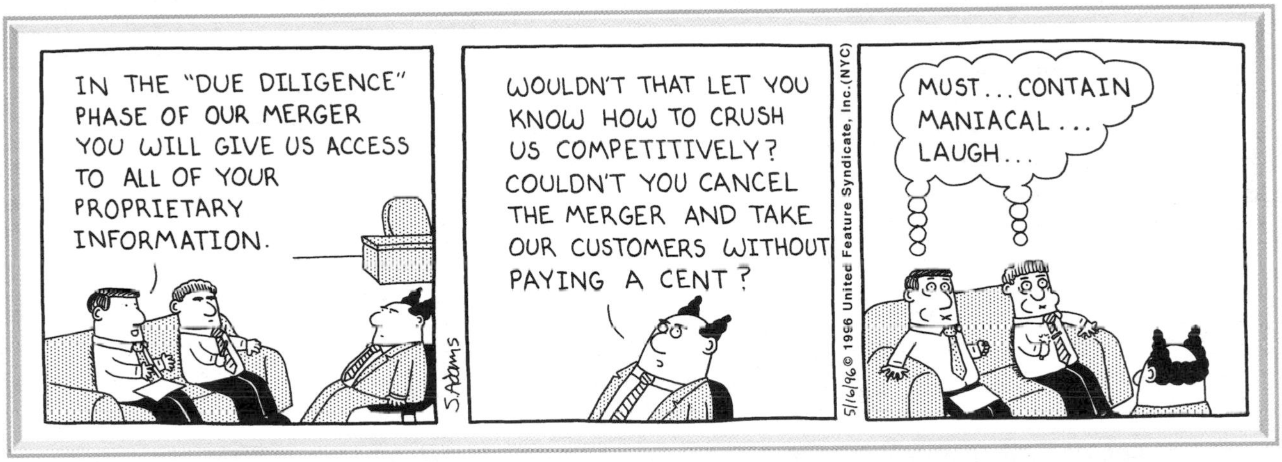
IN THE "DUE DILIGENCE" PHASE OF OUR MERGER YOU WILL GIVE US ACCESS TO ALL OF YOUR PROPRIETARY INFORMATION.
WOULDN'T THAT LET YOU KNOW HOW TO CRUSH US COMPETITIVELY? COULDN'T YOU CANCEL THE MERGER AND TAKE OUR CUSTOMERS WITHOUT PAYING A CENT?
MUST... CONTAIN MANIACAL... LAUGH...
S. Adams
5/16/96 © 1996 United Feature Syndicate, Inc.(NYC)

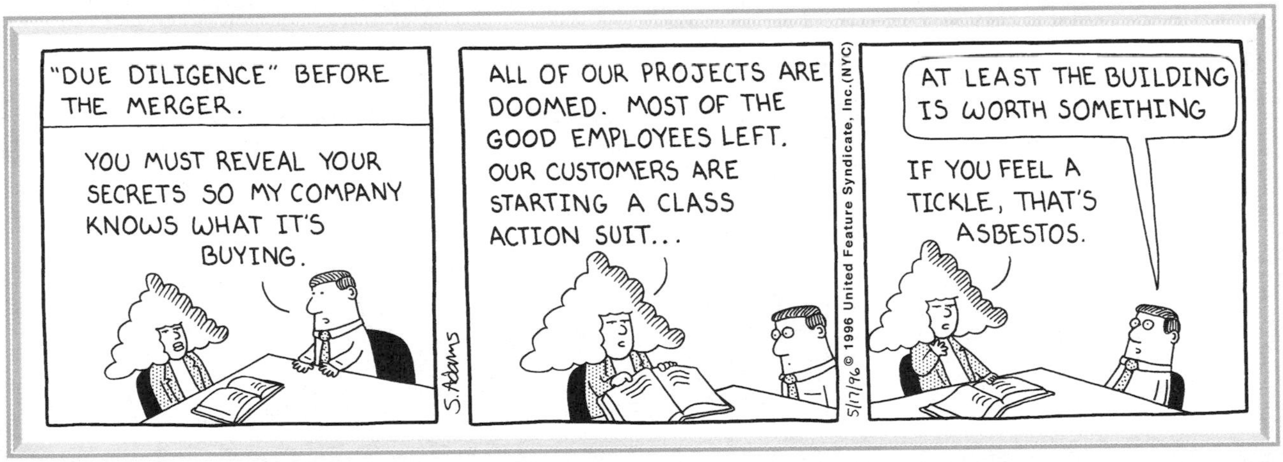
"DUE DILIGENCE" BEFORE THE MERGER.
YOU MUST REVEAL YOUR SECRETS SO MY COMPANY KNOWS WHAT IT'S BUYING.
ALL OF OUR PROJECTS ARE DOOMED. MOST OF THE GOOD EMPLOYEES LEFT. OUR CUSTOMERS ARE STARTING A CLASS ACTION SUIT...
AT LEAST THE BUILDING IS WORTH SOMETHING
IF YOU FEEL A TICKLE, THAT'S ASBESTOS.
S. Adams
5/17/96 © 1996 United Feature Syndicate, Inc.(NYC)

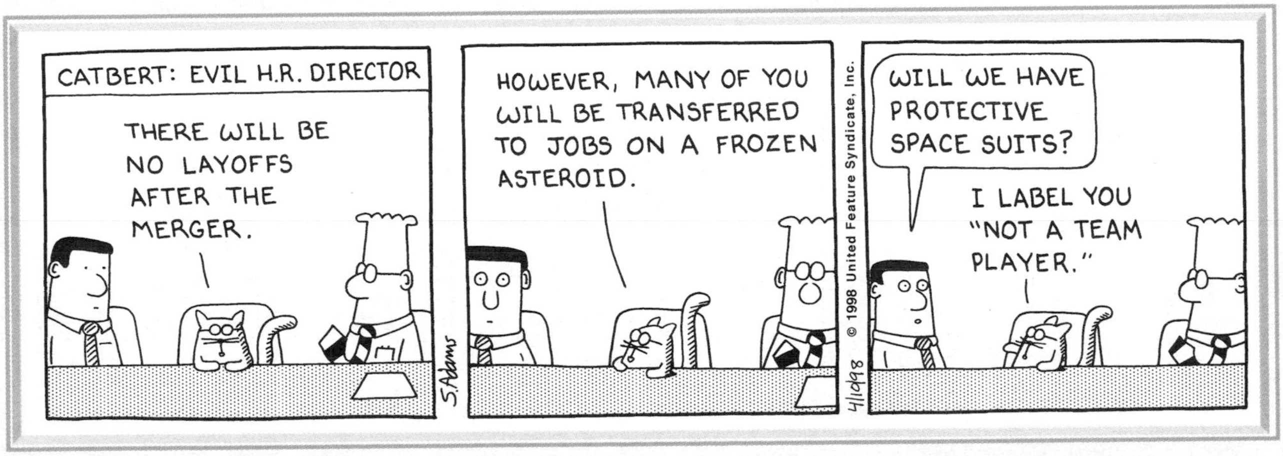
CATBERT: EVIL H.R. DIRECTOR
THERE WILL BE NO LAYOFFS AFTER THE MERGER.
HOWEVER, MANY OF YOU WILL BE TRANSFERRED TO JOBS ON A FROZEN ASTEROID.
WILL WE HAVE PROTECTIVE SPACE SUITS?
I LABEL YOU "NOT A TEAM PLAYER."
S. Adams
4/10/98 © 1998 United Feature Syndicate, Inc.

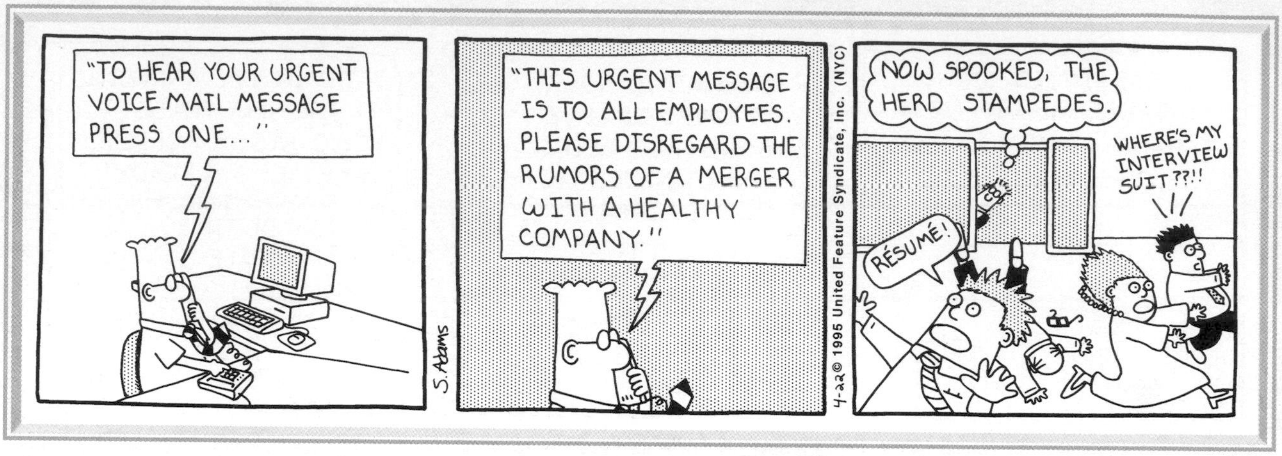
"TO HEAR YOUR URGENT VOICE MAIL MESSAGE PRESS ONE..."
S. Adams
"THIS URGENT MESSAGE IS TO ALL EMPLOYEES. PLEASE DISREGARD THE RUMORS OF A MERGER WITH A HEALTHY COMPANY."
4-22 © 1995 United Feature Syndicate, Inc. (NYC)
NOW SPOOKED, THE HERD STAMPEDES.
RÉSUMÉ!
WHERE'S MY INTERVIEW SUIT??!!

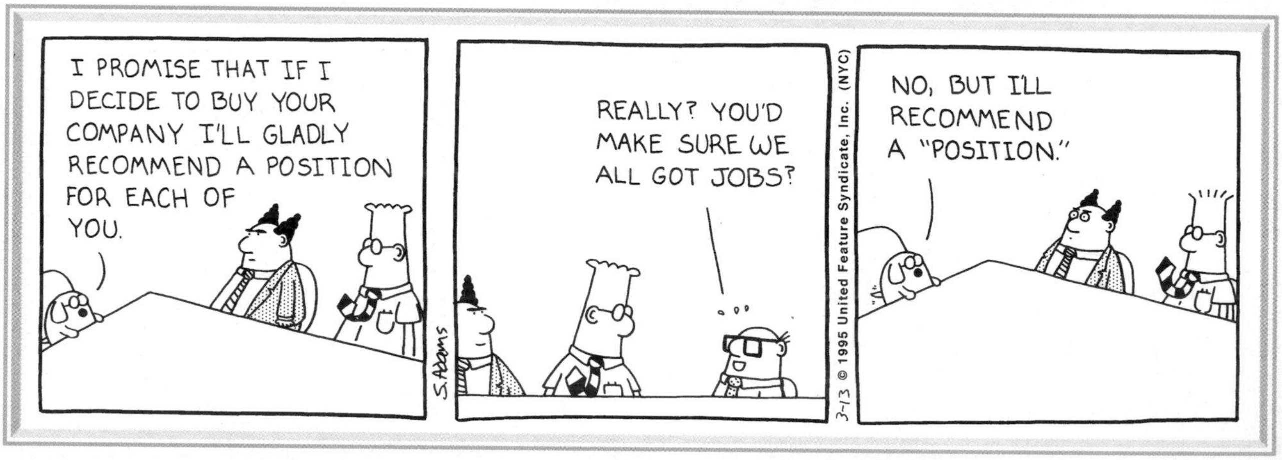
I PROMISE THAT IF I DECIDE TO BUY YOUR COMPANY I'LL GLADLY RECOMMEND A POSITION FOR EACH OF YOU.
S. Adams
REALLY? YOU'D MAKE SURE WE ALL GOT JOBS?
3-13 © 1995 United Feature Syndicate, Inc. (NYC)
NO, BUT I'LL RECOMMEND A "POSITION."

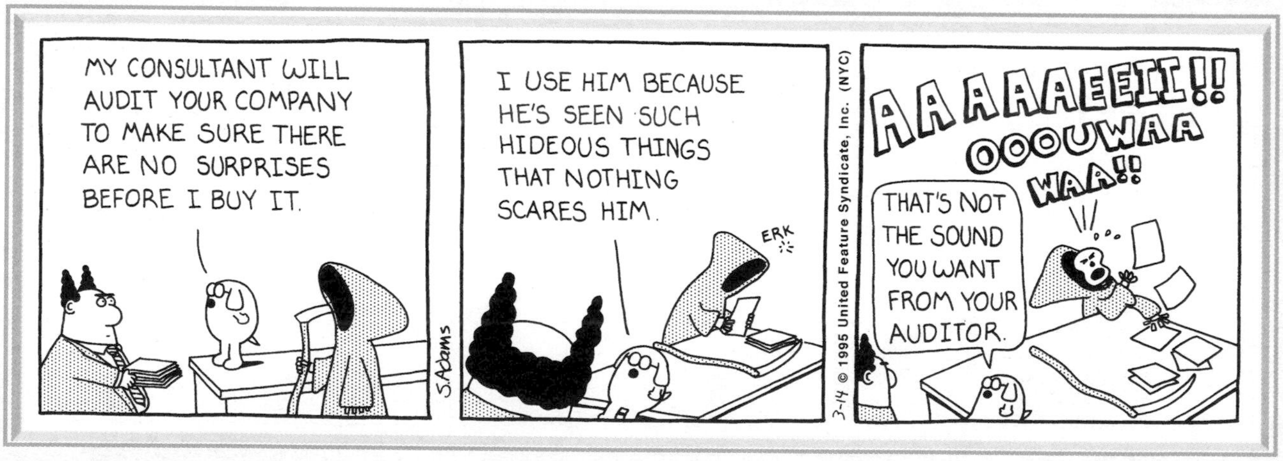
MY CONSULTANT WILL AUDIT YOUR COMPANY TO MAKE SURE THERE ARE NO SURPRISES BEFORE I BUY IT.
S. Adams
I USE HIM BECAUSE HE'S SEEN SUCH HIDEOUS THINGS THAT NOTHING SCARES HIM.
ERK
3-14 © 1995 United Feature Syndicate, Inc. (NYC)
AAAAAEEEII!!
OOOUWAA
WAA!!
THAT'S NOT THE SOUND YOU WANT FROM YOUR AUDITOR.

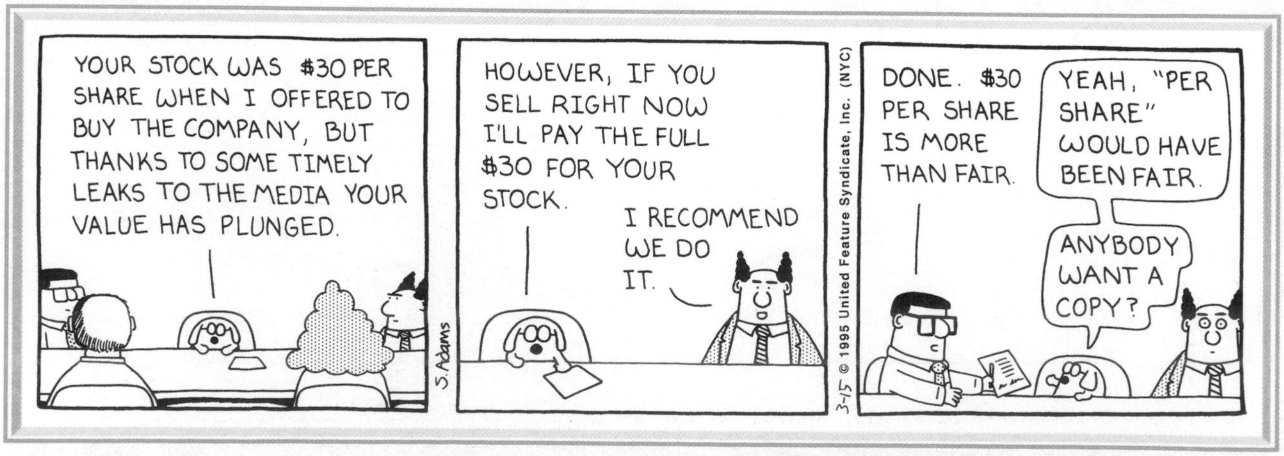
YOUR STOCK WAS $30 PER SHARE WHEN I OFFERED TO BUY THE COMPANY, BUT THANKS TO SOME TIMELY LEAKS TO THE MEDIA YOUR VALUE HAS PLUNGED.
S. Adams
HOWEVER, IF YOU SELL RIGHT NOW I'LL PAY THE FULL $30 FOR YOUR STOCK.
I RECOMMEND WE DO IT.
3-15 © 1995 United Feature Syndicate, Inc. (NYC)
DONE. $30 PER SHARE IS MORE THAN FAIR.
YEAH, "PER SHARE" WOULD HAVE BEEN FAIR.
ANYBODY WANT A COPY?

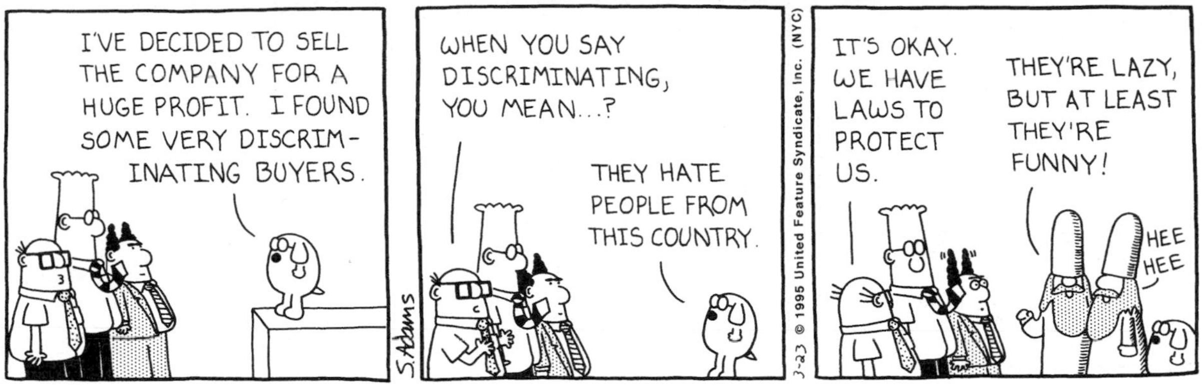
I'VE DECIDED TO SELL THE COMPANY FOR A HUGE PROFIT. I FOUND SOME VERY DISCRIMINATING BUYERS.
WHEN YOU SAY DISCRIMINATING, YOU MEAN...?
THEY HATE PEOPLE FROM THIS COUNTRY.
IT'S OKAY. WE HAVE LAWS TO PROTECT US.
THEY'RE LAZY, BUT AT LEAST THEY'RE FUNNY!
HEE HEE
S. Adams
3-23 © 1995 United Feature Syndicate, Inc. (NYC)

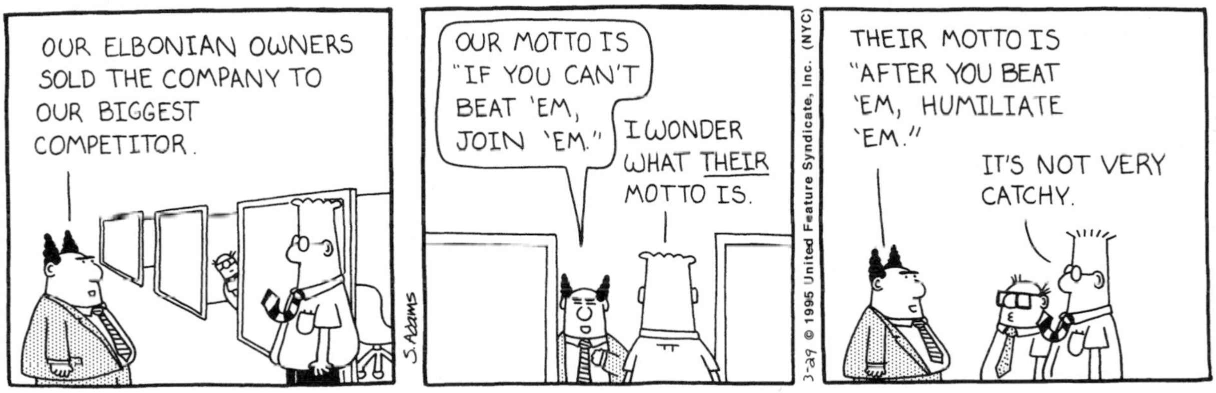
OUR ELBONIAN OWNERS SOLD THE COMPANY TO OUR BIGGEST COMPETITOR.
OUR MOTTO IS "IF YOU CAN'T BEAT 'EM, JOIN 'EM."
I WONDER WHAT THEIR MOTTO IS.
THEIR MOTTO IS "AFTER YOU BEAT 'EM, HUMILIATE 'EM."
IT'S NOT VERY CATCHY.
S. Adams
3-29 © 1995 United Feature Syndicate, Inc. (NYC)

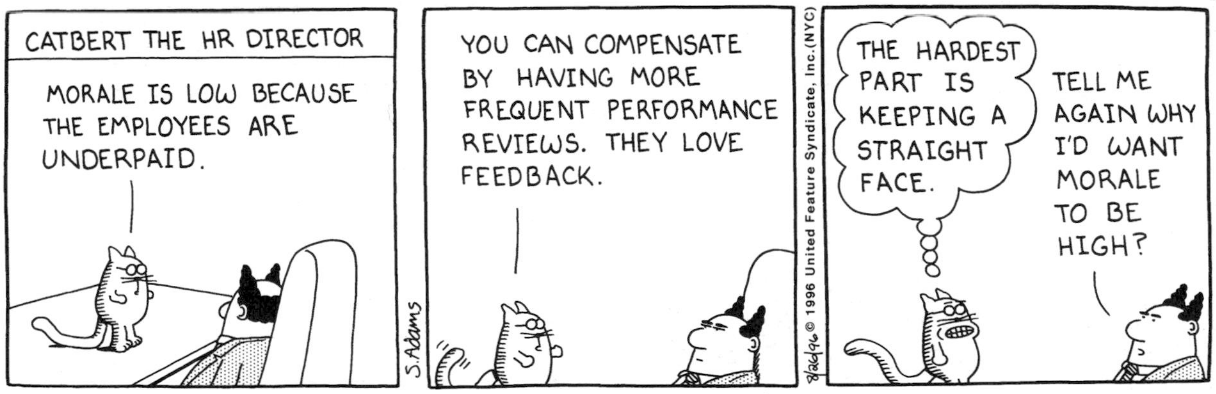
CATBERT THE HR DIRECTOR
MORALE IS LOW BECAUSE THE EMPLOYEES ARE UNDERPAID.
YOU CAN COMPENSATE BY HAVING MORE FREQUENT PERFORMANCE REVIEWS. THEY LOVE FEEDBACK.
THE HARDEST PART IS KEEPING A STRAIGHT FACE.
TELL ME AGAIN WHY I'D WANT MORALE TO BE HIGH?
S. Adams
© 1996 United Feature Syndicate, Inc.(NYC)

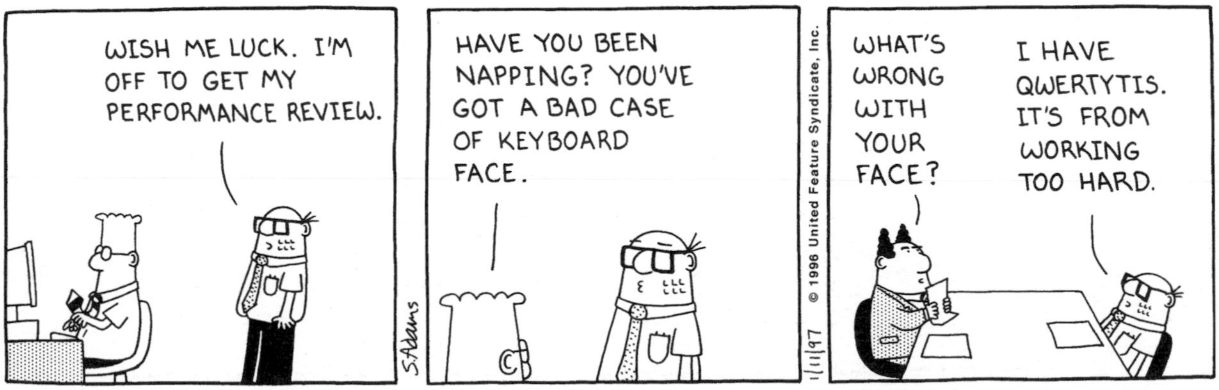
WISH ME LUCK. I'M OFF TO GET MY PERFORMANCE REVIEW.
HAVE YOU BEEN NAPPING? YOU'VE GOT A BAD CASE OF KEYBOARD FACE.
WHAT'S WRONG WITH YOUR FACE?
I HAVE QWERTYTIS. IT'S FROM WORKING TOO HARD.
S. Adams
1/11/97 © 1996 United Feature Syndicate, Inc.

PERFORMANCE REVIEWS

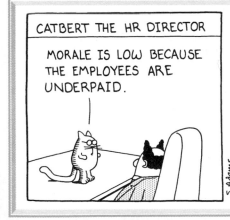

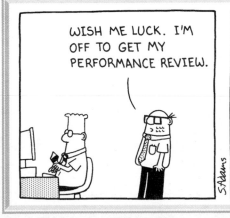

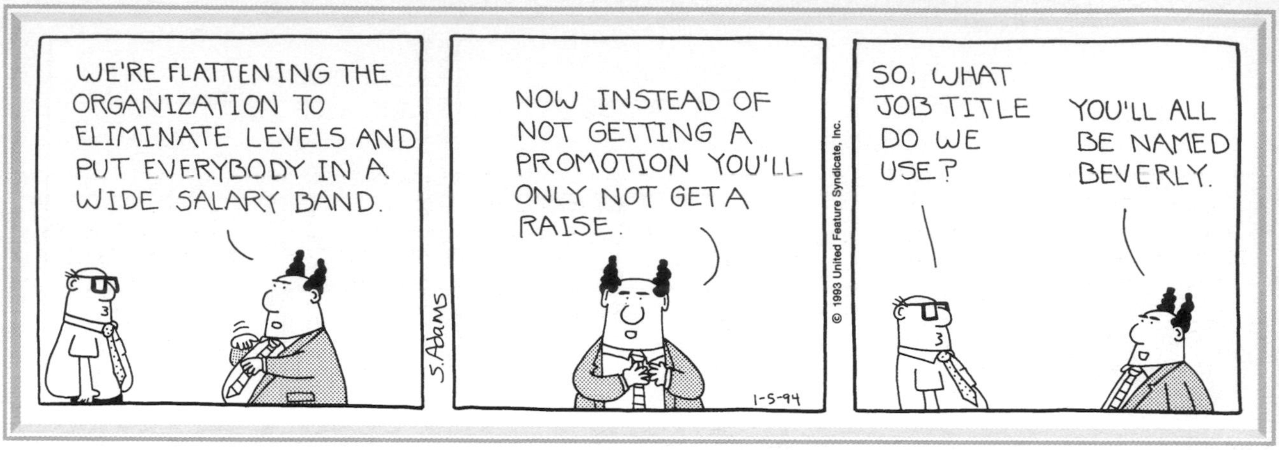
WE'RE FLATTENING THE ORGANIZATION TO ELIMINATE LEVELS AND PUT EVERYBODY IN A WIDE SALARY BAND.
NOW INSTEAD OF NOT GETTING A PROMOTION YOU'LL ONLY NOT GET A RAISE.
SO, WHAT JOB TITLE DO WE USE?
YOU'LL ALL BE NAMED BEVERLY.
S. Adams
1-5-94
© 1993 United Feature Syndicate, Inc.

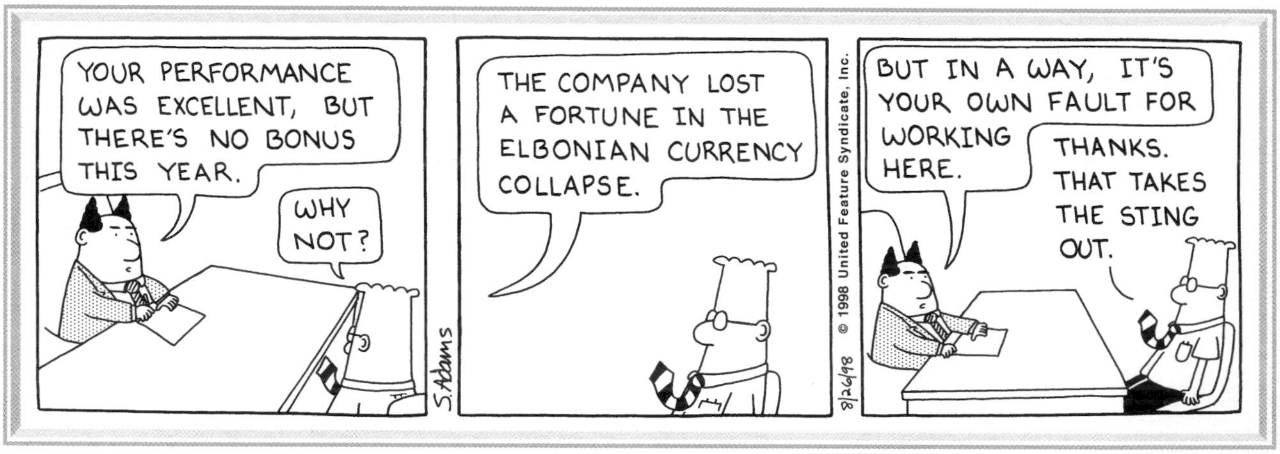
YOUR PERFORMANCE WAS EXCELLENT, BUT THERE'S NO BONUS THIS YEAR.
WHY NOT?
THE COMPANY LOST A FORTUNE IN THE ELBONIAN CURRENCY COLLAPSE.
BUT IN A WAY, IT'S YOUR OWN FAULT FOR WORKING HERE.
THANKS. THAT TAKES THE STING OUT.
S. Adams
8/26/98
© 1998 United Feature Syndicate, Inc.

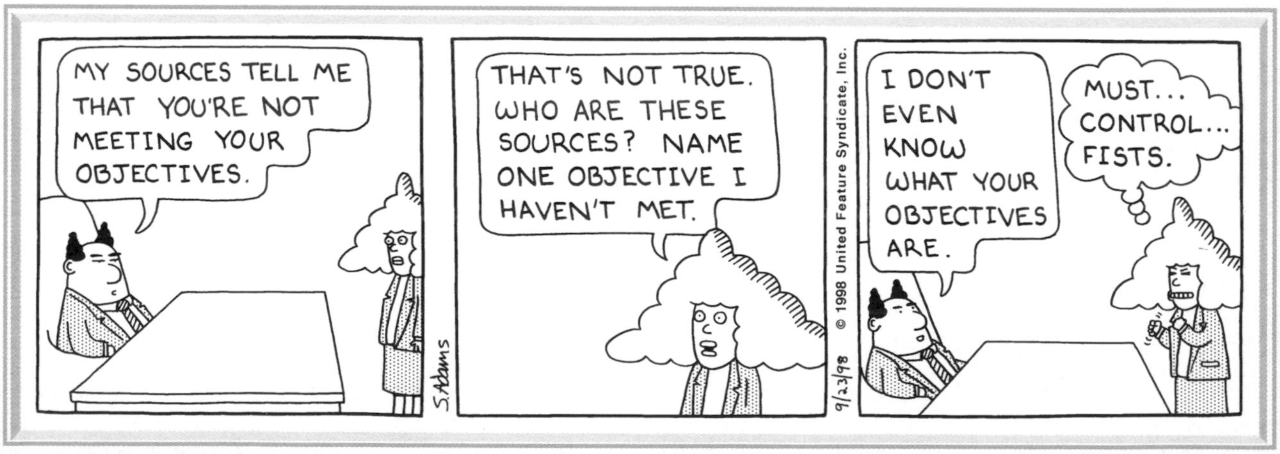
MY SOURCES TELL ME THAT YOU'RE NOT MEETING YOUR OBJECTIVES.
THAT'S NOT TRUE. WHO ARE THESE SOURCES? NAME ONE OBJECTIVE I HAVEN'T MET.
I DON'T EVEN KNOW WHAT YOUR OBJECTIVES ARE.
MUST... CONTROL... FISTS.
S. Adams
9/23/98
© 1998 United Feature Syndicate, Inc.

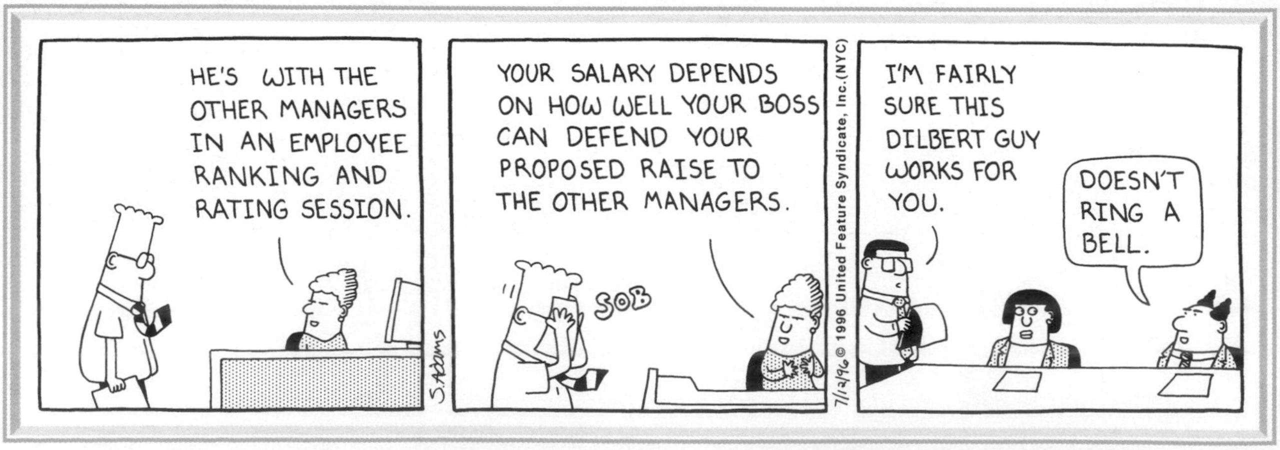
HE'S WITH THE OTHER MANAGERS IN AN EMPLOYEE RANKING AND RATING SESSION.
YOUR SALARY DEPENDS ON HOW WELL YOUR BOSS CAN DEFEND YOUR PROPOSED RAISE TO THE OTHER MANAGERS.
SOB
I'M FAIRLY SURE THIS DILBERT GUY WORKS FOR YOU.
DOESN'T RING A BELL.
S. Adams
7/12/96
© 1996 United Feature Syndicate, Inc.(NYC)

PERFORMANCE REVIEWS

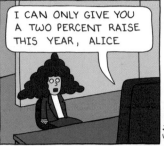

I CAN ONLY GIVE YOU A TWO PERCENT RAISE THIS YEAR, ALICE
BECAUSE YOUR JOB WAS NOT VERY CHALLENGING.
HOW COULD YOU POSSIBLY THINK IT WASN'T CHALLENGING?
YOU EXCEEDED ALL YOUR GOALS WITHOUT COMPLAINING.
COMPARE THAT TO WALLY'S PERFORMANCE. HE COMPLAINED ALL YEAR.
AND HE MISSED EVERY GOAL! NOW THAT'S A CHALLENGING JOB!
WALLY IS A FILTHY WEASEL !!!
MAYBE HIS HYGIENE ISN'T THE BEST, BUT HE WAS RIGHT WHEN HE SAID YOU WOULD STAB HIM IN THE BACK.
S. Adams
3/29/98 © 1998 United Feature Syndicate, Inc.

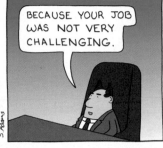

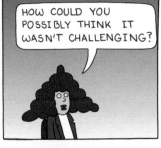

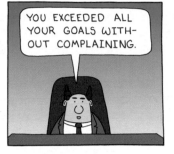

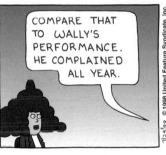

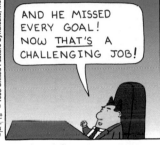

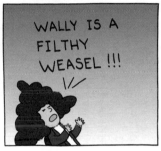

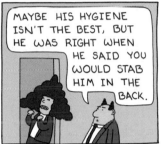

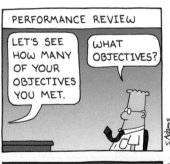

PERFORMANCE REVIEW
LET'S SEE HOW MANY OF YOUR OBJECTIVES YOU MET.
WHAT OBJECTIVES?
DIDN'T YOU KNOW YOU HAD OBJECTIVES?
I DON'T SEE HOW I WOULD HAVE HAD TIME TO WORK ON OBJECTIVES.
MY SCHEDULE WAS PACKED.
DOING WHAT?
EVERY MORNING YOU LEAVE THINGS ON MY CHAIR WITH NOTES THAT SAY "URGENT: HANDLE THIS."
NO I DON'T.
WALLY, CAN I SEE A SAMPLE OF YOUR HANDWRITING?
UH-OH.
S. Adams
8/2/98 © 1998 United Feature Syndicate, Inc.

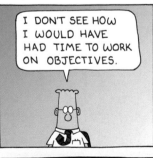

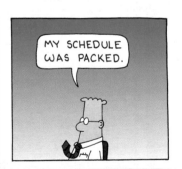

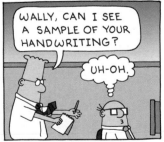

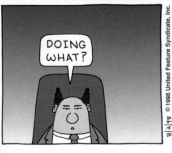

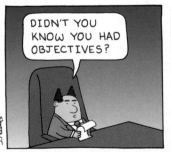

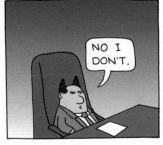

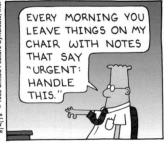

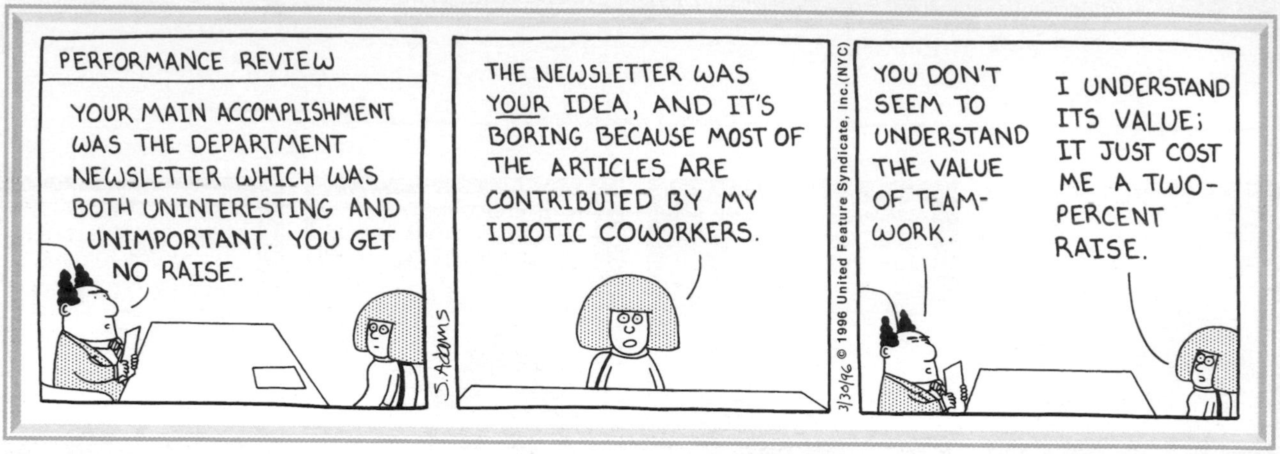
PERFORMANCE REVIEW
YOUR MAIN ACCOMPLISHMENT WAS THE DEPARTMENT NEWSLETTER WHICH WAS BOTH UNINTERESTING AND UNIMPORTANT. YOU GET NO RAISE.
THE NEWSLETTER WAS YOUR IDEA, AND IT'S BORING BECAUSE MOST OF THE ARTICLES ARE CONTRIBUTED BY MY IDIOTIC COWORKERS.
YOU DON'T SEEM TO UNDERSTAND THE VALUE OF TEAM-WORK.
I UNDERSTAND ITS VALUE; IT JUST COST ME A TWO-PERCENT RAISE.
S. Adams
3/30/96 © 1996 United Feature Syndicate, Inc.(NYC)

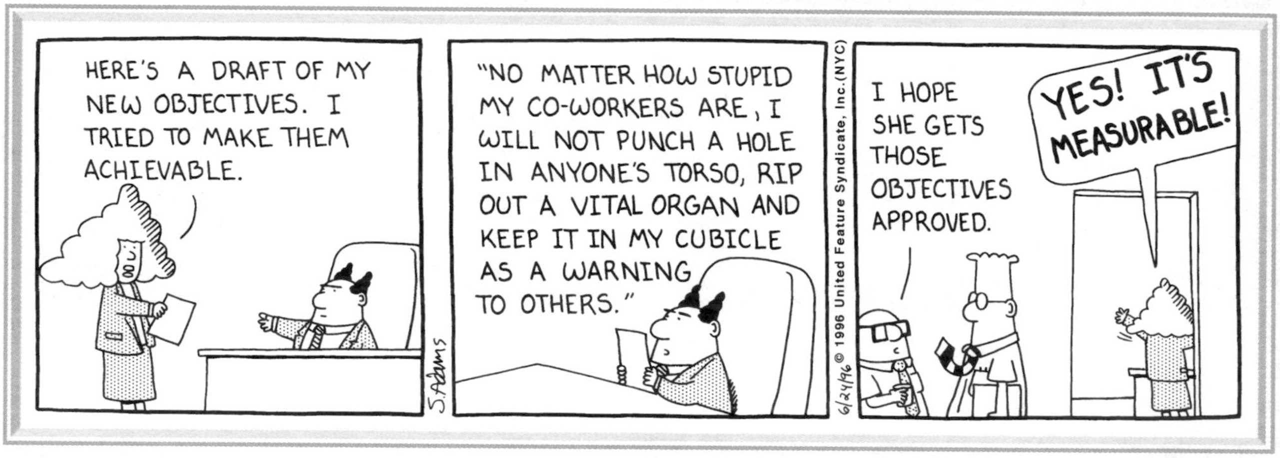
HERE'S A DRAFT OF MY NEW OBJECTIVES. I TRIED TO MAKE THEM ACHIEVABLE.
"NO MATTER HOW STUPID MY CO-WORKERS ARE, I WILL NOT PUNCH A HOLE IN ANYONE'S TORSO, RIP OUT A VITAL ORGAN AND KEEP IT IN MY CUBICLE AS A WARNING TO OTHERS."
I HOPE SHE GETS THOSE OBJECTIVES APPROVED.
YES! IT'S MEASURABLE!
S. Adams
6/24/96 © 1996 United Feature Syndicate, Inc.(NYC)

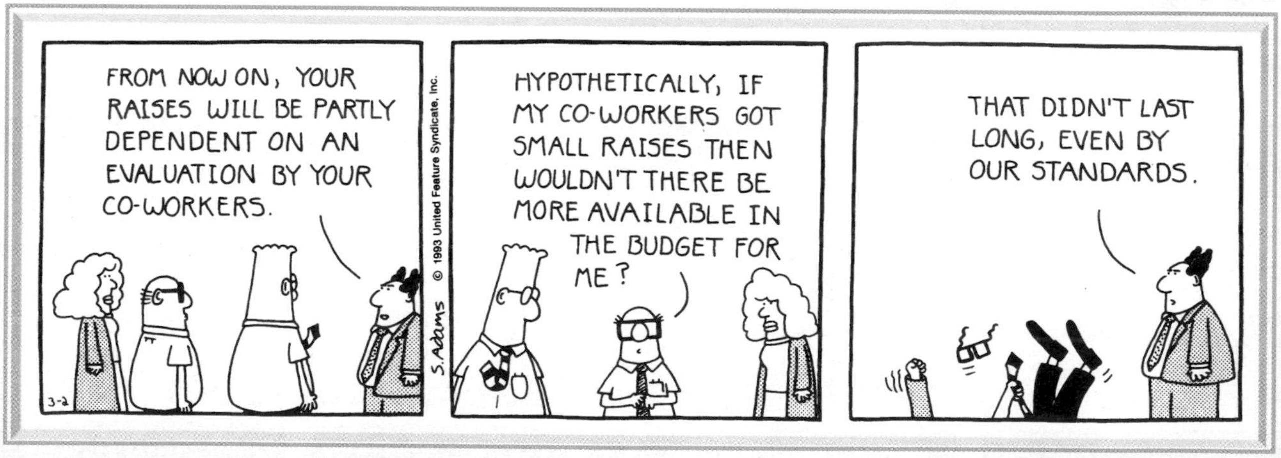
FROM NOW ON, YOUR RAISES WILL BE PARTLY DEPENDENT ON AN EVALUATION BY YOUR CO-WORKERS.
HYPOTHETICALLY, IF MY CO-WORKERS GOT SMALL RAISES THEN WOULDN'T THERE BE MORE AVAILABLE IN THE BUDGET FOR ME?
THAT DIDN'T LAST LONG, EVEN BY OUR STANDARDS.
S. Adams
© 1993 United Feature Syndicate, Inc.

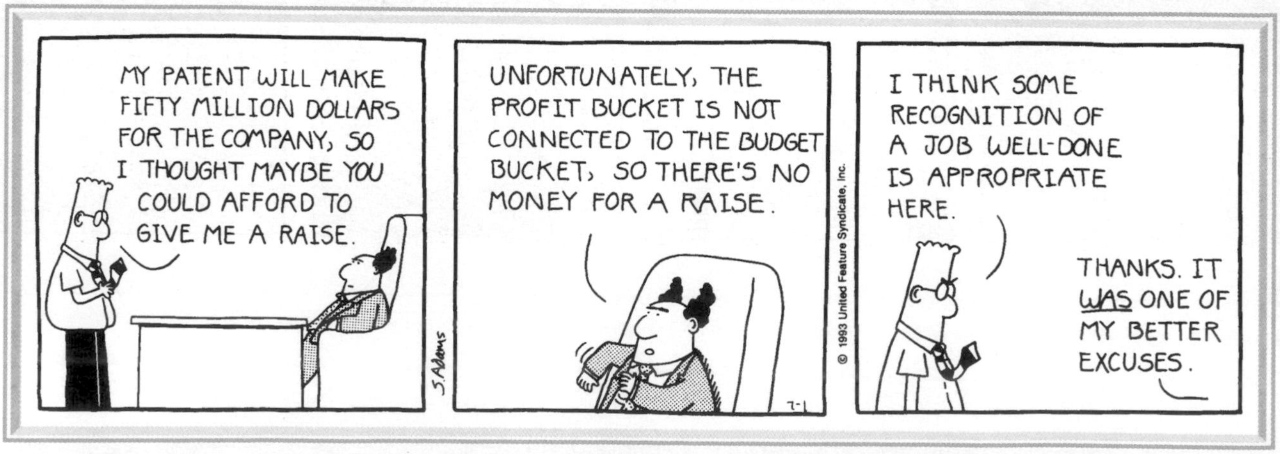
MY PATENT WILL MAKE FIFTY MILLION DOLLARS FOR THE COMPANY, SO I THOUGHT MAYBE YOU COULD AFFORD TO GIVE ME A RAISE.
UNFORTUNATELY, THE PROFIT BUCKET IS NOT CONNECTED TO THE BUDGET BUCKET, SO THERE'S NO MONEY FOR A RAISE.
I THINK SOME RECOGNITION OF A JOB WELL-DONE IS APPROPRIATE HERE.
THANKS. IT WAS ONE OF MY BETTER EXCUSES.
S. Adams
© 1993 United Feature Syndicate, Inc.

IT'S TIME FOR YOUR ANNUAL PERFORMANCE REVIEW.

THE PROCESS IS THE SAME AS USUAL.

MAKE YOUR ACCOMPLISHMENTS FIT THE TRENDY CATEGORIES ON THIS FORM.

"1. ESTIMATE THE CASH VALUE OF THE EMPOWERMENT YOU DISPLAYED THIS YEAR. CITE EXAMPLES."

TRY TO MAKE YOUR ACCOMPLISHMENTS MATCH THE RAISE I'VE ALREADY DECIDED FOR YOU.

WHY DON'T YOU JUST TELL ME WHAT YOU'VE DECIDED?

WHAT--AND RUIN THE MOTIVATIONAL VALUE OF THE PROCESS??

HOW DID I GET STUCK WITH ALL THE CYNICAL EMPLOYEES?

© 1993 United Feature Syndicate, Inc.

WRITE UP YOUR ACCOMPLISHMENTS SO I CAN DECIDE WHO GETS RAISES THIS YEAR.

ARE YOU SAYING OUR RAISES WILL DEPEND ON OUR ABILITY TO LIE ABOUT OUR ACHIEVEMENTS?

NO, THERE'S ALSO FAVORITISM.

AND DON'T FORGET THE IMPORTANCE OF MINIMIZING THE ACCOMPLISHMENTS OF OTHERS.

"THIS YEAR I SAVED A BILLION DOLLARS IN WAYS WHICH ARE IMPOSSIBLE TO VERIFY."

"WHILE THE OTHERS PLOTTED AGAINST YOU, I WAS APPLYING AN INVISIBLE RUST INHIBITOR TO YOUR CAR."

© 1995 United Feature Syndicate, Inc. 5-14

I CAN DROP THOSE OFF FOR YOU.

THANKS.

HAVE YOU NOTICED SHE'S THE ONLY ONE WHO EVER GETS A RAISE?

IT'S AS IF SHE HAS THE ACCOMPLISHMENTS OF THREE PEOPLE.

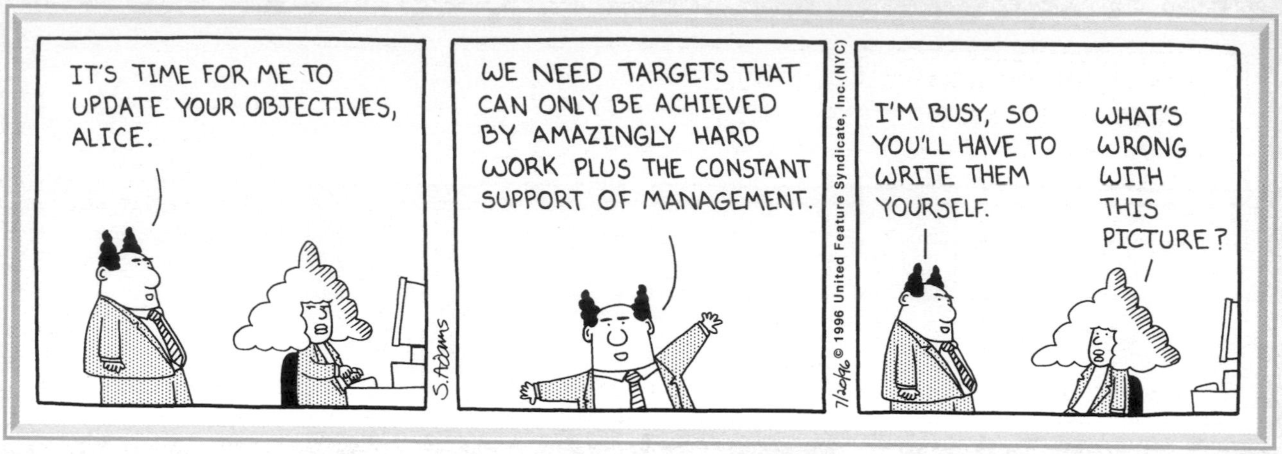
IT'S TIME FOR ME TO UPDATE YOUR OBJECTIVES, ALICE.
S. Adams
WE NEED TARGETS THAT CAN ONLY BE ACHIEVED BY AMAZINGLY HARD WORK PLUS THE CONSTANT SUPPORT OF MANAGEMENT.
7/20/96 © 1996 United Feature Syndicate, Inc.(NYC)
I'M BUSY, SO YOU'LL HAVE TO WRITE THEM YOURSELF.
WHAT'S WRONG WITH THIS PICTURE?

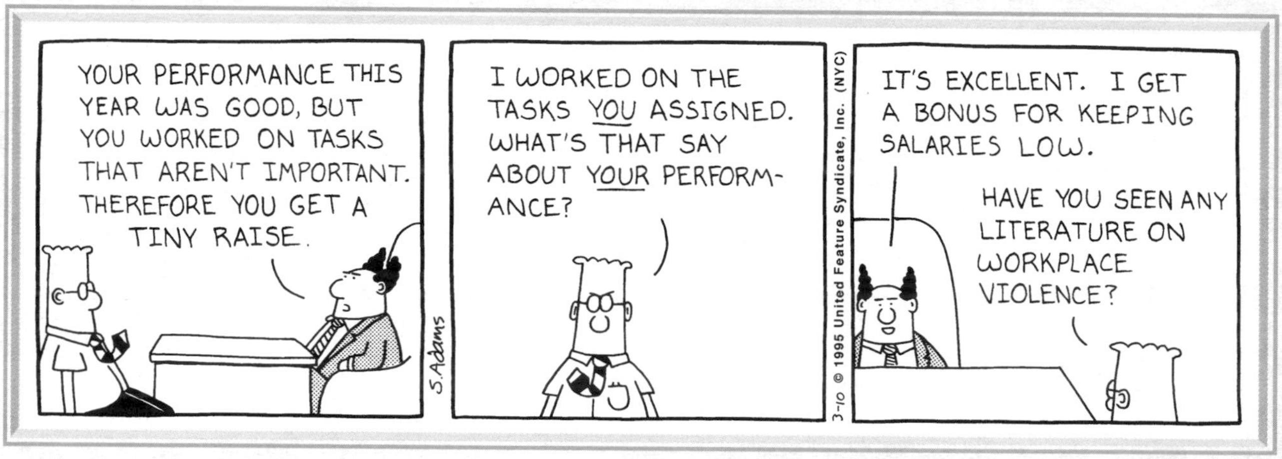
YOUR PERFORMANCE THIS YEAR WAS GOOD, BUT YOU WORKED ON TASKS THAT AREN'T IMPORTANT. THEREFORE YOU GET A TINY RAISE.
S. Adams
I WORKED ON THE TASKS YOU ASSIGNED. WHAT'S THAT SAY ABOUT YOUR PERFORMANCE?
3-10 © 1995 United Feature Syndicate, Inc. (NYC)
IT'S EXCELLENT. I GET A BONUS FOR KEEPING SALARIES LOW.
HAVE YOU SEEN ANY LITERATURE ON WORKPLACE VIOLENCE?

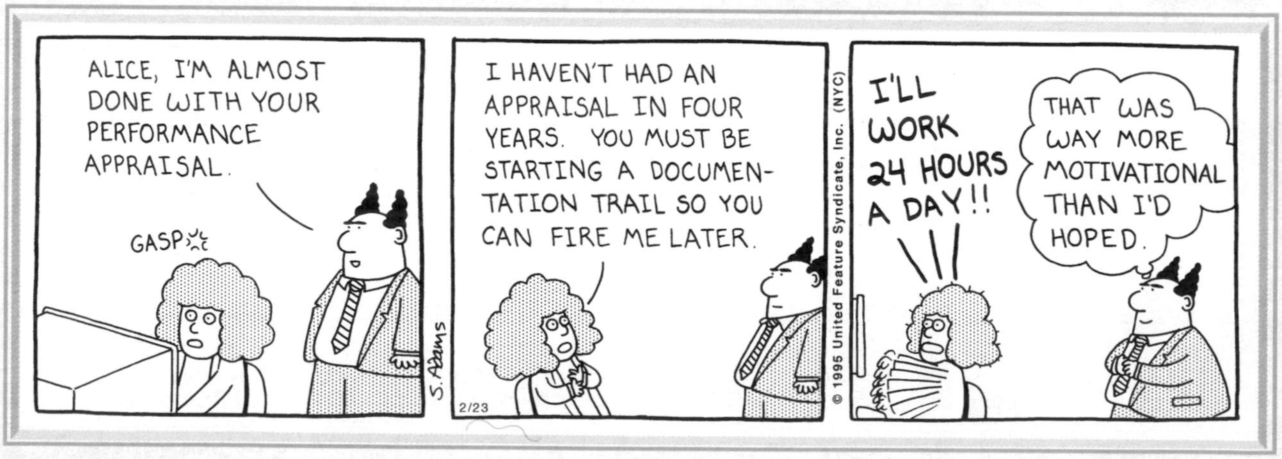
ALICE, I'M ALMOST DONE WITH YOUR PERFORMANCE APPRAISAL.
GASP
S. Adams
I HAVEN'T HAD AN APPRAISAL IN FOUR YEARS. YOU MUST BE STARTING A DOCUMENTATION TRAIL SO YOU CAN FIRE ME LATER.
2/23
© 1995 United Feature Syndicate, Inc. (NYC)
I'LL WORK 24 HOURS A DAY!!
THAT WAS WAY MORE MOTIVATIONAL THAN I'D HOPED.

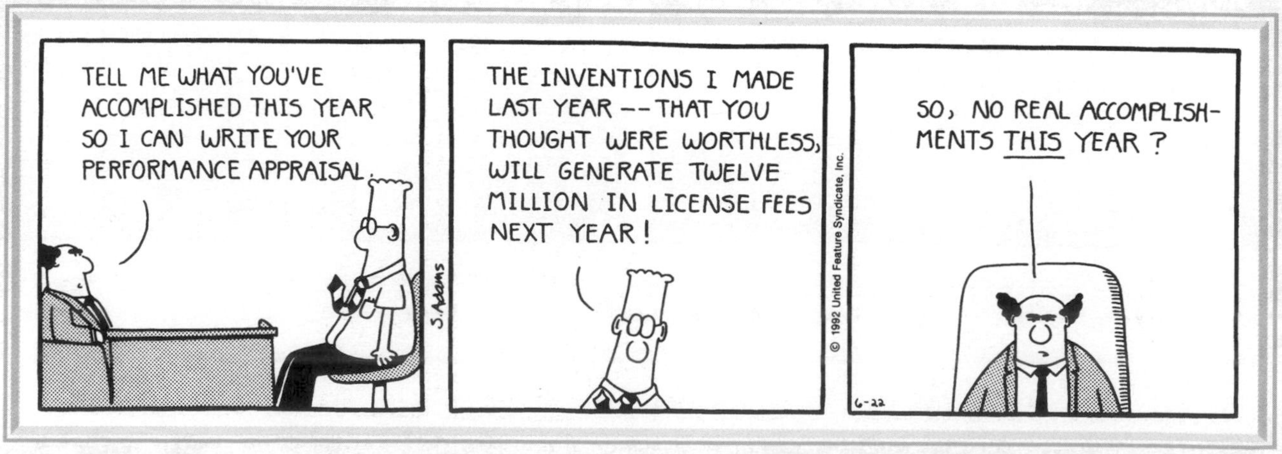
TELL ME WHAT YOU'VE ACCOMPLISHED THIS YEAR SO I CAN WRITE YOUR PERFORMANCE APPRAISAL.
S. Adams
THE INVENTIONS I MADE LAST YEAR -- THAT YOU THOUGHT WERE WORTHLESS, WILL GENERATE TWELVE MILLION IN LICENSE FEES NEXT YEAR!
© 1992 United Feature Syndicate, Inc.
SO, NO REAL ACCOMPLISHMENTS THIS YEAR?
6-22

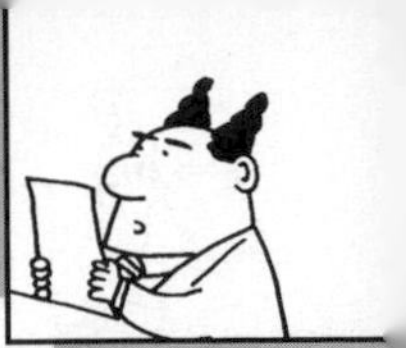

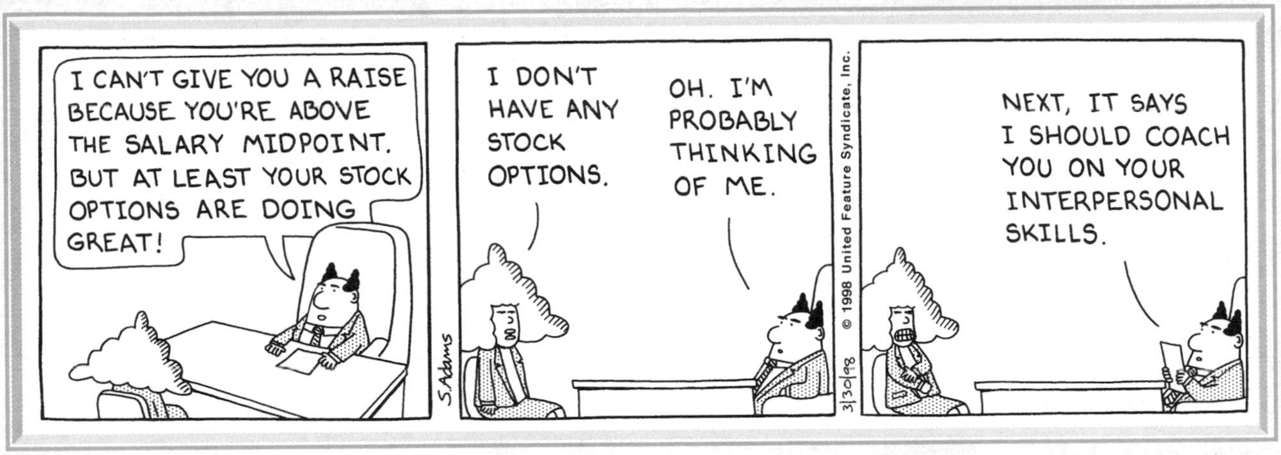
I CAN'T GIVE YOU A RAISE BECAUSE YOU'RE ABOVE THE SALARY MIDPOINT. BUT AT LEAST YOUR STOCK OPTIONS ARE DOING GREAT!
S. Adams
I DON'T HAVE ANY STOCK OPTIONS.
OH. I'M PROBABLY THINKING OF ME.
3/30/98 © 1998 United Feature Syndicate, Inc.
NEXT, IT SAYS I SHOULD COACH YOU ON YOUR INTERPERSONAL SKILLS.

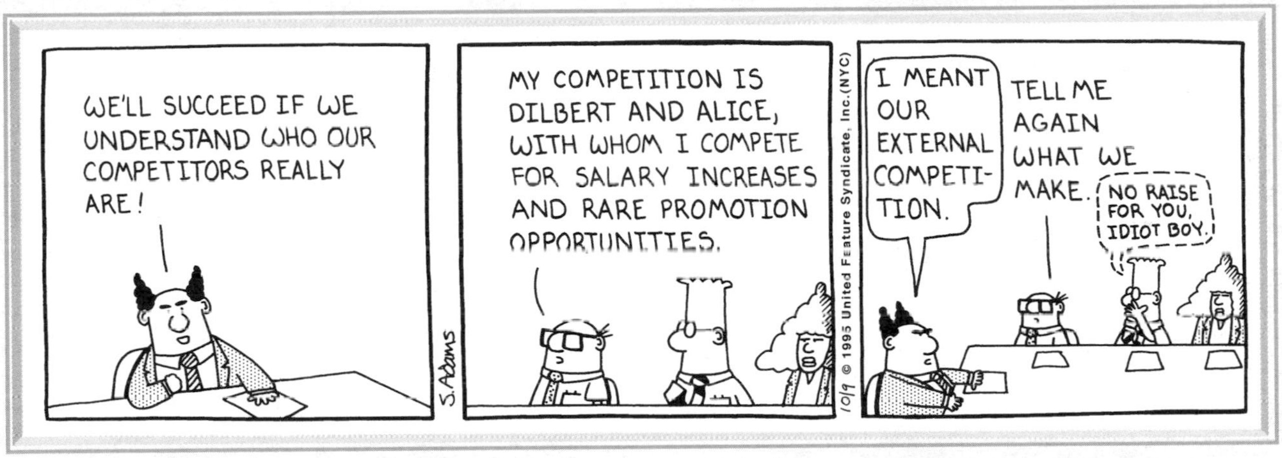
WE'LL SUCCEED IF WE UNDERSTAND WHO OUR COMPETITORS REALLY ARE!
S. Adams
MY COMPETITION IS DILBERT AND ALICE, WITH WHOM I COMPETE FOR SALARY INCREASES AND RARE PROMOTION OPPORTUNITIES.
10/9 © 1995 United Feature Syndicate, Inc.(NYC)
I MEANT OUR EXTERNAL COMPETITION.
TELL ME AGAIN WHAT WE MAKE.
NO RAISE FOR YOU, IDIOT BOY.

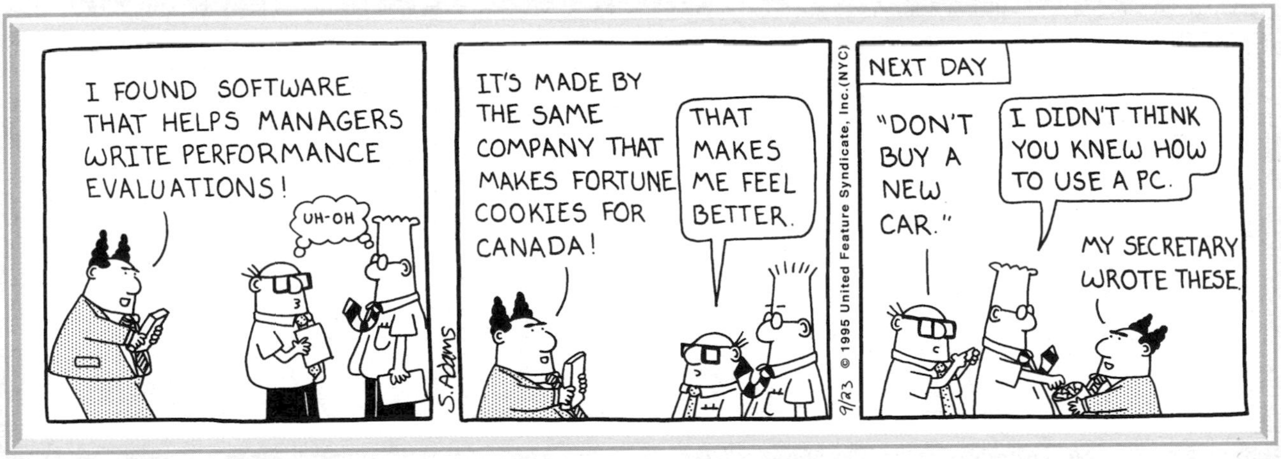
I FOUND SOFTWARE THAT HELPS MANAGERS WRITE PERFORMANCE EVALUATIONS!
UH-OH
S. Adams
IT'S MADE BY THE SAME COMPANY THAT MAKES FORTUNE COOKIES FOR CANADA!
THAT MAKES ME FEEL BETTER.
9/23 © 1995 United Feature Syndicate, Inc.(NYC)
NEXT DAY
"DON'T BUY A NEW CAR."
I DIDN'T THINK YOU KNEW HOW TO USE A PC.
MY SECRETARY WROTE THESE.

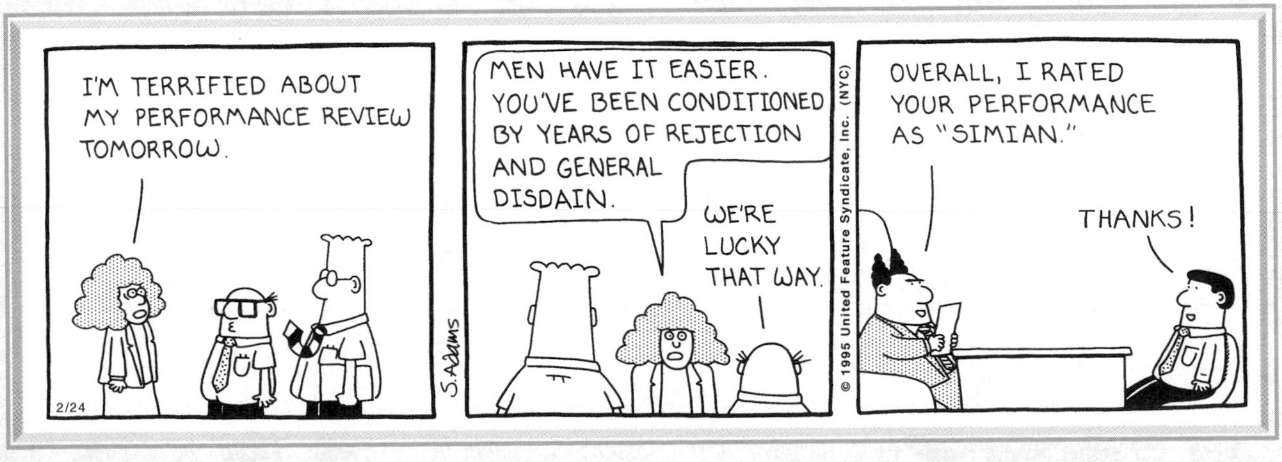
I'M TERRIFIED ABOUT MY PERFORMANCE REVIEW TOMORROW.
2/24
S. Adams
MEN HAVE IT EASIER. YOU'VE BEEN CONDITIONED BY YEARS OF REJECTION AND GENERAL DISDAIN.
WE'RE LUCKY THAT WAY.
© 1995 United Feature Syndicate, Inc. (NYC)
OVERALL, I RATED YOUR PERFORMANCE AS "SIMIAN."
THANKS!

PERFORMANCE REVIEWS

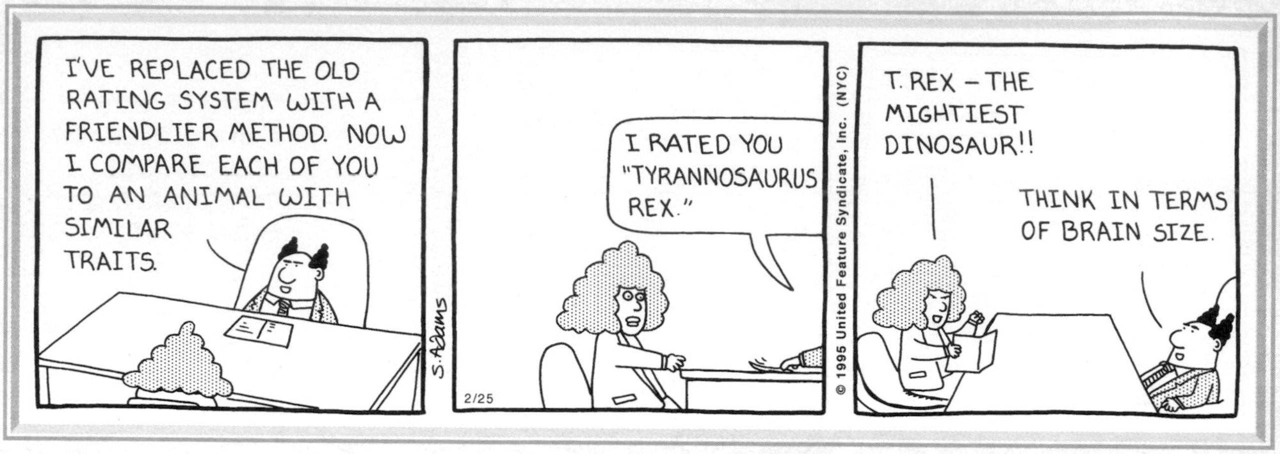
I'VE REPLACED THE OLD RATING SYSTEM WITH A FRIENDLIER METHOD. NOW I COMPARE EACH OF YOU TO AN ANIMAL WITH SIMILAR TRAITS.
I RATED YOU "TYRANNOSAURUS REX."
T. REX – THE MIGHTIEST DINOSAUR!!
THINK IN TERMS OF BRAIN SIZE.
S. Adams
2/25
© 1995 United Feature Syndicate, Inc. (NYC)

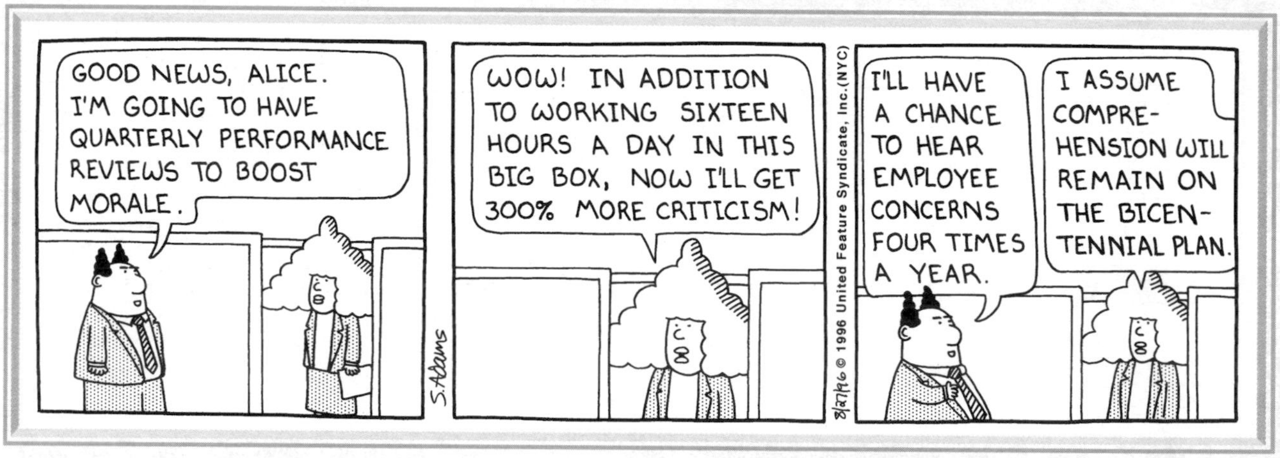
GOOD NEWS, ALICE. I'M GOING TO HAVE QUARTERLY PERFORMANCE REVIEWS TO BOOST MORALE.
WOW! IN ADDITION TO WORKING SIXTEEN HOURS A DAY IN THIS BIG BOX, NOW I'LL GET 300% MORE CRITICISM!
I'LL HAVE A CHANCE TO HEAR EMPLOYEE CONCERNS FOUR TIMES A YEAR.
I ASSUME COMPRE-HENSION WILL REMAIN ON THE BICEN-TENNIAL PLAN.
S. Adams
8/27/96 © 1996 United Feature Syndicate, Inc. (NYC)

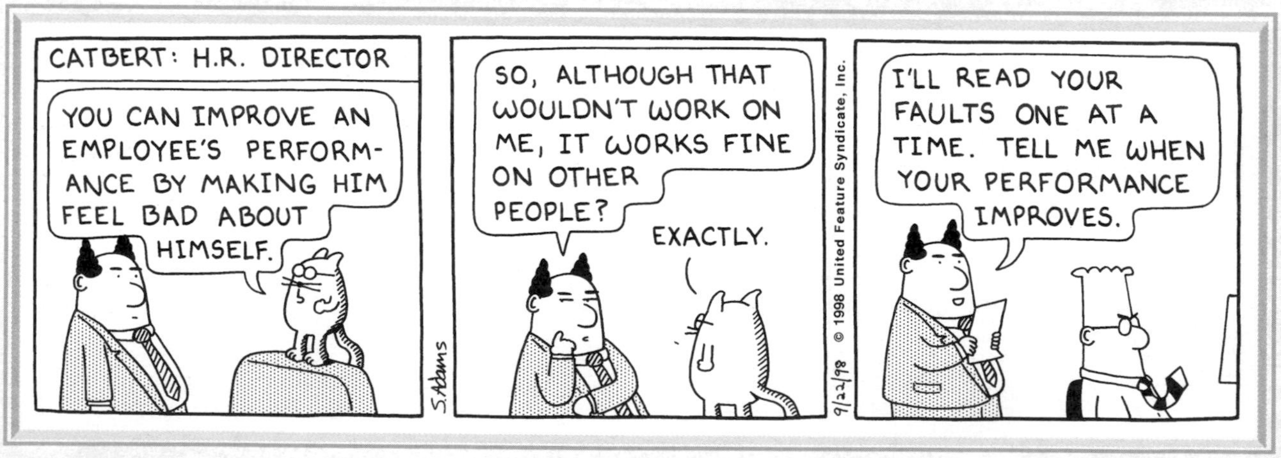
CATBERT: H.R. DIRECTOR
YOU CAN IMPROVE AN EMPLOYEE'S PERFORM-ANCE BY MAKING HIM FEEL BAD ABOUT HIMSELF.
SO, ALTHOUGH THAT WOULDN'T WORK ON ME, IT WORKS FINE ON OTHER PEOPLE?
EXACTLY.
I'LL READ YOUR FAULTS ONE AT A TIME. TELL ME WHEN YOUR PERFORMANCE IMPROVES.
S. Adams
9/22/98 © 1998 United Feature Syndicate, Inc.

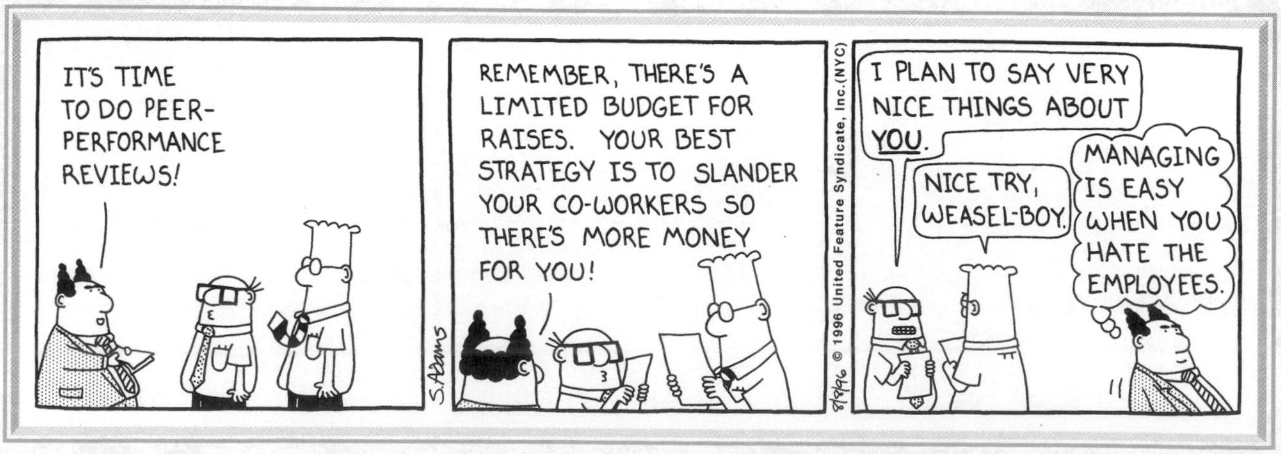
IT'S TIME TO DO PEER-PERFORMANCE REVIEWS!
REMEMBER, THERE'S A LIMITED BUDGET FOR RAISES. YOUR BEST STRATEGY IS TO SLANDER YOUR CO-WORKERS SO THERE'S MORE MONEY FOR YOU!
I PLAN TO SAY VERY NICE THINGS ABOUT YOU.
NICE TRY, WEASEL-BOY.
MANAGING IS EASY WHEN YOU HATE THE EMPLOYEES.
S. Adams
8/9/96 © 1996 United Feature Syndicate, Inc. (NYC)

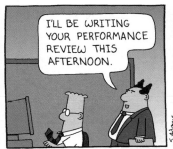

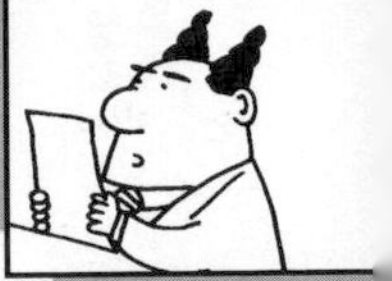

I'LL BE WRITING YOUR PERFORMANCE REVIEW THIS AFTERNOON.
BUT THIS MORNING I'M HELPING MY DAUGHTER SELL CUB GIRL COOKIES.
FOR YOUR SHOPPING CONVENIENCE I HAVE ASSIGNED A NAME TO EACH VOLUME LEVEL.
ZERO TO FOUR BOXES IS THE "DOWNSIZER" VOLUME...
FIVE TO EIGHT BOXES IS THE "LOW PERFORMER" VOLUME LEVEL.
LET'S SAY SIX HUNDRED BOXES.
AHH... THE "FAST TRACKER." AN EXCELLENT CHOICE.
WHAT'S YOUR DAUGHTER'S NAME?
OOH... GOTTA GO.
I ONLY BOUGHT TWELVE BOXES. NOW I'M THE "UNITED WAY" CHAIRPERSON.
I JUST SIGNED YOUR NAME FOR SIX HUNDRED MORE.
S. Adams
7/7/96
© 1996 United Feature Syndicate, Inc.

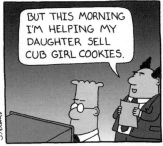

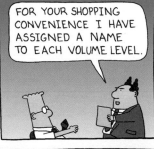

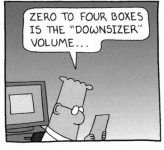

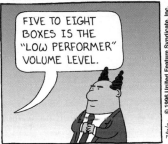

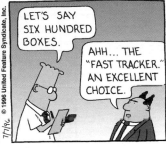

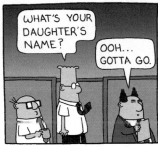

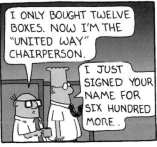

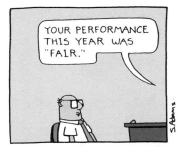

YOUR PERFORMANCE THIS YEAR WAS "FAIR."
BUT I'LL RAISE YOUR APPRAISAL TO "EXCELLENT" IF YOU'LL EAT A BUG.
SAY WHAT?
EAT A BUG.
I DIDN'T HAVE MUCH LUCK WITH THE OTHER MANAGEMENT TECH-NIQUES SO I'M KINDA WINGING IT NOW.
DO I GET TO PICK THE BUG?
IT'S WAY MORE MOTIVATIONAL IF I PICK THE BUG.
HOW DID YOUR EVALUATION GO?
MXLNT.
NEXT!
DO I GET A BUN?
YOU GUYS ARE NEVER HAPPY.
S. Adams
4-3

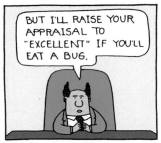

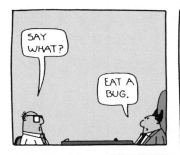

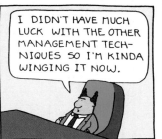

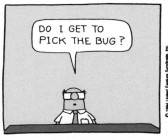

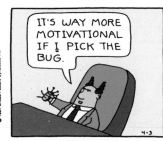

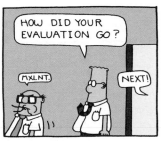

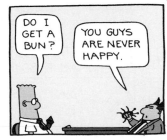

POLICIES

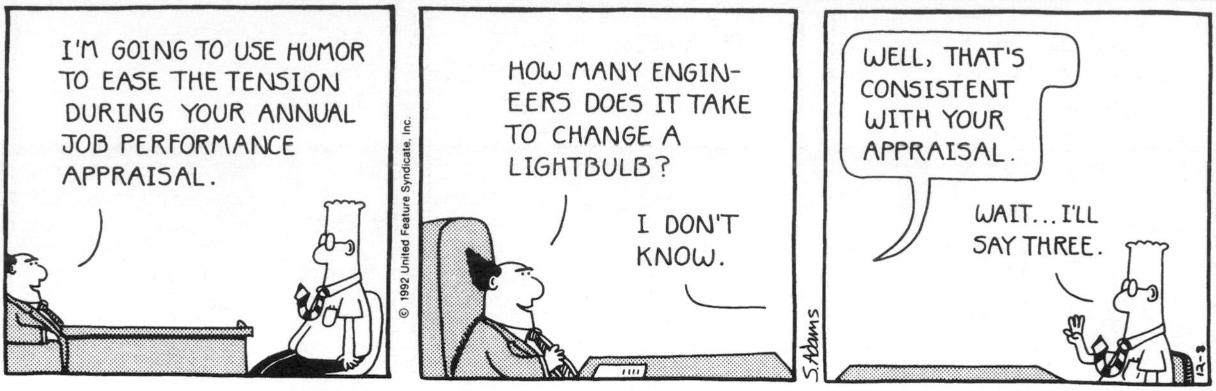
I'M GOING TO USE HUMOR TO EASE THE TENSION DURING YOUR ANNUAL JOB PERFORMANCE APPRAISAL.
© 1992 United Feature Syndicate, Inc.
HOW MANY ENGINEERS DOES IT TAKE TO CHANGE A LIGHTBULB?
I DON'T KNOW.
S.Adams
WELL, THAT'S CONSISTENT WITH YOUR APPRAISAL.
WAIT... I'LL SAY THREE.
12-8

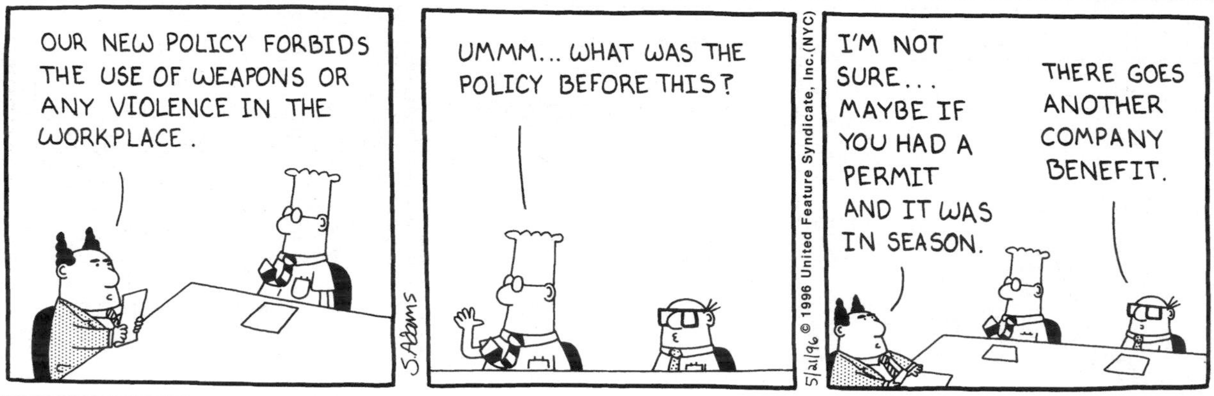
OUR NEW POLICY FORBIDS THE USE OF WEAPONS OR ANY VIOLENCE IN THE WORKPLACE.
S.Adams
UMMM... WHAT WAS THE POLICY BEFORE THIS?
5/21/96 © 1996 United Feature Syndicate, Inc.(NYC)
I'M NOT SURE... MAYBE IF YOU HAD A PERMIT AND IT WAS IN SEASON.
THERE GOES ANOTHER COMPANY BENEFIT.

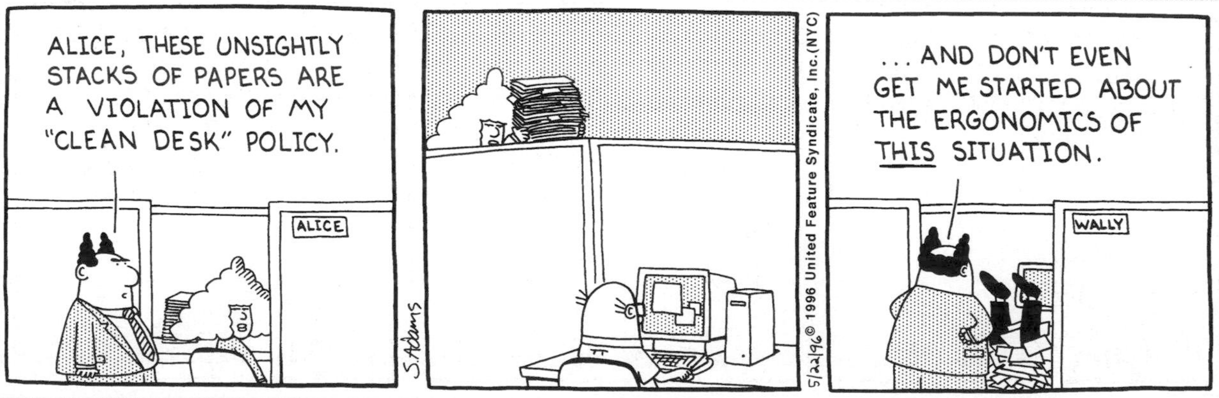
ALICE, THESE UNSIGHTLY STACKS OF PAPERS ARE A VIOLATION OF MY "CLEAN DESK" POLICY.
ALICE
S.Adams
5/22/96 © 1996 United Feature Syndicate, Inc.(NYC)
... AND DON'T EVEN GET ME STARTED ABOUT THE ERGONOMICS OF THIS SITUATION.
WALLY

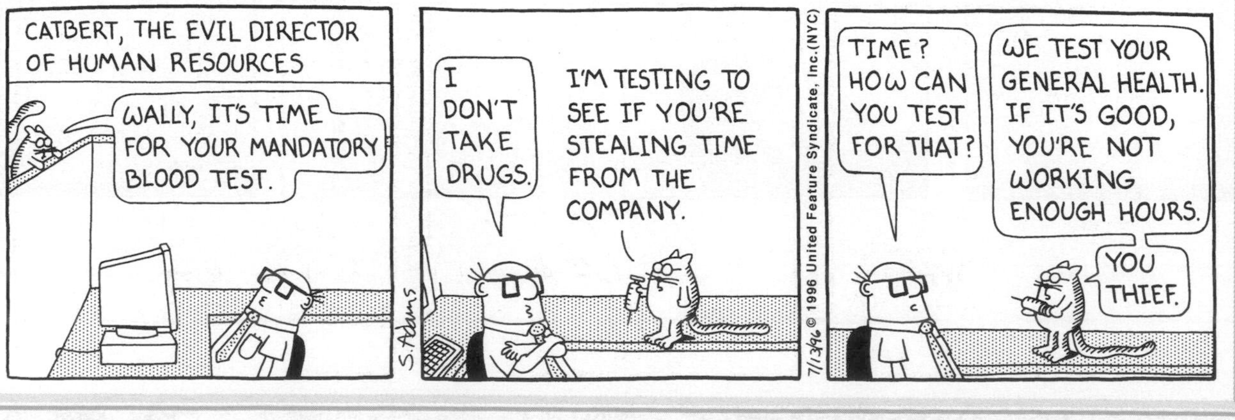
CATBERT, THE EVIL DIRECTOR OF HUMAN RESOURCES
WALLY, IT'S TIME FOR YOUR MANDATORY BLOOD TEST.
S.Adams
I DON'T TAKE DRUGS.
I'M TESTING TO SEE IF YOU'RE STEALING TIME FROM THE COMPANY.
7/13/96 © 1996 United Feature Syndicate, Inc.(NYC)
TIME? HOW CAN YOU TEST FOR THAT?
WE TEST YOUR GENERAL HEALTH. IF IT'S GOOD, YOU'RE NOT WORKING ENOUGH HOURS.
YOU THIEF.

Panel 1:
I'M WRITING AN E-MAIL TO PROTEST THE NEW POLICY OF MAKING THE EMPLOYEES EMPTY THEIR OWN TRASH AT NIGHT.

Panel 2:
IT'S STUPID TO HAVE HIGHLY PAID ENGINEERS DOING UNPRODUCTIVE TASKS WHEN WE COULD BE INVENTING THE FUTURE!

Panel 3:
ARE YOU COMING TO THE "QUALITY FAIRE"?

NO, THIS WILL TAKE ANOTHER HOUR.

© 1995 United Feature Syndicate, Inc. (NYC)

Panel 4:
CATBERT: H.R. DIRECTOR

"CONSISTENT WITH OUR EFFORT TO ELIMINATE PRIVACY AND DIGNITY...

Panel 5:
"...EMPLOYEES MUST SHARE HOTEL ROOMS ON ALL BUSINESS TRIPS."

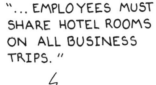

© 1998 United Feature Syndicate, Inc.

Panel 6:
AFTER THEY GET USED TO THIS, I'LL INTRODUCE THE TANDEM SHOWERING POLICY.

Panel 7:
I CAN'T BELIEVE THEY EXPECT US TO SIGN THESE NEW EMPLOYMENT AGREEMENT FORMS.

Panel 8:
ACCORDING TO THIS, ANYTHING WE EVEN THINK OF BECOMES THE COMPANY'S PROPERTY. I'M SURPRISED THEY DON'T CLAIM OUR FIRSTBORN SONS!

© 1996 United Feature Syndicate, Inc. (NYC)

Panel 9:
WHAT DO YOU SUPPOSE IT MEANS WHEN THEY COPYRIGHT OUR "DNA AND ALL DERIVATIVE WORKS"?

THEY'D MAKE AN EXCEPTION FOR YOU.

Panel 10:
WE'RE ANNOUNCING TWO NEW PROGRAMS FOR EMPLOYEES.

Panel 11:
THE FIRST IS A NEW DIGNITY ENHANCEMENT PROGRAM AND THE SECOND IS OUR NEW RANDOM DRUG TESTING INITIATIVE.

© 1995 United Feature Syndicate, Inc. (NYC)

Panel 12:
THE CLUE METER IS READING ZERO.

YOU EACH GET A HANDSOME COFFEE MUG AS PART OF THE KICK-OFF.

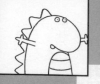

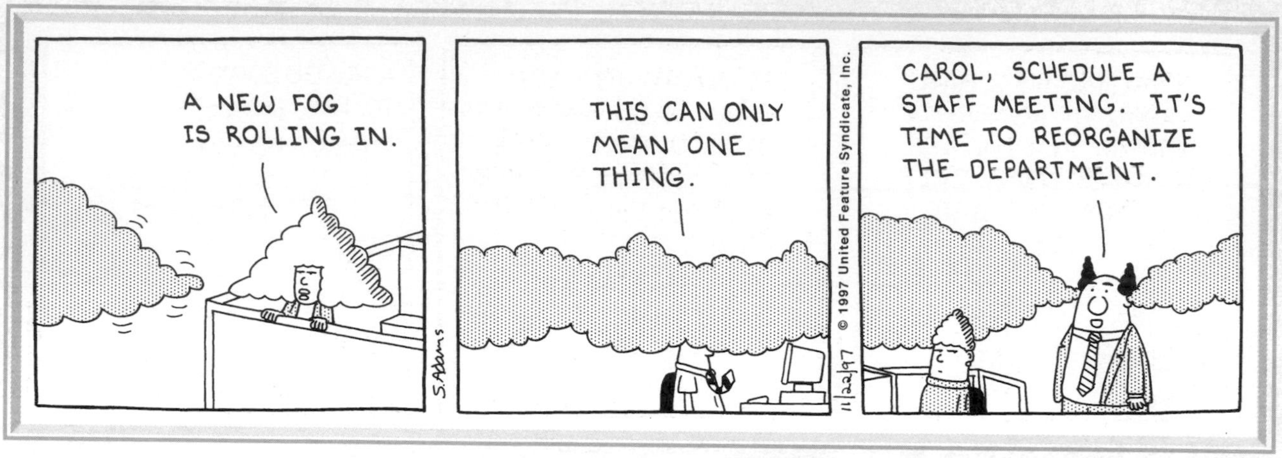
A NEW FOG IS ROLLING IN.
THIS CAN ONLY MEAN ONE THING.
CAROL, SCHEDULE A STAFF MEETING. IT'S TIME TO REORGANIZE THE DEPARTMENT.
© 1997 United Feature Syndicate, Inc.

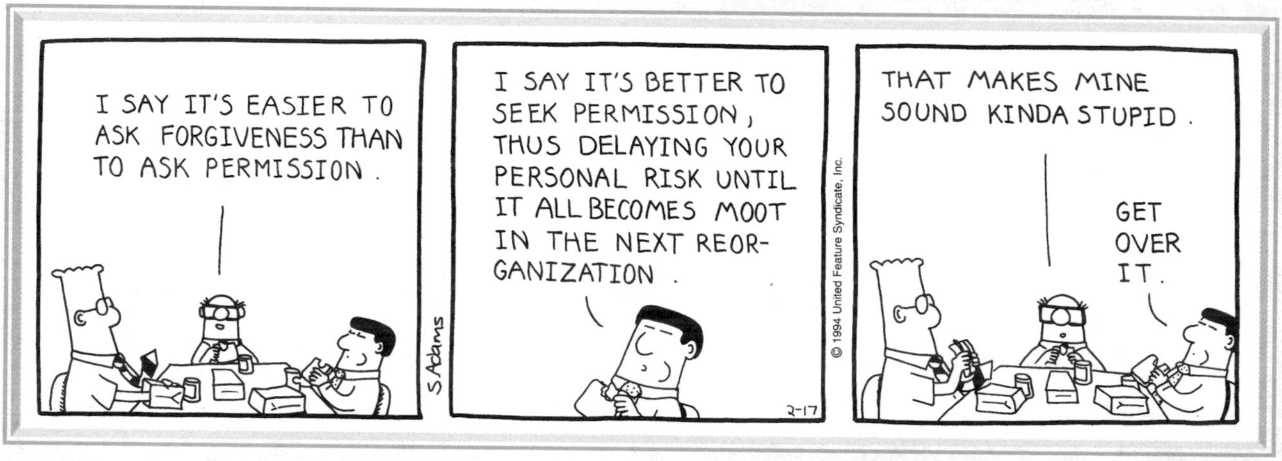
I SAY IT'S EASIER TO ASK FORGIVENESS THAN TO ASK PERMISSION.
I SAY IT'S BETTER TO SEEK PERMISSION, THUS DELAYING YOUR PERSONAL RISK UNTIL IT ALL BECOMES MOOT IN THE NEXT REORGANIZATION.
THAT MAKES MINE SOUND KINDA STUPID.
GET OVER IT.
© 1994 United Feature Syndicate, Inc.

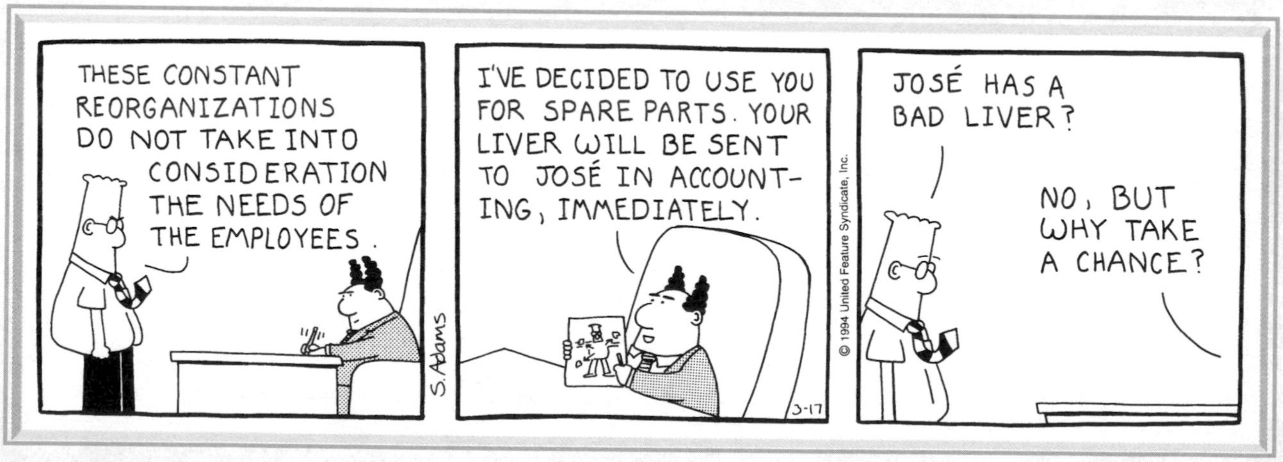
THESE CONSTANT REORGANIZATIONS DO NOT TAKE INTO CONSIDERATION THE NEEDS OF THE EMPLOYEES.
I'VE DECIDED TO USE YOU FOR SPARE PARTS. YOUR LIVER WILL BE SENT TO JOSÉ IN ACCOUNTING, IMMEDIATELY.
JOSÉ HAS A BAD LIVER?
NO, BUT WHY TAKE A CHANCE?
© 1994 United Feature Syndicate, Inc.

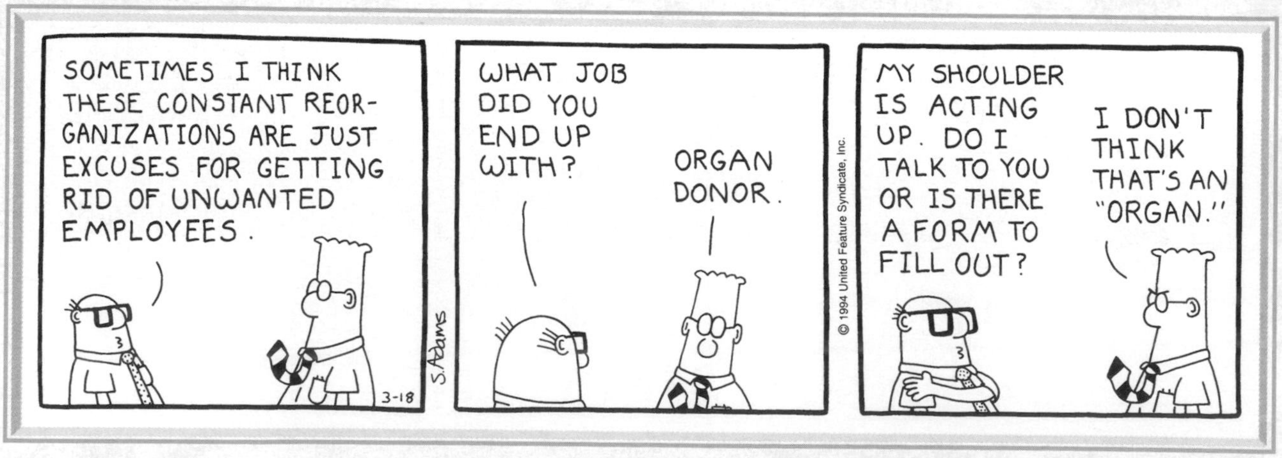
SOMETIMES I THINK THESE CONSTANT REORGANIZATIONS ARE JUST EXCUSES FOR GETTING RID OF UNWANTED EMPLOYEES.
WHAT JOB DID YOU END UP WITH?
ORGAN DONOR.
MY SHOULDER IS ACTING UP. DO I TALK TO YOU OR IS THERE A FORM TO FILL OUT?
I DON'T THINK THAT'S AN "ORGAN."
© 1994 United Feature Syndicate, Inc.

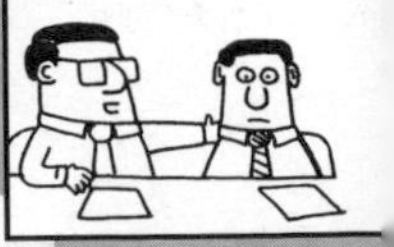

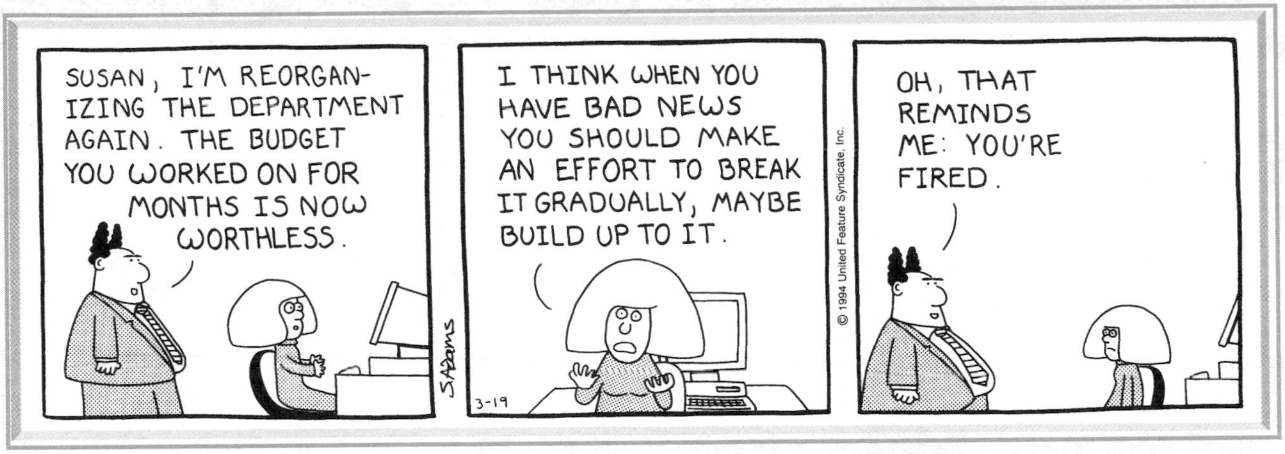
SUSAN, I'M REORGANIZING THE DEPARTMENT AGAIN. THE BUDGET YOU WORKED ON FOR MONTHS IS NOW WORTHLESS.
S.Adams 3-19
I THINK WHEN YOU HAVE BAD NEWS YOU SHOULD MAKE AN EFFORT TO BREAK IT GRADUALLY, MAYBE BUILD UP TO IT.
© 1994 United Feature Syndicate, Inc.
OH, THAT REMINDS ME: YOU'RE FIRED.

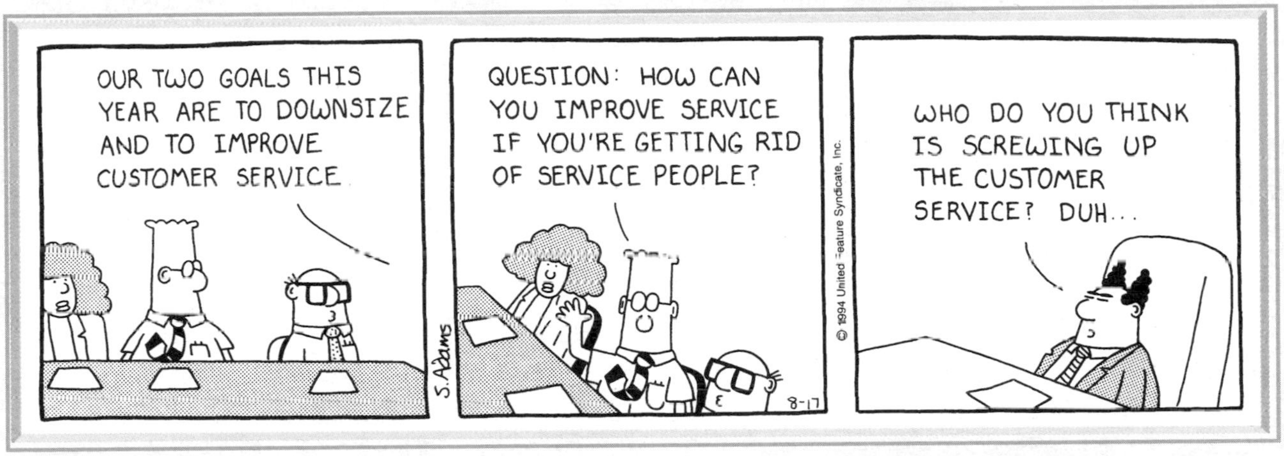
OUR TWO GOALS THIS YEAR ARE TO DOWNSIZE AND TO IMPROVE CUSTOMER SERVICE.
S.Adams
QUESTION: HOW CAN YOU IMPROVE SERVICE IF YOU'RE GETTING RID OF SERVICE PEOPLE?
8-17
© 1994 United Feature Syndicate, Inc.
WHO DO YOU THINK IS SCREWING UP THE CUSTOMER SERVICE? DUH...

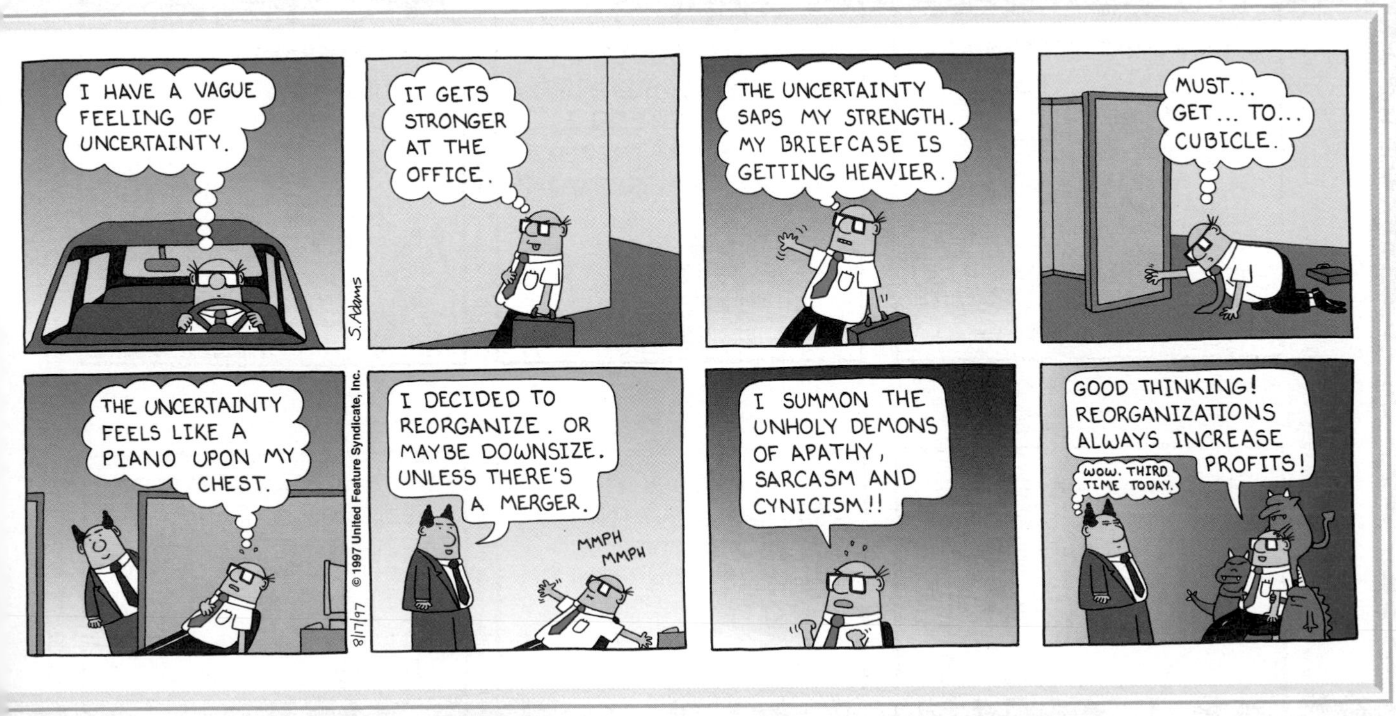
I HAVE A VAGUE FEELING OF UNCERTAINTY.
S.Adams
IT GETS STRONGER AT THE OFFICE.
THE UNCERTAINTY SAPS MY STRENGTH. MY BRIEFCASE IS GETTING HEAVIER.
MUST... GET... TO... CUBICLE.
THE UNCERTAINTY FEELS LIKE A PIANO UPON MY CHEST.
8/17/97 © 1997 United Feature Syndicate, Inc.
I DECIDED TO REORGANIZE. OR MAYBE DOWNSIZE. UNLESS THERE'S A MERGER.
MMPH MMPH
I SUMMON THE UNHOLY DEMONS OF APATHY, SARCASM AND CYNICISM!!
GOOD THINKING! REORGANIZATIONS ALWAYS INCREASE PROFITS!
WOW. THIRD TIME TODAY.

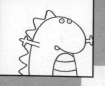

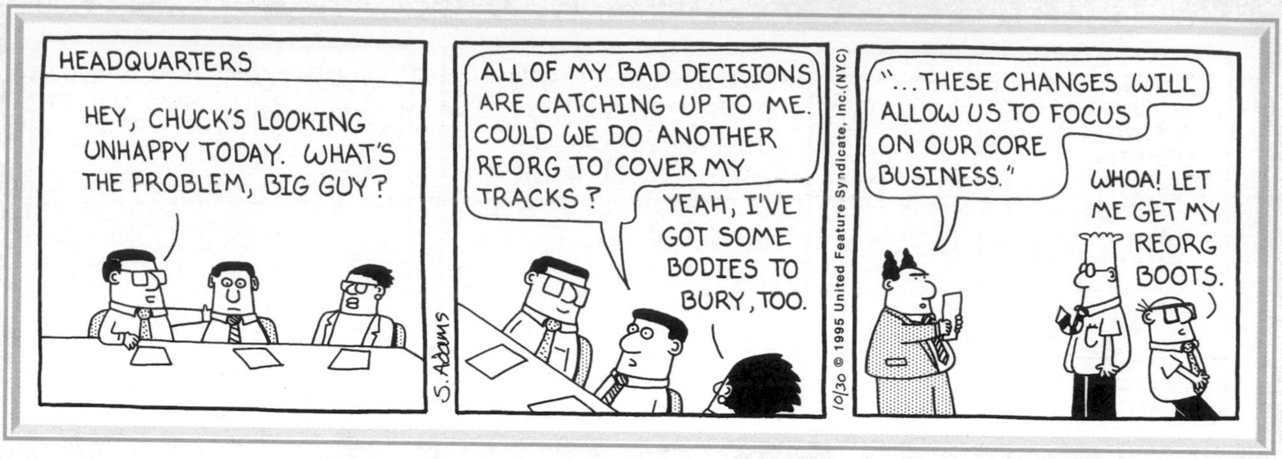
HEADQUARTERS
HEY, CHUCK'S LOOKING UNHAPPY TODAY. WHAT'S THE PROBLEM, BIG GUY?
ALL OF MY BAD DECISIONS ARE CATCHING UP TO ME. COULD WE DO ANOTHER REORG TO COVER MY TRACKS?
YEAH, I'VE GOT SOME BODIES TO BURY, TOO.
"...THESE CHANGES WILL ALLOW US TO FOCUS ON OUR CORE BUSINESS."
WHOA! LET ME GET MY REORG BOOTS.
S. Adams
10/30 © 1995 United Feature Syndicate, Inc.(NYC)

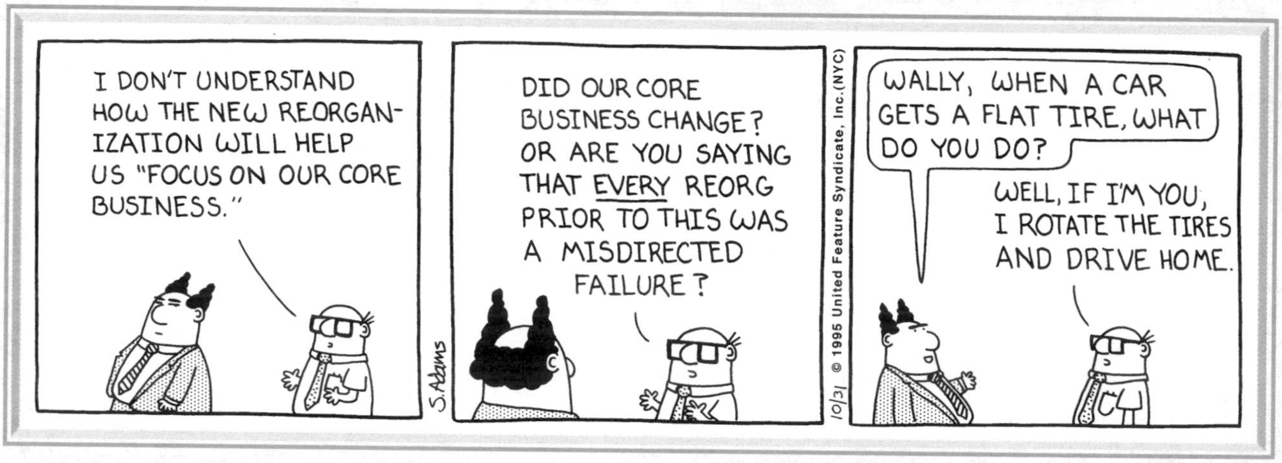
I DON'T UNDERSTAND HOW THE NEW REORGANIZATION WILL HELP US "FOCUS ON OUR CORE BUSINESS."
DID OUR CORE BUSINESS CHANGE? OR ARE YOU SAYING THAT EVERY REORG PRIOR TO THIS WAS A MISDIRECTED FAILURE?
WALLY, WHEN A CAR GETS A FLAT TIRE, WHAT DO YOU DO?
WELL, IF I'M YOU, I ROTATE THE TIRES AND DRIVE HOME.
S. Adams
10/31 © 1995 United Feature Syndicate, Inc.(NYC)

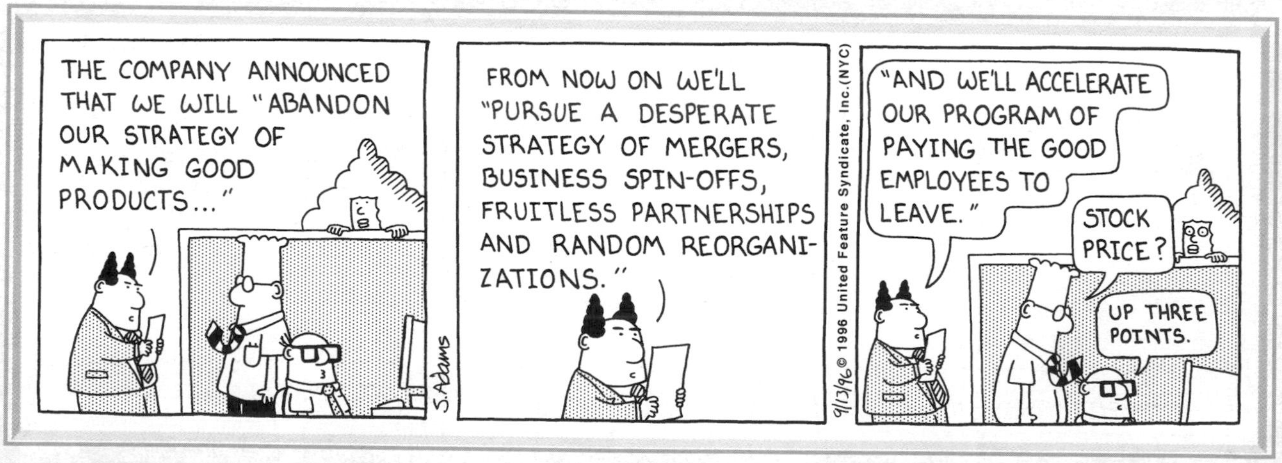
THE COMPANY ANNOUNCED THAT WE WILL "ABANDON OUR STRATEGY OF MAKING GOOD PRODUCTS..."
FROM NOW ON WE'LL "PURSUE A DESPERATE STRATEGY OF MERGERS, BUSINESS SPIN-OFFS, FRUITLESS PARTNERSHIPS AND RANDOM REORGANIZATIONS."
"AND WE'LL ACCELERATE OUR PROGRAM OF PAYING THE GOOD EMPLOYEES TO LEAVE."
STOCK PRICE?
UP THREE POINTS.
S. Adams
9/13/96 © 1996 United Feature Syndicate, Inc.(NYC)

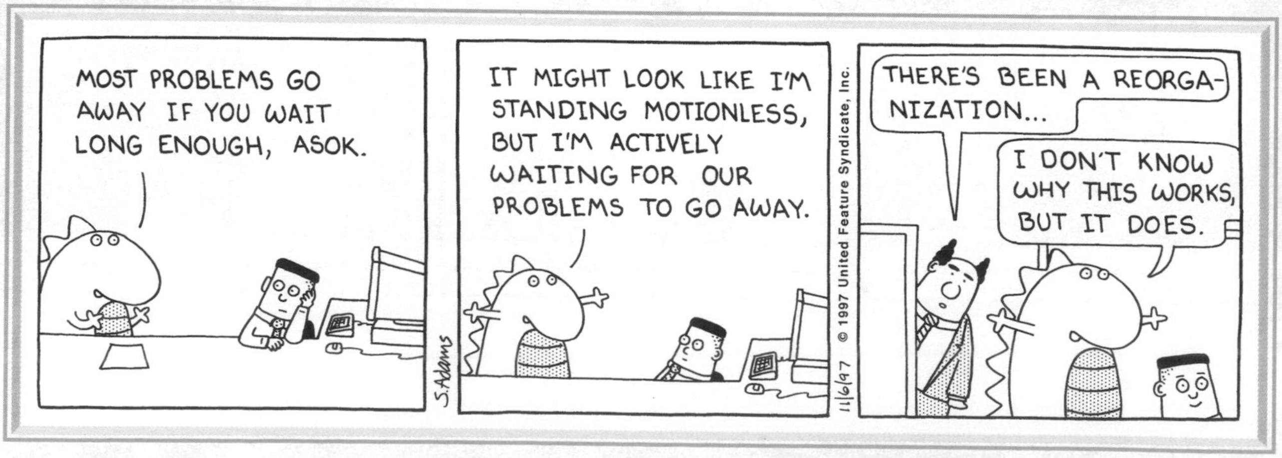
MOST PROBLEMS GO AWAY IF YOU WAIT LONG ENOUGH, ASOK.
IT MIGHT LOOK LIKE I'M STANDING MOTIONLESS, BUT I'M ACTIVELY WAITING FOR OUR PROBLEMS TO GO AWAY.
THERE'S BEEN A REORGANIZATION...
I DON'T KNOW WHY THIS WORKS, BUT IT DOES.
S. Adams
11/6/97 © 1997 United Feature Syndicate, Inc.

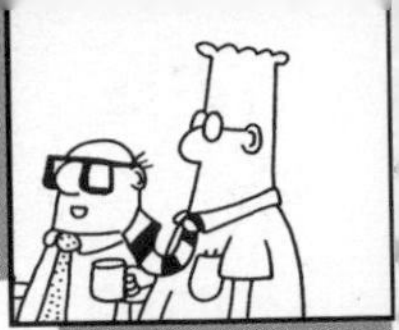

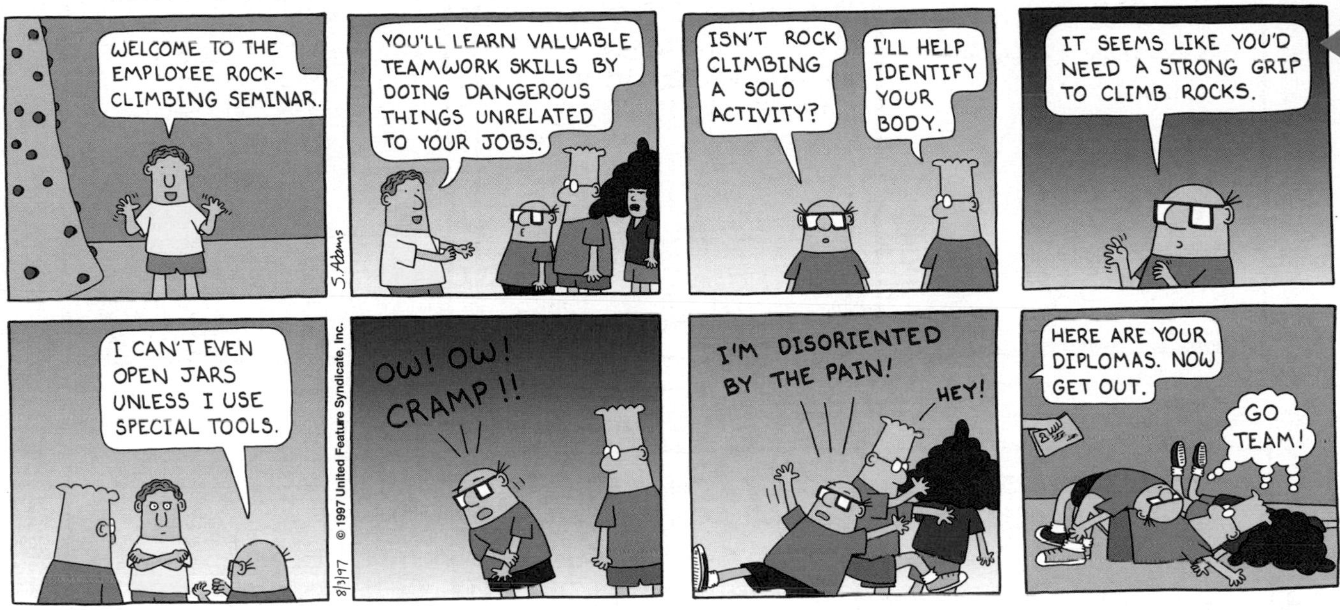
WELCOME TO THE EMPLOYEE ROCK-CLIMBING SEMINAR.
YOU'LL LEARN VALUABLE TEAMWORK SKILLS BY DOING DANGEROUS THINGS UNRELATED TO YOUR JOBS.
S. Adams
ISN'T ROCK CLIMBING A SOLO ACTIVITY?
I'LL HELP IDENTIFY YOUR BODY.
IT SEEMS LIKE YOU'D NEED A STRONG GRIP TO CLIMB ROCKS.
I CAN'T EVEN OPEN JARS UNLESS I USE SPECIAL TOOLS.
8/3/97 © 1997 United Feature Syndicate, Inc.
OW! OW! CRAMP!!
I'M DISORIENTED BY THE PAIN!
HEY!
HERE ARE YOUR DIPLOMAS. NOW GET OUT.
GO TEAM!

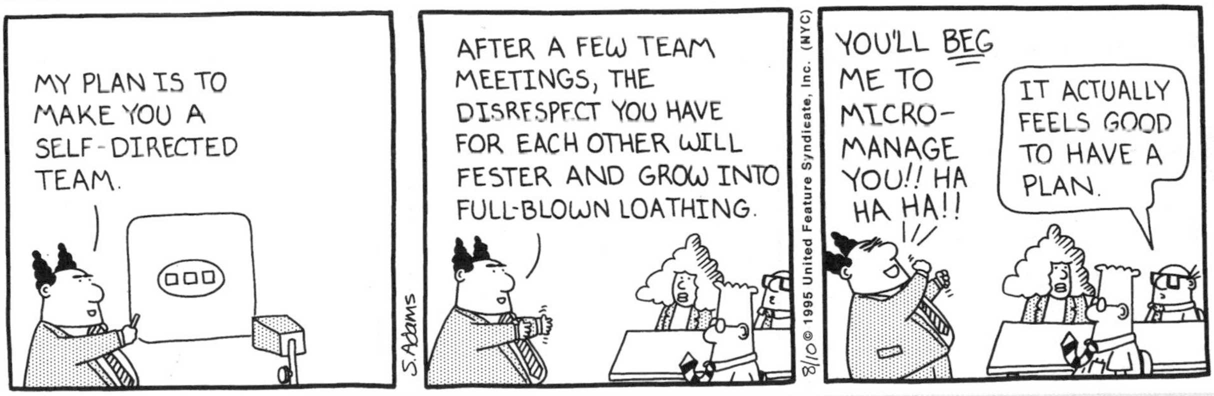
MY PLAN IS TO MAKE YOU A SELF-DIRECTED TEAM.
S. Adams
AFTER A FEW TEAM MEETINGS, THE DISRESPECT YOU HAVE FOR EACH OTHER WILL FESTER AND GROW INTO FULL-BLOWN LOATHING.
8/10 © 1995 United Feature Syndicate, Inc. (NYC)
YOU'LL BEG ME TO MICRO-MANAGE YOU!! HA HA HA!!
IT ACTUALLY FEELS GOOD TO HAVE A PLAN.

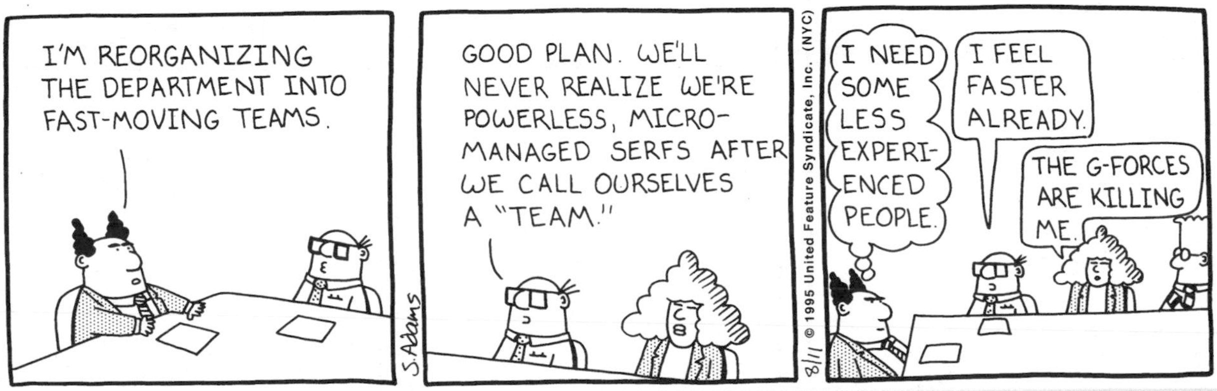
I'M REORGANIZING THE DEPARTMENT INTO FAST-MOVING TEAMS.
S. Adams
GOOD PLAN. WE'LL NEVER REALIZE WE'RE POWERLESS, MICRO-MANAGED SERFS AFTER WE CALL OURSELVES A "TEAM."
8/11 © 1995 United Feature Syndicate, Inc. (NYC)
I NEED SOME LESS EXPERI-ENCED PEOPLE.
I FEEL FASTER ALREADY.
THE G-FORCES ARE KILLING ME.

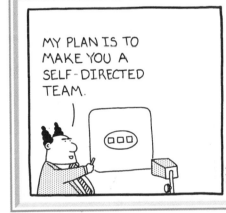

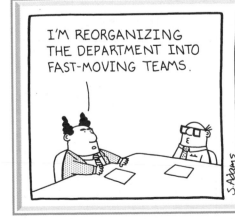

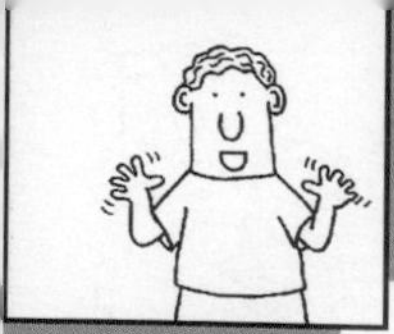

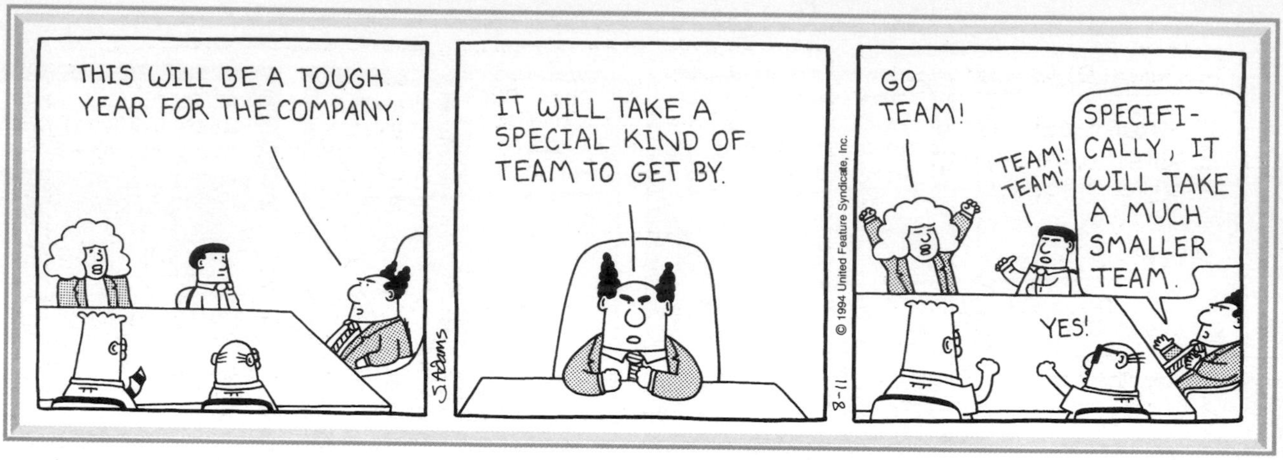
THIS WILL BE A TOUGH YEAR FOR THE COMPANY.
S.Adams
IT WILL TAKE A SPECIAL KIND OF TEAM TO GET BY.
8-11
© 1994 United Feature Syndicate, Inc.
GO TEAM!
TEAM! TEAM!
SPECIFI-CALLY, IT WILL TAKE A MUCH SMALLER TEAM.
YES!

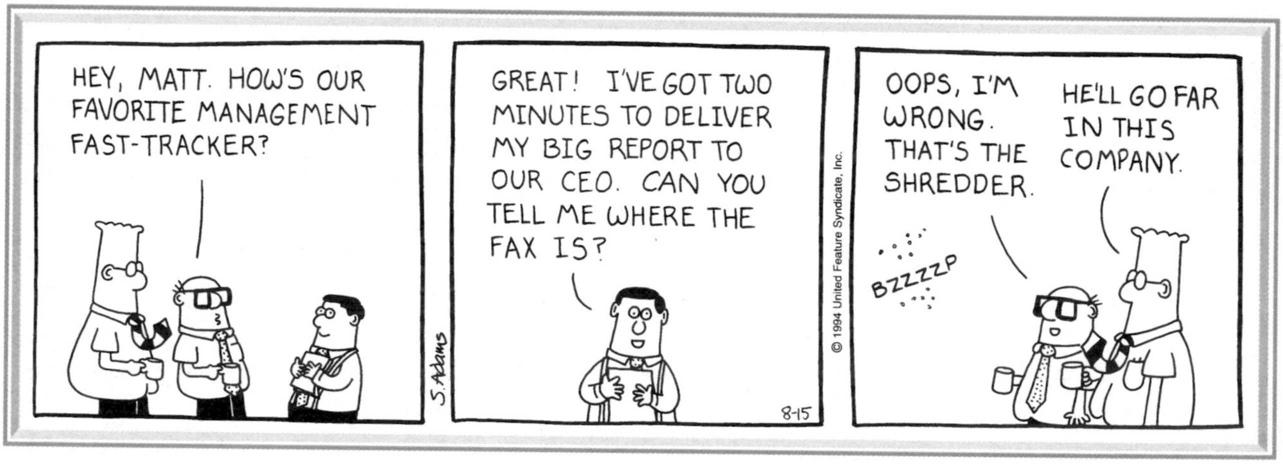
HEY, MATT. HOW'S OUR FAVORITE MANAGEMENT FAST-TRACKER?
S. Adams
GREAT! I'VE GOT TWO MINUTES TO DELIVER MY BIG REPORT TO OUR CEO. CAN YOU TELL ME WHERE THE FAX IS?
8-15
© 1994 United Feature Syndicate, Inc.
OOPS, I'M WRONG. THAT'S THE SHREDDER.
BZZZZP
HE'LL GO FAR IN THIS COMPANY.

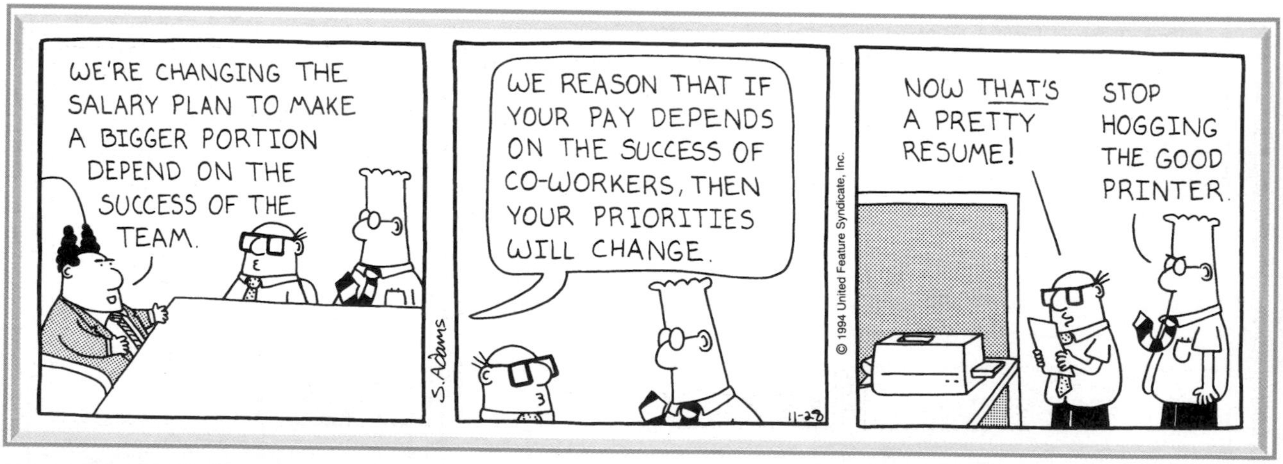
WE'RE CHANGING THE SALARY PLAN TO MAKE A BIGGER PORTION DEPEND ON THE SUCCESS OF THE TEAM.
S. Adams
WE REASON THAT IF YOUR PAY DEPENDS ON THE SUCCESS OF CO-WORKERS, THEN YOUR PRIORITIES WILL CHANGE.
11-28
© 1994 United Feature Syndicate, Inc.
NOW THAT'S A PRETTY RESUME!
STOP HOGGING THE GOOD PRINTER.

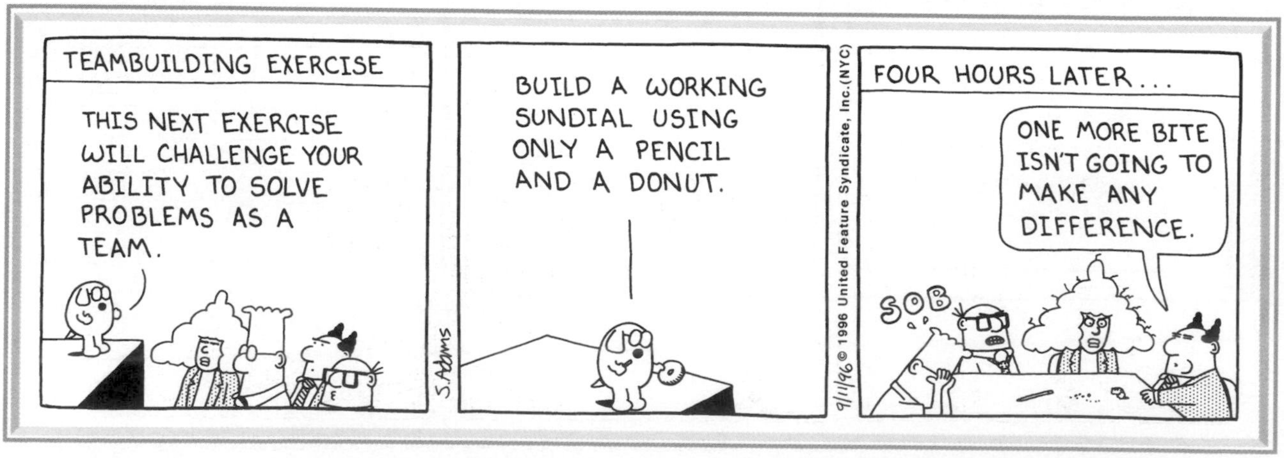
TEAMBUILDING EXERCISE
THIS NEXT EXERCISE WILL CHALLENGE YOUR ABILITY TO SOLVE PROBLEMS AS A TEAM.
S. Adams
BUILD A WORKING SUNDIAL USING ONLY A PENCIL AND A DONUT.
9/1/96 © 1996 United Feature Syndicate, Inc.(NYC)
FOUR HOURS LATER...
ONE MORE BITE ISN'T GOING TO MAKE ANY DIFFERENCE.
SOB

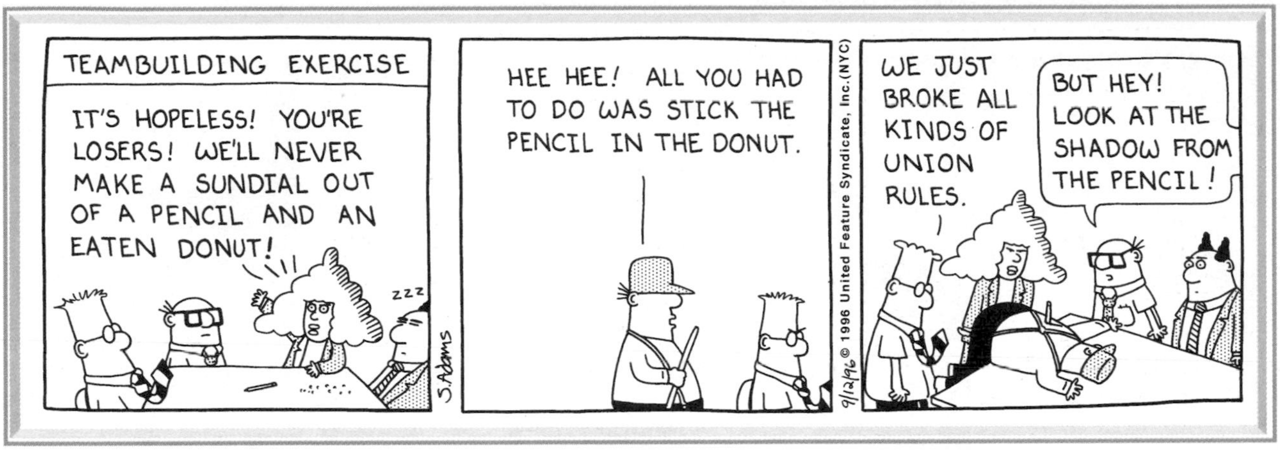
TEAMBUILDING EXERCISE
IT'S HOPELESS! YOU'RE LOSERS! WE'LL NEVER MAKE A SUNDIAL OUT OF A PENCIL AND AN EATEN DONUT!
ZZZ
S. Adams
HEE HEE! ALL YOU HAD TO DO WAS STICK THE PENCIL IN THE DONUT.
9/12/96 © 1996 United Feature Syndicate, Inc.(NYC)
WE JUST BROKE ALL KINDS OF UNION RULES.
BUT HEY! LOOK AT THE SHADOW FROM THE PENCIL!

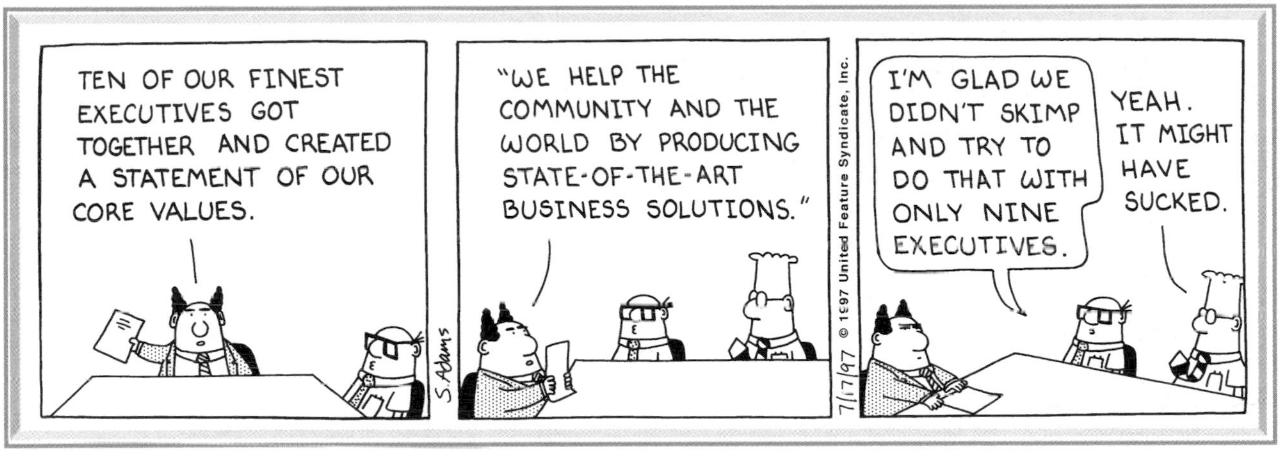
TEN OF OUR FINEST EXECUTIVES GOT TOGETHER AND CREATED A STATEMENT OF OUR CORE VALUES.
S. Adams
"WE HELP THE COMMUNITY AND THE WORLD BY PRODUCING STATE-OF-THE-ART BUSINESS SOLUTIONS."
7/17/97 © 1997 United Feature Syndicate, Inc.
I'M GLAD WE DIDN'T SKIMP AND TRY TO DO THAT WITH ONLY NINE EXECUTIVES.
YEAH. IT MIGHT HAVE SUCKED.

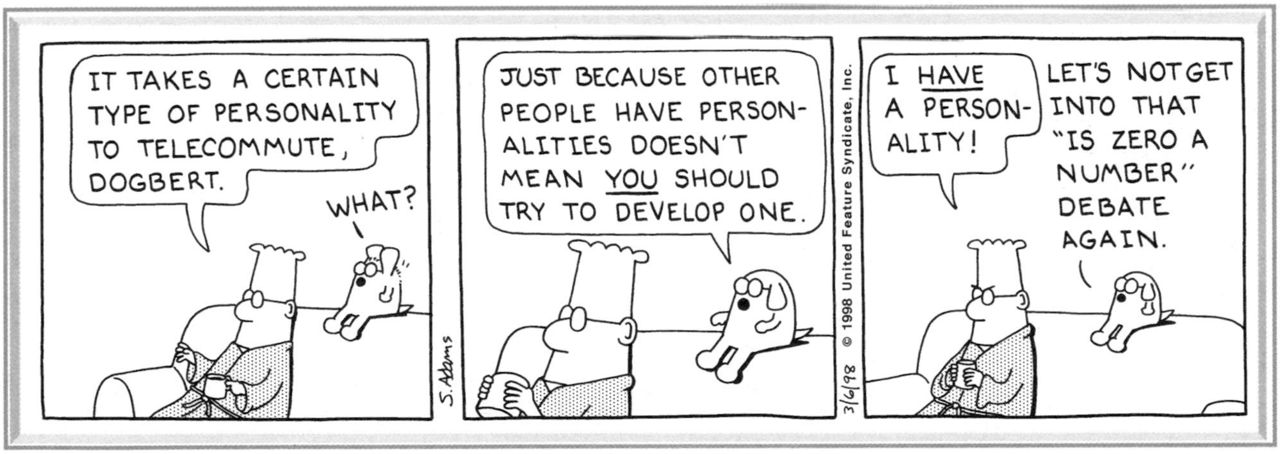
IT TAKES A CERTAIN TYPE OF PERSONALITY TO TELECOMMUTE, DOGBERT.
WHAT?
S. Adams
JUST BECAUSE OTHER PEOPLE HAVE PERSONALITIES DOESN'T MEAN YOU SHOULD TRY TO DEVELOP ONE.
3/6/98 © 1998 United Feature Syndicate, Inc.
I HAVE A PERSONALITY!
LET'S NOT GET INTO THAT "IS ZERO A NUMBER" DEBATE AGAIN.

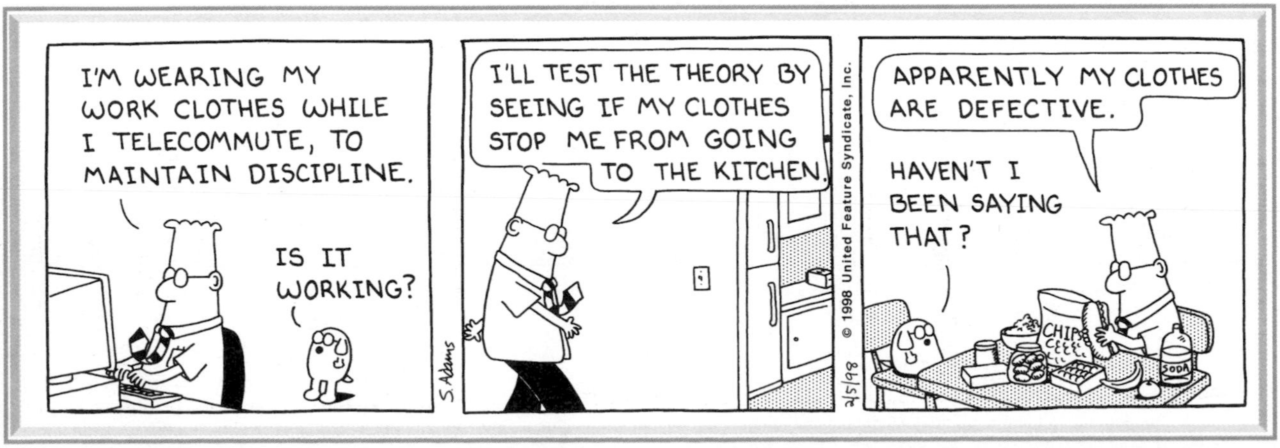
I'M WEARING MY WORK CLOTHES WHILE I TELECOMMUTE, TO MAINTAIN DISCIPLINE.
IS IT WORKING?
S. Adams
I'LL TEST THE THEORY BY SEEING IF MY CLOTHES STOP ME FROM GOING TO THE KITCHEN.
2/5/98 © 1998 United Feature Syndicate, Inc.
APPARENTLY MY CLOTHES ARE DEFECTIVE.
HAVEN'T I BEEN SAYING THAT?
CHIPS
SODA

TELECOMMUTING

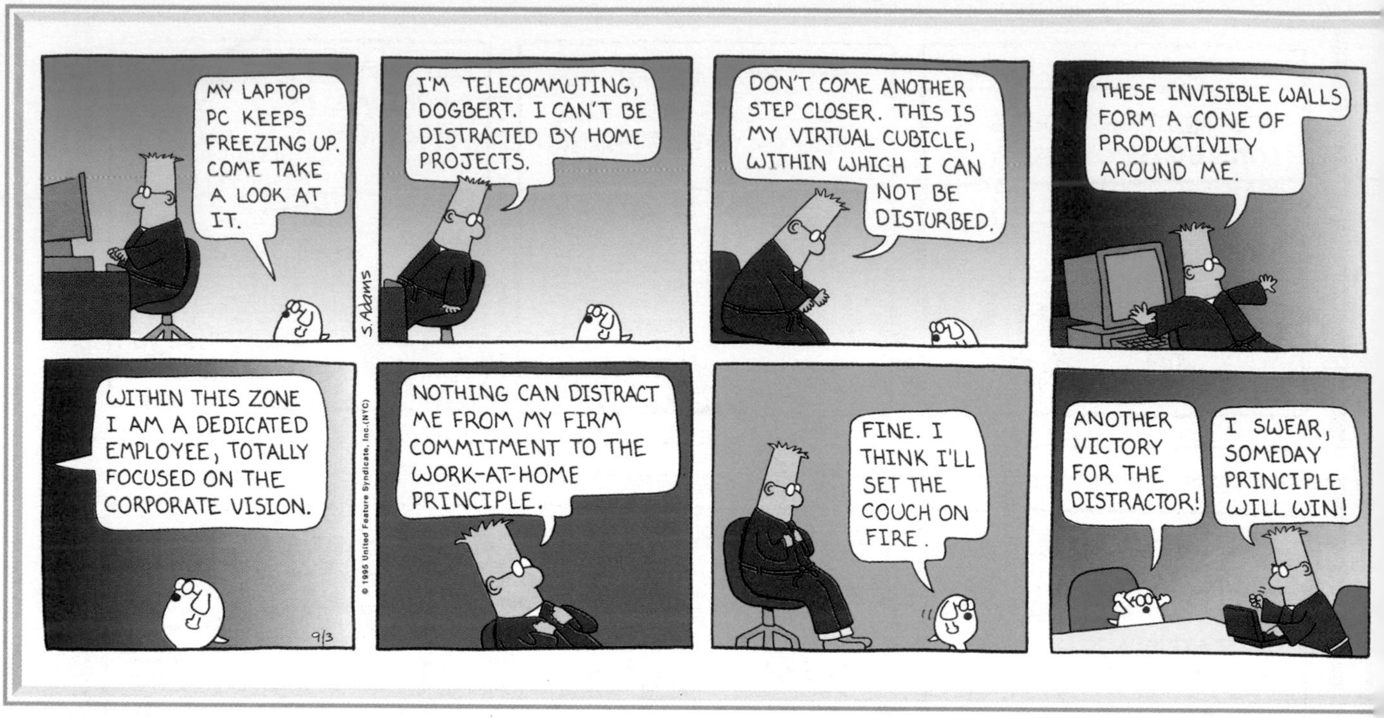
MY LAPTOP PC KEEPS FREEZING UP. COME TAKE A LOOK AT IT.
I'M TELECOMMUTING, DOGBERT. I CAN'T BE DISTRACTED BY HOME PROJECTS.
DON'T COME ANOTHER STEP CLOSER. THIS IS MY VIRTUAL CUBICLE, WITHIN WHICH I CAN NOT BE DISTURBED.
THESE INVISIBLE WALLS FORM A CONE OF PRODUCTIVITY AROUND ME.
WITHIN THIS ZONE I AM A DEDICATED EMPLOYEE, TOTALLY FOCUSED ON THE CORPORATE VISION.
NOTHING CAN DISTRACT ME FROM MY FIRM COMMITMENT TO THE WORK-AT-HOME PRINCIPLE.
FINE. I THINK I'LL SET THE COUCH ON FIRE.
ANOTHER VICTORY FOR THE DISTRACTOR!
I SWEAR, SOMEDAY PRINCIPLE WILL WIN!
S. Adams
© 1995 United Feature Syndicate, Inc.(NYC)
9/3

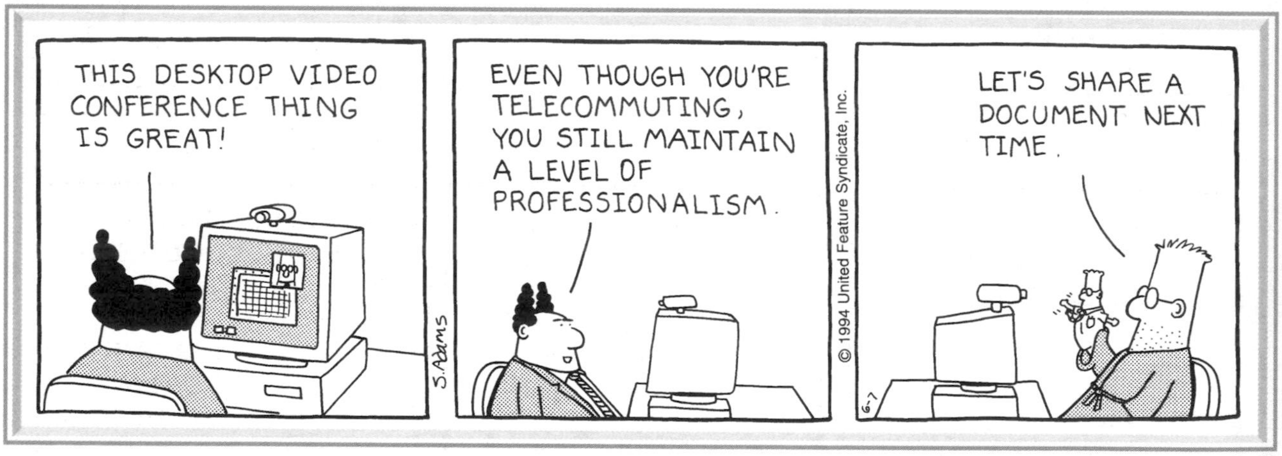
THIS DESKTOP VIDEO CONFERENCE THING IS GREAT!
EVEN THOUGH YOU'RE TELECOMMUTING, YOU STILL MAINTAIN A LEVEL OF PROFESSIONALISM.
LET'S SHARE A DOCUMENT NEXT TIME.
S. Adams
© 1994 United Feature Syndicate, Inc.
6-7

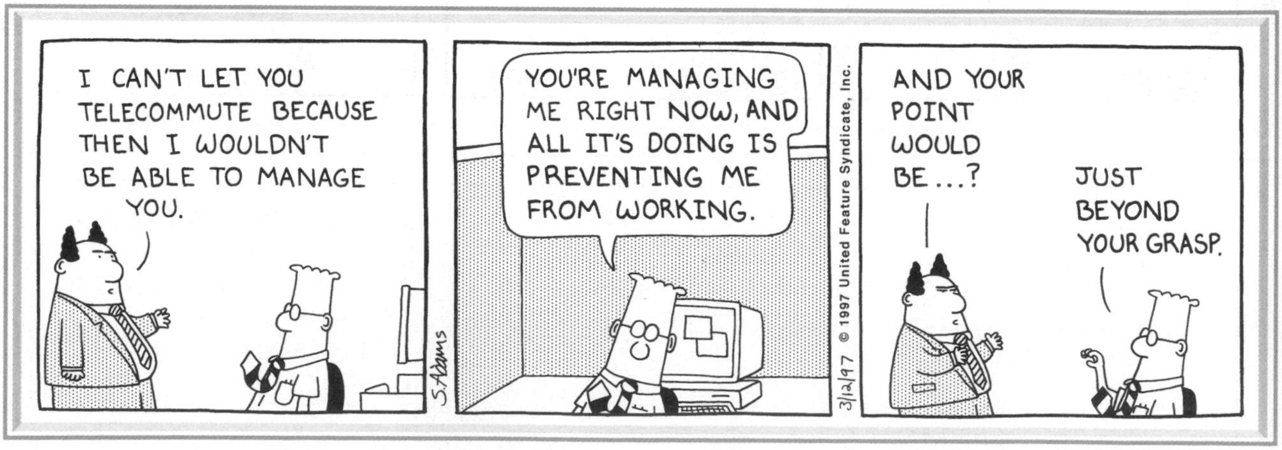
I CAN'T LET YOU TELECOMMUTE BECAUSE THEN I WOULDN'T BE ABLE TO MANAGE YOU.
YOU'RE MANAGING ME RIGHT NOW, AND ALL IT'S DOING IS PREVENTING ME FROM WORKING.
AND YOUR POINT WOULD BE...?
JUST BEYOND YOUR GRASP.
S. Adams
3/12/97 © 1997 United Feature Syndicate, Inc.

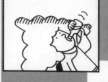

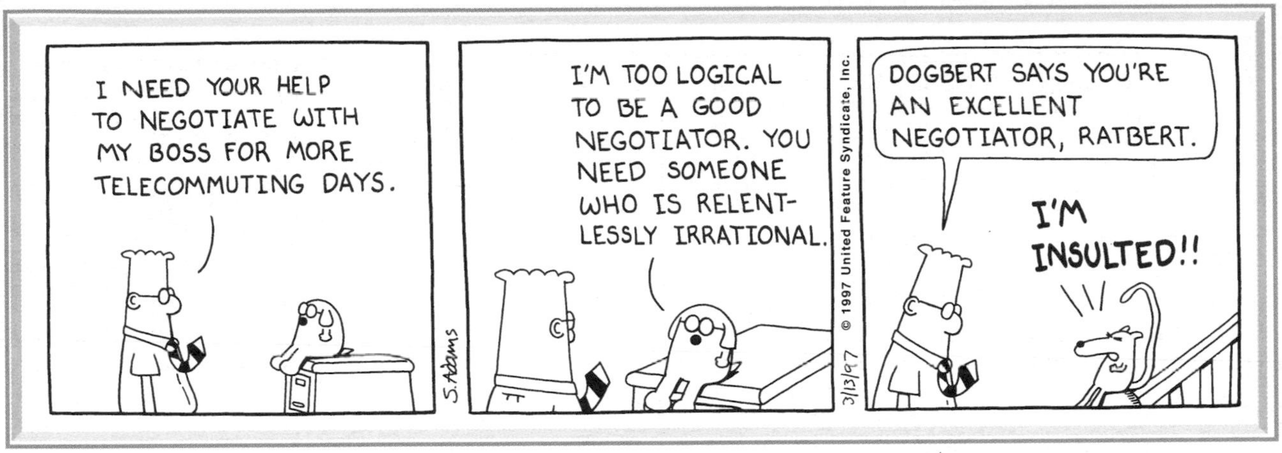
I NEED YOUR HELP TO NEGOTIATE WITH MY BOSS FOR MORE TELECOMMUTING DAYS.
I'M TOO LOGICAL TO BE A GOOD NEGOTIATOR. YOU NEED SOMEONE WHO IS RELENTLESSLY IRRATIONAL.
DOGBERT SAYS YOU'RE AN EXCELLENT NEGOTIATOR, RATBERT.
I'M INSULTED!!
S. Adams
© 1997 United Feature Syndicate, Inc.
3/13/97

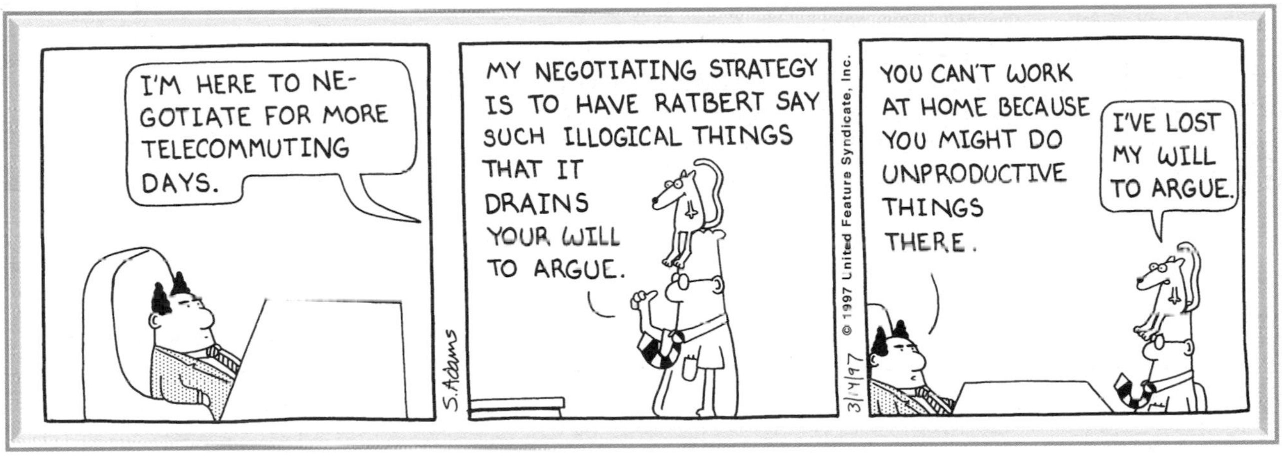
I'M HERE TO NEGOTIATE FOR MORE TELECOMMUTING DAYS.
MY NEGOTIATING STRATEGY IS TO HAVE RATBERT SAY SUCH ILLOGICAL THINGS THAT IT DRAINS YOUR WILL TO ARGUE.
YOU CAN'T WORK AT HOME BECAUSE YOU MIGHT DO UNPRODUCTIVE THINGS THERE.
I'VE LOST MY WILL TO ARGUE.
S. Adams
© 1997 United Feature Syndicate, Inc.
3/14/97

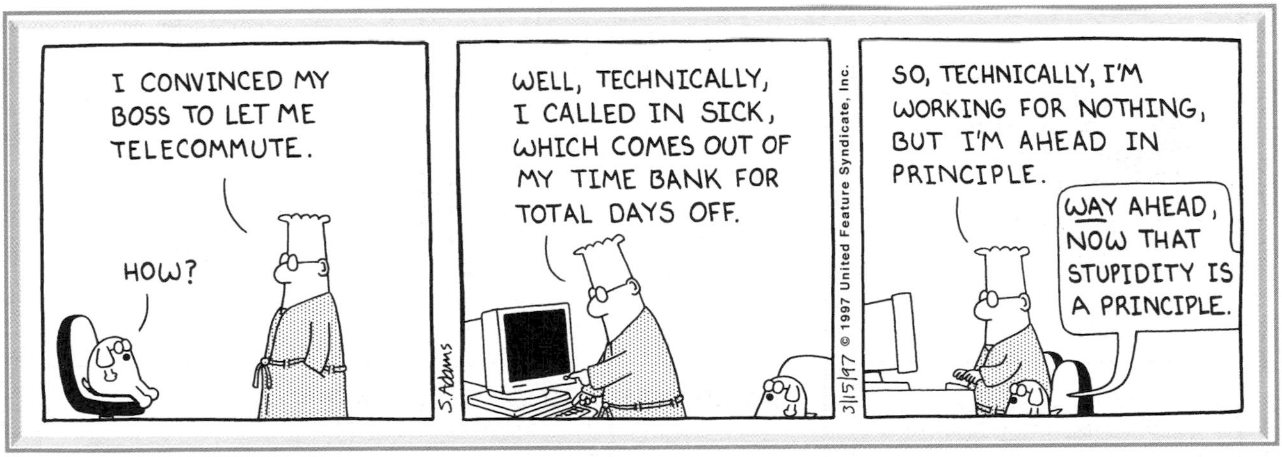
I CONVINCED MY BOSS TO LET ME TELECOMMUTE.
HOW?
WELL, TECHNICALLY, I CALLED IN SICK, WHICH COMES OUT OF MY TIME BANK FOR TOTAL DAYS OFF.
SO, TECHNICALLY, I'M WORKING FOR NOTHING, BUT I'M AHEAD IN PRINCIPLE.
WAY AHEAD, NOW THAT STUPIDITY IS A PRINCIPLE.
S. Adams
© 1997 United Feature Syndicate, Inc.
3/15/97

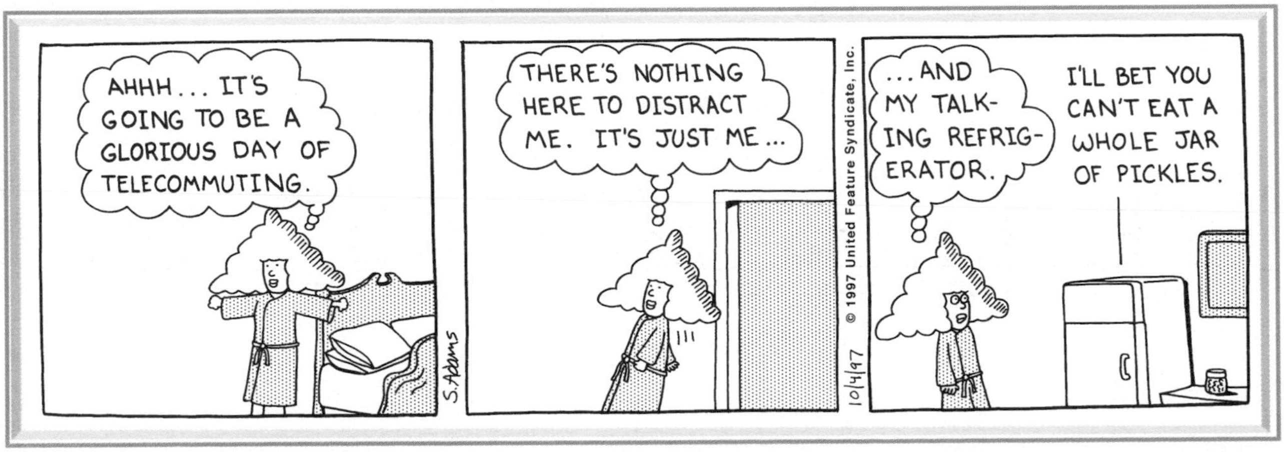
AHHH... IT'S GOING TO BE A GLORIOUS DAY OF TELECOMMUTING.
THERE'S NOTHING HERE TO DISTRACT ME. IT'S JUST ME...
...AND MY TALKING REFRIGERATOR.
I'LL BET YOU CAN'T EAT A WHOLE JAR OF PICKLES.
S. Adams
© 1997 United Feature Syndicate, Inc.
10/4/97

TELECOMMUTING

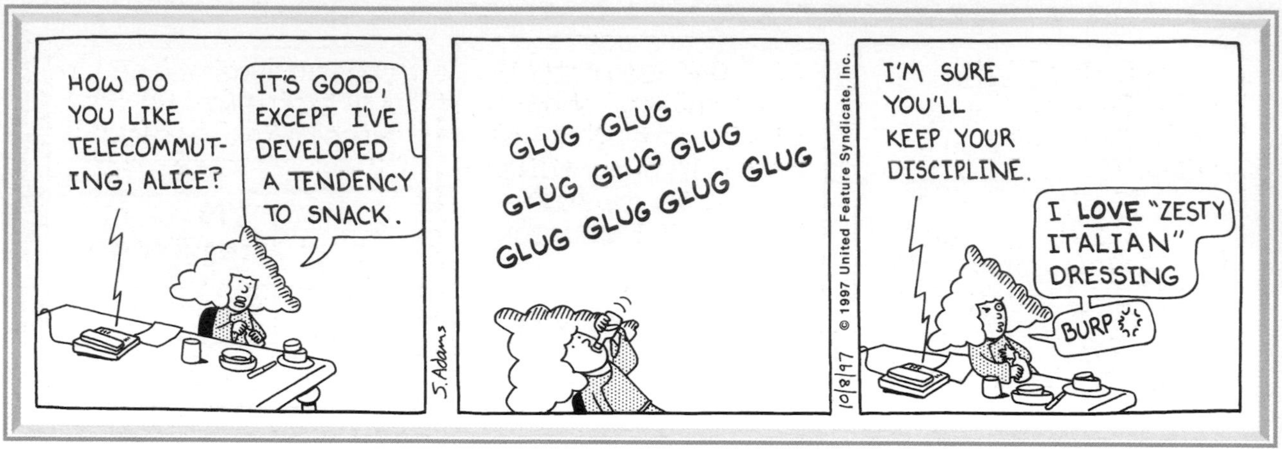
HOW DO YOU LIKE TELECOMMUT-ING, ALICE?
IT'S GOOD, EXCEPT I'VE DEVELOPED A TENDENCY TO SNACK.
GLUG GLUG GLUG GLUG GLUG GLUG GLUG GLUG GLUG
I'M SURE YOU'LL KEEP YOUR DISCIPLINE.
I LOVE "ZESTY ITALIAN" DRESSING
BURP
S. Adams
10/8/97 © 1997 United Feature Syndicate, Inc.

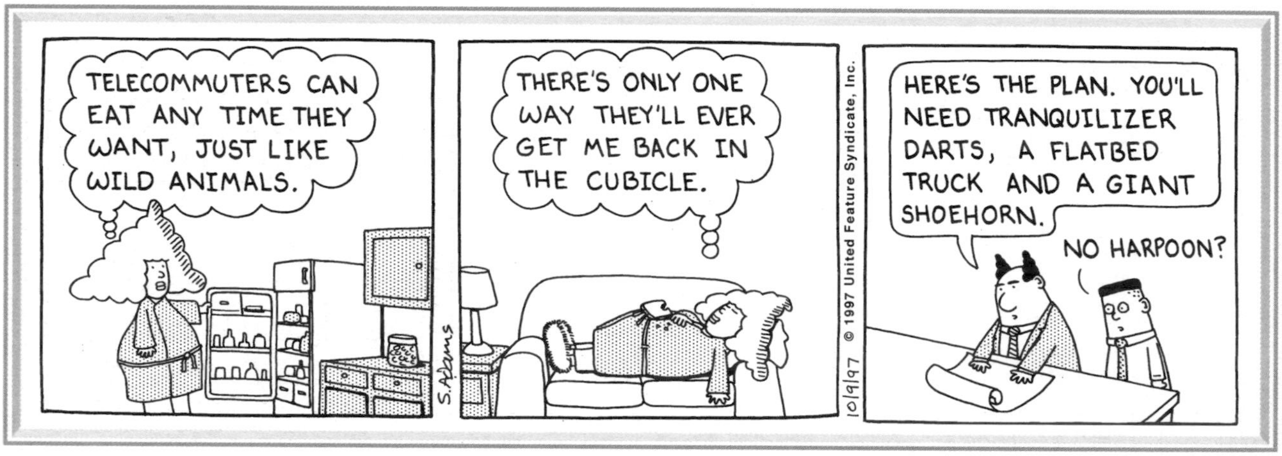
TELECOMMUTERS CAN EAT ANY TIME THEY WANT, JUST LIKE WILD ANIMALS.
THERE'S ONLY ONE WAY THEY'LL EVER GET ME BACK IN THE CUBICLE.
HERE'S THE PLAN. YOU'LL NEED TRANQUILIZER DARTS, A FLATBED TRUCK AND A GIANT SHOEHORN.
NO HARPOON?
S. Adams
10/9/97 © 1997 United Feature Syndicate, Inc.

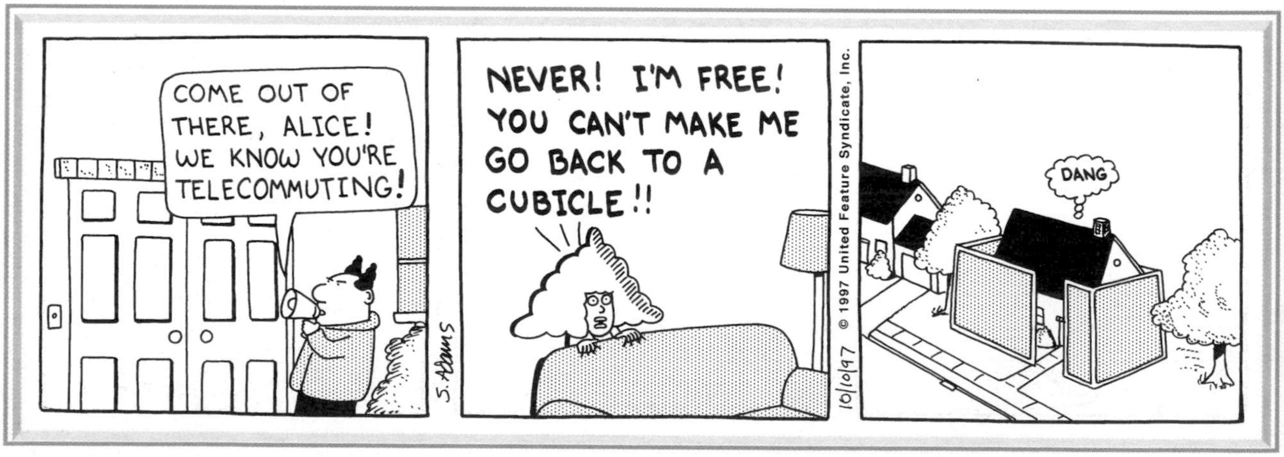
COME OUT OF THERE, ALICE! WE KNOW YOU'RE TELECOMMUTING!
NEVER! I'M FREE! YOU CAN'T MAKE ME GO BACK TO A CUBICLE!!
DANG
S. Adams
10/10/97 © 1997 United Feature Syndicate, Inc.

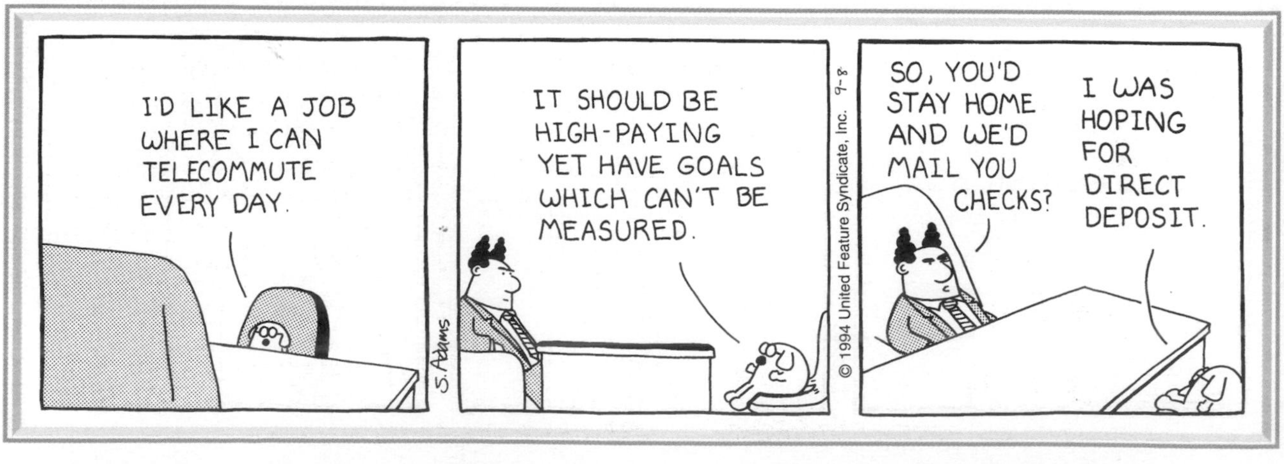
I'D LIKE A JOB WHERE I CAN TELECOMMUTE EVERY DAY.
IT SHOULD BE HIGH-PAYING YET HAVE GOALS WHICH CAN'T BE MEASURED.
SO, YOU'D STAY HOME AND WE'D MAIL YOU CHECKS?
I WAS HOPING FOR DIRECT DEPOSIT.
S. Adams
© 1994 United Feature Syndicate, Inc. 9-8

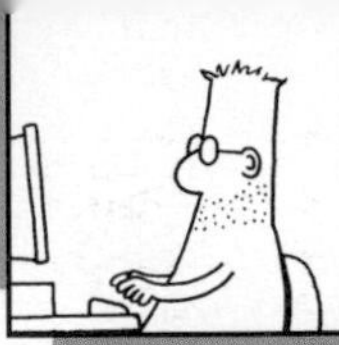

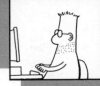

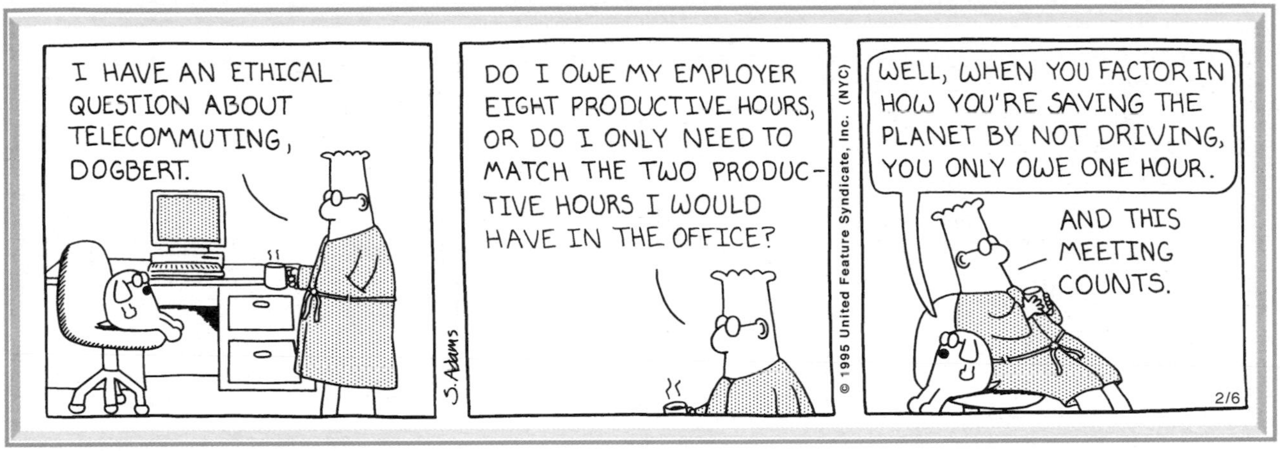
I HAVE AN ETHICAL QUESTION ABOUT TELECOMMUTING, DOGBERT.
S. Adams
DO I OWE MY EMPLOYER EIGHT PRODUCTIVE HOURS, OR DO I ONLY NEED TO MATCH THE TWO PRODUCTIVE HOURS I WOULD HAVE IN THE OFFICE?
© 1995 United Feature Syndicate, Inc. (NYC)
WELL, WHEN YOU FACTOR IN HOW YOU'RE SAVING THE PLANET BY NOT DRIVING, YOU ONLY OWE ONE HOUR.
AND THIS MEETING COUNTS.
2/6

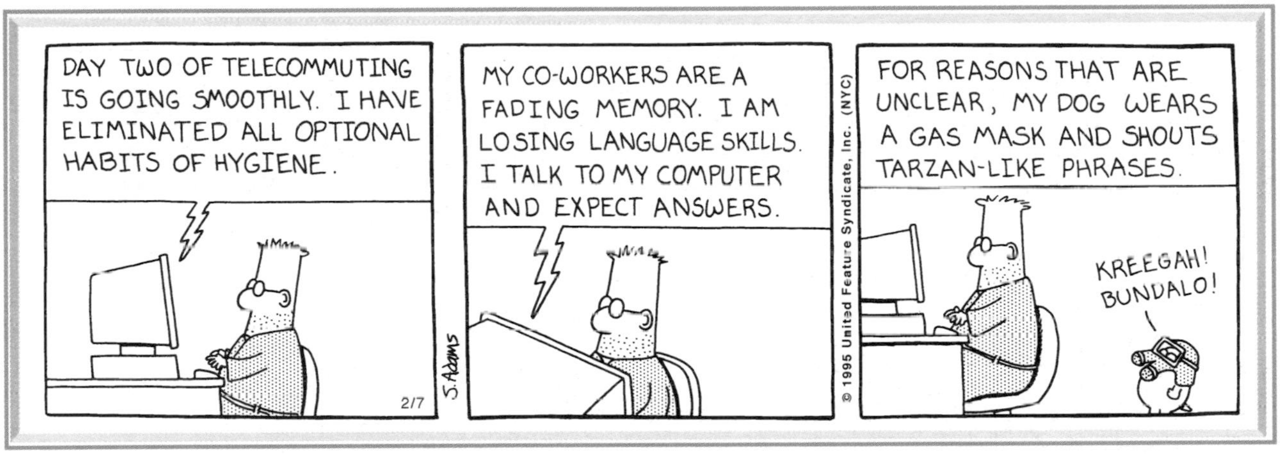
DAY TWO OF TELECOMMUTING IS GOING SMOOTHLY. I HAVE ELIMINATED ALL OPTIONAL HABITS OF HYGIENE.
2/7
S. Adams
MY CO-WORKERS ARE A FADING MEMORY. I AM LOSING LANGUAGE SKILLS. I TALK TO MY COMPUTER AND EXPECT ANSWERS.
© 1995 United Feature Syndicate, Inc. (NYC)
FOR REASONS THAT ARE UNCLEAR, MY DOG WEARS A GAS MASK AND SHOUTS TARZAN-LIKE PHRASES.
KREEGAH! BUNDALO!

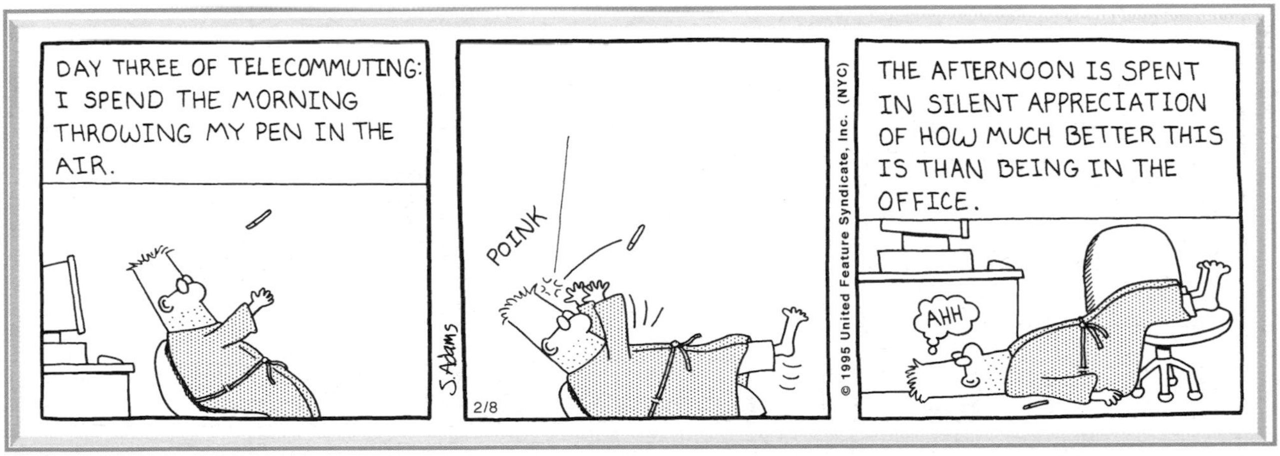
DAY THREE OF TELECOMMUTING: I SPEND THE MORNING THROWING MY PEN IN THE AIR.
S. Adams
POINK
2/8
© 1995 United Feature Syndicate, Inc. (NYC)
THE AFTERNOON IS SPENT IN SILENT APPRECIATION OF HOW MUCH BETTER THIS IS THAN BEING IN THE OFFICE.
AHH

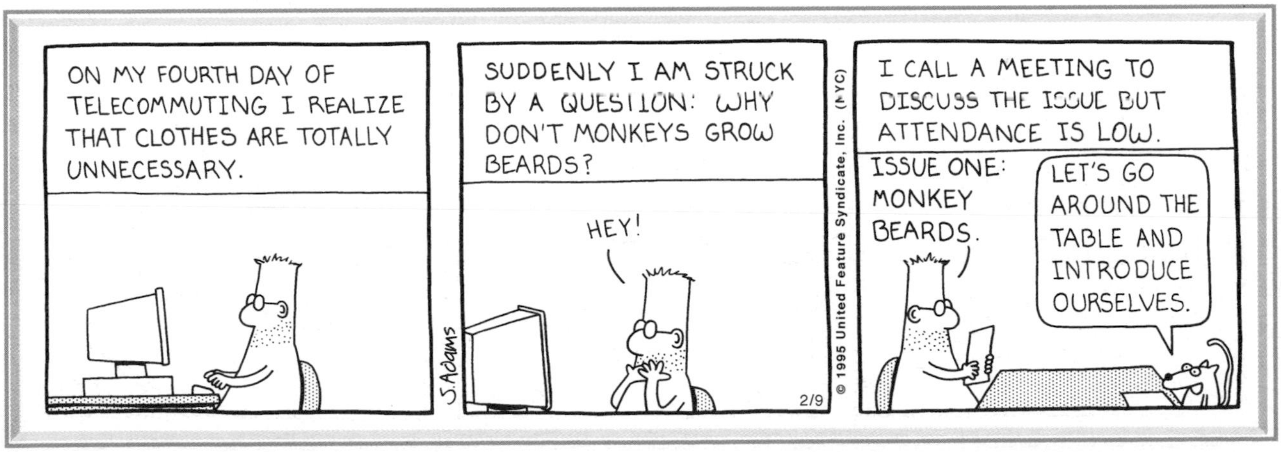
ON MY FOURTH DAY OF TELECOMMUTING I REALIZE THAT CLOTHES ARE TOTALLY UNNECESSARY.
S. Adams
SUDDENLY I AM STRUCK BY A QUESTION: WHY DON'T MONKEYS GROW BEARDS?
HEY!
2/9
© 1995 United Feature Syndicate, Inc. (NYC)
I CALL A MEETING TO DISCUSS THE ISSUE BUT ATTENDANCE IS LOW.
ISSUE ONE: MONKEY BEARDS.
LET'S GO AROUND THE TABLE AND INTRODUCE OURSELVES.

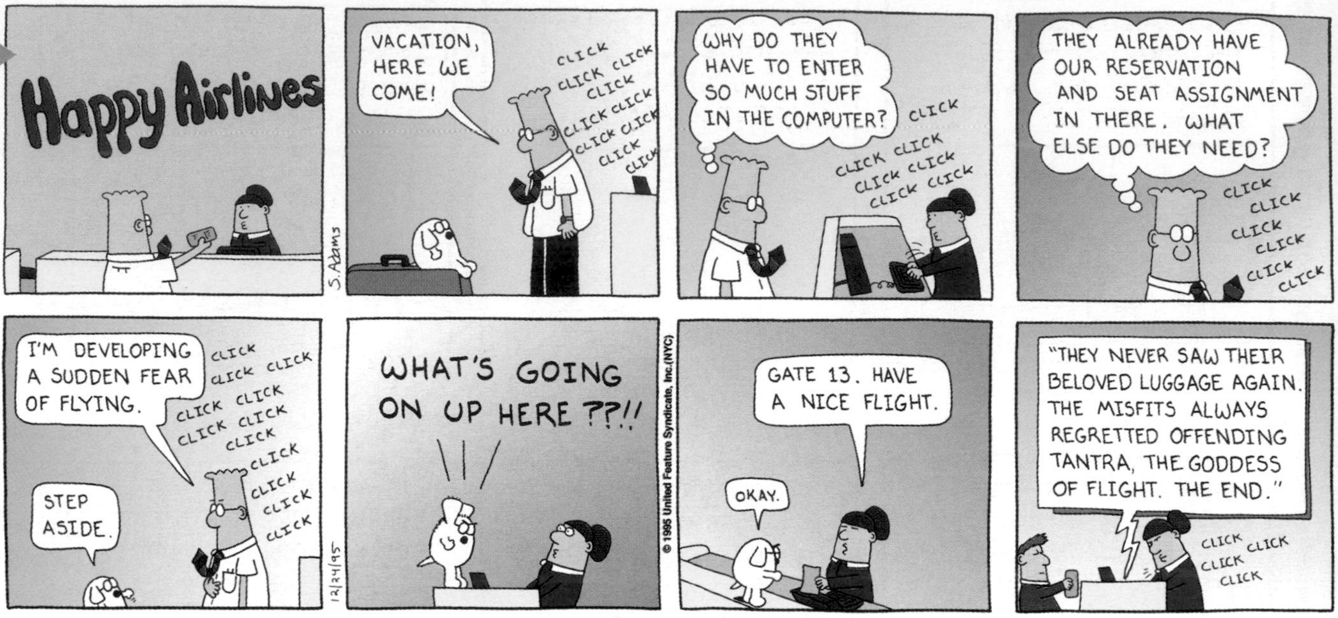
Happy Airlines
S. Adams
VACATION, HERE WE COME!
CLICK CLICK CLICK CLICK CLICK CLICK CLICK CLICK CLICK
WHY DO THEY HAVE TO ENTER SO MUCH STUFF IN THE COMPUTER?
CLICK CLICK CLICK CLICK CLICK CLICK CLICK
THEY ALREADY HAVE OUR RESERVATION AND SEAT ASSIGNMENT IN THERE. WHAT ELSE DO THEY NEED?
CLICK CLICK CLICK CLICK CLICK CLICK
I'M DEVELOPING A SUDDEN FEAR OF FLYING.
CLICK CLICK CLICK CLICK CLICK CLICK CLICK CLICK CLICK CLICK CLICK CLICK
STEP ASIDE.
12/24/95
WHAT'S GOING ON UP HERE ??!!
© 1995 United Feature Syndicate, Inc.(NYC)
GATE 13. HAVE A NICE FLIGHT.
OKAY.
"THEY NEVER SAW THEIR BELOVED LUGGAGE AGAIN. THE MISFITS ALWAYS REGRETTED OFFENDING TANTRA, THE GODDESS OF FLIGHT. THE END."
CLICK CLICK CLICK CLICK

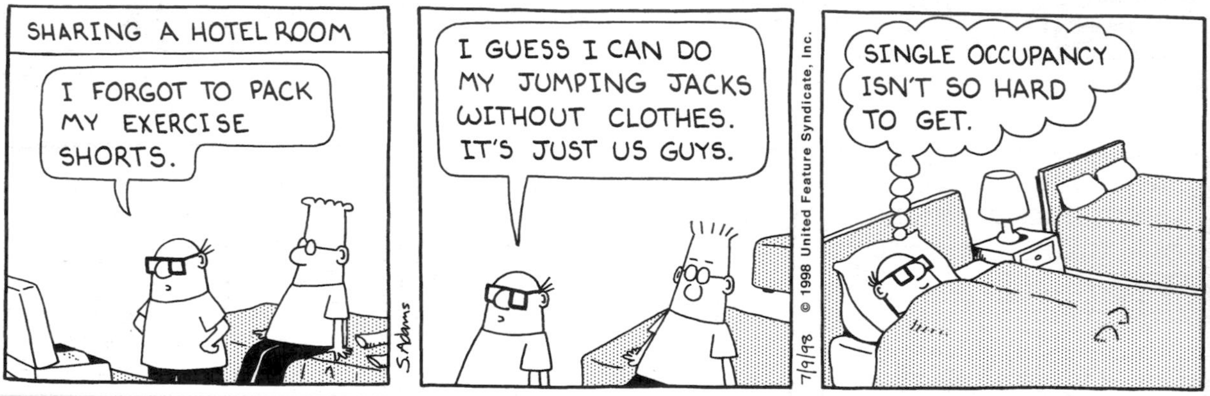
SHARING A HOTEL ROOM
I FORGOT TO PACK MY EXERCISE SHORTS.
S. Adams
I GUESS I CAN DO MY JUMPING JACKS WITHOUT CLOTHES. IT'S JUST US GUYS.
7/9/98 © 1998 United Feature Syndicate, Inc.
SINGLE OCCUPANCY ISN'T SO HARD TO GET.

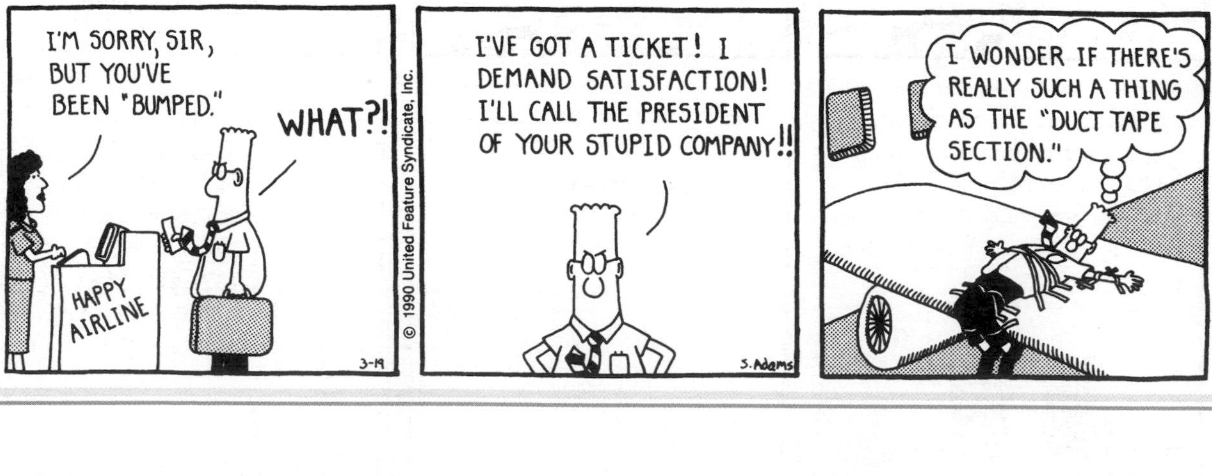
I'M SORRY, SIR, BUT YOU'VE BEEN "BUMPED."
WHAT?!
HAPPY AIRLINE
3-19
© 1990 United Feature Syndicate, Inc.
I'VE GOT A TICKET! I DEMAND SATISFACTION! I'LL CALL THE PRESIDENT OF YOUR STUPID COMPANY!!
S. Adams
I WONDER IF THERE'S REALLY SUCH A THING AS THE "DUCT TAPE SECTION."

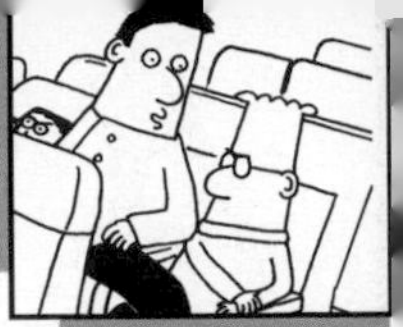

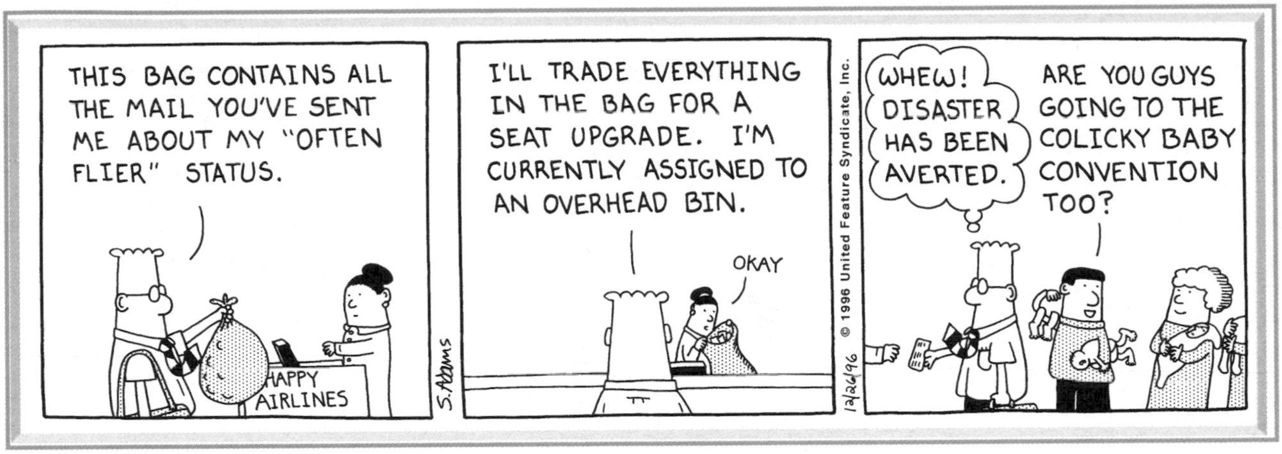
THIS BAG CONTAINS ALL THE MAIL YOU'VE SENT ME ABOUT MY "OFTEN FLIER" STATUS.
HAPPY AIRLINES
S. Adams
I'LL TRADE EVERYTHING IN THE BAG FOR A SEAT UPGRADE. I'M CURRENTLY ASSIGNED TO AN OVERHEAD BIN.
OKAY
© 1996 United Feature Syndicate, Inc.
12/26/96
WHEW! DISASTER HAS BEEN AVERTED.
ARE YOU GUYS GOING TO THE COLICKY BABY CONVENTION TOO?

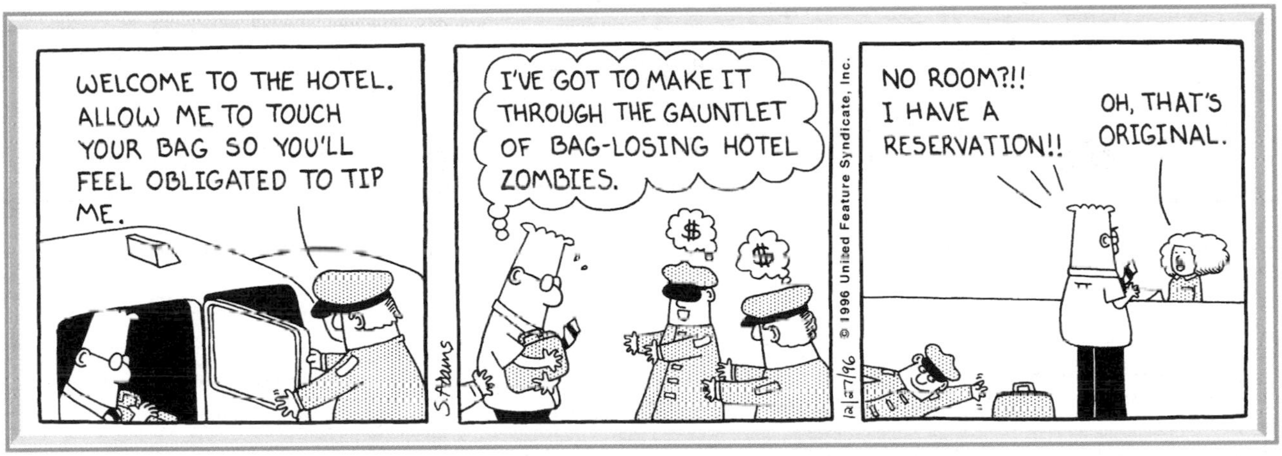
WELCOME TO THE HOTEL. ALLOW ME TO TOUCH YOUR BAG SO YOU'LL FEEL OBLIGATED TO TIP ME.
S. Adams
I'VE GOT TO MAKE IT THROUGH THE GAUNTLET OF BAG-LOSING HOTEL ZOMBIES.
$
$
© 1996 United Feature Syndicate, Inc.
12/27/96
NO ROOM?!! I HAVE A RESERVATION!!
OH, THAT'S ORIGINAL.

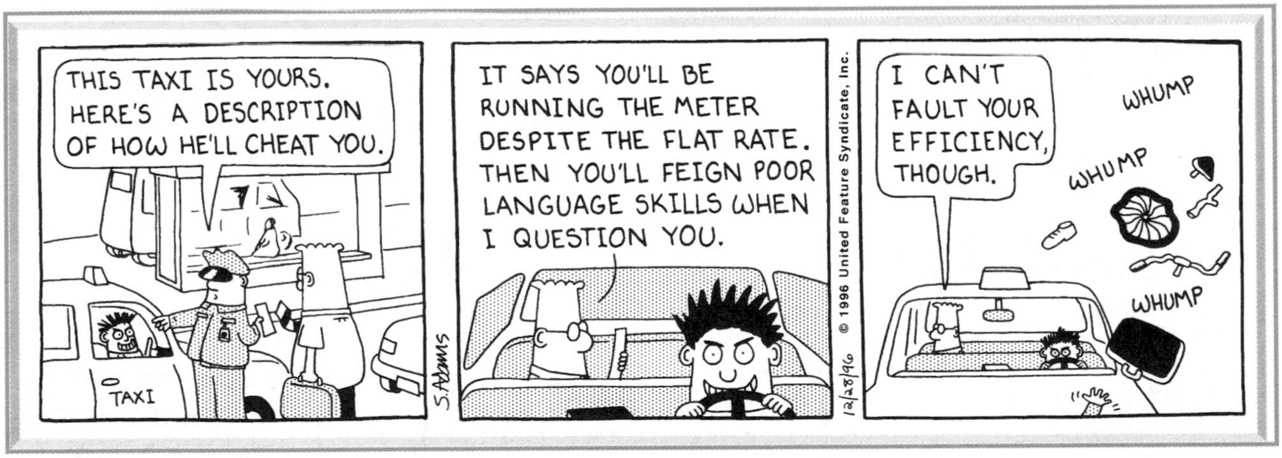
THIS TAXI IS YOURS. HERE'S A DESCRIPTION OF HOW HE'LL CHEAT YOU.
TAXI
S. Adams
IT SAYS YOU'LL BE RUNNING THE METER DESPITE THE FLAT RATE. THEN YOU'LL FEIGN POOR LANGUAGE SKILLS WHEN I QUESTION YOU.
© 1996 United Feature Syndicate, Inc.
12/28/96
I CAN'T FAULT YOUR EFFICIENCY, THOUGH.
WHUMP
WHUMP
WHUMP

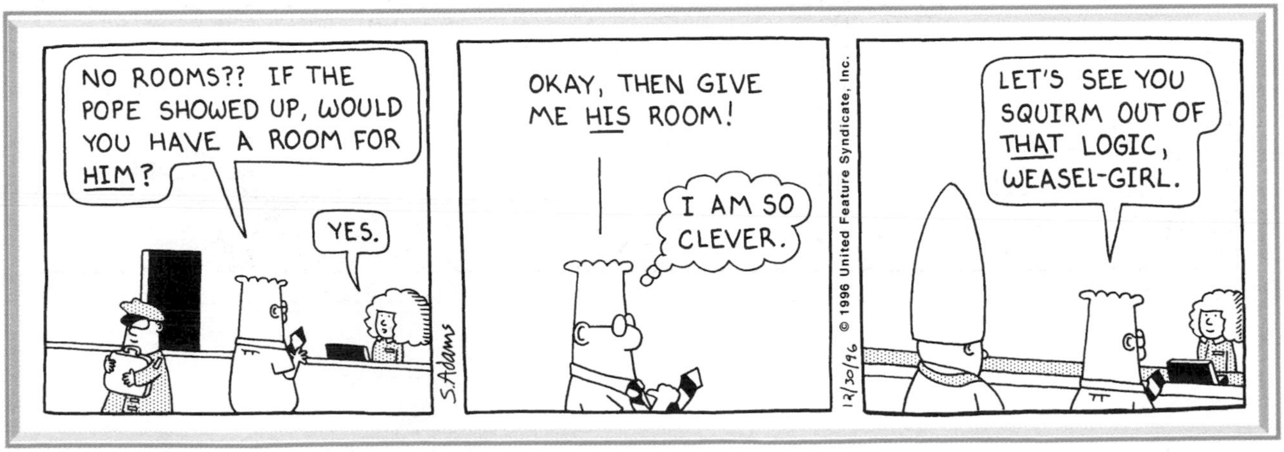
NO ROOMS?? IF THE POPE SHOWED UP, WOULD YOU HAVE A ROOM FOR HIM?
YES.
S. Adams
OKAY, THEN GIVE ME HIS ROOM!
I AM SO CLEVER.
© 1996 United Feature Syndicate, Inc.
12/30/96
LET'S SEE YOU SQUIRM OUT OF THAT LOGIC, WEASEL-GIRL.

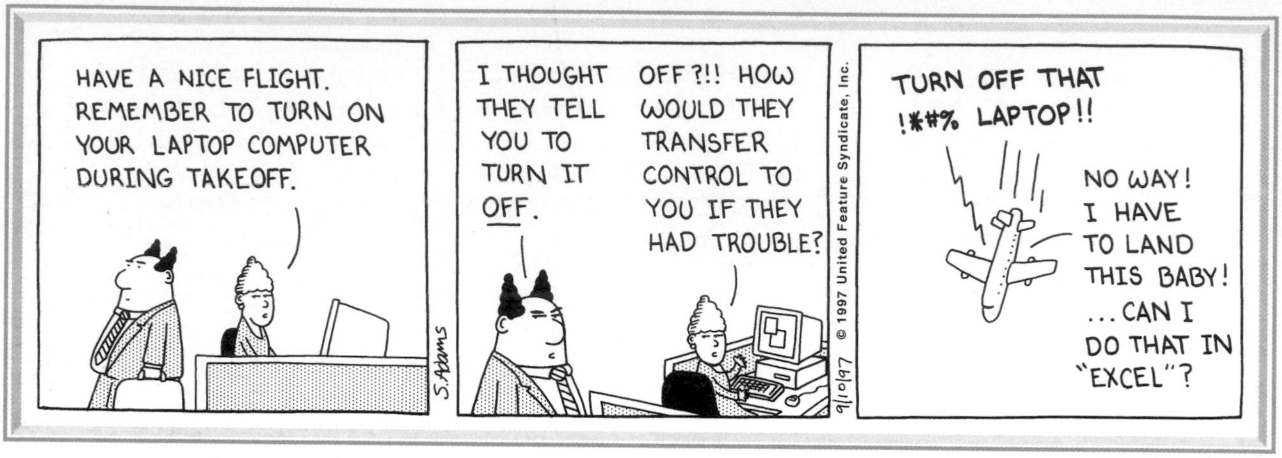

HAVE A NICE FLIGHT. REMEMBER TO TURN ON YOUR LAPTOP COMPUTER DURING TAKEOFF.
S. Adams
I THOUGHT THEY TELL YOU TO TURN IT OFF.
OFF?!! HOW WOULD THEY TRANSFER CONTROL TO YOU IF THEY HAD TROUBLE?
9/10/97
© 1997 United Feature Syndicate, Inc.
TURN OFF THAT !*#% LAPTOP!!
NO WAY! I HAVE TO LAND THIS BABY! ...CAN I DO THAT IN "EXCEL"?

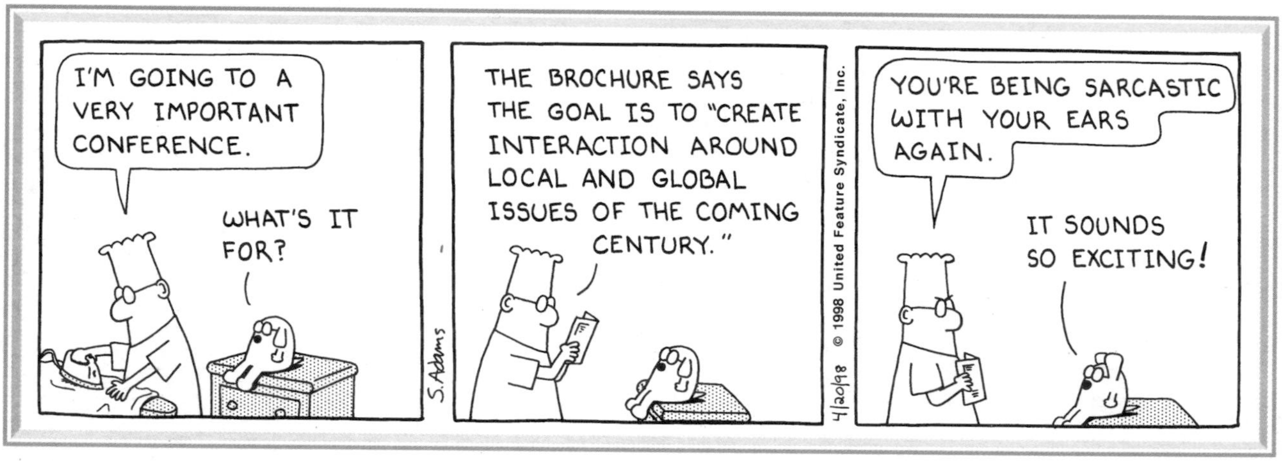

I'M GOING TO A VERY IMPORTANT CONFERENCE.
WHAT'S IT FOR?
S. Adams
THE BROCHURE SAYS THE GOAL IS TO "CREATE INTERACTION AROUND LOCAL AND GLOBAL ISSUES OF THE COMING CENTURY."
4/20/98
© 1998 United Feature Syndicate, Inc.
YOU'RE BEING SARCASTIC WITH YOUR EARS AGAIN.
IT SOUNDS SO EXCITING!

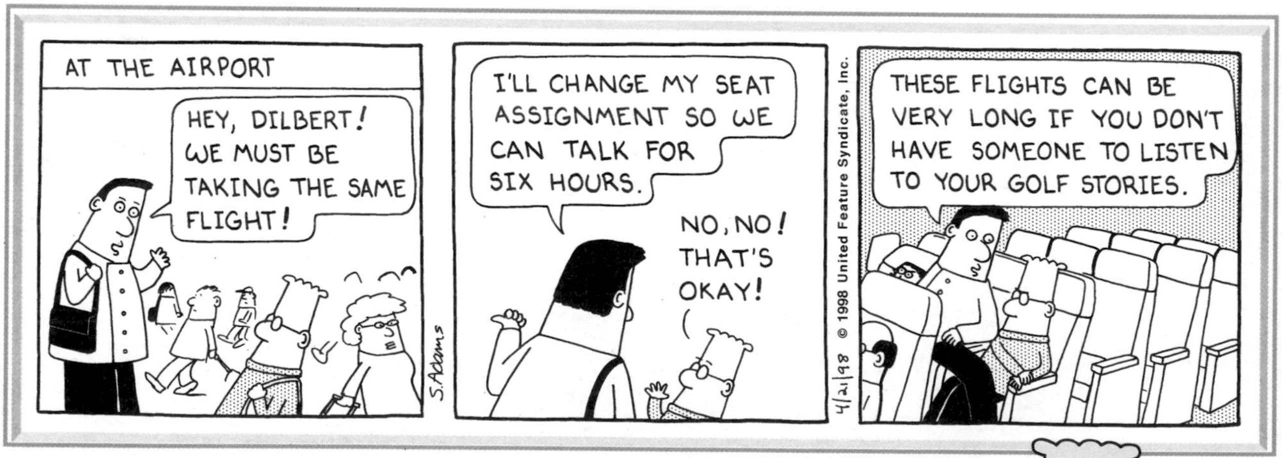

AT THE AIRPORT
HEY, DILBERT! WE MUST BE TAKING THE SAME FLIGHT!
S. Adams
I'LL CHANGE MY SEAT ASSIGNMENT SO WE CAN TALK FOR SIX HOURS.
NO, NO! THAT'S OKAY!
4/21/98
© 1998 United Feature Syndicate, Inc.
THESE FLIGHTS CAN BE VERY LONG IF YOU DON'T HAVE SOMEONE TO LISTEN TO YOUR GOLF STORIES.

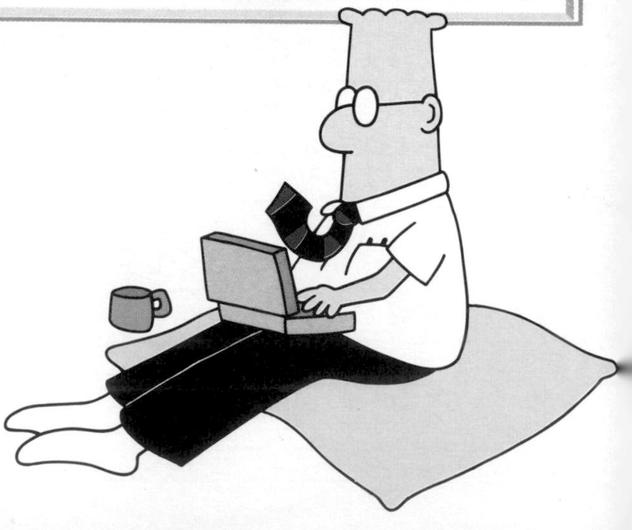